CompTIA® A+®
Complete
Study Guide
Exam 220-901
Exam 220-902
Third Edition

Quentin Docter

Emmett Dulaney

Toby Skandier

Senior Acquisitions Editor: Kenyon Brown
Development Editor: Gary Schwartz
Technical Editors: Robin Abernathy, Ian Seaton, Troy McMillan
Production Editor: Rebecca Anderson
Copy Editor: Judy Flynn
Editorial Manager: Mary Beth Wakefield
Production Manager: Kathleen Wisor
Associate Publisher: Jim Minatel
Media Supervising Producer: Rich Graves
Book Designers: Judy Fung and Bill Gibson
Proofreaders: Sarah Kaikini and Jen Larsen, Word One New York
Indexer: J & J Indexing
Project Coordinator, Cover: Brent Savage
Cover Designer: Wiley
Cover Image: © Getty Images Inc./Jeremy Woodhouse

Copyright © 2016 by John Wiley & Sons, Inc., Indianapolis, Indiana

Published simultaneously in Canada

ISBN: 978-1-119-13785-6
ISBN: 978-1-118-13787-0 (ebk.)
ISBN: 978-1-118-13786-3 (ebk.)

Manufactured in the United States of America

For general information on our other products and services or to obtain technical support, please contact our Customer Care Department within the U.S. at (877) 762-2974, outside the U.S. at (317) 572-3993 or fax (317) 572-4002.

Wiley publishes in a variety of print and electronic formats and by print-on-demand. Some material included with standard print versions of this book may not be included in e-books or in print on demand. If this book refers to media such as a CD or DVD that is not included in the version you purchased, you may download this material at http://booksupport.wiley.com. For more information about Wiley products, visit www.wiley.com.

Library of Congress Control Number: 2015951127

V007407_060418

For Kara, Abbie, Lauren, Reina, and Alina
—Quentin Docter

For Carl: Thanks for always looking after the baby.
—Emmett Dulaney

For Charlotte: Welcome to the world, baby.
—Toby Skandier

Acknowledgments

As we were putting this book together, I was reminded of the proverb that begins, "It takes a small village…" That beginning definitely holds true to create a book of this scope and size. From beginning to end, there are scores of dedicated professionals focused on delivering the best book possible to you, the readers.

First, I need to thank my coauthors, Emmett Dulaney and Toby Skandier. Their dedication to producing an excellent book that will best serve the needs of our readers is inspiring. Now, onto the rest of the team.

Kenyon Brown and Gary Schwartz kept us on track and moving forward, which was a challenge at times. Becca Anderson had the fun job of keeping us organized, which is akin to herding cats. Tech editors Robin Abernathy and Ian Seaton provided a great set of expert eyes and made excellent suggestions. Copyeditor Judy Flynn reminded me yet again that I am no master of the English language and saved me from butchering it (too badly). Many thanks also go out to proofreaders Sarah Kaikini and Jen Larsen at Word One, and our indexer Jack Lewis. Without their great contributions, this book would not have made it into your hands.

—Quentin Docter

I would like to thank my coauthors, Quentin Docter and Toby Skandier, without whom this book would have never happened. Thanks are also due to Gary Schwartz for keeping this book on schedule and working tirelessly to turn it into something usable.

—Emmett Dulaney

Yet another stellar project with Quentin and Emmett. While we haven't started finishing each other's sentences, we certainly have found our groove, I would say. That turns work into less thereof. Thank you, guys. Thanks also to our tireless editorial and production team. Keep up the great work!

—Toby Skandier

About the Authors

Quentin Docter (A+, Network+, IT Fundamentals, MCSE, CCNA, SCSA) is an IT consultant who started in the industry in 1994. Since then, he's worked as a tech and network support specialist, trainer, consultant, and webmaster. He has written several books for Sybex, including books on A+, Server+, IT Fundamentals, Windows, and Solaris 9 certifications as well as PC hardware and maintenance. Quentin can be reached at qdocter@yahoo.com.

Emmett Dulaney (A+, Network+, and Security+) is an associate professor and the former director of training for Mercury Technical Solution. He holds or has held 18 vendor certifications and is the author of over 30 books, including the *CompTIA Security+ Study Guide*. He specializes in certification and cross-platform integration, and he is a columnist for *Certification Magazine* and *Campus Technology*. Emmett can be reached at eadulaney@comcast.net.

Toby Skandier (A+, Network +, Cloud+, Storage+, Server+, JNCIS, MCSE, CCNP, and CCSI) began his career in 1985, and he is the founder of Talskan Technologies, LLC, a technical-education provider based in North Carolina. He has coauthored numerous books for Sybex, including *Network Administrator Street Smarts* and the best-selling *Network+ Study Guide*. Toby can be reached at tskandier@talskan.com.

Contents at a Glance

Introduction   *xxix*

Assessment Test   *lvii*

Part I   **220-901**   **1**

Chapter 1   Motherboards, Processors, and Memory   3

Chapter 2   Storage Devices and Power Supplies   71

Chapter 3   Peripherals and Expansion   113

Chapter 4   Display Devices   183

Chapter 5   Custom Configurations   219

Chapter 6   Networking Fundamentals   247

Chapter 7   Introduction to TCP/IP   297

Chapter 8   Installing Wireless and SOHO Networks   329

Chapter 9   Understanding Laptops   393

Chapter 10   Understanding Mobile Devices   455

Chapter 11   Installing and Configuring Printers   499

Chapter 12   Hardware and Network Troubleshooting   567

Part II   **220-902**   **659**

Chapter 13   Operating System Basics   661

Chapter 14   Operating System Administration   707

Chapter 15   Working with Windows 8/8.1   763

Chapter 16   Working with Windows 7   783

Chapter 17   Working with Windows Vista   827

Chapter 18   Working with Mac OS and Linux   867

Chapter 19   Security   893

Chapter 20   Network Services, Cloud Computing, and Virtualization   953

Chapter 21   Mobile Operating Systems and Connectivity   1003

Chapter 22   Troubleshooting Theory, OSs, and Security   1097

Chapter 23   Understanding Operational Procedures   1147
Appendix   A   Answers to Review Questions   1211
Appendix   B   Answers to Performance-Based Questions   1247

Index   *1269*

Contents

Introduction   *xxix*

Assessment Test   *lvii*

Part	**I**	**220-901**	**1**

Chapter	**1**	**Motherboards, Processors, and Memory**	**3**

Identifying Components of Motherboards   5
   System Board Form Factors   6
   System Board Components   8
Identifying Purposes and Characteristics of Processors   32
Identifying Purposes and Characteristics of Memory   38
   Important Memory Terms   38
   Types of Memory   43
   Memory Packaging   50
Identifying Purposes and Characteristics of Cooling Systems   54
   Fans   54
   Memory Cooling   58
   Hard Drive Cooling   58
   Chipset Cooling   58
   CPU Cooling   59
Summary   63
Exam Essentials   63
Review Questions   65
Performance-Based Question 1   69
Performance-Based Question 2   69

Chapter	**2**	**Storage Devices and Power Supplies**	**71**

Identifying Purposes and Characteristics of Storage Devices   72
   Hard Disk Drive Systems   72
   Solid-State Drives   77
   Optical Storage Drives   79
   Drive Interfaces and RAID   85
   Removable Storage and Media   89
   Installing, Removing, and Configuring Storage Devices   95
Identifying Purposes and Characteristics of Power Supplies   98
   Dual-Rail Architecture   99
   Power and Voltage Ratings   99

Power Connectors	100
Replacing Power Supplies	106
AC Adapters as Power Supplies	107
Summary	108
Exam Essentials	108
Review Questions	109
Performance-Based Question	112

Chapter 3	**Peripherals and Expansion**	**113**
	Installing and Configuring Expansion Cards	117
	Video	118
	Multimedia	119
	I/O	120
	Communications	120
	Adapter Configuration	126
	Identifying Characteristics of Connectors and Cables	126
	Device Connector Types	127
	Common Peripheral Cables and Their Interfaces	134
	Video Display Cables and Connectors	146
	Input Devices	157
	Mouse	158
	Touchpad	159
	Keyboard	161
	Scanner	163
	Barcode Reader	165
	Digitizer	166
	Biometric Devices	167
	Gamepads and Joysticks	168
	Motion Sensor	168
	Smart Card Reader	169
	Multimedia Input Devices	170
	Output Devices	173
	Printers	174
	Speakers	174
	Display Devices	174
	Input and Output Devices	174
	Touchscreens	175
	KVM Switch	175
	Smart TV	176
	Set-Top Box	177
	Summary	177
	Exam Essentials	178
	Review Questions	179
	Performance-Based Questions	182

Chapter	**4**	**Display Devices**	**183**
		Understanding Display Types and Settings	184
		Video Display Types	184
		Adjusting Display Settings	195
		Understanding Video Standards and Technologies	205
		Video Standards	205
		Advanced Video Resolutions and Concepts	207
		Summary	212
		Exam Essentials	213
		Review Questions	214
		Performance-Based Question	217
Chapter	**5**	**Custom Configurations**	**219**
		Standard Thick Clients	222
		Graphic and CAD/CAM Design Workstations	223
		CPU Enhancements	223
		Video Enhancements	224
		Maximized RAM	224
		Audio/Video Editing Workstations	225
		Video Enhancements	225
		Specialized Audio	226
		Specialized Hard Drives	226
		Virtualization Workstations	227
		CPU Enhancements	228
		Maximized RAM	228
		Gaming PCs	230
		CPU Enhancements	230
		Video Enhancements	231
		Specialized Audio	231
		Enhanced Cooling	232
		Home Theater PCs	232
		Video Enhancements	234
		Specialized Audio	234
		Special Chassis and TV Tuner	234
		Thin Clients	235
		Home Server PCs	236
		Media Streaming Capabilities	237
		File and Print Sharing Services	240
		Gigabit NIC	240
		RAID Array	241
		Summary	241
		Exam Essentials	241
		Review Questions	243
		Performance-Based Question	246

Chapter	6	**Networking Fundamentals**	**247**
		Understanding Networking Principles	249
		Understanding Networking Fundamentals	250
		Identifying Common Network Hardware	270
		Network Interface Cards (NICs)	270
		Cables and Connectors	272
		Networking Components	284
		Summary	289
		Exam Essentials	290
		Review Questions	292
		Performance-Based Question	295
Chapter	7	**Introduction to TCP/IP**	**297**
		Understanding TCP/IP	299
		TCP/IP Structure	300
		Understanding IP Addressing	308
		Summary	322
		Exam Essentials	323
		Review Questions	324
		Performance-Based Question	327
Chapter	8	**Installing Wireless and SOHO Networks**	**329**
		Understanding Wireless Networking	331
		802.11 Networking Standards	332
		802.11 Devices	338
		Wireless Encryption Methods	339
		Installing and Configuring SOHO Networks	341
		Choosing Connection Types	341
		Installing the Network	363
		Configuring a Wireless Router	373
		Summary	386
		Exam Essentials	387
		Review Questions	388
		Performance-Based Question	391
Chapter	9	**Understanding Laptops**	**393**
		Understanding Laptop Architecture	396
		Laptops vs. Desktops	396
		Laptop Case	398
		Motherboards and Processors	399
		Memory	402
		Storage	403
		Input Devices	406

Expansion Buses and Ports   414
Docking Stations   422
Power Systems   424
Laptop Displays   427
Cable Locks   431
Disassembling and Reassembling Laptops   432
Using the Right Tools   432
Replacing Laptop Components   434
Summary   448
Exam Essentials   448
Review Questions   450
Performance-Based Question   453

Chapter   10   Understanding Mobile Devices   455

Understanding Mobile Devices   457
Characteristics of Mobile Devices   458
Tablets   461
Smartphones   463
Phablets   469
e-Readers   471
GPS   473
Smart Cameras   476
Wearable Technology Devices   477
Connection Types   484
Mobile Device Accessories   490
Summary   492
Exam Essentials   492
Review Questions   494
Performance-Based Question   497

Chapter   11   Installing and Configuring Printers   499

Understanding Print Technologies and Imaging Processes   502
Impact Printers   503
Inkjet   505
Laser Printers   513
Thermal Printers   524
Virtual Printers   525
Installing and Configuring Printers   527
Printer Interface Components   527
Installing and Sharing Local Printers   532
Installing and Sharing Networked Printers   542
Performing Printer Maintenance
and Upgrades   550

Performing Printer Maintenance	551
Installing Printer Upgrades	556
Summary	559
Exam Essentials	560
Review Questions	562
Performance-Based Question	565

Chapter 12   Hardware and Network Troubleshooting   567

Troubleshooting Core Hardware Issues	574
Troubleshooting Motherboards, CPUs, RAM, and Power Problems	575
Troubleshooting Storage Device Problems	588
Troubleshooting Video Issues	593
Troubleshooting Mobile Devices, Printers, and Networking	595
Troubleshooting Common Mobile Device Issues	595
Troubleshooting Printer Problems	607
Troubleshooting Networking Problems	630
Summary	652
Exam Essentials	653
Review Questions	655
Performance-Based Question	658

Part II   220-902   659

Chapter 13   Operating System Basics   661

Understanding Operating Systems	662
Operating System Terms and Concepts	664
Minimum System Requirements	665
The Windows Interface	669
What's in a Window?	685
Updating Windows	689
Creating Restore Points	690
File Management	691
Going Virtual	698
Preparing for the Exam	699
Summary	702
Exam Essentials	702
Review Questions	703
Performance-Based Question	706

Chapter 14   Operating System Administration   707

Interacting with Operating Systems	709
Control Panel	709
The Command Prompt	721

Virtual Memory 733
Administrative Tools 734
    Task Manager 734
    MMC 739
    Computer Management 739
    Services 740
    Performance Monitor 740
    Task Scheduler 741
    Windows System Configuration Tools 742
    Power Management 748
Disk Management 749
    Getting Disks Ready to Store Files and Programs 749
    Backing Up the Data on Your Drives 753
    Checking the Health of Hard Disks and Optimizing
       Their Performance 753
    User Authentication 754
Summary 755
Exam Essentials 755
Review Questions 757
Performance-Based Question 761

Chapter   15   Working with Windows 8/8.1   763

Windows Editions 764
Installing Windows 8 769
    Unattended Installation/Image Deployment 773
    Remote Network Installation 773
    Multiboot Installation 774
    Repair Installation/Refresh/Restore 774
    Recovery Partition 774
Windows 8 Boot Methods 776
    Internal Hard Drive (Partition) 776
    External/Hot Swappable Drive 776
    Flash Drives 777
    Solid-State Drives 777
    Netboot 777
Summary 777
Exam Essentials 778
Review Questions 779
Performance-Based Question 782

Chapter   16   Working with Windows 7   783

Windows 7 Editions 785
Installing Windows 7 791
    Upgrading to Windows 7 792

Upgrading Editions of Windows 7 796
Installation/Upgrade Boot Options 797
The Windows 7 Boot Sequences 797
Key Boot Files 797
Windows 7 Features 798
Tools in Windows 7 798
Windows 7 Administrative Tools 804
Local Users and Groups 804
Local Security Policy 805
System Configuration 807
Component Services 808
Data Sources 808
Print Management 809
Windows Memory Diagnostics 810
Unique Control Panel Utilities 810
HomeGroup 810
RemoteApp and Desktop Connections 810
Troubleshooting 811
Networking and Windows 7 813
Configuring an Alternative IP Address in Windows 814
Network Card Properties 815
Configuring Windows Networking 816
Windows 7 System Performance and Optimization 817
Summary 819
Exam Essentials 819
Review Questions 821
Performance-Based Question 826

Chapter   17   Working with Windows Vista   827

Windows Vista Editions 829
Installing Windows Vista 832
Clean Install 832
Upgrading to Windows Vista 833
Transferring to Windows Vista 835
The Windows Vista Boot Sequences 835
Key Boot Files 835
Windows Vista Features 836
Tools in Windows Vista 836
Windows Vista Administrative Tools 840
Users and Groups 840
Local Security Policy 841
System Configuration 843
Component Services 845
Data Sources 845

Print Management 845
Windows Memory Diagnostics 846
Distinctive Utilities 847
Tablet PC Settings 847
Pen and Input Devices 848
Offline Files 849
Problem Reports and Solutions 850
Printers 852
Networking and Windows Vista 852
Vista System Performance and Optimization 855
Aero 856
User Account Control 857
Indexing 858
Sidebar 859
Summary 860
Exam Essentials 860
Review Questions 861
Performance-Based Question 865

Chapter   18   Working with Mac OS and Linux   867

Best Practices 868
Scheduled Backups 868
Scheduled Disk Maintenance 871
System Updates/App Store 871
Patch Management 871
Driver/Firmware Updates 873
Antivirus/Antimalware Updates 873
Tools 873
Features 874
Basic Linux Commands 877
Understanding the Syntax of Shell Commands 878
Discovering and Using Linux Commands 879
Becoming root (Superuser) 881
Managing Processes 881
Directory Navigation 883
Directory Listings 884
Changing Permissions and Ownership 885
Working with Files 886
Working with Directories 887
Networking Utilities 887
Summary 888
Exam Essentials 888
Review Questions 889
Performance-Based Question 892

Chapter 19	**Security**	**893**

Common Prevention Methods 896
Physical Security 897
Digital Security 899
User Education/AUP 905
Principle of Least Privilege 906
Email Filtering 906
Virtual Private Networks 906
Common Security Threats 907
Social Engineering 907
Password Attacks 908
Malware 909
Man-in-the-Middle Attacks 909
Rootkits 910
Phishing 910
Shoulder Surfing 911
Spyware 911
Viruses 912
Worms 917
Trojans 918
Ransomware 918
Spoofing 918
Zero-Day Attack 919
Zombie/Botnet 919
Non-Complaint Systems 920
Workstation Security Best Practices 920
Setting Strong Passwords 920
Requiring Passwords and Expiration 921
Account Management 921
Restricting User Permissions 921
Add Login Time Restrictions 921
Act on Failed Login Attempts 922
Changing Default Usernames 922
Disabling the Guest Account 922
Screensaver Required Password 922
Disable Autorun 922
Data Loss Prevention 923
Working with Windows OS Security Settings 923
Users and Groups 923
NTFS vs. Share Permissions 925
Shared Files and Folders 927
System Files and Folders 928
User Authentication 928
BitLocker and BitLocker To Go 929

EFS   929
Mobile Device Security   929
  Screen Locks   930
  Remote Wipes and Locator Applications   931
  Remote Backup   934
  Operating System Updates   934
Destruction and Disposal Methods   935
  Recycling or Repurposing Best Practices   936
  Low-Level Format vs. Standard Format   936
  Hard Drive Sanitation and Sanitation Methods   936
  Physical Destruction   937
Securing a SOHO Network (Wireless)   939
  Change Default Usernames and Passwords   940
  Changing the SSID   940
  Setting Encryption   940
  Disabling SSID Broadcast   940
  Enable MAC Filtering   940
  Antenna and Access Point Placement   941
  Radio Power Levels   941
  Assign Static IP Addresses   941
  WPS   942
Securing a SOHO Network (Wired)   942
  Change Default Usernames and Passwords   942
  Assign Static IP Addresses   943
  Disabling Ports   943
  Physical Security   943
Summary   945
Exam Essentials   945
Review Questions   947
Performance-Based Question   951

Chapter 20   Network Services, Cloud Computing, and
              Virtualization   953

Understanding Network Services   955
  Server Roles   956
  Internet Appliances   971
  Legacy and Embedded Systems   973
Understanding Cloud Computing and Virtualization   975
  Concepts of Cloud Computing   975
  Understanding Virtualization   984
Summary   996
Exam Essentials   996
Review Questions   998
Performance-Based Question   1001

Chapter	21	**Mobile Operating Systems and Connectivity**	**1003**
		Understanding Mobile Operating Systems	1006
		Comparing Mobile Operating Systems	1007
		Understanding Sensors and Calibration	1022
		Using Additional Mobile Operating System Features	1029
		Network Connectivity and Email	1036
		Understanding Cellular Data Connections	1037
		Establishing Wi-Fi Connectivity	1045
		Establishing Bluetooth Connectivity	1056
		Configuring Email Accounts	1069
		Mobile Device Synchronization	1082
		Syncing Apple iOS Devices	1083
		Syncing Android Devices	1088
		Software Installation Requirements	1089
		Summary	1092
		Exam Essentials	1092
		Review Questions	1093
		Performance-Based Question	1096
Chapter	22	**Troubleshooting Theory, OSs, and Security**	**1097**
		Understanding Troubleshooting Theory	1100
		Identifying the Problem	1101
		Establishing a Theory	1105
		Testing Solutions	1106
		Establishing a Plan of Action	1107
		Verifying Functionality	1109
		Documenting the Work	1109
		Troubleshooting Operating Systems	1110
		Common Symptoms	1110
		Operating System Tools	1118
		Troubleshooting Security Issues	1126
		Common Symptoms	1128
		Security Tools	1132
		Best Practices for Malware Removal	1136
		Troubleshooting Mobile Issues	1137
		Troubleshooting Mobile Security Issues	1139
		Summary	1142
		Exam Essentials	1142
		Review Questions	1143
		Performance-Based Question	1146
Chapter	23	**Understanding Operational Procedures**	**1147**
		Understanding Safety Procedures	1150
		Identifying Potential Safety Hazards	1151

Creating a Safe Workplace   1161
Understanding Environmental Controls   1170
    Managing the Physical Environment   1171
    Handling and Disposing of Computer Equipment   1177
Understanding Policies, Licensing,
    and Privacy   1186
    Managing Software Licenses   1186
    Managing Sensitive Information   1189
Demonstrating Professionalism   1191
    Communicating with Customers   1192
    Using Appropriate Behavior   1196
    Putting It All in Perspective   1202
Summary   1204
Exam Essentials   1204
Review Questions   1206
Performance-Based Question   1209

Appendix   A   Answers to Review Questions   1211

Chapter 1: Motherboards, Processors, and Memory   1212
Chapter 2: Storage Devices and Power Supplies   1214
Chapter 3: Peripherals and Expansion   1215
Chapter 4: Display Devices   1217
Chapter 5: Custom Configurations   1219
Chapter 6: Network Fundamentals   1221
Chapter 7: Introduction to TCP/IP   1222
Chapter 8: Installing Wireless and SOHO Networks   1224
Chapter 9: Understanding Laptops   1226
Chapter 10: Understanding Mobile Devices   1227
Chapter 11: Installing and Configuring Printers   1229
Chapter 12: Hardware and Network Troubleshooting   1230
Chapter 13: Operating System Basics   1232
Chapter 14: Operating System Administration   1233
Chapter 15: Working with Windows 8/8.1   1234
Chapter 16: Working with Windows 7   1235
Chapter 17: Working with Windows Vista   1236
Chapter 18: Working with Mac OS and Linux   1238
Chapter 19: Security   1239
Chapter 20: Network Services, Cloud Computing,
            and Virtualization   1240
Chapter 21: Mobile Operating
            Systems and Connectivity   1241
Chapter 22: Troubleshooting Theory,
            OSs, and Security   1243
Chapter 23: Understanding Operational Procedures   1244

Appendix	B	**Answers to Performance-Based Questions**	**1247**
		Chapter 1: Motherboards, Processors, and Memory	1248
		Chapter 2: Storage Devices and Power Supplies	1249
		Chapter 3: Peripherals and Expansion	1249
		Chapter 4: Display Devices	1249
		Chapter 5: Custom Configurations	1252
		Chapter 6: Network Fundamentals	1252
		Chapter 7: Introduction to TCP/IP	1254
		Chapter 8: Installing Wireless and SOHO Networks	1254
		Chapter 9: Understanding Laptops	1254
		Chapter 10: Understanding Mobile Devices	1256
		Chapter 11: Installing and Configuring Printers	1256
		Chapter 12: Hardware and Network Troubleshooting	1257
		Chapter 13: Operating System Basics	1257
		Chapter 14: Operating System Administration	1259
		Chapter 15: Working with Windows 8/8.1	1259
		Chapter 16: Working with Windows 7	1259
		Chapter 17: Working with Windows Vista	1262
		Chapter 18: Working with Mac OS and Linux	1264
		Chapter 19: Security	1264
		Chapter 20: Network Services, Cloud Computing, land Virtualization	1266
		Chapter 21: Mobile Operating Systems and Connectivity	1266
		Chapter 22: Troubleshooting Theory, OSs, and Security	1267
		Chapter 23: Understanding Operational Procedures	1267
		Index	*1269*

CompTIA.

Becoming a
CompTIA Certified
IT Professional is Easy

It's also the best way to reach greater
professional opportunities and rewards.

Why Get CompTIA Certified?

Growing Demand

Labor estimates predict some
technology fields will
experience growth of over 20%
by the year 2020.* CompTIA
certification qualifies the skills
required to join this workforce.

Higher Salaries

IT professionals with
certifications on their resume
command better jobs, earn
higher salaries and have more
doors open to new multiindustry
opportunities.

Verified Strengths

91% of hiring managers
indicate CompTIA certifications
are valuable in validating IT
expertise, making certification
the best way to demonstrate
your competency and
knowledge to employers.**

Universal Skills

CompTIA certifications are
vendor neutral—which means
that certified professionals can
proficiently work with an
extensive variety of hardware
and software found in most
organizations.

 **Learn** |  **Certify** |  **Work**

Learn	Certify	Work
Learn more about what the exam covers by reviewing the following:	Purchase a voucher at a Pearson VUE testing center or at CompTIAstore.com.	Congratulations on your CompTIA certification!

Learn more about what the exam covers by reviewing the following:

- Exam objectives for key study points.
- Sample questions for a general overview of what to expect on the exam and examples of question format.
- Visit online forums, like LinkedIn, to see what other IT professionals say about CompTIA exams.

Purchase a voucher at a Pearson VUE testing center or at CompTIAstore.com.

- Register for your exam at a Pearson VUE testing center.
- Visit pearsonvue.com/CompTIA to find the closest testing center to you.
- Schedule the exam online. You will be required to enter your voucher number or provide payment information at registration.
- Take your certification exam.

Congratulations on your CompTIA certification!

- Make sure to add your certification to your resume.
- Check out the CompTIA Certification Roadmap to plan your next career move.

Learn more: Certification.CompTIA.org/aplus

* Source: CompTIA 9th Annual Information Security Trends study: 500 U.S. IT and Business Executives Responsible for Security
** Source: CompTIA Employer Perceptions of IT Training and Certification
*** Source: 2013 IT Skills and Salary Report by CompTIA Authorized Partner

Introduction

Welcome to the CompTIA A+ Complete Study Guide. This is the third edition of our best-selling study guide for the A+ certification sponsored by CompTIA (Computing Technology Industry Association).

This book is written at an intermediate technical level; we assume that you already know how to *use* a personal computer and its basic peripherals, such as USB devices and printers, but we also recognize that you may be learning how to *service* some of that computer equipment for the first time. The exams cover basic computer service topics as well as some more advanced issues, and they cover some topics that anyone already working as a technician, whether with computers or not, should be familiar with. The exams are designed to test you on these topics in order to certify that you have enough knowledge to fix and upgrade some of the most widely used types of personal computers.

We've included review questions at the end of each chapter to give you a taste of what it's like to take the exams. If you're already working as a technical service or support technician, we recommend that you check out these questions first to gauge your level of knowledge. (You can also take the assessment test at the end of this introduction, which is designed to see how much you already know.)

Don't just study the questions and answers—the questions on the actual exams will be different from the practice ones included with this book. The exams are designed to test your knowledge of a concept or objective, so use this book to learn the objective behind the question.

You can mainly use the book to fill in the gaps in your current computer service knowledge. You may find, as many PC technicians have, that being well versed in all the technical aspects of the equipment is not enough to provide a satisfactory level of support—you must also have customer-relations skills. We include helpful hints to get the customers to help you help them.

What Is A+ Certification?

The A+ certification program was developed by the Computing Technology Industry Association (CompTIA) to provide an industry-wide means of certifying the competency of computer service technicians. The A+ certification is granted to those who have attained the level of knowledge and troubleshooting skills that are needed to provide capable support in the field of personal computers. It is similar to other certifications in the computer industry, such as the Cisco Certified Network Associate (CCNA) program and the Microsoft certification programs. The theory behind these certifications is that if you need to have service performed on any of their products, you would sooner call a technician who has been certified in one of the appropriate certification programs than just call the first "expert" in the phone book.

The A+ certification program was created to offer a wide-ranging certification, in the sense that it is intended to certify competence with personal computers and mobile devices from many different makers/vendors. You must pass two tests to become A+ certified:

- The A+ 220-901 exam, which covers basic computer concepts, PC hardware, basic networking, soft skills (such as customer service), and safety

- The A+ 220-902 exam, which covers operating systems, security, mobile devices, and troubleshooting

You don't have to take the 220-901 and the 220-902 exams at the same time. However, the A+ certification is not awarded until you've passed both tests.

Why Become A+ Certified?

There are several good reasons to get your A+ certification. The CompTIA Candidate's Information packet lists five major benefits:

- It demonstrates proof of professional achievement.

- It increases your marketability.

- It provides greater opportunity for advancement in your field.

- It is increasingly a requirement for some types of advanced training.

- It raises customer confidence in you and your company's services.

Provides Proof of Professional Achievement

The A+ certification is quickly becoming a status symbol in the computer service industry. Organizations that include members of the computer service industry are recognizing the benefits of A+ certification and are pushing for their members to become certified. And more people every day are putting the "A+ Certified Technician" emblem on their business cards.

Increases Your Marketability

A+ certification makes individuals more marketable to potential employers. A+ certified employees also may receive a higher base salary because employers won't have to spend as much money on vendor-specific training.

What Is an ASC?

More service companies are becoming CompTIA A+ Authorized Service Centers (ASCs). This means that over 50 percent of the technicians employed by such service centers are A+ certified. Customers and vendors alike recognize that ASCs employ the most qualified service technicians. As a result, an ASC gets more business than a nonauthorized service center. And, because more service centers want to reach the ASC level, they will give preference in hiring to a candidate who is A+ certified over one who is not.

Provides Opportunity for Advancement

Most raises and advancements are based on performance. A+ certified employees work faster and more efficiently and are thus more productive. The more productive employees are, the more money they make for their company. And, of course, the more money they make for the company, the more valuable they are to the company. So if an employee is A+ certified, their chances of being promoted are greater.

Fulfills Training Requirements

Most major computer hardware vendors recognize A+ certification. Some of these vendors apply A+ certification toward prerequisites in their own respective certification programs, which has the side benefit of reducing training costs for employers.

Raises Customer Confidence

As the A+ Certified Technician moniker becomes better known among computer owners, more of them will realize that the A+ technician is more qualified to work on their computer equipment than a noncertified technician.

How to Become A+ Certified

A+ certification is available to anyone who passes the tests. You don't have to work for any particular company. It's not a secret society. It is, however, an elite group. To become A+ certified, you must do two things:

- Pass the A+ 220-901 exam
- Pass the A+ 220-902 exam

The exams can be taken at any Pearson VUE testing center. If you pass both exams, you will get a certificate in the mail from CompTIA saying that you have passed, and you will also receive a lapel pin and business card.

To register for the tests, call Pearson VUE at (877) 551-PLUS (7587) or go to www.pearsonvue.com/comptia. You'll be asked for your name, Social Security number (an optional number may be assigned if you don't wish to provide your Social Security number), mailing address, phone number, employer, when and where you want to take the test, and your credit card number (arrangement for payment must be made at the time of registration).

Although you can save money by arranging to take more than one test at the same seating, there are no other discounts. If you have to repeat a test to get a passing grade, you must pay for each retake.

Tips for Taking the A+ Exam

Here are some general tips for taking your exam successfully:

- Bring two forms of ID with you. One must be a photo ID, such as a driver's license. The other can be a major credit card or a passport. Both forms must include a signature.

- Arrive early at the exam center so that you can relax and review your study materials, particularly tables and lists of exam-related information. When you enter the testing room, you will need to leave everything outside; you won't be able to bring any materials into the testing area.

- Read the questions carefully. Don't be tempted to jump to an early conclusion. Make sure that you know exactly what each question is asking.

- Don't leave any unanswered questions. Unanswered questions are scored against you. There will be questions with multiple correct responses. When there is more than one correct answer, a message at the bottom of the screen will prompt you to, for example, choose two. Be sure to read the messages displayed to know how many correct answers you must choose.

- When answering multiple-choice questions that you're not sure about, use a process of elimination to get rid of the obviously incorrect answers first. Doing so will improve your odds if you need to make an educated guess.

- On form-based tests (nonadaptive), because the hard questions will take the most time, save them for last. You can move forward and backward through the exam.

- For the latest pricing on the exams and updates to the registration procedures, visit CompTIA's website at www.comptia.org.

Who Should Read This Book?

If you are one of the many people who want to pass the A+ exams, and pass them confidently, then you should buy this book and use it to study for the exams.

This book was written to prepare you for the challenges of the real IT world, not just to pass the A+ exams. This study guide will do that by describing in detail the concepts on which you'll be tested.

What Does This Book Cover?

This book covers everything you need to know to pass the CompTIA A+ exams.

Part I of the book starts at Chapter 1 and concludes after Chapter 12. It will cover all of the topics on which you will be tested for Exam 220-901:

Chapter 1: Motherboards, Processors, and Memory   Chapter 1 details the characteristics of motherboards and their slots and built-in components. The CPU, RAM, and BIOS, which are attached to the motherboard, are also presented in Chapter 1.

Chapter 2: Storage Devices and Power Supplies   Chapter 2 presents the popular forms of storage devices in use today, including traditional hard drives, solid-state drives, flash drives, and memory cards. Capacities, form factors, and the makeup of these components are also discussed.

Chapter 3: Peripherals and Expansion   Chapter 3 covers installation and characteristics of expansion cards, the ports they and the motherboard present to the user, and the peripheral devices connected to these interfaces. Required cabling and its characteristics are also included.

Chapter 4: Display Devices   Chapter 4 runs the gamut of display devices and their characteristics. Everything from the familiar LCD and plasma panels to the cutting-edge organic LED is covered in this chapter.

Chapter 5: Custom Configurations   Chapter 5 presents information based on a newer objective outlining the specialized systems that we see more and more of in the field today. Examples include gaming PCs, graphic design and audio/video editing workstations, home theater PCs, and home servers.

Chapter 6: Networking Fundamentals   Chapter 6 covers characteristics of cable types and connectors, network devices, networking tools, and network topologies.

Chapter 7: Introduction to TCP/IP   Chapter 7 details the most common network protocol in use today. It covers TCP/IP structure, addressing (including IPv6), and common protocols in the suite.

Chapter 8: Installing Wireless and SOHO Networks   Chapter 8 contains two main sections. The first is on wireless networking standards and security, and the second discusses setting up a small office, home office (SOHO) network and choosing an Internet connection type.

Chapter 9: Understanding Laptops   Chapter 9 covers topics such as laptop-specific hardware, components within a laptop display, and laptop features.

Chapter 10: Understanding Mobile Devices   Chapter 10 covers topics related to mobile devices such as tablets, smartphones, e-readers, and wearable technology.

Chapter 11: Installing and Configuring Printers   Chapter 11 starts by discussing different printing technologies, such as impact, inkjet, and laser printers. It then moves on to cover installing printers and performing printer maintenance.

Chapter 12: Hardware and Network Troubleshooting   Chapter 12 covers the troubleshooting side of hardware and networking, including the need to identify and use the appropriate tools.

Part II of the book, Chapters 13 through 23, covers all of the topics on which you will be tested for Exam 220-902:

Chapter 13: Operating System Basics   Chapter 13 starts the examination of Microsoft Windows operating systems. CompTIA expects you to know how to administer three of them—Microsoft Windows 8/8.1, Windows 7, and Windows Vista. In addition, you will need to know about many of the various editions of each version.

Chapter 14: Operating System Administration   Chapter 14 continues the discussion begun in Chapter 13, and it looks at utilities and features that exist in each of the three versions of Windows operating systems that you need to know for the exam.

Chapter 15: Working with Windows 8/8.1   Chapter 15 focuses only on Windows 8/8.1. It's newest of the three versions of Windows operating systems tested on the 220-902 exam, and this chapter looks at its unique features.

Chapter 16: Working with Windows 7   Chapter 16 focuses only on Windows 7. This chapter looks at features unique to the Windows 7 Starter, Windows 7 Home Premium, Windows 7 Professional, Windows 7 Ultimate, and Windows 7 Enterprise editions.

Chapter 17: Working with Windows Vista   Chapter 17 examines Windows Vista and the features unique to the Windows Vista Home Basic, Windows Vista Home Premium, Windows Vista Business, Windows Vista Ultimate, and Windows Vista Enterprise editions.

Chapter 18: Working with Mac OS and Linux   Chapter 18 focuses on operating systems other than Microsoft Windows. It looks at Mac OS and Linux.

Chapter 19: Security   Just when you think this book couldn't get any better, we toss in a chapter devoted to security. This chapter looks at all of the security topics on the exam, and it includes information on social engineering, best practices, and securing SOHO networks—both wired and wireless.

Chapter 20: Network Services, Cloud Computing, and Virtualization   Chapter 20 focuses on the newest technologies related to networking with an emphasis on cloud computing and virtualization.

Chapter 21: Mobile Operating Systems and Connectivity   Chapter 21 details the similarities and differences between Apple- and Android-based mobile devices. This chapter provides extensive hands-on steps for configuring a variety of features and services on these devices.

Chapter 22: Troubleshooting Theory, OSs, and Security   If you collected a nickel every time someone requested a chapter on troubleshooting theory, you'd have enough to buy a decent pair of socks. Since CompTIA has an uncompromising view on the topic, you need to know the topic from the perspective of the objectives, and that is what you will find in Chapter 22.

Chapter 23: Understanding Operational Procedures   The last chapter in the book covers the "softer" side of working with computers. Topics include following safety procedures, understanding environmental impacts, practicing proper communication, and professionalism.

What's Included in the Book

We've included several learning tools throughout the book:

Assessment test   We have provided an assessment test that you can use to check your readiness for the exam at the end of this introduction. Take this test before you start reading the book; it will help you determine the areas on which you might need to brush up. The answers to the assessment test questions appear on a separate page after the last question of the test. Each answer includes an explanation and a note telling you the chapter in which the material appears.

Objective map and opening list of objectives   At the beginning of the book, we have included a detailed exam objective map showing you where each of the exam objectives is covered. In addition, each chapter opens with a list of the exam objectives it covers. Use these resources to see exactly where each of the exam topics is covered.

Exam essentials   Each chapter, just before the summary, includes a number of exam essentials. These are the key topics that you should take from the chapter in terms of areas on which you should focus when preparing for the exam.

Chapter review questions   To test your knowledge as you progress through the book, there are review questions at the end of each chapter. As you finish each chapter, answer the review questions and then check your answers—the correct answers and explanations are in Appendix A. You can go back to reread the section that deals with each question you got wrong to ensure that you answer correctly the next time that you're tested on the material.

Interactive Online Learning Environment and Test Bank

The interactive online learning environment that accompanies *CompTIA A+ Complete Study Guide Exam 220-901 and Exam 220-902* provides a test bank with study tools to help you prepare for the certification exams and increase your chances of passing them the first time! The test bank includes the following elements:

Sample tests   All of the questions in this book are provided, including the assessment test, which you'll find at the end of this introduction, and the chapter tests that include the review questions at the end of each chapter. In addition, there are four practice exams. Use these questions to test your knowledge of the study guide material. The online test bank runs on multiple devices.

Flashcards   Two sets of questions are provided in digital flashcard format (a question followed by a single correct answer). You can use the flashcards to reinforce your learning and provide last-minute test prep before the exam.

Glossary   The key terms from this book and their definitions are available as a fully searchable PDF.

Go to http://sybextestbanks.wiley.com to register and gain access to this interactive online learning environment and test bank with study tools.

How to Use This Book

If you want a solid foundation for preparing for the A+ exams, this is the book for you. We've spent countless hours putting together this book with the sole intention of helping you prepare for the exams.

This book is loaded with valuable information, and you will get the most out of your study time if you understand how we put the book together. Here's a list that describes how to approach studying:

1.   Take the assessment test immediately following this introduction. It's okay if you don't know any of the answers—that's what this book is for. Carefully read over the explanations for any question you get wrong, and make note of the chapters where that material is covered.

2.   Study each chapter carefully, making sure you fully understand the information and the exam objectives listed at the beginning of each one. Again, pay extra-close attention to any chapter that includes material covered in questions you missed on the assessment test.

3.   Read over the summary and exam essentials. These will highlight the sections from the chapter with which you need to be familiar before sitting for the exam.

4.   Answer all of the review questions at the end of each chapter. Specifically note any questions that confuse you, and study the corresponding sections of the book again. Don't just skim these questions! Make sure that you understand each answer completely.

5.   Go over the electronic flashcards. These help you prepare for the latest A+ exams, and they're really great study tools.

6.   Take the practice exams.

Performance-Based Questions

CompTIA includes performance-based questions on the A+ exams. These are not the traditional multiple-choice questions with which you're probably familiar. These questions
require the candidate to know how to perform a specific task or series of tasks. The candidate will be presented with a scenario and will be asked to complete a task. They will be
taken to a simulated environment where they will have to perform a series of steps and
will be graded on how well they complete the task.

The Sybex test engine does not include performance-based questions. However, at the
end of most chapters we have included a section called "Performance-Based Questions,"
which is designed to measure how well you understood the chapter topics. Some simply
ask you to complete a task for which there is only one correct response. Others are more
subjective, with multiple ways to complete the task. We will provide the most logical or
practical solution in Appendix B at the back of the book. Note that these may cover topic
areas not covered in the actual A+ performance-based questions. However, we feel that
being able to think logically is a great way to learn.

The CompTIA A+ Exam Objectives

The A+ exams consist of the 220-901 exam and the 220-902 exam. Following are the
detailed exam objectives for each test.

Exam objectives are subject to change at any time without prior notice and at
CompTIA's sole discretion. Please visit the A+ Certification page of CompTIA's website
(http://certification.comptia.org/getCertified/certifications/a.aspx) for the
most current listing of exam objectives.

A+ Certification Exam Objectives: 220-901

The following table lists the domains measured by this examination and the extent to
which they are represented on the exam:

Domain	Percentage of Exam
1.0 Hardware	34%
2.0 Networking	21%
3.0 Mobile Devices	17%
4.0 Hardware & Network Troubleshooting	28%

Objective	Chapter
1.0 Hardware	
1.1. Given a scenario, configure settings and use BIOS/UEFI tools on a PC	1

- Firmware upgrades—flash BIOS
- BIOS component information: RAM; hard drive; optical drive; CPU
- BIOS configurations: Boot sequence; enabling and disabling devices; date/time; clock speeds; virtualization support; BIOS security (passwords, drive encryption: TPM, lo-jack, secure boot)
- Built-in diagnostics
- Monitoring: Temperature monitoring; fan speeds; intrusion detection/notification; voltage; clock; bus speed

1

Objective	Chapter
1.2. Explain the importance of motherboard components, their purpose, and properties	1

- Sizes: ATX; Micro-ATX; Mini-ITX; ITX
- Expansion slots: PCI; PCI-X; PCIe; miniPCI
- RAM slots
- CPU sockets
- Chipsets: North Bridge; South Bridge
- CMOS battery
- Power connections and types
- Fan connectors
- Front/Top panel connectors: USB; audio; power button; power light; drive activity lights; reset button
- Bus speeds

1

Objective	Chapter
1.3. Compare and contrast RAM types and their features	1

- Types: DDR; DDR2; DDR3; SODIMM; DIMM; parity vs. non-parity; ECC vs. non-ECC; RAM configurations (single channel vs. dual channel vs. triple channel); single sided vs. double sided; buffered vs. unbuffered; RAM compatibility

1

Objective	Chapter
1.4. Install and configure PC expansion cards	3

- Sound cards
- Video cards
- Network cards
- USB cards
- FireWire cards
- Thunderbolt cards
- Storage cards
- Modem cards

3

Objective	Chapter
• Wireless/cellular cards	
• TV tuner cards	
• Video capture cards	
• Riser cards	

Objective	Chapter
1.5. Install and configure storage devices and use appropriate media	2
• Optical drives: CD-ROM/CD-RW; DVD-ROM/DVD-RW/DVD-RW DL; Blu-Ray; BD-R; BD-RE	2
• Magnetic hard disk drives: 5400 rpm; 7200 rpm; 10,000 rpm	
• Hot swappable drives	
• Solid state/flash drives: CompactFlash; SD; Micro-SD; Mini-SD; xD; SSD; hybrid; eMMC	
• RAID types: 0; 1; 5; 10	
• Tape drive	
• Media capacity: CD; CD-RW; DVD-RW; DVD; Blu-Ray; tape; DVD DL	

Objective	Chapter
1.6. Install various types of CPUs and apply the appropriate cooling methods	1
• Socket types	1
Intel: 775, 1155, 1156, 1366, 1150, 2011	
AMD: AM3, AM3+, FM1, FM2, FM2+	
• Characteristics: speeds; cores; cache size/type; hyperthreading; virtualization support; architecture (32-bit vs. 64-bit); integrated GPU; disable execute bit	
• Cooling: heat sink; fans; thermal paste; liquid-based;	
• fanless/passive	

Objective	Chapter
1.7. Compare and contrast various PC connection interfaces, their characteristics and purpose	3
• Physical connections	3
• USB 1.1 vs. 2.0 vs. 3.0:Connector types: A, B, mini, micro	
• FireWire 400 vs. FireWire 800	
• SATA1 vs. SATA2 vs. SATA3, eSATA	
• Other connector types: VGA; HDMI; DVI; Audio (analog, digital (optical connector)); RJ-45; RJ-11; Thunderbolt	
• Wireless connections: Bluetooth; RF; IR; NFC	
• Characteristics: analog; digital; distance limitations; data transfer speeds; quality; DRM; frequencies	

Objective	Chapter
1.8. Install a power supply based on given specifications	2
▪ Connector types and their voltages: SATA; Molex; 4/8-pin 12v; PCIe 6/8-pin; 20-pin; 24-pin	2
▪ Specifications: wattage; dual rail; size; number of connectors; ATX; Micro-ATX; dual-voltage options	
1.9. Given a scenario, select the appropriate components for a custom PC configuration, to meet customer specifications or needs	5
▪ Graphic/CAD/CAM design workstation: multicore processor, high-end video, maximum RAM	5
▪ Audio/video editing workstation: specialized audio and video card, large fast hard drive, dual monitors	
▪ Virtualization workstation: maximum RAM and CPU cores	
▪ Gaming PC: multicore processor, high-end video/specialized GPU, high definition sound card, high-end cooling	
▪ Home Theater PC: surround sound audio, HDMI output, HTPC compact form factor, TV tuner	
▪ Standard thick client: desktop applications, meets recommended requirements for selected OS	
▪ Thin client: basic applications, meets minimum requirements for selected OS; network connectivity	
▪ Home server PC: media streaming, file sharing, print sharing, Gigabit NIC, RAID array	
1.10. Compare and contrast types of display devices and their features	4
▪ Types: LCD (TN vs. IPS; fluorescent vs. LED backlighting); Plasma; Projector; OLED	4
▪ Refresh/frame rates	
▪ Resolution	
▪ Native resolution	
▪ Brightness/lumens	
▪ Analog vs. digital	
▪ Privacy/antiglare filters	
▪ Multiple displays	
▪ Aspect ratios: 16:9; 16:10; 4:3	
1.11. Identify common PC connector types and associated cables	3
▪ Display connector types: DVI-D; DVI-I; DVI-A; DisplayPort; RCA; HD15 (i.e. DE15 or DB15); BNC; miniHDMI; miniDin-6	

Objective	Chapter
▪ Display cable types: HDMI; DVI; VGA; component; composite; coaxial	3
▪ Device cables and connectors: SATA; eSATA; USB; Firewire (IEEE1394); PS/2; audio	
▪ Adapters and convertors: DVI to HDMI; USB A to USB B; USB to Ethernet; DVI to VGA; Thunderbolt to DVI; PS/2 to USB; HDMI to VGA	
1.12. Install and configure common peripheral devices	3
▪ Input devices: mouse; keyboard; scanner; barcode reader; biometric devices; game pads; joysticks; digitizer; motion sensor; touch pads; smart card readers; digital cameras; microphone; webcam; camcorder	3
▪ Output devices: printers; speakers; display devices	
▪ Input & output devices: touch screen; KVM; smart TV; set-top box; MIDI-enabled devices	
1.13. Install SOHO multifunction device / printers and configure appropriate settings	11
▪ Use appropriate drivers for a given operating system: Configuration settings (duplex; collate; orientation; quality)	11
▪ Device sharing: wired (USB; serial; Ethernet); Wireless (Bluetooth; 802.11(a, b, g, n, ac); Infrastructure vs. ad hoc); integrated print server (hardware); cloud printing/remote printing	
▪ Public/shared devices: sharing local/networked device via operating system settings (TCP/Bonjour/AirPrint); Data privacy (user authentication on the device; hard drive caching)	
1.14. Compare and contrast differences between the various print technologies and the associated imaging process	11
▪ Laser: imaging drum, fuser assembly, transfer belt, transfer roller, pickup rollers, separate pads, duplexing assembly. Imaging process: processing, charging, exposing, developing, transferring, fusing and cleaning.	11
▪ Inkjet: ink cartridge, print head, roller, feeder, duplexing assembly, carriage and belt; calibration.	
▪ Thermal: Feed assembly, heating element; special thermal paper	
▪ Impact: Print head, ribbon, tractor feed; impact paper	
▪ Virtual: print to file; print to PDF; print to XPS; print to image	
1.15. Given a scenario, perform appropriate printer maintenance	11
▪ Laser: replacing toner, applying maintenance kit, calibration, cleaning	11
▪ Thermal: replace paper, clean heating element, remove debris	
▪ Impact: replace ribbon, replace print head, replace paper	
▪ Inkjet: clean heads, replace cartridges, calibration, clear jams	

Objective	Chapter
2.0 Networking	
2.1. Identify the various types of network cables and connectors	6
▪ Fiber: Connectors: SC, ST, and LC	6
▪ Twisted Pair: Connectors: RJ-11, RJ-45; wiring standards: T568A, T568B	
▪ Coaxial: Connectors: BNC, F-connector	
2.2. Compare and contrast the characteristics of connectors and cabling	6
▪ Fiber: Types (single-mode vs. multi-mode); speed and transmission limitations	6
▪ Twisted pair: Types: STP, UTP, CAT3, CAT5, CAT5e, CAT6, CAT6e, CAT7, plenum, PVC; speed and transmission limitations; splitters and effects on signal quality	
▪ Coaxial: Types: RG-6, RG-59; speed and transmission limitations; splitters and effects on signal quality	
2.3. Explain the properties and characteristics of TCP/IP	7
▪ IPv4 vs. IPv6	7
▪ Public vs. private vs. APIPA/link local	
▪ Static vs. dynamic	
▪ Client-side DNS settings	
▪ Client-side DHCP	
▪ Subnet mask vs. CIDR	
▪ Gateway	
2.4. Explain common TCP and UDP ports, protocols, and their purpose	7
▪ Ports: 21 – FTP; 22 – SSH; 23 – TELNET; 25 – SMTP; 53 – DNS; 80 – HTTP; 110 – POP3; 143 – IMAP; 443 – HTTPS; 3389 – RDP; 137–139, 445 – SMB; 548 or 427 – AFP	7
▪ Protocols: DHCP; DNS; LDAP; SNMP; SMB; CIFS; SSH; AFP	
▪ TCP vs. UDP	
2.5. Compare and contrast various WiFi networking standards and encryption types	8
▪ Standards: 802.11 a/b/g/n/ac; speeds; distances; and frequencies	8
▪ Encryption types: WEP; WPA; WPA2; TKIP; AES	
2.6. Given a scenario, install and configure SOHO wireless/wired router and apply appropriate settings	8
▪ Channels	8
▪ Port forwarding, port triggering	

Objective	Chapter
• DHCP (on/off)	
• DMZ	
• NAT/DNAT	
• Basic QoS	
• Firmware	
• UPnP	
2.7. Compare and contrast Internet connection types, network types, and their features	8
• Internet connection types: cable; DSL; dial-up; fiber; satellite; ISDN; cellular (tethering; mobile hotspot); line of sight wireless Internet service	8
• Network types: LAN; WAN; PAN; MAN	
2.8. Compare and contrast network architecture devices, their functions, and features	6
• Hub	6
• Switch	
• Router	
• Access point	
• Bridge	
• Modem	
• Firewall	
• Patch panel	
• Repeaters/extenders	
• Ethernet over power	
• Power over Ethernet injector	
2.9. Given a scenario, use appropriate networking tools	12
• Crimper	12
• Cable stripper	
• Multimeter	
• Toner generator & probe	
• Cable tester	
• Loopback plug	
• Punchdown tool	
• WiFi analyzer	

3.0 Mobile Devices

3.1. Install and configure laptop hardware and components	9

Objective	Chapter
■ Expansion options: express card /34; express card /54;SODIMM; Flash; ports/adapters (Thunderbolt; DisplayPort; USB to RJ-45 dongle; USB to WiFi dongle; USB to Bluetooth; USB optical drive)	9
■ Hardware/device replacement: keyboard; hard drive (SSD vs. hybrid vs. magnetic disk; 1.8in vs. 2.5in); memory; smart card reader; optical drive; wireless card; Mini-PCIe; screen; DC jack; battery; touchpad; plastics/frames; speaker; system board; CPU	
3.2. Explain the functions of components within the display of a laptop	9
■ Types: LCD (TTL vs. IPS; fluorescent vs. LED backlighting); OLED	9
■ Wi-Fi antenna connector/placement	
■ Webcam	
■ Microphone	
■ Inverter	
■ Digitizer	
3.3. Given a scenario, use appropriate laptop features	9
■ Special function keys: dual displays; wireless (on/off); cellular (on/off); volume settings; screen brightness; Bluetooth (on/off); keyboard backlight; touch pad (on/off); screen orientation; media options (fast forward/rewind); GPS (on/off); airplane mode	9
■ Docking station	
■ Physical laptop lock and cable lock	
■ Rotating/removable screens	
3.4. Explain the characteristics of various types of other mobile devices	10
■ Tablets	10
■ Smart phones	
■ Wearable technology devices: smart watches; fitness monitors; glasses and headsets	
■ Phablets	
■ e-Readers	
■ Smart camera	
■ GPS	
3.5. Compare and contrast accessories & ports of other mobile devices	10
■ Connection types: NFC; proprietary vendor specific ports (communication/power); microUSB/miniUSB; Lightning; Bluetooth; IR; hotspot/tethering	10
■ Accessories: headsets; speakers; game pads; docking stations; extra battery packs/battery chargers; protective covers/water proofing; credit card readers; memory/MicroSD	

Objective	Chapter
4.0 Hardware and Network Troubleshooting	
4.1. Given a scenario, troubleshoot common problems related to motherboards, RAM, CPU and power with appropriate tools	12
▪ Common symptoms: unexpected shutdowns; system lockups; POST code beeps; blank screen on bootup; BIOS time and settings resets; attempts to boot to incorrect device; continuous reboots; no power; overheating; loud noise; intermittent device failure; fans spin—no power to other devices; indicator lights; smoke; burning smell; proprietary crash screens (BSOD/pin wheel); distended capacitors	12
▪ Tools: multimeter; power supply tester; loopback plugs; POST card/ USB	
4.2. Given a scenario, troubleshoot hard drives and RAID arrays with appropriate tools	12
▪ Common symptoms: read/write failure; slow performance; loud clicking noise; failure to boot; drive not recognized; OS not found; RAID not found; RAID stops working; proprietary crash screens (BSOD/pin wheel); S.M.A.R.T. errors	12
▪ Tools: screwdriver; external enclosures; CHKDSK; FORMAT; file recovery software; bootrec; diskpart; defragmentation tool	
4.3. Given a scenario, troubleshoot common video, projector and display issues	12
▪ Common symptoms: VGA mode; no image on screen; overheat shutdown; dead pixels; artifacts; color patterns incorrect; dim image; flickering image; distorted image; distorted geometry; burn-in; oversized images and icons	12
4.4. Given a scenario, troubleshoot wired and wireless networks with appropriate tools	12
▪ Common symptoms: no connectivity; APIPA/link local address; limited connectivity; local connectivity; intermittent connectivity; IP conflict; slow transfer speeds; low RF signal; SSID not found	12
▪ tools: cable tester; loopback plug; punch down tools; tone generator and probe; wire strippers; crimper; wireless locator	
▪ Command line tools: PING; IPCONFIG/IFCONFIG; TRACERT; NETSTAT; NBTSTAT; NET; NETDOM; NSLOOKUP	
4.5. Given a scenario, troubleshoot, and repair common mobile device issues while adhering to the appropriate procedures	12
▪ Common symptoms: no display; dim display; flickering display; sticking keys; intermittent wireless; battery not charging; ghost cursor/pointer drift; no power; num lock indicator lights; no wireless connectivity; no Bluetooth connectivity; cannot display to external monitor; touchscreen non-responsive; apps not loading; slow performance; unable to decrypt email; extremely short battery life; overheating; frozen system; no sound from speakers; GPS not functioning; swollen battery	12
▪ Disassembling processes for proper re-assembly: document and label cable and screw locations; organize parts; refer to manufacturer resources; use appropriate hand tools	

4.6. Given a scenario, troubleshoot printers with appropriate tools	12

- Common symptoms: streaks; faded prints; ghost images; toner not fused to the paper; creased paper; paper not feeding; paper jam; no connectivity; garbled characters on paper; vertical lines on page; backed up print queue; low memory errors; access denied; printer will not print; color prints in wrong print color; unable to install printer; error codes; printing blank pages; no image on printer display   **12**
- Tools: maintenance kit; toner vacuum; compressed air; printer spooler

A+ Certification Exam Objectives: 220-902

The following table lists the domains measured by this examination and the extent to which they are represented on the exam.

Domain	Percentage of Exam
1.0 Windows Operating Systems	29%
2.0 Other Operating Systems & Technologies	12%
3.0 Security	22%
4.0 Software Troubleshooting	24%
5.0 Operational Procedures	13%
Total	100%

Objective	Chapter
1.0 Windows Operating Systems	
1.1. Compare and contrast various features and requirements of Microsoft Operating Systems (Windows Vista, Windows 7, Windows 8, Windows 8.1).	15, 16, 17
■ Features: 32-bit vs. 64-bit; Aero; gadgets; user account control; bit-locker; shadow copy; system restore; ready boost; sidebar; compatibility mode; virtual XP mode; easy transfer; administrative tools; defender; Windows firewall; security center; event viewer; file structure and paths; category view vs. classic view; Side by side apps; Metro UI; pinning; One Drive; Windows store; multimonitor task bars; charms; start screen; power shell; Live sign in; action center	15, 16, 17
■ Upgrade paths—differences between in place upgrades; compatibility tools; Windows upgrade OS advisor	

Objective	Chapter
1.2. Given a scenario, install Windows PC operating systems using appropriate method	15, 16, 17
■ Boot methods: USB; CD-ROM; DVD; PXE; solid state/flash drives; netboot; external/hot swappable drive; internal hard drive (partition)	15, 16, 17
■ Type of installations: unattended installation; upgrade; clean install; repair installation; multiboot; remote network installation; image deployment; recovery partition; refresh/restore	
■ Partitioning: dynamic; basic; primary; extended; logical; GPT	
■ File system types/formatting: ExFAT; FAT32; NTFS; CDFS; NFS; ext3, ext4; quick format vs. full format	
■ Load alternate third party drivers when necessary	
■ Workgroup vs. Domain setup	
■ Time/date/region/language settings	
■ Driver installation, software and windows updates	
■ Factory recovery partition	
■ Properly formatted boot drive with the correct partition/format	
1.3. Given a scenario, apply appropriate Microsoft command line tools	14
■ TASKKILL; BOOTREC; SHUTDOWN; TASKLIST; MD; RD; CD; DEL; FORMAT; COPY; XCOPY; ROBOCOPY; DISKPART; SFC; CHKDSK; GPUPDATE; GPRE-SULT; DIR; EXIT; HELP; EXPAND; [command name] /?; commands available with standard privileges vs. administrative privileges	14
1.4. Given a scenario, use appropriate Microsoft operating system features and tools.	14
■ Administrative: computer management; device manager; local users and groups; local security policy; performance monitor; services; system configuration; task scheduler; component services; data sources; print management; Windows memory diagnostics; Windows firewall; advanced security	14
■ MSCONFIG: general; boot; services; startup; tools	
■ Task Manager: applications; processes; performance; networking; users	
■ Disk management: drive status; mounting; initializing; extending partitions; splitting partitions; shrink partitions; assigning/changing drive letters; adding drives; adding arrays; storage spaces	
■ Other: User State Migration tool (USMT); Windows Easy Transfer; Windows Upgrade Advisor	
■ System utilities: REGEDIT; COMMAND; SERVICES.MSC; MMC; MSTSC; NOTEPAD; EXPLORER; MSINFO32; DXDIAG; DEFRAG; System restore; Windows Update	
1.5. Given a scenario, use Windows Control Panel utilities	14

Objective	Chapter
■ Internet options: Connections; Security; General; Privacy; Programs; Advanced	14
■ Display/Display Settings: Resolution; Color depth; refresh rate	
■ User accounts	
■ Folder options: View hidden files; Hide extensions; general options; view options	
■ System: Performance (virtual memory); Remote settings; System protection	
■ Windows firewall	
■ Power options: Hibernate; power plans; Sleep/suspend; Standby	
■ Programs and features	
■ HomeGroup	
■ Devices and Printers	
■ Sound	
■ Troubleshooting	
■ Network and Sharing Center	
■ Device Manager	
1.6. Given a scenario, install and configure Windows networking on a client/desktop.	15, 16, 17
■ HomeGroup vs. Workgroup	15, 16, 17
■ Domain setup	
■ Network shares/administrative shares/mapping drives	
■ Printer sharing vs. network printer mapping	
■ Establish networking connections: VPN; dialups; wireless; wired; WWAN (cellular)	
■ Proxy settings	
■ Remote desktop connection	
■ Remote assistance	
■ Home vs. Work vs. Public network settings	
■ Firewall settings: exceptions; configuration; enabling/disabling Windows firewall	
■ Configuring an alternative IP address in Windows: IP addressing; subnet mask; DNS; gateway	
■ Network card properties: half duplex/full duplex/auto; speed; Wake-on-LAN; QoS; BIOS (on-board NIC)	
1.7. Perform common preventive maintenance procedures using the appropriate Windows OS tools	14
■ Best practices: scheduled backups; scheduled disk maintenance; Windows updates; patch management; driver/firmware updates; antivirus/antimalware updates	14
■ Tools: Backup; System Restore; recovery image; disk maintenance utilities	

Objective	Chapter
2.0 Other Operating Systems and Technologies	
2.1. Identify common features and functionality of the Mac OS and Linux operating systems	18
▪ Best practices: Scheduled backups; scheduled disk maintenance; system updates/App store; patch management; driver/firmware updates; antivirus/ antimalware updates	18
▪ Tools: Backup/Time Machine; Restore/snapshot; image recovery; disk maintenance utilities; shell/terminal; screen sharing; force quit	
▪ Features: Multiple desktops/Mission Control; Key Chain; Spot Light; iCloud; gestures; Finder; Remote Disc; Dock; Boot Camp	
▪ Basic Linux commands: ls; grep; cd; shutdown; pwd vs. passwd; mv; cp; rm; chmod; chown; iwconfig/ifconfig; ps; q; su/sudo; apt-get; vi; dd	
2.2. Given a scenario, setup and use client-side virtualization	20
▪ Purpose of virtual machines	20
▪ Resource requirements	
▪ Emulator requirements	
▪ Security requirements	
▪ Network requirements	
▪ Hypervisor	
2.3. Identify basic cloud concepts	20
▪ SaaS	20
▪ IaaS	
▪ PaaS	
▪ Public vs. Private vs. Hybrid vs. Community	
▪ Rapid elasticity	
▪ On-demand	
▪ Resource pooling	
▪ Measured service	
2.4. Summarize the properties and purpose of services provided by networked hosts	20
▪ Server roles: Web server, file server; print server; DHCP server; DNS server; proxy server; mail server; authentication server	20
▪ Internet appliance: UTM; IDS; IPS	
▪ Legacy / embedded systems	
2.5. Identify basic features of mobile operating systems	21

Objective	Chapter
▪ Android vs. iOS vs. Windows	21
▪ Open source vs. closed source/vendor specific	
▪ App source (play store, app store and store)	
▪ Screen orientation (accelerometer/gyroscope)	
▪ Screen calibration	
▪ GPS and geotracking	
▪ WiFi calling	
▪ Launcher/GUI	
▪ Virtual assistant	
▪ SDK/APK	
▪ Emergency notification	
▪ Mobile payment service	
2.6. Install and configure basic mobile device network connectivity and email	21
▪ Wireless / cellular data network (enable/disable): hotspot; tethering; airplane mode	21
▪ Bluetooth: enable Bluetooth; enable pairing; find device for pairing; enter appropriate pin code; test connectivity	
▪ Corporate and ISP email configuration: POP3; IMAP; port and SSL settings; Exchange, S/MIME	
▪ Integrated commercial provider email configuration: Google/Inbox; Yahoo; Outlook.com; iCloud	
▪ PRI updates/PRL updates/baseband updates	
▪ Radio firmware	
▪ IMEI vs. IMSI	
▪ VPN	
2.7. Summarize methods and data related to mobile device synchronization	21
▪ Types of data to synchronize: contacts; programs; email; pictures; music; videos; calendar; bookmarks; documents; location data; social media data; eBooks	21
▪ Synchronization methods: synchronize to the cloud; synchronize to the desktop	
▪ Mutual authentication for multiple services	
▪ Software requirements to install the application on the PC	
▪ Connection types to enable synchronization	
3.0 Security	
3.1. Identify common security threats and vulnerability	19

Objective	Chapter
■ Malware: spyware; viruses; worms; Trojans; rootkits; ransomware	19
■ Phishing	
■ Spear phishing	
■ Spoofing	
■ Social engineering	
■ Shoulder surfing	
■ Zero day attack	
■ Zombie/botnet	
■ Brute forcing	
■ Dictionary attacks	
■ Non-compliant systems	
■ Violations of security best practices	
■ Tailgating	
■ Man-in-the-middle	
3.2. Compare and contrast common prevention methods	19
■ Physical security: lock doors; mantrap; cable locks; securing physical documents/passwords/shredding; biometrics; ID badges; key fobs; RFID badge; smart card; tokens; privacy filters; entry control roster	19
■ Digital security: antivirus/antimalware; firewalls; user authentication/strong passwords; multifactor authentication; directory permissions; VPN; DLP; Disabling ports; Access control lists; smart card; email filtering; trusted/untrusted software sources	
■ User education/AUP	
■ Principle of least privilege	
3.3. Compare and contrast differences of basic Windows OS security settings	19
■ User and groups: administrator; power user; guest; standard user	19
■ NTFS vs. share permissions: allow vs. deny; moving vs. copying folders and files; file attributes	
■ Shared files and folders: administrative shares vs. local shares; permission propagation; inheritance	
■ System files and folders	
■ User authentication: single sign-on	
■ Run as administrator vs. standard user	
■ Bitlocker	
■ Bitlocker-to-Go	
■ EFS	

Objective	Chapter
3.4. Given a scenario, deploy and enforce security best practices to secure a workstation	19
■ Password best practices: Setting strong passwords; Password expiration; Changing default user names/passwords; Screensaver required password; BIOS/UEFI passwords; Requiring passwords ■ Account management: Restricting user permissions; Login time restrictions; Disabling guest account; Failed attempts lockout; Timeout/screen lock ■ Disable autorun ■ Data encryption ■ Patch/update management	19
3.5. Compare and contrast various methods for securing mobile devices	17
■ Screen locks: fingerprint lock; face lock; swipe lock; passcode lock ■ Remote wipes ■ Locator applications ■ Remote backup applications ■ Failed login attempts restrictions ■ Antivirus/antimalware ■ Patching/OS updates ■ Biometric authentication ■ Full device encryption ■ Multifactor authentication ■ Authenticator applications ■ Trusted sources vs. untrusted sources ■ Firewalls ■ Policies and procedures: BYOD vs. corporate owned; profile security requirements	17
3.6. Given a scenario, use appropriate data destruction and disposal methods	17
■ Physical destruction: shredder; drill/hammer; electromagnetic (degaussing); incineration; certificate of destruction ■ Recycling or repurposing best practices: Low level format vs. standard format; overwrite; drive wipe	17
3.7. Given a scenario; secure SOHO wired and wireless networks	17
■ Wireless specific: Changing default SSID; Setting encryption; Disabling SSID broadcast; Antenna and access point placement; Radio power levels; WPS ■ Change default usernames and passwords ■ Enable MAC filtering	17

Objective	Chapter
▪ Assign static IP addresses	17
▪ Firewall settings	
▪ Port forwarding/mapping	
▪ Disabling ports	
▪ Content filtering/parental controls	
▪ Update firmware	
▪ Physical security	

4.0 Software Troubleshooting

4.1. Given a scenario, troubleshoot PC operating system problems with appropriate tools	22
▪ Common symptoms: Proprietary crash screens (BSOD/pin wheel); failure to boot; improper shutdown; spontaneous shutdown/restart; device fails to start/detected; missing dll message; services fails to start; compatibility error; slow system performance; boots to safe mode; file fails to open; missing BOOTMGR; missing Boot Configuration Data; missing operating system; missing graphical interface; missing GRUB/LILO; kernel panic; graphical interface fails to load; multiple monitor misalignment/orientation	22
▪ Tools: BIOS/UEFI; SFC; logs; system recovery options; repair disks; pre-installation environments; MSCONFIG; DEFRAG; REGSRV32; REGEDIT; event viewer; safe mode; command prompt; uninstall/reinstall/repair	22
4.2. Given a scenario, troubleshoot common PC security issues with appropriate tools and best practices	22
▪ Common symptoms: pop-ups; browser redirection; security alerts; slow performance; internet connectivity issues; PC/OS lock up; application crash; OS update failures; rogue antivirus; spam; renamed system files; files disappearing; file permission changes; hijacked email (responses from users regarding email; automated replies from unknown sent mail); access denied; invalid certificate (trusted root CA)	22
▪ Tools: anti-virus software; anti-malware software; system recovery options; terminal; system restore/snapshot; pre-installation environments; event viewer; refresh/restore; MSCONFIG/safe boot	
▪ Best practices for malware removal: Identify malware symptoms; Quarantine infected system; Disable system restore (in Windows); Remediate infected systems (Update antimalware software; Scan and removal techniques (safe mode; pre-installation environment)); Schedule scans and run updates; Enable system restore and create restore point (in Windows); Educate end user	
4.3. Given a scenario, troubleshoot common mobile OS and application issues with appropriate tools	22

Objective	Chapter
• Common symptoms: dim display; intermittent wireless; no wireless connectivity; no Bluetooth connectivity; cannot broadcast to external monitor; touchscreen non-responsive; apps not loading; slow performance; unable to decrypt email; extremely short battery life; overheating; frozen system; no sound from speakers; inaccurate touch screen response; system lockout	22
• Tools: hard reset; soft reset; close running applications; reset to factory default; adjust configurations/settings; uninstall/reinstall apps; force stop	
4.4. Given a scenario, troubleshoot common mobile OS and application security issues with appropriate tools	22
• Common symptoms: signal drop/weak signal; power drain; slow data speeds; unintended WiFi connection; unintended Bluetooth pairing; leaked personal files/data; data transmission overlimit; unauthorized account access; unauthorized root access; unauthorized location tracking; unauthorized camera/microphone activation; high resource utilization	22
• Tools: antimalware; app scanner; factory reset/clean install; uninstall/reinstall apps; WiFi analyzer; force stop; cell tower analyzer; backup/restore (iTunes/iCloud/Apple Configurator; Google sync; One Drive)	
5.0 Operational Procedures	
5.1. Given a scenario, use appropriate safety procedures	23
• Equipment grounding	23
• Proper component handling and storage: antistatic bags; ESD straps; ESD mats; Self-grounding	
• Toxic waste handling: batteries; toner; CRT	
• Personal safety: disconnect power before repairing PC; remove jewelry; lifting techniques; weight limitations; electrical fire safety, cable management; safety goggles; air filter mask	
• Compliance with local government regulations	
5.2. Given a scenario with potential environmental impacts, apply the appropriate controls	23
• MSDS documentation for handling and disposal	23
• Temperature, humidity level awareness and proper ventilation	
• Power surges, brownouts, blackouts: battery backup; surge suppressor	
• Protection from airborne particles: enclosures; air filters/mask	
• Dust and debris: compressed air; vacuums	
• Compliance to local government regulations	
5.3. Summarize the process of addressing prohibited content/activity, and explain privacy, licensing, and policy concepts	23

Objective	Chapter
▪ Incident response: First response (identify; report through proper channels; data/device preservation); Use of documentation/documentation changes; Chain of custody (tracking of evidence/documenting process)	23
▪ Licensing/DRM/EULA: open source vs. commercial license; personal license vs. enterprise licenses	
▪ Personally Identifiable Information	
▪ Follow corporate end-user policies and security best practices	
5.4. Demonstrate proper communication techniques and professionalism	23
▪ Use proper language – avoid jargon, acronyms, slang when applicable	23
▪ Maintain a positive attitude / Project confidence	
▪ Actively listen (taking notes) and avoid interrupting the customer	
▪ Be culturally sensitive: use appropriate professional titles, when applicable	
▪ Be on time (if late contact the customer)	
▪ Avoid distractions: personal calls; texting/social media sites; talking to co-workers while interacting with customers; personal interruptions	
▪ Dealing with difficult customer or situation: do not argue with customers and/or be defensive; avoid dismissing customer problems; avoid being judgmental; clarify customer statements (ask open ended questions to narrow the scope of the problem, restate the issue or question to verify understanding); do not disclose experiences via social media	
▪ Set and meet expectations/timeline and communicate status with the customer: offer different repair/replacement options if available; provide proper documentation on the services provided; follow up with customer/user at a later date to verify satisfaction	
▪ Deal appropriately with customers confidential and private materials: located on a computer, desktop, printer, etc.	
5.5. Given a scenario, explain the troubleshooting theory.	23
▪ Always consider corporate policies, procedures and impacts before implementing changes.	23
▪ Identify the problem: Question the user and identify user changes to computer and perform backups before making changes	
▪ Establish a theory of probable cause (question the obvious): If necessary, conduct external or internal research based on symptoms	
▪ Test the theory to determine cause: Once theory is confirmed determine next steps to resolve problem; If theory is not confirmed re-establish new theory or escalate	
▪ Establish a plan of action to resolve the problem and implement the solution	
▪ Verify full system functionality and if applicable implement preventive measures	
▪ Document findings, actions and outcomes	

Exam objectives are subject to change at any time without prior notice at CompTIA's sole discretion. Please visit CompTIA's website (www.comptia.org) for the most current listing of exam objectives.

Assessment Test

1. Which of the following is *not* considered a system component that can be found inside a computer?

   A. CPU

   B. RAM

   C. PCIe graphics adapter

   D. Motherboard

2. Which of the following is a physical memory format installed directly in today's desktop computer systems?

   A. DIMM

   B. HDD

   C. SSD

   D. eMMC

3. Which of the following are components that can commonly be found on a motherboard? (Choose all that apply.)

   A. Slots

   B. Fan connectors

   C. Gyroscope

   D. Scanner

   E. HDD

4. What suffix indicates that the capacity of an optical disc is roughly twice that of its standard counterpart?

   A. DL

   B. R

   C. RW

   D. RE

5. What is the name of the standard power connector that has been used with larger drives since the first IBM personal computers were introduced?

   A. AT system connector

   B. Berg

   C. Molex

   D. ATX system connector

6. Except in the case of RAID 0, which two things do all types of RAID offer?

   A. Faster read speeds

   B. Faster write speeds

    C. Redundancy

    D. Fault tolerance

    E. Ability to restore automatically from tape after a drive failure

7. You are installing a new graphics adapter in a Windows 7 system. Which of the following expansion slots is designed for high-speed, 3D graphics adapters?

    A. USB

    B. FireWire

    C. PCI

    D. PCIe

8. A user complains that changing from a VGA graphics card to one that supports the latest HDMI revision has resulted in not being able to play back certain content from the computer. Some content does play back, however. What could be the problem?

    A. Digital signal required

    B. Resolution too low

    C. DRM

    D. VGA cable not compatible

9. Which of the following are modular ports used in data communications? (Choose two.)

    A. RG-6

    B. RJ-45

    C. RJ-11

    D. Thunderbolt

    E. RG-11

10. The _____ is the measurement of the number of pixels an LCD monitor can display without the image appearing distorted.

    A. Native resolution

    B. Contrast ratio

    C. Pixelation

    D. Base frequency

11. Which of the following is *not* a common monitor technology?

    A. LCD

    B. Plasma

    C. OLED

    D. Super PMOLED

12. What can be used at the check-in desk of a doctor's office to prevent patients from viewing confidential information?

   A. An antiglare filter

   B. A privacy filter

   C. An LED-backlit display

   D. A thin client

13. Which of the following is a standard computer that can access resources locally as well as from servers but requires no specialized enhancements?

   A. Gaming PC

   B. Home server

   C. Thin client

   D. Thick client

14. Which of the following is a requirement for virtualization workstations?

   A. Enhanced video

   B. Enhanced audio

   C. Maximum RAM and CPU cores

   D. RAID array

15. Which of the following is *not* a requirement for a home server PC?

   A. TV tuner

   B. Print and file sharing services

   C. Gigabit NIC

   D. RAID array

16. Which network connectivity device stops broadcasts from being sent to computers on a different network segment?

   A. Hub

   B. Switch

   C. Router

   D. Firewall

17. Which layer of the OSI model has the important role of providing error checking?

   A. Session layer

   B. Presentation layer

   C. Application layer

   D. Transport layer

18. On which port does FTP run by default?

   A. 21

   B. 25

   C. 63

   D. 89

19. Which of the following protocols can be used by a client to access email on a server?

   A. DNS

   B. FTP

   C. SMTP

   D. IMAP

20. Which of the following is a company that provides direct access to the Internet for home and business computer users?

   A. ASP

   B. ISP

   C. DNS

   D. DNP

21. What is the data throughput provided by one ISDN bearer channel?

   A. 16Kbps

   B. 56Kbps

   C. 64Kbps

   D. 128Kbps

22. Which LCD component in a laptop is responsible for providing brightness?

   A. Backlight

   B. Inverter

   C. Screen

   D. Backdrop

23. Your laptop has 2GB of installed memory and uses shared video memory. If the video card is using 512MB, how much is left for the rest of the system?

   A. 2GB

   B. 1.5GB

   C. 512MB

   D. Cannot determine

24. Which of the following standards supports both PCIe and USB 3.0?

   A. PC Card

   B. PlugCard

C. ExpandCard

D. ExpressCard

25. When using a capacitive touchscreen on a mobile device, what is the most common tool used to input data?

A. Keyboard

B. Trackball

C. Stylus

D. Finger

26. Which technology used by e-Readers gives them longer battery life than tablets?

A. Lithium-polymer battery

B. Low-power backlight

C. Electrophoretic ink

D. Capacitive touchscreen

27. What is the name of the mode that allows two NFC-enabled devices to transmit data to each other?

A. Emulation mode

B. Peer-to-peer mode

C. Reader/writer mode

D. Ad hoc mode

28. What is the function of the laser in a laser printer?

A. It heats up the toner so that it adheres to the page.

B. It charges the paper so that it will attract toner.

C. It creates an image of the page on the drum.

D. It cleans the drum before a page is printed.

29. What is the component called that stores the material that ends up printed to the page in a laser printer?

A. Toner cartridge

B. Ink cartridge

C. Laser module

D. Laser cartridge

30. What service was created by Apple to allow iPhones and iPads to print without installing printer drivers?

A. TCP printing

B. Bonjour

C. AirPrint

D. iPrint

31. Your laser printer has recently starting printing vertical white lines on the documents that it prints. What is the most likely cause of the problem?

  A. The print driver is faulty.

  B. The fuser is not heating properly.

  C. There is toner on the transfer corona wire.

  D. There is a scratch on the EP drum.

32. You are working with a Windows 7 computer that is assigned IP configuration information from a central server. You wish to refresh the IP information on the system manually. Which of the following commands would you use?

  A. `IPCONFIG /refresh`

  B. `IPCONFIG /all`

  C. `IPCONFIG /renew`

  D. `WINIPCFG /all`

33. One laser printer in your office experiences frequent paper jams. What is the most likely cause of the problem?

  A. Worn paper feed rollers.

  B. Faulty stepper motor.

  C. Faulty fuser assembly.

  D. The EP drum isn't advancing properly.

34. One of your network users was recently caught browsing pornographic websites at work. Which of the following servers could be installed to prohibit this activity?

  A. Web

  B. Security

  C. Proxy

  D. DNS

35. Google Docs is an example of what type of cloud service?

  A. SaaS

  B. IaaS

  C. PaaS

  D. GaaS

36. Which type of software is required to run client-side virtualization on your home network?

  A. Terminal emulation

  B. Process replication

  C. Hyperthreading

  D. Hypervisor

37. Which of the following are popular mobile-device operating systems? (Choose all that apply.)

   A. Android

   B. Windows 7

   C. Ubuntu

   D. iOS

38. Which of the following protocols can be used in close range to transfer data between a mobile device and a computer system or to allow media to stream from the mobile device to an audio system?

   A. SMTP

   B. Bluetooth

   C. NFC

   D. Pegasus

39. What term refers to copying data between a mobile device and a computer system to mirror such things as contacts, programs, pictures, and music?

   A. Calibration

   B. Remote wipe

   C. Pairing

   D. Synchronization

40. Which of the following computer components can retain a lethal electrical charge even after the device is unplugged? (Choose two.)

   A. Monitor

   B. Processor

   C. Power supply

   D. RAM

41. Roughly how much time spent communicating should be devoted to listening?

   A. 23 percent

   B. 40 percent

   C. 50 percent

   D. 80 percent

42. You have found prohibited content on a user's machine and need to follow proper procedures. What is the term used to describe the handling of evidence from discovery to delivery to the proper authorities?

   A. First response

   B. Chain of custody

   C. Data preservation

   D. Documentation flow changes

43. Which of the following is a security mechanism used by HTTPS to encrypt web traffic between a web client and server?

   A. IPSec

   B. SSL

   C. L2TP

   D. PPPoE

44. Which of the following are 4G technologies? (Choose all that apply.)

   A. LTE

   B. GSM

   C. CDMA

   D. WiMax

45. Which of the following standards is also known as CardBus?

   A. PCMCIA 1.0

   B. PCMCIA 2.0

   C. PCMCIA 5.0

   D. ExpressCard

46. When lifting heavy equipment, what is the proper technique?

   A. Get the heaviest part closest to your body and lift with your legs.

   B. Get the heaviest part closest to your body and lift with your back.

   C. Get the lightest part closest to your body and lift with your legs.

   D. Get the lightest part closest to your body and lift with your back.

47. Which of the following is a chip that is integrated into PATA drives, as opposed to being mounted on a daughter card?

   A. Controller

   B. CPU

   C. Host adapter

   D. IDE

48. After SATA was introduced, what was the retroactive term used for the original ATA specification?

   A. EIDE

   B. IDE

   C. PATA

   D. SCSI

49. Which of the following is a virtual machine manager—the software that allows the virtual machines to exist?

   A. Comptroller

   B. Shell

   C. Kernel

   D. Hypervisor

50. Which of the following would *not* be considered a standard permission in Windows using NTFS?

   A. Full Control

   B. Modify

   C. Allow

   D. Write

51. Which feature is designed to keep Windows current by automatically downloading updates such as patches and security fixes and installing these fixes automatically?

   A. Security Center

   B. Action Center

   C. Windows Update

   D. Windows Anytime

52. With dynamic storage, which of the following partition types are possible?

   A. Complex, bridged, or mirrored

   B. Simple, spanned, or striped

   C. Simple, complex, or interleaved

   D. Spanned, interleaved, or striped

53. You have been told to use Task Manager to change the priority of a process to Below Normal. This equates to a base priority of what?

   A. 2

   B. 4

   C. 6

   D. 8

54. Encrypting File System (EFS) is available in which editions of Windows 7? (Choose all that apply.)

   A. Professional

   B. Home Premium

   C. Enterprise

   D. Ultimate

   E. Business

55. Which of the following can provide electrical power over Ethernet cabling?

  A. PoE

  B. QoS

  C. DoS

  D. WoL

56. With which type of duplexing do communications travel in both directions but in only one direction at any given time?

  A. Full

  B. Half

  C. Auto

  D. Mechanical

57. Which applet in Windows Vista is the primary interface for configuring synchronization of offline files?

  A. Synchronization Wizard

  B. Action Center

  C. Merge

  D. Sync Center

58. Which Control Panel applet allows you to administer, as well as deploy, component services and configure behavior like security?

  A. SFC

  B. Data Sources

  C. Component Services

  D. DDR

59. In Windows, the Account Lockout Counter in an Account Lockout policy keeps track of the number of invalid attempts before lockout occurs. The default is 0 (meaning the feature is turned off), but it can be set from 1 to what?

  A. 9999

  B. 999

  C. 99

  D. 24

60. What Windows operating system tool can be used to block access from the network (be it internal or the Internet)?

  A. Windows Firewall

  B. Windows Defender

  C. Advanced Security

  D. Device Manager

61. Which of the following are programs that enter a system or network under the guise of another program? (Choose the best answer.)

   A. Worms

   B. Trojans

   C. Rootkits

   D. Spyware

62. Which of the following involves applying a strong magnetic field to initialize the media before tossing it away?

   A. Fraying

   B. Fracking

   C. Degaussing

   D. Spreading

63. Which term is synonymous with *MAC filtering*?

   A. Disabling Autorun

   B. Shredding

   C. Port disabling

   D. Network Lock

64. Which of the following is a copy of your system configuration at a given point in time?

   A. Restore point

   B. MBR

   C. Registry

   D. BOOT.INI

65. Which of the following could be described as a small, deviously ingenious program that replicates itself to other computers, generally causing those computers to behave abnormally? (Choose the best answer.)

   A. Rogue

   B. Redirector

   C. Virus

   D. Pop-up

Answers to Assessment Test

1. **C.** System components are essential for the basic functionality of a computer system. Many of the landmarks found on the motherboard can be considered system components, even expansion slots to a degree. What you plug into those slots, however, must be considered peripheral to the basic operation of the system. For more information, see Chapter 1.

2. **A.** Except for DIMMs, all options represent some form of secondary storage, all of which are covered in Chapter 2. For more information, see Chapter 1.

3. **A, B.** Motherboards commonly have RAM slots and expansion slots. Older motherboards even had CPU slots. Modern motherboards have connectors for powering cooling fans. Gyroscopes are most commonly found in mobile devices. Scanners are external devices. Although there might be one or more types of HDD interfaces built into the motherboard, the HDD itself is not. For more information, see Chapter 1.

4. **A.** DL stands for double or dual layer. With DVDs, the capacity almost doubles, but with Blu-ray discs, it actually does. For more information, see Chapter 2.

5. **C.** The standard peripheral power connector, or Molex connector, is commonly used on larger drives because it allows more current to flow to the drive than smaller peripheral connectors. For more information, see Chapter 2.

6. **C, D.** Except for RAID 0, all implementations of RAID offer a way to recover from the failure of at least one drive, which is an example of fault tolerance, through the implementation of some mechanism that stores redundant information for that purpose. Some RAID types offer faster read and/or write performance. RAID 1, for instance does not guarantee either. For more information, see Chapter 2.

7. **D.** Although technically PCI could be used for graphics adapters, PCIe supports high-speed, 3D graphic video cards. PCIe offers better performance than older graphics adapters. USB and FireWire can stream video, but they are not used for attachment of graphics adapters. For more information, see Chapter 3.

8. **C.** Digital rights management (DRM), using High-bandwidth Content Protection (HDCP), is supported by adapters and monitors that support HDMI and later versions of DVI. If the content is protected, HDMI in the adapter will use HDCP to encrypt the stream across the cable, and the monitor will use HDCP to decrypt it for playback. From the information given, it cannot be assumed that the monitor changed when the adapter did. As a result, the monitor might have an older DVI-D port that uses a passive converter to receive the HDMI cable's signal but that does not support HDCP. The signal over the HDMI cable is always digital. As a result, a VGA cable, which only supports analog signals, cannot be used when a DVI-D or HDMI interface is involved. HDMI supports all resolutions supported by a VGA interface. For more information, see Chapter 3.

9. **B, C.** RJ-11 ports are used in analog telephony, and they allow modems attached to computer serial ports to transmit modulated digital information across the public switched telephone network (PSTN). RJ-45 ports are used by various network interface controller (NIC) cards for attachment to networks such as Ethernet. RG-6 and RG-11 are coaxial cable types, and Thunderbolt connectors are not modular. For more information, see Chapter 3.

10. **A.** The native resolution refers to how many pixels an LCD screen can display (across and down) without distortion. The native resolution is based on the placement of the actual transistors that create the image by twisting the liquid crystals. The contrast ratio is the measurement between the darkest color and the lightest color that an LCD screen can display. For more information, see Chapter 4.

11. **D.** Although there *is* a Super AMOLED display, employing active-matrix technology, there is no corresponding "super" passive-matrix version. The other technologies exist and are discussed in further detail in Chapter 4.

12. **B.** Privacy filters are used to limit the viewing angle for a monitor. With such filters, the screen image becomes indiscernible when viewed at just a few degrees from center. For more information, see Chapter 4.

13. **D.** A thick client is any computer system with a standard configuration. The gaming PC has enhancements over thick clients to their CPU, video, audio, and cooling. The home server PC must have specialized capabilities and services along with a faster NIC than the thick client and a RAID array. The thin client is a lesser device in comparison to the thick client, but that cost-saving feature is its enhancement. These less expensive computers can connect over the network to servers for their operating system images and applications. For more information, see Chapter 5.

14. **C.** Virtualization workstations require more RAM than standard systems and need to be equipped with as many multicore processors as possible. Video and audio are not resources that need to be enhanced for such workstations. Although a RAID array is a wise addition whenever servers with valuable information are involved, a virtualization workstation does not require one. For more information, see Chapter 5.

15. **A.** A TV tuner card is a requirement for a home theater PC but not for a home server. The other options are among those features that are required. For more information, see Chapter 5.

16. **C.** A router does not pass along broadcasts to computers on other segments. Hubs and switches send broadcasts along because they do not segment traffic at the logical network address level. See Chapter 6 for more information.

17. **D.** A key role of the Transport layer is to provide error checking. The Transport layer also provides functions such as reliable end-to-end communications, segmentation and reassembly of larger messages, and combining smaller messages into a single larger message. See Chapter 6 for more information.

18. **A.** FTP listens on port 21. See Chapter 7 for more information.

19. **D.** The IMAP and POP3 protocols can be used to retrieve email from mail servers. See Chapter 7 for more information.

20. **B.** An Internet service provider (ISP) provides direct access to the Internet. See Chapter 8 for more information.

21. **C.** An ISDN B (bearer) channel provides 64Kbps data throughput. A home-based BRI ISDN provides two B channels. See Chapter 8 for more information.

22. A. The backlight provides light to the LCD screen. The inverter provides power to the backlight, and the screen displays the picture. See Chapter 9 for more information.

23. B. If the laptop is using shared video memory, then the system memory is shared with the video card. If the video card is using 512MB (half a gigabyte), then there is 1.5GB left for the system. See Chapter 9 for more information.

24. D. ExpressCard supports PCIe and USB 3.0. See Chapter 9 for more information.

25. D. Capacitive touchscreens react to slight changes in electrical charges. The human finger is used as an input device for capacitive touchscreens. For more information, see Chapter 10.

26. C. e-Readers use electrophoretic ink, also known as E Ink. E Ink uses less energy than other LCD displays, prolonging battery life. For more information, see Chapter 10.

27. B. Card emulation mode, reader/writer mode, and peer-to-peer mode are the three valid NFC communication modes. For two devices to transmit to each other, they will use peer-to-peer mode. For more information, see Chapter 10.

28. C. The laser creates an image on the photosensitive drum that is then transferred to the paper by the transfer corona. The fuser heats up the toner so that it adheres to the page. The transfer corona charges the page, and the eraser lamp cleans the drum before a page is printed. A rubber blade is also used to remove toner physically from the drum. See Chapter 11 for more information.

29. A. Laser printers use toner, which they melt to the page in the image of the text and graphics being printed. A toner cartridge holds the fine toner dust until it is used in the printing process. See Chapter 11 for more information.

30. C. AirPrint was created by Apple to let iPhones and iPads print without installing a printer driver. See Chapter 11 for more information.

31. C. Toner on the transfer corona wire is most likely the cause of white streaks on printouts. A scratch or a groove in the EP drum causes vertical black lines. If the fuser was not heating properly, toner would not bond to the paper and you would have smearing. Faulty print drivers will cause garbage to print or there will be no printing at all. See Chapter 12 for more information.

32. C. The IPCONFIG utility can be used with Windows computers to see the networking configuration values at the command line. It is one of the most commonly used command-line utilities that can be used in troubleshooting and network configurations. To renew IP configuration information, the IPCONFIG /renew command is used to force the DHCP server to renew the IP information assigned to the system. See Chapter 12 for more information.

33. A. The most likely cause of those listed is a worn paper feed roller. Stepper motors control the back-and-forth motion of a print head in an inkjet printer. If the fuser assembly were faulty, the images would smear. See Chapter 12 for more information.

34. C. A proxy server can be configured to block access to websites containing potentially objectionable material. See Chapter 20 for more information.

35. A. Google Docs is software, so it is an example of Software as a Service (SaaS). See Chapter 20 for more information.

36. D. The hypervisor is the key piece of software needed for virtualization. See Chapter 20 for more information.

37. A, D. Google's Android and Apple's iOS are two of the most popular operating systems for mobile devices on the market. The other two are not. Although some mobile operating systems are based on Linux or UNIX, Ubuntu is a Linux distribution not used for mobile devices. For more information, see Chapter 21.

38. B. Bluetooth allows you to pair a mobile device to a computer or to a device such as an automotive sound system or headset. Data can be transferred between devices, and media can be streamed from the mobile device. For more information, see Chapter 21.

39. D. Synchronizing a mobile device with a computer system allows you to mirror personal data between the devices, regardless of which one contains the most current data. Calibration refers to matching the device's and user's perceptions of where the user is touching the screen. Remote wipes allow you to remove personal data from a lost or stolen device. Pairing is what must be done in Bluetooth for two Bluetooth devices to connect and communicate. For more information, see Chapter 21.

40. A, C. Monitors and power supplies can retain significant electrical charges, even after they're unplugged. Don't open the back of a monitor or the power supply unless you are specifically trained to do so. See Chapter 23 for more information.

41. C. Roughly half the time spent communicating should be devoted to listening. See Chapter 23 for more information.

42. B. *Chain of custody* describes the procedure used to track handling and the location of evidence in the event of an incident such as discovering illegal or improper material on a user's computer. See Chapter 23 for more information.

43. B. HTTPS connections are secured using either Secure Sockets Layer (SSL) or Transport Layer Security (TLS).

44. A, D. WiMax and LTE are the two current 4G cellular technologies. GSM and CDMA are 3G technologies.

45. C. PCMCIA 5.0 is also known as CardBus.

46. A. When lifting heavy equipment, center the weight as close to your body as possible. Then, keep your back straight and lift with your legs.

47. A. A controller chip is responsible for encoding data to be stored on the disk platters as well as performing geometry translation for the BIOS. Translation is necessary because the true number of sectors per track of the hard disk drive system usually exceeds what is supported by the BIOS.

48. C. *IDE* (ATA-1) and *EIDE* (ATA-2 and later) were specific nicknames for the ATA series of standards. Although *ATA* is technically accurate, it refers to legacy IDE standards as well as newer SATA standards. Instead of using the term *ATA* to be synonymous with *IDE* and *EIDE*, as had been done in the past, the term *PATA* was coined, referring to the parallel nature of IDE communications. The term *PATA* differentiates the IDE and EIDE form of ATA from Serial ATA. SCSI is a related, yet completely different type of technology.

49. D. The hypervisor is a virtual machine manager—the software that allows the virtual machines to exist.

50. C. Standard permissions are collections of special permissions, including Full Control, Modify, Read & Execute, Read, and Write.

51. C. Windows includes Windows Update, a feature designed to keep Windows current by automatically downloading updates such as patches and security fixes and installing these fixes automatically.

52. B. Windows supports both basic and dynamic storage. Basic can have a primary and an extended partition, while dynamic can be simple, spanned, or striped.

53. C. For applications that don't need to drop all of the way down to Low, this equates to a base priority of 6.

54. A, C, D. EFS is available in the Professional, Enterprise, and Ultimate editions of Windows 7, allowing for encryption/decryption on files stored in NTFS volumes.

55. A. Power over Ethernet (PoE) is a handy technology to supply both power and an Ethernet connection. The purpose of Power over Ethernet (PoE) is pretty much described in its name: Electrical power is transmitted over twisted-pair Ethernet cable (along with data).

56. B. With half duplex, communications travel in both directions but in only one direction at any given time.

57. D. The Sync Center in Windows Vista is the primary interface for configuring synchronization.

58. C. Component Services allows you to administer as well as deploy component services and configure behavior like security.

59. B. It can be set from 1 to 999.

60. A. Windows Firewall (Start ➤ Control Panel ➤ Windows Firewall) is used to block access from the network (be it internal or the Internet).

61. B. Trojans are programs that enter a system or network under the guise of another program. While rootkits *may* do this, it is not their primary feature and thus not the best answer for this question.

62. C. Degaussing involves applying a strong magnetic field to initialize the media (this is also referred to as disk wiping). This process helps ensure that information doesn't fall into the wrong hands.

63. D. On a number of wireless devices, the term Network Lock is used in place of *MAC filtering*, and the two are synonymous.

64. A. A restore point is a copy of your system configuration at a given point in time. It's like a backup of your configuration but not necessarily your data.

65. C. A computer virus is a small, deviously ingenious program that replicates itself to other computers, generally causing those computers to behave abnormally. Generally speaking, a virus's main function is to reproduce.

CompTIA® A+®
Complete
Study Guide
Exam 220-901
Exam 220-902
Third Edition

Part I: 220-901

PART

I

Chapter

1

Motherboards, Processors, and Memory

THE FOLLOWING COMPTIA A+ 220-901 OBJECTIVES ARE COVERED IN THIS CHAPTER:

✓ **1.1 Given a scenario, configure settings and use BIOS/ UEFI tools on a PC.**

- Install firmware upgrades – flash BIOS

- BIOS component information: RAM, Hard drive, Optical drive, CPU, Boot sequence, Enabling and disabling devices, Date/time, Clock speeds, Virtualization support

- BIOS security (passwords, drive encryption: TPM, lo-jack, secure boot)

- Use built-in diagnostics

- Monitoring: Temperature monitoring, Fan speeds, Intrusion detection/notification, Voltage, Clock, Bus speed

✓ **1.2 Explain the importance of motherboard components, their purposes, and properties.**

- Sizes: ATX, Micro-ATX, Mini-ITX, ITX)

- Expansion slots: PCI, PCI-X, PCIe, miniPCI

- RAM slots

- CPU sockets

- Chipsets: Northbridge/Southbridge, CMOS battery

- Power connections and types

- Fan connectors

- Front/top panel connectors: USB, Audio, Power button, Power light, Drive activity lights, Reset button

- Bus speeds

✓ **1.3 Compare and contrast RAM types and features.**

- Types: DDR, DDR2, DDR3, SODIMM, DIMM, Parity vs. non-parity, ECC vs. non-ECC, RAM configurations (Single channel vs. dual channel vs. triple channel), Single sided vs. double sided, Buffered vs. unbuffered

- RAM compatibility and speed

✓ **1.6 Differentiate among various CPU types and features, and select the appropriate cooling method.**

- Socket types: Intel (775, 1155, 1156, 1366, 1150, 2011), AMD (AM3, AM3+, FM1, FM2, FM2+)

- Characteristics (Speeds, Cores, Cache size/type, Hyper-threading, Virtualization support, Architecture [32-bit vs. 64-bit], Integrated GPU, Disable execute bit)

- Cooling (Heat sink, Fans, Thermal paste, Liquid-based, Fanless/passive)

A personal computer (PC) is a computing device made up of many distinct electronic components that all function together in order to accomplish some useful task, such as adding up the numbers in a spreadsheet or helping you write a letter. Note that this definition describes a computer as having many distinct parts that work together. Most computers today are modular. That is, they have components that can be removed and replaced with another component of the same function but with different specifications in order to improve performance. Each component has a specific function. In this chapter, you will learn about the core components that make up a typical PC, what their functions are, and how they work together inside the PC.

Unless specifically mentioned otherwise, throughout this book the terms *PC* and *computer* are used interchangeably.

In this chapter, you will learn how to identify system components common to most personal computers, including the following:

- Motherboards
- Processors
- Memory
- Cooling systems

Identifying Components of Motherboards

The spine of the computer is the *motherboard*, otherwise known as the system board or mainboard. This is the *printed circuit board (PCB)*, which is a conductive series of pathways laminated to a nonconductive substrate that lines the bottom of the computer and is often of a uniform color, such as olive, brown, or blue. It is the most important component in the computer because it connects all of the other components together. Figure 1.1 shows a typical PC system board, as seen from above. All other components are attached to this circuit board. On the system board, you will find the central processing unit (CPU), underlying circuitry, expansion slots, video components, random access memory (RAM) slots, and a variety of other chips. We will be discussing each of these components throughout this book.

FIGURE 1.1 A typical system board

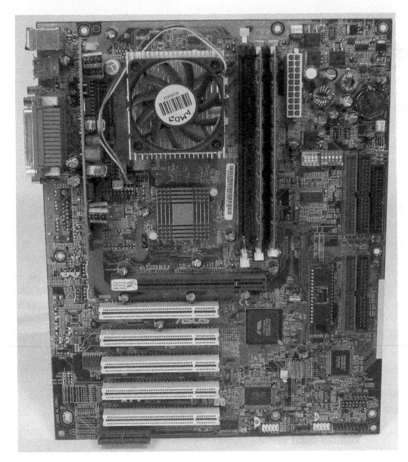

System Board Form Factors

System boards are classified by their form factor (design), such as ATX, micro ATX, and ITX. Exercise care and vigilance when acquiring a motherboard and case separately. Some cases are less accommodating than others, and they might not be physically compatible with the motherboard you choose.

Advanced Technology Extended

Intel developed the *Advanced Technology Extended (ATX)* motherboard in the mid-1990s to improve upon the classic AT-style motherboard architecture that had ruled the PC world for many years. The ATX motherboard has the processor and memory slots at right angles to the expansion cards. This arrangement puts the processor and memory in line with the fan output of the power supply, allowing the processor to run cooler. And because those components are not in line with the expansion cards, you can install full-length expansion cards—adapters that extend the full length of the inside of a standard computer case—in an ATX motherboard machine. ATX (and its derivatives) is the primary motherboard in use today. Standard ATX motherboards measure 12" × 9.6" (305mm × 244mm).

Micro ATX

A form factor that is designed to work in standard ATX cases, as well as its own smaller cases, is known as *micro ATX* (also referred to as µATX). Micro ATX follows the ATX principle of component placement for enhanced cooling over pre-ATX designs but with a smaller footprint. Some trade-offs come with this smaller form. For the compact use of space, you must give up quantity; that is, quantity of memory slots, motherboard headers, expansion slots, and integrated components. You also have fewer micro ATX chassis bays, although the same small-scale motherboard can fit into much larger cases if your original peripherals are still a requirement.

Be aware that micro ATX systems tend to be designed with power supplies of lower wattage in order to help keep power consumption and heat production down. This is generally acceptable with the standard, reduced micro ATX suite of components. As more off-board USB ports are added and larger cases are used with additional in-case peripherals, a larger power supply might be required.

Micro ATX motherboards share their width, mounting hole pattern, and rear interface pattern with ATX motherboards but are shallower and square, measuring 9.6" × 9.6" (244mm × 244mm). They were designed to be able to fit into full-size ATX cases. Figure 1.2 shows a full-size ATX motherboard next to a micro ATX motherboard.

FIGURE 1.2 ATX and micro ATX motherboards

Micro ATX

ATX

VIA Mini-ITX Form Factor Comparison by VIA Gallery from Hsintien, Taiwan - VIA Mini-ITX Form Factor Comparison uploaded by Kozuch. Licensed under CC BY 2.0 via Commons

ITX

The *ITX* line of motherboard form factors was developed by VIA as a low-power, small form factor (SFF) board for specialty uses, such as home-theater systems and embedded components. ITX itself is not an actual form factor but a family of form factors. The family consists of the following form factors:

- Mini-ITX—6.7″ × 6.7″ (170mm × 170mm)
- Nano-ITX—4.7″ × 4.7″ (120mm × 120mm)
- Pico-ITX—3.9″ × 2.8″ (100mm × 72mm)
- Mobile-ITX—2.4″ × 2.4″ (60mm × 60mm)

The *mini-ITX* motherboard has four mounting holes that line up with three or four of the holes in the ATX and micro ATX form factors. In mini-ITX boards, the rear interfaces are placed in the same location as those on the ATX motherboards. These features make mini-ITX boards compatible with ATX chassis. This is where the mounting compatibility ends because despite the PC compatibility of the other ITX form factors, they are used in embedded systems, such as set-top boxes, and lack the requisite mounting and interface specifications. Figure 1.3 shows the three larger forms of ITX motherboard.

FIGURE 1.3   ITX motherboards

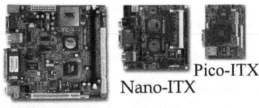

Mini-ITX   Nano-ITX   Pico-ITX

VIA Mainboards Form Factor Comparison by VIA Gallery from Hsintien, Taiwan - VIA Mainboards Form Factor Comparison uploaded by Kozuch. Licensed under CC BY 2.0 via Commons

System Board Components

Now that you understand the basic types of motherboards and their form factors, it's time to look at the components found on the motherboard and their locations relative to each other. Many of the following components can be found on a typical motherboard:

- Chipsets
- Expansion slots and buses
- Memory slots and external cache
- CPUs and their sockets
- Power connectors
- Onboard disk drive connectors

- Keyboard connectors
- Integrated peripheral ports and headers
- BIOS/firmware
- CMOS battery
- Front-panel connectors

In the following sections, you will learn about some of the most common components of a motherboard, what they do, and where they are located on the motherboard. We'll show what each component looks like so that you can identify it on most any motherboard that you run across. In the case of some components, this chapter provides only a brief introduction, with more detail to come in later chapters.

Before we can talk about specific components, however, you need to understand the concepts underlying serial and parallel connectivity, the two main categories of bus architecture.

Bus Architecture

There has been a quiet revolution taking place in the computer industry for quite some time now. Unlike in the early days of personal computing, when parallel communication pathways (made up of multiple synchronized wires or traces) dominated single-file serial connections, this revolution has brought a shift toward serial communications. Once engineers created transmitters and receivers capable of sustaining data rates many times those of parallel connections, they found no need to tie these pathways together in a parallel circuit. The downside of parallel communications is the loss of circuit length and throughput—how far the signal can travel and the amount of data moved per unit of time, respectively—due to the careful synchronization of the separate lines, the speed of which must be controlled to limit skewing the arrival of the individual signals at the receiving end.

The only limitation of serial circuits is in the capability of the transceivers, which tends to grow over time at a refreshing rate due to technical advancements. Examples of specifications that have heralded the migration toward the dominance of serial communications are Serial ATA (SATA), Universal Serial Bus (USB), IEEE 1394/FireWire, and Peripheral Component Interconnect Express (PCIe).

Parallel computer-system components work on the basis of a bus. A *bus*, in this sense, is a common collection of signal pathways over which related devices communicate within the computer system. Slots are incorporated at certain points in expansion buses of various architectures, such as PCI, to allow for the insertion of external devices, or adapters, usually with no regard as to which adapters are inserted into which slots; insertion is generally arbitrary. Other types of buses exist within the system to allow communication between the CPU and components with which data must be exchanged. Except for CPU slots and sockets and memory slots, there are no insertion points in such closed buses because no adapters exist for such an environment.

The term *bus* is also used in any parallel or bit-serial wiring implementation where multiple devices can be attached at the same time in parallel or in series (daisy-chained). Examples include Small Computer System Interface (SCSI), USB, and Ethernet.

The various buses throughout a given computer system can be rated by their bus speeds. The higher the bus speed, the higher the performance of which the bus is capable. In some cases, various buses must be synchronized for proper performance, such as the system bus and any expansion buses that run at the frontside-bus speed. Other times, one bus will reference another for its own speed. The internal bus speed of a CPU is derived from the frontside-bus clock, for instance. The buses presented throughout this chapter are accompanied by their speeds, where appropriate.

Chipsets

A *chipset* is a collection of chips or circuits that perform interface and peripheral functions for the processor. This collection of chips is usually the circuitry that provides interfaces for memory, expansion cards, and onboard peripherals, and it generally dictates how a motherboard will communicate with the installed peripherals.

Chipsets are usually given a name and model number by the original manufacturer. Typically, the manufacturer and model also tell you that your particular chipset has a certain set of features (for example, type of RAM supported, type and brand of onboard video, and so on).

Chipsets can be made up of one or several integrated circuit chips. Intel-based motherboards, for example, typically use two chips. To know for sure, you must check the manufacturer's documentation, especially because cooling mechanisms frequently obscure today's chipset chips, sometimes hindering visual brand and model identification.

Chipsets can be divided into two major functional groups, called Northbridge and Southbridge. Let's take a brief look at these groups and the functions they perform.

Northbridge

The *Northbridge* subset of a motherboard's chipset is the set of circuitry or chips that performs one very important function: management of high-speed peripheral communications. The Northbridge is responsible primarily for communications with integrated video using PCIe, for instance, and processor-to-memory communications. Therefore, it can be said that much of the true performance of a PC relies on the specifications of the Northbridge component and its communications capability with the peripherals it controls.

 When we use the term *Northbridge*, we are referring to a functional subset of a motherboard's chipset. There isn't actually a Northbridge brand of chipset.

The communications between the CPU and memory occur over what is known as the *frontside bus (FSB)*, which is just a set of signal pathways connecting the CPU and main memory, for instance. The clock signal that drives the FSB is used to drive communications by certain other devices, such as PCIe slots, making them local-bus technologies. The *backside bus (BSB)*, if present, is a set of signal pathways between the CPU and Level 2 or Level 3 (external) cache memory. The BSB uses the same clock signal that drives the FSB. If no backside bus exists, cache is placed on the frontside bus with the CPU and main memory.

The Northbridge is directly connected to the Southbridge (discussed next). It controls the Southbridge and helps to manage the communications between the Southbridge and the rest of the computer.

Southbridge

The *Southbridge* subset of the chipset is responsible for providing support to the slower onboard peripherals (PS/2, parallel ports, serial ports, Serial and Parallel ATA, and so on), managing their communications with the rest of the computer and the resources given to them. These components do not need to keep up with the external clock of the CPU and do not represent a bottleneck in the overall performance of the system. Any component that would impose such a restriction on the system should eventually be developed for FSB attachment.

In other words, if you're considering any component other than the CPU, memory and cache, or PCIe slots, the Southbridge is in charge. Most motherboards today have integrated PS/2, USB, LAN, analog and digital audio, and FireWire ports for the Southbridge to manage, for example, all of which are discussed in more detail later in this chapter or in Chapter 3, "Peripherals and Expansion." The Southbridge is also responsible for managing communications with the slower expansion buses, such as PCI, and legacy buses.

Figure 1.4 is a photo of the chipset of a motherboard, with the heat sink of the Northbridge at the top left, connected to the heat-spreading cover of the Southbridge at the bottom right.

FIGURE 1.4   A modern computer chipset

Figure 1.5 shows a schematic of a typical motherboard chipset (both Northbridge and Southbridge) and the components with which they interface. Notice which components interface with which parts of the chipset.

FIGURE 1.5 A schematic of a typical motherboard chipset

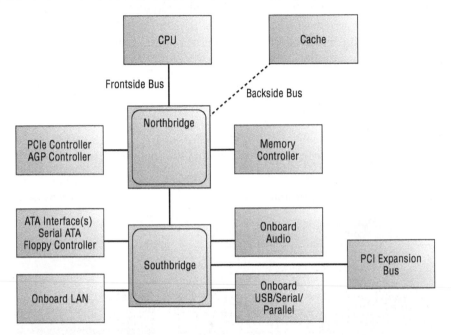

Expansion Slots

The most visible parts of any motherboard are the *expansion slots*. These are small plastic slots, usually from 1 to 6 inches long and approximately 1/2-inch wide. As their name suggests, these slots are used to install various devices in the computer to expand its capabilities. Some expansion devices that might be installed in these slots include video, network, sound, and disk interface cards.

If you look at the motherboard in your computer, you will more than likely see one of the main types of expansion slots used in computers today:

- PCI
- PCIe
- PCI-X

Each type differs in appearance and function. In the following sections, we will cover how to visually identify the different expansion slots on the motherboard. Personal Computer Memory Card International Association (PCMCIA) buses, such as PC Card, CardBus, Mini PCI, ExpressCard, and PCIe Mini, are more related to laptops than to desktop computers, and they are covered in Chapter 9, "Understanding Laptops."

PCI Expansion Slots

The motherboards of many computers in use today contain 32-bit *Peripheral Component Interconnect (PCI)* slots. They are easily recognizable because they are only around 3-inches long and classically white, although modern boards take liberties with the color. PCI slots became extremely popular with the advent of Pentium-class processors. Although popularity has shifted from PCI to PCIe, the PCI slot's service to the industry cannot be ignored; it has been an incredibly prolific architecture for many years.

PCI expansion buses operate at 33MHz or 66MHz (version 2.1) over a 32-bit (4-byte) channel, resulting in data rates of 133MBps and 266MBps, respectively, with 133MBps being the most common, server architectures excluded. PCI is a shared-bus topology, however, so mixing 33 MHz and 66MHz adapters in a 66MHz system will slow all adapters to 33MHz. Older servers might have featured 64-bit PCI slots as well, since version 1.0, which double the 32-bit data rates. See the sidebar in this chapter titled "Arriving at the Exact Answer" for help with understanding the math involved in frequencies and bit rates.

PCI slots and adapters are manufactured in 3.3V and 5V versions. Universal adapters are keyed to fit in slots based on either of the two voltages. The notch in the card edge of the common 5V slots and adapters is oriented toward the front of the motherboard, and the notch in the 3.3V adapters toward the rear. Figure 1.6 shows several PCI expansion slots. Note the 5V 32-bit slot in the foreground and the 3.3V 64-bit slots. Also notice that a universal 32-bit card, which has notches in both positions, is inserted into and operates fine in the 64-bit 3.3V slot in the background.

FIGURE 1.6 PCI expansion slots

Arriving at the Exact Answer

To get the math exactly right when dealing with frequencies and data rates ending in 33 and 66, you have to realize that every 33 has an associated one-third (1/3), and every 66 has an associated two-thirds (2/3). The extra quantities are left off of the final result but must be added back on to get the math exactly right. The good news is that omitting these small values from the equation still gets you close, and a bit of experience with the numbers leads to being able to make the connection on the fly.

PCI-X Expansion Slots

Visually indistinguishable from 64-bit PCI, because it uses the same slots, *PCI-Extended (PCI-X)* takes the 66MHz maximum frequency of PCI to new heights. Version 1.0 of the specification provided a 66MHz (533MBps) implementation as well as the most commonly deployed PCI-X offering, 133MHz (1066MBps). Version 2.0 introduced the current—and likely final—maximum, 533MHz. With an 8-byte (64-bit) bus, this translates to maximum throughput of 4266MBps, roughly 4.3GBps. Additionally, PCI-X version 2.0 supports a 266MHz (2133MBps) bus. Because PCI-X slots are physically compatible with PCI adapters, and because all PCI-X slots support the 66MHz minimum clock rate, PCI-X slots are compatible with 66MHz PCI adapters.

PCI-X is targeted at server platforms with its speed and support for hot-plugging, but it is still no match for the speeds available with PCIe, which all but obviates PCI-X today and made PCI-X version 2.0 obsolete not long after its release. PCI-X also suffers from the same shared-bus topology as PCI, resulting in all adapters falling back to the frequency of the slowest inserted adapter.

PCIe Expansion Slots

The latest expansion slot architecture that is being used by motherboards is *PCI Express (PCIe)*. It was designed to be a replacement for AGP, or accelerated graphics port, and PCI. PCIe has the advantage of being faster than AGP while maintaining the flexibility of PCI. PCIe has no plug compatibility with either AGP or PCI. As a result, modern PCIe motherboards can be found with regular PCI slots for backward compatibility, but AGP slots have not been included for many years.

PCIe is casually referred to as a bus architecture to simplify its comparison with other bus technologies. True expansion *buses* share total bandwidth among all slots, each of which taps into different points along the common bus lines. In contrast, PCIe uses a switching component with point-to-point connections to slots, giving each component full use of the corresponding bandwidth and producing more of a star topology versus a bus. Furthermore, unlike other expansion buses, which have parallel architectures, PCIe is a serial technology, striping data packets across multiple serial paths to achieve higher data rates.

PCIe uses the concept of *lanes*, which are the switched point-to-point signal paths between any two PCIe components. Each lane that the switch interconnects between any two intercommunicating devices comprises a separate pair of wires for both directions of traffic. Each PCIe pairing between cards requires a negotiation for the highest mutually supported number of lanes. The single lane or combined collection of lanes that the switch interconnects between devices is referred to as a *link*.

There are seven different link widths supported by PCIe, designated x1 (pronounced "by 1"), x2, x4, x8, x12, x16, and x32, with x1, x4, and x16 being the most common. The x8 link width is less common than these but more common than the others. A slot that supports a particular link width is of a physical size related to that width because the width is based on the number of lanes supported, requiring a related number of wires. As a result, a x8 slot is longer than a x1 slot but shorter than a x16 slot. Every PCIe slot has a 22-pin portion in common toward the rear of the motherboard, which you can see in Figure 1.7, in which the rear of the motherboard is to the left. These 22 pins comprise mostly voltage and ground leads.

FIGURE 1.7   PCIe expansion slots

There are four major versions of PCIe currently specified: 1.x, 2.x, 3.0, and 4.0. For the four versions, a single lane, and hence a x1 slot, operates in each direction (or transmits and receives from either communicating device's perspective), at a data rate of 250MBps (almost twice the rate of the most common PCI slot), 500MBps, approximately 1GBps, and roughly 2GBps, respectively.

An associated bidirectional link has a nominal throughput of double these rates. Use the doubled rate when comparing PCIe to other expansion buses because those other rates are for bidirectional communication. This means that the 500MBps bidirectional link of a x1 slot in the first version of PCIe was comparable to PCI's best, a 64-bit slot running at 66MHz and producing a throughput of 533MBps.

Combining lanes results in a linear multiplication of these rates. For example, a PCIe 1.1 x16 slot is capable of 4GBps of throughput in each direction, 16 times the 250MBps x1 rate. Bidirectionally, this fairly common slot produces a throughput of 8GBps. Later PCIe specifications increase this throughput even more.

> *Up-plugging* is defined in the PCIe specification as the ability to use a higher-capability slot for a lesser adapter. In other words, you can use a shorter (fewer-lane) card in a longer slot. For example, you can insert a x8 card into a x16 slot. The x8 card won't completely fill the slot, but it will work at x8 speeds if up-plugging is supported by the motherboard. Otherwise, the specification requires up-plugged devices to operate at only the x1 rate. This is something you should be aware of and investigate in advance. Down-plugging is possible only on open-ended slots, although not specifically allowed in the official specification. Even if you find or make (by cutting a groove in the end) an open-ended slot that accepts a longer card edge, the inserted adapter cannot operate faster than the slot's maximum rated capability because the required physical wiring to the PCIe switch in the Northbridge is not present.

Because of its high data rate, PCIe is the current choice of gaming aficionados. Additionally, technologies similar to NVIDIA's Scalable Link Interface (SLI) allow such users to combine preferably identical graphics adapters in appropriately spaced PCIe x16 slots with a hardware bridge to form a single virtual graphics adapter. The job of the bridge is to provide non-chipset communication among the adapters. The bridge is not a requirement for SLI to work, but performance suffers without it. SLI-ready motherboards allow two, three, or four PCIe graphics adapters to pool their graphics processing units (GPUs) and memory to feed graphics output to a single monitor attached to the adapter acting as SLI master. SLI implementation results in increased graphics performance over single-PCIe and non-PCIe implementations.

Refer back to Figure 1.7, which is a photo of an SLI-ready motherboard with three PCIe x16 slots (every other slot, starting with the top one), one PCIe x1 slot (second slot from the top), and two PCI slots (first and third slots from the bottom). Notice the latch and tab that secures the x16 adapters in place by their hooks. Any movement of these high-performance devices can result in temporary failure or poor performance.

Memory Slots and Cache

Memory or random access memory (RAM) slots are the next most notable slots on a motherboard. These slots are designed for the modules that hold memory chips that make up primary memory, which is used to store currently used data and instructions for the CPU. Many and varied types of memory are available for PCs today. In this chapter, you will become familiar with the appearance and specifications of the slots on the motherboard so that you can identify them.

For the most part, PCs today use memory chips arranged on a small circuit board. A *dual inline memory module (DIMM)* is one type of circuit board. Today's DIMMs differ in the number of conductors, or pins, that each particular physical form factor uses. Some common examples include 168-, 184-, and 240-pin configurations. In addition, laptop memory comes in smaller form factors known as *small outline DIMMs (SODIMMs)* and MicroDIMMs. The single inline memory module (SIMM) is an older memory form factor that began the trend of placing memory chips on modules. More detail on memory packaging and the technologies that use them can be found later in this chapter in the section "Identifying Purposes and Characteristics of Memory." Figure 1.8 shows the form factors for some once-popular memory modules. Notice how they basically look the same, but that the module sizes and keying notches are different.

FIGURE 1.8 Different memory module form factors

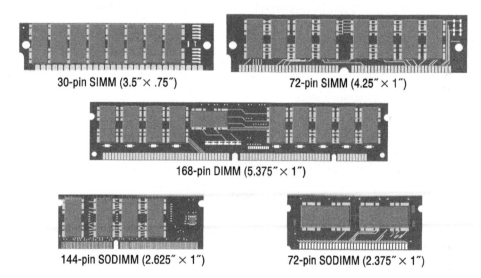

30-pin SIMM (3.5″ × .75″)　　72-pin SIMM (4.25″ × 1″)

168-pin DIMM (5.375″ × 1″)

144-pin SODIMM (2.625″ × 1″)　　72-pin SODIMM (2.375″ × 1″)

Memory slots are easy to identify on a motherboard. Classic DIMM slots were usually black and, like all memory slots, were placed very close together. DIMM slots with color-coding are more common these days, however. The color-coding of the slots acts as a guide to the installer of the memory. See the section "Single-, Dual-, and Triple-Channel Memory" later in this chapter for more on the purpose of this color-coding. Consult the motherboard's documentation to determine the specific modules allowed as well as their required orientation. The number of memory slots varies from motherboard to motherboard, but the structure of the different slots is similar. Metal pins in the bottom make contact with the metallic pins on each memory module. Small metal or plastic tabs on each side of the slot keep the memory module securely in its slot.

Table 1.1 identifies the types of memory slots that can be seen in various images throughout this chapter. All slots listed have the characteristic release-tabs at each end in common. The ATX motherboard in Figure 1.2 and the motherboard in Figure 1.4 exhibit dual-channel indicators, by way of dual-colored slots. Figure 1.9 shows only the memory slots from the ATX motherboard in Figure 1.2 as a reference.

TABLE 1.1 List of memory slots in Chapter 1 images

Image number	Type of memory slot
Figure 1.1	168-pin SDR SDRAM
Figure 1.2	184-pin DDR SDRAM
Figure 1.3 (mini-ITX)	184-pin DDR SDRAM
Figure 1.4 (partial visibility)	240-pin DDR2 SDRAM
Figure 1.12 (partial visibility)	168-pin SDR SDRAM
Figure 1.22	168-pin SDR SDRAM

FIGURE 1.9 DDR memory slots

Sometimes, the amount of primary memory installed is inadequate to service additional requests for memory resources from newly launched applications. When this condition occurs, the user may receive an "out of memory" error message and an application may fail to launch. One solution for this is to use the hard drive as additional RAM. This space on the hard drive is known as a *swap file* or a *paging file*. The technology in general is known as *virtual memory*. The swap file, PAGEFILE.SYS in modern Microsoft operating systems, is an optimized space that can deliver information to RAM at the request of the memory controller faster than if it came from the general storage pool of the drive. Note that virtual memory cannot be used directly from the hard drive; it must be paged into RAM as the oldest contents of RAM are paged out to the hard drive to make room. The memory controller, by the way, is the chip that manages access to RAM as well as adapters that have had a few hardware memory addresses reserved for their communication with the processor.

Nevertheless, relying too much on virtual memory (check your page fault statistics in the Reliability and Performance Monitor) results in the entire system slowing down noticeably. An inexpensive and highly effective solution is to add physical memory to the system, thus reducing its reliance on virtual memory. More information on virtual memory and its configuration can be found in Chapter 13, "Operating System Basics."

When it's not the amount of RAM in a system that you need to enhance but its speed, engineers can add *cache memory* between the CPU and RAM. Cache is a very fast form of memory forged from static RAM, which is discussed in detail in the section "Identifying Purposes and Characteristics of Memory" later in this chapter. Cache improves system performance by predicting what the CPU will ask for next and prefetching this information before being asked. This paradigm allows the cache to be smaller in size than the RAM itself. Only the most recently used data and code or that which is expected to be used next is stored in cache. Cache on the motherboard is known as external cache because it is external to the processor; it's also referred to as Level 2 cache (*L2 cache*). Level 1 cache (*L1 cache*), by comparison, is internal cache because it is built into the processor's silicon wafer, or *die*. The word *core* is often used interchangeably with the word *die*.

It is now common for chipmakers to use extra space in the processor's packaging to bring the L2 cache from the motherboard closer to the CPU. When L2 cache is present in the processor's packaging, but not on-die, the cache on the motherboard is referred to as Level 3 cache (*L3 cache*). Unfortunately, due to the de facto naming of cache levels, the term *L2 cache* alone is not a definitive description of where the cache is located. The terms *L1 cache* and *L3 cache* do not vary in their meaning, however.

The typical increasing order of capacity and distance from the processor die is L1 cache, L2 cache, L3 cache, RAM, and HDD/SSD (hard disk drive and solid-state drive—more on these in Chapter 2, "Storage Devices and Power Supplies"). This is also the typical decreasing order of speed. The following list includes representative capacities of these memory types. The cache capacities are for each core of the original Intel Core i7 processor. The other capacities are simply modern examples.

- L1 cache—64KB (32KB each for data and instructions)
- L2 cache—256KB
- L3 cache—4MB–12MB
- RAM—4–16GB
- HDD/SSD—100s–1000s of GB

Central Processing Unit and Processor Socket

The "brain" of any computer is the *central processing unit (CPU)*. There's no computer without a CPU. There are many different types of processors for computers—so many, in fact, that you will learn about them later in this chapter in the section "Identifying Purposes and Characteristics of Processors."

Typically, in today's computers, the processor is the easiest component to identify on the motherboard. It is usually the component that has either a fan or a heat sink (usually both) attached to it (as shown in Figure 1.10). These devices are used to draw away and disperse the heat that a processor generates. This is done because heat is the enemy of microelectronics. Theoretically, a Pentium (or higher) processor generates enough heat that, without the heat sink, it would permanently damage itself and the motherboard in a matter of hours or even minutes.

FIGURE 1.10   Two heat sinks, one with a fan

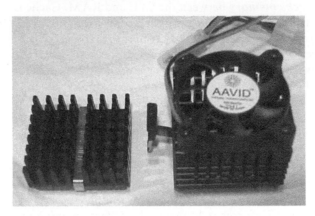

CPU sockets are almost as varied as the processors that they hold. Sockets are basically flat and have several columns and rows of holes or pins arranged in a square, as shown in Figure 1.11. The top socket is known as Socket A or Socket 462, made for earlier AMD processors such as the Athlon, and has holes to receive the pins on the CPU. This is known as a *pin grid array (PGA)* arrangement for a CPU socket. The holes and pins are in a row/column orientation, an array of pins. The bottom socket is known as Socket T or Socket *LGA 775*, and there are spring-loaded pins in the socket and a grid of lands on the CPU. The *land grid array (LGA)* is a newer technology that places the delicate pins (yet more sturdy than those on chips) on the cheaper motherboard instead of on the more expensive CPU, opposite to the way that the aging PGA does. The device with the pins has to be replaced if the pins become too damaged to function. The PGA and LGA are mentioned again later in this chapter in the section "Identifying Purposes and Characteristics of Processors."

Modern CPU sockets have a mechanism in place that reduces the need to apply considerable force to the CPU to install a processor, which was necessary in the early days of personal computing. Given the extra surface area on today's processors, excessive pressure applied in the wrong manner could damage the CPU packaging, its pins, or the motherboard itself. For CPUs based on the PGA concept, *zero insertion force (ZIF)* sockets are exceedingly popular. ZIF sockets use a plastic or metal lever on one of the two lateral edges to lock or release the mechanism that secures the CPU's pins in the socket. The CPU rides on the mobile top portion of the socket, and the socket's contacts that mate with the CPU's pins are in the fixed bottom portion of the socket. The image of Socket 462 shown in Figure 1.11 illustrates the ZIF locking mechanism at the edge of the socket along the bottom of the photo.

For processors based on the LGA concept, a socket with a different locking mechanism is used. Because there are no receptacles in either the motherboard or the CPU, there is no opportunity for a locking mechanism that holds the component with the pins in place. LGA-compatible sockets, as they're called despite the misnomer, have a lid that closes over the CPU and is locked in place by an L-shaped arm that borders two of the socket's edges. The nonlocking leg of the arm has a bend in the middle that latches the lid closed when the other leg of the arm is secured. The bottom image in Figure 1.11 shows an LGA socket with no CPU installed and the locking arm secured over the lid's tab (right-edge in the photo).

FIGURE 1.11   CPU socket examples

Table 1.2 lists some common socket/CPU relationships.

TABLE 1.2   Socket types and the processors they support

Socket	Processors
LGA 775 (Socket T)	Intel only: Pentium 4, Pentium 4 Extreme Edition (single core), Pentium D, Celeron D, Pentium Extreme Edition (dual core), Core 2 Duo, Core 2 Extreme, Core 2 Quad, Xeon, Celeron (4xx, Exxxx series).
LGA 1156 (Socket H)	Intel only: Celeron (G1xxx series), Core i3, Core i5, Core i7 (8xx series), Pentium (G6xxx series), Xeon (34xx series).
LGA 1155 (Socket H2)	Intel only: Replacement for LGA 1156 to support CPUs based on the Sandy Bridge (such as Celeron G4xx and G5xx) and eventual Ivy Bridge architectures.
LGA 1150 (Socket H3)	Replacement for LGA 1155 to support the Haswell and Broadwell processors, which rely on x8x and x9x desktop chipsets and C22x single-Xeon server chipsets.
LGA 1366 (Socket B)	Intel only: Core i7 (9xx series), Xeon (35xx, 36xx, 55xx, 56xx series), Intel Celeron P1053.
LGA 2011 (Socket R)	Replacement for LGA 1366. ■ Original LGA 2011-0 socket is used for Sandy Bridge-E (desktop Core i7-38xx, -39xx) and -EP (Xeon E5) as well as Ivy Bridge-E (desktop Core i7-48xx and -49xx) and -EP processors (Xeon E5 v2). ■ LGA 2011-1 is used for Ivy Bridge-EX (Xeon E7 v2) CPUs. ■ LGA 2011-v3 socket is used for Haswell-E (desktop, X99 chipset) and Haswell-EP (Xeon E5 v3) CPUs, supporting DDR4 memory. ■ The three sockets are not electrically compatible.
Socket AM3	AMD only: DDR3 capable CPUs only (thus not compatible with AM2+ CPUs), such as Phenom II, Athlon II, Sempron, Opteron 138x, and has the potential to accept AM3+ CPUs.
Socket AM3+	AMD only: Specified for CPUs based on the Bulldozer microarchitecture and designed to accept AM3 CPUs.
Socket FM1	AMD only: Designed to accept AMD Fusion Accelerated Processing Units (APUs), for desktops, which incorporate CPUs and GPUs, such as early A Series APUs.
Socket FM2	AMD only: A 904-pin desktop socket for Trinity and Richland APUs.
Socket FM2+	AMD only: A 906-pin desktop socket for Steamroller-based APUs Kaveri and Godavari. Accepts chips that fit socket FM2 as well, but the converse is not also true.

Power Connectors

In addition to these sockets and slots on the motherboard, a special connector (the 20-pin white block connector shown in Figure 1.12) allows the motherboard to be connected to the power supply to receive power. This connector is where the ATX power connector (mentioned in Chapter 2 in the section "Identifying Purposes and Characteristics of Power Supplies") plugs in.

FIGURE 1.12   An ATX power connector on a motherboard

Firmware

Firmware is the name given to any software that is encoded in hardware, usually a read-only memory (ROM) chip, and it can be run without extra instructions from the operating system. Most computers, large printers, and devices with no operating system use firmware in some sense. The best example of firmware is a computer's basic input/output system (BIOS) routine, which is burned into a chip. Also, some expansion cards, such as SCSI cards and graphics adapters, use their own firmware utilities for setting up peripherals.

BIOS and POST

One of the most important chips on the motherboard is the *basic input/output system (BIOS) chip*, also referred to as the ROM BIOS chip. This special memory chip contains the BIOS system software that boots the system and allows the operating system to interact with certain hardware in the computer in lieu of requiring a more complex device driver to do so. The BIOS chip is easily identified: If you have a brand-name computer, this chip might have on it the name of the manufacturer and usually the word *BIOS*. For clones, the chip usually has a sticker or printing on it from one of the major BIOS manufacturers (AMI, Phoenix/Award, Winbond, and so on). On later motherboards, the BIOS might be difficult to identify or it might even be integrated into the Southbridge, but the functionality remains regardless of how it's implemented.

The successor to the BIOS is the *Unified Extensible Firmware Interface (UEFI)*. The extensible features of the UEFI allow for the support of a vast array of systems and platforms by allowing the UEFI access to system resources for storage of additional modules that can be added at any time. In the following section, you'll see how a security feature known as Secure Boot would not be possible with the classic BIOS. It is the extensibility of the UEFI that makes such technology feasible.

BIOS

Figure 1.13 gives you an idea of what a modern BIOS might look like. Despite the 1998 copyright on the label, which refers only to the oldest code present on the chip, this particular chip can be found on motherboards produced as late as 2009. Notice also the Reset CMOS jumper at lower left and its configuration silkscreen at upper left. You might use this jumper to clear the CMOS memory, discussed shortly, when an unknown password, for example, is keeping you out of the BIOS configuration utility. The jumper in the photo is in the clear position, not the normal operating position. System boot-up is typically not possible in this state.

FIGURE 1.13   A BIOS chip on a motherboard

Most BIOS setup utilities have more to offer than a simple interface for making selections and saving the results. As always, you can enter the utility to check to see if the clock appears to be losing time, possibly due to a dying battery. (See Figure 1.14.) Today, these utilities also offer diagnostic routines that you can use to have the BIOS analyze the state and quality of the same components that it inspects during boot-up, but at a much deeper level. Consider the scenario where a computer is making noise and overheating. You can use the BIOS configuration utility to access built-in diagnostics to check the rotational speed of the motherboard fans. If the fans are running slower than expected, the noise could be related to the bearings of one or more fans, causing them to lose speed and, thus, cooling capacity.

FIGURE 1.14   A CR2032 CMOS battery

There is often also a page within the utility that gives you access to such bits of information as current live readings of the temperature of the CPU and the ambient temperature of the interior of the system unit. On such a page, you can set the temperature at which the BIOS sounds a warning tone and the temperature at which the BIOS shuts the system down to protect it. You can also monitor the instantaneous fan speeds, bus speeds, and voltage levels of the CPU and other vital landmarks to make sure that they are all within acceptable ranges. You might also be able to set a lower fan speed threshold at which the system warns you. In many cases, some of these levels can be altered to achieve such phenomena as overclocking, which is using the BIOS to set the system clock higher than what the CPU is rated for, or undervolting, which is lowering the voltage of the CPU and RAM, which reduces power consumption and heat production.

Some BIOS firmware can monitor the status of a contact on the motherboard for intrusion detection. If the feature in the BIOS is enabled and the sensor on the chassis is connected to the contact on the motherboard, the removal of the cover will be detected and logged by the BIOS. This can occur even if the system is off, thanks to the CMOS battery. At the next boot-up, the BIOS will notify you of the intrusion. No notification occurs over subsequent boots unless additional intrusion is detected.

The BIOS has always played a role in system security. Since the early days of the personal computer, the BIOS allowed the setting of two passwords—the user password and the supervisor, or access, password. The *user password* is required to leave the initial power-on screens and begin the process of booting an operating system. The *supervisor password* is required before entering the BIOS configuration utility. It is always a good idea to set the supervisor password, but the user password should not be set on public systems that need to boot on their own in case of an unforeseen power-cycle.

In later years, the role of the BIOS in system security grew substantially. Somehow, security needed to be extended to a point before the operating system was ready to take it over. The BIOS was a perfect candidate to supervise security and integrity in a platform-independent way. Coupled with the *Trusted Platform Module (TPM)*, a dedicated security coprocessor, or cryptoprocessor, the BIOS can be configured to boot the system only after authenticating the boot device. This authentication confirms that the hardware being booted to has been tied to the system containing the BIOS and TPM, a process known as *sealing*. Sealing the devices to the system also prohibits the devices from being used after removing them from the system. For further security, the keys created can be combined with a PIN or password that unlocks their use or with a USB flash drive that must be inserted before booting.

Microsoft's BitLocker uses the TPM to encrypt the entire drive. Normally, only user data can be encrypted, but BitLocker encrypts operating-system files, the Registry, the hibernation file, and so on, in addition to those files and folders that file-level encryption secures. If any changes have occurred to the Windows installation, the TPM does not release the keys required to decrypt and boot to the secured volume.

When a certain level of UEFI is used, the system firmware can also check digital signatures for each boot file it uses to confirm that it is the approved version and has not been tampered with. This technology is known as *Secure Boot.* The boot files checked include option ROMs (defined in the following section), the boot loader, and other operating-system boot files. Only if the signatures are valid will the firmware load and execute the associated software.

The problem can now arise that a particular operating system might not be supported by the database of known-good signatures stored in the firmware. In such a situation, the system manufacturer can supply an extension that the UEFI can use to support that operating system, not a task possible with traditional BIOS-based firmware.

POST

A major function of the BIOS is to perform a process known as a *power-on self-test (POST)*. POST is a series of system checks performed by the system BIOS and other high-end components, such as the SCSI BIOS and the video BIOS, known collectively as *option ROMs*. Among other things, the POST routine verifies the integrity of the BIOS itself. It also verifies and confirms the size of primary memory. During POST, the BIOS also analyzes and catalogs other forms of hardware, such as buses and boot devices, as well as managing the passing of control to the specialized BIOS routines mentioned earlier. The BIOS is responsible for offering the user a key sequence to enter the configuration routine as POST is beginning. Finally, once POST has completed successfully, the BIOS selects the boot device highest in the configured boot order and executes the master boot record (MBR) or similar construct on that device so that the MBR can call its associated operating system's boot loader and continue booting up.

The POST process can end with a beep code or displayed code that indicates the issue discovered. Each BIOS publisher has its own series of codes that can be generated. Figure 1.15 shows a simplified POST display during the initial boot sequence of a computer.

FIGURE 1.15 An example of a BIOS boot screen

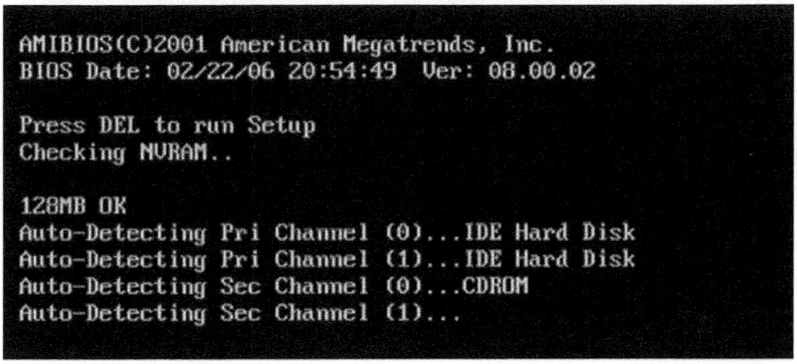

```
AMIBIOS(C)2001 American Megatrends, Inc.
BIOS Date: 02/22/06 20:54:49  Ver: 08.00.02

Press DEL to run Setup
Checking NVRAM..

128MB OK
Auto-Detecting Pri Channel (0)...IDE Hard Disk
Auto-Detecting Pri Channel (1)...IDE Hard Disk
Auto-Detecting Sec Channel (0)...CDROM
Auto-Detecting Sec Channel (1)...
```

Flashing the System BIOS

If ever you find that a hardware upgrade to your system is not recognized, even after the latest and correct drivers have been installed, perhaps a BIOS upgrade, also known as *flashing the BIOS*, is in order. Only certain hardware benefits from a BIOS upgrade, such as drives and a change of CPU or RAM types. Very often, this hardware is recognized immediately by the BIOS and has no associated driver that you must install. So, if your system doesn't recognize the new device, and there's no driver to install, the BIOS is a logical target.

Let's be clear about the fact that we are not talking about entering the BIOS setup utility and making changes to settings and subsequently saving your changes before exiting and rebooting. What we are referring to here is a replacement of the burned-in code within the BIOS itself. You might even notice after the upgrade that the BIOS setup utility looks different or has different pages and entries than before.

On older systems and certain newer ones, a loss of power during the upgrade results in catastrophe. The system becomes inoperable until you replace the BIOS chip, if possible, or the motherboard itself. Most new systems, however, have a fail-safe or two. This could be a portion of the BIOS that does not get flashed and has just enough code to boot the system and access the upgrade image. It could be a passive section to which the upgrade is installed and switched to only if the upgrade is successful. Sometimes this is controlled

continues

continued

onscreen. At other times, there may be a mechanism, such as a jumper, involved in the recovery of the BIOS after a power event occurs. The safest bet is to make sure that your laptop has plenty of battery power and is connected to AC power or your desktop is connected to an uninterruptible power supply (UPS).

In all cases, regardless of the BIOS maker, you should not consult BIOS companies—AMI, Award, Phoenix, and so forth. Instead, go back to the motherboard or system manufacturer; check its website, for example. The motherboard or system manufacturer vendors have personalized their BIOS code after licensing it from the BIOS publisher. The vendor will give you access to the latest code as well as the appropriate flashing utility for its implementation.

CMOS and CMOS Battery

Your PC has to keep certain settings when it's turned off and its power cord is unplugged:

- Date
- Time
- Hard drive/optical drive configuration
- Memory
- CPU settings, such as overclocking
- Integrated ports (settings as well as enable/disable)
- Boot sequence
- Power management
- Virtualization support
- Security (passwords, Trusted Platform Module settings, LoJack)

You added a new graphics adapter to your desktop computer, but the built-in display port continues to remain active, prohibiting the new interface from working. The solution here might be to alter your BIOS configuration to disable the internal graphics adapter, so that the new one will take over. Similar reconfiguration of your BIOS settings might be necessary when over-clocking—or changing the system clock speed—is desired, or when you want to set BIOS-based passwords or establish TPM-based whole-drive encryption, as with Microsoft's BitLocker (see Chapter 19, "Security"). While not so much utilized today, the system date and time can be altered in the BIOS configuration utility of your system; once, in the early days of personal computing, the date and time actually might have needed to be changed this way.

Your PC keeps these settings in a special memory chip called the *complementary metal oxide semiconductor (CMOS)* memory chip. Actually, CMOS (usually pronounced *see-moss*) is a manufacturing technology for integrated circuits. The first commonly used chip made from CMOS technology was a type of memory chip, the memory for the BIOS. As a result, the term *CMOS* stuck and is the accepted name for this memory chip.

The BIOS starts with its own default information and then reads information from the CMOS, such as which hard drive types are configured for this computer to use, which drive(s) it should search for boot sectors, and so on. Any overlapping information read from the CMOS overrides the default information from the BIOS. A lack of corresponding information in the CMOS does not delete information that the BIOS knows natively. This process is a merge, not a write-over. CMOS memory is usually *not* upgradable in terms of its capacity and might be integrated into the BIOS chip or the Southbridge.

To keep its settings, integrated circuit-based memory must have power constantly. When you shut off a computer, anything that is left in this type of memory is lost forever. The CMOS manufacturing technology produces chips with very low power requirements. As a result, today's electronic circuitry is more susceptible to damage from electrostatic discharge (ESD). Another ramification is that it doesn't take much of a power source to keep CMOS chips from losing their contents.

To prevent CMOS from losing its rather important information, motherboard manufacturers include a small battery called the *CMOS battery* to power the CMOS memory. The batteries come in different shapes and sizes, but they all perform the same function. Most CMOS batteries look like large watch batteries or small cylindrical batteries. Today's CMOS batteries are most often of a long-life, nonrechargeable lithium chemistry.

 When Absolute Software licensed the name LoJack, which was originally used as the name of a locating service for motor vehicles, the company replaced it as the name of its CompuTrace product, which allowed computing devices to be electronically tracked and controlled through a technology referred to as persistence. It's the ability to control devices that concerns many industry professionals. Because many laptop vendors incorporate the LoJack code and persistence into their BIOS firmware, there is a concern that attackers can redirect the service to rogue servers that can then gain control of legions of corporate systems. Furthermore, not all vendors incorporate the ability to disable this feature.

Front- and Top-Panel Connectors

From the time of the very first personal computer, there has been a minimum expectation as to the buttons and LEDs that should appear on the front of the case. In today's cases, buttons and LEDs have been added and placed on the top of the case or on a beveled edge between the top and the front. They have also been left on the front or have been used in a combination of these locations.

Users expect a *power button* to use to turn the computer on (these were on the side or back of very early PCs). The soft power feature available through the front power button, which is no more than a relay, allows access to multiple effects through the contact on the motherboard, based on how long the button is pressed. These effects can be changed through the BIOS or operating system. Users also expect a *power light*, often a green LED, to assure them that the button did its job. As time progressed, users were introduced to new things on the front panel of their computers. Each of these components depends on connectivity to the motherboard for its functionality. As a result, most motherboards have these standardized connections in common. The following list includes the majority of these landmarks (including the power button and power light, which were just discussed):

- Power button
- Power light
- Reset button
- Drive activity lights
- Audio jacks
- USB ports

So common are the various interfaces and indicators found on the front panel of today's computer chassis that the industry has standardized on a small number of connectors, making attachment to motherboards much simpler. Figure 1.16 shows a typical motherboard header. Consult the motherboard's documentation for a particular model's pin assignments.

FIGURE 1.16   The front-panel motherboard header

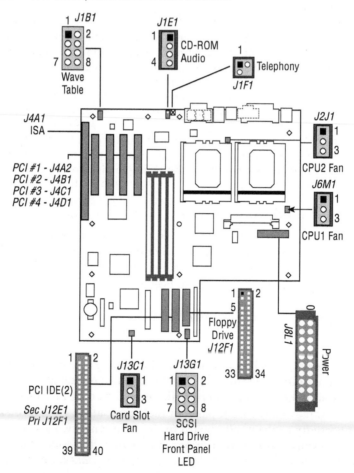

Reset Button

The *reset button* appeared as a way to reboot the computer from a cold startup point without removing power from the components. Keeping the machine powered tends to prolong the life of the electronics affected by power cycling. Pressing the reset button also gets around software lockups because the connection to the motherboard allows the system to restart from the hardware level. One disadvantage to power cycling is that certain circuits, such as memory chips, might need time to drain their charge for the reboot to be completely successful. This is why there is always a way to turn the computer off as well.

Drive Activity Light

In the early days of personal computing, the hard disk drive's LED had to be driven by the drive itself. Before long, the motherboard was equipped with drive headers, so adding pins to drive the *drive activity light* was no issue. These days, all motherboards supply this connectivity. The benefit of having one LED for all internal drives is that all the drives are represented on the front panel when only one LED is provided. The disadvantage might be that you cannot tell which drive is currently active. This tends to be a minor concern because you often know which drive you've accessed. If you haven't intentionally accessed any drive, it's likely the drive that holds the operating system or virtual-memory swap file is being accessed by the system itself. In contrast, external drives with removable media, such as optical drives, supply their own activity light on their faceplate.

Audio Jacks

Early generations of optical drives had to have a special cable attached to the rear of the drive. The cable was then attached to the sound card if audio CDs were to be heard through the speakers attached to the sound card. Sound emanating from a CD-ROM running an application, such as a game, did not have to take the same route and could travel through the same path from the drive as general data. The first enhancement to this arrangement came in the form of a front 3.5mm jack on the drive's faceplate that was intended for headphones but could also have speakers connected to it. The audio that normally ran across the special cable was rerouted to the front jack when something was plugged into it.

Many of today's motherboards have 10-position pin headers designed to connect to standardized front-panel audio modules. Some of these modules have legacy AC'97 analog ports on them while others have high-definition (HD) audio connections. Motherboards that accommodate both have a BIOS setting that allows you to choose which header you want to activate, with the HD setting most often being the default.

USB Ports

So many temporarily attached devices feature USB connectivity, such as USB keys (flash drives) and cameras, that front-panel connectivity is a must. Finding your way to the back of the system unit for a brief connection is hardly worth the effort in some cases. For many years, motherboards have supplied one or more 10-position headers for internal connectivity of front-panel USB ports. Because this header size is popular for many applications, only 9 positions tend to have pins protruding, while the 10th position acts as a key, showing up in different spots for each application to discourage the connection of the wrong cable.

Figure 1.17 shows USB headers on a motherboard. The labels "USB56" and "USB78" indicate that one block serves ports 5 and 6 while the other serves ports 7 and 8, all of which are arbitrary, based on the manufacturer's numbering convention.

FIGURE 1.17   Two motherboard USB headers

Identifying Purposes and Characteristics of Processors

Now that you've learned the basics of the motherboard, you need to learn about the most important component on the motherboard: the CPU. The role of the CPU, or central processing unit, is to control and direct all the activities of the computer using both external and internal buses. It is a processor chip consisting of an array of *millions* of transistors. Intel and Advanced Micro Devices (AMD) are the two largest PC-compatible CPU manufacturers. Their chips were featured in Table 1.1 during the discussion of the sockets into which they fit.

 The term *chip* has grown to describe the entire package that a technician might install in a socket. However, the word originally denoted the silicon wafer that is generally hidden within the carrier that you actually see. The external pins that you see are structures that can withstand insertion into a socket and are carefully threaded from the wafer's minuscule contacts. Just imagine how fragile the structures must be that you *don't* see.

Older CPUs are generally square, with contacts arranged in a pin grid array (PGA). Prior to 1981, chips were found in a rectangle with two rows of 20 pins known as a *dual in-line package (DIP)*; see Figure 1.18. There are still integrated circuits that use the DIP form factor. However, the DIP form factor is no longer used for PC CPUs. Most modern CPUs use the LGA form factor. Figure 1.11, earlier in this chapter, shows an LGA "socket" below a PGA socket. Additionally, the ATX motherboard in Figure 1.2 has a PGA socket, while the micro ATX motherboard has an LGA.

FIGURE 1.18   DIP and PGA

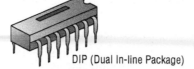

DIP (Dual In-line Package)

PGA (Pin Grid Array)

Intel and AMD both make extensive use of an inverted socket/processor combination of sorts. As mentioned earlier, the land grid array (LGA) packaging calls for the pins to be placed on the motherboard, while the mates for these pins are on the processor packaging. As with PGA, LGA is named for the landmarks on the processor, not the ones on the motherboard. As a result, the grid of metallic contact points, called *lands*, on the bottom of the CPU gives this format its name.

You can easily identify which component inside the computer is the CPU because it is a large square lying flat on the motherboard with a very large heat sink and fan (as shown earlier in Figure 1.10). Figure 1.19 points out the location of the CPU in relation to the other components on a typical ATX motherboard. Notice how prominent the CPU socket is.

FIGURE 1.19   The location of a CPU on a typical motherboard

Modern processors may feature the following characteristics:

Hyperthreading   This term refers to Intel's *Hyper-Threading Technology (HTT)*. HTT is a form of simultaneous multithreading (SMT). SMT takes advantage of a modern CPU's superscalar architecture. Superscalar processors can have multiple instructions operating on separate data in parallel.

HTT-capable processors appear to the operating system to be two processors. As a result, the operating system can schedule two processes at the same time, as in the case of symmetric multiprocessing (SMP), where two or more processors use the same system resources. In fact, the operating system must support SMP in order to take advantage of HTT. If the current process stalls because of missing data caused by, say, cache or branch prediction issues, the execution resources of the processor can be reallocated for a different process that is ready to go, reducing processor downtime.

HTT manifests itself in the Windows 8.x Task Manager by, for example, showing graphs for twice as many CPUs as the system has cores. These virtual CPUs are listed as logical processors (see Figure 1.20).

FIGURE 1.20 Logical processors in Windows

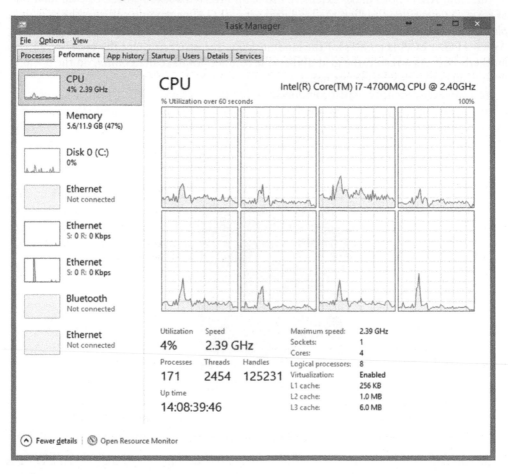

Which CPU Do You Have?

The surest way to determine which CPU your computer is using is to open the case and view the numbers stamped on the CPU, a process that today requires removal of the active heat sink. However, you may be able to get an idea without opening the case and removing the heat sink and fan because many manufacturers place a very obvious sticker somewhere on the case indicating the processor type. Failing this, you can always go to the manufacturer's website and look up the information on the model of computer you have.

If you have a no-name clone, look in the System Properties pages, found by right-clicking My Computer (Computer in Vista and Windows 7) and selecting Properties. The General tab, which is the default, contains this information. Even more detailed information can be found by running the System Information utility from Start ➢ Accessories ➢ System Tools or by entering **msinfo32.exe** in the Start ➢ Run dialog box.

Another way to determine a computer's CPU is to save your work, exit any open programs, and restart the computer. Watch closely as the computer boots back up. You should see a notation that tells you what chip you are using.

Multicore   A processor that exhibits a *multicore architecture* has multiple completely separate processor dies in the same package. The operating system and applications see multiple processors in the same way that they see multiple processors in separate sockets. As with HTT, the operating system must support SMP to benefit from the separate processors. In addition, SMP is not a benefit if the applications that are run on the SMP system are not written for parallel processing. Dual-core and quad-core processors are common specific examples of the multicore technology.

Don't be confused by Intel's Core 2 labeling. The numeric component does not imply that there are two cores. There was a Core series of 32-bit mobile processors that featured one (Solo) or two (Duo) processing cores on a single die (silicon wafer). The same dual-core die was used for both classes of Core CPU. The second core was disabled for Core Solo processors.

The 64-bit Core 2 product line can be thought of as a second generation of the Core series. Core 2, by the way, reunited Intel mobile and desktop computing—the Pentium 4 family had a separate Pentium M for mobile computing. Intel describes and markets the microcode of certain processors as "Core microarchitecture." As confusing as it may sound, the Core 2 processors are based on the Core microarchitecture; the Core processors are not. Core 2 processors come in Solo (mobile only), Duo, and four-core (Quad) implementations. Solo and Duo processors have a single die; Quad processors have two Duo dies. A more capable Extreme version exists for the Duo and Quad models.

Processors, such as certain models of AMD's Phenom series, can contain an odd number of multiple cores as well. The triple-core processor, which obviously contains three cores, is the most common implementation of multiple odd cores.

Throttling   CPU throttling allows for reducing the operating frequency of the CPU during times of less demand or during battery operation. CPU throttling is very common in processors for mobile devices, where heat generation and system-battery drain are key issues of full power usage. You might discover throttling in action when you use a utility that reports a lower CPU clock frequency than expected. If the load on the system does not require full-throttle operation, there is no need to push such a limit.

Speed   The speed of the processor is generally described in clock frequency (MHz or GHz). Since the dawn of the personal computer industry, motherboards have included oscillators, quartz crystals shaved down to a specific geometry so that engineers know exactly how they will react when a current is run through them. The phenomenon of a quartz crystal vibrating when exposed to a current is known as the *piezoelectric effect*. The crystal (XTL) known as the system clock keeps the time for the flow of data on the motherboard. How the frontside bus uses the clock leads to an *effective* clock rate known as the FSB speed. As shown in the section "Types of Memory" later in this chapter, the FSB speed is computed differently for different types of RAM (DDR, DDR2, and so forth). From here, the CPU multiplies the FSB speed to produce its own internal clock rate, producing the third *speed* mentioned thus far.

As a result of the foregoing tricks of physics and mathematics, there can be a discrepancy between the frontside bus frequency and the internal frequency that the CPU uses to latch data and instructions through its pipelines. This disagreement between the numbers comes from the fact that the CPU is capable of splitting the clock signal it receives from the external oscillator that drives the frontside bus into multiple regular signals for its own internal use. In fact, you might be able to purchase a number of processors rated for different (internal) speeds that are all compatible with a single motherboard that has a frontside bus rated, for instance, at 1333MHz. Furthermore, you might be able to adjust the internal clock rate of the CPU that you purchased through settings in the BIOS. The successful technician needs to be familiar with more basic information than this, however. The sidebar titled "Matching System Components" explains these basics.

Matching System Components

In a world of clock doubling, tripling, quadrupling, and so forth, it becomes increasingly important to pay attention to what you are buying when you purchase CPUs, memory, and motherboards a la carte. The only well-known relationship that exists in the marketplace among these components is the speed of the FSB (in MHz) and the throughput of the memory (in MBps). Because 8 bytes are transferred in parallel by a processor with a 64-bit (64 bits = 8 bytes) system data bus, you have to know the FSB rating before you choose the RAM for any particular modern motherboard. For example, an FSB of 800MHz requires memory rated at a throughput of 6400MBps (800 million cycles per second × 8 bytes per cycle).

Matching CPUs with motherboards or CPUs with memory requires consulting the documentation or packaging of the components. Generally, the CPU gets selected first. Once you know the CPU you want, the motherboard tends to come next. You must choose a motherboard that features a socket compatible with your chosen CPU. The FSB or Quick-Path Interconnect (QPI) used on the selected motherboard/CPU dictates the RAM that you should purchase.

32- and 64-bit processors   The set of data lines between the CPU and the primary memory of the system can be 32 or 64 bits wide, among other widths. The wider the bus, the more data that can be processed per unit of time, and hence, more work can be performed. Internal registers in the CPU might be only 32 bits wide, but with a 64-bit system bus, two separate pipelines can receive information simultaneously. For true 64-bit CPUs, which have 64-bit internal registers and can run x64 versions of Microsoft operating systems, the external system data bus will always be 64 bits wide or some larger multiple thereof.

Virtualization support   Many of today's CPUs support virtualization in hardware, which eases the burden on the system that software-based virtualization imposes. For more information on virtualization, see Chapter 20, "Network Services, Cloud Computing, and Virtualization." Unlike AMD's AMD-V (*V* for virtualization) technology, which is widely inclusive of AMD's CPUs, Intel's Virtualization Technology (VT) is used by Intel to segment its market for CPUs made concurrently. For example, you can find Intel VT on the Core 2 Duo processor in the E6000 series and most of the E8000 series but not in the E7000 series. In some cases, you must also first enable the virtualization support in the BIOS before it can be used. If you have an Intel processor and would like to check its support of VT, visit the following site to download the Intel Processor Identification utility:

```
downloadcenter.intel.com/Detail_Desc.aspx?ProductID=1881&DwnldID=7838
```

As shown in Figure 1.21, the CPU Technologies tab of this utility tells you if your CPU supports Intel VT.

FIGURE 1.21   Intel Processor Identification utility

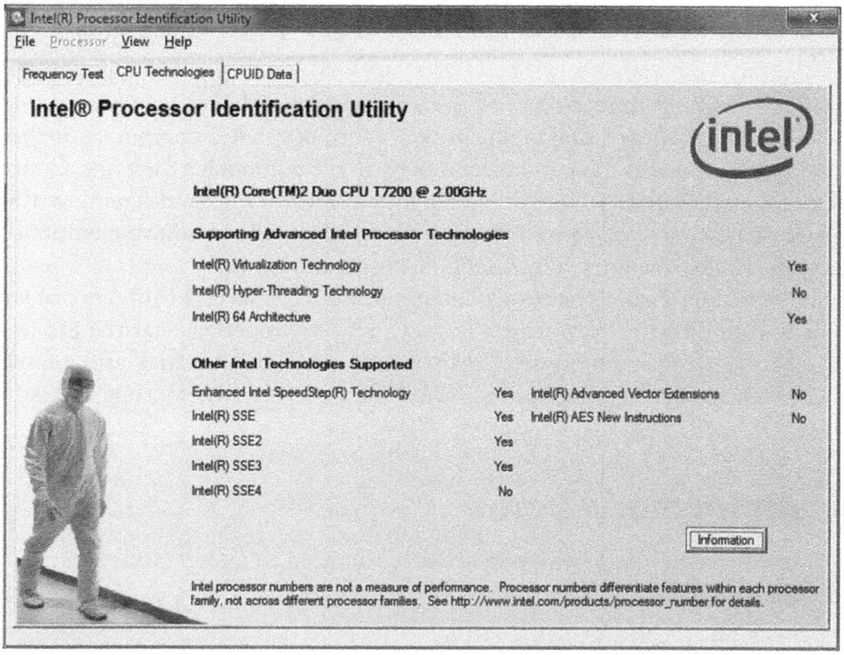

Integrated GPU Intel and AMD both have a line of low-power CPUs, originally aimed at the netbook and embedded markets, that have built-in graphics processing units (GPUs). Building in specialized functionality to CPUs is nothing new, but before now, math coprocessors were some of the most complex features added on to the die of CPUs. A GPU, then, which is normally a large chip on your graphics adapter, is quite a bit more complex than anything heretofore integrated into the CPU. Integrated GPUs take much of the burden off of the CPU itself in addition to minimizing the amount of off-package communication that must occur, which improves overall system performance. As if that were not enough, the CPUs in this class are quite a bit smaller than standard CPUs. The Intel Atom and AMD Fusion (now simply APU for Accelerated Processing Unit) lines of CPUs have built-in GPUs and open the door for other complex systems to be built into future processors.

Disable execute bit Modern CPUs respond to the operating system's setting of the *disable execute bit*, more accurately known as the *no-execute (NX) bit*, for an area of memory by refusing to execute any code placed into that memory location. The result is that malicious buffer overrun attacks are less likely to succeed. A similar, but non NX-based, support feature has been in existence since the Intel 80286 processor. Use of the NX bit provides more granular linear addressing. In contrast, the 286 applied protection to entire segments at a time. Windows began operating-system NX support with Windows XP, calling it Data Execution Prevention (DEP). Intel refers to the NX bit as the eXecute Disable (XD) bit.

Identifying Purposes and Characteristics of Memory

"More memory, more memory, I don't have enough memory!" Today, adding memory is one of the most popular, easy, and inexpensive ways to upgrade a computer. As the computer's CPU works, it stores data and instructions in the computer's memory. Contrary to what you might expect from an inexpensive solution, memory upgrades tend to afford the greatest performance increase as well, up to a point. Motherboards have memory limits; operating systems have memory limits; CPUs have memory limits.

To identify memory visually within a computer, look for several thin rows of small circuit boards sitting vertically, potentially packed tightly together near the processor. In situations where only one memory stick is installed, it will be that stick and a few empty slots that are tightly packed together. Figure 1.22 shows where memory is located in a system.

Important Memory Terms

There are a few technical terms and phrases that you need to understand with regard to memory and its function:

- Parity checking
- Error-correcting code (ECC)

- Single- and double-sided memory
- Single-, dual-, and triple-channel memory
- Buffered and unbuffered memory

FIGURE 1.22   Location of memory within a system

These terms are discussed in detail in the following sections.

Parity Checking and Memory Banks

Parity checking is a rudimentary error-checking scheme that offers no error correction. Parity checking works most often on a byte, or 8 bits, of data. A ninth bit is added at the transmitting end and removed at the receiving end so that it does not affect the actual data transmitted. If the receiving end does not agree with the parity that is set in a particular byte, a parity error results. The four most common parity schemes affecting this extra bit are known as even, odd, mark, and space. Even and odd parity are used in systems that actually compute parity. Mark (a term for a digital pulse, or 1 bit) and space (a term for the lack of a pulse, or a 0 bit) parity are used in systems that do not compute parity but expect to see a fixed bit value stored in the parity location. Systems that do not support or reserve the location required for the parity bit are said to implement *non-parity* memory.

The most basic model for implementing memory in a computer system uses eight memory chips to form a set. Each memory chip holds millions or billions of bits of information, each in its own *cell*. For every byte in memory, one bit is stored in each of the eight chips. A ninth chip is added to the set to support the parity bit in systems that require it. One or more of these sets, implemented as individual chips or as chips mounted on a memory module, form a *memory bank*.

A bank of memory is required for the computer system to recognize electrically that the minimum number of memory components or the proper number of additional memory components has been installed. The width of the system data bus, the external bus of the processor, dictates how many memory chips or modules are required to satisfy a bank. For example, one 32-bit, 72-pin SIMM (single inline memory module) satisfies a bank for an old 32-bit CPU, such as a 386 or 486 processor. Two such modules are required to satisfy a bank for a 64-bit processor, a Pentium, for instance. However, only a single 64-bit, 168-pin DIMM is required to satisfy the same Pentium processor. For those modules that have fewer than eight or nine chips mounted on them, more than 1 bit for every byte is being handled by some of the chips. For example, if you see three chips mounted, the two larger chips customarily handle 4 bits, a nybble, from each byte stored, and the third, smaller chip handles the single parity bit for each byte.

Even and odd parity schemes operate on each byte in the set of memory chips. In each case, the number of bits set to a value of 1 is counted up. If there are an even number of 1 bits in the byte (0, 2, 4, 6, or 8), even parity stores a 0 in the ninth bit, the parity bit; otherwise, it stores a 1 to even up the count. Odd parity does just the opposite, storing a 1 in the parity bit to make an even number of 1s odd and a 0 to keep an odd number of 1s odd. You can see that this is effective only for determining if there was a blatant error in the set of bits received, but there is no indication as to where the error is and how to fix it. Furthermore, the total 1-bit count is not important, only whether it's even or odd. Therefore, in either the even or odd scheme, if an even number of bits is altered in the same byte during transmission, the error goes undetected because flipping 2, 4, 6, or all 8 bits results in an even number of 1s remaining even and an odd number of 1s remaining odd.

Mark and space parity are used in systems that want to see 9 bits for every byte transmitted but don't compute the parity bit's value based on the bits in the byte. Mark parity always uses a 1 in the parity bit, and space parity always uses a 0. These schemes offer less error detection capability than the even and odd schemes because only changes in the parity bit can be detected. Again, parity checking is not error correction; it's error detection only, and not the best form of error detection at that. Nevertheless, an error can lock up the entire system and display a memory parity error. Enough of these errors and you need to replace the memory. Therefore, parity checking remains from the early days of computing as an effective indicator of large-scale memory and data-transmission failure, such as with serial interfaces attached to analog modems or networking console interfaces, but not so much for detecting random errors.

In the early days of personal computing, almost all memory was parity based. As quality has increased over the years, parity checking in the RAM subsystem has become more rare. As noted earlier, if parity checking is not supported, there will generally be fewer chips per module, usually one less per column of RAM.

Error Checking and Correction

The next step in the evolution of memory error detection is known as *error-correcting code (ECC)*. If memory supports ECC, check bits are generated and stored with the data. An algorithm is performed on the data and its check bits whenever the memory is accessed. If the result of the algorithm is all zeros, then the data is deemed valid and processing continues. ECC can detect single- and double-bit errors and actually correct single-bit errors. In other words, if a particular byte—group of 8 bits—contains errors in 2 of the 8 bits, ECC can recognize the error. If only 1 of the 8 bits is in error, ECC can correct the error.

Single- and Double-Sided Memory

Commonly speaking, the terms *single-sided memory* and *double-sided memory* refer to how some memory modules have chips on one side while others have chips on both sides. Double-sided memory is essentially treated by the system as two separate memory modules. Motherboards that support such memory have memory controllers that must switch between the two "sides" of the modules and, at any particular moment, can access only the side to which they have switched. Double-sided memory allows more memory to be inserted into a computer, using half the physical space of single-sided memory, which requires no switching by the memory controller.

Single-, Dual-, and Triple-Channel Memory

Standard memory controllers manage access to memory in chunks of the same size as the system bus's data width. This is considered communicating over a single channel. Most modern processors have a 64-bit system data bus. This means that a standard memory controller can transfer exactly 64 bits of information at a time. Communicating over a single channel is a bottleneck in an environment where the CPU and memory can both operate faster than the conduit between them. Up to a point, every channel added in parallel between the CPU and RAM serves to ease this constriction.

Memory controllers that support dual- and triple-channel memory implementation were developed in an effort to alleviate the bottleneck between the CPU and RAM. *Dual-channel memory* is the memory controller's coordination of two memory banks to work as a synchronized set during communication with the CPU, doubling the specified system bus width from the memory's perspective. *Triple-channel memory*, then, demands the coordination of three memory modules at a time.

The major difference between dual- and triple-channel architectures is that triple-channel memory employs a form of interleaving that reduces the amount of information transferred by each module. Nevertheless, there is an overall performance increase over that of dual-channel memory because of the ability to access more information per unit of time with triple-channel memory.

Because today's processors largely have 64-bit external data buses, and because one stick of memory satisfies this bus width, there is a 1:1 ratio between banks and modules. This means that implementing dual- and triple-channel memory in today's most popular computer systems requires that pairs or triads of memory modules be installed at a time.

Note, however, that it's the motherboard, not the memory, that implements dual- and triple-channel memory (more on this in a moment). *Single-channel memory*, in contrast, is the classic memory model that dictates only that a complete bank be satisfied whenever memory is initially installed or added. One bank supplies only half the width of the effective bus created by dual-channel support, for instance, which by definition pairs two banks at a time.

In almost all cases, multichannel implementations support single-channel installation, but poorer performance should be expected. The same loss of performance occurs when only two modules are installed in a triple-channel motherboard. Multichannel motherboards include slots of different colors, usually one of each color per set of slots. To use only a single channel, you populate slots of the same color, skipping neighboring slots to do so. Filling neighboring slots in a dual-channel motherboard takes advantage of its dual-channel capability.

Because of the special tricks that are played with memory subsystems to improve overall system performance, care must be taken during the installation of disparate memory modules. In the worst case, the computer will cease to function when modules of different speeds, different capacities, or different numbers of sides are placed together in slots of the same channel. If all of these parameters are identical, there should be no problem with pairing modules. Nevertheless, problems could still occur when modules from two different manufacturers or certain unsupported manufacturers are installed, all other parameters being the same. Technical support or documentation from the manufacturer of your motherboard should be able to help with such issues.

Although it's not the make-up of the memory that leads to dual-channel support but instead the technology on which the motherboard is based, some memory manufacturers still package and sell pairs and triplets of memory modules in an effort to give you peace of mind when you're buying memory for a system that implements dual- or triple-channel memory architecture. Keep in mind, the motherboard memory slots have the distinctive color-coding, not the memory modules.

Buffered and Unbuffered Memory

In technical terms, a *buffer* is a temporary storage area that takes some of the load off of the primary circuit. For instance, a network-interface buffer can store inbound packets when the CPU is currently unable to give undivided attention to the packets, or it can store outbound packets when available network bandwidth is low or the receiver has throttled its flow control. Buffers used in this sense are a form of hardware register. Registers are characterized by multiple cells, each of which stores a bit (binary digit) of information, accessed in parallel, at the same time.

In the high-end workstation and server market, there are two types of memory that are considered appropriate for the task at hand. The two types differ in the presence of a buffer or the lack thereof between the chips and the system's memory controller.

When the ECC memory mentioned earlier is referred to only as ECC, it is a form of *unbuffered* DIMM (see the section "Memory Packaging" later in this chapter for an explanation of DIMMs). Because *buffer* and *register* are interchangeable terms, in this context, this type of memory is also referred to as unregistered, and the modules are referred to as UDIMMs.

A common misconception could very well be that the term *unregistered* implies that there is an authority that provides certification for memory modules. Instead, the term refers to the hardware registers, or buffers, present in this type of memory module.

Buffered, or registered memory modules (RDIMMs), include specialized chips that act as buffers for all signals from the memory controller, except, in some cases, the data signals. By buffering these signals, the electrical load placed on the controller is reduced because the memory controller communicates in series with the register, instead of in parallel with the memory chips. The register performs the parallel communication with the chips.

Load-reduced DIMMs (LRDIMMs) are a form of registered DIMMs that increase performance by maintaining parallel communication, thus avoiding the performance hit of the conversion from serial to parallel.

The reduced electrical load on the memory controller leads to an increase in system stability when more modules are placed in a computer system. As a result, such systems can support more memory than those containing UDIMMs.

Before you jump to the conclusion that RDIMMs are, by definition, non-ECC, consider these points. The ECC function can be present with all forms of RDIMMs as well. UDIMMs may also be non-ECC. Nevertheless, the accepted industry naming convention is that the term *ECC*, alone, refers to UDIMMs. It would be correct to say, however, that UDIMMs and RDIMMs alike can be ECC or non-ECC based.

Types of Memory

Memory comes in many formats. Each one has a particular set of features and characteristics, making it best suited for a particular application. Some decisions about the application of the memory type are based on suitability; others are based on affordability to consumers or marketability to computer manufacturers. The following list gives you an idea of the vast array of memory types and subtypes:

- DRAM (dynamic random access memory)

    ADRAM (asynchronous DRAM)

    FPM DRAM (fast page mode DRAM)

    EDO DRAM (extended data out DRAM)

    BEDO DRAM (burst EDO DRAM)

    SDRAM (synchronous DRAM)

    SDR SDRAM (single data rate SDRAM)

    DDR SDRAM (double data rate SDRAM)

    DDR2 SDRAM (double data rate, version two, SDRAM)

    DDR3 SDRAM (double data rate, version three, SDRAM)

- SRAM (static random access memory)
- ROM (read-only memory)

I Can't Fill All My Memory Slots

As a reminder, most motherboard manufacturers document the quantity and types of modules that their equipment supports. Consult your documentation, whether in print or online, when you have questions about supported memory. Most manufacturers require that slower memory be inserted in lower-numbered memory slots. This is because such a system adapts to the first module it sees, looking at the lower-numbered slots first. Counterintuitively, however, it might be required that you install modules of larger capacity rather than smaller modules in lower-numbered slots.

Additionally, memory technology continues to advance after each generation of motherboard chipsets is announced. Don't be surprised when you attempt to install a single module of the highest available capacity in your motherboard and the system doesn't recognize the module, either by itself or with others. That capacity of module might not have been in existence when the motherboard's chipset was released. Sometimes, flashing the BIOS is all that is required. Consult the motherboard's documentation.

One common point of confusion, not related to capacity, when memory is installed is lack of recognition of four modules when two or three modules work fine, for example. In such a case, let's say your motherboard's memory controller supports a total of four modules. Recall that a double-sided module acts like two separate modules. If you are using double-sided memory, your motherboard might limit you to two such modules comprising four sides (essentially four virtual modules), even though you have four slots on the board. If instead you start with three single-sided modules, when you attempt to install a double-sided module in the fourth slot, you are essentially asking the motherboard to accept five modules, which it cannot.

Pay particular attention to all synchronous DRAM types. Note that the type of memory does not dictate the packaging of the memory. Conversely, however, you might notice one particular memory packaging holding the same type of memory every time you come across it. Nevertheless, there is no requirement to this end. Let's detail the intricacies of some of these memory types.

DRAM

DRAM is dynamic random access memory. This is what most people are talking about when they mention RAM. When you expand the memory in a computer, you are adding DRAM chips. You use DRAM to expand the memory in the computer because it's a cheaper type of memory. Dynamic RAM chips are cheaper to manufacture than most other types because they are less complex. *Dynamic* refers to the memory chips' need for a constant update signal (also called a refresh signal) in order to keep the information that is written there. If this signal is not received every so often, the information will bleed off and cease to exist. Currently, the most popular implementations of DRAM are based on synchronous DRAM and include DDR, DDR2, and DDR3. Before discussing these technologies, let's take a quick look at the legacy asynchronous memory types, none of which should appear on modern exams.

Asynchronous DRAM

Asynchronous DRAM (ADRAM) is characterized by its independence from the CPU's external clock. Asynchronous DRAM chips have codes on them that end in a numerical value that is related to (often 1/10 of the actual value of) the access time of the memory. Access time is essentially the difference between the time when the information is requested from memory and the time when the data is returned. Common access times attributed to asynchronous DRAM were in the 40- to 120-nanosecond (ns) vicinity. A lower access time is obviously better for overall performance.

Because ADRAM is not synchronized to the frontside bus, you would often have to insert wait states through the BIOS setup for a faster CPU to be able to use the same memory as a slower CPU. These wait states represented intervals in which the CPU had to mark time and do nothing while waiting for the memory subsystem to become ready again for subsequent access.

Common asynchronous DRAM technologies included fast page mode (FPM), extended data out (EDO), and burst EDO (BEDO). Feel free to investigate the details of these particular technologies, but a thorough discussion of these memory types is not necessary here. The A+ technician should be concerned with synchronous forms of RAM, which are the only types of memory being installed in mainstream computer systems today.

Synchronous DRAM

Synchronous DRAM (SDRAM) shares a common clock signal with the computer's system-bus clock, which provides the common signal that all local-bus components use for each step that they perform. This characteristic ties SDRAM to the speed of the FSB and hence the processor, eliminating the need to configure the CPU to wait for the memory to catch up.

Originally, *SDRAM* was the term used to refer to the only form of synchronous DRAM on the market. As the technology progressed, and more was being done with each clock signal on the FSB, various forms of SDRAM were developed. What was once called simply SDRAM needed a new name retroactively. Today, we use the term *single data rate SDRAM (SDR SDRAM)* to refer to this original type of SDRAM.

SDR SDRAM

SDR SDRAM is now considered a legacy RAM technology, and it is presented here only to provide a basis for the upcoming discussion of DDR and other more advanced RAM. With SDR SDRAM, every time the system clock ticks, 1 bit of data can be transmitted per data pin, limiting the bit rate per pin of SDRAM to the corresponding numerical value of the clock's frequency. With today's processors interfacing with memory using a parallel data-bus width of 8 bytes (hence the term *64-bit processor*), a 100MHz clock signal produces 800MBps. That's mega*bytes* per second, not mega*bits*. Such memory modules are referred to as PC100, named for the true FSB clock rate upon which they rely. PC100 was preceded by PC66 and succeeded by PC133, which used a 133MHz clock to produce 1066MBps of throughput.

Note that throughput in megabytes per second is easily computed as eight times the rating in the name. This trick works for the more advanced forms of SDRAM as well. The common thread is the 8-byte system data bus. Incidentally, you can double throughput results when implementing dual-channel memory.

DDR SDRAM

Double data rate (DDR) SDRAM earns its name by doubling the transfer rate of ordinary SDRAM; it does so by double-pumping the data, which means transferring a bit per pin on both the rising and falling edges of the clock signal. This obtains twice the transfer rate at the same FSB clock frequency. It's the increasing clock frequency that generates heating issues with newer components, so keeping the clock the same is an advantage. The same 100MHz clock gives a DDR SDRAM system the impression of a 200MHz clock compared to an SDR SDRAM system. For marketing purposes, and to aid in the comparison of disparate products (DDR vs. SDR, for example), the industry has settled on the practice of using this effective clock rate as the speed of the FSB.

Module Throughput Related to FSB Speed

There is always an 8:1 module-to-chip (or module-to-FSB-speed) numbering ratio because of the 8 bytes that are transferred at a time with 64-bit processors (*not* because of the ratio of 8 bits per byte). The formula in Figure 1.23 explains how this relationship works.

FIGURE 1.23   The 64-bit memory throughput formula

FSB in MHz	(cycles/second)
X 8 bytes	(bytes/cycle)
throughput	(bytes/second)

Because the actual system clock speed is rarely mentioned in marketing literature, on packaging, or store shelves for DDR and higher, you can use this advertised FSB frequency in your computations for DDR throughput. For example, with a 100MHz clock and two operations per cycle, motherboard makers will market their boards as having an FSB of 200MHz. Multiplying this effective rate by 8 bytes transferred per cycle, the data rate is 1600MBps. Because DDR made throughput a bit trickier to compute, the industry began using this final throughput figure to name the memory modules instead of the actual frequency, which was used when naming SDR modules. This makes the result seem many times better (and much more marketable), while it's really only twice (or so) as good, or close to it.

In this example, the module is referred to as PC1600, based on a throughput of 1600MBps. The chips that go into making PC1600 modules are named DDR200 for the effective FSB frequency of 200MHz. Stated differently, the industry uses DDR200 memory chips to manufacture PC1600 memory modules.

Let's make sure that you grasp the relationship between the speed of the FSB and the name for the related chips as well as the relationship between the name of the chips (or the speed of the FSB) and the name of the modules. Consider an FSB of 400MHz, meaning an actual clock signal of 200MHz, by the way—the FSB is double the actual clock for DDR, remember. It should be clear that this motherboard requires modules populated with DDR400 chips and that you'll find such modules marketed and sold as PC3200.

Let's try another. What do you need for a motherboard that features a 333MHz FSB (actual clock is 166MHz)? Well, just using the 8:1 rule mentioned earlier, you might be on the lookout for a PC2667 module. However, note that sometimes the numbers have to be played with a bit to come up with the industry's marketing terms. You'll have an easier time finding PC2700 modules that are designed specifically for a motherboard like yours, with an FSB of 333MHz. The label isn't always technically accurate, but round numbers sell better, perhaps. The important concept here is that if you find PC2700 modules and PC2667 modules, there's absolutely no difference; they both have a 2667MBps throughput rate. Go for the best deal; just make sure that the memory manufacturer is reputable.

DDR2 SDRAM

Think of the 2 in *DDR2* as yet another multiplier of 2 in the SDRAM technology, using a lower peak voltage to keep power consumption down (1.8V vs. the 2.5V of DDR). Still double-pumping, DDR2, like DDR, uses both sweeps of the clock signal for data transfer. Internally, DDR2 further splits each clock pulse in two, doubling the number of operations it can perform per FSB clock cycle. Through enhancements in the electrical interface and buffers, as well as through adding off-chip drivers, DDR2 nominally produces four times the throughput that SDR is capable of producing.

Continuing the DDR example, DDR2, using a 100MHz actual clock, transfers data in four operations per cycle (effective 400MHz FSB) and still 8 bytes per operation, for a total of 3200MBps. Just as with DDR, chips for DDR2 are named based on the perceived frequency. In this case, you would be using DDR2-400 chips. DDR2 carries on the effective-FSB frequency method for naming modules but cannot simply call them PC3200 modules because those already exist in the DDR world. DDR2 calls these modules PC2-3200 (note the dash to keep the numeric components separate).

As another example, it should make sense that PC2-5300 modules are populated with DDR2-667 chips. Recall that you might have to play with the numbers a bit. If you multiply the well-known FSB speed of 667MHz by 8 to figure out what modules you need, you might go searching for PC2-5333 modules. You might find someone advertising such modules, but most compatible modules will be labeled PC2-5300 for the same marketability mentioned earlier. They both support 5333MBps of throughput.

DDR3 SDRAM

The next generation of memory devices was designed to roughly double the performance of DDR2 products. Based on the functionality and characteristics of DDR2's proposed successor, most informed consumers and some members of the industry surely assumed the forthcoming name would be DDR4. This was not to be, however, and DDR3 was born. This naming convention proved that the 2 in DDR2 was not meant to be a multiplier but instead a revision mark of sorts. Well, if DDR2 was the second version of DDR, then DDR3 is the third. *DDR3* is a memory type that was designed to be twice as fast as the DDR2 memory that operates with the same system clock speed. Just as DDR2 was required to lower power consumption to make up for higher frequencies, DDR3 must do the same. In fact, the peak voltage for DDR3 is only 1.5V.

The most commonly found range of actual clock speeds for DDR3 tends to be from 133MHz at the low end to less than 300MHz. Because double-pumping continues with DDR3, and because four operations occur at each wave crest (eight operations per cycle), this frequency range translates to common FSB implementations from 1066MHz to more than 2000MHz in DDR3 systems. These memory devices are named following the conventions established earlier. Therefore, if you buy a motherboard with a 1600MHz FSB, you know immediately that you need a memory module populated with DDR3-1600 chips because the chips are always named for the FSB speed. Using the 8:1 module-to-chip/FSB naming rule, the modules that you need would be called PC3-12800, supporting a 12800MBps throughput.

The earliest DDR3 chips, however, were based on a 100MHz actual clock signal, so we can build on our earlier example, which was also based on an actual clock rate of 100MHz. With eight operations per cycle, the FSB on DDR3 motherboards is rated at 800MHz, quite a lot of efficiency while still not needing to change the original clock with which our examples began. Applying the 8:1 rule again, the resulting RAM modules for this motherboard are called PC3-6400 and support a throughput of 6400MBps, carrying chips called DDR3-800, again named for the FSB speed.

 Real World Scenario

Choosing the Right Memory for Your CPU

Picking out the right memory for your CPU and motherboard is all about understanding the minimum performance required for the CPU you choose. Sometimes, the motherboard you choose to mate with the CPU makes your decision for you. If you go with the cheaper motherboard, you might find that just a single channel of DDR2 is all you need to worry about. Otherwise, the more expensive boards might support dual- or triple-channel memory and require DDR3 modules. It's usually safe to assume that the higher price of admission gets you better performance. This is generally true on paper, but you might find that the higher-end setup doesn't knock your socks off the way you expected.

Let's say that you head down to your local computer store where motherboards, CPUs, memory, and other computer components are sold à la carte. You're interested in putting together your own system from scratch. Usually, you will have a CPU in mind that you would like to use in your new system. Assume you choose, for example, an Intel Core 2 Quad Q9650 processor. It's fast enough at 3GHz, but it calls for an older LGA 775 socket, meaning that you'll save a bit of money on that performance but you won't be approaching the state of the art. Nevertheless, the FSB with which this CPU is outfitted runs at a healthy 1333MHz, and its associated chipsets call for DDR3 memory. As a result, you will need to purchase one or more modules that contain DDR3-1333 chips, especially if you buy a motherboard that supports dual-channel memory. Therefore, you'll be buying PC3-10600 modules (multiplying 1333 by 8 and adjusting for marketing). Recall the 8:1 module-to-chip/FSB naming convention.

Perhaps you'd prefer the pricier Intel Core i7-990X Extreme Edition six-core processor. With a little research, you discover that Intel did away with the FSB by moving the memory controller out of the Northbridge and into the CPU. What remains is what Intel calls the QPI, or QuickPath Interconnect. QPI is a PCIe-like path that uses 20 bidirectional lanes to move data exceedingly fast between the CPU and RAM, requiring less capable RAM than FSB CPUs to do the same amount of work. The Core i7 requires a motherboard that has an LGA 1366 socket and supports a minimum of DDR3-1066 memory chips (chips, not modules). Therefore, you'll be buying at least one stick of your chosen capacity of PC3-8500 (multiplying 1066 by 8), two or three sticks if you decide to take advantage of the chip's ability to access as many as three channels of memory. These days, you'll have better luck starting with a minimum of PC3-10600 modules because PC3—8500s are becoming harder to find. The Core i7 is designed for desktop use; server-level processors that use the Intel QPI include the Xeon and Itanium.

To put each of the SDRAM types into perspective, consult Table 1.3, which summarizes how each technology in the SDRAM arena would achieve a transfer rate of 3200MBps, even if only theoretically.

TABLE 1.3   How some memory types transfer 3200MBps per channel

Memory Type	Actual/Effective (FSB) Clock Frequency (MHz)	Bytes per Transfer
DDR SDRAM PC3200	200/400	8
DDR2 SDRAM PC2-3200	100/400	8
DDR3 SDRAM PC3-3200*	50/400	8

*PC3-3200 does not exist and is too slow for DDR3.

SRAM

Static random access memory (SRAM) doesn't require a refresh signal like DRAM does. The chips are more complex and are thus more expensive. However, they are considerably faster. DRAM access times come in at 40 nanoseconds (ns) or more; SRAM has access times faster than 10ns. SRAM is classically used for cache memory.

ROM

ROM stands for read-only memory. It is called read-only because you could not write to the original form of this memory. Once information had been etched on a silicon chip and manufactured into the ROM package, the information couldn't be changed. Some form of ROM is normally used to store the computer's BIOS because this information normally does not change often.

The system ROM in the original IBM PC contained the power-on self-test (POST), BIOS, and cassette BASIC. Later, IBM computers and compatibles included everything but the cassette BASIC. The system ROM enables the computer to "pull itself up by its boot-straps," or *boot* (find and start the operating system).

Through the years, different forms of ROM were developed that could be altered, later ones more easily than earlier ones. The first generation was the programmable ROM (PROM), which could be written to for the first time in the field using a special program-ming device, but then no more. You may liken this to the burning of a CD-R.

The erasable PROM (EPROM) followed the PROM, and it could be erased using ultravio-let light and subsequently reprogrammed using the original programming device. These days, flash memory is a form of electronically erasable PROM (EEPROM). Of course, it does not require UV light to erase its contents, but rather a slightly higher than normal electrical pulse.

Although the names of these memory devices are different, they all contain ROM. Therefore, regardless which of these technologies is used to manufacture a BIOS chip, it's never incorrect to say that the result is a ROM chip.

Memory Packaging

First of all, it should be noted that each motherboard supports memory based on the speed of the frontside bus (or the CPU's QPI) and the memory's form factor. For example, if the motherboard's FSB is rated at a maximum speed of 1333MHz and you install memory that is rated at 1066MHz, the memory will operate at only 1066MHz, if it works at all, thus making the computer operate slower than it could. In their documentation, most mother-board manufacturers list which type(s) of memory they support as well as its maximum speeds and required pairings.

The memory slots on a motherboard are designed for particular module form factors or styles. RAM historically evolved from form factors no longer seen for such applications, such as dual inline package (DIP), single inline memory module (SIMM), and single inline pin pack-age (SIPP). The most popular form factors for primary memory modules today are as follows:

- DIMM (dual inline memory module)
- SODIMM (small outline dual inline memory module)

Note also that the various CPUs on the market tend to support only one form of physical memory packaging due to the memory controller in the Northbridge or CPU itself (QPI). For example, the Intel Pentium 4 class of processors was always paired with DIMMs. Laptops and smaller devices require SODIMMs or smaller memory packaging. So, in addition to coordinating the speed of the components, their form factor is an issue that must be addressed.

DIMM

One type of memory package is known as a DIMM, which stands for dual inline memory module. DIMMs are 64-bit memory modules that are used as a package for the SDRAM family: SDR, DDR, DDR2, and DDR3. The term *dual* refers to the fact that, unlike their SIMM predecessors, DIMMs differentiate the functionality of the pins on one side of the module from the corresponding pins on the other side. With 84 pins per side, this makes 168 independent pins on each standard SDR module, as shown with its two keying notches as well as the last pin labeled 84 on the right side in Figure 1.24. SDR SDRAM modules are no longer part of the CompTIA A+ objectives, and they are mentioned here as a foundation only.

FIGURE 1.24   An SDR dual inline memory module (DIMM)

The DIMM used for DDR memory has a total of 184 pins and a single keying notch, while the DIMM used for DDR2 has a total of 240 pins, one keying notch, and possibly an aluminum cover for both sides, called a *heat spreader* and designed like a heat sink to dissipate heat away from the memory chips and prevent overheating. The DDR3 DIMM is similar to that of DDR2. It has 240 pins and a single keying notch, but the notch is in a different location to avoid cross insertion. Not only is the DDR3 DIMM physically incompatible with DDR2 DIMM slots, it's also electrically incompatible.

Figure 1.25 shows a DDR2 module. A matched pair of DDR3 modules with heat spreaders, suitable for dual-channel use in a high-end graphics adapter or motherboard, is shown in Figure 1.26.

FIGURE 1.25   A DDR2 SDRAM module

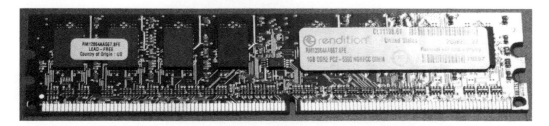

Figure 1.27 shows the subtle differences among various DIMM form factors.

FIGURE 1.26 A pair of DDR3 SDRAM modules

FIGURE 1.27 Aligned DIMM modules

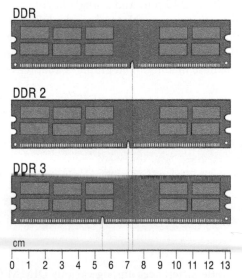

"Desktop DDR Memory Comparison" by Martini - Own work. Licensed under Public Domain via Wikimedia Commons

---

Inserting and Removing Memory Modules

The original single inline memory modules had to be inserted into their slots at a 45° angle. The installer then had to apply slight pressure as the module was maneuvered upright at a 90° angle to the motherboard where a locking mechanism would grip the module and prevent it from returning to its 45° position. This procedure created a pressure that reinforced the contact of the module with its slot. Releasing the clips on either end of the module unlocked it and allowed it to return to 45°, where it could be removed.

DIMM slots, by comparison, have no spring action. DIMMs are inserted straight into the slot with the locking tabs pulled away from the module. The locking tabs are at either end of the module, and they automatically snap into place, securing the module. Pulling the tabs away from the module releases the module from the slot, allowing it to be effortlessly removed.

SODIMM

Notebook computers and other computers that require much smaller components don't use standard RAM packages, such as DIMMs. Instead, they call for a much smaller memory form factor, such as a small outline DIMM. SODIMMs are available in many physical implementations, including the older 32-bit (72- and 100-pin) configuration and newer 64-bit (144-pin SDR SDRAM, 200-pin DDR/DDR2, and 204-pin DDR3) configurations.

All 64-bit modules have a single keying notch. The 144-pin module's notch is slightly off center. Note that although the 200 pin SODIMMs for DDR and DDR2 have slightly different keying, it's not so different that you don't need to pay close attention to differentiate the two. They are not, however, interchangeable. Figure 1.28 shows an example of a 144-pin, 64-bit SDR module. Figure 1.29 is a photo of a 200-pin DDR2 SODIMM.

FIGURE 1.28   144-pin SODIMM

FIGURE 1.29   200-pin DDR2 SODIMM

Identifying Purposes and Characteristics of Cooling Systems

It's a basic concept of physics: Electronic components turn electricity into work and heat. The excess heat must be dissipated or it will shorten the life of the components. In some cases (like with the CPU), the component will produce so much heat that it can destroy itself in a matter of seconds if there is not some way to remove this extra heat.

Air-cooling methods are used to cool the internal components of most PCs. With air cooling, the movement of air removes the heat from the component. Sometimes, large blocks of metal called heat sinks are attached to a heat-producing component in order to dissipate the heat more rapidly.

Fans

When you turn on a computer, you will often hear lots of whirring. Contrary to popular opinion, the majority of the noise isn't coming from the hard disk (unless it's about to go bad). Most of this noise is coming from the various fans inside the computer. Fans provide airflow within the computer.

Most PCs have a combination of these seven fans:

Front intake fan   This fan is used to bring fresh, cool air into the computer for cooling purposes.

Rear exhaust fan   This fan is used to take hot air out of the case.

Power supply exhaust fan   This fan is usually found at the back of the power supply, and it is used to cool the power supply. In addition, this fan draws air from inside the case into vents in the power supply. This pulls hot air through the power supply so that it can be blown out of the case. The front intake fan assists with this airflow. The rear exhaust fan supplements the power supply fan to achieve the same result outside of the power supply.

CPU fan   This fan is used to cool the processor. Typically, this fan is attached to a large heat sink, which is in turn attached directly to the processor.

Chipset fan   Some motherboard manufacturers replaced the heat sink on their onboard chipset with a heat sink and fan combination as the chipset became more advanced. This fan aids in the cooling of the onboard chipset (especially useful when overclocking—setting the system clock frequency higher than the default).

Video card chipset fan   As video cards get more complex and have higher performance, more video cards have cooling fans directly attached. Despite their name, these fans don't attach to a chipset in the same sense as to a chipset on a motherboard. The chipset here is the set of chips mounted on the adapter, including the GPU and graphics memory. On many late-model graphics adapters, the equivalent of a second slot is dedicated to cooling the adapter. The cooling half of the adapter has vents in the backplane bracket to exhaust the heated air.

Memory module fan   The more capable memory becomes of keeping up with the CPU, the hotter the memory runs. As an extra measure of safety, regardless of the presence of heat spreaders on the modules, an optional fan setup for your memory might be in order. See the upcoming section "Memory Cooling" for more information.

Motherboard Fan Power Connectors

It's important to be aware of the two main types of fan connections found on today's motherboards. One of these connectors has only three connections, while the other has four. The fan connectors and motherboard headers are interchangeable between the two pinouts, but if a chassis fan has four conductors, it's a sign that it's calling for connectivity to an extra +5VDC (volts direct current) connection that the most common three-pin header doesn't offer. A more rare three-pin chassis-fan connector features a +12VDC power connection for heavier-duty fans and a rotation pin used as an input to the motherboard for sensing the speed of the fan.

Four-pin CPU connections place the ground and power connections in pins 1 and 2, respectively, so that two-pin connectors can be used to power older fans. The four-pin header also offers a tachometer input signal from the fan on pin 3 so that the speed of the fan can be monitored by the BIOS and other utilities. Look for markings such as *CPU FAN IN* to identify this function. Pin 4 might be labeled *CPU FAN PWM* to denote the pulse-width modulation that can be used to send a signal to the fan to control its speed. This is the function lost when a three-pin connector is placed in the correct position on a four-pin header. Four-pin chassis-fan connectors can share the tachometer function but replace the speed control function with the extra 5V mentioned earlier.

Other power connections and types will be covered in Chapter 2, "Storage Devices and Power Supplies," including the Molex connector, which can be used to power chassis and CPU fans using an adapter or the built-in connector on mostly older fans manufactured

continues

continued

before the motherboard connectors were standardized. Figure 1.30 shows two three-pin chassis-fan headers on a motherboard.

FIGURE 1.30   Three-pin chassis-fan headers

Figure 1.31 shows a four-pin CPU fan header with an approaching three-pin connector from the fan. Note that the keying tab is lined up with the same three pins it's lined up with in the three-pin connectors.

FIGURE 1.31   A four-pin CPU fan header

This physical aspect and the similar pin functions are what make these connectors inter-changeable, provided the header's function matches the role of the fan being connected. Figure 1.32 shows the resulting unused pin on the four-pin header. Again, controlling the fan's speed is not supported in this configuration.

FIGURE 1.32   Position of a three-pin connector on a four-pin header

Ideally, the airflow inside a computer should resemble what is shown in Figure 1.33, where the back of the chassis is shown on the left in the image.

FIGURE 1.33   System unit airflow

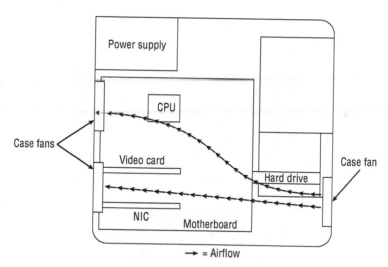

Note that you must pay attention to the orientation of the power supply's airflow. If the power supply fan is an exhaust fan, as assumed in this discussion, the front and rear fans will match their earlier descriptions: front, intake; rear, exhaust. If you run across a power supply that has an intake fan, the orientation of the supplemental chassis fans should be reversed as well. The rear chassis fan(s) should always be installed in the same orientation the power supply fan runs to avoid creating a small airflow circuit that circumvents the cross flow of air throughout the case. The front chassis fan and the rear fans should always be installed in reverse orientation to avoid having them fight against each other and thereby reduce the internal airflow. Reversing supplemental chassis fans is usually no harder than removing four screws and flipping the fan. Sometimes, the fan might just snap out, flip, and then snap back in, depending on the way it is rigged up.

Memory Cooling

If you are going to start overclocking your computer, you will want to do everything in your power to cool all of its components, and that includes the memory.

There are two methods of cooling memory: passive and active. The passive memory cooling method just uses the ambient case airflow to cool the memory through the use of enhanced heat dissipation. For this, you can buy either heat sinks or, as mentioned earlier, special "for memory chips only" devices known as heat spreaders. Recall that these are special aluminum or copper housings that wrap around memory chips and conduct the heat away from them.

Active cooling, on the other hand, usually involves forcing some kind of cooling medium (air or water) around the RAM chips themselves or around their heat sinks. Most often, active cooling methods are just high-speed fans directing air right over a set of heat spreaders.

Hard Drive Cooling

You might be thinking, "Hey, my hard drive is doing work all the time. Is there anything I can do to cool it off?" There are both active and passive cooling devices for hard drives. Most common, however, is the active cooling bay. You install a hard drive in a special device that fits into a 5'QF" expansion bay. This device contains fans that draw in cool air over the hard drive, thus cooling it. Figure 1.34 shows an example of one of these active hard drive coolers. As you might suspect, you can also get heat sinks for hard drives.

FIGURE 1.34   An active hard disk cooler

Chipset Cooling

Every motherboard has a chip or chipset that controls how the computer operates. As with other chips in the computer, the chipset is normally cooled by the ambient air movement in the case. However, when you overclock a computer, the chipset may need to be cooled more because it is working harder than it normally would be. Therefore, it is often desirable to replace the onboard chipset cooler with a more efficient one. Refer back to Figure 1.4 for a look at a modern chipset cooling solution.

CPU Cooling

Probably the greatest challenge in cooling is the computer's CPU. It is the component that generates the most heat in a computer (aside from some pretty insane GPUs out there). As a matter of fact, if a modern processor isn't actively cooled all of the time, it will generate enough heat to burn itself up in an instant. That's why most motherboards have an internal CPU heat sensor and a CPU_FAN sensor. If no cooling fan is active, these devices will shut down the computer before damage occurs.

There are a few different types of CPU cooling methods, but the most important can be grouped into three broad categories: air cooling, liquid cooling, and fanless and passive cooling methods.

Air Cooling

The parts inside most computers are cooled by air moving through the case. The CPU is no exception. However, because of the large amount of heat produced, the CPU must have (proportionately) the largest surface area exposed to the moving air in the case. Therefore, the heat sinks on the CPU are the largest of any inside the computer.

The CPU fan often blows air down through the body of the heat sink to force the heat into the ambient internal air where it can join the airflow circuit for removal from the case. However, in some cases, you might find that the heat sink extends up farther, using radiator-type fins, and the fan is placed at a right angle and to the side of the heat sink. This design moves the heat away from the heat sink immediately instead of pushing the air down through the heat sink. CPU fans can be purchased that have an adjustable rheostat to allow you to dial in as little airflow as you need, aiding in noise reduction but potentially leading to accidental overheating.

It should be noted that the highest-performing CPU coolers use copper plates in direct contact with the CPU. They also use high-speed and high-CFM cooling fans to dissipate the heat produced by the processor. CFM is short for cubic feet per minute, an airflow measurement of the volume of air that passes by a stationary object per minute.

Most new CPU heat sinks use tubing to transfer heat away from the CPU. With any cooling system, the more surface area exposed to the cooling method, the better the cooling. Plus the heat pipes can be used to transfer heat to a location away from the heat source before cooling. This is especially useful in cases where the form factor is small and with laptops, where open space is limited.

With advanced heat sinks and CPU cooling methods like this, it is important to improve the thermal transfer efficiency as much as possible. To that end, cooling engineers came up with a compound that helps to bridge the extremely small gaps between the CPU and the heat sink, which avoids superheated pockets of air that can lead to focal damage of the CPU. This product is known as thermal transfer compound, or simply thermal compound (alternatively, thermal grease or *thermal paste*), and it can be bought in small tubes. Single-use tubes are also available and alleviate the guesswork involved with how much you should apply. Watch out, though; this stuff makes quite a mess and doesn't want to come off your fingers very easily.

Apply the compound by placing a bead in the center of the heat sink, not on the CPU, because some heat sinks don't cover the entire CPU package. That might sound like a problem, but some CPUs don't have heat-producing components all the way out to the edges.

Some CPUs even have a raised area directly over the silicon die within the packaging, resulting in a smaller contact area between the components. You should apply less than you think you need because the pressure of attaching the heat sink to the CPU will spread the compound across the entire surface in a very thin layer. It's advisable to use a clean, lint-free applicator of your choosing to spread the compound around a bit as well, just to get the spreading started. You don't need to concern yourself with spreading it too thoroughly or too neatly because the pressure applied during attachment will equalize the compound quite well. During attachment, watch for oozing compound around the edges, clean it off immediately, and use less next time.

Improving and Maintaining CPU Cooling

In addition to using thermal compound, you can enhance the cooling efficiency of a CPU heat sink by lapping the heat sink, which smoothens the mating surface using a very fine sanding element, about 1000-grit in the finishing stage. Some vendors of the more expensive heat sinks will offer this service as an add-on.

If your CPU has been in service for an extended period of time, perhaps three years or more, it is a smart idea to remove the heat sink and old thermal compound and then apply fresh thermal compound and reattach the heat sink. Be careful, though; if your thermal paste has already turned into thermal "glue," you can wrench the processor right out of the socket, even with the release mechanism locked in place. Invariably, this damages the pins on the chip. Try running the computer for a couple of minutes to warm the paste and then try removing the heat sink again.

Counterintuitively, perhaps, you can remove a sealed heat sink from the processor by gently rotating the heat sink to break the paste's seal. Again, this can be made easier with heat. If the CPU has risen in the socket already, however, rotating the heat sink would be an extremely bad idea. Sometimes, after you realize that the CPU has risen a bit and that you need to release the mechanism holding it in to reseat it, you find that the release arm is not accessible with the heat sink in place. This is an unfortunate predicament that will present plenty of opportunity to learn.

If you've ever installed a brand-new heat sink onto a CPU, you've most likely used thermal compound or the thermal compound patch that was already applied to the heat sink for you. If your new heat sink has a patch of thermal compound preapplied, don't add more. If you ever remove the heat sink, don't try to reuse the patch or any other form of thermal compound. Clean it all off and start fresh.

Liquid Cooling

Liquid cooling is a technology whereby a special water block is used to conduct heat away from the processor (as well as from the chipset). Water is circulated through this block to a radiator, where it is cooled.

The theory is that you could achieve better cooling performance through the use of liquid cooling. For the most part, this is true. However, with traditional cooling methods (which use air and water), the lowest temperature you can achieve is room temperature. Plus, with liquid cooling, the pump is submerged in the coolant (generally speaking), so as it works, it produces heat, which adds to the overall liquid temperature.

The main benefit to liquid cooling is silence. There is only one fan needed: the fan on the radiator to cool the water. So a liquid-cooled system can run extremely quietly.

Liquid cooling, while more efficient than air cooling and much quieter, has its drawbacks. Most liquid-cooling systems are more expensive than supplemental fan sets and require less familiar components, such as a reservoir, pump, water block(s), hose, and radiator.

The relative complexity of installing liquid cooling systems, coupled with the perceived danger of liquids in close proximity to electronics, leads most computer owners to consider liquid cooling a novelty or a liability. The primary market for liquid cooling is the high-performance niche that engages in overclocking to some degree. However, developments in active air cooling, including extensive piping of heat away from the body of the heat sink, have kept advanced cooling methods out of the forefront. Nevertheless, advances in fluids with safer electrolytic properties and even viscosities keep liquid cooling viable.

In the next sections, you will notice a spate of seeming liquid-cooling methods. While these methods use liquid in the execution of their cooling duties, liquid to them is analogous to the heat used in cartridges to effect printing in inkjet printers. In other words, the following cooling systems are no more liquid-cooling methods than inkjet printers are thermal printers.

Fanless and Passive CPU Cooling Methods

Advancements in air cooling led to products like the Scythe Ninja series, which is a stack of thin aluminum fins with copper tubing running up through them. Some of the hottest-running CPUs can be passively cooled with a device like this, using only the existing air-movement scheme from your computer's case. Adding a fan to the side, however, adds to the cooling efficiency but also to the noise level, even though Scythe calls this line Ninja because of how quiet it is.

In addition to standard and advanced air-cooling methods, there are other methods of cooling a CPU (and other chips as well). Many of these are *fanless*, in that they do not include a fan but are still considered active because they require power to operate. Others require neither a fan nor power, making them *passive* methods. Some of these methods might appear somewhat unorthodox, but they often deliver extreme results.

 WARNING   Experimental methods can also result in permanent damage to your computer, so try them at your own risk.

Heat Pipes

Heat pipes are closed systems that employ some form of tubing filled with a liquid suitable for the applicable temperature range. Pure physics is used with this technology to achieve cooling to ambient temperatures; no outside mechanism is used. One end of the heat pipe is heated by the component being cooled. This causes the liquid at the heated end to evaporate and increase the relative pressure at that end of the heat pipe with respect to the cooler end. This pressure imbalance causes the heated vapor to equalize the pressure by migrating to the cooler end, where the vapor condenses and releases its heat, warming the nonheated end of the pipe. The cooler environment surrounding this end transfers the heat away from the pipe by convection. The condensed liquid drifts to the pipe's walls and is drawn back to the heated end of the heat pipe by gravity or by a wicking material or texture that lines the inside of the pipe. Once the liquid returns, the process repeats.

Heat pipes are found throughout the computing industry but are particularly beneficial in smaller devices, even as large as laptops. This is because heat pipes work in the absence of cavernous spaces that support airflow. A simple radiator of sorts at the cool end of the pipes, coupled with a simple fan, is enough to keep such devices running cool indefinitely.

Peltier Cooling Devices

Water- and air-cooling devices are extremely effective by themselves, but they are more effective when used with a device known as a *Peltier cooling element*. These devices, also known as thermoelectric coolers (TECs), facilitate the transfer of heat from one side of the element, made of one material, to the other side, made of a different material. Thus they have a hot side and a cold side. The cold side should always be against the CPU surface, and optimally, the hot side should be mated with a heat sink or water block for heat dissipation. Consequently, TECs are not meant to replace air-cooling mechanisms but to complement them.

One of the downsides to TECs is the likelihood of condensation because of the sub-ambient temperatures these devices produce. Closed-cell foams can be used to guard against damage from condensation.

Phase-Change Cooling

With phase-change cooling, the cooling effect from the change of a liquid to a gas is used to cool the inside of a PC. It is a very expensive method of cooling, but it does work. Most often, external air-conditioner-like pumps, coils, and evaporators cool the coolant, which is sent, ice cold, to the heat sink blocks on the processor and chipset. Think of it as a water-cooling system that chills the water below room temperature. Unfortunately, this is easily the noisiest cooling method in this discussion. Its results cannot be ignored, however; it is possible to get CPU temps in the range of −4° F (−20° C). Normal CPU temperatures hover between 104° F and 122° F (40° C and 50° C).

The major drawback to this method is that in higher-humidity conditions, condensation can be a problem. The moisture from the air condenses on the heat sink and can run off onto and under the processor, thus shorting out the electronics. Designers of phase-change cooling systems offer solutions to help ensure that this isn't a problem. Products in the form of foam; silicone adhesive; and greaseless, noncuring adhesives are available to seal the surface and perimeter of the processor. Additionally, manufacturers sell gaskets and shims that correspond to specific processors, all designed to protect your delicate and expensive components from damage.

Liquid Nitrogen and Helium Cooling

In the interest of completeness, there is a novel approach to super-cooling processors that is ill advised under all but the most extreme circumstances. By filling a vessel placed over the component to be cooled with a liquid form of nitrogen or, for an even more intense effect, helium, temperatures from −100° C to −240° C can be achieved. The results are short lived and only useful in overclocking with a view to setting records. The processor is not likely to survive the incident, due to the internal stress from the extreme temperature changes as well as the stress placed on the microscopic internal joints by the passage of excessive electrons.

Undervolting

Not an attachment, undervolting takes advantage of the property of physics whereby reduction in voltage has an exponential effect on the reduction of power consumption and associated heat production. Undervolting requires a BIOS (where the setting is made) and CPU combination that supports it.

You should monitor the system for unpredictable adverse effects. One of your troubleshooting steps might include returning the CPU voltage to normal and observing the results.

Summary

In this chapter, we took a tour of the system components of a PC. You learned about some of the elements that make up a PC, such as the motherboard, CPU, memory, BIOS/UEFI, and firmware. You'll learn about other PC components in the following chapters. You learned about the various methods used for cooling a PC. You also saw what many of these items look like and how they function.

Exam Essentials

Know the types of system boards.   Know the characteristics of and differences between ATX, micro ATX, and ITX motherboards.

Know the components of a motherboard.   Be able to describe motherboard components, such as chipsets, expansion slots, memory slots, external cache, CPUs, processor sockets, power connectors, BIOS/UEFI (firmware), and CMOS batteries.

Understand the purposes and characteristics of processors.   Be able to discuss the different processor packaging, old and new, and know the meaning of the terms *hyperthreading*, *cores*, *cache*, *speed*, *virtualization support*, and *integrated GPU*.

Understand the purposes and characteristics of memory. Know about the characteristics that set the various types of memory apart from one another. This includes the actual types of memory, such as DRAM (which includes several varieties), SRAM, ROM, and CMOS as well as memory packaging, such as DIMMs and SODIMMs. Also have a firm understanding of the different levels of cache memory as well as its purpose in general.

Understand the purposes and characteristics of cooling systems. Know the different ways internal components can be cooled and how overheating can be prevented.

Review Questions

The answers to the chapter review questions can be found in Appendix A.

1. Which computer component contains all of the circuitry necessary for other components or devices to communicate with one another?
   A. Motherboard
   B. Adapter card
   C. Hard drive
   D. Expansion bus

2. Which packaging is used for DDR SDRAM memory?
   A. 168-pin DIMM
   B. 72-pin SIMM
   C. 184-pin DIMM
   D. 240-pin DIMM

3. What memory chips would you find on a stick of PC3-16000?
   A. DDR-2000
   B. DDR3-2000
   C. DDR3-16000
   D. PC3-2000

4. Which motherboard design style features smaller size and lower power consumption?
   A. ATX
   B. AT
   C. Micro ATX
   D. ITX

5. Which of the following socket types is required for the Intel Core i7-9xx desktop series?
   A. LGA 1366
   B. LGA 1156
   C. LGA 1155
   D. LGA 775

6. Which of the following is a socket technology that is designed to ease insertion of modern CPUs?
   A. Socket 1366
   B. ZIF
   C. LPGA
   D. SPGA

7. Which of the following is *not* controlled by the Northbridge?
    A. PCIe
    B. SATA
    C. AGP
    D. Cache memory

8. Which of the following is used to store data and programs for repeated use? Information can be added and deleted at will, and it does *not* lose its data when power is removed.
    A. Hard drive
    B. RAM
    C. Internal cache memory
    D. ROM

9. Which socket type is required for an AMD Phenom II that uses DDR3 RAM?
    A. AM2
    B. AM2+
    C. AM3
    D. Socket 940

10. You press the front power button on a computer and the system boots. Later, you press it briefly and the system hibernates. When you press it again, the system resumes. You press and hold the button and the system shuts down. What is this feature called?
    A. Programmable power
    B. Soft power
    C. Relay power
    D. Hot power

11. Which of the following are the numbers of pins that can be found on DIMM modules used in desktop motherboards? (Choose two.)
    A. 180
    B. 184
    C. 200
    D. 204
    E. 232
    F. 240

12. To avoid software-based virtualization, which two components need to support hardware-based virtualization?
    A. Memory
    B. Hard drive
    C. CPU
    D. BIOS

13. You find out that a disgruntled ex-employee's computer has a boot password that must be entered before the operating system is ever loaded. There is also a password preventing your access to the BIOS utility. Which of the following motherboard components can most likely be used to return the computer to a state that will allow you to boot the system without knowing the password?

   A. Cable header

   B. Power supply connector

   C. Expansion slot

   D. Jumper

14. Your Core i5 fan has a four-pin connector, but your motherboard only has a single three-pin header with the CPU_FAN label. Which of the following will be the easiest solution to get the necessary cooling for your CPU?

   A. Plug the four-pin connector into the three-pin header.

   B. Buy an adapter.

   C. Leave the plug disconnected and just use the heat sink.

   D. Add an extra chassis fan.

15. What is the combined total speed of a PCIe 2.0 x16 slot?

   A. 500MBps

   B. 16Gbps

   C. 8GBps

   D. 16GBps

16. Which of the following allows you to perform the most complete restart of the computer without removing power?

   A. Start ➤ Restart

   B. Start ➤ Hibernate

   C. Reset button

   D. Power button

17. Which of the following is most helpful when flashing the BIOS on a desktop computer system?

   A. Floppy diskette drive

   B. Uninterruptible power supply

   C. An Internet connection

   D. The Windows administrator password

18. Intel and AMD have integrated which of the following into their Atom and APU processor lines that had not been integrated before?

   A. A GPU

   B. A math coprocessor

   C. The frontside bus

   D. The memory controller

19. You have just purchased a motherboard that has an LGA775 socket for an Intel Pentium 4 processor. What type of memory modules will you most likely need for this motherboard?

A. DIP

B. SIMM

C. RIMM

D. DIMM

20. What type of expansion slot is preferred today for high-performance graphics adapters?

A. AGP

B. PCIe

C. PCI

D. ISA

Performance-Based Question 1

You will encounter performance-based questions on the A+ exams. The questions on the exam require you to perform a specific task, and you will be graded on whether or not you were able to complete the task. The following requires you to think creatively in order to measure how well you understand this chapter's topics. You may or may not see similar questions on the actual A+ exams. To see how your answer compares to the authors', refer to Appendix B.

You have been asked to remove a dual inline memory module and insert one with a larger capacity in its place. Describe the process for doing so.

Performance-Based Question 2

Identify the component each arrow points to in the following image of an ATX motherboard.

Chapter

2

Storage Devices and Power Supplies

THE FOLLOWING COMPTIA A+ 220-901 EXAM OBJECTIVES ARE COVERED IN THIS CHAPTER:

✓ **1.5 Install and configure storage devices and use appropriate media.**

- Optical drives: CD-ROM / CD-RW, DVD-ROM / DVD-RW / DVD-RW DL, Blu-Ray, BD-R, BD-RE
- Magnetic hard disk drives: 5400 rpm, 7200 rpm, 10,000 rpm
- Hot swappable drives
- Solid state/flash drives: Compact flash, SD, Micro-SD, Mini-SD, xD, SSD, Hybrid, eMMC
- RAID types: 0, 1, 5, 10
- Tape drive
- Media capacity: CD, CD-RW, DVD-RW, DVD, Blu-Ray, Tape, DVD DL

✓ **1.8 Install a power supply based on given specifications.**

- Connector types and their voltages: SATA, Molex, 4/8-pin 12v, PCIe 6/8-pin, 20-pin, 24-pin
- Specifications: Wattage, Dual rail, Size, Number of connectors, ATX, Micro-ATX, Dual voltage options

As a PC technician, you need to know quite a bit about hardware. Given the importance and magnitude of this knowledge, the best way to approach it is in sections. The first chapter introduced the topic via the primary core components, and this chapter follows up where it left off. Specifically, this chapter focuses on storage devices and power supplies.

Identifying Purposes and Characteristics of Storage Devices

What good is a computer without a place to put everything? Storage media hold the data being accessed as well as the files that the system needs to operate and the data that needs to be saved. The many different types of storage media differ in terms of their capacity (how much they can store), access time (how fast the computer can access the information), and the physical type of media used.

Hard Disk Drive Systems

Hard disk drive (HDD) systems (or *hard drives* for short) are used for permanent storage and quick access. Hard drives typically reside inside the computer, where they are semi-permanently mounted with no external access (although there are external and removable hard drives) and can hold more information than other forms of storage. Hard drives use a *magnetic* storage medium, and they are known as conventional drives to differentiate them from newer solid-state storage media.

The hard disk drive system contains three critical components:

Controller   This component controls the drive. The controller chip controls how the drive operates and how the data is encoded onto the platters. It controls how the data sends signals to the various motors in the drive and receives signals from the sensors inside the drive. Most of today's hard disk drive technologies incorporate the controller and drive into one assembly. Today, the most common and well-known of these technologies is SATA.

Hard disk   This is the physical storage medium. Hard disk drive systems store information on small discs (from under 1 inch to 5 inches in diameter), also called *platters*, stacked together and placed in an enclosure.

Host bus adapter (HBA)   This is the translator, converting signals from the controller to signals that the computer can understand. Most motherboards today incorporate the host adapter into the motherboard's circuitry, offering headers for drive-cable connections. Legacy host adapters and certain modern adapters house the hard drive controller circuitry.

Figure 2.1 shows a hard disk drive and host adapter. The hard drive controller is integrated into the drive in this case, but it could be resident on the host adapter in other hard drive technologies. This particular example shows older technology because today's drives connect straight to the motherboard, in most cases, again with the HBA being integrated with the drive itself.

FIGURE 2.1   A hard disk drive system

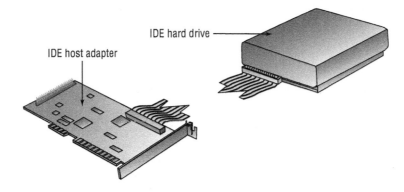

Figure 2.2 shows two 7-pin SATA headers on a motherboard.

FIGURE 2.2   SATA headers on a motherboard

"SATA ports" by en:User:Berkut - Transfered from English Wikipedia; en:File: SATA ports.jpg. Licensed under CC BY-SA 3.0 via Commons

These small headers in the photo connect SATA drives to the HBA circuitry in the Southbridge.

Anatomy of a Hard Drive

A hard drive is constructed in a cleanroom to avoid the introduction of contaminants into the hermetically sealed drive casing. Once the casing is sealed, most manufacturers seal one or more of the screws with a sticker warning that removal of or damage to the seal will result in voiding the drive's warranty. Even some of the smallest contaminants can damage the precision components if allowed inside the hard drive's external shell. The following is a list of the terms used to describe these components in the following paragraphs:

- Platters
- Read/write heads
- Tracks
- Sectors
- Cylinders
- Clusters (allocation units)

Inside the sealed case of the hard drive lie one or more platters, where the actual data is stored by the read/write heads. The heads are mounted on a mechanism that moves them in tandem across both surfaces of all platters. Older drives used a stepper motor to position the heads at discrete points along the surface of the platters, which spin at thousands of revolutions per minute on a spindle mounted to a hub. Newer drives use voice coils for a more analog movement, resulting in reduced data loss because the circuitry can sense where the data is located through a servo scheme, even if the data shifts due to changes in physical disc geometry. Figure 2.3 illustrates the key terms presented in this discussion. The four stacked discs shown in the illustration are platters.

FIGURE 2.3   Anatomy of a hard drive

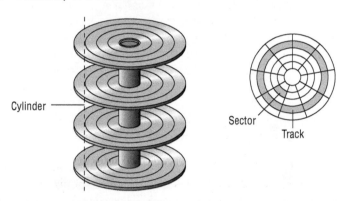

Factory preparation for newer drives, or low-level formatting in the field for legacy drives, maps the inherent flaws of the platters so that the drive controllers know not to place data in these compromised locations. Additionally, this phase in drive preparation creates concentric rings, or *tracks*, which are drawn magnetically around the surface of the platters. Sectors are then delineated within each of the tracks. *Sectors* are the magnetic domains that represent the smallest units of storage on the disk's platters. Magnetic-drive sectors commonly store only 512 bytes (½KB) of data each.

The capacity of a hard drive is a function of the number of sectors it contains. The controller for the hard drive knows exactly how the sectors are laid out within the disk assembly. It takes direction from the BIOS when writing information to and reading information from the drive. The BIOS, however, does not always understand the actual geometry of the drive. For example, the BIOS does not support more than 63 sectors per track. Nevertheless, many hard drives have tracks that contain many more than 63 sectors per track. As a result, a translation must occur from where the BIOS believes it is directing information to be written to where the information is actually written by the controller. When the BIOS detects the geometry of the drive, it is because the controller reports dimensions that the BIOS can understand. The same sort of trickery occurs when the BIOS reports to the operating system a linear address space for the operating system to use when requesting that data be written to or read from the drive through the BIOS.

The basic hard drive geometry consists of three components: the number of sectors that each track contains, the number of read/write heads in the disk assembly, and the number of cylinders in the assembly. This set of values is known as CHS (for cylinders/heads/sectors). The number of *cylinders* is the number of tracks that can be found on any single surface of any single platter. It is called a cylinder because the collection of all same-number tracks on all writable surfaces of the hard drive assembly looks like a geometric cylinder when connected together vertically. Therefore, cylinder 1, for instance, on an assembly that contains three platters comprises six tracks (one on each side of each platter), each labeled track 1 on its respective surface.

Because the number of cylinders indicates only the number of tracks on any one writable surface in the assembly, the number of writable surfaces must be factored into the equation to produce the total number of tracks in the entire assembly. This is where the number of heads comes in. There is a single head dedicated to each writable surface, two per platter. By multiplying the number of cylinders by the number of heads, you produce the total number of tracks throughout the disk assembly. By multiplying this product by the number of sectors per track, you discover the total number of sectors throughout the disk assembly. Dividing the result by 2 provides the number of kilobytes that the hard drive can store. This works because each sector holds 512 bytes, which is equivalent to ½KB. Each time you divide the result by 1024, you obtain a smaller number, but the unit of measure increases from kilobytes to megabytes, from megabytes to gigabytes, and so on. The equation in Figure 2.4 illustrates this computation:

For example, a drive labeled with the maximum allowed CHS geometry of 16383/16/63, respectively, results in only 7.9GB. Using the equation and multiplying the number of cylinders by the number of heads, you arrive at 262,128 total tracks on the drive. Multiplying this number by 63, the result is that there are 16,514,064 total sectors on the drive. Each sector holds ½KB, for a total capacity of 8,257,032KB. Dividing by 1024 to convert to MB and again by 1024 to convert to GB, the 7.9GB capacity is revealed. As a result, although drives larger than 8GB still display the 16383/16/63 CHS capacity for devices that must adhere to the CHS geometry, the CHS scheme cannot be used on today's larger drives at the risk of losing the vast majority of their capacity. The solution is to allow the operating system to reference logical blocks of ½KB sectors that can be individually addressed by a 48-bit value, resulting in 128PB of drive capacity, far above the largest drives being manufactured today. A PB is 1024TB; a TB is 1024GB.

FIGURE 2.4   Computing total sectors in CHS geometry

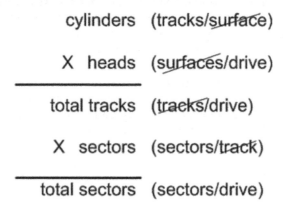

File systems laid down on the tracks and their sectors routinely group a configurable number of sectors into equal or larger sets called *clusters* or *allocation units*. This concept exists because operating system designers have to settle on a finite number of addressable units of storage and a fixed number of bits to address them uniquely. Because the units of storage can vary in size, however, the maximum amount of a drive's storage capacity can vary accordingly, but not unless logical drive capacities in excess of 2TB are implemented. Volumes based on the master boot record (MBR) structure are limited to 2TB total. Such volumes include those created on basic disks as well as simple and mirrored volumes on dynamic disks. Be aware that today's hard drives and volumes created with RAID can certainly exceed 2TB by combining multiple simple volumes into spanned or striped volumes, at which point maximum NTFS volume sizes—discussed at the end of this section—come into play. Keep in mind that larger clusters beget larger volumes, but they result in less efficient usage of space, a phenomenon that is discussed in the following paragraph.

No two files are allowed to occupy the same sector, so the opportunity exists for a waste of space that defragmenting cannot correct. Clusters exacerbate the problem by having a similar foible: The operating system does not allow any two files to occupy the same cluster. Thus the larger the cluster size, the larger the potential waste. So although you can increase the cluster size (generally to as large as 64KB, which corresponds to 128 sectors), you should keep in mind that unless you are storing a notable number of very large files, the waste will escalate astoundingly, perhaps negating or reversing your perceived storage-capacity increase. Nevertheless, if you have single files that are very large, say hundreds of megabytes or larger, then increased cluster sizes are for you.

For instance, assuming the 2TB maximum size for simple and mirrored dynamic volumes, a 64KB cluster size results in a maximum spanned or striped NTFS volume size of 64KB less than 256TB.

HDD Speeds

As the electronics within the HBA and controller get faster, they are capable of requesting data at higher and higher rates. If the platters are spinning at a constant rate, however, the information can only be accessed as fast as a given fixed rate. To make information available to the electronics more quickly, manufacturers increase the speed at which the platters spin from one generation of drives to the next, with multiple speeds coexisting in the marketplace for an unpredictable period, at least until the demand dies down for one or more speeds.

The following spin rates have been used in the industry for the platters in conventional magnetic hard disk drives:

- 5400 rpm
- 7200 rpm
- 10,000 rpm
- 12,000 rpm

While it is true that a higher revolutions per minute (rpm) rating results in the ability to move data more quickly, there are many applications that do not benefit from increased disk-access speeds. As a result, you should choose only faster drives, which are also usually more expensive per byte of capacity, when you have an application for this type of performance, such as for housing the partition where the operating system resides or for very disk-intensive programs. The lower speeds can be ideal in laptops, where heat production and battery usage can be issues with higher-speed drives.

Solid-State Drives

Conventional hard disk drive platters are still manufactured the same way that they have always been. They are metal or glass discs with a magnetic coating on their surface. The read/write heads change the magnetic orientation of each bit location, storing either a binary one or a binary zero. The same head senses the magnetic orientation of each location as the data is read from the disc.

Standard SSDs

In contrast, *solid-state drives (SSDs)* have no moving parts, but they use the same solid-state memory technology found in the other forms of flash memory. All solid-state memory is limited to a finite number of write (including erase) operations. Algorithms have been developed to spread the write operations over the entire device constantly. Such "wear leveling" increases the life of the SSD, but lack of longevity remains a disadvantage of this technology.

SSDs read contents more quickly, can consume less power and produce less heat, and are more reliable and less susceptible to damage from physical shock and heat production than their magnetic counterparts. However, the technology to build an SSD is still more expensive per byte, and SSDs are not yet available in capacities high enough to rival the upper limits of conventional hard disk drive technology. As of August 2015, for instance, the largest SSD on the market was 2TB, while the largest readily available conventional HDD was 8TB.

SSDs are separated into two broad categories: volatile DRAM-based and nonvolatile flash-based. Flash-based SSDs made with NAND memory (a transistor-based gate that has the opposite output to an AND gate) use considerably less power than HDDs. Those made with DRAM can use every bit as much power as conventional drives, however. The advantage of those made with the standard RAM modules used in desktop motherboards is that the modules can often be upgraded using larger modules, making a larger SSD overall.

When used as a replacement for traditional HDDs, SSDs are most often expected to behave in a similar fashion, mainly by retaining contents across a power cycle. With SSD, you can also expect to maintain or exceed the speed of the HDD. You can compensate for the volatility of DRAM-based SSDs by adding a backup power source, such as a battery or capacitor, or by keeping a nonvolatile backup of the drive's data that does not detract from the speed of the primary storage location. Flash-based SSDs, while faster during read operations than their HDD counterparts, can be made faster still by including a small amount of DRAM as a cache. DRAM-based SSDs are faster still.

Hybrid Drives

A cost-saving alternative to a standard SSD that can still provide a significant increase in performance over conventional HDDs is the *hybrid drive*. Hybrid drives can be implemented in two ways: a solid-state hybrid drive and a dual-drive storage solution. Both forms of hybrid drives can take advantage of solutions such as Intel's Smart Response Technology (SRT), which inform the drive system of the most used and highest-value data. The drive can then load a copy of such data into the SSD portion of the hybrid drive for faster read access.

It should be noted that systems on which data is accessed randomly do not benefit from hybrid drive technology. Any data that is accessed for the first time will also not be accessed from flash memory, and it will take as long to access it as if it were accessed from a traditional hard drive. Repeated use, however, will result in the monitoring software's flagging of the data for caching in the SSD.

Solid-State Hybrid Drive

The *solid-state hybrid drive (SSHD)* is a conventional HDD manufactured with a substantial amount of NAND-technology solid-state storage aboard. The SSHD is known to the operating system as a single drive, and individual access to the separate components is unavailable to the user.

Dual-Drive Solutions

Dual-drive storage solutions can also benefit from technologies such as Intel's SRT, but because they are implemented as two separate drives—one conventional HDD and one SSD—each with its own separate file system and drive letter, the user can also manually choose the data to move to the SSD for faster read access. Users can choose to implement dual-drive systems with SSDs of the same size as the HDD, resulting in a fuller caching scenario.

Optical Storage Drives

Most computers today have an optical storage drive, such as the latest *Blu-ray Disc (BD)* drive, a digital versatile disc (*DVD*, also called *digital video disc*) drive, or the legacy *compact disc* (*CD*) drive. Each type of optical drive can also be expected to support the technology that came before it. Such optical storage devices began earnestly replacing floppy diskette drives in the late 1990s. Although, like HDDs, these discs have greater data capacity and increased performance over floppies, they are not intended to replace hard disk drives. HDDs greatly exceed the capacity and performance of optical drives.

The CDs, DVDs, and BDs used for data storage are virtually the same as those used for permanent recorded audio and video. The way that data, audio, and video information is written to consumer-recordable versions makes them virtually indistinguishable from such professionally manufactured discs. Any differences that arise are due to the format used to encode the digital information on the disc. Despite the differences among the professional and consumer formats, newer players have no issue with any type of disc used. The encoding schemes used to store data on such discs are incompatible with the schemes used to record audio and video to the same discs.

CD-ROMs, DVD-ROMs, BD-ROMs, and Capacities

The amount of data that can be stored on the three primary formats of optical disc varies greatly, with each generation of disc exceeding the capacity of all previous generations. The following sections detail the science behind the capacities of all three formats.

CD-ROM

The *CD-ROM* (read-only memory) was designed for long-term storage of data. CD-ROMs are read-only, meaning that information written at the factory can't be erased or changed. CD-ROMs became very popular because they made a great software distribution medium. Programs are always getting larger and increasingly require more room to install, version after version. Instead of installing the program of the day using 100 floppy disks, you could use a single CD-ROM, which can hold approximately 650MB in its original, least-capable format. Although CDs capable of storing 700MB eventually became and continue to be the most common, discs with 800MB and 900MB capacities have been standardized as well. See Table 2.1 later in this chapter for a list of optical discs and their capacities.

DVD-ROM

For even more storage capacity, many computers feature some form of DVD or BD drive, such as the original DVD-ROM drive. The basic *DVD-ROM* disc is a single-sided disc that has a single layer of encoded information. These discs have a capacity of 4.7GB, many times the highest CD-ROM capacity. Simple multiplication can sometimes be used to arrive at the capacities of other DVD-ROM varieties. For example, when another media surface is added on the side of the disc where the label is often applied, a double-sided disc is created. Such double-sided discs have a capacity of 9.4GB, exactly twice that of a single-sided disc.

Practically speaking, the expected 9.4GB capacity from two independent layers isn't realized when those layers are placed on the same side of a DVD, resulting in only 8.5GB of usable space. (BDs do not have this issue; they make use of the full capacity of each layer.) The loss of capacity is due to the space between tracks on both layers being 10 percent wider than normal to facilitate burning one layer without affecting the other. This results in about 90 percent remaining capacity per layer. This technology is known as DVD DL (*DL* for dual-layer), attained by placing two media surfaces on the same side of the disc, one on top of the other, and using a more sophisticated mechanism that burns the inner layer without altering the semitransparent outer layer and vice versa, all from the same side of the disc. Add the DL technology to a double-sided disc, and you have a disc capable of holding 17.1GB of information—again twice the capacity of the single-sided version. Figure 2.5 shows an example of an early DVD-ROM drive, which also accepts CD-ROM discs. Modern 5¼″ optical drives are indistinguishable from older ones, aside from obvious markings concerning their capabilities.

FIGURE 2.5   An early DVD-ROM drive

BD-ROM

The next generation of optical storage technology was designed for modern high-definition video sources. The equipment used to read the resulting discs employs a violet laser, in contrast to the red laser used with standard DVD and CD technologies. Taking a bit of creative license with the color of the laser, the Blu-ray Disc Association named itself and the technology Blu-ray Disc (BD), after this visibly different characteristic. Blu-ray technology further increases the storage capacity of optical media without changing the form factor. On a 12cm disc, similar to those used for CD-ROMs and DVD-ROMs, BD derives a 25GB storage capacity from the basic disc. When you add a second layer to the same or opposite side of the disc, you attain 50GB of storage. The Blu-ray laser is of a shorter wavelength (405nm) than that of DVD (650nm) and CD (780nm) technologies. As a result, and through the use of refined optics, the laser can be focused on a much smaller area of the disc. This leads to a higher density of information being stored in the same area.

An interesting point to note is that designers of the Blu-ray technology do not have to stop with the common double-layer solution to increase capacity. Blu-ray discs with more than four layers on a side have been demonstrated, largely owing to the extremely accurate focus attainable with the Blu-ray laser.

In the interest of completeness, it should be mentioned that a high-definition technology directly related to DVD, because it comes from the same forum, and named HD DVD remains only as a footnote to the Blu-ray story. In February 2008, Toshiba, HD DVD's primary champion, gave up the fight, conceding to Blu-ray disc as the winner in the high-definition optical-disc race. HD DVD featured red- and blue-laser compatibility and 15GB data storage capacity.

Table 2.1 draws together the most popular optical-disc formats and lists their respective capacities. Some of these formats have already been introduced; others are presented in the upcoming section "Recordable Discs and Burners." Boldfaced capacities in the table are the commonly accepted values for their respective formats.

TABLE 2.1   Optical discs and their capacities

Disc Format	Capacity
CD SS (includes recordable versions)	650MB, **700MB**, 800MB, 900MB
DVD-R/RW SS, SL	4.71GB (**4.7GB**)
DVD+R/RW SS, SL	4.70GB (**4.7GB**)
DVD-R, DVD+R DS, SL	**9.4GB**
DVD-R SS, DL	8.54GB (**8.5GB**)
DVD+R SS, DL	8.55GB (**8.5GB**)
DVD+R DS, DL	17.1GB
BD-R/RE SS, SL	25GB
BD-R/RE SS, DL	50GB
BD-R/RE DS, DL	100GB

SS: single-sided; DS: double-sided; SL: single-layer; DL: dual-layer

Optical Drive Data Rates

CD-ROM drives are rated in terms of their data transfer speed. The first CD-ROM drives transferred data at the same speed as home audio CD players, 150KBps, referred to as 1X. Soon after, CD drives rated as 2X drives that would transfer data at 300KBps appeared. They increased the spin speed in order to increase the data transfer rate. This system of ratings continued up until the 8X speed was reached. At that point, the CDs were spinning so fast that there was a danger of them flying apart inside the drive. So, although future CD drives used the same rating (as in 16X, 32X, and so on), their rating was expressed in terms of theoretical maximum transfer rate; 52X is widely regarded as the highest multiplier for data CDs. Therefore, the drive isn't necessarily spinning faster, but through electronics and buffering advances, the transfer rates continued to increase.

The standard DVD-ROM 1X transfer rate is 1.4MBps, already nine times that of the comparably labeled CD-ROM. As a result, to surpass the transfer rate of a 52X CD-ROM drive, a DVD-ROM drive need only be rated 6X. DVD transfer rates of 16X at the upper end of the scale are common.

The 1X transfer rate for Blu-ray is 4.5MBps, roughly 3¼ times that of the comparable DVD multiplier and close to 30 times that of the 1X CD transfer rate. It takes 2X speeds to play commercial Blu-ray videos properly.

Recordable Discs and Burners

Years after the original factory-made CD-ROM discs and the drives that could read them were developed, the industry, strongly persuaded by consumer demand, developed discs that, through the use of associated drives, could be written to once and then used in the same fashion as the original CD-ROM discs. The firmware with which the drives were equipped could vary the power of the laser to achieve the desired result. At standard power, the laser allowed discs inserted in these drives to be read. Increasing the power of the laser allowed the crystalline media surface to be melted and changed in such a way that light would reflect or refract from the surface in microscopic increments. This characteristic enabled mimicking the way in which the original CD-ROM discs stored data.

Eventually, discs that could be written to, erased, and rewritten were developed. Drives that contained the firmware to recognize these discs and control the laser varied the laser's power in three levels. The original two levels closely matched those of the writable discs and drives. The third level, somewhere in between, could neutralize the crystalline material without writing new information to the disc. This medium level of power left the disc surface in a state similar to its original, unwritten state. Subsequent high-power laser usage could write new information to the neutralized locations.

The best algorithms for such drives, which are still available today, allow two types of disc erasure. The entire disc can be erased before new data is written (*erased* or *formatted*, in various application interfaces), or the data can be erased on the fly by one laser, just fractions of a second before new data is written to the same location by a second laser. If not properly implemented in a slow, determined fashion, the latter method can result in write errors because the crystalline material does not adequately return to its neutral state before the write operation. The downside to slowing down the process is obvious, and methods exist to allow a small level of encoding error without data loss. This need to move more slowly adds a third speed rating, the rewrite speed, to the existing read and write speed ratings of a drive. The following section delves more deeply into this concept. Updates to the drive's firmware can often increase or equalize these speeds.

Recordable CD Formats

CD-recordable (CD-R) and CD-rewritable (*CD-RW*) drives (also known as *CD burners*) are essentially CD-ROM drives that allow users to create (or *burn*) their own CD-ROMs. They look very similar to CD-ROM drives, but they feature a logo on the front panel that represents the drive's CD-R or CD-RW capability. Figure 2.6 shows the CD-R and CD-RW logos that you are likely to see on such drives.

FIGURE 2.6   CD-R and CD-RW logos

The difference between these two types of drives is that CD-R drives can write to a CD-R disc only once. A CD-RW drive can erase information from a CD-RW disc and rewrite to it multiple times. Also, CD-RW drives are rated according to their write, rewrite, and read times. Thus, instead of a single rating like 64X, as in the case of CD-ROM drives, CD-RW drives have a compound rating, such as 52X-32X-52X, which means that it writes at 52X, rewrites at 32X, and reads at 52X.

Recordable DVD Formats

A DVD burner is similar to a CD-R or CD-RW drive in how it operates: It can store large amounts of data on a special, writable DVD. Single-sided, dual-layer (DL) discs can be used to write 8.5GB of information to one single-sided disc. Common names for the variations of DVD burning technologies include DVD+R, DVD+RW, DVD-R, DVD-RW, DVD-RAM, DVD-R DL, and DVD+R DL. The "plus" standards come from the DVD+RW Alliance, while the "dash" counterparts are specifications of the DVD Forum. The number of sectors per disc varies between the "plus" and "dash" variants, so older drives might not support both types. The firmware in today's drives knows to check for all possible variations in encoding and capability. The "plus" variants have a better chance of interoperability, even without the disc being finalized.

A DVD-ROM or recordable drive looks very similar to a CD-ROM drive. The main difference is the presence of one of the various DVD logos on the front of the drive. CD-ROM and recordable CDs can usually be read and, if applicable, burned in DVD burners. Figure 2.7 and Figure 2.8 show the most popular data-oriented logos that you are likely to see when dealing with DVD drives suited for computers. Figure 2.7 shows the "dash" logos, while Figure 2.8 shows the "plus" logos.

FIGURE 2.7   DVD Forum logos

FIGURE 2.8   DVD+RW Alliance logos

Table 2.2 lists the main DVD formats used for storing and accessing data in computer systems as well as their characteristics.

TABLE 2.2   DVD formats and characteristics

Format	Characteristics
DVD-ROM	Purchased with data encoded; unable to be changed.
DVD-R, DVD+R	Purchased blank; able to be written to once and then treated like a DVD-ROM.
DVD-RW, DVD+RW	Purchased blank; able to be written to and erased multiple times; session usually must be closed for subsequent access to stored data.

Recordable BD Formats

The Blu-ray Disc Association duplicated the use of the R suffix to denote a disc capable of being recorded only once by the consumer. Instead of the familiar RW, however, the association settled on RE, short for re-recordable. As a result, watch for discs labeled BD-R and BD-RE. Dual-layer versions of these discs can be found as well.

The Blu-ray Disc Association decided against creating separate logos for each BD type, resolving instead to use only the logo shown in Figure 2.9. Discs are labeled most often in a sans-serif font with the actual type of the disc as well as this generic BD logo.

FIGURE 2.9   The Blu-ray Disc logo

Drive Interfaces and RAID

Storage devices come in many shapes and sizes. In addition to IDE/EIDE and SCSI, two of the older standards, there is now Serial ATA (*SATA*), and you can differentiate between internally and externally attached drives. The following sections look at storage devices from a number of those perspectives.

Parallel ATA (PATA) is nothing new. It is the name retroactively given to the ATA/IDE standards when SATA became available. PATA uses the classic 40-pin connector for parallel data communications, whereas SATA uses a more modern 7-pin card-edge connector for serial data transfer.

Serial AT Attachment Drives

At one time, *integrated drive electronics (IDE)* drives were the most common type of hard drive found in computers. Though often thought of in relation to hard drives, IDE was much more than a hard drive interface; it was also a popular interface for many other drive types, including optical drives and tape drives. Today, we call it IDE PATA and consider it to be a legacy technology. The industry now favors SATA instead.

Serial ATA began as an enhancement to the original ATA specifications, also known as IDE and, today, PATA. Technology is proving that the orderly progression of data in a single-file path is superior to placing multiple bits of data in parallel and trying to synchronize their transmission to the point that each bit arrives simultaneously. In other words, if you can build faster transceivers, serial transmissions are simpler to adapt to the faster rates than are parallel transmissions.

The first version of SATA, known as SATA 1.5Gbps (and also by the less-preferred terms SATA I and SATA 150), used an 8b/10b-encoding scheme that requires 2 non-data overhead bits for every 8 data bits. The result is a loss of 20 percent of the rated bandwidth. The silver lining, however, is that the math becomes quite easy. Normally, you have to divide by 8 to convert bits to bytes. With 8b/10b encoding, you divide by 10. Therefore, the 150MBps throughput for which this version of SATA was nicknamed is easily derived as 1/10 of the 1.5Gbps transfer rate. The original SATA specification also provided for hot swapping at the discretion of the motherboard and drive manufacturers.

Similar math works for SATA 3Gbps, also recklessly tagged as SATA II and SATA 300, and SATA 6Gbps, which is not approved for being called SATA III or SATA 600, but the damage is already done. Note that each subsequent version doubles the throughput of the previous version. Figure 2.10 shows a SATA connector on a data cable followed by the headers on a motherboard that will receive it. Note that identifiers silkscreened onto motherboards often enumerate such headers. The resulting numbers are not related to the SATA version that the header supports. Instead, such numbers serve to differentiate headers from one another and to map to firmware identifiers, often visible within the BIOS configuration utility.

The card-edge style connectors for data and power are arranged in such a manner on the back of SATA drives that no cables are required, although desktop and server systems almost certainly employ them. The same interface, however, can be used in laptops without the adapters needed to protect the delicate pins of the parallel interfaces found on the preceding generation of small form factor drives. The lack of adapter also leads to less space reserved in the bays for drives of the same size, giving designers and consumers the choice between smaller systems or more complex circuitry that can move into the newly available space.

FIGURE 2.10   SATA cable and headers

RAID

RAID stands for *Redundant Array of Independent Disks.* It's a way of combining the storage power of more than one hard disk for a special purpose, such as increased performance or fault tolerance. RAID can be implemented in software or in hardware, but hardware RAID is more efficient and offers higher performance but at an increased cost.

There are several types of RAID. The following are the most commonly used RAID levels:

RAID 0   Also known as *disk striping,* where a striped set of equal space from at least two drives creates a larger volume. This is in contrast to unequal space on multiple disks being used to create a simple *volume set*, which is not RAID 0. *RAID 0* is not RAID in every sense because it doesn't provide the fault tolerance implied by the *redundant* component of the name. Data is written across multiple drives, so one drive can be reading or writing while another drive's read-write head is moving. This makes for faster data access. However, if any one of the drives fails, all content is lost. Some form of redundancy or fault tolerance should be used in concert with RAID 0.

RAID 1   Also known as *disk mirroring*. *RAID 1* is a method of producing fault tolerance by writing all data simultaneously to two separate drives. If one drive fails, the other contains all of the data, and it will become the primary drive. However, disk mirroring doesn't help access speed, and the cost is double that of a single drive. If a separate host adapter is used for the second drive, the term *duplexing* is attributed to RAID 1. Only two drives can be used in a RAID 1 array.

RAID 5   Combines the benefits of both RAID 0 and RAID 1, creating a redundant striped volume set. Unlike RAID 1, however, *RAID 5* does not employ mirroring for redundancy. Each stripe places data on n-1 disks, and parity computed from the data is placed on the remaining disk. The parity is interleaved across all of the drives in the array so that neighboring stripes have parity on different disks. If one drive fails, the parity information for the stripes that lost data can be used with the remaining data from the working drives to derive what was on the failed drive and to rebuild the set once the drive is replaced.

The same process is used to continue to serve client requests until the drive can be replaced. This process can result in a noticeable performance decrease, one that is predictable because all drives contain the same amount of data and parity. Furthermore, the loss of an additional drive results in a catastrophic loss of all data in the array. Note that while live requests are served before the array is rebuilt, nothing needs to be computed for stripes that lost their parity. Recomputing parity for these stripes is required only when rebuilding the array. A minimum of three drives is required for RAID 5. The equivalent of one drive is lost for redundancy. The more drives in the array, the less of a percentage this single disk represents.

Although there are other implementations of RAID, such as RAID 3 and RAID 4, which place all parity on a single drive, resulting in varying performance changes upon drive loss, the three detailed here are by far the most prolific. RAID 6 is somewhat popular as well because it is essentially RAID 5 with the ability to lose two disks and still function. RAID 6 uses the equivalent of two parity disks as it stripes its data and distributed parity blocks across all disks in a fashion similar to that of RAID 5. A minimum of four disks is required to make a RAID 6 array.

There are also nested or hybrid implementations, such as *RAID 10* (also known as RAID 1+0), which adds fault tolerance to RAID 0 through the RAID 1 mirroring of each disk in the RAID 0 striped set. Its inverse, known as RAID 0+1, mirrors a complete striped set to another striped set just like it. Both of these implementations require a minimum of four drives and, because of the RAID 1 component, use half of your purchased storage space for mirroring.

Removable Storage and Media

Many additional types of storage are available for PCs today. Among the other types of storage available are tape backup devices, solid-state memory, and advanced optical drives. There are also external hard drives and optical drives as well as new storage media, such as USB keys that can store many gigabytes (more all the time, in fact) on a single small plastic device that can be carried on a lanyard around your neck or on a keychain.

Removable storage once meant something vastly different from what it means today. Sequential tape backup is one of the only remnants of the old forms of removable storage that can be seen in the market today. The more modern solution is random-access, solid-state removable storage. The following sections present details of tape backup and the newer removable storage solutions.

Tape Backup Devices

An older form of removable storage is the tape backup. Tape backup devices can be installed internally or externally and use either a digital or analog magnetic tape medium instead of disks for storage. They hold much more data than any other medium, but they are also much slower. They are primarily used for batch archival storage, not interactive storage.

With hard disks, it's not a matter of "if they fail"; it's "when they fail." So you must back up the information onto some other storage medium. Tape backup devices were once the most common choice in larger enterprises and networks because they were able to hold the most data and were the most reliable over the long term. Today, however, tape backup systems are seeing competition from writable and rewritable optical discs, which continue to advance in technology and size. Nevertheless, when an enterprise needs to back up large amounts of data on a regular basis, some form of tape media is the most popular choice. Table 2.3 lists the best known tape formats in order of market release dates, oldest first, and their capacities. Note that capacities are not associated with the format names but instead with models of tape within each format family.

TABLE 2.3   Sequential tape formats

Format Name	Representative Capacity
Quarter-inch Cartridge (QIC)	200KB to over a gigabyte
Digital Linear Tape (DLT)	Up to 800GB
Eight Millimeter (Data8, Exabyte)	Up to 60GB
Digital Audio Tape (DAT)/Digital Data Storage (DDS)	Up to 300GB, native
Linear Tape-Open (LTO)	Up to 2.5TB (up to 48TB planned)

Flash Memory

Once only for primary memory usage, the same components that sit on your motherboard as RAM can be found in various physical sizes and quantities among today's solid-state storage solutions. These include older removable and nonremovable flash memory mechanisms, Secure Digital (SD) and other memory cards, and USB flash drives. Each of these technologies has the potential to store reliably a staggering amount of information in a minute form factor. Manufacturers are using innovative packaging for some of these products to provide convenient transport options (such as keychain attachments) to users. Additionally, recall the SSD alternatives to magnetic hard drives mentioned earlier in this chapter.

For many years, modules and PC Card devices known as *flash memory* have offered low- to mid-capacity storage for devices. The name comes from the concept of easily being able to use electricity to alter the contents of the memory instantly. The original flash memory is still used in devices that require a nonvolatile means of storing critical data and code often used in booting the device, such as routers and switches.

For example, Cisco Systems uses flash memory in various forms to store its Internetwork Operating System (IOS), which is accessed from flash during boot-up and, in certain cases, throughout operation uptime and therefore during an administrator's configuration sessions. Lesser models store the IOS in compressed form in the flash memory device and then decompress the IOS into RAM, where it is used during configuration and operation. In this case, the flash memory is not accessed again after the boot-up process is complete, unless its contents are being changed, as in an IOS upgrade. Certain devices use externally removable PC Card technology as flash memory for similar purposes.

The following sections explain a bit more about today's most popular forms of flash memory, memory cards, and USB flash drives.

SD and Other Memory Cards

Today's smaller devices require some form of removable solid-state memory that can be used for temporary and permanent storage of digital information. Gone are the days of using microfloppies in your digital camera. Even the most popular video-camera media, such as mini-DVD and HDD, are giving way to solid-state multi-gigabyte models. These more modern electronics, as well as most contemporary digital still cameras, already use some form of removable memory card to store still images permanently or until they can be copied off or printed out. Of these, the *Secure Digital (SD)* format has emerged as the preeminent leader of the pack, which includes the older MultiMediaCard (MMC) format on which SD is based. Both of these cards measure 32mm by 24mm, and slots that receive them are often marked for both. The SD card is slightly thicker than the MMC and has a write-protect notch (and often a switch to open and close the notch), unlike MMC.

Even smaller devices, such as mobile phones, have an SD solution for them. One of these products, known as *miniSD*, is slightly thinner than SD and measures 21.5mm by 20mm. The other, *microSD*, is thinner yet and only 15mm by 11mm. Both of these reduced formats have adapters allowing them to be used in standard SD slots. Figure 2.11 is a photo of an SD card and a microSD card next to a ruler based on inches.

FIGURE 2.11   Typical SD cards

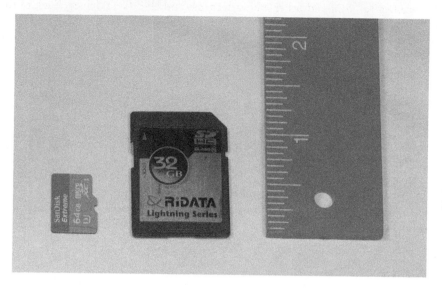

Table 2.4 lists additional memory card formats, the slots for some of which can be seen in the images that follow the table.

TABLE 2.4   Additional memory card formats

Format	Dimensions	Details	Year Introduced
CompactFlash (CF)	36mm by 43mm	Type I and Type II variants; Type II used by IBM for Microdrive	1994
xD-Picture Card	20mm by 25mm	Used primarily in digital cameras	2002

Figure 2.12 shows the memory-card slots of an HP PhotoSmart printer, which is capable of reading these devices and printing from them directly or creating a drive letter for access to the contents over its USB connection to the computer. Clockwise from the upper left, these slots accommodate CF/Microdrive, SmartMedia, Memory Stick (bottom right), and MMC/SD. The industry provides almost any adapter or converter to allow the various formats to work together.

FIGURE 2.12   Card slots in a printer

Many other devices exist for allowing access to memory cards. For example, 3½″ form factor devices can be purchased and installed in a standard front-access drive bay. One such device is shown in Figure 2.13. External card readers connected via USB, such as the one shown in Figure 2.14 (front first, then back), are widely available in many different configurations.

FIGURE 2.13   An internal card reader

Many of today's laptops have built-in memory card slots, such as the one shown in Figure 2.15.

Embedded Flash Memory

Based on the classic MMC flash card, embedded MMC (*eMMC*) stands for embedded MultiMediaCard. An eMMC drive can be permanently embedded on the primary circuit board of a cheaper or smaller mobile device. With its integrated controller logic, the eMMC drive can be made bootable as well. Although fostered beyond the time when development of the removable MMC card ceased, eMMC drives cannot compete outright with SSDs because the former does not have the latter's firmware and fast interfaces, such as SATA. Furthermore, SSDs use multiple flash memory chips as an array, similar to the way RAID uses multiple drives, to attain higher performance than an eMMC drive can.

FIGURE 2.14   A USB-attached card reader

FIGURE 2.15   Memory card slots in a laptop

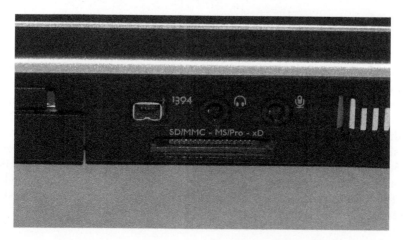

USB Flash Drives

USB flash drives are incredibly versatile and convenient devices that allow you to store large quantities of information in a very small form factor. Many such devices are merely extensions of the host's USB connector, extending out from the interface but adding little to its width, making them easy to transport, whether in a pocket or laptop bag. Figure 2.16 illustrates an example of one of these components and its relative size.

FIGURE 2.16   A USB flash drive

USB flash drives capitalize on the versatility of the USB interface, taking advantage of the Plug and Play feature and the physical connector strength. Upon insertion, these devices announce themselves to Windows File Explorer as removable drives, and they show up in the Explorer window with a drive letter. This software interface allows for drag-and-drop copying and most of the other Explorer functions performed on standard drives. Note that you might have to use the Disk Management utility (discussed in Chapter 13, "Operating System Basics") to assign a drive letter manually to a USB flash drive if it fails to acquire one itself. This can happen in certain cases, such as when the previous letter assigned to the drive has been taken by another device in the USB flash drive's absence.

Hot-Swappable Devices

Many of the removable storage devices mentioned are *hot swappable*. This means that you can insert and remove the device with the system powered on. Most USB-attached devices without a file system fall into this category. Non-hot-swappable devices, in contrast, either cannot have the system's power applied when they are inserted or removed or have some sort of additional conditions for their insertion or removal. One subset is occasionally referred to as cold swappable, the other as warm swappable. The system power must be off before you can insert or remove cold-swappable devices. An example of a cold-swappable device is anything connected to the PS/2-style mini-DIN connector, such as a keyboard or mouse. Insertion with the power on generally results in lack of recognition for the device and might damage the motherboard. AT keyboards and the full-sized DIN connector have the same restriction.

Warm-swappable devices include USB flash drives and external drives that have a file system. Windows and other operating systems tend to leave files open while accessing them and write cached changes to them at a later time, based on the algorithm in use by the software. Removing such a device without using the Safely Remove Hardware utility can result in data loss. However, after stopping the device with the utility, you can remove it without powering down the system, hence the *warm* component of the category's name. These are officially hot-swappable devices.

RAID systems benefit from devices and bays with a single connector that contains both power and data connections instead of two separate connectors. This is known as *Single Connector Attachment (SCA)*. SCA interfaces have ground leads that are longer than the power leads so that they make contact first and lose contact last. SATA power connectors are designed in a similar fashion for the same purpose. This arrangement ensures that no power leads make contact without their singular ground leads, which would often result in damage to the drive. Drives based on SCA are hot swappable. RAID systems that have to be taken offline before drives are changed out, but the system power can remain on, are examples of warm-swappable systems.

Installing, Removing, and Configuring Storage Devices

The removal and installation of storage devices, such as hard drives, CD/DVD drives, and tape drives, is pretty straightforward. There really isn't any deviation in the process of installing or exchanging the hardware. Fortunately, with today's operating systems, little to no configuration is required for such devices. The Plug and Play BIOS and operating system work together to recognize the devices. However, you still have to partition and format out-of-the-box hard drives before they will allow the installation of the operating system. Nevertheless, today's operating systems allow for a pain-free partition/format/setup experience by handling the entire process if you let them.

Removing Storage Devices

Removing any component is frequently easier than installing the same part. Consider the fact that most people could destroy a house, perhaps not safely enough to ensure their well-being, but they don't have to know the intricacies of construction to start smashing away. On the other hand, very few people are capable of building a house. Similarly, many could figure out how to remove a storage device, as long as they can get into the case to begin with, but only a few could start from scratch and successfully install one without tutelage.

In Exercise 2.1, you'll remove an internal storage device.

 This section details the removal of internal storage devices, and the section "Installing Storage Devices" details their installation. Be aware that external storage devices exist, but today's external storage devices are eSATA-, USB-, and FireWire-attached devices, making them completely Plug and Play. Only the software preparation of external hard drives is a consideration, but the same procedure for the software preparation of internal devices works for external devices as well. For this reason, these technologies have been removed from later versions of the A+ objectives.

EXERCISE 2.1

Removing an Internal Storage Device

1. With the power source removed from the system, ground yourself and the computer to the same source of ground.

2. Remove the cover from the system, exposing the internal components.

3. Unplug all connections from the storage device you wish to remove. These include data and power connections as well as any others, such as audio connections to the sound card or motherboard. The beveled Molex power connectors fit very tightly, so don't worry about how hard removing them seems to be. There is no clip to release. However, be sure to grip the connector, not the wires.

4. Gather the appropriate antistatic packaging for all static-sensitive components that will be reused in the future, including any adapter cards that the storage device plugs into.

5. Remove any obstructions that might hinder device removal, such as component cables attached to adapter cards or the adapter cards themselves, storing them in antistatic packaging so they can be reused.

6. Remove related adapter cards from the motherboard, storing them in antistatic packaging so they can be reused.

7. Remove the machine screws holding the storage device to the chassis. These could be on the side of the device or on the bottom.

8. Some devices, especially hard drives because they have no front access from the case, pull out of the chassis toward the rear of the case, while others, such as optical drives, generally pull out from the front. A gentle nudge from the rear of the device starts it on its way out the front. Go ahead and remove the device from the case. If you discover other components that obstruct the storage device's removal, repeat step 5.

Installing Storage Devices

An obvious difference among storage devices is their *form factor*. This is the term used to describe the physical dimensions of a storage device. Form factors commonly have the following characteristics:

- 3½″ wide vs. 5¼″ wide
- Half height vs. full height vs. 1″ high and more
- Any of the laptop specialty form factors

You will need to determine whether you have an open bay in the chassis to accommodate the form factor of the storage device that you want to install. Adapters exist that allow a device of small size to fit into a larger bay. For obvious reasons, the converse is not also true.

In Exercise 2.2, you'll install an internal storage device.

EXERCISE 2.2

Installing an Internal Storage Device

1. With the power source removed from the system, ground yourself and the computer to the same source of ground.

2. Remove the cover from the system, exposing the internal components.

3. Locate an available bay for your component, paying attention to your device's need for front access. If you do not see one, look around; some cases provide fastening points near the power supply or other open areas of the case. If you still do not see one, investigate the possibility of sacrificing a rarely or never used device to make room.

4. Remove any obstructions that might hinder device installation, such as component cables attached to adapter cards or the adapter cards themselves, storing them in antistatic packaging to be reused.

5. Find the proper screws for the storage device, and set any jumpers on the drive while it is in hand. Then insert the device into the bay. Keep in mind that some insert from the rear of the bay and some from the front.

6. Line up the screw holes in the device with the holes in the bay. Note that many devices rarely insert as far as they can before lining up with the chassis' holes, so don't be surprised when pushing the device all the way into the bay results in misalignment. Other devices that require front access stop themselves flush with the front of the case, and still others require you to secure them while holding them flush.

7. Use at least two screws on one side of the device. This keeps the device from sliding in the bay as well as from rotating, which happens when you use only one screw or one screw on each side. If the opposite side is accessible, go ahead and put at least one screw in the other side. Most devices allow for as many as four screws per side, but eight screws are not necessary in the vast majority of situations.

continues

8. Connect the data cable from the device to the adapter card or motherboard header. ATA devices, such as those that are designated as IDE drives (compatible hard drives and CD/DVD drives, for example) use a 40-pin connector.

9. Attach a power connector from the power supply to the device, bearing in mind that there are two connector styles that are not very close in appearance. You should have no trouble telling them apart. Be sure to insert the connector completely.

Identifying Purposes and Characteristics of Power Supplies

The computer's components would not be able to operate without power. The device in the computer that provides this power is the *power supply* (see Figure 2.17). A power supply converts 110V or 220V AC current into the DC voltages that a computer needs to operate. These are +3.3VDC, +5VDC, –5VDC (on older systems), +12VDC, and –12VDC. The jacket on the leads carrying each type of voltage has a different industry-standard color-coding for faster recognition. Black ground leads offer the reference that gives the voltage leads their respective magnitudes. The +3.3VDC voltage was first offered on ATX motherboards.

FIGURE 2.17   A power supply

The abbreviation *VDC* stands for *volts DC. DC* is short for *direct current.* Unlike alternating current (AC), DC does not alter the direction in which the electrons flow. AC for standard power distribution does so 50 or 60 times per second (50 or 60Hz, respectively).

Be aware that DC voltage is not safer than AC voltage, despite its common use in batteries and lower-power components. Direct current is more likely to cause a prolonged clamping of the muscles than AC, which is more likely to fibrillate the heart, which results in a deadly loss of coordination of the various cardiac muscles. Furthermore, power supplies contain transformers and capacitors that can discharge *lethal* amounts of current even when disconnected from the wall outlet for long periods. They are not meant to be serviced, especially by untrained personnel. *Do not* attempt to open them or do any work on them. Simply replace and recycle them when they go bad.

Dual-Rail Architecture

Some modern power supplies provide multiple 12V rails in an effort to supply more power overall to components that require 12VDC. For instance, in *dual-rail* power supplies, one rail might be dedicated to the CPU, while the other is used to supply power to all of the other components that need 12V.

The problem that can arise in high-powered systems is that although the collective power supplied by all rails is greater than that supplied by power supplies with a single rail, each rail provides less power on its own. As a result, it is easier to overdraw one of the multiple rails in such a system, causing a protective shutdown of the power supply. Care must be taken to balance the load on each of the rails if a total amperage greater than any one rail is to be supplied to attached components. Otherwise, if the total power required is less than any single rail can provide, there is no danger in overloading any one rail.

Power and Voltage Ratings

Power supplies are rated in watts. A watt is a unit of power. The higher the number, the more power your computer can draw from the power supply. Think of this rating as the "capacity" of the device to supply power. Most computers require power supplies in the 250- to 500-watt range. Higher wattage power supplies might be required for more advanced systems that employ power-hungry graphics technologies or multiple disk drives, for instance. It is important to consider the draw that the various components and subcomponents of your computer place on the power supply before choosing one or its replacement.

Of the connectors present in the classic power supplies, only the standard peripheral power connectors remain. In addition to these connectors, newer systems have a variety of replacement and additional connectors, such as dedicated power connectors for SATA and PCIe, more advanced power connectors for the motherboard, and even modular connections for these leads back to the power supply rather than a permanent wiring harness.

Some power supplies have a recessed, two-position slider switch, often a red one, on the rear that is exposed through the case. You can see the one for the power supply shown in Figure 2.17. *Dual voltage options* on such power supplies read 110 and 220, 115 and 230, or 120 and 240. This selector switch is used to adjust for the voltage level used in the country where the computer is in service. For example, in the United States, the power grid supplies anywhere from 110VAC to 120VAC. However, in Europe, for instance, the voltage supplied is double, ranging from 220VAC to 240VAC.

Although the voltage is the same as what is used in the United States to power high-voltage appliances such as electric ranges and clothes driers, the amperage is much lower. The point is, the switch is not there to allow multiple types of outlet to be used in the same country. If the wrong voltage is chosen in the United States, the power supply expects more voltage than it receives and might not power up at all. If the wrong voltage is selected in Europe, however, the power supply receives more voltage than it is set for. The result could be disastrous for the entire computer. Sparks could also ignite a fire that could destroy nearby property and endanger lives. Always check the switch before powering up a new or recently relocated computer. In the United States and other countries that use the same voltage, check the setting of this switch if the computer fails to power up.

Power Connectors

The connectors coming from the power supply are quite varied these days, but there are also some connectors that are considered legacy connectors that you might not see on modern power supplies. The following sections detail and illustrate the most common power connectors.

Classic Power Connectors

The classic connectors comprise outdated connectors as well as connectors still in use today despite being found in the original IBM PC.

AT System Connector

The original power connectors attached to the early PC motherboards were known collectively as the *AT system connector*. There are two six-wire connectors, labeled P8 and P9, as shown in Figure 2.18. They connect to an AT-style motherboard and deliver the power that feeds the electronic components on it. These connectors have small tabs on them that interlock with tabs on the motherboard's receptacle.

The P8 and P9 connectors must be installed correctly or you will damage the motherboard and possibly other components. To do this (on standard systems), place the connectors side by side with their black wires together, and then push the connectors together or separately onto the 12-pin receptacle on the motherboard. Although there is keying on these connectors, they both use the exact same keying structure. In other words, they can still be swapped with one another and inserted. When the black ground leads are placed together when the connectors are side by side, it is not possible to flip the pair 180 degrees and still insert the two connectors without physically defeating the keying. Most technicians would give up and figure out their mistake before any damage occurs if they always place the grounds together in the middle.

FIGURE 2.18   AT power supply system board connectors

 Although it's easy to remove this type of connector from the motherboard, the tabs on the connector make it difficult to reinstall it. Here's a hint: Place the connector at an almost right angle to the motherboard's connector, interlocking the tabs in their correct positions. Then tilt the connector to the vertical position. The connector will slide into place more easily.

It is important to note that only legacy computers with AT and baby AT motherboards use this type of power connector.

 Most computers today use some form of ATX power connector to provide power to the motherboard. Those connectors are described in later sections of this chapter.

Standard Peripheral Power Connector

The standard peripheral power connector is generally used to power different types of internal disk drives. This type of connector is also called a *Molex* connector. Figure 2.19

shows an example of a standard peripheral power connector. This power connector, though larger than the floppy drive power connector, uses the same wiring color code scheme as the floppy drive connector, although with a heavier gauge of wire. The added copper is for the additional current drawn by most devices that call for the Molex interface.

FIGURE 2.19   A standard peripheral power connector

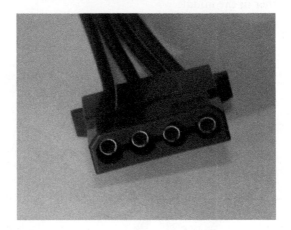

Modern Power Connectors

Modern components have exceeded the capabilities of some of the original power supply connectors. The Molex peripheral connector remains, but the P8/P9 motherboard connectors have been consolidated and augmented, and additional connectors have sprung up.

ATX, ATX12V, and EPS12V Connectors

With ATX motherboards came a new, single connector from the power supply. PCI Express has power requirements that even this connector could not satisfy, leading to different connectors with different versions of the more advanced ATX12V specifications, which have gone through four 1.x versions and already five 2.x versions. Throughout the versions of ATX12V, additional 4-, 6-, and 8-pin connectors supply power to components of the motherboard and its peripherals—such as network interfaces, PCIe cards, specialty server components, and the CPU itself—that require a +12V supply in addition to the +12V of the standard ATX connector. These additional connectors follow the ATX12V and EPS12V standards. The ATX connector was further expanded by an additional four pins in ATX12V 2.0.

The original ATX system connector (also known as the ATX motherboard power connector) feeds an ATX motherboard. It provides the six voltages required, plus it delivers them all through one connector: a single 20-pin connector. This connector is much easier to work with than the dual connectors of the AT power supply. Figure 2.20 shows an example of an ATX system connector.

FIGURE 2.20   ATX power connector

When the Pentium 4 processor was introduced, it required much more power than previous CPU models. Power measured in watts is a multiplicative function of voltage and current. To keep the voltage low meant that amperage would have to increase, but it wasn't feasible to supply such current from the power supply itself. Instead, it was decided to deliver 12V at lower amperage to a voltage regulator module (VRM) near the CPU. The higher current at a lower voltage was possible at that shorter distance from the CPU.

As a result of this shift, motherboard and power supply manufacturers needed to get this more varied power to the system board. The solution was the ATX12V 1.0 standard, which added two supplemental connectors. One was a single 6-pin auxiliary connector similar to the P8/P9 AT connectors that supplied additional +3.3V and +5V leads and their grounds. The other was a 4-pin square mini-version of the ATX connector, referred to as a P4 (for the processor that first required them) connector, which supplied two +12V leads and their grounds. EPS12V uses an 8-pin version, called the processor power connector, which doubles the P4's function with four +12V leads and four grounds. Figure 2.21 illustrates the P4 connector. The 8-pin processor power connector is similar but has two rows of 4 and, despite its uncanny resemblance, is keyed differently from the 8-pin PCIe power connector to be discussed shortly.

FIGURE 2.21   ATX12V P4 power connector

For servers and more advanced ATX motherboards that include PCIe slots, the 20-pin system connector proved inadequate. This led to the ATX12V 2.0 standard and the even higher-end EPS12V standard for servers. These specifications call for a 24-pin connector that adds further positive voltage leads directly to the system connector. The 24-pin connector looks like a larger version of the 20-pin connector. The corresponding pins of the 24-pin motherboard header are actually keyed to accept the 20-pin connector. Adapters are available if you find yourself with the wrong combination of motherboard and power supply. Many power supplies feature a 20-pin connector that snaps together with a separate 4-pin portion for flexibility, called a 20+4 connector, which can be seen in Figure 2.22. The 6-pin auxiliary connector disappeared with the ATX12V 2.0 specification and was never part of the EPS12V standard.

FIGURE 2.22   A 24-pin ATX12V 2.x connector in two parts

ATX12V 2.1 introduced a different 6-pin connector, which was shaped more like the P4 connector than the P8/P9-style auxiliary connector from the 1.x standards (see Figure 2.23). This 6-pin connector was specifically designed to give additional dedicated power to the PCIe adapters that required it. It provided a 75 W power source to such devices.

FIGURE 2.23   A 6-pin ATX12V 2.1 PCIe connector

ATX12V 2.2 replaced the 75W 6-pin connector with a 150W 8-pin connector, as shown in Figure 2.24. The plastic bridge between the top two pins on the left side in the photo keeps installers from inserting the connector into the EPS12V processor power header but clears the notched connector of a PCIe adapter. The individual pin keying should avoid this issue, but a heavy-handed installer could defeat that. The bridge also keeps the connector from inserting into a 6-pin PCIe header, which has identically keyed corresponding pins.

FIGURE 2.24   An 8-pin ATX12V 2.2 PCIe connector

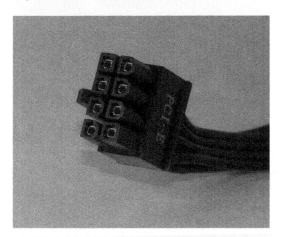

Proprietary Power Connectors

Although the internal peripheral devices have standard power connectors, manufacturers of computer systems sometimes take liberties with the power interface between the motherboard and power supply of their systems. In some cases, the same voltages required by a standard ATX power connector are supplied using one or more proprietary connectors. This makes it virtually impossible to replace power supplies and motherboards with other units "off the shelf." Manufacturers might do this to solve a design issue or simply to ensure repeat business.

SATA Power Connectors

SATA drives arrived on the market with their own power requirements in addition to their new data interfaces. Refer back to Figure 2.10 and imagine a larger but similar connector for power. You get the 15-pin SATA power connector, a variant of which is shown in Figure 2.25. The fully pinned connector is made up of three +3.3V, three +5V, and three +12V leads interleaved with two sets of three ground leads. Each of the five sets of three common pins is supplied by one of five single conductors coming from the power supply. The same colors are generally used for the conductors as with the Molex and Berg connectors. When the optional 3.3V lead is supplied, it is standard to see it delivered on an orange conductor.

FIGURE 2.25   SATA power connector

Note that in Figure 2.25, the first three pins are missing. These correspond to the 3.3V pins, which are not supplied by this connector. This configuration works fine and alludes to the SATA drives' ability to accept Molex connectors or adapters attached to Molex connectors, thus working without the optional 3.3V lead.

Replacing Power Supplies

Sometimes power supplies fail. Sometimes you grow out of your power supply and require more wattage than it can provide. Often, it is just as cost effective to buy a whole new case with the power supply included rather than dealing with the power supply alone. However, when you consider the fact that you must move everything from the old case to the new one, replacing the power supply becomes an attractive proposition. Doing so is not a difficult task.

Regardless of which path you choose, you must make sure the power connection of the power supply matches that of the motherboard to be used. Years ago, a new power supply with the single 20-pin ATX power connector wouldn't do a thing for you if you had a motherboard that had only the older P8/P9 connectors, although there are adapters that allow interconnection. Recall that the 24-pin ATXV2 2.x power supply connection can also be adapted to a motherboard with the 20-pin ATX connector.

Additionally, the physical size of the power supply should factor into your purchasing decision. If you buy a standard ATX-compatible power supply, it might not fit in the petite case you matched up to your micro-ATX motherboard. In that scenario, you should be on the lookout for a smaller form factor power supply to fit the smaller case. Odds are that the offerings that you find out there will tend to be a little lighter in the wattage department as well.

Exercise 2.3 details the process to remove an existing power supply. Use the reverse of this process to install the new power supply. Just keep in mind that you might need to procure the appropriate adapter if a power supply that matches your motherboard can no longer be found. There is no postinstallation configuration for the power supply, so there is nothing to cover along those lines. Many power supply manufacturers have utilities on their websites that allow you to perform a presale configuration so that you are assured of obtaining the most appropriate power supply for your power requirements.

EXERCISE 2.3

Removing a Power Supply

1. With the power source removed from the system, ground yourself and the computer to the same source of ground.

2. Remove the cover from the system, exposing the internal components.

3. After locating the power supply, which can come in a variety of formats and appear on the left or right side of the case, follow all wiring harnesses from the power supply to their termini, disconnecting each one.

4. Remove any obstructions that appear as if they might hinder removal of the power supply.

5. Using the dimensions of the power supply, detectable from the inside of the case, note which machine screws on the outside of the case correspond to the power supply. There are often four such screws in a nonsquare pattern. If your case has two side panels, and you removed only one, there will likely be one or more screws holding the other panel on that appear to be for the power supply. These do not need to be removed. If all case screws have been removed, pay attention to their location and do not use these holes when securing the new power supply.

6. Remove the screws that you identified as those that hold the power supply in place. Be aware that the power supply is not lightweight, so you should support it as you remove the final couple of screws.

7. Maneuver the power supply past any obstructions that did not have to be removed, and pull the power supply out of the case.

AC Adapters as Power Supplies

Just as the power supply in a desktop computer converts AC voltages to DC for the internal components to run on, the AC adapter of a laptop computer converts AC voltages to DC for the laptop's internal components. And AC adapters are rated in watts and selected for use with a specific voltage just as power supplies are rated. One difference is that AC adapters are also rated in terms of DC volts out to the laptop or other device, such as certain brands and models of printer.

Because both power supplies and AC adapters go bad on occasion, you should replace them both and not attempt to repair them yourself. When replacing an AC adapter, be sure to match the size, shape, and polarity of the tip with the adapter you are replacing. However, because the output DC voltage is specified for the AC adapter, be sure to replace it with one of equal output voltage, an issue not seen when replacing AT or ATX power supplies, which have standard outputs. Additionally, and as with power supplies, you can replace an AC adapter with a model that supplies more watts to the component because the component uses only what it needs.

You can read more on this subject later in Chapter 9, "Understanding Laptops."

Summary

In this chapter, you learned about two primary classes of personal computer components, specifically storage devices and power supplies. We covered storage devices such as hard drives (both conventional and solid state), optical drives, tape drives, and flash memory. We discussed power supply safety as well as the various connectors, and we compared and contrasted power supplies and AC adapters. You also learned how to remove, install, and configure storage devices and how to replace power supplies.

Exam Essentials

Be familiar with the components of a conventional hard drive system and the anatomy of a hard drive.   Most of today's hard drive systems consist of an integrated controller and disc assembly that communicates to the rest of the system through an external host adapter. The hard disk drives consist of many components that work together, some in a physical sense and others in a magnetic sense, to store data on the disc surfaces for later retrieval.

Get to know the newer solid-state drives.   SSDs continue to grow in popularity, and they will likely replace conventional drives as they become more reliable, offer larger capacities, and come down in price.

Understand the details surrounding optical storage.   From capacities to speeds, you should know what the varieties of optical storage offer as well as the specifics of the technologies this storage category comprises.

Be able to differentiate among removable storage options.   There are numerous tape and solid-state storage formats as well as a host of external and hot-swappable drives. Know the names of the options in each category.

Know about power supplies and their connectors.   Power supplies are made in AT, ATX, and proprietary form factors. Regardless of the type of power supply, they must offer connectors for motherboards and internal devices. Know the differences among the connectors and how power supplies are rated. Also understand why AC adapters are related to power supplies.

Know how to remove, install, and configure storage devices.   Know the difference between the data and power connectors used on storage devices. Know what it means to partition and format a hard drive. Be aware of the physical differences in storage device form factors.

Know how to remove, install, and configure power supplies.   Know the difference between the modern motherboard power headers, and know when an adapter might be required. Know the two most common device connectors coming from the power supply. Be familiar with how to fasten power supplies to the chassis as well as how to unfasten them.

Review Questions

The answers to the chapter review questions can be found in Appendix A.

1. What is the physical component where data is stored in a HDD?
    A. Read/write head
    B. Platter
    C. Sector
    D. Cluster

2. Which of the following is not one of the three major components of a hard disk drive system?
    A. Drive interface
    B. Controller
    C. Hard disk
    D. Host adapter

3. What is the largest NTFS volume size supported, assuming a 64KB cluster size as maximum?
    A. 256GB
    B. 2TB
    C. 128TB
    D. 256TB

4. Which technology is based on flash memory and is intended eventually to replace conventional hard disk drives that have moving discs and other mechanisms?
    A. USB flash drives
    B. Memory cards
    C. Solid-state drives
    D. Optical drives

5. A client is looking for a desktop drive technology that saves money over SSDs but offers performance increases over HDDs and can be used to house the operating system. Which of the following is the best to recommend?
    A. Dual-drive technology
    B. SSHD
    C. eMMC
    D. Magnetic-only drive

6. Which optical disc format supports a data capacity of 25GB?
    A. Double-sided, double-layer DVD+R
    B. Single-sided, single-layer Blu-ray disc
    C. Double-sided, single-layer DVD-R
    D. Double-sided, single-layer DVD+R

7. Which of the following best describes the concept of hot-swappable devices?

    A. Power does not need to be turned off before the device is inserted or removed.

    B. The device can be removed with power applied after it is properly stopped in the operating system.

    C. Care must be taken when swapping the device because it can be hot to the touch.

    D. The device can be swapped while still hot, immediately after powering down the system.

8. Of the following voltage pairings, which one accurately represents the input and output, respectively, of power supplies and AC adapters?

    A. AC in, AC out

    B. DC in, DC out

    C. AC in, DC out

    D. DC in, AC out

9. What are the output voltages that have been commonly produced by PC power supplies over the years? (Choose five.)

    A. +3.3VDC

    B. −3.3VDC

    C. +5VDC

    D. −5VDC

    E. +12VDC

    F. −12VDC

    G. +110VAC

    H. −110VAC

10. Which of the following statements about power supplies is true?

    A. You must make sure that the voltage selector switch on the back of the power supply is switched to the lower setting if the computer is going to be used in Europe.

    B. SATA hard drives most often use the same type of power connector that PATA hard drives use.

    C. Power supplies supply power to ATX-based motherboards with connectors known commonly as P8 and P9.

    D. Power supplies convert AC input to DC output.

11. Which of the following is not a consideration when installing an internal storage device?

    A. You should match the form factor of the drive or adapt it to an available drive bay or slot.

    B. You should secure the drive with at least two screws on one side and preferably two on each side.

    C. Due to the high revolutions at which modern hard drives spin, you must secure an external power source because the internal power supplies do not have the capacity.

    D. You need to be sure that the routing of the drive's ribbon cable, if applicable, does not obstruct the engineered flow of air across internal components.

12. What kind of media is most commonly used when large amounts of data need to be archived on a regular basis?

    A. Tape

    B. Optical disc

    C. External hard drive

    D. Network share

13. What does the *e* stand for in eMMC?

    A. Embedded

    B. Enhanced

    C. Extended

    D. External

14. Which of the following platter spin rates is not commonly associated with conventional magnetic hard disk drives?

    A. 5400 rpm

    B. 7200 rpm

    C. 10,000 rpm

    D. 12,000 rpm

15. Which of the following is not a consideration when upgrading power supplies?

    A. You might find that you do not have a matching motherboard connector on your new power supply.

    B. You might find that your case has a nonremovable power supply.

    C. You might find that your power rating is not adequate on the new power supply.

    D. You might find that you do not have enough of the appropriate connectors coming from the power supply for the devices that you have installed.

16. What does the red stripe on a ribbon cable indicate?

    A. Pin 16

    B. Pin 1

    C. The manufacturer's trademark

    D. Parity

17. Which of the following statements about dual-rail power supplies is LEAST true?

    A. Dual-rail power supplies have electrically separate 12VDC connections.

    B. Dual-rail power supplies typically support more cumulative amperage than single-rail supplies.

    C. Dual-rail power supplies are less likely to be overdrawn by connected components.

    D. Dual-rail power supplies feature most of the same connections as a single-rail supply.

18. Which of the following best describes a hybrid drive?

   A. A drive that has a SATA interface as well as one other

   B. A drive that has both HDD and SSD components

   C. A drive that can be used with Windows or Mac OS

   D. A drive that is partially internal and partially external

19. Which of the following is a concept that applies only to conventional magnetic hard disk drives and not newer solid-state drives?

   A. Storage capacity

   B. External attachment

   C. Access time

   D. 7200 rpm

20. When replacing a power supply, which of the following tends to vary among power supplies and must be chosen properly to support all connected devices?

   A. Wattage

   B. Voltage

   C. Amperage

   D. Resistance

Performance-Based Question

You will encounter performance-based questions on the A+ exams. The questions on the exam require you to perform a specific task, and you will be graded on whether or not you were able to complete the task. The following requires you to think creatively in order to measure how well you understand this chapter's topics. You may or may not see similar questions on the actual A+ exams. To see how your answer compares to the authors', refer to Appendix B.

Detail the process for removing a power supply from a computer chassis.

Chapter

3

Peripherals and Expansion

THE FOLLOWING COMPTIA A+ 220-901 OBJECTIVES ARE COVERED IN THIS CHAPTER:

✓ **1.4 Install and configure PC expansion cards.**

- Sound cards
- Video cards
- Network cards
- USB cards
- FireWire cards
- Thunderbolt cards
- Storage cards
- Modem cards
- Wireless/cellular cards
- TV tuner cards
- Video capture cards
- Riser cards

✓ **1.7 Compare and contrast various connection interfaces, their characteristics, and purpose.**

- Physical connections:
  - USB 1.1 vs. 2.0 vs. 3.0 (connector types: A, B, mini, micro)
  - FireWire 400 vs. FireWire 800
  - SATA1 vs. SATA2 vs. SATA3, eSATA
  - Other connector types (VGA, HDMI, DVI, Audio [analog, digital (optical connector)], RJ-45, RJ-11, Thunderbolt)
- Wireless connections:

- Bluetooth
- RF
- IR
- NFC
- Characteristics:
  - Analog
  - Digital
  - Distance limitations
  - Data transfer speeds
  - Quality
  - DRM
  - Frequencies

✓ **1.11 Identify connector types and associated cables.**

- Display connector types:
  - DVI-D
  - DVI-I
  - DVI-A
  - DisplayPort
  - RCA
  - HD15 (i.e., DE15 or DB15)
  - BNC
  - miniHDMI
  - miniDIN-6
- Display cable types:
  - HDMI
  - DVI
  - VGA
  - Component
  - Composite
  - Coaxial

- Device cables and connectors:
    - SATA
    - eSATA
    - USB
    - FireWire (IEEE1394)
    - PS/2
    - Audio
- Adapter and converters:
    - DVI to HDMI
    - USB A to USB B
    - USB to Ethernet
    - DVI to VGA
    - Thunderbolt to DVI
    - PS/2 to USB
    - HDMI to VGA

✓ **1.12 Install and configure common peripheral devices.**

- Input devices:
    - Mouse
    - Keyboard
    - Scanner
    - Barcode reader
    - Biometric devices
    - Game pads
    - Joysticks
    - Digitizer
    - Motion sensor
    - Touch pads
    - Smart card readers
    - Digital cameras
    - Microphone

- Webcam
- Camcorder
- MIDI enabled devices
- Output devices:
  - Printers
  - Speakers
  - Display devices
- Input & output devices:
  - Touch screen
  - KVM
  - Smart TV
  - Set-top box

With the core system components of the typical personal computer system under your belt, it is time to turn our attention to some of the available peripherals that can be connected to the computer. In doing so, we will also discuss the interfaces and cable assemblies associated with those peripherals.

Installing and Configuring Expansion Cards

An *expansion card* (also known as an *adapter card*) is simply a circuit board that you install into a computer to increase the capabilities of that computer. Expansion cards come in varying formats for different uses, but the important thing to note is that no matter what function a card has, the card being installed must match the bus type of the motherboard into which it is being installed. For example, you can install a PCI network card into a PCI expansion slot only.

For today's integrated components (those built into the motherboard), you might not need an adapter to achieve the related services, but you will still need to install drivers to make the integrated devices function with the operating system. As the trend toward more integrated components was maturing, many installers found most of the integrated components to be nonfunctional. A quick check in Device Manager showed a small collection of devices to be without their device drivers. Most motherboard manufacturers supply CD-ROM discs with their motherboards that contain all of the device drivers needed to get the built-in electronics recognized by the operating system. Execution of the disc's setup program generally results in all components working and Device Manager clearing its warnings.

The following are the four most common categories of expansion cards installed today:

- Video
- Multimedia
- I/O
- Communications

Let's take a quick look at each of these card types, their functions, and what some of them look like.

Video

A video adapter (more commonly called a graphics adapter or even more commonly a *video card*) is the expansion card that you put into a computer to allow the computer to display information on some kind of monitor. A video card is also responsible for converting the data sent to it by the CPU into the pixels, addresses, and other items required for display. Sometimes, video cards can include dedicated chips to perform some of these functions, thus accelerating the speed of display.

At a basic level, video adapters that have a PCI interface operate sufficiently. However, because AGP and PCIe slots offer more resources to the adapter, most manufacturers and computer owners prefer not to use PCI slots for video adapters. Although you might be able to find the rare motherboard that still offers an AGP slot, PCIe is the preferred expansion slot for video card attachment. The technology on which PCIe was designed performs better for video than those on which AGP and PCI are based. Figure 3.1 shows an example of a PCIe-based video card.

FIGURE 3.1   A video expansion card

Multimedia

The most basic and prolific multimedia adapter is the sound card. TV tuner cards and video capture cards are newer multimedia adapters that continue to gain in popularity due to decreasing cost and the rise of the Internet as a forum for creative sharing.

Sound Card

Just as there are devices to convert computer signals into printouts and video information, there are devices to convert those signals into sound. These devices are known as *sound cards*. Although sound cards started out as pluggable adapters, this functionality is one of the most common integrated technologies found on motherboards today. A sound card typically has small, round, 1/8″ jacks on the back of it for connecting microphones, headphones, and speakers as well as other sound equipment. Many sound cards used to have a DA15 game port, which can be used either for joysticks or MIDI controllers. Figure 3.2 shows an example of a legacy sound card with a DA15 game port.

FIGURE 3.2   A classic sound card

Sound cards today might come with an RCA jack (see the section "Audio/Video Jacks" later in this chapter). This is decidedly not for composite video. Instead, there is a digital audio specification known as the Sony/Philips Digital Interface (S/PDIF). Not only does this format allow you to transmit audio in digital clarity, but in addition to specifying an RCA jack and coaxial copper cabling, it specifies optical fiber connectors (TOSLINK) and cabling for electrically noisy environments, further increasing the transmission quality of the digital signal.

TV Tuner Cards and Video Capture Cards

The *TV tuner card* is a class of internal and external devices that allows you to connect a broadcast signal, such as home cable television, to your computer and display the output on the computer monitor. TV tuner cards come in analog, digital, and hybrid varieties. Most TV tuner cards act as video capture cards as well. A *video capture card* can also be a stand-alone device, and it is often used to save a video stream to the computer for later manipulation or sharing. Video-sharing sites on the Internet make video capture cards quite popular with enterprises and Internet socialites alike. TV tuner cards and video capture cards need and often come with software to aid in the processing of multimedia input.

I/O

I/O card is often used as a catchall phrase for any expansion card that enhances the system, allowing it to interface with devices that offer input to the system, output from the system, or both. The following are common examples of modern I/O cards:

- USB cards
- FireWire cards
- Thunderbolt cards
- Storage cards, such as eSATA

These cards are to be installed in a compatible slot on the motherboard. Their configuration is minimal, and it is usually completed through the Plug and Play process. Nevertheless, check the BIOS settings after installation for new entries in the menu structure. It's the job of the BIOS to track all of the hardware in the system and supply resources as needed. For example, a new Thunderbolt expansion card might allow you to configure whether attached Thunderbolt devices should be allowed to wake the system, how long of a delay should be observed before waking the system, and various settings for how to use memory and other resources.

Communications

Communications adapters give a computer the ability to transmit information to other devices that might be too distant to cable up to directly. Network adapters and modems are the two most popular types of communications adapters. Network adapters are generally used within the administrative domain of a home or enterprise and rely on other devices to relay their transmissions around the world. In contrast, modems allow direct domestic or international communication between two devices across the Public Switched Telephone Network (PSTN). Although there are other devices in the PSTN, the service provider's network appears as a cloud to the end stations, unlike the intermediate devices of a home or enterprise data network.

Network Interface Card (NIC)

A *network interface card (NIC)* is an expansion card that connects a computer to a network so that it can communicate with other computers on that network. *NIC* can also stand for *network interface controller*. It translates the data from the parallel data stream used inside the computer into the serial data stream that makes up the frames used on the network. It has a connector for the type of expansion bus on the motherboard (PCIe, PCI, and so on) as well as a connector for the type of network (such as fiber connectors, RJ-45 for UTP, antenna for wireless, or BNC for legacy coax). In addition to physically installing the NIC, you need to install drivers for the NIC in order for the computer to use the adapter to access the network. Figure 3.3 shows an example of a NIC.

FIGURE 3.3   A network interface card

   Some computers have NIC circuitry integrated into their motherboards. Therefore, a computer with an integrated NIC wouldn't need to have a NIC expansion card installed unless it was faster or you were using the second NIC for load balancing, security, or fault-tolerance applications.

If you have a system with either no or too few Ethernet interfaces, it's easy to find a *USB-to-Ethernet* adapter that uses an existing USB port to gain access to the energy needed to power the circuitry at the heart of the adapter's Ethernet interface. The USB port is also used as the communication pathway for the now-powered Ethernet interface to transmit and receive across a standard Ethernet network. Figure 3.4 shows an example of a USB-to-Ethernet adapter, with the Ethernet interface in the foreground.

FIGURE 3.4   A USB-to-Ethernet adapter

Ash Kyd/USB Ethernet adapter Licensed under CC BY-SA 4.0 via Commons

Another type of USB-to-Ethernet converter on the market is a device that produces the opposite effect and uses an Ethernet network to extend the range of USB ports and devices, which are unable to extend beyond a few meters on their own. There is an ongoing effort by various groups, such as the USB/IP Project, to advance the state of the art regarding the use of networks to extend USB connectivity. Other vendors create client-server platforms, such as USB over Network, to create an environment that supports USB access over the network.

Wireless NICs

Wireless NICs have the unique characteristic of requiring that you configure their connecting device before configuring the NIC. Wired NICs can generally create a link and begin operation just by being physically connected out of the box to a hub or switch. The wireless access point or ad hoc partner computer must also be configured before secure communication, at a minimum, can occur by using a wireless NIC. These terms will be explained in greater detail in Chapter 8, "Installing Wireless and SOHO Networks."

Cellular Cards

Almost every cellular service provider offers a line of adapters that can be installed into or inserted on the outside of desktop and laptop computers. Some advanced users have modified wireless access points to allow the insertion of such adapters into USB interfaces to act as the WAN gateway to obtain Internet access for their attached clients. In addition, depending on your service plan, most smartphones can be tethered to your computer and used as a cellular gateway. Very often, the cellular adapter comes with a setup program that configures the card for the service provider's network. From that point, anytime you are in a cellular service area, you can use the adapter to gain access to the Internet through the provider or by roaming on the network of a partner or competitor with which an agreement has been reached in that area.

Today, it's exceedingly common for cellular providers to offer devices like the one shown in Figure 3.5. Some of these devices use 3G or 4G cellular services to provide Internet access through the device. The LAN portion of the device creates an 802.11 wireless LAN to which 5, 10, or even more WiFi clients can attach.

FIGURE 3.5   A cellular hotspot

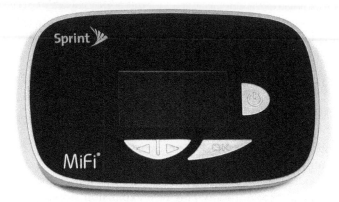

Modem

Any computer that connects to the Internet using an analog dial-up connection needs a modem, or *mo*dulator/*dem*odulator. A *modem* is a device that converts digital signals from a computer into analog signals that can be transmitted over phone lines and back again. These expansion card devices have one connector for the expansion bus being used (PCIe, PCI, and so on) and another for connection to the telephone line. Actually, as you can see in Figure 3.6, which shows an old ISA modem card, there might be two RJ-11 ports: one for connection to the telephone line and the other for connection to a telephone. This is primarily so that a phone can gain access to the same wall jack that the computer connects to without swapping their cords or using a separate splitter. Keep in mind, though, that you won't be able to use the phone while the computer is connected to the Internet.

FIGURE 3.6   An internal analog modem

Riser Cards

An alternative motherboard form factor, known as New Low-Profile Extended (NLX), or one of its offshoots has been used in some types of low-profile cases. NLX places the expansion slots sideways on a special *riser card* to use the reduced vertical space optimally. Adapter cards that normally plug into expansion slots vertically in other motherboards plug in parallel to the motherboard, so their second most demanding dimension does not affect case height. Figure 3.7 shows a motherboard with its riser card attached.

Riser technology also serves to free up valuable motherboard space for circuitry that cannot or should not be placed on adapters. Without the use of the riser, the motherboard would need to be made larger to accommodate the same circuitry. The term *riser* can also be used for any board that combines many functions into a single card, such as AMR and CNR (which were introduced in Chapter 1, "Motherboards, Processors, and Memory"), and don't actually allow the attachment of additional cards to themselves the way true risers do.

FIGURE 3.7 Both sides of a riser card with adapter

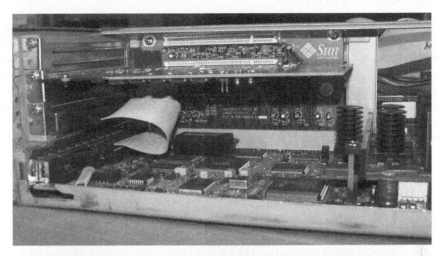

Adapter Configuration

Expansion cards might require configuration. However, most can be recognized automatically by a Plug and Play operating system. In other words, resources are handed out automatically without jumper settings or the installation of device drivers is handled or requested automatically. Supplying the drivers might be the only form of configuration required. For example, unlike older ISA adapters, PCI adapters take care of requesting their own resources through Plug and Play. This is especially true of simple I/O adapters, such as those that provide USB and FireWire ports.

Some modern adapters, however, require more specific configuration steps during installation. For example, two or more PCIe graphics adapters that support SLI (see Chapter 1) must be bridged together with special hardware that comes with the adapters. Although most sound cards tend to work with no specific configuration, advanced features will need to be implemented through the operating system or through utilities that came with the adapter. Wired network adapters tend to be easier to configure than wireless ones. Wireless adapters often require the installation of a screw-on antenna, which should be postponed until after the card is fully inserted and physically secured in the system. Software configuration that allows these cards to communicate with a wireless access point can be challenging for the novice. Nevertheless, even wired NICs might require static configuration of certain protocol settings, such as IP addressing, duplex, and speed, in order for them to be productive. The functions of TV and video capture cards are sometimes not native to the operating system and therefore come with advanced utilities that must be learned and configured before the adapters will work as expected.

In any event, consult the documentation provided with your adapter for additional configuration requirements or options. The more specialized the adapter, the more likely it will come with specialty-configuration utilities.

Identifying Characteristics of Connectors and Cables

Now that you've learned the various types of items found in a computer, let's discuss the various types of ports and cables used with computers. A *port* is a generic name for any connector on a computer or peripheral into which a cable can be plugged. A cable is simply a way of connecting a peripheral or other device to a computer using multiple copper or fiber-optic conductors inside a common wrapping or sheath. Typically, cables connect two ports: one on the computer and one on some other device.

Let's take a quick look at some of the different styles of port connector types as well as peripheral port and cable types. We'll begin by looking at peripheral port connector types.

Device Connector Types

Computer ports are interfaces that allow other devices to be connected to a computer. Their appearance varies widely, depending on their function. In the following sections, we'll examine the following types of peripheral ports:

- D-subminiature
- RJ-series
- Other types

D-subminiature Connectors

D-sub connectors, for a number of years the most common style of connector found on computers, are typically designated with DXn, where the letter X is replaced by a letter from A through E, which refer to the size of the connector, and the letter n is replaced by the number of pins or sockets in the connector. D-sub connectors are usually shaped like a trapezoid and have at least two rows of pins with no other keying structure or landmark, as you can see in Figure 3.8.

The "D" shape ensures that only one orientation is possible. If you try to connect them upside down or try to connect a male connector to another male connector, they just won't go together and the connection can't be made. By the way, male interfaces have pins, while female interfaces have sockets. Be on the lookout for the casual use of *DB* to represent any D-sub connector. This is very common and is accepted as an unwritten de facto standard.

FIGURE 3.8   D-sub ports and connectors

At the bottom left in Figure 3.8 is a DE15F 15-pin display-connector port, which may also be referred to as an HD15 or DB15 port. The other two interfaces are the classic parallel and serial ports.

RJ-Series

Registered jack (RJ) connectors are most often used in telecommunications. The two most common examples of RJ ports are RJ-11 and RJ-45. RJ-11 connectors are used most often on flat satin cables in telephone hookups; your home phone jack is probably an RJ-11 jack. The ports in older external and internal analog modems are RJ-11.

RJ-45 connectors, on the other hand, are larger and most commonly found on Ethernet networks that use twisted-pair cabling. Your Ethernet NIC likely has an RJ-45 jack on it. See Chapter 6, "Networking Fundamentals," for details on networking interfaces. Although RJ-45 is a widely accepted description for the larger connectors, it is not correct. Generically speaking, Ethernet interfaces are 8-pin modular connectors, or 8P8C connectors, meaning that there are eight pin positions and all eight of them are connected, or used. RJ-45 specifies the physical appearance of the connector and also how the contacts are wired from one end to the other. Surprisingly, the RJ-45 specification does not match the TIA T568A and T568B wiring standards used in data communications.

Figure 3.9 shows an RJ-11 jack on the left and an RJ-45 jack on the right. Notice the size difference. As you can see, RJ connectors are typically square with multiple gold contacts on the flat side. A small locking tab on the other side prevents the connector and cable from falling or being pulled out of the jack casually.

FIGURE 3.9   RJ ports

Other Types of Ports

There are many other types of ports that are used with computers today, including these:

- Universal Serial Bus (USB)
- IEEE 1394 (FireWire)
- Infrared
- Audio and video jacks
- PS/2 (6-pin mini-DIN)

Let's look at each one and how it is used.

Universal Serial Bus (USB)

Most computers built after 1997 have one or more flat ports in place of the original serial port. These ports are Universal Serial Bus (USB) ports, and they are used for connecting multiple (up to 127) peripherals to one computer through a single port (and the use of multiport peripheral hubs). USB version 1.x supports data rates as high as 12Mbps (1.5MBps). USB 2.0 supports data rates as high as 480Mbps (60MBps), 40 times that of its predecessor. USB 3.0 boasts data rates of 5Gbps, more than 10 times the rate of USB 2.0. Figure 3.10 shows an example of a set of Type A USB ports. Port types are explained in the section "Common Peripheral Cables and Their Interfaces" later in this chapter.

FIGURE 3.10   USB ports

USB 2.0 uses the same physical connection as the original USB, but it is much higher in transfer rates and requires a cable with more shielding that is less susceptible to noise. You can tell if a computer, hub, or cable supports USB 2.0 by looking for the red and blue "High Speed USB" graphic somewhere on the device or cable (or on its packaging). Super Speed USB 3.0 ports are also backward compatible but have additional contacts that only USB 3.0 cable connectors can access for increased performance.

Because of USB's higher transfer rate, flexibility, and ease of use, most devices now come standard with USB interfaces. For example, digital cameras feature USB and FireWire as the preferred interfaces.

IEEE 1394 (FireWire)

While not as prevalent as USB ports, one other port has crept into the mainstream and is included as a standard attachment in small numbers, often only one, on motherboards and laptops. That port is the *IEEE 1394* port (shown on a desktop PC in Figure 3.11 and on a laptop in Figure 3.12), more commonly known as a *FireWire* port. Its popularity is due to its ease of use, isochronous (synchronized clock) mode, and very high (400Mbps to 3.2Gbps and higher) transmission rates.

FIGURE 3.11   A 6-pin FireWire port on a PC

Originally developed by Apple, it was standardized by IEEE in 1995 as IEEE 1394. It is often used as a way to get digital video into a PC so that it can be edited with digital video editing tools. Security applications benefit from FireWire's higher power output, reducing the need for external power to devices such as security cameras. Audio/video enthusiasts also like this feature, and they rely on the capability of headend devices to control and synchronize the various media sources.

Look for a more thorough discussion of FireWire as a technology in the section "Common Peripheral Cables and Their Interfaces" later in this chapter.

FIGURE 3.12   A 4-pin FireWire port on a laptop

Infrared

Many years ago, increasing numbers of people became fed up with being tethered to their computers by cords. As a result, many computers (especially portable computing devices like laptops and PDAs) hit the market with infrared ports to send and receive data. Modern computers use radio frequency (RF) technologies, such as Bluetooth and WiFi, to accomplish the same and more. RF technologies such as Bluetooth and WiFi are presented in more detail, including their speed and distance limitations, in Chapter 8, and Near Field Communication (NFC) is covered in Chapter 10.

An infrared (*IR*) port is a small port on the computer that allows data to be sent and received using electromagnetic radiation in the infrared band. The infrared port itself is a small, dark square of plastic (usually a very dark maroon) and can typically be found on the front of a PC or on the side of a laptop or portable. Figure 3.13 shows an example of an infrared port.

FIGURE 3.13   An infrared port

Part of the reason for their fall from grace is that infrared ports send and receive data at a very slow rate (the maximum speed on PC infrared ports is less than 16Mbps). Most infrared ports support the Infrared Data Association (IrDA) standard, which outlines a standard way of transmitting and receiving information by infrared so that devices can communicate with one another.

 More information on the IrDA standard can be found at the organization's website: www.irda.org.

Note that although infrared is a wireless technology, it shares more characteristics with light than with radio waves. In fact, infrared pulses can be carried through the air or through optical fiber, just like visible light and laser light. As a result, most infrared communications, especially those that conform to the IrDA standards, are line-of-sight only and take place within a short distance (typically less than 4 meters). Infrared is generally used for point-to-point communications such as controlling the volume on a device with a handheld remote control.

IrDA is working on infrared standards that will push bit rates well into the Gbps range. Nevertheless, RF technologies that do not suffer from line-of-sight limitations might make advanced IrDA standards slow to take root.

Audio/Video Jacks

The *RCA* jack (shown in Figure 3.14) was developed by the RCA Victor Company in the late 1940s for use with its phonographs—the original record players. You bought a phonograph, connected the RCA plug on the back of your phonograph to the RCA jack on the back of your radio or television, and used the speaker and amplifier in the radio or television to listen to vinyl records. It made phonographs cheaper to produce, and it had the added bonus of making sure that everyone had an RCA Victor radio or television (or, at the very least, one with an RCA jack on the back). Either way, RCA made money.

FIGURE 3.14   An RCA jack (female) and RCA plug (male)

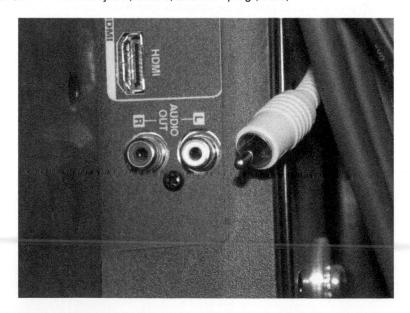

Today, RCA jacks and connectors (or plugs) are used to transmit both audio and video information. Typically, when you see a yellow-coded RCA connector on a PC video card (next to a DE15F VGA connector, perhaps), it's for composite video output (output to a television or VCR). However, digital audio can be implemented with S/PDIF, which can be deployed with an RCA jack. Figure 3.18, later in this chapter, shows an S/PDIF RCA jack. RCA jacks are considered coaxial because the outer circular conductor and the center pin that collectively make up the unbalanced single transmit/receive pair have the same axis of rotation; that is, *co-axial*. S/PDIF can also be implemented by TOSLINK fiber connectors. Toshiba's TOSLINK interface is a digital fiber-optic audio technology that is implemented with its own connector.

Although they aren't used for video, it bears mentioning that the 1/8″ stereo mini-jack and mating miniplug are still commonly used on computers these days for analog audio. Your sound card, microphone, and speakers have them. Figure 3.15 is a photo of a TOSLINK optical interface with a push-in/flip-up cover, pictured to the left of a set of standard analog minijacks.

FIGURE 3.15   The TOSLINK interface

In the spirit of covering interfaces that support both audio and video, don't forget the HDMI interface, which carries both over the same interface. Only CATV coaxial connections to TV cards can boast that on the PC. An RCA jack and cable carry either audio or video, not both simultaneously.

PS/2 (Keyboard and Mouse)

Another common port, as mentioned earlier, is the PS/2 port. A *PS/2 port* (also known as a mini-DIN 6 connector) is a mouse and keyboard interface port first found on the IBM PS/2 (hence the name). It is smaller than previous interfaces (the DIN 5 keyboard port and serial mouse connector), and thus its popularity increased quickly. Figure 3.16 shows examples of both PS/2 keyboard and mouse ports. When the color of the ports is visible, you can tell the difference because the keyboard port is usually purple and the mouse port is usually green. Also, typically there are small graphics of a keyboard and mouse, respectively, imprinted next to the ports.

FIGURE 3.16 PS/2 keyboard and mouse ports

Common Peripheral Cables and Their Interfaces

An *interface* is a method of connecting two dissimilar items together. A peripheral interface is a method of connecting a peripheral or accessory to a computer, including the specification of cabling, connector and port type, speed, and method of communication used.

The most common interfaces used in PCs today include (in no particular order):

- Drive interfaces
- USB
- IEEE 1394 (FireWire)
- RJ-45
- Audio (RCA and TOSLINK)
- PS/2

Let's look at the cabling and connectors used as well as the type(s) of peripherals that are connected to such interfaces.

Hard Disk Connectors

Almost every computer made today uses some type of disk drive to store data and programs until they are needed. All drives need some form of connection to the motherboard so that the computer can "talk" to the disk drive. Regardless of whether the connection is built into the motherboard (*onboard*)—it could reside on an adapter card (*off-board*)—the standard for the attachment is based on the drive's requirements. These connections are known as *drive interfaces*. The interfaces consist of circuitry and a port, or *header.*

Today, the headers that you will find on most motherboards are for Serial ATA (SATA), the speeds of which were discussed in Chapter 2. The SATA headers are vastly different from classic HDD headers. Figure 3.17 shows an example of the SATA data connector. Consult Chapter 2 for additional information on SATA and eSATA connectors and their flat data cables.

FIGURE 3.17   The Serial ATA connector

Common Ports and Connectors

For a computer to be useful and have as much functionality as possible, there must be a way to get the data into and out of it. Many different ports are available for this purpose. The following sections continue the discussion of port and connector types started earlier in the chapter, but it also introduces additional information on those already mentioned and other interfaces.

Briefly, the seven most common types of ports that you will see on a computer are Universal Serial Bus (USB), FireWire/IEEE 1394, eSATA, video, Ethernet, digital/analog sound in/out, and PS/2 keyboard and mouse. Figure 3.18 shows some of these and others on a docking station, or port replicator, for a laptop. From left to right, the interfaces shown are as follows:

- DC power in
- Analog modem RJ-11
- Ethernet NIC RJ-45
- S-video out—legacy
- DVI-D (dual-link) out
- SVGA out
- Parallel (on top)—legacy

- Standard serial—legacy
- Mouse (on top)
- Keyboard
- S/PDIF (out)
- USB

FIGURE 3.18   Peripheral ports and connectors

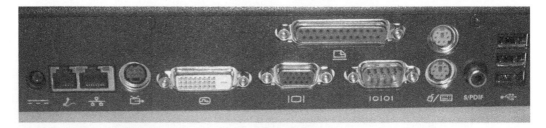

Analog Sound Jacks

Figure 3.19 shows another set of interfaces not seen in Figure 3.18, the sound card jacks. These jacks are known as 1/8″ (3.5mm) stereo minijacks, so called for their size and the fact that they make contact with both the left and right audio channels through their tip, rings (if they have any), and sleeve.

FIGURE 3.19   Sound card jacks

A six-jack setup capable of 8-channel audio is shown in the photo, also known as 7.1 surround sound. The 7 represents the seven full-bandwidth channels and the 1 represents the one low-frequency effects (LFE) channel, most often attached to the subwoofer. Each of the full-bandwidth channels is often represented by its own speaker in the system, but not necessarily. If there is a 1:1 channel-to-speaker representation, the eight speakers in 8-channel 7.1 are generally placed equidistant from the audience as follows, with all angles measured from front center (usually where the video source resides):

- One center speaker at 0 degrees (at the video source)
- Left and right front speakers at 22 to 30 degrees
- Left and right side speakers at 90 to 110 degrees
- Left and right rear speakers at 135 to 150 degrees
- One subwoofer possibly hidden anywhere in the room

The right column of jacks shown in Figure 3.19 represents the classic three minijacks found on sound cards. The middle one is a green output jack used for 2-channel audio, usually manifested as two full-bandwidth speakers, one each on the left and right channels. Both channels are provided by the single green *stereo* minijack. The other two are input interfaces; the top jack is the blue line-in interface, designed for audio sources that lack a specialized interface, such as less expensive musical keyboards and phonographs, for example, so audiophiles can convert their vinyl collections to digital. The bottom one is the pink microphone input jack.

If you understand the concept of 8-channel 7.1, then 4-channel 3.1 and 6-channel 5.1 will be simpler to understand. The left column of jacks in Figure 3.19 was added for dedicated surround sound use, and it comprises the orange jack at the top for the *center* and *subwoofer* channels (used for 3.1, 5.1, and 7.1), the black middle jack for the *rear* left and right surround channels (used for 5.1 and 7.1), and the gray jack at the bottom for the *side* left and right surround channels (used only for 7.1 surround sound). With 3.1, 5.1, and 7.1, the green jack is adopted for the *front* stereo channel. Technically, 3.1 is not surround sound because there are only front and center channels and no surround channels.

Most installers place the rear speakers in 5.1 at the rearmost position recommended for the 7.1 side speakers, about 110 degrees from front center. When you're migrating to 7.1, these rear speakers are repurposed as side speakers and new ones are installed as 7.1 rear speakers, at an angle starting from about 135 degrees.

Software can use these interfaces to allow you to record and play back audio content in file—MP3, for instance—or CD/DVD form. Note, however, that the jacks themselves are not distinctive in their physical characteristics. They are uniquely addressable, but it is up to the software's programming to assign their purpose. Most programmers, of course, respect the color code. As a case study, for motherboards that support surround sound but do not supply the black and orange jacks, you have to use the blue jack for both line-in and rear surround and the pink jack for both microphone and center/subwoofer. Depending on the software in use, you would need to swap one plug manually for another because the jack functions would change.

Universal Serial Bus (USB)

USB cables are used to connect a wide variety of peripherals to computers, including keyboards, mice, digital cameras, printers, and scanners. Not all USB cables maximize the potential of all USB ports. USB 1.x cables cannot provide USB 2.0 and 3.0 performance; USB 2.0 cables cannot provide USB 3.0 performance. Good or bad, depending on how you look at it, the interfaces accept all cable connectors. So, ensuring that your cable is built to the specification that you intend to use, whether version 2.0 or 3.0, is of utmost importance. Otherwise, the connected device will have to fall back to the maximum version supported by the cable. This is usually not an issue, except for the lost performance, but some high-performance devices will refuse to operate at reduced levels.

Table 3.1 details the differences in the maximum speeds defined by the three groups of USB specifications. Note that these speeds are not generally attainable due to a variety of factors, but USB 3.0 has the greatest likelihood of attaining its maximum rate because of its full-duplex nature. Note that all specifications are capable of *Low Speed* 1.5Mbps performance.

TABLE 3.1   USB speed limitations

Specification	Maximum Speed	Speed Trade Name
USB 1.0/1.1	12Mbps	Full Speed
USB 2.0	480Mbps	High Speed
USB 3.0	5Gbps (5000Mbps)	SuperSpeed

The USB technology is fairly straightforward. Essentially, it was designed to be Plug and Play—just plug in the peripheral and it should work, providing that the software is installed to support it. Many standard devices have drivers that are built into the common operating systems or automatically downloaded during installation. More complex devices come with drivers to be installed before the component is connected.

USB cable varies mostly based on the USB peripheral connector on the external-device end. Because there can be quite a number of USB devices on a single system, it helps to have a scheme to clarify their connectivity. The USB standard specifies two broad types of connectors. They are designated Type A and Type B connectors. A standard USB cable has some form of Type A connector on one end and some form of Type B connector on the other end. Figure 3.20 shows four USB 1.x/2.0 cable connectors. From left to right, they are as follows:

- Type A
- Standard Mini-B
- Type B
- Alternate Mini-B

Modern small form factor devices, including many phones and smaller digital cameras, use a Micro-B connector, shown in Figure 3.21, that is smaller than the standard Mini-B shown in Figure 3.20.

FIGURE 3.20 USB cables and connectors

FIGURE 3.21 USB Micro-B connector

The specification for USB 3.0, also known as SuperSpeed, recommends a standard blue color coding for all interfaces and cables as a way of differentiating them from legacy cables and interfaces. The connectors also feature five additional pins that are not accessible to 1.x/2.0 connectors and receptacles shown in Figure 3.18 and Figure 3.20.

One part of the USB interface specification that makes it so appealing is the fact that if your computer runs out of USB ports, you can simply plug a device known as a *USB hub* into one of your computer's USB ports, which will give you several more USB ports from one original port. Figure 3.22 shows an example of a USB hub.

FIGURE 3.22   A USB hub

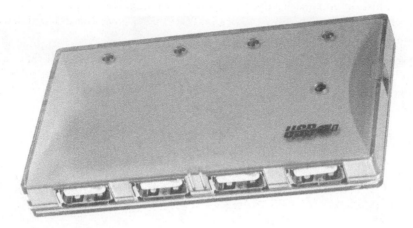

Be aware of the limitations in the USB specification. Table 3.2 details the cable-length limitations for each of the three families of USB. The third column simply shows the combined length of all six cables used with five hubs and a sixth cable connected to the component. If you use hubs, you should never use more than five hubs between the system and any component.

TABLE 3.2   USB cable-length limitations

Specification	Maximum Cable Length	Total Cable with Five Hubs
USB 1.0/1.1	3m	18m
USB 2.0	5m	30m
USB 3.0	3m	18m

In addition to the cable length difference between USB 2.0 and 3.0, there are a host of other differences between these specifications. The following items outline some of the primary differences.

Shielding   USB 3.0 requires that each pair in the cable assembly be shielded to withstand the electromagnetic interference (EMI) inherent with transmissions at higher frequencies.

Connectors   Although all connectors are compatible with all receptacles, to attain SuperSpeed performance, SuperSpeed connectors with five additional pins must be used on cables and receptacles. These pins do not obstruct the four legacy pins required for backward compatibility. Instead, they sit farther back and are accessible only to compatible interfaces.

Bursting and streaming   USB 2.0 does not support bursting, the low-duration, excessively fast transmission of data, nor does it support streaming, the continuous flow of data between two endpoints once the flow has begun. USB 3.0 supports continuous bursting as well as streaming.

Duplex   USB 2.0 is a half-duplex technology, meaning that all devices must share a common bandwidth, making overall performance appear subpar. USB 3.0, on the other hand, supports dual simplex communications pathways that collectively imitate full-duplex transmission, where devices at both ends of the cable can transmit simultaneously.

Media access method   USB 2.0 peripheral devices must wait until polled by the host before transmitting data. USB 3.0 endpoints use an asynchronous transmission mechanism, similar to that of Ethernet, where data is transmitted at will.

Host control   The host (computer system) is the only device in the USB 2.0 specification that can control power management. The endpoints are the only devices that can participate in error detection and recovery as well as flow control. USB 3.0 endpoints can all control when they enter low-power mode to conserve power. Error handling and flow control are performed on each link in USB 3.0, not just at the endpoints.

Power   USB 2.0 provides a maximum of 100 milliamperes (mA) of current at low power and 500mA at high power. USB 3.0 provides 150mA and 900mA, respectively, allowing for the direct powering of some of the same component types that FireWire is capable of powering but that USB 2.0 is not.

Through the use of a 7-bit identifier, providing $2^7 = 128$ possible addresses, no more than 127 devices, including hubs, should be connected back to a single USB host controller in the computer, not that you would ever want to approach this number. The 128th identifier, the highest address, is used for broadcasting to all endpoints. No interconnection of host controllers is allowed with USB; each one and its connected devices are isolated from other host controllers and their devices. As a result, USB ports are not considered networkable ports. Consult your system's documentation to find out if your USB ports operate on the same host controller.

From the perspective of the cable's plug, Type A is always oriented toward the system from the component. As a result, you might notice that the USB receptacle on the computer system that a component cables back to is the same as the receptacles on the USB hub that components cable back to. The USB hub is simply an extension of the system, and it becomes a component that cables back to the system. Each hub takes one of the 127 available addresses.

Type B plugs connect in the direction of the peripheral component. Therefore, you see a single Type B interface on the hub as well as on the peripheral endpoints to allow them to cable back to the system or another hub. Although they exist, USB cables with both ends of the same type, a sort of extension cable, are in violation of the USB specification. Collectively, these rules make cabling your USB subsystem quite straightforward.

Despite the letter of the standards and the seemingly locked-up logic of USB connectivity, it is occasionally necessary to alter the interface type at one end of a USB cable. For that reason, there is a variety of simple, passive converters on the market with a Type A interface on one side and a Type B interface on the other. Such devices allow some form of Type A connector on the cable to connect to a Type A port and a Type B connector to attach to a Type B port. These *USB A to USB B converters* should be purchased based on the compatibility of the two connectors on each end of the converter.

Typical USB connectors are keyed and will go into a USB port only one way. If the connector will not go into the port properly, try rotating it.

For more information on USB, check out www.usb.org.

IEEE 1394 (FireWire)

The IEEE 1394 interface is about two things, if nothing else: speed and efficiency. Its first iteration, now known as FireWire 400, has a maximum data throughput of 400Mbps in half duplex. Although the numbers imply that USB 2.0 at 480Mbps might outperform FireWire 400, the truth is that FireWire allows a closer saturation of the bandwidth by its devices due to its different encoding mechanism. USB devices are lucky to achieve half of their bus's rated bandwidth during sustained operation. The other major difference between the two technologies is the amount of power accessible to FireWire devices. Whereas USB provides less than an ampere of current at 5VDC, FireWire specifications allow for the provision of 1.5A at up to 30VDC (and slightly more in some implementations). This production of 45W of power allows for larger devices to be powered by the FireWire interface, obviating the need for separate external power.

The next iteration, FireWire 800 (specified under IEEE 1394b), has a maximum data throughput of 800Mbps and works in full duplex. FireWire 400 carries data over a maximum cable length of 4.5 meters with a maximum of 63 devices connected to each interface on the computer. Using new beta connectors and associated cabling, including a fiber-optic solution, FireWire 800 extends to 100 meters. When implemented over copper, FireWire 800, like FireWire 400, is limited to 4.5m cable runs. IEEE 1394b also allows for 1.6Gbps (S1600) and 3.2Gbps (S3200) implementations, but it's still, interestingly, referred to as FireWire 800. IEEE 1394c standardized the running of FireWire over the same Category 5e infrastructure that supports Ethernet, including the use of RJ-45 connectors. However, with the advent of more advanced technologies, not the least of which is Thunderbolt, IEEE 1394c may well prove to be a standard on paper only.

FireWire (also known as i.LINK in Sony's parlance) uses a very special type of six-wire cable, as shown on the left in Figure 3.23, for FireWire 400. Only four wires are used when power is not supplied by the interface. These interfaces are collectively known as *alpha connectors*. Notice the difference in the system end on the left and the component end on the right. It is difficult to mistake this cable for anything but a FireWire cable. FireWire 800 uses a nine-wire implementation with *beta connectors*. A beta connector and one of the FireWire logos (another is a stylized "1394") are shown on the left of Figure 3.35 later in this chapter. *Alpha* and *beta* originally referred to the different encoding methods used with FireWire 400 and FireWire 800.

FIGURE 3.23   A FireWire (IEEE 1394) 6- to 4-pin alpha cable

IEEE1394-4-6pin. Con licenza Pubblico dominio tramite Wikipedia

Although most people think of FireWire as a tool for connecting their digital camcorders to their computers, it's much more than that. Because of its high data transfer rate, it is being used more and more as a universal, high-speed data interface for things like hard drives, optical drives, and digital video editing equipment.

Because the FireWire specification was conceived to allow peripherals to be networked together in much the same fashion as intelligent hosts are networked together in LANs and WANs, a quick introduction to the concept of networking is in order (see Chapter 6 for more detail on networking concepts). A *topology* can be thought of as the layout of the nodes that make up the endpoints and connecting devices of the network. One of the most popular topologies today is the star topology, which uses a central concentrating device that is cabled directly to the endpoints. A tree structure is formed when these concentrating devices are interconnected to one another, each attached to its own set of endpoints. One or few concentrators appear at the first tier of the tree, sort of like the "root system" of the tree. These root devices are expected to carry more traffic than other concentrators because of their position in the hierarchy. In subsequent tiers, other concentrators branch off from the root and each other to complete the tree analogy.

The 1995 IEEE 1394 specification that is equivalent to FireWire 400 allows 1023 buses, each supporting 63 devices, to be bridged together. This networkable architecture supports more than 64,000 interconnected devices that can communicate directly with one another instead of communicating through a host computer in the way that USB is required to do. Star and tree topologies can be formed as long as no two devices are separated by more than 16 hops. A *hop* can be thought of as a link between any two end devices, repeaters, or bridges, resulting in a total maximum distance between devices of 72 meters.

Through an internal hub, a single end device can use two IEEE 1394 ports to connect to two different devices, creating a daisy-chained pathway that allows the other two devices to communicate with one another as well. The device in the middle, which can be the computer system or any peripheral device, affords a physical pathway between the other two devices but is not otherwise involved in their communication with one another. Contrast this function to that of the USB host which, prior to version 3.0, had to be involved in all transactions. USB 3.0 does not provide bridged networking the way that FireWire does, but it allows the devices to initiate communication and other transactions.

RCA

The RCA cable is a simple coaxial cable. There are two connectors, usually male, one on each end of the cable. There are two contacts on each connector, the ground ring and the positive data pin in the middle. The male connector connects to the female connector on the equipment. Figure 3.24 shows an example of an RCA cable. An RCA male to RCA female connector is also available; it's used to extend the reach of audio or video signals.

FIGURE 3.24   An RCA cable

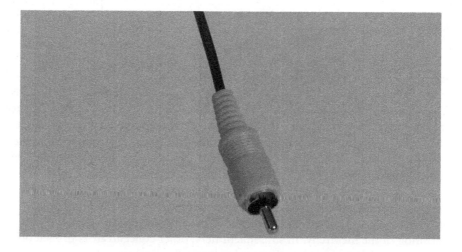

The RCA male connectors on a connection cable are sometimes plated in gold to increase their corrosion resistance and to improve longevity.

PS/2 (Keyboard and Mouse)

The most important input device for a PC is the keyboard. All PC motherboards contain some sort of connector that allows a keyboard to be connected directly to the motherboard through the case. There are two main types of wired keyboard connectors. At one time, these were the AT and PS/2 connectors. Today, the PS/2-style connector may be included but has largely been replaced by the USB port for wired keyboard attachment. The all-but-extinct original AT connector is round, about ½″ in diameter, in a 5-pin DIN configuration. Figure 3.25 shows an example of the AT-style keyboard connector.

FIGURE 3.25 An AT connector on a motherboard

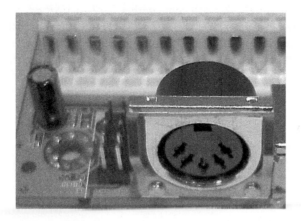

The PS/2 connector (as shown in Figure 3.26) is a smaller 6-pin mini-DIN connector. Until recently, PCs included a PS/2 keyboard connector as well as a PS/2 mouse connector right above it on the motherboard. Today, you might see a single double-use connector or none at all, in favor of USB or wireless attachment.

FIGURE 3.26 A PS/2-style keyboard connector on a motherboard

Wireless keyboard and mouse attachment is fairly popular today, and it is most often achieved with Bluetooth technology or a proprietary RF implementation.

> In past generations of motherboards, the PS/2 mouse and keyboard connectors have been color-coded to make connection of keyboards and mice easier because they are physically identical but functionally different. PS/2 mouse connectors are green (to match the standard green connectors on some mice), and the keyboard connectors are purple. If you have trouble remembering the difference, think of the fact that mice, not keyboards, exist in nature, and mice might get seasick and turn "green."

Some keyboards and mice today still come with a *PS/2-to-USB adapter* to change their USB connector into the PS/2 interface. Using the PS/2 connector that still comes with some motherboards saves one or two USB interfaces. Manufacturers sometimes opt for a single PS/2 connector with half purple and half green color codes, indicating that either device can be attached to the same interface. However, in these situations, only one of the two types of devices can be connected at a time. Figure 3.27 shows an example of a PS/2 keyboard cable.

FIGURE 3.27   A PS/2 keyboard cable

> Most often, PS/2 cables have only one connector because the other end is connected directly to the device being plugged in. The only exception is PS/2 extension cables used to extend the length of a PS/2 device's cable.

Video Display Cables and Connectors

While the analog VGA-spawned standards might keep the computing industry satisfied for years yet to come, the sector in the market driving development of non-VGA specifications has become increasingly more prevalent. These high-resolution, high-performance junkies approach video from the broadcast angle. They are interested in the increased quality of digital transmission. For them, the industry responded with technologies like DVI and HDMI. The computing market benefits from these technologies as well. DVI interfaces on graphics adapters and laptops became commonplace. In increasingly more cases, HDMI interfaces take adapters to the next generation.

Other consumers desire specialized methods to connect analog display devices by splitting out colors from the component to improve quality or simply to provide video output to displays not meant for computers. For this group, a couple of older standards remain viable: component video and composite video. The following sections present the details of these two specifications as well as DVI and HDMI.

DVI

In an effort to leave analog VGA standards and return to digital video, which can typically be transmitted farther and at higher quality than analog, a series of connectors known collectively as *Digital Visual (or Video) Interface (DVI)* was developed for the technology of the same name. These digital interfaces offer much higher performance than the original digital standards, such as CGA and EGA. At first glance, the DVI connector might look like a standard D-sub connector, but on closer inspection, it begins to look somewhat different. For one thing, it has quite a few pins, and for another, the pins it has are asymmetrical in their placement on the connector. Figure 3.28 illustrates the five types of connectors that the DVI standard specifies. Also look at an actual photo of the DVI-I interface in Figure 3.29 and the dual-link DVI-D interface in Figure 3.30.

FIGURE 3.28   Types of DVI connector

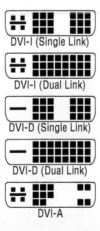

One thing to note about analog vs. digital display technologies is that all graphics adapters and all monitors deal with digital information. It is only the connectors and cabling that can be made to support analog transmission. Before DVI and HDMI encoding technologies were developed, consumer digital video display connectors could not afford the space to accommodate the number of pins that would have been required to transmit 16 or more bits of color information per pixel. For this reason, the relatively few conductors of the inferior analog signaling in VGA were appealing.

There are three main categories of DVI connectors:

DVI-A An analog-only connector. The source must produce analog output, and the monitor must understand analog input.

DVI-D A digital-only connector. The source must produce digital output, and the monitor must understand digital input.

DVI-I A combination analog/digital connector. The source and monitor must both support the same technology, but this cable works with either a digital or an analog signal.

The DVI-D and DVI-I connectors come in two varieties: single link and dual link. The dual-link options have more conductors—taking into account the six center conductors—than their single-link counterparts, which accommodate higher speed and signal quality. The additional link can be used to increase resolution from 1920×1080 to 2048×1536 for devices with a 16:9 aspect ratio or from WUXGA to WQXGA for devices with a 16:10 aspect ratio. Of course, both components, as well as the cable, must support the dual-link feature. Consult Chapter 4, "Display Devices," for more information on display standards.

DVI-A and DVI-I analog quality is superior to that of VGA, but it's still analog, meaning that it is more susceptible to noise. However, the DVI analog signal will travel farther than the VGA signal before degrading beyond usability. Nevertheless, the DVI-A and VGA interfaces are pin-compatible, meaning that a simple passive *DVI-to-VGA adapter*, as shown in Figure 3.29, is all that is necessary to convert between the two. As you can see, the analog portion of the connector, if it exists, comprises the four separate color and sync pins and the horizontal blade that they surround, which happens to be the analog ground lead that acts as a ground and physical support mechanism even for DVI-D connectors.

FIGURE 3.29 DVI-A–to–VGA adapter

FIGURE 3.29   *(continued)*

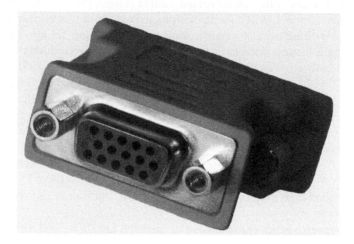

It's important to note that DVI-I cables and interfaces are designed to interconnect two analog or two digital devices; they cannot convert between analog and digital. DVI cables must support a signal of at least 4.5 meters, but better cable assemblies, stronger transmitters, and active boosters result in signals extending over longer distances.

HDMI

High-Definition Multimedia Interface (HDMI) is an all-digital technology that advances the work of DVI to include the same dual-link resolutions using a standard HDMI cable but with higher motion-picture frame rates and digital audio right on the same connector. HDMI cabling also supports an optional Consumer Electronics Control (CEC) feature that allows transmission of signals from a remote control unit to control multiple devices without separate cabling to carry infrared signals.

HDMI cables, known as Standard and High Speed, exist today in the consumer space. Standard cables are rated for 720p resolution as well as 1080i, but not 1080p. High Speed cables are capable of supporting not only 1080p, but also the newer 4K and 3D technologies.

In June 2006, revision 1.3 of the HDMI specification was released to support the bit rates necessary for HD DVD and Blu-ray disc. This version also introduced support for "deep color," or color depths of at least one billion colors, including 30-, 36-, and 48-bit color. However, not until version 1.4, which was released May 28, 2009, was the High Speed HDMI cable initially required.

With version 1.4 came HDMI capability for the controlling system—the television, for instance—to relay Ethernet frames between its connected components and the Internet, alleviating the need for each and every component to find its own access to the LAN for Internet access. Both Standard and High Speed cables are available with this Ethernet channel. Each device connected by such a cable must also support the HDMI Ethernet Channel specification, however.

Additional advances that were first seen in version 1.4 were 3D support, 4K resolution (but only at a 30Hz refresh rate), an increased 120Hz refresh rate for the 1080 resolutions, and an audio return channel (ARC) for televisions with built-in tuners to send audio back to an A/V receiver without using a separate output cable. Version 1.4 also introduced the anti-vibration Type E locking connector for the automotive-video industry and cables that can also withstand vibration as well as the hot/cold extremes that are common in the automotive world.

Version 2.0 of HDMI (2013) introduced no new cable requirements. In other words, the existing High Speed HDMI cable is fully capable of supporting all new version 2 enhancements. These enhancements include increasing the 4K refresh rate to 60Hz, a 21:9 theatrical widescreen aspect ratio, and 32-channel audio. Note that 7.1 surround sound comprises only eight channels, supporting the more lifelike Rec. 2020 color space and multiple video and audio streams to the same output device for multiple users. Version 2.0a, released in 2015, primarily added high dynamic range (HDR) video, but it does not require any new cables or connectors.

The HDMI connector is not the same as the one used for DVI. Nevertheless, the two technologies are electrically compatible. HDMI is compatible with DVI-D and DVI-I interfaces through proper adapters, but HDMI's audio and remote-control pass-through features are lost. Additionally, 3D video sources work only with HDMI. Figure 3.30 shows a *DVI-to-HDMI adapter* between DVI-D and the Type A 19-pin HDMI interface. The first image is the DVI-D interface, and the second is the HDMI interface on the other side of the adapter. Compare the DVI-D interface to the DVI-I interface of Figure 3.29, and note that the ground blade on the DVI-D connector is narrower than that of the DVI-A and DVI-I connectors. The DVI-D receptacle does not accept the other two plugs for this reason, as well as because the four analog pins around the blade have no sockets in the DVI-D receptacle.

FIGURE 3.30   HDMI-to-DVI adapter

Unlike DVI-D and, by extension DVI-I, DVI-A and VGA devices cannot be driven passively by HDMI ports directly. An *HDMI-to-VGA adapter* must be active in nature, either powered externally or through the HDMI interface itself.

There is also a Type B connector that has 29 pins and is intended to support higher resolution for the components that use it. HDMI version 1.3 specified a smaller 19-pin Type C connector for portable devices. The Type C connector, also referred to as a *miniHDMI connector*, is compatible with the Type A connector but it still requires an adapter due to its smaller size. HDMI version 1.4 specified two more interfaces: Type D and Type E. If Type C is a miniHDMI interface, then you might refer to the Type D connector as microHDMI. Figure 3.31 shows a Type D HDMI connector to the right of a Micro-B USB connector on a smartphone. Also compatible with Type A interfaces because they have the same 19 pins, Type D interfaces require but a simple adapter for conversion.

HDMI cables should meet the signal requirements of the latest specification. As a result, and as with DVI, the maximum cable length is somewhat variable. For HDMI, cable length depends heavily on the materials used to construct the cable. Passive cables tend to extend no farther than 15 meters, while adding electronics within the cable to create an active version results in lengths as long as 30 meters. Twisted-pair and fiber cabling options can extend cabling to 50 meters and 100 meters, respectively.

FIGURE 3.31 Type D HDMI interface

Component Video

When analog technologies outside the VGA realm are used for broadcast video, you are generally able to get better-quality video by splitting the red, green, and blue components in the signal into different streams right at the source. The technology known as *component video* performs a signal-splitting function similar to RGB separation. However, unlike

RGB separation, which requires full-bandwidth red, green, and blue signals as well as a fourth pathway for synchronization, the most popular implementation of component video uses one uncompressed signal and two compressed signals, reducing the overall bandwidth needed. These signals are delivered over coax either as red, green, and blue color-coded RCA plugs or similarly coded *BNC* connectors, the latter being seen mostly in broadcast-quality applications.

The uncompressed signal is called luma (Y), which is essentially the colorless version of the original signal that represents the "brightness" of the source feed as a grayscale image. The component-video source also creates two compressed color-difference signals known as Pb and Pr. These two chrominance (chroma, for short) signals are also known as B – Y and R – Y, respectively, because they are created by subtracting out the luma from the blue and red source signals. It might make sense, then, that the analog technology presented here is most often referred to and labeled as YPbPr. A digital version of this technology, usually found on high-end devices, replaces analog's Pb and Pr with Cb and Cr, respectively, and is most often labeled YCbCr. Figure 3.32 shows the three RCA connectors of a component video cable.

FIGURE 3.32   A component video cable

As a slightly technical aside, luma is a gamma-correcting, nonlinear display concept related to but not equivalent to luminance, which is a linear, non-gamma-corrected measure of light intensity. Display devices perform nonlinear gamma decompression, which means a complementary nonlinear gamma compression (correction) must have been performed by the transmitter for the resulting image to be displayed properly. Thus *luma*, not *luminance*, is the appropriate term when discussing component video. Furthermore, although *Y* is commonly used to represent luma, it actually stands for luminance. As a result, if you ever see a reference to Y′PbPr or Y′CbCr, the Y-prime refers correctly to luma. The more common, yet less correct, *Y* is used here to refer to luma.

Note that in the foregoing discussion, there is no mention of a green component-video signal. In fact, the often green-colored lead in the component-video cable carries the luma. There is no need for a separate green color-difference signal. Essentially, the luma signal is used as a colorless map for the detail of the image. The receiving display device adds the luma signal from the Y lead back to the blue and red color-difference signals that were received on the Pb and Pr leads, re-creating compressed versions of the full blue and red source signals. Whatever details in the luma version of the image have weak representation in the blue and red versions of the image are inferred to be green.

Therefore, you can conclude that by providing one full signal (Y) and two compressed signals (Pb and Pr) that are related to the full signal (Pb = B − Y and Pr = R − Y), you can transmit roughly the same information as three full signals (R, G, and B) but with less bandwidth. Incidentally, component video is capable of transmitting HD video at full 1080p (1920×1080, progressive-scan) resolution. However, the output device is at the mercy of the video source, which often is not manufactured to push 1080p over component outputs.

Composite Video

When the preceding component video technologies are not feasible, the last related standard, *composite video*, combines all luma and chroma leads into one. Composite video is truly the bottom of the analog-video barrel. However, the National Television System Committee (NTSC) signal received by over-the-air antennas or by cable-TV feeds is composite video, making it a very common video signal. Unfortunately, once the four signals are combined into one, the display equipment has no way of faithfully splitting them back out, leading to less than optimal quality but great cost efficiency.

A single yellow RCA jack, the composite video jack is rather common on computers and home and industrial video components. While still fairly decent in video quality, composite video is more susceptible to undesirable video phenomena and artifacts, such as aliasing, cross coloration, and dot crawl. If you have a three-connector cable on your home video equipment, such as a DVD player connected to a TV, odds are that the tips will be yellow, red, and white. The red and white leads are for left and right stereo audio; the yellow lead is your composite video.

DisplayPort

DisplayPort is a royalty-free digital display interface from the Video Electronics Standards Association (VESA) that uses less power than other digital interfaces and VGA. A simple adapter allows HDMI and DVI voltages to be lowered to those required by DisplayPort because it is functionally similar to HDMI and DVI. DisplayPort cables can extend 3 meters unless an active cable powers the run, in which case the cable can extend to 33 meters.

The DisplayPort (DP) connector latches itself to the receptacle with two tiny hooks in the same manner as micro-B USB connectors. A push-button mechanism serves to release the hooks for removal of the connector from the receptacle. Figure 3.33 shows the 20-pin DP interface at the end of a cable. Note the beveled keying at the bottom right corner of the connector.

FIGURE 3.33   A full-size DisplayPort connector

Displayport-cable by Belkin - `http://www.belkin.com/pressroom/releases/uploads/`
`01_07_08DisplayPortCable.html`. Licensed under CC BY-SA 3.0 via Wikimedia Commons

The DisplayPort standard also specifies a smaller connector, known as the *Mini DisplayPort (MDP) connector.* The MDP is electrically equivalent to the full-size DP connector and features a beveled keying structure, but it lacks the latching mechanism present in the DP connector. Although Figure 3.35 depicts a Thunderbolt port (designated by a lightning bolt with an arrowhead), you are essentially looking at the MDP port, repurposed for use as the more advanced Thunderbolt interface, discussed next. Figure 3.34 shows a Thunderbolt/MDP connector on the end of a cable.

FIGURE 3.34   A Thunderbolt/Mini DisplayPort connector

"Mini displayport" by Palthrow - Own work. Licensed under CC BY-SA 3.0 via Commons

Thunderbolt

The DisplayPort is being usurped by a smaller compatible—also digital—version called *Thunderbolt*, created in collaboration between Intel and Apple. Thunderbolt combines x4 PCI Express 2.0 with the DisplayPort 1.x technology. The most common Thunderbolt cable is a copper, powered active cable extending as far as 3m, which was designed to be less expensive than an active version of a DisplayPort cable of the same length. There are also supported optical cables in the specification that can reach as far as 60m but that terminate with the same copper MDP connector, by way of an embedded conversion chip.

Figure 3.35 shows a Thunderbolt interface on an Apple MacBook Pro. Note the standard lightning-bolt insignia by the port. To the left of the Thunderbolt port in the image is a 9-pin IEEE 1394b (FireWire) beta port. Despite its diminutive size, the Thunderbolt port has 20 pins around its connector bar, like its larger DisplayPort cousin. Of course, the functions of all of the pins do not directly correspond between the two interface types because Thunderbolt adds PCIe functionality.

FIGURE 3.35   A Thunderbolt interface

Thunderbolt as a Data Interface

Because Thunderbolt includes a separate I/O function from the DP video technology, it is rated for power and transfer rates in the same way as are technologies such as USB, FireWire, and eSATA. Both of the initial versions of Thunderbolt, v1 and v2, operate at 20Gbps of aggregate bandwidth. The v2 offering does so with more flexibility by combining the two 10Gbps channels instead of allowing each one to perform as either only transmit or only receive. Each Thunderbolt port provides a total of 18V and 9.9W of power to the one or more attached peripherals.

Additionally, and as is the case with USB and FireWire, Thunderbolt devices can be daisy-chained and connected via hubs. Daisy chains can extend six levels deep for each controller interface, and each interface can optionally drive a separate monitor, which should be placed alone on the controller's interface or at the end of a chain of components attached to the interface.

Thunderbolt Converters

Until the industry fully supports Thunderbolt on peripheral devices targeted by the technology, there is a need to be able to convert the ports on a computer to the standards that are most commonly supported by manufacturers of those peripherals.

Consumers can spend hundreds of dollars on hubs that split the system's Thunderbolt port into a variety of ports. A more modest alternative is one of a family of much less expensive converters that target specific applications. One such converter, a *Thunderbolt-to-DVI converter*, is shown in Figure 3.36. Note that standard converters allow a DisplayPort interface or Thunderbolt port on the system to drive a DVI monitor and not for a DVI port to drive a Thunderbolt or DP monitor. You can use simple, inexpensive passive converters when the monitor supports the same pin functions as does Thunderbolt, such as when the Thunderbolt port is connecting to a DVI-D interface on the monitor. Passive converters support resolutions as high as 1080p (1920×1080, progressive-scan).

FIGURE 3.36 A Thunderbolt/MDP-to-DVI converter

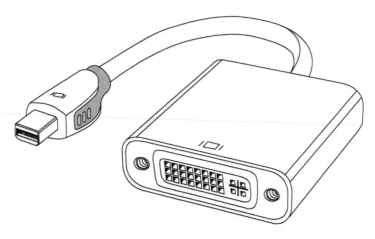

Converters are also available that connect Thunderbolt and DisplayPort connectors on the computer to analog VGA monitors. Still others are made to allow Thunderbolt ports to connect to digital HDMI monitors. Active converters that contain chips to perform the conversion are necessary in situations such as when the technology is not directly pin-compatible with Thunderbolt, as with VGA and DVI-A analog monitor inputs, for example. Active converters are only slightly more expensive than their passive counterparts but still only a fraction of the cost of Thunderbolt hubs. One other advantage of active connectors is that they can support resolutions of 4K (3840×2160) and higher.

Coaxial

Two main forms of coaxial cable are used to deliver video from a source to a monitor or television. One of them is terminated by RCA or BNC plugs and tends to serve a single frequency, while the other is terminated by F connectors, those seen in cable television (CATV) settings, and tends to require tuning/demodulation equipment to choose the frequency to display. The terms that refer to whether a single frequency or multiple frequencies are carried over a cable are *baseband* and *broadband*, respectively. Figure 3.37 shows an example of the F connector most commonly used in home and business CATV installations. This is a 75-ohm form of coax known as RG-6.

FIGURE 3.37   A CATV F connector and coaxial cable

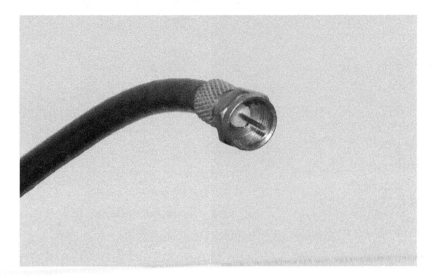

Digital Rights Management

Digital rights management (DRM) is a series of technologies aimed at protecting against the piracy of digital entertainment media. Graphics display standards such as DVI, HDMI, and DisplayPort support one or more forms of DRM. Early versions of DisplayPort included DisplayPort Content Protection (DPCP) from Philips. Later versions of DisplayPort and HDMI include Intel's High-bandwidth Digital Content Protection (HDCP).

HDCP operates by encrypting the stream of media over the connection between transmitter and receiver. Components must be licensed for HDCP by Digital Content Protection, LLC. In addition to sources and sinks—devices that can render the encrypted content for display—HDCP allows for repeaters that can decrypt the stream, adjust it for such features as increased resolution and amplified audio, and then re-encrypt it for transmission to the sink.

Input Devices

An *input device* is one that transfers information from outside the computer system to an internal storage location, such as system RAM, video RAM, flash memory, or disk storage. Without input devices, computers would be unable to change from their default boot-up state. The following sections detail different classes of input devices and a hub of sorts, used for switching between the most common of these devices. We will also demonstrate the similarities shared by devices that provide input to computer systems as well as their differences. Installation considerations will be presented where appropriate. The following input devices are covered in the subsequent sections:

- Mouse
- Touchpad
- Keyboard
- Scanner
- Barcode reader
- Digitizer
- Biometric devices
- Gamepads and joysticks
- Motion sensor
- Smart card reader
- Multimedia devices

Mouse

Although the computer mouse was born in the 1970s at Xerox's Palo Alto Research Center (PARC), it was in 1984 that Apple made the mouse an integral part of the personal computer with the introduction of the Macintosh. In its most basic form, the mouse is a hand-fitting device that uses some form of motion-detection mechanism to translate its own physical two-dimensional movement into onscreen cursor motion. Many variations of the mouse exist, including trackballs, tablets, touchpads, and pointing sticks. Figure 3.38 illustrates the most recognizable form of the mouse.

The motion-detection mechanism of the original Apple mouse was a simple ball that protruded from the bottom of the device so that when the bottom was placed against a flat surface that offered a slight amount of friction, the mouse would glide over the surface but the ball would roll, actuating two rollers that mapped the linear movement to a Cartesian plane and transmitted the results to the software interface. This method of motion detection remains available today, although it's fairly unpopular.

Later technologies used optical receptors to catch LED light reflected from specially made surfaces purchased with the devices and used like a mouse pad. A *mouse pad* is a special surface that improves mechanical mouse traction while offering very little resistance to the mouse itself. As optical science advanced for the mouse, lasers were used to allow a sharper image to be captured by the mouse, providing more sensitivity in motion detection. Certain surfaces don't lend themselves well to standard laser-mouse functionality, but a higher resolution version exists that can even track across the surface of glass. The mouse today can be wired to the computer system or connected wirelessly. Wireless versions use batteries to power them, and the optical varieties deplete these batteries more quickly than their mechanical counterparts.

FIGURE 3.38   A computer mouse

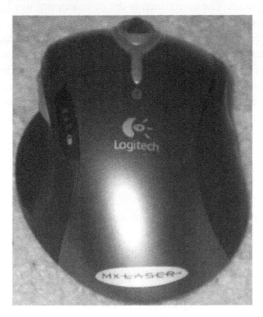

The final topic is one that is relevant for any mouse: buttons. The number of buttons that you need your mouse to have is dependent on the software interfaces you use. For the Macintosh, one button has always been sufficient, but for a Windows-based computer, at least two are recommended, hence the term *right-click*. Today, the mouse is commonly found to have a wheel on top to aid in scrolling and other specialty movement. The wheel has even developed a click in many models, sort of an additional button underneath the wheel. Buttons on the side of the mouse that can be programmed for whatever the user desires are more common today as well and can alarm the unsuspecting user the first time they grab such a mouse the wrong way.

Touchpads, which are flat panels below the spacebar, and pointing sticks, which are eraser-like protrusions in the middle of the keyboard, are found mainly on laptops. A trackball, however, is more like an inverted mouse, so let's look at how they compare. Both devices place the buttons on the top, which is where your fingers will be. A mouse places its tracking mechanism on the bottom, requiring that you move the entire assembly as an analogue for how you want the cursor on the screen to move. In contrast, a trackball places the tracking mechanism, usually a ball that is larger than that of a mouse, on the top with the buttons. You then have a device that need not be moved around on the desktop and can work in tight spaces and on surfaces that would be incompatible with the use of a mouse. The better trackballs place the ball and buttons in such a configuration that your hand rests ergonomically on the device, allowing effortless control of the onscreen cursor.

Touchpad

Many modern laptops have a built-in pointing device that can take the place of a mouse. *Touchpads* are flat panels, which are most often positioned in the same plane as the keyboard—between the spacebar and the user—sometimes with buttons that supply the left- and right-clicks of the mouse. The user controls the onscreen pointer by tracing its path on the surface of the touchpad, some of which include a tactile click feature that takes the place of the left-button click. Some touchpads also dedicate an edge to the right-click function.

Touchpads can be purchased as separate external devices for use with any computer that has an available port, often USB. These work with laptops and desktops alike. Regardless of the details surrounding the touchpad, Windows offers one or more tabs dedicated to the touchpad in the Mouse applet in Control Panel for use in configuring the various settings for it. Tabs added by the manufacturer of the hardware often include advanced configuration options, including those related to multitouch and motions.

Figure 3.39 shows a manufacturer's tab added to the Mouse applet in Control Panel. Figure 3.40 shows the additional configuration tabs produced by clicking the Options button shown in Figure 3.39.

FIGURE 3.39   Manufacturer tab in Mouse applet

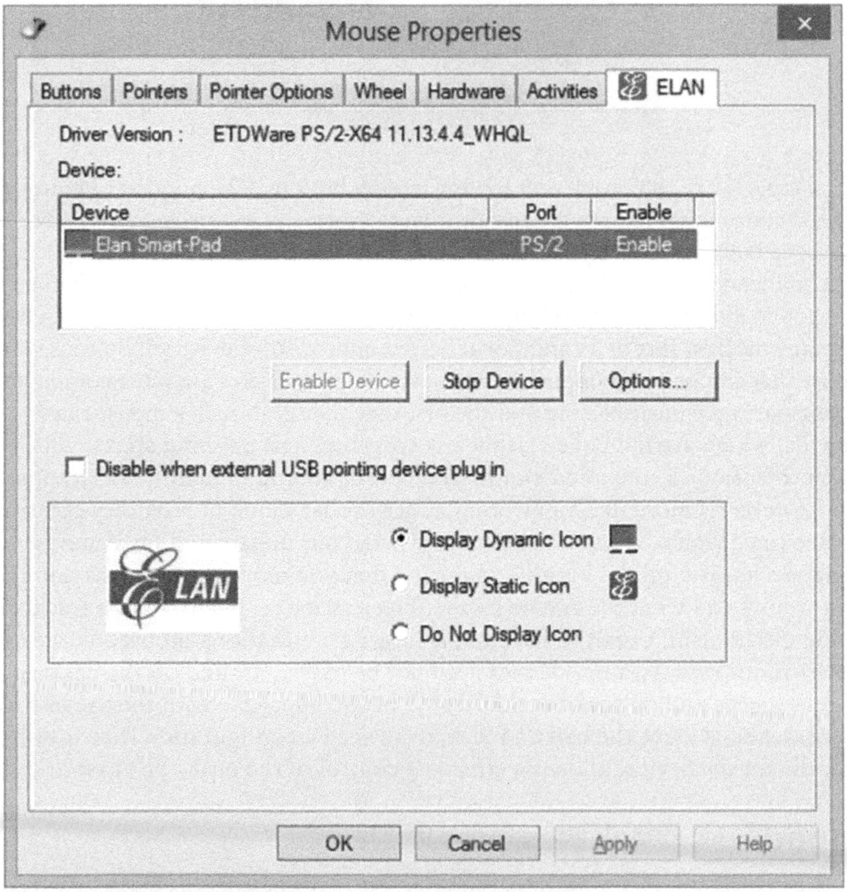

FIGURE 3.40   Manufacturer's custom tabs

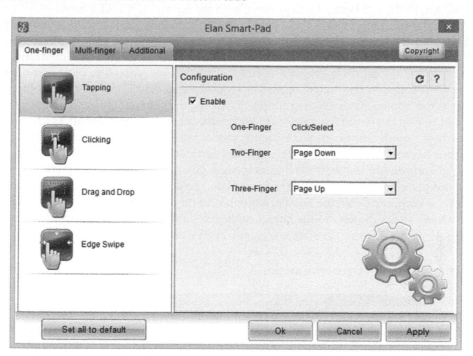

Keyboard

More ubiquitous than the mouse, the *keyboard* is easily the most popular input device, so much so that it's more of a necessity. Very few users would even think of beginning a computing session without a working keyboard. Fewer still would even know how. The U.S. English keyboard places keys in the same orientation as the QWERTY typewriter keyboards, which were developed in the 1860s.

In addition to the standard QWERTY layout, modern computer keyboards often have separate cursor-movement and numerical keypads. The numerical keys in a row above the alphabet keys send scan codes to the computer that are different from those sent by the numerical keypad. At the discretion of the programmer, any given application might require the use of only one of the two sets of numeric keys or allow the use of either. The IBM PC/AT keyboard had only 84 keys, lacking separate cursor-movement keys. These functions were superimposed on the numeric keypad only. The Num Lock key had to be toggled to switch between cursor movement and the numeric keypad. The 101-key keyboard did include these separate keys but still kept the Num Lock arrangement as well, and the popular 104-key Windows keyboard added Windows-specific keys to those 101 keys.

Keyboards have also added function keys (not to be confused with the common laptop key labeled *Fn*), which are often placed in a row across the top of the keyboard above the numerical row. Key functionality can be modified by using one or more combinations of the Ctrl, Alt, Shift, and laptop Fn keys along with the normal QWERTY keys.

Technically speaking, the keys on a keyboard complete individual circuits when each one is pressed. The completion of each circuit leads to a unique scan code that is sent to the keyboard connector on the computer system. The computer uses a keyboard controller chip or function to interpret the code as the corresponding key sequence. The computer then decides what action to take based on the key sequence and what it means to the computer and the active application, including simply displaying the character printed on the key.

In addition to the layout for a standard keyboard, other keyboard layouts exist, some not nearly as popular, however. For example, without changing the order of the keys, an ergonomic keyboard is designed to feel more comfortable to users as they type. The typical human's hands do not rest with the fingers straight down. Ergonomic keyboards, therefore, should not place keys flat and along the same plane. To accomplish that goal, manufacturers split the keyboard down the middle, angling keys on each side downward from the center. Doing so fits the keys to the fingers of the hands when they are in a relaxed state. Figure 3.41 shows an example of an ergonomic keyboard.

FIGURE 3.41   An ergonomic keyboard

My keyboard by ryaninc - Flickr. Licensed under CC BY 2.0 via Commons

The Dvorak Simplified Keyboard, patented in 1936, was designed to reduce fatigue in the hands of typists by placing characters that are more commonly used in the home row, among other physiologic enhancements. The QWERTY layout was designed to keep the hammers of a typewriter from becoming entangled. Although the Dvorak keyboard makes logical sense, especially in light of the historic decline in manufacturing and sales of the classic typewriter, the QWERTY keyboard remains dominant. One reason why the Dvorak keyboard has failed to take over might be the loss of productivity to a touch-typist as they retrain on the new format.

 Real World Scenario

Installing Your Mouse and Keyboard

In the early days of the mouse for the PC, the original AT keyboard was still in use. The 9-pin D-sub RS-232 serial ports the mouse used looked nothing like the 5-pin DIN to which the keyboard attached. Not long thereafter, the PS/2 product line blurred that distinction; indeed, it removed it. Because both interfaces are matching 6-pin mini-DIN connectors, care was paramount during installation. Standard industry color coding has simplified the installation process, but the ports are still easily interchanged during blind insertion. If you have visibility of the ports, remembering that the keyboard interface is coded purple and the mouse green takes much of the guesswork out of analyzing icons stamped into or printed on the case. Of course, graduation to USB-attached devices alleviates the hassle. Consult the accompanying documentation for the installation of all types of wireless input devices.

Scanner

One of the earliest input devices aside from the keyboard and mouse was the *scanner*. Today, most scanners feature USB, network (often as part of a multifunction device), or some form of wireless attachment. Look for a menu item in applications capable of scanning that specifies TWAIN (the generic term for the class of drivers associated with scanners), such as Select TWAIN Source. This selection allows you to choose from among multiple scanners before initiating the scan job.

Scanners use light to reflect off of a surface and measure the relative reflections of the different dots that make up the grid that the scanner is able to detect. The tighter the grid (the more dots per inch [DPI] supported), the higher the resolution of the resulting image. Charge coupled devices (CCDs) are a common choice in today's scanners. CCDs convert the light they receive into electrical impulses, which is then forwarded to the software producing the scan for further processing into an image that is a facsimile of the original object being scanned.

A flatbed scanner evokes the concept of a copier with the paper handling and printing mechanisms missing. This image is not far off, which is why copiers make wonderful scanners, as long as they can produce a digital image file. It's also why multifunction devices are so prolific; it takes very little to outfit a printer with a scanner component to be used for input to the computer and as a fax-scanning device. Inbound faxes can be printed, or the same digital interface that the scanner uses can be used to transfer the image electronically to software in the computer. Figure 3.42 shows the top flatbed scanner portion of a laser multifunction device that provides a way to print, scan, and fax.

FIGURE 3.42   A flatbed scanner

Figure 3.43 shows you one of numerous brands of portable document scanners. These handy little devices are scarcely more than a foot long and can make short work of scanning anything from a business card to a gas receipt to an 8.5" × 11" lodging folio. The associated software that comes with these scanners performs optical character recognition (OCR), and it can recognize the orientation of the text and glean pertinent information from the documents scanned to populate the internal database. From this database, you

can produce reports for such purposes as expenses, invoicing, and taxes. This model also offers the option to create a PDF during the scan instead.

FIGURE 3.43   A portable document scanner

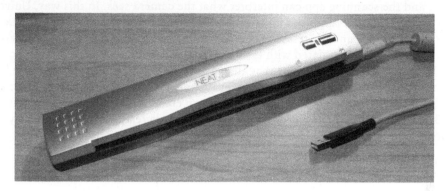

Barcode Reader

A *barcode reader* (or barcode *scanner*) is a specialized input device commonly used in retail and other industrial sectors that manage inventory. The systems to which the reader connects can be so specialized that they have no other input device. Barcode readers can use LEDs or lasers as light sources and can scan one- or two-dimensional barcodes.

Using a Barcode Reader in the VoIP Industry

The VoIP industry relies on barcode readers to quickly scan in the MAC addresses of hundreds or thousands of desk sets from labels on their neatly stacked boxes before their deployment. Depending on the brand of equipment, the MAC addresses might be read in to populate a spreadsheet that is later used as input to the call management system during the identification of which directory numbers will be assigned to which physical devices. The same job done by hand could have untold issues caused by user error.

Barcode readers can connect to the host system in a number of ways, but serial connections, such as USB, are fairly common. If the system uses proprietary software to receive the reader's input, the connection between the two might be proprietary as well. Classic software interfaces called for the reader to be plugged into the keyboard's PS/2 connector using a splitter, or "wedge," which allows the keyboard to remain connected. The scanner converts all output to keyboard scans so that the system treats the input as if it came from a keyboard. For certain readers, wireless communication with the host is also possible, using IR, RF, Bluetooth, WiFi, and more.

With today's smartphone technology being what it is, the built-in cameras can act as scanners, and the scanning app can interpret what the camera sees. In this way, Universal Product Code (UPC) barcodes and Quick Response (QR) codes and other 2D matrix barcodes can be input and processed. The smartphone can then use its Internet access to launch the application associated with the text, such as a web browser or an email client. A QR code is an encoded image that allows the scanning application to decode large amounts of text, and it can be used to represent simple text or popular strings, such as a website's URL, a phone number, a GEO location, an email address, or an SMS message. Figure 3.44 is a simple QR code that will direct a QR-code reader app to the www.sybex .com website.

FIGURE 3.44   A QR code

Digitizer

One way to reproduce incredibly good artwork faithfully in digital form for computer use is to place the analog artwork on top of a sensor and use a stylus to trace the artwork after choosing an onscreen "crayon" or "pen." The end result can be a work of art almost as good as the original. The device used to trace an analog source and turn it into a digital representation is a *digitizer*. Digitizing, in fact, is the act of turning any analog source—artwork, audio, video, slides and photographs—into a binary bit stream. As an input device, however, a digitizer or *digitizing tablet* takes pen strokes in the analog world and turns them into a digital rendering through the software controlling the digitizer. These devices are also commonly used to annotate presentations with the option to save or discard the annotations with each presentation. Figure 3.45 shows an example of a USB-attached digitizing tablet with choice of pen or mouse for input.

FIGURE 3.45   A digitizing tablet

Biometric Devices

Any device that measures one or more physical or behavioral features of an organism is considered a *biometric device*, or literally, a device that measures life. When the same device forwards this biometric information to the computer, it becomes an input device. The list includes fingerprint scanners, retinal and iris scanners, voice recognition devices, and facial recognition devices, to name a few. A computer can use this input to authenticate the user based on preestablished biometric information captured during user setup. Even cipher locks that authenticate personnel before allowing entry to secure environments can be replaced with biometric devices.

Because there are many manufacturers of biometric devices, the installation of any particular model is best performed while consulting the company's documentation. If the device is not built into the computer, at a minimum some form of interface, such as USB, must be used to attach the device, and software must be installed to lock the system until authentication occurs. Many offerings allow multiple forms of authentication to be required in sequence. An example of a highly secure approach to authentication with multiple factors would be a biometric scan, followed by a challenge that requires a code from a token card, followed finally by the opportunity to enter a password. This "something you are, something you have, and something you know" technique works to secure some of the world's most sensitive installations. Further discussion of the concept of multifactor authentication is beyond the scope of this book.

Gamepads and Joysticks

As long as there have been gaming applications for the personal computer, there have been standard and specialty controllers for some of those games. For the rest, the keyboard and mouse could be or had to be used for controlling the game. Two popular types of controllers have been the generic *joystick*, a controller with one or more buttons and a stick of varying length and girth, and the often proprietary *gamepad*, usually comprising function and directional buttons specific to the gaming console in use. Through the years, standardized PC connections have included the DA15 game port, also known as the joystick port, the RS-232 port, and the USB port. Figure 3.46 shows a wired joystick connected through the wireless controller for the Nintendo Wii video game console.

FIGURE 3.46   A proprietary gamepad

Motion Sensor

One of the first commercially viable motion sensors as an input device for a computing platform was found in the Nintendo Wii gaming system. Eventually, Sony's Move and

Microsoft's Kinect joined the Wii in the marketplace, with the two later entrants being add-ons to their manufacturers' existing game systems.

In the PC market, motion sensors as input devices are more likely to be seen as replacements for the mouse, trackball, trackpad, and other built-in pointing devices. One primary benefit of these devices, such as the Leap Motion Controller by Leap Motion, Inc., is that a user can control the movement of an onscreen cursor without physically laying a hand on any sort of component. Because such devices are not based on proven technology, the computer market does not seem to be flocking toward them—at least initially. But there might be hidden benefits in the end.

Repetitive strain injuries (RSIs) that stem from holding the hand against an object such as a mouse in a less than optimal position for extended periods of time do not occur when there is no contact. While there is no guarantee that users of motion sensors will not develop habits that may lead to RSIs, they will more likely exercise the same muscles and joints that would otherwise become damaged and begin pinching adjacent nerves. Even when handheld controllers are required, as in the case of the Wii system, the relative freedom from holding your hand in the same position for prolonged periods is a major benefit, despite holding it against the controller.

Smart Card Reader

As more and more organizations discover the value in multifactor authentication for access to their computing assets, smart card readers have become indispensable as an instrument of the "something you have" principle. For quite some time, the United States government and its military forces have relied on common access cards (CACs), which serve as visual identification cards as well as chip-based smart cards.

A *smart card reader* attaches to the system internally or externally by USB or sometimes through a dedicated adapter. FireWire was once supported, but it is no longer common for reader attachment. The reader provides power for the chip that is embedded in the smart card. These chips contain a combination of RAM, ROM, PROM, and a 16-bit CPU. Figure 3.47 shows the contacts of the integrated circuit chip (ICC) of a typical smart card.

It's increasingly common for merchants to install terminals that capture a patron's credit card for the duration of the transaction if an ICC is detected, in contrast to requiring that the customer insert and then quickly remove the card from the classic reader. These new ICC-friendly card readers can also be used with the traditional cards that have no chip embedded.

The chip on a smart card may contain one or more PKI certificates. Smart card readers used by the United States Department of Defense are able to access the CAC's ICC in order to use an identification certificate in the chip to verify the identity of the bearer. A PIN, however, may still be required to establish two-factor authentication. In other uses, card readers access digital-signature and encryption certificates to establish nonrepudiation and confidentiality for a user during electronic exchanges of information.

FIGURE 3.47   A smart card showing the ICC

Multimedia Input Devices

Multimedia input devices vary in functionality based on the type of input being gathered. Two broad categories of multimedia input are audio and video. Digital motion and still cameras are incredibly popular as a replacement for similar video products that do not transfer information to a computer, making sharing and collaboration so much easier than before. The following sections present information on these multimedia input devices:

- Webcams
- MIDI-enabled devices
- Digital cameras and camcorders
- Microphone

Webcams

Years ago, owing to the continued growth in the Internet's popularity, video camera–only devices known as *webcams* started their climb in popularity. Today, anyone who does a fair amount of instant messaging, whether professional or personal, has likely used or at least been introduced to webcams, often used in conjunction with messaging user interfaces.

Webcams make great security devices as well. Users can keep an eye on loved ones or property from anywhere that Internet access is available. Care must be taken, however, because the security that the webcam is intended to provide can backfire on the user if the webcam is not set up properly. Anyone who happens upon the web interface for the device can control its actions if there is no authentication enabled. Some webcams provide a light that illuminates when someone activates the camera. Nevertheless, it is possible to decouple the camera's operation and that of its light.

A webcam connects directly to the computer through an I/O interface, such as USB or WiFi, and it does not have any self-contained recording mechanism. Its sole purpose is to transfer its captured video directly to the host computer, usually for further transfer over the Internet, hence the term *web*. Webcams that have built-in wired and wireless NIC interfaces for direct network attachment are prevalent as well. A now maturing evolution of the webcam for laptops resulted in manufacturers building the device into the bezel of the display. Connectivity is generally through an internal USB or FireWire interface.

MIDI Devices

Microphones, audio playback, and audio synthesizing devices are common input components connected to a sound card or some form of serial port so that audio from these devices can be collected and processed. As an example, consider *Musical Instrument Digital Interface (MIDI)* devices, called controllers, which create messages describing, and thus synthesizing, the user's intended musical performance. These devices do not make sound that is recorded directly; they are merely designed to somewhat realistically fabricate the music the instruments that they represent might produce. MIDI files, therefore, are much smaller than files that contain digitized audio waveforms.

Modern MIDI controllers use 5-pin DIN connectors that look like the original AT keyboard connector. Controllers can be interconnected in one of two ways. The original method is to provide devices with two ports, an input and an output port, and daisy-chain them in a ring. This arrangement introduces a delay caused by devices processing and retransmitting messages that were not destined for them but instead for devices downstream from them. One solution is to replace the output port with one that merely replicates the input signal. If the receiving device is the intended destination, then the unnecessarily repeated message is ignored by downstream recipients. Otherwise, the actual recipient receives its message with far less delay. The second method of connection is another solution that reduces delay. A device with one input and multiple outputs interconnects many devices directly.

Regardless of the controller interconnection method, computers can receive MIDI controllers directly, such as through a sound card with a built-in MIDI interface or through the use of an external MIDI interface that originally connected to the computer's game port. Today,

USB and FireWire ports are more commonly used. Ethernet-attached interfaces also exist and require very little processing power to convert the MIDI messages into Ethernet frames.

Digital Cameras and Camcorders

A *digital camera* is a device that takes still pictures and records them to digital media of some sort for later access. A *camcorder* is a video capture device that performs a similar function to that of the digital camera but for moving video. Most of today's multimedia recording devices perform the functions of both the digital camera and the digital camcorder. Depending on the device, both pictures and video can be stored on the same or different media within the same device. In fact, the most basic smartphone can perform both of these functions, often with exceptional quality.

Early versions of digital cameras relied on the storage media of the day, 3~HF" floppy diskettes, for instance. Eventually, models with internal flash memory were developed, which led to hybrid models that also featured a memory card slot, resulting in the flexibility to grow the camera's storage capacity as the technology produced larger cards.

A similar evolution occurred in the world of camcorders. Originally, camcorders required one of a variety of analog tape formats on which to record. This gave way to digital tape formats and then to burnable optical discs, hard disk drives, and today's high-capacity flash storage devices. Once a removable memory card was added, the possibilities for what can be recorded and how much can be stored became nearly limitless. Figure 3.48 shows a digital camcorder on the left and a digital camera on the right.

FIGURE 3.48   A digital camera and camcorder

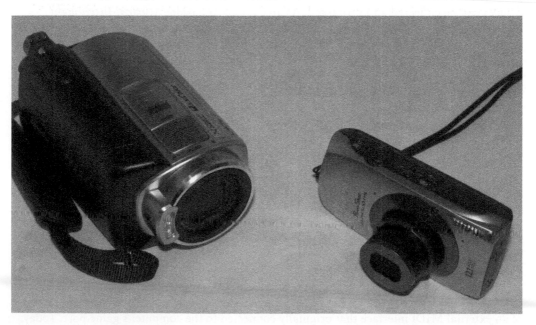

The mechanism by which the digital information is transferred to a computer varies somewhat among these devices. In some cases, a cable—USB, for instance—can be attached between the device and the computer. A drive icon might then appear in Windows File Explorer, or you might have a specific application for access to the content. In other cases, removable media is for recording, and this media is then removed and transferred directly to a reader on the computer system, be it an optical drive or card reader. Certain manufacturers have developed docking stations for their product line. The dock can remain attached to the computer system, and the device can be interfaced to the dock, usually by simply sitting it down on the docking station. In some cases, these stations also charge the device while it is docked.

Microphone

Although discussed throughout this chapter, the *microphone* has yet to be formally defined, a definition which is at once technical and simple. Microphones convert sound waves into varying electrical signals. The result can be recorded, transmitted, or altered in a variety of ways, including amplification.

When installing a microphone, you must match its connector with an available one on the computer. Modern choices include the classic analog pink TRS connector and USB. Wireless versions also exist, but their receiver might still be connected to a standard I/O port. Alternatively, the microphone could be paired with a built-in Bluetooth transceiver, in which case, installation amounts to the pairing process.

Configuring a microphone on a PC is most often performed through the Recording tab of the Sound applet in Control Panel. Options include setting the levels and choosing enhancements, such as noise suppression and echo cancellation. Specialized applications may also have internal configuration for the microphone, passing most details of the configuration back to the operating system.

Output Devices

The process for the installation and configuration of certain output devices varies almost as widely as the number of models within a given category. Nevertheless, certain high-level steps must be taken with nearly each such device. The devices in the following sections are each covered in eye-opening detail elsewhere in this book—two of the three have chapters dedicated to them alone:

- Printers (Chapter 11)
- Speakers
- Display devices (Chapter 4)

The following sections introduce each of the device categories and any specific issues that exist with their installation and configuration without delving too deeply just yet.

Printers

Often immediately behind your monitor in output-device importance, the one or more printers that you have attached to your computer become invaluable when you need to produce a hard copy for distribution or for inclusion in a report, for instance. Chapter 11 will detail the various printer families, such as impact, inkjet, and laser, as well as the details involved in their installation, including connectivity and driver installation. For now, this chapter provides copious information regarding the printer interfaces used today, such as USB and FireWire.

Speakers

The various audio-related discussions in this chapter present concepts surrounding speakers and their connection to the computer or other devices, such as surround sound processors or A/V receivers. Your operating system's audio controls have settings that can be manipulated, sometimes in very complex ways, to produce software configurations that derive the best performance from the speakers that you have installed.

Display Devices

The next chapter presents a wide array of pertinent information on this subject. This chapter also contains considerable interface and cabling information on video display technology. As output devices, the connectivity of display devices can be fixed, with a single type of connection to a video source, or variable, sometimes supporting the connection of multiple sources through similar or different interfaces. In the latter case, input selection is generally a fairly simple process, most often accessible directly from the display device's remote control. In the case of interfaces that have options, such as HDMI, a small amount of onscreen configuration might be in order. In most cases, however, configuration is Plug and Play in nature.

Input and Output Devices

Some devices refuse to be categorized as input or output devices, demanding instead to be considered both input and output devices. Take for example the following such devices:

- Touchscreen
- KVM switch
- Smart TV
- Set-top box

The following sections provide details of these devices and tips on installing and configuring them.

Touchscreens

Touchscreen technology converts stimuli of some sort, which are generated by actually touching the screen, to electrical impulses that travel over serial connections to the computer system. These input signals allow for the replacement of the mouse, both in terms of movement and in clicking. With onscreen keyboards, the external keyboard can be retired as well. However, standard computer systems are not the only application for touchscreen enhancement. This technology can also be seen in PDAs and smartphones, point-of-sale venues for such things as PIN entry and signature capture, handheld and bar-mounted games, ATMs, remote controls, appliances, and vehicles. The list continues to grow as technology advances.

For touchscreens, a handful of solutions exist for converting a touch to a signal. Some less-successful ones rely on warm hands, sound waves, or dust-free screens. The more successful screens have optical or electrical sensors that are quite a bit less fastidious. The two most popular technologies found on handheld devices are *resistive* and *capacitive*. *Capacitive interfaces* are generally smoother to the touch than resistive interfaces, and the pad of the finger or a special stylus that mimics this soft part of the fingertip can control them. *Resistive interfaces* usually have to be controlled by the fingernail or a plastic or metal stylus. In any event, the sensory system is added onto a standard monitor at some point, whether in the field by the user or in a more seamless fashion by the manufacturer.

Installing monitors with touch capability on standard computers entails not only attachment to the graphics adapter but also attachment to a serial interface. The most popular of these has become the USB port, much as it has for the mouse and keyboard.

Calibration is required upon first configuration and whenever there appears to be a misinterpretation by the system as to where the user has touched the screen. This calibration entails displaying a pattern that the user has to touch at certain points to let the system know where these landmarks are perceived to be.

KVM Switch

A KVM switch isn't an input or output device, per se, but it allows you to switch between sets of input and output devices. The *KVM switch* is named after the devices among which it allows you to switch. The initials stand for *keyboard*, *video*, and *mouse*. KVM switches come in a variety of models. You can select the switch that accommodates the types of interfaces that your components require. For example, your keyboard and mouse might attach with mini-DIN connectors or with USB connectors; your monitor might attach with a VGA, DVI, or HDMI connector.

The purpose of the switch is to allow you to have multiple systems attached to the same keyboard, monitor, and mouse. You can use these three devices with only one system at a time. Some switches have a dial that you turn to select which system attaches to the components, while others feature buttons for each system connected. Common uses of KVM switches include using the same components alternately for a desktop computer and a laptop docking station or having a server room with multiple servers but no need to interface with them simultaneously.

Figure 3.49 shows a four-system VGA/USB switch with analog audio switching as well. If DVI or PS/2 attachments are desired, for example, adapters are required. The buttons on the front (right side of the image) switch the common console connections (on the left side of the image) among the four systems, only three of which are currently attached. A maximum of one of the four LEDs beside the corresponding buttons is lit at a time—only for the system currently in control.

FIGURE 3.49   A KVM switch

Smart TV

The term *smart TV* was coined to describe a once budding class of monitors and televisions that have a built-in system for accessing network services. Today, the smart TV is almost as widespread as the networks to which they attach. The devices have gone from simply using the network to gain access to streaming online services to allowing users to browse the Web using remote controls or wireless keyboards and mice.

Smart TVs often have USB ports for the introduction of USB flash drives that contain entertainment media that the smart TV can recognize, and they offer a menu that allows the user to choose which file to access for playback on the TV. Many users combine the smart TV with a home media server to be able to stream movies and music across the wired or wireless LAN, which provides higher bit rates as compared to streaming similar media over the Internet.

Smart TVs are adept at installing themselves with minimal help from the home user, who may likely be a novice in the world of technical devices. At a minimum, however, the smart TV may require the user to choose from the available wireless networks within the range of the TV and to supply the chosen network's password for access. Otherwise, a wired Ethernet connection must be supplied along with power and possibly some form of television input signal. Final configuration can include any of a variety of standard television and display settings as well as basic and advanced network preferences.

Set-Top Box

The term *set-top box (STB)* is used to describe any of a variety of thin rectangular chassis that can sit or stack on classic CRT televisions but that most often reside today on shelves or furniture. One of the most common STBs is the cable converter box, which has developed into the modern digital video recorder (DVR). Optical-disc players and burners, home-theater PCs, and similar devices secure the STB's place in the combination input/output category.

Steps to install a set-top box are dependent on the type of STB in question. They range from choosing favorite and blocked channels to the same steps required to connect and configure a standard personal computer.

Summary

In this chapter, you learned about various types of expansion cards, the interfaces for which they are best known, and the peripherals to which they connect. The fact that some interfaces have gone through an evolution, changing in appearance and capabilities at times, was also presented. No discussion of expansion cards and interfaces would be complete without adding in the details of the cables needed, if any, to connect the cards to the peripherals; the discussion in this chapter is no exception.

This chapter also surveyed the details of peripherals from an output vs. input perspective, including specifics on the connections for display devices. Well-known input devices, such as the mouse and keyboard, and less conventional yet popular input devices were examined in this chapter. You also learned about the KVM switch, a device that allows you to share input and output devices among computers. The adapter cards highlighted in this chapter fall into four broad categories: video, multimedia, I/O, and communications.

Other output devices were presented, some with substantial detail while others that are covered in more detail elsewhere in this book were covered only briefly. Finally, you got a look at some of the most common hybrid devices that are capable of both input and output at once.

Exam Essentials

Familiarize yourself with installation and configuration of expansion cards.   The variety of expansion cards available leads to the need to know the similarities and differences among them. For example, they all need to be inserted into the system using an expansion slot. They all perform a specific function or set of functions, based on their type, but not all cards are configured in the same way. Some require more configuration than others, while some require no installer interaction at all.

Recognize and understand different peripheral connectors and converters.   Expansion cards and motherboards have external connectivity interfaces. The interfaces have connectors that adhere to some sort of standard for interconnecting with a cable or external device. Knowing these specific characteristics can help you differentiate among the capabilities of the interfaces available to you. Understanding when to use an adapter to convert one connector to another is crucial to achieving connectivity among differing interfaces.

Recognize and be able to describe display connectors specifically.   Although a type of peripheral connector, display connectors are in a class all their own. Technologies continue to be developed to merge display and other peripheral functions, such as serial I/O, but the differences among the various display interfaces are substantial enough for these connectors to warrant their own category.

Know the characteristics of cables used for peripheral attachment.   Whether the connection is internal or external to the computer system, each cable used has specific characteristics, no matter their resemblance to others. Some cables that look similar to others support higher speeds or longer distances. Some have power components, while others are completely passive in nature. Knowing the specific cables that go along with the expansion cards and their interfaces is extremely valuable and important.

Compare and contrast input devices.   Although input devices vary widely in their functionality, they all provide external input to the computer. Familiarize yourself with the specifics of the devices mentioned in this chapter, differentiating them by their function and applicability to a particular need.

Be able to differentiate among input, output, and hybrid devices.   The output-only devices listed and described in this chapter are less plentiful than the input devices. In fact, there are more combination input/output devices covered than output-only devices. Know the differences among them, and be able to explain why they fall into the category that they do.

Review Questions

The answers to the chapter review questions can be found in Appendix A.

1. You want to plug a keyboard into the back of a computer. You know that you need to plug the keyboard cable into a PS/2 port. Which style of port is the PS/2?

    A. RJ-11

    B. RJ-45

    C. DIN 5

    D. Mini-DIN 6

2. What is the maximum speed of USB 2.0 in Mbps?

    A. 1.5

    B. 12

    C. 60

    D. 480

3. Which of the following is both an input and an output device?

    A. Webcam

    B. Motion sensor

    C. Touchscreen

    D. Touchpad

4. What peripheral port type was originally developed by Apple and is currently regarded as the optimal interface for digital video transfers?

    A. DVD

    B. USB 2.0

    C. IEEE 1394

    D. IEEE 1284

5. What peripheral port type is expandable using a hub, operates at 1.5MBps, and is used to connect various devices (from printers to cameras) to PCs?

    A. DVD 1.0

    B. USB 1.1

    C. IEEE 1394

    D. IEEE 1284

6. Which peripheral port type was designed to transfer data at higher speeds over a D-sub interface?

    A. DVD

    B. USB

    C. IEEE 1394

    D. IEEE 1284

7. The surround sound mode known as 5.1 employs how many speakers when only one is used for each channel?

    A. One

    B. Five

    C. Six

    D. Seven

    E. Eight

8. Which of the following display interfaces is equivalent to DisplayPort with PCIe added in?

    A. Thunderbolt

    B. WHUXGA

    C. IEEE 1394c

    D. HDMI

9. Which of the following interfaces allows audio to be sent out over the same cabling infrastructure as video?

    A. VGA

    B. DVI

    C. HDMI

    D. Composite

10. How do you connect a DVI-A interface on a peripheral to a DVI-D interface on the computer?

    A. With a DVI-I cable.

    B. With a cable that is terminated on one end with a DVI-A connector and on the other end with a DVI-D connector.

    C. You wouldn't interconnect those two interfaces.

    D. With a standard DVI cable.

11. What kind of device uses unique physical traits of the user to authenticate their access to a secure system or location?

    A. Barcode reader

    B. Biometric device

    C. Keyboard

    D. Touchscreen

12. Why might you use a KVM switch?

    A. You have multiple Ethernet devices that need to communicate with one another.

    B. You need to be able to switch the voltage supplied to a particular device.

    C. You have a printer that is not attached to the network but you want multiple computers to be able to print to it.

    D. You have more than one server and don't want to buy certain external peripherals separately for each.

13. Which type of input device employs roughly the same connector as the original AT keyboard?

    A. Barcode reader

    B. PS/2 keyboard

    C. MIDI

    D. Touchscreen

14. What can you use to convert video to a format that can be uploaded to the Internet, among other things?

    A. A barcode reader

    B. A video capture card

    C. A TV tuner card

    D. A MIDI device

15. Which of the following is not an example of a connector for a standard peripheral input device?

    A. 1/8" jack

    B. Mini-DIN

    C. D-subminiature

    D. USB

16. Which category of adapters includes NICs?

    A. Multimedia

    B. I/O

    C. Communications

    D. Video

17. What category of adapter would you need to install to equip a system with one or more USB ports?

    A. Multimedia

    B. I/O

    C. Communications

    D. Video

18. What type of adapter has an RJ-11 jack built in?

    A. Modem

    B. Video

    C. Sound

    D. NIC

19. What type of pointing device features a ball and buttons on the top and a flat, steady surface on the bottom?

    A. Mouse

    B. Touchpad

    C. Trackball

    D. Trackpad

20. VGA-based video technologies use what type of signal between the adapter and monitor?

    A. Digital

    B. Analog

    C. Compressed

    D. Composite

Performance-Based Questions

You will encounter performance-based questions on the A+ exams. The questions on the exam require you to perform a specific task, and you will be graded on whether or not you were able to complete the task. The following requires you to think creatively in order to measure how well you understand this chapter's topics. You may or may not see similar questions on the actual A+ exams. To see how your answers compare to the authors', refer to Appendix B.

Looking at the back of a computer, you see interfaces of the following colors and shapes:

- Gray, flat 4-pin
- Blue, DE15
- Green, mini-DIN 6
- Purple, mini-DIN 6
- Green, 3.5mm TRS

One by one, match the following external devices and functions to these interfaces:

- VGA
- USB
- Mouse
- Keyboard
- Speaker

Chapter

4

Display Devices

THE FOLLOWING COMPTIA A+ 220-901 OBJECTIVES ARE COVERED IN THIS CHAPTER:

✓ **1.10 Given a scenario, evaluate types and features of display devices.**

- Types:
  - LCD:
  - TN vs. IPS
  - Fluorescent vs. LED backlighting
  - Plasma
  - Projector
  - OLED
  - Refresh/frame rates
  - Resolution
  - Native resolution
  - Brightness/lumens
  - Analog vs. digital
  - Privacy/antiglare filters
  - Multiple displays
- Aspect ratios:
  - 16:9
  - 16:10
  - 4:3

The primary method of getting information out of a computer is to use a computer video display unit (VDU). Display systems convert computer signals into text and pictures and display them on a TV-like screen. As a matter of fact, the first personal computers used television screens because it was simpler to use an existing display technology than to develop a new one.

This chapter introduces you to concepts surrounding display units used with personal computer systems. The previous chapter detailed the technology behind the adapters, interfaces, and connectors used in computer graphics. Other topics covered in this chapter include characteristics of display standards, such as the resolutions and color densities of VGA and the standards that sprung from it, and settings common to most display devices.

Understanding Display Types and Settings

Most display systems work the same way. First, the computer sends a signal to a device called the video adapter—an expansion board installed in an expansion bus slot or the equivalent circuitry integrated into the motherboard—telling it to display a particular graphic or character. The adapter then renders the character for the display; that is, it converts the single instruction into several instructions that tell the display device how to draw the graphic and sends the instructions to the display device based on the connection technology between the two. The primary differences after that are in the type of video adapter you are using (digital or analog) and the type of display (LCD, plasma, OLED, and so forth).

Video Display Types

To truly understand the video display arena, you must be introduced to a few terms and concepts with which you may be unfamiliar. The legacy digital transistor-transistor logic (TTL) and the analog technologies that began with video graphics array (VGA) were once the two broad categories of video technologies. These categories have nothing to do with the makeup of the VDU but instead with how the graphics adapter communicates with the VDU. You will read about many of the VGA technologies in later sections of this chapter. First, however, let's explore the different VDU types:

- Liquid crystal display
- Plasma

- OLED
- Projection systems

Liquid Crystal Displays

Portable computers were originally designed to be compact versions of their bigger desktop cousins. They crammed all of the components of the big desktop computers into a small, suitcase-like box called (laughably) a portable computer. You could also hear the term *luggable* in those days when referring to the same systems. No matter what the designers did to reduce the size of the computer, the display remained as large as those found on desktop versions; that is, until an inventor found that when he passed an electrical current through a semi-crystalline liquid, the crystals aligned themselves with the current. It was found that when transistors were combined with these liquid crystals, patterns could be formed. These patterns could be combined to represent numbers or letters. The first application of these *liquid crystal displays (LCDs)* was the LCD watch. It was rather bulky, but it was cool.

As LCD elements got smaller, the detail of the patterns became greater, until one day someone thought to make a computer screen out of several of these elements. This screen was very light compared to computer monitors of the day, and it consumed relatively little power. It could easily be added to a portable computer to reduce the weight by as much as 30 pounds. As the components got smaller, so did the computer, and the laptop computer was born.

For years now, LCDs have not been limited to just laptops; desktop versions of LCD displays and their offshoots are practically all that are seen today. Additionally, the home television market has been enjoying the LCD as a competitor of plasma for years. LCDs used with desktop computer systems use the same technology as their laptop counterparts but potentially on a much larger scale.

These external LCDs are available with either analog or digital interfaces. The analog interface is commonly a VGA interface, but it can also be a DVI-A interface. Internal digital signals from the computer are rendered, output as analog signals by the video card, and sent along the cable that terminates on and supports the analog connectors at each end. The analog signal is then converted back to a digital signal for processing by the display device. LCDs with a digital interface, on the other hand, require no analog modulation by the graphics adapter and demodulation by the display device. They require the video card to support digital output using a different interface, such as DVI-D or HDMI. The advantage is that because the video signal never changes from digital to analog, there is less of a chance of interference and no conversion-related quality loss. Digitally attached displays are generally sharper than their analog connected counterparts.

LCD Panel Construction

The two most popular methods of manufacturing LCD panels are *twisted nematic (TN)* and *in-plane switching (IPS)*. Each method has its strengths and weaknesses, but of the two, IPS is regarded as having the best color representation in all angles, while TN is faster and less expensive.

TN places two electrodes on opposite sides of a liquid crystal layer. The electrodes are attached to the inside of two polarizing surfaces, each rotated 90 degrees with respect to the other. When light enters one side and travels straight through, the other side blocks the light. The light must twist 90 degrees to be allowed through. Think of the crystals as thin rods. When an electrical field is generated by the electrodes, the crystals align lengthwise with the field, perpendicular to the electrodes, and they allow the light to pass straight through. The result is that the light is blocked from making it to the eye of the observer.

When the electrodes are off, the crystals rotate parallel to the them and are influenced by the coating on the electrodes to align to each one so they are rotated 90 degrees with respect to the crystals at the opposing electrode. The crystals are naturally influenced to remain parallel to adjacent crystals, but the influence of the electrodes to remain parallel to the crystals is stronger and causes the chain of crystals in between to twist gradually as they progress from one electrode to the other, following a helical path. The helix rotates the passing light 90 degrees so that it now aligns with the opposite polarizer and appears to pass through to the observer's eye.

TN exhibits the unfortunate characteristic of shifting the colors of the image as the observer views the screen from wide horizontal and vertical angles. At extreme angles, the light and dark shades appear to swap places, almost as a negative of the actual image. TN panels also tend to react to pressure when touched, blanching the area under a finger pressed against the screen, for instance. However, the faster response rates that lead to more fluid image changes make TN a favorite technology of gamers and action video enthusiasts.

IPS panels have electrodes that are positioned parallel to one another on the same side of the liquid crystal panel, creating an electrical "switch in the same plane." The two opposing outside polarizing layers are aligned in the same direction, so to create the helical structure with the crystals in the off state, the opposing glass panels have a 90-degree rotated internal coating. The coating influences adjacent crystals to align with the direction of the coating, as with TN. Unlike with TN, however, the parallel polarizer on the opposite side blocks the light when the electrodes are off.

Turning the electrodes on results in a parallel alignment of the crystals lengthwise from one electrode to the other, as they follow the electrical field being generated. This narrows the stack of crystals so that the light passes by them without twisting, thus passing through the similarly aligned polarizer on the opposite side.

IPS technology reproduces colors more accurately and does not suffer from the shifts in color when the screen is viewed from wide angles. These characteristics makes IPS ideal for those who require a true-to-life representation of the original colors of the image displayed. For that reason, as well as for their lack of reaction to being touched, IPS panels are more suitable for touchscreens, including those on handheld portable devices, such as smartphones. The drawbacks of slow response and lusterless display of black hues have been mitigated through the generations of IPS technological advancements. Nevertheless, IPS remains a more expensive solution that requires more power to operate than TN.

Table 4.1 summarizes the differences between TN and IPS, including their cost, image stability, and the power required to operate them.

TABLE 4.1   TN vs. IPS

Characteristic	TN	IPS
Cost	Less	More
Color accuracy	Less	More
Reaction to touch	More	Less
Viewing angle	Narrow	Wide
Power required	Less	More

Pixel Addressing

Two major types of LCD displays have been implemented over the years: active-matrix screens and passive-matrix screens. Another type, dual scan, is a passive-matrix variant. The main differences lie in the quality of the image. However, when used with computers, each type uses lighting behind the LCD panel (backlighting) to make the screen easier to view. Legacy LCD panels had one or more fluorescent bulbs as backlights. Modern LCD panels use LEDs to light the display more precisely by individually dedicating a separate light source to each pixel. The following discussions highlight the main differences among the pixel-addressing variants.

Active matrix   An active-matrix screen is made up of several independent LCD pixels. A transistor at each pixel location, when switched among various levels, activates two opposing electrodes that align the pixel's crystals and alter the passage of light at that location to produce hundreds or thousands of shades. The front electrode, at least, must be clear. This type of display is very crisp and easy to look at through nearly all oblique angles, and it does not require constant refreshing to maintain an image because transistors conduct current in only one direction and the pixel acts like a capacitor by holding its charge until it is refreshed with new information.

The major disadvantage of an active-matrix screen is that it requires larger amounts of power to operate all of the transistors—one for each red, green, and blue subpixel. Even with the backlight turned off, the screen can still consume battery power at an alarming rate, even more so when conventional fluorescent backlights are employed.

Passive matrix   A passive-matrix display does not have a dedicated transistor for each pixel or subpixel but instead a matrix of conductive traces. In simplified terms for a single pixel, when the display is instructed to change the crystalline alignment of a particular pixel, it sends a signal across the x- and y-coordinate traces that intersect at that pixel, thus turning it on. Figure 4.1 illustrates this concept.

FIGURE 4.1   A passive-matrix display

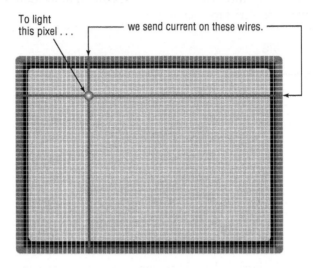

The circuits controlling the columns are synchronized to fire when that row's transistor is active and only for the pixels that should be affected on that row. Angles of visibility and response times (the time to change a pixel) suffer greatly with passive-matrix LCDs. Because neighboring pixels can be affected through a sort of "crosstalk," passive-matrix displays can look a bit "muddy."

Dual scan   Dual scan is a variation of the passive-matrix display. The classic passive-matrix screen is split in half to implement a dual-scan display. Each half of the display is refreshed separately, leading to increased quality. Although dual scan improves on the quality of conventional passive-matrix displays, it cannot rival the quality produced by active matrix.

The main differences between active matrix and typical passive matrix are image quality and viewing angle. Because the computer takes hundreds of milliseconds to change a pixel in passive-matrix displays (compared with tens of milliseconds or less in active-matrix displays), the response of the screen to rapid changes is poor, causing, for example, an effect known as *submarining*; that is, on a computer with a passive-matrix display, if you move the mouse pointer rapidly from one location to another, it will disappear from the first location and reappear in the new location without appearing anywhere in between. The poor response rate of passive-matrix displays also makes them suboptimal for displaying video.

If you watch the screen and gradually reposition yourself laterally, farther away from the center of a passive-matrix LCD, you eventually notice the display turning dark. In contrast, active-matrix LCDs have a viewing angle wider than 179 degrees. In fact, if you didn't know better, you'd think a passive-matrix display was a standard display with a privacy filter on it. A *privacy filter* is a panel that fits over the front of a display and, through a polarization affect, intentionally limits the viewing angle of the monitor. These same filters, as well as specialty versions, can act as *antiglare filters*, brightening and clarifying the image appearing on the monitor's screen.

We'll discuss additional concepts that apply to LCDs and other flat-panel displays later in this chapter.

Backlight Sources

A source of confusion for users and industry professionals alike, LED displays are merely LCD panels with light emitting diodes (LEDs) as light sources instead of the fluorescent bulbs used by legacy LCD monitors. No doubt, the new technology would not be nearly as marketable if they were referred to merely as LCDs. The general consumer would not rush to purchase a new display that goes by the same name as their current display. Nevertheless, calling these monitors LED displays is analogous to calling the conventional LCD monitors fluorescent displays; it's simply the backlight source, not the display technology.

Because there are many individually controlled LEDs in an LED display, most often as many as there are transistors in the LCD panel, the image can be intelligently backlit to enhance the quality of the picture. Additionally, there is no need for laptops with LED displays to convert the DC power coming into the laptop to the AC needed to power traditional fluorescent backlights because LEDs operate on DC power just like the rest of the laptop. As a result, these systems have no inverter board (discussed later in Chapter 9, "Understanding Laptops"), which are the DC-to-AC conversion devices present in traditionally backlit laptop displays. LED displays rival plasma displays in clarity and variations in luminance. This variation is referred to as *contrast ratio*, and it is discussed later in this chapter.

Plasma Displays

The word *plasma* refers to a cloud of ionized (charged) particles—atoms and molecules with electrons in an unstable state. This electrical imbalance is used to create light from the changes in energy levels as they achieve balance. Plasma display panels (PDPs) create just such a cloud from an inert gas, such as neon, by placing electrodes in front of and behind sealed chambers full of the gas and vaporized mercury. This technology of running a current through an inert gas to ionize it is shared with neon signs and fluorescent bulbs. Because of the pressurized nature of the gas in the chambers, PDPs are not optimal for high-altitude use, leading to LCDs being more popular for high-altitude applications, such as aboard aircraft, where PDPs can be heard to buzz the way fluorescent bulbs sometimes do.

Because of the emission of light that this process produces, plasma displays have more in common with legacy cathode ray tubes (CRTs) than they do with LCDs. In fact, as with CRTs, phosphors are responsible for the creation of light in the shade of the three primary colors—red, green, and blue. In this case, the pixels produce their own light (no backlight is required with plasma displays), also a feature shared with CRTs. The phosphor chemicals in CRTs and PDPs can be "used up" over time, reducing the overall image quality. The heat generated by CRTs and PDPs can lead to a loss of phosphorescence in the phosphor chemicals, which results in images burning into the screen. Advancements in the chemistry of plasma phosphors have reduced this tendency in recent years.

The refresh rate for plasma displays has always been in the 600Hz range, thus ensuring fluid video motion. See the section "Refresh Rate" later in this chapter for details on these concepts, but note that this rate is 10 times the classic standard refresh rate of 60Hz. The result is a display that produces the state of the art in video motion fluidity. Higher refresh rates in LCDs lead to an unwanted artificial or non-cinematic quality to video known as the "soap-opera effect." PDPs do not require compensation and should not suffer from this effect.

The Soap-opera Effect

When watching movies, most viewers appreciate the somewhat hazy, almost visually slurred quality described by some as "cinematic." The soap-opera effect (SOE) is a result of higher refresh rates and the intentional quality-enhancement feature of newer televisions called motion smoothing. Motion smoothing is a form of anti-blur compensation for the natural tendency of LCDs to blur their motion output. The end result is so smooth and clear that it reminds some of the lower-quality, lifelike cinematography seen in soap operas and some documentaries.

Detractors point to the hyperfluid, overly clear effect of the resulting output as being responsible for ruining the cinematic quality of movies watched on LCD monitors and on plasma displays that employ this feature. Sports lovers, however, tend to prefer such vivid clarity while watching their events. Although PDPs today offer the compensation feature, plasma does not benefit from it as much, so it should generally remain off for PDPs.

Instead of lowering the refresh rate back to 60Hz in LCDs, most manufacturers allow you to disable the motion smoothing manually. Some provide easily interpreted picture settings named "movie," "sports," and the like, adjusting compensation and other features as a package based on the user's selection.

PDPs can also produce deeper black colors than fluorescent-backlit LCD panels because the backlight cannot be completely blocked by the liquid crystal, thus producing hues that are more gray than black. LCDs backlit with LEDs, however, are able to dim selective areas or the entire image completely. Because of the relative cost-effectiveness to produce PDPs of the same size as a given LCD panel, plasma displays have historically enjoyed more popularity in the larger-monitor market. That advantage is all but gone today, resulting in more LCDs being sold today than plasma displays.

OLED Displays

Organic light emitting diode (OLED) displays, unlike LED displays, are really the image-producing parts of the display, not just the light source. In much the same way as a plasma cell places an excitable material between two electrodes, OLEDs are self-contained cells that use the same principle to create light. An organic light-emitting compound forms the heart of the OLED, and it is placed between an anode and a cathode, which produce a current that runs through the electroluminescent compound, causing it to emit light. An OLED, then, is the combination of the compound and the electrodes on each side of it. The electrode in the back of the OLED cell is usually opaque, allowing a rich black display when the OLED cell is not lit. The front electrode should be transparent to allow the emission of light from the OLED.

If thin-film electrodes and a flexible compound are used to produce the OLEDs, an OLED display can be made flexible, allowing it to function in novel applications where other display technologies could never work. Because of the thin, lightweight nature of the panels, OLED displays can both replace existing heavy full-color LED signs, like the ones you might see in Las Vegas or even at your local car dealer's lot, and carve out new markets, such as integration into clothing and multimedia advertisements on the sides of buses to replace and improve upon the static ads that are commonly seen.

LEDs create light and have been used in recent years for business, home, and automotive interior lighting and headlamps. OLEDs are LEDs, organic as they may be, and produce light as well. They, too, have already made their way into the interior lighting market. Because OLEDs create the image in an OLED display *and* supply the light source, there is no need for a backlight with its additional power and space requirements, unlike in the case of LCD panels. Additionally, the contrast ratio of OLED displays exceeds that of LCD panels, regardless of backlight source. This means that in darker surroundings, OLED displays produce better images than do LCD panels. Because OLEDs are highly reflective, however, quite a bit of research and development in optics has been required to produce filters and optical shielding for OLED displays. As unlikely as it seemed from early descriptions of OLED physics, true-black displays that are highly visible in all lighting conditions can now be developed using OLED technology. The foregoing discussion notwithstanding, double transparent-electrode OLEDs, with a sidelight for night viewing, have been demonstrated as a kind of "smart window."

As with LCD panels, OLED panels can be classified as active matrix (AMOLED) or passive matrix (PMOLED). As you might expect, AMOLED displays have better quality than PMOLED displays but, as a result, require more electrodes, a pair for each OLED. AMOLED displays have resolutions limited only by how small the OLEDs can be made, while the size and resolution of PMOLED displays are limited by other factors, such as the need to group the electrodes for the OLEDs.

The power to drive an OLED display is, on average, less than that required for LCDs. However, as the image progresses toward all white, the power consumption can increase to two or three times that of an LCD panel. Energy efficiency lies in future developments as well as the display of mostly darker images, which is a reason darker text on lighter backgrounds may give way to the reverse, both in applications and online. For OLEDs, the display of black occurs by default when the OLED is not lit and requires no power at all.

Although the early materials used in OLEDs have demonstrated drastically shorter life spans than those used in LCD and plasma panels, the technology is improving and has given rise to compounds that allow commercially produced OLEDs to remain viable long past the life expectancy of other technologies. The cost of such panels will continue to decrease so that purchases by more than just corporations and the elite can be expected.

Two important enhancements to AMOLED technology resulted in the development of the Super AMOLED and Super AMOLED Plus displays, both owing their existence to Samsung. The Super AMOLED display removes the standard touch sensor panel (TSP) found in the LCD and AMOLED displays and replaces it with an on-cell TSP that is flat and applied directly to the front of the AMOLED panel, adding a mere thousandth of a millimeter to the panel's thickness. The thinner TSP leads to a more visible screen in all lighting conditions and more sensitivity when used with touch panels.

The Super AMOLED Plus display uses the same TSP as the Super AMOLED display. One advantage that it has over Super AMOLED is that it employs 1.5 times as many elements (subpixels) in each pixel, leading to a crisper display. Another advantage is that Super AMOLED Plus is 18 percent more energy efficient compared with Super AMOLED. The Super AMOLED and Super AMOLED Plus displays also feature a longer lifetime than that of the standard AMOLED display.

Projection Systems

Another major category of display device is the video projection system, or projector. Portable *projectors* can be thought of as condensed video display units with a lighting system that projects the VDU's image onto a screen or other flat surface for group viewing. Interactive white boards have become popular over the past decade to allow presenters to project an image onto the board as they use virtual markers to draw electronically on the displayed image. Remote participants can see the slide on their terminal as well as the markups made by the presenter. The presenter can see the same markups because the board transmits them to the computer to which the projector is attached, causing them to be displayed by the projector in real time.

To accommodate using portable units at variable distances from the projection surface, a focusing mechanism is included on the lens. Other adjustments, such as keystone, trapezoid, and pincushion, are provided through a menu system on many models as well as a way to rotate the image 180 degrees for ceiling-mount applications.

Rear Projection

Another popular implementation of projection systems has been the rear-projection television, in which a projector is built into a cabinet behind a screen onto which a reverse image is projected so that an observer in front of the TV can view the image correctly. Early rear-projection TVs as well as ceiling-mounted home-theater units used CRT technology to drive three filtered light sources that worked together to create an RGB image.

Later rear-projection systems, including most modern portable projectors, implement LCD gates. These units shine a bright light through three LCD panels that adjust pixels in the same manner as an LCD monitor, except that the projected image is formed, as with the CRT projector, by synchronizing the combination and projection of the red, green, and blue images onto the same surface.

Digital light processing (DLP) is another popular technology that keeps rear-projection TVs on the market and benefits portable projectors as well, allowing some projectors to be extremely small. Special DLP chips, referred to as *optical semiconductors*, have roughly as many rotatable mirrors on their surface as pixels in the display resolution. A light source and colored filter wheel or colored light sources are used to switch rapidly among primary, and sometimes secondary, colors in synchronization with the chip's mirror positions, thousands of times per second.

Brightness

Projection systems are required to produce a lighted image and display it many feet away from the system. The inherent challenge to this paradigm is that ambient light tends to interfere with the image's projection. One solution to this problem is to increase the brightness of the image being projected. This brightness is measured in lumens. A *lumen (lm)* is a unit of measure for the total amount of visible light that the projector gives off, based solely on what the human eye can perceive and not on invisible wavelengths. When the rated brightness of the projector in lumens is focused on a larger area, the *lux*—a derivative of lumens measuring how much the projector lights up the surface on which it is focused—decreases; as you train the projector on a larger surface (farther away), the same lumens produce fewer lux.

The foregoing discussion notwithstanding, projection systems are rated and chosen for purchase based on lumens of brightness, usually once a maximum supported resolution has been chosen. Sometimes the brightness is even more of a selling point than the maximum resolution that the system supports because of the chosen environment in which it operates. Therefore, this is the rating that must be used to compare the capabilities of projection systems.

Some loose guidelines can help you choose the right projector for your application. Keep in mind that video versus static image projection requires more lumens, and 3D output requires roughly double the lumens of 2D projection. Additionally, use of a full-screen (4:3 aspect ratio) projector system in a business environment versus a widescreen (16:9) home theater projector requires approximately double the lumens of output at the low end and only 1.3 times at the high end.

For example, if you are able to completely control the lighting in the room where the projection system is used, producing little to no ambient light, a projector producing as little as 1,300 lumens is adequate in a home theater environment, while you would need one producing around 2,500 lumens in the office. However, if you can only get rid of most of the ambient light, such as by closing blinds and dimming overhead lights, the system should be able to produce 1,500 to 3,500 lumens in the home theater and 3,000 to 4,500 lumens in the office. If you have no control over a very well-lit area, you'll need 4,000 to 4,500 lumens in the home theater and 5,000 to 6,000 lumens in the business setting. These measurements assume a screen size of around 120″, regardless of aspect ratio.

By way of comparison, a 60W standard light bulb produces about 800 lumens. Output is not linear, however, because a 100W light bulb produces over double, at 1,700lm. Nevertheless, you couldn't get away with using a standard 100W incandescent bulb in a projector. The color production is not pure enough and constantly changes throughout its operation due to deposits of soot from the burning of its tungsten filament during the production of light. High-intensity discharge (HID) lamps like the ones found in projection systems do more with less by using a smaller electrical discharge to produce far more visible light. A strong quartz chamber holds the filament in a projector lamp and can be seen inside the outer bulb. It contains a metal halide (where the word *halogen* comes from) gas that glows bright white when the tungsten filament lights up. Depositing the soot on the inside of the projector bulb is avoided by using a chemical process that attracts the soot created back to the filament where it once again becomes part of the filament, extending its life and reducing changes in light output.

Expect to pay considerably more for projector bulbs than for standard bulbs of a comparable wattage. The metal halide gases used in projector bulbs are more expensive than the noble gases used in standard bulbs. Add to that the fact that the bulb itself might have to be handmade and you can understand the need for higher cost.

Cooling Down

Although it doesn't take long for the fan to stop running on its own, this is a phase that should never be skipped to save time. With projector bulbs being one of the priciest consumables in the world of technology, doing so may cost you more than a change in your travel arrangements. See the sidebar titled "Factor In Some Time" for some perspective.

 Real World Scenario

Factor In Some Time

A fellow instructor carried his own portable projector with him on the road. At the end of a week's class, he would power down the projector and get his laptop and other goodies packed away. Just before running out of the door, he would unplug the projector and pack it up. As with many instructors, this gentleman's presentations increased in density and length as he became more and more comfortable with the material.

Author Toby Skandier ran into him at a training center some time after this trend had begun. His presentation had been running later and later each Friday afternoon, edging him ever closer to his airline departure time. He admitted that he had gotten into the habit of yanking the power plug for his projector from the wall and quickly stuffing the unit into the carrying case before darting out the door. Not long after their meeting, Toby heard that his projector failed catastrophically. Replacing the bulb was not the solution.

One caveat with projectors is that you must never pull the electrical plug from the outlet until you hear the internal fan cut off. There is enough residual heat generated by the projector bulb that damage to the electronics or the bulb itself (discoloration or outright failure) can occur if the fan is not allowed to remove enough heat before it stops running. Without a connection to an electrical outlet, the fan stops immediately. The electronics have the appropriate level of heat shielding that the fan removes enough heat during normal operation to avoid damage to the shielded components.

Adjusting Display Settings

Although most monitors are automatically detected by the operating system and configured for the best quality that they and the graphics adapter support, sometimes manually changing display settings, such as for a new monitor or when adding a new adapter, becomes necessary. Let's start by defining a few important terms:

- Refresh rate
- Frame rate
- Resolution
- Multiple displays

Each of these terms relates to settings available through the operating system by way of display-option settings.

Refresh Rate

The *refresh rate* is technically the vertical scan frequency, and it specifies how many times in one second the image on the screen can be completely redrawn, if necessary. Measured in screen draws per second, or hertz (Hz), the refresh rate indicates how much effort is being put into checking for updates to the displayed image.

For LCD televisions, the refresh rate is generally fixed and not an adjustment to be made. LCD televisions that support 120Hz refresh rates are common, but it's easy to find those rated for 60Hz, 240Hz, and 480Hz as well. For computer monitors, you might be able to select among multiple refresh rates because you're in control of the circuitry driving the refresh rate, the graphics adapter. However, because LCDs do not illuminate phosphors, there is no concern of pixel decay (for which refreshing the pixel is necessary). Instead, higher refresh rates translate to more fluid video motion. Think of the refresh rate as how often a check is made to see if each pixel has been altered by the source. If a pixel should change before the next refresh, the monitor is unable to display the change in that pixel. Therefore, for gaming and home-theater systems, higher refresh rates are an advantage.

The refresh rate is selected for the monitor. Nevertheless, the refresh rate you select must be supported by both your graphics adapter and your monitor because the adapter drives the monitor. If a monitor supports only one refresh rate, it does not matter how many different rates your adapter supports—without overriding the defaults, you will be able to choose only the one common refresh rate. It is important to note that as the resolution you select increases, the higher supported refresh rates begin to disappear from the selection menu. If you want a higher refresh rate, you might have to compromise by choosing a lower resolution. Exercise 4.1 steps you through the process of changing the refresh rate in Windows 7.

EXERCISE 4.1

Changing the Refresh Rate in Windows 7

1. Right-click on a blank portion of the Desktop.
2. Click Screen Resolution, as shown in Figure 4.2.

continues

EXERCISE 4.1 *(continued)*

FIGURE 4.2   Selecting Screen Resolution

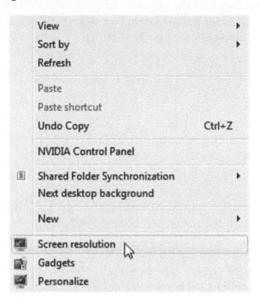

3.   Click the Advanced Settings link, as shown in Figure 4.3.

FIGURE 4.3   Selecting the Advanced Settings link

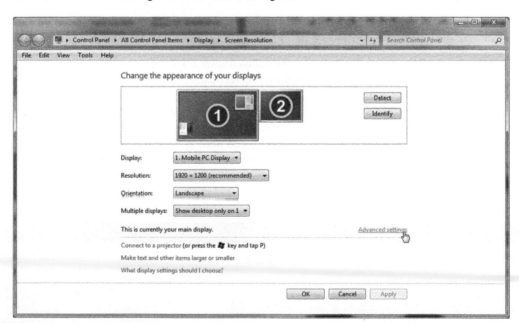

4.   Click the Monitor tab, as shown in Figure 4.4.

FIGURE 4.4   Monitor tab

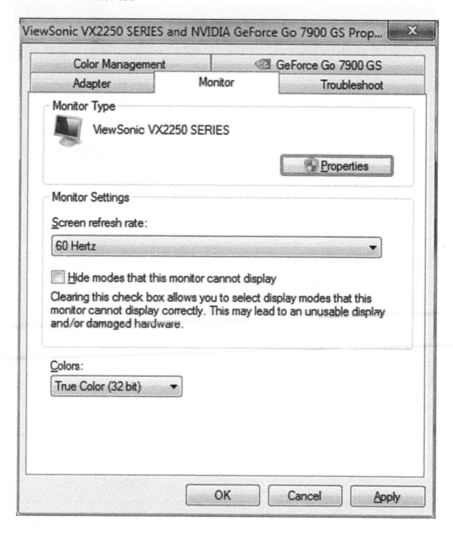

5.   Select the desired screen refresh rate from the drop-down menu, as shown in Figure 4.5.

continues

FIGURE 4.5 Selecting the screen refresh rate

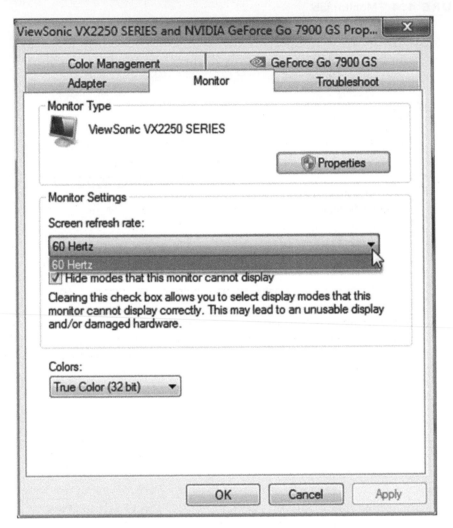

Just because a refresh rate appears in the properties dialog box, it does not mean that the associated monitor will be able to handle that rate. Figure 4.6 shows an internal message displayed by a monitor when a refresh rate that is out of range has been selected. Consider keeping the Hide Modes That This Monitor Cannot Display check box (see Figure 4.5) selected to avoid choosing a refresh rate not supported by your hardware.

FIGURE 4.6   An internal monitor error for an unsupported refresh rate

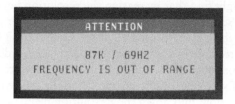

Frame Rate

When you're viewing video content, the refresh rate that you choose must be compatible or be made compatible with the frame rate at which the content was originally recorded or filmed. The *frame rate* is the measure of how many unique screens of content were recorded per second. If the playback of the content is not at the same rate, there will be a negative impact on the output if the difference in rates is not multiplicative.

For instance, content recorded at 30 frames per second (fps) and played back at 60Hz will look fine as is because exactly two copies of each frame can be displayed in the second it takes to redraw the screen 60 times. However, if the content were shot at 24fps—the most popular film recording rate—it would play back poorly at 60Hz. The recording would first need to be converted to 30fps, which happens to be the NTSC standard (the standard for PAL is 25fps), by a process known as 3:2 pulldown, which creates 10 frames out of 4 and then plays them in one second.

Although there are 60 frames being played in that one second, only 30 of them are unique; the other 30 are duplicates of those. Because frame rate only counts unique frames, this 60Hz signal gets credit for 30fps, just like the content that was recorded at that rate. In other words, refresh rate is a count of the screens of information displayed per second, even if each screen is duplicated, while frame rate is the measure of unique content only.

Resolution

Resolution is defined by how many software picture elements (pixels) are used to draw the screen. An advantage of higher resolutions is that more information can be displayed in the same screen area. A disadvantage is that the same objects and text displayed at a higher resolution appear smaller and might be harder to see. Up to a point, the added crispness of higher resolutions displayed on high-quality monitors compensates for the negative aspects. The resolution is described in terms of the visible image's dimensions, which indicate how many rows and columns of pixels are used to draw the screen. For example, a resolution of 1024×768 means 1024 pixels across (columns) and 768 pixels down (rows) were used to draw the pixel matrix. The video technology in this example would use $1024 \times 768 = 786,432$ pixels to draw the screen. Resolution is a software setting that is common among CRTs, LCDs, and projection systems as well as other display devices.

There are software and hardware resolutions. Setting the resolution for your monitor is fairly straightforward. If you are using an LCD, for best results you should use the monitor's native resolution, discussed later in this chapter. Some systems will scale the image to avoid distortion, but others will try to fill the screen with the image, resulting in distortion. On occasion, you might find that increasing the resolution beyond the native resolution results in the need to scroll the Desktop in order to view other portions of it. In such instances, you cannot see the entire Desktop all at the same time. The monitor has the last word in how the signal it receives from the adapter is displayed. Adjusting your display settings to those that are recommended for your monitor can alleviate this scrolling effect.

In Windows 7, follow Exercise 4.1 up to step 2. Click the image of the monitor for which you want to alter the resolution, pull down the Resolution menu, and then move the resolution slider up for higher resolutions, as shown in Figure 4.7, or down for lower resolutions.

FIGURE 4.7   Adjusting the resolution in Windows 7

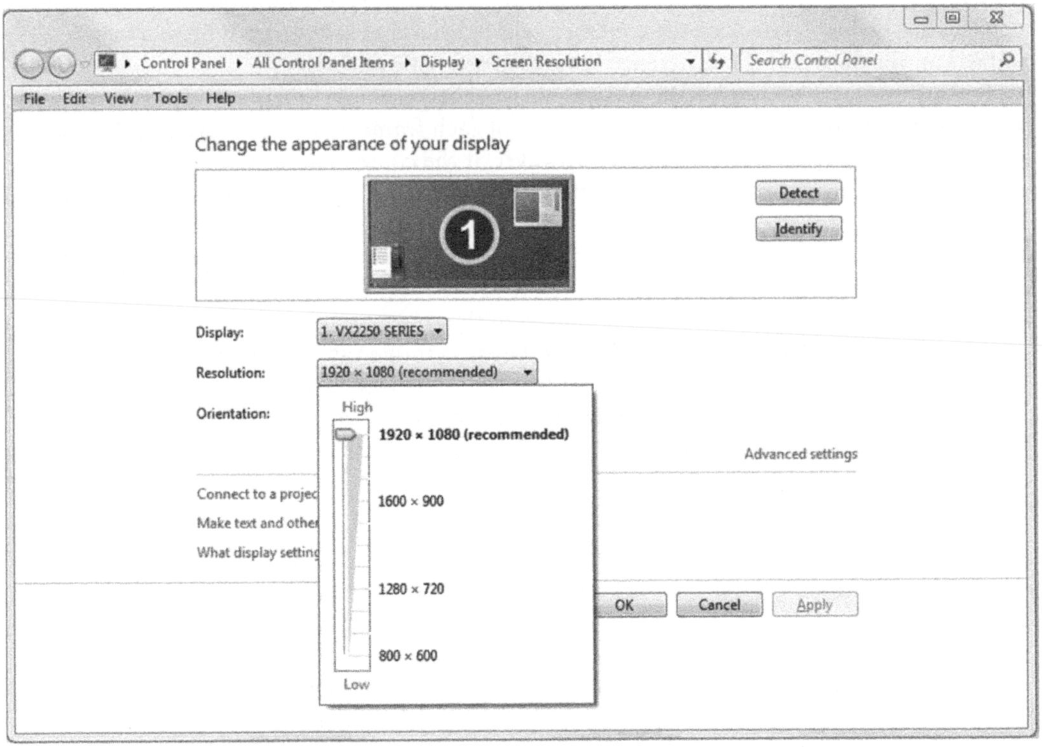

Some adapters come with their own utilities for changing settings such as the refresh rate and resolution. For example, Figure 4.8 shows two windows from the NVIDIA Control Panel. The first window has resolution, color depth, and refresh rate all in the same spot. The second window shows you the native resolution of the LCD and the current resolution selected. If they are different, you can have the utility immediately make the current resolution match the native resolution.

FIGURE 4.8   The NVIDIA Control Panel

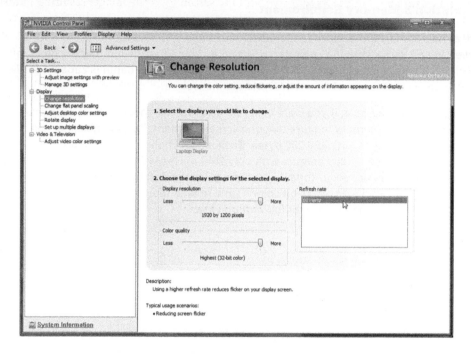

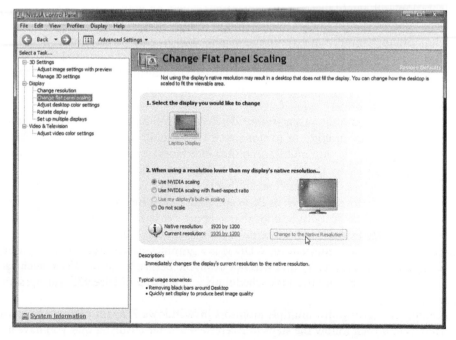

Resolution's Memory Requirement

Video memory is used to store rendered screen images. The memory required for a screen image varies with the color depth, which is defined as the number of colors in which each pixel can be displayed. A palette with a 24-bit color depth is capable of displaying each pixel in one of $2^{24} = 16,777,216$ distinct colors.

In the preceding example, if you were using 24-bit graphics, meaning that each pixel requires 24 bits of memory to store that one screen element, 786,432 pixels would require 18,874,368 bits, or 2,359,296 bytes. Because this boils down to 2.25MB, an early (bordering on ancient) video adapter with only 2MB of RAM would not be capable of such resolution at 24 bits per pixel. Today's adapters have absolutely no trouble displaying such a resolution with a 24- or 32-bit color depth. In fact, they store many screens at a time in order to allow the display of full-motion video.

Multiple Displays

Whether regularly or just on occasion, you may find yourself in a position where you need to use two monitors on the same computer simultaneously. For example, if you are giving a presentation and would like to have a presenter's view on your laptop's LCD but need to project a slide show onto a screen, you might need to connect an external projector to the laptop. Simply connecting an external display device does not guarantee that it will be recognized and work automatically. You might need to change the settings for the external device, such as the resolution or the device's virtual orientation with respect to the built-in display, which affects how you drag objects between the screens. Exercise 4.2 guides you through this process.

Microsoft calls its multimonitor feature *Dual View*. You have the option to extend your Desktop onto a second monitor or to clone your Desktop on the second monitor. You can use one graphics adapter with multiple monitor interfaces or multiple adapters. However, as of Vista, Windows Display Driver Model (WDDM) version 1.0 required that the same driver be used for all adapters. This doesn't mean that you cannot use two adapters that fit into different expansion slot types, such as PCIe and AGP. It just means that both cards have to use the same driver. Incidentally, laptops that support external monitors use the same driver for the external interface as for the internal LCD attachment. Version 1.1, introduced with Windows 7, relaxed this requirement. WDDM is a graphics-driver architecture that provides enhanced graphics functionality that was not available before Windows Vista, such as virtualized video memory, preemptive task scheduling, and sharing of Direct3D surfaces among processes.

To change the settings for multiple monitors in Windows 7, again perform Exercise 4.1 up to step 2, and then follow the steps in Exercise 4.2 after ensuring that you have a second monitor attached.

EXERCISE 4.2

Changing the Settings for Multiple Monitors

1. Click on the picture of the monitor with the number 2 on it, as shown in Figure 4.9.

FIGURE 4.9 Select Monitor #2

2. Pull down the menu labeled Multiple Displays, select Extend These Displays, and click Apply to produce an appropriate image of the second display's size and shape. Note that the Remove This Display option would not be available without completing step 1, but Extend These Displays still would be, as shown in Figure 4.10.

FIGURE 4.10 Multiple Displays options

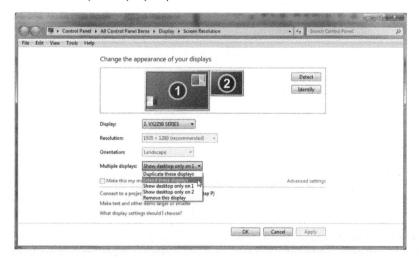

continues

3. Click Keep Changes in the pop-up dialog that appears before the 15-second timer expires, as shown in Figure 4.11.

FIGURE 4.11   Display Settings dialog

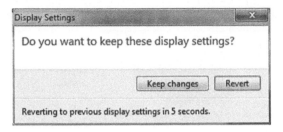

> **Display Settings**   ⊠
>
> Do you want to keep these display settings?
>
>   [Keep changes]   [Revert]
>
> Reverting to previous display settings in 5 seconds.

4. Click and drag the second monitor to the desired virtual position around the primary monitor, as shown in Figure 4.12. This affects the direction in which you drag objects from one display to the other.

FIGURE 4.12   Adjusting orientation of displays

5. While the second monitor is still selected, change its refresh rate and resolution, if necessary, as outlined previously. Note that if you would like for your Desktop to appear on the second monitor, you can check the Make This My Main Display box.

6. Click OK to save your changes and exit.

Understanding Video Standards and Technologies

The following sections introduce the various video standards, from the earlier digital standards to the later analog standards and the most current digital high-definition standards.

Pre-VGA standards are presented here to give perspective regarding display technology as a whole. Do not expect to be tested on any standards prior to VGA.

Video Standards

The early video standards differ in two major areas: the highest resolution supported and the maximum number of colors in their palette. The supported resolution and palette size are directly related to the amount of memory on the adapter, which is used to hold the rendered images to be displayed. Display adapters through the years can be divided into five primary groups:

- Monochrome
- CGA
- EGA
- VGA
- DVI, HDMI, and other modern digital video

See Chapter 3, "Peripherals and Expansion," for more information on DVI, HDMI, and other advanced video standards.

Because the amount of memory used to implement pre-VGA adapters was fixed, the resolution and number of colors supported by these cards was fixed as well. Newer standards, based on VGA analog technology and connectivity, were eventually developed using adapters with expandable memory or separately priced models with differing fixed memory. Adapters featuring variable amounts of memory resulted in selectable resolutions and color palettes. In time, 24-bit color palettes known as Truecolor and made up of almost 17 million colors, which approached the number of colors the human eye can distinguish, were implemented. As a result, in keeping with growing screen sizes, the latest commercial video standards continue to grow in resolution, their distinguishing trait, but generally not in palette size. These post-VGA resolutions are discussed later in this chapter in the section "Advanced Video Resolutions and Concepts."

Monochrome

The first video technology for PCs was monochrome (from the Latin *mono*, meaning one, and *chroma*, meaning color). This black-and-white video (actually, it was green or amber text on a black background) was fine for the main operating system of the day, DOS, which didn't have any need for color. Thus the video adapter was very basic. The first adapter, developed by IBM, was known as the Monochrome Display Adapter (MDA). It could display text but not graphics and used a resolution of 720×350 pixels.

The Hercules Graphics Card (HGC), introduced by Hercules Computer Technology, had a resolution of 720×350 and could display graphics as well as text. It did this by using two separate modes: a *text mode*, which allowed the adapter to optimize its resources for displaying predrawn characters from its onboard library, and a *graphics mode*, which optimized the adapter for drawing individual pixels for onscreen graphics. It could switch between these modes on the fly. These modes of operation have been included in all graphics adapters since the introduction of the HGC.

CGA

The next logical step for displays was to add a splash of color. IBM was the first with color, with the introduction of the Color Graphics Adapter (*CGA*). CGA displays 16-color text in resolutions of 320×200 (40 columns) and 640×200 (80 columns), but it displays 320×200 graphics with only 4 colors per mode. Each of the six possible modes has 3 fixed colors and a selectable 4th; each of the 4 colors comes from the 16 used for text. CGA's 640×200 graphics resolution has only 2 colors—black and one other color from the same palette of 16.

EGA

After a time, people wanted more colors and higher resolution, so IBM responded with the Enhanced Graphics Adapter (*EGA*). EGA could display 16 colors out of a palette of 64 with CGA resolutions as well as a high-resolution 640×350 mode. EGA marks the end of classic digital-video technology. The digital data pins on the 9-pin D-subminiature connector accounted for six of the nine pins. As a solution, analog technologies starting with VGA would all but stand alone in the market until the advent of DVI and HDMI, discussed in Chapter 3.

VGA

With the PS/2 line of computers, IBM wanted to answer the cry for "more resolution, more colors" by introducing its best video adapter to date: the Video Graphics Array (*VGA*). This video technology had a "whopping" 256KB of video memory on board and could display 16 colors at 640×480, 640×350, and 320×200 pixels or, using mode 13h of the VGA BIOS, 256 colors at 320×200 pixels. It became widely used and enjoyed a long reign as at least the base standard for color PC video. For many years, it was the starting point for computers as far as video is concerned. Until recently, however, your computer likely defaulted to this video technology's resolution and color palette only when there was an issue with the driver for your graphics adapter or when you entered Safe Mode. Today, even these modes appear with impressive graphics quality.

One unique feature of VGA (and its offshoots) is that it's an analog technology, unlike the preceding and subsequent standards. Technically, the electronics of all graphics adapters and monitors operate in the digital realm. The difference in VGA-based technologies is that graphics adapters output and monitors receive an analog signal over the cable. Conversely, MDA, CGA, EGA, HDMI, and DVI-D signals arrive at the monitor as digital pulse streams with no analog-to-digital conversion required.

VGA builds a dynamic palette of 256 colors, which are chosen from various shades and hues of an 18-bit palette of 262,114 colors. When only 16 colors are displayed, they are chosen from the 256 selected colors. VGA sold well mainly because users could choose from almost any color they wanted (or at least one that was close). The reason for moving away from the original digital signal is that for every power of 2 that the number of colors in the palette increases, you need at least one more pin on the connector. A minimum of 4 pins for 16 colors is not a big deal, but a minimum of 32 pins for 32-bit graphics become a bit unwieldy. The cable has to grow with the connector, as well, affecting transmission quality and cable length. VGA, on the other hand, requires only 3 pins, one each for red, green, and blue modulated analog color levels, not including the necessary complement of ground, sync, and other control signals. For this application, 12 to 14 of the 15 pins of a VGA connector are adequate.

One note about monitors that may seem rather obvious: You must use a video card that supports the type of monitor you are using. For example, you can't use a CGA monitor on a VGA adapter. Add-on adapters must also have a matching slot in the motherboard to accommodate them.

Advanced Video Resolutions and Concepts

The foregoing display technologies included hardware considerations and resolutions. Adjustments could be made to change the configuration of these technologies. Additional resolutions common in the computing world through the years and characteristics that cannot be adjusted but instead define the quality of the display device are presented in the following sections.

Resolutions

The following sections detail what might, at first, appear to be technologies based on new graphics adapters. However, advancements after the VGA adapter occurred only in the memory and firmware of the adapter, not the connector or its fundamental analog functionality. As a result, the following technologies are distinguished early on by supported resolutions and color palettes and later by resolutions alone. Subsequently, these resolutions have become supported by the newer digital standards with no change in their friendly names.

Super VGA

Until the late 1980s, IBM set most personal-computer video standards. IBM made the adapters, everyone bought them, and they became a standard. Some manufacturers didn't like this monopoly and set up the Video Electronics Standards Association (VESA) to try to enhance IBM's video technology and make the enhanced technology an open standard. The initial result of this work was Super VGA (*SVGA*). This new standard was indeed an enhancement because it could support 16 colors at a resolution of 800×600 (the VESA standard), but it soon expanded to support 1024×768 pixels with 256 colors.

Since that time, *SVGA* has been a term used loosely for any resolution and color palette to exceed that of standard VGA. This even includes the resolution presented next, XGA. New names still continue to be introduced, mainly as a marketing tool to tout the new resolution du jour. While display devices must be manufactured to support a certain display resolution, one of the benefits of analog video technology was that later VGA monitors could advance along with the graphics adapter, in terms of the color palette. The analog signal is what dictates the color palette, and the standard for the signal has not changed since its VGA origin. This makes VGA monitors' color limitations a nonissue. Such a topic makes sense only in reference to graphics adapters.

XGA

IBM introduced a new technology in 1990 known as the Extended Graphics Array (*XGA*). This technology was available only as a Micro Channel Architecture (MCA) expansion board (versus ISA or EISA, for instance). XGA could support 256 colors at 1024×768 pixels or 65,536 colors at 800×600 pixels. It was a different design, optimized for GUIs of the day, such as Windows and OS/2. It was also an *interlaced* technology when operating at the 1024×768 resolution, meaning that rather than scan every line one at a time on each pass to create the image, it scanned every other line on each pass, using the phenomenon known as "persistence of vision" to produce what appears to our eyes as a continuous image.

The *i* in *1080i* refers to interlaced—versus progressive (*1080p*) scanning.

The advertised refresh rate specifies the frequency with which all odd or all even rows are scanned. The drawback to interlacing is that the refresh rate used on a CRT has to be twice the minimum comfort level for refreshing an entire screen. Otherwise, the human eye will interpret the uncomfortably noticeable decay of the pixels as flicker. Therefore, a refresh rate of 120Hz would result in a comfortable effective refresh rate of 60Hz. Unfortunately, 84Hz was a popular refresh rate for interlaced display signals, resulting in an entire screen being redrawn only 42 times per second, a rate below the minimum comfort level.

More Recent Video Standards

Any standard other than the ones already mentioned are probably extensions of SVGA or XGA. It has become quite easy to predict the approximate or exact resolution of a video specification based on its name. Whenever a known technology is preceded by the letter W, you can assume roughly the same vertical resolution but a wider horizontal resolution to accommodate 16:10 widescreen monitor formats (16:9 for LCD and plasma televisions). Preceding the technology with the letter *Q* indicates that the horizontal and vertical resolutions were each doubled, making a final number of pixels 4 times (quadruple) the original. To imply 4 times each, for a final resolution enhancement of 16 times, the letter *H*, for *hexadecatuple* is used.

Therefore, if XGA has a resolution of 1024×768, then Quad XGA (QXGA) will have a resolution of 2048×1536. If Ultra XGA (UXGA) has a resolution of 1600×1200 and an aspect ratio of 4:3, then Wide Ultra XGA (WUXGA) has a resolution of 1920×1200 and a 16:10 aspect ratio. Clearly, there have been a large number of seemingly minute increases in resolution column and row sizes. However, consider that at 1024×768, for instance, the screen will display a total of 786,432 pixels. At 1280×1024, comparatively, the number of pixels increases to 1,310,720—nearly double the number of pixels for what doesn't sound like much of a difference in resolution. As mentioned, you need better technology and more video memory to display even slightly higher resolutions.

> The term *aspect ratio* refers to the relationship between the horizontal and vertical pixel counts that a monitor can display. For example, for a display that supports 4:3 ratios, such as 1024×768, if you divide the first number by 4 and multiply the result by 3, the product is equal to the second number. Additionally, if you divide the first number by the second number, the result is approximately 1.3, the same as 4 ÷ 3. Displays with a 16:10 aspect ratio have measurements that result in a dividend of 16 ÷ 10 = 1.6.
>
> Because the ATSC (Advanced Television Systems Committee) standard for widescreen aspect ratios is 16:9 (1.778), computer monitors are trending more toward this same aspect ratio. As a result, the popular 1920×1200, 16:10 resolution is being supplanted by the common 1920×1080, 16:9 resolution.

Table 6.2 lists the various video technologies, their resolutions, and the maximum color palette they support, if specified as part of the standard. All resolutions, VGA and higher, have a 4:3 aspect ratio unless otherwise noted.

TABLE 4.2   Video display technology comparison

Name	Resolutions	Colors
Monochrome Display Adapter (MDA)	720×350	Mono (text only)
Hercules Graphics Card (HGC)	720×350	Mono (text and graphics)
Color Graphics Adapter (CGA)	320×200	4
	640×200	2

continues

TABLE 4.2   Video display technology comparison *(continued)*

Name	Resolutions	Colors
Enhanced Graphics Adapter (EGA)	640×350	16
Video Graphics Array (VGA)	640×480	16
	320×200	256
ATSC 480i/480p, 4:3 or 16:9	704×480	Not specified
Super VGA (SVGA)	800×600	16
Extended Graphics Array (XGA)	800×600	65,536
	1024×768	256
Widescreen XGA (WXGA), 16:10	1280×800	Not specified
Super XGA (SXGA), 5:4	1280×1024	Not specified
ATSC 720p, 16:9	1280×720	Not specified
SXGA+	1400×1050	Not specified
WSXGA+, 16:10	1680×1050	Not specified
Ultra XGA (UXGA)	1600×1200	Not specified
WUXGA, 16:10	1920×1200	Not specified
ATSC 1080i/1080p, 16:9	1920×1080	Not specified
Quad XGA (QXGA)	2048×1536	Not specified
WQXGA, 16:10	2560×1600	Not specified
UHD 4K	3840×2160	Not specified
WQUXGA, 16:10	3840×2400	Not specified
WHUXGA, 16:10	7680×4800	Not specified

Starting with SXGA, the more advanced resolutions can be paired with 32-bit graphics, which specifies the 24-bit Truecolor palette of 16,777,216 colors and uses the other 8 bits for enhanced noncolor features, if at all. In some cases, using 32 bits to store 24 bits of color information per pixel increases performance because the bit boundaries are divisible by a power of 2; 32 is a power of 2, but 24 is not. That being said, however, unlike with the older standards, the color palette is not officially part of the newer specifications.

Nonadjustable Characteristics

The following sections discuss features that are more selling points for display units and not configurable settings.

Native Resolution

One of the peculiarities of LCD, plasma, OLED, and other flat-panel displays is that they have a single fixed resolution, known as the *native resolution*. Unlike CRT monitors, which can display a crisp image at many resolutions within a supported range, flat-panel monitors have trouble displaying most resolutions other than their native resolution.

The native resolution comes from the placement of the transistors in the hardware display matrix of the monitor. For a native resolution of 1680×1050, for example, there are 1,764,000 transistors (LCDs) or cells (PDPs and OLED displays) arranged in a grid of 1680 columns and 1050 rows. Trying to display a resolution other than 1680×1050 through the operating system tends to result in the monitor interpolating the resolution to fit the differing number of software pixels to the 1,764,000 transistors, often resulting in a distortion of the image on the screen.

The distortion can take various forms, such as blurred text, elliptical circles, and so forth. SXGA (1280×1024) was once one of the most popular native resolutions for larger LCD computer monitors before use of widescreen monitors became pervasive. For widescreen aspects, especially for widescreen LCD displays of 15.4″ and larger, WSXGA+ (1680×1050) was one of the original popular native resolutions. The ATSC 1080p resolution (1920×1080) is highly common today across all display technologies, largely replacing the popular computer-graphics version, WUXGA (1920×1200).

Contrast Ratio

The *contrast ratio* is the measure of the ratio of the luminance of the brightest color to that of the darkest color that the screen is capable of producing. Do not confuse contrast ratio with *contrast*. Contrast ratios are generally fixed measurements that become selling points for the monitors. Contrast, on the other hand, is an adjustable setting on all monitors (usually found alongside brightness) that changes the relative brightness of adjacent pixels. The more contrast, the sharper and edgier the image. Reducing the contrast too much can make the image appear washed out. This discussion is not about contrast but instead it's about contrast ratio.

One of the original problems with LCD displays, and a continuing problem with cheaper versions, is that they have low contrast ratios. Only LED-backlit LCD panels rival the high contrast ratios that plasma displays have always demonstrated. A display with a low contrast ratio won't show a "true black" very well, and the other colors will look washed out when you have a light source nearby. Try to use the device in full sunshine and you're not going to see much of anything, although the overall brightness level is the true key in such surroundings. Also, lower contrast ratios mean that you'll have a harder time viewing images from the side as compared to being directly in front of the display.

Ratios for smaller LCD monitors and televisions typically start out around 500:1. Common ratios for larger units range from 20,000:1 to 100,000:1. In the early days of monitors that used LEDs as backlights, 1,000,000:1 was exceedingly common. Today, vendors advertise 10,000,000:1 and "infinite" as contrast ratios. Anything higher than 32,000:1 is likely a dynamic contrast ratio. Plasma displays have always been expected to have contrast ratios of around 5000:1 or better.

Once considered a caveat, a dynamic ratio is realized by reducing power to the backlight for darker images. The downside was that the original backlight being a single fluorescent bulb meant that the signal to the brighter LCD pixels had to be amplified to compensate for the uniform dimming of the backlight. This occasionally resulted in overcompensation manifested as areas of extreme brightness, often artificial in appearance. This practice tends to wash out the lighter colors and make white seem like it's glowing, which is hardly useful to the user. Today's LED backlights, however, are controlled either in zones made up of a small number of pixels or individually per pixel, resulting in trustworthy high dynamic contrast ratios.

The environment where the monitor will be used must be taken into account when considering whether to place a lot of emphasis on contrast ratio. In darker areas, a high contrast ratio will be more noticeable. In brighter surroundings, widely varying contrast ratios do not make as much of a difference. For these environments, a monitor capable of higher levels of brightness is more imperative.

One caveat to contrast ratios that remains is that there is no vendor-neutral regulatory measurement. The contrast ratio claimed by one manufacturer can take into account variables that another manufacturer does not. A manufacturer can boost the ratio simply by increasing how bright the monitor can go, the portion of the monitor tested, or the conditions in the room where the test was performed. This doesn't do anything to help the display of darker colors, though. So, although the contrast ratio is certainly a selling point, don't just take it at face value. Look for independent comparison reviews that use multiple methods of measuring contrast ratio or compare displays in person to see which one works better for the situation in which you intend to use it.

Summary

In this chapter, you read about various display technologies and settings. The primary categories of video display units were mentioned and explained: LCD, OLED, plasma, and projector. Concepts unique to each of these categories were explored. Additionally, the similarities among them were highlighted. We identified names and characteristics of display resolutions and explained the process of configuring settings such as resolution, refresh rate, and multimonitor support in Windows.

Exam Essentials

Be able to compare and contrast the main categories of display technology.   Although video display units all have roughly the same purpose—to display images created by the computer and rendered by the graphics adapter—LCDs, plasmas, OLEDs, and projectors go about the task in slightly different ways.

Be familiar with the key terms and concepts of display units.   Make sure that you can differentiate among terms such as *resolution, refresh rates* and *frame rates,* and *brightness,* and be familiar with terms used in other settings that might be found on the monitor or in the operating system.

Understand the key concepts behind LCD and other flat-panel technology.   You need to be familiar with active and passive matrix; resolution standards, such as XGA and UXGA; and terms such as *contrast ratio* and *native resolution.*

Be able to discuss and differentiate the various features of LCD monitors.   Familiarize yourself with the construction of LCD panels, including the difference between TN and IPS construction technologies. Also be able to discuss the difference and characteristics of backlighting performed by fluorescent bulbs versus LEDs.

Familiarize yourself with the steps that must be taken to configure display settings in Windows.   Most of the settings based on the operating system are found in roughly the same place. However, nuances found in the details of configuring these settings make it important for you to familiarize yourself with specific configuration procedures.

Review Questions

The answers to the chapter review questions can be found in Appendix A.

1. Which of the following would be the best choice as a personal display technology if a user wants to save desk space and not have to deal with interference from nearby speakers?

    A. CRT

    B. HDMI

    C. LCD

    D. Projector

2. Which of the following have been common methods to backlight an LCD monitor? (Choose two.)

    A. RGB OLEDs

    B. LEDs

    C. Incandescent bulbs

    D. Halogen bulbs

    E. Fluorescent bulbs

3. Which of the following is true regarding a monitor's refresh rate?

    A. As long as the graphics adapter can refresh the image at a particular rate, the attached monitor can accommodate that refresh rate.

    B. The refresh rate is normally expressed in MHz.

    C. The refresh rate is normally selected by using the controls on the front panel of the monitor.

    D. As you lower the resolution, the maximum refresh rate allowed tends to increase.

4. Which statement about LCD monitors is most accurate?

    A. The concept of refresh rate has no meaning with regard to LCDs.

    B. Those based on IPS technology suffer from color shifts when viewed from the edges.

    C. Those based on TN technology are preferred by gamers.

    D. The electric fields generate a magnetic field that eventually must be removed.

5. If you are unable to display a given resolution on a monitor, which of the following might explain why?

    A. The graphics adapter does not have enough memory installed.

    B. The video display unit does not have enough memory installed.

    C. You are using an LCD with a single, fixed resolution.

    D. You have the refresh rate set too high.

6. Which video technology has a resolution of 1280×1024?

A. SVGA

B. SXGA

C. WSXGA

D. UXGA

7. What does a *Q* in video resolution names, such as QXGA, refer to?

A. Both the horizontal and vertical components of the resolution have been quadrupled.

B. The resolution is cut to one-fourth.

C. The technology is faster.

D. Both the horizontal and vertical components of the resolution have been doubled.

8. What is contrast ratio?

A. The ratio of luminance between the darkest and lightest colors that can be displayed

B. A term that was used with CRTs but has no meaning with LCDs

C. The ratio of luminance between two adjacent pixels

D. Something that can be corrected through degaussing

9. Which of the following display types physically creates the image displayed in a manner most similar to OLED displays?

A. Fluorescent-based LCD

B. LED-based LCD

C. IPS-based LCD

D. Plasma

10. When approaching an older LCD panel from the side, you don't realize there is actually an image displayed on it until you are almost in front of it. Which options might explain why you could not detect the image from the side? (Choose two.)

A. Older LCDs were equipped with a motion sensor.

B. Multiple monitors are in use, and the LCD is the secondary monitor, resulting in its poor oblique visibility.

C. The user has a privacy filter in place.

D. The monitor employs active-matrix pixel addressing.

E. It is a passive-matrix LCD panel.

11. On which properties tab do you select the refresh rate to use between the graphics adapter and monitor in Windows Vista?

A. Adapter

B. Monitor

C. Advanced

D. Display Settings

12. When you're in a hurry to pack everything up and head to the airport after a presentation using a video projector, which of the following should you avoid doing immediately?

   A. Unplugging the projector's power cable

   B. Unplugging the projector's video cable from your laptop

   C. Powering down the projector

   D. Turning off your laptop

13. What might cause your display to appear in a resolution of 640×480?

   A. You have your resolution set to SVGA.

   B. You added memory to your graphics adapter but have not informed the BIOS of the new memory.

   C. You have your resolution set to XGA.

   D. You have booted into Safe Mode.

14. Which of the following results can occur with improper display settings?

   A. The computer spontaneously reboots.

   B. The graphics adapter automatically chooses to use the highest supported resolution.

   C. You might have to scroll to see parts of the Desktop.

   D. The mouse cursor changes or permanently disappears.

15. What is the single, fixed resolution of an LCD called?

   A. Native resolution

   B. Default resolution

   C. Refresh rate

   D. Burned-in resolution

16. Which of the following is possible to do with multimonitor settings?

   A. Connect multiple monitors to your computer only by using a graphics adapter with two video interfaces.

   B. Cause two different Desktops to merge onto the same monitor.

   C. Connect two laptops together so they display the same Desktop.

   D. Display different parts of your Desktop on different monitors.

17. Which of the following types of LCD has the best performance characteristics?

   A. Active matrix

   B. Passive matrix

   C. Dual matrix

   D. Dual scan

18. Which of the following resolutions is an example of a 16:10 aspect ratio?

   A. 1280×1024

   B. 1920×1200

   C. 800×600

   D. 2048×1536

19. Which of the following is true with regard to the difference between refresh rate and frame rate?

   A. Monitors are rated only in refresh rate or frame rate, but never both.

   B. Content is recorded at a specific refresh rate, and output on a monitor at a specific frame rate.

   C. Refresh rate can be higher than frame rate, in terms of screens of information displayed per second, when considered for any given video output.

   D. The frame rate of a monitor is adjustable, while the refresh rate is fixed.

20. What is the unit of measure used by manufacturers of projectors to indicate the brightness of their product?

   A. Lux

   B. Lumens

   C. Watts

   D. Candelas

Performance-Based Question

You will encounter performance-based questions on the A+ exams. The questions on the exam require you to perform a specific task, and you will be graded on whether or not you were able to complete the task. The following requires you to think creatively in order to measure how well you understand this chapter's topics. You may or may not see similar questions on the actual A+ exams. To see how your answers compare to the authors', refer to Appendix B.

List the steps necessary to extend your main display to a second monitor and adjust their orientation with respect to one another.

Chapter

5

Custom Configurations

THE FOLLOWING COMPTIA A+ 220-901 OBJECTIVES ARE COVERED IN THIS CHAPTER:

✓ **1.9 Given a scenario, select the appropriate components for a custom PC configuration to meet customer specifications or needs.**

- Graphic / CAD / CAM design workstation
    - Multicore processor
    - High-end video
    - Maximum RAM
- Audio/Video editing workstation
    - Specialized audio and video card
    - Large fast hard drive
    - Dual monitors
- Virtualization workstation
    - Maximum RAM and CPU cores
- Gaming PC
    - Multicore processor
    - High-end video/specialized GPU
    - High definition sound card
    - High-end cooling
- Home Theater PC
    - Surround sound audio
    - HDMI output
    - HTPC compact form factor
    - TV tuner

- Standard thick client
  - Desktop applications
  - Meets recommended requirements for running selected OS
- Thin client
  - Basic applications
  - Meets minimum requirements for running selected OS
  - Network connectivity
- Home Server PC
  - Media streaming
  - File sharing
  - Print sharing
  - Gigabit NIC
  - RAID array

Not all computers are right for every situation. There are small Chromebooks that are ideal for portability and web browsing, but they would fail miserably when used for mathematical modeling of complex systems. Supercomputers that are up to the modeling task would have to be completely disassembled to be transported anywhere, and they would probably break the bank for most home users. While these are extreme examples, dozens more exist that shine a light on the need for custom configurations to perform specific jobs.

This chapter introduces you to some of the custom configurations, which have become so popular that they are tantamount to standards, enough so that they can be discussed in a finite way. Because of the situations in which you might find yourself, such concepts have become requisite knowledge for the A+ certified technician. For example, you might be given a list of requirements from a client and need to translate that into the optimal system for their needs. Or the A+ exam might give you a scenario with specifications, and you'll need to determine the best answer. The following specialized systems are covered in this chapter:

- Standard thick clients
- Graphic and CAD/CAM design workstations
- Audio/video editing workstations
- Virtualization workstations
- Gaming PCs
- Home theater PCs
- Thin clients
- Home server PCs

As much as computer systems have become specialized, their core components don't differ dramatically in functionality from one type of system to the next. For example, a hard drive is designed to store files, regardless of whether it's a small one in a Chromebook or if it's in a gigantic and super-fast video editing workstation. Because of this, you might feel like this chapter talks about much of the same hardware over and over, but that is by design. Many hardware components are in multiple configurations; the size and speed of those components may differ among custom configuration types. Software is much the same; an operating system provides an interface between other software applications and the hardware, regardless of the device on which is it running. Other types of hardware and software are so specialized that they only apply to a single custom configuration from the previous list. The following types of hardware (and software) are discussed in the sections to come:

- CPU enhancements
- Video enhancements
- Maximized RAM
- Specialized audio
- Specialized drives
- NIC enhancements
- Additional specialized devices or software
    - Enhanced cooling
    - Special chassis
    - TV tuner requirement
    - Application specifics

On the A+ exam, you may be given a scenario and asked to choose the right PC configuration to meet customer needs. Each of the next eight sections on different configurations gives you the information needed to choose the right configuration based on a given scenario. For example, if given a scenario where the user will be designing magazines, he or she will need a graphic or CAD/CAM workstation. Or, if the user wants to store all of the family's important files in a central location, they might consider a home server PC.

Standard Thick Clients

A standard *thick client* is not really a custom configuration; it's the standard configuration on which custom configurations are based. In other words, a thick client is a standard client computer system. For most end user scenarios, this is the type of client that they need unless they are performing specialized duties requiring extra hardware or software.

As a typical client computer, it must meet the recommended requirements for the selected operating system as well as be able to run standard desktop applications such as a productivity suite, like Microsoft Office. Because it's a client, however, the ability to attach to a network and accept a configuration that attaches it to one or more servers is implied. Although most computers today exhibit such capabilities, they cannot be assumed.

Each operating system requires a minimum set of hardware features to support its installation. Each additional desktop application installed requires its own set of features concurrent with, or on top of, those required for the operating system. For example, the operating system requires a certain amount of RAM for its installation and a certain amount of hard drive space. A typical application might be able to run with the same amount of RAM, but it will most certainly require enough additional hard-drive space to store its related files.

Keep in mind that minimum specifications are just that, the minimum. Better performance is realized by using recommended specifications or higher.

Graphic and CAD/CAM Design Workstations

Some users will be designers of graphical content, such as posters, advertisements, magazines, product packaging, and other graphic media. Others will be engineers or architects designing homes or commercial buildings. When faced with a scenario in which these types of users need a workstation, know that the systems used in the design of graphical content need a particular emphasis placed on the following three areas:

- CPU enhancements
- Video enhancements
- Maximized RAM

CPU Enhancements

Sometimes it's a matter of how powerful a computer's CPU is. At other times, having multiple lesser CPUs that can work independently on a number of separate tasks is more important. Many of today's PCs have either of these characteristics or a combination of both. Nevertheless, there are enough computers being produced that have neither. As a result, it is necessary to gauge the purpose of the machine when choosing the CPU profile of a computer.

Graphic design workstations and *computer-aided design/computer-aided manufacturing (CAD/CAM) workstations* are computers used for similar yet distinct reasons. Graphic design workstations are used by desktop publishers in the creation of high-quality copy consisting of professional text and graphical images. This output is used in advertising, marketing, and other forms of specialized documentation. CAD/CAM workstations are used in the design of engineering and architectural documentation, including blueprints in both two and three dimensions. Such systems place quite a load on their CPUs. Systems with average CPUs can become overwhelmed by the amount of processing required by professional graphical software. For this reason, such systems must be designed with CPUs of above-average performance.

The best type of CPU for these types of systems will often be a multicore processor. This is because, with multiple cores, each core can execute instructions independently, which greatly speeds up the system's performance. With today's technology, a quad-core processor should be considered at a minimum. If the user has extremely high needs, then a 12- or 16-core processor might be better, but also consider that these CPUs will be incredibly expensive by comparison.

When selecting a multicore processor, the amount of cache is also a very important consideration. Each core should have a sufficient amount of L1 and L2 cache dedicated to it, and L3 cache will be shared among them. A 16-core processor with 40MB of cache will greatly outperform a 16-core processor with only a 16MB cache.

Graphic Design Workstations

Computers used by graphic-design artists must process a constant flow of colors and detailed shapes, the combination of which can put a strain on the CPU, RAM, and video components.

CAD/CAM Workstations

CAD/CAM systems can carry the designer's vision from conception to design in a 100-percent digital setting. Three-dimensional drawings are also common with this technology. These designs drive or aid in the production of 3D models. Software used for such projects requires a high number of CPU cycles during the rendering of the designs before display on the monitor or output to a printer or plotter. Such systems have been used for decades by professionals in the architecture, surveying, and engineering fields as well as by design engineers in manufacturing firms.

The output of computerized numerical control (CNC) systems used in the manufacturing process following the use of CAD/CAM workstations in the design phase is far different from displays on monitors or printouts. CNC systems take a set of coded instructions and render them into machine or tool movements. The result is often a programmable cutting away of parts of the raw material to produce a finished product. Examples are automotive parts, such as metallic engine parts or wheel rims, crowns and other dental structures, and works of art from various materials.

Video Enhancements

Possibly an obvious requirement for such systems, graphics adapters with better graphics processing units (GPUs) and additional RAM on board have the capability to keep up with the demand of graphic design applications. Such applications place an unacceptable load on the CPU and system RAM when specialized processors and adequate RAM are not present on the graphics adapter. The video system is an area in which the best technology (that is within the budget) should be purchased.

Maximized RAM

Although such systems take advantage of enhanced video subsystems, all applications still require CPUs to process their instructions and RAM to hold these instructions during processing. Graphics applications tend to be particularly CPU and RAM hungry. Maximizing the amount of RAM that can be accessed by the CPU and operating system will result in better overall performance by graphic design workstations.

Before upgrading your RAM, always check to see what type of RAM is compatible with the motherboard, how many slots are available, and how the slots work together. For example, if there is an open slot, you might be able to upgrade the total system RAM by just adding a new stick; in some cases, the new RAM must be exactly the same type as the existing RAM for them to work together. In other cases, you may need to remove the old RAM and replace it with new RAM. Check your documentation!

Audio/Video Editing Workstations

Professionals who edit multimedia material require workstations that excel in three areas:

- Video enhancements
- Specialized audio
- Specialized hard drives

The following sections assume the use of nonlinear editing (NLE) schemes for video. NLE differs from linear editing by storing the video to be edited on a local drive instead of editing being performed in real time as the source video is fed into the computer. NLE requires workstations with much higher RAM capacity and disk space than does linear editing. Although maximizing RAM is a benefit to these systems, doing so is considered secondary to the three areas of enhancement mentioned in the preceding list.

Video Enhancements

Although a high-performance video subsystem is a benefit for computer systems used by audio/video (A/V) editors, it is not the most important video enhancement for such systems. *Audio/video editing workstations* benefit most from a graphics adapter with multiple video interfaces that can be used simultaneously. These adapters are not rare, but it is still possible to find high-end adapters with only one interface, which are not ideal for A/V editing systems.

Having dual monitors is a must. When editing multimedia content, or even generalized documents, it is imperative that editors have multiple views of the same or similar files. The editor of such material often needs to view different parts of the same file. Additionally, many A/V editing software suites allow, and often encourage or require, the editor to use multiple utilities simultaneously. For example, in video editing, many packages optimize their desktop arrangement when multiple monitors are detected, allowing less horizontal scrolling through timelines. The ability to extend the desktop across multiple monitors is valuable in such situations. For more on setting up this feature, see the section "Multiple Displays" in Chapter 4, "Display Devices."

To improve video-editing performance, insist on a graphics adapter that supports CUDA and OpenCL. CUDA is NVIDIA's Compute Unified Device Architecture, a parallel computing architecture for breaking down larger processing tasks into smaller tasks and processing them simultaneously on a GPU. Open Computing Language (OpenCL) is a similar, yet cross-platform, open standard. Programmers can specify high-level function calls in a programming language with which they are more familiar instead of writing specific instructions for the microcode of the processor at hand. The overall performance increase of macro-style application programming interfaces (APIs) like these is an advantage of the technologies as well. The rendering of 2D and 3D graphics occurs much more quickly and in a more fluid manner with one of these technologies. CUDA is optimized for NVIDIA

GPUs, while OpenCL is less specific, more universal, and perhaps, as a result, less ideal when used with the same NVIDIA GPUs that CUDA supports.

Furthermore, depending on the visual quality of the content being edited, the professional's workstation might require a graphics adapter and monitor capable of higher resolution than is readily available in the consumer marketplace. If the accuracy of what the editor sees on the monitor must be as true to life as possible, a specialty monitor might be the best choice for the project. Such monitors are expensive, but they provide the best resolution and color representation when compared to other high-quality monitors available today.

Specialized Audio

The most basic audio controllers in today's computer systems are not very different from those in the original sound cards from the 1980s. They still use an analog codec with a simple two-channel arrangement. Editors of audio information who are expected to perform quality work often require six to eight channels of audio. Many of today's motherboards come equipped with 5.1 or 7.1 analog audio. (See the section "Analog Sound Jacks" in Chapter 3, "Peripherals and Expansion.") Although analog audio is not entirely incompatible with quality work, digital audio is preferred the vast majority of the time. In some cases, an add-on adapter supporting such audio might be required to support an A/V editing workstation.

In addition to audio output, many A/V editors will require the ability to input custom music from an electronic musical keyboard or other device. A term you will hear in relation to this is the *musical instrument digital interface (MIDI)* standard. Old sound cards would sometimes have a MIDI port, which was used to connect the keyboard to the computer. Nowadays, those connections are most often made via USB. Nonetheless, you will still see the term *MIDI compatible* used with a lot of digital musical devices.

Specialized Hard Drives

Graphics editing workstations and other systems running drive-intensive NLE software benefit from uncoupling the drive that contains the operating system and applications from the one that houses the media files. This greatly reduces the need for multitasking by a single drive. With the data drive as the input source for video encoding, consider using the system drive as an output destination during the encoding if a third drive is not available. Just remember to move the resulting files to the data drive once the encoding is complete.

Not only should you use separate drives for system and data files, you should also make sure that the data drive is large and fast. SATA 6Gbps drives that spin at 7,200rpm and faster are recommended for these applications. Solid-state hard drives can also be considered because they're very fast, but their biggest limitation for A/V editing is lack of size. Editors cannot afford delays and the non-real-time video playback caused by buffering due to inefficient hard-drive subsystems. If you decide to use an external hard drive, whether for convenience or portability, or because of the fact that an extremely powerful laptop is being used as an A/V editing workstation, use an eSATA connection when possible. Doing so ensures that there will be no loss in performance over internal SATA drives due to conversion delays or slower interfaces, such as USB 2.0.

 For external hard drives, Thunderbolt and USB 3.1 devices can be used too, as they provide similar performance to eSATA.

If you cannot find a drive that has the capacity that you require, you should consider implementing RAID 0, disk striping without parity. Doing so has two advantages: You can pay less for the total space you end up with, and RAID 0 improves read and write speeds because multiple drives are active simultaneously. Don't confuse spanned volume sets with RAID 0. Simple volume sets do not read and write to all drives in the set simultaneously; data simply spills over to the next drive when the preceding one is full. The only advantage volume sets share with RAID 0 is the ability to store files larger than a single drive. Consult Chapter 2, "Storage Devices and Power Supplies," for more information on SATA and various RAID levels.

If you would also like to add fault tolerance and prevent data loss, go with RAID 5, which has much of the read/write benefit of RAID 0 with the added assurance that losing a single drive won't result in data loss. RAID should be implemented in hardware when possible to avoid overtaxing the operating system, which has to implement or help implement software RAID itself.

Virtualization Workstations

Hardware virtualization has taken the industry by storm. It's the core technology that enables cloud computing. Entire companies exist to provide software and algorithms of varying effectiveness for the purpose of minimizing the hardware footprint required to implement multiple servers and workstations. Although virtualization as a technology subculture is discussed in greater detail later in this book, in this chapter we will investigate the unique requirements for the workstation that will host the guest operating systems and their applications.

A typical use case for a virtualization workstation might exist in a software development environment. Developers might need to ensure that their programs work on different operating systems, and virtualization allows them to do that with one physical computer.

 Virtualization is discussed in depth in Chapter 20, "Network Services, Cloud Computing, and Virtualization."

Without getting into too much detail, virtualization allows for multiple guest OSs to run on the same computer at the same time, along with a host OS. Each virtual machine (VM) running on a host system appears to come along with its own resources. A quick look in the Device Manager utility of a guest operating system leads you to believe it has its own components and does not require or interfere with any resources on the host. This is not entirely true, however. The following list includes some of the more important components that are shared by the host and all guest operating systems:

- CPU cycles
- System memory
- Drive storage space
- System-wide network bandwidth

Because of these requirements, *virtualization workstations* must exceed the specifications of standard workstations in two primary areas:

- CPU enhancements
- Maximized RAM

Depending on the specific guest systems and processes that the workstation will host, it may be necessary to increase the hard drive capacity of the workstation and possibly the number and speed of network cards as well. Because this is only a possibility, increased drive or network capacity is not considered a primary enhancement for virtualization workstations.

CPU Enhancements

Because the physical host's processor is shared by all operating systems running, virtual or not, it behooves you to implement virtual machines on a host with as many CPUs or CPU cores as possible. In virtualization, each core in a multicore processor can be considered its own individual processor and therefore assigned duties separately by the VMs running on them. Consequently, the more CPUs you can install in a workstation, each with as many cores as possible, the more dedicated CPU cycles you can assign to each virtual machine.

Maximized RAM

As you create a virtual machine, even before a guest operating system is installed in the VM, you must decide how much RAM the guest system will require. The same minimum requirements for installing an operating system on a conventional machine apply to the installation of that operating system on a virtual machine.

The RAM you dedicate to that VM is not used until the VM is booted. Once it is booted, though, that RAM is typically unavailable to the host operating system. As a result, you must ensure that the virtualization workstation is equipped with enough RAM to handle its own needs as well as those of all guests that could run simultaneously. As with a conventional system running a single operating system at a time, you generally want to supply each VM with additional RAM to keep it humming along nicely.

This cumulative RAM must be accounted for in the physical configuration of the virtualization workstation. In most cases, this will result in maximizing the amount of RAM installed in the computer. The maximum installed RAM hinges on three primary constraints:

- The CPU's address-bus width
- The operating system's maximum supported RAM
- The motherboard's maximum supported RAM

The smallest of these constraints dictates the maximum RAM you will be able to use in the workstation. Attention to each of these limitations should be exercised in the selection of the workstation to be used to host guest operating systems and their applications. Considering the limitations of operating systems leads to preferring the use of server versions over client versions and the use of x64 versions over x86 versions.

 Real World Scenario

What's It Going to Take?

The folks at a medium-sized organization decided to try their hand at virtualization because the IT manager heard that they could save money on future infrastructure and "go green" at the same time. They already had all of the server operating systems they needed; they were currently installed on separate machines. The manager envisioned removing the KVM switch and having a single machine in the server room.

The technician in charge did almost everything right. He chose the company's most powerful server and created five virtual machines. The hard drive was large enough that there was plenty of room for the host operating system and the five VMs. The technician knew the minimum requirements for running each of the operating systems and made sure that each VM was configured with plenty of RAM. The dual-core CPU installed in the system was more than powerful enough to handle each operating system.

After a combination of clean installations and image transfers into the VMs, the server was ready to test. The host booted and ran beautifully as always. The first VM was started and was found to be accessible over the network. It served client requests and created a barely noticeable draw on performance. It was the second VM that sparked the realization that the manager and technician missed a crucial point. The processor and the RAM settings for each individual VM were sufficient for the host and at most one VM, but when any second VM was added to the mix, the combined drain on the CPU and RAM was untenable. "What's it going to take to be able to run these servers simultaneously?" the technician wondered.

The solution was to replace the server motherboard with a model that supported an eight-core Intel i7 Extreme Edition processor and to maximize the RAM based on what the new motherboard supported. The result was an impressive system with five virtual servers, each of which displayed impressive performance statistics. Before long, the expense of the server was returned in power savings. Eventually, additional savings will be realized when the original physical hardware for the five servers would have had to be replaced.

Gaming PCs

Early video games designed for the PC market were able to run on the average end user's computer system. As is true with all software, there is a push/pull relationship between PC-based games and the hardware they run on. Over time, the hardware improved and challenged the producers of gaming software. Inspired by the possibilities, the programmers pushed the limits of the hardware, encouraging hardware engineers to create more room for software growth. Today's advanced PC-based gaming software cannot be expected to run on an average system. Specialized *gaming PCs*, computers optimized for running modern video games, fill a niche in the marketplace, leading to a continually growing segment of the personal-computer market.

 Keep in mind that when we are talking about gaming systems, we're not talking about solitaire or free Internet games. Nearly every computer can do that. The games to which we're referring are the high-end, multiplayer games, such as the *Call of Duty* series, *League of Legends*, *World of Warcraft*, and several others. In many newer games, the video quality is practically cinema-like. Of course, this list will change over time as these titles age and new ones take their place!

Gaming enthusiasts often turn to specialized game consoles for the best performance, but with the right specifications, a personal computer can give modern consoles a run for their money, possibly even eclipsing their performance. If you encounter a scenario in which you need to build a gaming PC that will light up the eyes of the most difficult-to-please gamer, four areas of enhancement must be considered:

- CPU enhancements
- Video enhancements
- Specialized audio
- Enhanced cooling

CPU Enhancements

Unlike with A/V editing, gaming requires millions of decisions to be made by the CPU every second. It's not enough that the graphics subsystem can keep up with the action; the CPU must be able to create that action. Some gamers find that they do fine with a high-end stock CPU; many of the mid-level to higher-end multicore processors will suffice. Others require that the CPUs perform above their specified rating. They find that overclocking the CPU by making changes in the BIOS to the clock frequency used by the system gains them the requisite performance that allows them to remain competitive against or to dominate competitors. Overclocking was discussed in Chapter 1, "Motherboards, Processors, and Memory," but to reiterate, it means that you are running your CPU at a clock speed greater than the manufacturer's rating to increase performance.

However, this increased performance comes at a price: Their CPU will almost certainly not live as long as if they had used the default maximum speed determined by the manufacturer and detected by the BIOS. Nothing can completely negate the internal damage caused by pushing electrons through the processor's cores faster than they should be allowed. Nevertheless, the CPU would scarcely survive days or even hours with standard cooling techniques. Enhancing the cooling system, discussed shortly, is the key to stretching the CPU's life back out to a duration that approaches its original expectancy.

Overclocking your CPU voids all manufacturer warranties, and it is generally not recommended.

Video Enhancements

Video games have evolved from text-based and simple two-dimensional graphics-based applications into highly complex software that requires everything from real-time high-resolution, high-definition rendering to three-dimensional modeling. Technologies like NVIDIA's SLI and ATI's Crossfire are extremely beneficial for such graphics-intensive applications. SLI was discussed in Chapter 1.

No longer can gaming software rely mostly on the system's CPU to process its code and deliver the end result to the graphics adapter for output to the monitor. Video cards for gaming systems essentially require their own dedicated graphics processing unit (GPU). No longer can this software store a screen or two at a time in the graphics adapter's memory, allowing for video adapters with only a few hundred MB of RAM. Today's gaming applications can be resource-hungry powerhouses capable of displaying fluid video at 40 to 60 frames per second. To keep up with such demands, the RAM installed on relatively decent graphics adapters has breached the 4GB mark, a capacity not long ago reserved for primary system memory. In fact, if users want to spend thousands of dollars on a video card, they could get one with 12GB or 16GB RAM as well.

In the same way that CUDA- and OpenCL-capable GPUs benefit workstations used for video editing, these same standards are indispensable in the world of modern gaming software. Not all GPUs support these standards. Thus, another selling point emerges for high-end graphics adapters.

Of course, all of the internal system enhancements in the world are for naught if the monitor you choose cannot keep up with the speed of the adapter or its resolutions and 3D capability. Quite a bit of care must be exercised when comparison shopping for an adequate gaming monitor.

Specialized Audio

Today's video games continue the genre of interactive multimedia spectacles. Not only can your video work in both directions, using cameras to record the image or motion of the player, your audio as well. It's exceedingly common to find a gamer shouting into a microphone boom on a headset as they guide their character through the virtual world of high-definition video and high-definition digital audio. A lesser audio controller is not acceptable in today's PC gaming world. Technologies such as S/PDIF and HDMI produce high-quality, high-definition digital audio for the gaming enthusiast. Of course, HDMI provides for state-of-the-art digital video as well.

Enhanced Cooling

As mentioned earlier, the practices of speed junkies, such as modern PC gamers, can lead to a processor's early demise. Although a shorter lifespan for an overclocked CPU isn't a given, operators of such systems use standard and experimental cooling methods to reduce the self-destructive effects of the increased heat output from the CPU. Refer back to the section "CPU Cooling" in Chapter 1 for more information on cooling techniques that give overclocked CPUs a fighting chance. Of course, experimental cooling techniques such as immersion of the system in mineral oil and indirect application of liquid nitrogen or helium to the CPU continue to garner attention from enthusiasts. It remains to be seen, however, if some of these techniques have a shot at making it in the marketplace.

Today's high-end graphics adapters come equipped with their own cooling mechanisms designed to keep them properly cooled under even extreme circumstances. Nevertheless, the use of high-end adapters in advanced ways leads to additional concerns. Graphics adapters that rob a second slot for their cooling mechanism to have space to exhaust heated air through the backplane might be unwelcome in a smaller chassis that has only a single slot to spare. Also, the gaming-PC builder's decision to include two or more ganged adapters (video cards that are two expansion slots wide and take up two expansion slots but attached together as one unit) in one system (SLI or Crossfire) challenges the engineered cooling circuit. When many large adapters are placed in the path of cooler air brought in through one end of the chassis for the purpose of replacing the warmer internal air of the chassis, the overall ambient internal temperature increases.

Figure 5.1 shows the inside of an NVIDIA gaming computer that has a liquid cooling system in it.

Home Theater PCs

Several years ago, most home theater systems consisted of separate components controlled individually. It might have felt like the user needed an advanced degree in electronic engineering just to set the whole thing up properly. Today though, *home theater PCs (HTPCs)* are becoming more popular as specialized computing appliances used to control the entire home entertainment experience.

An HTPC might have multiple capabilities, such as storing large amounts of video media and streaming it to an output device, streaming it directly from the Internet, or acting as an A/V tuner and receiver, mating input sources with output devices. The versatility of an HTPC makes it a logical choice for people desiring to exercise more control over their existing set-top boxes, most of which do not even offer the option of flexible storage. HTPCs are personal computers with operating systems that allow easy access to local storage, allowing the user to add whatever media they want whenever they feel the need.

FIGURE 5.1   Gaming system with liquid cooling

The average PC can be turned into a device with similar functionality, but a computer designed for use as such should be built on a chassis that adheres to the HTPC form factor; the average computer would not. In fact, the following list comprises the specializations inherent in true HTPCs:

- Video enhancements
- Specialized audio
- Special chassis
- TV tuner requirement

Video Enhancements

High-definition monitors are as commonplace as television displays in the home today. HTPCs, then, must go a step beyond, or at least not fall a step behind. Because High-Definition Multimedia Interface (HDMI) is an established standard that is capable of the highest-quality audio, video resolution, and video refresh rates offered by consumer electronics, and because nearly all manufacturers have adopted HDMI, it is the logical choice for connectivity in the HTPC market. Considering the simple, small form factor plug and interface inherent in HDMI, more cumbersome video-only choices, such as DVI and YPbPr component video, lose favor on a number of fronts.

Graphics adapters present in HTPCs should have one or more HDMI interfaces. Ideally, the adapter will have both input and output HDMI interfaces, giving the PC the capability to combine and mix signals as well as interconnect sources and output devices. Additionally, internally streamed video will be presented over the HDMI interface to the monitor. Keep in mind that the monitor used should be state of the art to keep up with the output capabilities of the HTPC.

Specialized Audio

Recall that HDMI is capable of eight-channel 7.1 surround sound, which is ideal for the home theater. The fact that the HTPC should be equipped with HDMI interfaces means that surround-sound audio is almost an afterthought. Nevertheless, high-end digital audio should be near the top of the wish list for HTPC specifications. If it's not attained through HDMI, then copper or optical S/PDIF should be employed. At the very least, the HTPC should be equipped with 7.1 analog surround sound (characterized by a sound card with a full complement of six 3.5mm stereo minijacks).

Special Chassis and TV Tuner

As mentioned earlier, HTPCs have their own specialized computer case form factor. These machines should be able to blend well with other home theater appliances, such as digital video recorders (DVRs) from a cable company or satellite provider, or look totally fine taking their place. Quite often these cases will be black, sit horizontally like old-school desktop computers, and have touchscreen interfaces and big stereo-like volume or selector knobs. Many of them look like A/V receivers. Figure 5.2 shows an example of an HTPC case.

Creating a machine that takes up minimal space (perhaps even capable of being mounted on a wall beside or behind the monitor) without compromising storage capacity and performance requires the use of today's smallest components. The following list comprises some of the components that you might use when building your own HTPC from separate parts.

- HTPC chassis, typically with dimensions such as 17″ × 17″ × 7″ and 150W HTPC power supply
- Motherboard, typically mini-ITX (6.7″ × 6.7″) with integrated HDMI video

- HDD or SSD, usually 2½″ portable form factor, larger capacity if storage of multimedia content is likely
- RAM: DIMMs for mini-ITX motherboard; SODIMMs for many pre-built models
- Blu-ray drive minimum
- PCIe or USB TV tuner card, optionally with capture feature

FIGURE 5.2   HTPC case

Many prebuilt offerings exist with all of the components standard. You need only to choose the model with the specifications that match your needs. Barebones systems exist as well, allowing you to provide your own hard drive and RAM modules. Many such units contain smaller ITX boards, such as nano- or pico-ITX, which are not compatible with most do-it-yourself chassis.

TV tuner cards are available as system add-ons and not commonly as integrated motherboard components. HTPCs that will be used only for streaming video from Internet sources and playing music do not require a TV tuner card. Otherwise, such a card might allow one or more sources, including one source split into two inputs, to be watched or recorded.

Thin Clients

In situations where an enterprise is interested in saving copious amounts in infrastructure cost, thin clients can be used to achieve their goal. A *thin client* is any machine that divests itself of all or most local storage and varying levels of RAM and processing power without necessarily giving up all ability to process instructions and data. In the extreme, a thin client resembles a dumb terminal, which only displays output to the monitor and relays input from the mouse and keyboard back to the server. The primary difference between these ultra-thin clients and dumb terminals is that the clients feature a true network connection and contain enough intelligence to locate the server before turning over processing control.

The ramification of having clients with low processing and storage capabilities is that there must be one or more servers with increased corresponding capacities. Unfortunately, this leads to a single or centralized point of failure in the infrastructure that can impact productivity to an unacceptable level. Thin clients have no offline capability, requiring constant network connectivity. Workforces that require employees to be independent or mobile with their computing power lean away from thin clients as well, opting for laptops and similar technology.

Some thin clients will have local storage and be capable of running basic applications, which are executed locally. These types of systems must, of course, be able to accommodate the storage and processing needs of those applications and an operating system. Thin client OSs can be very simple and designed specifically for a thin client, such as Thinstation, Windows Embedded Standard (WES7), and Lenovo Terminal Operating System (LeTOS), or they can be more robust such as full versions of Windows. Simple thin client designs featuring flash-based storage and small quantities of small form factor RAM exist, reducing the need for such systems to resemble thick clients at all.

Home Server PCs

You may encounter a scenario where you (or a client) want to have many of the features of a server but you don't want to mess with a server operating system such as Windows Server or Linux. A home server PC might be the right solution.

Home server PCs are essentially powerful client systems with a standard, non-server OS. They differ from enterprise servers to the point that they qualify as custom configurations. For many generations, desktop operating systems have run server services and have been capable of allowing other clients to have limited access, but not enough access to accommodate a large number of users.

In addition, because the home server PC is the center of the home network, fault tolerance considerations should be entertained, which is decidedly not the case for standard home systems.

Recall that fault tolerance differs from redundancy in that fault tolerance seeks to retain accessibility during the failure while redundancy simply ensures recoverability after the failure. Redundancy, in the form of a data backup, does not ensure the continued accessibility of the data, but RAID, for example, seeks to do so. Even the most basic home system should be backed up regularly to avoid total data loss, but only servers in the home environment should be considered for the added expense of fault tolerance.

Home server PCs can be built from the same components that go into today's higher-performance systems. Attention needs to be paid to certain enhanced features, however. The following list outlines these differences:

- Media streaming capabilities
- File sharing services
- Print sharing services
- Gigabit NIC
- RAID array

Media Streaming Capabilities

A popular use for a home server is to stream music, photos, and videos to other devices, including those that are not PCs. With Windows 7 and newer, you can enable media streaming services and configure the computer to stream media. Of course, third-party applications and utilities are also a possibility.

Starting with Windows 7, Microsoft introduced HomeGroups, which are a lot like workgroups but with a smaller scope and different security requirements. HomeGroups work hand in hand with libraries, another feature introduced in Windows 7. Anything that can be included in a library (documents, pictures, videos, and music) can be shared among the devices in the password-protected HomeGroup. Additionally, HomeGroups can share installed printers among the member computers. Chapter 16, "Working with Windows 7," discusses HomeGroups in more detail.

You can prepare a Windows 7 computer to stream media through Windows Media Player by accessing the media streaming configuration through the advanced settings of the Network And Sharing Center in Control Panel. Exercise 5.1 walks you through the process.

EXERCISE 5.1

Configuring Windows 7 for Media Streaming

1. Open Control Panel, and in the upper-right corner where it says View By, change it to Small Icons or Large Icons. Click on the Network And Sharing Center applet to open it.

2. Click the Change Advanced Sharing Settings link in the left frame, shown in Figure 5.3.

FIGURE 5.3   Click the Change Advanced Sharing Settings link.

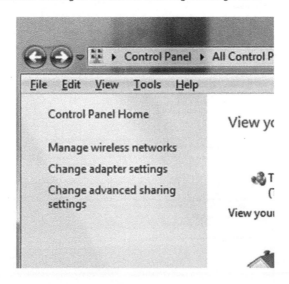

continues

3. Click the down arrow to the right of Home Or Work, as shown in Figure 5.4, to expand that configuration section.

FIGURE 5.4   Changing sharing options

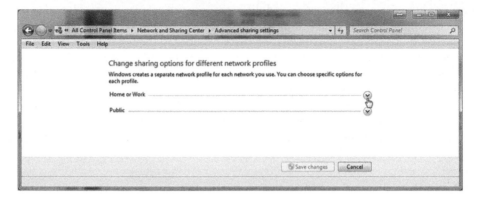

4. In the Media Streaming section, click the Choose Media Streaming Options link, which is shown at the bottom of Figure 5.5.

FIGURE 5.5   Changing advanced sharing settings

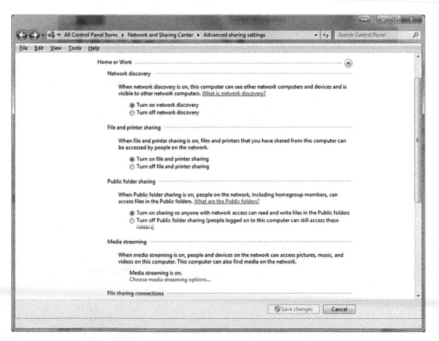

5. If media streaming is not turned on, you will need to click the Turn on Media Streaming box to proceed to step 6.

6. In the Media Streaming Options dialog, pull down the buttons labeled Blocked and change them to Allowed for each computer on the network that you want to be able to stream from the local PC. An example is shown in Figure 5.6.

FIGURE 5.6   Media streaming options

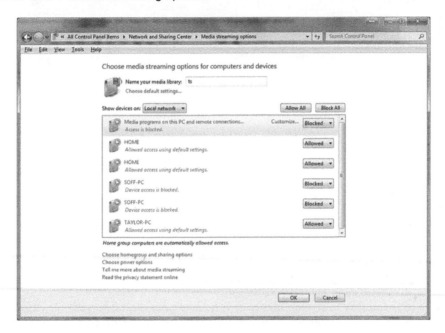

7. Click OK to leave the Media Streaming Options dialog, and then close the Network And Sharing Center dialog.

8. Open Windows Media Player (for example, Start ➤ All Programs ➤ Windows Media Player) and switch to Library mode, if necessary. (You can do this by using the grid icon with the arrow pointing left in Now Playing mode, by pressing the Alt key and choosing View ➤ Library, or by pressing Ctrl+1).

9. Make sure streaming is enabled by clicking Stream ➤ Turn On Media Streaming (or Turn On Media Streaming With HomeGroup, as shown in Figure 5.7). This option is hidden if streaming is already on.

10. On one of the remote systems, start Windows Media Player.

11. Scroll down, if necessary, in the left frame until you see Other Libraries (as is shown at the bottom of Figure 5.7).

12. Expand the remote library that you just shared, and see if you can play music, watch videos or recorded TV, or view pictures.

continues

FIGURE 5.7   Streaming settings

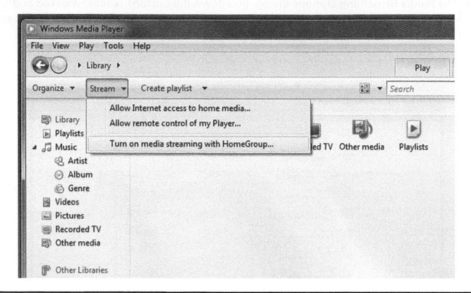

File and Print Sharing Services

In addition to the ability to stream files to remote machines, home servers are expected to allow the static transfer of files to or from the server's hard drive or array. Streaming and file sharing are similar concepts, but streaming occurs in one direction from the server and does not affect the client's file system. File sharing can go in both directions, and it adds to the client's file system during downloads. The server acts as a repository for uploaded files that can then be downloaded from any other machine in the home network.

The difference between home servers and enterprise servers is that all clients in a home environment tend to have equal access to the file server's data store. Enterprise file servers have data stores that are isolated from users that do not have permission to access them. Print servers in the home and enterprise behave in a similar fashion. Each printer attached to the home server should be accessible to anyone on the home network.

File and print sharing are available through classic file sharing in Windows as well as through HomeGroups in Windows 7 and newer.

Gigabit NIC

The home server should be attached to a wired switched port in an Ethernet switch or in the wireless access point. The NIC and the switch port should be capable of gigabit speeds. Providing such speed ensures that clients using 100Mbps Fast Ethernet ports and across the wireless network will not create a bottleneck in their attempt to share the server's resources. Running client NICs at gigabit speeds should be avoided, even though the capability is ubiquitous. Running all devices on the network at gigabit speeds guarantees that each device that is attached will attempt to saturate the server's gigabit interface with its own traffic.

RAID Array

Because some of the data stored on a home server represents the only copy, such as data that is streamed to all clients or the data included in a crucial backup of client systems, it must be protected from accidental loss. Because the data that comprises the streaming content, shared data store, and client backup sets can become quite expansive, a large storage capacity is desirable. Even a recoverable server outage results in a home network that is temporarily unusable by any client, so fault tolerance should be included. RAID provides the answer to all of these needs.

When a hardware RAID solution is used in the home server PC, the server's operating system is not taxed with the arduous task of managing the array, and additional RAID levels might also be available. The RAID array can extend to many terabytes in size, many times the size of a single drive, and it should include hot-swappable drives so that it can be rebuilt on the fly while still servicing client requests during the loss of a single drive.

Summary

In this chapter, you were introduced to seven custom configurations and how a standard thick client differs from them. The seven systems are graphic and CAD/CAM design workstations, audio/video editing workstations, virtualization workstations, gaming PCs, home theater PCs, thin clients, and home server PCs.

You learned how some of these systems have very specific needs while others share common requirements for components not found in a standard desktop system. These needs include CPU enhancements, video enhancements, maximized RAM, specialized audio, specialized drives, NIC enhancements, enhanced cooling, special chassis, a TV tuner requirement, and specifics related to applications.

Exam Essentials

Be able to describe graphic and CAD/CAM design workstations and list their components.   CAD/CAM workstations are designed to create blueprints and advanced designs. These workstations require powerful processors (often multicore), high-end video, and maximum RAM to be able to provide the performance required to allow efficient graphic design and modeling.

Be able to describe audio/video editing workstations and list their components. If a user wants to create high-quality audio or video files, they need an A/V workstation. A/V workstations call for specialized audio and video, large and fast hard drives, and multiple monitors to allow editors to play back their media smoothly while being able to see all of the controls of their utilities and applications.

Be able to describe virtualization workstations and list their components. Some users, particularly developers, can benefit from workstations that can host multiple operating systems at one time, and virtualization is a technology that enables this. Virtualization workstations need plenty of RAM and CPU cores to share among the guest operating systems while still allowing the host to run efficiently and error free.

Be able to describe gaming PCs and list their components. For hardcore gaming enthusiasts, a gaming PC that makes use of high-performance multicore CPUs and powerful GPUs to deliver the ultimate gaming experience is required. Rounding out the experience is awesome sound production, which comes at the price of increased heat production due to the faster-running components. As a result, enhanced cooling mechanisms must be employed.

Be able to describe home theater PCs and list their components. For the best movie theatre-like experience in the home, use a home theater PC, which can replacing or augment other set-top boxes. Surround sound, HDMI, and a TV tuner allow such systems to run the show. The components are placed in a chassis that conforms to the HTPC form factor.

Be able to describe thin clients and list their components. Thin clients are used in situations where costs are to be kept to a minimum but users still need to run applications like they would on a workstation. Because of this, thin clients should still conform to the basic specifications required to run a client OS and basic applications. However, it is possible to go a step further and have the server run all software and feed the client no more information than a dumb terminal would receive. The primary difference is that it is fed over an Ethernet connection instead of a classic serial interface.

Be able to describe home server PCs and list their components. If multiple users on a home network need to share files or other resources, a home server PC can be beneficial. Home server PCs are expected to support media streaming as well as file and print sharing. To stay ahead of the client demand, the server should be connected to a Gigabit Ethernet interface. To ensure fault tolerance, RAID is recommended for home server PCs.

Review Questions

The answers to the chapter review questions can be found in Appendix A.

1. You have been asked to set up a workstation for a new graphic designer at your company. Which of the following is *not* a requirement for a graphic design workstation?

   A. Fast hard drive

   B. Maximum RAM

   C. Powerful CPU

   D. High-end video

2. You have been hired as a consultant for a video editing company that needs all new workstations for its six editors. Which of the following is required when constructing an A/V editing workstation?

   A. Gigabit NIC

   B. Powerful processor

   C. Maximum RAM

   D. Fast hard drive

3. Danielle has been asked to configure virtualization at her company. She recommends that her manager buy multicore processors. What justification should she give as to why virtualization workstations require as many CPU cores as possible?

   A. Each virtual machine has one or more cores installed directly in it.

   B. Each virtual machine makes use of actual CPU resources for processing instructions and data.

   C. Fault tolerance dictates that if one CPU core fails, there should be one or more in line to take its place.

   D. Because each guest operating system runs in its own space, multiple cores are required to store the collective data.

4. Your friend Joe plays video game tournaments online, and he read in an online forum that he should overclock his CPU for better speed. You tell him that if he does that, he needs better cooling. Why is high-end cooling a requirement for gaming PCs?

   A. Gaming PCs tend to overclock their CPUs and run multiple high-performance GPUs.

   B. Gaming controllers have components for tactile realism that generate copious amounts of heat.

   C. Digital sound cards generate more heat than analog sound cards.

   D. Placing that many hard drives in such a small space generates too much heat.

5. Marcus, a network technician, has been asked to build an HTPC for his manager. Which of the following is *not* a common requirement that Marcus should consider for this custom configuration?

   A. Surround sound

   B. HDMI

    C. Micro-ATX case

    D. TV tuner

6. Which type of system simply needs to run standard versions of Windows and desktop applications?

    A. Thin client

    B. Thick client

    C. Home server PC

    D. Virtualization workstation

7. Which of the following descriptions most closely matches that of a thin client?

    A. A high-resolution monitor, keyboard, and mouse

    B. A computer with a low-profile case

    C. A laptop

    D. A dumb terminal with a NIC

8. You have recently installed a home server PC in your home so that all of your family members can share media. You have a router and network cabling that supports Gigabit Ethernet. Why should you equip a home server PC with a gigabit NIC?

    A. All systems, including the server, should communicate at the same speed.

    B. The server should not be allowed to communicate at the higher speeds of the rest of the network or it will be overused.

    C. The server should exceed the communication speed of the clients to avoid a bottleneck.

    D. The operating system that home servers run is not compatible with Gigabit Ethernet.

9. An engineer on your network is complaining that his CAD workstation is slow and he wants a processor upgrade. Which of the following reasons is justification for having a powerful processor in a CAD/CAM workstation?

    A. Only powerful processors can stream graphical information efficiently.

    B. Manufacturing equipment is generally faster than design equipment, which needs faster processors to keep up.

    C. Graphics adapters used in CAD/CAM do not have their own processors, so the CPU performs this job as well.

    D. The algorithms used in rendering graphics can be processor intensive.

10. A video editor at your company wants a second monitor, claiming that only having one monitor limits her ability to work. Why do A/V editing workstations benefit from more than one monitor?

    A. Their software often has enough controls across their width that one monitor seems cramped.

    B. While one graphics adapter works on one rendering project, the other can simply display a normal desktop.

    C. Once the editing is complete, the second monitor is used to present the results to others on the team.

    D. Additional monitors are used for remote collaboration among other editors.

11. You are configuring a virtualization workstation for your home use. Which of the following is required for your new system?
    A. Multiple host operating systems
    B. Maximum RAM allowed
    C. File sharing services
    D. Multiple NICs

12. Robin has been asked to lead training for new technicians at a local PC distributor specializing in gaming PCs. For which one of the following should she not recommend upgraded parts?
    A. High-end cooling
    B. A RAID array
    C. High-end video
    D. Better sound card

13. Which of the following system types does *not* require a CPU enhancement of any sort?
    A. A/V editing workstation
    B. Gaming PC
    C. Graphic design workstation
    D. Virtualization workstation

14. Maria is setting up an HTPC and wants to know which type of video cables to purchase. Which of the following is the recommended video output technology for home theater PCs?
    A. DVI
    B. WUXGA
    C. HDMI
    D. YCbCr

15. Which of the following is a common feature of a standard thick client?
    A. Has enhanced video capabilities
    B. Has a high-performance hard drive
    C. Has as much RAM installed as is possible
    D. Can run a full version of Windows

16. Your network uses thin clients. A new technician is amazed that the computers have no hard drives and asks, "If the operating system is not resident on the client, where is it found?"
    A. On a DVD inserted at bootup
    B. On a USB flash drive
    C. On the server for session-by-session client use
    D. Embedded in a flash module on the motherboard

17. Peter is configuring a home server PC. Which of the following should be his least-important priority to include in his home server PC?
    A. File and print sharing
    B. Maximum RAM

    C.   Gigabit NIC

    D.   Media streaming

    E.   RAID array

18. All of the following systems benefit from increased RAM *except*_____. (Choose two.)

    A.   Home theater PC

    B.   Virtualization workstation

    C.   Graphic design workstation

    D.   Gaming PC

19. Which of the following uses would *not* require a custom configuration for a PC?

    A.   A computer running Windows 7 Ultimate with 1TB of data and 250GB of applications installed

    B.   A computer running WHS 2011

    C.   A design computer used to drive a lathe that makes automotive rims

    D.   A computer to replace a BD player and DVR

20. Which of the following system types does *not* benefit from video enhancements?

    A.   CAD/CAM design workstation

    B.   Home server PC

    C.   A/V editing workstation

    D.   Home theater PC

Performance-Based Question

You will encounter performance-based questions on the A+ exams. The questions on the exam require you to perform a specific task, and you will be graded on whether or not you were able to complete the task. The following requires you to think creatively in order to measure how well you understand this chapter's topics. You may or may not see similar questions on the actual A+ exams. To see how your answer compares to the authors', refer to Appendix B.

List the steps required to stream video from one Windows 7 computer to another in the same house. Assume that the two computers are members of the same HomeGroup.

Chapter 6

Networking Fundamentals

THE FOLLOWING COMPTIA A+ 220-901 EXAM OBJECTIVES ARE COVERED IN THIS CHAPTER:

✓ **2.1 Identify the various types of network cables and connectors.**

- Fiber
    - Connectors: SC, ST, and LC
- Twisted Pair
    - Connectors: RJ-11, RJ-45
    - Wiring standards: T568A, T568B
- Coaxial
    - Connectors: BNC, F-connector

✓ **2.2 Compare and contrast the characteristics of connectors and cabling.**

- Fiber
    - Types (single-mode vs. multi-mode)
    - Speed and transmission limitations
- Twisted Pair
    - Types: STP, UTP, CAT3, CAT5, CAT5e, CAT6, CAT6e, CAT 7, plenum, PVC
    - Speed and transmission limitations
    - Splitters and effects on signal quality
- Coaxial
    - Types: RG-6, RG-59
    - Speed and transmission limitations
    - Splitters and effects on signal quality

✓ **2.7 Compare and contrast Internet connection types, network types, and their features.**

- Network Types
  - LAN
  - WAN
  - PAN
  - MAN

✓ **2.8 Compare and contrast network architecture devices, their functions, and features.**

- Hub
- Switch
- Router
- Access point
- Bridge
- Modem
- Firewall
- Patch panel
- Repeaters/extenders
- Ethernet over Power
- Power over Ethernet injector

Looking around most homes or offices today, it's hard to imagine a world without networks. Nearly every place of business has some sort of network. Wireless home networks have exploded in popularity in the last few years, and it seems that everywhere you go, you can see a dozen wireless networks from your smartphone, tablet, or laptop.

It didn't used to be that way. Even when we're not thinking about networking, it's still likely that we're doing it with the ubiquitous Internet-enabled smartphones in our pockets and purses. We take for granted a lot of what we have gained in technology over the past few years, much less the past several decades.

Twenty-five years ago, if you wanted to send a memo to everyone in your company, you had to use a photocopier and interoffice mail. Delivery to a remote office could take days. Today, one mistaken click of the Reply All button can result in instantaneous embarrassment. Email is an example of one form of communication that became available with the introduction and growth of networks.

This chapter focuses on the basic concepts of how a network works, including the way it sends information, the hardware used, and the common types of networks you might encounter. It used to be that in order to be a PC technician, you needed to focus on only one individual (but large) computer at a time. In today's environment, though, you will in all likelihood need to understand combinations of hardware, software, and network infrastructure in order to be successful.

If the material in this chapter interests you, you might consider studying for, and eventually taking, CompTIA's Network+ exam. It is a non-company-specific networking certification similar to A+ but for network-related topics. You can study for it using Sybex's *CompTIA Network+ Study Guide* materials, available at www.wiley.com/WileyCDA/Section/id-420431.html.

Understanding Networking Principles

Stand-alone personal computers, first introduced in the late 1970s, gave users the ability to create documents, spreadsheets, and other types of data and save them for future use. For the small-business user or home-computer enthusiast, this was great. For larger companies, however, it was not enough. Larger companies had greater needs to share information between offices and sometimes over great distances. Stand-alone computers were insufficient for the following reasons:

- Their small hard-drive capacities were insufficient.
- To print, each computer required a printer attached locally.
- Sharing documents was cumbersome. People grew tired of having to save to a floppy and then take that disk to the recipient. (This procedure was called *sneakernet.*)
- There was no email. Instead, there was interoffice mail, which was slow and sometimes unreliable.

To address these problems, networks were born. A *network* links two or more computers together to communicate and share resources. Their success was a revelation to the computer industry as well as to businesses. Now departments could be linked internally to offer better performance and increase efficiency.

You have probably heard the term *networking* in a business context, where people come together and exchange names for future contact and access to more resources. The same is true with a computer network. A computer network allows computers to link to each other's resources. For example, in a network, every computer does not need a printer connected locally in order to print. Instead, you can connect a printer to one computer or you can connect it directly to the network and allow all of the other computers to access it. Because they allow users to share resources, networks can increase productivity as well as decrease cash outlay for new hardware and software.

In the following sections, we will discuss the fundamentals of networking as well as the types of networks that you are likely to encounter.

Understanding Networking Fundamentals

In many cases, networking today has become a relatively simple plug-and-play process. Wireless network cards can automatically detect and join networks, and then you're seconds away from surfing the Web or sending email. Of course, not all networks are that simple. Getting your network running may require a lot of configuration, and one messed-up setting can cause the whole thing to fail.

Just as there is a lot of information you should know about how to configure your network, there is a lot of background information you should understand about *how* networks work. The following sections cover the fundamentals, and armed with this information, you can then move on to how to make it work *right*.

LANs, WANs, PANs, and MANs

Local area networks (LANs) were introduced to connect computers in a single office or building. *Wide area networks (WANs)* expanded the LANs to include networks outside the local environment and also to distribute resources across great distances. Generally, it's safe to think of a WAN as multiple, disbursed LANs connected together. Today, LANs exist in many homes (wireless networks) and nearly all businesses. WANs are becoming more common as businesses become more mobile and as more of them span greater distances. Historically, only larger corporations used WANs, but many smaller companies with remote locations now use them as well.

Having two types of network categories just didn't feel like enough, so the industry introduced two more terms: the personal area network and the metropolitan area network. The *personal area network (PAN)* is a very small-scale network designed around one person within a very limited boundary area. The term generally refers to networks that use Bluetooth technology. On a larger scale is the *metropolitan area network (MAN)*, which is bigger than a LAN but not quite as big as a WAN.

It is important to understand these concepts as a service professional because when you're repairing computers, you are likely to come in contact with problems that are associated with the computer's connection to a network. Understanding the basic structure of the network can often help you solve a problem.

LANs

The 1970s brought us the minicomputer, which was a smaller version of large mainframe computers. Whereas the mainframe used *centralized processing* (all programs ran on the same computer), the minicomputer used *distributed processing* to access programs across other computers. As depicted in Figure 6.1, distributed processing allows a user at one computer to use a program on another computer as a *back end* to process and store information. The user's computer is the *front end*, where data entry and minor processing functions are performed. This arrangement allowed programs to be distributed across computers rather than be centralized. This was also the first time network cables rather than phone lines were used to connect computers.

FIGURE 6.1   Distributed processing

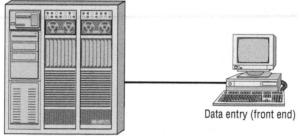

Data processing and storage (back end)

Data entry (front end)

By the 1980s, offices were beginning to buy PCs in large numbers. Portables were also introduced, allowing computing to become mobile. Neither PCs nor portables, however, were efficient in sharing information. As timeliness and security became more important, floppy disks were just not cutting it. Offices needed to find a way to implement a better means to share and access resources. This led to the introduction of the first type of PC local area network (LAN): ShareNet by Novell, which had both hardware and software components. LANs simply link computers in order to share resources within a closed environment. The first simple LANs were constructed a lot like the LAN in Figure 6.2.

FIGURE 6.2   A simple LAN

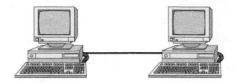

After the introduction of ShareNet, more LANs sprouted. The earliest LANs could not cover large distances. Most of them could only stretch across a single floor of the office and could support no more than 30 computers. Furthermore, they were still very rudimentary and only a few software programs supported them. The first software programs that ran on a LAN were not capable of being used by more than one user at a time (this constraint was known as *file locking*). Nowadays, multiple users often concurrently access a program or file. Most of the time, the only limitations will be restrictions at the record level if two users are trying to modify a database record at the same time.

WANs

By the late 1980s, networks were expanding to cover large geographical areas and were supporting thousands of users. Wide area networks (WANs), first implemented with mainframes at massive government expense, started attracting PC users as networks went to this new level. Employees of businesses with offices across the country communicated as if they were only desks apart. Soon the whole world saw a change in the way of doing business, across not only a few miles but across countries. Whereas LANs are limited to single buildings, WANs can span buildings, states, countries, and even continental boundaries. Figure 6.3 shows an example of a simple WAN.

FIGURE 6.3   A simple WAN

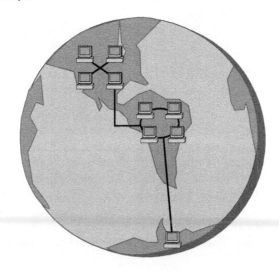

The networks of today and tomorrow are no longer limited by the inability of LANs to cover distance and handle mobility. WANs play an important role in the future development of corporate networks worldwide.

PANs

The term PAN is most commonly associated with Bluetooth networks. In 1998, a consortium of companies formed the Bluetooth Special Interest Group (SIG) and formally adopted the name *Bluetooth* for its technology. The name comes from a tenth-century Danish king named Harald Blåtand, known as Harold Bluetooth in English. (One can only imagine how he got that name.) King Blåtand had successfully unified warring factions in the areas of Norway, Sweden, and Denmark. The makers of Bluetooth were trying to unite disparate technology industries, namely computing, mobile communications, and the auto industry.

 Although the most common use of a PAN is in association with Bluetooth, a PAN can also be created with other technologies, such as infrared.

Current membership in the Bluetooth SIG includes Microsoft, Intel, Apple, IBM, Toshiba, and several cell phone manufacturers. The technical specification IEEE 802.15.1 describes a *wireless personal area network (WPAN)* based on Bluetooth version 1.1.

The first Bluetooth device on the market was an Ericsson headset and cell phone adapter, which arrived on the scene in 2000. While mobile phones and accessories are still the most common type of Bluetooth device, you will find many more, including wireless keyboards, mice, and printers. Figure 6.4 shows a Bluetooth USB adapter.

FIGURE 6.4 Bluetooth USB adapter

 If you want to learn more about Bluetooth you can visit www.bluetooth.com.

One of the defining features of a Bluetooth WPAN is its temporary nature. With traditional Wi-Fi, you need a central communication point, such as a wireless router or access point to connect more than two devices together. (This is referred to as *infrastructure*.) Bluetooth networks are formed on an ad hoc basis, meaning that whenever two Bluetooth devices get close enough to each other, they can communicate directly with each other—no central communication point is required. This dynamically created network is called a *piconet*.

A Bluetooth-enabled device can communicate with up to seven other devices in one piconet. Two or more piconets can be linked together in a *scatternet*. In a scatternet, one or more devices would serve as a bridge between the piconets.

MANs

For those networks that are larger than a LAN but confined to a relatively small geographical area, there is the term *metropolitan area network (MAN)*. A MAN is generally defined as a network that spans a city or a large campus. For example, if a city decides to install wireless hotspots in various places, that network could be considered a MAN.

One of the questions a lot of people ask is, "Is there really a difference between a MAN and a WAN?" There is definitely some gray area here; in many cases they are virtually identical. Perhaps the biggest difference is who has responsibility for managing the connectivity. In a MAN, a central IT organization such as the campus or city IT staff is responsible. In a WAN, it's implied that you will be using publicly available communication lines and there will be a phone company or other service provider involved.

Primary Network Components

Technically speaking, two or more computers connected together constitute a network. But networks are rarely that simple. When you're looking at the devices or resources available on a network, there are three types of components of which you should be aware:

- Servers
- Clients or workstations
- Resources

Every network requires two more items to tie these three components together: a network operating system (NOS) and some kind of shared medium. These components are covered later in their own sections.

Blurring the Lines

In the 1980s and 1990s, LANs and WANs were often differentiated by their connection speeds. For example, if you had a 10Mbps or faster connection to other computers, you were often considered to be on a LAN. WANs were often connected to each other by very expensive T1 connections, which have a maximum bandwidth of 1,544Mbps.

As with all other technologies, networking capacity has exploded. In today's office network, wired connections slower than 100Mbps are considered archaic. Connections of 1Gbps are fairly common. WAN connectivity, although still slower than LAN connectivity, can easily be several times faster than the T1. Because of the speed increases in WAN connectivity, the old practice of categorizing your network based on connection speed is outdated.

Today, the most common way to classify a network is based on geographical distance. If your network is in one central location, whether that is one office, one floor of an office building, or maybe even one entire building, it's usually considered a LAN. If your network is spread out among multiple distant locations, it's a WAN.

Servers

Servers come in many shapes and sizes. They are a core component of the network, providing a link to the resources necessary to perform any task. The link that the server provides could be to a resource existing on the server itself or a resource on a client computer. The server is the critical enabler, offering directions to the client computers regarding where to go to get what they need.

Servers offer networks the capability of centralizing the control of resources and security, thereby reducing administrative difficulties. They can be used to distribute processes for balancing the load on computers and can thus increase speed and performance. They can also compartmentalize files for improved reliability. That way, if one server goes down, not all of the files are lost.

Servers can perform several different critical roles on a network. For example, servers that provide files to the users on the network are called *file servers*. Likewise, servers that host printing services for users are called *print servers*. (Servers can be used for other tasks as well, such as authentication, remote access services, administration, email, and so on.) Networks can include multipurpose and single-purpose servers. A multipurpose server can be, for example, both a file server and a print server at the same time. If the server is a single-purpose server, it is a file server only or a print server only. Another distinction we use in categorizing servers is whether they are dedicated or nondedicated:

Dedicated servers   A *dedicated server* is assigned to provide specific applications or services for the network and nothing else. Because a dedicated server specializes in only a few tasks, it requires fewer resources than a nondedicated server might require from the computer that is hosting it. This savings may translate to efficiency and can thus be considered as having a beneficial impact on network performance. A web server is an example of a dedicated server: It is dedicated to the task of serving up web pages and nothing else.

Nondedicated servers   Nondedicated servers are assigned to provide one or more network services *and* local access. A *nondedicated server* is expected to be slightly more flexible in its day-to-day use than a dedicated server. Nondedicated servers can be used to direct network traffic and perform administrative actions, but they also are often used to serve as a front end for the administrator to work with other applications or services or to perform services for more than one network. For example, a dedicated web server might serve out one or more websites, whereas a nondedicated web server serves out websites but might also function as a print server on the local network or as the administrator's workstation.

The nondedicated server is not what some would consider a true server because it can act as a workstation as well as a server. The workgroup server at your office is an example of a nondedicated server. It might be a combination file, print, and email server. Plus, because of its nature, a nondedicated server could also function well in a peer-to-peer environment. It could be used as a workstation in addition to being a file, print, and email server.

We will talk in more depth about server roles in Chapter 20, "Network Services, Cloud Computing, and Virtualization."

Many networks use both dedicated and nondedicated servers to incorporate the best of both worlds, offering improved network performance with the dedicated servers and flexibility with the nondedicated servers.

Workstations

Workstations are the computers on which the network users do their work, performing activities such as word processing, database design, graphic design, email, and other office or personal tasks. Workstations are basically everyday computers, except for the fact that they are connected to a network that offers additional resources. Workstations can range from diskless computer systems to desktops or laptops. In network terms, workstations are also known as *client computers*. As clients, they are allowed to communicate with the servers in the network to use the network's resources.

It takes several items to make a workstation into a network client. You must install a *network interface card (NIC)*, a special expansion card that allows the PC to talk on a network. You must connect it to a cabling system that connects to other computers (unless your NIC supports wireless networking). And you must install special software, called *client software*, which allows the computer to talk to the servers and request resources from them. Once all this has been accomplished, the computer is "on the network."

Network client software comes with all operating systems today. When you configure your computer to participate in the network, the operating system utilizes this software.

To the client, the server may be nothing more than just another drive letter. However, because it is in a network environment, the client can use the server as a doorway to more storage or more applications or to communicate with other computers or other networks. To users, being on a network changes a few things:

▪ They can store more information because they can store data on other computers on the network.

▪ They can share and receive information from other users, perhaps even collaborating on the same document.

- They can use programs that would be too large or complex for their computer to use by itself.
- They can use hardware not attached directly to their computer, such as a printer.

Real World Scenario

Is That a Server or a Workstation?

This is one of the things that author Quentin Docter does when teaching novice technicians. In the room, there will be a standard-looking mini-tower desktop computer. He points to it and asks, "Is that a server or a workstation?" A lot of techs will look at it and say it's a workstation because it is a desktop computer. The real answer is, "It depends."

Although many people have a perception that servers are ultra-fancy, rack-mounted devices, that isn't necessarily true. It's true that servers typically need more powerful hardware than do workstations because of their role on the network, but that doesn't have to be the case. (Granted, having servers that are less powerful than your workstations doesn't make logical sense.) What really differentiates a workstation from a server is what operating system it has installed and what role it plays on the network.

For example, if that system has Windows Server 2012 R2 installed on it, you can be pretty sure that it's a server. If it has Windows 7 or Windows 8.1, it's more than likely going to be a client, but not always. Computers with operating systems such as Windows 7 can be both clients on the network and nondedicated servers, as would be the case if you share your local printer with others on the network.

The moral of the story? Don't assume a computer's role simply by looking at it. You need to understand what is on it and its role on the network to make that determination.

Network Resources

We now have the server to share the resources and the workstation to use them, but what about the resources themselves? A *resource* (as far as the network is concerned) is any item that can be used on a network. Resources can include a broad range of items, but the following items are among the most important:

- Printers and other peripherals
- Disk storage and file access
- Applications

When only a few printers (and all of the associated consumables) have to be purchased for the entire office, the costs are dramatically lower than the costs for supplying printers at every workstation.

Networks also give users more storage space to store their files. Client computers can't always handle the overhead involved in storing large files (for example, database files) because they are already heavily involved in users' day-to-day work activities. Because servers in a network can be dedicated to only certain functions, a server can be allocated to store all of the larger files that are used every day, freeing up disk space on client computers. In addition, if users store their files on a server, the administrator can back up the server periodically to ensure that if something happens to a user's files, those files can be recovered.

Files that all users need to access (such as emergency contact lists and company policies) can also be stored on a server. Having one copy of these files in a central location saves disk space as opposed to storing the files locally on everyone's system.

Applications (programs) no longer need to be on every computer in the office. If the server is capable of handling the overhead that an application requires, the application can reside on the server and be used by workstations through a network connection.

> The sharing of applications over a network requires a special arrangement with the application vendor, who may wish to set the price of the application according to the number of users who will be using it. The arrangement allowing multiple users to use a single installation of an application is called a *site license*.

Being on a Network Brings Responsibilities

You are part of a community when you are on a network, which means that you need to take responsibility for your actions. First, a network is only as secure as the users who use it. You cannot randomly delete files or move documents from server to server. You do not own your email, so anyone in your company's management team can choose to read it. In addition, sending something to the printer does not necessarily mean that it will print immediately—your document may not be the first in line to be printed at the shared printer. Plus, if your workstation has also been set up as a nondedicated server, you cannot turn it off.

Network Operating Systems (NOSs)

PCs use a disk operating system that controls the file system and how the applications communicate with the hard disk. Networks use a *network operating system (NOS)* to control the communication with resources and the flow of data across the network. The NOS runs on the server. Some of the more popular NOSs are UNIX and Linux and Microsoft's Windows Server series (Server 2012, Server 2008, and so on). Several other companies offer network operating systems as well.

Network Resource Access

We have discussed two major components of a typical network—servers and workstations—and we've also talked briefly about network resources. Let's dive in a bit deeper on how those resources are accessed on a network.

There are generally two resource access models: peer-to-peer and client-server. It is important to choose the appropriate model. How do you decide what type of resource model is needed? You must first think about the following questions:

- What is the size of the organization?
- How much security does the company require?
- What software or hardware does the resource require?
- How much administration does it need?
- How much will it cost?
- Will this resource meet the needs of the organization today and in the future?
- Will additional training be needed?

Networks cannot just be put together at the drop of a hat. A lot of planning is required before implementation of a network to ensure that whatever design is chosen will be effective and efficient, and not just for today but for the future as well. The forethought of the designer will lead to the best network with the least amount of administrative overhead. In each network, it is important that a plan be developed to answer the previous questions. The answers will help the designer choose the type of resource model to use.

Peer-to-Peer Networks

In a peer-to-peer network, the computers act as both service providers and service requestors. An example of a peer-to-peer resource model is shown in Figure 6.5.

FIGURE 6.5   The peer-to-peer resource model

The peer-to-peer model is great for small, simple, inexpensive networks. This model can be set up almost instantly, with little extra hardware required. Many versions of Windows (Windows 8, Windows 7, Vista) as well as Linux and Mac OS are popular operating system environments that support the peer-to-peer resource model. Peer-to-peer networks are also referred to as *workgroups*.

Generally speaking, there is no centralized administration or control in the peer-to-peer resource model. Every station has unique control over the resources that the computer owns, and each station must be administered separately. However, this very lack of centralized control can make administering the network difficult; for the same reason, the network isn't very secure. Each user needs to manage separate passwords for each computer on which they wish to access resources, as well as set up and manage the network shares on their own computer. Moreover, because each computer is acting as both a workstation and server, it may not be easy to locate resources. The person who is in charge of a file may have moved it without anyone's knowledge. Also, the users who work under this arrangement need more training because they are not only users but also administrators.

Will this type of network meet the needs of the organization today and in the future? Peer-to-peer resource models are generally considered the right choice for small companies that don't expect future growth. Small companies that expect growth, on the other hand, should not choose this type of model.

A rule of thumb is that if you have no more than 10 computers and centralized security is not a key priority, a workgroup may be a good choice for you.

Client-Server Resource Model

The client-server (also known as server-based) model is better than the peer-to-peer model for large networks (say, more than 10 computers) that need a more secure environment and centralized control. Server-based networks use one or more dedicated, centralized servers. All administrative functions and resource sharing are performed from this point. This makes it easier to share resources, perform backups, and support an almost unlimited number of users. This model also offers better security. However, the server needs more hardware than a typical workstation/server computer in a peer-to-peer resource model. In addition, it requires specialized software (the NOS) to manage the server's role in the environment. With the addition of a server and the NOS, server-based networks can easily cost more than peer-to-peer resource models. However, for large networks, it's the only choice. An example of a client-server resource model is shown in Figure 6.6.

FIGURE 6.6   The client-server resource model

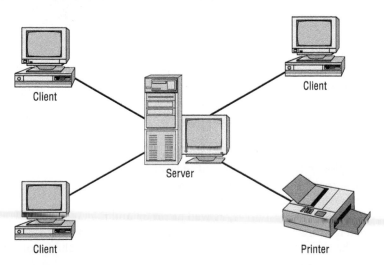

Server-based networks are often known as *domains*. The key characteristic of a server-based network is that security is centrally administered. When you log in to the network, the login request is passed to the server responsible for security, sometimes known as a *domain controller*. (Microsoft uses the term *domain controller*, whereas other vendors of server products do not.) This is different from the peer-to-peer model, where each individual workstation validates users. In a peer-to-peer model, if the user jsmith wants to be able to log in to different workstations, she needs to have a user account set up on each machine. This can quickly become an administrative nightmare! In a domain, all user accounts are stored on the server. User jsmith needs only one account and can log on to any of the workstations in the domain.

Client-server resource models are the desired models for companies that are continually growing, need to support a large environment, or need centralized security. Server-based networks offer the flexibility to add more resources and clients almost indefinitely into the future. Hardware costs may be more, but with the centralized administration, managing resources becomes less time consuming. Also, only a few administrators need to be trained, and users are responsible for only their own work environment.

If you are looking for an inexpensive, simple network with little setup required, and there is no need for the company to grow in the future, then the peer-to-peer network is the way to go. If you are looking for a network to support many users (more than 10 computers), strong security, and centralized administration, consider the server-based network your only choice.

Whatever you decide, always take the time to plan your network before installing it. A network is not something you can just throw together. You don't want to find out a few months down the road that the type of network you chose does not meet the needs of the company—this could be a time-consuming and costly mistake.

Network Topologies

A *topology* is a way of laying out the network. When you plan and install a network, you need to choose the right topology for your situation. Each type differs from the others by its cost, ease of installation, fault tolerance (how the topology handles problems such as cable breaks), and ease of reconfiguration (such as adding a new workstation to the existing network).

There are five primary topologies:

- Bus
- Star
- Ring
- Mesh
- Hybrid

Each topology has advantages and disadvantages. After the following sections, check out Table 6.1, which summarizes the advantages and disadvantages of each topology.

Bus Topology

A *bus topology* is the simplest. It consists of a single cable that runs to every workstation, as shown in Figure 6.7. This topology uses the least amount of cabling. Each computer shares the same data and address path. With a bus topology, messages pass through the trunk, and each workstation checks to see if a message is addressed to it. If the address of the message matches the workstation's address, the network adapter retrieves it. If not, the message is ignored.

FIGURE 6.7   The bus topology

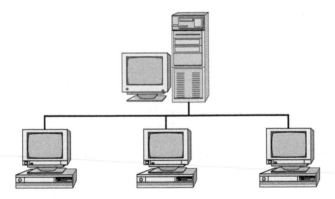

Cable systems that use the bus topology are easy to install. You run a cable from the first computer to the last computer. All of the remaining computers attach to the cable somewhere in between. Because of the simplicity of installation, and because of the low cost of the cable, bus topology cabling systems are the cheapest to install.

Although the bus topology uses the least amount of cabling, it is difficult to add a workstation. If you want to add another workstation, you have to reroute the cable completely and possibly run two additional lengths of it. Also, if any one of the cables breaks, the entire network is disrupted. Therefore, such a system is expensive to maintain and can be difficult to troubleshoot. You will rarely run across physical bus networks in use today.

Star Topology

A *star topology* branches each network device off a central device called a *hub* or a *switch*, making it easy to add a new workstation. If a workstation goes down, it does not affect the entire network; if the central device goes down, the entire network goes with it. Because of this, the hub (or switch) is called a *single point of failure*. Figure 6.8 shows a simple star network.

FIGURE 6.8   The star topology

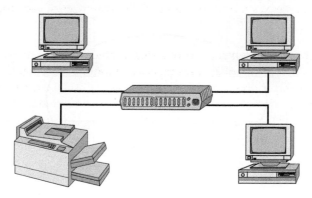

Star topologies are very easy to install. A cable is run from each workstation to the hub. The hub is placed in a central location in the office (for example, a utility closet). Star topologies are more expensive to install than bus networks because several more cables need to be installed, plus the hubs. But the ease of reconfiguration and fault tolerance (one cable failing does not bring down the entire network) far outweigh the drawbacks. This is the most commonly installed network topology in use today.

 Although the hub is the central portion of a star topology, many networks use a device known as a switch instead of a hub. Switches are more advanced than hubs, and they provide better performance than hubs for only a small price increase. Colloquially though, many administrators use the terms *hub* and *switch* interchangeably.

Ring Topology

In a *ring topology*, each computer connects to two other computers, joining them in a circle and creating a unidirectional path where messages move from workstation to workstation. Each entity participating in the ring reads a message and then regenerates it and hands it to its neighbor on a different network cable. See Figure 6.9 for an example of a ring topology.

The ring makes it difficult to add new computers. Unlike a star topology network, the ring topology network will go down if one entity is removed from the ring. Physical ring topology systems rarely exist anymore, mainly because the hardware involved was fairly expensive and the fault tolerance was very low.

 You might have heard of an older network architecture called Token Ring. Contrary to its name, it does *not* use a physical ring. It actually uses a physical star topology, but the traffic flows in a logical ring from one computer to the next.

FIGURE 6.9   The ring topology

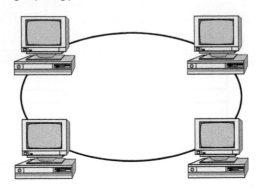

Mesh Topology

The *mesh topology* is the most complex in terms of physical design. In this topology, each device is connected to every other device (see Figure 6.10). This topology is rarely found in LANs, mainly because of the complexity of the cabling. If there are x computers, there will be $(x \times (x - 1)) \div 2$ cables in the network. For example, if you have five computers in a mesh network, it will use $5 \times (5 - 1) \div 2 = 10$ cables. This complexity is compounded when you add another workstation. For example, your 5-computer, 10-cable network will jump to 15 cables if you add just one more computer. Imagine how the person doing the cabling would feel if you told them they had to cable 50 computers in a mesh network—they'd have to come up with $50 \times (50 - 1) \div 2 = 1,225$ cables!

FIGURE 6.10   The mesh topology

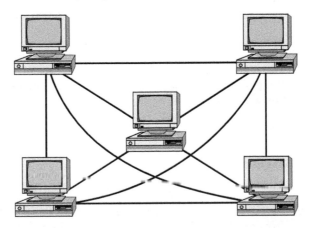

Because of its design, the physical mesh topology is expensive to install and maintain. Cables must be run from each device to every other device. The advantage you gain is high fault tolerance. With a mesh topology, there will always be a way to get the data from source to destination. The data may not be able to take the direct route, but it can take an alternate, indirect route. For this reason, the mesh topology is often used to connect multiple sites across WAN links. It uses devices called *routers* to search multiple routes through the mesh and determine the best path. However, the mesh topology does become inefficient with five or more entities because of the number of connections that need to be maintained.

Hybrid Topology

The *hybrid topology* is simply a mix of the other topologies. It would be impossible to illustrate it because there are many combinations. In fact, most networks today are not only hybrid but heterogeneous (they include a mix of components of different types and brands). The hybrid network may be more expensive than some types of network topologies, but it takes the best features of all of the other topologies and exploits them.

Table 6.1 summarizes the advantages and disadvantages of each type of network topology.

TABLE 6.1   Topologies—advantages and disadvantages

Topology	Advantages	Disadvantages
Bus	Cheap. Easy to install.	Difficult to reconfigure. A break in the bus disables the entire network.
Star	Cheap. Very easy to install and reconfigure. More resilient to a single cable failure.	More expensive than bus.
Ring	Efficient. Easy to install.	Reconfiguration is difficult. Very expensive.
Mesh	Best fault tolerance.	Reconfiguration is extremely difficult, extremely expensive, and very complex.
Hybrid	Gives a combination of the best features of each topology used.	Complex (less so than mesh, however).

Rules of Communication

Regardless of the type of network you choose to implement, the computers on that network need to know how to talk to each other. To facilitate communication across a network, computers use a common language called a protocol. We'll cover protocols more in Chapter 7, "Introduction to TCP/IP," but essentially they are languages much like English is a language. Within each language, there are rules that need to be followed so that both computers understand the right communication behavior.

To use a human example, within English there are grammar rules. If you put a bunch of English words together in a way that doesn't make sense, no one will understand you. If you just decide to omit verbs from your language, you're going to be challenged to get your point across. And if everyone talks at the same time, the conversation can be hard to follow.

Computers need standards to follow to keep their communication clear. Different standards are used to describe the rules that computers need to follow to communicate with each other. The most important communication framework, and the backbone of all networking, is the OSI model.

The OSI model is not specifically listed in the CompTIA A+ exam objectives. However, it's a critical piece of networking knowledge and a framework with which all technicians should be familiar.

OSI Model

The International Organization for Standardization (ISO) published the *Open Systems Interconnection (OSI)* model in 1984 to provide a common way of describing network protocols. The ISO put together a seven-layer model providing a relationship between the stages of communication, with each layer adding to the layer above or below it.

This OSI model is a theoretical model governing computer communication. Even though at one point an "OSI protocol" was developed, it never gained wide acceptance. You will never find a network that is running the "OSI protocol."

Here's how the theory behind the OSI model works: As a transmission takes place, the higher layers pass data through the lower layers. As the data passes through a layer, that layer tacks its information (also called a *header*) onto the beginning of the information being transmitted until it reaches the bottom layer. A layer may also add a trailer to the end of the data. The bottom layer sends the information out on the wire (or in the air, in the case of wireless).

At the receiving end, the bottom layer receives and reads the information in the header, removes the header and any associated trailer related to its layer, and then passes the remainder to the next highest layer. This procedure continues until the topmost layer receives the data that the sending computer sent.

The OSI model layers are listed here from top to bottom, with descriptions of what each of the layers is responsible for:

7—Application layer   Allows access to network services. This is the layer at which file services, print services, and other applications operate.

6—Presentation layer   Determines the "look," or format, of the data. This layer performs protocol conversion and manages data compression, data translation, and encryption. The character set information also is determined at this level. (The character set determines which numbers represent which alphanumeric characters.)

5—Session layer   Allows applications on different computers to establish, maintain, and end a session. A *session* is one virtual conversation. For example, all of the procedures needed to transfer a single file make up one session. Once the session is over, a new process begins. This layer enables network procedures, such as identifying passwords, logons, and network monitoring.

4—Transport layer   This layer controls the data flow and troubleshoots any problems with transmitting or receiving datagrams. It also takes large messages and segments them into smaller ones and takes smaller segments and combines them into a single, larger message, depending on which way the traffic is flowing. Finally, the TCP protocol (one of the two options at this layer) has the important job of verifying that the destination host has received all packets, providing error checking and reliable end-to-end communications.

3—Network layer   This layer is responsible for logical addressing of messages. At this layer, the data is organized into chunks called *packets*. The Network layer is something like the traffic cop. It is able to judge the best network path for the data based on network conditions, priority, and other variables. This layer manages traffic through packet switching, routing, and controlling congestion of data.

2—Data Link layer   Arranges data into chunks called *frames*. Included in these chunks is control information indicating the beginning and end of the datastream. This layer is very important because it makes transmission easier and more manageable and it allows for error checking within the data frames. The Data Link layer also describes the unique physical address (also known as the *MAC address*) for each NIC. The Data Link layer is actually subdivided into two sections: Media Access Control (MAC) and Logical Link Control (LLC).

1—Physical layer   Describes how the data gets transmitted over a communication medium. This layer defines how long each piece of data is and the translation of each into the electrical pulses or light impulses that are sent over the wires, or the radio waves that are sent through the air. It decides whether data travels unidirectionally or bidirectionally across the hardware. It also relates electrical, optical, mechanical, and functional interfaces to the cable.

Figure 6.11 shows the complete OSI model. Note the relationship of each layer to the others and the function of each layer.

FIGURE 6.11   The OSI model

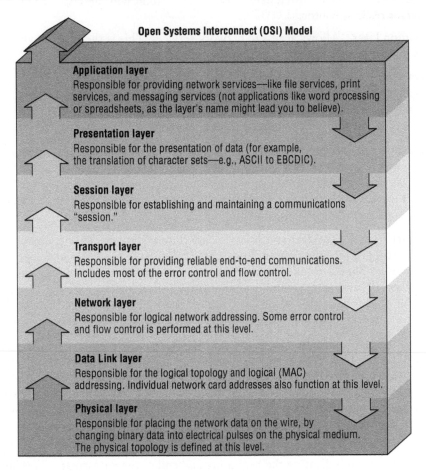

Open Systems Interconnect (OSI) Model

Application layer
Responsible for providing network services—like file services, print services, and messaging services (not applications like word processing or spreadsheets, as the layer's name might lead you to believe).

Presentation layer
Responsible for the presentation of data (for example, the translation of character sets—e.g., ASCII to EBCDIC).

Session layer
Responsible for establishing and maintaining a communications "session."

Transport layer
Responsible for providing reliable end-to-end communications. Includes most of the error control and flow control.

Network layer
Responsible for logical network addressing. Some error control and flow control is performed at this level.

Data Link layer
Responsible for the logical topology and logical (MAC) addressing. Individual network card addresses also function at this level.

Physical layer
Responsible for placing the network data on the wire, by changing binary data into electrical pulses on the physical medium. The physical topology is defined at this level.

A helpful mnemonic device to remember the OSI layers in order is "All People Seem To Need Data Processing."

IEEE 802 Standards

Continuing with our theme of communication, it's time to introduce one final group of standards. You've already learned that a protocol is like a language; think of the IEEE 802 standards as syntax, or the rules that govern who communicates, when they do it, and how they do it.

The Institute of Electrical and Electronics Engineers (IEEE) formed a subcommittee to create standards for network types. These standards specify certain types of networks, although not every network protocol is covered by the IEEE 802 committee specifications. This model contains several categories, but the following are the most popularly referenced:

- 802.2 Logical Link Control
- 802.3 CSMA/CD (Ethernet) LAN
- 802.5 Token Ring LAN
- 802.6 Metropolitan Area Network
- 802.11 Wireless Networks

The IEEE 802 standards were designed primarily for enhancements to the bottom three layers of the OSI model. The IEEE 802 standard breaks the Data Link layer into two sub-layers: a Logical Link Control (LLC) sublayer and a Media Access Control (MAC) sublayer. In the Logical Link Control sublayer, data link communications are managed. The Media Access Control sublayer watches out for data collisions and manages physical addresses, also referred to as MAC addresses.

You've most likely heard of 802.11g or 802.11n wireless networking. The rules for communicating with all versions of 802.11 are defined by the IEEE standard. Another very well-known standard is 802.3 CSMA/CD. You might know it by its more popular name, Ethernet.

The original 802.3 CSMA/CD standard defines a bus topology network that uses a 50-ohm coaxial baseband cable and carries transmissions at 10Mbps. This standard groups data bits into frames and uses the Carrier Sense Multiple Access with Collision Detection (CSMA/CD) cable access method to put data on the cable. Currently, the 802.3 standard has been amended to include speeds up to 10Gbps.

Breaking the CSMA/CD acronym apart may help illustrate how it works. First, there is the Carrier Sense (CS) part, which means that computers on the network are listening to the wire at all times. Multiple Access (MA) means that multiple computers have access to the line at the same time. This is analogous to having five people on a conference call. Everyone is listening, and everyone in theory can try to talk at the same time. Of course, when more than one person talks at once, there is a communication error. In CSMA/CD, when two machines transmit at the same time, a data *collision* takes place and the intended recipients receive none of the data. This is where the Collision Detection (CD) portion of the acronym comes in; the collision is detected and each sender knows they need to send again. Each sender then waits for a short, random period of time and tries to transmit again. This process repeats until transmission takes place successfully. The CSMA/CD technology is considered a *contention-based* access method.

The only major downside to 802.3 is that with large networks (more than 100 computers on the same segment), the number of collisions increases to the point where more collisions than transmissions are taking place.

Other examples exist, such as 802.5 token ring, which defines a logical ring on a physical star. On a token ring network, an access packet called a *token* circles the network. If you have the token, you can send data; otherwise you wait for your turn. It's not important to memorize all of the different IEEE standards for the test. Just know that different ones exist, governing how to transmit data on the wire and making sure that all computers co-exist peacefully.

Identifying Common Network Hardware

We have looked at the types of networks, network topologies, and the way communications are handled. That's all of the logical stuff. To really get computers to talk to each other requires hardware. Every computer on the network needs to have a network adapter of some type. In many cases, you also need some sort of cable to hook them together. (Wireless networking is the exception, but at the back end of a wireless network there are still components wired together.) And finally, you might also need connectivity devices to attach several computers or networks to each other.

Network Interface Cards (NICs)

The *network interface card (NIC)*, also referred to as a network adapter card, provides the physical interface between computer and cabling. It prepares data, sends data, and controls the flow of data. It can also receive and translate data into bytes for the CPU to understand. NICs come in many shapes and sizes.

Different NICs are distinguished by the PC bus type and the network for which they are used. The following sections describe the role of NICs and how to evaluate them.

Compatibility

The first thing you need to determine is whether the NIC will fit the bus type of your PC. If you have more than one type of bus in your PC (for example, a combination PCI/PCI Express), use a NIC that fits into the fastest type (the PCI Express, in this case). This is especially important in servers because the NIC can quickly become a bottleneck if this guideline isn't followed.

More and more computers are using NICs that have USB interfaces. For the rare laptop computer that doesn't otherwise have a NIC built into it, these small portable cards are very handy.

A USB network card can also be handy for troubleshooting. If a laptop isn't connecting to the network properly with its built-in card, you may be able to use the USB NIC to see if it's an issue with the card or perhaps a software problem.

Network Interface Card Performance

The most important goal of the NIC is to optimize network performance and minimize the amount of time needed to transfer data packets across the network. The key is to ensure that you get the fastest card that you can for the type of network that you're on. For example, if your wireless network supports 802.11b/g/n, make sure to get an 802.11n card because it's the fastest.

Sending and Controlling Data

For two computers to send and receive data, the cards must agree on several things:

- The maximum size of the data frames
- The amount of data sent before giving confirmation
- The time needed between transmissions
- The amount of time to wait before sending confirmation
- The speed at which data transmits

If the cards can agree, the data is sent successfully. If the cards cannot agree, the data is not sent.

To send data on the network successfully, all NICs need to use the same media access method (such as CSMA/CD or token passing) and be connected to the same piece of cable. This usually isn't a problem because the vast majority of network cards sold today are Ethernet. If you were to try to use cards of different types (for example, one Ethernet and one token ring), neither of them would be able to communicate with the other unless you had a separate hardware device between them that could translate.

In addition, NICs can send data using either full-duplex or half-duplex mode. *Half-duplex communication* means that between the sender and receiver, only one of them can transmit at any one time. In *full-duplex communication*, a computer can send and receive data simultaneously. The main advantage of full-duplex over half-duplex communication is performance. NICs (specifically Fast Ethernet NICs) can operate twice as fast (200Mbps) in full-duplex mode as they do normally in half-duplex mode (100Mbps). In addition, collisions are avoided, which speeds up performance as well.

Normally you aren't going to have to worry about how your NIC sends or controls data. Just make sure to get the fastest NIC that is compatible with your network. Do know that the negotiations discussed here are happening in the background, though.

NIC Configuration

Each card must have a unique hardware address, called a *MAC address*. If two NICs on the same network have the same hardware address, neither one will be able to communicate. For this reason, the IEEE has established a standard for hardware addresses and assigns blocks of these addresses to NIC manufacturers, who then hard-wire the addresses into the cards.

Although it is possible for NIC manufacturers to produce multiple NICs with the same MAC address, it happens very rarely. If you do encounter this type of problem, contact the hardware manufacturer.

NIC Drivers

For the computer to use the NIC, it is very important to install the proper device drivers. These drivers are pieces of software that communicate directly with the operating system, specifically the network redirector and adapter interface. Drivers are specific to each NIC and operating system, and they operate in the Media Access Control sublayer of the Data Link layer of the OSI model.

Cables and Connectors

When the data is passing through the OSI model and reaches the Physical layer, it must find its way onto the medium that is used to transfer data physically from computer to computer. This medium is called the *cable* (or in the case of wireless networks, the air). It is the NIC's role to prepare the data for transmission, but it is the cable's role to move the data properly to its intended destination. There are three main types of physical cabling to discuss: coaxial cable, twisted-pair cable, and fiber-optic cable. (Wireless communications will be covered in Chapter 8, "Installing Wireless and SOHO Networks.") The three cabling types will be discussed in the following sections.

Coaxial

Coaxial cable (or coax) contains a center conductor core made of copper, which is surrounded by a plastic jacket with a braided shield over it (as shown in Figure 6.12). Either Teflon or a plastic coating covers this metal shield.

FIGURE 6.12   Coaxial cable

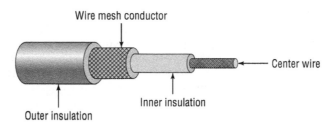

Wire mesh conductor

Center wire

Inner insulation

Outer insulation

Common network cables are covered with a plastic called *polyvinyl chloride (PVC)*. While PVC is flexible, fairly durable, and inexpensive, it has a nasty side effect in that it produces poisonous gas when burned. An alternative is a Teflon-type covering that is frequently referred to as a *plenum-rated* coating. That simply means that the coating does not produce toxic gas when burned and is rated for use in ventilation plenums that carry breathable air. This type of cable is more expensive, but it may be mandated by electrical code whenever cable is hidden in walls or ceilings.

Plenum rating can apply to all types of network cabling.

Coax Cable Specifications

Coaxial cable is available in various specifications that are rated according to the Radio Guide (RG) system, which was originally developed by the US military. The thicker the copper, the farther a signal can travel—and with that comes a higher cost and a less-flexible cable.

When coax cable was popular for networking, there were two standards that had fairly high use: RG-8 (thicknet) and RG-58A/U (thinnet). Thicknet had a maximum segment distance of 500 meters and was used primarily for network backbones. Thinnet was more often used in a conventional physical bus. A thinnet segment could span 185 meters. Both thicknet and thinnet had impedance of 50 ohms. Table 6.2 shows the different types of RG cabling and their uses.

TABLE 6.2 Coax RG types

RG #	Popular Name	Ethernet Implementation	Type of Cable
RG-6	Satellite/cable TV, cable modems	N/A	Solid copper
RG-8	Thicknet	10Base5	Solid copper
RG-58 U	N/A	None	Solid copper
RG-58 A/U	Thinnet	10Base2	Stranded copper
RG-59	Cable television	N/A	Solid copper

Explaining Ethernet Naming Standards

In Table 6.2, you will notice two terms that might be new to you: *10Base5* and *10Base2*. These are Ethernet naming standards. The number at the beginning tells you the maximum speed that the standard supports, which is 10Mbps in this case. The word *Base* refers to the type of transmission, either baseband (one signal at a time per cable) or broadband (multiple signals at the same time on one cable). Legend has it that the 5 and the 2 refer to the approximate maximum transmission distance (in hundreds of meters) for each specification. Later in the chapter, you will see *10BaseT*, which refers to twisted-pair cabling.

Coaxial networking has all but gone the way of the dinosaur. The only two coaxial cable types used today are RG-6 and RG-59. Of the two, RG-6 has a thicker core (1.0mm), can run longer distances (up to 304 meters, or 1000 feet), and support digital signals. RG-59 (0.762mm core) is considered adequate for analog cable TV but not digital and has a maximum distance of about 228 meters (750 feet). The maximum speed for each depends on the quality of the cable and the standard on which it's being used. Both have impedance of 75 ohms.

Coax Connector Types

Thicknet was a bear to use. Not only was it highly inflexible, but you also needed to use a connector called a *vampire tap*. A vampire tap is so named because a metal tooth sinks into the cable, thus making the connection with the inner conductor. The tap is connected to an external transceiver that in turn has a 15-pin AUI connector (also called *DIX* or *DB15* connector) to which you attach a cable that connects to the station. The transceiver is shown in Figure 6.13. On the right side, you will see the thicknet cable running through the portion of the unit that contains the vampire tap. DIX got its name from the companies that worked on this format—Digital, Intel, and Xerox.

FIGURE 6.13   Thicknet transceiver and cable inside a vampire tap

Thicknet transceiver licensed Under CC By-Sa 2.5 via Wikimedia Commons.
http://commons.wikimedia.org/wiki/File:ThicknetTransceiver.jpg#/media/
File:ThicknetTransceiver.jpg

Thinnet coax was much easier to use. Generally, thinnet cables used a *BNC connector* (see Figure 6.14) to attach to a T-shaped connector that attached to the workstation. The other side of the T-connector would either continue on with another thinnet segment or be capped off with a terminator. It is beyond the scope of this book to settle the long-standing argument over the meaning of the abbreviation

BNC. We have heard Bayonet Connector, Bayonet Nut Connector, and British Naval Connector—among others. What is relevant is that the BNC connector locks securely with a quarter-twist motion.

FIGURE 6.14   Male and female BNC connectors, T-connector, and terminator

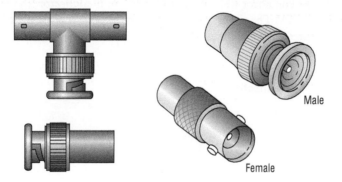

Male

Female

Another type of connector that you will see in use with coax is a *splitter*. As its name implies, a splitter takes a single signal (say that three times fast) and splits it into multiple replicas of the same signal. You might use this for cable TV—one line may run into your house, but the signal ultimately needs to get split for three televisions. This type of configuration will work for cable TV or cable Internet. Figure 6.15 shows a one-to-two coax splitter. You can also buy splitters that split one input into three or more outputs.

FIGURE 6.15   A coax splitter

Keep in mind that a coax signal is designed to go from one sender to one receiver, so splitting it can cause some issues. Splitting the signal causes it to weaken, meaning that signal quality could be lower, and it might not travel the same distance as a non-split signal. To avoid problems, don't over-split the cable, and purchase a good quality or amplified splitter.

The last type of coax connector we will cover is called an *F-connector* (shown in Figure 6.16), and it is used with cable TV. The exposed end of the copper cable is pushed into the receptacle, and the connector is threaded so that it can screw into place.

FIGURE 6.16   An F-connector

Twisted Pair

Twisted pair is the most popular type of cabling to use because of its flexibility and low cost. It consists of several pairs of wire twisted around each other within an insulated jacket, as shown in Figure 6.17.

FIGURE 6.17   Unshielded twisted-pair cable

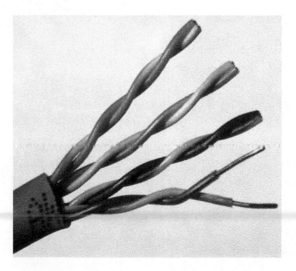

There are two different types of twisted-pair: *shielded twisted-pair (STP)* and *unshielded twisted-pair (UTP)*. Both types of cable have two or four pairs of twisted wires going through them. The difference is that STP has an extra layer of braided foil shielding surrounding the wires to decrease electrical interference, as shown in Figure 6.18. (In Figure 6.18, the individual wire pairs are shielded as well.) UTP has a PVC or plenum coating but no outer foil shield to protect it from interference.

FIGURE 6.18   Shielded twisted-pair cable

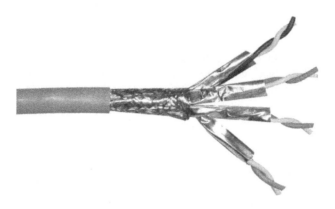

 You will often hear people refer to UTP cables as Ethernet cables. As you learned earlier in this chapter, Ethernet is an access method based on the IEEE 802.3 standard and not related to a specific cable type. So while technically it's incorrect, there's no harm in using the term to refer to the cable.

Twisted-Pair Cable Specifications

There aren't any STP standards that you really need to know about, either for the test or real-life situations. UTP is a different animal. It comes in several grades to offer different levels of performance and protection against electrical interference:

- Category 1 contains two twisted pairs. It is for voice-only transmissions, and it is in many legacy phone systems today.
- Category 2 is the lowest-grade cable that can have four pairs of wires. (Every other CAT rating since CAT-2 has four pairs.) It can handle data transmission at speeds up to 4Mbps.
- Category 3 is able to transmit data at speeds up to 10Mbps. It was popular for 10BaseT installations before CAT-5 came out.
- Category 4 is able to transmit data at speeds up to 16Mbps.

- Category 5 is able to transmit data at speeds up to 100Mbps.

- Category 5e is able to transmit data at speeds up to 1Gbps. The enhancement over CAT-5 is that the four twisted pairs of copper wire are physically separated and contain more twists per foot. This provides maximum interference protection.

- Category 6 is able to transmit data at speeds up to 10Gbps, but only up to a distance of 55 meters. Its four twisted pairs of copper wire are oriented differently than in CAT-5e. This is the lowest grade of cable you should ever use as a backbone to connect different parts of a network together, such as those on different floors of a building.

- Category 6a can also handle 10Gbps speed, but at longer distances (up to 100 meters) than CAT-6 can.

- Category 7 is an incremental upgrade over CAT-6e. Its most notable feature is that every wire pair is shielded, which provides better resistance to crosstalk and external noise. It can handle 10Gbps at up to 100 meters. You might hear it also called Class F cabling.

CompTIA (and many others) usually shortens the word *category* to CAT and use the form CAT-5 to refer to Category 5, for example. This is a common way to refer to these categories, and you can feel free to use these terms interchangeably. If you are buying cable today, you shouldn't buy anything older than CAT-5e.

Before the CAT-6a standard was finalized, several cable vendors started selling CAT-6e cable. Much like CAT-5e was an enhanced version of CAT-5, CAT-6e was supposed to be an enhanced version of CAT-6. The thing is, there was never an official CAT-6e specification officially established—if you buy CAT-6e, there is no guarantee of the type of performance that you will get. The official standard is CAT-6a.

The standard maximum transmission distance for UTP is 100 meters (328 feet). Do note, however, that if you want to run 10GBaseT over CAT-6, you won't get that much distance—about 55 meters under ideal conditions.

Twisted-Pair Connector Types

Twisted-pair cabling uses a connector type called an *RJ (registered jack)* connector. You are probably familiar with RJ connectors. Most landline phones connect with an RJ-11 connector. The connector used with UTP cable is called RJ-45. The RJ-11 has room for two pairs (four wires), and the RJ-45 has room for four pairs (eight wires).

In almost every case, UTP uses RJ connectors; a crimper is used to attach an RJ connector to a cable. Higher-quality crimping tools have interchangeable dies for both types of connectors. (Crimpers are discussed in Chapter 12, "Hardware and Network Troubleshooting.") Figure 6.19 shows an RJ-11 and an RJ-45 connector.

FIGURE 6.19   RJ-11 and RJ-45 connectors

You will also find RJ-45 splitters (often called Ethernet splitters) in the marketplace. The idea is similar to a coax splitter, but functionally they are very different. Coax signals are carried over one wire, while twisted pair uses either two pairs of wires (for 100Mbps or slower connections) or all four pairs of wires (for Gigabit Ethernet and faster). An Ethernet splitter will take the incoming signal on two pairs and then split it, so on the output end it produces two sets of signals using two pairs each. Because of this, Ethernet splitters are limited to 100Mbps connections.

It is not recommended that you use Ethernet splitters on a network. If you need to connect multiple computers together using UTP, use a hub or a switch. We talk about both of these devices later in this chapter.

Wiring Standards

Twisted-pair cables are unique in today's network environment in that they use multiple physical wires. Those eight wires need to be in the right places in the RJ-45 connector or it's very likely that the cable will not work properly. To ensure consistency in the industry, two standards have been developed: 568A and 568B.

Older implementations using UTP used only two pairs of wires, and those two pairs were matched to pins 1, 2, 3, and 6 in the connector. Newer applications such as Voice over IP and Gigabit Ethernet use all four pairs of wires, so you need to make sure that they're all where they're supposed to be.

If you're creating a regular network *patch cable* to connect a computer to a hub or switch, both sides need to have the same pinout. For that, follow either the 568A standard shown in Figure 6.20 or the 568B standard shown in Figure 6.21. Although there are no differences in terms of how the standards perform, some companies prefer one over the other.

FIGURE 6.20   568A standard

Pin	Pair	Wire	Color
1	3	1	white/green
2	3	2	green
3	2	1	white/orange
4	1	2	blue
5	1	1	white/blue
6	2	2	orange
7	4	1	white/brown
8	4	2	brown

If you are going to create a cable to connect a computer to another computer directly, or you're going to make a connection from hub to hub, switch to switch, hub to switch, or a computer directly to a router, you need what's called a *crossover cable*. In a crossover cable, pin 1 to pin 3 and pin 2 to pin 6 are crossed on *one side of the cable only.* This is to get the "send" pins matched up with the "receive" pins on the other side, and vice versa. For easier visualization, look at Figure 6.21.

FIGURE 6.21   568B standard

Pin	Pair	Wire	Color
1	2	1	white/orange
2	2	2	orange
3	3	1	white/green
4	1	2	blue
5	1	1	white/blue
6	3	2	green
7	4	1	white/brown
8	4	2	brown

The key thing to remember is that a patch (straight-through) cable is the same on both ends. A crossover cable is different on each end. You should know the order of the colors for both standards.

Fiber-Optic

Fiber-optic cabling has been called one of the best advances in cabling. It consists of a thin, flexible glass or plastic fiber surrounded by a rubberized outer coating (see Figure 6.22). It provides transmission speeds from 100Mbps to 10Gbps and a maximum distance of several miles. Because it uses pulses of light instead of electric voltages to transmit data, it is immune to electrical interference and to wiretapping.

FIGURE 6.22 Fiber-optic cable

Optical fiber cable by Buy_on_turbosquid_optical.jpg: Cable master derivative work: Srleffler (talk) - Buy_on_turbosquid_optical.jpg
http://commons.wikimedia.org/wiki/File:Optical_fiber_cable.jpg#/media/File:Optical_fiber_cable.jpg

Fiber-optic cable is still not as popular as UTP for local area networks, however, because of its high cost of installation. Fiber-optic cabling is often used in networks that need extremely fast transmission rates or transmissions over long distances or in networks that have had problems with electrical interference in the past.

Fiber-Optic Cable Specifications

Fiber-optic cable comes in two varieties: single-mode or multimode. The term *mode* refers to the bundles of light that enter the fiber-optic cable. *Single-mode fiber (SMF)* cable uses only a single mode of light to propagate through the fiber cable, whereas *multimode fiber* allows multiple modes (paths) of light to propagate simultaneously. In multimode fiber-optic cable, the light bounces off the cable walls as it travels through the cable, which causes the signal to weaken more quickly.

Multimode fiber is most often used as horizontal cable. It permits multiple modes of light to propagate through the cable, which shortens cable distances but delivers more available bandwidth. Devices that use MMF cable typically use light-emitting diodes (LEDs) to generate the light that travels through the cable; however, lasers with multimode fiber-optic cable are now being used in higher-bandwidth network devices such as Gigabit Ethernet. MMF can transmit up to 10Gbps for up to 550 meters (1,804 feet, or just over one-third of a mile), depending on the standard used.

Single-mode fiber cable is commonly used as backbone cabling. It is also usually the cable type used in phone systems. Light travels through single-mode fiber-optic cable using only a single mode, meaning that it travels straight down the fiber and does not bounce off the cable walls. Because only a single mode of light travels through the cable, single-mode fiber-optic cable supports lower bandwidth at longer distances than does multimode fiber-optic cable. Devices that use single-mode fiber-optic cable typically use lasers to generate the light that travels through the cable. SMF can transmit up to 10Gbps for up to 40 kilometers (25.85 miles), depending on the standard used.

We have talked about several different types of cables, and it's possible that you will be asked to know maximum distances and transmission speeds on the A+ exam. Table 6.3 summarizes the most common cable types, the specifications with which they are used, and their characteristics.

TABLE 6.3   Common cable types and characteristics

Cable type	Ethernet Specification	Maximum Speed	Maximum Distance	Notes
RG-6 coax	*	*	304 meters	Digital cable/satellite television.
RG-8 coax	10Base5	10Mbps	500 meters	Thicknet.
RG-58 coax	10Base2	10Mbps	185 meters	Thinnet.
RG-59 coax	*	*	228 meters	Analog cable TV.
CAT-3 UTP	10BaseT	10Mbps	100 meters	
CAT-5 UTP or STP	100BaseT	100Mbps	100 meters	100Mbps and less use two pairs of wires.
CAT-5e UTP	1000BaseT	1Gbps	100 meters	1Gbps and higher use four pairs of wires.
CAT-6 UTP	10GBaseT	10Gbps	55 meters	Can support 1Gbps up to 100 meters.
CAT-6a UTP	10GBaseT	10Gbps	100 meters	
CAT-7 UTP	10GBaseT	10Gbps	100 meters	Every wire pair is individually shielded.
MMF Fiber	1000BaseLX or 1000BaseSX	1Gbps	550 meters	For fiber, maximum length depends on fiber size and quality.
MMF Fiber	10GBaseSR or 10GBase SW	10Gbps	300 meters	
SMF Fiber	10GBaseER or 10GBase EW	10Gbps	40 kilometers	

*RG-6 and RG-59 coax cables can be used with many different specifications, and the maximum speed depends on cable quality and specification.

Fiber-Optic Connector Type

There are literally dozens of fiber-optic connectors out there because it seemed that every producer wanted its proprietary design to become "the standard." Three of the most commonly used ones are ST, SC, and LC.

The *straight tip (ST)* fiber-optic connector, developed by AT&T, is probably the most widely used fiber-optic connector. It uses a BNC attachment mechanism that makes connections and disconnections fairly easy. The ease of use of the ST is one of the attributes that make this connector so popular. Figure 6.23 shows an ST connector.

FIGURE 6.23 ST connectors

The *subscriber connector (SC)*, also sometimes known as a *square connector*, is shown in Figure 6.24. SCs are latched connectors, making it virtually impossible for you to pull out the connector without releasing its latch, usually by pressing a button or release. SCs work with either single-mode or multimode optical fibers. They aren't as popular as ST connectors for LAN connections.

FIGURE 6.24 A sample SC

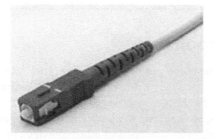

The last type of connector with which you need to be familiar is the *local connector (LC)*, which was developed by Lucent Technologies. It is a mini form factor (MFF) connector, especially popular for use with Fibre-Channel adapters, fast storage area networks, and Gigabit Ethernet adapters (see Figure 6.25).

FIGURE 6.25   LC fiber connector

The prices of network cables differ dramatically between copper and fiber cables. Exercise 6.1 asks you to investigate the difference for yourself.

EXERCISE 6.1

Pricing Network Cables

1.   Visit a major electronics retailer website (such as www.frys.com or an online retailer of your choice).

2.   Search for a CAT-6a patch cable. Price the difference between a 7-foot, 25-foot, and 50-foot cable.

3.   Search for the same lengths of CAT-7 patch cables. Note the price difference. (At the time of writing, they were about twice as expensive as CAT-6a cables.)

4.   Search for fiber-optic cables. Notice, first, that most of them are much shorter in length than commercially available UTP cables. What is the price difference? Do you notice price differences between fiber cables with different types of connectors?

Networking Components

Network cabling can link one computer to another, but most networks are far grander in scale than two simple machines. There are a variety of networking devices that provide connectivity to the network, make the network bigger, and offer auxiliary services to end users.

In the following sections, we're going to classify additional networking components into two broad categories: connectivity devices and auxiliary devices.

Connectivity Devices

We all know that if you want to be part of a computer network, you need to attach to that network somehow. Using network cables is one way to accomplish this, but not everyone is in a position to just plug a cable in and go. In addition, if you want to grow your network beyond a few simple connections, you need to use a special class of networking devices known as *connectivity devices*. These devices allow communications to break the boundaries of local networks and really provide the backbone for nearly all computer networks, regardless of size.

There are several categories of connectivity devices. These connectivity devices make it possible for users to connect to networks and to lengthen networks to almost unlimited distances. We will now discuss the most important and frequently used connectivity devices.

Modems

If you want to connect to a network or the Internet using plain old phone lines and a dial-up connection, a *modem* is the device you'll need. Modems got their name because they modulate and demodulate (mo-dem) digital signals that computers use into analog signals that can be passed over telephone lines. In the early to mid-1990s, modems were practically the only device available to get onto the Internet. Many companies also used them to allow users who were not in the office to dial into the local network.

While modems did provide flexibility, of course you needed to be near a phone line, and speed was an issue. The fastest modems transferred data at 56Kbps. At the time that felt lightning quick, but fortunately our species has moved well beyond that technology. It's horrifically slow by today's standards and therefore rarely used.

Access Points

Technically speaking, an access point is any point that allows a user on to a network. The term is commonly used in reference to a *wireless access point*, which lets users connect to your network via an 802.11 technology. We'll get deeper into wireless access points and how to configure them in Chapter 8.

Repeaters and Extenders

A *repeater*, or *extender*, is a small, powered device that receives a signal, amplifies it, and sends it on its way. The whole purpose of a repeater is to extend the functional distance of a cable run. For example, you know that UTP is limited to 100 meters, but what if you need to make a cable run that is 160 meters long? (One answer could be to use fiber, but pretend that's not an option!) You could run two lengths of cable with a repeater in the center and it would work. Repeaters and extenders work at the Physical layer (Layer 1) of the OSI model.

Hubs

A *hub* is a device used to link several computers together. Hubs are very simple devices that possess no real intelligence. They simply repeat any signal that comes in on one port and copy it to the other ports (a process that is also called *broadcasting*). You'll sometimes hear them referred to as multiport repeaters. They work at Layer 1 of the OSI model just as repeaters do.

There are two types of hubs: active and passive. *Passive hubs* connect all ports together electrically but do not have their own power source. *Active hubs* use electronics to amplify and clean up the signal before it is broadcast to the other ports. Active hubs can therefore be used to extend the length of a network, whereas passive hubs cannot.

Patch Panels

A *patch panel* is essentially a large hub that is rack mounted. It houses multiple cable connections but possesses no network intelligence. Its sole purpose is to connect cables together. Short patch cables are used to plug into the front-panel connectors, and there are longer, more permanent cables on the back side. Figure 6.26 shows three rack-mounted devices. The top one is a 24-port patch panel. Underneath that is a 24-port switch, and then a Dell server is shown.

FIGURE 6.26   A patch panel, switch, and server

Bridges

Bridges operate in the Data Link layer (Layer 2) of the OSI model. They join similar topologies, and they are used to divide network segments into multiple collision domains. Bridges isolate network traffic, preventing unwanted traffic from entering a segment when there are no recipients on that segment.

For example, with 100 people on one Ethernet segment, performance will be mediocre because of the design of Ethernet and the number of workstations that are fighting to transmit. If you use a bridge to divide the segment into two segments of 50 workstations each, the traffic will be much lower on either side and performance will improve.

Bridges are not able to distinguish one protocol from another because higher levels of the OSI model are not available to them. If a bridge is aware of the destination MAC address, it can forward packets to the correct segment; otherwise, it forwards the packets to all segments.

Because bridges work at the Data Link layer, they are aware of only hard-ware (MAC) addresses. They are not aware of and do not deal with IP addresses.

Bridges are more intelligent than repeaters, but they are unable to move data across multiple networks simultaneously.

The main disadvantage of bridges is that they forward broadcast packets. Broadcasts are addressed to all computers, so the bridge just does its job and forwards the packets. Bridges also cannot perform intelligent path selection, meaning that the path from the sender to the destination will always be the same regardless of network conditions. To stop broadcasts or perform intelligent path selection, you need a router.

Switches

Switches work at Layer 2 as do bridges, and they provide centralized connectivity just like hubs. They often look similar to hubs, so it's easy to confuse them. There are big performance differences, though. Hubs pass along all traffic, but switches examine the Layer 2 header of the incoming packet and forward it properly to the right port and only that port. This greatly reduces overhead and thus improves performance because there is essentially a virtual connection between sender and receiver. The only downside is that switches forward broadcasts because they are addressed to everyone.

If it helps you to remember their functions, a hub is essentially a multiport repeater, whereas a switch functions like a multiport bridge and, in some cases, a multiport router.

Nearly every hub or switch that you will see has one or more status indicator lights on it. If there is a connection to a port of the switch, a light either above the connector or on an LED panel elsewhere on the device will light up. If traffic is crossing the port, the light may flash, or there may be a secondary light that will light up. Many devices can also detect a problem in the connection. If a normal connection produces a green light, a bad connection might produce an amber one.

Routers

Routers are highly intelligent devices that connect multiple network types and determine the best path for sending data. They can route packets across multiple networks and use *routing tables* to store network addresses to determine the best destination. Routers operate at the Network layer (Layer 3) of the OSI model. Because of this, they make their decisions on what to do with traffic based on logical addresses, such as an IP address.

Routers have a few key functions:

- They connect multiple networks to each other, which none of the other devices we have discussed do.

- Routers do not forward broadcasts. (Switches and bridges break up collision domains, whereas routers break up broadcast domains.)

- Routers are normally used to connect one LAN to another. Typically, when a WAN is set up, at least two routers are used.

In the last few years, wireless routers have become all the rage for small business and home networks. They possess all of the functionality of routers historically associated with networking, but they are relatively inexpensive. We'll talk more about these routers in Chapter 8.

Auxiliary Devices

The devices we just talked about are specialized to provide connectivity. This next group of devices adds in features outside of connectivity that can help network users, specifically by protecting them from malicious attacks, providing network connections over power lines, and providing power over Ethernet cables.

A *firewall* is a hardware or software solution that serves as your network's security guard. They're probably the most important device on networks that are connected to the Internet. Firewalls can protect you in two ways: they protect your network resources from hackers lurking in the dark corners of the Internet, and they can simultaneously prevent computers on your network from accessing undesirable content on the Internet. At a basic level, firewalls filter packets based on rules defined by the network administrator.

Firewalls can be stand-alone "black boxes," software installed on a server or router, or some combination of hardware and software. Most firewalls will have at least two network connections: one to the Internet, or *public side*, and one to the internal network, or *private side*. Some firewalls have a third network port for a second semi-internal network. This port is used to connect servers that can be considered both public and private, such as web and email servers. This intermediary network is known as a *demilitarized zone (DMZ)*.

Firewalls can be network based in that they protect a group of computers (or an entire network), or they can be host based. A host-based firewall (such as Windows Firewall) protects only the individual computer on which it's installed.

A firewall is configured to allow only packets that pass specific security restrictions to get through. By default, most firewalls are configured as *default deny*, which means that all traffic is blocked unless specifically authorized by the administrator. The basic method of configuring firewalls is to use an *access control list (ACL)*. The ACL is the set of rules that determines which traffic gets through the firewall and which traffic is blocked. ACLs are typically configured to block traffic by IP address, port number, domain name, or some combination of all three.

Ethernet over Power

Occasionally, you will find yourself in a spot where it's not possible to run cables for a network connection and wireless is a problem as well. For example, perhaps you are installing a device that only has a wired RJ-45 port but you can't get a cable to it. *Ethernet over power* can help make that connection by using electrical outlets; an adapter is shown in Figure 6.27.

FIGURE 6.27   Ethernet over power adapter

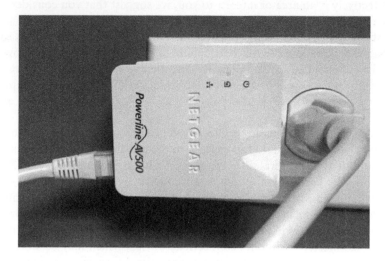

For Ethernet over power to work, both devices must be on the same electrical circuit, such as would be the case for a house or a small building. To connect the devices, plug both in and then press a button on the side of each device. They will search the electrical circuit for the signal from the other and negotiate the connection. As you can see in Figure 6.27, an Ethernet cable also connects to the device. You can plug that cable into a device directly or into a connectivity device such as a hub or a switch.

Power over Ethernet

If you can run an Ethernet signal over power lines, why can't you run electricity over network cables? As it turns out, you can with *Power over Ethernet (PoE)*. This technology is extremely useful in situations where you need a wireless access point in a relatively remote location that does not have any power outlets. For it to work, the access point and the device it plugs into (such as a switch) both need to support PoE. In a configuration such as this, the switch would be considered an *endspan* PoE device, because it's at the end of the network connection. If the switch in question doesn't support PoE, you can get a device that sits between the switch and the access point (called a *midspan* device) whose sole purpose is to supply power via the Ethernet connection. Appropriately, these midspan devices are called *Power over Ethernet injectors*.

Summary

In this chapter, we covered a broad variety of networking topics. This chapter contains everything that you need to get you ready for the networking questions on the A+ 220-901 exam. At the same time, the A+ exam (and consequently this chapter) barely scratches the surface of the things that you can learn about networking. If making computers talk to each other effectively is an area of interest to you, we suggest that you consider studying for the CompTIA Network+ exam after you pass your A+ tests.

First, we started with networking fundamentals. Much of the discussion of fundamentals was about understanding the concepts behind networking so that you know how to set them up. Topics included LANs versus WANs; clients, servers, and resources; network operating systems; peer-to-peer and server-based resource models; network topologies such as bus, star, and ring; and theoretical networking models and standards, such as the OSI model and IEEE standards.

Next, you learned about hardware devices used in networking. Each computer needs a network adapter (NIC) of some sort to connect to the network. On a wired network, cables are required, and there are several different types, including coaxial, STP, UTP, and fiber-optic. Each cable type has its own specific connector.

Finally, we discussed various types of network connectivity hardware and auxiliary devices and their use. Some users may need a modem or access point to get onto your network. All wired computers will plug into a connectivity device such as a hub or a switch, which in turn is connected to another connectivity device, which may be a bridge or a router. Other devices on your network, such as firewalls, Ethernet over power, and PoE injectors provide additional services.

Exam Essentials

Know the difference between workgroups and domains.   A workgroup is often referred to as a peer-to-peer network, and there is no centralized administration. A domain is a server-based network; the server (often called a domain controller) manages user accounts and security for the network. Workgroups are best suited for networks with 10 or fewer computers and low security requirements.

Know the difference between a LAN, a WAN, a PAN, and a MAN.   A LAN is a local area network, which typically means a network in one centralized location. A WAN is a wide area network, which means several LANs in remote locations connected to each other.

A PAN is a small Bluetooth network. A network that spans an area such as a city or a campus is a MAN.

Understand the difference between a patch (straight-through) cable and a crossover cable.   Patch cables are used to connect hosts to a switch or a hub. Crossover cables switch pins 1 and 3 and 2 and 6 on one end. They are used to connect hubs to hubs, switches to switches, hosts to hosts, and hosts to routers.

Know what hubs, switches, and routers are.   These are all network connectivity devices. Hubs and switches are used to connect several computers or groups of computers to each other. Routers are more complex devices that are often used to connect network segments or networks to each other.

Know what types of cables are used in networking and the connectors for each.   Common network cables include coaxial, STP, UTP (Category 5/5e, Category 6/6a, and Category 7), and fiber-optic. Coax cables use BNC connectors, STP and UTP use RJ-45 connectors, and fiber-optic uses ST, SC, and LC connectors. (You may also be tested on phone connectors, which are called RJ-11.)

Understand network topologies.   Network topologies are bus, star, ring, mesh, and hybrid.

Review Questions

The answers to the chapter review questions can be found in Appendix A.

1. _____ is immune to electromagnetic or radio-frequency interference.

   A. Twisted-pair cabling

   B. CSMA/CD

   C. Broadband coaxial cabling

   D. Fiber-optic cabling

2. Which IEEE 802 standard defines a bus topology using coaxial baseband cable and is able to transmit at 10Mbps?

   A. 802.1

   B. 802.2

   C. 802.3

   D. 802.5

3. Which OSI layer signals "all clear" by making sure that the data segments are error free?

   A. Application layer

   B. Session layer

   C. Transport layer

   D. Network layer

4. _____ is the type of media access method used by NICs that listen to or sense the cable to check for traffic and send only when they hear that no one else is transmitting.

   A. Token passing

   B. CSMA/CD

   C. CSMA/CA

   D. Demand priority

5. What model is used to provide a common way to describe network protocols?

   A. OSI

   B. ISO

   C. IEEE

   D. CSMA/CD

6. A physical star topology consists of several workstations that branch off a central device called a(n) _____ .

   A. NIC

   B. Bridge

    C. Router

    D. Hub

7. Of all the network cabling options, _____ offers the longest possible segment length.

    A. Unshielded twisted-pair

    B. Coaxial

    C. Fiber-optic

    D. Shielded twisted-pair

8. What devices transfer packets across multiple networks and use tables to store network addresses to determine the best destination?

    A. Routers

    B. Bridges

    C. Hubs

    D. Switches

9. In which network design do users access resources from other workstations rather than from a central location?

    A. Client-server

    B. Star

    C. Ring

    D. Peer-to-peer

10. Which of the following wireless communication standards is often described in terms of a wireless personal area network?

    A. Bluetooth

    B. Infrared

    C. Cellular

    D. Ethernet

11. Which of the following statements are *not* associated with a star network? (Choose all that apply.)

    A. A single cable break can cause complete network disruption.

    B. All devices connect to a central device.

    C. It uses a single backbone computer to connect all network devices.

    D. It uses a dual-ring configuration.

12. If you are going to run a network cable in the space above the drop ceiling in your office, which type of cable should you use?

    A. Plenum

    B. PVC

    C. Coaxial

    D. Fiber-optic

13. Which of the following connector types is an MFF connector?

    A. BNC

    B. ST

    C. SC

    D. LC

14. What Ethernet specification would you be running if you needed to make a connection of 10Gbps over a distance of five kilometers?

    A. 10GBaseER

    B. 10GBaseT

    C. 10GBaseSR

    D. 10GBaseLR

15. You have been asked to configure a full mesh network with seven computers. How many connections will this require?

    A. 6

    B. 7

    C. 21

    D. 42

16. Which tool is used by technicians to connect an RJ-45 connector to the end of a cable?

    A. Punch-down tool

    B. Crimper

    C. Cable tester

    D. Loopback plug

17. What type of device will block unwanted traffic from your network using a set of rules called an ACL?

    A. Router

    B. Firewall

    C. Internet appliance

    D. NAS

18. What type of coaxial cable is recommended for digital television cable signals?

    A. RG-6

    B. RG-8

    C. RG-58

    D. RG-59

19. Which of the following devices work at Layer 2 of the OSI model? (Choose two.)

    A. Hub

    B. Router

    C. Bridge

    D. Switch

20. Transmitting at 10Gbps, how far can signals on an MMF cable travel?

    A. 100 meters

    B. 550 meters

    C. 1 kilometer

    D. 40 kilometers

Performance-Based Question

You will encounter performance-based questions on the A+ exams. The questions on the exam require you to perform a specific task, and you will be graded on whether or not you were able to complete the task. The following requires you to think creatively in order to measure how well you understand this chapter's topics. You may or may not see similar questions on the actual A+ exams. To see how your answer compares to the authors', refer to Appendix B.

Draw three examples of physical network topologies, and explain how each works.

Chapter

7

Introduction to TCP/IP

THE FOLLOWING COMPTIA A+ 220–901 EXAM OBJECTIVES ARE COVERED IN THIS CHAPTER:

✓ **2.3 Explain properties and characteristics of TCP/IP.**

- IPv4 vs. IPv6
- Public vs. private vs. APIPA/link local
- Static vs. dynamic
- Client-side DNS settings
- Client-side DHCP
- Subnet mask vs. CIDR
- Gateway

✓ **2.4 Explain common TCP and UDP ports, protocols, and their purpose.**

- Ports
  - 21—FTP
  - 22—SSH
  - 23—Telnet
  - 25—SMTP
  - 53—DNS
  - 80—HTTP
  - 110—POP3
  - 143—IMAP
  - 443—HTTPS
  - 3389—RDP
  - 137–139, 445—SMB
  - 548 or 427—AFP

- Protocols
  - DHCP
  - DNS
  - LDAP
  - SNMP
  - SMB
  - CIFS
  - SSH
  - AFP
- TCP vs. UDP

Networking protocols are a lot like human languages in that they are the language that computers speak when talking to each other. If computers don't speak the same language, they won't be able to talk. To complicate matters, there are dozens of different languages out there that computers can use. Just like humans, computers can understand and use multiple languages. Imagine that you are on the street and someone comes up to you and speaks in Spanish. If you know Spanish, you will likely reply in kind. It doesn't matter if both of you know English as well because you've already established that you can communicate. On the other hand, it's going to be a pretty quick conversation if you don't know Spanish. This same concept applies to computers that are trying to communicate. They must have a network protocol in common in order for the conversation to be successful.

Throughout the years, hundreds of network protocols have been developed. As the use of networking exploded, various companies developed their own networking hardware, software, and proprietary protocols. Some were incorporated as an integral part of the network operating system, such as Banyan VINES. One-time networking giant Novell had IPX/SPX. Microsoft developed NetBEUI. Apple created AppleTalk. Others included DECnet, SNA, and XNS. While a few achieved long-term success, most have faded into oblivion. The one protocol suite that has survived is TCP/IP. While it has some structural advantages such as its modularity, it didn't necessarily succeed because it was inherently superior to other protocols. It succeeded because it is the protocol of the Internet.

This chapter focuses on the TCP/IP protocol suite. It is the protocol suite used on the Internet, but it's also the protocol suite used by the vast majority of home and business networks today. We'll start by taking a quick look at the history of TCP/IP and the model on which it's based. Then we'll dive deeper into TCP/IP structure and the individual protocols it comprises. From there, we'll spend some time on IP addressing, including IPv4 and IPv6. Entire books have been written on TCP/IP—so there's no way we could cover it entirely in one chapter. Instead, we'll give you the foundation that you need to understand it well and work effectively with it in the field.

Understanding TCP/IP

As we mentioned in the introduction, computers use a protocol as a common language for communication. A *protocol* is a set of rules that govern communications, much like a language in human terms. Of the myriad protocols out there, the key ones to understand are the protocols in the TCP/IP suite, which is a collection of different protocols that work together to deliver connectivity. Consequently, they're the only ones listed on the A+ exam objectives. In the following sections, we'll start with a look at its overall structure and then move into key protocols within the suite.

TCP/IP Structure

The *Transmission Control Protocol/Internet Protocol (TCP/IP)* suite is the most popular network protocol in use today, thanks mostly to the rise of the Internet. While the protocol suite is named after two of its hardest-working protocols, *Transmission Control Protocol (TCP)* and *Internet Protocol (IP)*, TCP/IP actually contains dozens of protocols working together to help computers communicate with one another.

 TCP/IP is the protocol used on the Internet.

TCP/IP is robust and flexible. For example, if you want to ensure that the packets are delivered from one computer to another, TCP/IP can do that. If speed is more important than guaranteed delivery, then TCP/IP can ensure that too. The protocol can work on disparate operating systems such as UNIX, Mac OS X, Windows, iOS, and Android. It can also support a variety of programs, applications, and required network functions. Much of its flexibility comes from its modular nature.

You're familiar with the seven-layer OSI model that we discussed in Chapter 6, "Networking Fundamentals." Every protocol that's created needs to accomplish the tasks (or at least the key tasks) outlined in that model. The structure of TCP/IP is based on a similar model created by the United States Department of Defense; that is, the *Department of Defense (DOD) model*. The DOD model has four layers that map to the seven OSI layers, as shown in Figure 7.1.

FIGURE 7.1   The DOD and OSI models

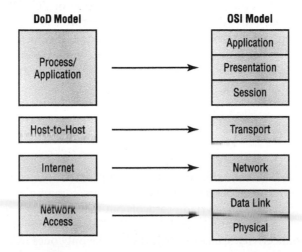

The overall functionality between these two models is virtually identical; the layers just have different names. For example, the Process/Application layer of the DOD model is designed to combine the functionality of the top three layers of the OSI model. Therefore, any protocol designed against the Process/Application layer would need to be able to perform all of the functions associated with the Application, Presentation, and Session layers in the OSI model.

TCP/IP's modular nature and common protocols are shown in Figure 7.2.

FIGURE 7.2   TCP/IP protocol suite

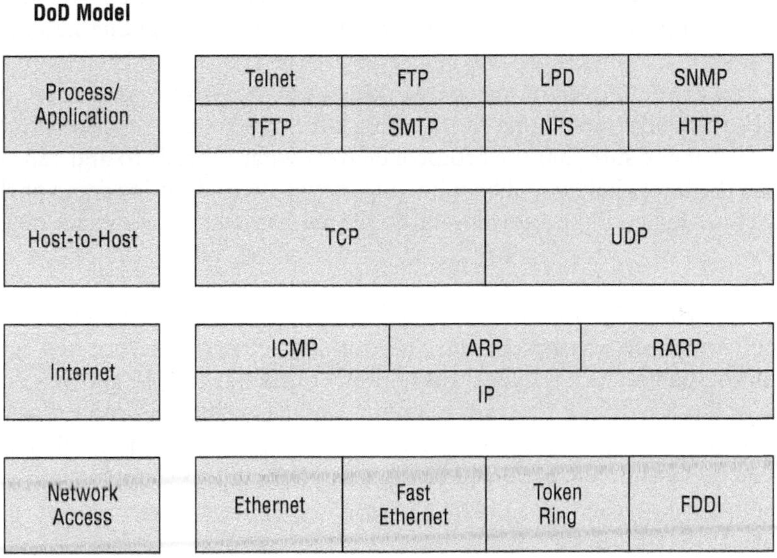

DoD Model

| Process/Application | Telnet | FTP | LPD | SNMP |
| | TFTP | SMTP | NFS | HTTP |

| Host-to-Host | TCP | | UDP | |

| Internet | ICMP | ARP | | RARP |
| | IP | | | |

| Network Access | Ethernet | Fast Ethernet | Token Ring | FDDI |

The majority of TCP/IP protocols are located at the Process/Application layer. These include some protocols with which you may already be familiar, such as *Hypertext Transfer Protocol (HTTP)*, *File Transfer Protocol (FTP)*, *Simple Mail Transfer Protocol (SMTP)*, *Post Office Protocol (POP)*, and others.

At the Host-to-Host layer, there are only two protocols: TCP and *User Datagram Protocol (UDP)*. Most applications will use one or the other to transmit data, although some can use both but will do so for different tasks.

The most important protocol at the Internet layer is IP. This is the backbone of TCP/IP. Other protocols at this layer work in conjunction with IP, such as *Internet Control Message Protocol (ICMP)* and *Address Resolution Protocol (ARP)*.

You'll notice that the Network Access layer doesn't have any protocols as such. This layer describes the type of network access method that you are using, such as Ethernet, Wi-Fi, or others.

Process/Application Layer Protocols

As we mentioned in the previous section, most of the protocols within the TCP/IP suite are at the Process/Application layer. This is the layer of differentiation and flexibility. For example, if you want to browse the Internet, the HTTP protocol is designed for that. FTP is optimized for file downloads, and Remote Desktop Protocol (RDP) allows you to connect to a remote computer and manage programs.

Before we get into the protocols themselves, let's take a quick look into a few key points on the TCP/IP suite's flexibility. There are literally dozens of protocols at the Process/Application layer, and they have been created over time as networking needs arose. Take HTTP, for example. The first official version was developed in 1991, nearly 20 years after TCP/IP was first implemented. Before this protocol was created, there weren't any effective client-server request-response protocols at this layer. HTTP let the client (web browser) ask the web server for a page, and the web server would return it. Going one step further, there was a need for secure transactions over HTTP, hence the creation of HTTPS in 1994. As new applications are developed or new networking needs are discovered, developers can build an application or protocol that fits into this layer to provide the needed functionality. They just need to make sure that the protocol delivers what it needs to and can communicate with the layers below it. The following sections will describe some of the more common Process/Application protocols—and the ones listed in the A+ exam objectives.

AFP

The *Apple Filing Protocol (AFP)* was developed in the 1980s for use with the AppleTalk network protocol. AppleTalk was a proprietary networking protocol developed by Apple for use on Macintosh computers. AFP is a file transfer protocol similar to FTP and Server Message Block (SMB). It was the default file transfer protocol on Mac OS until Apple changed to SMB2 in 2013. Converting to the industry-standard SMB protocol helped enhance interoperability between Macs and PCs. SMB will be discussed later in this chapter.

CIFS

Common Internet File System (CIFS) is a Microsoft-developed enhancement of the SMB protocol, which was also developed by Microsoft. The intent behind CIFS is that it can be used to share files and printers between computers, regardless of the operating system that they run. It's been the default file and print sharing protocol on Windows-based computers since Windows 2000.

DHCP

Dynamic Host Configuration Protocol (DHCP) dynamically assigns IP addresses and other IP configuration information to network clients. Configuring your network clients to receive their IP addresses from a DHCP server reduces network administration headaches. We'll cover the mechanics of how DHCP works later in this chapter when we talk about IP addressing.

DNS

You probably use *Domain Name System (DNS)* every day whether you realize it or not. Its purpose is to resolve hostnames to IP addresses. For example, let's say that you open your web browser and type in a Uniform Resource Locator (URL) such as http://www.sybex.com. Your computer needs to know the IP address of the server that hosts that website in order for you to connect to it. Through a DNS server, your computer resolves the URL to an IP address so communication can happen. DNS as a service is discussed in more detail later in this chapter.

FTP

The *File Transfer Protocol (FTP)* is optimized to do what it says it does—transfer files. This includes both uploading and downloading files from one host to another. FTP is both a protocol and an application. Specifically, FTP lets you copy files, list and manipulate directories, and view file contents. You can't use it to execute applications remotely.

Whenever a user attempts to access an FTP site, they will be asked to log in. If it's a public site, you can often just use the login name *anonymous* and then provide your email address as the password. Of course, there's no rule saying that you have to give your real email address if you don't want to. If the FTP site is secured, you will need a legitimate login name and password to access it. If you are using a browser such as Internet Explorer, Chrome, Firefox, or Edge to connect via FTP, the correct syntax in the address window is `ftp://username:password@ftp.ftpsite.com`.

In Windows XP and later, you can type a URL such as the one in the FTP example into the Run box to connect as well.

HTTP

The most commonly used Process/Application layer protocol is HTTP. It manages the communication between a web server and client and lets you connect to and view all of the content that you enjoy on the Internet. All of the information transmitted by HTTP is plain text, which means that it's not secure. Because of this, it's not a good choice for transmitting sensitive or personal information such as usernames and passwords or for transmitting banking information.

HTTPS

To encrypt traffic between a web server and client securely, *Hypertext Transfer Protocol Secure (HTTPS)* can be used. HTTPS connections are secured using either *Secure Sockets Layer (SSL)* or *Transport Layer Security (TLS)*.

From the client side, the most common issue that you will encounter when HTTPS is in use on a website is that users may not know the proper context. To access most websites, you use `http://` in the address bar. To get to a site using HTTPS, you need to use `https://` instead.

 Real World Scenario

How Secure Is It?

You have probably heard before that you should not enter personal information (such as a credit card number) into an unsecure website. But what does that really mean?

First, know what to look for. If you are entering information into a website form and the address of the site begins with just `http://`, you're just asking for someone to steal the information! The HTTP protocol transmits data in plain text, meaning that there is no encryption at all between your computer and the server. On the other hand, HTTPS encrypts the data transmissions as they cross the wire.

---

continues

continued

> To use HTTPS, the website needs to obtain an SSL certificate from a reputable certificate authority which verifies the identity of the website. So the good news is that if you are accessing a site with https:// in the header, you know that the site is what it says it is (and not a Trojan horse) and that transmissions between your computer and that site are encrypted. Once the data is on the website's server though, HTTPS is no longer relevant and other protection methods are needed to keep your data secure.

Occasionally, you might visit a website that uses HTTPS and get a pop-up error message saying that the certificate has expired or could not be validated. This is most likely a case of the certificate legitimately expiring, but it could be that it's a Trojan horse website. Proceed with caution!

IMAP

Internet Message Access Protocol (IMAP) is a secure protocol designed to download email. Its current version is version 4, or IMAP4. It's the client-side email management protocol of choice, having replaced the unsecure POP3. Most current email clients, such as Microsoft Outlook and Gmail, are configured to be able to use either IMAP4 or POP3.

IMAP4 has some definite advantages over POP3. First, IMAP4 works in connected and disconnected modes. With POP3, the client makes a connection to the email server, downloads the email, and then terminates the connection. IMAP4 allows the client to remain connected to the email server after the download, meaning that as soon as another email enters the inbox, IMAP4 notifies the email client, which can then download it. Second, it also lets you store the email on the server, as opposed to POP3, which requires you to download it. Third, IMAP4 allows multiple clients to be simultaneously connected to the same inbox. This can be useful for smartphone users who have both Outlook on their workstation and their smartphone email client operational at the same time or for cases where multiple users monitor the same mailbox, such as on a customer service account. IMAP4 allows each connected user or client to see changes made to messages on the server in real time.

LDAP

The *Lightweight Directory Access Protocol (LDAP)* is a directory services protocol based on the X.500 standard. LDAP is designed to access information stored in an information directory typically known as an LDAP directory or LDAP database.

On your network, you probably have a lot of information such as employee phone books and email addresses, client contact lists, and infrastructure and configuration data for the network and network applications. This information might not get updated frequently, but you might need to access it from anywhere on the network, or you might have a network application that needs access to this data. LDAP provides you with the access, regardless of the client platform from which you're working. You can also use access control lists (ACLs) to set up who can read and change entries in the database using LDAP. A common analogy is that LDAP provides access to and the structure behind your network's phone book.

POP3

For a long time, *Post Office Protocol 3 (POP3)* had been the preferred protocol for downloading email. It's being replaced by IMAP4 because IMAP4 includes security and more features than POP3.

RDP

Developed by Microsoft, the *Remote Desktop Protocol (RDP)* allows users to connect to remote computers and run programs on them. When you use RDP, you see the desktop of the computer you've signed into on your screen. It's like you're really there, even though you're not.

When you use RDP, the computer at which you are seated is the client and the computer you're logging into is the server. The server uses its own video driver to create video output and sends the output to the client using RDP. Conversely, all keyboard and mouse input from the client is encrypted and sent to the server for processing. RDP also supports sound, drive, port, and network printer redirection. In a nutshell, this means that if you could see, hear, or do it sitting at the remote computer, you could see, hear, or do it at the RDP client too.

Services using this protocol can be great for telecommuters. It's also very handy for technical support folks, who can log into and assume control over a remote computer. It's a lot easier to troubleshoot and fix problems when you can see what's going on and "drive"!

SFTP

The *Secure File Transfer Protocol (SFTP)* is used as an alternative to FTP when you need to transfer files over a secure, encrypted connection.

SMB

Server Message Block (SMB) is a protocol originally developed by IBM but then enhanced by Microsoft, IBM, Intel, and others. It's used to provide shared access to files, printers, and other network resources. In a way, it functions a bit like FTP only with a few more options, such as the ability to connect to printers, and more management commands.

SMTP

We've already looked at a few protocols that are for downloading or receiving email. *Simple Mail Transfer Protocol (SMTP)* is the protocol most commonly used to send email messages. Because it's designed to send only, it's referred to as a *push protocol*. SMTP is the protocol used to send email from mail server to mail server as well as from a mail server to an email client. An email client locates its email server by querying the DNS server for a mail exchange (MX) record. After the server is located, SMTP is used to push the message to the email server, which will then process the message for delivery.

SNMP

Simple Network Management Protocol (SNMP) gathers and manages network performance information.

On your network, you might have several connectivity devices such as routers and switches. A management device called an *SNMP server* can be set up to collect data from these devices (called *agents*) and ensure that your network is operating properly. Although it's mostly used to monitor connectivity devices, many other network devices are SNMP compatible as well. The most current version is SNMPv3.

SSH

Secure Shell (SSH) can be used to set up a secure Telnet session for remote logins or for remotely executing programs and transferring files. Because it's secure, it was originally designed to be a replacement for the unsecure `telnet` command. A common client interface using SSH is called OpenSSH (www.openssh.com).

Telnet

It seems as though *Telnet* has been around since the beginning of time as a terminal emulation protocol. Someone using Telnet can log into another machine and "see" the remote computer in a window on their screen. Although this vision is text only, the user can manage files on that remote machine just as if they were logged in locally.

The problem with `telnet` and other unsecure remote management interfaces (such as `rcp` and `ftp`) is that the data they transmit, including passwords, is sent in plain text. Anyone eavesdropping on the line can intercept the packets and thus obtain usernames and passwords. SSH overcomes this by encrypting the traffic, including usernames and passwords.

Host-to-Host Layer Protocols

After the myriad protocols at the Process/Application layer, the simplicity of the Host-to-Host layer is welcome. At this layer there are two alternatives within the TCP/IP suite: TCP and UDP. The major difference between the two is that TCP guarantees packet delivery through the use of a virtual circuit and data acknowledgements and UDP does not. Because of this, TCP is often referred to as *connection oriented*, whereas UDP is *connectionless*. Because UDP is connectionless, it does tend to be somewhat faster, but we're talking about milliseconds here.

Another key concept to understand about TCP and UDP is the use of *port numbers*. Imagine a web server that is managing connections from incoming users who are viewing web content and others who are downloading files. TCP and UDP use port numbers to keep track of these conversations and make sure that the data gets to the right application and right end user. Conversely, when a client makes a request of a server, it needs to do so on a specific port to make sure that the right application on the server hears the request. For example, web servers are listening for HTTP requests on port 80, so web browsers need to make their requests on that port.

A good analogy for understanding port numbers is to think of cable or satellite television. In this analogy, the IP address is your house. The cable company needs to know where to send the data. But once the data is in your house, which channel are you going to receive it on? If you want sports, that might be on one channel, but weather is on a different channel, and the cooking show is on yet another. Those channels are analogous to ports. You know that if you want a cooking show, you need to turn to channel 923 (or whatever). Similarly, the client computer on a network knows that if it needs to ask a question in HTTP, it needs to do it on port 80.

There are 65,536 ports numbered from 0 to 65535. Ports 0 through 1023 are called the *well-known ports* and are assigned to commonly used services, and 1024 through 49151 are called the *registered ports*. Anything from 49152 to 65535 is free to be used by application vendors. Fortunately, you don't need to memorize them all.

 TCP/IP applications combine the host's IP address with the port number in order to communicate. This combination is known as a *socket*.

Table 7.1 shows the ports used by some of the more common protocols. You should know each of these for the A+ exam.

TABLE 7.1   Common port numbers

Service	Protocol	Port(s)
FTP	TCP	20, 21
SSH	TCP	22
Telnet	TCP	23
SMTP	TCP	25
DNS	TCP/UDP	53
HTTP	TCP	80
DHCP	UDP	67, 68
POP3	TCP	110
SMB/CIFS	TCP	137–139, 445
IMAP4	TCP	143
SNMP	UDP	161
LDAP	TCP	389
AFP	TCP	427, 548
HTTPS	TCP	443
RDP	TCP	3389

A complete list of registered port numbers can be found at www.iana.org.

Internet Layer Protocols

At the Internet layer, there's one key protocol and a few helpful support protocols. The main workhorse of TCP/IP is the Internet Protocol (IP), and it can be found at this layer. IP is responsible for managing logical network addresses and ultimately getting data from point A to point B, even if there are dozens of points in between. We'll cover IP addressing more in the next section.

There are three support protocols of which you should be aware at this layer as well. *Internet Control Message Protocol (ICMP)* is responsible for delivering error messages. If you're familiar with the ping utility, you'll know that it utilizes ICMP to send and receive packets. *Address Resolution Protocol (ARP)* resolves logical IP addresses to physical MAC addresses built into network cards. Reverse ARP (RARP) resolves MAC addresses to IP addresses.

Understanding IP Addressing

To communicate on a TCP/IP network, each device needs to have a unique IP address. Any device with an IP address is referred to as a *host*. This can include servers, workstations, printers, and routers. If you can assign it an IP address, it's a host. As an administrator, you can assign the host's IP configuration information manually, or you can have it automatically assigned by a DHCP server.

 The information in this section will cover IPv4. IPv6 will be covered in its own separate section.

An IPv4 address is a 32-bit hierarchical address that identifies a host on the network. It's typically written in dotted-decimal notation, such as 192.168.10.55. Each of the numbers in this example represents 8 bits (or 1 byte) of the address, also known as an *octet*. The same address written in binary (how the computer thinks about it) would be 11000000 10101000 00001010 00110111. As you can see, the dotted-decimal version is a much more convenient way to write these numbers!

The addresses are said to be hierarchical, as opposed to "flat," because the numbers at the beginning of the address identify groups of computers that belong to the same network. Because of the hierarchical address structure, we're able to do really cool things like route packets between local networks and on the Internet.

A great example of hierarchical addressing is your street address. Let's say that you live in apartment 4B at 123 Main Street, Anytown, Kansas, USA. If someone sent you a letter via snail mail, the hierarchy of your address helps the postal service and carrier deliver it to the right place. First and broadest is USA. Kansas helps narrow it down a bit, and Anytown narrows it down more. Eventually we get to your street, the right number on your street, and then the right apartment. If the address space were flat (for example, Kansas didn't mean anything more specific than Main Street), or you could use any name you wanted for your state, it would be really hard to get the letter to the right spot.

Take this analogy back to IP addresses. They're set up to organize networks logically in order to make delivery between them possible and then to identify an individual node within a network. If this structure weren't in place, a huge, multi-network space like the Internet probably wouldn't be possible. It would simply be too unwieldy to manage.

Another example of a hierarchical addressing scheme is telephone numbers. The first three digits, the area code, group all telephone numbers with that area code into one logical network. The second grouping of three numbers defines a local calling area, and the last grouping of numbers is the unique identifier within that local calling area.

A Quick Binary Tutorial

As we mentioned earlier, each IP address is written in four octets in dotted-decimal notation, but each octet represents 8 bits. A binary bit is a value with two possible states: on equals 1 and off equals 0. If the bit is turned on, it has a decimal value based upon its position within the octet. An off bit always equals zero. Take a look at Figure 7.3, which will help illustrate what we mean.

FIGURE 7.3   Binary values

Position in octet	8	7	6	5	4	3	2	1
Bit on	1	1	1	1	1	1	1	1
Has the decimal value of . . .	128	64	32	16	8	4	2	1
Mathematically	2^7	2^6	2^5	2^4	2^3	2^2	2^1	2^0

If all of the bits in an octet are off, or 00000000, the corresponding decimal value is 0. If all bits in an octet are on, you would have 11111111, which is 255 in decimal.

When you're working with IPv4 addressing, all numbers will be between 0 and 255.

Where it starts to get more entertaining is when you have combinations of zeroes and ones. For example, 10000001 is equal to 129 (128 + 1), and 00101010 is equal to 42 (32 + 8 + 2).

As you work with IPv4 addresses, you'll see certain patterns emerge. For example, you may be able to count quickly from left to right in an octet pattern, such as 128, 192, 224, 240, 248, 252, 254, and 255. That's what you get if you have (starting from the left) 1, 2, 3, and so forth up to 8 bits on in sequence in the octet.

It's beyond the scope of this book to get into too much detail on binary-to-decimal conversion, but this primer should get you started.

Parts of the IP Address

Each IP address is made up of two components: the *network ID* and the *host ID*. The network portion of the address always comes before the host portion. Because of the way IP addresses are structured, the network portion does not have to be a specific fixed length. In other words, some computers will use 8 of the 32 bits for the network portion and the other 24 for the host portion, while other computers might use 24 bits for the network portion and the remaining 8 bits for the host portion. Here are a few rules that you should know about when working with IP addresses:

- All host addresses on a network must be unique.

- On a routed network (such as the Internet), all network addresses must be unique as well.

- Neither the network ID nor the host ID can be set to all 0s. A host ID portion of all 0s means "this network."

- Neither the network ID nor the host ID can be set to all 1s. A host ID portion of all 1s means "all hosts on this network," commonly known as a broadcast address.

Computers are able to differentiate where the network ID ends and the host address begins through the use of a *subnet mask*. This is a value written just like an IP address and may look something like 255.255.255.0. Any bit that is set to a 1 in the subnet mask makes the corresponding bit in the IP address part of the network ID (regardless of whether the bit in the IP address is on or off). When setting bits to 1 in a subnet mask, you always have to turn them on sequentially from left to right, so that the bits representing the network address are always contiguous and come first. The rest of the address will be the host ID. The number 255 is the highest number you will ever see in IP addressing, and it means that all bits in the octet are set to 1.

Here's an example based on two numbers that we have used in this chapter. Look at the IP address of 192.168.10.55. Let's assume that the subnet mask in use with this address is 255.255.255.0. This indicates that the first three octets are the network portion of the address and the last octet is the host portion, therefore the network portion of this ID is 192.168.10 and the host portion is 55.

To communicate using IPv4, each computer is *required* to have an IP address and correct subnet mask. A third component, called a *default gateway*, identifies the IP address of the device that will allow the host to connect outside of the local network. This is typically your router, and it's required if you want to communicate with computers outside of your local network.

IPv4 Address Classes

The designers of TCP/IP designated classes of networks based on the first three bits of the IP address. As you will see, classes differ in how many networks of each class can exist and the number of unique hosts that each network can accommodate. Here are some characteristics of the three classes of addresses that you will commonly deal with:

Class A Class A networks are defined as those with the first bit set as 0 (decimal values from 0 to 127) and are designed for very large networks. The default network portion for Class A networks is the first 8 bits, leaving 24 bits for host identification. Because the network portion is only 8 bits long (and 0 and 127 are reserved), there are only 126 Class A network addresses available. The remaining 24 bits of the address allow each Class A network to hold as many as 16,777,214 hosts. Examples of Class A networks include the networks for telecommunications giants Level 3 Communications and AT&T and organizations such as General Electric, IBM, Hewlett-Packard, Apple, Xerox, Ford, MIT, and the United States Department of Defense. All possible Class A networks are in use; no more are available.

The number of networks available is determined by the formula 2^n, where n represents the number of bits being used. In the Class A example, 7 bits are available by default (because the first one is always set as 0 by design), so there are 2^7 networks available, which is 128. However, the network addresses of 0 and 127 are also reserved, so it's really 126.

The number of hosts available is determined by the formula $2^n - 2$, because a host address of all 0s or all 1s is not allowed. Remember, all 0s means "this network" and all 1s are broadcast addresses. So, in a default Class A network, there can be $2^{24} - 2$ hosts, or 16,777,214.

Class B Class B networks always have the first two bits set at 10 (decimal values from 128 to 191) and are designed for medium-sized networks. The default network portion for Class B networks is the first 16 bits, leaving 16 bits for host identification. This allows for 16,384 (2^{14}) networks, each with as many as 65,534 ($2^{16} - 2$) hosts attached. Examples of Class B networks include the networks of Microsoft, ExxonMobil, and Purdue University. Class B networks are generally regarded as unavailable, but address-conservation techniques have made some of these addresses available from time to time over the years.

Class C Class C networks have the first three bits set at 110 (decimal values from 192 to 223) and are designed for smaller networks. The default network portion for Class C networks is the first 24 bits, leaving 8 bits for host identification. This allows for 2,097,152 (2^{21}) networks, but each network can have a maximum of only 254 ($2^8 - 2$) hosts. Most companies have Class C network addresses. A few class C networks are still available.

The address assignment examples in this chapter refer to addresses that are used on the Internet. For example, MIT has the network address of 18.0.0.0. No one else on the Internet can use addresses in that network's range. But if you are using IP addresses on an internal network that never connects to the Internet, you are free to use whatever addresses you would like.

Table 7.2 shows the IPv4 classes, their ranges, and their default subnet masks.

TABLE 7.2 IPv4 address classes

Class	First Octet	Default Subnet Mask	Comments
A	1–127	255.0.0.0	For very large networks; 127 reserved for the loopback address
B	128–191	255.255.0.0	For medium-sized networks
C	192–223	255.255.255.0	For smaller networks with fewer hosts
D	224–239	N/A	Reserved for multicasts (sending messages to multiple systems)
E	240–255	N/A	Reserved for testing

The network addresses 0 and 127 are reserved and not available for use. Specifically, the address 127.0.0.1 is called the *loopback address*, and it's used for troubleshooting network adapters. We'll talk more about this in Chapter 12, "Hardware and Network Troubleshooting."

The IP address can be written in shorthand to show how many bits are being used for the network portion of the address. For example, you might see something like 10.0.0.0/8. The /8 on the end indicates that the first 8 bits are the network portion of the address, and the other 24 are the host portion. Another example is 192.168.1.0/24, which is a Class C network with a default subnet mask.

Classless Inter-Domain Routing

The default subnet masks for each class of address are by no means the only subnet masks that can be used. In fact, if they were, it would severely limit the number of possible TCP/IP networks available. To resolve this and provide additional addressing flexibility, there is *classless inter-domain routing (CIDR)*. This is just a fancy of way of saying, "You don't have to use the default subnet masks." From a practical standpoint, CIDR minimizes the concept of IP address classes and primarily focuses on the number of bits that are used as part of the network address.

Taking a look at the defaults can help illustrate how CIDR works. If you have a Class A default mask of 255.0.0.0, that is 11111111.00000000.00000000.00000000 in binary. A Class B default mask of 255.255.0.0 is 11111111.11111111.00000000.00000000 in binary. There's no rule that says you have to use an entire octet of bits to represent the network portion of the address. The only rule is that you have to add 1s in a subnet mask from left to right. What if you wanted to have a mask of 255.240.0.0 (11111111.1111000 0.00000000.00000000); can you do that? The answer is yes, and that is essentially what CIDR does. Table 7.3 shows you every available subnet mask and its equivalent slash notation.

TABLE 7.3 CIDR values

Subnet Mask	Notation
255.0.0.0	/8
255.128.0.0	/9
255.192.0.0	/10
255.224.0.0	/11
255.240.0.0	/12
255.248.0.0	/13
255.252.0.0	/14
255.254.0.0	/15
255.255.0.0	/16
255.255.128.0	/17
255.255.192.0	/18
255.255.224.0	/19
255.255.240.0	/20
255.255.248.0	/21
255.255.252.0	/22
255.255.254.0	/23
255.255.255.0	/24
255.255.255.128	/25 *continues*

TABLE 7.3 CIDR values *(continued)*

Subnet Mask	Notation
255.255.255.192	/26
255.255.255.224	/27
255.255.255.240	/28
255.255.255.248	/29
255.255.255.252	/30

Earlier, we said that CIDR minimizes the impact of classes, but there are still some restrictions. The /8 through /15 notations can be used only with Class A network addresses; /16 through /23 can be used with Class A and B network addresses; /24 through /30 can be used with Class A, B, and C network addresses. You can't use anything more than /30 because you always need at least 2 bits for hosts.

Now that you know that you *can* do it, the question is, *why* would you do it? The answer is that it provides you with the flexibility to configure your network.

Here's an example. Say that your default network address is 10.0.0.0/8. That means that you have 24 bits left for hosts on that one network, so you can have just over 16.7 million hosts. How realistic is it that one company will have that many hosts? It's not realistic at all, and that doesn't even bring up the issue that the network infrastructure wouldn't be able to handle physically having that many hosts on one network. However, let's say that you work for a large corporation with about 15 divisions and some of them have up to 3,000 hosts. That's plausible. What you can do is to set up your network so that each division has its own smaller portion of the network (a subnet) big enough for its needs. To hold 3,000 hosts and have a bit of room for expansion, you need 12 bits ($2^{12} - 2 = 4{,}094$), meaning that you have 20 bits left over for the network address. Thus, your new configuration could be 10.0.0.0/20.

DHCP and DNS

Two critical TCP/IP services about which you need to be aware are Dynamic Host Configuration Protocol (DHCP) and Domain Name System (DNS). Both are services that need to be installed on a server and both provide key functionality to network clients.

A DHCP server is configured to provide IP configuration information to clients automatically, in what is called a lease. It's called that because the information is not permanently granted to the client computer and the client must periodically request a renewed lease or a new lease. The following configuration information is typically provided in a lease:

- IP address
- Subnet mask

- Default gateway (the "door" to the outside world)
- DNS server address

DHCP servers can provide a lot more than the items on this list, but these are the most common. When a DHCP-configured client boots up, it sends out a broadcast on the network (called a *DHCP DISCOVER*) requesting a DHCP server. The DHCP server initially responds to the request and then fulfills the request by returning configuration information to the client.

The alternative to DHCP, of course, is for an administrator to enter the IP configuration information manually for each host. This is called *static IP addressing*, and it is administratively intensive as compared to DHCP's dynamic addressing. Some hosts on the network need to have static IP addresses, such as routers, servers, printers, and perhaps some specific workstations. Computers need to access these devices consistently, and the best way to do that is to ensure that they're where they are expected to be (from an address standpoint)! If you use static IP addressing, be sure to exclude the static addresses from the range of addresses that the DHCP server can provide. Or, on the DHCP server, you can specify that certain hosts will always receive the same IP address, which is called a reservation.

To use DHCP, all that you need to do from the client side is configure it to obtain IP addressing information automatically. It's usually as simple as clicking a radio button. No additional configuration is required, because the client broadcasts request messages searching for the DHCP server.

DNS has one function on the network, and that is to resolve hostnames to IP addresses. This sounds simple enough, but it has profound implications.

Think about using the Internet. You open your browser, and in the address bar, you type the name of your favorite website, something like www·google·com, and press Enter. The first question your computer asks is, "Who is that?" Your machine requires an IP address to connect to the website. The DNS server provides the answer, "That is 72.14.205.104." Now that your computer knows the address of the website you want, it's able to traverse the Internet to find it.

Each DNS server has a database where it stores hostname-to-IP-address pairs. If the DNS server does not know the address of the host you are seeking, it has the ability to query other DNS servers to help answer the request.

Think about the implications of that for just a minute. We all probably use Google several times a day, but in all honesty how many of us know its IP address? It's certainly not something we are likely to have memorized. Much less, how could you possibly memorize the IP addresses of all of the websites that you regularly visit? Because of DNS, it's easy to find resources. Whether you want to find Coca-Cola, Toyota, Amazon, or thousands of other companies, it's usually pretty easy to figure out how. Type in the name with a .com on the end of it and you're usually right. The only reason this is successful is because DNS is there to perform resolution of that name to the corresponding IP address.

DNS works the same way on an intranet (a local network not attached to the Internet) as it does on the Internet. The only difference is that instead of helping you find www.google.com, it may help you find Jenny's print server or Joe's file server. From a client-side perspective, all you need to do is configure the host with the address of a legitimate DNS server and you should be good to go.

Public vs. Private IP Addresses

All of the addresses that are used on the Internet are called public addresses. They must be purchased, and only one computer can use any given public address at one time. The problem that presented itself was that the world was soon to run out of public IP addresses while the use of TCP/IP was growing. Additionally, the structure of IP addressing made it impossible to "create" or add any new addresses to the system.

To address this, a solution was devised to allow for the use of TCP/IP without requiring the assignment of a public address. The solution was to use private addresses. Private addresses are not routable on the Internet. They were intended for use on private networks only. Because they weren't intended for use on the Internet, it freed us from the requirement that all addresses be globally unique. This essentially created an infinite number of IP addresses that companies could use within their own network walls.

While this solution helped alleviate the problem of running out of addresses, it created a new one. The private addresses that all of these computers have aren't globally unique, but they need to be in order to access the Internet.

A service called *Network Address Translation (NAT)* was created to solve this problem. NAT runs on your router and handles the translation of private, nonroutable IP addresses into public IP addresses. There are three ranges reserved for private, nonroutable IP addresses, as shown in Table 7.4.

TABLE 7.4   Private IP address ranges

Class	IP Address Range	Default Subnet Mask	Number of Hosts
A	10.0.0.0–10.255.255.255	255.0.0.0	16.7 million
B	172.16.0.0–172.31.255.255	255.240.0.0	1 million
C	192.168.0.0–192.168.255.255	255.255.0.0	65,536

 Real World Scenario

Private IP Addresses and Subnet Masks

When you look at the default subnet masks for the private IP address ranges, you might think, "Wait a minute. Those masks aren't the same as the default subnet masks for the address class," and you are correct.

To understand how TCP/IP addresses work, it's often helpful to start with the concept of address classes, because it helps you break the information into chunks, making it easier to understand. In the real world though, most network administrators don't think in terms of classes, and routers certainly don't operate based on classes. Communication and routing on a network all happens in binary. Experienced network admins will think in terms like, "I am dealing with a 10.0.0.0/16 network." They know the address and the length of the subnet mask.

Earlier in this chapter, you learned about the concept of CIDR, which basically ignores the artificial boundaries of address classes. It uses a concept called variable length subnet masking (VLSM), which might sound complicated, but it just means that the length of the subnet mask determines the structure of the network. (And by structure, we mean the network addresses and the number of networks and hosts that you can have on a network.)

How does this relate back to private IP address ranges? You'll notice that the Class A address range is 10.0.0.0/8, which has a "default" mask for a Class A address. 172.16.0.0/12 is an address in the Class B range, but it does not use the "default" /16 mask. If it did use a /16 mask, then the administrator would have only the remaining 16 bits to use for additional subnets and hosts. As it is, the administrator has 20 bits to play with, which provides much greater flexibility in designing the network. The same concept applies to 192.168.0.0/16. The administrator has 16 free bits to create subnets and host ranges, whereas the "default" /24 mask would leave only 8 bits, and not a lot of flexibility.

There are three things that you should take away from this sidebar:

- Know the subnet masks in Table 7.4 and understand that they are different than the default masks for that class of address.

- Know that you are not limited to using the default masks or class rules.

- It's all about the binary.

The A+ exam may test you on the basics of IP addressing and subnetting, which we have covered in this book. If you pursue more advanced certifications, such as the CompTIA Network+ or the Cisco series of certifications, you will be expected to know IP addressing and subnetting in depth. If you are interested in learning more (after you pass the A+ exam, of course), check out *CompTIA Network+ Study Guide* by Todd Lammle (Sybex, 2015).

These private addresses cannot be used on the Internet and cannot be routed externally. The fact that they are not routable on the Internet is actually an advantage because a network administrator can use them essentially to hide an entire network from the Internet.

This is how it works: The network administrator sets up a NAT-enabled router, which functions as the default gateway to the Internet. The external interface of the router has a public IP address assigned to it that has been provided by the ISP, such as 155.120.100.1. The internal interface of the router will have an administrator-assigned private IP address within one of these ranges, such as 192.168.1.1. All computers on the internal network will then also need to be on the 192.168.1.0 network. To the outside world, any request coming from the internal network will appear to come from 155.120.100.1. The NAT router translates all incoming packets and sends them to the appropriate client. This type of setup is very common today.

By definition, NAT is actually a one-to-one private-to-public IP address translation protocol. There is a type of NAT called NAT Overload, also known as *Port Address Translation (PAT)*, which allows for many private IP addresses to use one public IP address on the Internet.

You may look at your own computer, which has an address in a private range, and wonder, "If it's not routable on the Internet, then how am I on the Internet?" Remember, the NAT router technically makes the Internet request on your computer's behalf, and the NAT router is using a public IP address.

Don't make the mistake of thinking that your internal network can't be hacked if it is using private addresses through NAT. It can. Hackers just have to use more tools and try a little harder to uncover your internal structure. Even if you're using NAT, you still need protective features such as firewalls and anti-malware software.

Automatic Private IP Addressing

Automatic Private IP Addressing (APIPA) is a TCP/IP standard used to automatically configure IP-based hosts that are unable to reach a DHCP server. APIPA addresses are in the 169.254.0.0 range with a subnet mask of 255.255.0.0. If you see a computer that has an IP address beginning with 169.254, you know that it has configured itself.

Typically, the only time that you will see this is when a computer is supposed to receive configuration information from a DHCP server but for some reason that server is unavailable. Even while configured with this address, the client will continue to broadcast for a DHCP server so that it can be given a real address once the server becomes available.

APIPA is also sometimes known as *zero configuration networking* or *address autoconfiguration*. Both of these terms are marketing efforts, created to remove the perceived difficulty of configuring a TCP/IP network. While TCP/IP has generally been considered difficult to configure (compared to other protocols), APIPA can make it so that a TCP/IP network can run with no configuration at all! For example, say that you are setting up a small local area network that has no need to communicate with any networks outside of itself. To accomplish this, you can use APIPA to your advantage. Set the client computers to receive DHCP addresses automatically, but don't set up a DHCP server. The clients will configure themselves and be able to communicate with each other using TCP/IP. The only downside is that this will create a little more broadcast traffic on your network. This solution is only really effective for a nonrouted network of fewer than 100 computers. Considering that most networks today need Internet access, it's unlikely that you'll run across a network configuration like this.

 Real World Scenario

Help! I Can't Get to the Internet!

This is something that you will probably hear a lot: A user on your network calls and complains that they can't get their email or get to the Internet. Everything was fine yesterday, but since this morning they have had no connectivity. Of course, they haven't done anything to or changed their computer at all! No one else on the network appears to be affected.

If the computer is otherwise running normally, the first step should always be to run an `ipconfig` command to look at the IP address configured on the system. More often than not, the user will report back that their IP address is "169 dot 254 dot something dot something." The last two somethings don't really matter—it's the first two numbers that should have your attention. APIPA.

Knowing that the computer is a DHCP client, you know that it's not connecting to the DHCP server for some reason. After getting to the workstation, check the easy stuff first. Are the cables plugged in (if it's wired)? Are there lights on the NIC? Even if they appear to be plugged in, unplug and reconnect them. If that doesn't work, try a different cable. Those simple steps will solve the vast majority of these types of problems. If not, then it's on to more advanced troubleshooting steps! (More TCP/IP troubleshooting is covered in Chapter 12.)

IPv6

The present incarnation of TCP/IP that is used on the Internet was originally developed in 1973. Considering how fast technology evolves, it's pretty amazing to think that the protocol still enjoys immense popularity nearly 40 years later. This version is known as IPv4.

There are a few problems with IPv4 though. One is that we're quickly running out of available network addresses, and the other is that TCP/IP can be somewhat tricky to configure.

If you've dealt with configuring custom subnet masks, you may nod your head at the configuration part, but you might be wondering how we can run out of addresses. After all, IPv4 has 32 bits of addressing space, which allows for nearly 4.3 billion addresses! With the way it's structured, only about 250 million of those addresses are actually usable, and all of those are pretty much spoken for.

A new version of TCP/IP has been developed, and it's called IPv6. Instead of a 32-bit address, it provides for 128-bit addresses. That provides for 3.4×10^{38} addresses, which theoretically should be more than enough that they will never run out globally. (Famous last words, right?)

IPv6 also has many standard features that are optional (but useful) in IPv4. While the addresses may be more difficult to remember, the automatic configuration and enhanced flexibility make the new version sparkle compared to the old one. Best of all, it's backward compatible with and can run on the computer at the same time as IPv4, so networks can migrate to IPv6 without a complete restructure.

Understanding IPv6 Addressing

Understanding the IPv6 addressing scheme is probably the most challenging part of the protocol enhancement. The first thing you'll notice is that, of course, the address space is longer. The second is that IPv6 uses hexadecimal notation instead of the familiar dotted decimal of IPv4. Its 128-bit address structure looks something like what is shown in Figure 7.4.

FIGURE 7.4   IPv6 address

```
2001:0db8:3c4d:0012:0000:0000:1234:56ab
———————————|—_—|————————————————
Global prefix    Subnet        Interface ID
```

The new address is composed of eight 16-bit fields, each represented by four hexadecimal digits and separated by colons. The letters in an IPv6 address are not case sensitive. IPv6 uses three types of addresses: *unicast*, *anycast*, and *multicast*. A unicast address identifies a single node on the network. An anycast address refers to one that has been assigned to multiple nodes. A packet addressed to an anycast address will be delivered to the closest node. Sometimes you will hear this referred to as one-to-nearest addressing. Finally, a multicast address is one used by multiple hosts, and is used to communicate to groups of computers. IPv6 does not employ broadcast addresses. Multicasts handle that functionality. Each network interface can be assigned one or more addresses.

Just by looking at them, it's impossible to tell the difference between unicast and anycast addresses. Their structure is the same; it's their functionality that's different. The first four fields, or 64 bits, refer to the network and subnetwork. The last four fields are the interface ID, which is analogous to the host portion of the IPv4 address. Typically, the first 56 bits within the address are the routing (or global) prefix and the next 8 bits refer to the subnet ID. It's also possible to have shorter routing prefixes though, such as 48 bits, meaning that the subnet ID will be longer.

The Interface ID portion of the address can be created in one of four ways. It can be created automatically using the interface's MAC address, procured from a DHCPv6 server, assigned randomly, or configured manually.

Multicast addresses can take different forms. All multicast addresses use the first 8 bits as the prefix.

Working with IPv6 Addresses

In IPv4, the subnet mask determines the length of the network portion of the address. The network address was often written in an abbreviated form, such as 169.254.0.0/16. The /16 indicates that the first 16 bits are for the network portion and that corresponds to a subnet mask of 255.255.0.0. While IPv6 doesn't use a subnet mask, the same convention for stating the network length holds true. An IPv6 network address could be written as 2001:db8:3c4d::/48. The number after the slash indicates how many bits are in the routing prefix.

Because the addresses are quite long, there are a few ways that you can write them in shorthand; in the world of IPv6, it's all about eliminating extra zeroes. For example, take the address 2001:0db8:3c4d:0012:0000:0000:1234:56ab. The first common way to shorten it is to remove all of the leading zeroes. Thus it could also be written as 2001:db8:3c4d:12:0:0:1234:56ab. The second accepted shortcut is to replace consecutive groups of zeroes with a double colon. So now the example address becomes 2001:db8:3c4d:12::1234:56ab. It's still long, but not quite as long as the original address.

> The double-colon shortcut can be used only once in an address. For example, in the 2001:db8:3c4d:12::1234:56ab address, you can count the number of fields (six) and know that the double colon represents two fields of all zeroes. If, for example, you tried to write an address like 2001::1ab4::5468, you would have a big problem. You would know that there are five fields of zeroes, but you would have no way to identify where exactly the 1ab4 portion of the address falls in relation to the all-zero fields.

An increasingly common occurrence is a mixed IPv4-IPv6 network. As mentioned earlier, IPv6 is backward compatible. In the address space, this is accomplished by setting the first 80 bits to 0, the next 16 bits all to 1, and the final 32 bits to the IPv4 address. In IPv6 format, the IPv4 address looks something like ::ffff:c0a8:173. You will often see the same address written as ::ffff:192.168.1.115 to enable easy identification of the IPv4 address.

There are a few more addresses with which you need to be familiar. In IPv4, the autoconfiguration (APIPA) address range was 169.254.0.0/16. IPv6 accomplishes the same task with the *link local* address fe80::/10. Every IPv6-enabled interface is required to have a link local address, and they are nonroutable. The IPv4 loopback address of 127.0.0.1 has been replaced with ::1/128 (typically written as just ::1). Global addresses (for Internet use) are 2000::/3, and multicast addresses are FF00::/8. Figure 7.5 shows the output of an ipconfig command, and you can see the IPv4 address configuration as well as the IPv6 link local address. Table 7.5 summarizes the IPv6 address ranges with which you should be familiar.

TABLE 7.5   IPv6 address ranges

Address	Use
0:0:0:0:0:0:0:0	Equals::, and is equivalent to 0.0.0.0 in IPv4. It usually means that the host is not configured.
0:0:0:0:0:0:0:1	Also written as ::1. Equivalent to the loopback address of 127.0.0.1 in IPv4.
2000::/3	Global unicast address range for use on the Internet.
FC00::/7	Unique local unicast address range.
FE80::/10	Link local unicast range.
FF00::/8	Multicast range.

FIGURE 7.5   `ipconfig` output with IPv4 and IPv6 addresses

Summary

In this chapter, you learned about the protocol suite used on the Internet, TCP/IP. It's by far the most common protocol in worldwide use today. We started with TCP/IP structure. It's a modular suite that follows the DOD model, with different protocols performing unique tasks at each layer. We looked at individual protocols and their functions at the Process/Application, Host-to-Host, and Internet layers. We also discussed ports and well-known port numbers for common protocols.

Next you learned about IP addressing. We started with a brief tutorial on converting binary numbers to decimal to make them easier to read. Then we looked at the different address classes, CIDR, DHCP and DNS, public vs. private IP addresses, APIPA, and NAT. Each of these services and concepts plays a unique role in managing TCP/IP on your network.

We finished the chapter by looking at the next generation of TCP/IP, IPv6. We talked about the seemingly infinite number of addresses as well as the fact that addresses are written in hexadecimal, which might take some getting used to—even for experienced technicians. Finally, we looked at working with IPv6 addresses, including shorthand notation and special addresses to be aware of.

Exam Essentials

Understand how IPv4 addressing works.   IP addresses are 32-bit addresses written as four octets in dotted-decimal notation, such as 192.168.5.18. To communicate on an IP network, a host also needs a subnet mask, which may look something like 255.255.255.0.

Understand how IPv6 addressing works.   IPv6 addresses are 128-bit addresses written as eight fields of four hexadecimal characters, such as 2001:0db8:3c4d:0012: 0000:0000:1234:56ab. Using shorthand conventions, this address can also be written as 2001:db8:3c4d:12::1234:56ab.

Know what DHCP and DNS do.   On TCP/IP networks, the DHCP server can provide IP configuration information to hosts. A DNS server resolves hostnames to IP addresses.

Know common TCP/IP ports.   Some common protocol and port pairings that you should know are HTTP (80), FTP (20 and 21), POP3 (110), SMTP (25), Telnet (23), and HTTPS (443).

Be able to identify IP address classes.   Know how to identify Class A, B, and C IP addresses. Class A addresses will have a *first octet* in the 1 to 126 range. B is from 128 to 191, and C is from 192 to 223.

Know the private IP addresses ranges.   Private IP addresses will be in one of three ranges: 10.0.0.0/8, 172.16.0.0/16, or 192.168.0.0/16.

Know about the APIPA range.   IP addresses in the 169.254.0.0/16 range are APIPA addresses.

Know the difference between unicast, anycast, and multicast in IPv6.   Unicast addresses are for a single node on the network. Anycast can represent a small group of systems. An anycast message will be delivered to the closest node. Multicast messages are delivered to all computers within a group.

Recognize the special classes of IPv6 addresses.   The loopback address is ::1. Global unicast addresses are in the 2000::/3 range. Unique local unicast addresses are in the FC00::/7 range, link local addresses are FE80::/10, and FF00::/8 addresses are multicast.

Review Questions

The answers to the chapter review questions can be found in Appendix A.

1. You have just set up a network that will use the TCP/IP protocol, and you want client computers to obtain IP configuration information automatically. Which type of server do you need for this?

   A. DNS

   B. DHCP

   C. Domain controller

   D. IP configuration server

2. You have a computer with the IP address 171.226.18.1. What class is this address?

   A. Class A

   B. Class B

   C. Class C

   D. Not a valid IP address

3. Which TCP/IP protocol uses port 80?

   A. HTTP

   B. HTTPS

   C. Telnet

   D. POP3

4. What is the maximum number of IPv6 addresses that can be assigned to one IPv6 interface?

   A. One (unicast)

   B. Two (unicast and anycast)

   C. Three (unicast, anycast, and multicast)

   D. None of the above

5. Which of the following are valid examples of IPv6 addresses? (Choose all that apply.)

   A. 2001:0db8:3c4d:0012:0000:0000:1234:56ab

   B. ::ffff:c0a8:173

   C. 2001:db8:3c4d:12:1234:56ab

   D. 2001::1ab4::5468

6. Which of the following IP addresses would not be valid for a DNS server on the Internet?

   A. 10.25.11.33

   B. 18.33.66.254

   C. 155.118.63.11

   D. 192.186.12.2

7. The workstations on your network are configured to use a DHCP server. One of the workstations can't communicate with other computers. Its IP address is 169.254.1.18. What could be the problem?

   A. The subnet mask is wrong.

   B. It has a private IP address.

   C. The default gateway is wrong.

   D. It can't reach the DHCP server.

8. Which of the following protocols is responsible for sending email?

   A. IMAP4

   B. POP3

   C. SMTP

   D. SNMP

9. What port does the RDP protocol work on?

   A. 53

   B. 143

   C. 389

   D. 3389

10. Which two TCP/IP protocols work at the Host-to-Host layer of the DOD model? (Choose two.)

    A. IP

    B. ARP

    C. TCP

    D. UDP

11. What are two advantages that TCP has over UDP? (Choose two.)

    A. Acknowledged delivery

    B. Faster delivery

    C. Lower overhead

    D. Virtual circuits

12. Your friend is concerned about the security of making an online purchase. What should you tell her to look for in the address bar of the web browser?

    A. HTTP

    B. HTTPS

    C. SSH

    D. SFTP

13. You are manually configuring a TCP/IP host. Another administrator gives you the router's IP address. What is the TCP/IP term for this?

    A. Default gateway

    B. Subnet mask

    C. DNS server

    D. DHCP server

14. Your network is running IPv4. Which of the configuration options are mandatory for your host to communicate on the network? (Choose two.)

    A. IP address

    B. Subnet mask

    C. Default gateway

    D. DNS server address

15. Which of the following protocols is used for secure delivery of email?

    A. SMTP

    B. SNMP

    C. POP3

    D. IMAP4

16. Which protocol was developed to be a secure alternative to Telnet?

    A. SMB

    B. SSH

    C. SNMP

    D. SFTP

17. Which of the following protocols uses TCP port 23?

    A. Telnet

    B. SSH

    C. FTP

    D. DNS

18. Which of the following is an IPv6 broadcast address?

    A. ::1

    B. FE80::

    C. FF00::

    D. ::FFFF

    E. None of the above

19. You are setting up a small network that will not connect to the Internet. You want computers to be able to locate each other by using hostnames. What service will do this?

   A. DNS

   B. DHCP

   C. FTP

   D. APIPA

20. Which of the following protocols is responsible for resolving IP addresses to hardware addresses?

   A. DNS

   B. DHCP

   C. ARP

   D. RARP

Performance-Based Question

You will encounter performance-based questions on the A+ exams. The questions on the exam require you to perform a specific task, and you will be graded on whether or not you were able to complete the task. The following requires you to think creatively in order to measure how well you understand this chapter's topics. You may or may not see similar questions on the actual A+ exams. To see how your answers compare to the authors', refer to Appendix B.

   You need to use Internet Explorer 8 to connect to the ftp.domain.com FTP site. The username is *jsmith* and the password is *getfiles*. What would you type into the address window to access this ftp site?

Chapter

8

Installing Wireless and SOHO Networks

THE FOLLOWING COMPTIA A+ 220-901 EXAM OBJECTIVES ARE COVERED IN THIS CHAPTER:

✓ **2.5   Compare and contrast various WiFi networking standards and encryption types.**

- Standards
    - 802.11 a/b/g/n/ac
    - Speeds, distances, and frequencies
- Encryption types
    - WEP, WPA, WPA2, TKIP, AES

✓ **2.6   Given a scenario, install and configure a SOHO wireless/wired router and apply appropriate settings.**

- Channels
- Port forwarding, port triggering
- DHCP (on/off)
- DMZ
- NAT / DNAT
- Basic QoS
- Firmware
- UPnP

✓ **2.7   Compare and contrast Internet connection types, network types, and their features.**

- Internet Connection Types
    - Cable
    - DSL

- Dial-up
- Fiber
- Satellite
- ISDN
- Cellular
    - Tethering
    - Mobile hotspot
- Line-of-sight wireless Internet service

Over the last two chapters, we've talked a lot about foundational networking knowledge. We've discussed theoretical networking models, physical topologies, cables and connectors, and connectivity devices. We also spent an entire chapter devoted to the most common protocol of all, TCP/IP. The one critical technology that we haven't covered yet is wireless networking.

Because of the unique technology of wireless networking and its huge spike in popularity, it feels appropriate to talk about it as a separate entity. That said, it's important to remember that wireless networking is just like wired networking only without the wires. You still need to figure out how to get resources connected to each other and give the right people access while keeping the bad people at bay. You're now just playing the game with slightly different rules and many new challenges.

We'll start this chapter off with the last of our key networking "theory" discussions, this one on wireless networking standards and encryption methods. From there, we'll move on to setting up and configuring small networks. This is really where the rubber meets the road. Understanding the theory and technical specifications of networking is fine, but the true value in all of this knowledge comes in being able to make good recommendations and implement the right network for your client's needs.

Understanding Wireless Networking

No area of networking has experienced as rapid an ascent as wireless networking over the last several years. What used to be slow and unreliable is now fast and pretty stable, not to mention convenient. It seems like everywhere you go these days there are Internet cafés or fast-food restaurants with wireless hotspots. Nearly every mobile phone sold today has Internet capabilities. No matter where you go, you're likely just seconds away from being connected to the Internet.

The most common term you'll hear thrown around referring to wireless networking today is *Wi-Fi*. While the term was originally coined as a marketing name for 802.11b, it's now used as a nickname referring to the family of IEEE 802.11 standards. That family comprises the primary wireless networking technology in use today, but there are other wireless technologies out there too. You might hear about Bluetooth, cellular, infrared, or others. Each of these standards has its strengths and weaknesses and fills a computing role. The A+ exam covers only 802.11 though, so that's primarily what we'll focus on here.

As a technician, it will fall to you to provide users with access to networks and the Internet. You must make sure that their computers and mobile devices can connect and they can get their email and that downtime is something that resides only in history books. To be able to make that a reality, you must understand as much as you can about networking and the topics discussed in the following sections, where we'll take an in-depth look at the 802.11 standards. After that, we'll spend some time on wireless security features as well.

802.11 Networking Standards

In the United States, wireless LAN (WLAN) standards are created and managed by the Institute of Electrical and Electronics Engineers (IEEE). The most commonly used WLAN standards used today are in the IEEE 802.11 family. Eventually, 802.11 will likely be made obsolete by newer standards, but that is some time off. IEEE 802.11 was ratified in 1997 and was the first standardized WLAN implementation. There are over 20 802.11 standards defined, but you will only see a few in common operation: 802.11a, b, g, n, and ac. As mentioned in the introduction to this chapter, there are several wireless technologies on the market, but 802.11 is the one currently best suited for WLANs.

In concept, an 802.11 network is similar to an Ethernet network, only wireless. At the center of Ethernet networks is a connectivity device such as a hub, switch, or router, and all computers are connected to it. Wireless networks are configured in a similar fashion, except that they use a wireless router or wireless access point instead of a wired connectivity device. In order to connect to the wireless hub or router, the client needs to know the *service-set identifier (SSID)* of the network. *SSID* is a fancy term for the wireless network's name. Wireless access points may connect to other wireless access points, but eventually they connect back to a wired connection with the rest of the network.

802.11 networks use the *Carrier Sense Multiple Access/Collision Avoidance (CSMA/CA)* access method instead of Ethernet's Carrier Sense Multiple Access/Collision Detection (CSMA/CD). Packet collisions are generally avoided, but when they do happen, the sender will need to wait a random period of time (called a *back-off time*) before transmitting again.

Since the original 802.11 standard was published in 1997, several upgrades and extensions of the standard have been released.

802.11

The original *802.11* standard defines WLANs transmitting at 1Mbps or 2Mbps bandwidths using the 2.4GHz frequency spectrum and using either frequency-hopping spread spectrum (FHSS) or direct-sequence spread spectrum (DSSS) for data encoding.

802.11a

The *802.11a* standard provides WLAN bandwidth of up to 54Mbps in the 5GHz frequency spectrum. The 802.11a standard also uses a more efficient encoding system, orthogonal frequency division multiplexing (OFDM), rather than FHSS or DSSS.

This standard was ratified in 1999, but devices didn't hit the market until 2001. Thanks to its encoding system, it was significantly faster than 802.11b (discussed next) but never gained widespread popularity. They were ratified as standards right around the same time, but 802.11b devices beat it to market and were significantly cheaper.

802.11b

The *802.11b* standard was ratified in 1999 as well, but device makers were much quicker to market, making this the de facto wireless networking standard for several years. 802.11b provides for bandwidths of up to 11Mbps (with fallback rates of 5.5, 2, and 1Mbps) in the 2.4GHz range. The 802.11b standard uses DSSS for data encoding. You will occasionally still see 802.11b devices in the wild, but they are relatively uncommon today. When you encounter them, encourage the users to upgrade to something faster. They will appreciate the increase in speed!

> The 802.11b and 802.11a standards are incompatible for two reasons: frequency and modulation. 802.11b operates in the 2.4GHz frequency and uses DSSS. 802.11a runs at 5GHz and uses OFDM.

802.11g

Ratified in 2003, the *802.11g* standard provides for bandwidths of 54Mbps in the 2.4GHz frequency spectrum using OFDM or DSSS encoding. Because it operates in the same frequency and can use the same modulation as 802.11b, the two standards are compatible. Because of the backward compatibility and speed upgrades, 802.11g replaced 802.11b as the industry standard for several years, and it is still popular today.

> Devices on the market that can operate with both 802.11b and 802.11g standards are labeled as 802.11b/g.

As we mentioned, 802.11g devices are backward compatible with legacy 802.11b devices, and both can be used on the same network. That was initially a huge selling point for 802.11g hardware and helped it gain popularity very quickly. However, there are some interoperability concerns of which you should be aware. 802.11b devices are not capable of understanding OFDM transmissions; therefore, they are not able to tell when the 802.11g access point is free or busy. To counteract this problem, when an 802.11b device is associated with an 802.11g access point, the access point reverts back to DSSS modulation to provide backward compatibility. This means that all devices connected to that access point will run at a maximum of 11Mbps. To optimize performance, you should upgrade to all 802.11g devices and set the access point to G-only.

One additional concept that you need to know about when working with 2.4GHz wireless networking is channels. We've said before that b/g works in the 2.4GHz range. Within this range, the FCC has defined 14 different 22MHz communication channels. An illustration of this is shown in Figure 8.1.

FIGURE 8.1 2.4GHz communication channels

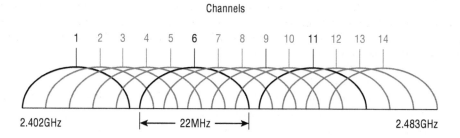

Although 14 channels have been defined for use in the United States, you're only allowed to configure your wireless networking devices to the first 11. When you install a wireless access point and wireless NICs, they will all auto-configure their channel and this will probably work okay for you. If you are experiencing interference, changing the channel might help. And if you have multiple, overlapping wireless access points, you will need to have non-overlapping channels to avoid communications problems. (We'll talk about this more in the section, "Installing and Configuring SOHO Networks," later in this chapter.) Two channels will not overlap if there are four channels between them. If you need to use three non-overlapping channels, your only choices are 1, 6, and 11.

802.11n

Continuing the evolution in Wi-Fi is *802.11n*, which was ratified in 2010. The standard claims to support bandwidth up to 600Mbps, but in reality the typical throughput is about 300Mbps to 450Mbps. That's still pretty fast. It works in both the 2.4GHz and 5GHz ranges.

802.11n achieves faster throughput in a couple of ways. Some of the enhancements include the use of 40MHz channels, multiple-input multiple-output (MIMO), and channel bonding. Remember how 802.11g uses 22MHz channels? 802.11n combines two channels to double (basically) the throughput. Imagine being able to take two garden hoses and combine them into one bigger hose. That's kind of what channel bonding does. MIMO means using multiple antennas rather than a single antenna to communicate information. (802.11n devices can support up to eight antennas, or four streams, because each antenna only sends or receives.) Channel bonding also allows the device to communicate simultaneously at 2.4GHz and 5GHz and bond the data streams, which increases throughput.

One big advantage of 802.11n is that it is backward compatible with 802.11a/b/g. This is because 802.11n is capable of simultaneously servicing 802.11b/g/n clients operating in the 2.4GHz range as well as 802.11a/n clients operating in the 5GHz range.

Not As Much Freedom As You Might Think

In the 5GHz spectrum, there are 25 non-overlapping 20MHz communications channels, 24 of which can be used for Wi-Fi networks. On the surface, this sounds much better than the 3 non-overlapping channels available in the 2.4GHz spectrum!

To increase throughput, 802.11n (and 802.11ac, discussed in the next section) bond channels together. When 20MHz channels are bonded into 40MHz channels, this reduces the number of non-overlapping channels to 12. To complicate matters further, weather, commercial, and military radar operate in the 5GHz range as well, and Wi-Fi needs to avoid conflicting with them.

To avoid conflicts, wireless routers use a technology named *dynamic frequency selection (DFS)*, which will detect radar interference and dynamically adjust to a different frequency range to avoid the problem. If your installation is in an area that does not receive interference from radar signals, you will have 12 non-overlapping 40MHz channels. Otherwise, only 4 non-overlapping, non-DFS 40MHz channels remain available for bonding.

If you're curious (and it's highly unlikely that you will be tested on this), the four non-overlapping non-DFS 40MHz channels are numbered: 36 and 40, 44 and 48, 149 and 153, and 157, and 161. We'll explain this a bit more in the section on 802.11ac.

802.11ac

Technology is always marching forward and getting faster and cheaper, and wireless networking is no different. In January 2014, *802.11ac* was approved as the newest Wi-Fi standard. In many ways, it's a more powerful version of 802.11n in that it carries over many of the same features while adding in only a few new ones. It's the first commercial wireless standard that claims to offer the speed of Gigabit Ethernet.

802.11n introduced channel bonding and MIMO, and 802.11ac takes those concepts further. Instead of bonding two channels, 802.11ac can bond up to eight for a 160MHz bandwidth. This results in a 333-percent speed increase. And 802.11ac doubles the MIMO capabilities of 802.11n to eight streams, resulting in another 100 percent speed increase. The theoretical maximum speed of 802.11ac is a ridiculous 6,900Mbps, but most current devices can get to about 1,300Mbps. Common maximum throughput is just under Gigabit Ethernet speeds, at around 800Mbps. You might see devices in the marketplace that claim to offer speeds over 2Gbps, but the reality is that you're unlikely to get those speeds in anything less than pristine, laboratory-like conditions with all top-of-the-line hardware. In other words, don't count on it being that fast.

Back to DFS

Remember that Wi-Fi installations using the 5GHz range need to steer clear of radar signals to avoid conflicts. Radar for airplanes and weather stations has priority over your Wi-Fi network. (Sorry!)

802.11ac obtains its insanely fast performance mostly through channel bonding. If you will recall, 802.11n can bond 20MHz channels into 40MHz ones, whereas 802.11ac can take the same channels and bond them further into either 80MHz or 160MHz channels.

Ignoring DFS for a moment, there are a maximum of six non-overlapping 80MHz channels and two non-overlapping 160MHz channels available in the 5GHz spectrum. You can't ignore DFS though, and it takes the maximum number of non-overlapping 80MHz channels down to two and eliminates any possible 160MHz channels.

Why is this important to know? Well, mostly because it explains why you're probably not going to get gigabit speeds out of 802.11ac. And for companies or other organizations that want to upgrade to 802.11ac, there are only two non-overlapping channels to use at 80MHz. This makes it difficult (if not impossible) to deploy in anything other than a relatively small office. The other option is to use 40MHz channels just like 802.11n, but then the performance boost of 802.11ac is small and not likely to justify the higher cost of equipment. Figure 8.2 illustrates the available channels in the 5GHz frequency. The channels in the UNII-1 and UNII-3 are the ones that are completely available for Wi-Fi network use. UNII-2 and UNII-2 Extended channels are the DFS ones. (UNII stands for Unlicensed National Information Infrastructure, and is sometimes abbreviated as U-NII.)

FIGURE 8.2   Channel availability in the 5GHz spectrum

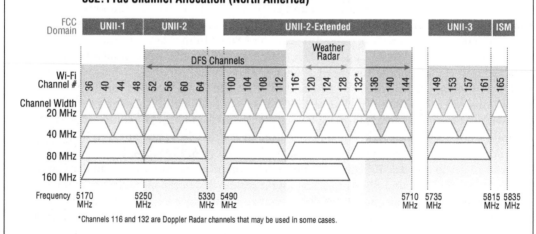

*Channels 116 and 132 are Doppler Radar channels that may be used in some cases.

The most important new feature of 802.11ac is beamforming, which can allow for range increases by sending the wireless signal in the specific direction of the client as opposed to broadcasting it omnidirectionally. Beamforming helps overcome the fact that the range for a 5GHz signal is inherently shorter than one for a 2.4GHz signal. Not all 802.11ac routers support beamforming though, so you might have some range limitations depending on your hardware. And even if the router does support the technology, the maximum distance still won't be any more than what you will get out of 802.11n.

Table 8.1 summarizes the 802.11 standards we discussed here. You'll notice that 802.11ac operates in the 5GHz range and uses OFDM modulation, meaning that it is not backward compatible with 802.11b. That's okay though—as we said earlier, it's probably best to retire those old and slow devices anyway. Many 802.11ac wireless routers are branded as dual-band, meaning they can operate in the 2.4GHz frequency as well for support of older 802.11g and 802.11n devices. If you are running a mixed environment and want to upgrade to an 802.11ac router, check the specifications carefully to see what it supports.

TABLE 8.1   802.11 standards

Type	Frequency	Maximum Throughput	Modulation	Indoor Range	Outdoor Range
—	2.4GHz	2Mbps	FHSS/DSSS	20m	100m
a	5GHz	54Mbps	OFDM	35m	120m
b	2.4GHz	11Mbps	DSSS	40m	140m
g	2.4GHz	54Mbps	DSSS/OFDM	40m	140m
n	5GHz/2.4GHz	600Mbps	OFDM/DSSS	70m	250m
ac	5GHz	1300Mbps	OFDM	35m	140m

The ranges provided in Table 8.1 are approximate and may differ based on your environment. For example, thick walls and steel beams will dramatically reduce your range. In addition, the maximum data rates for 802.11n and 802.11ac can be debated. Some equipment (and experts) will quote the theoretical maximum, whereas others will give more realistic throughput numbers. This wasn't an issue pre-802.11n, but the newer technologies use fancier techniques to achieve maximum speeds, and we don't always have hardware that can produce the speeds that scientists can draw up on a whiteboard.

Also keep in mind that when discussing ranges, the further away from the WAP you get, the lower your connection speed will be. For example, to get 54Mbps out of your 802.11g router, you need to be within about 100 feet of it. At the far end of its range, your throughput will be only about 6Mbps. Another key is how many clients are attached to the WAP. More clients means less bandwidth for each client. If you have ever used the Wi-Fi in an airport or a busy hotel, you know exactly what we mean. These principles hold true for all 802.11 technologies.

Modulation Techniques

We have mentioned three signal modulation techniques used in the 802.11 standards. Here is how the three in common use today work:

Frequency-hopping spread spectrum (FHSS)   FHSS accomplishes communication by hopping the transmission over a range of predefined frequencies. The changing, or hopping, is synchronized between both ends and appears to be a single transmission channel to both ends.

Direct-sequence spread spectrum (DSSS)   DSSS accomplishes communication by adding the data that is to be transmitted to a higher-speed transmission. The higher-speed transmission contains redundant information to ensure data accuracy. Each packet can then be reconstructed in the event of a disruption.

Orthogonal frequency division multiplexing (OFDM)   OFDM accomplishes communication by breaking the data into subsignals and transmitting them simultaneously. These transmissions occur on different frequencies or subbands.

The mathematics and theories of these transmission technologies are beyond the scope of this book and far beyond the scope of this exam.

There are many other commercial devices that transmit at the frequencies at which 802.11 operates. When this happens, there can be a lot of interference. Older Bluetooth devices, cordless phones, cell phones, other WLANs, and microwave ovens can all create interference problems for 802.11 networks, particularly in the 2.4GHz range.

802.11 Devices

If you think about a standard wired network and the devices required on such a network, you can easily determine what types of devices are available for 802.11 networks. Wireless network cards come in a variety of shapes and sizes, including PCI, PCIe, USB, and CardBus models and wireless print servers for your printers. As for connectivity devices, the most common are wireless routers (as shown in Figure 8.3) and a type of hub called a *wireless access point (WAP)*. WAPs look nearly identical to wireless routers and provide central connectivity like wireless routers, but they don't have nearly as many features. The main one most people worry about is Internet connection sharing. You can share an Internet connection using a wireless router but not with a WAP.

FIGURE 8.3   Wireless router

Most wireless routers and WAPs also have wired ports for RJ-45 connectors. The router shown in Figure 8.3 has four wired connections, but they are on the back side of the device (meaning you can't see them in the figure).

Wireless Encryption Methods

The growth of wireless systems has created several opportunities for attackers. These systems are relatively new, they use well-established communications mechanisms, and they're easily intercepted. Wireless controllers such as 802.11 routers use SSIDs to allow communications with a specific access point. The SSID is basically the network name. Because by default wireless routers will broadcast their SSID, all someone with a wireless client needs to do is search for an available signal. If it's not secured, they can connect within a few seconds.

You can configure the router to not broadcast and then manually set up your clients with the SSID of the device. But using this type of SSID configuration doesn't prevent your wireless network from being compromised. If anything, it just makes it harder for legitimate users to connect to your network.

We'll discuss more on SSIDs and configuring your wireless routers to be more secure than their default settings in the section "Installing and Configuring SOHO Networks" later in this chapter.

A more effective way of securing your network is to use one of the several encryption methods available. Examples of these are WEP, WPA, and WPA2, which we discuss next.

WEP

Wired Equivalent Privacy (WEP) was one of the first security standards for wireless devices. WEP encrypts data to provide data security. It uses a static key; the client needs to know the right key to gain communication through a WEP-enabled device. The keys are commonly 10, 26, or 58 hexadecimal characters long.

You may see the use of the notation WEP.*x*, which refers to the key size; 64-bit and 128-bit are the most widely used, and 256-bit keys are supported by some vendors (WEP.64, WEP.128, and WEP.256). WEP.64 uses a 10-character key. WEP.128 uses 26 characters, and WEP.256 uses 58.

The protocol has always been under scrutiny for not being as secure as initially intended. WEP is vulnerable due to the nature of static keys and weaknesses in the encryption algorithm. These weaknesses allow the algorithm to potentially be cracked in a very short amount of time—no more than two or three minutes. This makes WEP one of the more vulnerable protocols available for security.

Because of security weaknesses and the availability of newer protocols, WEP should not be used widely. You will likely see it as the default security setting on many routers, even with all of its shortcomings. It's still better than nothing though, and it does an adequate job of keeping casual snoops at bay.

WPA

Wi-Fi Protected Access (WPA) is an improvement on WEP that was first available in 1999 but did not see widespread acceptance until around 2003. Once it became widely available, the Wi-Fi Alliance recommended that networks no longer use WEP in favor of WPA.

This standard was the first to implement some of the features defined in the IEEE 802.11i security specification. Most notably among them was the use of the *Temporal Key Integrity Protocol (TKIP)*. Whereas WEP used a static 40- or 128-bit key, TKIP uses a 128-bit dynamic per-packet key. It generates a new key for each packet sent. WPA also introduced message integrity checking.

When WPA was introduced to the market, it was intended to be a temporary solution to wireless security. The provisions of 802.11i had already been drafted, and a standard that employed all of the security recommendations was in development. The upgraded standard would eventually be known as WPA2.

Both WPA and WPA2 (discussed next) have two variants: personal and enterprise. For a small office or home office network with just one wireless router or access point, personal is the choice to make. With personal, the device itself handles the authentication. For larger networks, enterprise is recommended because it consolidates authentication administration. Enterprise requires the use of a separate central authentication server, such as a Remote Authentication Dial-in User Service (RADIUS) server.

WPA2

Even though their names might make you assume that WPA and WPA2 are very similar, they are quite different in structure. *Wi-Fi Protected Access 2 (WPA2)* is a huge improvement over WEP and WPA. As mentioned earlier, it implements all of the required elements of the 802.11i security standard. Most notably, it uses Counter Mode CBC-MAC Protocol (CCMP), which is a protocol based on the *Advanced Encryption Standard (AES)* security algorithm. CCMP was created to address the shortcomings of TKIP, so consequently it's much stronger than TKIP.

The terms *CCMP* and *AES* tend to be interchangeable in common parlance. You might also see it written as *AES-CCMP*.

Since 2006, wireless devices have been required to support WPA2 to be certified as Wi-Fi compliant. Of the wireless security options available today, it provides the strongest encryption and data protection.

Installing and Configuring SOHO Networks

Nearly every small office has a network, and it seems like most homes these days have one or more computers that need access to the Internet. As a technician, you may be asked to set up or troubleshoot any number of these types of networks, often collectively referred to as *small office, home office (SOHO) networks*. This part of the chapter will give you the background you need to feel comfortable that you can get the job done. Most of the principles we talk about here apply to larger networks as well, so they're helpful if you're in a corporate environment too.

Before we get into installation and configuration, though, it's critical to introduce a topic that permeates this whole discussion: *planning*. Before installing a network or making changes to it, *always* plan ahead. We'll talk specifically about how to do that, but always keep planning in the back of your mind. Planning ahead of time will help you avoid many problems you could potentially run into, which will save you time in the long run.

In the following sections, we'll look at choosing connection types, network planning and installation, and configuring a wireless router.

Choosing Connection Types

You already know that for computers to talk to each other, they need to be connected in some way. This can be with physical wires or through the air with one of several wireless technologies. The type of connection you choose depends on the purpose of the connection and the needs of the user or users.

You also need to think about the future. Remember that planning concept? When choosing a connection type, think about not only what the needs are today, but what the needs of the individual or organization could be. There is no sense in going overboard and recommending a top-of-the-line expensive solution if it's not needed, but you do want to plan for expansion if that's a possibility.

For our purposes here, we'll break the connection types into two categories. First we'll look at connections designed to facilitate Internet access, and then we'll look at internal network connections.

Choosing an Internet Connection

Internet connections can be broadly broken into two categories: dial-up and broadband. It used to be that you had to weigh the pros and cons and figure out which one was best for your situation. Today, the choice is easy. Go broadband. The only time you would want to use dial-up is if broadband isn't available, and if that's the case, we're sorry!

Your Internet connection will give you online service through an *Internet service provider (ISP)*. The type of service you want will often determine who your ISP choices are.

For example, if you want cable Internet, your choices are limited to your local cable companies and a few national providers. We'll outline some of the features of each type of service and discuss why you might or might not recommend a specific connection type based on the situation.

Dial-Up/POTS

One of the oldest ways of communicating with ISPs and remote networks is through dial-up connections. Although this is still possible, dial-up is not used much anymore due to limitations on modem speed, which top out at 56Kbps. Dial-up uses modems that operate over regular phone lines—that is, the *plain old telephone service (POTS)*—and cannot compare to speeds possible with DSL and cable modems. Reputable sources claim that dial-up Internet connections dropped from 74 percent of all US residential Internet connections in 2000 to three percent in 2014. Three-percent of Americans equals about nine million people, and that still feels like a lot. Most of the people who still use dial-up do it because it's cheaper than broadband or high-speed access isn't available where they live.

The biggest advantage to dial-up is that it's cheap and relatively easy to configure. The only hardware you need is a modem and a phone cable. You dial in to a server (such as an ISP's server), provide a username and a password, and you're on the Internet.

Companies also have the option to grant users dial-up access to their networks. As with Internet connections, this option used to be a lot more popular than it is today. Microsoft offered a server-side product to facilitate this called the Routing and Remote Access Service (RRAS), as did many other companies. ISPs and Remote Access Service (RAS) servers would use the Data Link layer Point-to-Point Protocol (PPP) to establish and maintain the connection.

> The historical term for a dial-up server is a RAS server, as used in the preceding paragraph. When Microsoft launched Windows 2000, it added routing to its RAS capabilities and renamed it RRAS. Industry wide, however, the term *RAS* is still widely used.

It seems that dial-up is considered to be a relic from the Stone Age of Internet access. But there are some reasons it might be the right solution:

- The only hardware it requires is a modem and a phone cord.
- It's relatively easy to set up and configure.
- It's the cheapest online solution (usually $10 to $20 per month).
- You can use it wherever there is phone service, which is just about everywhere.

Of course, there are reasons a dial-up connection might not be appropriate. The big one is speed. If your client needs to download files or has substantial data requirements, dial-up is probably too slow. In addition, with limited bandwidth, it's really good only for one computer. It *is* possible to share a dial-up Internet connection by using software tools, but it's also possible to push a stalled car up a muddy hill. Neither option sounds like much fun.

DSL

One of the two most popular broadband choices for home use is *Digital Subscriber Line (DSL)*. It utilizes existing phone lines and provides fairly reliable high-speed access. To use DSL, you need a DSL modem (shown in Figure 8.4) and a network card in your computer. The ISP usually provides the DSL modem, but you can also purchase them in a variety of electronics stores. You use an Ethernet cable with an RJ-45 connector to plug your network card into the DSL modem (Figure 8.5) and the phone cord to plug the DSL modem into the phone outlet. If you need to plug a land line into the same phone jack as your DSL modem, you will need a DSL splitter (such as the one shown in Figure 8.6) and plug the splitter into the wall.

FIGURE 8.4   A DSL modem

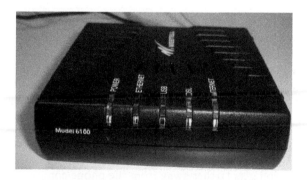

FIGURE 8.5   The back of the DSL modem

FIGURE 8.6   A DSL splitter

 Instead of plugging your computer directly into the DSL modem, you can plug your computer into a router (such as a wireless router) and then plug the router into the DSL modem. Most phone companies will tell you that you can't (or shouldn't) do this, but if you want to connect multiple computers to the Internet and don't mind sharing the bandwidth, there is no reason not to.

There are actually several different forms of DSL, including *high bit-rate DSL (HDSL)*, *symmetric DSL (SDSL)*, *very high bit-rate DSL (VDSL)*, and *asymmetric DSL (ADSL)*. Table 8.2 summarizes the general speeds of each. Keep in mind that the maximum speeds decrease as the installation gets farther away from the phone company's equipment.

TABLE 8.2   DSL standards and approximate speeds

Standard	Download Speed	Upload Speed
ADSL	Up to 8Mbps	Up to 1Mbps
SDSL	Up to 2.5Mbps	Up to 2.5Mbps
HDSL	Up to 42Mbps	Up to 8Mbps
VDSL	Up to 52Mbps	Up to 16Mbps

The most popular in-home form of DSL is ADSL. It's asymmetrical because it supports download speeds that are faster than upload speeds. Dividing up the total available bandwidth this way makes sense because most Internet traffic is downloaded, not uploaded. Imagine a 10-lane highway. If you knew that 8 out of 10 cars that drove the highway went south, wouldn't you make eight lanes southbound and only two lanes northbound? That is essentially what ADSL does.

ADSL and your voice communications can work at the same time over the phone line because they use different frequencies on the same wire. Regular phone communications use frequencies from 0 to 4kHz, whereas ADSL uses frequencies in the 25.875kHz to 138kHz range for upstream traffic and in the 138kHz to 1,104kHz range for downstream traffic. Figure 8.7 illustrates this.

FIGURE 8.7   Voice telephone and ADSL frequencies used

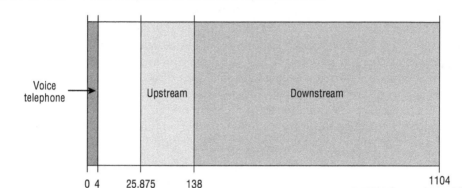

The first ADSL standard was approved in 1998 and offered maximum download speeds of 8Mbps and upload speeds of 1Mbps. The newest standard (ADSL2+, approved in 2008) supports speeds up to 24Mbps download and 3.3Mbps upload. Most ADSL communications are full-duplex.

Many ISPs have moved from ADSL to VDSL, which offers 52Mbps downloads and 16Mbps uploads over telephone wires. In practice, service providers will offer many plans with different speeds, starting at about 10Mbps to 12Mbps download and 1Mbps upload. If you want more speed, you will pay more for it. In addition, just because you pay for a certain speed doesn't mean you will get it. The farther away you are from the phone exchange, the slower your speed will be. Line quality also affects speed, because poorer lines have more attenuation (signal loss).

One major advantage that DSL providers tout is that with DSL you do not share bandwidth with other customers, whereas that may not be true with cable modems.

To summarize, here are some advantages to using DSL:

- It's *much* faster than dial-up.

- Your bandwidth is not shared with other users.

- It's generally very reliable (depending on your ISP).

There are some potential disadvantages as well:

- DSL may not be available in your area. There are distance limitations as to how far away from the phone company's central office you can be to get DSL. Usually this isn't a problem in metro areas, but it could be a problem in rural areas.

- DSL requires more hardware than dial-up: a network card, network cable, a DSL modem, a phone cord, and sometimes a splitter. A DSL modem package usually comes with a network cable and splitter, but many ISPs will make you pay for that package.

- The cost is higher. Lower-speed packages often start off at around $20 to $30 per month, but the ones they advertise with the great data rates can easily run you $100 a month or more.

- If you are in a house or building with older wiring, the older phone lines may not be able to support the full speed you pay for.

That said, DSL is a popular choice for both small businesses and residential offices. If it's available, it's easy to get the phone company to bundle your service with your land line and bill you at the same time. Often you'll also get a package discount for having multiple services. Most important, you can hook the DSL modem up to your router or wireless router and share the Internet connection among several computers. The phone companies don't like the fact that you can do this (they want you to pay for more access), but as of now there's not a lot they can do about it.

To see if DSL is available in your area, go to www.dslreports.com. You can also talk to your local telephone service provider.

With many people using their cell phones as their home phones and land lines slowly fading into history, you may wonder if this causes a problem if you want DSL. Not really. Many phone providers will provide you with DSL without a land line (called *naked DSL*). Of course, you are going to have to pay a surcharge for the use of the phone lines if you don't already use one.

Cable

The other half of the popular home-broadband duet is the *cable modem*. These provide high-speed Internet access through your cable service, much like DSL does over phone lines. You plug your computer into the cable modem using a standard Ethernet cable, just as you would plug into a DSL modem. The only difference is that the other connection goes into a cable TV jack instead of the phone jack. Cable Internet provides broadband Internet access via a specification known as Data Over Cable Service Internet Specification (DOCSIS). Anyone who can get a cable TV connection should be able to get the service.

As advertised, cable Internet connections are faster than DSL connections. You'll see a wide variety of claimed speeds; some cable companies offer packages with download speeds up to 30Mbps, 50Mbps, or even 100Mbps and uploads of 5Mbps. (For business customers, download speeds can be 400Mbps.) If it's that fast, why wouldn't everyone choose it?

While cable generally is faster, a big caveat to these speeds is that they are not guaranteed and they can vary.

One of the reasons that speeds may vary is that you are sharing available bandwidth within your distribution network. The size of the network varies, but it's usually between 100 and 2,000 customers. Some of them may have cable modems too, and access can be slower during peak usage times. Another reason is that cable companies make liberal use of bandwidth throttling. If you read the fine print on some of their packages that promise the fast speeds, one of the technical details is that they boost your download speed for the first 10MB or 20MB of a file transfer, and then they throttle your speed back down to your normal rate.

To see how this could affect everyone's speed on the shared bandwidth, let's think about a simplified example. Let's say that two users (Sally and John) are sharing a connection that has a maximum capacity of 40Mbps. For the sake of argument, let's assume that they are the only two users and that they share the bandwidth equally. That would mean normally each person gets 20Mbps of bandwidth. If Sally gets a boost that allows her to download 30Mbps, for however long, that leaves John with only 10Mbps of available bandwidth. If John is used to having 20Mbps, that 10Mbps is going to seem awfully slow.

While it may seem as though we are down on cable modems, you just need to understand exactly what you and your customers are getting. In practice, the speeds of a cable modem are pretty comparable to those of DSL. Both have pros and cons when it comes to reliability and speed of service, but a lot of that varies by service provider and isn't necessarily reflective of the technology. When it comes right down to it, the choice you make between DSL and cable (if both are available in your area) may depend on which company you get the best package deal from: phone and DSL through your telephone company or cable TV and cable modem from your cable provider.

To summarize, here are the advantages to using cable:

- It's *much* faster than dial-up, and it can be faster than DSL (particularly for uploads).

- You're not required to have or use a telephone land line.

- It's generally very reliable (depending on your ISP).

As with anything else, there are possible disadvantages:

- Cable may not be available in your area. In metro areas this normally isn't a problem, but it could be in rural areas.

- Cable requires more hardware than dial-up: a network card, network cable, and a cable modem. Most ISPs will charge you a one-time fee or a monthly lease fee for the cable modem.

- Your bandwidth is shared with everyone on your network segment, usually a neighborhood-sized group of homes. Everyone shares the available bandwidth. During peak times, your access speed may slow down.

- Security could be an issue. Essentially you are on a LAN with all the neighbors in your cable segment. Thus, if you (or your cable company) don't protect your connection, theoretically you could see your neighbors' computers and they could see yours. The cable companies have made strides in this area and it usually isn't a problem anymore, but know that it is a possibility.

- The cost is higher. Lower-speed packages often start off at around $20 to $30 per month, but the ones they advertise with the great data rates can easily run you $100 a month or more.

Cable modems can be connected directly to a computer but can also be connected to a router or wireless router just as a DSL modem. Therefore, you can share an Internet connection over a cable modem.

 For detailed information about cable Internet availability and performance, check out www.highspeedinternet.net.

Integrated Services Digital Network (ISDN)

Integrated Services Digital Network (ISDN) is a digital, point-to-point network capable of maximum transmission speeds of about 2Mbps, although speeds of 128Kbps are more common. ISDN uses the same two-pair UTP wiring as POTS (but it can transmit data at much higher speeds). That's where the similarity ends. What makes ISDN different from a regular POTS line is how it uses the copper wiring. Instead of carrying an analog (voice) signal, it carries digital signals. While not nearly as fast as other broadband services, it still is considered a broadband type of access.

A computer connects to an ISDN line via an *ISDN terminal adapter* (often referred to as an *ISDN TA* or an *ISDN modem*). Like DSL and cable modems, an ISDN terminal adapter is not an actual modem because it does not convert a digital signal to an analog signal; ISDN signals are digital. Computers also need a *network terminator* to connect to the ISDN TA, but most TAs have them built in. If you have multiple users on the network who need Internet access through the ISDN line, you need an ISDN router.

An ISDN line has two types of channels. The data is carried on a channel called a *Bearer channel*, or *B channel*, which can carry 64Kbps of data. The second type of channel is used for call setup and link management and is known as the *signal channel*, or *D channel*. This channel has only 16Kbps of bandwidth. A typical 144Kbps *basic rate interface (BRI)* ISDN line has two B channels and one D channel. One B channel can be used for a voice call while the other is being used for data transmissions, or both can be used for data. When the B channels are combined to maximize data throughput (which is common), the process is called *bonding* or *inverse multiplexing*. Multiple BRI ISDN lines can also be bonded together to form higher throughput channels.

BRI ISDN is also known as 2B+D because of the number and type of channels used. BRI ISDN is more common in Europe than it is in the United States.

You can also obtain a *primary rate interface (PRI)*, also known as 23B+D, which means it has 23 B channels and 1 D channel. The total bandwidth of a 23B+D ISDN line is 1,536Kbps (23 B channels × 64Kbps per channel + 64Kbps for the D channel). This is typically carried on a dedicated T1 connection and is fairly popular in the United States.

The main advantages of ISDN are as follows:

- The connection is faster than dial-up.

- It runs over phone lines.

- It's flexible. Each B channel can support voice or data. If you have a BRI ISDN connection, you can have two separate voice conversations happening at once, two data streams, a voice conversation and a data stream, or both channels bridged into one data stream.

- Support for video teleconferencing is easy to obtain.

- There is no conversion from digital to analog.

However, ISDN does have a few disadvantages:

- It's more expensive than POTS.

- You need an ISDN modem and perhaps an ISDN router.

- ISDN is a type of dial-up connection and therefore the connection must be initiated before use.

BRI ISDN connections were starting to become popular in home applications in the mid- to late-1990s as an alternative to dial-up before broadband really took off. Today you'll rarely see it used in a home, but it's occasionally used in an office. You will find PRI ISDN to be more common in office environments. BRI rates start at about $20 to $40 per month, while PRI solutions typically start in the $300-per-month range.

If you need a dedicated Internet connection, which will serve as an Internet-only connection, then one of the other broadband services is likely a better choice. If you want a line that can support both Internet and voice and provide flexibility to go between the two, then ISDN could be the right solution (although VoIP could be as well—but that is beyond the scope of this chapter).

Fiber-Optic Internet

Fiber-optic cable is pretty impressive with the speed and bandwidth it delivers. For nearly all of fiber-optic cable's existence, it's been used mostly for high-speed telecommunications and network backbones. This is because it is much more expensive than copper to install and operate. The cables themselves are pricier, and so is the hardware at the end of the cables.

Technology follows this inevitable path of getting cheaper the longer it exists, and fiber is really starting to embrace its destiny. Some phone and media companies are now offering fiber-optic Internet connections for home subscribers.

An example of one such option is FiOS, offered by Verizon. It offers *Fiber-to-the-Home (FTTH)* service, which means that the cables are 100-percent fiber from their data centers to your home. At the time we were writing this book, the fastest speeds offered for home users were 75Mbps download and 75Mbps upload. Businesses can get 150Mbps down and 150Mbps up. That means you could download a two-hour HD movie in about four minutes. That's sick. What's even better is that other providers are claiming to offer 1Gbps implementations.

Other companies may offer a service called *Fiber-to-the-Node (FTTN)*, sometimes called Fiber to the Curb. This runs fiber to the phone or cable company's utility box near the street and then runs copper from there to your house. Maximum speeds for this type of service are around 25Mbps. These options are probably best suited for small businesses or home offices with significant data requirements, unless online gaming is *really* important to you.

> Some cable companies promise a high-speed, fiber-optic connection for your TV cable as well as cable Internet service. In the vast majority of cases, the fiber is FTTN, and the fiber runs only from their network to the junction box at the entrance to your neighborhood or possibly to your curb. From there, the cable is coaxial copper. If you're paying for a fiber connection, be sure you're actually *getting* a fiber connection.

Are there any downsides to a fiber Internet connection? Really only two come to mind. The first is availability. It's still pretty spotty on where you can get it. The second is price. That great 150Mbps connection will run you about $200 a month.

Satellite

One type of broadband Internet connection that does not get much fanfare is satellite Internet. *Satellite Internet* is not much like any other type of broadband connection. Instead of a cabled connection, it uses a satellite dish to receive data from an orbiting satellite and relay station that is connected to the Internet. Satellite connections are typically a lot slower than wired broadband connections, with downloads often maxing out at around 10Mbps to 15Mbps and uploads at 1Mbps to 2Mbps.

The need for a satellite dish and the reliance upon its technology is one of the major drawbacks to satellite Internet. People who own satellite dishes will tell you that there are occasional problems due to weather and satellite alignment. You must keep the satellite dish aimed precisely at the satellite or your signal strength (and thus your connection reliability and speed) will suffer. Plus, cloudy or stormy days can cause interference with the signal, especially if there are high winds that could blow the satellite dish out of alignment. Receivers are typically small satellite dishes (like the ones used for DirecTV or DishNetwork) but can also be portable satellite modems (modems the size of a briefcase) or portable satellite phones.

> Satellite Internet is often referred to as "line-of-sight" wireless because it does require a clear line of sight between the user and the transmitter.

Another drawback to satellite technology is the delay (also called *propagation delay*), or *latency*. The delay occurs because of the length of time required to transmit the data and receive a response via the satellite. This delay (between 250 and 350 milliseconds) comes from the time it takes the data to travel the approximately 35,000 kilometers into space and return. To compare it with other types of broadband signals, cable and DSL have a delay between customer and ISP of 10 to 30 milliseconds. With standard web and email traffic, this delay, while slightly annoying, is acceptable. However, with technologies like VoIP and live Internet gaming, the delay is intolerable.

> Online gamers are especially sensitive to propagation delay. They often refer to it as *ping time*. The higher the ping time (in milliseconds), the worse the response time in the game. It sometimes means the difference between winning and losing an online game.

Of course, satellite also has advantages or no one would use it. First, satellite connections are incredibly useful when you are in an area where it's difficult or impossible to run a cable or if your Internet access needs are mobile and cellular data rates just don't cut it.

The second advantage is due to the nature of the connection. This type of connection is called *point-to-multipoint* because one satellite can provide a signal to a number of receivers simultaneously. It's used in a variety of applications from telecommunications and handheld GPSs to television and radio broadcasts and a host of others.

Here are a few considerations to keep in mind regarding satellite:

It's expensive compared to other broadband access.   The top packages that offer 15Mbps downloads will cost you over $100 a month. That kind of download speed will only cost you about $30 or so for DSL or cable. The low-end satellite packages, with download speeds of around 5Mbps, will run you around $30–40 per month. And, many providers set thresholds on the amount of data you can download per month. Going over that amount can result in extra charges and/or speed throttling. Your speed will be decreased for a certain period, and you will pay more for that data as well!

Installation can be tricky.   When installing a satellite system, you need to ensure that the satellite dish on the ground is pointed at precisely the right spot in the sky. This can be tricky to do if you're not trained, but some have a utility that helps you see how close you are to being right on (you're getting warmer. . . warmer).

Line of sight is required.   Satellite communications also require line of sight. A tree between you and your orbiting partner will cause problems. Rain and other atmospheric conditions can cause problems as well.

Latency can be a problem.   Because of the long distance the message must travel, satellites can be subject to long latency times. While it happens with wired connections, it disproportionately affects satellite transmissions. Have you ever watched a national news channel when a reporter is reporting from some location halfway across the world? The anchor behind the desk will ask a question, and the reporter will nod, and nod, and finally about five excruciating seconds after the anchor is done, the reporter will start to answer. That's latency.

🌐 Real World Scenario

All in the Name of Entertainment

Several years ago (and we do mean several) as a teenager, one of the authors worked for a local television station during the summers. Each summer, the television station would broadcast a Senior PGA golf tournament that was held on a nearby mountain course.

Before the tournament, the crew would spend three days setting up the control truck, cameras, and link back to the station. (It was a network with TV cameras instead of workstations!) Because of the remote location, the crew had to set up a satellite uplink to get the signals back to civilization. From the control truck, a transmitter was pointed at a relay station on the side of the mountain, which in turn was pointed at a satellite orbiting the earth. It took a team of four engineers to get it set up. Two engineers would stay at the truck, and two others would board ATVs and journey up the remote mountainside. Once in position, they would set up the relay station, which looked a lot like a keg of beer with a few antennas. The engineers at the truck would adjust their directional microwave transmitter until the relay station received a strong signal. Then the engineers on the mountainside would perform the arduous task of pointing their transmitter at the satellite.

It was a long and tedious process, and that's really the point of the story. Satellite was the *only* option available to complete the network, but satellite networks can be a challenge to set up and configure.

Cellular (Cellular WAN)

The cell phone, once a clunky brick-like status symbol of the well-to-do, is now pervasive in our society. It seems that everyone—from kindergarteners to 80-year-old grandmothers—has a cell. The industry has revolutionized the way we communicate and, some say, contributed to furthering an attention-deficit-disorder-like, instant-gratification-hungry society. In fact, the line between cell phones and computers has blurred significantly with all of the new smartphones on the market. It used to be that the Internet was reserved for "real" computers, but now anyone can be online at almost any time.

Regardless of your feelings about cell phones, whether you are fanatical about checking in every time you visit a local eatery to ensure you're the "mayor" or you long for the good old days when you could escape your phone because it had a functional radius as long as your cord, you need to understand the basics of cell technology.

CELLULAR TECHNICAL SPECIFICATIONS

For years, there have been two major cell standards used around the world. The *Global System for Mobile Communications (GSM)* is the most popular, boasting over 1.5 billion users in 210 countries. The other standard is *code division multiple access (CDMA)*, which was developed by Qualcomm and is available only in the United States.

Both are considered *3G (or third-generation)* mobile technologies, and each has its advantages. GSM was introduced first, and when CDMA was launched, it was much faster than GSM. GSM eventually caught up, though, and the two now have relatively similar data rates. The biggest issue is that GSM and CDMA are not compatible with each other. Whatever technology you get is based on the provider you sign up with. Sprint and Verizon use CDMA, and AT&T and T-Mobile use GSM. That means that if you have a CMDA phone through Verizon, you can't switch (with that phone) to AT&T. And, your CDMA phone won't work outside the United States.

Now we have 4G technology available, which is the new global standard designed to make 3G obsolete. The biggest enhancement in *4G LTE (Long-Term Evolution)* over 3G is speed. Whereas with 3G technology you were limited to about 500Kbps downloads, some 4G LTE networks will give you download speeds of 10 to 20Mbps and upload speeds of 3 to 10Mbps. (The theoretical maximum for LTE is 300Mbps download and 75Mbps upload.) The range of 4G LTE depends on the tower and obstructions in the way. The optimal cell size is about 3.1 miles (5km) in rural areas, and you can get reasonable performance for about 19 miles (30km).

What Is 4G?

Whenever you turn on the TV, you can't help but be bombarded with commercials (if you don't fast-forward through them) from cell providers pitching the fastest or widest or whatever-est 4G LTE network. What does it all mean?

To be specific, 4G refers to a generation of standards for mobile devices (such as phones and tablets) and telecommunication services that fulfill the International Mobile Telecommunications Advanced (IMT-Advanced) specifications as adopted by the International Telecommunication Union (ITU). In more practical terms, it's simply a standard for wireless telephone, Internet, video, and mobile TV. To meet IMT-Advanced standards, the service must provide peak data rates of at least 100Mbps for high-mobility communication (such as trains or cars) and 1Gbps for low-mobility communication. One major difference between 4G and 3G is that 4G is designed to use IP instead of traditional telephone circuits. It's designed to provide mobile broadband access.

The first 4G devices that came on the market did not offer anything close to the speeds specified by the ITU. Mobile manufacturers branded them 4G anyway, and there wasn't much the ITU could do to stop it. The result was that the world became inundated with 4G LTE advertising.

There are a two competing 4G standards: WiMax and LTE. WiMax is the marketing name given to the IEEE 802.16 standard for wireless MAN technology. LTE is what's used by mobile providers. As of the writing of this book, it's not even a close competition—LTE is clearly dominating.

Believe it or not, there actually were 1G and 2G standards as well. You probably just never heard anything about them. You might have heard of 3G, and now 4G is on the market. Just wait, and a few years from now everyone will probably be clamoring for the new 5G device, whatever that may be!

TETHERING

In regular life, *tethering* means connecting two things together. In computing, it means hooking your laptop up to your cell phone and using the cell phone's connection and data plan to get on the Internet. Technically speaking, the device that's being used for the connection can get on the Internet using a wired connection, Wi-Fi, or Bluetooth as well, but the cell phone and laptop example is the most common scenario. The cellular-enabled device that is making the Internet connection is often known as a mobile hotspot.

Several mobile carriers prohibit the use of your mobile phone for tethering, unless explicitly permitted in your data plan.

MOBILE HOTSPOTS

Many cell phone providers offer network cards (or they will incorrectly call them modems) that allow your laptop computer or other device to connect to the Internet from anywhere you can get a cell signal. Some will bundle that service with your normal monthly cell service at no additional charge, while others will charge you an incremental fee. The term you'll hear a lot in connection with this is *MiFi*. Figure 8.8 shows a Verizon MiFi hotspot.

FIGURE 8.8   MiFi hotspot

A MiFi card such as this allows you to connect up to eight Wi-Fi-enabled devices (usually 802.11g/n) as a MiFi cloud to get Internet access. Some MiFi cards allow up to 10 connections. The MiFi card then makes the connection back to the cell phone provider.

After you purchase a MiFi device, you first connect it to your laptop via USB cable for activation and setup. Once that step is complete, you can go entirely wireless. MiFi supports Wi-Fi security such as WEP, WPA, and WPA2.

Table 8.3 summarizes the connection types we have discussed in this chapter.

TABLE 8.3   Common Internet connection types and speeds

Connection Type	Approximate Basic Package Cost	Download Speed Range	Description
Dial-up	$10–20	Up to 56Kbps	Plain old telephone service. A regular analog phone line.
DSL	$20–30	Up to 50Mbps	Inexpensive broadband Internet access method with wide availability, using telephone lines.
Cable	$20–30	Up to 50Mbps	Inexpensive broadband Internet access method with wide availability, using cable television lines.
ISDN	$20–40	Up to 1.5Mbps	Integrated Services Digital Network. Once popular for home office Internet connections.
Fiber	$40–50	Up to 1Gbps	Incredibly fast and just as expensive.
Cellular	$30–50	Up to 20Mbps	Great range; supported by cell phone providers. Best for a very limited number of devices.
Satellite	$30–40	Up to 15Mbps	Great for rural areas without cabled broadband methods. More expensive than DSL or cable.

 Real World Scenario

Sometimes, the Choices Are Limited

Before you decide which broadband connection sounds the most appealing to you, you should also factor in something very important: what is available in your area. DSL is available at different rates of connectivity based on distance from a central station. If you live far enough from a central station, or near a central station that has not been updated lately (such as in the middle of rural America), DSL may not be an option.

continues

continued

Similarly, not all cable providers are willing to take the steps necessary to run a connection in all situations. One of the authors once had a small business in a section of an old industrial building. The cable provider said the office where the modem was desired was too far from their nearest pole and there was nothing that could be done about it. He offered to pay the expense to have an additional pole placed closer to the location, but they would not discuss it further.

Make certain you know the available options—not just the technological options—before you spend too much time determining what is best for you.

Choosing Internal Network Connections

Along with deciding how your computers will get to the outside world, you need to think about how your computers will communicate with each other on your internal network. The choices you make will depend on the speed you need, distance and security requirements, and cost involved with installation and maintenance. It may also depend some on the abilities of the installer or administrative staff. You may have someone who is quite capable of making replacement Category 6 cables but for whom making replacement fiber-optic cables is a much more daunting task. Your choices for internal connections can be lumped into two groups: wired and wireless.

Many networks today are a hybrid of wired and wireless connections. Understand the fundamentals of how each works separately; then you can understand how they work together. Every wireless connection eventually connects back to a wired network point somehow.

Wired Network Connections

Wired connections form the backbone of nearly every network in existence. Even as wireless becomes more popular, the importance of wired connections still remains strong. In general, wired networks are faster and more secure than their wireless counterparts.

When it comes to choosing a wired network connection type, you need to think about speed, distance, and cost. You learned about several types of wired connections in Chapter 6, "Networking Fundamentals," such as coaxial, UTP, STP, and fiber-optic, but the only two you'll want to go with today are twisted pair and fiber. You'll run one of the two (or maybe a combination of the two), with UTP being by far the most common choice, as an Ethernet star network. Table 8.4 shows a summary of the more common Ethernet standards along with the cable used, speed, and maximum distance.

TABLE 8.4   Common Ethernet standards

Standard	Cables Used	Maximum Speed	Maximum Distance
10BaseT	UTP CAT-3 and above	10Mbps	100m (~300 feet)
100BaseTX	UTP CAT-5 and above	100Mbps	100m
100BaseFX	Multi-mode fiber	100Mbps	2,000m
1000BaseT	UTP CAT-5e and above	1Gbps	100m
10GBaseT	UTP CAT-6a and above	10Gbps	100m
10GBaseSR	Multi-mode fiber	10Gbps	300m
10GBaseLR	Single-mode fiber	10Gbps	10km (6.2 miles)
10GBaseER	Single-mode fiber	10Gbps	40km (~25 miles)

Looking at Table 8.4, you might have noticed that the number in the standard corresponds to the maximum speed in megabytes (unless it says 10G, where the G is for gigabytes). This can help you remember what the standard's maximum speed is without a lot of rote memorization. For example, if you see 100Base anything, you know the maximum speed is 100Mbps. The letter *T* always indicates twisted pair, and *F* is always fiber.

The first question you need to ask yourself is, "How fast does this network need to be?" There really is no point installing a 10BaseT network these days because even the slowest wireless LAN speeds can deliver that. For most networks, 100Mbps is probably sufficient. If the company has higher throughput requirements, then you can start looking into Gigabit Ethernet (1Gbps) or faster (10Gbps).

The second question is then, "What is the maximum distance I'll need to run any one cable?" In most office environments, you can configure your network in such a way that 100 meters will get you from any connectivity device to the end user. If you need to go longer than that, you'll definitely need fiber for that connection unless you want to mess with repeaters.

As you're thinking about what type of cable you will go with, also consider the hardware you'll need. If you are going to run fiber to the desktop, you'll need fiber network cards, routers, and switches. If you are running UTP, you need network cards, routers, and switches with RJ-45 connectors. If you're going to run Gigabit, all devices that you want to run at that speed need to support it.

The third question to ask yourself is, "How big of a deal is security?" Most of the time, the answer lies somewhere between "very" and "extremely"! Copper cable is pretty secure, but it does emit a signal that can be intercepted, meaning people can tap into your transmissions (hence the term *wiretap*). Fiber-optic cables are immune to wiretapping. Normally this isn't a big deal because copper cables don't exactly broadcast your data all over as a wireless connection does. But if security is of the utmost concern, then fiber is the way to go.

Fourth, "Is there a lot of electrical interference in the area?" Transmissions across a copper cable can be ravaged by the effects of electromagnetic interference (EMI). Fiber is immune to those effects.

Finally, ask yourself about cost. Fiber cables and hardware are more expensive than their copper counterparts. Table 8.5 summarizes your cable choices and provides characteristics of each.

TABLE 8.5   Cable types and characteristics

Characteristics	Twisted Pair	Fiber-Optic
Transmission rate	CAT-5: 100Mbps CAT-5e: 1Gbps CAT-6a and CAT-7: 10Gbps	100Mbps to 10Gbps
Maximum length	100 meters (328 feet)	About 25 miles
Flexibility	Very flexible	Fair
Ease of installation	Very easy	Difficult
Connector	RJ-45	Special (SC, ST, and others)
Interference (security)	Susceptible	Not susceptible
Overall cost	Inexpensive	Expensive
NIC cost	100Mbps: $15–$40 1Gbps: $30 and up	$100–$150; easily $600–$800 for server NICs
10m cable cost	CAT-5/5e: $8–$12 CAT-6: $12–$15	Depends on mode and connector type, but generally $20–$40
8-port switch cost	100Mbps: $30–$100 1Gbps: $70–$400	$350 and up

Understand that the costs shown in Table 8.5 are approximate and are for illustrative purposes only. The cost for this equipment in your area may differ. Fiber has gotten considerably cheaper in the last 5 to 10 years, but it's still far more expensive than copper.

Fiber-optic cabling has some obvious advantages over copper, but as you can see it may be prohibitively expensive to run fiber to the desktop. What a lot of organizations will do is use fiber sparingly, where it is needed the most, and then run copper to the desktop. Fiber will be used in the server room and perhaps between floors of a building as well as any place where a very long cable run is needed.

Wireless Network Connections

People love wireless networks for one major reason: convenience. Wireless connections enable a sense of freedom in users. They're not stuck to their desk; they can work from anywhere! (We're not sure if this is actually a good thing or not.) Wireless isn't typically as fast and it tends to be a bit more expensive than wired copper networks, but the convenience factor far outweighs the others.

WIRELESS LAN (WLAN)

When thinking about using wireless for network communications, the only real technology option available today is IEEE 802.11. Bluetooth and infrared (which we'll cover in just a bit) can help mobile devices communicate, but they aren't designed for full wireless LAN (WLAN) use. Your choice becomes which 802.11 standard you want to use.

So how do you choose which one is right for your situation? You can apply the same thinking you would for a wired network in that you need to consider speed, distance, security, and cost. Generally speaking though, with wireless it's best to start with the most robust technology and work your way backwards.

Security concerns on wireless networks are similar regardless of your choice. You're broadcasting network signals through air; there will be some security concerns. It comes down to range, speed, and cost.

In today's environment it's silly to consider 802.11a only or 802.11b only. Deciding that you are going to install an 802.11b network from the ground up at this point is a bit like saying you are going to use 10BaseT. You could, but why? In fact, it will be a challenge to even find 802.11b-only devices for your network. Most devices that support 802.11b are branded as 802.11b/g (or 802.11g/b), meaning they support both network types. 802.11a never really got too popular even when it *was* the best technology, so why use it now?

That brings us to your most likely choices: 802.11g, 802.11n, and 802.11ac. 802.11g is heading toward belonging only in history books, but considering its relatively decent speed, it will stick around for a while. Still, it probably isn't best to design a new network from the ground up based on that technology. For 802.11n, devices are plentiful, and it's backward compatible with 802.11b/g. (If you happen to have 802.11a devices, then 802.11n still makes sense. But really, you should upgrade those devices!) 802.11ac is the newest and fastest, but it will cost you more and you might not get significantly better performance than

802.11n. It will come down to cost. Network cards will run you anywhere from $20 to $100, and you can get wireless access points and wireless routers for as little as around $20 to $40. Shop around to see what kind of deal you can get. Exercise 8.1 has you do just that.

EXERCISE 8.1

The Cost of Networking

1. Visit the website for an electronics store. If you're unfamiliar with any, try www.bestbuy.com or www.frys.com.

2. Find an 802.11ac wireless router. How much is it?

3. Find an older standard. See if you can find an 802.11b one. If not, go for 802.11g. How much is it?

4. Now price out wired network cards. Find a fiber-optic card, and price that versus an Ethernet card that offers similar speeds. Also look at the price of a 25m CAT-6 (or CAT-5) cable versus a 5m fiber-optic cable. How much difference is there?

BLUETOOTH

Bluetooth is not designed to be a WLAN but rather a wireless personal area network (PAN). In other words, it's not the right technology to use if you want to set up a wireless network for your office. It is, however, a great technology to use if you have wireless devices that you want your computer to be able to communicate with. Examples include smartphones, mice, keyboards, headsets, and printers.

Nearly every laptop comes with built-in Wi-Fi capabilities, and most also come Bluetooth enabled. If not, you will need to use a USB Bluetooth adapter to use your Bluetooth devices. Almost all smartphones and other mobile devices today support Bluetooth.

There are several Bluetooth standards that have been introduced into the market. Version 1.2 was adopted in 2003 and supported data rates of up to 1Mbps. Newer versions have increased speed and compatibility with technologies such as Wi-Fi, LTE, and IPv6 as well as reduced power requirements and increased security. The newest version is Bluetooth v4.2, which was released in December 2014. Bluetooth currently supports maximum data rates of 24Mbps. It can achieve these rates by using available 802.11 signals as a transmission medium. Otherwise, the maximum transmission speed of Bluetooth is about 3Mbps. Table 8.6 summarizes the Bluetooth versions and maximum data rates.

TABLE 8.6 Bluetooth versions and data rates

Version	Data rate
1.2	1Mbps
2.0 + EDR	3Mbps

Version	Data rate
3.0 + HS	24Mbps
4.0	24Mbps

There are three classes of Bluetooth devices, which differ in their transmission range and power usage; the specifications are shown in Table 8.7. Most mobile Bluetooth devices are Class 2 devices, which have a maximum range of 10 meters (33 feet) and power usage of 2.5mW. When studying Bluetooth, it's easy to get the versions and classes mixed up. Remember that they are independent of each other. Most devices you see will be Class 2, regardless of the Bluetooth version they support. Also, remember that the version affects the data rate but not the maximum distance.

TABLE 8.7   Bluetooth device classes and specifications

Class	Distance	Power usage
1	100m	100mW
2	10m	2.5mW
3	1m	1mW

Like 802.11b/g/n, Bluetooth uses the unlicensed 2.4GHz range for communication. To avoid interference, Bluetooth can "signal hop" at different frequencies to avoid conflicts with devices using other technologies in the area. Thanks to technology improvements, interference with Wi-Fi is unlikely, but it can still occur.

One of the unusual features of Bluetooth networks is their temporary nature. With Wi-Fi, you need a central communication point, such as a WAP or router. Bluetooth networks are formed on an ad hoc basis, meaning that whenever two Bluetooth devices get close enough to each other, they can communicate directly with each other. This dynamically created network is called a *piconet*. A Bluetooth-enabled device can communicate with up to seven other devices in one piconet.

INFRARED

Infrared waves have been around since the beginning of time. They are longer than light waves but shorter than microwaves. The most common use of infrared technology is the television remote control, although infrared is also used in night-vision goggles and medical and scientific imaging.

In 1993 the *Infrared Data Association (IrDA)* was formed as a technical consortium to support "interoperable, low-cost infrared data interconnection standards that support a walk-up, point-to-point user model." The key terms here are *walk-up* and *point-to-point*, meaning you need to be at very close range to use infrared and it's designed for one-to-one communication. Infrared requires line-of-sight, and generally speaking, the two devices need to be pointed at each other to work. If you point your remote away from the television, how well does it work?

 More information on the IrDA standard can be found at the organization's website: http://www.irda.org.

Some laptops have a built-in infrared port, which is a small, dark square of plastic, usually black or dark maroon. For easy access, infrared ports are located on the front or sides of devices that have them. Figure 8.9 shows an example of an infrared port.

FIGURE 8.9   Infrared port

Current IrDA specifications allow transmission of data up to 1Gbps, and IrDA claims that 5Gbps and 10Gbps standards are in the works. Because infrared does not use radio waves, there are no concerns of interference or signal conflicts. Atmospheric conditions can play a role in disrupting infrared waves, but considering that the maximum functional range of an IrDA device is about 1 meter, weather is not likely to cause you any problems.

Security is not an issue with infrared. The maximum range is about 1 meter with an angle of about 30 degrees, and the signal does not go through walls, so hacking prospects are limited. If someone is making an attempt to intercept an infrared signal, it's going to be pretty obvious. The data is directional, and you choose when and where to send it.

Different Infrared Technologies

You might have read the 1-meter distance limitation in the section on infrared and thought, "But my television remote works at longer distances than that," and you are right. Television and other consumer electronics remote controls are not governed by IrDA. They use a different infrared technology, based on the RC-5 protocol developed by Philips in the late 1980s. The maximum functional distance of these remote controls is about 15 to 20 feet, depending on the device.

Computer communications standards using infrared are managed by IrDA, and the maximum distance is about 1 meter. There are methods that IR manufacturers can use to modify this, but the general specification guarantees data rates at only 1 meter.

Installing the Network

Before you run your first cable or place your first wireless router, know exactly where everything is supposed to go on the network. The only way you'll be able to do this is to plan ahead. If you have planned the installation before you begin, the actual physical work of installing the network will be much easier.

Keys to Planning a Network

Every network is going to be somewhat different, but there are some general things to keep in mind as you go through your planning process:

Get a map.   Understand the layout of the space in which you're installing the network. Get a map of the office or draw one yourself. Add distances or a scale if possible so you can determine how far you'll need to run cables or how many wireless access points you'll need. Label power locations and their capacity. Mark any potential obstacles or hazards that you may run into when you try to run cable, such as your fluorescent lights, water pipes, or cinder block walls.

Locate your server(s).   If you are installing a small network, you may not have to worry about this. But if you have a network with one or more dedicated servers, decide where they will be located. They need to be in a secured location where only authorized people have access to them. This can be anything from a small closet to an elaborate server room with raised, antistatic floors. Just make sure it's temperature controlled because server closets tend to get very hot, and we know that heat and computers don't mix well.

Identify where client computers will be.   If you are setting up an office in a cubicle farm, just assume one computer (or more, depending on the cubicle type) per cube. This will help you determine where you need shared network resources as well as cable placement.

Locate network resources.   If your network users are going to share resources such as printers, where will they be located? If there are dozens or even hundreds of users, you may need multiple printer locations or *printer banks*. Locate these and other shared resources in enough places so that users don't have to walk from one end of the office to the other just to pick up printouts.

Determine how you are going to connect.   If you are going to go all wireless, you can start figuring out how many wireless routers or access points you'll need. If you are going to have wired connections, start determining how long the cable runs will be. Remember that UTP has a maximum segment distance of 100 meters. If you have to go up from a patch panel, into a ceiling, and down through a wall or conduit, take that into account too!

Designate additional connectivity areas if needed.   If you are running cables and some systems are outside of your maximum cable length, you will need to install a repeater of some sort. The best choice is probably a switch, which repeats signals. If you have several hundred computers, though, and you want to separate out networks, then a router is the best choice. These connectivity locations can be just a small closet. Other times, if no space is available, some administrators will put the switch in the drop ceiling. Although there is nothing wrong with this (as long as it's secured), it can be challenging to find power up there and it does make it more difficult to add to that switch. Finally, if there's no way to run power into the area where you need the switch, you could buy one that uses *Power over Ethernet (PoE)*, which is covered in Chapter 6. Generally the number of ports these devices support is limited, but it beats having no connectivity at all.

Physical Installation

You shouldn't begin to physically install the network until all of your plans are complete and you've double-checked them. There are few things more annoying than getting halfway through an installation and determining that your plans need to change drastically. Here we'll look at installation of three groups of items: network cards, cables, and connectivity devices.

Installing and Configuring Network Interface Cards

In the old days (1980s) of personal computers, NICs were a pain to install. Not only did you have to configure the hardware manually, you had to configure the network protocol stack manually. This usually involved a configuration program of some kind and was very cumbersome. Fortunately, installing a NIC today is pretty straightforward.

INSTALLING A NIC

Before you can begin communicating on your network, you must have a NIC installed in the machine. Installing a NIC is a fairly simple task if you have installed any expansion card before; a NIC is just a special type of expansion card. In Exercise 8.2, you will learn how to install a NIC.

EXERCISE 8.2

Installing a NIC in Windows 7

1. Power off the PC, remove the case and the metal or plastic blank covering the expansion slot opening, and insert the expansion card into an open slot.

2. Secure the expansion card with the screw provided.

3. Put the case back on the computer and power it up (you can run software configuration at this step, if necessary). If there are conflicts, change any parameters so that the NIC doesn't conflict with any existing hardware.

Note that these first three steps may not be necessary if you have an onboard NIC.

4. Install a driver for the NIC for the type of operating system that you have. Windows Plug and Play (PnP) will recognize the NIC and install the driver automatically. It may also ask you to provide a copy of the necessary driver if it does not recognize the type of NIC you have installed. If Windows does not start the installation routine immediately, open Control Panel, and choose Add A Device under Hardware And Sound. A list of hardware devices will appear. Choose the NIC and continue the installation.

5. After installing a NIC, you must hook the card to the network using the appropriate cable (if using wired connections). Attach this patch cable to the connector on the NIC and to a port in the wall (or connectivity device), thus connecting your PC to the rest of the network.

CONFIGURING A NIC

Now that your NIC is installed, it's time to configure it with the right IP address and TCP/IP configuration information. There are two ways to do this. The first is to automatically obtain IP configuration information from a Dynamic Host Configuration Protocol (DHCP) server, if one is available on the network. The other way is to manually enter in the configuration information yourself.

 Real World Scenario

Easy Configuration

Imagine that you have found yourself in a situation in which you have a small network of no more than 10 computers and do not have a DHCP server. You want to minimize the administrative hassle of configuring TCP/IP, so you want your computers to configure themselves automatically. What do you do?

The answer is to set the NIC up to get its IP information from the DHCP server anyway. Microsoft Windows operating systems will automatically configure themselves with an Automatic Private IP Addressing (APIPA) address if they are unable to locate a DHCP server. With an APIPA address, computers on the local network will be able to communicate with one another. The limitation is that the computers will *not* be able to communicate with any remote devices (those not on the local network) and will not be able to get on the Internet.

To configure your NIC in Windows 7, open Control Panel in Category view and click View Network Status And Tasks under Network And Internet. In the left pane, click Change Adapter Settings. You'll see the name of a connection, such as Local Area Connection. Right-click that, and click Properties. Figure 8.10 shows you what the Properties screen will look like.

FIGURE 8.10 Wireless Network Connection properties

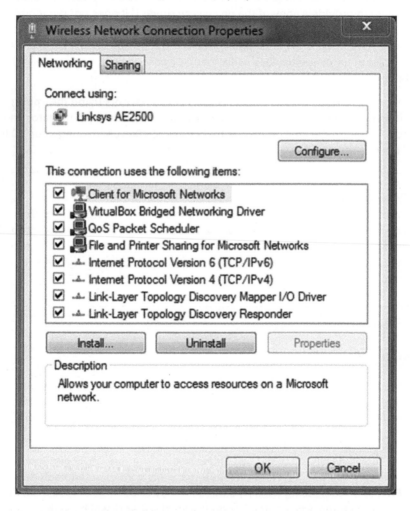

On that screen, highlight Internet Protocol Version 4 (TCP/IPv4) and click Properties. This will take you to a screen similar to the one in Figure 8.11.

FIGURE 8.11   TCP/IP properties

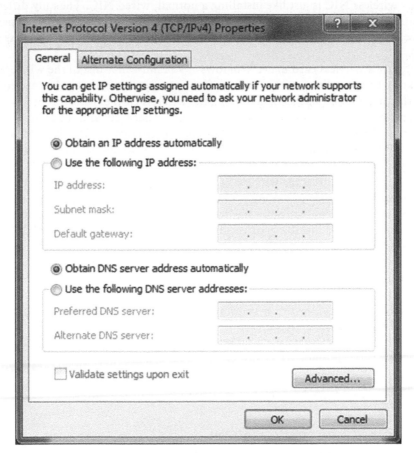

As you can see in Figure 8.11, this computer is configured to obtain its information from a DHCP server. (If you have a wireless router, as many people do on their home networks, it can function as a DHCP server. We'll talk more about that in a few sections.) If you wanted to configure the client manually, you would click Use The Following IP Address and enter in the correct information. To supply the client with a DNS server address manually, click Use The Following DNS Server Addresses.

If you manually configure the IP address, you must also configure the DNS server address manually. Otherwise, the client will not have access to a DNS server. Client computers can broadcast to find a DHCP server, but they cannot broadcast to find a DNS server.

WIRELESS CARD INSTALLATION

Installing a wireless NIC is just like installing a normal, wired NIC. The only difference is in the configuration of the NIC. You must configure the NIC to connect to your preferred wireless network (by its SSID) and configure any security settings (such as wireless encryption keys).

To configure a wireless card under Windows 7, you must first install the wireless card. For a desktop, this usually means powering off the computer, removing the case cover, and inserting the card into an open slot (assuming the wireless card expansion card type and bus slot type match). Then you can power the computer back up, and the computer should recognize that a new card was installed and prompt you to install the driver. Most desktops also have USB ports for installation of wireless NICs. The process will be nearly identical to the one you followed in Exercise 8.2.

On a laptop, simply insert the wireless PC Card or USB NIC into any open PC Card slot or USB port with the laptop powered up. Once you have done this, Windows PnP will recognize the card and ask you to install the driver. (Note that some NIC manufacturers ask you to insert the CD and install the drivers before physically installing the NIC. Not doing so could cause installation issues. Always check your documentation!) Nearly every laptop processor chipset made today (such as the Intel Core i5) comes with integrated wireless, so no external adapter needs to be added. USB-attached NICs are an option for desktop computers as well.

Once the NIC is in and the driver is installed, you may have to reboot (but only in very unique cases). Then the wireless card should be ready to use.

Bear in mind that these are general steps. Always consult the documentation that comes with the hardware to ensure that there isn't a special step that is unique to that card.

WIRELESS CONNECTION CONFIGURATION

Now that your wireless card is installed in your computer, you can configure the connection so you can use it. Windows versions from XP on are beautiful for wireless use because they have utilities for connecting to wireless networks built into the operating system. Windows uses the Wireless Zero Configuration Service (also called Wireless Auto Configuration or WLAN AutoConfig) to automatically connect to wireless access points using IEEE 802.11 standards.

To configure a wireless connection, you can simply bring a Windows (XP or newer) laptop or computer within range of a wireless access point and Windows will detect and alert you to the presence of the access point. Alternatively, if you would like control over the connection, in Windows 7, you can choose Start ➤ Control Panel ➤ Network And Internet and then choose Connect To A Network. You will get a screen similar to the one shown in Figure 8.12.

If you have a wireless signal strength indicator in the system tray next to the clock, you can click on it and see the same screen as is shown in Figure 8.12.

FIGURE 8.12 Available wireless connections

From this screen you can view the SSIDs of the available wireless networks, including the one to which you are connected (the one that says "Connected" next to it). The bars in the far-right column indicate the relative signal strength of each connection. The more green bars showing, the stronger the signal and the better (and faster) the connection.

 If the connection shows a lock icon next to the signal indicator, it is a secured wireless network and you will need to enter some sort of password to gain access to it. It can be dangerous to join unsecured networks; you have no way of knowing who is on them or what are their intentions. Wireless attacks on unsecured networks are becoming more common, so be careful with joining unsecured networks!

To connect to any network, double-click it and Windows will try to connect. You'll see a window similar to the one in Figure 8.13 that shows you the connection attempt is in progress. Once you are connected, Windows will display "Connected" next to that connection.

FIGURE 8.13   Connecting to a wireless network

The weaker the signal, the longer the connection will take. Authentication will also slow down the initial connection time.

Installing Network Cables

Network cables are not the most fun thing to install. Proper installation of network cables generally means running them through ceilings and walls and making a mess of the office. Thank goodness for wireless!

Be sure to use plenum cable if you are running cables through spaces where there is air ventilation, such as drop ceilings. PVC-coated cables will produce poisonous gas when burned. Also be sure that you have the proper permission to run the cables and that you aren't violating any building codes.

If you are installing a wired network in an existing office space, you may want to look into hiring out the cable installation to a third party. You'll find many companies that have the tools needed to properly install a wired network.

When installing a wired network yourself, always be aware of the maximum cable lengths, as outlined in Table 8.4. In addition, utilize cable troughs in ceilings and walls or another conduit in walls to keep your cables organized. Figure 8.14 shows a cable trough; they come in a variety of lengths and quality.

FIGURE 8.14 Cable trough

Finally, if you must run cables across the floor in a walkway (which isn't recommended), use a floor cable guard to avoid creating a trip hazard and to protect your cables. A floor cable guard is shown in Figure 8.15.

FIGURE 8.15 Floor cable guard

When running cables through a ceiling, never run the cables directly across fluorescent lights. These lights emit electromagnetic radiation (EMI) that can interfere with network communications. Utilize your cable troughs to keep cables in one place and away from lights. Also remember that fiber-optic cables are immune to EMI!

Installing and Configuring Wireless Access Points and Wireless Routers

Instead of using switches and hubs, wireless networks use either a *wireless access point (WAP)* or a *wireless router* to provide central connectivity. A WAP functions essentially like a wireless hub, whereas wireless routers provide more functionality, similar to that of a wired router. Based on looks alone, they are pretty much identical, and physically installing them is similar. The differences come in configuring them because they will have different options.

In the following sections, we're going to talk about installing and configuring WAPs and wireless routers interchangeably; just remember that a lot of the features available in a wireless router may not be available in a WAP.

PHYSICALLY INSTALLING A WIRELESS ACCESS POINT OR ROUTER

After unwrapping the device from its packaging (and reading the instructions, of course), you must choose a place for it. If it is supplying wireless access to your home network and the Internet, locate it where you can receive access in the most places. Keep in mind that the more walls the signal has to travel through, the lower the signal strength.

In addition, you may choose to have some computers plug directly into the device using a UTP cable. If so, it makes sense to locate the device near the computer or computers you will want to physically connect.

Place the WAP in the center of your home, close to a network connection. Or if you have only one computer, place it close to the broadband Internet connection you are using (i.e., the cable modem or DSL line).

In many offices, WAPs and wireless routers are often placed in the ceiling, with the antennae pointed downward through holes in the ceiling tiles. You can purchase metal plates designed to replace ceiling tiles to hold these devices. The plates have holes precut in them for the antennae to stick through, are designed to securely hold the device and easily open for maintenance, and often lock for physical security. There are also Wi-Fi ceiling antennas you can purchase that basically look like a little dome hanging from the ceiling.

For wireless connectivity devices placed in a ceiling (or other places with no easy access to an electrical outlet), *Power over Ethernet (PoE)* is a very handy technology to supply both power and an Ethernet connection.

Once you have chosen the location, plug the unit into a wall outlet and connect the two antennae that come with the unit (as needed; many newer devices contain built-in antennae). They will screw onto two bungs on the back of the unit. Once the unit is plugged in, you need to connect it to the rest of your network.

If you are connecting directly to the Internet through a cable modem or DSL or to a wired hub or router, you will most likely plug the cable into the Internet socket of the device, provided it has one. If not, you can use any of the other wired ports on the back of the device to connect to the rest of your network. Make sure that you get a link light on that connection.

At this point, the device is configured for a home network, with a few basic caveats. First, the default SSID (for example, Linksys) will be used, along with the default administrative password and the default IP addressing scheme. Also, there will be no encryption on the connection. This is known as an *open access point*. Even if you have nothing to protect except for the Internet connection, you shouldn't just leave encryption turned off. It just makes you an easy and inviting target for neighbors who want to siphon off your bandwidth or even worse. Many wireless manufacturers have made their devices so easy to configure that for most networks it is Plug and Play.

If you have personal data on your home network and more than one computer, you should never keep the default settings. Anyone could snoop your access point from the road in front of or behind your house and possibly get on your home network. It's too easy for identity theft!

From a computer on the home network, insert the device's setup CD into the computer's CD-ROM drive. It will automatically start and present you with a wizard that will walk you through setting the name of the SSID of this new access point as well as changing the default setup password, setting any security keys for this connection, and generally configuring the unit for your network's specific configuration. Then you're done!

Configuring a Wireless Router

Each wireless router manufacturer uses different software, but you can usually configure their parameters with the built-in, web-based configuration utility that's included with the product. While the software is convenient, you still need to know which options to configure and how those configurations will affect users on your networks. The items that require configuration depend on the choices you make about your wireless network. We will divide the configuration section into two parts: basic configuration and security options and then additional services.

Basic Configuration

The Wi-Fi Alliance (www.wi-fi.org) is the authoritative expert in the field of wireless LANs. It lists five critical steps to setting up a secured wireless router:

1. Change the router's SSID.
2. Change the administrator username and password. Make sure it's a strong password.
3. Select AES or WPA2.
4. Choose a high-quality security passphrase.
5. From the clients, select WPA2 and enter the security passphrase to connect.

The parameter that needs immediate attention is the SSID. An SSID is a unique name given to the wireless network. All hardware that is to participate on the network must be configured to use the same SSID. Essentially, the SSID is the network name. When you are using Windows to connect to a wireless network, all available wireless networks will be listed by their SSID when you select View Available Wireless Networks.

When you first install the wireless network, the default SSID is used and there is no security enabled. In other words, it's pretty easy to find your network (Linksys), and anyone within range of your signal can get on your network with no password required. This is obviously a security risk, so you want to change that.

For the rest of this example, we'll use a Linksys EA3500 wireless router. First, you need to log in to your device. The default internal address of this router is 192.168.1.1, so to log in, open Internet Explorer (or your preferred Internet browser) and type **192.168.1.1** into the address bar. (Some routers use 192.168.0.1 as a default; check your router's documentation if you are unsure about what your router uses.) You'll get a screen similar to the one in Figure 8.16.

FIGURE 8.16 Logging in to the wireless router

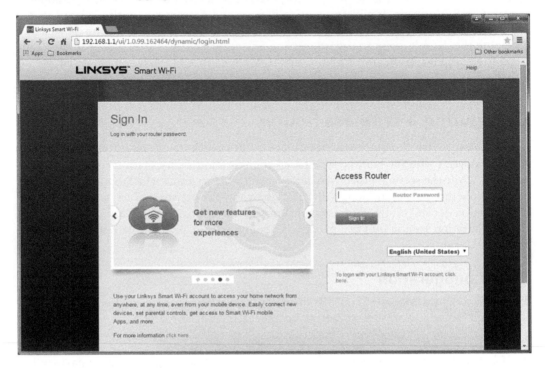

Some wireless router installation programs will install an icon on your desktop to use for management. Clicking the icon will take you to the management program.

You should have already set up the username and password using the CD provided with the device. If not, look in the manual for the default username and password. You'll definitely want to change these as soon as possible. Once you're logged in, the first screen you'll see is similar to the one in Figure 8.17. On this screen, you can see sections along the left-hand side that allow you to configure various router settings. On this router, the Connectivity section has an Internet Settings tab that identifies how you configure your incoming connection from the ISP. In most cases, your cable or DSL provider will just have you use DHCP to get an external IP address from its DHCP server, but there are options to configure this manually as well.

Next, configure the parameters that are crucial for operation according to the Wi-Fi Alliance. On this router, the SSID and passwords are configured on the Basic tab of the Connectivity settings, as shown in Figure 8.18.

FIGURE 8.17   Basic setup screen

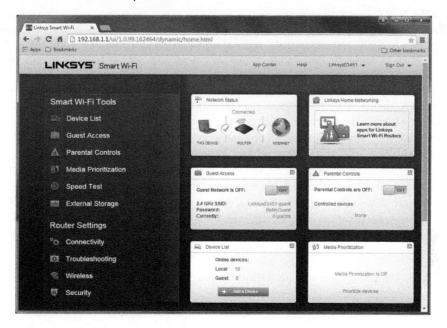

FIGURE 8.18   Basic wireless settings tab

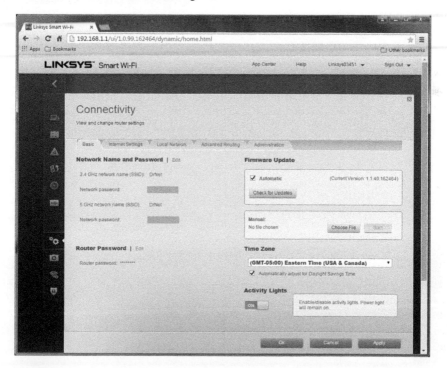

Figure 8.18 also shows the option to check for firmware updates, and in this case those updates will be automatic. After you install a router, change the SSID and passwords, and set up security, you should update the firmware to ensure that it's the most current version. Using older firmware versions could present security risks.

You can see the network name (SSID) as well as the password required by clients to join the network. (We blocked out the password for pretty obvious reasons, because this router screen shows it in plain text.) You can change either of these parameters by clicking the Edit link to the right of Network Name And Password. The router's administrative password is also changed from this screen, in the Router Password section. Click Edit and set the password as needed. Make sure it's very different than the password needed to join the network! These steps take care of the SSID, admin password, and security phrase. While we're in Connectivity, we're going to click the Local Network tab to configure our internal network settings, as shown in Figure 8.19.

FIGURE 8.19   Internal Network Settings screen

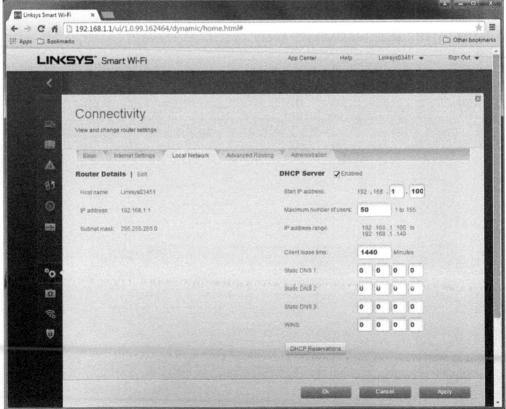

Here, you configure your router's hostname, internal IP address (in this case 192.168.1.1), and subnet mask. On this router, DHCP is also configured on this screen. If you want the device to act as a DHCP server for internal clients, enable it here, specify the starting IP address, and specify the maximum number of DHCP users. (Author's note: I just realized that I have my router set up to allow 50 DHCP leases at once. In my home, I have about a dozen devices that connect to my network and need a DHCP lease, so having it set to 50 is overkill. I should probably change that!) Disabling DHCP means that clients will have to use a static IP address.

> Most wireless routers (like the one used in this example) have a help section to describe each setting on the configuration pages. So if you're not totally sure what a setting does, click the Help link (at the top of the screen in this case) to find out what the setting does. If not, there's always the manual or online help!

The last critical setting you need to make is to enable wireless encryption. If you don't do this, all signals sent from the wireless router to client computers will be in plain text and anyone can join the network without a security password. It's a really bad thing to leave disabled. On this particular router, it would make sense to configure security via the Security section, but that's not true. (Who says things need to be logical?) Here, click the Wireless section, as shown in Figure 8.20.

FIGURE 8.20   Wireless settings, including encryption

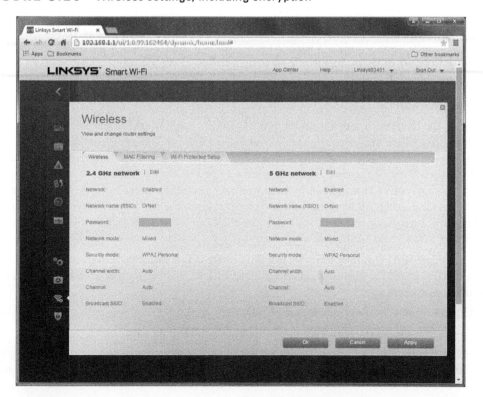

This router happens to be 802.11n, so it has sections for both a 2.4GHz and 5GHz network. If there were only devices of one type, it would make sense to disable the other network. In this case, though, we are talking about security, and you can see that it's set to WPA2 Personal. To change the setting, click Edit next to the network type. The other WPA2 choice you generally have is WPA2 Enterprise, which is more secure than Personal. For a business network, regardless of the size, Enterprise is the way to go. In order to use Enterprise, though, you need a separate security server called a RADIUS server.

Another tab shown on Figure 8.20 is the MAC Filtering tab. On that tab, you can configure the router to allow connections only from clients with certain MAC addresses. (Recall that MAC addresses are hardware addresses built into NICs.) This is a light-duty security measure you can use on your network, but it's easily defeated by an attacker with the ability to spoof a MAC address.

For your wireless router to use WPA2 Enterprise, remember that you need to have a RADIUS server on your network. The A+ exam won't test you on how to configure RADIUS. For now just know what it is, which is an authentication server. Other exams, such as Network+, will test you on how to configure RADIUS.

With that, the router-side setup recommendations have been taken care of. Now it's just a matter of setting up the clients with the same security method and entering in the passphrase. Before we move on to specific security options, there are a few more basic setup concepts we need to cover.

Wireless Channels

Earlier in the chapter in the section on 802.11g, we brought up the concept of wireless channels. There are 11 configurable channels in the 2.4GHz range, which is what 802.11b/g uses to communicate. If you look back at Figure 8.20, you'll see that the channel is set to auto. Most of the time, you won't have a need to change that.

But let's say you're in a situation where you have too many users for one WAP to adequately service (about 30 or more) or your physical layout is too large and you need multiple access points. Now you need to have more than one access point. In a situation like this, here's how you should configure it:

- Set up the WAPs so they have overlapping ranges. The minimum overlap is 10 percent, and 20 percent is recommended. This way, if users roam from one area to another, they don't lose their signal.
- Configure the WAPs with the same SSID.
- Configure the WAPs with non-overlapping channels.

2.4GHz channels need to be at least five numbers apart to not overlap. So, for example, channels 2 and 7 do not overlap, nor do 4 and 10. There are 11 configurable channels, so you can have a maximum of three overlapping ranges on the same SSID, configured with channels 1, 6, and 11, and not have any interference. Wireless clients are configured to auto-detect a channel by default, but they can be forced to use a specific channel as well.

On the example router we were using, you could also configure the 5GHz network. In this case, you can choose from 20MHz or 40MHz channel widths, as well as choose the channel. Figure 8.21 shows the channels available. Each of the 20MHz channels shown is non-overlapping.

FIGURE 8.21 5GHz channels available to select

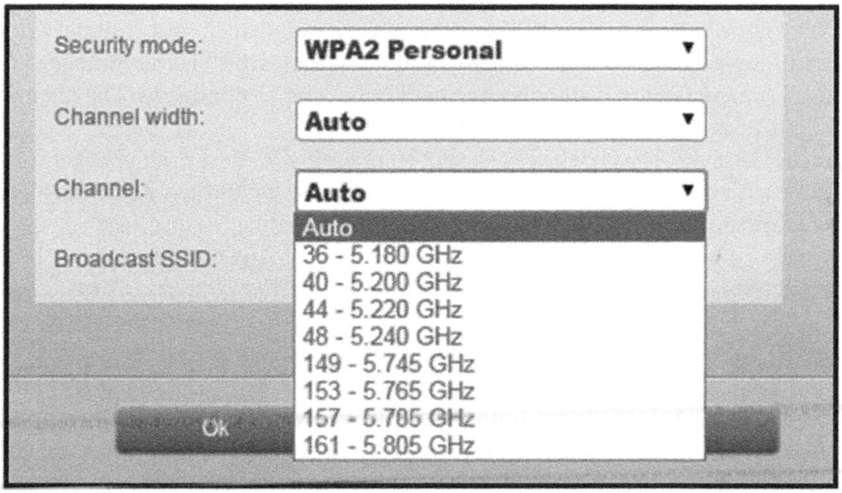

Security mode:	**WPA2 Personal** ▾
Channel width:	**Auto** ▾
Channel:	**Auto** ▾
	Auto
Broadcast SSID:	36 - 5.180 GHz
	40 - 5.200 GHz
	44 - 5.220 GHz
	48 - 5.240 GHz
	149 - 5.745 GHz
	153 - 5.765 GHz
	157 - 5.785 GHz
	161 - 5.805 GHz

Ok

Network Address Translation (NAT)

Network Address Translation (NAT) is a very cool service that translates private IP addresses on your internal network to a public IP address on the Internet. If you are using your wireless router to allow one or more clients to access the Internet but you have only one external public IP address, your router is using NAT.

Most routers have NAT enabled by default, and there might not be any specific configuration options for it. That's true in the case of the EA3500 router we've been using as an example. You can enable or disable it on the Advanced Routing tab in Connectivity, but otherwise the only options you can configure are the internal IP addresses that the router hands out to clients.

To be technically correct, NAT is specifically a one-to-one translation of a private IP address to a public IP address. If you have multiple client computers with private addresses accessing the Internet using one public address (called many-to-one), that is a specific form of NAT known as overloading, Port Address Translation (PAT), or *port forwarding*. The A+ exam does not test you on the differences between NAT and PAT, but other tests do, such as the Network+ exam.

Another type of NAT is called *Dynamic Network Address Translation (DNAT)*, which translates a group of private addresses to a pool of routable addresses. This is used to make a resource that's on a private network available for consumption on public networks by appearing to give it a publicly available address. For example, if a web server were behind a NAT-enabled router and did not have its own public IP address, it would be inaccessible to the Internet. DNAT can make it accessible.

Universal Plug and Play

Universal Plug and Play (UPnP) is a standard designed to simplify the process of connecting devices to a network and enable those devices to automatically announce their presence to other devices on the network. If you remember when Plug and Play was new to computers, it was revolutionary. You simply plugged in a peripheral (such as a USB network card or mouse) and it was detected automatically and it worked. UPnP is the same idea, but for networking. From a standards standpoint, there's not a lot to configure. The client needs to be a DHCP client and the service uses UDP port 1900.

The concept is great. It lets devices connect to the network and discover each other automatically with the Simple Service Discovery Protocol. It can be used for any networked device you can think of, from routers and printers to smartphones and security cameras.

The problem is, UPnP has no authentication mechanism. Any device or user is trusted and can join the network. That is obviously a problem. The security consulting firm Rapid7 did a six-month research study in early 2013 and found that over 6,900 network-aware products, made by 1,500 different companies, responded to public UPnP requests. In total, they found nearly 81 million individual devices responded to requests. The United States Department of Homeland Security and many others immediately began requesting people to disable UPnP.

Since that time, the UPnP forum (www.upnp.org) has released statements saying that the security holes have been patched and that the system is more secure than ever. As of the time of writing, skeptics still abound and UPnP does not appear to be a safe option. Regardless of if and when it gets fixed, the reputation of UPnP is not a good one.

The biggest risk is for open UPnP connections to be exploited by unknown systems on the Internet. Therefore, you should configure your router to not allow UPnP connections from its external connection. Many ISPs have also taken steps to help prevent issues. If you're concerned about devices on your network posing security risks via UPnP, visit www.rapid7.com/resources/free-security-software-downloads/universal-plug-and-play-jan-2013.jsp to download and run the UPnP exploit scanner. If you're unsure about your router, disable UPnP just to be safe.

 Real World Scenario

Sharing an Internet Connection

Wireless routers have many advantages over wireless access points. One of the biggest advantages is the ability to share an Internet connection. By sharing a connection, you pay for only one connection but you can connect as many computers as you would like (or as many as are reasonable) to your wireless router. Here is how to do that.

First, ensure that your DSL modem or cable modem is connected properly. Then, connect your wireless router to your cable modem or DSL modem using a UTP cable (CAT-5e or better). In most cases, the wireless router will have a wired Internet port on the back of it. Connect the cable here and plug it into your broadband modem. Finally, you can connect computers to your wireless router.

Many ISPs, in an attempt to prohibit this sort of behavior, will restrict access through the modem to one MAC address. This isn't a problem. You can do one of two things. The first option is, when you first make your connection to the ISP, just make sure your computer is already connected through your router. The ISP will see the MAC address of the router and assume that is your computer. The second option is that most wireless routers will allow you to clone your computer's MAC address (see Figure 8.22). Your router will simply tell the ISP that it has the same MAC address as your computer, which was previously connected directly to the cable or DSL modem. ISPs may not like it, but sharing a wireless Internet connection is very economical option for a small office or home network.

FIGURE 8.22 Option to clone a MAC address

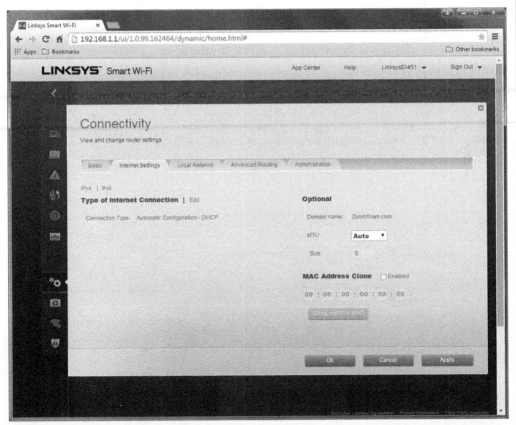

Additional Wireless Router Services

Wireless routers offer many more services than we've been able to cover to this point, and most of them are out of the scope of A+ exam training. That includes configuring your router as a firewall, but that topic is so important for networking that we feel the need to give you a primer anyway. (Besides, port forwarding and port triggering *are* exam objectives, and those are firewall concepts.) So, we want to finish off this chapter with two more important concepts related to routers: firewalls and QoS.

Understanding Firewall Basics

Before we get into configuring your wireless router as a firewall, let's be sure you know what firewalls can do for you. A *firewall* is a hardware or software solution that serves as your network's security guard. For networks that are connected to the Internet, they're probably the most important device on the network. Firewalls can protect you in two ways. They protect your network resources from hackers lurking in the dark corners of the Internet, and they can simultaneously prevent computers on your network from accessing undesirable content on the Internet. At a basic level, firewalls filter packets based on rules defined by the network administrator.

Firewalls can be stand-alone "black boxes," software installed on a server or router, or some combination of hardware and software. Most firewalls will have at least two network connections: one to the Internet, or *public side*, and one to the internal network, or *private side*. Some firewalls have a third network port for a second semi-internal network. This port is used to connect servers that can be considered both public and private, such as web and email servers. This intermediary network is known as a *demilitarized zone (DMZ)*, an example of which is shown in Figure 8.23. Personal software-based firewalls will run on computers with only one NIC.

FIGURE 8.23   A network with a demilitarized zone (DMZ)

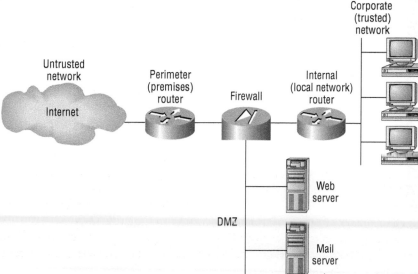

Types of Firewalls

We've already stated that firewalls can be software- or hardware-based or a combination of both. Keeping that in mind, there are two general categories of firewalls: network-based and host-based.

Network-based firewalls   A *network-based firewall* is what companies use to protect their private network from public networks. The defining characteristic of this type of firewall is that it's designed to protect an entire network of computers instead of just one system. It's generally a stand-alone hardware device with specialized software installed on it to protect your network.

Host-based firewalls   In contrast to network-based firewalls, a *host-based firewall* is implemented on a single machine so it protects only that one machine. This type of firewall is usually a software implementation because you don't need any additional hardware in your personal computer to run it. All current Windows client operating systems come with Windows Firewall, which is a great example of a host-based solution. Norton Security and many other security products come with software firewalls too. Host-based firewalls are generally not as secure as network firewalls, but for small businesses or home use, they're an adequate, cheap solution.

How Firewalls Work

Firewalls are configured to allow only packets that pass specific security restrictions to get through them. They can also permit, deny, encrypt, decrypt, and proxy all traffic that flows through them, most commonly between the public and private parts of a network. The network administrator decides on and sets up the rules a firewall follows when deciding to forward data packets or reject them.

The default configuration of a firewall is generally *default deny*, which means that all traffic is blocked unless specifically authorized by the administrator. While this is very secure, it's also time consuming to configure the device to allow legitimate traffic to flow through it. The other option is *default allow*, which means all traffic is allowed through unless the administrator denies it. If you have a default allow firewall and don't configure it, you might as well not have a firewall at all.

The basic method of configuring firewalls is to use an *access control list (ACL)*. The ACL is the set of rules that determines which traffic gets through the firewall and which traffic is blocked. ACLs are typically configured to block traffic by IP address, port number, domain name, or some combination of all three.

Packets that meet the criteria in the ACL are passed through the firewall to their destination. For example, let's say you have a computer on your internal network that is set up as a web server. To allow Internet clients to access the system, you need to allow data on port 80 (HTTP) to get to that computer.

Another concept you need to understand is *port triggering*. It allows traffic to enter the network on a specific port after a computer makes an outbound request on that specific port. For example, if a computer on your internal network makes an outbound Telnet request (port 23), subsequent inbound traffic destined for the originating computer on port 23 would be allowed through.

Configuring Your Wireless Firewall

Nearly every wireless router sold today provides you with some level of firewall protection. On the router used in this example, the firewall options are on two separate tabs. Enabling the firewall and setting a few basic options is done from the Security section, as shown in Figure 8.24. More advanced options, such as configuring port forwarding and port triggering, are on the DMZ and Apps And Gaming tabs.

FIGURE 8.24   Enabling the firewall

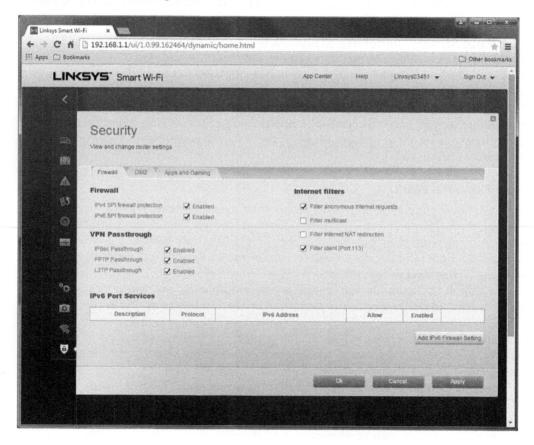

Quality of Service (QoS)

Quality of Service (QoS) is a strategy that allows an administrator to control traffic to maintain a certain service level. By using QoS, an administrator can set different priorities for one or more types of network traffic based on different applications, data flows, or users. For example, if the engineering group needs to have a certain amount of guaranteed network bandwidth, QoS can make that happen. This is not typically implemented on small or home office networks but rather for larger enterprise networks.

QoS focuses on dealing with five different types of problems that can affect data on a network:

- Delay, usually caused by congested routes that prevent critical data from arriving on time
- Dropped packets, which often causes delay
- Error, or corrupted data
- Jitter, or variation in packet delay in a data stream
- Out-of-order delivery, which can cause performance issues in time-sensitive applications such as VoIP.

Before each session, a QoS level is established as part of a service-level agreement (SLA). This is a simply priority setting. Higher-level numbers indicate higher priority, and administrators can set priority levels 0 through 5. Table 8.8 shows the eight levels of QoS.

TABLE 8.8   QoS levels

Level	Description
0	Best effort
1	Background
2	Standard
3	Excellent load (business-critical applications)
4	Controlled load (streaming media)
5	Interactive voice and video (less than 100ms latency)
6	Layer 3 network control reserved traffic (less than 10ms latency)
7	Layer 2 network control reserved traffic (lowest latency)

As more and more real-time business-critical applications hit the market, QoS will become a bigger topic.

 Real World Scenario

Knowing How to Install and Configure a SOHO Router

If you are given the scenario in real life or on the A+ exam, you should know how to install and configure a SOHO router. In today's environment, most installations for small offices and home networks will involve wireless routers. Throughout this chapter you have

continues

continued

learned everything you need to know to purchase the best device for different situations and how to set it up once you get it out of the box. Let's review here though.

The first decision to make is which router technology to purchase. With wireless, it's generally best to go with the best technology available because speeds have been increasing rapidly over the last several years. It seems like 802.11ac provides great speed, but you might not be able to use all of its capacity due to channel bonding limitations. Therefore, 802.11n might be just fine, and possibly cheaper.

Next, how will the office get on the Internet? The two most obvious choices are DSL and cable internet. Find the best solution (which often means the least expensive), and set it up through the service provider. In fact, you may want to do this first because it will probably take the provider at least a few days to get it set up on their end and you want it to be ready when you install the network.

Then, as needed, plan the internal network layout. Is it all wireless or will there be wired connections? Do you need to run cables? Will there be a server closet or other central connectivity point? Once you're certain of your configuration, you can begin installation.

When installing the router, always remember these key steps:

1. Change the default SSID.
2. Change the administrator username and password to something highly secure.
3. Configure the best security possible, such as WEP2 (AES).
4. Set a strong passphrase for clients to join the network.

After those steps are complete, you can configure the clients to join the network by setting their security appropriately, finding the SSID, and entering the passphrase. Follow these guidelines and you will be able to properly install a network, regardless of the scenario presented.

Summary

In this chapter, you learned about wireless networking and configuring a small office, home office (SOHO) network. We started with wireless networking. We introduced the key wireless networking standards 802.11a, 802.11b, 802.11g, 802.11n, and 802.11ac and talked about their characteristics, such as speed, distances, frequencies, and modulation. Then, we moved into wireless security. Important security protocols to remember are WEP, WPA, and WPA2.

Next, you learned the fundamentals of installing a small network. We started this section off looking at the myriad possibilities for Internet connections, from the archaic dial-up to broadband options such as DSL, cable modems, fiber, ISDN, and satellite. After that, we talked about choosing internal network connections in both wired and wireless environments.

From there, we dove into physical network installation. The first critical step is planning. Don't be the one who forgets that! After covering elements of good planning, we looked at how to install network adapters, cabling, and connectivity devices.

Finally, we looked at how to configure a router. The Wi-Fi Alliance has some great practical steps on how to configure a secure wireless network, such as changing the SSID, setting passwords, and enabling security. We also looked at other basic configuration options, such as DHCP, communication channels, and NAT. After that, we finished up by looking at your wireless router as a firewall and taking a quick look at basic QoS.

Exam Essentials

Know the different 802.11 standards.   Standards you should be familiar with are 802.11a, 802.11b, 802.11g, 802.11n, and 802.11ac. 802.11a transmits up to 54Mbps in the 5GHz range. 802.11b transmits up to 11Mbps in the 2.4GHz range. 802.11g is backward compatible with 802.11b and transmits 54Mbps in the 2.4GHz range. 802.11n is backward compatible with all of the older versions and can achieve throughput of 600Mbps communicating in both the 2.4GHz and 5GHz ranges. The newest one is 802.11ac, which promises gigabit speeds in the 5GHz range.

Understand security protocols used for wireless networking.   Listed in order from least to most secure, the common wireless security protocols include WEP, WPA, and WPA2. WPA uses TKIP and WPA2 uses AES.

Know the different types of available broadband connections.   Broadband connections include DSL, cable, satellite, ISDN, cellular, and fiber optic.

Know the three non-overlapping 2.4GHz wireless channels.   If you need three non-overlapping channels, you must use channels 1, 6, and 11.

Review Questions

The answers to the chapter review questions can be found in Appendix A.

1. Which of the following wireless IEEE standards operate on the 2.4GHz radio frequency and are directly compatible with each other? (Choose two.)

   A. 802.11a

   B. 802.11b

   C. 802.11ac

   D. 802.11g

2. What is the primary function of the SSID?

   A. Secure communication between a web server and browser

   B. Secure communication between a server and remote host

   C. A parameter used to identify a network and configure a wireless connection

   D. A type of password used to secure a wireless connection

3. Which two of the following are features that allow 802.11ac to achieve higher data throughput? (Choose two.)

   A. MIMO

   B. Beamforming

   C. Channel bonding

   D. Code division multiplexing

4. What is the most secure wireless encryption standard for 802.11 networks?

   A. WEP

   B. WPA

   C. WPA2

   D. SAFER+

5. What level of QoS is designated for interactive voice and video?

   A. 1

   B. 4

   C. 5

   D. 6

6. You have just installed a wireless router on your home network. Which of the following should you do to make it highly secure? (Choose two.)

   A. Change the default administrator name and password.

   B. Change the SSID.

   C. Enable WEP.

D. Configure it to channel 11.

7. You are setting up a small office network for a client. Which Internet service would you recommend to provide the best speed?

A. DSL

B. Dial-up

C. Satellite

D. BRI ISDN

E. PRI ISDN

8. Which service allows users with private IP addresses to access the Internet using a public IP address?

A. DHCP

B. DNS

C. DMZ

D. NAT

9. You are installing a single 802.11g wireless network. The office space is large enough that you need three WAPs. What channels should you configure the WAPs on to avoid communication issues?

A. 2, 5, and 7

B. 1, 8, and 14

C. 1, 6, and 11

D. 3, 6, and 9

10. You are setting up a wireless network. Which wireless standards would give the users over 40Mbps throughput? (Choose three.)

A. 802.11ac

B. 802.11b

C. 802.11g

D. 802.11n

11. You have been asked to configure a network for a small office. The wireless router is installed, and now you need to connect the client computers. What do you enter on the client computers to connect to the router?

A. The administrator password

B. The security passphrase

C. The client's MAC address

D. The default router password

12. Which of the following wireless communication methods has an operational range of 1 meter with a viewing angle of 30 degrees?

    A. Bluetooth

    B. Infrared

    C. WiMAX

    D. Satellite

13. Which of the following are advantages to using dial-up Internet service? (Choose two.)

    A. High speed

    B. Broad availability

    C. Low cost

    D. High security

14. Which of the following security standards was the first to introduce a dynamic 128-bit per-packet security key?

    A. WEP

    B. TKIP

    C. AES

    D. CCMP

15. You are running an 802.11g wireless router in mixed mode. You have three 802.11g wireless NICs using the router. A new user connects using an 802.11b wireless NIC. What will happen?

    A. The user with 802.11b will access the network at 11Mbps while the users with 802.11g will access the network at 54Mbps.

    B. The user with 802.11b will not be able to communicate on the network.

    C. The user with 802.11b will access the network at 11Mbps. The users with 802.11g will access the network at 54Mbps unless they are communicating with the 802.11b device, which will be at 11Mbps.

    D. All users will access the network at 11Mbps.

16. When enabled, which feature of a wireless router allows only specified computers to access the network?

    A. Port forwarding

    B. WPS

    C. SSID

    D. MAC filtering

17. A firewall operates by using a set of rules known as what?

    A. SLA

    B. ACL

    C. Default deny

    D. DMZ

18. You have set up a wireless router on your network and configured it to use AES. What configuration option do you need to choose on the client computers?

   A. WEP

   B. WPA

   C. WPA2

   D. TKIP

19. Besides 802.11 standards, which wireless communication method works in the 2.4GHz range?

   A. Bluetooth

   B. Infrared

   C. Satellite

   D. Cellular

20. Which of the following broadband technologies provides two dedicated, digital data channels that can be combined for greater throughput?

   A. DSL

   B. Cable

   C. Satellite

   D. BRI ISDN

   E. PRI ISDN

Performance-Based Question

You will encounter performance-based questions on the A+ exams. The questions on the exam require you to perform a specific task, and you will be graded on whether or not you were able to complete the task. The following requires you to think creatively in order to measure how well you understand this chapter's topics. You may or may not see similar questions on the actual A+ exams. To see how your answers compare to the authors', refer to Appendix B.

You just purchased a new PCI network card for a Windows 7 desktop computer. How would you install it?

Chapter

9

Understanding Laptops

THE FOLLOWING COMPTIA A+ EXAM 220-901 OBJECTIVES ARE COVERED IN THIS CHAPTER:

✓ **3.1 Install and configure laptop hardware and components.**

- Expansion options
  - Express card/34
  - Express card/54
  - SODIMM
  - Flash
  - Ports/Adapters
    - Thunderbolt
    - DisplayPort
    - USB to RJ-45 dongle
    - USB to Wi-Fi dongle
    - USB to Bluetooth
    - USB Optical Drive
- Hardware/device replacement
  - Keyboard
  - Hard Drive
    - SSD vs. Hybrid vs. Magnetic disk
    - 1.8in vs. 2.5in
  - Memory
  - Smart card reader
  - Optical drive
  - Wireless card
  - Mini-PCIe
  - Screen
  - DC jack

- Battery
- Touchpad
- Plastics/frames
- Speaker
- System board
- CPU

✓ **3.2 Explain the function of components within the display of a laptop.**

- Types
  - LCD
    - TTL vs. IPS
    - Fluorescent vs. LED backlighting
  - OLED
- Wi-Fi antenna connector/placement
- Webcam
- Microphone
- Inverter
- Digitizer

✓ **3.3 Given a scenario, use appropriate laptop features.**

- Special function keys
  - Dual displays
  - Wireless (on/off)
  - Cellular (on/off)
  - Volume settings
  - Screen brightness
  - Bluetooth (on/off)
  - Keyboard backlight
  - Touchpad (on/off)
  - Screen orientation
  - Media options (fast-forward/rewind)
  - GPS (on/off)
  - Airplane mode
- Docking station
- Physical laptop lock and cable lock
- Rotating/removable screens

As recently as the early 1990s, portable computers were luxuries that were affordable to only the wealthy or the select few businesspeople who traveled extensively. As with all other technologies, though, portable systems have gotten smaller, lighter (more portable), more powerful, and less expensive. Because the technology and price disparity between the two platforms has decreased significantly, laptops have outsold desktops since the mid-2000s.

Every indication is that the movement toward mobile computing will continue, so you definitely need to be well versed in portable technologies, which contain both nifty features and frustrating quirks. For this discussion, assume that a *portable computer* is any computer that contains all of the functionality of a desktop computer system but is portable. Most people define *portability* in terms of weight and size. So that we can discuss things on the same level, let's define portable as less than 10 pounds and smaller than an average desktop computer.

Of course, laptops are not the only types of portable computers in the market today. There are Chromebooks, tablets, and a variety of handheld smartphones that can also lay claim to being called computers. For the purpose of this chapter, we'll focus primarily on laptops, but many of the principles will be applicable to other, smaller portable computers as well. For specific material on smaller mobile devices, see Chapter 10, "Understanding Mobile Devices."

The original portable computers were hardly portable, hence the unofficial term *luggable*. They were the size of a small suitcase and could weigh 50 pounds. Not only were they greatly inferior to desktops in technology, they were also outrageously expensive. It's no wonder few people purchased them. Compaq, Kaypro, IBM, and Osborne made some of the first luggable computers.

Laptops were the next type of portable computer. They contain a built-in keyboard, pointing device, and LCD screen in a clamshell design. They are also called *notebook* computers because they resemble large notebooks. Most portable computers in use today are laptop computers.

In this chapter, you will learn about laptop computer architecture and how it differs from desktop computer architecture, including specific laptop hardware technologies. We'll then talk about management features unique to laptops and how to replace laptop components.

Understanding Laptop Architecture

Laptops are similar to desktop computers in architecture in that they contain many parts that perform similar functions. However, the parts that make up a laptop are completely different from those in desktop computers. The obvious major difference is size; laptops are space challenged. Another primary concern is heat. Restricted space means less airflow, meaning parts can heat up and overheat faster.

To overcome space limitations, laptop parts are physically much smaller and lighter, and they must fit into the compact space of a laptop's case. It might not sound like much, but there really is a major difference between a 4.5-pound laptop and a 5.5-pound laptop if you're hauling it around in its carrying case all day. Also, laptop parts are designed to consume less power and to shut themselves off when not being used, although many desktops also have components that go into a low-power state when not active, such as video circuitry. Finally, most laptop components are proprietary—the motherboard is especially proprietary, and the LCD screen from one laptop will not necessarily fit on another.

Manufacturers have also pushed smaller and smaller portables out as technology has improved. For example, in 2007 the first netbooks were introduced. A netbook is an extremely small laptop computer that is lighter in weight and more scaled down in features than a standard laptop. The term *netbook* is rarely used today, but Chromebooks are an example of that type of technology. Users are attracted to Chromebooks because of their enhanced portability and affordability. The features that remain are ideal for Internet access and emailing. However, many users would find them insufficient for mainstream usage.

In the following sections, you will learn about the various components that make up laptops and how they differ from desktop computer components. If you don't remember exactly what each component does, it may help you to refer back to earlier hardware chapters occasionally as you read this chapter.

Laptops vs. Desktops

If you've ever shopped for a laptop, you have no doubt noticed that the prices of desktop PCs are often quite a bit lower than those for notebook computers, yet the desktops are faster and more powerful. If you've ever wondered what makes a laptop so much different than a PC, here are the primary differences between laptops and desktops:

Portability   This is probably the most obvious difference. Laptops are designed to be portable. They run on batteries, so you aren't tied to one spot at home or at the office. Networking options are available that allow you to connect to a network wirelessly and do work from just about anywhere, including malls, airports, coffee shops, and so on. As anyone who's tried to bring their full-tower PC to a LAN party can tell you, desktops just aren't that portable.

Cost   Laptops tend to cost more than desktop computers with similar features. The primary reason is that portability requires small components and unique proprietary designs so that those components fit into the small size necessary. Miniature versions of components cost more money than standard-sized (desktop) versions. The cost discrepancy between desktops and laptops has shrunk considerably in the last few years, but it still exists.

Performance   By and large, laptops are always going to lose out somewhere in the performance department. Compromises must often be made between performance and portability, and considering that portability is the major feature of a laptop, performance is what usually suffers. While it is possible to have a laptop and a desktop with comparable performance, the amount of money one would have to spend for a "desktop replacement" laptop is considerable. This is not to say that a laptop can't outperform a desktop, it's just that the "bang for the buck" factor is higher in a desktop.

Expandability   Because desktop computers were designed to be modular, their capabilities can be upgraded quite easily. It is next to impossible to upgrade the processor or motherboard on most laptops. Other than memory and hard drives, most laptop upgrades consist of adding an external device through one of the laptop's ports, such as a USB port.

Quality of construction   Considering how much abuse laptops get, it is much more important that the materials used to construct the laptop case and other components be extremely durable. Durability is important in a desktop too, but it won't be tested as much as in a laptop.

Building Your Own

This anecdote comes from one of the authors: "During an A+ course, I gave the class the assignment to go out on the Web and put together the most powerful and complete computer they could for under a thousand dollars. The class was for non-degree-seeking adults, so nothing was graded; it was simply to provide experience with spec'ing out and pricing the parts that go into making a complete system.

"One of the students had her eye on a new laptop for personal use. Because she noticed the trend toward being able to build a desktop computer for less than she could buy one, the student assumed the same about laptops. Unfortunately, I had not specifically mentioned the fact that there are no standards for building complete laptop clones, unlike with desktops.

"You can't reliably build your own laptop. Because laptop components are designed to exacting specifications to fit properly inside one manufacturer's notebook, there generally are no universal motherboards, video boards, and so on for laptops. Memory and hard drives are the exception. You can get different brands of memory and hard drives for laptops, but you can't buy a motherboard from one company and the video circuitry from another. Even things as common as optical drives are usually designed to work only with a specific brand or model."

Now that we've illustrated the primary differences between laptops and desktops, let's examine the parts of the laptop and what they do.

Laptop Case

A typical laptop case is made up of three main parts:

- The display—usually an LCD or LED display
- The case frame, which is the metal reinforcing structure inside the laptop that provides rigidity and strength and to which most components are mounted
- The case, or the plastic cover that surrounds the components and provides protection from the elements

The cases are typically made of some type of plastic (usually ABS plastic or ABS composite) to provide for reduced weight as well as strength.

Some notebooks have cases made of a strong, lightweight metal, such as aluminum or titanium. However, the majority of laptop cases are made of plastic.

Laptop cases are made in what is known as a clamshell design. In a clamshell design, the laptop has two halves, hinged together at the back. Usually, the display is the top half (along with a webcam and possibly a microphone) and everything else is in the bottom half.

Occasionally, part of the laptop's case or the device's frame (occasionally referred to as *plastics*) will crack and need to be replaced. However, you usually can't just replace the cracked section. Most often, you must remove every component from inside the laptop's case and swap the components over to the new one. This is a labor-intensive process because the screws in laptops are often very small and hard to reach. Often, repairing a cracked case may cost several hundred dollars in labor alone. Most times, people who have cracked laptop cases wait until something else needs to be repaired before having the case fixed. Or, they just wait until it's time to upgrade to a new system. The decision on when to repair or replace the laptop boils down to a few factors. The primary one is if the user can live with the damage. While they can be annoying, most case problems don't inhibit the operation of the machine. The secondary factor is money. The user (or company) needs to decide if it's really worth spending the money needed to fix the issue immediately.

In the A+ objectives, you will see the words *plastics* and *frames* used together. These terms are basically interchangeable with the term *laptop case*. It just depends on whom you talk to. In real life, the term *plastics* is used infrequently, probably because it sounds kind of weird and not all cases are plastic. Know that the terms all mean basically the same thing, and use the one that best suits your tastes.

Motherboards and Processors

As with desktop computers, the motherboard of a laptop is the backbone structure to which all internal components connect. However, with a laptop, almost all components must be integrated onto the motherboard, including onboard circuitry for the serial, parallel, USB, IEEE 1394, video, expansion, and network ports of the laptop. With desktop systems, the option remains to not integrate such components. Because of the similarities between laptop and desktop components, some material in the next few sections will be familiar to you if you have read Chapter 1, "Motherboards, Processors, and Memory."

Laptop Motherboards

The primary differences between a laptop motherboard and a desktop motherboard are the lack of standards and the much smaller form factor. As mentioned earlier, most motherboards are designed along with the laptop case so that all the components will fit inside. Therefore, the motherboard is nearly always proprietary, and that's what we mean by "lack of standards." They use the technologies you're used to such as USB and 802.11, but it's very unlikely that you're going to be able to swap a motherboard from one laptop to another, even if both laptops are from the same manufacturer. Figure 9.1 shows an example of a laptop motherboard. Its unusual shape is designed to help it fit into a specific style of case with the other necessary components.

FIGURE 9.1   A laptop motherboard

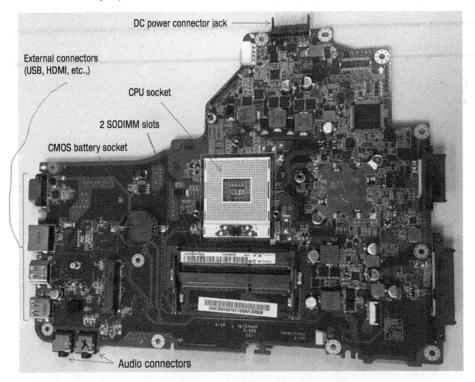

To save space, components of the video circuitry (and possibly other circuits as well) are placed on a thin circuit board that connects directly to the motherboard. This circuit board is often known as a riser card or a *daughterboard*; an example is shown in Figure 9.2.

FIGURE 9.2   A laptop daughterboard

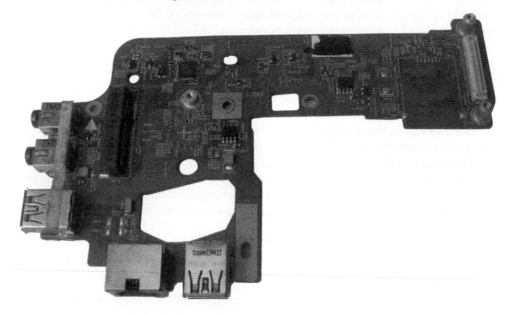

Having components performing different functions (such as video, audio, and networking) integrated on the same board is a mixed bag. On one hand, it saves a lot of space. On the other hand, if one part goes bad, you have to replace the entire board, which is more expensive than just replacing one expansion card.

Laptop Processors

Just as with desktop computers, the processor is the brain of the laptop computer. And just like everything else, compared to desktop hardware devices, laptop hardware devices are smaller and not quite as powerful. The spread between the speed of a laptop CPU and that of a desktop motherboard can be a gigahertz or more. In the past, this performance difference was significant, but laptop processors today are pretty fast, and many people think they perform just fine. It's up to the user to determine if the difference in speed hurts their usage experience.

Laptops have less space, and thus, heat is a major concern. Add to that the fact that the processor is the hottest-running component, and you can see where cooling can be an issue. To help combat this heat problem, laptop processors are engineered with the following features:

Streamlined connection to the motherboard   Nearly all desktop processors mount using pin connectors, whether on the CPU or on the motherboard (as is the case with LGA sockets). Pins and sockets are big and bulky, meaning they're not a laptop's friends. Laptop processors are generally either soldered directly to the motherboard or attached using the Micro-FCBGA (Flip Chip Ball Grid Array) standard, which uses balls instead of pins. In most cases, this means that the processor cannot be removed, meaning no processor upgrades are possible.

Lower voltages and clock speeds   To combat heat, you can either slow the processor down (run it at a lower speed) or give it less juice (run it at a lower voltage). Again, performance will suffer compared to a desktop processor, but lowering heat is the goal here.

Active sleep and slowdown modes   Most laptops will run the processor in a lower power state when on battery power in an effort to extend the life of the battery. This is known as *processor throttling.* The motherboard works closely with the operating system to determine if the processor really needs to run at full speed. If it doesn't, it's slowed down to save energy and to reduce heat. When more processing power is needed, the CPU is throttled back up.

One of the best features of many laptop processors is that they include built-in wireless networking. One of the earliest laptop-specific chipsets that gained a ton of popularity was the Pentium M chip made by Intel. The Pentium M consists of three separate components:

- The Mobile Intel Express chipset (such as the Mobile Intel 915GM Express or the Mobile Intel 910GML), which is the graphics memory controller hub

- The Intel/PRO Wireless Network Connection, providing an integrated wireless LAN connection

- The Intel Centrino chipset, which is the "brain" of the chipset, designed to run on lower power than the desktop processor

While the Pentium M chip is old news now, its design still impacts laptop designs today. Depending on the manufacturer, motherboard, and processor used, the features described as part of the Pentium M will be built into the motherboard rather than the processor itself. Regardless of where it's built into, it's a great set of features to have for mobile computers!

While many portable computers will have processors that have just as many features as their desktop counterparts, others will simply use stripped-down versions of desktop processors such an Intel Core series processor. While there's nothing wrong with this, it makes sense that components specifically designed for notebooks fit the application better than components that have been retrofitted for notebook use. Consider an analogy to the automobile industry: It's better to design a convertible from the ground up than simply to cut the top off an existing coupe or sedan.

Memory

Notebooks don't use standard desktop computer memory chips because they're too big. In fact, for most of the history of laptops, there were no standard types of memory chips. If you wanted to add memory to your laptop, you had to order it from the laptop manufacturer. Of course, because you could get memory from only one supplier, you got the privilege of paying a premium over and above a similar-sized desktop memory chip.

However, there are now two common types of laptop memory packages: SODIMM and MicroDIMM. Nevertheless, modern laptop manufacturers may still opt to go the proprietary route due to design considerations that favor a custom solution. To see what kind of memory your laptop uses, check either the manual or the manufacturer's website. You can also check third-party memory producers' websites (such as www.crucial.com).

SODIMM

The most common memory form factor for laptops is called a Small Outline DIMM (SODIMM). They're much smaller than standard DIMMs, measuring about 67 millimeters (2.6″) long and 32 millimeters (1.25″) tall. SODIMMs are available in a variety of configurations, including 32-bit (72-pin) and 64-bit (144-pin SDRAM, 200-pin DDR, 200-pin DDR2, and 204-pin DDR3) options. Figure 9.3 shows a DDR3 SODIMM under desktop DDR2 memory for a size comparison.

FIGURE 9.3   Desktop DIMM and laptop SODIMM

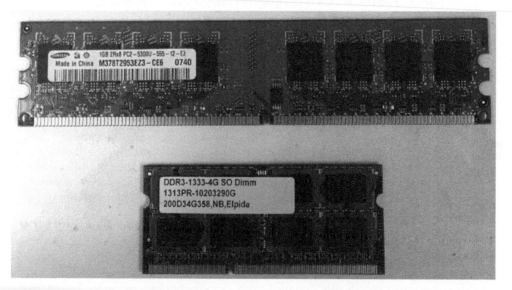

   You'll also see *SODIMM* spelled as *SO–DIMM*.

Just as with desktop computers, make sure the SODIMM you want to put into the laptop is compatible with the motherboard. The same standards that apply to desktop memory compatibility apply to laptops. This means that you can find DDR, DDR2, and DDR3 SODIMMs for laptops. DDR has all but topped out at 1GB per module, while DDR2 and DDR3 SODIMM modules can be purchased in sizes up to 8GB (at the time this book was being written), which lags desktop DIMM capacity by a bit.

MicroDIMM

Although it's been around a while, the MicroDIMM is a newer form factor for laptop memory modules. The MicroDIMM is an extremely small RAM form factor. In fact, it is over 50 percent smaller than a SODIMM—only about 45.5mm (about 1.75″) long and 30mm (about 1.2″, a bit bigger than a U.S. quarter) wide. Another major difference is that the MicroDIMM does not have any notches on the bottom. Figure 9.4 shows a 172-pin MicroDIMM; notice that it's a lot closer to being square-shaped than the RAM shown in Figure 9.3, in addition to being a lot smaller. It was designed for the ultralight and portable subnotebook style of computer. Popular MicroDIMM form factors include 64-bit modules with 172 or 214 pins for DDR2.

FIGURE 9.4 172-pin MicroDIMM

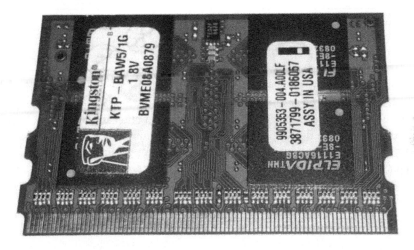

Storage

Storage is important for every computer made. If you can't retrieve important files when you need them, the computer isn't very useful. While the trend is moving toward storing more data online (in the "cloud"), there's still considerable need for built-in storage. For laptops, this typically means two types of devices: hard drives and optical drives.

Laptop Hard Drives

Laptops don't have the room for the full-sized 3.5″ hard drives that desktop computers use. Instead, they use a hard drive with either a 2.5″ or 1.8″ form factor that is less than ½″

thick. These drives share the same controller technologies as desktop computers; however, they use smaller connectors. Figure 9.5 shows an example of a standard hard drive compared to a laptop hard drive.

FIGURE 9.5   A desktop hard drive (left) compared to a laptop hard drive (right)

Newer advances in hard drive technology have greatly helped laptop speed and battery performance. Perhaps the most important technology development is that of the *solid-state drive (SSD)*. Unlike conventional magnetic hard drives, that use spinning platters, SSDs have no moving parts. They use the same solid-state memory technology found in the other forms of flash memory; think of them as bigger versions of the flash drives that are so common. Otherwise, they perform just like a traditional magnetic HDD.

Connecting an SSD in a desktop is usually just like connecting a regular HDD: they have the same PATA/SATA and power connectors. Laptops often have a specialized connector and a single cable that handles both data and power, as shown in Figure 9.6. Most manufacturers also make them in the same physical dimensions as traditional hard drives, even though they could be made much smaller, like removable flash drives. (This is probably to preserve the "look" of a hard drive so as to not confuse consumers or technicians.)

As you might expect, SSDs have several advantages over their mechanical counterparts:

- Faster startup and read times
- Less power consumption and heat produced
- Silent operation
- Generally more reliable because of lack of moving parts
- Less susceptible to damage from physical shock and heat production
- Higher data density per square centimeter

Disadvantages of SSDs are as follows:

- The technology to build an SSD is more expensive per byte.

FIGURE 9.6   2.5″ SSD, motherboard connector, and cable

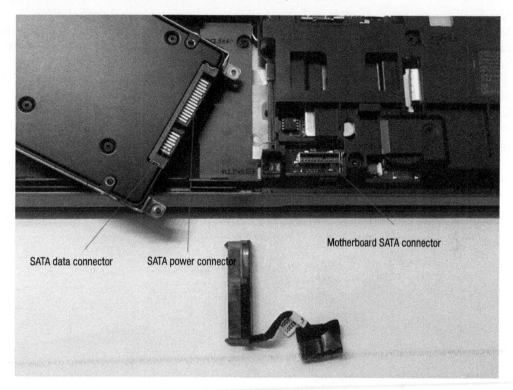

SATA data connector   SATA power connector   Motherboard SATA connector

- Overall storage space will be much smaller than an HDD.

- All solid-state memory is limited to a finite number of write (including erase) operations. Lack of longevity could be an issue, but improvements in technology have practically eliminated this limitation versus older SSDs. It probably will never be an issue for home users, but it could pop up in data centers or similar uses where there are massive amounts of data transactions.

- When they fail, they tend to do so without warning.

To summarize, SSDs are faster, produce less heat, and are more shock resistant, which is perfect for laptops. They are more expensive than conventional hard drives, but that's the trade-off you have to make for better performance.

A third type of hard drive on the market is called a *hybrid hard drive*. As you might expect based on the name, it combines the features of a standard hard drive with those of an SSD. It contains moving platters and some high-speed flash memory. The intent is that the frequently used files will be stored in flash memory, making for faster access, while other files are stored on the magnetic plates. Pretty much everything about a hybrid drive is a fusion of the other two technologies. Performance, size, and price will all fall somewhere within the HDD to SSD spectrum.

Laptop Optical Drives

Nearly all laptops have a hard drive, but not all laptops have an internal optical drive. Many times, there just isn't room for one. If that's the case, you can attach an external optical drive via an expansion port such as USB. It might be a bit slower than an internal drive, but it's better than not having one at all.

Optical drives on laptops are necessarily smaller than their desktop counterparts as well. Figure 9.7 shows an example of a desktop DVD-ROM drive compared to a laptop CD-ROM drive. Note that the laptop drive is very small, but it has the same functionality as a desktop unit. The drive mechanism and circuits have all been miniaturized to save space. As a result, the functionality is basically the same, but the cost is usually higher. Anytime a component's functionality remains the same while its size decreases, you will notice an increase in price over the standard-sized item.

FIGURE 9.7   A desktop DVD drive (left) compared to a laptop CD drive (right)

 CD, DVD, and Blu-ray burners are great to have with laptops as backup devices. Simply copy the contents of the hard drive (or just important files) to the optical discs and store them in a safe location.

Input Devices

Because of the small size of laptops, getting data into them presents unique challenges to designers. They must design a keyboard that fits within the case of the laptop. They must also design some sort of pointing device that can be used with graphical interfaces like Windows.

The primary challenge in both cases is to design these peripherals so that they fit within the design constraints of the laptop (low power and small form factor) while remaining usable.

Keyboards

A standard-sized desktop keyboard wasn't designed to be portable. It wouldn't fit well with the portable nature of a laptop. That usually means laptop keys are not normal size; they must be smaller and packed together more tightly. People who learned to type on a typewriter or regular computer often have a difficult time adjusting to a laptop keyboard.

Laptop keyboards are built into the lower portion of the clamshell. Sometimes, they can be removed easily to access peripherals below them like memory and hard drives, as in the Lenovo ThinkPad series.

Special Function Keys

Because of the much smaller space available for keys, some laptop keys (like the number pad, Home, Insert, PgUp, and PgDn keys) are consolidated into special multifunction keys. These keys are accessed through the standard keys by using a special *function (Fn)* key. It's typically near the Windows key on the keyboard and can be labeled in lettering of an alternate color (usually blue) that matches the lettering of the labels for alternate functions on other keys. To use a multifunction key, you press and hold the Fn key (as you would the Shift, Ctrl, and Alt keys) and then tap the key labeled with the function you want and release the Fn key. Figure 9.8 shows an example of a function key.

FIGURE 9.8   Function (Fn) key

The function key combinations can control many laptop functions, but the most common are video, audio and media, and network connectivity. The specific keys used and functions provided will vary by laptop model, but there are usually icons on the keys that perform the functions to help you figure out what does what.

Video adjustments come in two varieties: changing the video output and dimming or brightening the screen. Dimming and brightening the screen is pretty straightforward, but the video output function can throw people off. Remember that nearly every laptop has a video connector on the back or the side to plug in an external monitor or a projector. You will need to use the video toggle key to get this external port to work. Usually there are three or four states: laptop only, external output only, duplicate, or extend the desktop (some models won't have extend the desktop). Figure 9.9 shows examples of the keys that handle video functions.

FIGURE 9.9   Video adjustment keys F4 (LCD toggle), F7 (dim), and F8 (brighten)

Note that the LCD toggle (the F4 key in Figure 9.9 and Figure 9.10) has the same symbol on it as the external video connector. The dimming key has a sun with an arrow pointing down, and the brightening key has a sun with an arrow pointing up. (Some manufacturers will use a small sun on the dimming key and a large sun on the brightening key, as you see in Figure 9.10 on the F9 and F10 keys.)

FIGURE 9.10   Audio adjustment keys F6 (quieter), F7 (louder), and F8 (microphone mute)

The audio settings can often be adjusted using the function keys too. To lower the volume, look for an icon with a speaker with only one "wave" coming out of it. The volume is increased with the speaker with several waves, the mute button will have a speaker with an *X* or a circle with a line through it, and the microphone mute will show a microphone with the same. Figure 9.10 shows an example. Media settings such as rewinding and fast-forwarding might be included too. If you look at Figure 9.9, the sample laptop has a touch strip above the keyboard with rewind, play/pause, and fast-forward (not shown) buttons.

Finally, there are the network connectivity settings. There aren't really a lot of choices here; it's a matter of turning the connection on or off. Options for your laptop might include any or all of the following: Wireless Networking (Wi-Fi), Bluetooth, Cellular, Airplane mode, and GPS. There are several scenarios in which you might need to turn these services off quickly. Taking off or landing in an airplane is one of the most obvious ones. You might want to do some work, but there are restrictions as to what you can have turned on and when. Another situation might be if you are in a public place on public Wi-Fi and you suspect that someone might be trying to use the network to attack your computer. Turning Wi-Fi off will stop the attack. Finally, sometimes the communications just seem to "hang," that is, they stop working at random times. If the connection isn't working, turning it off and back on might reset it to a working condition.

Sometimes, the Fn keys handle disabling these options. At other times, separate buttons or switches near the keyboard handle them. For example, Figure 9.11 shows three examples of Wi-Fi toggle switches. From the top down, there is one on the front of a laptop, one above the keyboard, and one as an Fn option on the F2 key. The switch in the one above the keyboard looks like an indicator light only, but the strip is touch-sensitive. The symbol for Wi-Fi usually looks like a small antenna. If you're using Bluetooth, the symbol will be Bluetooth's trademarked *B*. Cellular options usually show bars (like what you see on a phone), airplane mode has an airplane icon, and GPS looks like the "pins" that you see which mark locations on online maps. (Honestly, it's pretty uncommon to see GPS built in to a laptop, but it does happen.)

FIGURE 9.11   Network card toggle switches on laptops

The point is, look around if you don't see the right function key on the keyboard itself. It's bound to be there somewhere.

Some laptops include a backlight for the keyboard as well. These can also be dimmed or brightened, or turned off and on, with the use of a function key. For example, the right combination might be Fn+Z. Keep in mind that on laptop models with an ambient light sensor, such as the MacBook Pro, the backlight settings will be controlled automatically by the operating system; you won't be able to turn it off unless it's already on.

Pointing Devices

In addition to using the keyboard, you must have a method of controlling the onscreen pointer in the Windows (or other graphical) interface. Most laptops today include multiple USB ports for connecting a mouse, and you can choose from a wide range of wired or wireless full-size or smaller mice. There are several additional methods for managing the Windows pointer. Here are some of the more common ones:

- Trackball
- Touchpad
- Point stick
- Touchscreen

Because of different pointing-device preferences, some laptops include multiple pointing devices to appeal to a wider variety of people.

Trackball

Many early laptops used trackballs as pointing devices. A *trackball* is essentially the same as a mouse turned upside down. The onscreen pointer moves in the same direction and at the same speed that you move the trackball with your thumb or fingers.

Trackballs are cheap to produce. However, the primary problem with trackballs is that they do not last as long as other types of pointing devices; a trackball picks up dirt and oil from operators' fingers, and those substances clog the rollers on the trackball and prevent it from functioning properly.

Touchpad

To overcome the problems of trackballs, a newer technology that has become known as the Touchpad was developed. *Touchpad* is actually the trade name of a product. However, the trade name is now used to describe an entire genre of products that are similar in function.

A Touchpad is a device that has a pad of touch-sensitive material. The user draws with their finger on the Touchpad, and the onscreen pointer follows the finger motions. Included with the Touchpad are two buttons for left- or right-clicking (although with some Touchpads, you can perform the functions of the left-click by tapping on the Touchpad, and Macs will have one button). Figure 9.12 shows a Touchpad.

FIGURE 9.12 Laptop Touchpad

One problem people have with a touchpad is the location. You'll notice that the touchpad is conveniently placed right below the laptop keyboard, which happens to be where your palms rest when you type. Sometimes this will cause problems, because you can inadvertently cause your mouse cursor to do random things like jump across the screen. Most touchpads today have settings to allow you to control the sensitivity, and they will also differentiate between a palm touching them and a finger. In addition, if you have a sensitive touchpad that is giving you trouble, you can disable it altogether. Exercise 9.1 shows you how to do that in Windows 7. The specific steps to disable the touchpad will differ by manufacturer. The steps in Exercise 9.1 were performed on an HP ProBook laptop. On other laptops, this feature may be in the mouse Properties window. Consult the laptop documentation if you are unable to locate the setting.

EXERCISE 9.1

Disabling a Touchpad in Windows 7

1. Open the Hardware And Sound window within Control Panel. You can do so by clicking Start ➤ Control Panel, and if you are in Category view, by clicking Hardware And Sound, as shown in Figure 9.13.

continues

FIGURE 9.13   Hardware And Sound

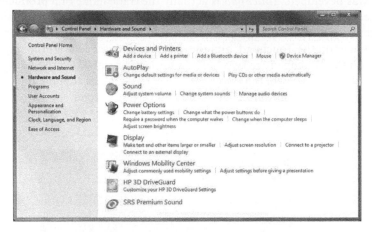

2.   Click Mouse near the top of the screen, and then go to the Device Settings tab, as shown in Figure 9.14.

FIGURE 9.14   Device Settings tab of the Mouse Properties window

3. Highlight your touchpad. In this example, it's named LuxPad. If you are curious to view the configuration options, click the Settings button to get a screen similar to the one shown in Figure 9.15.

FIGURE 9.15 Touchpad configuration options

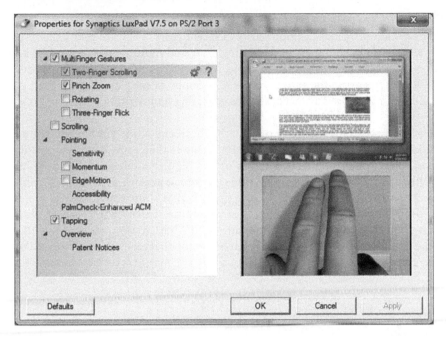

4. On the Device Settings tab, and with your touchpad highlighted, click the Disable button.

5. Click OK to close this window.

Although touchpads are primarily used with laptop computers, you can also buy external touchpads that connect to a computer just as you would connect a mouse.

Point Stick

With the introduction of the ThinkPad series of laptops, IBM introduced a new feature known as the Touchpoint, generically known as a *point stick*. (ThinkPads are now produced by Lenovo.) The point stick is a pointing device that uses a small rubber-tipped stick. When you push the point stick in a particular direction, the onscreen pointer goes in the same direction. The harder you push, the faster the onscreen pointer moves. The point allows fingertip control of the onscreen pointer, without the reliability problems associated with trackballs.

Point sticks have their own problems, however. Often, the stick does not return to center properly, causing the pointer to drift when not in use. You might also notice the rubber cover for the stick becoming a bit gummy with extended use. Most manufacturers supply replacement covers of varying textures with new systems. Some later systems employ a concave version of the cover and updated workings that tend to minimize a lot of these concerns.

Touchscreen

Touchscreens have exploded in popularity in recent years. They are pretty much standard fare for smartphones, and they are becoming more and more popular for tablet and laptop computers as well. The idea is pretty simple; it looks like any other display device, but you can touch the screen and the system senses it. It can be as simple as registering a click, like a mouse, or it can be more advanced, such as capturing handwriting and saving it as a digital note.

Although the technical details of how touchscreens work are beyond the scope of this chapter, there are a few things to know. One is that some touchscreens will work with any object touching them, whereas others require a conductive input, such as your finger. iPhones are a great example of this, to which anyone who lives in cold climates and wears gloves can attest. The second thing is that some touchscreens are coated with a film that is sensitive to touch. Cleaning these screens with regular glass cleaner can ruin the touchscreen nature of the device. It's best to clean those devices only with a damp cloth as needed. The third is that some touchscreens need to be calibrated in order to properly interpret the user's input. See the manufacturer's documentation for details.

Expansion Buses and Ports

Although laptop computers are less expandable than their desktop counterparts, they can be expanded to some extent. Laptops have expansion ports similar to those found on desktop computers as well as a couple that are found only on laptops.

ExpressCard

ExpressCard was launched by the Personal Computer Memory Card International Association (PCMCIA) as a way to support USB 2.0, USB 3.0, and PCI Express (hence the *Express* in the term *ExpressCard*) connectivity for portable computers. In 2009, the ExpressCard 2.0 version was launched. It has the same size connector but upgrades the technology to support faster speeds. With ExpressCard technology, portable computers can be adapted to support faster versions of technologies that they might not natively support. For example, ExpressCard expansion cards can be used to provide Gigabit Ethernet, IEEE 1394b (FireWire), eSATA, and other types of connections. There are also ExpressCard mobile broadband modems, SSDs, NICs, and sound cards. ExpressCard speeds are shown in Table 9.1. The maximum speeds shown are theoretical maximums; the performance won't match these speeds in actual use.

TABLE 9.1   ExpressCard Speeds

Version	Mode	Maximum Speed
ExpressCard 1.x	USB 2.0	480Mbps
ExpressCard 1.x	PCIe 1.0 x1	2.5Gbps
ExpressCard 2.0	PCIe 2.0 x1 or USB 3.0	5Gbps

ExpressCard replaces the older *PC Card* (also called *CardBus*) technology, also created by PCMCIA.

ExpressCard adapters are 75mm in length and 5mm thick. The standard ExpressCard, known as ExpressCard/34, is only 34mm wide. A 54mm-wide version, known appropriately as ExpressCard/54, is still only 34mm at its insertion point, but 22mm from that end, it expands to 54mm to accommodate more internal electronics, as shown in Figure 9.16. The additional space allows for better heat dissipation and the support of applications such as 1.8″ disk drives, card readers, and CompactFlash readers. A Universal ExpressCard host slot is wide enough to fit either an ExpressCard/54 or an ExpressCard/34 adapter; notice that both of them have 26-pin connectors. (Slots designed for an ExpressCard/34 device cannot accommodate its wider cousins.) Universal ExpressCard slots also appear to be able to accept a CardBus adapter, but the card inserts not even an inch before stopping on the internal guide that assures correct ExpressCard/34 insertion. ExpressCard shares with CardBus the use of 3.3V to power some cards but swaps the 5V versions for a new, lower 1.5V offering.

You may see the term *ExpressBus* used in reference to this technology. Despite the source, it's not a valid term.

Mini PCIe

Mini PCIe technology replaced Mini PCI, much like PCIe has replaced PCI in desktop computers. Nearly all laptops built today (and most built since 2005) use Mini PCIe slots for expansion cards. These cards reside inside the case of the laptop and are connected via a 52-pin edge connector. Mini PCIe cards come in two sizes. The full size cards are similar in size to ExpressCard devices without the external cover, measuring 30mm wide and 51mm long. Half-size cards (one is shown in Figure 9.17, with the connector at the bottom) are 30mm wide and 27mm long. Like ExpressCard 2.0, Mini PCIe cards support USB (2.0 and 3.0) and PCIe x1 functionality, and at the same speeds. Additionally, Mini PCIe cards have the 1.5V and 3.3V power options in common with ExpressCard.

FIGURE 9.16   ExpressCard /34, ExpressCard /54, and legacy CardBus expansion cards

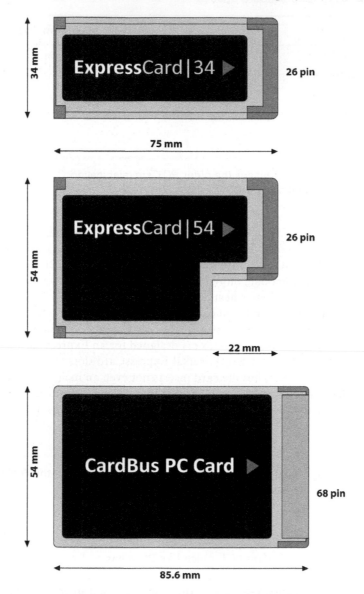

"PCCard-ExpressCard ZP." Licensed under CC BY 2.5 via Wikimedia Commons
http://commons.wikimedia.org/wiki/File:PCCard-ExpressCard_ZP.svg#/media/
File:PCCard-ExpressCard_ZP.svg

FIGURE 9.17 Mini PCIe card in a laptop

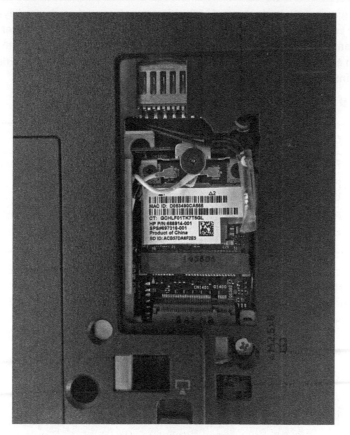

The Next Generation of Laptop Expansion Cards

As of early 2015, many laptop vendors are moving away from Mini PCIe to a newer form factor called M.2, which is a faster technology that uses a 22-mm-wide, 66-pin card edge connector.

M.2 was originally developed under the name Next Generation Form Factor (NGFF) and was born from the desire to standardize small form factor SSD hard drives. M.2 supports more than hard drives, though; you will find M.2 cards that provide Wi-Fi, Bluetooth, GPS, and NFC connectivity as well as PCIe and SATA connections.

continues

continued

One interesting connectivity feature of M.2 is that the slots and cards are keyed such that only a specific type of card can fit into a certain slot. The keys are given letter names to distinguish them from each other, starting with the letter A and moving up the alphabet as the location of the key moves across the expansion card. Table 9.2 explains the slot names, some interface types supported, and common uses.

TABLE 9.2   M.2 keying characteristics

Key	Common Interfaces	Uses
A	PCIe x2, USB 2.0	Wi-Fi, Bluetooth, and cellular cards
B	PCIe x2, SATA, USB 2.0, USB 3.0, audio	SATA and PCIe x2 SSDs
E	PCIe x2, USB 2.0	Wi-Fi, Bluetooth, and cellular cards
M	PCIe x4, SATA	PCIe x4 SSDs

Let's look at some examples. Figure 9.18 shows four different M.2 cards. From left to right, they are an A- and E-keyed Wi-Fi card, two B- and M-keyed SSDs, and an M-keyed SSD. Of the four, only the M-keyed SSD can get the fastest speeds (up to 1.8Gbps), because it supports PCIe x4. Current SSDs on the market will be keyed B, M, or B+M. A B-keyed or M-keyed SSD won't fit in a B+M socket. A B+M keyed drive will fit into a B socket or an M socket, however.

FIGURE 9.18   Four M.2 cards

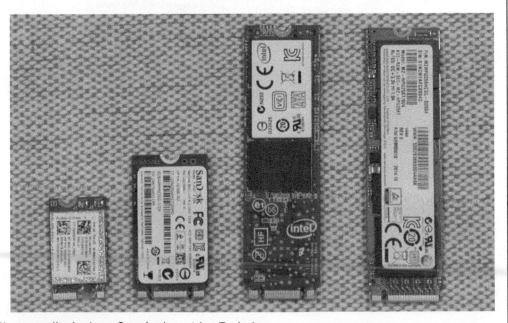

Photo credit: Andrew Cunningham / Ars Technica

Another interesting feature of the cards is that they are also named based on their size. For example, you will see card designations such as 1630, 2242, 2280, 22110, or 3042. Those numbers refer to the width and length (in millimeters) of the card. In Figure 9.18, you see a 1630, a 2242, and two 2280 cards.

Figure 9.19 shows a motherboard with two M.2 slots. The one on the left is E-keyed and the one on the right is B-keyed. The left slot is designed for an E-keyed Wi-Fi NIC, and the right one for a B-keyed SSD.

FIGURE 9.19   Two M.2 slots

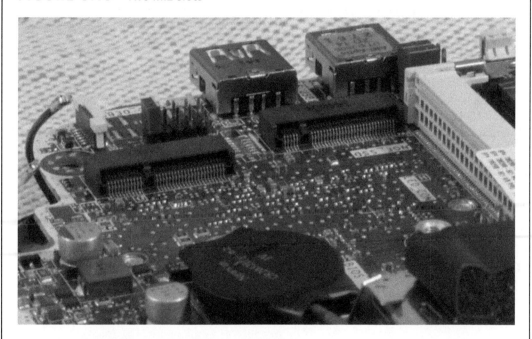

Photo credit: Andrew Cunningham / Ars Technica

As of the time of writing, M.2 devices are not as easy to find on the market as are Mini PCIe cards, but that will change over time. M.2 seems to be the future (for now), and they will increase in popularity over the coming years.

USB Ports

Like desktops, laptops use USB ports for expansion. Because of the lack of internal expansion in laptops, the majority of peripherals for laptops are USB expansion devices.

By now, you probably know that there are USB expansion devices of almost every type; USB is known for its versatility. One quick example is that the USB port is the most common type for portable storage devices known as flash drives. These handy little sticks can hold up to 1TB of data (at the time of this writing), and they make it easy to transfer large files from one computer to another if a network is unavailable. They are continually increasing in capacity.

You can also get USB devices that act as adaptors to other types of connections or provide extended functionality. These are very handy if the laptop doesn't have the connector or functionality built in. Here are some examples:

- USB to RJ-45
- USB to Wi-Fi
- USB to Bluetooth
- USB to HDMI
- USB to Thunderbolt
- USB to DisplayPort
- USB optical drives
- USB smart card readers

These adapters are often called dongles. Figure 9.20 shows a simple USB Bluetooth adapter as well as a USB to RJ-45 dongle. A USB optical drive is handy because it can be moved from laptop to laptop, and if you don't need it, you can leave it at the office or home and not have to carry the extra weight around. Just plug it in and the operating system will detect and configure it. USB smart card readers are becoming more popular as well, because they are rarely built in to laptop cases. A smart card is a credit-card-sized plastic card with embedded circuits in it that can be used to store or process data. They can be used in security applications embedded into credit cards themselves. If you have ever seen a credit card with what looks like a microchip built in to it, that's a smart card.

FIGURE 9.20 USB Bluetooth adapter and USB to RJ-45 dongle

For more information about USB ports and their function, refer to Chapter 3, "Peripherals and Expansion."

DisplayPort and Thunderbolt

The Video Electronics Standards Association (VESA) introduced *DisplayPort* in 2008. It was designed to be an industry standard and to replace VGA and DVI. It's also backward compatible with VGA and DVI by using adapters. A display port on a laptop is shown in Figure 9.21. A display port is intended to be for video devices only, but like HDMI and USB, it can transmit audio and video simultaneously.

FIGURE 9.21   Display port

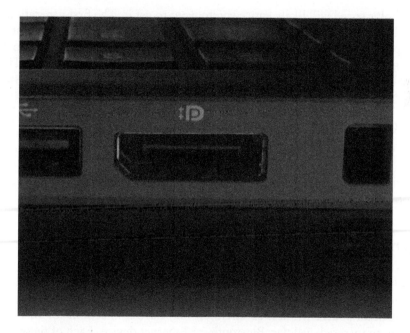

Thunderbolt was developed as an offshoot of the display port technology. The short history is that Apple announced a mini DisplayPort (MDP) standard in late 2008 and that the standard would have no licensing fee. In early 2009, VESA responded by saying that MDP would be included in the upcoming DisplayPort 1.2 specification. Apple was not pleased about this and teamed up with Intel to rework the specification. They added in support for PCIe, renamed it Thunderbolt, and launched it in 2011. Thunderbolt supports not only video devices but also several other types of peripherals. In terms of versatility, it's really only second to USB. You will find video devices, hard drives (both HDD and SSD), printers, laptop docking stations, audio devices, and PCIe expansion enclosures that use Thunderbolt.

All Apple laptops made right now contain a Thunderbolt port; other laptops can too if the manufacturer licenses the technology from Apple. It looks a lot like a display port, only smaller, and has the characteristic lightning bolt icon, as shown in Figure 9.22.

FIGURE 9.22   Thunderbolt port

Thunderbolt's speed will likely entice you to want to get it. The first generation of the technology boasted a 10Gbps data rate, which is just as fast as the newest USB standard, USB 3.1 SuperSpeed+. Thunderbolt 2, which was released in late 2013, joins two 10Gbps channels together for 20Gbps throughput. Apple has also announced plans for Thunderbolt 3, which will again double the throughput, to 40Gbps. Apple says it expects to start shipping products with Thunderbolt 3 connectors in late 2015 or early 2016.

Mouse/Keyboard Port

Just in case you don't like using your laptop's built-in keyboard or pointing device, some laptops come with a combination PS/2 *keyboard/mouse port* that allows you to connect either an external keyboard or an external mouse. These ports are quickly fading away, as most laptop manufacturers assume that you will use your USB ports for external keyboards and mice.

Communications Ports

Laptops are built to make computing mobile. And in a world where it seems that you always need to be in touch with others while you're on the go, it makes sense that laptops have a variety of communication methods. Nearly all new laptops come equipped with some version of an 802.11 wireless card. Others may have connections for an analog dial-up modem or an infrared, cellular, Bluetooth, or Ethernet device. Each of these can also be added to laptops through a USB or ExpressCard connection.

Docking Stations

Some laptops are designed to be desktop replacements. That is, they will replace a standard desktop computer for day-to-day use and are thus more fully featured than other laptops. These laptops often have a proprietary docking port. A docking port (as shown in Figure 9.23) is about 2.5 inches wide and is used to connect the laptop to a special laptop-only peripheral known as a *docking station*. A docking station (shown in Figure 9.24) is basically an extension of the motherboard of a laptop. Because a docking station is designed to stay behind when the laptop is removed, it can contain things like a full-sized drive bay and expansion bus slots. Also, the docking station can function as a port replicator.

FIGURE 9.23 A docking port

FIGURE 9.24 The back and front of a docking station

A port replicator reproduces the functions of the ports on the back of a laptop so that peripherals such as monitors, keyboards, printers, and so on that don't travel with the laptop can remain connected to the dock and don't all have to be unplugged physically each time the laptop is taken away. Figure 9.24 shows the back and front of a docking station; some of the ports on the back are only available on the docking station and not on the laptop. Finally, there may be accessory bays (also called media bays). These external bays allow you to plug your full-sized devices into them and take your laptop with you (for example, a full-sized hard drive that connects to an external USB or FireWire port). As a point of clarification (or perhaps confusion), media bays and accessory bays are sometimes used to refer to laptop drive bays.

Docking ports and docking stations are *proprietary.* That is, the port works only with docking stations designed by the laptop's manufacturer and vice versa.

Power Systems

Because portable computers have unique characteristics as a result of their portability, they have unique power systems as well. Portable computers can use either of two power sources: batteries or adapted power from an AC or DC source. Regardless of the source of their power, laptops utilize DC power to energize their internal components. Therefore, any AC power source needs to be rectified (converted) to DC. Most laptop display backlights, on the other hand, require high-voltage, low-amperage AC power. To avoid a separate external AC input, an inverter is used to convert the DC power that is supplied for the rest of the system to AC for the backlight. In case it's not obvious, converters and inverters perform opposite functions, more or less.

Batteries

There are many different battery chemistries that come in various sizes and shapes. Nickel cadmium (NiCd), lithium-ion (Li-ion), and nickel-metal hydride (NiMH) have been the most popular chemistries for laptop batteries. A newer battery chemistry, lithium-polymer (Li-poly), has been gaining in prominence over recent years for smaller devices. Figure 9.25 is a photo of a Li-ion battery for an HP laptop.

Battery chemistries can be compared by energy density and power density. Energy density measures how much energy a battery can hold. Power density measures how quickly the stored energy can be accessed, focusing on access in bursts, not prolonged runtime. An analogy to the storage and distribution of liquids might help solidify these concepts. A gallon bucket has a higher "energy density" and "power density" than a pint bottle; the bucket holds more and can pour its contents more quickly. Another common metric for battery comparison is rate of self-discharge, or how fast an unused battery reduces its stored charge.

FIGURE 9.25   A laptop Li-ion battery

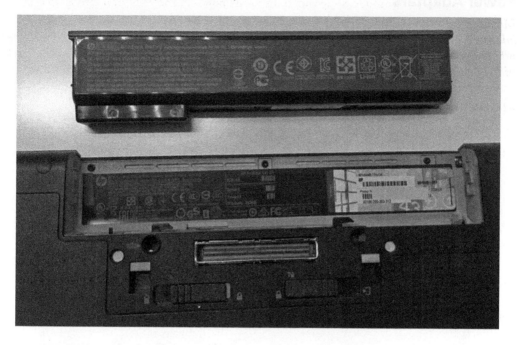

 **Real World Scenario**

Is That Battery Really Dead?

Some batteries, such as nickel cadmium (NiCd) ones, suffer from a performance-affecting chemical memory loss. Others, such as lithium-ion, don't suffer from this affliction but do suffer from so-called digital memory loss that plagues the built-in gauges that monitor the charge left in the battery. This effect can be observed in software gauges that read the battery's charge level. The digital memory effect manifests itself as a sudden loss of power when the gauges register, say, 30-percent remaining capacity. The fix, much like the fix for chemical memory in NiCd batteries, is to allow a full discharge once a month or so. This is called *battery calibration* and can be performed right in the device while it's using the battery. Other than this occasional full discharge, Li-ion batteries last longer when you partially discharge them and then recharge them, making them ideal for laptops and personal handheld devices, such as smartphones, that tend to get used sporadically on battery power before being plugged back in to charge.

Power Adapters

Most notebook computers can also use AC power with a special adapter (called an *AC adapter*) that converts AC power input to DC output. The adapter can be integrated into the notebook, but more often it's a separate "brick" with two cords, one that plugs into the back of the laptop and another that plugs into a wall outlet. Figure 9.26 is a photo of the latter.

FIGURE 9.26   A laptop AC adapter

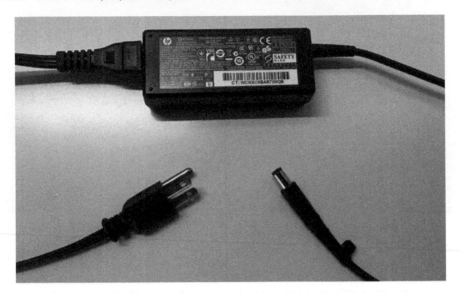

Another power accessory that is often used is a *DC adapter*, which allows a user to plug the laptop into the DC power source (usually called an auxiliary power outlet) inside a car or on an airplane. These adapters allow people who travel frequently to use their laptops while on the road (literally).

Use caution when selecting a replacement AC adapter for your laptop. You should choose one rated for the same or higher wattage than the original. You must also pay special attention to the polarity of the plug that interfaces with the laptop. If the laptop requires the positive lead to be the center conductor, for instance, then you must take care not to reverse the polarity. Look for symbols like the ones shown in Figure 9.27, and make sure the new power supply is the same as the old one.

FIGURE 9.27   Polarity symbols

positive polarity   negative polarity

Regarding the input voltage of the adapter, care must also be taken to match the adapter to the power grid of the surrounding region. Some adapters have a fixed AC input requirement. Purchasing the wrong unit can result in lack of functionality or damage to the laptop. Other adapters are autoswitching, meaning that they are able to switch the input voltage they expect automatically based on the voltage supplied by the wall outlet. These units are often labeled with voltage-input ranges, such as 100V to 240V, and frequency ranges, such as 50Hz to 60Hz, and are able to accommodate deployment in practically any country around the world. Nevertheless, you should still ascertain whether some sort of converter is required, even for autoswitching adapters.

Laptop Displays

The display system is the primary component in the top half of the clamshell case. (The wireless antenna often resides here too, and we'll get to that in just a bit.) Much like all other laptop components, the display is more or less a smaller version of its desktop counterpart. What is unique to laptop displays, though, is that for some time, the technology used in them was actually more advanced than what was commonly used in desktops. This is due to liquid crystal display (LCD) technology.

Before LCD technology, computer displays used cathode-ray tube (CRT) technology (like old-school televisions) and were big, bulky, and hardly mobile. We talked about LCD standards and concepts (in addition to other video technologies) in Chapter 4, "Display Devices," so there's not really a need to dive into the technical specs again. Instead, we'll focus here on the different components that are required to make these types of displays work on a laptop.

Some laptops feature screens that rotate orientation depending on how they are held (much like smartphones and tablets), or the screens themselves will rotate horizontally or be entirely removable. Rotating and removable screens cost more money, so consider your needs or the needs of the user when recommending such features.

Video Card

The video card in a laptop or desktop with an LCD monitor does the same thing a video card supporting a CRT monitor would do. It's responsible for generating and managing the image sent to the screen. The big difference is that most LCD monitors are digital, meaning that you need a video card that puts out a digital image. Laptop manufacturers put video cards that are compatible with the display in laptops, but with desktops it can get a bit confusing. Figure 9.28 shows the faceplate of a standard desktop video card with three ports (from left to right): S-video/composite, digital video interface (DVI), and analog (VGA).

FIGURE 9.28   Video card

The video card in Figure 9.28 is obviously for a desktop. Most laptop manufacturers choose to integrate the LCD circuitry on the motherboard to save space.

You can find digital-to-analog video converters on the market if you need to plug in an older analog monitor to a DVI port.

 **Real World Scenario**

Video Memory Sharing

If your video card is built into your motherboard, odds are that it doesn't have its own memory but shares system memory with the processor. Note that there is nothing wrong with this type of setup; in fact, it often brings the cost of the laptop down. It's just that instead of having 4GB of RAM and 512MB of video RAM (for example), you would have only 4GB total. So if your video card were using 512MB, the system would be left with only 3.5GB.

How much of a difference does all of this make? Well, it depends on what you're doing with your laptop. If you're using it for the Internet and light work, probably not much difference. If you're working with more video-intensive applications, using a computer with shared memory might slow you down some. This usually brings up two questions: What's the optimal balance? And where do I change this?

To answer the first question, again, it depends on what you are doing. If you perform more video-intensive operations (or if you're gaming), then you might want to set aside more memory for the video card. If you're not as concerned with rapid pixilation, then less is fine. Which brings us to the second question: Where do you set it? Shared memory is configured in the system BIOS. Each BIOS is different, so be sure to consult your owner's manual if you have any questions. Keep in mind that some BIOSs will allow you to set aside only a certain amount of memory—say, 512MB—for video memory

How does this affect your computer when you upgrade the memory? First, keep in mind that some of your memory will be taken by the video card, so you might want to upgrade to more memory than you originally had planned. Second, after upgrading the memory, you will need to go into the BIOS and reconfigure how much memory you want allocated to the video card.

Backlight

LCD displays do not produce light, so to generate brightness, LCD displays have a *backlight*. A backlight is a small lamp placed behind, above, or to the side of an LCD display. The light from the lamp is diffused across the screen, producing brightness. The typical laptop display uses a *cold cathode fluorescent lamp (CCFL)* as its backlight. As their name implies, they are fluorescent lights, and they're generally about 8 inches long and slimmer than a pencil. You might see laptops claiming to have 2-CCFL, which just means that they have two backlights. This can result in a laptop with a brighter screen. CCFLs generate little heat, which is always a good thing to avoid with laptops.

Another backlight technology uses LEDs instead of CCFLs. Instead of CCFL tubes, they have strips of LED lights, and most LEDs do not need an inverter. Smaller devices, such as tablets and phones, almost exclusively use LED backlighting, which is smaller and consumes less power than CCFLs.

Inverter

Fluorescent lighting, and LCD backlights in particular, require fairly high-voltage, high-frequency energy. Another component is needed to provide the right kind of energy, and that's the *inverter.*

The inverter is a small circuit board installed behind the LCD panel that takes DC current and inverts it to AC for the backlight. If you are having problems with flickering screens or dimness, it's more likely that the inverter is the problem and not the backlight itself.

There are two things to keep in mind if you are going to replace an inverter. One, they store and convert energy, so they have the potential to discharge that energy. To an inexperienced technician, they can be dangerous. Two, make sure the replacement inverter was made to work with the LCD backlight that you have. If they weren't made for each other, you might have problems with a dim screen or poor display quality.

 Inverters can discharge energy, which can cause severe injury to you. Be careful when working with them!

Screen

The screen on a laptop does what you might expect—it produces the image that you see. The overall quality of the picture depends a lot on the quality of the screen and the technology your laptop uses. Current popular options include LCD, LED, and OLED.

There are two types of LCD technologies listed in the exam objectives: TN and IPS. *Twisted Nematic (TN)* is the older of the two, and it is relatively inexpensive and low power. The issue with TN LCD screens is that when you start viewing them at wider angles, the picture quality suffers greatly. *In-Plane Switching (IPS)* LCD monitors provide better color representation as well as wider-angle viewing, but they tend to be a bit more expensive and have somewhat slower response times.

For more information on display technologies, see Chapter 4.

Digitizer

A *digitizer* is a device that can be written or drawn on, and the content will be converted from analog input to digital images on the computer. Digitizers take input from a user's finger or a writing utensil, such as a stylus. When built in to the display, they might be the glass of the display itself, or they might be implemented as an overlay for the display. For touchscreen devices, the digitizer might be the primary method of input. For other devices, such as a laptop with a touchscreen, users might find the digitizer helpful for capturing drawings or handwritten notes.

 Other types of digitizers are not built into the screen and may be pads on the palm rest of a laptop or next to the touch pad or peripheral USB devices that look like notepads.

Webcam and Microphone

Webcams are nearly universal on laptops today. The most common placement is right above the display on the laptop. Most laptops with webcams will also have a smaller circle to the left of the lens, which has a light that turns on to illuminate the user when the webcam is on. Some people are a bit paranoid about their webcams, and they will put a piece of Scotch tape over the camera when it's not in use.

If you're going to use a webcam to conduct a video call with someone, it helps if they can hear you too. That's where the microphone comes into play. Microphones can be built in to the monitor as well. The webcam shown in Figure 9.29 has the illumination light to the left and the microphone inputs on both sides of the lens. Microphones can also be built in to the bottom half of the clamshell, either above the keyboard or somewhere on the front bezel.

FIGURE 9.29 Webcam and microphone

Wi-Fi Antenna

The vast majority of laptops produced today include built-in Wi-Fi capabilities. Considering how popular wireless networking is today, it only makes sense to include 802.11 functionality without needing to use an expansion card. With laptops that include built-in Wi-Fi, the wireless antenna is generally run through the upper half of the clamshell case. This is to get the antenna higher up and improve signal reception. The wiring will run down the side of the display and through the hinge of the laptop case and plug in somewhere on the motherboard.

The Wi-Fi antenna won't affect what you see on the screen, but if you start digging around in the display, know that you'll likely be messing with your wireless capabilities as well.

Cable Locks

Portability defines what makes laptops truly useful. They're not as fast or as strong as their desktop cousins, but the fact that we can easily haul them around wherever we go gives them a special status within our hearts. It also presents less-scrupulous types with ample opportunity to quickly make away with our prized possessions and personal data. Laptop theft is a major concern for companies and individual owners alike.

One way that you can help to physically secure your laptop is through the use of a cable lock, sometimes called a Kensington lock (named after a company that makes them) or a K-lock. Essentially, a cable lock anchors your device to a physical structure, making it nearly impossible for someone to walk off with it. Figure 9.30 shows a cable with a number combination lock. With others, small keys are used to unlock the lock. If you grew up using a bicycle lock, these will look really familiar.

FIGURE 9.30   Cable lock

Here's how it works. First, find a secure structure, such as the permanent metal supports of your workstation at work. Then, wrap the lock cord around the structure, putting the lock through the loop at the other end. Finally, secure the lock into your cable lock hole on the back or side of your laptop (Figure 9.31), and you're secure. If you forget your combination or lose your key, you're most likely going to have to cut through the cord, which will require a large cable cutter or a hack saw.

FIGURE 9.31   Cable lock insertion point

If someone wants your laptop bad enough, they can break the case and dislodge your lock. Having the lock in place will deter most people looking to make off with it though.

Disassembling and Reassembling Laptops

Desktop computers often have a lot of empty space inside their cases. This lets air circulate and also gives the technician some room to maneuver when troubleshooting internal hardware. Space is at a premium in laptops, and rarely is any wasted. With a desktop computer, if you end up having an extra screw left over after putting it together, it's probably not a big deal. With laptops, every screw matters, and you'll sometimes find yourself trying to identify visually miniscule differences between screws to make sure that you get them back into the right places.

Even though repairing a laptop poses unique issues, most of the general troubleshooting and safety tips that you use when troubleshooting a desktop still apply. For example, always make sure that you have a clean and well-lit work space and be cautious of electrostatic discharge (ESD). General safety tips and ESD prevention is covered in Chapter 23, "Understanding Operational Procedures." Here we'll get into specific objectives for tearing apart laptops.

 Throughout this section, we'll use the word *laptop* almost exclusively. The principles covered here apply to nearly all portable devices, though, such as notebooks and handhelds.

Using the Right Tools

It's doubtful that any technician goes into a job thinking, "Hey, I'm going to use the wrong tools just to see what happens." With laptops, though, it's especially important to ensure that you have exactly the tools you'll need for the job. Two critical camps of materials you need are the manufacturer's documentation and the right hand tools.

Using the Manufacturer's Documentation

Most technicians won't bat an eye at whipping out their cordless screwdriver and getting into a desktop's case. The biggest difference between most desktops is how you get inside the case. Once it's opened, everything inside is pretty standard fare.

Laptops are a different story. Even experienced technicians will tell you to not remove a single screw until you have the documentation handy unless you're incredibly familiar with that particular laptop. Most laptop manufacturers give you access to repair manuals on their website; Table 9.3 lists the service and support websites for some of the top laptop manufacturers.

TABLE 9.3 Laptop manufacturers' service and support websites

Company	URL
Asus	http://www.service.asus.com
Dell	http://www.dell.com/support
HP	http://support.hp.com
Lenovo	http://support.lenovo.com
Sony	http://esupport.sony.com/en/vaio
Toshiba	http://support.toshiba.com

Once you are at the right website, search for the manual using the laptop's model number.

Some laptop manufacturers have a policy that if you open the case of a laptop, the warranty is voided. Be sure to understand your warranty status and implications of cracking the case before you do it.

Using the Right Hand Tools

Once you have the manual in hand or on your screen, you need to gather the right hand tools for the job. For some laptops, you only need the basics, such as small Phillips-head and flat-head screwdrivers. For others, you may need a Torx driver. Gather the tools you need and prepare to open the case. A small flashlight might also come in handy.

Real World Scenario

The Consequences of Using the Wrong Tools

It's been said once, but it's important to say it again: Always use the right tool for the job when repairing laptops. If the documentation says that you need a T-10 Torx driver, make sure that you have a T-10 Torx driver.

Not using the right tools can result in the stripping of the screw head. If you strip a screw head in a desktop, you might have alternative methods of removing the screw. Laptops are far less forgiving. If you strip a screw head and are unable to turn the screw, you may never be able to remove it. That could result in needing to scrap the device.

Organization and Documentation

Before you crack open the case of your laptop, have an organization and documentation plan in place. Know where you are going to put the parts. Have a container set aside for the screws. You can purchase small plastic containers that have several compartments in them with lids that snap tightly shut, into which you can place screws. You can also use containers designed to organize prescription pills. The bottom of an egg carton works well too, provided that you don't need to be mobile to fix the laptop.

For documentation, many technicians find it handy to draw a map of the computer they're getting into, such as the one shown in Figure 9.32. It can be as complex as you want it to be, as long as it makes sense to you.

FIGURE 9.32   Laptop repair "road map"

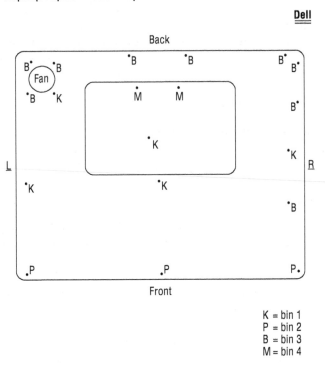

The drawing in Figure 9.32 shows the locations of the screws, and it also calls out where the screws should be placed once they're removed. Again, this type of documentation can be as simple or complex as you want it to be, as long as it makes sense and helps you stay organized.

Replacing Laptop Components

You have your manual, screwdrivers, and screw container handy and are ready to go. Now you just need to figure out how to get to the defective component to replace it. It would be nice if we could just tell you one simple way to do this for all laptops, but that's not going to happen. Internal laptop structure, components that can be replaced, and how to get to those components varies widely between models. It's impractical to list steps to remove all of these devices because the steps we would list here will only help you if you're working on the same model of laptop we're using for an example.

The list of components that may be replaceable could include input devices such as the keyboard and Touchpad; storage devices, including hard drives and optical drives; core components such as memory, the processor, and the motherboard; expansion options, including wireless cards and Mini PCIe cards; and integrated components such as the screen, case (plastics/frames), smart card reader, speakers, battery, and DC jack. Again, depending on the make and model of the laptop on which you're working, the list of replaceable components might be longer or shorter.

In the following sections, we're going to assume that you've figured out what's defective and needs to be replaced. We'll stay away from describing components and what they do, unless it's not been covered elsewhere in the book. The model we're going to use in the examples in the rest of this chapter is a Dell Latitude C640. Admittedly, this particular model is a bit dated, but all of the procedures we're going to walk you through will still be similar for newer systems. For other models, please consult the manufacturer's documentation.

Replacing Hard Drives and Memory

Hard drives and memory are the two most common components people usually upgrade in a laptop. We'll look at how to accomplish replacing both of them.

Replacing Hard Drives

External storage devices are more popular now than ever . On the small end, you can get postage-stamp-sized SD cards or ultra-portable thumb drives that hold from a few gigabytes to a terabyte each. If you need more storage, you can get external hard drives that hold several terabytes and connect to your laptop using a USB cable.

Even with all of those options, a laptop still needs an internal hard drive. Exercise 9.2 shows you how to remove and replace an internal hard drive.

We could start off each of these exercises by saying, "Check your documentation," because that is realistically what you're going to have to do for the specific model of laptop on which you will be working. Obviously, each of these exercises is intended to be an example of how to replace a part. Instead of telling you to check your documentation each time for the exact steps, we'll assume that it's understood.

If you don't have a laptop to use for the exercises, or you want to see laptops being repaired in a video, you can find many such videos online. Two good sites to check out are www.ifixit.com and www.youtube.com. Just search for the item you want to repair or replace, and see if there's a video for it!

EXERCISE 9.2

Replacing a Laptop Hard Drive

1. Turn off the computer.

2. Disconnect the computer and any peripherals from their power sources, and remove any installed batteries.

3. Locate the hard drive door and remove the screw holding it in place.

4. Lift the hard drive door until it clicks.

5. Slide the hard drive out to remove it, as shown in Figure 9.33.

FIGURE 9.33   Sliding out the hard drive

6. Remove the two screws holding the hard drive to the hard drive door; you can see them in Figure 9.34.

7. Attach a new hard drive to the hard drive door.

8. Slide the new hard drive back into the hard drive bay.

9. Snap the hard drive door back into place, and insert and tighten the screw to hold the door in place.

Replacing Memory

No matter how much memory your laptop has, it's probably not enough. Most laptops share their system memory with the video card, meaning that memory on a laptop might not go as far as you think.

FIGURE 9.34   Hard drive secured to the door

Not long ago, there weren't any standards for the physical size of laptop memory. Manufacturers weren't in a hurry to conform to each other either. After all, if they were the only ones producing memory for their systems, then they could pretty much charge what they wanted.

Fortunately, standards do exist today, and most manufacturers will use memory that conforms to SODIMM (or MicroDIMM) standards. Only occasionally will you run into a laptop that uses proprietary memory modules. Your documentation will tell you what type of memory your system takes. Exercise 9.3 shows you how to access the memory bay so that you can upgrade or replace memory chips.

EXERCISE 9.3

Replacing Laptop Memory

1. Turn off the computer.

2. Disconnect the computer and any peripherals from their power sources, and remove any installed batteries.

3. Remove the screws holding the memory door in place. You will see the memory module, as shown in Figure 9.35. Note that some laptops will have the memory module located under the keyboard, so you will have to get the keyboard off first to replace the memory.

4. Use your fingers to gently separate the plastic tabs holding the memory module in place. The module should pop up so that you can grab it.

continues

5.   Align the notch in the new memory module to the one in the connector.

6.   Insert the new memory module into the socket at a 45-degree angle. Once full contact is made, press the module down. It should click into place.

7.   Replace the memory door and fasten the screws.

FIGURE 9.35   SODIMMs in a laptop

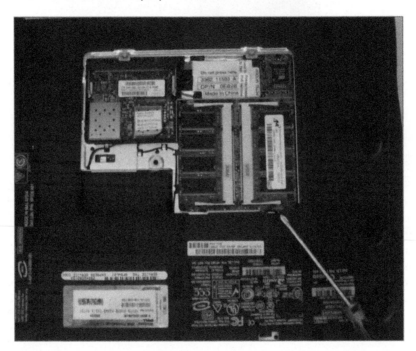

Replacing Internal Laptop Expansion Cards

As we covered earlier in the chapter, laptops have their own proprietary architecture for internal expansion. The most common standard is Mini PCIe, and it's covered in detail in the section "Expansion Buses and Ports" earlier in this chapter.

Most laptops will come with only one internal Mini PCIe port, and common devices include SATA controllers, network cards, sound cards, and modems.

Figure 9.36 shows you the Type IIIA Mini PCI (an older technology than Mini PCIe) network card installed in this laptop, which happens to be in the same bay as the system memory module. The connector is on the top side of the figure.

Removing the Mini PCI (or a Mini PCIe) card is just like removing the memory module, except that this one has antenna cables that you need to disconnect first. After that, spread the retaining clips just as you would for the memory, and the card will pop up. Replace it with a new card the same way that you would replace a memory module.

FIGURE 9.36   Mini PCI card installed in a laptop

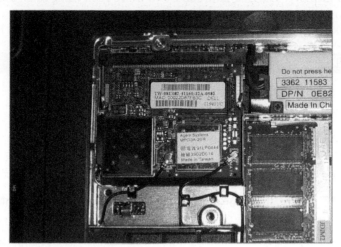

Upgrading Wireless and Video Systems

What do wireless network cards and video cards have in common in laptops? Most of the time, they're integrated into your system motherboard. If either one fails, you need to replace the entire motherboard. A few laptops have these components as separate *field-replaceable units (FRUs)*, and you can remove them as needed. The only way to know for sure is to consult your trusty service manual. The following sections look at some ways that you may be able to upgrade these devices.

Upgrading Wireless Network Cards

Wireless network cards and laptops are a perfect match for each other, much like peanut butter and chocolate. You can have one without the other, but what's the point, really?

Most network cards are built into the motherboard chipset of laptops. In other words, if it fails, you likely need to replace the motherboard. Network cards are special, though, in that you have many other, easier ways to upgrade if you so desire.

You can find several external portable network cards on the market. You often have choices that range from network cards that look like a thumb drive and have a USB connector to slightly bulkier ExpressCard network cards. These are even valid options if your built-in network card is still working but you want to upgrade. For example, if you have an older laptop with an 802.11b network card in it but you want to upgrade to 802.11n, it may be more economical to purchase an external card and use it in your system. Windows should disable the old device automatically to avoid conflicts, but if not, you can do it manually through Device Manager.

Upgrading Laptop Video C-ards

Odds are that the laptop you're using has an integrated video card. If the video card fails, you're likely looking at a motherboard replacement. Some laptops do have a replaceable video card. If it fails or if you choose to upgrade it, the procedure will probably resemble replacing system memory. The Dell Latitude C640 we've been using as an example has a built-in video card, so there's no way to upgrade that specific device. For an example of what it might take to replace a video card, we'll use a Dell Inspiron 6000 in Exercise 9.4.

EXERCISE 9.4

Removing a Laptop Video Card

1. Turn off the computer.

2. Disconnect the computer and any peripherals from their power sources, and remove any installed batteries.

3. Remove the Mini PCI card and the optical drive.

4. Remove the hard drive, the hinge cover, the keyboard, the display assembly, and the palm rest.

5. Loosen the two captive screws holding the video card/thermal cooling assembly in place.

6. Lift up on the video card/thermal cooling assembly to remove it from the motherboard.

Replacing LCD Components

Besides the video card, many of the LCD components (the screen, backlight, and inverter) in a laptop can be replaced. Replacing these components often means removing the LCD display from the main chassis of the laptop. When doing so, just be careful of the video circuitry that connects the two and of the wireless network card antenna wires, which are usually threaded through one of the laptop case hinges.

WARNING Be particularly careful working with inverters. They can store and discharge energy, which can cause severe injury to you!

Replacing Other Internal Components

By now you have probably gotten the idea that in order to know how to replace components inside your laptop, you need to check the laptop's manual. The upshot is that nearly every component that you can think of replacing in a desktop computer is also replaceable in a laptop. It just might require a bit more work to fix the laptop than it would to fix a desktop.

As a rule of thumb, you can either access components from the bottom of your laptop, such as the memory and Mini PCIe card, or you're going to need to remove the keyboard to access the components from the top.

Because the keyboard is often the gateway to the guts of a laptop, we will include an example of removing it. We'll also include a few other examples of components that you may need to replace in your line of work. Exercise 9.5 shows you how to remove a keyboard.

Laptop keyboards aren't as easy to switch out as desktop keyboards. If your laptop keyboard has failed, however, you can very easily attach an external keyboard to it. Of course, if your goal is to remove the keyboard to get to the laptop's guts, then you need to perform surgery like the example in Exercise 9.5.

EXERCISE 9.5

Removing a Laptop Keyboard

1. Turn off the computer.

2. Disconnect the computer and any peripherals from their power sources, and remove any installed batteries.

3. Remove the hard drive.

4. On the bottom of the laptop, remove the five screws marked with the letter *K*.

5. Turn the laptop over and open the display.

6. Remove the center control cover by inserting a small flat-edged screwdriver into the notch at the right end of the center control cover and prying it loose, as shown in Figure 9.37.

FIGURE 9.37 Removing the control cover

continues

7. To release the keyboard, use a small flat-edged screwdriver to pry up on its right edge near the blank key, as shown in Figure 9.38.

FIGURE 9.38   Removing the keyboard

8. Lift the keyboard up about an inch and rotate it forward so that the keys are facing on the palm rest. Don't pull the keyboard too far or you might damage the connector cable.

9. Pull up on the keyboard connector to disconnect it from the keyboard interface connector on the motherboard, as shown in Figure 9.39.

FIGURE 9.39   Disconnecting the keyboard

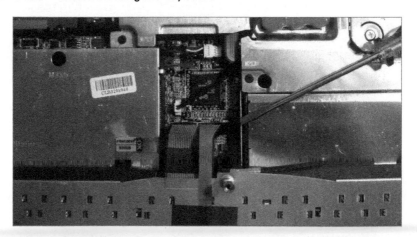

10. Set the keyboard aside.

Now that the keyboard is off, you can remove several other components with relative ease. Exercise 9.6 looks at removing the processor cooling assembly and the processor.

EXERCISE 9.6

Removing the Processor Cooling Assembly and Processor

1. Turn off the computer.

2. Disconnect the computer and any peripherals from their power sources, and remove any installed batteries.

3. Remove the hard drive.

4. Remove the keyboard.

5. Loosen the four captive screws (shown in Figure 9.40) that hold the cooling assembly in place.

FIGURE 9.40 Four screws holding the cooling assembly in place

6. Insert a small screwdriver into the recess in the front left side of the assembly and pry the assembly from the motherboard. If this is the first time removing the assembly, it might take some force because it's likely glued to the processor. Set the assembly aside.

7. Use a small flat-edged screwdriver to loosen the processor's ZIF socket (shown in Figure 9.41) by rotating the cam screw counterclockwise until it reaches the cam stop. (It should take about a one-quarter turn.)

8. Use a microprocessor extraction tool to remove the microprocessor. If you don't have an extraction tool, you can try to use your hands. Make sure that you're grounded first, and always pull straight up to avoid bending pins.

continues

FIGURE 9.41   Loosening the ZIF socket

9. Set the processor aside on an antistatic mat or place it in an antistatic bag.

The last internal device we'll look at removing is the CMOS battery. If the BIOS isn't maintaining system information such as the date and time or boot sequence, you will want to replace this component. Exercise 9.7 shows you how to replace the CMOS battery.

 Many laptops use the same type of round, silver watch-style batteries that desktop motherboards use. Others use packaged batteries that more closely resemble cell phone batteries, such as this laptop.

EXERCISE 9.7

Replacing the CMOS Battery

1. Turn off the computer.

2. Disconnect the computer and any peripherals from their power sources, and remove any installed batteries.

3. Remove the hard drive.

4. Remove the keyboard.

5. Disconnect the CMOS battery from the motherboard, as shown in Figure 9.42.

6. Pry the battery from its seat (shown in Figure 9.43) with a small flat-edged screwdriver. Note that it's adhered to the EMI shield below it, so removing it might require some force.

FIGURE 9.42   Disconnecting the CMOS battery

FIGURE 9.43   Prying the battery out

continues

EXERCISE 9.7 *(continued)*

7. Connect the new battery to the appropriate connector on the motherboard.

8. Peel away the backing from the adhesive bottom of the new CMOS battery. Press the battery into the battery tray.

9. Upgrade the BIOS using a flash BIOS CD.

Flashing the system BIOS is usually a pretty straightforward process. You can get a BIOS update from the manufacturer and burn it to a CD. Once you have the CD, you just need to boot the laptop from the CD and the disc will automatically flash the BIOS. Exercise 9.8 shows you the steps to flash the BIOS on this model.

EXERCISE 9.8

Flashing the System BIOS

1. Turn off the computer.

2. Ensure that the computer is plugged into AC power and that the main battery is installed properly.

3. Turn on the computer, and press F2 to enter the BIOS setup.

4. Reset the system boot order to ensure that the system boots from the CD first.

5. Insert the flash BIOS update CD, and reboot the computer. The disc will flash the BIOS and automatically reboot.

6. Upon reboot, press F2 again to enter the BIOS setup. Verify that the settings are correct, and change the boot sequence to your preferred setting.

7. Remove the flash BIOS CD.

Removing External Hardware

In the grand scheme of things, there are two types of peripherals: internal and external. We've already discussed removing internal hardware, and compared to that, removing external components is very easy. If you have USB-type devices plugged in, removing them is as easy as disconnecting them, but other peripherals require a bit more work.

Devices that can be removed when the computer is powered on are called hot-swappable devices. If you need to turn the computer off first, then the device is not hot swappable. There are several different hot-swappable peripherals, including mice, keyboards, some hard drives, network cards, printers, and others. Good examples of non-hot-swappable devices include motherboards and internal hard drives. Odds are if it's internal to your computer case, then it's not hot-swappable. Always be sure to check your hardware documentation to see if it's safe to plug in or disconnect the device with the system powered on.

WARNING Although most of the time you can just remove a USB device, make sure that it's not in use when you remove it.

In Exercise 9.9, we will show you the recommended method to remove a device.

EXERCISE 9.9

Removing External Devices

1. You need to stop the device first (this is good policy even for USB devices), using the Safely Remove Hardware icon in the system tray (it looks like a card with a green arrow or green check over it, depending on your version of Windows) as shown in Figure 9.44.

FIGURE 9.44 System tray with the Safely Remove Hardware icon (on the left)

2. Once you've clicked the icon, you will get a screen similar to the one shown in Figure 9.45.

FIGURE 9.45 Safely removing hardware

3. Highlight the device you want to remove, and click Stop. (Or in this case, click Eject USB Disk.) Windows will then notify you that it's safe to remove the device. If it's a cabled device or USB, just detach it. Other types of hardware in some laptops require you to release a latch.

Adding an external device to a laptop generally means that the computer will automatically recognize and enable the device for you, unless there's no compatible driver available. In cases like these, Windows will tell you that it detected new hardware and ask you to provide an appropriate driver.

Summary

In this chapter, you learned about the various laptop issues that the A+ technician faces. We discussed differences between laptops and desktops, including the various components that make up a laptop and how they differ in appearance and function from those on a desktop.

Input devices, expansion buses, and interfaces found in laptops were presented in detail. We also discussed special laptop function keys and the components of an LCD screen.

Then we looked at repairing and replacing laptop components. We started off by quickly talking about finding laptop documentation and using the right tools. We then discussed organization and documentation.

Next, we discussed replacing hard drives and memory and also looked at upgrading internal expansion cards. After that, we explored upgrading wireless adapters, video cards, and other internal components. Finally, we explained how to remove an external device safely from your laptop.

Exam Essentials

Know the differences between laptop processors and desktop processors.   Laptops have less room in them, so it makes sense that laptop processors are smaller than their desktop brethren. They also operate at lower voltages, have more advanced power-down or sleep modes, and are often soldered directly to the motherboard. Finally, chipsets, such as the Intel Pentium M chipset, also include built-in video processing and networking capabilities.

Understand the differences between laptop memory standards and desktop memory standards.   Continuing a main theme of this chapter, memory in laptops needs to be smaller than in desktops, and so it is. The two main standards for laptop memory are SODIMM and MicroDIMM.

Understand the various power sources for laptops.   You should know that the Li-ion battery is the preferred rechargeable power source for laptops and that active power supplies that plug into AC and DC power sources are available. Additionally, knowing the difference between autoswitching and fixed power supplies is essential.

Know the various input devices and expansion buses and ports found on laptop computers.   Although many of these technologies are available in desktop computers as well, the science behind outfitting laptops with similar functionality presents unique details that the A+ technician should know. ExpressCard-based expansion buses have their own specific traits, with which you should be familiar.

Know where to get service manuals for laptops.   Service manuals can be downloaded from the laptop manufacturers' websites.

Be familiar with the components of an LCD. LCDs are made up of the video card, back-light, inverter, and screen.

Know how to replace hardware devices from laptops. Laptop components are typically accessed either from the bottom of the case or by removing the keyboard and accessing them from the top. Each laptop is different, so be sure to consult your documentation.

Review Questions

The answers to the chapter review questions can be found in Appendix A.

1. A client has a laptop with which you are unfamiliar. You are asked to perform a memory upgrade. How can you obtain the service manual for this laptop computer?

   A. By pressing F1 while in Windows

   B. By pressing F2 while the system is booting up

   C. By reading the paper copy that comes with the laptop

   D. By searching the manufacturer's website

2. Which of the following is *not* a benefit of laptop design?

   A. Portability

   B. Increased performance

   C. Desktop replacement

   D. Higher-quality construction

3. Which of the following are components of an LCD? (Choose two.)

   A. Inverter

   B. Screen

   C. CRT

   D. Backdrop

4. Which laptop input device was released with the IBM ThinkPad (now distributed by Lenovo) series of laptops?

   A. Touchpad

   B. Mouse

   C. Point stick

   D. Trackball

5. One of the users on your network needs to travel, and she wants to work on the airplane. Which laptop accessory will allow her to power her laptop from the airplane?

   A. AC adapter

   B. DC adapter

   C. Battery converter

   D. Airplane mode

6. How many pins does a DDR2 MicroDIMM memory module have?

   A. 72

   B. 144

   C. 172

   D. 198

7. _____ is the fastest and most modern interface used as an expansion method for external peripherals, such as mice, webcams, scanners, and printers It is popular on laptops and desktops alike.

    A. Parallel

    B. PS/2

    C. USB

    D. ATA

8. You are sitting in a coffee shop and using the public wireless network. You suddenly notice suspicious activity on your laptop. Which laptop feature should you use?

    A. Wi-Fi toggle

    B. Cellular toggle

    C. Bluetooth toggle

    D. Laptop lock

9. There has recently been a string of hardware thefts in your office building. What should you recommend that your users implement to help avoid this problem?

    A. Enable GPS tracking

    B. Use a docking station

    C. Use a cable lock

    D. Use the screensaver lock

10. You have a user who needs to upgrade his laptop. Due to how often he collaborates with others, he wants to be sure that the viewing angle is as wide as possible. Which technology should you look for?

    A. Fluorescent backlight

    B. LED backlight

    C. LCD IPS

    D. LCD TN

11. Which of the following expansion buses uses serial communications and is capable of operating in USB and PCIe modes?

    A. ExpressCard

    B. CardBus

    C. Mini PCI

    D. FireWire

12. A user on your network wants to be able to draw images on his screen and have the laptop capture them. What type of device does he need?

    A. Inverter

    B. Capturer

    C. Digitizer

    D. Touchpad

13. Which of the following technologies allows for data transfers of up to 20Gbps?

   A. USB 3.0

   B. USB 3.1

   C. DisplayPort

   D. Thunderbolt

14. You have a user who needs to keep desktop devices such as keyboard, monitor, and mouse permanently connected so that they can be used by an attached laptop. What type of device do you recommend that they use?

   A. Docking station

   B. Keyboard, video, mouse (KVM) switch

   C. Print server

   D. USB hub

15. The process by which the processor slows down to conserve power is officially called _____.

   A. Underclocking

   B. Cooling

   C. Disengaging

   D. Throttling

16. You need to replace a failed AC adapter for a client's laptop. When replacing the adapter, which of the following purchases is acceptable to obtain the same or better results?

   A. An AC adapter with a higher voltage rating than the original

   B. An AC adapter with a higher wattage rating than the original

   C. A DC adapter with the same voltage rating as the original

   D. An AC adapter with a lower voltage and wattage rating than the original

17. What should you do for a Li-ion battery that appears to charge fully but does not last as long as the battery's meter indicates that it will last?

   A. Replace the battery.

   B. Exercise the battery.

   C. Calibrate the battery.

   D. Short the terminals to discharge the battery.

18. How do laptop hard drives differ from desktop hard drives?

   A. Laptop hard drives use completely different standards from those used by desktop hard drives for communication with the host.

   B. Laptop hard drives are solid state; desktop hard drives have spinning platters.

   C. Laptop hard drives require a separate power connection; desktop hard drives are powered through the drive interface.

   D. The most common form factor of a laptop hard drive is about an inch smaller than that of a desktop hard drive.

19. One of your network users has an older laptop with no Bluetooth support. He recently received a Bluetooth headset that he needs to use with his laptop. What is the least expensive way to make the headset compatible with his laptop?

    A. Buy a Wi-Fi–compatible headset.

    B. Buy a USB Bluetooth adapter.

    C. Buy a Mini PCIe Bluetooth adapter.

    D. Replace the laptop.

20. Which of the following memory types has the smallest form factor?

    A. RIMM

    B. DIMM

    C. MicroDIMM

    D. SODIMM

Performance-Based Question

You will encounter performance-based questions on the A+ exams. The questions on the exam require you to perform a specific task, and you will be graded on whether or not you were able to complete the task. The following requires you to think creatively in order to measure how well you understand this chapter's topics. You may or may not see similar questions on the actual A+ exams. To see how your answer compares to the authors', refer to Appendix B.

The hard drive on a Dell Latitude C640 computer failed. You have an extra hard drive of the exact same type. What would you do to replace it?

Chapter

10

Understanding Mobile Devices

THE FOLLOWING COMPTIA A+ EXAM 220-901 OBJECTIVES ARE COVERED IN THIS CHAPTER:

✓ **3.4 Explain the characteristics of various types of other mobile devices.**

- Tablets
- Smart phones
- Wearable technology devices
  - Smart watches
  - Fitness monitors
  - Glasses and headsets
- Phablets
- e-Readers
- Smart camera
- GPS

✓ **3.5 Compare and contrast accessories & ports of other mobile devices.**

- Connection types
  - NFC
  - Proprietary vendor specific ports (communication/power)
  - microUSB/miniUSB
  - Lightning
  - Bluetooth
  - IR
  - Hotspot / tethering

- Accessories
  - Headsets
  - Speakers
  - Game pads
  - Docking stations
  - Extra battery packs/battery chargers
  - Protective covers / water proofing
  - Credit card readers
  - Memory/MicroSD

For about 20 years, laptop computers enjoyed a status as the most popular mobile computing device available. Desktop computers were more powerful and cheaper, but with a laptop, users weren't tethered to a desk. Even though the first laptops weren't exactly easy to lug around, they were still preferable to desktops for users on the go. Technology kept improving, components kept getting smaller, and prices kept falling, which made laptops explode in popularity. As of the mid-2000s, more laptops were sold than desktops each year.

Technology has an inevitable way of progressing. The radio was the most popular source of information and entertainment until the television came along. Black-and-white televisions were cutting edge until color models were developed. Today, televisions don't resemble their ancestors at all. The same can pretty much be said of the mobile devices in the market today. Technology has progressed, components are getting smaller, and so are the devices that we legitimately call computers. In stark contrast to the computers of yesteryear, today's mobile devices can be so small that the likelihood of misplacing them is a real and ongoing concern.

This chapter covers the characteristics of modern mobile devices. Examples include tablets and smartphones, along with wearable technology, which could be the next big wave of computing devices. Along with the various types of mobile devices, we will discuss the common accessories and ports used to make connectivity easier. For now, it's cutting-edge technology. No doubt that 20 years from now, this chapter will seem as outdated as one that were to gush about the promise of mobile desktops today!

Understanding Mobile Devices

To be totally fair, laptop computers are mobile devices. Calling this chapter "Computers Smaller Than Laptops" or referring to the devices in this chapter in this manner would get tedious in a hurry. So instead we call them mobile devices, which we hope that you will all agree (at least for this chapter) are computers smaller than laptops.

In this chapter, we start off by discussing characteristics that make mobile devices what they are. Then we'll explain the characteristics of the following types of mobile devices:

- Tablets
- Smartphones
- Phablets
- e-Readers

- GPS
- Smart cameras
- Wearable technology

We will finish by discussing connection types related to mobile devices and specific accessories that users may find helpful.

Characteristics of Mobile Devices

If you were asked to define the primary characteristic of mobile devices, you would probably answer, "They are small," and you wouldn't be wrong. There are three overarching characteristics of mobile devices that make working with them unique versus working with laptops or desktops: field servicing, input, and secondary storage. We'll discuss each one in turn.

Field Servicing and Upgrading

Ever since the dawn of the portable computer, manufacturers and service providers have based a percentage of their success on warranties and "house calls" to repair devices on the fritz. It's a fact that quasi-permanent components, such as displays and motherboards, are widely considered replaceable only with identical components in laptops and similar devices. However, technically minded users could take it upon themselves to expand the capabilities of their own system by, for instance, upgrading the hard drive, increasing RAM, using expansion cards and flash devices, attaching wired peripherals, and inserting discs.

Although the ability to repair and expand the functionality of portable devices in the field has become all but obviated, it has been shown with current and past generations of mobile devices that users are not averse to giving up expandability and replaceable parts as long as functionality and convenience outshine the loss.

Although many Android and other non-Apple devices allow the replacement of batteries and the use of removable memory cards as primary storage, even this basic level of access is removed in Apple's mobile devices, including its iPad line of tablet computers. In an effort to produce a sleeker mobile phone, even Android devices have been developed without user access to the battery. For Apple, however, in addition to producing a nice compact package, it is all part of keeping the technology as closed to adulteration as possible. Supporters of this practice recognize the resulting long-term quality. Detractors lament the lack of options.

To service closed mobile devices of any size, it may be necessary to seek out an authorized repair facility and take or send your device to them for service. Attempting your own repairs can void any remaining warranty, and it can possibly render the device unusable. For example, a special tool is required to open Apple's devices. You cannot simply dig between the seams of the case to pop the device open. Even if you get such a device to open, there is no standard consumer pipeline for parts, whether for repair or upgrading. If you want to try the repair yourself, you could be on your own. You may be able to find helpful videos on YouTube or www.ifixit.com to provide some guidance, though.

Anyone who has been around the business for more than just a few years has likely seen their fair share of components and systems with no user-serviceable parts. For these situations, an authorized technician can be dispatched to your location, home or work, with the appropriate tools, parts, and skills to field-service the system for you. On a slightly different, perhaps more subtle, note the bottom line here is that many of today's mobile devices, including some of the larger tablet-style devices, have no field-serviceable parts inside, let alone user-serviceable parts. In some extremes, special work environments similar to the original clean manufacturing environment have to be established for servicing.

Input Methods

With decreased size comes increased interaction difficulties. Human interfaces can become only so small without the use of projection or virtualization. In other words, a computer the size of a postage stamp is fine as long as it can project a full-sized keyboard and a 60″ display, for example. Using microscopic real interfaces would not sell much product. Thus, the conundrum is that users want smaller devices, but they do not want to have to wear a jeweler's loupe or big-screen virtualization glasses to interact with their petite devices.

As long as the size of the devices remains within the realm of human visibility and interaction, modern technology allows for some pretty convenient methods of user input. Nearly all devices, from tablet size down, are equipped with touchscreens, supplying onscreen keyboards and other virtual input interfaces. On top of that, more and more of the screens are developing the ability to detect more than one contact point.

 We discuss touchscreens more in the section "Tablets" later in this chapter as well as in Chapter 21, "Mobile Operating Systems and Connectivity."

Generically, this technology is referred to in the industry as *multi-touch*, and it is available on all Apple devices with touch input, including the touch pads of the Apple laptops. Apple, through its acquisition of a company called Fingerworks, holds patents for the capacitive multi-touch technology featured on its products. Today, multi-touch is more about functionality than novelty. Nevertheless, the markets for both business and pleasure exist for multi-touch.

Certainly, touchscreens with the ability to sense hundreds of separate points of contact can allow large-scale collaboration or fun at parties. Imagine a coffee table that can allow you to pull out a jigsaw puzzle with the touch of an icon, remembering where you and three friends left off. Imagine all of you being able to manipulate pieces independently and simultaneously and being able to send the puzzle away again as quickly as you brought it out, so that you can watch the game on the same surface. This technology exists, and it is for sale today. Early examples were built on Microsoft's PixelSense technology, including the Samsung SUR40. Companies like Ideum build multi-touch platform tables, including a monster 84″ ultra-high definition 4K display with 100 touch points.

On a smaller scale, our mobile devices allow us to pinch and stretch images on the screen by placing multiple fingers on that screen at the same time. Even touch pads on laptops can be made to differentiate any number of fingers being used at the same time, each producing a different result, including pointing and clicking, scrolling and right-clicking, and dragging—all one-handed with no need to press a key or mouse button while gesturing.

HTC created an early touchscreen software interface called *TouchFLO* that has matured into HTC Sense, and it is still in use today on its Android and Windows line of mobile devices. TouchFLO is not multi-touch capable, nor does it specify the physical technology behind the touchscreen, only the software application for it. Theoretically then, TouchFLO and multi-touch could be combined.

The primary contribution of TouchFLO was the introduction of an interface that the user perceives as multiple screens, each of which is accessible by an intuitive finger gesture on the screen to spin around to a subsequent page. On various devices using this concept, neighboring pages have been constructed side by side or above and below one another. Apple's mobile devices employ gestures owing to the contributions of TouchFLO, bringing the potential of combining TouchFLO-like technology and multi-touch to bear.

Users of early HTC devices with resistive touchscreen technology met with difficulty and discord when flowing to another screen. The matte texture of the early resistive screens was not conducive to smooth gesturing. Capacitive touchscreen technology is a welcome addition to such a user interface, making gestures smooth and even more intuitive than ever.

Secondary Storage

Computers of all sizes and capabilities use similar forms of RAM for primary storage—the storage location for currently running instructions and data. Secondary storage—the usually nonvolatile location where these instructions and data are stored on a more permanent basis—is another story. Larger systems still favor conventional hard disk drives—with magnetic spinning disks, larger overall capacity, and less cost per byte—over the newer solid-state drives, although SSDs are quickly gaining in popularity. This discussion was presented first in Chapter 2, "Storage Devices and Power Supplies."

The primary concern with smaller devices is the shock they tend to take as the user makes their way through a typical day. Simply strapping a phone to your hip and taking the metro to work presents a multitude of opportunities for a spinning disk to meet with catastrophe. The result would be the frequent loss of user information from a device counted on more and more as technology advances.

Just as many telephony subscribers have migrated from a home landline that stays put to a mobile phone that follows them everywhere, many casual consumers are content to use their mobile device as their primary or only computing system, taking it wherever they go. As a result, the data must survive conditions more brutal than most laptops because laptops are most often shut down before being transported.

The most popular solution is to equip mobile devices with solid-state drives (SSDs) in place of traditional magnetic disk drives. There are no moving parts, the drive stays cooler and resists higher temperature extremes, and SSDs require less power to run than their conventional counterparts.

Tablets

The *tablet computer* has been available for longer than you probably think. GRiD Systems released the first commercial tablet, called the GRiDPad, in 1989 (see Figure 10.1). It ran the MS-DOS operating system and had a touchscreen input. You can see some of its other characteristics in Table 10.1. Its display size isn't atypical for a tablet today, but it's pretty heavy by even today's laptop standards (much less a tablet!).

TABLE 10.1 GRiDPad specifications

Feature	Specification
CPU	Intel 80C86 @ 10MHz
RAM	1MB internal
Display	10" LCD, 640×400 graphics
Storage	Two RAM card slots
Ports	RS-232 (serial), mini-DIN keyboard
OS	MS-DOS 3.3
Weight	4.5lbs

FIGURE 10.1 GRiDPad Tablet from 1989

Photo credit: http://oldcomputers.net

The defining characteristic of a tablet computer has always been the touchscreen. Touchscreens come in two varieties: resistive and capacitive. Resistive touchscreens respond to pressure, and they are highly accurate in detecting the position of the touch. These types of touchscreens require the use of a stylus or other hard object, such as a fingernail. Capacitive touchscreens are a little less accurate but more responsive. They respond to changes in electrical current, and as such, the human fingertip works great as the facilitator of input.

More modern tablets were hitting the market in the year 2000, when Microsoft showed off the Tablet PC at the popular technology conference, Comdex. For as innovative as it was, the Tablet PC never sold very well. More tablets came along. Many were laptops with screens that would rotate and then fold over the top of the keyboard (like the one shown in Figure 10.2), so they could be used as a traditional laptop or a tablet. When used like a tablet, they were said to be in *slate mode*.

FIGURE 10.2 HP Tablet PC from 2006

HP Tablet PC running Windows XP (Tablet PC edition) (2006) by Janto Dreijer—Own work. Licensed under Public Domain via Wikimedia Commons:
https://commons.wikimedia.org/wiki/File:HP_Tablet_PC_running_Windows_XP_
(Tablet_PC_edition)_(2006).jpg

The watershed moment for tablets came in 2007 when Apple launched the iPad, running the iOS operating system. The iPad became instantly popular, following in the footsteps of the iPod and growing up together with the iPhone. Tablets today typically run either iOS or Google's Android OS, with Microsoft Windows–based tablets in third place.

 We will cover iOS and Android in depth in Chapter 21.

Today, tablets are still known for their touchscreens, although you can easily find keyboard accessories that attach to the tablet. Some are for temporary use, and others look a little more permanent and make the tablet look like a small clamshell-style laptop. Listing the characteristics of all tablets in a forum like this isn't practical, but Table 10.2 gives you some specifications for a popular tablet at the time of this writing. Screen sizes typically fall anywhere between about 7" and 12.2", although you can find much larger ones with 24" displays as well. All tablets come equipped with Wi-Fi and Bluetooth, and many have cellular capabilities as well.

TABLE 10.2 Microsoft Surface Pro 3 specifications

Feature	Specification
CPU	Intel Core i5 1.9GHz
RAM	8GB
Display	12", 2160×1440 resolution
Storage	128GB SDD
Ports	USB 3.0, microSD
OS	Windows 8.1 Pro
Weight	28.8oz

Tablets running iOS or Android come with an installed web browser and some apps, and you can download additional apps from their respective stores (App Store or Google Play). Windows-based tablets can run apps designed for current versions of Windows, or you can download apps from the Windows Store.

Smartphones

The *smartphone* is by far the most popular computer device in the world today. Whereas households might have one or maybe two desktop or laptop computers each, it seems like everyone from grandparents to preschoolers has their own smartphone. From highly industrialized nations to developing countries, smartphones have permeated every corner of the globe.

Any mobile phone with its own processor and operating system can be considered a smartphone. Touchscreens are ubiquitous, and nearly all devices also come with features such as a web browser, email access, media player, GPS, PDA capability, camera, and various apps. They are able to connect wirelessly via cellular, Wi-Fi, Bluetooth, and in many cases, near field communication (NFC) or infrared (IR). Their small screen size, generally less than 5", makes them poorly suited for business applications such as creating documents or spreadsheets, but they are the perfect size to carry around and read email, text, listen to music, and surf the Internet. Some people even actually use them to make phone calls.

Apps can be downloaded from the same app stores that we mentioned in the section on tablets. The vast majority of apps for an OS can run on either tablets or smartphones, but always be sure to check compatibility before purchasing an app.

The IBM Simon Personal Communicator released by BellSouth in 1994, and shown in Figure 10.3, is considered to be the first ever smartphone. By today's standards, it was pretty remedial, but back then it was revolutionary (although perhaps a bit ahead of its time). It included a touchscreen with a stylus, its own OS, and a few basic apps. You can see the basic specifications in Table 10.3. BellSouth sold about 50,000 units (at the low price of $899 with a two-year contract!) during the six months or so that it was for sale. In part because of its size, weight (just over a pound), and expense, the device didn't gain widespread popularity.

TABLE 10.3 Simon Personal Communicator specifications

Feature	Specification
CPU	Vadem 16MHz
RAM	1MB
Display	4.5" × 1.4" monochrome backlit LCD
Storage	1MB
Connectivity	Cellular, 2400bps modem, fax, PCMCIA type 2
OS	Datalight ROM-DOS
Dimensions	0" × 2.5" × 1.5"
Weight	18oz

FIGURE 10.3 Simon Personal Communicator

IBM's "Simon Personal Communicator" by Bcos47—http://commons.wikimedia.org/wiki/
File:IBM_SImon_in_charging_station.png. Licensed under Public Domain via Wikimedia
Commons.

Japan was the first country to see widespread smartphone adoption in 1999, with
a phone released by telecom giant NTT DoCoMo. By 2001, it's estimated that NTT
DoCoMo had 40 million subscribers. The technology didn't really start to take off in the
United States until after 2003, when a company called Research In Motion (RIM) launched

the modern BlackBerry. The early BlackBerry 6210 is shown in Figure 10.4. The built-in hardware keyboard was a key defining feature; indeed, even as recently as 2014, BlackBerry was still releasing phones with physical keyboards to please their loyal buyers.

FIGURE 10.4   BlackBerry 6210

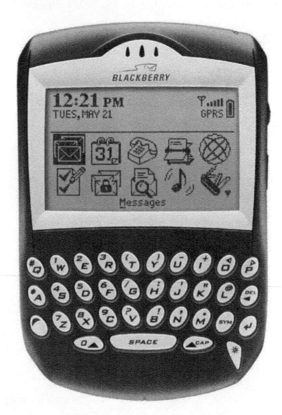

The defining year for smartphones came in 2007 with Apple's release of the iPhone, running the iOS operating system. It was the first popular device with a capacitive touchscreen and an onscreen keyboard that users could operate with their fingers. An Android-based phone was launched a year later, in 2008, in the form of the HTC Dream. It wasn't quite as advanced as the iPhone, but it had similar capabilities. Although iPhones and Android-based phones are each slightly better at certain tasks, today they are more or less compa rable in technology.

Google's Android OS and Apple's iOS are discussed in depth in Chapter 21.

In terms of current usage, Android-based smartphones dominate market share, with Apple second and Windows-based phones a distant third. BlackBerry devices are rare nowadays. Figure 10.5 and Table 10.4 show comparisons of selected iPhone versions. In Figure 10.5, you can see the sizes as well as the available colors. There are so many different Android smartphones in the market that it would be unrealistic to try to compare them all. The biggest manufacturers are Samsung, HTC, LG, Sony, and Motorola.

TABLE 10.4   Selected iPhone specifications

Feature	1st Gen	4	5	6	6 Plus
Release Date	June 2007	June 2010	Sept. 2012	Sept. 2014	Sept. 2014
Initial OS	iPhone OS 1.0	iOS 4	iOS 6	iOS 8	iOS 8
Display Size	3.5"	3.5"	4"	4.7"	5.5"
Weight	4.8oz	4.8oz	4.0oz	4.6oz	6.1oz
Storage	4GB, 8GB, or 16GB	8GB, 16GB, or 32GB	16GB, 32GB, or 64GB	16GB, 64GB, or 128GB	16GB, 64GB, or 128GB
Processor Speed	620MHz	1GHz	1.3GHz dual core	1.4GHz dual core	1.4GHz dual core
802.11 spec	b/g	b/g/n	a/b/g/n	a/b/g/n/ac	a/b/g/n/ac
Camera	2 megapixel (MP) f/2.8	5MP f/2.8, 720p HD video	8MP f/2.4, 1080p HD video	8MP f/2.2, 1080p HD video	8MP f/2.2, 1080p HD video with optical image stabilization
Battery life (hours of standby)	250	300	225	250	384
Other	No GPS	Added gyroscope	5s added Touch ID	NFC	NFC

FIGURE 10.5   A visual iPhone history

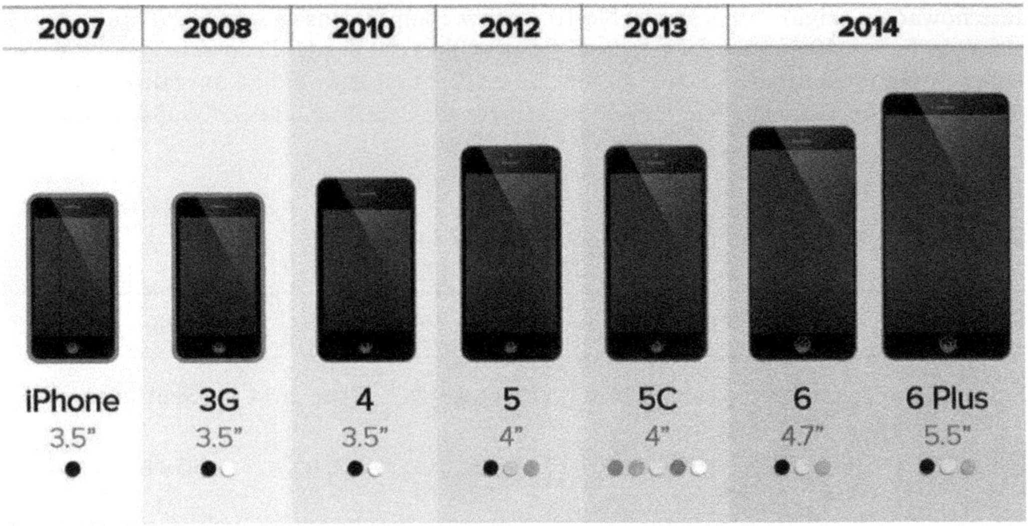

2007	2008	2010	2012	2013	2014	
iPhone	3G	4	5	5C	6	6 Plus
3.5"	3.5"	3.5"	4"	4"	4.7"	5.5"

Photo credit: theshayna.com

Real World Scenario

The Fall of a Giant

The naturalist Charles Darwin is famously quoted as saying, "It's not the strongest of the species that survives, but the one that is most adaptable to change." That may be true in nature, but it is most certainly true in the rapidly evolving world of technology.

In 1999, a Canadian telecommunications company named Research In Motion (RIM) introduced what many consider to be the predecessor to the first modern smartphone. The first BlackBerry was basically a two-way pager with email support, but within a few years it would support mobile calls, email, text messaging, Internet faxing, and web browsing. With the focus on providing mobile email, BlackBerry quickly gained a significant presence in the mobile space.

One of the primary features of the BlackBerry was that it had a full keyboard. It wasn't full-sized, but each letter had its own key, which made typing emails and texts significantly easier than on the cell phones in use at the time. Over the course of its history, the physical keyboard became both a symbol of BlackBerry as well as part of its downfall. Similarly to Apple, RIM produced both the hardware and the software together. The hardware devices ran the Java-based BlackBerry OS.

BlackBerry devices went through several revisions much like their competitors, with the addition of new features. However, RIM was not as able to adapt quickly to changing market conditions as its competitors, and it went from being a strong player to being mostly irrelevant in the mobile space. As of 2009, BlackBerry commanded about a 20 percent share of the global mobile market and a 43-percent share in the United States. In 2011, the global figure had dropped to about 10 percent, and by 2014 it was down to below 2 percent. The introduction of the iPhone severely hurt sales, and the launch of Android a year later just made things worse. Critics complained that the BlackBerry had a dated look and feel, and it wasn't as good at browsing the Internet. The BlackBerry App World had some apps but not enough, and developing new ones was expensive. Moreover, RIM held a strong belief that consumers would not want to use a virtual keyboard, and it turned out they were wrong. The company did eventually introduce touchscreen smartphones, some with and some without physical keyboards, but by that time, the damage had already been done.

In 2013, RIM changed its name to BlackBerry, released the BlackBerry 10 OS (based on the UNIX-like QNX platform), and announced that BlackBerry would stop producing operating systems. As of the summer of 2015, rumors abound about what will happen to BlackBerry, including the rumor that another company will acquire it.

BlackBerry is a great case study for what happens to a technology company when it bets on the wrong trends or when it focuses on the wrong consumer benefits and the rest of the industry leapfrogs it in what seems to be an instant.

Phablets

Throughout the 1990s and early 2000s, miniaturization was the biggest trend in mobile phones. First there were brick designs, then flip phones, and then sliding phones—each one getting smaller and smaller. Several popular movies and television shows made fun of the trend by showing characters using impossibly small devices, and some wondered if or when we would see the day when phones were simply a small microchip implanted inside a person's head.

Something funny happened on the road to cellular phone implants though, and that was the smartphone. Smartphones made the device so much, well, smarter, than a regular phone. Among other things, they incorporated Internet access and video players, and users wanted to be able to clearly see the content. So instead of devices getting smaller, they started getting bigger. You saw an example of this with iPhones in Figure 10.5.

At the same time, tablet computers were becoming more popular and smaller. It was inevitable that, at some point, a device would blur the line between smartphone and tablet, and that device is the phablet. Technically, a *phablet* is a smartphone with a display size between 5" and 7".

One of the first smartphones with a screen in the phablet range was the Android-based Dell Streak 5, released in 2010 and shown in Figure 10.6. Technologically speaking, it was equipped about as well as one could expect for the time. It had a multi-touch capacitive touchscreen, plenty of storage, a fast enough CPU, Wi-Fi and Bluetooth (in addition to cellular), and two cameras. (The specifications are outlined in Table 10.5.) The downsides were that it was bulky, had a relatively poor display quality, and ran an OS that wasn't really designed for a mobile device. It didn't achieve great commercial success.

FIGURE 10.6   Dell Streak 5 phablet

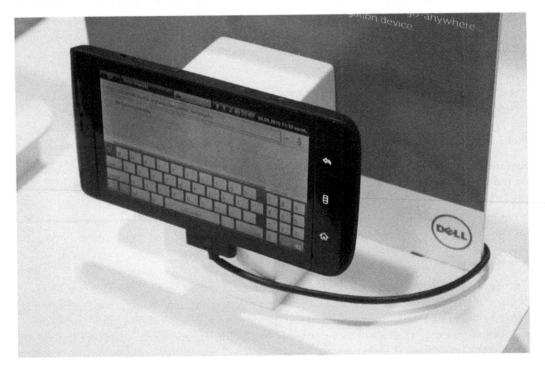

IFA 2010 Internationale Funkausstellung Berlin 57 by Bin im Garten—Own work. Licensed under CC BY-SA 3.0 via Wikimedia Commons:
https://commons.wikimedia.org/wiki/File:IFA_2010_Internationale_Funkausstellung_Berlin_57.JPG

Within about a year, Samsung released the Galaxy Note, a relatively svelte Android-based phone with a 5.3" screen, better resolution, faster processor, and better OS (see Table 10.5). Although critics were skeptical of the Galaxy Note, it took off in popularity and really spawned the phablet category. Apple didn't enter the phablet market until 2014 with the iPhone 6 Plus (the details of which are shown in Table 10.4).

TABLE 10.5   Comparison of early phablets

Feature	Dell Streak 5	Samsung Galaxy Note
Release date	June 2010	October 2011
Initial OS	Android 1.6 Donut	Android 2.3.6 Gingerbread
Display size	5″	5.3″
Display resolution	800×480 pixels	1280×800 pixels
Weight	7.8oz	6.3oz
Storage	1.63GB expandable to 32GB	16GB or 32GB
Processor speed	1GHz	1.4GHz or 1.5GHz
Camera	5MP, 720p HD video	8MP, 1080p HD video

From about 2011 to 2014, *phablet* was a hot buzzword in tech circles; in fact, Reuters called 2013 "The Year of the Phablet." *The New York Times* forecast that phablets would become the dominant computer device of the future. Maybe that will come true, but the enthusiasm for the device overlooks its biggest downside. For a phone replacement, it's a bit too big to be conveniently stuffed into a pocket, and for many users it's too large to be comfortably used with one hand. So while the larger phones remain popular, it's possible that they have reached their high-water mark.

The term *phablet* isn't used as often today; they're simply seen as large phones. In fact, a recent search of the term *phablet* on a few popular electronics retailers' websites returned no phones but only a few accessories. At the end of the day, a phablet is simply a big smartphone, and it has all of the same features that you would expect from that type of device.

e-Readers

An *e-reader* is a device similar to a tablet in size but optimized for the reading digital books, magazines, and newspapers. The main characteristics that differentiate an e-reader from a tablet are the type of display, smaller on-board storage, and longer battery life.

Most e-readers use a technology called electrophoretic ink, or E Ink, which is a proprietary type of electronic paper. Although E Ink is available in color, many consider its best applications to be in grayscales or pure black and white. While e-readers might not look as fancy as tablets, there are two clear advantages of E Ink displays:

- Lower energy use than other LCD displays, which greatly prolongs battery life; many e-readers can go several weeks between charges.

- Much easier to read in bright conditions, such as sunlight.

Although the term *E Ink* is used to discuss a general technology, the term is a trademark of E Ink Holdings, Inc. (www.eink.com). E Ink is also marketed under the name Vizplex. Other competitors exist in this field, but Vizplex products lead the market.

The most popular e-reader is the Amazon Kindle, shown in Figure 10.7. Others include the Barnes & Noble Nook, Kobo Aura and Kobo Glo, Onyx BOOX, PocketBook, and the Sony DPT-S1, which has a large 13.3" screen. Specifications differ by manufacturer and model, but generally speaking, e-readers have about a 6" touch-screen, 2GB to 4GB storage, Wi-Fi connectivity, and weigh 6oz. to 8oz. Some relatively common features are a built-in web browser, a backlight for reading in dim-light settings, and a microSD memory card reader. Most e-readers have a file system that allows users to store their titles in folders (Kobo calls them shelves). Users either subscribe to a service for a certain amount of monthly content, or they pay for each item that they choose to download.

The Kindle Fire series devices run a version of Android and are considered tablets, not e-readers. The Fire uses a traditional LCD display and not E Ink.

FIGURE 10.7 A basic fourth-generation Kindle

"Kindle4" by Difbobatl—Own work. Licensed under CC BY-SA 3.0 via Wikimedia Commons: https://commons.wikimedia.org/wiki/File:Kindle4.jpg#/media/File:Kindle4.jpg

Based on market sales data, it would appear that the e-reader peak was in about 2011. Since then, sales have slowly declined, possibly due to the overlap between tablets and e-readers. Tablets with e-reader apps give the user much more flexibility than a simple e-reader. e-Readers are much less expensive though, and they fill a specific niche for those who read a lot.

GPS

Global positioning system (GPS) is a satellite-based navigation system that provides location and time services. It's great technology for those who are perpetually lost, want to know the best way to get somewhere, or want or need to track down someone else.

The most common commercial use for GPS is navigation; you can get your current location and directions to where you want to go. Other uses include tracking; law enforcement can monitor inmates with location devices, or parents can locate their children via their smartphones. Oil and gas companies use GPS in their geological surveys, and farmers can use GPS-enabled machines to plant crops automatically. There are three major components to GPS: the satellite constellation, the ground control network, and the receiver. The ground control network monitors satellite health and signal integrity. We'll look at the other two components next.

GPS Satellites

The United States Department of Defense (DOD) developed GPS starting in the early 1970s with the goal of creating the best navigation system possible. The first GPS satellite launched in 1978, and now the United States government manages 32 total GPS satellites covering the globe. Twenty-four are active satellites for the service and the rest are backups. Satellites are launched into an orbit of about 12,550 miles above the earth, and old satellites are replaced with new ones when an old one reaches its life expectancy or fails. GPS is free to use for commercial purposes.

There are additional global satellite-based navigation systems managed by other government entities. Collectively, they are called Global Navigation Satellite Systems (GNSSs). All of the systems are outlined in Table 10.6; as you might expect, no two systems are compatible with each other.

TABLE 10.6 Global Navigation Satellite Systems

Name	Managed By	Number of Satellites
Global Positioning System (GPS)	United States	24
Global Navigation Satellite System (GLONASS)	Russia	24
Galileo Positioning System	European Space Agency	30

TABLE 10.6   Global Navigation Satellite Systems *(continued)*

Name	Managed By	Number of Satellites
BeiDou Navigation Satellite System (BDS)	China	35
Indian Regional Navigation Satellite System (IRNSS)	India	7

At first glance, it might seem like there are an excessive number of satellites required to run a navigation service. GPS systems were designed to require multiple satellites. Receivers use a process called *triangulation*, which they use to calculate the distance between themselves and the satellites (based on the time it takes to receive a signal) to determine their location. They require input from four satellites to provide location and elevation or three to provide location. Most GNSSs provide two levels of service, one more precise than the other. For example, GPS provides two levels:

▪ Standard Positioning Service (SPS) for civil use, accurate to within 100m horizontally and 156m vertically. Uses Coarse Acquisition (C/A) code.

▪ Precise Positioning Service (PPS) for Department of Defense and ally use, accurate to within 22m horizontally and 27.7m vertically. Uses Precise (P) code.

The accuracy numbers listed in this section are the official specifications of GPS, which were calculated when the service was launched. For many years, GPS used a feature called Selective Availability (SA), which was an intentional degradation of public signals, implemented for national security reasons. (The government didn't want potential enemies to be able to use GPS.) In 2000, the United States government discontinued the use of SA. Now, commercial GPS is accurate to within about 10 to 15 meters in most cases. Under ideal conditions, it can be accurate to within a centimeter. Much of the accuracy depends on the quality of the receiver.

The two service levels are separated by transmitting on different frequencies, named L1 and L2. L1 transmits at 1575.42MHz, and it contains unencrypted civilian C/A code as well as military Precise (P) code. L2 (1227.60MHz) only transmits encrypted P code, referred to as Y code. In the United States, SPS is free to use; the receiver just needs to manage C/A code. PPS requires special permission from the United States DoD as well as special equipment that can receive P and Y code and decrypt Y code. Galileo, in the European Union, provides free open (standard) service, but charges users a fee for the high data throughput commercial (premium) service. Both offer encrypted signals with controlled access for government use.

GPS Receivers

GPS receivers come in all shapes and sizes. Common forms are wearable watches and wristbands, stand-alone GPS devices (like the Garmin device shown in Figure 10.8), and ones built into automobiles. Most smartphones, phablets, and tablets support GPS as well (sometimes under the name Location Services), and more and more laptops are coming with built-in GPS capabilities. You can also find GPS devices that come on a collar for pets. Most stand-alone GPS devices feature capacitive touchscreens. The Garmin device shown in Figure 10.8 has a 4.5″ touchscreen; 5″ devices are common as of the time of this writing. It also contains an SD memory card slot for expansion. Popular brands of automobile GPS devices are Garmin, TomTom, and Magellan.

FIGURE 10.8   Garmin Nuvi GPS

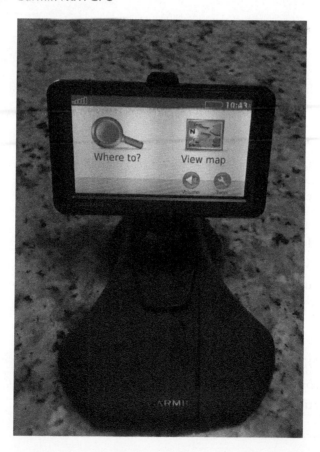

Smart Cameras

Although most people use their phones as cameras these days, there's still a big market for higher-quality digital cameras. Most of these cameras record video as well. Newer cameras, called *smart cameras*, have built-in wireless network connectivity for easy picture and video transfers. A recent example is the Samsung NX500, released in February 2015 and pictured in Figure 10.9. Another similar model is the Sony A6000.

FIGURE 10.9   Samsung NX500 smart camera

The NX500 includes the following features:

- Samsung DRIMe Vs processor
- 28-megapixel image sensor with up to 21x optical zoom
- 4K Ultra High Definition video recording
- 3" touchscreen monitor/viewfinder, which rotates up above the camera 180 degrees for selfies
- SD/SDHC/SDXC flash memory
- Wireless support for Wi-Fi 802.11b/g/n, Bluetooth, and NFC
- Wired connections: USB 2.0, HDMI
- Weighs 10oz

The list of specifications is for illustrative purposes only; don't feel the need to memorize the specs of this specific camera. You should have a feel for a typical smart camera's features, especially in relation to network connectivity. The newer smart cameras will have Wi-Fi, Bluetooth, and possibly NFC built-in. There will be a menu on the screen to connect it to a Wi-Fi network, just as you would a smartphone or any other mobile device.

Wearable Technology Devices

Devices that we can call computers keep getting smaller and smaller. It's no wonder then that manufacturers have designed wearable computers that can provide great functionality to users. Three types of wearable technology are smart watches, fitness monitors, and glasses and headsets.

Smart Watches

A classic American newspaper comic strip named *Dick Tracy*, created by Chester Gould, made its debut in 1931. It featured a hard-nosed detective named Dick Tracy, who by 1946 had the coolest technologically advanced gadget: a *smart watch*. It wasn't called a smart watch in the comic strip, but a two-way wrist radio based on a walkie-talkie. If you search for "Dick Tracy and his watch," you'll probably recognize the device instantly. It's clearly the inspiration for the smart watches of today. In fact, in 2015 Apple CEO Tim Cook said that Tracy's watch was the impetus to make the Apple Watch.

Throughout the 1990s and into the 2000s, many devices came on the market claiming to be smart watches. They were basically computerized wristwatches that offered some functionality, such as a calculator, but had no connection to cellular phones. By 2009, smart watches had the ability to connect to cell phones and a few models had built-in cellular capabilities themselves. Most of these early prototypes ran some version of Linux, although Microsoft dabbled in the area as did Palm, Inc., which was famous for the Palm Pilot PDA and made the Palm OS.

Modern smart watches run their own OS, often are able to make and receive cellular calls, provide touchscreen capability, function as media players, have a camera, run apps, and include many of the same sensors as those found in a smartphone. In many respects, several smart watches are basically low-powered smartphones but strapped to the user's wrist; others are designed to be an extension of a user's phone. They are generally charged via a micro USB connection. Some of the more popular brands of smart watches and their features are listed in Table 10.7. The Samsung Gear series is one of the longest running smart watches, and it is one of the more popular Android-based options. In April 2015, the Apple Watch was launched to much fanfare because that's what usually happens when Apple releases new toys. Pebble watches are lower-priced entries, but they have the advantage of being able to sync with both Android-based smartphones and iPhones.

TABLE 10.7   Selected smart watches

Feature	Apple Watch	Samsung Gear S	LG Watch Urbane LTE	Sony SmartWatch 3	Mororola Moto 360	Pebble Time
Release date	April 2015	Oct 2014	March 2015	Oct 2014	Sept 2014	May 2015
OS	WatchOS	Tizen	LG Wearable Platform	Android Wear	Android Wear	Pebble OS
Display Size	1.5"	2"	1.3"	1.6"	1.56"	1.26"
Weight	Varies	2.36oz	4.06oz	2.7oz	1.7oz	1.5oz
Storage	8GB	4GB	4GB	4GB	4GB	4GB
Processor	Apple S1	1GHz Dual Core	1.2GHZ Quad Core	1.2 GHz Quad Core	1GHz	100MHz
Wi-Fi	b/g/n	b/g/n	b/g/n	Yes	No	No
Bluetooth	v4.0 LE	v4.1 LE	v4.0 LE	v4.0 LE	v4.0 LE	v4.0 LE
Other	NFC	3G, GPS	LTE, GPS, NFC	GPS, NFC	Wireless charging	

The Apple Watch is interesting to explore a bit more because of the different available features. Apple is always very interested in getting the user experience just right. Over the last decade or so, whether or not its technology was as good as its competitors, Apple has always tried to "out cool" people. The Apple Watch is no different. Here are some interesting features of the Apple Watch:

▪ Apple made sure to focus on style. There are two sizes of Apple Watch available, a 42mm version and a 38mm version, each with its own set of styled bands. Basic styles are Sport, Milanese Loop, Classic Buckle, Leather Loops, Modern Buckle, and Link Bracelet. Some special edition bands with 18-karat cases cost as much as $17,000. This is the primary physical element that users can customize. Some of the choices and different watch faces (which are customizable too) are shown in Figure 10.10.

▪ Apple developed a new OS for the Watch, called WatchOS. It's more or less on par with iOS 8, but of course it includes features more tailored to the smaller device. WatchOS 2 is expected to be released at the same time as iOS 9.

- Apple made sure to market a device that has plenty of storage, with 8GB. Interestingly, Apple made limitations to how much memory can be used for different features. For example, music is limited to 2GB, which will allow users to store approximately 200 songs. Users can only store 75MB of photos, and the rest of the memory is reserved for the OS.

- GPS is not built in, but it will use the GPS in the paired phone if it's nearby.

- NFC is built in, so the user can use the Apple Pay feature.

- Watches get a lot of their functionality from a paired iPhone. For example, Apple Watches can run apps, but the apps are stored on the paired iPhone and only transmitted to the watch when the app is used. In addition, the Apple Watch itself is not able to take calls directly, but when paired with a user's iPhone, the user can take the calls via the Apple Watch. Notifications are pushed to the Apple Watch, so the user can simply look at their wrist as opposed to searching for their phone.

FIGURE 10.10 Several Apple Watch styles

Long story short, the Apple Watch is really an extension of the iPhone, located conveniently on the wrist.

Fitness Monitors

The CompTIA A+ exam objectives list fitness monitors as their own class of wearable technology, but in many cases the functionality they provide is also provided by smart watches.

A *fitness monitor* is normally worn on the wrist, and it tracks a user's movements and heart rate. Some fitness monitors will be able to track sleep patterns and have a clock, alarm, and other features like an electronic or smart watch. All fitness monitors have the ability to sync to a device such as a smartphone, laptop, or desktop. For example, the fitness monitor will likely come with a smartphone app that lets the user track calories and see heart rate, steps taken, flights of stairs climbed, and other physical activity. The app lets the user track performance over time and set goals, and it gives updates on progress toward those goals.

There are over a dozen brands of fitness monitors on the market today. The most popular brands are Fitbit and Jawbone, but others include Polar, Garmin, Basis, Misfit, Nike, and Withings. Each brand has several options available, from basic step counters (pedometers) to deluxe models that track steps, flights of stairs climbed, and sleep patterns and have built-in wrist heart rate monitors. The wrist-based heart rate monitor is a relatively new feature in this category, and it doesn't seem to be quite as accurate as more traditional chest strap heart rate monitors. But given the convenience of 24/7 heart rate monitoring without the need to wear a chest strap, people who choose to wear one are willing to make that sacrifice. Some nicer models will also sync with a smartphone and display notifications or texts.

Let's use a Fitbit as an example; the Fitbit Flex, a mid-level activity monitor, is pictured in Figure 10.11. In the upper row is the Flex itself along with the wrist strap. The device in the middle is a Bluetooth receiver, and the USB charger is on the bottom. The Flex contains a three-axis accelerometer, a vibration motor, a Bluetooth v4.0 transceiver, and a lithium-polymer battery. A full charge on the battery lasts about five days. The display is very simple: five lights. The five lights can tell the user how close they are to achieving their goals and the battery life remaining. Wristbands come in a variety of colors.

FIGURE 10.11   Fitbit Flex, wrist strap, Bluetooth USB dongle, and USB charging cable

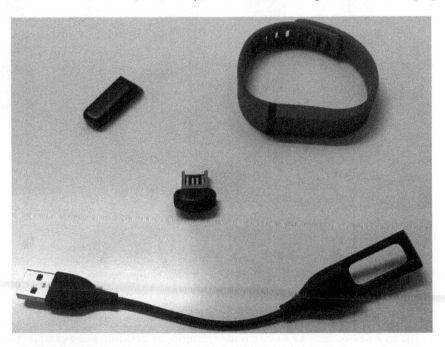

Because the Flex only has the accelerometer, it can track steps taken but it does not track stairs climbed. To track sleep with this particular model, the user needs to tap it five times to put the device into sleep mode and then tap it five times again when they wake up. It will sync using Bluetooth to a smartphone, or to a desktop or laptop computer if the computer has the Bluetooth transceiver plugged in. Figure 10.12 shows you the Fitbit app dashboard.

FIGURE 10.12 Fitbit dashboard

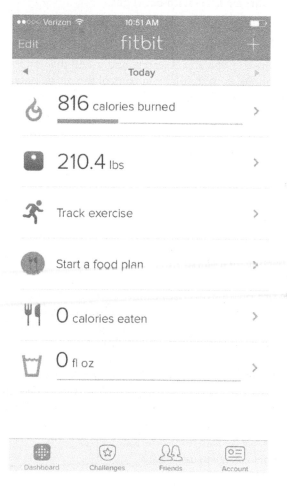

Within the dashboard, you can set goals, enter data, and see progress. Fitbit, Jawbone, and a few others also sell Bluetooth-enabled scales with the ability to measure weight and body fat percentage, which will sync to your phone as well.

The Fitbit Surge, the high-end Fitbit at the time of this writing, contains the following:

- GPS
- Three-axis accelerometer
- Three-axis gyroscope

- Digital compass
- Optical heart rate monitor (OHRM)
- Altimeter
- Ambient light sensor
- Vibration motor
- Touchscreen monochrome LCD with backlight
- Bluetooth v4.0 transceiver
- Lithium-polymer battery with up to seven-day life

The Surge is about the size of a smart watch, and it will display text and call notifications from the synced phone as well as let you control the music on your phone. Of course, different manufacturers and models have different features; there are plenty of options to choose from to meet every user's needs.

Glasses and Headsets

It's hard to think of any computer product that has generated more controversy in recent years than Google Glass. Some see the glasses-mounted computer as an amazing technological step forward, while others view it as a highly intrusive technology that should be permanently banned.

The idea that Google pushed was relatively benign. The company wanted to produce a wearable computer that enhanced the user experience without the user having to think about the device or become distracted by it. Thus it created a device that basically has the functionality of a smartphone (without the ability to make cellular calls itself) but that was small enough to be worn on an eyeglasses frame. Users see an *augmented reality (AR)* projected display a few inches from their face that was equivalent to looking at a 25" screen from about 8 feet away. There's a touchpad on the side of the device that lets users scroll through menus and make selections. Other inputs can be made by voice command through a microphone or other built-in sensors such as the accelerometer, gyroscope, magnetometer, proximity sensor, and ambient light sensor. Oh, and it has a camera mounted on it. Yes, it's the camera that caused the controversy. Figure 10.13 shows Google Glass being worn. Google also produced a version that fits onto prescription glasses frames.

Table 10.8 outlines some of the technical specifications of Google Glass.

TABLE 10.8 Google Glass specs

Feature	Specification
Release Date	To "Glass Explorers" in April 2013
Price	$1,500
Weight	1.51oz

Feature	Specification
Operating System	Android 4.4.2 KitKat
CPU	OMAP 4430 Dual Core
RAM	2GB
Storage	16GB, 12GB usable
Display	Prism projector, equivalent to a 25" screen viewed from 8 feet
Camera	5MP, 720p HD video
Connectivity	802.11b/g, Bluetooth, micro USB

FIGURE 10.13   Google Glass

"Google Glass detail" by Antonio Zugaldia—www.flickr.com/photos/azugaldia/
7457645618. Licensed under CC BY 3.0 via Wikimedia Commons—https://commons.
wikimedia.org/wiki/File:Google_Glass_detail.jpg

Google Glass, as of the time of this writing, has never been available to the general public. A certain number of trial users, called Glass Explorers, were allowed to purchase the item for $1,500 and provide feedback to Google on their usage experience. Even though the device had limited distribution, it caused a great deal of controversy.

Many complained that the device, with its mounted camera, is an invasion of privacy. In theory, the wearer could take pictures or record video without other people knowing about it. (By default, turning on video recording lights up features on Glass, making it pretty obvious that the wearer is recording. But non-users don't necessarily know this, and in theory an app could be created to disable the lights.) Indeed, an app was created that allowed wearers to take pictures by just winking. Several establishments in the United States posted signs prohibiting Google Glass from being worn inside, such as restaurants, movie theatres, and casinos. In some countries, the device can be considered illegal spy equipment. Apps could be created to identify faces (imagine walking down the street and seeing a total stranger, but then seeing their name pop up attached to their Facebook profile) or track finger movements to steal passwords or ATM PINs.

In addition to privacy concerns, there are safety concerns. For example, wearing Google Glass while driving an automobile could be considered a safety hazard, much like using a smartphone while driving. Another safety concern could be for users, who on occasion have reportedly been accosted for wearing the device. With all of the potential ramifications, many experts in the tech industry wonder if a product like Glass will ever receive mainstream acceptance.

It's likely that Glass and similar products may be more accepted for commercial applications. For example, surgeons could use it during an operation, and commercial delivery drivers, law enforcement personnel, military personnel, manufacturing supervisors, and journalists might find some use for it.

Other companies have created a few similar, wearable smart glasses as well, such as EyeTap, Golden-i, Microsoft HoloLens, Vuzix, and the Epson Moverio.

Connection Types

Mobile devices allow users to roam about freely without the worry of being constantly plugged in, but they are not islands unto themselves. They still need to recharge and communicate with other devices. Therefore, they require connections to power sources, networks, and peripherals. Just as in the rest of the networking world, there are two connection classifications: wired and wireless.

Wired Connections

Because space is at a premium, manufacturers of mobile devices need to get creative with the size and shape of each component. Consequently, you will see several different types of proprietary, vendor-specific ports or connectors designed for power or communication. Wired connections are almost always used for recharging, and they are often used for syncing devices as well.

Regardless of the connector type used on the device side, the other end of the cable will nearly always be a USB male type A connector so that it can easily plug into a laptop or other device. Figure 10.14 shows five common USB connectors.

FIGURE 10.14   USB connectors: micro, mini, type B, female type A, male type A

5 cm

By Techtonic (edited from USB types.jpg) [Public domain], via Wikimedia Commons

Many companies choose to design their devices with a built-in micro USB or mini USB connector. Others modify the standard USB connector slightly, as Samsung has done with the connector for the S5 smartphone and other devices. The cable is shown in Figure 10.15. A standard micro USB cable will work to charge the phone, but charging and syncing won't be as fast as it is with the Samsung cable.

FIGURE 10.15   Samsung compound micro USB charging cable

Apple products nearly always have their own proprietary connectors. Figure 10.16 shows the connector for an iPod Shuffle, the 30-pin Apple connector used by many iPods and iPhones up to the 4s, the *Lightning connector* used by the iPhone 5 series and iPhone 6 series, and a USB type A connector for comparison.

FIGURE 10.16   Apple iPod Shuffle, iPhone 4, and iPhone 5/6, and USB type A connectors

If you are not sure which connector to use, always check the product documentation. A quick Internet search will likely find the answer as well.

Wireless Connections

Wireless connections are convenient in ways that wired connections never will be. You don't need to haul a cable around, and in many cases the wireless connection can be in use for things like syncing even without your intervention. The four connection types mentioned in the CompTIA A+ exam objectives for this section are Bluetooth, IR, NFC, and hotspot/tethering. Don't forget that many of the mobile devices that we've covered in this chapter are capable of Wi-Fi and cellular connections as well. Look again at Chapter 8, "Installing Wireless and SOHO Networks," for a review of Wi-Fi and cellular specifications.

Bluetooth

Bluetooth is used quite often for connecting mobile accessories to a device, particularly headsets, full-size keyboards, and mice. It's also used for syncing. Bluetooth specifications are covered in Chapter 8. The vast majority of mobile devices are Bluetooth Class 2 devices, meaning that they have a maximum communication distance of 10 meters.

When setting up a Bluetooth connection between a mobile device and an accessory, you will most often be required to connect the two devices logically in a process called *pairing*. Pairing is basically a discovery and authentication process that validates the communication link. The exact process for Bluetooth pairing will differ by your mobile OS and the device to which you are connecting. In general, though, remember that these are the steps:

1.   Turn on the Bluetooth device.

     a.   Enable Bluetooth.

     b.   Enable pairing.

2.   Use your mobile device to locate and select the Bluetooth device.

3. Enter the Bluetooth device's passcode.

4. Confirm pairing on the Bluetooth device by pressing a button or a combination of buttons.

5. Test connectivity.

 More information on Bluetooth pairing, including two pairing exercises, is provided in Chapter 21, "Mobile Operating Systems and Connectivity."

Infrared

While most mobile devices support Bluetooth, *infrared (IR)* is less common, especially in smartphones. Samsung, HTC, and LG all include IR support, whereas the iPhone does not. If the phone does not include built-in IR, you can buy IR-capable accessories that plug into the headphone jack. IR specifications are also covered in Chapter 8.

Remember that IR is a short-distance, line-of-sight, point-to-point communication method. It's usually used to transfer small amounts of data from one device to another. The maximum functional distance of IR in mobile devices is about 1 meter, with a viewing angle of about 30 degrees.

 Television remote controls, which have a functional range of about 15 to 20 feet, use a different infrared technology than most mobile devices use.

Near Field Communication

Near field communication (NFC) is a wireless technology that has become more and more popular over the last several years. With Apple's introduction of the iPhone 6, nearly every smartphone manufacturer today equips its phones with NFC. Many tablets have NFC as well, except for the iPad, which does not at the time of this writing.

NFC uses radio frequency (RF) signals, and NFC devices can operate in three different modes:

- NFC card emulation mode, which lets the device act as a smart card. This is useful for making payments at the site of a merchant who uses NFC.

- NFC reader/writer mode, which allows the device to read information stored in an NFC tag on a label or poster.

- NFC peer-to-peer mode, which allows for ad hoc data transfer between two NFC-enabled devices.

Data rates are rather slow compared to other wireless methods, as NFC operates at 106Kbps, 212Kbps, and 424Kbps. It transmits at 13.56MHz. NFC always involves an initiator and a target. Let's say that you wanted to read an NFC tag in a poster. You would move your phone close to the tag, and the phone would generate a small RF field that would power the target. Data could then be read from the tag. Tags currently hold up to 4KB of data.

In peer-to-peer mode, NFC data is transmitted in the NFC Data Exchange Format (NDEF), using the Simple NDEF Exchange Protocol (SNEP). SNEP uses the Layer 2 Logical Link Control Protocol (LLCP), which is connection based, to provide reliable data delivery.

To use NFC, a user simply moves their device within range (about 4" or 10cm) of another NFC-enabled device. Then, using an app, the device will be able to perform the desired transaction, such as making a payment, reading information, or transferring data from one device to another.

NFC uses two different coding mechanisms to send data. At the 106Kbps speed, it uses a modified Miller coding (delay encoding) scheme, whereas at faster speeds it uses Manchester coding (phase encoding). Neither method is encrypted, so it is possible to hack NFC communications using man-in-the-middle or relay attacks. Because of the limited distance of the RF signals though, hacking is pretty hard to do. The potential attacker would need to be within a few meters to attempt it.

The mobile payment feature of NFC is growing in popularity. More merchants are accepting it, and Apple got into the NFC payment arena in 2014 with the launch of Apple Pay, which can be used from iPhones, iPads, and the Apple Watch. In 2015, Google introduced Android Pay, which is an update to the older Google Wallet app. It's fair to question its security though, considering that NFC does not support encryption.

When using Apple Pay, users with iPhones with Touch ID simply need to get the phone within range of the receiving device and have their finger or thumb on the Touch ID button. The phone will transmit its secure element identifier (SEID), and the Touch ID will act as a mode of verification; without it, the transaction will not succeed. If you have an iPhone 6 or 6 Plus, you can see your SEID by going to Settings ➢ General ➢ About ➢ SEID. The Android Pay feature is similar.

There have been some reports in the news about Apple Pay being unsecure. It's true that data breaches have happened regarding Apple Pay accounts, but it's been due to data stolen from merchants, not the Apple Pay mechanism.

Hotspots

Imagine yourself in a situation where you're in an office building that doesn't have Wi-Fi and you need to send an important document from your laptop to a key client? What can you do? If you have a cellular-enabled device such as a smartphone, you may be able to turn that phone into a *mobile hotspot*. By doing so, you can share your cellular Internet connection with Wi-Fi enabled devices such as a laptop or tablet.

> In order to use your smartphone as a mobile hotspot, your service contract with your provider must allow it. Not all do! Be sure to check with your provider before trying to enable a hotspot.

Enabling an iPhone to be a mobile hotspot is done via Settings ➢ Personal Hotspot. The Personal Hotspot screen is shown in Figure 10.17. A password to join the network is provided (and can be changed) as well as instructions on how to join. On Android, you enable a mobile hotspot by checking the box next to Portable Wi-Fi Hotspot in Settings ➤ Wireless & Networks ➤ Tethering & Portable Hotspot. The option below that, Portable Wi-Fi Hotspot Settings, allows you to change the network SSID, security method (use WPA2!), and password.

FIGURE 10.17   Enabled personal hotspot

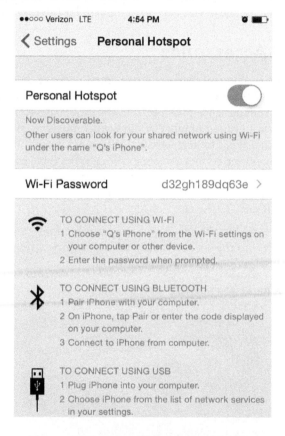

There are three downsides to using your cellphone as a hotspot:

- **Speed** Multiple devices are now using one cellular connection.

- **Cost** You're using your cellular data plan, which could result in additional charges if you go over your data limit. Unless you know that you have plenty of capacity in your plan, use a hotspot sparingly.

- **Security** You may have noticed in Figure 10.17 that there was a password but no security options. iOS 7 and newer do use WPA2 security, but of course any wireless network has the potential to be hacked. Older iOS versions were susceptible to brute-force security attacks.

Some mobile providers limit the number of devices that can join the mobile hotspot. For example, Verizon limits it to 5 devices for a 3G phone and 10 devices for 4G LTE phones.

Tethering

Tethering is connecting a device to a mobile hotspot. The term used to be reserved only for when you were connected via USB cable, as opposed to connecting via wireless. Some devices will not function as a mobile hotspot but will allow you to tether a laptop (or other device) to it with a USB cable so the mobile device can share the cellular Internet connection.

Mobile Device Accessories

Mobile devices pack a ton of useful features into a small package, but they don't account for every need right out of the box. At times, you will need to purchase additional accessories to get the best user experience possible from the mobile device. Considering that most mobile devices have a limited number of physical connectors, you're going to be rather limited on the number and types of accessories that you can attach. For example, iPhones only have two ports: the power connector (either the 30-pin Apple connector or Lightning) and a speaker/headphone jack. Any wired accessory must plug into one of those two ports, or you'll need something like a Lightning to female USB adapter. Here are some common accessories that you will see:

Headsets   Headsets are used for hands-free phone conversations and listening to music. Headsets can either plug into the speaker/headphone jack or be wireless. Most wireless headsets are Bluetooth. Figure 10.18 shows a Bluetooth headset.

FIGURE 10.18   A Bluetooth headset

"Bluetooth headset." Licensed under CC BY-SA 3.0 via Wikimedia Commons: https://commons.wikimedia.org/wiki/File:Bluetooth_headset.jpg

Speakers   If you want to share music with friends, or listen without needing to stuff something into your ear, speakers are good to have. Speakers generally use the speaker/headphone jack, but Bluetooth speakers exist as well.

Game pads   A good game controller can make your mobile device feel a bit more like a gaming console. Most of the game pads will look like standard video gaming console controllers and connect via Bluetooth. Popular models include iControlPad, Gametel, SteelSeries Free, GameKlip, and PowerA Moga.

Docking stations   Docking stations for laptops and tablets are great because they give you a more permanent home for your device, with more ports and likely a full-size monitor, keyboard, and mouse. Many laptop and tablet docking stations will also have extra hard disk storage space. Docking stations for smartphones are more likely to be simple charging stations, many times with a built-in speaker system and clock.

Battery packs and chargers   Battery life is a critical mobile currency. Without battery power, you're in trouble unless there's a power outlet in sight. Battery chargers help you charge the battery, of course, but you can also purchase extra external battery packs for many devices. Some smartphone battery packs simply plug into the charging port on the phone, whereas others are designed to be a protective cover with extra battery life included. They will make your phone bigger and bulkier, but that's the trade-off you make for more battery life. A final option is a power bank. They are small battery packs, usually about 3″ long and less than an inch wide, that you charge up using a USB cable and take with you. When your mobile device needs charging, just plug it into the power bank.

Protective covers   If you have a mobile device, get a protective cover. The devices are relatively fragile, considering they are constantly moved from place to place; shoved into pockets, purses, and bags; and occasionally dropped. Most protective covers will help keep the screen from cracking if the device gets dropped; some offer better protection than others, and yet others are waterproof. Just don't go without one.

Credit card readers   If you need to make mobile sales, you will need a credit card reader and an app to make the transactions. Many mobile credit card readers are small devices that plug into the speaker/headphone jack, like the PayPal Here shown in Figure 10.19. You swipe the credit card through the device and then complete the transaction on the screen. Other, larger and more expensive readers are available as well.

FIGURE 10.19   PayPal Here mobile credit card reader

Memory cards and readers   Mobile devices often make use of small form factor memory cards, such as Secure Digital (SD), miniSD, or microSD cards. Higher capacity versions of these cards are SDHC, SDXC, miniSDHC, microSDHC, and microSDXC. The standard versions can hold up to 4GB in storage, HC up to 32GB, and XC up to 2TB. Mobile devices may have memory card slots built in, or you can purchase an external reader.

Summary

In this chapter, you learned about the characteristics of various types of mobile devices, those that are smaller than laptops. You also learned about common mobile accessories and connection types.

   The mobile devices covered were tablets, smartphones, phablets, e-Readers, smart watches, fitness monitors, glasses and headsets, smart cameras, and GPS devices.

   Connection types can be wired or wireless. The wired connections you should know are proprietary vendor-specific ports, micro USB, mini USB, and Lightning. Wireless connections with which you should be familiar are Bluetooth, infrared, near field communication (NFC), and using cellular to create a hotspot.

   Common accessories include headsets, speakers, game pads, docking stations, battery packs and chargers, protective covers, credit card readers, and memory cards and readers.

Exam Essentials

Know the characteristics of tablets.   Tablet computers are usually smaller than laptops and have a touchscreen interface.

Understand the difference between a phablet and a smartphone.   Phablets are basically large smartphones, with screens between 5″ and 7″ in size.

Know how wearable technology devices work.   Some smart watches are basically like smaller smartphones, and they can make cellular calls. Others are extensions of the smartphone in a convenient location.

Know how GPS works.   GPS receivers require connections to satellites in order to function. Know the various global GNSSs and in general how GPS works.

Know what wired connection types mobile devices frequently use.   Many mobile devices have proprietary power or communications ports due to their small size. Almost all proprietary ports use USB though. Micro and mini USB are also popular. Lightning is Apple's latest (as of this writing) iPhone power connector.

Know what wireless connection types mobile devices frequently use.   Most mobile devices are equipped with Wi-Fi capabilities, along with Bluetooth, IR, and NFC. Many devices also have cellular capabilities, and they can function as mobile hotspots.

Know some common accessories for mobile devices.   Common accessories include headsets, speakers, game pads, docking stations, extra battery packs, battery chargers, protective covers, credit card readers, and memory cards and readers.

Review Questions

1. Which of the following is the most common input method for mobile devices?
   A. Stylus
   B. Resistive touchscreen
   C. Capacitive touchscreen
   D. Keyboard and mouse

2. Which of the following is the operating system used by Apple Watch?
   A. WatchOS
   B. iOS
   C. OS X
   D. Apple OS

3. *Multi-touch* refers to which feature of a touchscreen device?
   A. The ability to touch multiple parts of the screen at once to provide input.
   B. The ability to touch the screen multiple times consecutively as part of the same input stream.
   C. The ability for multiple people to use the touchscreen device.
   D. The ability to use a stylus or a finger as an input device.

4. The type of display that Google Glass presents to its users is called what?
   A. Retinal projection
   B. VR
   C. AR
   D. OCR

5. Which of the following devices was the first commercial tablet computer in the marketplace?
   A. Microsoft Surface Pro
   B. Tablet PC
   C. iPad
   D. GRiDPad

6. With which iPhone version was the Lightning connector introduced?
   A. iPhone 4
   B. iPhone 5
   C. iPhone 5s
   D. iPhone 6

7. You have a mobile touchscreen device with a screen size of 11″. What is the most likely classification of this device?

   A. Tablet

   B. Phablet

   C. Smartphone

   D. GPS

8. Most smartphone Bluetooth accessories have a communication range of approximately how far?

   A. 10 centimeters

   B. 10 meters

   C. 100 meters

   D. 1 kilometer

9. Apps for Android-based smartphones and tablets can be downloaded from which store?

   A. App Store

   B. Google Play

   C. Android Store

   D. Windows Store

10. Which of the following wireless communication methods has the shortest operational range?

    A. Wi-Fi

    B. Bluetooth

    C. NFC

    D. IR

11. What is the typical screen size for a phablet?

    A. Smaller than 5″

    B. From 5″ to 7″

    C. From 7″ to 12″

    D. Larger than 12″

12. Which wireless communication method has an operational range of about 1 meter?

    A. Wi-Fi

    B. Bluetooth

    C. NFC

    D. IR

13. Which of the following are advantages of e-readers using E Ink over tablets? (Choose two.)

   A. More vivid colors

   B. Longer battery life

   C. Easier to read in bright light

   D. Better screen resolution

14. Which of the following best describes the concept of tethering?

   A. When a cellular device uses another device's Wi-Fi connection to get on the Internet

   B. When a Bluetooth device uses another device's Wi-Fi connection to get on the Internet

   C. When a Wi-Fi device uses another device's Bluetooth connection to get on the Internet

   D. When a Wi-Fi device uses another device's cellular connection to get on the Internet

15. What is the number of active satellites used by GPS?

   A. 12

   B. 24

   C. 30

   D. 36

16. What is the fastest data transfer speeds currently supported by NFC?

   A. 106Kbps

   B. 212Kbps

   C. 424Kbps

   D. 636Kbps

17. What is the name of the Russian-managed GNSS?

   A. GLONASS

   B. Galileo

   C. BDS

   D. IRNSS

18. Which of the following is the name of the protocol used to transmit data in NFC peer-to-peer mode?

   A. NDEF

   B. NFCP

   C. LLCP

   D. SNEP

19. Which GPS component is responsible for triangulation?

   A. Satellites

   B. Ground control network

   C. Receiver

   D. All three combined

20. How much data can a micro SDXC memory card hold?

   A. 4GB

   B. 32GB

   C. 128GB

   D. 2TB

Performance-Based Question

You will encounter performance-based questions on the A+ exams. The questions on the exam require you to perform a specific task, and you will be graded on whether or not you were able to complete the task. The following requires you to think creatively in order to measure how well you understand this chapter's topics. You may or may not see similar questions on the actual A+ exams. To see how your answer compares to the authors', refer to Appendix B.

Explain the five steps needed to perform pairing of a smartphone with a Bluetooth device.

Installing and Configuring Printers

THE FOLLOWING COMPTIA A+ 220-901 EXAM OBJECTIVES ARE COVERED IN THIS CHAPTER:

✓ **1.13 Install SOHO multifunction device/printers and configure appropriate settings.**

- Use appropriate printer drivers for a given operating system
    - Configuration settings
        - Duplex
        - Collate
        - Orientation
        - Quality
- Device sharing
    - Wired
        - USB
        - Serial
        - Ethernet
    - Wireless
        - Bluetooth
        - 802.11(a,b,g,n,ac)
        - Infrastructure vs. adhoc
    - Integrated print server (hardware)
    - Cloud printing/remote printing
- Public/shared devices
    - Sharing local/networked devices via Operating System settings

- TCP/Bonjour/AirPrint
- Data privacy
  - User authentication on the device
  - Hard drive caching

✓ **1.14   Compare and contrast differences between the various print technologies and the associated imaging process.**

- Laser
  - Imaging drum, fuser assembly, transfer belt, transfer roller, pickup rollers, separate pads, duplexing assembly
  - Imaging process: processing, charging, exposing, developing, transferring, fusing and cleaning
- Inkjet
  - Ink cartridge, print head, roller, feeder, duplexing assembly, carriage and belt
  - Calibration
- Thermal
  - Feed assembly, heating element
  - Special thermal paper
- Impact
  - Print head, ribbon, tractor feed
  - Impact paper
- Virtual
  - Print to file
  - Print to PDF
  - Print to XPS
  - Print to image

✓ **1.15   Given a scenario, perform appropriate printer maintenance.**

- Laser
  - Replacing toner, applying maintenance kit, calibration, cleaning

- Thermal
  - Replace paper, clean heating element, remove debris
- Impact
  - Replace ribbon, replace print head, replace paper
- Inkjet
  - Clean heads, replace cartridges, calibration, clear jams

Let's face it. No matter how much we try to get away from it, our society is dependent on paper. When we conduct business, we use different types of paper documents, such as contracts, letters, and, of course, money. And because most of those documents are created on computers, printers are inherently important. Even with electronic business being the norm in many situations, you will likely still have daily situations that require an old-fashioned hard copy of something.

Printers are electromechanical output devices that are used to put information from the computer onto paper. They have been around since the introduction of the computer. Other than the display monitor, the printer is the most popular peripheral purchased for a computer because a lot of people want to have paper copies of the documents that they create.

In this chapter, we will discuss the details of each major type of printing technology, including impact printers, inkjet printers, laser printers, thermal printers, and virtual printers. Once we cover the different types, we'll talk about installing and configuring printers and finish up with a section on printer maintenance.

Take special note of the section on laser printers. The A+ exams test these subjects in detail, so we'll cover them in depth.

Printer troubleshooting is covered in Chapter 12, "Hardware and Network Troubleshooting."

Understanding Print Technologies and Imaging Processes

Several types of printers are available on the market today. As with all other computer components, there have been significant advancements in printer technology over the years. Most of the time, when faced with the decision of purchasing a printer, you're going to be weighing performance versus cost. Some of the higher-quality technologies, such as color laser printing, are rather expensive for the home user. Other technologies are less expensive but don't provide the same level of quality.

In the following sections, you will learn about the various types of print technologies that you will see as a technician as well as their basic components and how they function. Specifically, we are going to look at five classifications of printing: impact, inkjet, laser, thermal, and virtual.

Impact Printers

The most basic type of printer is in the category known as *impact printers*. Impact printers, as their name suggests, use some form of impact and an inked *ribbon* to make an imprint on the paper. Impact printers also use a paper feed mechanism called a *tractor feed* that requires special paper. Perhaps you've seen it before—it's continuous feed paper with holes running down both edges.

There are two major types of impact printers: daisy wheel and dot matrix. Each type has its own service and maintenance issues.

Daisy-Wheel Printers

The first type of impact printer we're going to discuss is the *daisy-wheel printer*. This is one of the oldest printing technologies in use. These impact printers contain a wheel (called the daisy wheel because it looks like a daisy) with raised letters and symbols on each "petal" (see Figure 11.1). When the printer needs to print a character, it sends a signal to the mechanism that contains the wheel. This mechanism is called the *print head*. The print head rotates the daisy wheel until the required character is in place. An electromechanical hammer (called a *solenoid*) then strikes the back of the petal containing the character. The character pushes up against an inked ribbon that ultimately strikes the paper, making the impression of the requested character.

FIGURE 11.1 A daisy-wheel printer mechanism

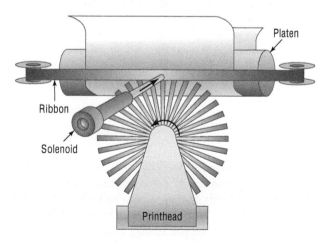

Daisy-wheel printers were among the first types of impact printer developed. Their speed is rated by the number of *characters per second (cps)* they can print. The earliest printers could print only two to four characters per second. Aside from their poor speed, the main disadvantage of this type of printer is that it makes a lot of noise when printing—so much so, in fact, that special enclosures were developed to contain the noise. There is also no concept of using multiple fonts; the font is whatever the character on the wheel looks like.

The daisy-wheel printer has a few advantages, of course. First, because it is an impact printer, you can print on multipart forms (like carbonless receipts), assuming that they can be fed into the printer properly. Sometimes, you will hear this type of paper referred to as *impact paper*. Second, it is relatively inexpensive compared to the price of a laser printer of the same vintage. Finally, the print quality is easily readable; the level of quality was given a name: *letter quality (LQ)*. Today, LQ might refer to quality that's better than an old-school typewriter (if you're familiar with them) but not up to inkjet standards.

Dot-Matrix Printers

The other type of impact printer that we'll discuss is the *dot-matrix printer*. These printers work in a manner similar to daisy-wheel printers, but instead of a spinning, character-imprinted wheel, the print head contains a row of pins (short, sturdy stalks of hard wire). These pins are triggered in patterns that form letters and numbers as the print head moves across the paper (see Figure 11.2).

FIGURE 11.2   Formation of images in a dot-matrix printer

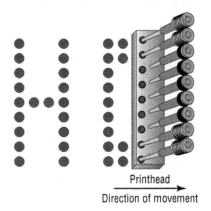

Printhead

→

Direction of movement

The pins in the print head are wrapped with coils of wire to create a solenoid and are held in the rest position by a combination of a small magnet and a spring. To trigger a particular pin, the printer controller sends a signal to the print head, which energizes the wires around the appropriate print wire. This turns the print wire into an electromagnet, which repels the print pin, forcing it against the ink ribbon and making a dot on the paper. The arrangement of the dots in columns and rows creates the letters and numbers that you see on the page. Figure 11.2 shows this process.

The main disadvantage of dot-matrix printers is their image quality, which can be quite poor compared to the quality produced with a daisy wheel. Dot-matrix printers use patterns of dots to make letters and images, and the early dot-matrix printers used only nine pins to make those patterns. The output quality of such printers is referred to as *draft quality*—good mainly for providing your initial text to a correspondent or reviser. Each letter looked fuzzy because the dots were spaced as far as they could be and still be perceived as a letter or image. As more pins were crammed into the print head (17-pin and 24-pin models were eventually developed), the quality increased because the dots were closer together. Dot-matrix technology ultimately improved to the point that a letter printed on a dot-matrix printer was *almost* indistinguishable from daisy-wheel output. This level of quality is known as *near letter quality (NLQ)*.

Dot-matrix printers are noisy, but the print wires and print head are covered by a plastic dust cover, making them quieter than daisy-wheel printers. They also use a more efficient printing technology, so the print speed is faster (typically starting around 72cps). Some dot-matrix printers (like the Epson DFX series) can print at close to a page per second! Finally, because dot-matrix printers are also impact printers, they can use multipart forms. Because of these advantages, dot-matrix printers quickly made daisy-wheel printers obsolete.

Most impact printers have an option to adjust how close the print head rests from the ribbon. So if your printing is too light, you may be able to adjust the print head closer to the ribbon. If it's too dark or you get smeared printing, you may be able to move the print head back.

Inkjet

One of the most popular types of printers in use today is the *inkjet printer*. As opposed to impact printers, which strike the page, these printers spray ink on the page to form the image. Inkjet printers typically use a reservoir of ink, a pump, and a nozzle to accomplish this. Older ones were messy, noisy, and inefficient, but the technology is good enough now that you see plenty of photo printers using inkjet technology. You might also hear these types of printers referred to as bubble-jet printers, but that term is copyrighted by Canon. The main difference is that in a *bubble-jet printer*, droplets of ink are sprayed onto a page and form patterns that resemble the items being printed. You can think of it as spraying droplets of ink in a very high-definition dot-matrix pattern, although printer manufacturers would likely scoff at the comparison to an older technology.

In the following sections, you will learn the parts of an inkjet printer as well as how inkjet printers work.

Parts of a Typical Inkjet Printer

Inkjet printers are simple devices. They contain very few parts (even fewer than dot-matrix printers) and, as such, are inexpensive to manufacture. It's common today to have a $40 to $50 inkjet printer with print quality that rivals that of basic laser printers.

The printer parts can be divided into the following categories:

- Print head/ink cartridge
- Head carriage, belt, and stepper motor
- Paper-feed mechanism
- Control, interface, and power circuitry

Print Head/Ink Cartridge

The first part of an inkjet printer is the one that people see the most: the *print head*. This part of a printer contains many small nozzles (usually 100 to 200) that spray the ink in small droplets onto the page. Many times, the print head is part of the *ink cartridge*, which contains a reservoir of ink and the print head in a removable package. Most color inkjet printers include multiple print heads, one for each of the CMYK(cyan, magenta, yellow, and black) print inks. The print cartridge must be replaced as the ink supply runs out.

Inside the ink cartridge are several small chambers. At the top of each chamber are a metal plate and a tube leading to the ink supply. At the bottom of each chamber is a small pinhole. These pinholes are used to spray ink on the page to form characters and images as patterns of dots, similar to the way a dot-matrix printer works but with much higher resolution.

There are two methods of spraying the ink out of the cartridge. Hewlett-Packard (HP) popularized the first method: When a particular chamber needs to spray ink, an electric signal is sent to the heating element, energizing it. The elements heat up quickly, causing the ink to vaporize. Because of the expanding ink vapor, the ink is pushed out of the pinhole and forms a bubble. As the vapor expands, the bubble eventually gets large enough to break off into a droplet. The rest of the ink is pulled back into the chamber by the surface tension of the ink. When another drop needs to be sprayed, the process begins again. The second method, developed by Epson, uses a piezoelectric element (either a small rod or a unit that looks like a miniature drum head) that flexes when energized. The outward flex pushes the ink from the nozzle; on the return, it sucks more ink from the reservoir.

When the printer is done printing, the print head moves back to its maintenance station. The *maintenance station* contains a small suction pump and ink-absorbing pad. To keep the ink flowing freely, before each print cycle, the maintenance station pulls ink through the ink nozzles using vacuum suction. The pad absorbs this expelled ink. The station serves two functions: to provide a place for the print head to rest when the printer isn't printing and to keep the print head in working order.

Head Carriage, Belt, and Stepper Motor

Another major component of the inkjet printer is the head carriage and the associated parts that make it move. The *print head carriage* is the component of an inkjet printer that moves back and forth during printing. It contains the physical as well as electronic connections for the print head and (in some cases) the ink reservoir. Figure 11.3 shows an example of a head carriage. Note the clips that keep the ink cartridge in place and the electronic connections for the ink cartridge. These connections cause the nozzles to fire, and if they aren't kept clean, you may have printing problems.

FIGURE 11.3   A print head carriage (holding two ink cartridges) in an inkjet printer

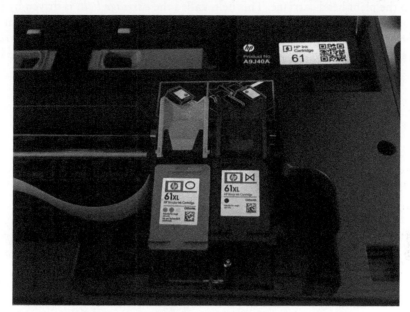

The stepper motor and belt make the print head carriage move. A *stepper motor* is a precisely made electric motor that can move in the same very small increments each time it is activated. That way, it can move to the same position(s) time after time. The motor that makes the print head carriage move is also often called the *carriage motor* or *carriage stepper motor*. Figure 11.4 shows an example of a stepper motor.

FIGURE 11.4   A carriage stepper motor

In addition to the motor, a belt is placed around two small wheels or pulleys and attached to the print head carriage. This belt, called the *carriage belt*, is driven by the carriage motor and moves the print head back and forth across the page while it prints. To keep the print head carriage aligned and stable while it traverses the page, the carriage rests on a small metal *stabilizer bar*. Figure 11.5 shows the stabilizer bar, carriage belt, and pulleys.

FIGURE 11.5   Stabilizer bar, carriage belt, and pulleys in an inkjet printer

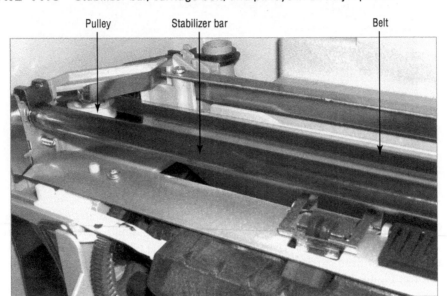

Paper-Feed Mechanism

In addition to getting the ink onto the paper, the printer must have a way to get the paper into the printer. That's where the paper-feed mechanism comes in. The *paper-feed mechanism* picks up paper from the paper drawer and feeds it into the printer. This component consists of several smaller assemblies. First are the *pickup rollers* (see Figure 11.6), which are several rubber rollers with a slightly flat spot; they rub against the paper as they rotate and feed the paper into the printer. They work against small cork or rubber patches known as *separator pads* (see Figure 11.7), which help keep the rest of the paper in place so that only one sheet goes into the printer. The pickup rollers are turned on a shaft by the *pickup stepper motor*.

Clean pickup rollers (and other rubber rollers) with mild soap and water and not alcohol. Alcohol can dry out the rollers, making them brittle and ineffective.

FIGURE 11.6   Inkjet pickup rollers

FIGURE 11.7   Inkjet separator pads

Sometimes the paper that is fed into an inkjet printer is placed into a *paper tray*, which is simply a small plastic tray in the front of the printer that holds the paper until it is fed into the printer by the paper-feed mechanism. On smaller printers, the paper is placed vertically into a *paper feeder* at the back of the printer; it uses gravity, in combination with feed rollers and separator pads, to get the paper into the printer. No real rhyme or reason dictates which manufacturers use these different parts; some models use them, and some don't. Generally, more expensive printers use paper trays because they hold more paper. Figure 11.8 shows an example of a paper tray on an inkjet printer.

FIGURE 11.8   A paper tray on an inkjet printer

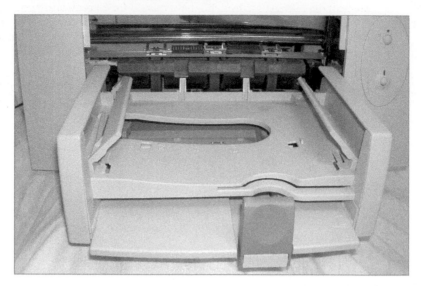

The final parts of the paper-feed mechanism are the *paper-feed sensors*. These components tell the printer when it is out of paper as well as when a paper jam has occurred during the paper-feed process. Figure 11.9 shows an example of a paper-feed sensor. Being able to identify the parts of an inkjet printer is an important skill for an A+ candidate. In Exercise 11.1, you will identify the parts of an inkjet printer. For this exercise, you'll need an inkjet printer.

FIGURE 11.9   A paper-feed sensor on an inkjet printer

Many of the exercises in this chapter require printer hardware. If you don't have the proper hardware on which to practice, you can find many helpful videos online showing how to identify parts and install and perform maintenance on printers. Sites such as ifixit.com and youtube.com are good places to start.

EXERCISE 11.1

Identifying the Parts of an Inkjet Printer

1. Unplug the inkjet printer from the power source and the computer.

2. Open the top cover to expose the inner print mechanism.

3. Locate and identify the paper tray.

4. Locate and identify the paper-feed sensor.

5. Locate and identify the pickup roller(s).

6. Locate and identify the separator pad(s).

7. Locate and identify the print head and carriage assembly.

Control, Interface, and Power Circuitry

The final component group is the electronic circuitry for printer control, printer interfaces, and printer power. The *printer control circuits* are usually on a small circuit board that contains all of the circuitry to run the stepper motors the way the printer needs them to work (back and forth, load paper and then stop, and so on). These circuits are also responsible for monitoring the health of the printer and for reporting that information back to the PC.

The second power component, the interface circuitry (commonly called a port), makes the physical connection to whatever signal is coming from the computer (USB, serial, network, infrared, and so on) and also connects the physical interface to the control circuitry. The interface circuitry converts the signals from the interface into the datastream that the printer uses.

The last set of circuits the printer uses is the *power circuits*. Essentially, these conductive pathways convert 110V (in the United States) or 220V (in most of the rest of the world) from a standard wall outlet into the voltages that the inkjet printer uses, usually 12V and 5V, and distribute those voltages to the other printer circuits and devices that need it. This is accomplished through the use of a *transformer*. A transformer, in this case, takes the 110V AC current and changes it to 12V DC (among others). This transformer can be either internal (incorporated into the body of the printer) or external. Either design can be used in today's inkjets, although the integrated design is preferred because it is simpler and doesn't show the bulky transformer.

The Inkjet Printing Process

Before you print to an inkjet printer, you must ensure that the device is calibrated. *Calibration* is the process by which a device is brought within functional specifications. For example, inkjet printers need their print heads aligned so that they print evenly and don't print funny-looking letters and unevenly spaced lines. The process is part of the installation for all inkjet printers. Printers will typically run a calibration routine every time you install new ink cartridges. You will only need to manually initiate a calibration if the printing alignment appears off.

Just as with other types of printing, the inkjet printing process consists of a set of steps that the printer must follow in order to put the data onto the page being printed. The following steps take place whenever you click the Print button in your favorite software (like Microsoft Word or Internet Explorer):

1. You click the Print button (or similar) that initiates the printing process.

2. The software from which you are printing sends the data to be printed to the printer driver that you have selected.

 The function and use of the printer driver are discussed later in this chapter.

3. The printer driver uses a page-description language to convert the data being printed into the format that the printer can understand. The driver also ensures that the printer is ready to print.

4. The printer driver sends the information to the printer via whatever connection method is being used (USB, network, serial, and so on).

5. The printer stores the received data in its onboard *print buffer* memory. A print buffer is a small amount of memory (typically 512KB to 16MB) used to store print jobs as they are received from the printing computer. This buffer allows several jobs to be printed at once and helps printing to be completed quickly.

6. If the printer has not printed in a while, the printer's control circuits activate a cleaning cycle. A *cleaning cycle* is a set of steps the inkjet printer goes through to purge the print heads of any dried ink. It uses a special suction cup and sucking action to pull ink through the print head, dislodging any dried ink or clearing stuck passageways.

7. Once the printer is ready to print, the control circuitry activates the paper-feed motor. This causes a sheet of paper to be fed into the printer until the paper activates the paper-feed sensor, which stops the feed until the print head is in the right position and the leading edge of the paper is under the print head. If the paper doesn't reach the paper-feed sensor in a specified amount of time after the stepper motor has been activated, the Out Of Paper light is turned on and a message is sent to the computer.

8. Once the paper is positioned properly, the print head stepper motor uses the print head belt and carriage to move the print head across the page, little by little. The motor is moved one small step, and the print head sprays the dots of ink on the paper in the pattern dictated by the control circuitry. Typically, this is either a pattern of black dots or a pattern of CMYK inks that are mixed to make colors. Then the stepper motor moves the print head another small step; the process repeats all the way across the page. This process is so quick, however, that the entire series of starts and stops across the page looks like one smooth motion.

9. At the end of a pass across the page, the paper-feed stepper motor advances the page a small amount. Then the print head repeats step 8. Depending on the model, either the print head returns to the beginning of the line and prints again in the same direction only or it moves backward across the page so that printing occurs in both directions. This process continues until the page is finished.

10. Once the page is finished, the feed-stepper motor is actuated and ejects the page from the printer into the output tray. If more pages need to print, the process for printing the next page begins again at step 7.

11. Once printing is complete and the final page has been ejected from the printer, the print head is *parked* (locked into rest position) and the print process is finished.

Some nicer models of inkjet printers will have a *duplexing assembly* attached to them, usually at the back of the printer. It's used for two-sided printing. After the first page is printed, it's fed into the duplexing assembly, turned over, and fed back into the paper feed assembly. Then the second page can be printed on the back side of the original piece of paper. It's a fancy attachment that gives your inkjet more functionality.

Laser Printers

Laser printers and inkjet printers are referred to as *page printers* because they receive their print job instructions one page at a time rather than receiving instructions one line at a time. There are two major types of page printers that use the electrophotographic (EP) print process. The first uses a laser to scan the image onto a photosensitive drum, and the second uses an array of light-emitting diodes (LEDs) to create the image on the drum. Even though they write the image in different ways, both types still follow the EP print process. Since the A+ exam focuses on the EP print process and not on differences between laser and LED, we'll focus on the same here.

Xerox, Hewlett-Packard, and Canon were pioneers in developing the laser printer technology we use today. Scientists at Xerox developed the electrophotographic (EP) process in 1971. HP introduced the first successful desktop laser printer in 1984 using Canon hardware that used the EP process. This technology uses a combination of static electric charges, laser light, and a black powdery ink-like substance called *toner*. Printers that use this technology are called EP process laser printers, or just *laser printers*. Every laser printer technology has its foundations in the EP printer process.

Let's discuss the basic components of the EP laser printer and how they operate so that you can understand the way an EP laser printer works.

Basic Components

Most printers that use the EP process contain nine standard assemblies: the toner cartridge, laser scanner, high-voltage power supply, DC power supply, paper transport assembly (including paper-pickup rollers and paper-registration rollers), transfer corona, fusing assembly, printer controller circuitry, and ozone filter. Let's discuss each of the components individually, along with a duplexing assembly, before we examine how they all work together to make the printer function.

The Toner Cartridge

The EP toner cartridge (see Figure 11.10), as its name suggests, holds the toner. Toner is a black carbon substance mixed with polyester resins to make it flow better and iron oxide particles to make it sensitive to electrical charges. These two components make the toner capable of being attracted to the photosensitive drum and of melting into the paper. In addition to these components, toner contains a medium called the developer (also called the carrier), which carries the toner until it is used by the EP process. The toner cartridge also contains the EP print drum. This drum is coated with a photosensitive material that can hold a static charge when not exposed to light but *cannot* hold a charge when it *is* exposed to light—a curious phenomenon and one that EP printers exploit for the purpose of making images. Finally, the drum assembly contains a cleaning blade that continuously scrapes the used toner off the photosensitive drum to keep it clean.

FIGURE 11.10   An EP toner cartridge

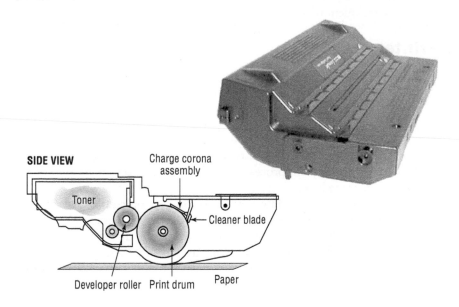

SIDE VIEW — Toner — Charge corona assembly — Cleaner blade — Developer roller — Print drum — Paper

WARNING   Exposing a photosensitive drum to dust or light can damage it, but touching it will most likely render the drum inoperable! It's best to just not mess around with them.

NOTE   In most laser printers, *toner cartridge* means an EP toner cartridge that contains toner and a photosensitive drum in one plastic case. In some laser printers, however, the toner and photosensitive drum can be replaced separately instead of as a single unit. If you ask for a toner cartridge for one of these printers, all you will receive is a cylinder full of toner. Consult the printer's manual to find out which kind of toner cartridge your laser printer uses.

Never ship a printer anywhere with a toner cartridge installed! The jostling that happens during shipping could cause toner to spill out of the cartridge and all over the inside of the printer. This will be a huge mess to clean up! If the printer is a laser printer, remove the toner cartridge first. You can put it in a sealed, airtight bag to ship if needed. If it's an LED page printer, there is a method to remove the photosensitive drum and toner cartridge (check your manual for details).

The Laser Scanning Assembly

As we mentioned earlier, the EP photosensitive drum can hold a charge if it's not exposed to light. It is dark inside an EP printer, except when the laser scanning assembly shines on particular areas of the photosensitive drum. When it does that, the drum discharges, but only in the area that has been exposed. As the drum rotates, the laser scanning assembly scans the laser across the photosensitive drum, writing the image onto it. Figure 11.11 shows the laser scanning assembly.

FIGURE 11.11   The EP laser scanning assembly (side view and simplified top view)

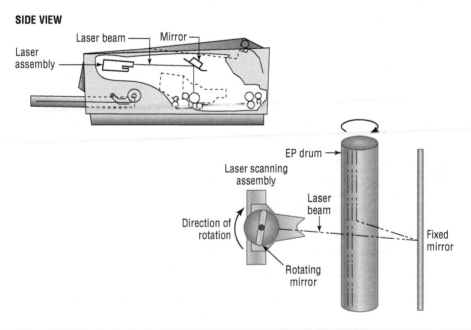

SIDE VIEW

Laser beam — Mirror
Laser assembly

EP drum
Laser scanning assembly
Laser beam
Direction of rotation
Fixed mirror
Rotating mirror

Laser light is damaging to human eyes. Therefore, the laser is kept in an enclosure and will operate only when the laser printer's cover is closed.

High-Voltage Power Supply (HVPS)

The EP process requires high-voltage electricity. The high-voltage power supply (HVPS) provides the high voltages used during the EP process. This component converts AC current from a standard wall outlet (120V and 60Hz) into higher voltages that the printer can use. This high voltage is used to energize both the charging corona and the transfer corona.

WARNING   Anything with the words *high voltage* in it should make you pause before opening a device and getting your hands into it. The HVPS can hurt or kill you if you're working inside a laser printer and don't know what you're doing.

DC Power Supply (DCPS)

The high voltages used in the EP process can't power the other components in the printer (the logic circuitry and motors). These components require low voltages, between +5VDC and +24VDC. The DC power supply (DCPS) converts house current into three voltages: +5VDC and −5VDC for the logic circuitry and +24VDC for the paper-transport motors. This component also runs the fan that cools the internal components of the printer.

Paper-Transport Assembly

The paper-transport assembly is responsible for moving the paper through the printer. It consists of a motor and several rubberized rollers that each performs a different function.

The first type of roller found in most laser printers is the *feed roller*, or *paper-pickup roller* (see Figure 11.12). This D-shaped roller, when activated, rotates against the paper and pushes one sheet into the printer. This roller works in conjunction with a special rubber separator pad to prevent more than one sheet from being fed into the printer at a time.

FIGURE 11.12   Paper-transport rollers

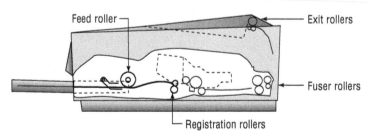

Another type of roller that is used in the printer is the *registration roller* (also shown in Figure 11.12). There are actually two registration rollers, which work together. These rollers synchronize the paper movement with the image-formation process in the EP cartridge. The rollers don't feed the paper past the EP cartridge until the cartridge is ready for it.

Both of these rollers are operated with a special electric motor known as an *electronic stepper motor*. This type of motor can accurately move in very small increments. It powers all of the paper-transport rollers as well as the fuser rollers.

The Transfer Corona Assembly

When the laser writes the images on the photosensitive drum, the toner then sticks to the exposed areas; we'll cover this in the section "Electrophotographic (EP) Print Process." How does the toner get from the photosensitive drum onto the paper? The *transfer corona assembly* (see Figure 11.13) is given a high-voltage charge, which is transferred to the paper, which in turn pulls the toner from the photosensitive drum.

FIGURE 11.13   The transfer corona assembly

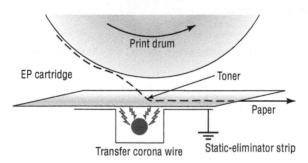

Included in the transfer corona assembly is a *static-charge eliminator strip* that drains away the charge imparted to the paper by the corona. If you didn't drain away the charge, the paper would stick to the EP cartridge and jam the printer.

There are two types of transfer corona assemblies: those that contain a transfer *corona wire* and those that contain a transfer *corona roller*. The transfer corona wire is a small-diameter wire that is charged by the HVPS. The wire is located in a special notch in the floor of the laser printer (under the EP print cartridge). The transfer corona roller performs the same function as the transfer corona wire, but it's a roller rather than a wire. Because the transfer corona roller is directly in contact with the paper, it supports higher speeds. For this reason, the transfer corona wire is infrequently used in laser printers today.

Fusing Assembly

The toner in the EP toner cartridge will stick to just about anything, including paper. This is true because the toner has a negative static charge and most objects have a net positive charge. However, these toner particles can be removed by brushing any object across the page. This could be a problem if you want the images and letters to stay on the paper permanently!

To solve this problem, EP laser printers incorporate a device known as a *fuser* (see Figure 11.14), which uses two rollers that apply pressure and heat to fuse the plastic toner particles to the paper. You may have noticed that pages from either a laser printer or a copier (which uses a similar device) come out warm. This is because of the fuser.

FIGURE 11.14   The fuser

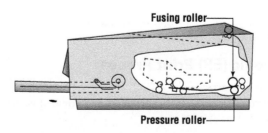

The fuser is made up of three main parts: a halogen heating lamp, a Teflon-coated aluminum-fusing roller, and a rubberized pressure roller. The fuser uses the halogen lamp to heat the fusing roller to between 329° F (165° C) and 392° F (200° C). As the paper passes between the two rollers, the pressure roller pushes the paper against the fusing roller, which melts the toner into the paper.

 The fuser can cause severe burns! Be careful when working with it.

Printer Controller Circuitry

Another component in the laser printer that we need to discuss is the *printer controller assembly*. This large circuit board converts signals from the computer into signals for the various assemblies in the laser printer using a process known as *rasterizing*. This circuit board is usually mounted under the printer. The board has connectors for each type of interface and cables to each assembly.

When a computer prints to a laser printer, it sends a signal through a cable to the printer controller assembly. The controller assembly formats the information into a page's worth of line-by-line commands for the laser scanner. The controller sends commands to each of the components, telling them to wake up and begin the EP print process.

Ozone Filter

Your laser printer uses various high-voltage biases inside the case. As anyone who has been outside during a lightning storm can tell you, high voltages create ozone. Ozone is a chemically reactive gas that is created by the high-voltage coronas (charging and transfer) inside the printer. Because ozone is chemically reactive and can severely reduce the life of laser printer components, many older laser printers contain a filter to remove ozone gas from inside the printer as it is produced. This filter must be removed and cleaned with compressed air periodically (cleaning it whenever the toner cartridge is replaced is usually sufficient). Most newer laser printers don't have ozone filters. This is because these printers don't use transfer corona wires but instead use transfer corona rollers, which dramatically reduce ozone emissions.

Duplexing Assembly

Any laser printer worth its money today can print on both sides of the paper (as can some nicer models of inkjet printers, mentioned earlier). This is accomplished through the use of a *duplexing assembly*. Usually located inside or on the back of the printer, the assembly is responsible for taking the paper, turning it over, and feeding back into the printer so the second side can be printed.

Electrophotographic (EP) Print Process

The *EP print process* is the process by which an EP laser printer forms images on paper. It consists of seven major steps, each designed for a specific goal. Although many different manufacturers call these steps different things or place them in a different order, the basic process is still the same. Here are the steps in the order you will see them on the exam:

1. Processing
2. Charging
3. Exposing (writing)
4. Developing
5. Transferring
6. Fusing
7. Cleaning

Before any of these steps can begin, however, the controller must sense that the printer is ready to start printing (toner cartridge installed, fuser warmed to temperature, and all covers in place). Printing cannot take place until the printer is in its ready state, usually indicated by an illuminated Ready LED light or a display that says something like 00 READY (on HP printers). The computer sends the print job to the printer, which begins processing the data as the first step to creating output.

Step 1: Processing

The processing step comprises two parts: receiving the image and creating the image. The computer sends the print job to the printer, which receives it via its print interface (USB, wireless, etc.). Then, the printer needs to create the print job in such a way that it can accurately produce the output.

If you think back to our discussion of dot-matrix printing earlier in this chapter, you might recall that dot-matrix printers produce images by creating one strip of dots at a time across the page. Laser printers use the same concept of rendering one horizontal strip at a time to create the image. Each strip across the page is called a *scan line* or a *raster line*.

A component of the laser printer called the *Raster Image Processor (RIP)* manages raster creation. Its responsibility is to generate an image of the final page in memory. How the raster gets created is dependent upon the page description language that your system is using, such as PostScript (PS) or Printer Control Language (PCL). Ultimately, this collection of lines is what gets written to the photosensitive drum and onto the paper.

Step 2: Charging

The next step in the EP process is *charging* (see Figure 11.15). In this step, a special wire or roller (called a *charging corona*) within the EP toner cartridge (above the photo sensitive drum) gets high voltage from the HVPS. It uses this high voltage to apply a strong, uniform negative charge (around −600VDC) to the surface of the photosensitive drum.

FIGURE 11.15   The charging step of the EP process

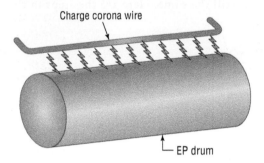

Step 3: Exposing (Writing)

Next is exposing the drum to the image, often referred to as the *writing* or *exposing* step. In this step, the laser is turned on and scans the drum from side to side, flashing on and off according to the bits of information that the printer controller sends it as it communicates the individual bits of the image. Wherever the laser beam touches, the photosensitive drum's charge is severely reduced from –600VDC to a slight negative charge (around –100VDC). As the drum rotates, a pattern of exposed areas is formed, representing the image to be printed. Figure 11.16 shows this process.

FIGURE 11.16   The writing step of the EP process

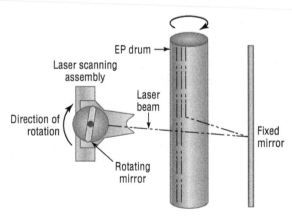

At this point, the controller sends a signal to the pickup roller to feed a piece of paper into the printer, where it stops at the registration rollers.

Step 4: Developing

Now that the surface of the drum holds an electrical representation of the image being printed, its discrete electrical charges need to be converted into something that can be transferred to a piece of paper. The EP process step that accomplishes this is *developing* (see Figure 11.17). In this step, toner is transferred to the areas that were exposed in the writing step.

FIGURE 11.17 The developing step of the EP process

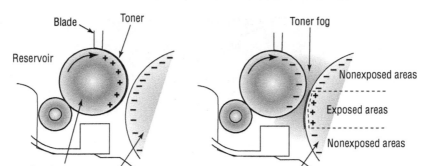

A metallic roller called the *developing roller* inside an EP cartridge acquires a −600VDC charge (called a *bias voltage*) from the HVPS. The toner sticks to this roller because there is a magnet located inside the roller and because of the electrostatic charges between the toner and the developing roller. While the developing roller rotates toward the photosensitive drum, the toner acquires the charge of the roller (−600VDC). When the toner comes between the developing roller and the photosensitive drum, the toner is attracted to the areas that have been exposed by the laser (because these areas have a lesser charge, −100VDC). The toner also is repelled from the unexposed areas (because they are at the same −600VDC charge and like charges repel). This toner transfer creates a fog of toner between the EP drum and the developing roller.

The photosensitive drum now has toner stuck to it where the laser has written. The photosensitive drum continues to rotate until the developed image is ready to be transferred to paper in the next step.

Step 5: Transferring

At this point in the EP process, the developed image is rotating into position. The controller notifies the registration rollers that the paper should be fed through. The registration rollers move the paper underneath the photosensitive drum, and the process of transferring the image can begin; this is the *transferring* step.

The controller sends a signal to the charging corona wire or roller (depending on which one the printer has) and tells it to turn on. The corona wire/roller then acquires a strong *positive* charge (+600VDC) and applies that charge to the paper. Thus charged, the paper pulls the toner from the photosensitive drum at the line of contact between the roller and the paper because the paper and toner have opposite charges. Once the registration rollers move the paper past the corona wire, the static-eliminator strip removes all charge from that line of the paper. Figure 11.18 details this step. If the strip didn't bleed this charge away, the paper would attract itself to the toner cartridge and cause a paper jam.

FIGURE 11.18   The transferring step of the EP process

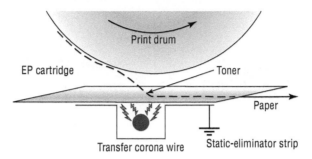

The toner is now held in place by weak electrostatic charges and gravity. It will not stay there, however, unless it is made permanent, which is the reason for the fusing step.

Step 6: Fusing

The penultimate step before the printer produces the finished product is called *fusing*. Here the toner image is made permanent. The registration rollers push the paper toward the fuser rollers. Once the fuser grabs the paper, the registration rollers push for only a short time longer. The fuser is now in control of moving the paper.

As the paper passes through the fuser, the 350° F fuser roller melts the polyester resin of the toner, and the rubberized pressure roller presses it permanently into the paper (see Figure 11.19). The paper continues through the fuser and eventually exits the printer.

Once the paper completely exits the fuser, it trips a sensor that tells the printer to finish the EP process with the cleaning step.

FIGURE 11.19   The fusing step of the EP process

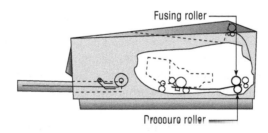

Step 7: Cleaning

In the last part of the laser print process, a rubber blade inside the EP cartridge scrapes any toner left on the drum into a used toner receptacle inside the EP cartridge, and a fluorescent lamp discharges any remaining charge on the photosensitive drum. (Remember that the drum, being photosensitive, loses its charge when exposed to light.) This step is called *cleaning* (see Figure 11.20).

FIGURE 11.20   The cleaning step of the EP process

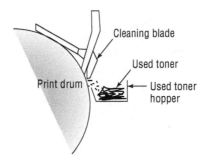

The EP cartridge is constantly cleaning the drum. It may take more than one rotation of the photosensitive drum to make an image on the paper. The cleaning step keeps the drum fresh for each use. If you didn't clean the drum, you would see ghosts of previous pages printed along with your image.

 The amount of toner removed in the cleaning process is quite small, and the cartridge will run out of toner before the used toner receptacle fills up. The toner that's in the receptacle is useless because the print process has already chemically altered it. In addition, it's considered a hazardous substance. Recycle the print cartridge, and don't pay attention to the leftover toner.

At this point, the printer can print another page, and the EP process can begin again.

Summary of the EP Print Process

Figure 11.21 provides a diagram of all of the parts involved in the EP printing process. Here's a summary of the process, which you should commit to memory:

1. The printer receives and processes the image and stores a page in memory.

2. The printer places a uniform –600VDC charge on the photosensitive drum by means of a charging corona.

3. The laser "paints" an image onto the photosensitive drum, discharging the image areas to a much lower voltage (–100VDC).

4. The developing roller in the toner cartridge has charged (–600VDC) toner stuck to it. As it rolls the toner toward the photosensitive drum, the toner is attracted to (and sticks to) the areas of the photosensitive drum that the laser has discharged.

5. The image is then transferred from the drum to the paper at its line of contact by means of the transfer corona wire (or corona roller) with a +600VDC charge. The static-eliminator strip removes the high, positive charge from the paper, and the paper, now holding the image, moves on.

6. The paper then enters the fuser, where a fuser roller and the pressure roller make the image permanent. The paper exits the printer.

7. The printer uses a rubber scraper to clean the photosensitive drum. At that point, it is ready to print the next page or it returns to the ready state.

FIGURE 11.21   The EP print process

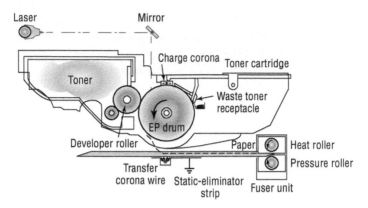

Thermal Printers

The types of printers that you have learned about so far in this chapter account for 90 percent of all printers that are used with home or office computers and that you will see as a repair technician. The remaining 10 percent consist of other types of printers that primarily differ by the method they use to put colored material on the paper to represent what is being printed. Examples of these include solid ink, dye sublimation, and thermal printers. Keep in mind that, for the most part, these printers operate like other printers in many ways: They all have a paper-feed mechanism (sheet-fed or roll); they all require consumables such as ink or toner and paper; they all use the same interfaces, for the most part, as other types of printers; and they are usually about the same size.

Thermal printing technology is used in many point-of-sale terminals and older fax machines (newer fax machines usually use inkjet or laser technology). They print on a kind of special, waxy paper that comes on a roll; the paper turns black when heat passes over it. *Thermal printers* work by using a print head that is the width of the paper. When it needs to print, a heating element heats certain spots on the print head. The paper below the heated print head turns black in those spots. As the paper moves through the printer, the pattern of blackened spots forms an image on the page of what is being printed. Another type of thermal printer uses a heat-sensitive ribbon instead of heat-sensitive paper. A thermal print head melts wax-based ink from the ribbon onto the paper. These are called thermal transfer or thermal wax-transfer printers.

Thermal direct printers typically have long lives because they have few moving parts. The only unique part that you might not be as familiar with is the paper feed assembly, which oftentimes needs to accommodate a roll of paper instead of sheets. The paper is somewhat expensive, doesn't last long (especially if it is left in a very warm place, like a closed car in summer), and produces poorer-quality images than the paper used by most of the other printing technologies.

Virtual Printers

All of the print technologies that we have covered so far are physical technologies; that is, they do something to the paper to produce an image, by using ink, toner, or heat. The final technology that we need to cover is *virtual printing*, which sends the desired output to a file instead of to paper. From the end user's standpoint, starting the print process is the same. They click Print in their application and the process starts. From there though, instead of sending the output to an electromechanical device, a new file containing the output is generated.

Printing to a file is nothing new; this option has been around for probably 20 years or more. You open the document (or other file) that you wanted to print, select Print, and a print window similar to the one shown in Figure 11.22 opens. Once there, you check the Print To File box, and then click OK. Then, choose where to save the file (just as saving any other file), and after you chose a destination, you are done. Some programs or operating systems would even let you print to an image (such as JPG) instead of a file, but the process works the same way.

FIGURE 11.22   Print To File option

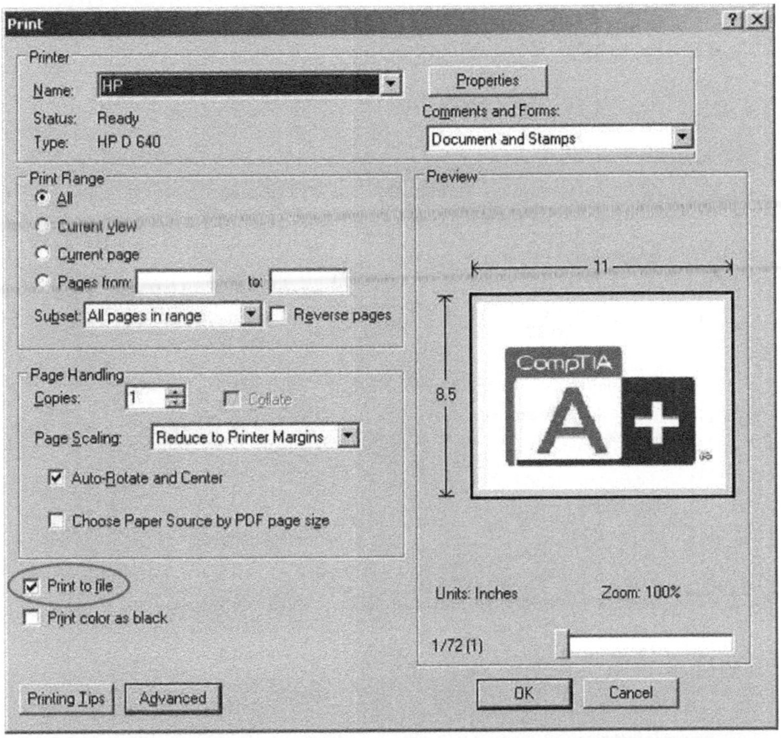

It used to be that people only chose this option when the printer was not available. You could print your output to a file, take the file to a different machine that had a printer available, and print the file from that machine. Now, you might ask, why wouldn't you just take the original file from the first computer to the second and print it from the application? That would make sense, but this method allowed you to print from a second computer that didn't have the application in which you created the file installed on it. There was one big caveat; you had to be printing to the same type of printer using the same print driver as you used to publish the electronic print file; otherwise, it wouldn't work. The upshot was that it was rarely, if ever, used.

Another option has emerged though, and this one is actually useful! Instead of printing to a generic file format that can be later used to produce a paper copy, you can print to a PDF file. Basically, you are just creating a PDF file using your application's print function.

To print to PDF from Windows, you need to install an application that installs support for printing to PDF (the Windows operating system does not currently support this natively). There are no shortage of apps in the market that will do this; for example Adobe Acrobat (www.adobe.com), CutePDF Writer (www.cutepdf.com), and Nitro PDF (www.gonitro.com) will do the trick. When you install one of these apps, it will add the option to print to PDF as one of your available printers. After it's installed, open an app, choose the print option, and you will get a screen similar to the one shown in Figure 11.23.

FIGURE 11.23   Printing to PDF

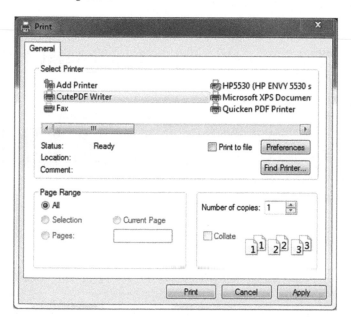

Select CutePDF Writer (or your version of it), and click Print. A window will pop up asking where you want to save the file. Save it and a PDF file is created for you. It's as easy as that.

Current versions of Microsoft Office products also let you create a PDF file automatically. For example, in Word, you can choose File ➤ Save As, and one of your options in the drop-down menu will be PDF format. Another way is to click File ➤ Save & Send and choose Send As PDF.

As we mentioned earlier, Windows does not come with the Print To PDF option by default. It does, however, come with the Print To XPS option (you can see the Microsoft XPS Document Printer option on the right side of Figure 11.23). An *Open XML Paper Specification (XPS)* file is Microsoft's version of a PDF. It's designed to be an open standard, like PDF, but it hasn't really taken off in terms of popularity. In fact, with Windows 8, Microsoft included support for *OpenXPS (OXPS)*, which is incompatible with the XPS reader included with Windows 7. In addition, Windows 8 includes a native PDF reader, so it seems that Microsoft isn't heavily invested in supporting the XPS format itself.

Let's go back to printing to an image for a minute. If your program doesn't support printing to an image but you need the output of the file in an image format (JPG, TIF, PNG, or other), you can print the file as a PDF first, and then convert it to an image file. There are dozens of free image file converters on the Web.

To summarize, there are four potential options for printing to a virtual printer: print to file, print to image, print to PDF, and print to XPS. Of the four, the only one that you will likely find to be useful is print to PDF.

Installing and Configuring Printers

Odds are that if someone owns a computer, they own a printer as well. If they don't, they have easy access to a printer at a library, work, or some other place. Many retailers and computer manufacturers make it incredibly easy to buy a printer because they often bundle a printer with a computer system as an incentive to get you to buy.

The A+ 220-901 exam will test your knowledge of the procedures to install printers. We're going to break this section into two parts: printer interface components and installing and sharing printers.

Printer Interface Components

A printer's *interface* is the collection of hardware and software that allows the printer to communicate with a computer. The hardware interface is commonly called a port. Each printer has at least one interface, but some printers have several to make them more flexible in a multiplatform environment. If a printer has several interfaces, it can usually switch between them on the fly so that several computers can print at the same time.

An interface incorporates several components, including its interface type and the *interface software*. Each aspect must be matched on both the printer and the computer. For example, if you have an older HP LaserJet 4L, it only has a parallel port. Therefore, you must use a parallel cable as well as the correct software for the platform being used (for example, a Macintosh HP LaserJet 4L driver if you connect it to a Macintosh computer).

Interface Types

When we say *interface types*, we're talking about the ports used in getting the printed information from the computer to the printer. There are two major classifications here: wired and wireless. Wired examples are serial, parallel, USB, and Ethernet. Wireless options include 802.11 and Bluetooth. You've learned about these connections in earlier chapters, but now you will learn how they apply to printers.

Serial

When computers send data serially, they send it 1 bit at a time, one after another. The bits stand in line like people at a movie theater, waiting to get in. Old-time serial (RS-232) connections were painfully slow, but new serial technology (FireWire, Thunderbolt, and others) makes it a more viable option than parallel. While it's quite common to see USB (another type of serial connection) printers on the market, it's rare to find any other types of serial printers out there.

Parallel

When a printer uses parallel communication, it is receiving data 8 bits at a time over eight separate wires (one for each bit). Parallel communication was the most popular way of communicating from computer to printer for many years, mainly because it was faster than serial. In fact, the *parallel port* became so synonymous with printing that a lot of companies simply started referring to parallel ports as printer ports. Today though, parallel printers are becoming uncommon. The vast majority of wired printers that you see will be USB or Ethernet.

A parallel cable consists of a male DB25 connector that connects to the computer and a male 36-pin Centronics connector that connects to the printer. Most of the cables are shorter than 10′. Parallel cables should be IEEE 1284 compliant.

WARNING   Keep printer cable lengths shorter than 10′. Some people try to run printer cables more than 50′. If the length is greater than 10′, communications can become unreliable due to crosstalk.

Universal Serial Bus (USB)

The most popular type of wired printer interface as this book is being written is the Universal Serial Bus (USB). In fact, it is the most popular interface for just about every peripheral. The convenience for printers is that it has a higher transfer rate than older serial or parallel connections, and it automatically recognizes new devices. And of course, USB is physically very easy to connect.

Ethernet

Many printers sold today have a wired Ethernet interface that allows them to be hooked directly to an Ethernet cable. These printers have an internal network interface card (NIC) and ROM-based software that allow them to communicate on the network with servers and workstations.

As with any other networking device, the type of network interface used on the printer depends on the type of network to which the printer is being attached. It's likely that the only connection type that you will run into is RJ-45 for an Ethernet connection.

Wireless

The latest boon in printer interface technology is wireless. Clearly, people love their Wi-Fi because it enables them to roam around an office and still remain connected to one another and to their network. It logically follows that someone came up with the brilliant idea that it would be nice if printers could be that mobile as well—after all, many are on carts with wheels. Some printers have built-in Wi-Fi interfaces, while others can accept wireless network cards. Wi-Fi enabled printers support nearly all 802.11 standards (a, b, g, n, ac), and the availability of devices will mirror the current popularity of each standard.

The wireless technology that is especially popular among peripheral manufacturers is *Bluetooth*. Bluetooth is a short-range wireless technology; most devices are specified to work within 10 meters (33 feet). Printers such as the HP Officejet 100 mobile printer have Bluetooth capability.

When printing with a Bluetooth-enabled device (like a smartphone or tablet) and a Bluetooth-enabled printer, all you need to do is get within range of the device (that is, move closer), select the print driver from the device, and choose Print. The information is transmitted wirelessly through the air using radio waves and is received by the device.

> When Wi-Fi is used to connect printers to a network on a more permanent basis, it is known as *infrastructure mode*. Wi-Fi and Bluetooth can be used to connect a printer temporarily to a single computer (or mobile device), and the connection does not have permanent status. This type of configuration is known as an *ad hoc* network connection.

Interface Software

Now that we've looked at the ways that you can connect your printer, it's time to face a grim reality: Computers and printers don't know how to talk to each other. They need help. That help comes in the form of interface software used to translate software commands into commands that the printer can understand.

There are two major components of interface software: the page-description language and the driver software. The page-description language (PDL) determines how efficient the printer is at converting the information to be printed into signals that the printer can understand. The driver software understands and controls the printer and must be written to communicate between a specific operating system and specific printer. It is very important that you use the correct interface software for your printer. If you use either the wrong page-description language or the wrong driver software, the printer will print garbage—or possibly nothing at all.

Page-Description Languages

A *page-description language* works just as its name implies: It describes the whole page being printed by sending commands that describe the text as well as the margins and other settings. The controller in the printer interprets these commands and turns them into laser pulses (or pin strikes). There are several printer communication languages in existence, but the three most common ones are PostScript, Printer Command Language (PCL), and Graphics Device Interface (GDI).

The first page-description language was PostScript. Developed by Adobe, it was first used in the Apple LaserWriter printer. It made printing graphics fast and simple. Here's how PostScript works: The PostScript printer driver describes the page in terms of "draw" and "position" commands. The page is divided into a very fine grid (as fine as the resolution of the printer). When you want to print a square, a communication like the following takes place:

```
POSITION 1,42%DRAW 10%POSITION 1,64%DRAW10D% . . .
```

These commands tell the printer to draw a line on the page from line 42 to line 64 (vertically). In other words, a page-description language tells the printer to draw a line on the page, gives it the starting and ending points, and that's that. Rather than send the printer the location of each and every dot in the line and an instruction at each and every location to print that location's individual dot, PostScript can get the line drawn with fewer than five instructions. As you can see, PostScript uses commands that are more or less in English. The commands are interpreted by the processor on the printer's controller and converted into the print-control signals.

PCL was developed by Hewlett-Packard in 1984 and originally intended for use with inkjet printers as a competitor to PostScript. Since then, its role has been expanded to virtually every printer type, and it's a de facto industry standard.

GDI is actually a Windows component and is not specific to printers. Instead, it's a series of components that govern how images are presented to both monitors and printers. GDI printers work by using computer processing power instead of their own. The printed image is rendered to a bitmap on the computer and then sent to the printer. This means that the printer hardware doesn't need to be as powerful, which results in a less expensive printer. Generally speaking, the least expensive laser printers on the market are GDI printers.

 Many newer printers can handle both PS and PCL (and GDI) and will automatically translate for you. Therefore, it's less likely that you'll install the wrong print driver than it was several years ago.

The main advantage of page-description languages is that they move some of the processing from the computer to the printer. With text-only documents, they offer little benefit. However, with documents that have large amounts of graphics or that use numerous fonts, page-description languages make the processing of those print jobs happen much faster. This makes them an ideal choice for laser printers, although nearly every type of printer uses them.

If you're working with an older laser printer and it's printing garbage, check the driver. It might have the letters *PS* or *PCL* at the end of the name. If a PS driver is installed for a printer that wants PCL (or vice versa), garbage output could be the result.

 Real World Scenario

Life Without a Page-Description Language

Page-description languages make printing an efficient process. But what about when they are not used? In situations like this, the computer sends all of the instructions the printer needs in a serial stream, like so: Position 1, print nothing; Position 2, strike pins 1 and 3; Position 3, print nothing. This type of description language works well for dot-matrix printers, but it can be inefficient for laser printers. For example, if you wanted to print a page using a standard page-description language and there was only one character on the page, there would be a lot of signal wasted on the "print nothing" commands.

With graphics, the commands to draw a shape on the page are relatively complex. For example, to draw a square, the computer (or printer) has to calculate the size of the square and convert that into lots of "strike pin *x*" (or "turn on laser") and "print nothing" commands. This is where the other types of page-description languages come into the picture.

Driver Software

The *driver software* controls how the printer processes the print job. When you install a printer driver for the printer you are using, it allows the computer to print to that printer correctly (assuming that you have the correct interface configured between the computer and printer). The driver must be written specifically for the operating system the computer is using and for the printer being used. In other words, Mac clients need a different driver than Windows clients do, even to print to the same printer.

If you're working with a Windows-based operating system, Microsoft refers to the software that is installed on the computer and lets you print as the "printer." The physical device where the paper comes out is referred to as the "print device." Here, when we say "printer," we mean the physical device.

When you need to print, you select the printer driver for your printer from a preconfigured list. The driver that you select has been configured for the type, brand, and model of printer as well as the computer port to which it is connected. You can also select which paper tray the printer should use as well as any other features the printer has (if applicable). Also, each printer driver is configured to use a particular page-description language.

WARNING   If the wrong printer driver is selected, the computer will send commands in the wrong language. If that occurs, the printer will print several pages full of garbage (even if only one page of information was sent). This "garbage" isn't garbage at all but the printer page-description language commands printed literally as text instead of being interpreted as control commands.

Installing and Sharing Local Printers

Although every device is different, there are certain accepted methods used for installing almost all of them. The following procedure works for installing many kinds of devices:

1. Attach the device using a local port (generally USB, but maybe parallel) and connect the power.
2. Install and update the device driver and calibrate the device.
3. Configure options and settings.
4. Print a test page.
5. Verify compatibility with the operating system and applications.
6. Educate users about basic functionality.

TIP   Before installing any device, read your device's installation instructions. There are exceptions to every rule.

Step 1: Attach the Device Using a Local Port and Connect the Power

When installing a printer, you must first take the device out of its packaging and set it up on a flat, stable surface. Then, with the device powered off, connect it to the host computer. Today, the vast majority of local printers are USB, but you will occasionally find ones that use different ports as well.

Once you have connected the device, connect power to it using whatever supplied power adapter comes with it. Some devices have their own built-in power supply and just need an AC power cord connecting the device to the wall outlet, while others rely on an external transformer and power supply. Finally, turn on the device.

Step 2: Install and Update the Device Driver and Calibrate the Device

Once you have connected and powered up the device, boot up the computer and wait for Windows to recognize the device. Windows will pop up a screen similar to the one shown in Figure 11.24, and you will choose Add A Local Printer. This wizard will allow you to configure the driver for the printer (depending on the device). You can insert the driver CD or DVD that comes with the device and the wizard will guide you through the device driver installation. If Windows fails to recognize the device, you can use the Add A Printer Wizard (in Windows 7 and Windows 8/8.1) or the Add Printer Wizard (in older Windows versions) to troubleshoot the installation and to install the device drivers.

FIGURE 11.24 Adding a printer in Windows 7

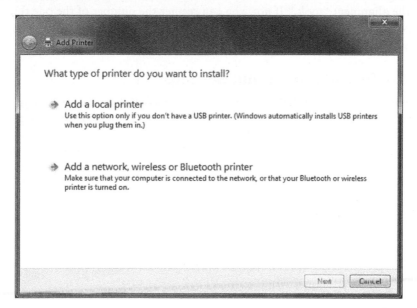

 This might go without saying at this point, but it bears repeating: You need the right driver—one that matches both your printer and your operating system—for everything to work right.

Once the driver is installed, the device will function. But some devices, such as inkjet printers, must be calibrated. If the printer requires this step, it will tell you. You'll need to walk through a few steps before the printer will print, but instructions will be provided either on your computer screen or on the printer's display.

 When working with print media, it is especially important to calibrate all of your hardware, including your monitor, scanner, printer, and digital camera, to ensure color matching.

Each manufacturer's process is different, but a typical alignment/calibration works like this:

1. During software installation, the installation wizard asks you if you would like to calibrate now, to which you will respond Yes or OK.

2. The printer prints out a sheet with multiple sets of numbered lines. Each set of lines represents an alignment instance.

3. The software will ask you which set(s) looks the best. Enter the number and click OK or Continue.

4. Some alignment routines end at this point. Others will reprint the alignment page and see if the alignment "took." If not, you can reenter the number of the one that looks the best.

5. Click Finish to end the alignment routine.

Step 3: Configure Options and Settings

Once you have installed the software and calibrated the device, you can configure any options that you would like for the printer. All of the settings and how to change them can be found online or in your user manual.

Where you configure specific printer properties depends a lot on the printer itself. As a rule of thumb, you're looking for the Printer Properties or Printing Preferences applet. In Windows 7, if you click Start and then Devices And Printers, you will get a window similar to the one shown in Figure 11.25. At the top there is an option to add a device or a printer. If you double-click the printer icon, you will get another window (like the one in Figure 11.26) that lets you get to the printer's configuration options.

FIGURE 11.25 Devices And Printers

If you don't see the options you're looking for, be sure to highlight the printer first.

FIGURE 11.26   Printer information and options

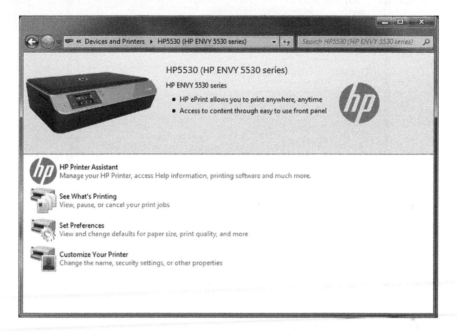

Various configuration features can be set from each menu option. In this example, there are three options in which you would probably be most interested. The first one, See What's Printing, lets you look at and manage the print queue. This is something we'll talk about more in Chapter 12. The second one, Set Preferences, gives you a number of settings related to print output. The third one, Customize Your Printer, is where you find the printer's properties, shown in Figure 11.27.

From the Printer Properties dialog box, you can configure nearly any option that you want to for your printer. The Properties dialog box will be pretty much the same for any printer that you install, and we'll cover a few options here in a minute. First though, notice the Preferences button on the General tab. Clicking this will produce a new window like the one in Figure 11.28. That window will have configuration options based on your specific model of printer.

Now back to the Properties dialog box. The printer's Properties dialog box is less about how the printer does its job and more about how people can access the printer. From the Properties dialog box, you can share the printer, set up the port that it's on, configure when the printer will be available throughout the day, and specify who can use it. Let's take a look at a few key tabs. We've already taken a look at the General tab, which has the Preferences button as well as the all-important Print Test Page button. It's handy for troubleshooting!

FIGURE 11.27 Printer Properties dialog box

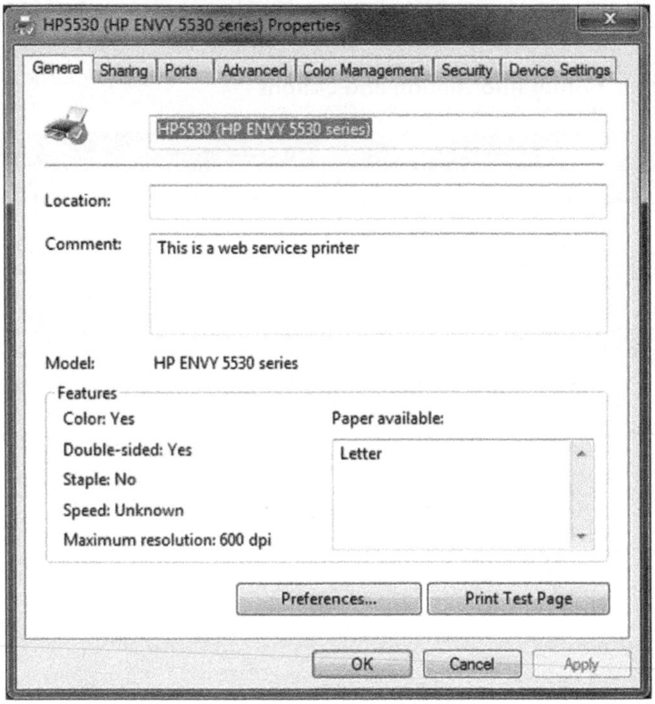

FIGURE 11.28 Printing Preferences window

Figure 11.29 shows the Sharing tab. If you want other users to be able to print to this printer, you need to share it. Notice the warnings above the Share This Printer check box. Those are important to remember. When you share the printer, you give it a share name. Network users can map the printer through their own Add Printer Wizard (choosing a networked printer) and by using the standard *computer_name**share_name* convention. User permissions are managed through the Security tab.

FIGURE 11.29   Printer Properties Sharing tab

One other important feature to call out on this tab is the Additional Drivers button. This one provides a description that is fairly self-explanatory.

Figure 11.30 shows the Ports tab. Here you can configure your printer port and add and delete ports. There's also a check box to enable printer pooling. This would be used if you have multiple physical printers that operate under the same printer name.

If you're going to configure a printer pool, remember that all of the output can appear on any of the devices that are part of that pool. Make sure that all of the printers in that pool are in the same physical location! Otherwise, you will have people wandering all over the office trying to find their printouts. That might be entertaining for you, but not so much for them.

FIGURE 11.30 Printer Properties Ports tab

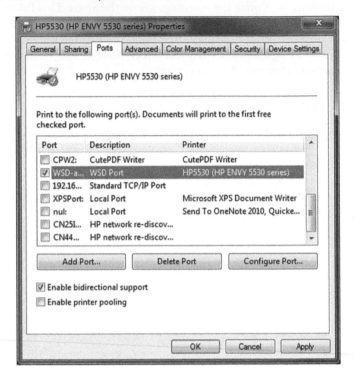

Figure 11.31 shows the important Advanced tab of the printer Properties dialog box. On this tab, you can configure the printer to be available during only certain hours of the day. This might be useful if you're trying to curtail after-hours printing of non-work-related documents, for example. You can also configure the spool settings. For faster printing, you should always spool the jobs instead of printing directly to the printer. However, if the printer is printing garbage, you can try printing directly to it to see if the spooler is causing the problem.

Regarding the check boxes at the bottom, you will always want to print spooled documents first because that speeds up the printing process. If you need to maintain an electronic copy of all printed files, check the Keep Printed Documents check box. Keep in mind that this will eat up a lot of hard disk space.

Finally, the Printing Defaults button takes you to the Printing Preferences window (shown earlier in Figure 11.28). Print Processor lets you select alternate methods of processing print jobs (not usually needed), and Separator Page lets you specify a file to use as a separator page (a document that prints out at the beginning of each separate print job, usually with the user's name on it), which can be useful if you have several (or several dozen) users sharing one printer.

FIGURE 11.31   Printer Properties Advanced tab

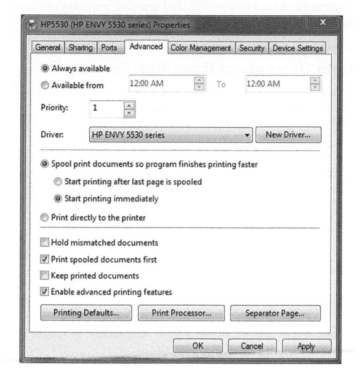

Step 4: Print a Test Page

Once you have configured your printer, you are finished and can print a test page to test its output. Windows has a built-in function for doing just that. To print a test page, right-click the icon for the printer you installed from within the Devices And Printers window and click Printer properties. On the General tab of the Printer properties (shown in Figure 11.27), there will be a Print Test Page button. Click that button and Windows will send a test page to the printer. If the page prints, your printer is working. If not, double-check all of your connections. If they appear to be in order, then read ahead to Chapter 12 for troubleshooting tips.

Step 5: Verify Compatibility with Operating System and Applications

Once your printer is installed and you have printed a test page, everything else should work well, right? That's usually true, but it's good practice to verify compatibility with applications before you consider the device fully installed.

With printers, this process is rather straightforward. Open the application you're wondering about and print something. For example, open up Microsoft Word, type in some gibberish (or open a real document if you want), and print it out. If you are running non-Microsoft applications (such as a computer-aided drafting program or accounting software) and have questions about their compatibility with the printer, try printing from those programs as well.

Step 6: Educate Users about Basic Functionality

Most users today know how to print, but not everyone knows how to install the right printer or how to print efficiently. This can be a significant issue in work environments.

Say your workplace has 10 different printers, and you just installed number 11. First, your company should use a naming process to identify the printers in a way that makes sense. Calling a printer HPLJ4 on a network does little to help users understand where that printer is in the building. After installing the printer, offer installation assistance to those who might want to use the device. Show users how to install the printer in Windows (or if printer installation is automated, let them know that they have a new printer and where it is). Also, let the users know the various options available on that printer. Can it print double-sided? If so, you can save a lot of paper. Show users how to configure that. Is it a color printer? Do users really need color for rough drafts of documents or presentations? Show users how to print in black and white on a color printer to save the expensive color ink or toner cartridges.

On the printer we've used as an example in this chapter, most of the options involving print output are located in Preferences (look back at Figure 11.28). Two of them are on the Printing Shortcut tab: Duplex (or Print On Both Sides) and Print Quality (Best, Normal, Draft). Orientation (Portrait or Landscape) is set on the Layout tab. This printer does not have a collate feature, which is used if you are printing several copies of a longer document. Collation will let you select whether you want it to print pages in order (1, 2, 3. . . 1, 2, 3. . . and so on) or multiple copies of the same page at once (1, 1, 1. . . 2, 2, 2. . . and so forth).

In Exercise 11.2, we'll step through the process of installing a USB printer in Windows 7; the process will work in Windows XP and Vista as well.

EXERCISE 11.2

Installing a USB Printer in Windows 7

For this exercise, you will need the following items:

- A USB printer
- A USB printer cable
- The software driver CD or DVD that came with the printer
- A computer with a free USB port and a CD-ROM drive

1. Turn on the computer.
2. Plug the printer into the wall outlet and turn it on.

3. Insert the CD into the computer's CD-ROM drive. The driver CD's autorun feature should automatically start the installation program. If not, click Start ➤ Run and type in **D:\setup** or **D:\install** (if your CD-ROM drive letter is different, substitute that letter for *D*).

4. Follow the prompts in the installation program to install the driver.

5. Once the software has been installed, plug one end of the USB cable into the printer and the other end into the free USB port. Some installation programs will prompt you for this step.

6. Windows will automatically detect the new printer, install the driver, and configure it automatically. Windows will display a balloon in the lower-right corner of the screen saying "Your hardware is now installed and is ready to use." If Windows doesn't properly detect the printer, open Add A Printer to begin the installation process again, and manually specify the location of the print driver (such as the CD-ROM).

7. Print a test page to see if the printer can communicate and print properly.

 Real World Scenario

Which Printer Did That Go To?

One of the authors used to work at a satellite office in Salt Lake City for a company whose headquarters were in Houston. Because of printer problems, a new network printer had been installed and it had a different network name from the previous printer.

At the end of the month, one of the accountants printed her monthly reconciliation report, which typically ran about 400 pages. (A hard copy was required for regulatory reasons.) Puzzled when it didn't come out of the printer, she printed it again. And again. And again. After the fourth failed attempt, and several hours later, she decided to ask someone in IT what the problem was.

It turns out that she had mapped (installed) the new network printer but had gotten a few letters wrong in the printer name. Instead of being at her office, all of her print jobs were sent to a printer in the Houston office. And of course, there were people in Houston trying to print similar reports and who just kept refilling the printer with paper because they didn't want to cut someone else's report off in the middle.

While this wasn't a catastrophic failure, it was annoying. She had unintentionally wasted three reams of paper, the associated toner, and hours of printer life. It wasn't a malicious act, and she was a literate computer user, but it's illustrative of the need to educate and help users with installing and configuring devices. Had the printer been mapped correctly the first time, the waste could have been avoided.

Installing and Sharing Networked Printers

The previous section was about installing a printer attached to your local computer. There are advantages to that approach, such as being able to manage and control your own printer, not to mention having a printer at your own desk. That doesn't happen often in the business world these days!

There are some big disadvantages as well. First, it means that all users who need to print to your device may need local accounts on your computer, unless you are on a domain or have configured a homegroup. If so, you will need to manage security for these accounts and the printer. Second, your computer is the print server. The *print server* is the device that hosts the printer and processes the necessary printer commands. This can slow your system down. Third, because your computer is the print server, if for any reason it's turned off, no one will be able to print to that device.

There is another option, though. Instead of needing a specific computer to be the print server, why not make the print server part of the printer itself, or make it a separate network device that hosts the printers? That is exactly the principle behind network printing. Next, we will cover two types of network printing, local network printing and cloud printing, as well as talk about data privacy concerns with printing to public or shared printers.

Local Network Printing

The key to local network printing is that you are moving the print server from your computer to another location, accessible to other users on the network. Therefore, the print server needs a direct attachment to the network, via either a wired (RJ-45) or wireless connection. There are two major varieties of print servers that you will find. The first is incorporated into the printer itself (called an *integrated print server*), and the second is a separate hardware print server. If you are using a stand-alone print server, the printers attach to the print server, either physically or logically. In most cases, if a printer is capable of connecting directly to a network, it has the ability to be its own print server.

Installing and using a networked printer is very similar to installing and using a local printer. You need to ensure that both devices are plugged in, turned on, and attached to the network (either with an RJ-45 Ethernet connection or by using wireless). Probably the biggest difference is that when you install it, you need to tell your computer that you are adding a networked printer instead of a local one. For example, in Windows 7, when you open the Add Printer utility (shown in Figure 11.24), you choose Add A Network, Wireless, Or Bluetooth Printer instead of Add A Local Printer. From there, you will be asked to install the printer driver, just as you would if the printer were directly attached to your computer. Once it's installed, you use it just as you would use a local printer, including setting the configuration options that we looked at in earlier sections. Every computer on the local network should be able to see and add the printer in the same way.

 The print server needs to have drivers available (installed) for all of the types of clients that will connect to its printers. For example, if the network has Mac, Linux, and Windows 7 clients, the server will need to have all three drivers. If not, users may not be able to install the printer properly and not be able to print.

There are a few other ways that you can add shared networked printers, and they are by using TCP, Bonjour, and AirPrint.

TCP Printing

Printers that are network aware need IP addresses, so it makes sense that you can add a networked printer by using TCP/IP, also known as *TCP printing*. Exercise 11.3 walks you through the general process of installing a TCP printer, using Windows 7 as an example.

EXERCISE 11.3

Installing a TCP Printer in Windows 7

1. Connect the printer to the network and power it on.

2. Configure the printer with an IP address if it does not already have one. Most network-aware printers will have their own display panel where you can configure or verify network settings. The IP address needs to be on the same subnet as the computer trying to add the printer.

3. From your Windows 7 computer, start Add A Printer.

4. Choose Add A Network, Wireless, Or Bluetooth Printer and click Next.

5. On the next screen, the system will search for printers. You can let it search, or you can stop it and click the link that says "The Printer That I Want Isn't Listed." That will give you a screen similar to the one shown in Figure 11.32.

FIGURE 11.32 Adding a TCP printer

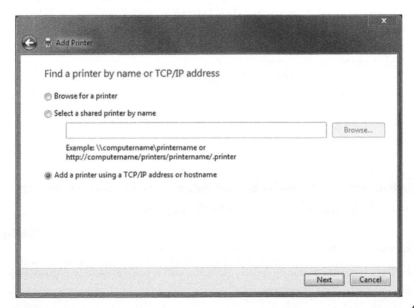

continues

6. Choose Add A Printer Using A TCP/IP Address Or Hostname and click Next.

7. Enter the IP address (or hostname) of the printer that you want to add, add a port name (it's just for identification), and click Next.

8. Select the make and model of your printer from the list.

9. You will be prompted to install the driver; continue installing the printer as you would any other local or networked printer.

Some installations will ask you which TCP printing protocol you want to use: RAW or LPR. RAW (also called the Standard TCP/IP Port Monitor) is the default, and it uses TCP port 9100 by default. It also uses the SNMP protocol for bidirectional communication between the computer and the printer. LPR is older, and the protocol is included for use with legacy systems. It's limited to source ports 721–731 and the destination port 515.

After the printer is installed, it will appear in your Devices And Printers window just as any other printer would.

There are a few advantages to using TCP printing. First, it sends the print jobs directly to the printer, so your system does not need to act as the print server or spend processing time dealing with formatting the print job. Second, it allows clients with different OSs, such as Linux or OS X, to add printers without worrying about intra-OS conflicts.

Bonjour

Apple introduced Bonjour in 2002 (then under the name Rendezvous) as an implementation of zero configuration networking. It's designed to enable automatic discovery of devices and services on local networks using TCP/IP as well as to provide hostname resolution. Currently, it comes installed by default on Apple's OS X and iOS operating systems. Bonjour makes it easy to discover and install printers that have been shared by other Bonjour-enabled clients on the network.

Even though Apple developed Bonjour, it does work on other operating systems. For example, it comes with iTunes and the Safari browser, so if you have either of those installed on your, say, Windows computer, odds are that you have Bonjour as well. Once installed, the Bonjour service starts automatically and scans the network looking for shared devices. Exercise 11.4 shows you how to see if Bonjour is installed in Windows.

EXERCISE 11.4

Determining if Bonjour Is Installed in Windows

1. Click Start, and in the Search box, type `services.msc` and press Enter. The Services window will open.

2. Sort the list by name, and look for the Bonjour service, as shown in Figure 11.33.

FIGURE 11.33 Bonjour service is set to start automatically

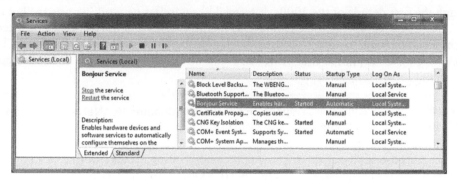

Bonjour only works on a single broadcast domain, meaning that it will not find a printer or other device if it's on the other side of a router from your computer. All major printer manufacturers support Bonjour technology.

If you are using a Mac, adding a Bonjour printer is easy. You open System Preferences ➤ Print And Scan, click the plus sign under Printers to open the Add Printer window, and look for the printer on the list. If the Mac doesn't have the driver available, you will be asked to provide it. Otherwise, you're done.

In order to add or share a Bonjour printer from Windows, you need to download Bonjour Print Services for Windows. It's found on Apple's support site at https:// support.apple.com/kb/dl999.

AirPrint

The one big complaint that Apple aficionados had about Bonjour was that it didn't support printing from iPhones or iPads. In 2010, Apple introduced *AirPrint* to meet that need.

The idea behind AirPrint is quite simple. Mobile devices can automatically detect AirPrint-enabled printers on their local network and print to them without requiring the installation of a driver. To be fair, what Apple really did was eliminate the need for a specific printer driver to be installed on the client and replaced it with the AirPrint concept. Then it was up to the printer manufacturers to develop their own drivers that talked to AirPrint. HP was happy to oblige with its Photosmart Plus series, and other manufacturers soon followed. The list of AirPrint-enabled printers is available at https://support.apple .com/en-us/HT201311. From the end-user standpoint though, no driver is required.

There really is no installation process, and printing is easy. Just be sure that your mobile device is on the same local network as an AirPrint printer. When you attempt to print from your device, select the printer to which you want to print, and it should work.

 You can also purchase AirPrint servers, which are small print servers that allow you to connect almost any printer to the network and make them Air-Print compatible.

Cloud Printing

Through the first decade of the 2000s, it seemed like wireless networking was the hot new trend in computing. Now that technology has matured a bit, and the *cloud* has replaced it as the trend du jour. Not everyone knows what the cloud is or what the cloud does, but they think they are supposed to have it. The cloud would be a sad place if it didn't support printing, but fortunately for us it does.

> We will provide details on the cloud in Chapter 20, "Network Services, Cloud Computing, and Virtualization."

For the purpose of this chapter, know that cloud printing means printing to a remote device, one that is not necessarily located on your local network. Essentially, you are using the Internet to send the print job from your device to the printer from which you want the output to come, and the printer can be located practically anywhere in the world. To use cloud printing, you need to work through a cloud printing service, such as Google Cloud Print, HP ePrint, or others. Some printers are cloud-ready, but you can often get older devices to work on the cloud as well.

Cloud services will have their own steps on how to activate printing, but in Exercise 11.5 we will go through an example using Google Cloud Print.

EXERCISE 11.5

Enabling Google Cloud Print

1. If you do not already have a Google account, you will need to create one.

2. Log in to your Google account and visit https://www.google.com/cloudprint/#printers, as shown in Figure 11.34. You can see in the figure that you have options to add a classic printer or a cloud-ready printer.

FIGURE 11.34   Getting Started with Google Cloud Print

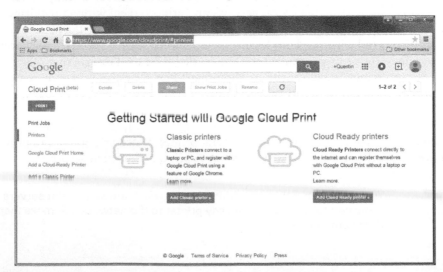

3. For this example, we will add a cloud-ready printer. Click the blue button that says Add A Cloud Ready Printer.

4. You will be directed to an information page, which lists cloud-ready printers. Find your brand on the left side, and click it to see instructions on how to add the printer, similar to what is shown in Figure 11.35.

FIGURE 11.35   Adding an HP cloud-ready printer

5. If you scroll down in the instructions for an HP printer, it will say to make sure that you have an active HP ePrint email address, and then they provide a link to click to associate your printer with Google Cloud Print. Follow those steps and when you click the link, you will see a screen similar to the one shown in Figure 11.36.

FIGURE 11.36   Enter the printer's email address

continues

EXERCISE 11.5 *(continued)*

6.   Enter the printer's email address, and click Connect My Printer.

7.   After a moment, you will see that the printer has been registered with Google Cloud Print.

After registering your printer, you can print from Google Cloud Print, as shown in Figure 11.37. Notice that the printer is now installed in the right pane. Exercise 11.6 shows you how to print to Google Cloud Print using the Chrome browser.

FIGURE 11.37   Printer registered with Google Cloud Print

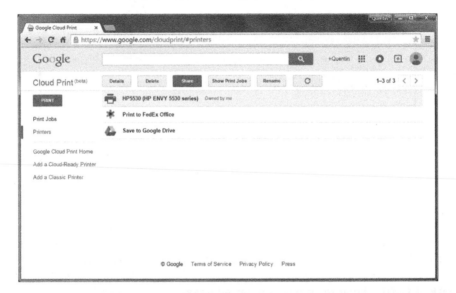

EXERCISE 11.6

Printing from Google Cloud Print

1.   Open Google Cloud Print, as shown in Figure 11.37.

2.   Click the red Print button. You will be asked if you want to upload a file to print or choose other ways to print. If the file is on your machine, choose the first option. If you are looking to print from Chrome or another Google Cloud Print–enabled app, choose the second. In this example, we will choose the first.

3.   A new window pops up with a link to select a file from your computer. Click the link and choose a file. You will be taken back to the list of available printers.

4.   Click the printer to which you'd like to print. You will see print options such as collate, color, number of copies, size, orientation, pages to print, and quality, similar to what is shown in Figure 11.38. Choose your options and click Print.

FIGURE 11.38   Google Cloud Print options

The steps involved to print directly from client computers differ based on the client you are using. Table 11.1 provides information to get you started in the right direction.

TABLE 11.1   Google Cloud Print OS client options

Client	Option
Windows	Go to `https://tools.google.com/dlpage/cloudprintdriver` to download the print client. After installation, Google Cloud Printer will appear in your list of printers when you print from an application.
Mac OS X	Download Cloud Printer from the Mac App Store.
Android	Android should natively support Google Cloud Print; if not, download the Google Drive Android app from Google Play, or use a third-party app such as PrinterShare Mobile Print or Easy Cloud Print.
iOS	Download PrintCentral Pro, gCloud Print, or other apps from iTunes.

Earlier we mentioned HP's ePrint capability as well. Of course, this only works if you purchased an HP cloud-ready printer. If it's cloud-ready, it will have an icon on it that looks like a printer with a wireless signal coming from it (the bottom icon on the right side of Figure 11.39), and you can configure it with an email address @hpeprint.com. Printer settings, including the email address and security related to who can print to the printer, can be managed at www.hpconnected.com. If you have access, it's very easy to print. Simply email what you want printed to the email address of your printer, and it will print.

FIGURE 11.39   HP ePrint information

Data Privacy Concerns

When printing to a public printer, or one that is shared in a common workspace, there may be data privacy concerns. For example, employees in Human Resources might need to print confidential personnel files, or someone in the Mergers group might have a highly restricted contract to print.

Several printer manufacturers, including Brother, Canon, HP, and Xerox, offer a feature called Secure Printing (or Private Printing) on many of their office printers. When users print, they need to go into the printer preferences (or a similar place) and indicate that it's a secure print job. They are then asked to enter a PIN and, finally, print the document. The document will not print until they physically go to the printer and enter the PIN.

Another security issue is storing print jobs on print servers. Print jobs are cached on the print server, and they can be saved indefinitely. We looked at the check box to keep printed documents in Figure 11.31. If you are configuring a printer for a public area, do not select this option. If you're printing to a public printer (such as at a hotel), and you can see the printer properties, check to make sure that this option is not selected. That will help ensure that your files will not be cached on the hotel computer's hard drive.

Performing Printer Maintenance and Upgrades

Considering the amount of work they do, printers last a pretty long time. Some printers handle over 100,000 pages per month, yet they're usually pretty reliable devices. You can help your printers live long and fulfilling lives by performing the right maintenance, and smoothly running printers always make your officemates happy. After all, going to get your print job from the printer and discovering that the printer is in the shop is a very frustrating experience! In addition, there may be ways that you can upgrade a slower printer or add functionality without breaking the bank. In the following sections, we'll look at performing printer maintenance and upgrading your printers.

Performing Printer Maintenance

Regardless of the type of printer you use, giving it a regular check-up is a good idea. You're probably familiar with some of the activities that fall under maintenance, such as replacing paper, ink, or toner cartridges. We'll look at those as well as some additional, more involved maintenance procedures.

Replacing Consumables

To maintain a printer properly, you need to replace consumables such as toner or ink cartridges, assemblies, filters, and rollers on occasion. Trying to cut costs by buying cheaper supplies rarely pays off.

Whenever purchasing supplies for your printer, always get supplies from the manufacturer or from an authorized reseller. This way, you'll be sure that the parts are of high quality. Using unauthorized parts can damage your printer and possibly void your warranty.

Printer Paper

Most people don't give much thought to the kind of paper they use in their printers. It's a factor that can have a tremendous effect on the quality of the hard-copy printout, however, and the topic is more complex than people think. For example, if the wrong paper is used, it can cause frequent paper jams and possibly even damage components.

Several aspects of paper can be measured; each gives an indication as to the paper's quality. The first factor is *composition*. Paper is made from a variety of substances. Paper used to be made from cotton and was called rag stock. It can also be made from wood pulp, which is cheaper. Most paper today is made from the latter or a combination of the two.

Another aspect of paper is the property known as *basis weight* (or simply *weight* for short). The weight of a particular type of paper is the actual weight, in pounds, of a ream (500 sheets) of the standard size of that paper made of that material. For regular bond paper, that size is 17×22.

The final paper property we'll discuss is the *caliper* (or thickness) of an individual sheet of paper. If the paper is too thick, it may jam in feed mechanisms that have several curves in the paper path. (On the other hand, a paper that's too thin may not feed at all.)

These are just three of the categories we use to judge the quality of paper. Because there are so many different types and brands of printers as well as paper, it would be impossible to give the specifications for the "perfect" paper. However, the documentation for any printer will give specifications for the paper that should be used in that printer.

Many impact printers need to use special paper that has tractor feed perforations on the side or they will not work properly. When replacing tractor feed paper, it's very easy to get it misaligned, and it will feed crookedly and ultimately jam the printer. Similarly, thermal printers also require special paper that needs to be loaded properly. In many cases, if you load it upside down, the unit will not produce images. By comparison, adding paper to a laser or inkjet printer is usually very easy!

> For best results, store paper in an area where it will not get wet or be exposed to excessive humidity.

Ink and Toner

The area in which using recommended supplies is the biggest concern is ink and toner cartridges. Using the wrong ink or toner supplies is the easiest way to ruin a perfectly good printer.

Dot-matrix printers use a cloth or polyester ribbon soaked in ink and coiled up inside a plastic case. This assembly is called a *printer ribbon* (or *ribbon cartridge*). Once the ribbon has run out of ink, it must be discarded and replaced. Ribbon cartridges are developed closely with their respective printers. For this reason, ribbons should be purchased from the same manufacturer as the printer. The wrong ribbon could jam in the printer as well as cause quality problems.

> It is possible to re-ink a ribbon. Some vendors sell a bottle of ink solution that can be poured into the plastic casing, where the cloth ribbon will soak up the solution. This can be a messy process, and you should do this only if the manufacturer recommends it.

Inkjet cartridges have a liquid ink reservoir. The ink in these cartridges is sealed inside. Once the ink runs out, the cartridge must be removed and discarded. A new, full one is installed in its place. Because the ink cartridge contains the printing mechanism as well as ink, it's like getting a new printer every time you replace the ink cartridge.

In some inkjet printers, the ink cartridge and the print head are in separate assemblies. This way, the ink can be replaced when it runs out, and the print head can be used several times. This works fine if the printer is designed to work this way. However, some people think that they can do this on their integrated cartridge/print head system, using special ink cartridge refill kits. These kits consist of a syringe filled with ink and a long needle. The needle is used to puncture the top of an empty ink cartridge, and the syringe is then used to refill the reservoir.

> *Do not use ink cartridge refill kits!* There are several problems with these kits (the ones you see advertised with a syringe and a needle). First, the kits don't use the same kind of ink that was originally in the ink cartridges. The new ink may be thinner, causing it to run out or not print properly. Also, the print head is oftentimes supposed to be replaced around this same time. Refilling the cartridge doesn't replace the print head, so you'll have print-quality problems. Finally, the hole the syringe leaves cannot be plugged and may allow ink to leak out. These problems can happen with do-it-yourself kits as well as with cartridges refilled by office supply stores or private printer supply sellers. Here's the bottom line: *Buy new ink cartridges from the printer manufacturer.* Yes, they are a bit more expensive, but in the long run you will save money because you won't have any of the problems described here.

The final type of consumable is toner. Each model of laser printer uses a specific toner cartridge. You should check the printer's manual to see which toner cartridge your printer needs. Many businesses will recycle your toner or ink cartridges for you, refill them, and sell them back to you at a discount. Don't buy them. While some businesses that perform this "service" are more legitimate than others, using recycled parts is more dangerous to your hardware than using new parts. The reason for this is that refilled cartridges are more likely to break or leak than new parts, and this leakage could cause extensive damage to the inside of your printer. And again, using secondhand parts can void your warranty, so you're left with a broken printer that you have to pay for. Avoid problems like this by buying new parts.

 Real World Scenario

Think Before You Refill

Just as with ink cartridges, you should always buy the exact model of toner cartridge recommended by the manufacturer. The toner cartridges have been designed specifically for a particular model. Additionally, *never* refill toner cartridges, for most of the same reasons we don't recommend refilling ink cartridges. The printout quality will be poor, and the fact that you're just refilling the toner means that you might *not* be replacing the photosensitive drum (which is usually inside the cartridge), and the drum might *need* to be replaced. Simply replacing refilled toner cartridges with proper, name-brand toner cartridges has solved most laser printer quality problems that we have run across. We keep recommending the right ones, but clients keep coming back with the refilled ones. The result is that we take our clients' money to solve their print-quality problems when all it involves is a toner cartridge, our (usually repeat) advice to buy the proper cartridge next time, and the obligatory minimum charge for a half hour of labor (even though the job of replacing the cartridge takes all of 5 minutes!).

 Always properly recycle your used ink and toner cartridges. Just don't buy recycled cartridges!

Performing Scheduled Maintenance

When shopping for a printer, one of the characteristics you should look for is the printer's capacity, which is often quoted in monthly volume. This is particularly important if the printer will be serving in a high-load capacity. Every printer needs periodic maintenance, but printers that can handle a lot of traffic typically need it less frequently. Check the printer specifications to see how often scheduled maintenance is suggested. Never, ever fall behind on performing scheduled maintenance on a printer.

Many laser printers have LCD displays that provide useful information, such as error messages or notices that you need to replace a toner cartridge. The LCD display will also tell you when the printer needs scheduled maintenance. How does it know? Printers keep track of the number of pages they print, and when the page limit is reached, they display a message, usually something simple like *Perform user maintenance*. The printer will still print, but you should perform the maintenance.

Being the astute technician that you are, you clean the printer with the recommended cleaning kit or install the maintenance kit that you purchased from the manufacturer. Now, how do you get the maintenance message to go away? Reset the page count using a menu option. For example, on many HP laser printers, you press the Menu button until you get to the Configuration menu. Once there, you press the Item key until the display shows *Service Message = ON*. Then press the plus key (+) to change the message to *Service Message = OFF*. Bring the printer back online, and you're ready to go.

When performing maintenance on an impact printer, always carefully inspect the print head for damage. Replace damaged print heads with authorized parts from the manufacturer.

Performing routine maintenance will keep the printer clean, make it last longer, and help prevent annoying paper jams.

Using Cleaning Solutions

With all of the ink or toner they use, printers get dirty. If printers get too dirty or if the print heads get dirty, you'll notice print problems. No one wants this to happen.

Most printers have a self-cleaning utility that is activated through a menu option or by pressing a combination of buttons on the printer itself. It's recommended that you run the cleaning sequence every time you replace the toner or ink cartridges. If you experience print-quality problems, such as lines in the output, run the cleaning routine.

Sometimes, the self-cleaning routines aren't enough to clear up the problem. If you are having print-quality issues, you might want to consider purchasing a cleaning or maintenance kit, which frequently comes with a cleaning solution.

Cleaning kits are often designed for one specific type of printer and should be used only on that type of printer. For example, don't apply an inkjet cleaning solution to a laser printer.

Each cleaning kit comes with its own instructions for use. Exercise 11.7 walks you through the steps of using an inkjet cleaning solution. Note that the steps for your printer might differ slightly; please consult your manual for specific instructions. After using a cleaning kit on a laser or inkjet printer, it's best to perform a calibration per the printer's instructions.

EXERCISE 11.7

Using an Inkjet Cleaning Solution

1. Power on the printer, and open the top cover to expose the area containing the print cartridges.

2. Initiate a self-cleaning cycle. When the print head moves from its resting place, pull the AC power plug. This lets you freely move the print heads without damaging them.

3. Locate the sponge pads on which to apply the cleaning solution. They'll be in the area where the print heads normally park. Use a cotton swab or paper towel to gently soak up any excess ink in the pads.

4. Using the supplied syringe, apply the cleaning solution to the sponge pads until they are saturated.

5. Plug the printer back into the wall outlet, and turn it on. The print heads will park themselves.

6. Turn the printer back off. Let the solution sit for at least 3 hours.

7. Power the printer back on, and run three printer cleaning cycles. Print a nozzle check pattern (or a test page) after each cleaning cycle to monitor the cleaning progress.

That should take care of it! If not, again, refer to your printer's manual for more instructions.

Thermal printers require special attention because they contain a heating element. Always unplug the device and ensure that it's cooled off before trying to clean it. Thermal printer cleaning cards, cleaning pens, and kits are widely available in the marketplace. If you need to remove any debris (from any printer), use compressed air or a specialized computer vacuum.

Ensuring a Suitable Environment

Printers won't complain if the weather outside is too hot or too cold, but they are susceptible to environmental issues. Here are some things to watch out for in your printer's environment:

Heat   Laser printers can generate a lot of heat. Because of this, ensure that your laser printer is in a well-ventilated area. Resist the temptation to put the laser printer in the little cubbyhole in your desk; overheating will reduce the shelf life of your printer.

Humidity   High humidity can cause printer paper to stick together. Sticky paper leads to paper jams. Humidity over 80 or 90 percent can cause issues.

Light   The laser printer's toner cartridge contains a photosensitive drum. Exposing that drum to light could ruin the drum. While the drum is encased in plastic, it's best to avoid exposing the printer or toner cartridges to extreme light sources. Under no circumstance should you open the toner cartridge, unless you're ready to get rid of it as well as clean up a big mess.

Ozone   Laser printers that use corona wires produce ozone as a by-product of the printing process. In offices, ozone can cause respiratory problems in small concentrations, and it can be seriously dangerous to people in large amounts. Ozone is also a very effective oxidizer and can cause damage to printer components.

Fortunately, laser printers don't produce large amounts of ozone, and most laser printers have an ozone filter. Ozone is another reason to ensure that your printer area has good ventilation. Also, replace the ozone filter periodically; check your printer's manual for recommendations on when to do this.

Ammonia   A printer doesn't produce ammonia, but it is contained in many cleaning products. Ammonia can greatly reduce the printer's ability to neutralize ozone and can cause permanent damage to toner cartridges. It's best to avoid using ammonia-based cleaners near laser printers.

Installing Printer Upgrades

The printer market encompasses a dizzying array of products. You can find portable printers, photo printers, cheap black-and-white printers for under $30, high-end color laser printers for over $5,000, and everything in between. Most of the cheaper printers do not have upgrade options, but higher-end printers will have upgrade options, including memory, network cards, and firmware.

Installing Printer Memory

When purchasing a memory upgrade for your printer, you need to make sure of two things. First, buy only memory that is compatible with your printer model. Most printers today use a standard computer dual in-line memory module (DIMM), but check your manual or the manufacturer's website to be sure. If you're not sure, purchasing the memory through the manufacturer's website (or an authorized reseller) is a good way to go. Second, be sure that your printer is capable of a memory upgrade. It's possible that the amount of memory in your printer is at the maximum that it can handle.

Once you have obtained the memory, it's time to perform the upgrade. The specific steps required to install the memory will depend on your printer. Check the manual or the manufacturer's website for instructions tailored to your model.

Exercise 11.8 walks you through the general steps for installing memory into a laser printer.

EXERCISE 11.8

Installing Memory into a Laser Printer

1. Turn off the printer.

2. Disconnect all cables from the printer (power and interface cables).

3. Find the area in which you need to install the memory.

   On most HP LaserJet printers, this is in the back, on a piece of hardware called the formatter board. Tabs near the top and bottom of the board hold the formatter board in. Remove the formatter board from the printer. Other brands have different configurations. For example, on many Xerox laser printers you remove a panel on the top of the unit (underneath the paper output tray) to get to the memory.

If your printer requires you to remove a component (such as the formatter board) to upgrade the memory, place that component on a grounded surface, such as an anti-static work mat.

4. If you are replacing an existing memory module, remove the old module, being careful not to break off the latches at the end of the module that hold it in.

5. Insert the new memory module, making sure that any alignment notches on the memory module are lined up with the device before inserting the memory module.

6. Replace the removable component (if necessary).

7. Reconnect the power and interface cables.

8. Power on the printer.

9. Follow the printer manual's instructions on running a self-test to ensure that the memory is recognized.

Some printers require that you manually enable the added memory. Here are the steps to do that in Windows:

1. Open the Devices And Printers (in Windows 7 and 8) or Printers (in Windows Vista) window.

2. Right-click the printer and choose Properties.

3. On the Device Settings tab, click the Printer Memory button in the Installable Options section.

4. Select the amount of memory that is now installed.

5. Click OK.

Installing a Network Interface Card

Installing a NIC directly into a printer has become popular as more and more people need their printers to be on the network but don't want to hassle with a host computer. The NIC in a printer is similar to the NIC in a computer, with a couple of important differences. First, the NIC in a printer has a small processor on it to perform the management of the NIC interface (functions that the software on a host computer would do). This software is usually referred to as a print server, but be careful because that term can also refer to a physical computer that hosts many printers. Second, the NIC in a printer is proprietary, for the most part. The same manufacturer makes the printer and the NIC.

When a person on the network prints to a printer with a NIC, they are printing right to the printer and not going through any third-party device (although in some situations, that is desirable and possible with NICs). Because of its dedicated nature, the NIC option installed in a printer makes printing to that printer faster and more efficient—that NIC is dedicated to receiving print jobs and sending printer status to clients.

Most printer NICs come with management software installed that allows clients to check their print jobs' status as well as toner levels from any computer on the network. You access the configuration options by typing the IP address of the printer into your web browser and generally entering an authorized username and password.

Your manual is the best place to check to see if you can install a print server. Specific steps for installing the print server will also be in the manual or on the manufacturer's website. Generally speaking, it's very similar to installing a NIC into a computer.

Upgrading Printer Firmware

As with upgrading memory, methods to upgrade a printer's firmware depend on the model of printer you have. Most of the time, upgrading a printer's firmware is a matter of downloading and/or installing a free file from the manufacturer's website. Printer firmware upgrades are generally done from the machine hosting the printer (again, usually called the print server).

Firmware is usually upgraded for one of two reasons. One, if you are having compatibility issues, a firmware upgrade might solve them. Two, firmware upgrades can offer newer features that are not available on previous versions.

Installing Other Upgrades

While we've covered some of the most important upgrades, most printers (especially laser printers) can be upgraded with additional capabilities as well. Each manufacturer, with the documentation for each printer, includes a list of all of the accessories, options, and upgrades available. The following options can be included on that list:

- Hard drives
- Trays and feeders
- Finishers

Hard Drives

For a printer to print properly, the type style, or *font*, being printed must be downloaded to the printer along with the job being printed. Desktop publishing and graphic design businesses that print color pages on slower color printers are always looking for ways to speed up their print jobs, so they install multiple fonts into the onboard memory of the printer to make them *printer-resident fonts*. There's a problem, however: most printers have a limited amount of storage space for these fonts. To solve this problem, printer manufacturers made it possible for hard drives to be added to many printers. The hard drives can be used to store many fonts used during the print process and are also used to store a large document file while it is being processed for printing.

Trays and Feeders

One option that is popular in office environments is the addition of paper trays. Most laser and inkjet printers come with at least one paper tray (usually 500 sheets or fewer). The addition of a paper tray allows a printer to print more sheets between paper refills, thus reducing its operating cost. In addition, some printers can accommodate multiple paper trays, which can be loaded with different types of paper, stationery, and envelopes. The benefit is that you can print a letter and an envelope from the same printer without having to leave your desk or change the paper in the printer.

Related to trays is the option of *feeders*. Some types of paper products need to be watched as they are printed to make sure that the printing happens properly. One example is envelopes: You usually can't put a stack of envelopes in a printer because they won't line up straight or they may get jammed. An accessory that you might add for this purpose is the *envelope feeder*. An envelope feeder typically attaches to the front of a laser printer and feeds in envelopes, one at a time. It can hold usually between 100 and 200 envelopes.

Finishers

A printer's *finisher* does just what its name implies: It finishes the document being printed. It does this by folding, stapling, hole punching, sorting, or collating the sets of documents being printed into their final form. So rather than printing out a bunch of paper sheets and then having to collate and staple them, you can have the finisher do it. This particular option, while not cheap, is becoming more popular on laser printers to turn them into multifunction copiers. As a matter of fact, many copiers are now digital and can do all the same things that a laser printer can do but much faster and for a much cheaper cost per page.

Summary

In this chapter, we discussed how different types of printers work as well as the most common methods of connecting them to computers. You learned how computers use page-description languages to format data before they send it to printers and drivers to talk to them. You also learned about the various types of consumable supplies and how they relate to each type of printer.

The most basic category of printer currently in use is the impact printer. Impact printers form images by striking something against a ribbon, which in turn makes a mark on the paper. You learned how these printers work and the service concepts associated with them.

One of the most popular types of printer today is the inkjet printer, so named because of the mechanism used to put ink on the paper.

The most complex type of printer is the laser printer. The A+ 220-901 exam covers this type of printer more than any other. You learned about the steps in the electrophotographic

(EP) process, the process that explains how laser printers print. We also explained the various components that make up this printer and how they work together.

Virtual printing has become more popular in recent years, with people choosing to output electronic PDF files instead of physical paper.

You then learned about the interfaces used to connect printers to PCs and how to install and share a printer. Proper steps include connecting the device, installing the driver, configuring options, validating application and operating system compatibility, and educating users on how to use the device. Installing the device is the first step, but you're not done until you ensure that it works properly and that users know how to access it.

Installing network printers usually involves a few more steps than are needed to install local printers, and the device is connected to the network instead of to a host. Cloud printing is becoming more popular with the flexibility it offers, but installing cloud printers is an entirely different process than installing local and networked printers.

Finally, we looked at how to perform printer maintenance, including the importance of using recommended supplies and various types of upgrades you can install in printers.

Exam Essentials

Know the differences between types of printer technologies (for example, laser, inkjet, thermal, impact).   Laser printers use a laser and toner to create the page. Inkjet printers spray ink onto the page. Thermal printers use heat to form the characters on the page. Impact printers use a mechanical device to strike a ribbon, thus forming an image on the page.

Know the names, purposes, and characteristics of interfaces used by printers, including port and cable types.   Most printers today use the same interfaces, no matter what their type. Printers use serial, parallel, USB, Ethernet, Wi-Fi, Bluetooth, or infrared to connect to their host computers. By far the most common is USB.

Know how to install and configure printers.   The basic procedure is as follows:

1. Attach the device using a local or network port and connect the power.
2. Install and update the device driver and calibrate the device.
3. Configure options and default settings.
4. Print a test page.
5. Verify compatibility with the operating system and applications.
6. Educate users about basic functionality.

Know the seven steps in the laser printing print sequence.   The seven steps are processing, charging, exposing, developing, transferring, fusing, and cleaning.

Understand the importance of using recommended supplies.   Using consumables (paper, ink, toner) that are recommended for your printer is important. Using bad supplies could ruin your printer and void your warranty.

Understand how to upgrade printer memory and firmware.   Printer memory is upgraded by installing an additional or replacement memory module. To do this, you must remove a panel from the printer. The specific steps depend on your printer model. Firmware is upgraded by downloading a file from the manufacturer's website and installing it. Some printers require that you manually enable the added memory.

Know what environmental hazards to watch out for around printers.   Heat, excessive light, ozone, and ammonia are all bad things for printers to be around.

Review Questions

The answers to the chapter review questions can be found in Appendix A.

1. Which voltage is applied to the paper to transfer the toner to the paper in an EP process laser printer?

   A. +600VDC

   B. −600VDC

   C. +6000VDC

   D. −6000VDC

2. Which types of printers are referred to as page printers because they receive their print job instructions one page at a time? (Choose two.)

   A. Daisy wheel

   B. Dot matrix

   C. Inkjet

   D. Laser

   E. Thermal

3. Which of the following is *not* an advantage of a Universal Serial Bus (USB) printer interface?

   A. It has a higher transfer rate than a serial connection.

   B. It has a higher transfer rate than a parallel connection.

   C. It automatically recognizes new devices.

   D. It allows the printer to communicate with networks, servers, and workstations.

4. Which type of printers can be used with multipart forms?

   A. Inkjet printers

   B. Laser printers

   C. Thermal printers

   D. Dot-matrix printers

5. Which step in the EP print process uses a laser to discharge selected areas of the photosensitive drum, thus forming an image on the drum?

   A. Writing

   B. Transferring

   C. Developing

   D. Cleaning

6. Which of the following are page-description languages? (Choose two.)

   A. Page Description Language (PDL)

   B. PostScript

    C. PageScript

    D. Printer Control Language (PCL)

7. What voltage does the corona wire or corona roller hold?

    A. +600VDC

    B. –600VDC

    C. 0VDC

    D. –100VDC

8. Which device in an inkjet printer contains the print head?

    A. Toner cartridge

    B. Ink cartridge

    C. Daisy wheel

    D. Paper tray

9. What is the correct order of the steps in the EP print process?

    A. Developing, exposing, transferring, fusing, charging, cleaning, processing

    B. Charging, processing, exposing, developing, transferring, fusing, cleaning

    C. Processing, transferring, exposing, developing, charging, cleaning, fusing

    D. Processing, charging, exposing, developing, transferring, fusing, cleaning

10. Most printers that use the electrophotographic process contain how many standard assemblies?

    A. Five

    B. Six

    C. Four

    D. Nine

11. What is typically included in the EP laser printer toner cartridge? (Choose three.)

    A. Toner

    B. Print drum

    C. Laser

    D. Cleaning blade

12. What happens during the developing stage of laser printing?

    A. An electrostatic charge is applied to the drum to attract toner particles.

    B. Heat is applied to the paper to melt the toner.

    C. The laser creates an image of the page on the drum.

    D. An electrostatic charge is applied to the paper to attract toner particles.

13. Which of the following are possible interfaces for printers? (Choose three.)

    A. Parallel

    B. PS/2

    C. USB

    D. Network

14. You have just installed a new printer. After it is installed, it prints only garbled text. Which of the following is likely the problem?

    A. Wrong IP address

    B. Worn print head

    C. Incorrect print drivers

    D. Unsupported printer

15. Which printer contains a wheel that looks like a flower with raised letters and symbols on each petal?

    A. Inkjet printers

    B. Daisy-wheel printer

    C. Dot-matrix printer

    D. Laser printer

16. What part of a laser printer supplies the voltages for charging and transferring corona assemblies?

    A. High-voltage power supply (HVPS)

    B. DC power supply (DCPS)

    C. Controller circuitry

    D. Transfer corona

17. Which printer part gets the toner from the photosensitive drum onto the paper?

    A. Laser-scanning assembly

    B. Fusing assembly

    C. Corona assembly

    D. Drum

18. Which step in the laser printer printing process occurs immediately after the exposing phase?

    A. Charging

    B. Fusing

    C. Transferring

    D. Developing

19. Which laser printer component permanently presses the toner into the paper?

    A. Transfer corona

    B. Fuser assembly

    C.   Printer controller circuitry

    D.   Paper transport assembly

20. Which of the following most accurately describes how to obtain a firmware upgrade for your laser printer?

    A.   Download the firmware upgrade for free from the manufacturer's website.

    B.   Pay to download the firmware upgrade from the manufacturer's website.

    C.   Have a certified laser printer technician come to your site and install a new firmware chip.

    D.   Contact the manufacturer of the printer, and they will send you the firmware upgrade on a CD.

Performance-Based Question

You will encounter performance-based questions on the A+ exams. The questions on the exam require you to perform a specific task, and you will be graded on whether or not you were able to complete the task. The following requires you to think creatively in order to measure how well you understand this chapter's topics. You may or may not see similar questions on the actual A+ exams. To see how your answer compares to the authors', refer to Appendix B.

Your network has several inkjet printers in use. A user is complaining that their documents are consistently printing with extra smudges along the lines of print on one of them. What steps would you take to clean the printer?

Chapter

12

Hardware and Network Troubleshooting

THE FOLLOWING COMPTIA A+ EXAM 220-901 OBJECTIVES ARE COVERED IN THIS CHAPTER:

✓ **2.9 Given a scenario, use appropriate networking tools.**

- Crimper
- Cable stripper
- Multimeter
- Tone generator & probe
- Cable tester
- Loopback plug
- Punchdown tool
- WiFi analyzer

✓ **4.1 Given a scenario, troubleshoot common problems related to motherboards, RAM, CPU, and power with appropriate tools.**

- Common symptoms
  - Unexpected shutdowns
  - System lockups
  - POST code beeps
  - Blank screen on bootup
  - BIOS time and settings resets
  - Attempts to boot to incorrect device
  - Continuous reboots
  - No power

- Overheating
- Loud noise
- Intermittent device failure
- Fans spin – no power to other devices
- Indicator lights
- Smoke
- Burning smell
- Proprietary crash screens (BSOD/pin wheel)
- Distended capacitors
- Tools
  - Multimeter
  - Power supply tester
  - Loopback plugs
  - POST card / USB

✓ **4.2 Given a scenario, troubleshoot hard drives and RAID arrays with appropriate tools.**

- Common symptoms
  - Read/write failure
  - Slow performance
  - Loud clicking noise
  - Failure to boot
  - Drive not recognized
  - OS not found
  - RAID not found
  - RAID stops working
  - Proprietary crash screens (BSOD/pin wheel)
  - S.M.A.R.T errors
- Tools
  - Screwdriver
  - External enclosures

- CHKDSK
- FORMAT
- File recovery software
- Bootrec
- Diskpart
- Defragmentation tool

✓ **4.3   Given a scenario, troubleshoot common video, projector, and display issues.**

- Common symptoms
  - VGA mode
  - No image on screen
  - Overheat shutdown
  - Dead pixels
  - Artifacts
  - Color patterns incorrect
  - Dim image
  - Flickering image
  - Distorted image
  - Distorted geometry
  - Burn-in
  - Oversized images and icons

✓ **4.4   Given a scenario, troubleshoot wired and wireless networks with appropriate tools.**

- Common symptoms
  - No connectivity
  - APIPA/link local address
  - Limited connectivity
  - Local connectivity
  - Intermittent connectivity
  - IP conflict

- Slow transfer speeds
- Low RF signal
- SSID not found
- Tools
  - Cable tester
  - Loopback plug
  - Punch down tools
  - Tone generator and probe
  - Wire strippers
  - Crimper
  - Wireless locator
- Command line tools
  - PING
  - IPCONFIG/IFCONFIG
  - TRACERT
  - NETSTAT
  - NBTSTAT
  - NET
  - NETDOM
  - NSLOOKUP

✓ **4.5 Given a scenario, troubleshoot and repair common mobile device issues while adhering to the appropriate procedures.**

- Common symptoms
  - No display
  - Dim display
  - Flickering display
  - Sticking keys
  - Intermittent wireless
  - Battery not charging
  - Ghost cursor/pointer drift

- No power
- Numlock indicator lights
- No wireless connectivity
- No Bluetooth connectivity
- Cannot display to external monitor
- Touchscreen non-responsive
- Apps not loading
- Slow performance
- Unable to decrypt email
- Extremely short battery life
- Overheating
- Frozen system
- No sound from speakers
- GPS not functioning
- Swollen battery
- Disassembling processes for proper re-assembly
  - Document and label cable and screw locations
  - Organize parts
  - Refer to manufacturer documentation
  - Use appropriate hand tools

✓ **4.6   Given a scenario, troubleshoot printers with appropriate tools.**

- Common symptoms
  - Streaks
  - Faded prints
  - Ghost images
  - Toner not fused to the paper
  - Creased paper
  - Paper not feeding
  - Paper jam

- No connectivity
- Garbled characters on paper
- Vertical lines on page
- Backed up print queue
- Low memory errors
- Access denied
- Printer will not print
- Color prints in wrong print color
- Unable to install printer
- Error codes
- Printing blank pages
- No image on printer display
- Tools
  - Maintenance kit
  - Toner vacuum
  - Compressed air
  - Printer spooler

Troubleshooting can be hard. With all of the integration between software applications and hardware components, it can be challenging to understand where one stops and the other starts, or how their interoperation affects one another. To top it all off, you're probably going to be working in an environment that requires you to understand not just one computer but a network full of workstations, servers, switches, routers, and other devices and how they should play nicely together. Situations will arise that make even the most experienced technicians shake their heads in frustration.

Sometimes, you will hear people say things like, "It just takes practice and experience to become good at troubleshooting." Those words are of little comfort to someone who is relatively new and facing a challenging problem. Yes experience does help, but even newer technicians can be effective troubleshooters if they understand the fundamentals and follow a logical process.

Objective 5.5 of the second A+ exam (the 220-902 exam) asks you to understand the steps of troubleshooting theory. That will be great background for you to have. However, because hardware troubleshooting is an objective of the 220-901 exam, we need to cover the topic before diving into the theory. It may feel a bit like we're putting the cart before the horse, but we'll give you some high-level pointers now to get you started before addressing specific issues.

The best way to tackle any problem is to take a systematic approach to resolving it. This applies to the hardware and networking issues that we'll talk about here as well as the software and security issues that we will cover in Chapter 22, "Troubleshooting Theory, OSs, and Security." Troubleshooting becomes a lot easier if you follow logical procedures to help you develop experience. The first thing to do is always to check the easy stuff, such as physical cables and connections. You would be amazed at how many times the simple question, "Is it plugged in?" resolves hardware problems. Second, see if anything has recently changed or if there are any recent incidents that might have caused the problem. For example, if someone's laptop won't boot up, you might not have a clue as to why. But if they tell you that they just dropped it down the stairs, you might have a better idea of where to start. Finally, narrow down the scope of the problem. Find out exactly what works and what doesn't. Knowing where the problem starts and stops helps you to focus your troubleshooting efforts.

For more specifics on troubleshooting theory and methods, see Chapter 22.

There's one last thing to remember before getting into the details of specific problems: In order to troubleshoot anything, you need to have a base level of knowledge. For example, if you've never opened the hood of a car, it will be a bit challenging for you to figure out why your car won't start in the morning. If you're not a medical professional, you might not know why that body part hurts or how to make it feel better. In the same vein, if you don't know how data is stored and accessed on a computer, it's unlikely that you'll be able to fix related computer problems. So before you get too heavy into troubleshooting, make sure you understand how the systems on which you are working are supposed to function in the first place!

Because this chapter comes after the hardware and networking chapters, we're going to assume that you've read them already. Therefore, we're not going to get into a lot of detail about how things work—it's assumed that you know those details by now. (If you're still not certain, this book is a great reference manual!) Instead, we'll talk more about what happens when things don't work the way they're supposed to: what signs to look for and what to do to fix the problem. The first part of this chapter will cover key internal hardware components. After that, we'll look at issues specific to mobile devices and printers and then finish off the chapter with a section on network troubleshooting.

Troubleshooting Core Hardware Issues

To many who are not familiar with computers, that whirring, humming box sitting under or on their desk is an enigma. They know what shows up on the screen, where the power button is, where to put DVDs, and what not to spill on their keyboard. But the insides are shrouded in mystery.

Fortunately for them, we're around. We can tell the difference between a hard drive and a motherboard and have a pretty good idea of what each part inside that box is supposed to do. When the computer doesn't work like it's supposed to, we can whip out our trusty screwdriver, crack the case, and perform surgery. And most of the time, we can get the system running just as good as new.

In the following sections, we're going to focus our troubleshooting efforts on the key hardware components inside the case, but we're also going to include monitors (which are attached to video cards inside the case, so close enough for our purposes). We will start off with motherboards, processors, memory, and power. Then we will look at storage devices and finish off the discussion with video and display issues.

The following sections will focus primarily on desktop computers. Laptop issues will be covered in their own section later in this chapter.

Troubleshooting Motherboards, CPUs, RAM, and Power Problems

These components are the brains, backbone, and nervous system of your computer. Without a network card, you won't be able to surf the Web. Without a processor, well, you won't be able to surf the Web—or do much of anything else for that matter. So we'll get started with these components.

As you continue to learn and increase your troubleshooting experience, your value will increase as well. This is because, if nothing else, it will take you less time to accomplish common repairs. Your ability to troubleshoot from past experiences and gut feelings will make you more efficient and more valuable, which in turn will allow you to advance and earn a better income. We will give you some guidelines that you can use to evaluate common hardware issues that you're sure to face.

Identifying Hardware Symptoms and Causes

Before we get into specific components, let's take a few minutes to talk about hardware symptoms and their causes at a general level. This discussion can apply to a lot of different hardware components.

Some hardware issues are pretty easy to identify. If there are flames shooting out of the back of your computer, then it's probably the power supply. If the power light on your monitor doesn't turn on, it's the monitor itself, the power cord, or your power source. Other hardware symptoms are a bit more ambiguous. We'll now look at some hardware-related symptoms and their possible causes.

Excessive Heat

Electronic components produce heat; it's a fact of life. While they're designed to withstand a certain amount of the heat that's produced, excessive heat can drastically shorten the life of components. There are two common ways to reduce heat-related problems in computers: heat sinks and cooling systems, such as case fans.

Any component with its own processor will have a heat sink. Typically these look like big, finned hunks of aluminum or another metal attached to the processor. Their job is to dissipate heat from the component so that it doesn't become too hot. Never run a processor without a heat sink!

 WARNING One way to ensure that your processor dies quickly is to overclock it. Overclocking is running the processor faster than it was designed to run. While it may work in the short run, it's never a good idea to do this!

Case fans are designed to take hot air from inside the case and blow it out of the case. There are many different designs, from simple motors to high-tech liquid-cooled models. Put your hand up to the back of your computer at the power supply fan and you should feel warm air. If there's nothing coming out, you either need to clean your fan out or replace your power supply. Some cases come with additional cooling fans to help dissipate heat. If your case has one, you should feel warm air coming from it as well.

Computers are like human beings: They have similar tolerances to heat and cold. In general, anything comfortable to us is comfortable to computers, although they do tend to like it colder than many of us do. They need lots of clean, moving air to keep them functioning.

We've mentioned dust before and now is a good time to bring it up again. Dust, dirt, grime, paint, smoke, and other airborne particles can become caked on the inside of the components. This is most common in automotive and manufacturing environments. The contaminants create a film that coats the components, causing them to overheat and/ or conduct electricity on their surface. Blowing out these exposed systems with a can of compressed air from time to time can prevent damage to the components. While you're cleaning the components, be sure to clean any cooling fans in the power supply or on the heat sink.

To clean the power supply fan, blow the air from the inside of the case. When you do this, the fan will blow the contaminants out the cooling vents. If you spray from the vents toward the inside of the box, you'll be blowing the dust and grime inside the case or back into the fan motor.

One way to ensure that dust and grime don't find their way into your computer is to always leave the *blanks* (or slot covers) in the empty slots on the back of your box. Blanks are the pieces of metal or plastic that come with the case and cover the expansion slot openings. They are designed to keep dirt, dust, and other foreign matter from the inside of the computer. They also maintain proper airflow within the case to ensure that the computer doesn't overheat.

Noise

Have you ever been working on a computer and heard a noise that resembles fingernails on a chalkboard? If so, you will always remember that sound, along with the impending feeling of doom as the computer stops working.

Some noises on a computer are normal. The POST beep (which we'll talk about in a few pages) is a good sound. The whirring of a mechanical hard drive and power supply fan are familiar sounds. Some techs get so used to their "normal" system noises that if anything is slightly off pitch, they go digging for problems even if none are readily apparent.

Creeping Chips

The inside of a computer is a harsh environment. The temperature inside the case of many computers is well over 100° F! When you turn on your computer, it heats up. Turn it off, and it cools down. After several hundred such cycles, some components can't handle the stress, and they begin to move out of their sockets. This phenomenon is known as *chip creep*, and it can be really frustrating.

Chip creep can affect any socketed device, including ICs, RAM chips, and expansion cards. The solution to chip creep is simple: Open the case, and reseat the devices. It's surprising how often this is the solution to phantom problems of all sorts, particularly intermittent device failures, random reboots, and unexpected shutdowns.

For the most part, the components that can produce noise problems are those that move. Mechanical hard drives have motors that spin the platters. Power supply fans spin. CD and DVD drives spin the disks. If you're hearing excessive noise, these are the likely culprits.

If you hear a whining sound and it seems to be fairly constant, it's more than likely a fan. Either it needs to be cleaned (desperately) or replaced. Power supplies that are failing can also sound louder and quieter intermittently because a fan will run at alternating speeds.

The "fingernails on a chalkboard" squealing could be an indicator that the heads in a mechanical hard drive have crashed into the platter. This thankfully doesn't seem to be as common today as it used to be, but it still happens. Note that this type of sound can also be caused by a power supply fan's motor binding up. A rhythmic ticking sound is also likely to be caused by a mechanical hard drive.

Problems with the CD-ROM or DVD-ROM drive tend to be the easiest to diagnose. Those drives aren't constantly spinning unless you put some media in them. If you put a disc in and the drive makes a terrible noise, you have a good idea what's causing the problem.

So what do you do if you hear a terrible noise from the computer? If it's still responsive, shut it down normally as soon as possible. If it's not responsive, then shut off the power as quickly as you can. Examine the power supply to see if there are any obvious problems such as excessive dust, and clean it as needed. Power the system back on. If the noise was caused by the hard drive, odds are that the drive has failed and the system won't boot normally. You may need to replace some parts.

If the noise is mildly annoying but doesn't sound drastic, boot up the computer with the case off and listen. By getting up close and personal with the system, you can often tell where the noise is coming from and then troubleshoot or fix the appropriate part.

WARNING   Never touch internal components when the case is off and the power is on! Doing so could result in a severe electrical shock to you and/or the components.

Odors and Smoke

Bad smells or smoke coming from your computer are never good things. While it normally gets pretty warm inside a computer case, it should never be hot enough inside there to melt plastic components, but it does happen from time to time. And power problems can sometimes cause components to get hot enough to smoke.

If you smell an odd odor or see smoke coming from a computer, shut it down immediately. Open the case and start looking for visible signs of damage. Things to look for include melted plastic components and burn marks on circuit boards. If components appear to be damaged, it's best to replace them before returning the computer to service.

If you have scorch marks on a component, say a video card or a motherboard, it could be that the specific component went bad. It could also be a sign of a problem with the power supply. If you replace the component and a similar problem occurs, definitely replace the power supply.

Status Light Indicators

Many hardware devices have status light indicators that can help you identify operational features or problems with a device. Obviously, when you power on a system, you expect the power light to come on. If it doesn't, you have a problem. The same holds true for other external devices, such as wireless routers, external hard drives, and printers. In situations in which the power light doesn't come on and the device has no power, always obey the first rule of troubleshooting: Check your connections first!

Beyond power indicators, several types of devices have additional lights that can help you troubleshoot. If you have a hub, switch, or other connectivity device, you should have an indicator for each port that lights up when there is a connection. Some devices will give you a green light for a good connection and a yellow or red light if they detect a problem. A lot of connectivity devices will also have an indicator that blinks or flashes when traffic is going through the port. Sometimes it's the same light that indicates a connection, but at other times it's a separate indicator. The same holds true for NICs. They usually have a connectivity light and a transmission light. If no lights are illuminated, it can indicate a lack of connection.

Many computers also have hard drive activity lights. When disk reads or writes occur, the light will blink, otherwise it will be off. A hard drive indicator that is constantly on is generally not a good sign; it could indicate that the hard drive is constantly busy or that the system is frozen, either of which is bad.

Most keyboards will have status lights for the Caps Lock and Num Lock keys. If you believe a system is locked up, try pressing the Caps Lock or Num Lock key on the keyboard to see if the lights change. If they don't, that's a sign that the system is unresponsive. If no lights ever illuminate on the keyboard, it could be that the keyboard is disconnected or that there is a system power issue.

If you have a device with lights and you're not sure what they mean, it's best to check the manual or the manufacturer's website to learn about them.

The manufacturer's website is generally a great place to go for troubleshooting tips!

Alerts

An alert is a message generated by a hardware device. In some cases, the device has a display panel that will tell you what the alert is. A good example of this is an office printer. Many have an LCD display that can tell you if something is wrong. Other devices, particularly rack-mounted servers or connectivity devices, will have status lights that indicate that there's an issue.

Other alerts will pop up on the computer screen. If the device is attached to a specific computer, the alert will generally pop up on that computer's screen. Some devices can be configured to send an alert to a specific user account or system administrator, so the administrator will get the alert regardless of which computer they are currently logged into.

 Operating system errors and alerts are generally logged in an event log, such as Windows Event Viewer. Troubleshooting operating system errors is an objective on the 220-902 exam, and we cover Event Viewer in Chapter 22.

Visible Damage

The good news about visible damage is that you can usually figure out which component is damaged pretty quickly. The bad news is that it often means you need to replace parts.

Visible damage to the outside of the case or the monitor casing might not matter much as long as the device still works. But if you're looking inside a case and see burn marks or melted components, that's a sure sign of a problem. Replace damaged circuit boards or melted plastic components immediately. After replacing the part, it's a good idea to monitor the new component for a while too. It could be the power supply causing the problem. If the new part fries quickly too, it's time to replace the power supply as well.

POST Routines

Every computer has a diagnostic program built into its basic input/output system (BIOS) called the *power-on self-test (POST)*. When you turn on the computer, it executes this set of diagnostics. Many steps are involved in the POST, but they happen very quickly, they're invisible to the user, and they vary among BIOS vendors. The steps include checking the CPU, checking the RAM, checking for the presence of a video card, and verifying basic hardware functionality. The main reason to be aware of the POST's existence is that if it encounters a problem, the boot process stops. Being able to determine at what point the problem occurred could help you troubleshoot.

If the computer doesn't perform the POST as it should, one way to determine the source of a problem is to listen for a *beep code*. This is a series of beeps from the computer's speaker. A successful POST generally produces a single beep. If there's more than one beep, the number, duration, and pattern of the beeps can sometimes tell you what component is causing the problem. However, the beeps differ depending on the BIOS manufacturer and version, so you must look up the beep code in a chart for your particular BIOS. AMI BIOS, for example, relies on the number of beeps and uses patterns of short and long beeps.

Another way to determine a problem during the POST routine is to use a *POST card*. This is a circuit board that fits into an expansion slot (PCI or PCIe) in the motherboard and reports numeric codes as the boot process progresses. Each of those codes corresponds to a particular component being checked. If the POST card stops at a certain number, you can look up that number in the manual for the card to determine the problem. Figure 12.1 shows an example of a PCI POST card. You will find newer POST cards that have a USB connection on them, which makes them easier to use. You don't have to crack the case to check for POST errors, and they can be used to test laptops as well.

FIGURE 12.1   PCI POST card

POST card 98usd by Rumlin—Own work. Licensed under CC BY-SA 3.0 via Wikimedia Commons http://commons.wikimedia.org/wiki/File:POST_card_98usd.jpg#/media/ File:POST_card_98usd.jpg

Motherboard manufacturers tend to use different beep codes to indicate different error messages. If you're getting a beep code during POST, check the Internet for information on what the beep code means. A good reference site is BIOS Central; for example, you can find AMI BIOS beep codes at www.bioscentral.com/beepcodes/amibeep.htm You can also visit the manufacturer's website.

Identifying BIOS Issues

Because we just talked about the POST routine, which is a function of the BIOS, let's look at a few other BIOS issues as well. First, computer BIOSs don't go bad; they just become out-of-date. This isn't necessarily a critical issue—they will continue to support the hardware that came with the box. It *does*, however, become an issue when the BIOS doesn't support some component that you would like to install—a larger hard drive, for instance.

Most of today's BIOSs are written to an EEPROM and can be updated through the use of software. This process is called "flashing the BIOS." Each manufacturer has its own method for accomplishing this. Check the documentation for complete details.

WARNING
If you make a mistake in the upgrade process, the computer can become unbootable. If this happens, your only option may be to ship the box to a manufacturer-approved service center. Be careful!

A fairly common issue with the BIOS is when it fails to retain your computer's settings, such as time and date and hard drive configuration. The BIOS uses a small battery (much like a watch battery) on the motherboard to help it retain settings when the system power is off. If this battery fails, the BIOS won't retain its settings. Simply replace the battery to solve the problem.

Finally, remember that your BIOS also contains the boot sequence for your system. You probably boot to the first hard drive in your system (the one that contains the OS boot files), but you can also set your BIOS to boot from a secondary hard drive, the optical drive, or the network. If your computer can't find a proper boot device, it could be that it's attempting to boot from the wrong device. Check the BIOS to see if you need to change the boot sequence. To do this, reboot the system, and look for the message telling you to press a certain key to enter the BIOS (usually something like F2). Once you're in the BIOS, find the menu with the boot sequence (like the one shown in Figure 12.2) and set it to the desired order. If the changes don't hold the next time you reboot, check the battery!

FIGURE 12.2 BIOS boot sequence settings

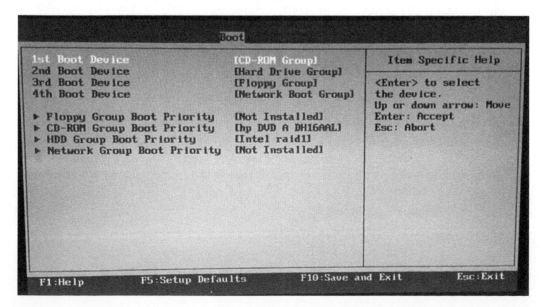

There may be times that you want to boot to an alternate device such as the optical drive. During the part of the boot process when the BIOS entry key is shown, most systems will also show you an alternate key to press (such as the spacebar) to boot from the CD-ROM. This can be very helpful when troubleshooting a system that won't load the OS properly, as long as you have the installation disc handy.

Identifying Motherboard and CPU Problems

Most motherboard and CPU problems manifest themselves by the system appearing to be completely dead. However, "completely dead" can be a symptom of a wide variety of problems, not only with the CPU or motherboard but also with the RAM or the power supply. At other times, a failing motherboard or CPU will cause the system to lock up completely, or "hang," requiring a hard reboot, or the failing motherboard or CPU may cause continuous reboots. A POST card may be helpful in narrowing down the exact component that is faulty.

When a motherboard fails, it's usually because it has been damaged. Most technicians can't repair motherboard damage; the motherboard must be replaced. Motherboards can become damaged due to physical trauma, exposure to electrostatic discharge (ESD), or short-circuiting. To minimize the risk, observe the following rules:

- Handle a motherboard as little as possible, and keep it in an antistatic bag whenever it's removed from the PC case.

- Keep all liquids well away from the motherboard; water can cause a short circuit.

- Wear an antistatic wrist strap when handling or touching a motherboard.

- When installing a motherboard in a case, make sure you use brass standoffs with paper or plastic washers to prevent any stray solder around the screw holes from causing a short circuit with the metal of the screw.

A CPU may fail because of physical trauma or short-circuiting, but the most common cause for a CPU not to work is overheating, and most overheating issues are due to installation failures. This means that the heat sink and/or fan must be installed properly along with the processor. With a PGA- or LGA-style CPU, ensure that the CPU is oriented correctly in the socket. With an older SECC- or ZIF-style CPU, make sure the CPU is completely inserted into its slot or socket.

Identifying I/O Port and Cable Problems

Input/output (I/O) ports are most often built into the motherboard and include legacy parallel and serial, USB, and FireWire ports. All of them are used to connect external peripherals to the motherboard. When a port doesn't appear to be functioning, make sure the following conditions are met:

- The cables are snugly connected.

- The port has not been disabled in BIOS Setup.

- The port has not been disabled in Device Manager in Windows.

- No pins are broken or bent on the male end of the port or on the cable being plugged into it.

If you suspect that it's the port, you can purchase a loopback plug to test its functionality. If you suspect that the cable, rather than the port, may be the problem, swap out the cable with a known good one. If you don't have an extra cable, you can test the existing cable with a multimeter by setting it to ohms and checking the resistance between one end of the cable and the other.

Use a pin-out diagram, if available, to determine which pin matches up to which at the other end. There is often—but not always—an inverse relationship between the ends. In other words, at one end pin 1 is at the left, and at the other end it's at the right on the same row of pins. You see this characteristic with D-sub connectors where one end of the cable is male and the other end is female.

Distended Capacitors

Many motherboards have capacitors on them, which store electricity. They are short cylindrical tubes. Figure 12.3 shows three of them on the left side of the motherboard. Sometimes, when capacitors fail, they will bulge and brownish-red electrolyte residue may seep out of the vents in the top. These are called *distended capacitors*. If a capacitor fails, the motherboard will not work. You have a few options. The first and probably best option is to replace the motherboard. Whatever you do, do *not* touch the residue coming from a distended capacitor! The second option is to drain the energy from the failed capacitor and replace it. Only do this if you have specialized training on how to deal safely with capacitors because they can cause lethal shocks.

FIGURE 12.3   Capacitors on a motherboard

Identifying Memory Issues

Isolating memory issues on a computer is one of the more difficult tasks to do properly because so many memory problems manifest themselves as software issues. For example, memory problems can cause applications to fail and produce error messages such as general protection faults (GPFs). Memory issues can also cause a fatal error in your operating system, producing the infamous Blue Screen of Death (BSOD) in Windows or the rotating pinwheel in OS X, which we will discuss later, in Chapter 22. Sometimes these are caused by the physical memory failing. At other times, they are caused by bad programming, when an application writes into a memory space reserved for the operating system or another application.

In short, memory problems can cause system lockups, unexpected shutdowns or reboots, or the errors mentioned in the preceding paragraph. They can be challenging to pin down. If you do get an error message related to memory, be sure to write down the memory address if the error message gives you one. If the error happens again, write down the memory address again. If it's the same or a similar address, then it's very possible that the physical memory is failing. You can also use one of several hardware- or software-based RAM testers to see if your memory is working properly.

Memory issues can also be caused by the virtual memory, which is an area of the hard drive set aside to emulate memory. The operating system creates and manages a paging file on the hard drive to act as memory when the system needs more than what the physical RAM can provide; oftentimes, this paging file is dynamic in size. If the hard drive runs out of room for the paging file, memory issues can appear. As a rule of thumb, ensure that at least 10 percent of the hard drive space is free. (Virtual memory is discussed further in Chapter 14, "Operating System Administration.")

Identifying Power Supply and Cooling Problems

Power supply problems can manifest themselves in two ways. In the first, you will see an obvious problem such as an electrical flash or possibly a fire. In the second, the system doesn't respond in any way when the power is turned on. Hopefully you don't have to deal with many of the first type!

Recall from Chapter 2, "Storage Devices and Power Supplies," that power supplies have a voltage switch on the back to change from 110v–120v power to 220v–240v power to meet different countries' power specifications. If a computer has been moved from one country to another, make sure that it's on the right setting before you plug it in and try to power it up!

When the system doesn't respond when you try to power it up, try a new power cable and make sure the outlet is functional. If those check out, open the case, remove the power supply, and replace it with a new one. Partial failures, or intermittent power supply problems, are much less simple. A completely failed power supply gives the same symptoms as a malfunctioning wall socket, uninterruptible power supply (UPS), or power strip; a power cord that is not securely seated; or some motherboard shorts (such as those caused by an improperly seated expansion card, memory stick, CPU, and the like). You want to rule out those items before you replace the power supply and find that you still have the same problem as when you started. At other times, the power supply fan might spin but the rest of the system does not appear to get power. This can be a power supply issue or possibly a motherboard (POST) issue. Be aware that different cases have different types of on/off switches. The process of replacing a power supply is a lot easier if you purchase a replacement with the same mechanism.

 Real World Scenario

Hot, Hot, Hot

Several years ago, the company with which one of the authors was working got in a batch of hardware that it had purchased from another company. He and another tech were building Frankensteins out of the plethora of parts they had.

They put RAM into one of the systems and powered it on. Immediately there was an electrical arc from the RAM to the motherboard, so they shut it back off. The arc was present for a split second, and they had the box powered down within a second or two after that.

The RAM module had a pretty obvious burn mark on it, so the author went to take it out and promptly scorched his fingers when he touched it. It was searing hot! They let it cool down for about 20 minutes before going back to take it out. The moral of the story: Be careful not to burn yourself on fried components.

Incidentally, they put a new motherboard and new RAM into the same case and powered it up only to see the exact same thing happen. Fried. (Fortunately, the author was smart enough not to burn himself a second time!) The verdict? Bad power supply. After replacing the power supply and trying a third motherboard and RAM combination, they had a functioning system.

If you're curious as to the state of your power supply, you can buy hardware-based power supply testers online starting at about $10 and running up to several hundred dollars. Multimeters are also effective devices for testing your power supplies.

Never try to repair or disassemble a power supply. They contain capacitors that can store a lethal amount of electricity, even when they are powered off and have been unplugged. The high risk of electrocution and the relatively low cost of a new power supply makes working on them something to avoid.

Identifying Cooling Issues

A PC that works for a few minutes and then locks up is probably experiencing overheating because of a heat sink or fan not functioning properly. To troubleshoot overheating, first check all fans inside the PC to ensure that they're operating, and make sure that any heat sinks are firmly attached to their chips.

In a properly designed, properly assembled PC case, air flows in a specific path driven by the power supply fan and using the power supply's vent holes. Make sure that you know the direction of flow and that there are limited obstructions and no dust buildup. Cases are also designed to cool by making the air flow in a certain way. Therefore, operating a PC with the cover removed can make a PC more susceptible to overheating, even though it's "getting more air."

Similarly, operating a PC with expansion-slot covers removed can inhibit a PC's ability to cool itself properly because the extra holes change the airflow pattern from what was intended by its design.

Although CPUs are the most common component to overheat, occasionally other chips on the motherboard, such as the chipset or chips on other devices, particularly video cards, may also overheat. Extra heat sinks or fans may be installed to cool these chips.

Liquid cooling systems have their own set of issues. The pump that moves the liquid through the tubing and heat sinks can become obstructed or simply fail. If this happens, the liquid's temperature will eventually equalize with that of the CPU and other components, resulting in their damage. Dust in the heat sinks has the same effect as with nonliquid cooling systems, so keep these components as clean as you would with any such components. Check regularly for signs of leaks that might be starting, and try to catch them before they result in damage to the system.

Exercise 12.1 walks you through the steps of troubleshooting a few specific hardware problems. The exercise will probably end up being a mental one for you, unless you have the exact problem that we're describing here. As practice, you can write down the steps that you would take to solve the problem and then check to see how close you came to our steps. Clearly, there are several ways to approach a problem, so you might use a slightly different process, but the general approach should be similar. Finally, when you have found the problem, you can stop. As you go through each step, assume that it didn't solve the issue so you need to move on to the next step.

For additional troubleshooting experience, you can watch videos on YouTube or iFixIt.com. There are many great examples for hundreds of different types of problems!

EXERCISE 12.1

Troubleshooting Practice

Issue One: Blank screen on bootup. You turn the computer on, and there's nothing on the screen.

1. Check to make sure the monitor is on. Is its power light on?

    Seriously. Check it. Sometimes 5 seconds of checking the obvious can save you an hour of wasted time.

2. Is the monitor getting a signal?

    Some monitors will go into sleep mode if they don't get a signal. Check the connections. If all the connections are good and you're not getting a signal, it could be the video card.

3. Did the system POST properly? Did you get a POST beep or a beep code?

    No POST likely indicates a bigger problem than just the video card or the monitor. If you do get a POST beep but never see anything, try a different monitor.

4. Did you ever see anything on the screen? BIOS information? Did the OS start to load and then it went blank?

    The key to troubleshooting an ambiguous situation like this is to ask yourself, "What is the last thing that worked as it was supposed to?" That will help you determine what you need to fix.

Issue Two: The power supply fan spins, but no other devices have power.

1. Did you hear a POST beep or a beep code?

    Odds are you that didn't get any sounds, but it's always good to reboot and double-check.

2. Disconnect all internal and external peripherals so that the only component drawing power is the motherboard (with CPU and RAM, of course). Does it POST then?

    If you disconnect everything and it still doesn't POST, odds are that your motherboard is fried. If it POSTs, then start plugging components back in one at a time, starting with your hard drive and other internal devices and working your way to the external peripherals. You'll eventually get to the part that's causing the problem.

3. If you have a power supply tester or multimeter, now would be a good time to make sure that the power supply is working properly. There's no sense in replacing components, such as the motherboard, if the power supply is just going to fry them!

    Again, with all troubleshooting, it's imperative to narrow down the problem to isolate the cause. If you can do that, then fixing it should be the easy part.

Troubleshooting Storage Device Problems

Storage devices present unique problems simply due to their nature. Most of them are devices with moving parts, which means that they are more prone to mechanical failure than a motherboard or a stick of RAM. (SSDs are the exception.) In the following sections, we'll discuss hard disk problems, including RAID arrays. Then we'll take a quick look at optical drive issues.

Identifying Hard Disk System Problems

Hard disk system problems usually stem from one of three causes:

- The adapter (that is, the SATA or PATA interface) is bad.
- The disk is bad.
- The adapter and disk are connected incorrectly.

The first and last causes are easy to identify, because in either case, the symptom will be obvious: the drive won't work. You won't be able to get the computer to communicate with the disk drive.

However, if the problem is a bad disk drive, the symptoms aren't as obvious. As long as the POST routines can communicate with the disk drive, they're usually satisfied. But the POST routines may not uncover problems related to storing information. Even with healthy POST results, you may find that you're permitted to save information to a bad disk, but when you try to read it back, you get errors. Or the computer may not boot as quickly as it used to because the disk drive can't read the boot information successfully every time.

Software utilities used to manage hard drives include CHKDSK, FORMAT, BOOTREC, DISKPART, and DEFRAG (disk defragmenter). These are covered in detail in Chapter 14.

Let's take a look at some specific hard-drive related issues, the likely culprits, and actions to take:

Loud clicking or scratching noises   You will only hear these coming from mechanical drives, and they are usually caused by a physical malfunction within the drive itself. If the drive is still usable, back up the information on it as soon as possible. The drive is going to stop working in short order. It's time to brandish the screwdriver and replace the hard drive.

Slow performance or read/write failures   A failing hard drive might exhibit these symptoms. They can also be a symptom of the hard drive being too full. Hard drives move information around a lot, especially temporary files. If the drive doesn't have enough free space (at least 10 percent), it can slow down dramatically. The solution here is to remove files or old applications to free up space and look at defragmenting the hard drive. If problems persist, consider formatting the hard drive and reinstalling the OS. If the issues don't go away, assume that the hard drive is on its last legs.

Boot problems   This could be any of a number of problems, such as a complete failure to boot, the hard drive not being recognized by the BIOS, or the OS not being found. Failure to boot at all likely means the drive is dead. Do your due diligence and reseat your connections and make sure that the BIOS recognizes the drive before replacing it. Most BIOSs today auto-detect the hard drive. If that auto-detection fails, it's bad news for the hard drive unless there's a cable, connection, or jumper issue (for example, if you just added a new hard drive, the master/slave jumper could be set incorrectly). Finally, if the system boots fine but it can't find the OS, it could indicate a problem with the Master Boot Record (MBR). You can boot from a bootable disk and repair the MBR with BOOTREC /FIXMBR (Windows Vista and newer).

   Failed reads and writes from hard drives can also cause the operating system to crash, resulting in a BSOD or pinwheel error.

S.M.A.R.T.

As of 2004, nearly every hard drive has been built with *Self-Monitoring, Analysis, and Reporting Technology (S.M.A.R.T.)* software installed on them, which monitors hard drive reliability and theoretically can warn you in the event of an imminent failure. The idea behind S.M.A.R.T. is great. Who wouldn't want to know when their hard drive was going to fail so they could back up the drive? In practice, though, it seems to help manufacturers locate persistent issues by identifying hard drive design flaws more than it helps end users avoid catastrophic data losses. Helping hard drive manufacturers do a better job isn't a bad thing, but S.M.A.R.T. hasn't enjoyed widespread commercial success with end users. This can largely be attributed to three factors:

- Windows OSs don't come with a built-in graphical utility to parse the data.

- The 70 metrics provided by S.M.A.R.T. aren't always easy to understand, and there has been little guidance as to which metric or metrics are most closely associated with impending drive failure.

- Manufacturers have not consistently defined the metrics among themselves; there are no industry-wide analysis applications or standards for this technology.

Let's address the three issues in order. First, you can download one of several graphical tools from the Internet if you want to run S.M.A.R.T. diagnostics on a hard drive. Table 12.1 gives you a few options. Each one has a free option, and they all offer a variety of hard drive diagnostic capabilities.

TABLE 12.1 S.M.A.R.T. software utilities

Name	Website
GSmartControl	gsmartcontrol.sourceforge.net
SpeedFan	www.almico.com/speedfan.php
HD Tune	www.hdtune.com
Crystal Disk Info	http://crystalmark.info/software/CrystalDiskInfo/index-e.html

Second, yes there are a lot of metrics that S.M.A.R.T. reports, and not all of them make sense in English. Figure 12.4 shows the output from GSmartControl. Looking at it, you can tell that three metrics appear to be problematic because they are highlighted in pink (warning) or red (failed). The question is, which metrics are most likely to predict drive failure?

FIGURE 12.4 S.M.A.R.T. report from GSmartControl

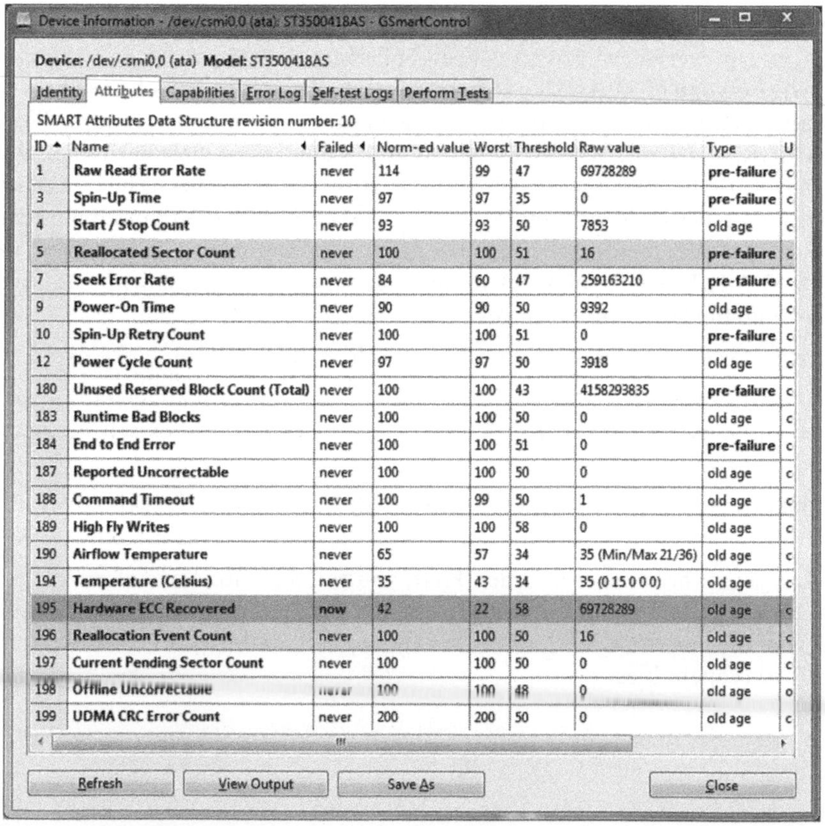

In 2014, Google and cloud service provider Backblaze ran large-scale tests to determine which metrics most strongly correlated with drive failure. Their results showed five metrics, which are highlighted in Table 12.2.

TABLE 12.2   S.M.A.R.T. metrics most correlated with hard drive failure

ID	Attribute Name	Description
05	Reallocated sector count	The number of bad sectors that have been found and remapped during read/write processes. Any nonzero number could indicate a problem.
187	Reported uncorrectable errors	The number of errors that could not be recovered using hardware error correction.
188	Command timeout	The number of failed hard drive read/write operations due to disk timeout.
197	Current pending sector count	The number of unstable sectors waiting to be remapped.
198	Uncorrectable sector count	The total number of bad sectors when reading from or writing to a sector.

Interestingly enough, metrics related to higher temperatures or the number of reboots did not correlate to drive failure. The old adage that you should leave your computer running to make the hard drive last longer wasn't verified by the research. In addition, over half of the drives in the study failed without recording a sector error, and over 30 percent of the drives failed with no S.M.A.R.T. error whatsoever.

What does that mean for the drive shown in Figure 12.4, which has errors on ID 5? Maybe not much. The same drive passed that ID when scanned with SpeedFan (see Figure 12.5). The safe conclusion is that S.M.A.R.T. can provide useful diagnostics on a hard drive's health, but it's by no means a guaranteed problem finder.

As for the last issue, there being little consistency between hard drive manufacturers, that's an annoyance but not a critical issue. All it really means is that you can't compare data from one drive manufacturer with that of another. It's likely that if you're running S.M.A.R.T. data on a hard drive, you're primarily concerned with that drive's performance and not how it compares to other hard drives anyway. If you have a situation where you're worried about a drive, you can benchmark its performance and track it over time, or you can just replace it.

RAID Issues

If you are using a Redundant Array of Independent Disks (RAID) system, you have additional challenges to deal with. First, you have more disks, so the chance of having a single failure increases. Second, you more than likely have one or more additional hard disk

FIGURE 12.5 SpeedFan S.M.A.R.T. output

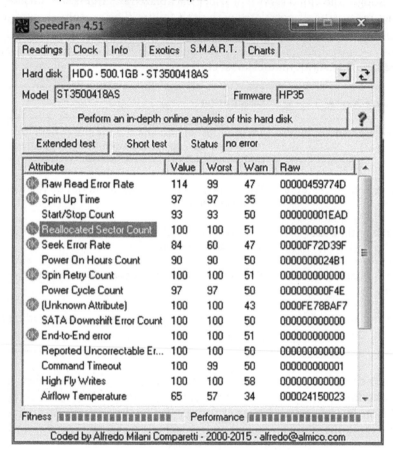

controllers, so again you introduce more parts that can fail. Third, there will likely be a software component that manages the RAID array.

Boiling it down, though, dealing with RAID issues is just like dealing with a single hard drive issue, except that you have more parts that make up the single storage unit. If your RAID array isn't found or stops working, try to narrow down the issue. Is it one disk that's failed, or is the whole system down, indicating a problem with a controller or the software? Along with external enclosures, which require a separate connection to the computer, most external RAID systems have status indicators and troubleshooting utilities to help you identify problems. Definitely use those to your advantage.

Finally, the problem could be dependent on the type of RAID you're using. If you are using RAID 0 (disk striping), you actually have more points of failure than a single device, meaning that you're at a greater risk of failure versus using just one hard drive. One drive failure will cause the entire set to fail. RAID 1 (disk mirroring) increases your fault tolerance; if one drive fails, the other has an exact replica of the data. You'll need to replace the failed drive, but unless both drives unexpectedly fail, you shouldn't lose any data. If you're using RAID 5 (disk striping with parity), a single drive failure usually means that your data will be fine, provided you replace the failed drive. RAID 10 is a mirrored striped set. As long as one drive in each mirrored pair is functional (just like in RAID 1), you shouldn't lose any data.

If your hard drive fails completely and you need to get critical data off of it, there are third-party companies that provide file recovery software and services. These services are generally very expensive. (And you should have been backing up the drive in the first place!)

Identifying Optical Drive Issues

Optical drive (CD-ROM, DVD, and Blu-ray) problems are normally media related. Although compact disc technology is pretty reliable, it's not perfect. One factor to consider is the cleanliness of the disc. On many occasions, if a disc is unreadable, cleaning it with an approved cleaner and a lint-free cleaning towel will fix the problem. The next step might be to use a commercially available scratch-removal kit. If that fails, you always have the option to send the disc to a company that specializes in data recovery.

If the operating system doesn't see the drive, start troubleshooting by determining whether the drive is receiving power. If the tray will eject, you can assume there is power to it. Next, check BIOS Setup (SATA or PATA drives) to make sure that the drive has been detected. If not, check the master/slave jumper on the drive, and make sure that the PATA adapter is set to Auto, CD-ROM, or ATAPI in BIOS Setup. Once inside the case, ensure that the ribbon cable is properly aligned with pin 1 and that both the drive and mother-board ends are securely connected.

To play movies, a DVD or Blu-ray drive must have MPEG decoding capability. This is usually built into the drive, video card, or sound card these days, but it may require a soft-ware decoder. If DVD or Blu-ray data discs will read but not play movies, suspect a problem with the MPEG decoding.

If an optical drive works normally but doesn't perform its special capability (for exam-ple, it won't burn discs), perhaps you need to install software to work with it. For example, with CD-RW drives, unless you're using an operating system that supports CD writing, you must install CD-writing software to write to CDs.

Troubleshooting Video Issues

Troubleshooting video problems is usually fairly straightforward because there are a lim-ited number of issues that you might face. You can sum up nearly all video problems with two simple statements:

- There is either no video or bad video.
- Either the video card or the monitor/projector is to blame.

In the vast majority of cases when you have a video problem, a good troubleshooting step is to check the monitor by transferring it to another machine that you know is working. See if it works there. If the problem persists, you know it's the monitor. If it goes away, you know it's the video card (or possibly the driver). Is the video card seated properly? Is the newest driver installed?

 Remember that CompTIA recommends that you not work on a CRT monitor because of the electrical charge stored within.

Let's take a look at some common symptoms and their causes:

Booting into VGA mode   Video graphics array (VGA), as you will recall from Chapter 4, "Display Devices," is a basic mode for displaying video. Pretty much all you get is 640×480 with 16 colors. (That used to be awesome!) When your system refuses to boot into anything other than VGA mode, it indicates one of two problems. Either the video card is set to a resolution that it can't handle, or the video card driver isn't loading properly. When in VGA mode, reset the video resolution to something you know the card can handle and reboot. If that doesn't solve it, reinstall the driver. If it still doesn't work, replace the video card.

No image on the screen   Troubleshooting this one is usually pretty easy. Try another monitor or try this monitor on another computer. That will narrow it down pretty quickly. Remember, if it's not the monitor it's probably the video card. (Don't forget to make sure that the system POSTed properly!)

Monitor that keeps shutting down   Monitors have their own internal power supply, and they can overheat. Overheating was more common with CRT displays than LCDs, but it still happens. Make sure the air vents on the back of the monitor are dust and debris free. If the problem persists, it's best to replace the monitor.

Dead pixels or artifacts   These two problems are definitely monitor related. Dead pixels are spots on the screen that never "fire," or light up. You can check for these by setting the background to white and seeing if any spots don't light up. With artifacts, no matter what you have on your screen, you can still see the outlines of a different image. That image has been "burned" into the monitor (sometimes simply referred to as *burn-in*) and isn't going away. In either case, the only solution is to replace the monitor.

Incorrect colors   This too is most likely a monitor issue, but you should confirm it by switching monitors. This can happen when the LCD monitor's controller board starts to fail and doesn't perform color mapping correctly. It also used to happen on CRTs, and you used a process called *degaussing* (decreasing or eliminating an unwanted magnetic field), which was done through a utility built into the menu on the monitor, to try to fix the problem. Finally, this can also happen if the pins on the connector are damaged or if the connector isn't plugged all the way in. If switching the monitor makes the problems go away, it's probably time to replace the monitor.

Dim or flickering images   In LCD monitors, these issues are most commonly caused by the backlight starting to fail. In those cases, replace the backlight.

Distorted images   This used to be more of a problem on CRT monitors if they were near a motor or other device that produced a magnetic field. Sometimes, the image would be wavy, and at other times it might look like it was getting stretched to one side of the screen. If your office is a cubicle farm, desk fans can be a major culprit. If you can eliminate the possibility of any sort of external interference, and you've confirmed that it's the monitor and not the video card, then replace the monitor.

Distorted geometry   In Chapter 4, we discussed the concepts of resolution and aspect ratio. Older, square-ish CRT monitors had a 4:3 aspect ratio, and newer widescreen HD displays are either 16:9 or 16:10. The point is, if you set your resolution such that it doesn't match the monitor's geometry, you may get distorted geometry problems. When this happens, the screen will look stretched or squeezed, depending on how you set it. Just choose a different resolution and the problem should go away.

Oversized images and icons   Oversized images and icons are also related to screen resolution; it usually means that your resolution is set too low for the monitor or projector you are using. Increase the resolution, and the issue should disappear.

Other graphics issues can be attributed to the memory installed on the video card. This is the storage location of the screens of information in a queue to be displayed by the monitor. Problems with the memory modules on the video card have a direct correlation to how well it works. It follows, then, that certain unacceptable video-quality issues (such as jerky refresh speeds or lags) can be remedied by adding memory to a video card. Doing so generally results in an increase in both quality and performance. If you can't add memory to the video card, you can upgrade to a new one.

Troubleshooting Mobile Devices, Printers, and Networking

Now that we've taken a whirlwind tour of troubleshooting the inside of a computer, it's time to change our focus. First, we will cover unique challenges to troubleshooting mobile devices. They have most of the same components as desktop computers, so a lot of what we've already covered still applies. Because of their small size and features, though, they introduce a whole host of new potential problems. After we discuss mobile issues, we'll move into troubleshooting two services that most computer users are fond of: printing and networking.

Troubleshooting Common Mobile Device Issues

Mobile devices, for the most part, are essentially the same types of devices as desktops, but troubleshooting the two can feel very different. While the general troubleshooting philosophies never change—steps such as gathering information, isolating the problem, and then testing one fix at a time—the space and configuration limitations can make troubleshooting smaller devices more frustrating.

Before getting into specific mobile device issues, remember that good troubleshooting means acting in a methodical manner. You need to find out if the device or software ever worked, what happened before the problem occurred, and what changes were made (if any). Then you must try to isolate the problem and test one fix at a time.

We will take a look at five areas where mobile devices could have different problems than their desktop counterparts: power, video, input, wireless networking, and responsiveness. Much of what we cover here will be more closely related to laptops than smaller mobile devices, but the concepts generally apply to mobile computers of all sizes.

Working on Laptops

For whatever reason, it's easier to lose screws and other small pieces when working on laptops than it is with desktops. Don't forget these key concepts when working on laptops:

- Document and label screw and cable locations.

- Have a clear organization method for your parts and screws.

- Refer to the manufacturer's documentation.

- Use the appropriate hand tools.

For a review of these four concepts, see Chapter 9, "Understanding Laptops."

Power Issues

Is it plugged in? Everyone hates getting asked that question if their computer doesn't work. But it's the critical first question to ask. After all, if it's not plugged in, who knows whether or not it will work? You can't assume that the battery is working (or is attached) as it's supposed to be. Always check power and connections first!

 If the laptop works while it's plugged in but not while it's on battery power, the battery itself may be the culprit. As batteries get older, they are not able to hold as much of a charge, and in some cases, they are not able to hold a charge at all. If the battery won't charge while the laptop is plugged in, try removing the battery and reinserting it. If it still won't charge, you might want to replace the battery.

Most laptop power adapters have a light on them indicating that they're plugged in. If there's no light, check to make sure that the outlet is working, or switch outlets. Also, most laptops have a power-ready indicator light when plugged into a wall outlet as well. Check to see if it's lit. If the outlet is fine, try another power adapter. They do fail on occasion.

Smaller mobile devices will have a lightning bolt next to their battery icon or an animated filling battery when charging. If the device doesn't appear to charge, the same culprits apply: it could be the outlet, the adapter, or the device itself.

If you're working on a DC adapter, the same concepts apply. Check for lights, try another adapter if you have one, or try changing plugs if possible. For example, if you're using a DC outlet in a car, many newer models have secondary power sources, such as ones in the console between the seats.

Another thing to remember when troubleshooting power problems is to remove all external peripherals. Strip your laptop down to the base computer so that there isn't a short or other power drain coming from an external device.

 Windows has built-in power management features to help conserve laptop battery life. In Windows, open the Power Options applet in Control Panel. Once there, you can configure different power-saving settings to maximize the battery life of your laptop.

Smaller devices have greater potential to overheat than do their larger brethren. Space is at a premium, so all of the components are packed tightly together, which means less room for each component to breathe. Manufacturers realize this, of course, so they use components that generate less heat. Overheating can still be a problem though. If your mobile device is overheating, turn it off to let it cool down. It could be from overuse, or perhaps it did not have proper ventilation (for example, if it was stuffed into someone's pocket or purse). If the overheating is persistent, you have a few options. The first is to test or replace the battery, as that's the most likely culprit. If overheating still happens, you may have to replace the device.

Another issue that small devices can have is an extremely short battery life. We're not talking about when people complain that their laptop only runs for an hour-and-a-half when they are playing a DVD while surfing the Internet and talking to their friends on their Bluetooth headset over a social media instant messenger. No, that's bound to drain your battery quickly. What we're referring to here is when a laptop battery only lasts for an hour or so after a full charge with normal usage, or if a mobile phone battery is only able to power the device for 30 minutes or so. These things happen.

If it's a laptop, you can try to perform a battery calibration, as we discussed in Chapter 9. For all mobile devices, you can try to drain the battery completely and then charge it fully before turning the device back on. If these options don't work, then it's likely that the battery needs to be replaced.

The last power issue that we need to discuss is a swollen battery. As the term *swollen battery* suggests, the battery physically swells in size. It can be caused by a number of things, including manufacturer defects, age, misuse, using the wrong adapter for charging, or leaving the laptop constantly plugged into a wall outlet. Inside the battery, the individual cells become overcharged, causing them to swell.

If you have a swollen battery, turn the device off immediately and make sure that it's not plugged into a charger. If the battery is removable, you can try to remove it if you wish, but be very careful. Swollen batteries are more prone to explosions than normal ones because the casing is already compromised. If you are able to remove it, place it into a safe container, just in case there are further issues. If the battery is not removable, it's time for a new device. In either case, take the battery or device to a proper recycling center to dispose of it. Never just throw it in the trash because it can explode and harm sanitation workers, as well as cause significant damage to the environment.

Video Difficulties

The video card (built into the motherboard on most mobile devices) and the display unit are usually the cause of video problems. Video problems on small computers can also occur if the connection between the motherboard and the LCD screen becomes damaged. On laptops, this connection typically passes through the hinges of the case, which is the weakest part.

The coverage for video problems follows the section on power problems for a reason: Make sure the computer is on before diagnosing the issue as a video problem!

Here are a few things to try for laptops:

- Plug in an external monitor that you know works. On most laptops, you need to press the function key and another key known as the LCD cutoff switch (often F4 or F8) to direct the video output to an external monitor. This is called toggling the display. You might need to do this a few times. Figure 12.6 shows a laptop keyboard where F4 is the appropriate toggle key. Look for the symbol that looks like a VGA video connector.

FIGURE 12.6   Video adjustment keys F4 (LCD toggle), F9 (dim), and F10 (brighten)

- Check the *LCD cutoff switch*. Remember the *function*+F4 idea? Try toggling it a few times, waiting a few seconds between each press of the toggle key to let the display power up. Most laptops have three or four display states: LCD only, external only, both displays, and extend screen (where the second screen becomes an extension of the first monitor). Raise or lower the brightness level. This is usually done with a function key combination as well, such as Fn+F9 or Fn+F10. Check your keyboard for function keys that have a sun on them.
- If you have a handheld computer, try turning the backlight feature on or off. For specifics on how to do this, check your manual.

If the display is not working, you can order a new one from the manufacturer—although it may be cheaper to just buy a new device. If the computer won't output a screen image to an external monitor or projector, it means one of two things (assuming you know that the monitor or projector works): Either the external VGA port is shot, or the function keys aren't working. In either case, you likely need to replace the motherboard if you want the display to appear on an external device.

Dim or flickering displays on laptops are usually caused by a faulty backlight in the display panel. A failing inverter can cause these problems too.

Input Problems

Laptop keyboards aren't as easy to switch out as desktop keyboards. You can, however, very easily attach an external keyboard to your laptop if the keys on your laptop don't appear to work. If you have an ancient laptop or keyboard with a PS/2 connector, most electronics stores will have USB-to-PS/2 or PS/2-to-USB converters.

If the keyboard doesn't seem to respond at all, try pressing the Num Lock and Caps Lock keys to see if they toggle the Num Lock and Caps Lock lights on and off. If the lights don't respond, the keyboard isn't functioning properly. Try rebooting the system. (You will probably have to press and hold the power button for 5 seconds, and the system will shut off. Wait 10 seconds, and press the power button again to turn it back on.) If that doesn't fix the problem, you probably have faulty hardware.

Another problem unique to laptop keyboards is the *Fn key*. (It can be your friend or your enemy.) You can identify it on your laptop keyboard because it's in the lower-left corner and has the letters *Fn* on it (often in blue), as shown in Figure 12.7. If the Fn key is "stuck" on, the only keys that will work are those with functions on them. If you look at other keys on your laptop, several of them will have blue lettering too. Those are the functions that the keys may perform if you press and hold the Fn key before pressing the function key that you want. If the Fn key is stuck on, try toggling it just as you would a Caps Lock or Num Lock key.

FIGURE 12.7   The Fn key on a laptop

If another key on your laptop keyboard is stuck, you need to determine if the contact is having problems or if the key itself is stuck. If the key is not physically stuck but the laptop thinks it is, rebooting generally solves the problem. If the key physically sticks, you can try blowing out underneath the key with compressed air, or use a cotton swab slightly dampened with water (or rubbing alcohol) to clean underneath the key. Make sure to clean the entire surface underneath the sticking key. If none of this resolves the issue, you might need to replace the keyboard.

One of the conveniences that users often take advantage of in laptops is a built-in pointing device. Most laptops have touchpads or point sticks that function much like a mouse. They're nice because you don't need to carry an external mouse around with you. While these types of devices are usually considered very handy, some people find them annoying. For example, when you are typing your palm might rest on the touchpad, causing erratic pointer behavior. This is referred to as a *ghost cursor* because it seems like the cursor just randomly jumps all over the screen. You can turn the touchpad off through Control Panel. While understanding that you can turn it off on purpose, remember that it can be turned off accidentally as well. Check to make sure that it's enabled. Some laptops allow you to disable or change the sensitivity of the touchpoint as well, just as you can adjust the sensitivity of your mouse.

Another potential issue is pointer drift, where the mouse cursor will slowly drift in one direction even though you are not trying to make it move. This issue is generally related to the point stick not centering properly after it's been used. If you have pointer drift, try using the point stick and moving it back and forth a few times to get it to re-center itself. You can also try rebooting. If the problem persists, either disable or replace the point stick.

Networking Troubles

Nearly every mobile device sold is equipped with integrated wireless networking, and most have Bluetooth built in as well. In many cases, the wireless antenna is run into the LCD panel. This allows the antenna to stand up higher and pick up a better signal.

If your wireless networking isn't working, check to make sure that the LEDs on your network card are functioning. If there are no lights, it could indicate a problem with the card itself or, on some cards, that there is no connection or signal. First, make sure the wireless card is enabled through Windows. You generally do this in Windows by right-clicking My Network Places, selecting Properties, right-clicking the wireless network connection, and selecting Properties to look at the network card properties. However, some network cards have their own proprietary configuration software. You can also often check here by clicking a tab (often called Wireless Networks) to see if you're getting a signal and, if so, the strength of that signal.

A weak signal is the most common cause of intermittent wireless networking connection problems. If you have intermittent connectivity and keep getting dropped, see if you can get closer to the WAP or remove obstructions between you and the WAP. Failing network cards and connectivity devices can also cause intermittent wireless networking connection failures.

Most laptops also come with an external switch or button on the front or side or above the keyboard that can toggle the network card on and off. Be sure that this is set to the On position! Figure 12.8 shows a toggle above the keyboard (it's the one on the left that looks like an antenna).

FIGURE 12.8 Network card toggle switch above the keyboard

  If you have a USB network adapter, try unplugging it and plugging it back in. Make sure that Windows recognizes the card properly.

When the wireless connection fails but the network card appears to be working, try plugging it in. Most laptops with wireless cards also have wired RJ-45 network ports. Plug the card in and see if you get lights, and see if the network works.

🌐 Real World Scenario

Potential Wireless and Wired Conflicts

A short time ago, a friend of ours was frustrated because he couldn't get to the network in his office with his laptop plugged into his docking station. He had used the laptop at home the night before and gotten on his wireless network without a problem. But this day, his wired connection would not work. He checked his cables (always your first step!) and saw that there were lights (a good sign). He had tried to access both the Internet and intranet sites but to no avail.

We opened a command prompt and ran IPCONFIG. He didn't have an IP address, but we noticed that his built-in wireless card was listed and active.

What he needed to do was to disable his built-in wireless card. He had enabled the wireless to work at home, and it was still enabled. Because it was enabled, the wireless card

continues

continued

was trying to obtain an IP address, and it refused to let the wired "portion" of the card pick up an address from the company DHCP server (there was no wireless in the building). After disabling his wireless card, his wired connection picked up an IP address, and all was well.

Most laptop network cards have a wired connection in addition to their wireless capabilities. For some of them, the wired connection will not work if the wireless is enabled. It's an attempt to prevent conflicts if both connection types are active.

The principles behind troubleshooting network or Bluetooth connectivity issues on mobile phones and tablets is the same as on laptops. The big difference is that you can't try an external network card if your internal one is failing. The first thing to check is that the network connection or Bluetooth is enabled, which also means double-checking that airplane mode is not turned on. On Android and iOS devices, this is done through Settings. Figure 12.9 shows iOS network settings and Figure 12.10 shows Android network settings. Toggle the connection off and then back on to reset it; oftentimes, that will resolve connectivity issues.

FIGURE 12.9 iOS network settings

FIGURE 12.10 Android network settings

Another way to access network settings in iOS is from the Control Center. You can do this from both the lock screen and the home screen. Simply swipe your finger up from the very bottom of the iPhone's touchscreen, and you will get the Control Center, similar to what's shown in Figure 12.11.

FIGURE 12.11   iPhone Control Center

Responsiveness Issues

Responsiveness issues are most common on smaller mobile devices such as phones and tablets. For the most part, we expect these devices to run automatically without any problems, but when they decide to stop working, it can be tricky figuring out why. Here are six common responsiveness scenarios you might run into, and the steps to take to resolve them:

Apps not loading   Sometimes you will tap on an app and nothing happens. Of course you tap it again, and still nothing. After a dozen or so taps, you might just give up. It could be one of three things. The touchscreen has stopped responding, something has corrupted the app, or the memory has become corrupted. Try another app to help narrow down the problem. If that doesn't work, try powering the device off and back on again, and then try the app once more. If that doesn't resolve the problem, look to see if there is an updated version of the app that you need to install. If not, simply uninstall and reinstall the app.

Frozen system   This is one step further than just one app not working. If the touchscreen is completely non-responsive and the system is entirely frozen, all you really can do is to power it off and then back on. You might need to hold the power button down for several seconds to force the device to power off. If the power button does not work, you can reset an iPhone by pressing and holding the power button and the sleep/wake button simultaneously for about 10 seconds. The Apple logo will appear, and the phone should reset.

If that doesn't work, then you need to restore the phone to factory settings. Note that doing this will cause all data on the phone to disappear, which is one reason it's always good to have the phone sync so that you have a backup! If the restore process also fails, then it's time to have the device repaired by a service technician or replaced.

Slow performance   This happens when the device is really slow but isn't completely locked up. First, isolate the issue. Is it one app or overall performance? It could be that apps are running in the background and need to be closed. Shutting down those apps or powering the device off and then back on is a good step. You can also check to see how much memory is available. If it's very little, you might uninstall some items to see if that improves performance.

If it's one app giving you problems instead of the entire device, look for updates to the app, or delete and reinstall the app.

Finally, if none of these steps work, perform a restore to factory settings. If the problems persist, it's time for a new device.

Unable to decrypt email   Security certificates and public and private keys are used to accomplish encryption and decryption. Security certificates are obtained through a certificate authority (CA), similar to how secure websites get set up so that you know they're legitimate. The entire process for enabling encryption and decryption is beyond the scope of this chapter, but you do need to know two key points. First, you need a certificate to enable encryption, and second, public keys are used to encrypt messages and private keys are used to decrypt the same message. In other words, if you want to send Mary an encrypted message, you will use Mary's public key to encrypt it. The only key that can properly decrypt the message is Mary's private key

Android and iOS both support the *Secure/Multipurpose Internet Mail Extensions (S/MIME)* standard for public key encryption.

If you can't decrypt email, it is most likely because S/MIME settings are not properly enabled on your email account, which means installing the certificate (and by extension, your private key) on your mobile device. Exercise 12.2 walks you through the general steps to enable S/MIME on iOS, using iOS 8 as an example. The exercise assumes that you already have obtained a security certificate through a CA.

EXERCISE 12.2

Enabling S/MIME on iOS 8

1. Transfer the security certificate to your iOS device. You need the .p12 file; download it directly from your CA or email the .p12 file to yourself.

2. Open the .p12 file. iOS will automatically try to install it as a profile.

3. If it didn't install automatically in step 2, click Install.

4. If you get a warning that the profile is unsigned, click OK.

5. Enter the passcode for the device, and then enter the passcode for the .p12 file. Click Next.

6. Click Done to complete the certificate installation.

7. On your iOS device, open Settings ➢ Mail ➢ Contacts ➢ Calendars.

8. Tap Exchange, and then tap your email account.

9. At the bottom of your account settings, tap Advanced Settings.

10. Enable S/MIME, as shown in Figure 12.12.

FIGURE 12.12 Advanced Settings for email

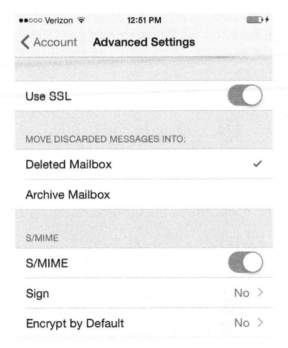

11. Turn on Sign and Encrypt By Default if you would like.

12. Close out of Advanced Settings.

If you are sending an encrypted email to someone who is on the same Exchange server as you, Exchange will locate their public key (certificate) to perform the encryption. If the recipient is not on the same Exchange server as you, you will need to install their certificate on your device. You will know that the email is encrypted if there is a lock icon next to the recipient's email address; if it's not configured properly, the recipient's email address will appear in red and have an unlocked lock icon next to it.

No sound from speakers   Make sure that your device is not set to silent operation. Most mobile devices will have a switch on the side that sets them to silent or vibrate mode, and that will mute your device from making a noise when you get a call or a message. Also check your volume settings, which are in Settings ➤ Sounds, as well as the control center, shown in Figure 12.11. If the speakers have failed on a mobile device, it's time for a new device.

GPS not functioning   iPhones and other devices have an amazing array of kinetic sensors built in. For example, the iPhone 6 has a gyroscope, accelerometer, linear acceleration sensor, magnetometer, altitude sensor, and gravity sensor. These sensors let your device act like a GPS and compass, and they also detect movements that many apps take advantage of, such as tilting or shaking the device. GPS must be enabled to use it. On an iPhone, you do so through Location Services, which is under Settings ➤ Privacy ➤ Location Services as shown in Figure 12.13. Then, you have to give each app permission to use the service, which is also done on the same screen. In Android, location access settings are configured under Settings ➤ Location and then Location, Location Services, or Location Reporting, depending on the Android version.

FIGURE 12.13   Location Services

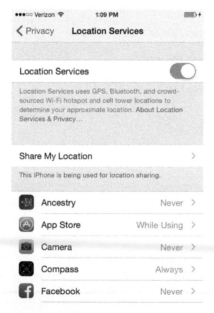

If GPS is not working, check to ensure that the device has either a cellular or a Wi-Fi connection. Location Services doesn't work without one of those two enabled. It's possible for any of the kinetic sensors to fail, including those that enable GPS services. If the settings are properly enabled and GPS still does not work, the only way to resolve this problem is to send it in for service or replace the device.

Troubleshooting Printer Problems

Other than the monitor (which every computer needs), the most popular peripheral purchased for computers today is the printer. Printers are also the most complex peripheral as far as troubleshooting is concerned; this arises from complications in putting ink to paper. There are several different ways that this can be accomplished, but the end result is all pretty much the same.

Different types of printers work in different ways, so you would expect that laser printers might have different issues than impact printers. Because problems are often dependent upon the type of printer you're using, we've chosen to break down this discussion by printer type. We'll start with a quick review of the technology and then get into specific issues. At the end, we'll look at the process of managing the print spooler, which is the same regardless of the printer type in use.

Printer manufacturer websites are great places to look to find troubleshooting information. They often provide descriptions of problems and detailed instructions for resolving the issue. Most printers also come with management software that you can install on your computer, which may be able to assist you in troubleshooting any issues that you have.

For a more detailed description of each type of printer's components and inner workings, see Chapter 11, "Installing and Configuring Printers."

Help! I can't install my printer!

Before you can print, you must of course install the printer on the computer you want to print from. Sometimes though, installing the printer can be problematic. The first common issue you will run into is if the printer isn't found during the installation process. If this is the case, check to make sure that the printer is on and connected to either the computer or the network. Wireless network printers are notorious for not being "found." If needed, reseat the connections and try again, or see if you can connect the printer using a different method (for example, USB instead of wireless).

The second common issue is if the printer driver won't install. Be sure that any other instances of that type of printer aren't already installed on the computer. If you just removed the old printer driver, reboot before reinstalling the new one. And finally, download and install the newest driver from the manufacturer's web site.

Dot-Matrix Printer Problems

Dot-matrix printers are impact printers, meaning that they rely upon making a physical impact in order to print. A dot-matrix printer contains a print head, which has a row of short, sturdy pins made of a hard wire. The pins in the print head are wrapped with coils of wire to create a solenoid and are held in the rest position by a combination of a small magnet and a spring. To trigger a particular pin, the printer controller sends a signal to the print head, which energizes the wires around the appropriate print wire. This turns the print wire into an electromagnet, which repels the print pin, forcing it against the ink ribbon and making a dot on the paper.

Although this might sound complex, dot-matrix printers are relatively simple devices. Therefore, only a few problems usually arise. We will cover the most common problems and their solutions here.

Low Print Quality

Problems with print quality are easy to identify. When the printed page comes out of the printer, the characters may be too light or have dots missing from them. Table 12.3 details some of the most common print quality problems, their causes, and their solutions.

TABLE 12.3   Common dot-matrix print quality problems

Characteristics	Cause	Solution
Consistently faded or light characters	Worn-out printer ribbon	See if you can adjust the print head to be closer to the ribbon. If not (or if it doesn't help), replace the ribbon with a new, vendor-recommended ribbon.
Print lines that go from dark to light as the print head moves across the page	Printer ribbon-advance gear slipping	Replace the ribbon-advance gear or mechanism.
A small, blank line running through a line of print (consistently)	Print head pin stuck inside the print head	Replace the print head.
A small, blank line running through a line of print (intermittently)	A broken, loose, or shorting print head cable	Secure or replace the print head cable.
A small, dark line running through a line of print	Print head pin stuck in the out position	Replace the print head. (Pushing the pin in may damage the print head.)
Printer making a printing noise, but no print appears on the page	Worn, missing, or improperly installed ribbon cartridge	Replace the ribbon cartridge correctly.
Printer printing garbage	Cable partially unhooked, wrong driver selected, or bad printer control board (PCB)	Hook up the cable correctly, select the correct driver, or replace the PCB (respectively).

Printout Jams Inside the Printer

Printer jams (aka "the printer crinkled my paper") are very frustrating because they always seem to happen more than halfway through your 50-page print job, requiring you to take time to remove the jam before the rest of your pages can print. A paper jam happens when something prevents the paper from advancing through the printer evenly. There are generally three causes of printer jams: an obstructed paper path, stripped drive gears, and using the wrong paper.

Obstructed paper paths are often difficult to find. Usually it means disassembling the printer to find the bit of crumpled-up paper or other foreign substance that's blocking the paper path. A common obstruction is a piece of the "perf"—the perforated sides of tractor-feed paper—that has torn off and gotten crumpled up and then lodged in the paper path. It may be necessary to remove the platen roller and feed mechanism to get at the obstruction.

Stripped drive gears cause the paper to feed improperly, causing it to crinkle and cause jams. Using the wrong paper, such as thick paper when the platen has been set for thin paper, can also cause jams. When loading new paper, always be sure that the platen is properly adjusted.

Use extra caution when printing peel-off labels in dot-matrix printers. If a label or even a whole sheet of labels becomes misaligned or jammed, *do not* roll the roller backward to realign the sheet. The small plastic paper guide that most dot-matrix printers use to control the forward movement of the paper through the printer will peel the label right off its backing if you reverse the direction of the paper. Once the label is free, it can easily get stuck under the platen, causing paper jams. A label stuck under the platen is almost impossible to remove without disassembling the paper-feed assembly. If a label is misaligned, try realigning the whole sheet of labels *slowly* using the feed roller (with the power off), moving it in very small increments.

Stepper Motor Problems

Printers use stepper motors to move the print head back and forth as well as to advance the paper. The carriage motor is responsible for the back-and-forth motion while the main motor advances the paper. These motors get damaged when they are forced in any direction while the power is on. This includes moving the print head over to install a printer ribbon as well as moving the paper-feed roller to align paper. These motors are very sensitive to stray voltages. If you are rotating one of these motors by hand, you are essentially turning it into a small generator and thus damaging it.

A damaged stepper motor is easy to detect. Damage to the stepper motor will cause it to lose precision and move farther with each step. If the main motor is damaged (which is more likely to happen), lines of print will be unevenly spaced. If the print head motor goes bad, characters will be scrunched together. If a stepper motor is damaged badly enough, it won't move at all in any direction; it may even make high-pitched squealing noises. If any of these symptoms appear, it's time to replace one of these motors.

Stepper motors are usually expensive to replace—about half the cost of a new printer! Damage to them is easy to avoid; the biggest key is to not force them to move when the power is on.

Inkjet Printer Problems

An inkjet printer has many of the same types of parts as a dot-matrix printer. In this sense, it's almost as if the inkjet technology is simply an extension of the technology used in dot-matrix printers. The parts on an inkjet can be divided into four categories:

- Print head/ink cartridge
- Print head carriage, belt, and stepper motor
- Paper-feed mechanism
- Control, interface, and power circuitry

Perhaps the most obvious difference between inkjet and dot-matrix printers is that dot-matrix printers often use tractor-feed paper while inkjets use normal paper. The differences don't end there, though. Inkjet printers work by spraying ink (often in the form of a bubble) onto a page. The pattern of the bubbles forms images on the paper.

Inkjet printers are the most common type of printer found in homes because they are inexpensive and produce good-quality images. For this reason, you need to understand the most common problems with these printers so that your company can service them effectively. Let's take a look at some of the most common problems with inkjet printers and their solutions.

Print Quality

The majority of inkjet printer problems are quality problems. Ninety-nine percent of these can be traced to a faulty ink cartridge. With most inkjet printers, the ink cartridge contains the print head and the ink. The major problem with this assembly can be described by "If you don't use it, you lose it." The ink will dry out in the small nozzles and block them if they are not used at least once a week.

An example of a quality problem is when you have thin, blank lines present in every line of text on the page. This is caused by a plugged hole in at least one of the small, pinhole ink nozzles in the print cartridge. Another common problem is faded printing. Replacing the ink cartridge generally solves these issues.

WARNING As we warned in Chapter 11, some people try to save a buck by refilling their ink cartridge when they need to replace it. If you are one of them, *stop!* Don't refill your ink cartridges! Almost all ink cartridges are *not* designed to be refilled. They are designed to be used once and thrown away. By refilling them, you make a hole in them—ink can leak out, and the printer will need to be cleaned. The ink will probably also be of the wrong type, and print quality can suffer. Finally, using a refilled cartridge may void the printer's warranty.

If an ink cartridge becomes damaged or develops a hole, it can put too much ink on the page and the letters will smear. Again, the solution is to replace the ink cartridge. (You should be aware, however, that a very small amount of smearing is normal if the pages are laid on top of each other immediately after printing.)

One final print quality problem that does not directly involve the ink cartridge occurs when the print quickly goes from dark to light and then prints nothing. As we already mentioned, ink cartridges dry out if not used. That's why the manufacturers include a small suction pump inside the printer that primes the ink cartridge before each print cycle. If this priming pump is broken or malfunctioning, this problem will manifest itself and the pump will need to be replaced.

If the problem of the ink quickly going from dark to light and then disappearing ever happens to you and you really need to print a couple of pages, try this trick. First, take the ink cartridge out of the printer. Then squirt some window cleaner on a paper towel and gently tap the print head against the wet paper towel. The force of the tap plus the solvents in the window cleaner should dislodge any dried ink, and the ink will flow freely again. Just be careful to not rub the paper towel across the print head because this could damage the nozzles.

After you install a new cartridge into many inkjet printers, the print heads in that cartridge must be aligned. *Print head alignment* is the process by which the print head is calibrated for use. A special utility that comes with the printer software is used to do this. You run the alignment utility, and the printer prints several vertical and horizontal lines with numbers next to them. It then shows you a screen and asks you to choose the horizontal and vertical lines that are the most "in line." Once you enter the numbers, the software understands whether the print head(s) are out of alignment, which direction, and by how much. The software then makes slight modifications to the print driver software to tell it how much to offset when printing. Occasionally, alignment must be done several times to get the images to align properly.

Most new inkjet printers automatically align the print head, and no interaction is required on your part. Even if this is the case, your printer software may have an option for you to be able to align the print heads manually.

Color Output Problems

Sometimes, when you print a color document, the colors might not be the same colors that you expected based on what you saw on the screen. A few different issues could cause this problem. First, ink could be bleeding from adjacent areas of the picture, causing the color to be off. A leaking cartridge can cause this, as can using the wrong type of paper for your printer.

If you know that you're using the right paper, try cleaning the print cartridges using the software utility that should have been included with the printer software. Once you do that, print a test page to confirm that the colors are correct. On most color printers, the test page will print colors in a pattern from left to right that mirrors the way the ink cartridges are installed. That brings us to our second potential problem: the ink cartridges are installed in the wrong spot. (This is for printers with multiple color ink cartridges.) That should be easy to check. Obviously, if that's the problem, put the color cartridges where they're supposed to be!

Third, if the ink that comes out of the cartridge doesn't match the label on the cartridge, try the self-cleaning utility. If that doesn't help, replace the cartridge. Finally, if one of the colors doesn't come out at all and self-cleaning doesn't help, just replace the cartridge.

Paper Jams

Inkjet printers have pretty simple paper paths. Therefore, paper jams due to obstructions are less likely than they are on dot-matrix printers. They are still possible, however, so an obstruction shouldn't be overlooked as a possible cause of jamming.

Paper jams in inkjet printers are usually due to one of two things:

- A worn pickup roller
- The wrong type of paper

The pickup roller usually has one or two D-shaped rollers mounted on a rotating shaft. When the shaft rotates, one edge of the D roller rubs against the paper, pushing it into the printer. When the roller gets worn, it gets smooth and doesn't exert enough friction against the paper to push it into the printer.

If the paper used in the printer is too smooth, it can cause the same problem. Pickup rollers use friction, and smooth paper doesn't offer much friction. If the paper is too rough, on the other hand, it acts like sandpaper on the rollers, wearing them smooth. Here's a rule of thumb for paper smoothness: paper slightly smoother than a new dollar bill will work fine.

Creased paper is a common culprit in paper jams. The printer can crease the paper if there are obstructions in the paper path or problems with the paper-feed mechanism.

Paper-Feeding Problems

You will normally see one of two paper-feeding options on an inkjet printer. The first is that the paper is stored in a paper tray on the front of the printer. The second, which is more common on smaller and cheaper models, is for the paper to be fed in vertically from the back of the printer in a paper feeder. Both types may also have manual feed or envelope feed options.

Regardless of the feed style, the printer will have a paper-feed mechanism, which picks up the paper and feeds it into the printer. Inside the paper-feed mechanism are pickup rollers, which are small rubber rollers that rub up against the paper and feed it into the printer. They press up against small rubber or cork patches known as *separator pads*. These help to keep the rest of the paper in the tray so that only one sheet gets picked up at a time. A pickup stepper motor turns the pickup rollers.

If your printer fails to pick up paper, it could indicate that the pickup rollers are too worn. If your printer is always picking up multiple sheets of paper, it could be a couple of things, such as problems with the separator pads or your paper being too "sticky," damp, or rough. Some printers that use vertical paper feeders have a lever with which you can adjust the amount of tension between the pickup rollers and the separator pads. If your printer is consistently pulling multiple sheets of paper, you might want to try to increase the tension using this lever.

The final component is the paper-feed sensor. This sensor is designed to tell the printer when it's out of paper, and it rarely fails. When it does, the printer will refuse to print because it thinks it is out of paper. Cleaning the sensor might help, but if not, you should replace the printer.

Stepper Motor Problems

Inkjet printers use stepper motors, just like dot-matrix printers. On an inkjet, the print head carriage is the component containing the print head that moves back and forth. A carriage stepper motor and an attached belt (the carriage belt) are responsible for the movement. So the print head carriage stays horizontally stable, it rests on a metal stabilizer bar. Another stepper motor is responsible for advancing the paper.

Stepper motor problems on an inkjet will look similar to the ones on a dot-matrix printer. That is, if the main motor is damaged, lines of print will be unevenly spaced, and if the print head motor goes bad, characters will be scrunched together. A lot of damage may cause the stepper motor to not move at all and possibly make high-pitched squealing noises. If any of these symptoms appear, it's time to replace one of these motors. As with dot-matrix printers, stepper motors can be expensive. It may make more economical sense to replace the printer.

Power Problems

Inkjet printers have internal power circuits that convert the electricity from the outlet into voltages that the printer can use, typically 12V and 5V. The specific device that does this is called the transformer. If the transformer fails, the printer will not power up. If this happens, it's time to get a new printer.

Laser Printer Problems

The process that laser printers use to print, called the electrophotographic (EP) printing process, is the most complex process of all commonly used printers. You should have already memorized the seven-step EP process for the 220-901 A+ exam, but perhaps you've forgotten a bit. Table 12.4 gives you the seven steps and a short description of what happens in each step.

 The descriptions in Table 12.4 are summaries of the EP printing process. For detailed descriptions, see Chapter 11.

TABLE 12.4 The EP printing process

Step	Action
Processing	The page to be printed gets rendered, one horizontal strip at a time. The image is stored in memory for printing.
Charging	The charging corona gets a high voltage from the high-voltage power supply (HVPS). It uses the voltage to apply a strong uniform negative charge (−600VDC) to the photosensitive drum.
Exposing (writing)	The laser scans the drum. Wherever it touches the drum, the charge is reduced from −600VDC to around −100VDC. The pattern formed on the drum will be the image that is printed.
Developing	The developing roller acquires a −600VDC charge from the HVPS and picks up toner, which gets the same −600VDC charge. As the developing toner rolls by the photosensitive drum, the toner is attracted to the lesser-charged (−100VDC) areas on the photosensitive drum and sticks to it in those areas.
Transferring	The charging corona wire or roller acquires a strong positive charge (+600VDC) and transfers it to the paper. As the photosensitive drum with ink on it rolls by, the ink is attracted to the paper.
Fusing	The 350° F fuser roller melts the toner paper and the rubberized pressure roller presses the melted toner into the paper, making the image permanent.
Cleaning	A rubber blade scrapes any remaining toner off the drum and a fluorescent lamp discharges any remaining charge on the photosensitive drum.

Looking at the steps involved in laser printing, it's pretty easy to tell that laser printers are the most complex printers that we have discussed. The good news, though, is that most laser printer problems are easily identifiable and have specific fixes. Let's discuss the most common laser and page printer problems and their solutions.

Don't forget to perform periodic preventative maintenance on your laser printers. It can help eliminate many potential problems before they happen. Preventative maintenance includes cleaning the printer and using manufacturer-recommended maintenance kits.

Power Problems

If you turn your laser printer on and it doesn't respond normally, there could be a problem with the power it's receiving. Of course, the first thing to do is to ensure that it's plugged in!

A laser printer's DC power supply provides three different DC voltages to printer components. This can all be checked at a power interface labeled J210, which is a 20-pin female interface. Pin 1 will be in the lower-left corner, and the pins along the bottom will all be odd numbers, increasing from left to right.

    Printer voltages can be tested with a multimeter.

Using the multimeter, you should find the following voltages:

- Pin 1 +5v
- Pin 5 −5v
- Pin 9 +24v

If none of the voltages are reading properly, then you probably need to replace the fuse in the DC power supply. If one or more (but not all) of the voltages aren't reading properly, then the first thing to do is to remove all optional hardware in the printer (including memory) and test again. If the readings are still bad, it's likely you need to replace the DC power supply.

No Connectivity (IP Issues)

You can connect many laser printers directly to your network by using a network cable (such as Category 5e or 6a) or by using a wireless network adapter with the printer. In cases like these, the printer acts as its own print server (typically print server software is built into the printer), and it can speed up printing because you don't have a separate print server translating and then sending the directions to the printer.

For printers such as these, no connectivity can be a sign of improperly configured IP settings such as the IP address. While each printer is somewhat different, you can manually configure most laser printers' IP settings a number of ways:

- Through the printer's LCD control panel. For example, on several HP LaserJet models, you press Menu, navigate to the Network Config menu, select TCP/IP Config, select Manual, and then enter the IP address. You would then also configure the subnet mask and default gateway.
- By using Telnet to connect to the printer's management software from your computer.
- By using the management software that came with your printer.

You can also configure most IP printers to obtain an IP address automatically from a Dynamic Host Configuration Protocol (DHCP) server. Whenever the printer is powered up, it will contact the server to get its IP configuration information just like any other client on the network. While this may be convenient, it's usually not a good idea to assign dynamic IP addresses to printers. Client computers will have their printer mapped to a specific IP address; if that address is changed, you will have a lot of people complaining about no connectivity. If you are using the DHCP server to manage all of your network's IP addresses, be sure to reserve a static address for the printers.

To see the setting of a printer's IP address, print a configuration page from the printer's control panel. Then post the IP information near the printer so that users can easily connect to it.

Nothing Prints

You tell your computer to print, but nothing comes out of the printer. That problem is probably the most challenging to solve because several different things could cause it. Are you the only one affected by the problem, or are others having the same issue? Is the printer plugged in, powered on, and online? As with any troubleshooting, check your connections first.

Sometimes when nothing prints, you get a clue as to what the problem is. The printer may give you an "out of memory" error or something similar. Another possibility is that the printer will say "processing data" (or something similar) on its LCD display and nothing will print. It's likely that the printer has run out of memory while trying to process the print job. If your printer is exhibiting these symptoms, it's best to power the printer off and then power it back on.

Be aware that large print jobs may cause the printer to say "processing data" for several minutes before the print job starts. There is nothing wrong with this, although it's possible that your printer could stand a memory upgrade. But if the printer exhibits this behavior for a long time, say 20 or 30 minutes, it may be best to cycle the power.

Paper Jams

Laser printers today run at copier speeds. Because of this, their most common problem is paper jams. Paper can get jammed in a printer for several reasons. First, feed jams happen when the paper-feed rollers get worn (similar to feed jams in inkjet printers). The solution to this problem is easy: replace the worn rollers.

Another cause of feed jams is related to the drive gear of the pickup roller. The drive gear (or clutch) may be broken or have teeth missing. Again, the solution is to replace it. To determine if the problem is a broken gear or worn rollers, print a test page, but leave the paper tray out. Look into the paper-feed opening with a flashlight and see if the paper pickup roller(s) are turning evenly and don't skip. If they turn evenly, the problem is probably worn rollers.

If worn pickup rollers are causing your paper-feed jams, there is something that you can do to get your printer working while you're waiting for the replacement pickup rollers. Scuff the feed rollers with a Scotch-Brite pot scrubber pad (or something similar) to roughen them up. This trick works only once. After that, the rollers aren't thick enough to touch the paper.

Worn exit rollers can also cause paper jams. These rollers guide the paper out of the printer into the paper-receiving tray. If they are worn or damaged, the paper may catch on its way out of the printer. These types of jams are characterized by a paper jam that occurs just as the paper is getting to the exit rollers. If the paper jams, open the rear door and see where the paper is located. If the paper is very close to the exit rollers, they are probably the problem.

The solution is to replace all of the exit rollers. You must replace all of them at the same time because even one worn exit roller can cause the paper to jam. Besides, they're inexpensive. Don't skimp on these parts if you need to have them replaced.

Paper jams can also be the fault of the paper. If your printer consistently tries to feed multiple pages into the printer, the paper isn't dry enough. If you live in an area with high humidity, this could be a problem. We've heard some solutions that are pretty far out but that work (like keeping the paper in a Tupperware-type airtight container or microwaving it to remove moisture). The best all-around solution, however, is humidity control and keeping the paper wrapped until it's needed. Keep the humidity around 50 percent or lower (but above 25 percent if you can, in order to avoid problems with electrostatic discharge).

 Real World Scenario

Printer Triage

One of the authors relates the following story. He was in the local hospital ER a while ago having his hand examined (he had cut it pretty badly on some glass). The receptionist asked him a few questions, filled out a report in the medical database on her computer, and printed it. When the paper starting coming out of the laser printer, she grabbed it and "ripped" it from the printer as you might do if the paper were in an old typewriter! The printer's exit rollers complained bitterly and made a noise that made him cringe. She did this for every sheet of paper she printed.

The following week, that printer came in for service because it was jamming repeatedly. The problem? Worn exit rollers.

He had a word with the person in charge of computer repair at that hospital and saved them from many future repairs. The lesson? Printers don't have to be treated with kid gloves, but using them properly can prolong life and reduce the need for service repairs.

Finally, a grounded metal strip called the *static-eliminator strip* inside the printer drains the transfer corona charge away from the paper after it has been used to transfer toner from the EP cartridge. If that strip is missing, broken, or damaged, the charge will remain on the paper and may cause it to stick to the EP cartridge, causing a jam. If the paper jams after reaching the transfer corona assembly, this may be the cause.

Blank Pages

There's nothing more annoying than printing a 10-page contract and receiving 10 pages of blank paper from the printer. Blank pages are a somewhat common occurrence in laser printers. Somehow, the toner isn't being put on the paper. There are three major causes of blank pages:

- The toner cartridge
- The transfer corona assembly
- The high-voltage power supply (HVPS)

TONER CARTRIDGE

The toner cartridge is the source of most quality problems because it contains most of the image-formation pieces for laser printers. Let's start with the obvious. A blank page or faded prints will come out of the printer if there is no toner or low toner in the cartridge. It might sound simple, but some people think these things last forever. Many laser printers give some sort of warning if the toner cartridge is low, but it's easy to check. Just open the printer, remove the toner cartridge, and shake it. You will be able to hear if there's toner inside the cartridge. If it's empty, replace it with a known, good, manufacturer-recommended toner cartridge. If it is not yet empty, shaking it redistributes the toner and may provide better printing for some time.

When you're shaking a toner cartridge, loose toner can fall out of the cartridge and get on your clothing. Always hold the toner cartridge away from your body when shaking it.

Another issue that crops up rather often is the problem of using refilled or reconditioned toner cartridges. During their recycling process, these cartridges may be filled with the wrong kind of toner (for example, one with an incorrect composition). This can cause toner to be repelled from the EP drum instead of being attracted to it. Thus there's no toner on the page because there was no toner on the EP drum to begin with. The solution once again is to replace the toner cartridge with the type recommended by the manufacturer.

A third problem related to toner cartridges happens when someone installs a new toner cartridge and forgets to remove the sealing tape that is present to keep the toner in the cartridge during shipping. The solution to this problem is as easy as it is obvious: Remove the toner cartridge from the printer, remove the sealing tape, and reinstall the cartridge.

Most of the time if you have dust or debris in a printer, you can go ahead and use compressed air to blow it away. Don't do that with toner though, because it will make a huge mess. If you have a toner spill, use a specialized toner vacuum to pick it up. Also, never use a damp cloth to try to clean up a toner spill. If a cloth is needed, use a dry one.

TRANSFER CORONA ASSEMBLY

The second cause of the blank-page problem is a damaged or missing transfer corona wire or damaged transfer corona roller. If a wire is lost or damaged, the developed image won't transfer from the EP drum to the paper. Thus no image appears on the printout. To determine if this is causing your problem, do the first half of the self-test (described later in this chapter in the section called "Self-Tests"). If there is an image on the drum but not on the paper, you know that the transfer corona assembly isn't doing its job.

To check if the transfer corona assembly is causing the problem, open the cover and examine the wire (or roller, if your printer uses one). The corona wire is hard to see, so you may need a flashlight. You will know if it's broken or missing just by looking at it (it will either be in pieces or just not be there). If it's not broken or missing, the problem may be related to the high-voltage power supply.

The transfer corona wire (or roller) is a relatively inexpensive part, and it can easily be replaced with the removal of two screws and some patience.

HIGH-VOLTAGE POWER SUPPLY (HVPS)

The HVPS supplies high-voltage, low-current power to both the charging and transfer corona assemblies in laser printers. If it's broken, neither corona will work properly. If the self-test shows an image on the drum but none on the paper, and the transfer corona assembly is present and not damaged, then the HVPS is at fault.

All-Black Pages

Only slightly more annoying than 10 blank pages are 10 black pages. This happens when the charging unit (the charging corona wire or charging corona roller) in the toner cartridge malfunctions and fails to place a charge on the EP drum. Because the drum is grounded, it has no charge. Anything with a charge (like toner) will stick to it. As the drum rotates, all of the toner is transferred to the page and a black page is formed.

This problem wastes quite a bit of toner, but it can be fixed easily. The solution (again) is to replace the toner cartridge with a known, good manufacturer-recommended one. If that doesn't solve the problem, then the HVPS is at fault (it's not providing the high voltage that the charging corona needs to function).

Repetitive Small Marks or Defects

Repetitive marks occur frequently in heavily used (as well as older) laser printers. Toner spilled inside the printer may be causing the problem. It can also be caused by a crack or chip in the EP drum (this mainly happens with recycled cartridges), which can accumulate toner. In both cases, some of the toner gets stuck onto one of the rollers. Once this happens, every time the roller rotates and touches a piece of paper, it leaves toner smudges spaced a roller circumference apart.

The solution is relatively simple: Clean or replace the offending roller. To help you figure out which roller is causing the problem, the service manuals contain a chart like the one shown in Figure 12.14. (Some larger printers will also have the roller layout printed inside the service door.) To use the chart, place the printed page next to it.

Align the first occurrence of the smudge with the top arrow. The next smudge will line up with one of the other arrows. The arrow it lines up with tells you which roller is causing the problem.

FIGURE 12.14 Laser printer roller circumference chart

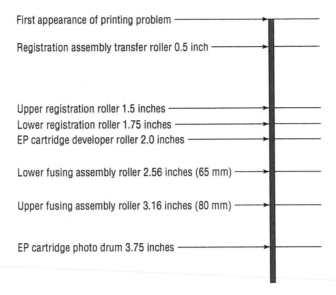

First appearance of printing problem

Registration assembly transfer roller 0.5 inch

Upper registration roller 1.5 inches

Lower registration roller 1.75 inches

EP cartridge developer roller 2.0 inches

Lower fusing assembly roller 2.56 inches (65 mm)

Upper fusing assembly roller 3.16 inches (80 mm)

EP cartridge photo drum 3.75 inches

Remember that the chart in Figure 12.14 is only an example. Your printer may have different-sized rollers and thus need a different chart. Check your printer's service documentation for a chart like this. It is valuable in determining which roller is causing a smudge.

Vertical White Lines on the Page

Vertical white lines running down all or part of the page are a relatively common problem on older printers, especially ones that don't see much maintenance. Foreign matter (more than likely toner) caught on the transfer corona wire causes this. The dirty spots keep the toner from being transmitted to the paper (at those locations, that is), with the result that streaks form as the paper progresses past the transfer corona wire.

The solution is to clean the corona wires. LaserJet Series II printers contain a small corona wire brush to help with this procedure. It's usually a small, green-handled brush located near the transfer corona wire. To use it, remove the toner cartridge and run the brush in the charging corona groove on top of the toner cartridge. Replace the cartridge, and use the brush to remove any foreign deposits on the transfer corona. Be sure to put it back in its holder when you're finished.

Vertical Black Lines on the Page

A groove or scratch in the EP drum can cause the problem of vertical black lines running down all or part of the page. Because a scratch is lower than the surface, it doesn't receive as much (if any) of a charge as the other areas. The result is that toner sticks to it as though it were discharged. The groove may go around the circumference of the drum, so the line may go all the way down the page.

Another possible cause of vertical black lines is a dirty charging corona wire. A dirty charging corona wire prevents a sufficient charge from being placed on the EP drum. Because the charge on the EP drum is almost zero, toner sticks to the areas that correspond to the dirty areas on the charging corona.

The solution to the first problem is, as always, to replace the toner cartridge (or EP drum, if your printer uses a separate EP drum and toner). You can also solve the second problem with a new toner cartridge, but in this case that would be an extreme solution. It's easier to clean the charging corona with the brush supplied with the cartridge.

Image Smudging

If you can pick up a sheet from a laser printer, run your thumb across it, and have the image come off on your thumb, you have a fuser problem. The fuser isn't heating the toner and fusing it into the paper. This could be caused by a number of things—but all of them can be handled by a fuser replacement. For example, if the halogen light inside the heating roller has burned out, that would cause the problem. The solution is to replace the fuser. The fuser can be replaced with a rebuilt unit, if you prefer. Rebuilt fusers are almost as good as new ones, and some even come with guarantees. Plus, they cost less.

 The whole fuser may not need to be replaced. Fuser components can be ordered from parts suppliers and can be rebuilt by you. For example, if the fuser has a bad lamp, you can order a lamp and replace it in the fuser.

A similar problem occurs when small areas of smudging repeat themselves down the page. Dents or cold spots in the fuser heat roller cause this problem. The only solution is to replace either the fuser assembly or the heat roller.

Ghosting

Ghosting is what you have when you can see light images of previously printed pages on the current page. This is caused by one of two things: a broken cleaning blade or bad erasure lamps. A broken cleaning blade causes old toner to build up on the EP drum and consequently presents itself in the next printed image. If the erasure lamps are bad, then the previous electrostatic discharges aren't completely wiped away. When the EP drum rotates toward the developing roller, some toner sticks to the slightly discharged areas.

If the problem is caused by a broken cleaner blade, you can replace the toner cartridge. If it's caused by bad erasure lamps, you'll need to replace them. Because the toner cartridge is the least expensive cure, you should try that first. Usually, replacing the toner cartridge will solve the ghosting problem. If it doesn't, you will have to replace the erasure lamps.

Printer Prints Pages of Garbage

This has happened to everyone at least once. You print a one-page letter, but instead of the letter you have 10 pages of what looks like garbage (or garbled characters) or many more pages with one character per page come out of the printer. This problem comes from one of two different sources: the printer driver software or the formatter board.

PRINTER DRIVER

The correct printer driver needs to be installed for the printer and operating system. For example, if you have an HP LaserJet III and a Windows 7 computer, then you need to install an HP LaserJet III driver made for Windows 7. Once the driver has been installed, it must be configured for the correct page-description language: PCL or PostScript. Most HP LaserJet printers use PCL (but can be configured for PostScript). Determine what page-description language your printer has been configured for, and set the printer driver to the same setting. If this is not done, you will get garbage out of the printer.

Most printers that have LCD displays will indicate that they are in Post-Script mode with a *PS* or *PostScript* somewhere in the display.

If the problem is the wrong driver setting, the garbage that the printer prints will look like English. That is, the words will be readable, but they won't make any sense.

FORMATTER BOARD

The other cause of several pages of garbage being printed is a bad formatter board. This circuit board takes the information the printer receives from the computer and turns it into commands for the various components in the printer. Usually, problems with the formatter board produce wavy lines of print or random patterns of dots on the page.

It's relatively easy to replace the formatter board in a laser printer. Usually, this board is installed under the printer and can be removed by loosening two screws and pulling it out. Typically, replacing the formatter board also replaces the printer interface, which is another possible source of garbage printouts.

Example Printer Testing: HP LaserJet

Now that we've defined some of the possible sources of problems with laser printers, let's discuss a few of the testing procedures that you use with them. We'll discuss HP LaserJet laser printers because they are the most popular brand of laser printer, but the topics covered here apply to other brands of laser printers as well.

We'll look at two ways to troubleshoot laser printers: self-tests and error codes (for laser printers with LCD displays).

SELF-TESTS

You can perform three tests to narrow down which assembly is causing the problem: the engine self-test, the engine half self-test, or the secret self-test. These tests, which the printer runs on its own when directed by the user, are internal diagnostics for printers, and they are included with most laser printers.

Engine Self-Test   The engine self-test tests the print engine of the LaserJet, bypassing the formatter board. This test causes the printer to print a single page with vertical lines running its length. If an engine self-test can be performed, you know that the laser print engine can print successfully. To perform an engine self-test, you must press the printer's self-test button, which is hidden behind a small cover on the side of the printer (see Figure 12.15). The location of the button varies from printer to printer, so you may have to refer to the printer manual. Using a pencil or probe, press the button, and the print engine will start printing the test page.

FIGURE 12.15   Print engine self-test button location. The location may vary on different printers.

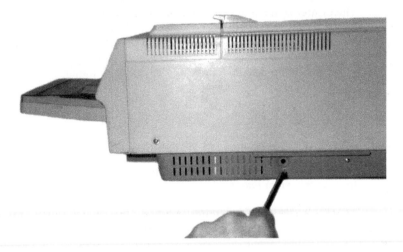

Half Self-Test   A print engine half self-test is performed the same way as the self-test, but you interrupt it halfway through the print cycle by opening the cover. This test is useful in determining which part of the print process is causing the printer to malfunction. If you stop the print process and part of a developed image is on the EP drum and part has been transferred to the paper, you know that the pickup rollers, registration rollers, laser scanner, charging roller, EP drum, and transfer roller are all working correctly. You can stop the half self-test at various points in the print process to determine the source of a malfunction.

Secret self-test   To activate this test, you must first put the printer into service mode. To accomplish this, turn on the printer while simultaneously holding down the On Line, Continue, and Enter buttons (that's the first secret part, because nobody knows it unless somebody tells them). When the screen comes up blank, release the keys and press, in order, Continue and then Enter. The printer will perform an internal self-test and then display 00 READY. At this point, you are ready to initiate the rest of the secret self-test. Take the printer offline by pressing the On Line button, press the Test button on the front panel, and hold the button until you see the 04 Self Test message. Then release the Test button. This will cause the printer to print one self-test page. (If you want a continuous printout, instead of releasing the Test button at the 04 Self Test message, keep holding the Test button. The printer will print continuous self-test pages until you power it off or press On Line or until it runs out of paper.)

ERROR CODES

In addition to the self-tests, you have another tool for troubleshooting HP laser printers. Error codes are a way for the LaserJet to tell the user (and a service technician) what's wrong. Table 12.5 details some of the most common codes displayed on an HP LaserJet.

TABLE 12.5 HP LaserJet error messages

Message	Description
00 Ready	The printer is in standby mode and ready to print.
02 Warming Up	The fuser is being warmed up before the 00 Ready state.
05 Self-Test	A full self-test has been initiated from the front panel.
11 Paper Out	The paper tray sensor is reporting that there is no paper in the paper tray. The printer will not print as long as this error exists.
13 Paper Jam	A piece of paper is caught in the paper path. To fix this problem, open the cover and clear the jam (including all pieces of paper causing the jam). Close the cover to resume printing. The printer will not print as long as this error exists.
14 No EP Cart	There is no EP cartridge (toner cartridge) installed in the printer. The printer will not print as long as this error exists.
15 Engine Test	An engine self-test is in progress.
16 Toner Low	The toner cartridge is almost out of toner. Replacement will be necessary soon.
50 Service	A fuser error has occurred. This problem is most commonly caused by fuser lamp failure. Power off the printer, and replace the fuser to solve the problem. The printer will not print as long as this error exists.
51 Error	There is a laser-scanning assembly problem. Test and replace, if necessary. The printer will not print as long as this error exists.
52 Error	The scanner motor in the laser scanning assembly is malfunctioning. Test and replace as per the service manual. The printer will not print as long as this error exists.
55 Error	There is a communication problem between the formatter and the DC controller. Test and replace as per the service manual. The printer will not print as long as this error exists.

When There Is No Display

Several times in the printer troubleshooting section, we have mentioned the LCD screen or printer display. Nearly every laser printer and many inkjet printers have them, and they are useful for configuring the device as well as relaying information to you. But what about when the screen itself doesn't work?

The screen assembly on a laser printer needs several components to work properly, including the formatter board, engine controller board, and cables connecting the display to each. If any of those components have failed, you could end up with a blank display. It could also be a failed low-voltage power supply (LVPS).

The way to troubleshoot this is to run an engine self-test, which we have already discussed. If there is no output from the engine self-test, then you have a problem with the power supply. If the test works, the device will print a page of lines, and you know that the LVPS is fine. Then it's most likely the display itself, the printer's memory (DIMMs), or the formatter board causing the problem.

Troubleshooting Tips for HP LaserJet Printers

Printer technicians usually use a set of troubleshooting steps to help them solve HP LaserJet printing problems. Let's detail each of them to bring our discussion of laser printer troubleshooting to a close:

1. **Is the exhaust fan operational?** This is the first component to receive power when the printer is turned on. If you can feel air coming out of the exhaust fan, this confirms that AC voltage is present and power is turned on, that +5VDC and +24VDC are being generated by the AC power supply (ACPS), and that the DC controller is functional. If there is no power to the printer (no lights, fan not operating), the ACPS is at fault. Replacement involves removing all printer covers and removing four screws. You can purchase a new ACPS module, but it is usually cheaper to replace it with a rebuilt unit.

 If you are into electronics, you can probably rebuild the ACPS yourself simply and cheaply. The main rectifier is usually the part that fails in these units; it can easily be replaced if you know what you're doing.

2. **Do the control panel LEDs work?** If so, the formatter board can communicate with the control panel. If the LEDs do not light, it could mean that the formatter board is bad, the control panel is bad, or the wires connecting the two are broken or shorting out.

3. **Does the main motor rotate at power up?** Turn off the power. Remove the covers from the sides of the printer. Turn the printer back on and carefully watch and listen for main motor rotation. If you see and hear the main motor rotating, this indicates that a

toner cartridge is installed, all photo sensors are functional, all motors are functional, and the printer can move paper (assuming that there are no obstructions).

4. **Does the fuser heat lamp light after the main motor finishes its rotation?** You will need to remove the covers to see this. The heat lamp should light after the main motor rotation and stay lit until the control panel says 00 Ready.

5. **Can the printer perform an engine test print?** A sheet of vertical lines indicates that the print engine works. This test print bypasses the formatter board and indicates whether the print problem resides in the engine. If the test print is successful, you can rule out the engine as a source of the problem. If the test print fails, you will have to troubleshoot the printer further to determine which engine component is causing the problem.

6. **Can the printer perform a control panel self-test?** This is the final test to ensure printer operation. If you can press the Test Page control panel button and receive a test printout, this means that the entire printer is working properly. The only possibilities for problems are outside the printer (interfaces, cables, and software problems).

Most printers will print a test page, which contains both colors and patterns, based on their capabilities. Although the exact style of pattern may vary, the idea is the same for all printers. You're checking to ensure that the printer can do what it's capable of. Many test patterns will measure gradients and resolution as well as letter qualities at various font sizes. Color printers will also print color sections, whereas black-and-white printers will often produce patterns in grayscale. If you are experiencing print-quality issues, running a test pattern is a good way to check to see what's wrong with the printer.

Managing Print Jobs

Most people know how to send a job to the printer. Clicking File and then Print, or pressing Ctrl+P on your keyboard, generally does the trick. But once the job gets sent to the printer, what do you do if it doesn't print?

Keep in mind that in a networked environment, users need the proper permissions both to install and to print to the printer. Not having permission will result in denied access.

When you send a job to the printer, that print job ends up in a line with all other documents sent to that printer. The line of all print jobs is called the *print queue*. In most cases, the printer will print jobs on a first-come, first-served basis. (There are exceptions if you've enabled printing priorities in Printer Properties.) Once you send the job to the printer in

Windows, a small printer icon will appear in the system tray in the lower-right corner of your desktop, near the clock. By double-clicking it (or by right-clicking it and selecting the printer name), you will end up looking at the jobs in the print queue, like the one shown in Figure 12.16.

FIGURE 12.16   Print jobs in the print queue in Windows

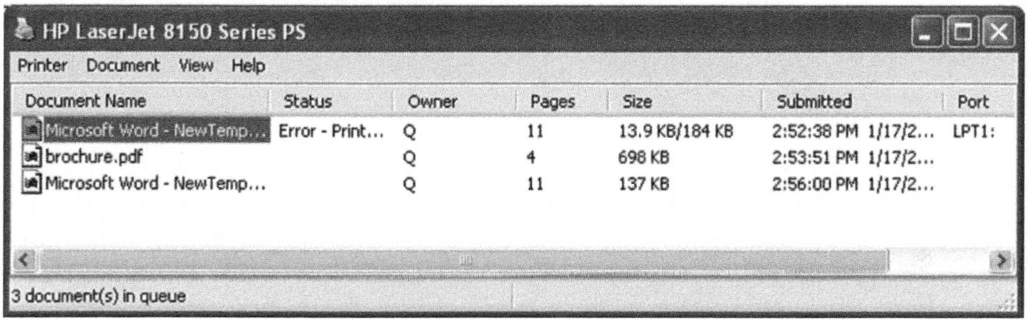

Document Name	Status	Owner	Pages	Size	Submitted	Port
Microsoft Word - NewTemp...	Error - Print...	Q	11	13.9 KB/184 KB	2:52:38 PM 1/17/2...	LPT1:
brochure.pdf		Q	4	698 KB	2:53:51 PM 1/17/2...	
Microsoft Word - NewTemp...		Q	11	137 KB	2:56:00 PM 1/17/2...	

3 document(s) in queue

In Figure 12.16, you can see that the first document submitted has an error, which may explain why it hasn't printed. All of the other documents in the queue are blocked until the job with the error is cleared. You can clear it one of two ways. Either right-click on the document and choose Cancel or from the Document menu, shown in Figure 12.17, choose Cancel.

FIGURE 12.17   Printer Document menu in Windows

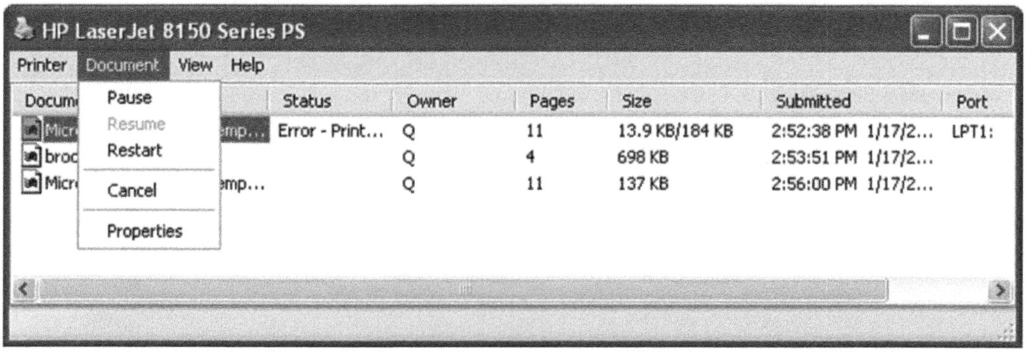

Docum	Pause		Status	Owner	Pages	Size	Submitted	Port
Micr	Resume	mp...	Error - Print...	Q	11	13.9 KB/184 KB	2:52:38 PM 1/17/2...	LPT1:
broc	Restart			Q	4	698 KB	2:53:51 PM 1/17/2...	
Micr	Cancel	mp...		Q	11	137 KB	2:56:00 PM 1/17/2...	
	Properties							

Note that from the menu that you see in Figure 12.17, you can pause, resume, restart, and cancel print jobs as well as see properties of the selected print job. If you wanted to pause or cancel all jobs going to a printer, you would do that from the Printer menu, as shown in Figure 12.18.

FIGURE 12.18 Printer menu in Windows

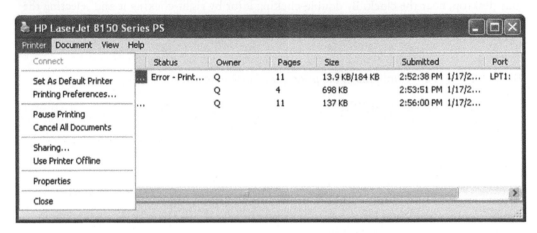

Once you have cleared the print job causing the problem, the next job will move to the top of the queue. It should show its status as Printing, like the one shown in Figure 12.19. But what if it shows that it's printing but it still isn't working? (We're assuming that the printer is powered on, connected properly, and online.) It could be a problem with the print spooler.

FIGURE 12.19 Print job printing correctly

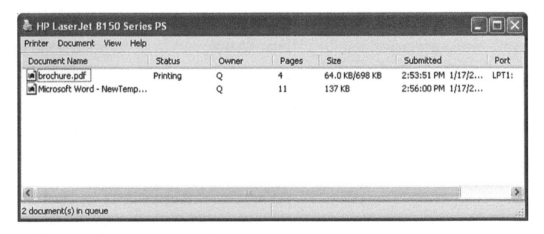

 If print jobs are processed very slowly, or if you are continually seeing "low memory" error messages, it might be a good time to upgrade the memory in the printer.

Managing the Print Spooler

The *print spooler* is a service that formats print jobs in a language that the printer understands. Think of it as a holding area where the print jobs are prepared for the printer. In Windows, the spooler is a service that's started automatically when Windows loads.

If jobs aren't printing and there's no apparent reason why, it could be that the print spooler has stalled. To fix the problem, you need to stop and restart the print spooler. Exercise 12.3 walks you through stopping and restarting the spooler in Windows 7.

EXERCISE 12.3

Stopping and Restarting the Print Spooler in Windows 7

1. Open Computer Management, and navigate to Services (right-click the Computer icon and choose Manage; if necessary, click the arrow next to Services And Applications to expand the list).

2. Find the Print Spooler service, which is selected in Figure 12.20.

FIGURE 12.20 Locating the Print Spooler service

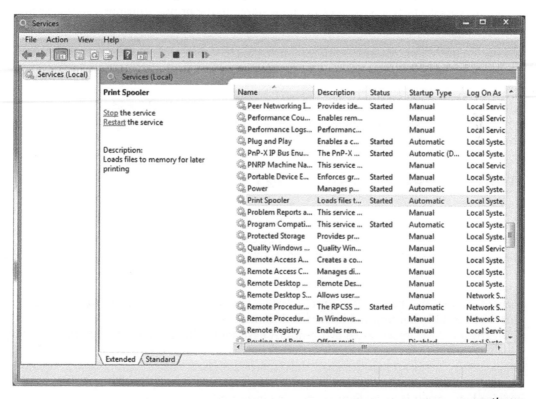

continues

3. Stop the spooler. There are several ways you can do this. You can right-click the service name and choose Stop, click the Stop square above the list of services, or click Stop under where it says Print Spooler to the left of the services list.

4. Restart the spooler by right-clicking the service name and choosing Start or by clicking the Start arrow above the list of services. After it's restarted, the service's Status column should display Started.

5. Close Computer Management.

If you have a different version of Windows, the steps to stop and restart the spooler are the same as in Exercise 12.3; the only difference might be in how you get to Computer Management.

Printing a Test Page

If your printer isn't spitting out print jobs, it may be a good idea to print a test page and see if that works. The test page information is stored in the printer's memory, so there's no formatting or translating of jobs required. It's simply a test to make sure that your printer hears your computer.

When you install a printer, one of the last questions it asks is if you want to print a test page. If there's any question, go ahead and do it. If the printer is already installed, you can print a test page from the printer's Properties window (right-click the printer and choose Printer Properties). Just click the Print Test Page button and it should work. If nothing happens, double-check your connections and stop and restart the print spooler. If garbage prints, there is likely a problem with the printer or the print driver.

Troubleshooting Networking Problems

As a technician, you are going to be called on to solve a variety of issues, including hardware, software, and networking problems. Networking problems can sometimes be the most tricky to solve considering that it could be either a software or a hardware problem or a combination of the two causing your connectivity issue.

The first adage for troubleshooting any hardware problem is to check your connections. That holds true for networking as well, but then your troubleshooting will need to go far deeper than that in a hurry. As with troubleshooting anything else, follow a logical procedure when troubleshooting and be sure to document your work.

Nearly all of the issues tested by CompTIA have something to do with connectivity, which makes sense because that's what networking is all about. Connectivity issues, when not caused by hardware, are generally the result of a messed-up configuration. And because the most common protocol in use today, TCP/IP, has a lot of configuration options, you can imagine how easy it is to configure something incorrectly.

In the following sections, we'll look at connectivity issues and how to resolve them. We'll also review several tools that we've talked about elsewhere in the book but are handy for network troubleshooting as well.

CompTIA 220-901 objective 4.4 combines wired and wireless networking. We'll cover them together and note when specific differences exist.

Resolving Connectivity Issues

The whole purpose of using a network is to connect to other resources, right? So when networks don't work like they're supposed to, users tend to get a bit upset. With the explosion of wireless networking over the last several years, our job as technicians has only gotten more complicated. Let's take a look at some common issues that you might run across and how to deal with them.

No Connectivity

Let's start with the most dire situation: no connectivity. Taking a step back to look at the big picture, think about all of the components that go into networking. On the client side, you need a network card and drivers, operating system, protocol, and the right configuration. Then you have a cable of some sort or a wireless connection. At the other end is a switch or wireless router. That device connects to other devices, and so forth. The point is, if someone is complaining of no connectivity, there could be one of several different things causing it. So start with the basics.

The most common issue that prevents network connectivity on a wired network is a bad or unplugged patch cable. Cleaning crews and the rollers on the bottoms of chairs are the most common threats to patch cables. In most cases, wall jacks are placed 4 to 10 feet away from the desktop. The patch cables are normally lying exposed under the user's desk, and from time to time damage is done to the cable or it's inadvertently snagged and unplugged. Tightly cinching the cable while tying it up out of the way is no better a solution. Slack must be left in the cable to allow for some amount of equipment movement and to avoid altering the electrical characteristics of the cable. When you troubleshoot connectivity, start with the most rudimentary explanations first. Make sure that the patch cable is tightly plugged in, and then look at the card and check if any lights are on. If there are lights on, use the NIC's documentation to help troubleshoot. More often than not, shutting down the machine, unplugging the patch and power cables for a moment, and then reattaching them and rebooting the PC will fix an unresponsive NIC.

A properly connected NIC should typically have one light illuminated (the link light). If the link light is not illuminated, it indicates a problem with the NIC, the patch cable, or the device to which the patch cable is connecting (hub, switch, server, and so on). Other lights that may be illuminated include a speed light, duplex light, and/or activity light.

If you don't have any lights, you don't have a connection. It could be that the cable is bad or that it's not plugged in on the other side, or it could also be a problem with the NIC or the connectivity device on the other side. Is this the only computer having problems? If everyone else in the same area is having the same problem, that points to a central issue.

Most wireless network cards also have indicators on them that can help you troubleshoot. For example, a wireless card might have a connection light and an activity light, much like a wired network card. On one particular card we've used, the lights will alternate blinking if the card isn't attached to a network. Once it attaches, the connection light will be solid and the link light will blink when it's busy. Other cards may operate in a slightly different manner, so be sure to consult your documentation.

If you don't have any lights, try reseating your cables and rebooting. It might also help to reseat the card. If you're using a USB or ExpressCard wireless adapter, this is pretty easy. If it's inside your desktop, it will require a little surgery. If it's integrated into your laptop, you could have serious issues. Try rebooting first. If that doesn't help, see if you can use an expansion NIC and make that one light up.

Let's assume that you have lights and that no one else is having a problem. (Yes, it's just you.) This means that the network hardware is probably okay, so it's time to check the configuration. Open a command prompt, type IPCONFIG, and press Enter. You should get an IP address. (If it starts with 169.254.*x.x*, that's an APIPA address. We'll talk about those next.) If you don't have a valid IP address, that's the problem.

The UNIX, Linux, and OS X version of IPCONFIG is IFCONFIG.

Remember that in order to communicate on a network using TCP/IP (IPv4), you need to have a unique IP address and a valid subnet mask. If you want to communicate on a network outside of your own local network, you also need a default gateway.

If you do have a valid IP address, it's time to see how far your connectivity reaches. With your command prompt open, use the PING command to ping a known, remote working host. If that doesn't work, start working backward. Can you ping the outside port of your router? The inside port? A local host? (Some technicians recommend pinging your loopback address first with PING 127.0.0.1 and then working your way out to see where the connectivity ends. Either way is fine. The advantage to starting with the loopback is that if it doesn't work, you know nothing else will either.) Using this methodology, you'll be able to figure out where your connectivity truly begins and ends.

The ping utility is useful for troubleshooting several types of connectivity problems that you might encounter. For example, if you can ping an IP address but not a hostname, then you know it's a DNS error. If you can ping a hostname (such as a remote web server) but you can't get to it with your web browser, then you know it's a problem with your browser or HTTP or port 80, which may possibly involve the router configuration (like a blocked port).

APIPA and Link Local Addresses

As we talked about in Chapter 7, "Introduction to TCP/IP," Automatic Private IP Addressing (APIPA) is a service that auto-configures your network card with an IP address. APIPA kicks in only if your computer is set to receive an IP address from the Dynamic Host Configuration Protocol (DHCP) server and that server doesn't respond. You can always tell an APIPA address because it will be in the format of 169.254.*x*.*x*.

When you have an APIPA address, you will be able to communicate with other computers that also have an APIPA address but not with any other resources. The solution is to figure out why you're not getting an answer from the DHCP server and fix that problem.

Link local addresses are the IPv6 version of APIPA, and link local addresses always start with fe80:: (they are in the fe80::/10 range). They will work to communicate with computers on a local network, but they will not work through a router. If the only IP address that your computer has is a link local one, you're not going to communicate outside of your network. The resolution is the same as it is for APIPA.

IP Address Conflicts

Every host on a network needs to have a unique IP address. If two or more hosts have the same address, communication problems will occur. The good news is that nearly every operating system today will warn you if it detects an IP address conflict with your computer. The bad news is it won't fix it by itself.

The communication problems will vary. In some cases, the computer will seem nearly fine, with intermittent connectivity issues. In others, it will appear as if you have no connectivity.

The most common cause of this is if someone configures a computer with a static IP address that's part of the DHCP server's range. The DHCP server, not knowing that the address has been statically assigned somewhere, doles out the address and now there's a conflict. Rebooting the computer won't help, and neither will releasing the address and getting a new lease from the DHCP server—it's just going to hand out the same address again because it doesn't know that there's a problem.

As the administrator, you need to track down the offending user. A common way to do this is to use a packet sniffer to look at network traffic and determine the computer name or MAC address associated with the IP address in question. Most administrators don't keep network maps of MAC addresses, but everyone should have a network map with hostnames. If not, it could be a long, tedious process to check everyone's computer to find the culprit.

 Usually the person who manually configured their address didn't intend to cause any problems. This would be a good time to show your professionalism and communication skills and educate the user as to why they shouldn't have done what they did.

Limited or Local Connectivity

In a way, limited connectivity problems are a bit of a blessing. You can immediately rule out client-side hardware issues because they can connect to some resources. You just need to figure out why they can't connect to others. This is most likely caused by one of two things: a configuration issue or a connectivity device (such as a router) problem.

Check the local configuration first. Use IPCONFIG /ALL to ensure that the computer's IP address, subnet mask, and default gateway are all configured properly. After that, use the ping utility to see the range of connectivity. In situations like this, it's also good to check with other users in the area. Are they having the same connectivity issues? If so, it's more likely to be a central problem rather than one with the client computer.

Intermittent Connectivity

Under this heading, we're going to consider intermittent connectivity, slow transfer speeds, and low radio frequency (RF) signals because they are all pretty similar.

On a wired network, if you run into slow speeds or intermittent connectivity, it's likely a load issue. There's too much traffic for the network to handle, and the network is bogging down. (You obviously don't need to worry about RF signals on a wired network.) Solutions include adding a switch, replacing your hubs with switches, and even creating virtual LANs (VLANs) with switches. If the network infrastructure is old (for example, if it's running on Category 3 cable or you only have 10Mbps switches), then it might be time for an upgrade.

Wireless networks can get overloaded too. It's recommended that no more than 30 or so client computers use one wireless access point (WAP) or wireless router. Any more than that can cause intermittent access problems. The most common reason that users on wireless networks experience any of these issues though is distance. The further away from the WAP the user gets, the weaker the signal becomes. When the signal weakens, the transfer rates drop dramatically. For example, the signal from an 802.11g wireless router has a maximum range of about 300 feet barring any obstructions. At that distance though, 802.11g will support transfer rates of only 6Mbps—far less than the 54Mbps the users think they're getting! The solution here is to move closer or install more access points. Depending on the configuration of your working environment, you could also consider adding a directional antenna to the WAP. It will increase the distance the signal travels, but only in a limited direction.

SSID Not Found

This is obviously a wireless problem, because wired networks don't use service-set identifiers (SSIDs). If a client can't find an SSID for a network it had previously joined, it's possible that the router's SSID has been changed. If you're going to change an SSID, be sure to alert all users or technicians who might be affected. A second potential cause could be that the router is configured to not broadcast SSIDs. Some administrators will stop this broadcast, believing that doing so will increase the network security. It really doesn't, because any semi-decent hacker with a wireless packet sniffer will pick it up—what it does best, though, is make it difficult for legitimate users to join the network. With all of that said, CompTIA A+ exam objectives list disabling SSID broadcasts as a security measure, so be aware of that. Just don't expect it to secure the wireless network in real life.

A third potential cause is that the user's computer is too far out of range. Get closer to the access point or wireless router and the signal should appear.

Using Network Troubleshooting Tools

The CompTIA A+ 220-901 exam will test you on your knowledge of troubleshooting tools for networks. There are two categories of tools that you need to know: hardware tools and software commands.

Hardware and Cabling Tools

We covered several different types of cables and their properties in Chapter 6, "Networking Fundamentals." Here we will look at some tools that can be used to make or test network cables as well as a few tools to troubleshoot network connectivity issues.

CRIMPER

A *crimper* is a very handy tool for helping you put connectors on the end of a cable. Most crimpers will be a combination tool that strips and snips wires as well as crimps the connector on to the end. Figure 12.21 shows you one of these tools. You can also buy tools that are just cable strippers and cable snippers, but usually the point of cutting and stripping a cable is to put a connector on the end of it, so why not just get a crimper that does it all?

FIGURE 12.21   A UTP crimper

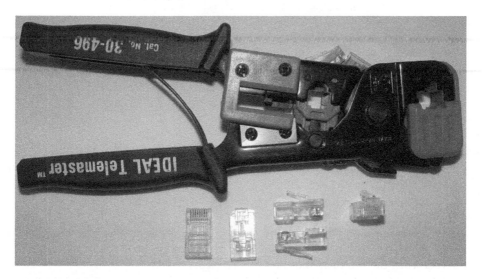

MULTIMETER

Multimeters are versatile electronic measuring tools. A *multimeter* can measure voltage, current, and resistance on a wire. There are a wide variety of types and qualities on the market, everywhere from economical $10 versions to ones that cost several thousand dollars. Figure 12.22 shows a basic multimeter.

FIGURE 12.22 A multimeter

TONER PROBE

If you need to trace a wire in a wall from one location to another, a *toner probe* is the tool for you. Shown in Figure 12.23, it consists of two pieces: a tone generator and a probe. Because it's so good at tracking, you will sometimes hear this referred to as a "fox and hound."

To use a toner probe, attach one end to one end of the cable, such as the end at the computer. Then go to the patch panel with the other end of the probe to locate the cable. These are lifesavers when the cables are not properly labeled.

CABLE TESTER

Cable testers are indispensable tools for any network technician. Usually you would use a cable tester before you install a cable to make sure it works. Of course, you can test them after they've been run as well. A decent cable tester will tell you the type of cable, and more elaborate models will have connectors for multiple types of cables. Figure 12.24 shows a TRENDnet cable tester.

FIGURE 12.23   A toner probe

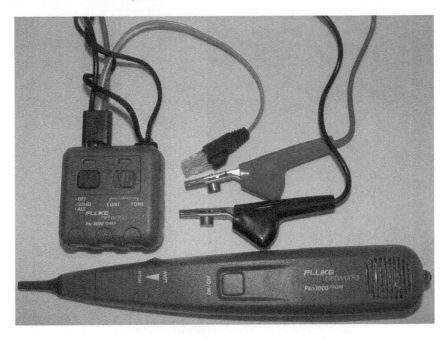

FIGURE 12.24   TRENDnet cable tester

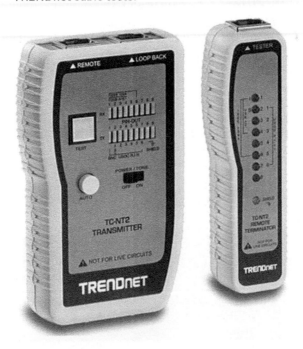

PUNCH-DOWN TOOL

If you're working on a larger network installation, you might use a punch-down tool. It's not a testing tool but one that allows you to connect (that is, punch down) the exposed ends of a wire into wiring harnesses, such as a 110 block (used many times in connectivity closets to help simplify the tangled mess of cables). Figure 12.25 shows the tool and its changeable bit.

FIGURE 12.25 A punch-down tool

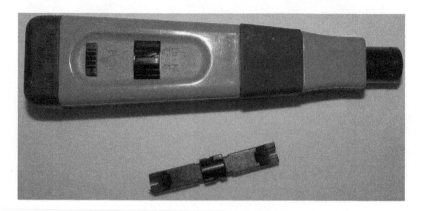

LOOPBACK PLUG

A loopback plug is for testing the ability of a network adapter to send and receive. The plug gets plugged into the NIC, and then a loopback test is performed using troubleshooting software. You can then tell if the card is working properly or not. Figure 12.26 shows an Ethernet loopback plug, but they are made for fiber-optic NICs as well.

FIGURE 12.26 An Ethernet loopback plug

WIRELESS LOCATOR

The one hardware tool that we didn't talk much about earlier is a wireless locator. Specific tools for locating Wi-Fi networks and analyzing their traffic are indispensable today. A wireless locator or a Wi-Fi analyzer can be either a handheld hardware device, such as the one shown in Figure 12.27, or specialized software that is installed on a laptop and whose purpose is to detect and analyze Wi-Fi signals. Anyone interested in wardriving will definitely have one of these, but they're also handy for locating wireless hot spots.

FIGURE 12.27   RF Explorer handheld wireless locator

Software Commands

Troubleshooting networks often involves using a combination of hardware tools and software commands. Usually, the software commands are easier to deal with because you don't need to dig around physically in a mess of wires to figure out what's going on. The downside to the software commands is that there can be a number of options that you need to memorize. In the following sections, we'll cover the networking command-line tools, which you are expected to know for this exam: PING, IPCONFIG/IFCONFIG, TRACERT, NETSTAT, NBTSTAT, NET, NETDOM, and NSLOOKUP.

PING COMMAND

The PING command is one of the most useful commands in the TCP/IP protocol. It sends a series of packets to another system, which in turn sends back a response. This utility can be extremely useful for troubleshooting problems with remote hosts. Pings are also called ICMP echo requests/replies because they use Internet Control Message Protocol (ICMP).

The PING command indicates whether the host can be reached and how long it took for the host to send a return packet. Across wide area network links, the time value will be much larger than across healthy LAN links.

The syntax for PING is ping *hostname* or ping *IP address*. Figure 12.28 shows what a ping should look like.

FIGURE 12.28 A successful ping

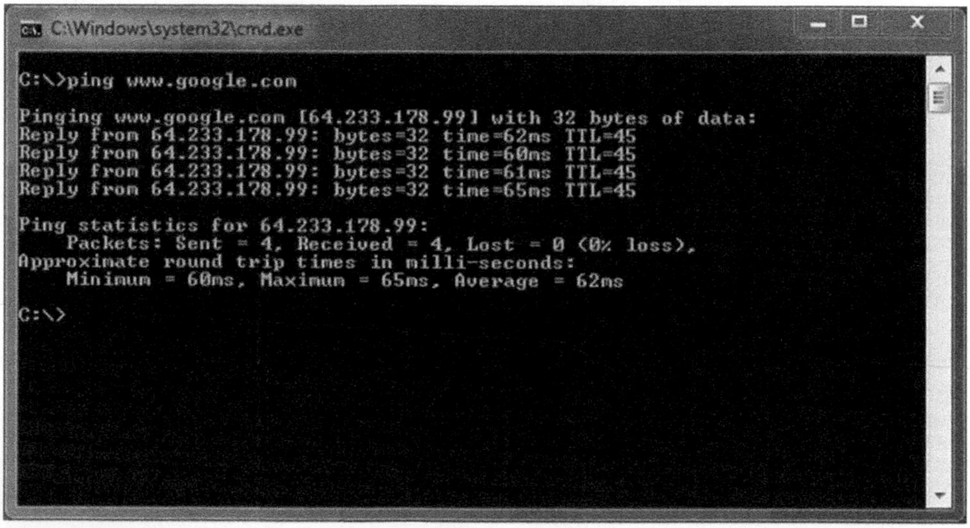

```
C:\>ping www.google.com

Pinging www.google.com [64.233.178.99] with 32 bytes of data:
Reply from 64.233.178.99: bytes=32 time=62ms TTL=45
Reply from 64.233.178.99: bytes=32 time=60ms TTL=45
Reply from 64.233.178.99: bytes=32 time=61ms TTL=45
Reply from 64.233.178.99: bytes=32 time=65ms TTL=45

Ping statistics for 64.233.178.99:
    Packets: Sent = 4, Received = 4, Lost = 0 (0% loss),
Approximate round trip times in milli-seconds:
    Minimum = 60ms, Maximum = 65ms, Average = 62ms

C:\>
```

As you can see, by pinging with the hostname, we found the host's IP address thanks to DNS. The time is how long in milliseconds it took to receive the response. On a LAN, you want this to be 10 milliseconds (ms) or less, but 60ms to 65ms for an Internet ping isn't too bad.

There are several options for the PING command, and you can see them all by typing ping /? at the command prompt. Table 12.6 lists some of the more useful ones.

TABLE 12.6 PING options

Option	Function
-t	Persistent ping. Will ping the remote host until stopped by the client (by using Ctrl+C).
-n *count*	Specifies the number of echo requests to send.

Option	Function
-l *size*	Specifies the packet size to send.
ping -4 / ping -6	Use either the IPv4 or IPv6 network explicitly.

> Some webmasters have configured their routers to block pings in order to avoid problems such as someone trying to eat up bandwidth with a *ping of death* (sending a persistent ping with a huge buffer to overwhelm the recipient). Therefore, if you ping a website, it's possible that you won't get a response even though the site is functional.

IPCONFIG COMMAND

With Windows-based operating systems, you can determine the network settings on the client's network interface cards, as well as any that a DHCP server has leased to your computer, by typing the following at a command prompt: **IPCONFIG /ALL**.

IPCONFIG /ALL also gives you full details on the duration of your current lease. You can verify whether a DHCP client has connectivity to a DHCP server by releasing the client's IP address and then attempting to lease an IP address. You can conduct this test by typing the following sequence of commands from the DHCP client at a command prompt:

```
ipconfig /release
ipconfig /renew
```

IPCONFIG is one of the first tools to use when experiencing problems accessing resources because it will show you whether an address has been issued to the machine. If the address displayed falls within the 169.254.*x.x* category, this means that the client was unable to reach the DHCP server and has defaulted to Automatic Private IP Addressing (APIPA), which will prevent the network card from communicating outside its subnet, if not altogether. Table 12.7 lists useful switches for IPCONFIG.

TABLE 12.7   IPCONFIG switches

Switch	Purpose
/ALL	Shows full configuration information
/RELEASE	Releases the IP address, if you are getting addresses from a Dynamic Host Configuration Protocol (DHCP) server
/RELEASE6	Releases the IPv6 addresses

continues

TABLE 12.7 IPCONFIG switches *(continued)*

Switch	Purpose
/RENEW	Obtains a new IP address from a DHCP server
/RENEW6	Obtains a new IPv6 address from a DHCP server
/FLUSHDNS	Flushes the Domain Name System (DNS) server name resolver cache

In the UNIX, Linux, and Mac OS X worlds, a utility similar to ipconfig is ifconfig.

Figure 12.29 shows output from IPCONFIG, and Figure 12.30 shows you the output from IPCONFIG /ALL.

FIGURE 12.29 IPCONFIG output

```
C:\Windows\system32\cmd.exe                                    _ □ X

C:\>ipconfig

Windows IP Configuration

Wireless LAN adapter Wireless Network Connection 3:

    Media State . . . . . . . . . . . . : Media disconnected
    Connection-specific DNS Suffix  . :

Wireless LAN adapter Wireless Network Connection:

    Connection-specific DNS Suffix  . : ZoomTown.com
    Link-local IPv6 Address . . . . . : fe80::9907:2be8:16b3:e9c1%12
    IPv4 Address. . . . . . . . . . . : 192.168.1.142
    Subnet Mask . . . . . . . . . . . : 255.255.255.0
    Default Gateway . . . . . . . . . : 192.168.1.1

Ethernet adapter Local Area Connection:

    Media State . . . . . . . . . . . . : Media disconnected
    Connection-specific DNS Suffix  . :

Ethernet adapter VirtualBox Host-Only Network:

    Connection-specific DNS Suffix  . :
    Link-local IPv6 Address . . . . . : fe80::81:e66f:7e0e:3133%16
    IPv4 Address. . . . . . . . . . . : 192.168.56.1
    Subnet Mask . . . . . . . . . . . : 255.255.255.0
    Default Gateway . . . . . . . . . :

C:\>
```

FIGURE 12.30   IPCONFIG /ALL output

```
C:\Windows\system32\cmd.exe                                          _  □  X

C:\>ipconfig /all

Windows IP Configuration

    Host Name . . . . . . . . . . . . : Q-HP
    Primary Dns Suffix  . . . . . . . :
    Node Type . . . . . . . . . . . . : Hybrid
    IP Routing Enabled. . . . . . . . : No
    WINS Proxy Enabled. . . . . . . . : No
    DNS Suffix Search List. . . . . . : zoomtown.com

Wireless LAN adapter Wireless Network Connection 3:

    Media State . . . . . . . . . . . : Media disconnected
    Connection-specific DNS Suffix  . :
    Description . . . . . . . . . . . : Microsoft Virtual WiFi Miniport Adapter
    Physical Address. . . . . . . . . : C0-C1-C0-6C-92-4A
    DHCP Enabled. . . . . . . . . . . : Yes
    Autoconfiguration Enabled . . . . : Yes

Wireless LAN adapter Wireless Network Connection:

    Connection-specific DNS Suffix  . : ZoomTown.com
    Description . . . . . . . . . . . : Linksys AE2500
    Physical Address. . . . . . . . . : C0-C1-C0-6C-92-4A
    DHCP Enabled. . . . . . . . . . . : Yes
    Autoconfiguration Enabled . . . . : Yes
    Link-local IPv6 Address . . . . . : fe80::9907:2be8:16b3:e9c1%12(Preferred)
    IPv4 Address. . . . . . . . . . . : 192.168.1.142(Preferred)
    Subnet Mask . . . . . . . . . . . : 255.255.255.0
    Lease Obtained. . . . . . . . . . : Sunday, May 17, 2015 10:39:08 AM
    Lease Expires . . . . . . . . . . : Monday, May 25, 2015 7:45:32 AM
    Default Gateway . . . . . . . . . : 192.168.1.1
    DHCP Server . . . . . . . . . . . : 192.168.1.1
    DHCPv6 IAID . . . . . . . . . . . : 331399616
    DHCPv6 Client DUID. . . . . . . . : 00-01-00-01-13-8F-AC-A5-40-61-86-E4-5A-9A

    DNS Servers . . . . . . . . . . . : 192.168.1.1
    NetBIOS over Tcpip. . . . . . . . : Enabled
    Connection-specific DNS Suffix Search List :
                                        zoomtown.com

Ethernet adapter Local Area Connection:

    Media State . . . . . . . . . . . : Media disconnected
    Connection-specific DNS Suffix  . :
    Description . . . . . . . . . . . : Realtek PCIe GBE Family Controller
    Physical Address. . . . . . . . . : 40-61-86-E4-5A-9A
    DHCP Enabled. . . . . . . . . . . : Yes
    Autoconfiguration Enabled . . . . : Yes

Ethernet adapter VirtualBox Host-Only Network:

    Connection-specific DNS Suffix  . :
    Description . . . . . . . . . . . : VirtualBox Host-Only Ethernet Adapter
    Physical Address. . . . . . . . . : 08-00-27-00-5C-61
    DHCP Enabled. . . . . . . . . . . : No
    Autoconfiguration Enabled . . . . : Yes
    Link-local IPv6 Address . . . . . : fe80::81:e66f:7e0e:3133%16(Preferred)
    IPv4 Address. . . . . . . . . . . : 192.168.56.1(Preferred)
    Subnet Mask . . . . . . . . . . . : 255.255.255.0
    Default Gateway . . . . . . . . . :
    DHCPv6 IAID . . . . . . . . . . . : 419954727
    DHCPv6 Client DUID. . . . . . . . : 00-01-00-01-13-8F-AC-A5-40-61-86-E4-5A-9A

    DNS Servers . . . . . . . . . . . : fec0:0:0:ffff::1%1
                                        fec0:0:0:ffff::2%1
                                        fec0:0:0:ffff::3%1
    NetBIOS over Tcpip. . . . . . . . : Enabled

C:\>
```

In Exercise 12.4, you will renew an IP address on a Windows 7/Vista system within the graphical interface. Exercise 12.5 shows you how to renew your lease from the command line.

EXERCISE 12.4

Renew an IP Address in Windows 7/Vista

1. From the Start menu, right-click Network to open the Network dialog box and select Properties and then Sharing Center. (This exercise assumes the use of Windows 7 or Vista and dynamic IP assignments from a DHCP server.)

2. In the left pane, click Manage Network Connections (in Windows 7 this is Change Adapter Settings). This will open a new window displaying your network connections.

3. Right-click your connection and choose Status. On the General tab of the network connection's status properties, you will see information such as whether you are connected, the speed of the connection, and how long the connection has been active.

4. Click the Details button. This expands the information by also showing you the physical (MAC) address and lease information, among other things.

5. Back at the General tab, click the Diagnose button. This will diagnose any network problems and attempt to establish or renew the connection (in Windows Vista, you need to click Reset The Network Adapter For Local Area Connection to release/renew the DHCP lease.) If the network (DHCP) is functioning properly, a notification that it finished will appear in a short time. If not, Windows will attempt to repair the connection.

While Windows provides this interface to troubleshoot connection problems, some administrators still prefer the reliability of a command-line interface. Exercise 12.5 shows you how to perform a similar action using the command line.

EXERCISE 12.5

Renew an IP Address from the Command Line

1. Open a command prompt (choose Start ▸ Run, and then type **CMD**). (This exercise assumes that you are using Windows 7 or Windows Vista and dynamic IP assignments from a DHCP server.)

2. Type **IPCONFIG** and view the abbreviated list of information.

3. Type **IPCONFIG /ALL** to see the full list. Notice the date and time on the lease for the IP address.

4. Type **IPCONFIG /RENEW** followed by **IPCONFIG /ALL**. The date and time on the lease for the IP address should be the current date and time.

5. Close the command-prompt window by typing **EXIT** and pressing Enter.

TRACERT COMMAND

TRACERT (trace route) is a Windows-based command-line utility that enables you to verify the route to a remote host. Execute the command TRACERT *hostname*, where *hostname* is the computer name or IP address of the computer whose route you want to trace. Tracert returns the different IP addresses the packet was routed through to reach the final destination. The results also include the number of hops needed to reach the destination. If you execute the TRACERT command without any options, you see a help file that describes all of the TRACERT switches.

 TRACEROUTE can be used on UNIX/Linux machines, and it performs the same task as TRACERT.

This utility determines the intermediary steps involved in communicating with another IP host. It provides a road map of all the routing an IP packet takes to get from host A to host B.

Timing information from TRACERT can be useful for detecting a malfunctioning or overloaded router. Figure 12.31 shows what a TRACERT output looks like. In addition to TRACERT, there are many graphical third-party network-tracing utilities available on the market.

FIGURE 12.31   TRACERT output

```
C:\Windows\system32\cmd.exe

C:\>tracert www.google.com

Tracing route to www.google.com [74.125.198.106]
over a maximum of 30 hops:

  1    <1 ms    <1 ms    <1 ms  Linksys03451 [192.168.1.1]
  2     1 ms     1 ms     1 ms  192.168.200.1
  3    26 ms    24 ms    31 ms  RO1-DSL-208-102-248-1.fuse.net [208.102.248.1]
  4    23 ms    28 ms    26 ms  172.17.114.18
  5    79 ms    79 ms    81 ms  EV-ZT-1.EVE2.core.fuse.net [216.68.14.58]
  6    96 ms    94 ms    38 ms  216.68.14.63
  7    42 ms    37 ms    38 ms  72.14.223.8
  8    39 ms    42 ms    41 ms  209.85.252.46
  9    42 ms    41 ms    41 ms  209.85.143.112
 10    46 ms    45 ms    45 ms  209.85.143.115
 11    73 ms    69 ms    68 ms  209.85.143.99
 12    67 ms    67 ms    68 ms  209.85.252.119
 13     *        *        *     Request timed out.
 14    68 ms    68 ms   146 ms  og-in-f106.1e100.net [74.125.198.106]

Trace complete.

C:\>
```

NETSTAT COMMAND

The NETSTAT command is used to check out the inbound and outbound TCP/IP connections on your machine. It can also be used to view packet statistics, such as how many packets have been sent and received and the number of errors.

When used without any options, the NETSTAT command produces output similar to what you see in Figure 12.32, which shows all of the outbound TCP/IP connections.

FIGURE 12.32 NETSTAT output

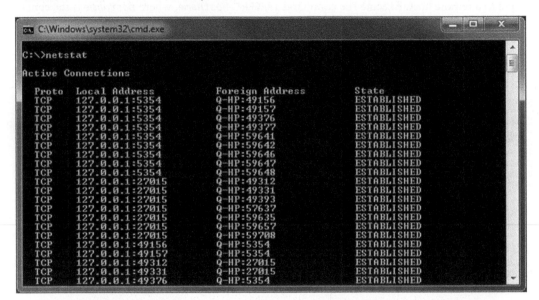

There are several useful command-line options for NETSTAT, as shown in Table 12.8.

TABLE 12.8 NETSTAT options

Option	Function
-a	Displays all connections and listening ports.
-b	Displays the executable involved in creating each connection or listening port. In some cases, well-known executables host multiple independent components, and in these cases the sequence of components involved in creating the connection or listening port is displayed. In this case, the executable name is in brackets at the bottom [ ]. At the top is the component it called, in sequence, until TCP/IP was reached. Note that this option can be time consuming, and it will fail unless you have sufficient permissions.
-e	Displays Ethernet statistics. This may be combined with the -s option.
-f	Displays fully qualified domain names (FQDNs) for foreign addresses.

Option	Function
-n	Displays addresses and port numbers in numerical form.
-o	Displays the owning process ID associated with each connection.
-p proto	Shows connections for the protocol specified by proto; proto may be any of the following: TCP, UDP, TCPv6, or UDPv6. If used with the -s option to display per-protocol statistics, *proto* may be IP, IPv6, ICMP, ICMPv6, TCP, TCPv6, UDP, or UDPv6.
-r	Displays the routing table.
-s	Displays per-protocol statistics. By default, statistics are shown for IP, IPv6, ICMP, ICMPv6, TCP, TCPv6, UDP, and UDPv6; the -p option may be used to specify a subset of the default.

NBTSTAT COMMAND

NBTSTAT is a command that shows NetBIOS over TCP/IP information. While not used as often as other entries in this category, it can be useful when trying to diagnose a problem with NetBIOS name resolution. The /? parameter can be used to see the available switches. Sample output from this command is shown in Figure 12.33.

FIGURE 12.33   NBTSTAT −n output

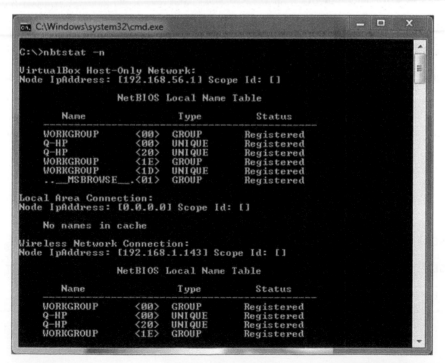

NET Command

Depending on the version of Windows you are using, NET can be one of the most powerful commands at your disposal. While all Windows versions include a NET command, its capabilities differ based on whether it is used on a server or workstation and the version of the operating system.

While always command-line based, this tool allows you to do almost anything that you want with the operating system.

Table 12.9 shows common NET switches.

TABLE 12.9   NET switches

Switch	Purpose
NET ACCOUNTS	Set account options (password age, length, and so on).
NET COMPUTER	Add and delete computer accounts.
NET CONFIG	See network-related configuration.
NET CONTINUE, NET PAUSE, NET START, NET STATISTICS, and NET STOP	Control services.
NET FILE	Close open files.
NET GROUP and NET LOCALGROUP	Create, delete, and change groups.
NET HELP	See general help.
NET HELPMSG	See specific message help.
NET NAME	See the name of the current machine and user.
NET PRINT	Interact with print queues and print jobs.
NET SEND	Send a message to user(s).
NET SESSION	See session statistics.
NET SHARE	Create a share.
NET TIME	Set the time to that of another computer.
NET USE	Connect to a share.
NET USER	Add, delete, and see information about a user.
NET VIEW	See available resources.

These commands are invaluable troubleshooting aids when you cannot get the graphical interface to display properly. You can also use them when interacting with hidden ($) and administrative shares that do not appear within the graphical interface.

The NET command used with the SHARE parameter enables you to create shares from the command prompt, using this syntax:

```
NET SHARE <share_name>=<drive_letter>:<path>
```

To share the C:\EVAN directory as SALES, you would use the following command:

```
NET SHARE SALES=C:\EVAN
```

You can use other parameters with NET SHARE to set other options. Table 12.10 summarizes the most commonly used parameters, and Exercise 12.6 will give you some experience with the NET SHARE command.

TABLE 12.10   NET SHARE parameters

Parameter	Purpose
/DELETE	Stop sharing a folder.
/REMARK	Add a comment for browsers.
/UNLIMITED	Set the user limit to Maximum Allowed.
/USERS	Set a specific user limit.

EXERCISE 12.6

Using the NET SHARE command in Windows

1. Click the Start button, type **CMD** in the Search Programs And Files box, and press Enter to open a command prompt.

2. To see what is currently shared on your computer, type **NET SHARE** and press Enter. You will see output similar to what's shown in Figure 12.34. Notice that the C:\ and D:\ drives are shared by default. This is normal, and they are hidden shares (the $ at the end of the share name makes it hidden), meaning that other users on the network won't see them.

continues

EXERCISE 12.6 *(continued)*

FIGURE 12.34   Shares on the local computer

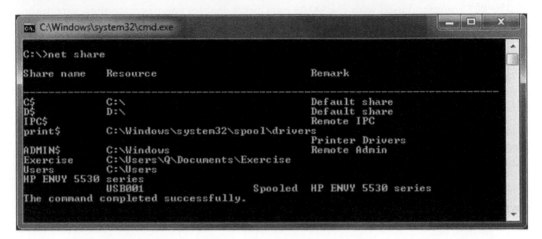

3. You will now share the C:\TEMP folder with the share name *files4u*. To do this, type **NET SHARE files4u=c:\temp** and press Enter. The system should respond with files4u was shared successfully.

4. To verify that it was shared, type **NET SHARE** and press Enter. You can see the new share in Figure 12.35. Users on the network can now access your drive as *computername*\files4u.

FIGURE 12.35   NET SHARE output with a new shared drive

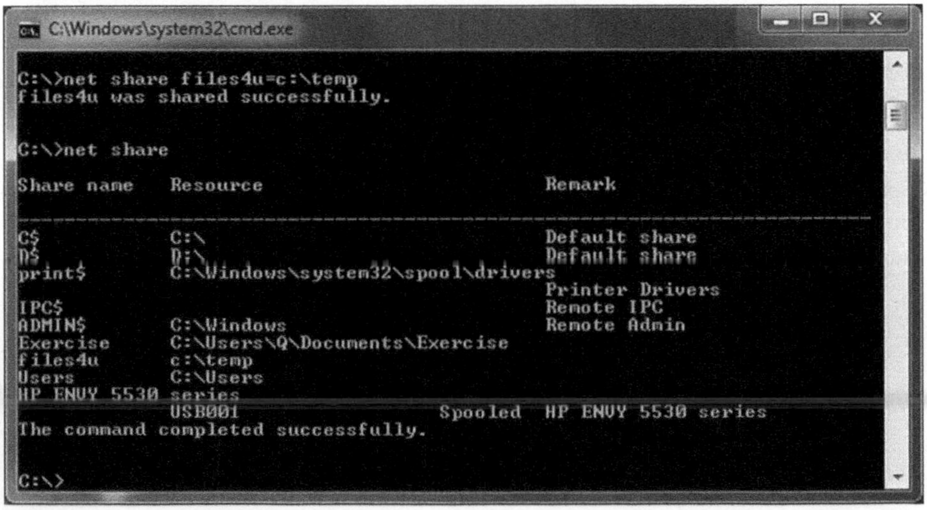

5. (optional) To stop sharing files4u, type **NET SHARE files4u /DELETE** at the command prompt and press Enter.

6. (optional) To verify that the folder is no longer shared, type **NET SHARE** and press Enter.

The NET /? command is basically a catch-all help request. It will instruct you to use the NET command in which you are interested for more information.

NETDOM Command

NETDOM is a tool first included with Windows Server 2008 that provides Active Directory management capabilities, specifically domain and trust management. In order to run NETDOM, you must have administrative privileges. NETDOM allows an administrator to perform the following tasks:

- Rename a computer that is a member of a domain.

- Join a client computer (Windows XP or newer) to a Windows domain.

- Manage computer accounts within a domain, such as adding or removing computers, changing the organizational unit (OU) for the computer, or moving a computer from one domain to another.

- Establishing and managing trust relationships between domains.

Most of the actions for which NETDOM is used are relatively advanced Windows Server administrator functions, so it's a bit surprising to see this command on the A+ exam. For the purposes of the exam, think of NETDOM as the command you would use to manage computer accounts (*not* user accounts) and membership in domains.

NSLOOKUP COMMAND

One of the key things that must take place to use TCP/IP effectively is that a hostname must resolve to an IP address—an action usually performed by a DNS server.

NSLOOKUP is a command that enables you to verify entries on a DNS server. You can use the NSLOOKUP command in two modes: interactive and noninteractive. In interactive mode, you start a session with the DNS server in which you can make several requests. In noninteractive mode, you specify a command that makes a single query of the DNS server. If you want to make another query, you must type another noninteractive command.

To start nslookup in interactive mode (which is what most admins use because it allows them to make multiple requests without typing NSLOOKUP several times), type **NSLOOKUP** at the command prompt and press Enter. You will receive a greater than prompt (>) and can then type in the command that you want to run. You can also type **HELP** or ? to bring up the list of possible commands, as shown in Figure 12.36. To exit nslookup and return to a command prompt, type **EXIT** and press Enter.

FIGURE 12.36   Starting NSLOOKUP and using help

```
C:\Windows\system32\cmd.exe - nslookup

C:\>nslookup
Default Server:  Linksys03451
Address:  192.168.1.1

> help
Commands:     (identifiers are shown in uppercase, [] means optional)
NAME             - print info about the host/domain NAME using default server
NAME1 NAME2      - as above, but use NAME2 as server
help or ?        - print info on common commands
set OPTION       - set an option
    all              - print options, current server and host
    [no]debug        - print debugging information
    [no]d2           - print exhaustive debugging information
    [no]defname      - append domain name to each query
    [no]recurse      - ask for recursive answer to query
    [no]search       - use domain search list
    [no]vc           - always use a virtual circuit
    domain=NAME      - set default domain name to NAME
    srchlist=N1[/N2/.../N6] - set domain to N1 and search list to N1,N2, etc.
    root=NAME        - set root server to NAME
    retry=X          - set number of retries to X
    timeout=X        - set initial time-out interval to X seconds
    type=X           - set query type (ex. A,AAAA,A+AAAA,ANY,CNAME,MX,NS,PTR,
SOA,SRV)
    querytype=X      - same as type
    class=X          - set query class (ex. IN (Internet), ANY)
    [no]msxfr        - use MS fast zone transfer
    ixfrver=X        - current version to use in IXFR transfer request
server NAME      - set default server to NAME, using current default server
lserver NAME     - set default server to NAME, using initial server
root             - set current default server to the root
ls [opt] DOMAIN [> FILE] - list addresses in DOMAIN (optional: output to FILE)
    -a           - list canonical names and aliases
    -d           - list all records
    -t TYPE      - list records of the given RFC record type (ex. A,CNAME,MX,NS,
PTR etc.)
view FILE            - sort an 'ls' output file and view it with pg
exit             - exit the program

>
```

To run NSLOOKUP in noninteractive mode, you would use the NSLOOKUP command option you want to run at the command prompt. Examples would be NSLOOKUP /SET TIMEOUT=<3> or NSLOOKUP /VIEW:*DOMAIN*.

Summary

In this chapter, we discussed hardware and network troubleshooting. First we looked at general hardware troubleshooting. We investigated the causes for hardware problems, such as excessive heat, and signs of problems, such as noise, odors, and visible damage. We also discussed alerts and status lights.

After the discussion of general hardware, we talked about issues specific to internal components, including the motherboard, CPU, RAM, power supply, storage systems, and video cards. Next we covered problems that are unique to laptop computers. Because of their compact nature, they have unique issues relating to heat, power, and input and output. Laptops also typically have built-in wireless networking, which is a blessing but occasionally needs to be fixed.

We followed that with a discussion on troubleshooting printers. Specifically, we discussed problems with three major classes of printers, including dot matrix, inkjet, and laser, and then we talked about managing print jobs, the print spooler, and printing a test page.

Finally, we ended the chapter with a section on troubleshooting issues that are specific to networking. We talked about connectivity issues and looked at tools and commands that you can use to troubleshoot network problems.

Exam Essentials

Understand what happens during the POST routine. During the power-on self-test (POST), the BIOS checks to ensure that the base hardware is installed and working. Generally, one POST beep is good. Any more than that and you might have an error.

Understand the types of symptoms that misbehaving hardware can cause. Hardware problems cause symptoms that include excessive heat, noise, odors, and visible damage. Some devices can also warn of problems with status light indicators or alerts.

Know how to stop and restart the print spooler. Open the Services applet of Computer Management. Find Print Spooler on the right side. Right-click it and click Stop, or highlight it and click the Stop square above the list of services. To restart it, right-click and select Start or click the Start triangle above the list of services.

Understand what to do for laptop video issues. If you have no video, you can try an external monitor or try toggling the LCD cutoff switch. For screens that are too dim or too bright, you can raise and lower the brightness by using the Fn key plus the appropriate function key on your keyboard.

Know what to check if your wireless networking card isn't working. Make sure the card has lights indicating that it's working. You might also have an external toggle switch to turn the card on and off. Finally, if your computer has an external RJ-45 connection, you can plug it in and see if it works when wired.

Know how to set IP addresses on a printer. The IP address can often be obtained automatically from a DHCP server, but this is not recommended for corporate networks. Instead, you may be able to use the printer's control panel, Telnet, or printer management software to configure the IP address.

Know what could cause the printer to print garbage. Most often, the print driver causes this. Deleting and reinstalling it should fix the problem. A defective formatter board can also cause it.

Understand what could cause print-quality issues on a dot-matrix printer.   Print-quality issues are generally related to either the ribbon or the print head. The specific problem you are having will help determine the culprit.

Know what can cause unevenly spaced lines or characters on a dot-matrix or inkjet printer.   A failing stepper motor usually causes this. For line spacing problems, it's the main stepper motor. For character spacing, it will be the carriage stepper motor.

Know what causes printers to have paper jams.   In a dot-matrix printer, jams are usually caused by material getting into the rollers, such as extra perf from the tractor-feed paper. On inkjets and laser printers, worn pickup rollers often cause this problem.

Know what the IPCONFIG, PING, and TRACERT commands are used for.   Both IPCONFIG and PING are network troubleshooting commands. You can use IPCONFIG to view your computer's IP configuration and PING to test connectivity between two network hosts. TRACERT allows you to view the network path a packet takes from the host to the destination.

Know what the NETSTAT, NBTSTAT, NET, NETDOM, and NSLOOKUP commands are used for.   NETSTAT shows network statistics, NBTSTAT shows NetBIOS over TCP/IP information, NET allows you to perform network management tasks such as sharing folders, NETDOM is used for network domain administration, and NSLOOKUP allows you to query a DNS server.

Understand what various networking hardware tools are used for.   A cable tester allows you to verify that a cable works, loopback plugs test the functionality of network cards, punch-down tools connect wires to frames such as a 110 block, tone generators allow you trace a cable from one point to another, wire strippers and crimpers are for cutting and putting the ends on network cables, and a wireless locator helps you find wireless network signals.

Review Questions

The answers to the chapter review questions can be found in Appendix A.

1. If the video on your laptop is not working, what should you do to troubleshoot it? (Choose two.)
   A. Toggle the video function key.
   B. Try using an external monitor.
   C. Remove the display unit and reattach it.
   D. Power the system off and back on.

2. While inspecting a motherboard, you notice a discolored area. What usually causes this?
   A. Spilled liquid
   B. Improper manufacture
   C. Power surge
   D. Underclocking

3. You need to connect a client computer to a shared network drive from the command prompt. Which command should you use?
   A. NET USE
   B. NETSTAT
   C. NSLOOKUP
   D. IPCONFIG

4. Every computer has a diagnostic program built into its BIOS called the _____.
   A. CMOS
   B. BIOS
   C. POST
   D. DNS

5. While troubleshooting a client computer, you decide to obtain a new IP address from the DHCP server. After releasing the existing address, which command do you use to get new IP information from the DHCP server?
   A. IPCONFIG /REFRESH
   B. IPCONFIG /RENEW
   C. IFCONFIG /RELEASE
   D. IFCONFIG /START

6. Users are complaining that their print jobs are not printing. You open the print queue and see 50 jobs lined up. The printer is connected properly and online. What should you do?

   A. Open Printer Troubleshooting and have it diagnose the problem.

   B. Stop and restart the print spooler.

   C. Delete and reinstall the printer.

   D. Delete and reinstall Windows.

7. What two devices are commonly used to cool components within a PC? (Choose two.)

   A. Fans

   B. Compressed air

   C. Freon

   D. Heat sinks

8. You are having problems with the video card in one of your computers. Where could you check for troubleshooting information?

   A. Another computer with the same video card

   B. The video card manufacturer's website

   C. The manual that came with the card

   D. The server log

9. Your laser printer keeps printing vertical black lines on its output pages. What is the most likely cause of the problem?

   A. There is a groove or scratch in the EP drum.

   B. The EP drum-cleaning blade is broken.

   C. The printer is low on toner.

   D. The transfer corona wire is not working properly.

10. The display on your laptop appears warped and fuzzy. You plug in an external monitor, and the image on it is fine. What is the most likely cause of the problem?

    A. The video card

    B. The LCD display

    C. The motherboard

    D. The video driver

11. You have an inkjet printer. Recently, papers are being printed with excessive amounts of ink, and the ink is smearing. What is the most likely cause of the problem?

    A. A faulty ink cartridge

    B. A corrupt print driver

    C. A faulty fuser

    D. Too much humidity in the air

12. You are working with a system that is assigned IP configuration information from a central server. You wish to view the IP information on the system. Which of the following commands would you use from the command prompt?

   A. IPCONFIG /REFRESH

   B. IPCONFIG /ALL

   C. IPCONFIG /RENEW

   D. WINIPCFG /ALL

13. When you print documents on your laser printer, you see residue from previous images on the output. What two things are the most likely causes of this problem? (Choose two.)

   A. A faulty transfer corona wire

   B. An overheating printer

   C. A bad erasure lamp

   D. A broken cleaning blade

14. You turn a computer on, but nothing shows up on the monitor. Instead of one beep, you hear one long beep followed by three short beeps. What is the problem?

   A. The video card is dead.

   B. The motherboard is dead.

   C. The BIOS is not functioning.

   D. Not enough information; you need to look up the beep code to determine the problem.

15. Which of the following Windows command-line utilities is used to verify the route a data packet takes to a remote host?

   A. Trace

   B. Tracert

   C. TraceRoute

   D. Tracepacket

16. You turn a computer on and it doesn't boot up properly. From inside the case, you hear a rhythmic ticking sound. What is most likely the problem?

   A. The motherboard

   B. The power supply fan

   C. The hard drive

   D. The video card

17. You support an old dot-matrix printer at work. When the printer prints, there is always a blank horizontal line in the middle of each line of output. What is the most likely cause of the problem?

   A. The print ribbon is old and needs to be replaced.

   B. The print ribbon is not advancing properly.

    C. The print head needs to be replaced.

    D. The wrong print driver is installed.

18. A user calls saying that his laptop won't power on. He charged it all night, so he knows that the battery is fine. What should you have him do first?

    A. Plug the laptop in using an AC adapter and try to power it on.

    B. Replace the battery with a spare and try to power it on.

    C. Toggle the battery power switch on the front of the laptop, and then try to power it on.

    D. Send the laptop in for service.

19. You suspect a faulty network card on a client machine. Which tool can you use to test your hypothesis?

    A. Wireless locator

    B. Cable tester

    C. Toner probe

    D. Loopback plug

20. You are troubleshooting a server and discover that one of the hard drives in the RAID 0 array has failed. Which statement is true?

    A. You need to replace the failed drive, but the data is okay because it is configured as a mirror.

    B. You need to replace the failed drive, but the data is okay because it is configured as a disk stripe with parity.

    C. You need to replace the failed drive, and the data on the array is lost.

    D. You do not need to replace the failed drive; the system will function normally.

Performance-Based Question

You will encounter performance-based questions on the A+ exam. The questions on the exam require you to perform a specific task, and you will be graded on whether or not you were able to complete the task. The following requires you to think creatively in order to measure how well you understand this chapter's topics. You may or may not see similar questions on the actual A+ exams. To see how your answers compare to the authors', refer to Appendix B.

    Your network users are sending print jobs to the printer, but they are stacking up in the queue and not printing. The printer appears to be online and has paper. How would you stop and restart the print spooler in Windows 7?

Part II: 220-902

Chapter

13

Operating System Basics

THE FOLLOWING A+ 220-902 EXAM OBJECTIVES ARE COVERED IN THIS CHAPTER:

✓ **1.1 Compare and contrast various features and requirements of Microsoft Operating Systems (Windows Vista, Windows 7, Windows 8, Windows 8.1).**

   - Features: 32-bit vs. 64-bit; Aero, gadgets, user account control, system restore, sidebar, compatibility mode, administrative tools, security center, event viewer, file structure and paths, category view vs. classic view

✓ **1.4 Given a scenario, use appropriate Microsoft operating system features and tools.**

   - System utilities: NOTEPAD

✓ **1.7 Perform common preventive maintenance procedures using the appropriate Windows OS tools.**

   - Best practices: Windows updates
   - Tools: System restore

✓ **2.2 Given a scenario, setup and use client-side virtualization.**

   - Purpose of virtual machines
   - Resource requirements
   - Emulator requirements
   - Security requirements
   - Network requirements
   - Hypervisor

✓ **3.3 Compare and contrast differences of basic Windows OS security settings.**

   - NTFS vs. Share permissions: File attributes
   - System files and folders

The previous chapters focused mainly on the hardware and physical elements of the computing environment. We looked at the physical components, or hardware, of personal computers and laptops as well as networking, printers, and operational procedures. That completes the coverage of the topics on the 220-901 exam. This chapter marks a departure from that.

In this chapter—and several to come—the focus is on operating systems (OSs). To be specific, the focus is on Microsoft Windows operating systems, which you must know well for the 220-902 certification exam.

Understanding Operating Systems

Computers are pretty much useless without software. A piece of hardware might just as well be used as a paperweight or doorstop unless you have an easy way to interface with it. Software provides that way. While there are many types of software, or programs, the most important one you'll ever deal with is the operating system. Operating systems have many different, complex functions, but two of them jump out as being critical: interfacing with the hardware and providing a platform on which other applications can run.

Here are three major distinctions of software about which you should be aware:

Operating system (OS)   The *operating system* provides a consistent environment for other software to execute commands. The OS provides users with an interface with the computer so that they can send commands (input) and receive feedback or results (output). To do this, the OS must communicate with the computer hardware to perform the following tasks, as illustrated in Figure 13.1:

- Disk and file management
- Device access
- Memory management
- Output format

Once the OS has organized these basic resources, users can give the computer instructions through input devices (such as a keyboard or a mouse). Some of these commands are built into the OS, whereas others are issued through the use of applications. The OS becomes the center through which the system hardware, other software, and the user communicate; the rest of the components of the system work together through the OS, which coordinates their communication.

FIGURE 13.1   The operating system interacts with resources.

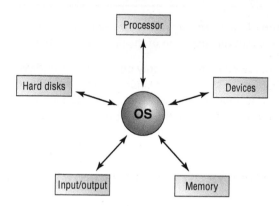

Application   Used to accomplish a particular task, an *application* is software that is written to supplement the commands available to a particular OS. Each application is specifically compiled (configured) for the OS on which it will run. For this reason, the application relies on the OS to do many of its basic tasks. Examples of applications include complex programs such as Microsoft Word and Internet Explorer as well as simple programs such as a command-line FTP program. Whether they are complex or simple, when accessing devices and memory, the programs can simply request that the OS do it for them. This arrangement saves substantially on programming overhead because much of the executable code is *shared*; that is, it is written into the operating system and can therefore be used by multiple applications running on that OS.

Driver   *Drivers* are extremely specific software written for the purpose of instructing a particular OS on how to access a piece of hardware. Each modem or printer has unique features and configuration settings, and the driver allows the OS to understand how the hardware works and what it is able to do.

In the following sections, we'll look at some terms and concepts central to all operating systems. Then we'll move into specific discussions of Windows operating systems.

 Real World Scenario

Are These the Only Versions of Windows?

In the workplace, it is likely that you will encounter some different versions of the Windows operating systems beyond just Windows 8/8.1, Windows 7, and Windows Vista. Windows XP, for example, is still used in some settings even though support for it has

continues

continued

lapsed. On the other end of the spectrum, Windows 10 is sure to gain traction in the workplace over the years that this iteration of the A+ exams is available.

Know that this version of the exam focuses only on the three Windows operating systems mentioned here as well as Mac OS and Linux (addressed in Chapter 18, "Working with Mac OS and Linux"). It is highly recommended that you become familiar with all operating systems your job requires, but these are the ones that you will need to know for the A+ certification exam.

Operating System Terms and Concepts

Before we get too far into our discussion of PC operating systems, it will be useful to define a few key terms. The following are some terms that you will come across as you study this chapter and work in the computer industry:

Version   A *version* is a particular revision of a piece of software, normally described by a number that tells you how new the product is in relation to other versions of the product.

Source   The *source code* is the actual code that defines how a piece of software works. Computer operating systems can be *open source*, meaning that the OS can be examined and modified by anyone, or they can be *closed source*, meaning that only an owner or developer can modify or examine the code.

 A word often used interchangeably with *closed source* is *proprietary*.

Shell   A *shell* is a program that runs on top of the OS and allows the user to issue commands through a set of menus or another interface (which may or may not be graphical). Shells make an OS easier to use by changing the user interface.

Graphical user interface (GUI)   A *graphical user interface*, or *GUI*, is a method by which a person communicates with a computer using graphical images, icons, and methods other than text. GUIs allow a user to use a mouse, touchpad, or another mechanism (in addition to the keyboard) to interact with the computer to issue commands.

Network   A *network* is any group of computers that have a communication link between them. Networks allow computers to share information and resources quickly and securely.

Cooperative multitasking   *Cooperative multitasking* is a multitasking method that depends on the application itself to be responsible for using the processor and then freeing it for access by other applications. This is the way very early versions of Windows managed multiple applications. If any application locked up while using the processor, the application was unable to free the processor to do other tasks and the entire system locked, usually forcing a reboot.

Preemptive multitasking   *Preemptive multitasking* is a multitasking method in which the OS allots each application a certain amount of processor time and then forcibly takes back control and gives another application or task access to the processor. This means that if an application crashes, the OS takes control of the processor away from the locked application and passes it on to the next application, which should be unaffected. Although unstable programs still lock, only the locked application will stall—not the entire system. This is what is used today in modern operating systems.

Multithreading   *Multithreading* is the ability of a single application to have multiple requests in to the processor at one time. This results in faster application performance because it allows a program to do many things at once.

32-bit   A *32-bit operating system* is one that cannot only run on 32-bit processors but can utilize the capabilities of the processor fully. While this may sound simple, the truth of the matter is that it took many years after the 32-bit processor became available before operating systems (which were 16-bit at the time) were able to utilize their features. Just as you should not drive racecars on a country road, you cannot mix 64-bit software with 32-bit hardware.

64-bit   A *64-bit operating system* is one that is written to utilize the instructions possible with 64-bit processors. Originally, these were more common with servers than desktops, but they have now become ubiquitous in the market with both Intel and AMD processors. As mentioned earlier, you cannot mix 64-bit software with 32-bit hardware (but you can run most 32-bit software on 64-bit hardware).

x86   The term *x86* is commonly used to refer to operating systems intended to run on the Intel processor because Intel initially identified its 32-bit processors with numbers ending in 86 prior to switching to the Pentium line.

x64   The term *x64* is commonly used to denote operating systems that can run on 64-bit processors. This is also commonly referred to as AMD64 since AMD defined the 64-bit instruction set used today.

Minimum System Requirements

In the chapters to come, we'll explore how to install and upgrade each of the operating systems that you need to know for the exam. However, the hardware requirements of the operating system that you are thinking of installing can prevent you from even considering these options. Before you can begin to install an OS, there are several items that you must consider. You must perform the following tasks before you even start to think about undertaking the installation. These items essentially set the stage for the procedure that you are about to perform:

- Determining hardware compatibility and minimum requirements
- Determining installation options
- Determining the installation method
- Preparing the computer for installation

Let's begin our discussion by talking about hardware compatibility issues and the requirements for installing the various versions of Windows.

Determining Hardware Compatibility and Minimum Requirements

Before you can begin to install any version of Windows, it is important that you determine whether the hardware that you will be using is supported by the Windows version that you will be running. That is, will the version of Windows have problems running any of the device drivers for the hardware that you have?

To answer this question, Microsoft developed several versions of its *Hardware Compatibility List (HCL)*. These HCLs were intended to be a list of all the hardware that worked with Windows and the versions of Windows with which the hardware worked. Several years ago, Microsoft expanded the idea of the HCL to include software as well, and a list that includes both hardware and software can hardly be called a Hardware Compatibility List. The new term used for this purpose was the *Windows Catalog*, which replaced HCLs. This eventually gave way to the *Compatibility Center.* The one for Windows 8/8.1 can be found at the following location:

www.microsoft.com/en-us/windows/compatibility/CompatCenter/
Home?Language=en-US

The point is, before you install Windows, you should check all of your computer's components against this list and make sure that each item is compatible with the version of Windows that you plan to install. Just because a product is not on the list does not mean that it will not work; it merely means that it has not been tested. The list represents tested software and hardware that vendors have stated are compatible, but it is by no means all-inclusive.

In addition to general compatibility, it is important that your computer have enough "oomph" to run the version of Windows that you plan to install. For that matter, it is important for your computer to have enough resources to run any software that you plan to use. Toward that end, Microsoft (as well as other software publishers) releases a list of both minimum and recommended hardware specifications that you should follow when installing Windows.

"Minimum specifications" are the absolute minimum requirements for hardware your that system should meet in order to install and run the OS version you have chosen. "Recommended hardware specifications" are what you should have in your system in order to realize usable performance. Always try to have the recommended hardware (or better) in your system. If you don't, you may have to upgrade your hardware before you upgrade your OS if you're running anything beyond a minimal environment. Table 13.1 lists the minimum hardware specifications for Windows 8 and Windows 8.1. Note that in addition to these minimum requirements, the hardware chosen must be compatible with the selected version of Windows. Also, be aware that additional hardware may be required if certain features are installed (for example, a TV tuner is required to play and record live TV).

TABLE 13.1 Windows 8 and Windows 8.1 minimum system requirements

Hardware	32-bit	64-bit
Processor	1GHz with support for PAE, NX, and SSE2	1GHz with support for PAE, NX, and SSE2
Memory	1GB	2GB
Free hard disk space	16GB	20GB
Video	Microsoft DirectX 9 graphics device with WDDM driver	Microsoft DirectX 9 graphics device with WDDM driver

Table 13.2 lists the minimum system requirements for Windows 7. It should be noted that Windows XP Mode requires an additional 1GB RAM and 15GB hard drive space.

TABLE 13.2 Windows 7 minimum system requirements

Hardware	Minimum Supported for All Versions
Processor	1GHz
Memory	1GB for 32-bit; 2GB for 64-bit
Free hard disk space	16GB free for 32-bit; 20GB free for 64-bit
CD-ROM or DVD drive	DVD-ROM
Video	DirectX 9 with WDDM 1.0 (or higher) driver
Mouse	Required (but not listed as a requirement)
Keyboard	Required (but not listed as a requirement)
Internet access	Not listed as a requirement

Table 13.3 lists the minimum system requirements for various versions of Windows Vista.

TABLE 13.3 Windows Vista minimum system requirements

Hardware	Minimum Supported for All Versions	Home Basic Recommendation	Home Premium/Business/Enterprise/Ultimate Recommendation
Processor	800MHz	1GHz 32-bit (x86) or 64-bit (x64) processor	1GHz 32-bit (x86) or 64-bit (x64) processor
Memory	512MB	512MB	1GB
Free hard disk space	15GB free on a 20GB drive	15GB free on a 20GB drive	15GB free on a 40GB drive
CD-ROM or DVD	CD-ROM	DVD-ROM	DVD-ROM
Video	DirectX 9-class graphics card and 32MB graphics memory	Support for DirectX 9 graphics and 32MB graphics memory	Support for DirectX 9 with WDDM driver, 128MB of graphics memory, Pixel Shader 2.0 in hardware, 32 bits per pixel
Mouse	Required (but not listed as a requirement)	Required (but not listed as a requirement)	Required (but not listed as a requirement)
Keyboard	Required (but not listed as a requirement)	Required (but not listed as a requirement)	Required (but not listed as a requirement)
Internet access	Not listed as a requirement	Required	Required

If there is one thing to be learned from Table 13.1, Table 13.2, and Table 13.3, it is that Microsoft is nothing if not optimistic. For your own sanity, though, we strongly suggest that you always take the minimum requirements with a grain of salt. They are, after all, *minimum* requirements. Even the recommended requirements should be considered minimum requirements. The bottom line is to make sure that you have a good margin between your system's performance and the minimum requirements listed. Always run Windows on more hardware rather than less!

Other hardware—sound cards, network cards, modems, video cards, and so on—may or may not work with Windows. If the device is fairly recent, you can be relatively certain that it was built to work with the newest version of Windows. But if it is older, you may need to find out who made the hardware and check their website to see if there are drivers available for the version of Windows that you are installing.

Windows Upgrade Assistant and Upgrade Advisor

The easiest way to see if your current hardware can run another version of Windows is to download the utility that Microsoft creates for checking what you have. For Windows 7, this was called Upgrade Advisor. For Windows 8 and Windows 8.1, it has been renamed Upgrade Assistant and can be accessed at the following location:

```
http://windows.microsoft.com/is-is/windows-8/upgrade-assistant-download-
online-faq
```

There's one more thing to consider when evaluating installation methods. Some methods only work if you're performing a clean installation and not an upgrade. We'll discuss this in greater detail in Chapter 15, "Working with Windows 8/8.1."

The Windows Interface

The interface of a machine running Windows 7 is shown in Figure 13.2. If you've worked with older versions of Windows (such as Windows XP), you'll notice that it looks similar to the older interfaces. While there are some differences, most of the basic tasks are accomplished in almost identical fashion on everything from a Windows 95 workstation computer on up. Also, although the tools that are used often vary between the different OSs, the way that you use those tools remains remarkably consistent across platforms.

FIGURE 13.2   The Windows 7 interface

Between the older interfaces and Windows 7, Microsoft released Windows Vista and the Aero interface. This was a departure from the usual, as Figure 13.3 shows, and not one that met with as warm a reception as Microsoft had hoped.

FIGURE 13.3 The Windows Vista interface

Borrowing from the best of each of these, Microsoft came up with a new user interface for Windows 8, as shown in Figure 13.4. This was originally called the Metro interface, but the name was changed after its release to the new Windows UI (or the Windows 8 UI).

We will begin with an overview of the common elements of the Windows GUI. We will then look at some tasks that are similar across Windows operating systems. You are encouraged to follow along by exploring each of the elements as they are discussed.

As you follow along, you may notice that there are numerous icons and options that we do not mention. Quite honestly, there are too many to cover, and they're beyond the scope of this chapter. For now, simply ignore them or browse through them on your own and then return to the text.

FIGURE 13.4 The Windows 8 interface

The Desktop

The *Desktop* is the virtual desk on which all of your other programs and utilities run. By default, in all but Windows 8/8.1, it contains the *Start menu*, the *Taskbar*, and a number of *icons* (Windows 8/8.1 has all of these features, but Microsoft has chosen not to display them in the same way as in other versions.) The Desktop can also contain additional elements, such as shortcuts or links to web page content. Because it is the foundation on which everything else sits, the way that the Desktop is configured can have a major effect on how the GUI looks and how convenient it is for users. Windows 8/8.1 hid the Start menu on the Desktop in favor of a graphical tiled interface. Now when you click the lower-left corner of the Desktop (where you would expect the Start menu to be), the Start screen menu comes up. (Right-clicking the Windows icon in Windows 8.1 displays a set of operating system functions.)

You can change the background patterns, screensaver, color scheme, and size of elements on the Desktop by right-clicking in any area of the Desktop that doesn't contain an icon. The menu that appears, similar to the one shown for Windows 7 in Figure 13.5, allows you to do several things, such as create new Desktop items, change how your icons are arranged, or select a special command called Properties or Personalize.

FIGURE 13.5   The Windows 7 Desktop context menu

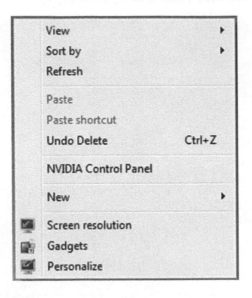

The Three Clicks in Windows

When it comes to interacting with a mouse in Windows, there are three possibilities:

- *Primary mouse click*: A single click (typically the left mouse button) is used to select an object or place a cursor.

- *Double-click*: Two primary mouse clicks in quick succession. Used to open a program through an icon or for other application-specific functions.

- *Secondary mouse click (or alternate click):* Most mice have two buttons. Clicking once on the secondary button (usually the one on the right, although that can be modified) is interpreted differently from a left mouse click. Generally, this click displays a context-sensitive menu in Windows from which you can perform tasks or view object properties.

When you right-click the Desktop and choose Personalize and then Display, you will see the Display Properties screen (for Windows 7) shown in Figure 13.6.

This screen will differ slightly based on the operating system, but you either click the various options at the top to move to the different screens of information about the way Windows looks (pre–Windows 7) or choose the options on the left to do the same (post–Windows 7). While the options will differ based on the operating system, the main ones in the Display Properties window of most are listed here:

FIGURE 13.6   The Windows 7 Display Properties screen

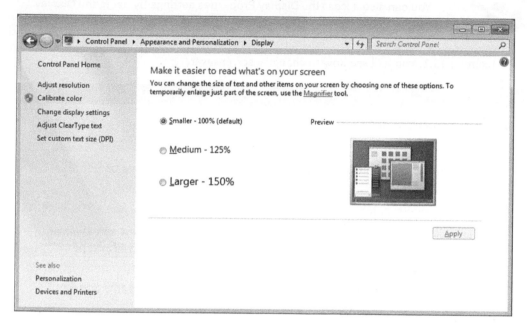

Personalization (or Themes)   Used to select a theme that enables you to customize the look and feel of your machine quickly. Selecting a *theme* sets several items at once, such as a picture to display on the Desktop, the look of icons, sounds to use, and so on. All of these options can also be selected individually through the other Desktop Properties tabs. For example, if you're more comfortable with the look and feel of previous versions of Windows, you can select the Windows Classic theme.

Desktop Background   The Background tab is used to select a picture to display on the Desktop. In addition, you can configure other items through the Customize Desktop button or Personalization dialog. Examples include changing which default icons to display on the Desktop and configuring web content for the Desktop.

Screen Saver   Sets up an automatic screensaver to display on your screen if your computer has been inactive for a certain period of time. Originally used to prevent burn-in of monitors, screensavers are now generally used for entertainment or to password-protect users' desktops. The Screen Saver tab also gives you access to other power settings.

Window Color (and Appearance)   Used to select a color scheme for the Desktop or to change the color or size of other Desktop elements.

Change Display Settings   Used to set the color depth or screen size. Also contains the Advanced button, which leads to graphics driver and monitor configuration settings.

You can also access the Display Properties settings by using the Display icon under Control Panel.

In Exercise 13.1, you will see how to change a screensaver.

EXERCISE 13.1

Changing a Screensaver

1. Right-click the Desktop.

2. Choose Personalize from the context menu (or Properties, depending on your operating system).

3. Click the Screen Saver tab.

4. Choose Ribbons or another screensaver. Click Preview to see the new screensaver. Move the mouse to cancel the screensaver and return to the Display Properties dialog box.

5. Click the OK button or the Apply button. (OK performs two tasks—Apply and Exit Window—whereas Apply leaves the window open.)

The Taskbar

The *Taskbar* (see Figure 13.7) is another standard component of the Windows interface. Note that although the colors and feel of the Desktop components, including the Taskbar, have changed throughout the operating system versions, the components themselves are the same. Outside of Windows 8, the Taskbar contains two major items: the Start menu and the *system tray* (systray). The Start menu is on the left side of the Taskbar and is easily identifiable: It is a button that has the word *Start* on it, or in the case of Windows 7/Vista, it is the large Windows icon. The *system tray* is located on the right side of the Taskbar and contains only a clock by default, but other Windows utilities (for example, screensavers or antivirus utilities) may put their icons there to indicate that they are running and to provide the user with a quick way to access their features.

FIGURE 13.7 The Windows 8.1 Taskbar

Windows also uses the middle area of the Taskbar. When you open a new window or program, it gets a button on the Taskbar with an icon that represents the window or program as well as the name of the window or program. To bring that window or program to the front (or to maximize it if it was minimized), click its button on the Taskbar. As the middle area of the Taskbar fills with buttons, the buttons become smaller so that they can all be displayed.

A special area on the Taskbar to the right of the Start button is known as the *Quick Launch* area, and icons of commonly used programs can appear here, allowing the programs to be started with a single click. If the icons are in the Quick Launch area—as opposed to on the Desktop, or elsewhere—they are always visible and accessible. In Windows 7, the Quick Launch area was replaced with a mechanism where commonly used programs can be pinned to the Taskbar. This concept of pinning is continued with Windows 8/8.1, and if you ever need to remove a pinned application, you simply open the jump list (which, as the name implies, takes you directly to the entity to which it is configured) for that application and choose to unpin the program from the Taskbar.

Last, you can increase the size of the Taskbar by moving the mouse pointer to the top of it and pausing until the pointer turns into a double-headed arrow. Once this happens, click the mouse and move it up to make the Taskbar bigger. Or move it down to make the Taskbar smaller. You can also click the Taskbar and drag it to the top or side of the screen.

In Windows, once you've configured the Taskbar position and layout to your liking, you can configure it so that it can't be changed accidentally. To do so, right-click the Taskbar and select Lock The Taskbar. To unlock the Taskbar and make changes, right-click the Taskbar and select Lock The Taskbar again.

You can make the Taskbar automatically hide itself when it isn't being used (thus freeing that space for use by the Desktop or other windows). In Exercise 13.2, we will show you how to do this.

EXERCISE 13.2

Auto-Hiding the Taskbar

1. Right-click the Taskbar.

2. Choose Properties. This will bring up the Taskbar And Start Menu Properties dialog box.

3. Check the Auto-Hide The Taskbar option on the Taskbar tab.

4. Click OK.

5. The Taskbar retracts as soon as you click OK.

6. Move the mouse pointer to the bottom of the screen, and the Taskbar will pop up and be available for normal use.

In addition to the Taskbar, Windows Vista includes the Sidebar, shown in Figure 13.8. This provides a quick interface that allows you to access common utilities (such as the headlines) and *gadgets*. While the Sidebar existed only for Windows Vista, the concept of gadgets persists and they can be placed directly on the Desktop in other Windows versions.

FIGURE 13.8   The Windows Vista Sidebar

The Start Menu

Back when Microsoft officially introduced Windows 95, it bought the rights to use the Rolling Stones's song "Start Me Up" in its advertisements and at the introduction party. Microsoft chose that particular song because the Start menu was the central point of focus in the new Windows interface, as it was in all subsequent versions until Windows 8.

To display the Start menu, you can press the Windows key on your keyboard at any time. You can also click the Start button in the Taskbar in Windows 7 or Windows Vista.

You'll see a Start menu similar to the one shown in Figure 13.9. There are slight differences between the Start menu in Windows 7 and the one it Windows Vista, but they all behave the same. With Windows 8/8.1, you point to the lower-left corner of the Start screen until the Start button appears and then right-click it (see Figure 13.10); it then appears as a pop-up menu. Regardless of the operating system, the Start menu serves the function of providing quick access to important features and programs.

FIGURE 13.9   Sample Windows 7 Start menu

There was considerable backlash by the user community over the removal of the Start menu in Windows 8, and a number of third-party vendors developed alternatives and marketed them to fill this demand.

FIGURE 13.10 The button to access the Windows 8 Start screen appears when you point the lower left

From the Start menu, you can select any of the various options the menu presents. An arrow pointing to the right indicates that a submenu is available. To select a submenu, move the mouse pointer over the submenu title and pause. The submenu will appear; you don't even have to click. (You have to click to choose an option on the submenu, though.) We'll discuss each of the Start menu's submenu options and how to use them.

All Programs Submenu

The All Programs submenu holds icons for the program groups. When you select this submenu, you will be shown a submenu for each program group. In Windows 7 and Windows Vista, the look is again a little different, but the functionality is the same. You can navigate through this menu and its submenus and click the icon for the program you wish to start.

 You can check which OS you are using by right-clicking the My Computer icon on the Desktop and selecting Properties. The OS type and version are displayed. Note that the My Computer/This PC icon may not appear on the Desktop by default (if the icon does not appear on the Desktop, you can find it on the Start menu instead in versions of Windows other than Windows 8/8.1). You can add the icon to the Desktop by using the Personalization dialog, or you can click Start and then right-click the Computer option and select Properties in Windows Vista or Windows 7.

The most common way to add programs to this submenu is by using an application's installation program. Additionally, items can be added by dragging and dropping icons onto these menus. Windows 8 adds these to the Start screen.

Recent Items Submenu (Windows Vista and Windows 7 Only)

The Recent Items submenu has only one function: to keep track of the last data files you opened. Whenever you open a file, a shortcut to it is automatically added to this menu. To open the document again, click the shortcut in the Documents menu to open it in its associated application.

 To clear the list of documents shown in the Recent Items submenu in Windows Vista/7, open the Taskbar And Start Menu Properties screen. Then use the Clear button on the Advanced tab.

Search Box

What used to be an actual menu item in previous versions of Windows is now a dynamic item with which you can interact. In Windows 8, this is a magnifying glass icon on the Start screen. In Windows 7 and Windows Vista, the Search menu choice has disappeared, but you can search by typing into the Search box that always appears in the upper-right corner of Windows File Explorer (technically, searching is still available from the Start menu in the Search Programs And Files bar, but File Explorer's Search feature works better). You can search through file content by typing the filter *contents:* followed by the word/phrase/text you are seeking. More important, though, to find commands quickly, start typing into the Start menu find field and the system displays matching commands. This is sometimes the quickest way of getting to a particular command, especially when you can't remember the exact name (for example, the Disk Management tools can be accessed by typing **nfts**; the command appears as Create And Format Hard Disk Partitions).

Help And Support Command

Windows has always included a very good Help system. When you click Help And Support, the Help And Support Center home page opens. This screen may have been slightly customized by a hardware vendor if the operating system was preinstalled on your machine. However, all of the options and available tools will still be present.

 A quick way to access Help is to press the F1 key.

The Run Command

It is possible to run commands and utilities from the search box or from Run (if it is first enabled in the Customize Start Menu dialog). When it's enabled, you can use the Run command to start programs if they don't have a shortcut on the Desktop or in the Programs/All Programs submenu. When you choose Run from the Start menu, a pop-up window appears. To execute a particular program, type its name in the Open field. If you don't know the exact path, you can browse to find the file by clicking the Browse button. Once you have typed in the executable name, click OK to run the program.

To open a command prompt, you can type **CMD** or **COMMAND** in the Run box and click OK. You might need to run this as Administrator if you want to change system settings. From the Start menu, type **cmd** in the search field and then type Ctrl+Shift+Enter to run as Administrator.

Applications can easily be started from the Run window; often you will find it faster to open programs this way than to search for their icons in the Start menu maze. In Exercise 13.3, you will see how to start a program from the Run window.

EXERCISE 13.3

Starting a Program from the Run Window

1.   Click Start ➤ Run.

2.   In the Open field, type **notepad**.

3.   Click OK. Notepad will open in a new window.

If the program that you want to start has been run from the Run window before, you can find it on the Open field's drop-down list. Click the down arrow to display the list, and then select the program that you want by clicking its name and then OK.

While this functionality still exists in Windows Vista and Windows 7, it is a bit different. A blank dialog box appears at the bottom of the Start menu with the default phrase Start Search within. Type the name of the command that you want to run in there, and press Enter. Windows will look for the executable and run it.

Shut Down Command

Windows operating systems are very complex. At any one time, many files are open in memory. If you accidentally hit the power switch and turn off the computer while these files are open, there is a good chance that they will be corrupted. For this reason, Microsoft has added the Shut Down command under the Start menu (which can also appear as an icon of an on/off button without a label). When you select this option, Windows presents you with several choices. Exactly which options are available depends on the Windows version that you are running.

Icons

Icons are shortcuts that allow a user to open a program or a utility without knowing where that program is located or how it needs to be configured. Icons consist of several major elements:

▪   Icon label

▪   Icon graphic

▪   Program location or path

The label and graphic of the icon typically tells the user the name of the program and gives a visual hint about what that program does. The icon for the Solitaire program, for instance, is labeled *Solitaire*, and its icon graphic is a deck of cards. By right-clicking an icon once, you make it the active icon and a drop-down menu appears. One of the selections is Properties. Clicking Properties brings up the icon's attributes (see Figure 13.11), and it is the only way to see exactly which program an icon is configured to start and where the program's executable is located. You can also specify whether to run the program in a normal window or maximized or minimized.

FIGURE 13.11   The Properties window of an application with its icon above it

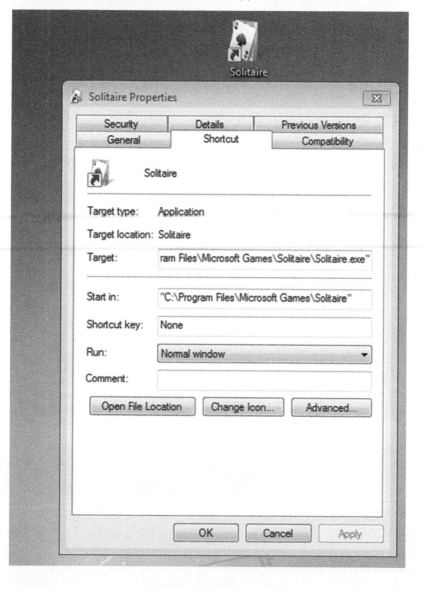

Additional functionality has been added to an icon's properties to allow for backward compatibility with older versions of Windows (known as *compatibility mode*). To configure this, click the Compatibility tab and specify the version of Windows for which you want to configure compatibility. Note that you cannot configure compatibility if the program is part of the version of Windows that you are using. Figure 13.12 shows the settings available for an older program.

FIGURE 13.12   The Compatibility settings possible with an older program

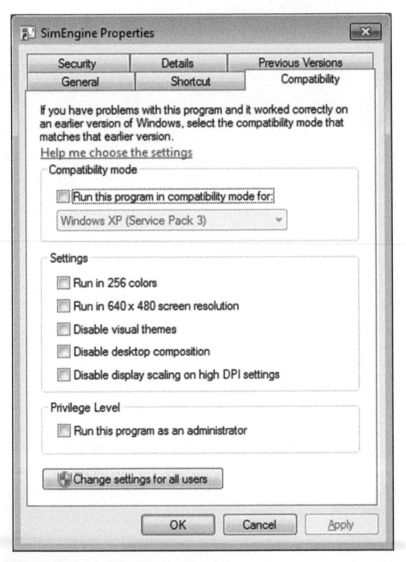

This feature is helpful if you own programs that used to work in older versions of Windows but no longer run under the current Windows version. In addition, you can specify different display settings that might be required by older programs.

Standard Desktop Icons

In addition to the options in your Start menu, a number of icons are placed directly on the Desktop in Windows. The Recycle Bin icon is one of these. Along with the Recycle Bin icon, two of the most important icons are Computer and Network. However, although they are important, they no longer appear by default on the Desktop. You can add them if you wish (in Windows 7, for example, choose Personalization from Control Panel, and then choose Change Desktop Icons).

THE COMPUTER ICON

If you double-click the Computer icon, it displays a list of all of the disk drives installed in your computer. In addition to displaying disk drives, it displays a list of other devices attached to the computer, such as scanners, cameras, and mobile devices. The disk devices are sorted into categories such as Hard Disk Drives, Devices With Removable Storage, Scanners And Cameras, and so on.

You can delve deeper into each disk drive or device by double-clicking its icon. The contents are displayed in the same window.

In addition to allowing you access to your computer's files, the My Computer icon on the Desktop lets you view your machine's configuration and hardware, also called the System Properties.

Within Windows, right-clicking Computer in the Start menu allows you to choose Properties and see the same information (choosing Manage, instead of Properties, brings up the Computer Management interface, in which you can make a plethora of changes).

NETWORK

Another icon in Windows relates to accessing other computers to which the local computer is connected, and it's called Network (known as My Network Places in previous versions).

Opening Network lets you browse for and access computers and shared resources (printers, scanners, media devices, and so on) to which your computer can connect. This might be another computer in a workgroup, HomeGroup, or domain as well as shared resources.

 For the exam, know that the three types of networks from which you can choose are Workgroup, HomeGroup, and Domain. Other chapters in this book focus more on networking specifics and how to set up each type.

Through the properties of Network, you can configure your network connections, including LAN and dial-up connections (should you still live in an area where a now antiquated dial-up connection is required for Internet access).

You can choose Network from the Start menu or you can add it—and other common icons—to the Windows 8.1/8/7/Vista Desktop by choosing Start ➤ Control Panel, clicking Appearance And Personalization, and then clicking Personalization. Choose Change Desktop Icons from the choices on the left to open the dialog box shown in Figure 13.13.

FIGURE 13.13   Common icons can easily be added to the Desktop.

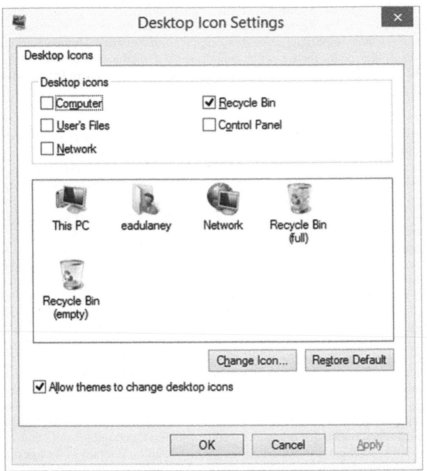

THE RECYCLE BIN

All files, directories, and programs in Windows are represented by icons, and these icons are generally referred to as *objects*. When you want to remove an object from Windows, you do so by deleting it. Deleting doesn't just remove the object, though; it also removes the ability of the system to access the information or application that the object represents. For this reason, Windows includes a special directory where all deleted files are placed: the Recycle Bin. The Recycle Bin holds the files until it is emptied or until you fill it, and it gives users the opportunity to recover files that they delete accidentally. By right-clicking the Recycle Bin icon, you can see how much disk space is allocated, and some larger files that cannot fit in the Recycle Bin will be erased after a warning.

You can retrieve a file that you have deleted by opening the Recycle Bin icon and then dragging the file from the Recycle Bin to where you want to restore it. Alternatively, you can right-click a file and select Restore, and the file will be restored to the location from which it was deleted.

In versions of Windows that this exam tests you on, the "deleted" files are stored in a folder called \\$Recycle.Bin. This was not the case in all previous versions of Windows.

To erase files permanently, you need to empty the Recycle Bin, thereby deleting any items in it and freeing the hard drive space they took up. If you want to delete only specific files, you can select them in the Recycle Bin, right-click, and choose Delete. You can also permanently erase files (bypassing the Recycle Bin) by holding down the Shift key as you delete them (by dragging the file and dropping it in the Recycle Bin, pressing the Del key, or clicking Delete on the file's context menu). If the Recycle Bin has files in it, its icon looks like a full trash can; when there are no files in it, it looks like an empty trash can.

What's in a Window?

We have now looked at the nature of the Desktop, the Taskbar, the Start menu, and icons. Each of these items was created for the primary purpose of making access to user applications easier, and these applications are in turn used and managed through the use of *windows*, the rectangular application environments for which the Windows family of operating systems is named. We will now examine how windows work and what they are made of.

A *program window* is a rectangular area created on the screen when an application is opened within Windows. This window can have a number of different forms, but most windows include at least a few basic elements.

Elements of a Window

Several basic elements are present in a standard window. Figure 13.14 shows the control box, title bar, Minimize/Maximize button, Restore button, Close button, and resizable border in a text editor called Notepad (NOTEPAD.EXE) that has all of the basic window elements—and little else.

The basic window elements are as follows:

Control box   Located in the upper-left corner of the window, the control box is used to control the state of the application. It can be used to maximize, minimize, and close the application. Clicking it once brings into view a selection menu. Double-clicking it closes the window and shuts down the application.

Minimize and Maximize/Restore buttons   Used to change the state of the window on the Desktop. They are discussed in the section "States of a Window" later in this chapter.

FIGURE 13.14 The basic elements of a window, as seen in Notepad

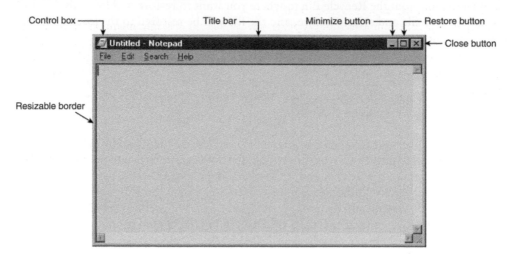

Close button Used to easily end a program and return any resources that it was using to the system. It essentially does the same thing as double-clicking the control box, but with one fewer click.

Title bar The area between the control box and the Minimize button. It states the name of the program and, in some cases, gives information about the particular document being accessed by that program. The color of the title bar indicates whether the window is the active window. Clicking and holding on it is an easy way to move the window on the screen.

Menu bar Used to present useful commands within an application in an easily accessible format. Clicking one of the menu choices displays a list of related options from which you may choose.

Active window The window that is currently being used. It has two attributes. First, any keystrokes that are entered are directed into the active window by default. Second, any other windows that overlap the active window are pushed behind it.

Border A thin line that surrounds the window in its restored down state and allows it to be resized.

Not every element is found in every window because application programmers can choose to eliminate or modify each item. Still, in most cases, they will be consistent, with the rest of the window filled in with menus, toolbars, a workspace, or other application-specific elements. For instance, Microsoft Word, the program with which this book was written, adds a Ribbon control. It also has a menu bar, a number of optional toolbars, scroll bars at the right and bottom of the window, and a status bar at the very bottom. Application windows can become quite cluttered.

Notepad is a very simple Windows program. It has only a single menu bar and the basic elements seen previously in Figure 13.14. It also starts a simple editor, where you can edit a file that already exists or create a new one. Figure 13.15 shows a Microsoft Word window. Both Word and Notepad are used to create and edit documents, but Word is far more configurable and powerful and therefore has many more optional components available within its window.

FIGURE 13.15   A window with many more components, as seen in Microsoft Word

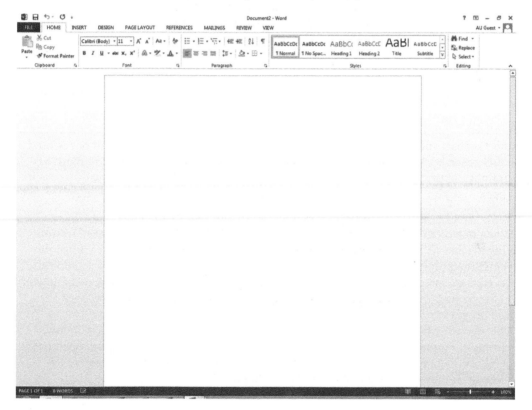

States of a Window

There is more to the Windows interface than the specific parts of a window. Windows also are movable, stackable, and resizable, and they can be hidden behind other windows (often unintentionally!).

When an application window has been launched, it exists in one of three states:

Maximized   A maximized window takes up all of the available space on the screen. When it is in front of other programs, it is the only thing visible—even the Desktop is hidden. It takes up the entire space of the Desktop, and the middle button in the upper-right corner displays two rectangles rather than one. The sides of the window no longer have borders. The window is flush with the edges of the screen. Maximizing a window provides the maximum workspace possible for that window's application, and the user can actively access the window. In general, maximized mode is the preferred window size for most word processing, graphics-creation, and other types of user applications.

Restored   A restored window can be used interactively, and it is identical in function to a maximized window, with the simple difference that it does not necessarily take up the entire screen. Restored windows can be very small, or they can take up as much space as maximized windows. Generally, how large the restored window becomes is the user's choice. Restored windows display a Maximize button (the middle button in the upper-right corner) with a single rectangle in it; this is used to maximize the window. Restored windows have a border.

Minimized   Minimized program windows are represented by nothing but an icon and title on the Taskbar, and they are not usable until they have been either maximized or restored. The difference between a minimized program and a closed program is that a minimized program is out of the way, but it is still taking up resources and is therefore ready to use if you need it. It also leaves the content of the window in the same place when you return to it as when you minimized it.

When one program is open and you need to open another (or maybe you need to stop playing a game because your boss has entered the room), you have two choices. First you can close the program currently in use and simply choose to reopen it later. If you do this, however, the contents of the window (your current game, for example) will be lost and you will have to start over. Once the program has been closed, you can move on to open the second program.

The second option is to minimize the active window. Minimizing the game window, for example, removes the open window from the screen and leaves the program open but displays nothing more than an icon and title on the Taskbar. Later, you can restore the window to its previous size and finish the game in progress.

Keep in mind that applications in the background are still running. Therefore, if you minimize your game, you might return to find that you've been eaten by whatever monster you were running from in the game. A program running while minimized can be a good thing, however, if you're running a useful utility such as a long search or a disk defrag.

Updating Windows

Windows includes *Windows Update*, a feature designed to keep Windows current by automatically downloading and installing updates such as patches and security fixes.

By default, Windows Update will run automatically when any administrator user is logged in. If you want to run it manually, however, you can always do so. Here is an overview of how Windows Update works:

1. Windows Update starts (either by itself or manually).

2. Windows Update goes online to check to see what updates are available. It compares the update list to the updates that have already been applied to the computer or have been refused by the administrator.

3. If updates are available, they may be downloaded automatically in the background.

4. Once the updates are downloaded, Windows Update notifies you that the download is complete and asks you if you want to install them, assuming you have that behavior configured (settings can be used to control the behavior).

 Often, major updates to Windows are called *service packs*.

If you choose not to install the updates right away, Windows will do so for you when you shut off the computer. Instead of shutting off right away, Windows Update will install the updates first and then perform a proper shutdown.

By default, Windows Update is enabled. But there might be times when you want to configure it. Exercise 13.4 steps through the process of configuring Windows Update in Windows 8.1/8/7/Vista.

EXERCISE 13.4

Configuring Windows Update

1. Click the Start button, and choose All Programs. Scroll down the list and choose Windows Update.

2. Click the Change Settings entry on the left to open the Choose How Windows Can Install Updates window.

3. Choose the option that best suits your needs. You have four choices:
   - Install Updates Automatically (Recommended)
   - Download Updates But Let Me Choose Whether To Install Them
   - Check For Updates But Let Me Choose Whether To Download And Install Them
   - Never Check For Updates (Not Recommended)

4. Click OK. You will be prompted by User Account Control (UAC) to verify that you want to make that change.

Microsoft has an update server, Windows Server Update Services (WSUS), for large organizations that controls the update process for all hosts in the company.

Creating Restore Points

Almost everyone, no matter how hard they've tried to keep their computer running properly, will experience a computer crash at some point. Many of the ways to get your computer back up and running (such as reinstalling the operating system) take a lot of time. In Windows, System Restore allows you to create restore points to make recovery of the operating system easier.

A *restore point* is a copy of your system configuration at a given point in time. Restore points are created one of three ways:

1. Windows creates them automatically by default.

2. You can manually create them yourself (which is highly recommended before you make any significant changes to the system, such as installing new drivers).

3. During the installation of some programs, a restore point is created before the installation; that way, if the install fails, you can "roll back" the system to a preinstallation configuration.

Restore points are useful for when Windows fails to boot but the computer appears to be fine otherwise or if Windows doesn't seem to be acting right and you think it was because of a recent configuration change.

To open System Restore, click Start ➢ All Programs ➢ Accessories ➢ System Tools ➢ System Restore. In Windows 7, it will open a screen like the one shown in Figure 13.16.

FIGURE 13.16 System Restore

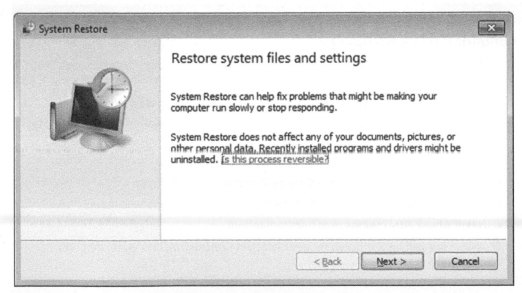

If you need to use a restore point and Windows won't boot, you can reboot into Safe Mode. After Safe Mode loads, you will have the option to work in Safe Mode or use System Restore. Choose System Restore, and you'll be presented with the restore points (if any) that you can use.

This tool can be used to configure System Restore settings. You can also get to the same place by opening the System control panel (right-clicking Computer and choosing Properties) and selecting the System Restore tab.

It is possible for you to turn off System Restore. Don't do this unless you really don't care if your computer crashes and you can't recover it without a reinstall. The other option is to select how much disk space is available for System Restore. The less disk space you make available, the fewer the number of restore points you will be able to retain. If you have multiple hard drives, you can allocate a different amount of space per hard drive.

Exercise 13.5 demonstrates how to create a restore point manually in Windows.

EXERCISE 13.5

Manually Creating a Restore Point in Windows

1. Assuming that you are using Category view, click Start ➤ Control Panel ➤ System And Security ➤ System ➤ System Protection.

2. If prompted, type in the administrator password (and account name, if needed), or confirm that you want to continue.

3. Choose the System Protection tab, and then click Create.

4. Fill in a description for the restore point, and then click Create (you cannot click Create without putting text in for a description).

5. When the process is finished, click OK and then exit out of the Control Panel windows.

A factory recovery partition may exist on a machine. A vendor has a great deal of freedom with what it puts here, but usually it contains copies of drivers and preinstalled programs. This partition—if it exists—may serve as a last resort for stabilizing a system if all else has failed.

File Management

File management is the process by which a computer stores data and retrieves it from storage. Although some of the file-management interfaces across Windows may have a different look and feel, the process of managing files is similar across the board.

Files and Folders

For a program to run, it must be able to read information off the hard disk and write information back to the hard disk. To be able to organize and access information—especially in larger new systems that may have thousands of files—it is necessary to have a structure and an ordering process.

Windows provides this process by allowing you to create *directories*, also known as *folders*, in which to organize files. Windows also regulates the way that files are named and the properties of files. The filename for each file created in Windows has to follow certain rules, and any program that accesses files through Windows must also comply with these rules:

- Each file has a filename of up to 255 characters.

- Certain characters, such as a question mark (?) and slash (\ or /), are reserved for other uses and cannot be used in the filename. Periods are used to separate the filename from the extension, and the backslash is used to separate the directories in a path from the filename.

- A filename extension (generally three or four characters) can be added to identify the file's type.

- Filenames are not case sensitive. (You can create files with names that use both upper- and lowercase letters, but to identify the file within the file system, it is not necessary to adhere to the capitalization in the filename.) Thus, you cannot have a file named working.txt and another called WORKING.TXT in the same directory. To Windows, these filenames are identical, and you can't have two files with the same filename in the same directory. We'll get into more detail on this topic a little later.

In Windows 3.*x* and DOS, filenames were limited to eight characters and a three-character extension, separated by a period. This is also called the 8.3 file-naming convention. With Windows 95, long filenames were introduced, which allowed the 255-character filename convention.

The Windows file system is arranged like a filing cabinet. In a filing cabinet, paper is placed into folders, which are internal dividers, which are in a drawer of the filing cabinet. In the Windows file system, individual files are placed in subdirectories that are inside directories, which are stored on different disks or different partitions.

Windows also protects against duplicate filenames, so no two files on the system can have exactly the same name and path. A *path* indicates the location of the file on the disk; it is composed of the letter of the logical drive on which the file is located and, if the file is located in a directory or subdirectory, the names of those directories. For instance, if a file named AUTOEXEC.BAT is located in the root of the C: drive—meaning it is not within a directory—the path to the file is C:\AUTOEXEC.BAT. If, as another example, a file called FDISK.EXE is located in the Command directory under Windows under the root of C:, then the path to this file is C:\WINDOWS\COMMAND\FDISK.EXE.

The *root directory* of any drive is the place where the hierarchy of folders for that drive begins. On a C: drive, for instance, C:\ is the root directory of the drive.

Common filename extensions that you may encounter are .EXE for executable files (applications), .DLL for dynamic linked library (DLL) files, .SYS for system files, .LOG for log files, .DRV for driver files, and .TXT for text files. Note that DLL files contain additional functions and commands that applications can use and share. In addition, specific filename extensions are used for the documents created with each application. For example, the filenames for documents created in Microsoft Word have a .DOC or .DOCX extension. You'll also encounter extensions such as .MPG for video files, .MP3 for music files, .PNG and .TIF for graphics files, .HTM and .HTML for web pages, and so on. Being familiar with different filename extensions is helpful in working with the Windows file system.

Capabilities of EXPLORER

Although it is technically possible to use the command-line utilities provided within the command prompt to manage your files, this generally is not the most efficient way to accomplish most tasks. The ability to use drag-and-drop techniques and other graphical tools to manage the file system makes the process far simpler, and *EXPLORER* is a utility that allows you to accomplish a number of important file-related tasks from a single graphical interface.

Here are some of the tasks you can accomplish using EXPLORER:

- View files and directories
- Open programs or data files
- Create directories and files
- Copy objects to other locations
- Move objects to other locations
- Delete or rename objects
- Change file attributes

You can access many of these functions by right-clicking a file or folder and selecting the appropriate option, such as Copy or Delete, from the context menu.

Navigating and Using EXPLORER

Using EXPLORER is simple. A few basic instructions are all you need to start working with it. First, the EXPLORER interface has a number of parts, each of which serves a specific purpose. The top area of EXPLORER is dominated by a set of menus and toolbars that give you easy access to common commands. The main section of the window is divided into two panes: The left pane displays the drives and folders available, and the right pane displays the contents of the currently selected drive or folder. The following list includes some common actions in Explorer:

Expanding a folder   You can double-click a folder in the left pane to expand it (show its subfolders in the left pane) and display its contents in the right pane. Clicking the plus sign (+) to the left of a folder expands the folder without changing the display in the right pane.

Collapsing a folder   Clicking the minus sign (–) next to a folder collapses it.

Selecting a file   If you click the file in the right pane, Windows highlights the file by marking it with a darker color.

Selecting multiple files   The Ctrl or Shift keys allow you to select multiple files at once. Holding down Ctrl while clicking individual files selects each new file while leaving the currently selected file(s) selected as well. Holding down Shift while selecting two files selects both of them and all of the files in between.

Opening a file   Double-clicking a file in the right pane opens the program if the file is an application; if it is a data file, it will open using the application for which the filename extension is configured.

Changing the view type   Windows has several different view types: Extra Large Icons, Medium Icons, Large Icons, Small Icons, List, Details, Content, and Tiles. The choices vary a bit between the Windows versions (Vista, for example, does not have Content, but the others are the same). You can move between these views by clicking the View menu and selecting the view that you prefer. By default, in Windows 7, the menu isn't visible until you press the Alt key.

Finding specific files   You access this option by using the Search button or bar. You can search for files based on their name, file size, file type, and other attributes.

When you're searching, you can also use wildcards. *Wildcards* are characters that act as placeholders for a character or set of characters, allowing, for instance, a search for all files with a .TXT filename extension. To perform such a search, you'd type an asterisk (*****) as a stand-in for the filename: ***.TXT**. An asterisk takes the place of any number of characters in a search. A question mark (?) takes the place of a single number or letter. For example, AUTOEX??.BAT would return the file AUTOEXEC.BAT as part of its results.

Creating new objects   To create a new file, folder, or other object, navigate to the location where you want to create the object, and then right-click in the right pane (without selecting a file or directory). In the menu that appears, select New and then choose the object that you want to create.

Deleting objects   Select the object and press the Del key on the keyboard, or right-click the object and select Delete from the menu that appears.

The simplicity of deleting in Windows makes it likely that you or one of the people you support will delete or misplace a file or a number of files that are still needed. In such a case, the Recycle Bin (mentioned earlier) is a lifesaver.

Besides simplifying most file-management commands as shown here, EXPLORER allows you to complete a number of disk-management tasks easily. You can format and label removable media.

Changing File Attributes

File attributes determine what specific users can do to files or directories. For example, if a file or directory is flagged with the Read Only attribute, then users can read the file or directory but cannot make changes to it or delete it. Attributes include Read Only, Hidden, System, and Archive as well as Compression, Indexing, and Encryption. Not all attributes are available with all versions of Windows. We'll look at this subject in more detail in a moment.

Some attributes date back to DOS—such as Read Only, Hidden, System, and Archive. All others, such as Compression, Indexing, and Encryption, are a part of NTFS.

You can view and change file attributes either by entering **ATTRIB** at the command prompt or by changing the properties of a file or directory. To access the properties of a file or directory in the Windows GUI, right-click the file or directory and select Properties. You can view and configure the Read Only and Hidden file attributes on the General tab. To view and configure additional attributes, click Advanced.

System files are usually flagged with the Hidden attribute, meaning that they don't appear when a user displays a directory listing. You should not change this attribute on a system file unless absolutely necessary. System files are required for the OS to function. If they are visible, users might delete them (perhaps thinking they can clear some disk space by deleting files they don't recognize). Needless to say, that would be a bad thing!

File System Advanced Attributes

Windows may use the New Technology File System (NTFS), which gives you a number of options that are not available on earlier file systems such as FAT and FAT32. A number of these options are implemented through the use of the Advanced Attributes window, shown in Figure 13.17. To reach these options in Windows, right-click the folder or file that you wish to modify and select Properties from the menu. On the main Properties page of the folder or file, click the Advanced button in the lower-right corner.

FAT32 does not have as many options as NTFS, such as Encryption and Compression. These attributes are available only on NTFS partitions.

On the Advanced Attributes window, you have access to the following settings:

Archiving   The archiving option can be used to tell the system whether or not the file has changed since the last time it was backed up. Technically, it is known as the Archive Needed attribute; if this bit is on, the file should be backed up. If it is not selected, a current version of the file is already backed up.

Indexing   Windows implements a feature called the *Indexing Service* to catalog and improve the search capabilities of your drive. Once files are indexed, you can search for them more quickly by name, date, or other attributes. Setting the index option on a folder causes a prompt to appear, asking whether you want the existing files in the folder to be indexed as well. If you choose to do this, Windows will automatically reset this attribute on subfolders and files. If not, only new files created in the directory are indexed.

Compression   The versions of Windows that you need to know for the exam support advanced *compression* options, which were first introduced in Windows NT. NTFS files and folders can be dynamically compressed and uncompressed, often saving a great deal of space on the drive. As with indexing, when you turn on compression for a folder, you'll be prompted as to whether you want the existing files in the folder to be compressed. If you choose to do this, Windows automatically compresses the subfolders and files. If not, only new files created in the directory are compressed.

FIGURE 13.17   The Advanced Attributes window

Compression works best on such files as word processing documents and uncompressed images. Word files and Microsoft Paint bitmaps can be compressed up to 80 percent. Files that are already packed well do not compress as effectively; EXE and ZIP files generally compress only about 2 percent. Similarly, GIF and JPEG images are already compressed (which is why they are used in Internet web pages), so they compress a little or not at all.

Encryption   *Encryption* lets you secure files so that no one else can view them; you encrypt files by encoding them with a key to which only you have access. This can be useful if you're worried about extremely sensitive information, but in general encryption is not necessary on the network. NTFS local file security is usually enough to provide users with access to what they need and prevent others from getting to what they shouldn't. If you want to encrypt a file, go through the same process that you would for indexing or compression.

> Encryption and compression are mutually exclusive—you can set one but not both features on a file or folder. Not all features are available in all editions of every operating system. If a user forgets their password or is unable to access the network to authenticate their account, they will not be able to open encrypted files. By default, if the user's account is lost or deleted, the only other user who can decrypt the file is the Administrator account.

File Permissions

Windows also supports the use of *file permissions* because these OSs use NTFS, which includes file-level file system security (along with share-level security). Permissions serve the purpose of controlling who has access and what type of access they have to what files or folders. Several permissions are available, such as Read, Write, Execute, Delete, Change Permissions, Take Ownership, Full Control, and more. The list is quite extensive. For a complete list, consult the Windows Help files.

Assigning special permissions individually could be a tedious task. To make it easier for administrators to assign multiple permissions at once, Windows incorporates standard permissions. *Standard permissions* are collections of special permissions, including Full Control, Modify, Read & Execute, Read, and Write. As we said, each of these standard permissions automatically assigns multiple special permissions at once. To see which special permissions are assigned by the different standard permissions refer to http://technet .microsoft.com/en-us/library/cc732880.

Note that you can assign permissions to individual users or to groups. You assign standard permissions on the Security tab of a file or folder, which you access through the file or folder's properties.

Being able to set file permissions is a great reason to use NTFS. In Exercise 13.6, we will show you how to examine file permissions.

EXERCISE 13.6

Examining File Permissions

1. Open Windows File Explorer.

2. Right-click a file or folder and choose Properties.

3. Select and then examine the Security tab.

continues

4. You'll see the users and/or groups to which permissions have been assigned. Select a user or group in the list, and examine the list of standard permissions. (To add a new user or group, click Add and follow the prompts.) Any standard permissions that are checked in the Allow column are applied. If a check box is grayed out, this means that the permission was inherited. To revoke a set of standard permissions, click the appropriate check box in the Deny column. If you click the check box in the Deny column for the Full Control permission, all other standard permissions are also denied.

5. Click Advanced to examine advanced options.

6. Click Cancel twice to close the file or folder's properties.

Be sure that you don't accidentally make any changes that you didn't intend to make. Changing permissions without understanding the ramifications can have negative consequences, such as losing access to files or folders. It is a best practice to assign Deny permissions sparingly. Unchecking Allow is better (you may need to turn off Inheritance).

Going Virtual

Thanks to the ability to create virtual machines (VMs), it is becoming far less common to need dual-boot machines today than in the past. Using VMs, you can run multiple operating systems (or multiple instances of the same operating system) on the same hardware at the same time and not need to reboot the system each time you want a different OS.

The *hypervisor* is a virtual machine manager—the software that allows the virtual machines to exist. In the Microsoft client OS realm, the built-in hypervisor in Windows Vista is the Microsoft Virtual PC, the Windows Virtual PC in Windows 7, and Hyper-V in Windows 8. Other options include VMware and Xen, which are two other well-known hypervisors.

There have been a number of virtualization-specific threats that have cropped up focusing on the hypervisor, but updates fixed the issues as they became known. The solution to most virtual machine threats is always to apply the most recent updates and keep the system(s) up-to-date.

An excellent resource from Microsoft on desktop virtualization can be found here:

https://www.microsoft.com/en-us/windows/enterprise/products-and-technologies/virtualization/default.aspx

The virtual desktop is often called a *virtual desktop interface (VDI)*, and that term encompasses the software and hardware needed to create the virtual environment.

Virtual desktops are often used with remote administration, allowing a remote administrator to work on the workstation with or without the knowledge of the user sitting in front of the machine.

The resource requirements for virtualization are largely based upon what environments you are creating. The hardware on the machine must have enough memory, hard drive space, and processor capability to support the virtualization. You also need the software to make virtualization possible. XP Mode was mentioned earlier in this chapter, and it is a free emulator that Microsoft supplied for Windows 7 as a pre-configured virtual machine, which is run in the Windows Virtual PC emulator (the hypervisor). A number of others are also available. In most cases, the motherboard and associated BIOS settings need no alteration to provide services to these virtual machines. Some of the newer virtualization products, however (such as Microsoft's Hyper-V), require that the motherboard support *hardware-assisted virtualization*. The benefit derived from using hardware-assisted virtualization is that it allows the hypervisor (the virtualization product) to allocate memory and CPU dynamically to the VMs as required. XP Mode is not supported—or available—with Windows 8/8.1; in discontinuing support for Windows XP, Microsoft no longer wants users running it even in a virtual environment.

 VMware Player allows you to work in multiple environments on one system. For more information, go to www.vmware.com/products/player/.

Preparing for the Exam

The next four chapters delve further into operating systems and the tools, utilities, and features available with each. There is also additional coverage, as applicable, in the chapters on troubleshooting. For purposes of exam study, Table 13.4 offers a complete list of the features for each of the Windows operating systems that you need to know for this exam. It also signifies whether that feature is available in each of those operating systems and which chapter in this book has more coverage of that particular topic.

TABLE 13.4   Windows features

Feature	Purpose	Windows Vista	Windows 7	Windows 8/8.1	More Information
Aero	Default interface for Windows Vista	Yes			Chapter 17
Gadgets	Mini programs created for Vista. Still available with other OSes but as relevant	Yes	Yes, but degradated	Yes, but degradated	Chapter 17
User Account Control	Controls changes to OS settings	Yes	Yes	Yes	Chapter 16

TABLE 13.4 Windows features *(continued)*

Feature	Purpose	Windows Vista	Windows 7	Windows 8/8.1	More Information
Bit-Locker	Encrypts drives. Available in each OS, but not in every edition	Yes	Yes	Yes	Chapter 16
Shadow Copy	Makes snapshots that can be reverted back to	Yes	Yes	Yes	Chapter 16
System Restore	Allows restore of system files and settings	Yes	Yes	Yes	Chapter 16
Ready Boost	Use removable drive as cache	Yes	Yes	Yes	Chapter 16
Sidebar	Vertical bar for holding gadgets	Yes	No	No	Chapters 13, 17
Compatibility Mode	Allows legacy programs to run	Yes	Yes	Yes	Chapters 13, 16, 17
Virtual XP mode	Allows older programs to think they are running on Windows XP	Yes	Yes	No	Chapters 13, 16
Easy Transfer	Transfer data files from one OS to another	Yes	Yes	Yes	Chapters 13, 16
Administrative Tools	Allows administrative tasks to be run on the computer	Yes	Yes	Yes	Chapter 14
Defender	Looks for Malware	Yes	Yes	Yes	Chapters 16, 17
Windows firewall	Blocks unwanted traffic	Yes	Yes	Yes	Chapters 16, 17
Security center	Allows configuration of security-related items	Yes	Became Action Center	Action Center	Chapter 15
Event Viewer	Allows viewing of the log files	Yes	Yes	Yes	Chapter 14
File structure and paths	Allows orderly creation of folders and files	Yes	Yes	Yes	Chapter 13

Feature	Purpose	Windows Vista	Windows 7	Windows 8/8.1	More Information
Category view vs. Classic view	Two possible ways to view the Control Panel	Yes	Yes	Yes	Chapter 14
Side by side apps	Allows you to position windows on the desktop and Windows will remember the size and position	No	Yes, as Aero Snap	Yes	Chapter 16
Metro UI	The interface released with Windows 8.	No	No	Yes	Chapter 15
Pinning	Connecting an app to the Taskbar	No	Yes	Yes	Chapters 13, 15, 16
One Drive	Allows cloud storage	No	Not pre-installed	Yes	Chapter 15
Windows store	A convenient location to purchase Windows apps	No	No	Yes	Chapter 15
Multimonitor task bars	Taskbars appear in Windows in multiple monitors	No	No	Yes	Chapter 15
Charms	Commonly used apps/features such as Search and Share	No	No	Yes	Chapter 15
Start Screen	A portion of the Metro UI from which you can choose common options	No	No	Yes	Chapter 15
Power Shell	A scripting language that can be used to automate tasks	Yes	Yes	Yes	Chapter 15
Live sign in	A single sign-on feature	No	No	Yes	Chapter 15
Action Center	A central location for dealing with problems, security, and maintenance	Known as Security Center	Yes	Yes	Chapters 15, 16

Summary

In this chapter, you learned about Windows, the basics of the Windows structure, and window management. Because Windows is a graphical system, the key to success in learning to use it is to explore the system to find out what it can do. You will then be better prepared to decipher later what a user has done.

First, we covered the Windows interface. Next, we covered what the component that gives Windows its name (the window) actually is and how windows are used.

Finally, we covered some basic Windows management concepts, including using file systems and managing files as well as understanding directory structure. We discussed using approved hardware, updating Windows, and creating restore points.

With the basic knowledge gained in this chapter, you are now ready to learn how to interact with the most commonly used tools, the subject of the following chapter.

Exam Essentials

Know what file systems are available in Windows and the differences between them.   The most commonly used file system on Windows hard drives is NTFS. FAT32 is older and perhaps a bit quicker for smaller hard drives, but NTFS adds a plethora of important features, including security and auditing.

Understand how to manage files in Windows.   Nearly all file management is accomplished through Windows File Explorer, including moving, copying, renaming, and deleting files and changing file attributes, advanced attributes, and permissions.

Know where files are located.   The various versions of Windows that you need to know for this exam store files in multiple locations. You should be able to identify the location of those files mentioned in this chapter and be able to identify items such as where the Recycle Bin files are on each Windows operating system.

Review Questions

The answers to the chapter review questions can be found in Appendix A.

1. Which of the following can you type at a Start menu in Windows to open a command prompt? (Choose two.)

   A. RUN

   B. CMD

   C. COMMAND

   D. OPEN

2. Which part of the operating system can be described as extremely specific software written for the purpose of instructing the OS on how to access a piece of hardware?

   A. Source

   B. Application

   C. Kernel

   D. Driver

3. The Taskbar can be increased in size by _____.

   A. Right-clicking the mouse and dragging the Taskbar to make it bigger

   B. Left-clicking the mouse and double-clicking the Taskbar

   C. Moving the mouse pointer to the top of the Taskbar, pausing until the pointer turns into a double-headed arrow, and then clicking and dragging

   D. Highlighting the Taskbar and double-clicking in the center

4. Which of the following file attributes are available to files on a FAT32 partition?

   A. Hidden, Read Only, Archive, System

   B. Compression, Hidden, Archive, Encryption, Read Only

   C. Read Only, Hidden, System, Encryption

   D. Indexing, Read Only, Hidden, System, Compression

5. The Windows File Explorer program can be used to do which of the following? (Choose two.)

   A. Browse the Internet

   B. Copy and move files

   C. Change file attributes

   D. Create backup jobs

6. Standard permissions are _____.

   A. The same as special permissions

   B. Only the Read, Write, and Execute permissions

    C.   Permissions assigned to users but not to groups

    D.   Permissions grouped together for easy assignment

7. Which of the following is a program that runs on top of the OS and allows the user to issue commands through a set of menus or some other graphical interface?

    A.   Taskbar

    B.   Shell

    C.   GUI

    D.   Source

8. If a program doesn't have a shortcut on the Desktop or in the Programs submenu, you can start it by _____. (Choose the best answer.)

    A.   Using the Shut Down command

    B.   Typing **CMD** in the Start Run box

    C.   Using the RUN command and typing in the name of the program

    D.   Typing **CMD** in the Start box followed by the program name

9. What operating system feature offers the ability for a single application to have multiple requests into the processor at one time?

    A.   Multiuser mode

    B.   Dystopia

    C.   Preemption

    D.   Multithreading

10. In Windows, a deleted file can be retrieved using which of the following?

    A.   My Computer icon

    B.   Recycle Bin

    C.   Control Panel

    D.   Settings panel

11. To turn off a Windows 7 machine, you should _____.

    A.   Run the Shut Down (Turn Off) command at a command prompt.

    B.   Turn off the switch and unplug the machine.

    C.   Press Ctrl+Alt+Del.

    D.   Select Start ➢ Shut Down, and choose Shut Down.

12. What is the minimum amount of memory recommended for a 32-bit installation of Windows 8.1?

    A.   128MB

    B.   256MB

   C. 512MB

   D. 1GB

13. What is the minimum amount of free hard drive space recommended for the installation of Windows Vista Home Basic?

   A. 1.5GB

   B. 15GB

   C. 30GB

   D. 60GB

14. What is the minimum recommended memory for a 32-bit installation of Windows 7?

   A. 512MB

   B. 1GB

   C. 2GB

   D. 4GB

15. In Windows, a quick way to access Help is to press which keyboard key?

   A. F12

   B. The Windows button on the keyboard

   C. F1

   D. Alt

16. Which of the following was installed to the Desktop by default only in Windows Vista?

   A. Gadgets

   B. Sidebar

   C. System tray

   D. Recycle Bin

17. Which of the following is located on the rightmost portion of the Taskbar?

   A. Start menu

   B. Quick Launch

   C. System tray

   D. Shutdown options

18. In addition to right-clicking on the Desktop, how else can you access the Display Properties settings?

   A. Using the Display icon under Control Panel

   B. Using the System icon under Control Panel

   C. Pressing Ctrl+Alt+Esc

   D. Pressing Ctrl+Alt+Tab

19. Which of the following is the name of the graphical interface included with Windows Vista?

    A. Start

    B. Aero

    C. KDE

    D. GNOME

20. What is the minimum recommended memory for a 64-bit installation of Windows 7?

    A. 512MB

    B. 1GB

    C. 2GB

    D. 4GB

Performance-Based Question

You will encounter performance-based questions on the A+ exams. The questions on the exam require you to perform a specific task, and you will be graded on whether or not you were able to complete the task. The following requires you to think creatively in order to measure how well you understand this chapter's topics. You may or may not see similar questions on the actual A+ exams. To see how your answer compares to the authors', refer to Appendix B.

You have been told that a number of workstations in your department may be upgraded in the near future, and you've been assigned the task of logging on to each locally and collecting basic data on the workstations. All workstations on this floor run Windows 7. How would you most efficiently collect the following information?

Windows Edition:

Service Pack installed:

Processor:

Installed Memory:

Total paging file size for all drives:

Chapter 14

Operating System Administration

THE FOLLOWING COMPTIA A+ 220-902 EXAM OBJECTIVES ARE COVERED IN THIS CHAPTER:

✓ **1.1 Compare and contrast various features and requirements of Microsoft Operating Systems (Windows Vista, Windows 7, Windows 8, Windows 8.1).**

- Features: User account control, compatibility mode, administrative tools, security center, event viewer, file structure and paths, category view vs. classic view

✓ **1.2 Given a scenario, install Windows PC operating systems using appropriate methods.**

- Partitioning: Dynamic, Basic, Primary, Extended, Logical, GPT
- Filesystem types/formatting: ExFAT, FAT32, NTFS, CDFS, NFS, ext3, ext4, Quick format vs. full format
- Load alternate third-party drivers when necessary
- Workgroup vs. Domain setup
- Time/date/region/language settings
- Driver installation, software, and Windows updates
- Factory recovery partition
- Properly formatted boot drive with the correct partitions/format

✓ **1.3 Given a scenario, apply appropriate Microsoft command-line tools.**

- TASKKILL, BOOTREC, SHUTDOWN, TASKLIST, MD, RD, CD, DEL, FORMAT, COPY, XCOPY, ROBOCOPY, DISKPART, SFC, CHKDSK, GPUPDATE, GPRESULT, DIR, EXIT, HELP, EXPAND, [command name] /?, Commands available with standard privileges vs. administrative privileges

✓ **1.4 Given a scenario, use appropriate Microsoft operating system features and tools.**

- Administrative: Computer management, Device manager, Performance monitor, Services, Task Scheduler

- MSCONFIG: General, Boot, Services, Startup, Tools

- Task Manager: Applications, Processes, Performance, Networking, Users

- Disk management: Drive Status, Mounting, Initializing, Extending partitions, Splitting partitions, Shrink partitions, Assigning drive letters, Adding drives, Adding Arrays, Storage spaces

- System utilities: REGEDIT, COMMAND, SERVICES.MSC, MMC, MSTSC, EXPLORER, MSINFO32, DXDIAG

✓ **1.5 Given a scenario, use Windows Control Panel utilities.**

- Internet options (Connections, Security, General, Privacy, Programs, Advanced)

- Display/Display Settings (Resolution, Color depth, Refresh rate)

- User accounts

- Folder options (View hidden files, Hide extensions, General options, View options)

- System Performance (virtual memory), Remote settings, System protection

- Windows firewall

- Power options (Hibernate, Power plans, Sleep/suspend, Standby)

- Programs and features

✓ **1.7 Perform common preventive maintenance procedures using the appropriate Windows OS tools.**

- Best practices (Scheduled backups, Scheduled disk maintenance, Scheduled defragmentation)

- Tools (Backup, Disk maintenance utilities)

The previous chapter introduced the basic components of the Windows operating systems. This chapter builds upon that and focuses more on the administration of those operating systems. All of the content is generic to the three Windows operating systems on which you'll be tested in the 220–902 certification exam: Windows 8/8.1, Windows 7, and Windows Vista.

In the three chapters that follow, we will dive into specifics for each of the three end-user operating systems, one per OS.

Interacting with Operating Systems

In the following sections, we will look at the Microsoft GUI from the ground up. In Chapter 13, "Operating System Basics," we took a detailed look at its key components, and we will build on that with an exploration of basic tasks common across Windows 8/8.1, Windows 7, and Windows Vista.

Control Panel

Although, for the most part, the Windows system is functional from the time it is installed, Microsoft realized that if someone were going to use computers regularly, they would probably want to be able to customize their environment so that it would be better suited to their needs—or at least more fun to use. As a result, the Windows environment has a large number of utilities that are intended to give you control over the look and feel of the operating system.

This is, of course, an excellent idea. It is also a bit more freedom than some less-than-cautious users seem to be capable of handling, and you will undoubtedly serve a number of customers who call you in to restore their configuration after botched attempts at changing one setting or another.

More than likely, you will also have to reinstall Windows yourself a few times because of accidents that occur while you are studying or testing the system's limits. This is actually a good thing because no competent computer technician can say that they have never had to reinstall because of an error. You can't really know how to fix Windows until you are experienced at breaking it. So it is extremely important to experiment and find out what can be changed in the Windows environment, what results from those changes, and how to undo any unwanted results. To this end, we will examine the most common configuration utility in Windows: Control Panel. The names of some of the applets, icons, categories, and tasks are different in various versions of Windows; different names are indicated in parentheses. Also, not all applets are available in all versions. You'll see some of the more popular applets described in Table 14.1.

TABLE 14.1   Selected Windows Control Panel applets

Applet Name	Function
Add A Device (Add Hardware)	Adds and configures new hardware.
Programs and Features	Changes, adds, or deletes software.
Administrative Tools	Performs administrative tasks on the computer.
Date And Time	Sets the system time and configures options such as time zone.
Display (Personalization)	Configures screensavers, colors, display options, and monitor drivers.
Folder Options	Configures the look and feel of how folders are displayed in Windows File Explorer.
Fonts	Adds and removes fonts.
Internet Options	Sets a number of Internet connectivity options.
Hardware And Sound (Sound; Scanners And Cameras) (Multimedia)	Configures audio, video, or audio and video options.
Network And Internet; Network And Sharing Center	Sets options for connecting to other computers.
Phone And Modem	Sets options for using phone lines to dial out to a network or the Internet.
Power Options	Configures different power schemes to adjust power consumption.
Devices And Printers (Printers)	Configures printer settings and print defaults.
System	Allows you to view and configure various system elements. We'll look at this in more detail later in this chapter.

In the current version of Windows, when you first open Control Panel, it appears in Category view, as shown in Figure 14.1. Control Panel programs have been organized into different categories, and this view provides you with the categories from which you can choose. Once you choose a category, you can pick a task and the appropriate Control Panel program is opened for you, or you can select one of the Control Panel programs that is part of the category. However, you can change this view to Classic view (or Small/Large Icons in Windows 7 and Windows 8), which displays all of the Control Panel programs in a list, as in older versions of Windows. The specific wording of the CompTIA objective for this exam reads, "Given a scenario, use Control Panel utilities (the items are organized by 'classic view/large icons' in Windows)." Because of this, we *strongly* suggest that administrators change to this view. To do so, click Switch To Classic View in the left pane or View By in the drop-down box in the right corner in Windows 7 and Windows 8. Throughout this chapter, when we refer to accessing Control Panel programs, we will assume that you have changed the view to the Classic/Icons view.

FIGURE 14.1   The Control Panel in Category view in Windows 8.1.

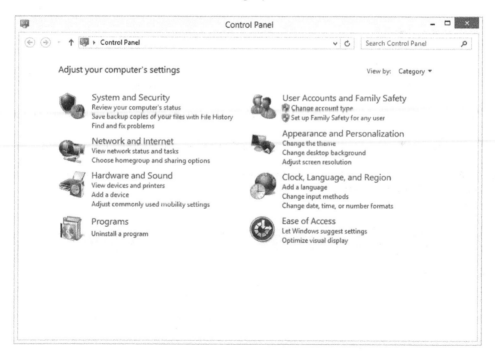

For a quick look at how the Control Panel programs work, in Exercise 14.1, you'll examine some of the settings in the Date And Time applet (TIMEDATE.CPL).

Filenames appearing in parentheses, such as TIMEDATE.CPL in the preceding paragraph, can be used to start the utility without needing to go through the Control Panel dialog boxes.

The Date And Time applet is used to configure the system time, date, and time zone settings, which can be important for files that require accurate time stamps or to users who don't have a watch. Because it is a simple program, it's a perfect example to use. Current versions of Windows have an Internet Time tab, which enables you to synchronize time on the computer with an Internet time server (the options in Windows 8.1 are shown in Figure 14.2).

FIGURE 14.2   System time can be configured to be retrieved from an Internet time server.

EXERCISE 14.1

Changing the Time Zone

1. Click Start ➢ Control Panel.

2. From Control Panel, double-click the Date And Time icon (by default, the programs are listed alphabetically).

3. Click the Time Zone tab, and use the drop-down menu to select (GMT –03:30) New-foundland.

4. Hop a plane to Newfoundland, secure in the knowledge that you will know what time it is once you get there.

5. If you skipped step 4, change the time zone back to where it should be before closing the window.

The Regional and Language Options

Regional settings are configured through the Control Panel applet called Region in Windows 8/8.1, Region And Language in Windows 7, and Regional And Language Options in Windows Vista. From this applet (INTL.CPL), you can choose what format is used for numbers (see Figure 14.3), the layout of the keyboard you are using, your geographic location, and the language to be used for non-Unicode programs.

FIGURE 14.3 Set the format used for numbers with the options in the Region applet.

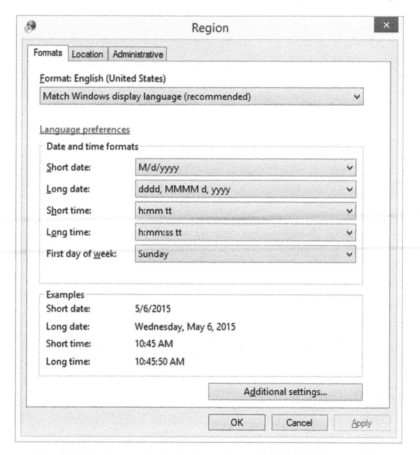

The ability to support so many languages is provided through the use of the Unicode standard. In Unicode, and the Unicode Character Set (UCS), each character has a 16-bit value. This allows the same character to be interpreted/represented by 65,536 different entities.

If you click Additional Settings, you can go beyond the date and time formats and also configure number and currency, as shown in Figure 14.4.

FIGURE 14.4 Set the number and currency settings for the system as well.

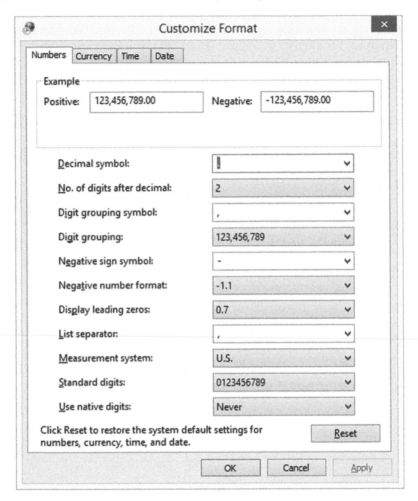

The Internet Options Applet

The Internet Options applet (INETCPL.CPL) brings up the Internet properties, shown in Figure 14.5. The tabs here include General, Security, Privacy, Content, Connections, Programs, and Advanced. This applet is used when you want to configure the browser environment and such things as the programs used to work with files found online.

The Folder Options Applet

Some of the more important files that you will need to work on are hidden by default as a security precaution. To make certain folders or files visible, you need to change the display properties of Windows File Explorer. We will show you how to do this in Exercise 14.2.

FIGURE 14.5 The Internet properties are accessed through the Internet Options applet.

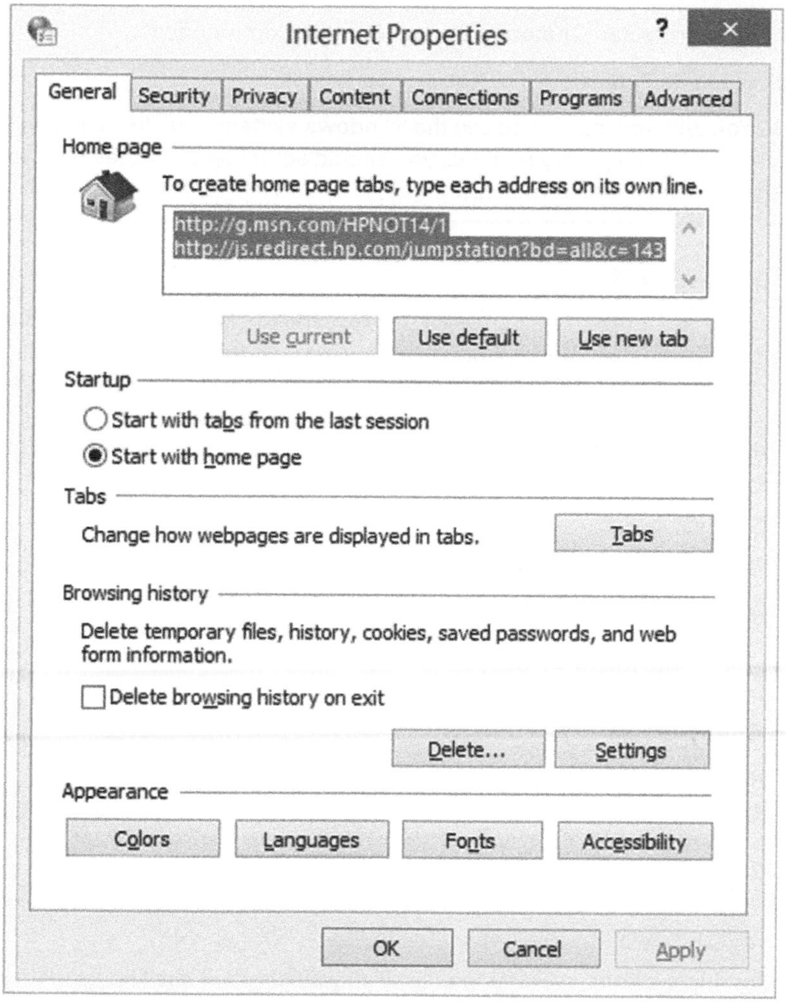

EXERCISE 14.2

Showing Hidden Files and Folders

1. Open Windows File Explorer on a Windows system.

2. Browse to the root of the C: drive and note the entries that are there.

3. If it is available, choose View and check the box for the Hidden Items option so that they are now visible.

4. Note the entries that now appear but did not previously.

5. Open the Folder Options applet and choose the View tab if needed.

continues

6. Deselect Hide Protected Operating System Files (Recommended).

7. Uncheck Hide File Extensions For Known File Types.

8. Click OK. You will now be able to see the Windows system files discussed in the following sections. For security reasons, you should set these attributes back to the defaults after you've read this chapter.

The System Applet

The System applet in Control Panel (see Figure 14.6 for the Windows 8.1 System applet) is one of the most important, and it's nearly all business. It usually appears with System Properties in the title bar. From within this one relatively innocuous panel (SYSDM.CPL), you can make a large number of configuration changes to a Windows machine. The different versions of Windows have different options available in this applet, but they can include some of the following options:

- Network Identification
- Device Manager
- Hardware
- User Profiles
- Environment Variables
- Startup And Recovery
- Performance
- System Restore
- Remote
- Computer Name
- Advanced

In the following sections, we will look a bit more closely at the functionality of the tabs.

Computer Name

This tab is used to define whether the machine is in a workgroup or a domain environment. We talk more about networking in a separate chapter, but in general terms, here's the difference between a workgroup and a domain:

Workgroup Loosely associated computers, each of which is its own security authority, that share a common workgroup name.

Domain A group of computers that are tightly connected or associated and share a common domain name. Has a single authority (called a *domain controller*) that manages security for all of the computers.

FIGURE 14.6   The System Properties Control Panel applet on a Windows 8.1 computer with the Advanced tab selected

Hardware

This tab includes a number of tools, all of which allow you to change how the hardware on your machine is used. To minimize the risks involved with adding third-party software to your machine, Microsoft came up with a technique called *driver signing*. Installing new hardware drivers onto the system is a situation in which both viruses and badly written software can threaten your system's health. To minimize the risks, you can choose to use only drivers that have been signed. The signing process is meant to ensure that you are getting drivers that have been checked with Windows and that those drivers have not been modified maliciously.

WARNING   Even in a Plug and Play system, it is important to unplug a device properly if you wish to remove it while the system is running. If you don't do this, it's possible that nothing will go wrong, but you can sometimes damage the device or cause the system to become unstable.

For the exam, understand that loading alternate third-party drivers when necessary can be a solution to problems. Know, as well, that it is preferred that those drivers be signed.

When you purchase a hardware device, odds are that it's been in the box for a while. By the time it gets made, packaged, stored, delivered to the store, stored again at the retailer, and then purchased by you, it's entirely likely that the company that made the device has updated the driver—even possibly a few times if there have been a lot of reported problems.

When you install a device, always go to the manufacturer's website to see if a newer driver is available. The old driver might work fine, but the newest driver is the one most likely to be bug free and have all of the most current bells and whistles for your device.

Advanced

The Advanced tab has several subheadings, each of which can be configured separately. The following options are among those on this tab.

Performance   Although it is hidden in the backwaters of Windows's system configuration settings, the Performance option holds some important settings that you may need to configure on a system. To access it, on the Advanced tab, click Settings in the Performance area.

In the Performance window, you can set the size of your virtual memory and how the system handles the allocation of processor time. In Windows, you also use Performance to configure visual effects for the GUI.

How resources are allocated to the processor is normally not something that you will need to modify. It is set by default to optimize the system for foreground applications, making the system most responsive to the user who is running programs. This is generally best, but it means that any applications (databases, network services, and so on) that are run by the system are given less time by the system.

If the Windows machine will be working primarily as a network server, you may want to change the Performance option to Background Services. Otherwise, leave it as is.

Environment Variables   There are two types of *environment variables*, and you can access either one by clicking the Environment Variables button:

User Variables   Specifies settings that are specific to an individual user and do not affect others who log on to the machine.

System Variables   Set for all users on the machine. System variables are used to provide information needed by the system when running applications or performing system tasks.

System and user variables were extremely important in the early days of DOS and Windows. Their importance has been more subdued with recent Windows versions, but this is the interface where TEMP variables, the location of the OS, and other important settings for Windows can be found.

User Profiles   In Windows, every user is automatically given a user profile when they log on to the workstation. This profile contains information about their settings and preferences. Although it does not happen often, occasionally a user profile becomes corrupted or needs to be destroyed. Alternatively, if a particular profile is set up appropriately, you can copy it so that it is available for other users. To do either of these tasks, use the User Profiles settings to select the user profile with which you wish to work. You will be given three options:

Delete   Removes the user's profile entirely. When that user logs on again, they will be given a fresh profile taken from the system default. Any settings that they have added will be lost, as will any profile-related problems that they have caused.

Change Type   Allows you to configure a profile as local (the default) or roaming. If a user works at two machines, each machine will use a different profile. Updates to one machine will not be reflected on the other. If you have a network, roaming profiles can be configured to allow a user to have a single profile anywhere on the network. Further discussion of this topic is beyond the scope of this book.

Copy To   Copies a profile from one user to another. Often the source profile is a template set up to provide a standard configuration.

Startup And Recovery   The Windows Startup And Recovery options are relatively straightforward. They involve two areas: what to do during system startup and what to do in case of unexpected system shutdown:

System Startup   The System Startup option defaults to the Windows OS you installed, but you can change this default behavior if you like. Unless you are *dual-booting*, only one option is available, but if you have another OS installed, you can change the Windows boot manager to load that as the default. You can also reduce the time the menu is displayed or remove the menu entirely.

 If you choose to disable the menu completely on a dual-boot system, you will find that doing so may cause you annoyance in the future when you want to boot into a different OS but no longer have a choice to do so. Thus, you should always let the boot menu appear for at least 2 to 5 seconds if you are dual-booting.

System Failure   A number of options are available in the Startup And Recovery screen for use in case of problems. These include writing an event about the problem, sending out an alert to the network, and saving information about the problem to disk. These options come into play only in case of a major system problem, though.

System Protection

The System Protection tab lets you disable/enable and configure the System Restore feature. When it's enabled on one or more drives, the operating system monitors the changes that you make on your drives. From time to time it creates what is called a *restore point*. Then, if you have a system crash, it can restore your data back to the restore point. You can turn on System Restore for all drives on your system or for individual drives. Note that turning off System Restore on the system drive (the drive on which the OS is installed) automatically turns it off on all drives.

For more on System Restore, see the section "Creating Restore Points" in Chapter 13.

Remote

The Remote tab lets you enable or disable Remote Assistance and Remote Desktop. Remote Assistance permits people to access the system in response to requests issued by the local user using the Windows Remote Assistance tool. Remote Desktop permits people to log into the system at any time using the Remote Desktop Connection tool. This can help an administrator or other support person troubleshoot problems with the machine from a remote location.

Remote Assistance is enabled by default. It is handled at two levels. Having just Remote Assistance turned on allows the person connecting to view the computer's screen. To let that person take over the computer and be able to control the keyboard and mouse, click Advanced, and then in the Remote Control section, click Allow This Computer To Be Controlled Remotely. You can also configure Remote Desktop here.

The Action Center Applet

The Action Center applet (WSCUI.CPL)—known as Security Center in Windows Vista—is used to manage the firewall, automatic updates, and virus protection. From here, you can manage settings for Internet options as well and see any maintenance or troubleshooting issues to which you need to attend. The Firewall and Internet options are not available from this menu in Windows 7 or Windows 8, but Performance and Troubleshooting were added.

The Windows Firewall Applet

As the name implies, the Windows Firewall applet (FIREWALL.CPL) can be used to manage the firewall included with the operating system. In addition to local configuration, the settings can be managed by the system administrator, an application vendor, or another third party.

The Power Options Applet

The Power Options applet (POWERCFG.CPL) allows you to configure a power plan dictating when devices, namely the display device and the computer, will turn off or be put to sleep. Through the advanced settings, you can configure the need to enter a password to revive the devices as well as configure wireless adapter settings, Internet options (namely JavaScript), and the system cooling policy.

The Command Prompt

Although the exam focuses on the Windows operating systems, it tests a great number of concepts that carry over from the Microsoft Disk Operating System (MS-DOS). MS-DOS was never meant to be extremely user friendly. Its roots are in CP/M, which in turn has its roots in Unix. Both of these older OSs are command-line based, and so is MS-DOS. In other words, they all use long strings of commands typed in at the computer keyboard to perform operations. Some people prefer this type of interaction with the computer, including many folks with technical backgrounds. Although Windows has left the full command-line interface behind, it still contains a bit of DOS, and you get to it through the command prompt.

Although you can't tell from looking at it, the Windows command prompt is actually a Windows program that is intentionally *designed* to have the look and feel of a DOS command line. Because it is, despite its appearance, a Windows program, the command prompt provides all of the stability and configurability you expect from Windows. You can access a command prompt by running CMD.EXE.

A number of diagnostic utilities are often run at the command prompt, and they can be broken into two categories: networking and operating system. Those associated with networking appear in other chapters, but the focus here is on those associated with the operating system.

The OS command-line tools that you are expected to know for this exam are TASKKILL, BOOTREC, SHUTDOWN, TASKLIST, MD, RD, CD, DEL, FORMAT, COPY, XCOPY, ROBOCOPY, DISKPART, SFC, CHKDSK, GPUPDATE, GPRESULT, DIR, EXIT, HELP, EXPAND, and /?. They are discussed in the sections that follow along with the commands available with standard privileges as opposed to those with administrative privileges.

TASKKILL Command

The TASKKILL.EXE utility is used to terminate processes. Those processes can be identified by either name or process ID number (PID). The process can exist on the machine where the administrator is sitting (the default) or on another machine, in which case you signify the other system by using the /S switch.

The /IM *name* switch is used to specify an (image) name of a process to kill, and it can include the wildcard (*) characters. If the process ID number is used in place of the name, then the /PID switch is needed. The processes in question are the same, and they can be killed through Task Manager. There are two signals that can be sent: the default is SIGTERM (a gentle kill, related to code 15) and the /F switch issues a SIGKILL (a terminate at all cost kill, related to code 9).

BOOTREC Command

The BOOTREC.EXE utility can be run in Windows 8/8.1, Windows 7, or Windows Vista to interact with the Master Boot Record (MBR), boot sector, or Boot Configuration Data (BCD) store. It cannot be used with previous versions of Windows (such as XP) because they utilized a different boot structure.

To run the tool, you must boot from the installation disk, choose the Repair Your Computer option, and enter the *System Recovery Options*. Choose Command Prompt from System Recovery Options and then type **BOOTREC.EXE**.

The options for BOOTREC are /Fixboot (to write a new boot sector), /Fixmbr (to write a new MBR), /RebuildBCD (to rebuild the BCD store), and /ScanOS (to scan all disks for installations the Boot Manager menu is not listing).

Newer versions of Windows (Vista, 7, and 8.*x*) include the option of using GPT (GUID Partition Table) in place of MBR for 64-bit versions. All versions can read drives with GPT and use the data, but they can only boot from them if they are running 64-bit versions of the OS.

SHUTDOWN Command

The SHUTDOWN.EXE utility can be used to schedule a shutdown (complete or a restart) locally or remotely. A variety of reasons can be specified and announced to users for the shutdown.

TASKLIST Command

The TASKLIST.EXE utility is used at the command line to see a list of all the running processes (and their process ID number), similar to what you see in the GUI by using Task Manager. By default, it shows the processes on the current machine, but the /S switch can be used to see the processes on a remote machine. /SVC will show the services hosted in each process, and you can use /U if you need to run the command as another user. (/P allows you to specify a password associated with that user.)

CD/MD/RD Commands

The CD, MD, and RD commands are used to change (or display), make, and remove directories, respectively. They're shorthand versions of the CHDIR, MKDIR, and RMDIR commands. Table 14.2 lists their usage and switches.

TABLE 14.2   CD/MD/RD usage and switches

Command	Purpose
CD [path]	Changes to the specified directory.
CD /D [drive:][path]	Changes to the specified directory on the drive.
CD ..	Changes to the directory that is up one level.
CD\	Changes to the root directory of the drive.
MD [drive:][path]	Makes a directory in the specified path. If you don't specify a path, the directory will be created in your current directory.

Command	Purpose
RD *[drive:][path]*	Removes (deletes) the specified directory.
RD /S *[drive:][path]*	Removes all directories and files in the specified directory, including the specified directory itself.
RD /Q *[drive:][path]*	Quiet mode. You won't be asked whether you're sure you want to delete the specified directory when you use /S.

Now that you've looked at the available switches, let's use them in Exercise 14.3.

EXERCISE 14.3

Command-Line Directory Management

1. Open a command prompt. To do this, click Start ➢ Run, type **CMD** in the Open field, and click OK.

2. Change to the root of your C: drive by typing **CD /D C:** and pressing Enter. (Note: If you are already in C:, all you have to do is type **CD** and press Enter.)

3. Create a directory called C14 by typing **MD C14** and pressing Enter.

4. Change to the C14 directory by typing **CD C14** and pressing Enter.

5. Create several layers of subdirectories at once. Type **MD A1\B2\C3\D4** and press Enter.

Notice that these commands created each of the directories that you specified. You now have a directory structure that looks like this: **C:\C14\A1\B2\C3\D4**.

6. Change back to your root directory by typing **CD**.

7. Attempt to delete the C14 directory by typing **RD C14** and pressing Enter.

Windows won't let you delete the directory because the directory is not empty. This is a safety measure. Now let's really delete it.

8. Delete the C14 directory and all of its subdirectories by typing **RD /S C14** and pressing Enter. You will be asked whether you're sure that you want to delete the directory. If you are, type **Y** and press Enter. To close the command prompt window, type **EXIT**.

Note that if you had used the /Q option in addition to /S, your system wouldn't have asked whether you were sure; it would have just deleted the directories.

DEL Command

The DEL command is used to delete files and directories at the command line. Wildcards can be used with it and ERASE performs the same operations.

FORMAT Command

The FORMAT command is used to wipe data off disks and prepare them for new use. Before a hard disk can be formatted, it must have partitions created on it. (Partitioning was done in the DOS days with the FDISK command, but that command does not exist in current versions of Windows, having been replaced with DISKPART.) The syntax for FORMAT is as follows:

```
FORMAT [volume] [switches]
```

The *volume* parameter describes the drive letter (for example, D:), mount point, or volume name. Table 14.3 lists some common FORMAT switches.

TABLE 14.3 FORMAT switches

Switch	Purpose
/FS:[*filesystem*]	Specifies the type of filesystem to use (FAT, FAT32, or NTFS).
/V:[*label*]	Specifies the new volume label.
/Q	Executes a quick format.

There are other options as well to specify allocation sizes, the number of sectors per track, and the number of tracks per disk size. However, we don't recommend that you use these unless you have a very specific need. The defaults are just fine.

Thus, if you wanted to format your D: drive as NTFS, with a name of HDD2, you would type the following:

```
FORMAT D: /FS:NTFS /V:HDD2
```

WARNING Before you format any drive, be sure that you have it backed up or are prepared to lose whatever is on it!

COPY Command

The COPY command does what it says: It makes a copy of a file in a second location. (To copy a file and then remove it from its original location, use the MOVE command.) Here's the syntax for COPY:

```
COPY [filename] [destination]
```

It's pretty straightforward. There are several switches for COPY, but in practice they are rarely used. The three most commonly used ones are /A, which indicates an ASCII text file; /V, which verifies that the files are written correctly after the copy; and /Y, which suppresses the prompt asking whether you're sure that you want to overwrite files if they exist in the destination directory.

The COPY command cannot be used to copy directories. Use XCOPY for that function.

One useful tip is to use wildcards. For example, in DOS (or at the command prompt), the asterisk (*) is a wildcard that means *everything*. So you could type **COPY *.EXE** to copy all files that have an .EXE filename extension, or you could type **COPY *.*** to copy all files in your current directory. The other popular wildcard is the question mark (?) which does not mean everything but instead means one thing: **COPY ABC?.EXE** would only copy EXE files with four-letter names of which the first three letters are ABC.

XCOPY Command

If you are comfortable with the COPY command, learning XCOPY shouldn't pose too many problems. It's basically an extension of COPY with one notable exception—it's designed to copy directories as well as files. The syntax is as follows:

XCOPY [source] [destination][switches]

There are 26 XCOPY switches; some of the more commonly used ones are listed in Table 14.4.

TABLE 14.4   XCOPY switches

Switch	Purpose
/A	Copies only files that have the Archive attribute set and does not clear the attribute. (Useful for making a quick backup of files while not disrupting a normal backup routine.)
/E	Copies directories and subdirectories, including empty directories.
/F	Displays full source and destination filenames when copying.
/G	Allows copying of encrypted files to a destination that does not support encryption.
/H	Copies hidden and system files as well.
/K	Copies attributes. (By default, XCOPY resets the Read-Only attribute.)

TABLE 14.4   XCOPY switches *(continued)*

Switch	Purpose
/O	Copies file ownership and ACL information (NTFS permissions).
/R	Overwrites read-only files.
/S	Copies directories and subdirectories but not empty directories.
/U	Copies only files that already exist in the destination.
/V	Verifies the size of each new file.

Perhaps the most important switch is /O. If you use XCOPY to copy files from one location to another, the filesystem creates new versions of the files in the new location without changing the old files. In NTFS, when a new file is created, it inherits permissions from its new parent directory. This could cause problems if you copy files. (Users who didn't have access to the file before might have access now.) If you want to retain the original permissions, use XCOPY /O.

ROBOCOPY Command

The ROBOCOPY utility (Robust File Copy for Windows) is included with recent versions of Windows and has the big advantage of being able to accept a plethora of specifications and keep NTFS permissions intact in its operations. The /MIR switch, for example, can be used to mirror a complete directory tree.

An excellent TechNet article on how to use ROBOCOPY can be found at the following location: https://technet.microsoft.com/en-us/magazine/ee851678.aspx

DISKPART Command

The DISKPART utility shows the partitions and lets you manage them on the computer's hard drives. Because of the enormous power it holds, membership in the Administrators local group (or equivalent) is required to run DISKPART.

SFC Command

The System File Checker (SFC) is a command-line-based utility that checks and verifies the versions of system files on your computer. If system files are corrupted, the SFC will replace the corrupted files with correct versions.

The syntax for the SFC command is as follows:

```
SFC [switch]
```

Table 14.5 lists the switches available for SFC.

TABLE 14.5   SFC switches

Switch	Purpose
/SCANFILE	Scans a file that you specify and fixes problems if they are found.
/SCANNOW	Immediately scans all protected system files.
/VERIFYONLY	Scans protected system files and does not make any repairs or changes.
/VERIFYFILE	Identifies the integrity of the file specified, and makes any repairs or changes.
/OFFBOOTDIR	Repairs an offline boot directory.
/OFFFWINDIR	Repairs an offline windows directory.

To run the SFC, you must be logged in as an administrator or have administrative privileges. If the System File Checker discovers a corrupted system file, it will automatically overwrite the file by using a copy held in another directory. The most recent Windows versions store the files in a large number of discrete folders beneath C:\WINDOWS\WINSXS (where they are protected by the system and only TrustedInstaller is allowed direct access to them—the cache is not rebuildable).

> The C:\WINDOWS\SYSTEM32 directory is where many of the Windows system files reside.

If you attempt to run SFC from a standard command prompt, you will be told that you must be an administrator running a console session in order to continue. Rather than opening a standard command prompt, choose Start ➤ All Programs ➤ Accessories, then right-click Command Prompt and choose Run As Administrator. The UAC will prompt you to continue, and then you can run SFC without a problem.

CHKDSK Command

You can use the Windows Chkdsk utility to create and display status reports for the hard disk. Chkdsk can also correct filesystem problems (such as cross-linked files) and scan for and attempt to repair disk errors. You can manually start Chkdsk by right-clicking the problem disk and selecting Properties. This will bring up the Properties dialog box for that disk, which shows the current status of the selected disk drive.

By clicking the Tools tab at the top of the dialog box and then clicking the Check Now button in the Error-Checking section, you can start Chkdsk. Exercise 14.4 walks you through starting Chkdsk in the GUI, while Exercise 14.5 does the same from the command line.

EXERCISE 14.4

Running Chkdsk within Windows

1. Open Windows File Explorer by holding down the Windows key and pressing E.

2. Right-click C: and choose Properties.

3. Click the Tools tab, and then click the Check Now button.

4. Choose your options: You can automatically fix filesystem errors and/or scan for and attempt recovery of bad sectors.

5. After you have selected your options, click Start. With the boot disk (usually C), an error box will appear informing you that Windows can't check the disk while it is in use.

EXERCISE 14.5

Running Chkdsk at the Command Line

1. Open an administrative command prompt in Windows 8 by right-clicking the Start icon and choosing Control Prompt (Admin) from the pop-up menu. In another operating system, run **CMD** with administrator privileges.

2. Type **CHKDSK /f** and press Enter. The system will now scan for, and fix, filesystem errors.

GPUPDATE Command

This utility is used to update Group Policy settings. It refreshes, or changes, both local and Active Directory–based policies and replaces some of the functionality that previously existed with SECEDIT.

GPRESULT Command

The GPRESULT command is used to show the Resultant Set of Policy (RSoP) report/values for a remote user and computer. Bear in mind that configuration settings occur at any number of places: They are set for a computer, a user, a local workstation, the domain, and so on. Often one of the big unknowns is which set of configuration settings takes precedence and which is overridden.

With GPRESULT, it is possible to ascertain which settings apply.

DIR Command

The DIR command is used to display a list of the files and folders/subdirectories within a directory. When you use it without any parameters, it will not only show you that information, but also the volume label and serial number along with the amount of free space, in bytes, remaining on the disk.

Wildcards discussed with COPY also work with this command, and there are a plethora of parameters that can be used to customize the results or the display. Table 14.6 lists some of the most common switches available for DIR.

TABLE 14.6   Common DIR switches

Switch	Purpose
/A	Allows you to specify the attributes of files you are seeking (hidden, system, and so on).
/O	Allows you to specify a different display order (alphabetic is the default).
/L	Returns the results unsorted and in lowercase format.
/S	Recursively searches through subdirectories as well as the current directory.
/T	Sorts the files according to time order.
/P	Displays the results one page/screen at a time.
/Q	Shows file ownership.

EXIT Command

The EXIT command is used to get you out of what you are currently in. If you are running a batch script, it will exit that batch script. If you are in the command interpreter, it will close the command interpreter.

EXPAND

The EXPAND command can be used to expand one or more compressed files—usually from update files such as security patches or critical updates. If you use the -R option, you can rename the files that are expanded, and -D can be used to just display a list of the files in the source file.

HELP and the */?* Command

The HELP command does what it says: it gives you help. Actually, if you just type **HELP** and press Enter, your computer gives you a list of system commands that you can type. To get more information, type the name of a command that you want to learn about after typing HELP. For example, type **HELP RD** and press Enter, and you will get information about the RD command.

You can also get the same help information by typing /? after the command.

The /? switch is slightly faster and provides more information than the HELP command. The HELP command provides information for only system commands (it does not include network commands). For example, if you type **HELP IPCONFIG** at a command prompt, you get no useful information (except to try /?); however, typing **IPCONFIG /?** provides the help file for the IPCONFIG command.

Commands with Standard Privileges vs. Administrative Privileges

By default, any user can open a command prompt and begin typing in the names of command-line commands. There are, however, certain commands that can be dangerous when run and, as a safety precaution, require administrative privileges. SFC was mentioned earlier, for example, as requiring administrative privileges.

With Windows Vista and Windows 7, rather than opening a standard command prompt, choose Start ➤ All Programs ➤ Accessories, then right-click Command Prompt and choose Run As Administrator. The UAC will prompt you to continue, and then you can run SFC without a problem. With Windows 8, there are two choices on the Start menu, as shown in Figure 14.7. The latter allows you to open the command prompt with administrative privileges.

FIGURE 14.7 You can open a command prompt with or without admin privileges in Windows 8.1.

In most cases, if you try to run a utility that requires administrative privileges and you are not currently in a console session that has them, an error message will notify you of this.

The Windows Registry

Windows configuration information is stored in a special configuration database known as the *Registry*. This centralized database contains environmental settings for various Windows programs. It also contains registration information that details which types of filename extensions are associated with which applications. So, when you double-click a file in Windows File Explorer, the associated application runs and opens the file that you double-clicked.

The Registry was introduced with Windows 95. Most OSs up until Windows 95 were configured through text files, which can be edited with almost any text editor. However, the Registry database is contained in a special binary file that can be edited only with the special Registry Editor provided with Windows.

Current versions of Windows have what appear to be two applications that can be used to edit the Registry: REGEDIT and REGEDT32 (with no /), but in reality, REGEDT32 opens REGEDIT. They work similarly, but each has slightly different options for navigation and browsing.

The Registry is broken down into a series of separate areas called *hives*. The keys in each hive are divided into two basic sections—user settings and computer settings. In Windows, a number of files are created corresponding to each of the different hives. The names of most of these files do not have extensions, and their names are SYSTEM, SOFTWARE, SECURITY, SAM, and DEFAULT. One additional file whose name does have an extension is NTUSER.DAT.

The basic hives of the Registry are as follows:

HKEY_CLASSES_ROOT   Includes information about which filename extensions map to particular applications.

HKEY_CURRENT_USER   Holds all configuration information specific to a particular user, such as their Desktop settings and history information.

HKEY_LOCAL_MACHINE   Includes nearly all configuration information about the actual computer hardware and software.

HKEY_USERS   Includes information about all users who have logged on to the system. The HKEY_CURRENT_USER hive is actually a subkey of this hive.

HKEY_CURRENT_CONFIG   Provides quick access to a number of commonly needed keys that are otherwise buried deep in the HKEY_LOCAL_MACHINE structure.

Modifying a Registry Entry

If you need to modify the Registry, you can modify the values in the database or create new entries or keys. You will find the options for adding a new element to the Registry under the Edit menu. To edit an existing value, double-click the entry and modify it as needed. You need administrative-level access to modify the Registry.

Windows uses the Registry extensively to store all kinds of information. Indeed, the Registry holds most, if not all, of the configuration information for Windows. Modifying the Registry in Windows is a potentially danger- ous task. Control Panel and other configuration tools are provided so that you have graphical tools for modifying system settings. Directly modifying the Registry can have unforeseen—and unpleasant—results. You should modify the Registry only when told to do so by an extremely trustworthy source or if you are absolutely certain that you have the knowledge to do so without wreaking havoc in the Registry.

Restoring the Registry

Windows stores Registry information in files on the hard drive. You can restore this information using the Last Known Good Configuration option, which restores the Registry from a backup of its last functional state. This can be used if—and only if—you have not logged in again since a change was made (otherwise, the Last Known Good Configuration option is useless).

To use this option, press **F8** during startup and then select Last Known Good Configuration from the menu that appears. You can also back up the Registry files to the systemroot\repair directory by using the Windows Backup program, or you can save them to tape during a normal *backup*. To repair the Registry from a backup, overwrite the Registry files in systemroot\system32\config.

🌐 Real World Scenario

Beware of Editing the Registry

Just in case it hasn't sunk in yet, be careful editing the Registry. There is no Undo button, nor do you have the safety net of choosing not to save your edits before you close. Once you make the change, it's made—for better or for worse.

There have been countless examples throughout our careers of people going in to edit the Registry without really knowing what they were doing. In many cases, making small changes to the Registry, without having a viable backup, means having to reinstall Windows. At the very least, this is inconvenient.

Windows can help in this regard if you are in a networked environment with Windows- based servers. You can create system policies that prevent users from performing certain tasks, and the most important task to restrict is running Registry editors.

Remember that a system restore will restore the Registry to the state it was in when a restore point was saved. As a very last-resort option for system recovery, Windows uses the WinRE recovery environment to do a complete PC restore. It is your goal to make sure you never need to use this.

Virtual Memory

Another thing that you may need to configure is *virtual memory*. Virtual memory uses what's called a swap file, or paging file. A *swap file* is actually hard drive space into which idle pieces of programs are placed while other active parts of programs are kept in or swapped into main memory. The programs running in Windows believe that their information is still in RAM, but Windows has moved the data into near-line storage on the solid-state drive (SSD) or hard drive. When the application needs the information again, it is swapped back into RAM so that the processor can use it.

Random access memory (RAM) is the computer's physical memory. The more RAM you put into the machine, the more items it can remember without looking anything up. And the larger the swap file, the fewer times the machine has swapped out the contents of what it is holding in memory. The maximum possible size of your swap file depends on the amount of disk space that you have available on the drive where the swap file is placed. Windows configures the minimum and maximum swap file size automatically, but if you want Windows to handle the size of the swap file dynamically, you have to change the default setting by selecting System Managed Size in the Virtual Memory dialog box. We'll show you how to get there in a moment.

In Windows, the swap file is called `PAGEFILE.SYS`, and it's located in the root directory of the drive on which you installed the OS files. The swap file is a hidden file; to see the file in Windows File Explorer, you must have the folder options configured to show hidden files. Typically, there's no reason to view the swap file in the filesystem because you'll use Control Panel to configure it. However, you may want to check its size, and in that case you'd use Windows File Explorer.

 The moral of the story: As with most things virtual, a swap file is not nearly as good as actual RAM, but it is better than nothing!

To modify the default Virtual Memory settings, follow these steps: Click Start ➢ Control Panel. Double-click the System icon, and select Advanced System Settings from the left panel. In the Performance area, click Settings. Next, click the Advanced tab (yes, another Advanced tab), and then, in the Virtual Memory area, click Change. Note that in addition to changing the swap file's size and how Windows handles it, you can specify the drive on which you want to place the file.

 You should place the swap file on a drive with plenty of empty space. As a general rule, try to keep 20 percent of your drive space free for the overhead of various elements of the OS, like the swap file. Do not set the swap file to an extremely small size. If you make the swap file too small, the system can become unbootable, or at least unstable. In general, the swap file should be at least 1.5x the amount of RAM in the machine.

Administrative Tools

Microsoft has included a number of tools with each iteration of Windows to simplify system administration. While some tools have very specific purposes and are used only on rare occasions, you will come to rely on a number of them and access them on a regular basis. It is this latter set that we will examine in the following sections.

Task Manager

Task Manager lets you shut down nonresponsive applications selectively in all Windows versions. In current versions of Windows, it can do so much more, allowing you to see which processes and applications are using the most system resources, view network usage, see connected users, and so on. To display Task Manager, press Ctrl+Alt+Delete and click the Task Manager button or option. You can also right-click on an empty spot in the Taskbar and choose it from the pop-up menu that appears.

> To get to Task Manager directly in any of the Windows versions that include it, you can press Ctrl+Shift+Esc.

Depending on the Windows version, Task Manager has various tabs. Figure 14.8 shows the common default display in Windows 8.1, but other versions vary from the seven shown here to six: Applications, Processes, Services, Performance, Networking, and Users.

Let's look at these tabs in more detail:

Applications   The Applications tab lets you see which tasks are open on the machine. You also see the status of each task, which can be either Running or Not Responding. If a task/application has stopped responding (that is, it's hung), you can select the task in the list and click End Task. Doing so closes the program, and you can try to open it again. Often, although certainly not always, if an application hangs, you have to reboot the computer to prevent the same thing from happening again shortly after you restart the application. You can also use the Applications tab to switch to a different task or create new tasks. In Windows 8/8.1, much of what appeared in Applications was split between the Processes and Details tabs while an App History tab was added that, as the name implies, displays usage settings for applications and the currently logged-in user account.

Processes/Details   In Windows Vista and Windows 7, the Processes tab lets you see the names of all the processes running on the machine, whereas with Windows 8/8.1, this tab now shows what Applications once did (and a little more). To illustrate this difference, Figure 14.9 shows the Processes tab in Windows 7, while Figure 14.10 shows it in Windows 8.1.

FIGURE 14.8   The default Task Manager in Windows 8.1

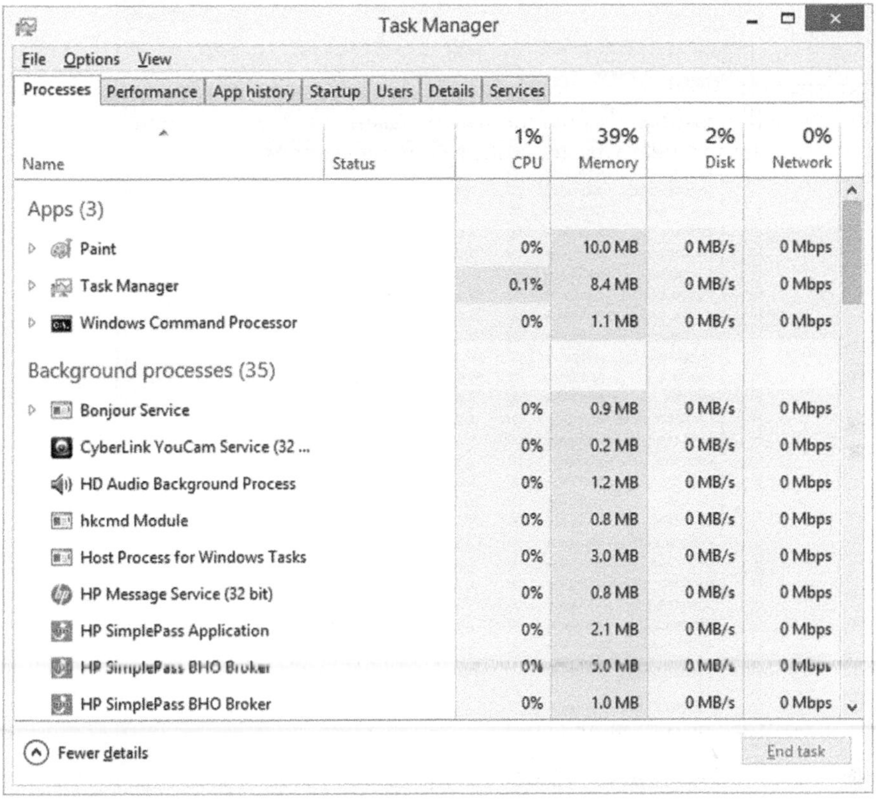

In Windows Vista/7, you also see the user account that's running each process as well as how much CPU and RAM resources each process is using. Starting with Windows 8, this information was moved to the Details tab, as shown in Figure 14.11.

To end a process, select it in the list and click End Process. Be careful with this choice because ending some processes can cause Windows to shut down. If you don't know what a particular process does, you can look for it in any search engine and find a number of sites that will explain it.

You can also change the priority of a process in Task Manager's Processes tab for Windows Vista and Windows 7 (or on the Details tab in Windows 8) by right-clicking on the name of the process and choosing Set Priority. The six priorities, from lowest to highest, are as follows:

Low   For applications that need to complete sometime but that you don't want interfering with other applications. On a numerical scale from 0 to 31, this equates to a base priority of 4.

FIGURE 14.9   The Processes tab of Task Manager in Windows 7

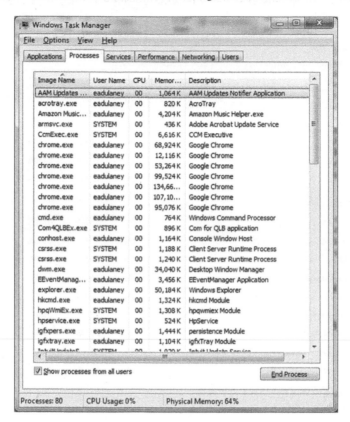

Below Normal   For applications that don't need to drop all the way down to Low. This equates to a base priority of 6.

Normal   The default priority for most applications. This equates to a base priority of 8.

Above Normal   For applications that don't need to boost all the way to High. This equates to a base priority of 10.

High   For applications that must complete soon, when you don't want other applications to interfere with the applications' performance. This equates to a base priority of 13.

Realtime   For applications that must have the processor's attention to handle time-critical tasks. Applications can be run at this priority only by a member of the Administrators group. This equates to a base priority of 24.

If you decide to change the priority of an application, you'll be warned that doing so may make it unstable. You can generally ignore this option when changing the priority to Low, Below Normal, Above Normal, or High, but you should heed this warning when changing applications to the Realtime priority. Realtime means that the processor gives precedence to this process over all others—over security processes, over spooling, over everything—and this is sure to make the system unstable.

FIGURE 14.10   The Processes tab of Task Manager in Windows 8.1

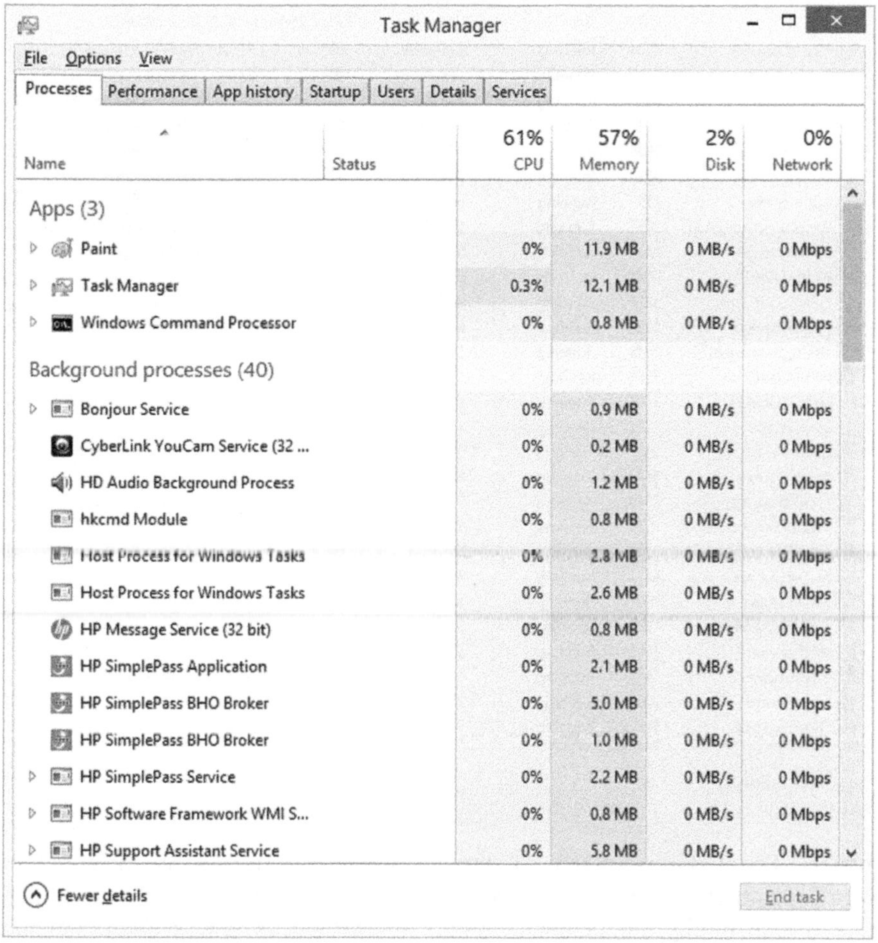

Task Manager changes the priority only for that instance of the running application. The next time the process is started, priorities revert back to that of the base (typically Normal).

Services   The Services tab lists the name of each running service as well as the process ID associated with it and its description, status, and group. A button labeled Services appears on this tab, and clicking it will open the Microsoft Management Console (MMC) snap-in for Services, where you can configure each service. Within Task Manager, right-clicking a service will open a context menu listing three choices: Start Service, Stop Service, and Go To Process (this takes you to the Processes or Details tab).

FIGURE 14.11 The Details tab of Task Manager in Windows 8.1

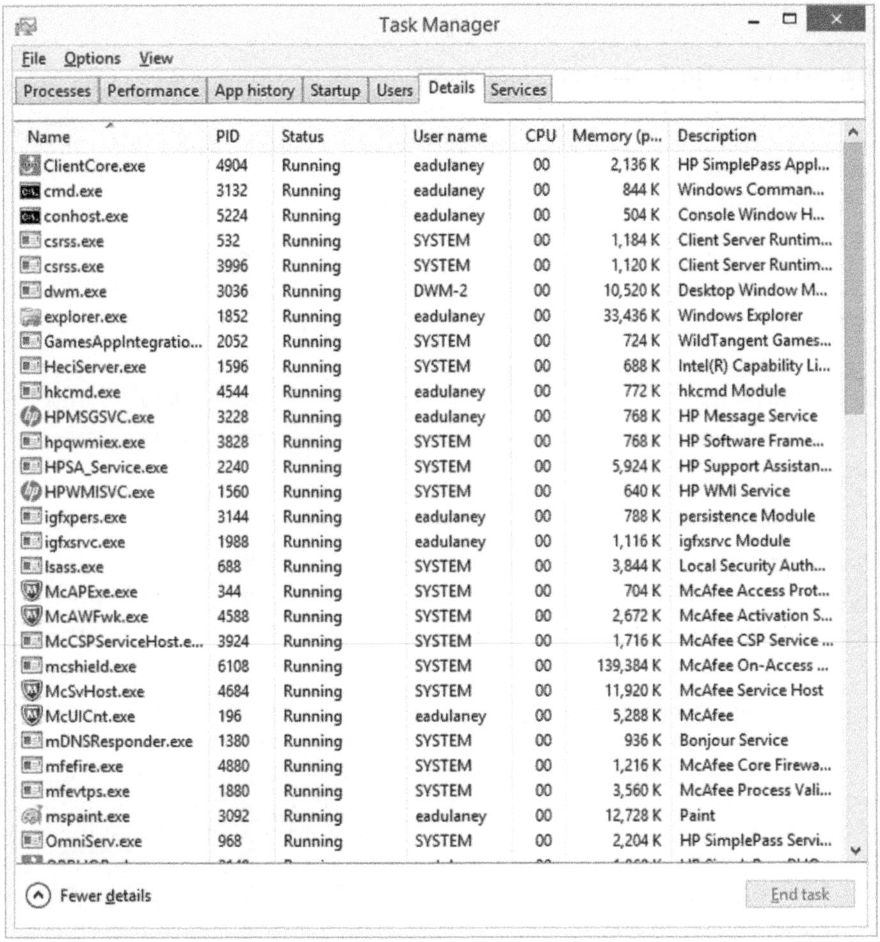
Task Manager
File Options View
Processes Performance App history Startup Users Details Services
Name PID Status User name CPU Memory (p... Description
ClientCore.exe 4904 Running eadulaney 00 2,136 K HP SimplePass Appl...
cmd.exe 3132 Running eadulaney 00 844 K Windows Comman...
conhost.exe 5224 Running eadulaney 00 504 K Console Window H...
csrss.exe 532 Running SYSTEM 00 1,184 K Client Server Runtim...
csrss.exe 3996 Running SYSTEM 00 1,120 K Client Server Runtim...
dwm.exe 3036 Running DWM-2 00 10,520 K Desktop Window M...
explorer.exe 1852 Running eadulaney 00 33,436 K Windows Explorer
GamesAppIntegratio... 2052 Running SYSTEM 00 724 K WildTangent Games...
HeciServer.exe 1596 Running SYSTEM 00 688 K Intel(R) Capability Li...
hkcmd.exe 4544 Running eadulaney 00 772 K hkcmd Module
HPMSGSVC.exe 3228 Running eadulaney 00 768 K HP Message Service
hpqwmiex.exe 3828 Running SYSTEM 00 768 K HP Software Frame...
HPSA_Service.exe 2240 Running SYSTEM 00 5,924 K HP Support Assistan...
HPWMISVC.exe 1560 Running SYSTEM 00 640 K HP WMI Service
igfxpers.exe 3144 Running eadulaney 00 788 K persistence Module
igfxsrvc.exe 1988 Running eadulaney 00 1,116 K igfxsrvc Module
lsass.exe 688 Running SYSTEM 00 3,844 K Local Security Auth...
McAPExe.exe 344 Running SYSTEM 00 704 K McAfee Access Prot...
McAWFwk.exe 4588 Running SYSTEM 00 2,672 K McAfee Activation S...
McCSPServiceHost.e... 3924 Running SYSTEM 00 1,716 K McAfee CSP Service ...
mcshield.exe 6108 Running SYSTEM 00 139,384 K McAfee On-Access ...
McSvHost.exe 4684 Running SYSTEM 00 11,920 K McAfee Service Host
McUICnt.exe 196 Running eadulaney 00 5,288 K McAfee
mDNSResponder.exe 1380 Running SYSTEM 00 936 K Bonjour Service
mfefire.exe 4880 Running SYSTEM 00 1,216 K McAfee Core Firewa...
mfevtps.exe 1880 Running SYSTEM 00 3,560 K McAfee Process Vali...
mspaint.exe 3092 Running eadulaney 00 12,728 K Paint
OmniServ.exe 968 Running SYSTEM 00 2,204 K HP SimplePass Servi...
Fewer details
End task

Performance The Performance tab will display a variety of information, including overall CPU usage percentage, a graphical display of CPU usage history, page-file usage in MB, and a graphical display of physical memory. This tab also provides you with additional memory-related information such as physical and kernel memory usage as well as the total number of handles, threads, and processes. Total, limit, and peak commit-charge information also appears. Some of the items are beyond the scope of this book, but it's good to know that you can use the Performance tab to keep track of system performance. Note that the number of processes, CPU usage percentage, and commit-charge information always appears at the bottom of the Task Manager window, regardless of which tab you have currently selected.

Networking In Windows Vista and Windows 7, the Networking tab provides you with a graphical display of the performance of your network connection. It also tells you the network adapter name, link speed, and state. If you have more than one network adapter installed in the machine, you can select the appropriate adapter to see graphical usage data for that adapter. Bluetooth would show up on this screen as well.

With Windows 8, this information is provided on the Performance tab.

Users   The Users tab provides you with information about the users connected to the local machine. You'll see the username, ID, status, client name, and session type. You can right-click the name of any connected user to perform a variety of functions, including sending the user a message, disconnecting the user, logging off the user, and initiating a remote-control session to the user's machine.

Startup (Windows 8/8.1)   The Startup tab lists the name of services configured to begin at startup as well as the publisher, status, and startup impact. From this tab, you can select any service and choose to disable it. This functionality is provided by MSCONFIG in Windows Vista and Windows 7.

Use Task Manager whenever the system seems bogged down by an unresponsive application.

MMC

Microsoft created the Microsoft Management Console (MMC) interface as a front end in which you can run administrative tools. Many administrators don't even know that applications they use regularly run within an MMC.

Computer Management

Windows includes a piece of software to manage computer settings: the Computer Management Console. The Computer Management Console can manage more than just the installed hardware devices; it can manage all of the services running on a computer in addition to Device Manager, which functions almost identically to the one that has existed since Windows 9x. It also contains *Event Viewer* to show any system errors and events as well as methods to configure the software components of all of the computer's hardware.

To access the Computer Management Console, you can go through Administrative Tools in Control Panel or just right-click the Computer/My Computer icon and choosing Manage (in Windows 8, it is on the Start menu).

After you are in Computer Management, you will see all of the tools available. This is one power-packed interface, which includes the following system tools:

Device Manager   Lets you manage hardware devices.

Event Viewer   A link to the tool that allows you to view application error logs, security audit records, and system errors. This tool is shown in Figure 14.12 as it would appear in Windows 8.1.

Shared Folders   Allows you to manage all of your computer's shared folders.

Local Users And Groups   Allows you to create and manage local user and group accounts.

FIGURE 14.12   Event Viewer's opening screen

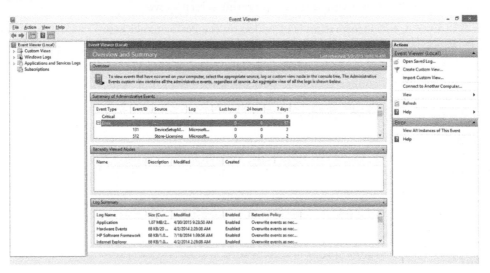

Performance (Windows 7 and Windows 8)/Reliability And Performance (Windows Vista)   Shows you how your system hardware is performing, and alerts you if system performance goes under a threshold that you set.

Computer Management also has the Storage area, which lets you manage removable media, defragment your hard drives, or manage partitions through the Disk Management utility. Finally, you can manage system services and applications through Computer Management as well.

Services

This tool (SERVICES.MSC) is an MMC snap-in that allows you to interact with the services running on the computer. Select Start ➤ Control Panel ➤ Administrative Tools, and choose Services. You will then see those that are configured on the system. The status of the services will typically either be started or stopped, and you can right-click and make a choice from the context menu: Start, Stop, Pause, Resume, or Restart. Services can be started automatically or manually or be disabled. If you right-click a service and choose Properties from the menu, you can choose the startup type as well as see the path to the executable and any dependencies.

Performance Monitor

Performance Monitor differs a bit in different versions of Windows, but it has the same purpose throughout: to display performance counters. It will collect counter information and then send that information to a console or event log.

Performance Monitor's objects and counters are very specific; you can use Performance Monitor as a general troubleshooting tool as well as a security troubleshooting tool. For instance, you can see where resources are being utilized and from where the activity is coming.

The name differs a bit between Windows versions: It is Called Reliability and Performance Monitor in Windows Vista, Performance Monitor in Windows 7/8/8.1, and so on. In Exercise 14.6, you will see how to work with Performance Monitor.

EXERCISE 14.6

Working with Performance Monitor

1. Select Start, type **perfmon,** and then press Enter. Make sure that you select Performance Monitor (as opposed to System Monitor or other default that may come to the forefront).

2. Choose the Performance Monitor section under Monitoring Tools.

3. Click the plus sign [+] or right-click in the graphical display area and select Add Counters.

4. Expand the Processor section, and select the %Processor Time object. Click Add>> and then click OK.

5. Open Windows File Explorer and type * into the search box and press Enter. Quickly change to Performance Monitor, and watch the impact of this search on the processor. This action is time consuming and therefore will help you notice the changes that take place in Performance Monitor.

6. Run the same operation again, but this time change your view within Performance Monitor to Histogram (click the button directly to the left of the plus sign [+]).

7. Run the same operation again, and change your view within Performance Monitor to Report.

8. Exit Performance Monitor.

Task Scheduler

Accessible either beneath Computer Management or via Start ➤ All Programs ➤ Accessories ➤ System Tools, the Task Scheduler (which may appear as Schedule Tasks in Windows 8.*x* Administrative Tools) allows you to configure an application to run automatically or at any regular interval (see Figure 14.13). There are a number of terms used to describe the options for configuring tasks: *action* (what the task actually does), *condition* (an optional requirement that must be met before a task runs), *setting* (any property that affects the behavior of a task), and *trigger* (the required condition for the task to run).

For example, you could configure a report to run automatically (action) every Tuesday (trigger) when the system has been idle for 10 minutes (condition), and only when requested (setting).

FIGURE 14.13   Windows Task Scheduler in Windows 8.1

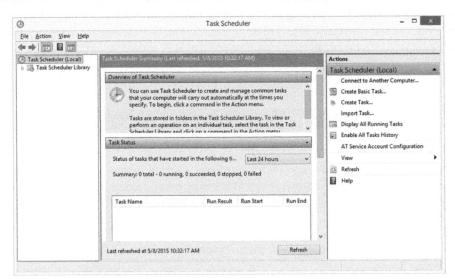

Windows System Configuration Tools

The MSCONFIG system configuration tool differs a bit in its tabs based on the Windows version you are running. Nonetheless, the key ones are General, Boot, Services, Startup, and Tools. Figure 14.14 shows the General tab for Windows 7 Enterprise. From here, you can configure the startup options.

FIGURE 14.14   MSCONFIG General tab in Windows 7

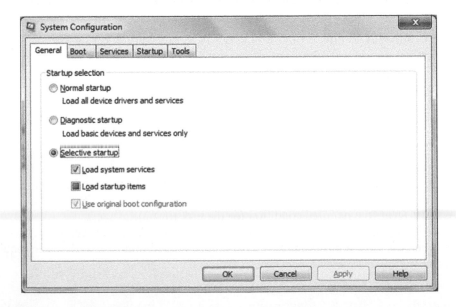

Figure 14.15 shows the Boot tab for Windows 7 Enterprise. Note that from here, you can configure the next boot to be into Safe mode and you can turn on the boot information so that you can see drivers as they load – quite useful when a system keeps hanging during boot.

FIGURE 14.15   MSCONFIG Boot tab in Windows 7

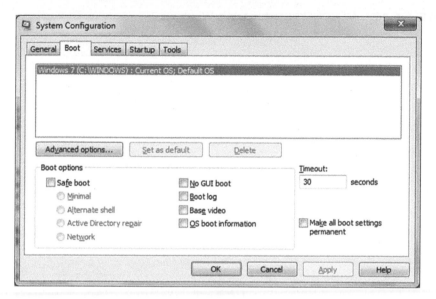

Figure 14.16 shows the Services tab for Windows 7 Enterprise. At this tab you can view the services installed on the system and their current status (running or stopped). You can also enable or disable services as necessary.

FIGURE 14.16   MSCONFIG Services tab in Windows 7

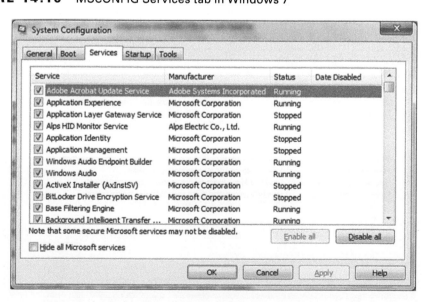

Figure 14.17 shows the Startup tab for Windows 7 Enterprise. At this tab you can turn on or off items to startup – allowing for much simpler configuration that editing the Registry. In the figure, note that Skype is still available on this machine but not currently configured to start automatically with each boot.

FIGURE 14.17   MSCONFIG Startup tab in Windows 7

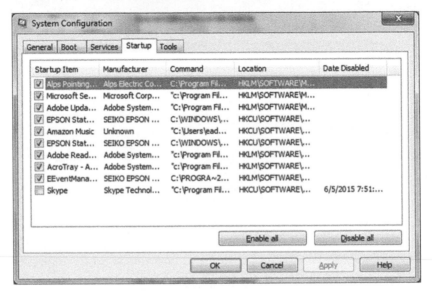

Figure 14.18 shows the Tools tab for Windows 7 Enterprise. At this tab you can launch a number of administrative tools to configure various Windows features.

FIGURE 14.18   MSCONFIG Tools tab in Windows 7

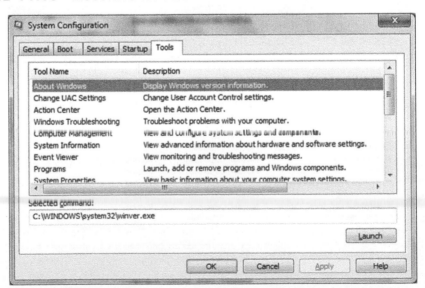

Although it has been said already, it must be stated again that the tabs differ slightly based on the operating system version. The CompTIA objectives related to this tool were walked through in this discussion.

The Msinfo32 tool, shown in Figure 14.19, displays a fairly thorough list of settings on the machine. You cannot change any values from here, but you can search, export, save, and run a number of utilities (accessed through the Tools menu option). There are several command-line options that can be used when starting Msinfo32, and Table 14.7 summarizes them.

FIGURE 14.19 The Msinfo32 interface shows configuration values for the system.

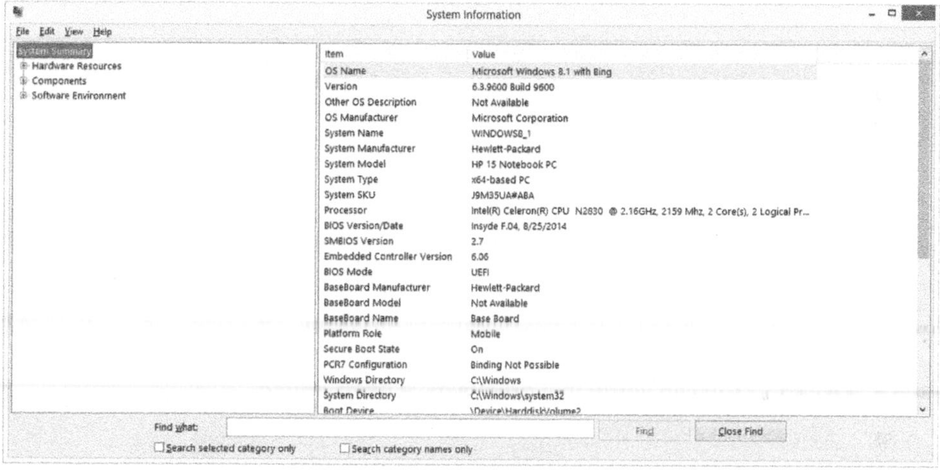

TABLE 14.7 Msinfo32 command-line options

Option	Function
/computer	Allows you to specify a remote computer on which to run the utility
/nfo	Creates a file and saves it with an .NFO filename extension
/report	Creates a file and saves it with an .TXT filename extension

Another utility to know is the *DxDiag* (DirectX Diagnostic) tool, shown in Figure 14.20. This tool allows you to test DirectX functionality. When you start it, you can also verify that Microsoft has signed your drivers, as shown in Figure 14.21. DirectX is a collection of application programming interfaces (APIs) related to multimedia.

FIGURE 14.20 The DxDiag tool lets you test functionality with DirectX components.

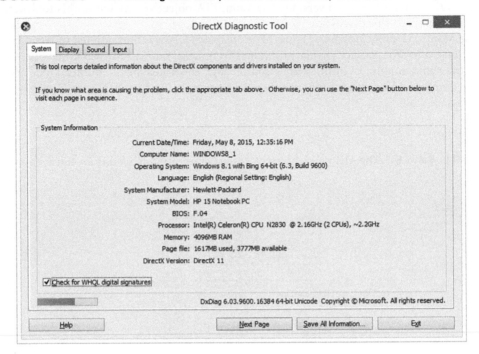

FIGURE 14.21 You can verify that drivers have been signed.

Finally, *MSTSC* (Remote Desktop Connection) is used to configure remote desktop connections. It offers a glut of options, as shown in Figure 14.22. It can be started from the command line using the options shown in the help screen, or it can be configured through the graphical interface (much easier) shown in Figure 14.23.

FIGURE 14.22   Command-line options for MSTSC

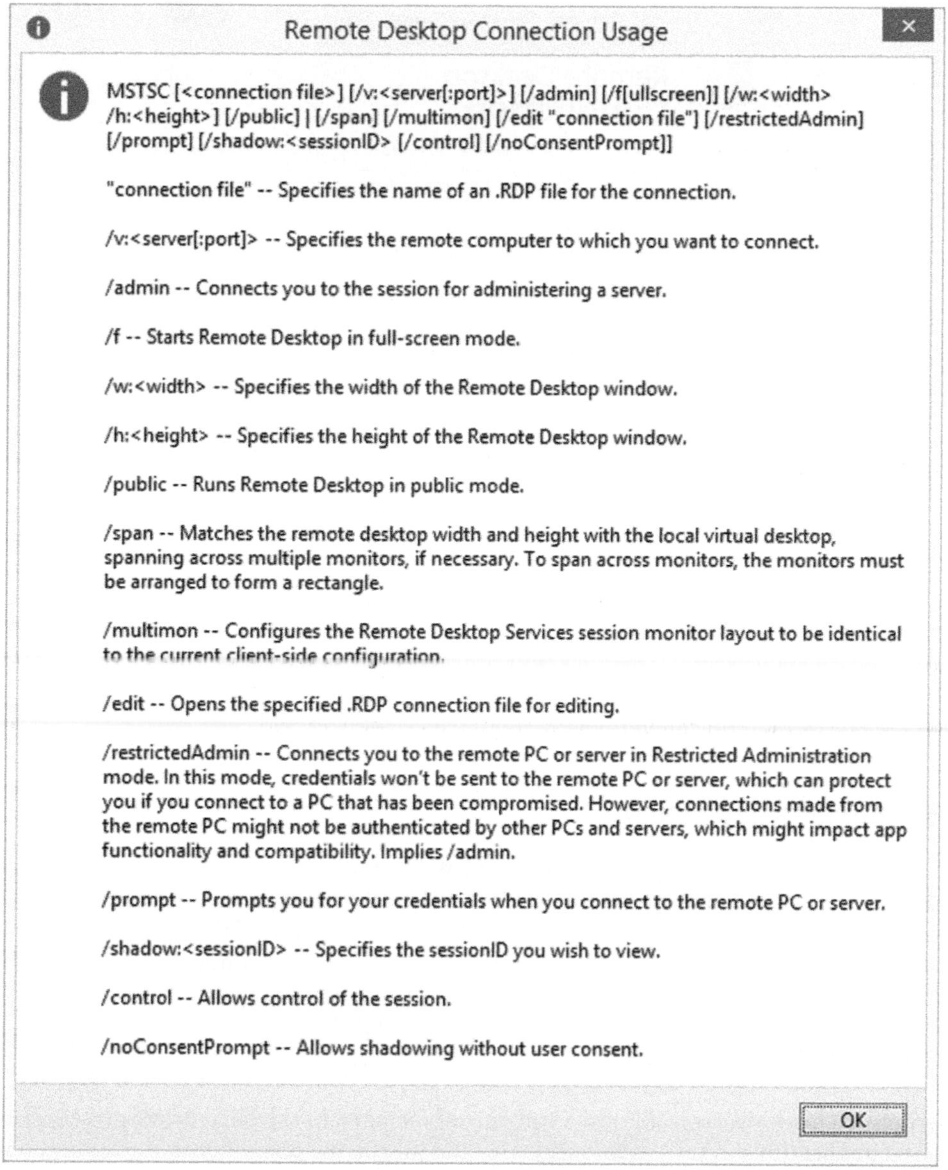

Remote Desktop Connection Usage   ×

MSTSC [<connection file>] [/v:<server[:port]>] [/admin] [/f[ullscreen]] [/w:<width>
/h:<height>] [/public] | [/span] [/multimon] [/edit "connection file"] [/restrictedAdmin]
[/prompt] [/shadow:<sessionID> [/control] [/noConsentPrompt]]

"connection file" -- Specifies the name of an .RDP file for the connection.

/v:<server[:port]> -- Specifies the remote computer to which you want to connect.

/admin -- Connects you to the session for administering a server.

/f -- Starts Remote Desktop in full-screen mode.

/w:<width> -- Specifies the width of the Remote Desktop window.

/h:<height> -- Specifies the height of the Remote Desktop window.

/public -- Runs Remote Desktop in public mode.

/span -- Matches the remote desktop width and height with the local virtual desktop,
spanning across multiple monitors, if necessary. To span across monitors, the monitors must
be arranged to form a rectangle.

/multimon -- Configures the Remote Desktop Services session monitor layout to be identical
to the current client-side configuration.

/edit -- Opens the specified .RDP connection file for editing.

/restrictedAdmin -- Connects you to the remote PC or server in Restricted Administration
mode. In this mode, credentials won't be sent to the remote PC or server, which can protect
you if you connect to a PC that has been compromised. However, connections made from
the remote PC might not be authenticated by other PCs and servers, which might impact app
functionality and compatibility. Implies /admin.

/prompt -- Prompts you for your credentials when you connect to the remote PC or server.

/shadow:<sessionID> -- Specifies the sessionID you wish to view.

/control -- Allows control of the session.

/noConsentPrompt -- Allows shadowing without user consent.

OK

FIGURE 14.23 Graphical configuration options for MSTSC

Power Management

The Advanced Configuration Power Interface (ACPI) must be supported by the system BIOS in order to work properly. With ACPI, it is the BIOS that provides the operating system with the necessary methods for controlling the hardware. This is in contrast to Advanced Power Management (APM), which only gave a limited amount of power to the operating system and let the BIOS do all the real work. Because of this, it is not uncommon to find legacy systems that can support APM but not ACPI.

There are three main states of power management common in most operating systems:

Hibernate   This state saves all of the contents of memory to the hard drive, preserves all data and applications exactly where they are, and allows the computer to power off completely. When the system comes out of hibernation, it returns to its previous state.

Sleep   In some operating systems, *Sleep* is used interchangeably with *Hibernate*, but that should not be the case. In Windows, Sleep puts the system in a low-power state, while Hibernate turns it off.

Shutdown/Turn Off   As the name implies, this shuts everything down and then turns the system off. It can be performed where it stays off or where it shuts down and then powers back on (Restart). The latter option is often used when updates need to be applied.

 Whether you see Shut Down or Turn Off Computer in Windows Vista has a lot to do with the way your user interface is configured (Classic view, for example). Regardless of the name of the option, it performs the same function.

If you are interested in saving power with a system that is not accessed often, one option is to employ Wake on LAN (WoL). Wake on LAN is an Ethernet standard implemented via a card that allows a "sleeping" machine to awaken when it receives a wakeup signal. Wake on LAN cards have more problems than standard network cards. In our opinion, this is because they're always on. In some cases, you'll be unable to get the card working again unless you unplug the PC's power supply and reset the card.

Sleep timers allow you to configure a system to sleep for certain periods of time to conserve power. While not included with the operating system, a number of downloadable programs can be found that will turn the machine off at a certain time or after some specified condition is met.

Disk Management

Where there are files, there are disks. That is to say, all of the files and programs that we've talked about so far reside on disks. Disks are physical storage devices, and they also need to be managed. There are several aspects to disk management. One is concerned with getting disks ready to be able to store files and programs; another deals with backing up your data. Yet another involves checking the health of disks and optimizing their performance. We'll look at these aspects in more detail.

Getting Disks Ready to Store Files and Programs

For a hard disk to be able to hold files and programs, it has to be partitioned and formatted. Partitioning is the process of creating logical divisions on a hard drive. A hard drive can have one or more partitions. Formatting is the process of creating and configuring a file allocation table (FAT) and creating the root directory. New Technology Filesystem (NTFS) is available with all of the versions of Windows you need to know about for the exam, but others are also recognized and supported. The file table for the NTFS is called the *Master File Table (MFT)*.

The following is a list of the major filesystems that are, or have been, used and the differences among them:

File allocation table (FAT)   *FAT* is the acronym for the file table used to keep track of where files are within the filesystem. It's also the name given to this type of filesystem, introduced in 1981. The filesystems for many OSs have been built on the design of FAT, but without its limitations. A FAT filesystem uses the *8.3 naming convention* (eight letters for the name, a period, and then a three-letter file identifier). This later became known as *FAT16* (to differentiate it from FAT32) because it used a 16-bit binary number to hold cluster-numbering information. Because of that number, the largest FAT disk partition that could be created was approximately 2GB.

Virtual FAT (VFAT)   This is an extension of the FAT filesystem that was introduced with Windows 95. It augmented the 8.3 file-naming convention and allowed filenames with up to 255 characters. It created two names for each file: a long name and an 8.3-compatible name so that older programs could still access files. When VFAT was incorporated into Windows 95, it used 32-bit code for improved disk access while keeping the 16-bit naming system for backward compatibility with FAT. It also had the 2GB disk partition limitation.

FAT32   This filesystem was introduced along with Windows 95 OEM Service Release 2. As disk sizes grew, so did the need to be able to format a partition larger than 2GB. FAT32 was based more on VFAT than on FAT16. It allowed for 32-bit cluster addressing, which in turn provided for a maximum partition size of 2 terabytes (2048GB). It also included smaller cluster sizes to avoid wasted space. FAT32 support is included in current Windows versions.

New Technology File System (NTFS)   Introduced along with Windows NT, NTFS is available with all current versions of Windows. NTFS is a much more advanced filesystem in almost every way than all versions of the FAT filesystem. It includes such features as individual file security and *compression* and RAID support as well as support for extremely large file and partition sizes and disk transaction monitoring. It is the filesystem of choice for higher-performance computing.

CD-ROM File System (CDFS)   While not a filesystem that can be used on a hard drive, CDFS is the filesystem of choice for CD media, and it has been used with 32-bit Windows versions since Windows 95. A CD mounted with the CDFS driver appears as a collection.

Extended File Allocation Table (ExFAT)   Microsoft created ExFAT, and it is a proprietary filesystem of choice for flash drives where NTFS cannot be used (because of overhead) and FAT32 is not acceptable (due to filesystem limitations). It is ideal for SD cards that hold a lot of information, and it is supported in all current versions of Windows.

Network File System (NFS)   NFS was created by Sun Microsystems a number of decades ago, and it is widely used in Unix and then Linux environments. Starting with Windows 7, Microsoft includes support for NFS with Windows (but it is not always installed). Windows versions prior to Windows 7 (Vista) can install Windows Services for Unix to gain this support.

Extended File System (ext)   Not natively supported with Windows, ext3 (Third Extended File System) became the default filesystem for many distributions of Linux due to its journaling capabilities. Enhancements were added to it to create ext4 (Fourth Extended File System), which is used with Android and other operating systems. It is possible to use ext4 with Windows, but doing so requires making some sacrifices in features for the sake of compatibility.

When you're installing any Windows OS, you will be asked first to format the drive using one of these disk technologies. Choose the disk technology based on what the computer will be doing and which OS you are installing.

To format a partition, you can use the FORMAT command. FORMAT.EXE is available with all versions of Windows. You can run FORMAT from a command prompt or by right-clicking a drive in Windows File Explorer and selecting Format. However, when you install Windows, it performs the process of partitioning and formatting for you if a partitioned and formatted drive does not already exist. You can usually choose between a *quick format* or a *full format*. With a quick format, a new file table is created on the hard disk, but files are not fully overwritten or erased from the disk. A quick format is much faster since the normal format fully erases any and all existing data on the hard disk (a time-consuming process).

WARNING   Be extremely careful with the Format command! When you format a drive, treasured data can be lost. Make sure you back up the data that you want to save first.

In Windows, you can manage your hard drives through the Disk Management component. To access Disk Management, open Control Panel, double-click Administrative Tools, and double-click Computer Management. Then double-click Disk Management.

The Disk Management screen lets you view a host of information regarding all of the drives installed in your system, including CD-ROM and DVD drives. The list of devices in the top portion of the screen shows you additional information for each partition on each drive, such as the filesystem used, status, free space, and so on. If you right-click a partition in either area, you can perform a variety of functions, such as formatting the partition and changing the name and drive-letter assignment. For additional options and information, you can also access the properties of a partition by right-clicking it and selecting Properties.

Windows supports both basic and dynamic storage. Basic storage can have a primary and an extended partition, while dynamic storage can be simple, spanned, or striped. The partition from which the operating system boots must be designated as *active*. Only one partition on a disk may be marked active. With basic storage, Windows drives can be partitioned with *primary* or *extended* partitions. The difference is that extended partitions can be divided into one or more logical drives and primary partitions cannot be further subdivided. Each hard disk can be divided into a total of four partitions, either four primary partitions or three primary partitions and one extended partition.

Finally, there is the concept of a *logical partition*. In reality, all partitions are logical in the sense that they don't necessarily correspond to one physical disk. One disk can have several logical divisions (partitions). A logical partition is any partition that has a drive letter.

Sometimes, you will also hear of a logical partition as one that spans multiple physical disks. For example, a network drive that you know as drive H: might actually be located on several physical disks on a server. To the user, all that is seen is one drive, or H:.

Given a scenario, there are many instances in which an administrator would turn to Disk Management (shown in Figure 14.24) during the course of trying to find the right storage solution. Note that drive status is readily identified in the fifth column and it is possible to perform a plethora of tasks from this interface.

FIGURE 14.24 Disk Management in Windows 7

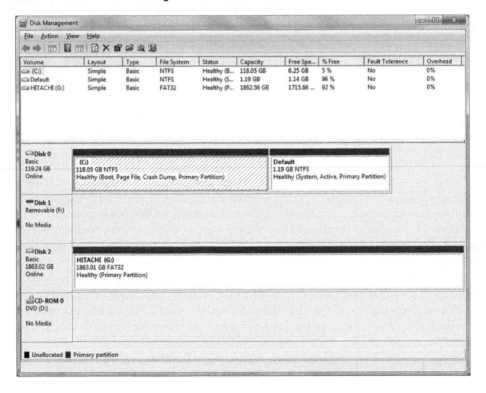

The popup menu that comes from right-clicking on any volume allows you to change the drive letter or paths, format, extend, shrink, delete, or add a mirror. The popup menu that comes from right-clicking on any drive allows you to create a new spanned, striped, mirrored, or RAID-5 volume. You can also convert to a dynamic or GPT disk.

Adding drives, arrays, and storage spaces are all accomplished through Disk Management, as has been discussed previously, along with mounting/initializing, and splitting/extending partitions.

Backing Up the Data on Your Drives

Another very important aspect of disk management is backing up the data on your drives. Sooner or later, you can count on running into a situation where a hard drive fails or data becomes corrupted. Without a backup copy of your data, you are facing a world of trouble trying to re-create it, if that's even possible or economically feasible. You also shouldn't rely on the Recycle Bin. Although it is a good utility to occasionally restore a file or directory that a user has accidentally deleted, it will not help you if your drives and the data on them become unusable.

Toward that end, Windows has a built-in backup feature called, you guessed it, Backup. To access Backup in Windows 7, click Start ➤ Control Panel ➤ Backup And Restore, and then either click Set Up Backup or select another backup from which to restore files. This will open the Backup Wizard.

The Backup utility in each of the different versions of Windows has different capabilities, with newer versions having greater capabilities. In general, you can either run a wizard to create a backup job or manually specify the files to back up. You can also run backup jobs or schedule them to run at specific time at a specific interval. With Windows 8/8.1, the Backup program morphed into File History (with a little System Image Backup added as well).

Refer to the Windows Help system in your version of Windows for in-depth information on how to use the backup utility and features relevant to you.

Checking the Health of Hard Disks and Optimizing Their Performance

As time goes on, it's important to check the health of Windows computers' hard disks and to optimize their performance. Windows provides you with several tools to do so, some of which we've already mentioned in this chapter. One important tool is Disk Defragmenter, which has existed in almost all versions of Windows.

When files are written to a hard drive, they're not always written contiguously, or with all of the data in a single location. Files are stored on the disk in numbered blocks similar to PO boxes—when they are written, they are written to free blocks. As a result, file data is spread out over the disk, and the time it takes to retrieve files from the disk increases. Defragmenting a disk involves analyzing the disk and then consolidating fragmented files and folders so that they occupy a contiguous space (consecutive blocks), thus increasing performance during file retrieval.

To access Disk Defragmenter, click Start ➤ Programs/All Programs ➤ Accessories ➤ System Tools ➤ Disk Defragmenter. In the list of drives, select the drive that you want to defragment and then click Analyze. When the analysis is finished, Disk Defragmenter tells you how much the drive is fragmented and whether defragmentation is recommended. If it is, click Defragment. Be aware that for large disks with a lot of fragmented files, this process can take quite some time to finish.

In Windows, you can also access Disk Defragmenter through the properties of any partition listed in Disk Management (or, even easier, any disk
root under Computer in Windows File Explorer). Click the Tools tab, and
then click Defragment.

Administrative Shares vs. Local Shares

Administrative shares are created on servers running Windows on the network for administrative purposes. These shares can differ slightly based on which OS is running, but they
end with a dollar sign ($) to make them hidden. There is one for each volume on a hard
drive (C$, D$, and so forth) as well as admin$ (the root folder – usually C:\WINDOWS), and
print$ (where the print drivers are located). These are created for use by administrators
and usually require administrator privileges to access.

Local shares, as the name implies, are those that are created locally and are visible with
the icon of a hand beneath them.

As the name implies, network shares are those that exist on the network, but they can
be mapped to appear as if they are local. The **NET USE** command can be used to establish
network connections at a command prompt, for example. If you want to connect to a shared
network drive and make it your M drive, the syntax **NET USE M: ***server\share* will accomplish this. Drives can also be mapped using Disk Management, discussed in Chapter 14.

One common use of this command is to connect to a shared printer (**NET USE LPT1:
***printername*).

Sharing printers was one of the primary reasons why networking became
popular in the workplace and it still continues to be an important reason
today. Know that you can map to any printer on the network but it still
must be shared for you to be able to use it.

User Authentication

One of the big problems that larger systems must deal with is the need for users to access
multiple systems or applications. This may require a user to remember multiple accounts
and passwords. The purpose of a *single sign-on (SSO)* is to give users access to all of the
applications and systems that they need when they log on. This is becoming a reality in
many environments, including Kerberos, Microsoft Active Directory, Novell eDirectory,
and some certificate model implementations.

Single sign-on is both a blessing and a curse. It's a blessing in that once
the user is authenticated, they can access all of the resources on the network and browse multiple directories. It's a curse in that it removes the
doors that otherwise exist between the user and various resources.

In the case of Kerberos, a single token allows any "Kerberized" applications to accept a user as valid. The important thing to remember in this process is that each application that wants to use SSO must be able to accept and process the token presented by Kerberos.

A server that runs Active Directory (AD) retains information about all access rights for all users and groups in the network. When a user logs on to the system, AD issues the user a globally unique identifier (GUID). Applications that support AD can use this GUID to provide access control.

Using AD simplifies the sign-on process for users and lowers the support requirements for administrators. Access can be established through groups, and it can be enforced through group memberships. Active Directory can be implemented using a Windows Server (such as Windows Server 2012) computer. All users will then log in to the Windows domain using their centrally created AD account. On a decentralized network, SSO passwords are stored on each server and can represent a security risk. It's important to enforce password changes and make sure that passwords are updated throughout the organization on a frequent basis.

While single sign-on is not the opposite of multi-factor authentication, it is often mistakenly thought of this way. One-, two-, and three-factor authentication merely refers to the number of items a user must supply to authenticate. Authentication can be based on something they have (a smart card), something they know (a password), something unique (biometric factor), and so forth. After factor authentication is done, then single sign-on can still apply throughout the user's session.

Summary

In this chapter, you learned about some of the tools that can be used with Windows. We covered basic Windows management concepts, including managing disks, using filesystems, and understanding directory structure. Keeping your computer healthy will save you a lot of stress. Examples that we discussed included performing backups.

With the basic knowledge gained in this chapter, you are now ready to learn how to interact with the most popular operating systems in use today. These topics are covered in the next three chapters.

Exam Essentials

Know what the critical Windows interfaces are and how to use them. This list includes the Desktop, Taskbar, Start menu, icons, windows, Control Panel, the command prompt, Computer, Network, the system tray, and the Registry editor.

Know what filesystems are available in Windows and the differences between them.   The most commonly used filesystem on Windows hard drives is NTFS. FAT32 is older and perhaps a bit quicker for smaller hard drives, but NTFS adds a plethora of important features, including security and auditing.

Understand what each of the following commands does: CMD, COPY, XCOPY, /?, MD, CD, and RD.   Many utilities that come with Windows help you navigate through or manage files and directories from a command prompt. The CMD command opens a command line, where you can type the rest of the commands. If you're not sure which utility to use, /? will provide the information. The MD, CD, and RD commands make, change, and delete (remove) directories, respectively. Both COPY and XCOPY are used to copy files.

Know the main administrative tools.   You should know the primary graphical tools for troubleshooting Windows and working with the operating system. These include the disk management tools, Administrative Tools, Device Manager, Task Manager, System Information, System Restore, and Task Scheduler.

Review Questions

The answers to the chapter review questions can be found in Appendix A.

1. Which of the following utilities is used to update Group Policy settings and replaces some of the functionality that previously existed with SECEDIT?

    A. CLOBBER

    B. GPUPDATE

    C. CONSOLIDATE

    D. EXTRACT

2. In Windows, which of the following is the filesystem of choice for CD media?

    A. NTFS

    B. JFS

    C. FAT32

    D. CDFS

3. Which utility can be used to schedule a remote shutdown?

    A. TaskMgr

    B. Kill

    C. Shutdown

    D. Netstat

4. You have been told to use the /FIXBOOT switch to write a new boot sector on a Windows 7 machine. Which command does this switch work with?

    A. BOOTREC

    B. SFC

    C. BCEDIT

    D. ROBOCOPY

5. Which of the following filesystems is a proprietary one created by Microsoft for use with large flash drives?

    A. GPT

    B. NFS

    C. ext3

    D. ExFAT

6. Which command lists all running processes at the command line?

    A. WLIST

    B. ALIST

    C. PLIST

    D. TASKLIST

7. Virtual memory is configured through which system tool?
   - **A.** Taskbar
   - **B.** System applet
   - **C.** Memory Manager
   - **D.** Virtual Configuration

8. Within the Services snap-in, services can be in any state except which of the following?
   - **A.** Started automatically
   - **B.** Started manually
   - **C.** Disabled
   - **D.** Detached

9. What can you do if a program is not responding to any commands and appears to be locked up?
   - **A.** Open the System Control Panel applet, and choose Performance to see what process is causing the problem.
   - **B.** Add more memory.
   - **C.** Press Ctrl+Alt+Del to reboot the computer.
   - **D.** Open Task Manager, select the appropriate task, and click End Task.

10. Which of the following can be used to configure a remote connection?
    - **A.** REGEDIT
    - **B.** MSTSC
    - **C.** REGSRV32
    - **D.** SPL

11. Which tool is shown in the following screen shot (Figure 14.25)?
    - **A.** DxDiag
    - **B.** Msinfo
    - **C.** Msconfig
    - **D.** Msinfo32

12. Which type of resource do you configure in Device Manager?
    - **A.** Hardware
    - **B.** Files and folders
    - **C.** Applications
    - **D.** Memory

13. To back up the files on your disks in Windows 7, which Windows program can you use?
    - **A.** Disk Management
    - **B.** Backup
    - **C.** My Computer
    - **D.** No backup program in Windows

FIGURE 14.25   Standard Windows Utility

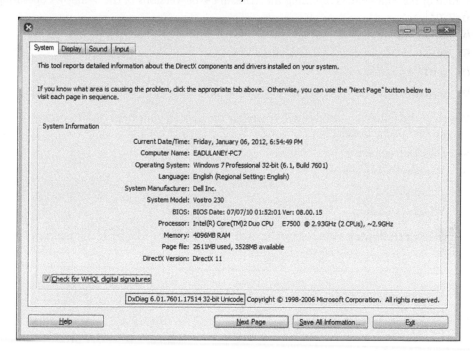

14. You believe that your system files are corrupted in Windows. You run System File Checker. What do you do to make System File Checker automatically repair your system files if repair is needed?

- **A.** Run SFC /AUTOREPAIR
- **B.** Run SFC /REPAIR
- **C.** Run SFC /REVERT
- **D.** Run SFC /SCANNOW

15. Which of the following partitions is specifically the partition from which the operating system boots?

- **A.** Primary partition
- **B.** Extended partition
- **C.** Active partition
- **D.** Logical partition

16. Which of the following Registry hives contains information about the computer's hardware?

- **A.** HKEY_CURRENT_MACHINE
- **B.** HKEY_LOCAL_MACHINE
- **C.** HKEY_MACHINE
- **D.** HKEY_RESOURCES

17. Which of the following is replacing the MBR in 64-bit versions of the Windows operating system?

   A. LILO

   B. NFS

   C. GPT

   D. GRUB

18. Which of the following utilities will rearrange the files on your hard disk to occupy contiguous chunks of space?

   A. Disk Defragmenter

   B. Windows File Explorer

   C. Scandisk

   D. Windows Backup

19. Which of the following switches can be used with ROBOCOPY to mirror a complete directory tree?

   A. /S

   B. /MIR

   C. /CDT

   D. /AH

20. Which of the following tools allows you to test DirectX functionality?

   A. Msinfo32

   B. Ping

   C. Telnet

   D. DxDiag

Performance-Based Question

You will encounter performance-based questions on the A+ exams. The questions on the exam require you to perform a specific task, and you will be graded on whether or not you were able to complete the task. The following requires you to think creatively in order to measure how well you understand this chapter's topics. You may or may not see similar questions on the actual A+ exams. To see how your answers compare to the authors', refer to Appendix B.

You are working at a company that has standardized on Windows 7 workstations for all. The phone rings and it is your superior. He tells you that his workstation is running incredibly slow, and it is almost to the point where is it is unusable. When you ask what he is running, he reports that he has exited out of everything but the operating system. You suspect there are background processes tying up the CPU and memory. What utility can you have him use to look for such culprits?

Chapter

15

Working with Windows 8/8.1

THE FOLLOWING COMPTIA A+ 220-902 EXAM OBJECTIVES ARE COVERED IN THIS CHAPTER:

✓ **1.1 Compare and contrast various features and requirements of Microsoft Operating Systems (Windows 8, Windows 8.1).**

- Features: Side-by-side apps; Metro UI, Pinning, One Drive, Windows store, Multimonitor task bars, Charms, Start Screen, Power Shell, Live sign in, Action Center

- Upgrade paths – differences between in place upgrades, compatibility tools, Windows upgrade OS advisor

✓ **1.2 Given a scenario, install Windows PC operating systems using appropriate methods.**

- Boot methods: Solid state/flash drives, Netboot, External/hot swappable drive, Internal hard drive (partition)

- Types of installations: Unattended installation, Upgrade, Clean install, Repair installation, Multiboot, Remote network installation, Image deployment, Recovery partition, Refresh/restore

The preceding two chapters looked at Windows operating systems in general, and the focus of this chapter is on Windows 8/8.1. The next two chapters will similarly focus on Windows 7 and then Windows Vista to round out the coverage of the three operating systems you need to know for the 220-902 exam.

The leap from one operating system to another can be either an evolutionary change or a revolutionary change. Windows 8 was a revolutionary change from the operating systems that came before it in the adoption of a tablet-friendly interface implemented on all devices. The interface was designed to accommodate touch gestures on a touchscreen, but it did not make their existence mandatory: you can still navigate with a keyboard, mouse, and touchpad.

Windows 8.1 was released as an update to replace Windows 8 and to make running the operating system on a system without a touchscreen easier. The changes from 8 to 8.1 were evolutionary, as opposed to revolutionary, and they could arguably fall under the category of a patch (or a step backward to adapt to hardware). The biggest noticeable difference is that during boot, the OS checks to see if it is on a touch-capable device. If it is not, it boots to the desktop view (which looks like Windows 7) instead of to the Start screen (which is still there just the same).

Because the differences are minimal, this chapter discusses them as if they are the same and uses "Windows 8" to signify both. We'll point out where there is a substantial difference between Windows 8 and Windows 8.1; there are only a few areas where they differ.

Windows Editions

Windows 8 was released in four different editions: Windows 8 (commonly called "core"), Windows 8 Pro (similar to Windows 7 Professional and Windows 7 Ultimate in terms of features), Windows 8 Enterprise (for volume licensing), and Windows 8 RT (for preinstallation on tablets). The RT version includes touch-optimized versions of Microsoft Office. All of the versions include the Start screen, Desktop, Windows Store, secure boot, and drive encryption. Only the Pro and Enterprise versions support BitLocker and Encrypting File System (EFS).

The minimum hardware requirements for a 32-bit installation are a 1GHz (or faster) processor, 1GB of RAM, 16GB of hard drive space, and a DirectX 9 graphics device with WDDM driver. For 64-bit installations, this rises to 2GB of RAM and 20GB of hard drive space. Naturally, for touch capabilities, you need a monitor that supports touch, and you need an Internet connection to be able to access the Windows Store if you should need software from there.

Windows 8 RT runs on an ARM (Advanced RISC Machine) processor, not on x86/x64 processors. This is important because programs and upgrades written for the x86/x64 processors will not work on RT.

Table 15.1 lists a number of features associated with the Windows 8 operating system that CompTIA wants you to know for the exam, along with a brief description of each.

TABLE 15.1   Windows 8 features

Feature	Significance
Metro UI	When the new interface was released with Windows 8, it was called the Metro UI. This name did not last long; it came to be known as the new Windows UI or the Windows 8 UI.
	Figure 15.1 shows an example of the interface, in this case the Windows Start screen.

FIGURE 15.1   The Windows 8 UI

Pinning	If you have favorite apps, you can "pin" (add) them to the Start screen or the Desktop so that you can get to them quickly or see updates to their tiles at a glance. To add an app to the Taskbar, right-click and choose Pin To Taskbar (or choose to unpin it if you want to remove it). Choosing Pin To Start places it on the Start screen instead of on the Taskbar.
OneDrive	CompTIA refers to this as two words (One Drive), but Microsoft refers to it as one (OneDrive). Either way, it is the online/cloud storage account that comes with your Microsoft account. You can save files there from applications or move them there (and back again) using File Explorer (previously called Windows Explorer). There is a limited amount of storage given to each account for free, and you can purchase more as you need it.

Feature	Significance
Windows Store	The Windows Store is an online site, requiring Windows 8 or higher, from which you can download apps, games, software, and so on. Once they're downloaded, you can install them, pin them, and use them.
Multimonitor Taskbars	Multiple monitors have been available with Windows for some time, but not until Windows 8 has it been possible to have a Taskbar appear in each monitor.
Charms	Windows 8 introduced charms to the OS. These are controls that are available on the side of the screen for every Windows Store app. They consist of Search, Share, Start, Devices, and Settings.
Start screen	The Windows Start screen, shown in Figure 15.1, is the central location where you can access your most commonly used data and sites.
PowerShell	Windows PowerShell (one word per Microsoft and two per CompTIA) has been around for several years and was available with previous versions of Windows as well. It can be thought of as a greatly enhanced command interface where you can write script files based on the .NET programming framework. Figure 15.2 shows an example of the interface and the results of the get-process command.

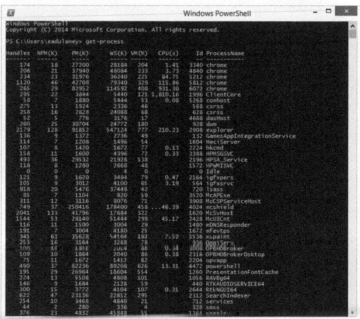

FIGURE 15.2   Windows PowerShell

Some common commands that can be used in PowerShell can be found at
https://technet.microsoft.com/en-us/magazine/2006.12.powershell.aspx.

Feature	Significance
Live sign-in	In a non-domain-based environment, it is possible to use your Microsoft account (MSN, Hotmail, Outlook, and so forth) username and password to log in to your Windows 8–based PC. This is intended to serve as a single sign-on, allowing you to not only interact with the OS but also to download apps from the Windows Store, sync files with OneDrive, and so on. As an alternative to this, you can still create a local account and use it to log in, but you will need to authenticate with cloud-based services when/if you connect to them.
Action Center	Also available in Windows 7, Action Center (Control Panel ➤ System and Security ➤ Action Center) is a central dialog for dealing with problems, security, and maintenance. Figure 15.3 shows an example of the interface on a system with expired virus protection.

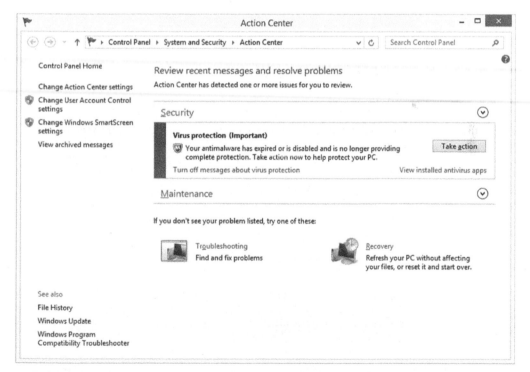

FIGURE 15.3   The Action Center

The Windows Start screen, with its tiled look, provides a main location where you can access everything. Depending on whether you have a touch-enabled device or not, how you interact with this screen will differ. Table 15.2 lists common actions and ways of navigating the Start screen based on whether you are using touch gestures or a keyboard and mouse.

TABLE 15.2 Navigating Windows 8 Start screen

Action	With Touch Gestures	With Keyboard and Mouse
Open an app	Tap the app. Figure 15.4 shows the tile representing the Calendar app.	Click on the app.

FIGURE 15.4 A tile/icon for an app

Return to Start screen from an app	Tap the Start button in the lower left-corner of the screen.	Press the Windows key on the keyboard.
Display the charms	 Swipe from the right edge of the screen. Figure 15.5 shows the charms.	Point to the upper-right or lower-right corner of the Start screen.

FIGURE 15.5 The Windows 8 charms

Action	With Touch Gestures	With Keyboard and Mouse
Display the Start menu	 Tap the Desktop tile and then press and release the Start button. Figure 15.6 shows the Start button.	Point to the lower-left corner of the Start screen to display the Start button, and then right-click it.

FIGURE 15.6   The Start button

| See all apps on your computer | Swipe to the left until the down arrow appears, and then tap the arrow in the lower-left corner of the Start screen (shown in Figure 15.7). A list of the apps will appear, by name and in alphabetical order. | Point to the lower-left area of the Start screen, and then click the down arrow. |

FIGURE 15.7   The down arrow

| Switch between open apps | Swipe in and out from the left edge of the screen to see a list of open apps, and then tap on one. | Point to the upper-left corner of the Start screen to see a list of open apps, and then click on one. |

On the Start screen, you can start typing the name of any app, setting, or file and the OS will attempt to find what you are looking for and narrow your options to that. You can also search by using the Search icon (which looks like a magnifying glass) in the upper-right corner of the Start Screen, as shown in Figure 15.8.

FIGURE 15.8   The Search icon appears on the Start screen.

Installing Windows 8

As with any operating system installation, the two primary methods of installing Windows 8 are either a clean install or an upgrade. With a *clean install*, no traces of any previous operating system are kept, and the main concern is that the hardware meets (or preferably, exceeds) the minimum requirements. Clean installs are usually done with new hardware and virtual machines (and, to a limited extent, multiple boot installations).

With an *upgrade*, the focus is on keeping something from the previous operating system that was installed earlier on the machine. That "something" can be user accounts, data, apps, or almost anything else.

 If you're keeping any existing data, it is an upgrade. Otherwise, it is a clean install.

When the upgrade is done without removing the existing operating system (the norm), this is known as an *in-place upgrade*. Windows 8.1 can do an in-place upgrade only from Windows 7 or Windows 8, and Table 15.3 shows the upgrade possibilities.

TABLE 15.3   Windows 8 upgrade options

Existing Operating System	Windows 8 Core	Windows 8 Pro	Windows 8 Enterprise
Windows 7 Starter	Yes	Yes	No
Windows 7 Home Basic	Yes	Yes	No
Windows 7 Home Premium	Yes	Yes	No
Windows 7 Professional	No	Yes	Yes
Windows 7 Ultimate	No	Yes	No
Windows 7 Enterprise	No	No	Yes

Since Windows RT 8 is designed for preinstallation on tablets, there is not an upgrade path for it.

The easiest way to see if your current hardware can run Windows 8.1 is to download and run the *Windows 8.1 Upgrade Assistant*. Figure 15.9 shows the opening screen, and Figure 15.10 shows an example of the results it found when run on a Windows 7 laptop.

FIGURE 15.9   The opening screen of the Windows Upgrade Assistant

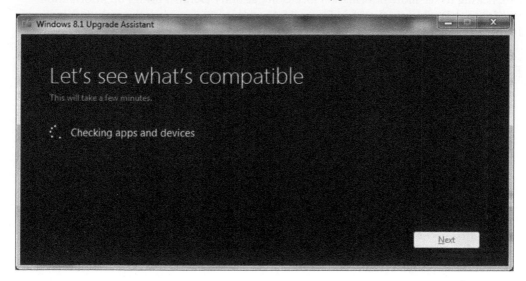

FIGURE 15.10   An example of the Windows Upgrade Assistant results

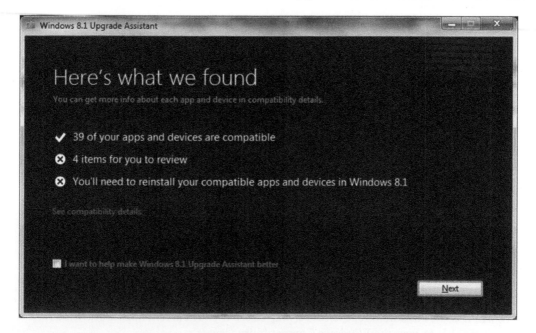

Clicking to see more information (See Compatibility Details) brings up information similar to that which is shown in Figure 15.11, and it lets you work through each issue individually.

FIGURE 15.11   The compatibility details offer more information.

A tutorial and link to download the Windows 8.1 Upgrade Assistant are available at `http://windows.microsoft.com/en-us/windows-8/upgrade-from-windows-7-tutorial`.

When it comes to software, the easiest way to see if your current apps work with Windows 8.1 is to visit the Windows Compatibility Center at:

www.microsoft.com/en-us/windows/compatibility/CompatCenter/Home

As mentioned, Windows 8 can be installed as an upgrade or a clean installation—accomplished with the Custom option (think custom = clean). When you choose Custom, you can choose whether or not to format the hard disk. If you choose not to format the hard disk, the old operating system is placed in a folder named Windows.old to allow you to attempt to return to the old operating system if needed. After 28 days, any files placed in the Windows.old folder are automatically deleted.

 When formatting is involved, it is a clean install.

Regardless of whether you are doing an install or an upgrade, there are a number of ways to approach doing it and CompTIA has placed them into several categories, which we will walk through next.

Unattended Installation/Image Deployment

An *unattended installation*, as the name implies, is one in which you don't need to be sitting in front of the machine to complete the operation. The heart of an unattended installation is utilizing *image deployment*, which is sort of like copying an ideal image over from one machine to another. Microsoft makes tools available with which to create images, and the core deployment tools are in the Windows Assessment and Deployment Kit (usually referred to as the Windows ADK). Expanding on these core tools is the Microsoft Deployment Toolkit (commonly called MDT), which simplifies the process and reduces the time each install takes.

 You can download the Microsoft Deployment Toolkit from www.microsoft .com/en-us/download/details.aspx?id=40796.

With the toolkit, you create a reference image for deployment to the physical machines. Once it's created, you can edit this image with the System Preparation Tool (Sysprep) and create a Windows Imaging (WIM) file to roll out. To simplify matters, the initial image is usually created on a virtual platform to help rule out hardware-related issues.

Complete documentation on using the MDT for Windows deployment can be found at:

https://technet.microsoft.com/en-us/library/dn744280.aspx

Remote Network Installation

An install can be started many ways—with a USB drive, a DVD, and so on—and an image and setup files can also be located on and installed from a network, thus saving you from having to keep all of the files on the local machine. Often called a PXE-initiated boot (for Pre-Execution Environment), the workstation involved in the installation can retrieve the files from the network, as needed, and configure variables accordingly.

Multiboot Installation

If there is sufficient space on a machine, and the hardware will support it, you can have more than one operating system and choose which one to run when you boot. A rule of thumb from Microsoft is that you should always install older operating systems first and then work forward (have Windows Vista on before installing Windows 7 and then Windows 8, for example); if you go in the other direction, an earlier version of Windows may not recognize the startup files and will overwrite them, rendering the system inoperable.

To change which operating system to boot to, go to Control Panel ➤ System and Security ➤ System, and click Advanced System Settings. On the Advanced tab, chose Settings (under Startup And Recovery). Under System Start-Up, choose the default operating system that you want to use when the computer restarts.

If you install Windows on a system with multiple hard drives, you can use diskpart to verify that images are pointing to their intended drives. The system partition (containing BCD) usually appears as 0, but the system can assign different numbers, and different computers that have identical hardware configurations can end up having different disk numbers assigned to them.

Repair Installation/Refresh/Restore

When a problem pops up with the Windows 8 operating system, you can boot into the Windows Recovery Environment (Windows RE) and repair it by choosing to refresh, reset, or restore it. *Refreshing* it keeps personal files and settings along with the default apps and those that you installed from the Windows Store.

Resetting reinstalls Windows and deletes all but the default apps (meaning that you lose your personal files and settings). *Restoring* allows you to just undo recent system changes.

Depending on the type of repair operation that you perform, you may or may not need the Windows 8 product key to continue. This is a 25-character code used for Windows activation (primarily to keep you from installing it on more PCs than you have licenses for).

Recovery Partition

A *recovery partition* is an area of the hard drive set aside to hold files that can be used to recover the operating system in the event of a failure. You can copy the information from this partition to another location (usually a USB drive) to use in the event that the partition fails. In Exercise 15.1, we will walk through creating a USB recovery drive.

EXERCISE 15.1: CREATING A USB RECOVERY DRIVE

1. If you are using a mouse/keyboard, point to the lower-right corner of the screen and then click Search. If you are using a touchscreen, swipe in from the right edge of the screen and tap Search.

2. Type **Recovery**, and choose Create A Recovery Drive when the option pops up.

3. Click Next to copy the contents of the recovery partition to the recovery drive.

4. Insert a USB drive when prompted, as shown in Figure 15.12. Note the massive size of this file and that everything currently on the USB drive will be deleted.

FIGURE 15.12   Creating a recovery drive

5. Click Next.

6. Click Create.

7. After the process is finished, you can choose if you want to keep the recovery partition on your machine (in which case, you just click Finish) or delete it (in which case, you click Delete). The latter is recommended only when you need to free up the disk space.

Windows 8 Boot Methods

Windows 8 can be booted from a number of sources. To simplify matters, we've lumped them into categories constituting the ones that you need to know for the A+ exam.

Internal Hard Drive (Partition)

The most common method of booting the operating system—the traditional method of so doing—is to boot from an internal hard drive. In this case, the files are installed on a partition. A hard drive can be divided into multiple partitions, and it is not uncommon to have one for the system and one for data or recovery. By definition, a *system partition* is one that contains the Boot (BCD) folder that tells the computer where to look to start Windows, while the *boot partition* (which can be the same as the system partition) contains the actual files used to start Windows, and a *recovery partition* includes recovery tools (like Windows RE tools or a recovery image).

The boot files are the same as for Windows 7 and Windows Vista, and they load in the following order:

BOOTMGR   The Windows Boot Manager (BOOTMGR) bootstraps the system. In other words, this file starts the loading of an OS on the computer.

BCD   The Boot Configuration Data (BCD) holds information about OSs installed on the computer, such as the location of the OS files.

WINLOAD.EXE   Loads the operating system kernel (NTOSKRNL.EXE).

WINRESUME.EXE   If the system is not starting fresh but resuming a previous session, then WINRESUME.EXE is called by the BOOTMGR.

NTOSKRNL.EXE   The Windows OS kernel.

System files   In addition to the previously listed files, Windows needs a number of files from its system directories (that is, SYSTEM and SYSTEM32), such as the hardware abstraction layer (HAL.DLL), session manager (SMSS.EXE), user session (WINLOGON.EXE), and security subsystem (LSASS.EXE).

External/Hot Swappable Drive

Rather than booting from an internal drive, it is possible to install and boot Windows from an external drive *if* your BIOS supports it (and looks for the external drive in the boot order). You need to image/clone the operating system to the external drive and then change the boot order. Since many external drives are USB, one simple solution is to use Windows To Go, which is discussed with flash drives in the next section.

    As silly as it sounds, bear in mind when taking the exam that an external drive will not boot if it is not found at startup.

Flash Drives

Microsoft created *Windows To Go (WTG)* to allow Windows 8/8.1 to be installed on any USB-bootable device: flash drive, external hard drive, and so forth. It is officially included only with the Enterprise version, but workarounds can be found on the Web to work with lesser versions.

With Windows To Go, an image of the OS is known as a workspace, and you can use BitLocker with WTG to secure the workspace further. WTG works with both USB 2.0 and USB 3.0 ports, but it requires USB 3.0 drives. Because of the size of the OS, it is recommended that USB drives used for WTG not be less than 20GB in size.

One exam-worthy note is that WTG does not support OS upgrades. It was created for use by enterprise departments, and there is no current model for upgrading WTG in place.

Solid-State Drives

Just as Windows 8 can run from USB, internal, and external drives, it can also run on *solid-state drives (SSDs),* as long as they meet the standard minimum requirements for size (a minimum of 16GB, in this case). Microsoft recommends that WinSAT.exe be used with the formal option to optimize Windows for the SSD (this reduces the number of write operations that Windows makes).

Netboot

The process of booting the OS from the network, performing a *netboot,* is commonly done with a thin client. This can be done with Windows 8 using Microsoft Desktop Virtualization. This is a useful option for environments where hardware is kept to a minimum.

After using DHCP to obtain network configuration parameters from a server, the thin client can locate a PXE boot server to send it the files that it needs to boot. The PXE server can be the same server as the DHCP server or a different one dedicated to the task.

Summary

This chapter focused on Windows 8/8.1. This is one of the three operating systems covered on the exam, and CompTIA expects you to be familiar with it and able to answer questions on everything from installing it to managing it.

We looked at the various editions of Windows 8, how to install it, and the Windows 8 boot options. The key operating system boot files are the same for this version of Windows, Window 7, and Windows Vista (which are explored in the next two chapters).

Exam Essentials

Know what types of installations are possible with Windows 8. You should know which operating systems can be upgraded to Windows 8 and which require a clean installation.

Understand the difference between an upgrade and a clean install. You should know that a clean installation replaces the operating system that was previously there (if there was one) and often includes a format. An upgrade, on the other hand, keeps some of the existing values, such as user accounts and user files.

Know the editions of Windows 8. Windows 8 was released in four different editions: Windows 8 (commonly called "core"), Windows 8 Pro (similar to Windows 7 Professional and Windows 7 Ultimate in terms of features), Windows 8 Enterprise (for volume licensing), and Windows 8 RT (for preinstallation on tablets).

Review Questions

The answers to the chapter review questions can be found in Appendix A.

1. When Windows 8 was initially released, what was the interface called?
   A. Starter
   B. Aero
   C. Charm
   D. Metro

2. Which versions of Windows 8 support EFS? (Choose all that apply.)
   A. Enterprise
   B. Pro
   C. RT
   D. Core

3. What is the minimum amount of hard drive space needed for a 32-bit installation of Windows 8?
   A. 16GB
   B. 20GB
   C. 24GB
   D. 28GB

4. For a 64-bit installation of Windows 8, how much RAM is considered the minimum requirement?
   A. 1GB
   B. 2GB
   C. 4GB
   D. 8GB

5. Which of the following is the online/cloud storage account (to which you can save or move files) that comes with your Microsoft account?
   A. eDirectory
   B. Cloud+
   C. OneDrive
   D. PostBox

6. Previous versions of Windows included Windows Explorer. What is this utility called in Windows 8?
   A. Voyeur
   B. Magellan

    C. Navigator

    D. File Explorer

7. Which of the following is an online site, requiring Windows 8 or higher, where you can download apps, games, software, and so forth?

    A. Windows Store

    B. Windows Transfer

    C. Windows Anytime

    D. Windows Roller

8. Which of the following are controls that are available on the side of the screen and consist of Search, Share, Start, Devices, and Settings?

    A. Ornaments

    B. Sidecars

    C. Gestures

    D. Charms

9. PowerShell script files are based on which programming framework?

    A. API

    B. PHP

    C. .NET

    D. ASP

10. Windows 7 Ultimate can be upgraded to which versions of Windows 8? (Choose all that apply.)

    A. Enterprise

    B. Pro

    C. RT

    D. Core

11. Which tool can evaluate your current system and determine if it can be upgraded to Windows 8?

    A. Windows Compatibility Advisor

    B. Windows Upgrade Wizard

    C. Windows Administrative Tools

    D. Windows Upgrade Assistant

12. Which tool from Microsoft simplifies the process of creating a Windows 8 image for upgrading multiple machines and reduces the time each install takes?

    A. MDT

    B. MAP

   C. MAB

   D. WVE

13. If Windows is installed on a system with multiple hard drives, what tool can be used to verify that images are pointing to their intended drives?

   A. GRUB

   B. LILO

   C. diskpart

   D. Sysprep

14. Which of the following was created to allow Windows 8 to boot from flash drives?

   A. BitLocker

   B. Windows To Go

   C. OneDrive

   D. Load2Go

15. You are installing Windows 8 on a solid-state drive (SSD). Which of the following can be used to reduce the number of write operations Windows makes and thus optimize Windows for the SSD?

   A. MSD tiny

   B. diskpart ssd

   C. WinSAT formal

   D. MCAT now

16. Which partition is the one that contains the hardware-specific files needed to load Windows?

   A. Recovery

   B. Data

   C. Windows

   D. System

17. Which versions of Windows 8 include Windows To Go? (Choose all that apply.)

   A. Enterprise

   B. Pro

   C. RT

   D. Core

18. Which repair option keeps personal files and settings along with the default apps and those that you installed from the Windows Store?

   A. Reset

   B. Restore

    C. Refresh

    D. Replace

19. How many characters are in a Windows 8 product key?

    A. 25

    B. 32

    C. 64

    D. 128

20. In a drive path, what does the system partition usually appear as?

    A. A

    B. H

    C. 1

    D. 0

Performance-Based Question

You will encounter performance-based questions on the A+ exams. The questions on the exam require you to perform a specific task, and you will be graded on whether or not you were able to complete the task. The following requires you to think creatively in order to measure how well you understand this chapter's topics. You may or may not see similar questions on the actual A+ exams. To see how your answers compare to the authors', refer to Appendix B.

You have been assigned to write a PowerShell script that will find other scripts in a user profile directory and all of its subdirectories. Which PowerShell variable should you use since %UserProfile% is an environment variable and will not run in PowerShell?

Chapter 16

Working with Windows 7

THE FOLLOWING COMPTIA A+ 220-902 EXAM OBJECTIVES ARE COVERED IN THIS CHAPTER:

✓ **1.1 Compare and contrast various features and requirements of Microsoft Operating Systems (Windows 7).**

- Features: 32-bit vs. 64-bit; Aero, gadgets, user account control, bit-locker, shadow copy, system restore, ready boost, compatibility mode, easy transfer, administrative tools, defender, Windows firewall, Action Center

- Upgrade paths – differences between in place upgrades, compatibility tools, Windows upgrade OS advisor

✓ **1.2 Given a scenario, install Windows PC operating systems using appropriate methods.**

- Boot methods: USB, CD-ROM, DVD, PXE

- Types of installations: Upgrade, Clean install, Image deployment

✓ **1.4 Given a scenario, use appropriate Microsoft operating system features and tools.**

- Administrative: Local Users and groups, Local security policy, System configuration, Component services, Data sources, Print management, Windows memory diagnostics, Windows firewall, Advanced security

- Other: User State Migration Tool (USMT), Windows Easy Transfer

✓ **1.5 Given a scenario, use Windows Control Panel utilities.**

- HomeGroup

✓ **1.6 Given a scenario, install and configure Windows networking on a client/desktop.**

- HomeGroup vs. WorkGroup

- Network shares/administrative shares/mapping drives

- Printer sharing vs. network printer mapping

- Establish network connections: VPN, Dialups, Wireless, Wired, WWAN (Cellular)

- Proxy settings

- Remote Desktop Connection

- Home vs. Work vs. Public network settings

- Firewall settings: Exceptions, Configuration, Enabling/disabling Windows firewall

- Configuring an alternate IP address in Windows: IP addressing, Subnet mask, DNS, Gateway

- Network card properties: Half duplex/full duplex/auto, Speed, Wake-on-LAN, QoS, BIOS (on-board NIC)

In the previous three chapters, we looked at operating systems in general and then focused on Windows 8/8.1. This chapter focuses on Windows 7 exclusively: the second of the three operating systems that you need to know well for the 220-902 exam.

Some of the tools covered in this chapter have been touched on in previous chapters, but care has been taken to avoid redundancy whenever possible. Be certain that you know the specifics of Windows 7 and the differences in how this operating system stands out from its predecessors.

Windows 7 Editions

Windows 7 was released in six different editions, only three of which were made available in the retail channel: Windows 7 Home Premium, Windows 7 Professional, and Windows 7 Ultimate. In addition to these, there is also Windows 7 Enterprise, which offers the same features as Ultimate (more than Professional), and it is licensed with a Software Assurance contract and not available in the retail channel. Windows 7 Starter was created for OEMs to install on netbooks. The sixth edition, Windows 7 Home Basic, was marketed only in emerging technology countries.

Table 16.1 lists the five domestic editions of Windows 7 for feature comparison purposes.

TABLE 16.1   Windows 7 features and editions

Edition	Maximum RAM Supported	Maximum Physical CPUs Supported (Multiple Cores)	Notes
Starter	2GB (x86)	1	Lacks support for Aero, cannot join a Windows Server domain, no parental controls, Remote Desktop client only, can join HomeGroup but not create
Home Premium	16GB	1	Includes support for multitouch, cannot join a Windows Server domain, Remote Desktop client only, can join or create HomeGroup

TABLE 16.1   Windows 7 features and editions *(continued)*

Edition	Maximum RAM Supported	Maximum Physical CPUs Supported (Multiple Cores)	Notes
Professional	192GB	2	Can join a Windows server domain, includes Remote Desktop Server, includes EFS, includes Windows XP Mode, can create HomeGroup if not domain joined, supports offline files/folders and Group Policy
Enterprise	192GB	2	Includes BitLocker, not available in retail or OEM channels (volume licensing only), includes Multilingual User Interface (MUI), can create HomeGroup if not domain joined, supports offline files/folders and Group Policy
Ultimate	192GB	2	Includes BitLocker, available in retail and OEM channels, includes MUI, can create HomeGroup if not domain joined, supports offline files/folders and Group Policy. Functionally identical to Enterprise.

There are 32-bit and 64-bit versions available for each of the editions listed except Starter. Except where indicated, the RAM support in the table is for the 64-bit versions. As a successor to Windows Vista, Microsoft released Windows 7 with the key goals of overcoming the sluggishness in Vista as well as the incompatibilities with applications written for previous versions.

There are some features of the operating system that are available, or not available, only as certain conditions exist. For example, Parental Controls ceases to be available if the workstation is part of a domain.

Table 16.2 lists a number of features associated with the Windows 7 operating system that CompTIA wants you to know for the exam, along with a brief description of each.

If you don't know what edition of Windows 7 is running on a particular machine, you can click Start and type **winver** in the search box. The screen that is returned will identify the edition as well as the service pack installed. Figure 16.1 shows an example of this screen.

FIGURE 16.1   The Winver dialog box shows the current operating system and service pack.

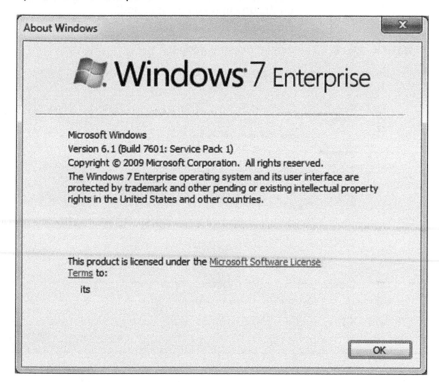

TABLE 16.2   Windows 7 features

Feature	Significance
Aero	The Aero interface offers a "glass" design that includes translucent windows. It was new with Windows Vista and is available in every edition of Windows 7 except Starter.

TABLE 16.2 Windows 7 features *(continued)*

Feature	Significance
Gadgets	These are mini programs, introduced with Windows Vista, which can be placed on the Desktop, allowing them to run quickly and personalize the PC (clock, weather, and so on). Windows 7 renamed these Windows Desktop Gadgets (right-click on the Desktop, click Gadgets in the context menu, and then double-click on the one that you want to add). Figure 16.2 shows an example of the gadgets.

FIGURE 16.2 The default desktop gadgets.

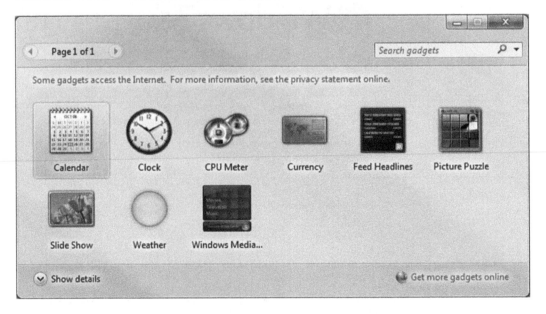

Sidebar	Windows Vista had an area known as the Sidebar that was designed for gadgets and could be placed on the Desktop. Windows 7 did away with the Sidebar, and the gadgets are now placed directly on the Desktop. Interestingly enough, though, SIDEBAR .EXE is the program that runs if any gadgets are running.
User Account Control	The UAC is intended to prevent unintentional/unauthorized changes to the computer either by prompting for permission to continue or requiring the administrator password before continuing. Changes to this from Windows Vista allow for more granular control over how UAC intercedes.

Feature	Significance
BitLocker	BitLocker allows you to use drive encryption to protect files, including those needed for startup and logon. This is available only with Windows 7 in the Enterprise and Ultimate editions and is shown in Figure 16.3.

FIGURE 16.3   Windows BitLocker can encrypt files and folders.

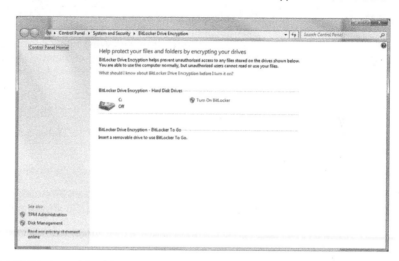

For removable drives, BitLocker To Go provides the same encryption technology to help prevent unauthorized access to the files stored on them.

Feature	Significance
Shadow Copy	The Volume Shadow Copy Service creates copies from which you can recover should a file be accidentally deleted or overwritten. Windows 7 adds to Vista by including an interface for configuring storage used by volume shadow copies. The Properties dialog box for a file contains a Previous Versions tab that can be used to return to another version of the file.
ReadyBoost	This feature allows you to use free space on a removable drive to speed up a system by caching content. In Windows 7, it can work with a USB drive, flash memory, SD card, or CompactFlash drive. Up to eight devices can employ ReadyBoost in Windows 7 (each needing a minimum of 256MB of free space). ReadyBoost is configured from the ReadyBoost tab of the Properties for the removable media device.

TABLE 16.2 Windows 7 features *(continued)*

Feature	Significance
Compatibility Mode	Program Compatibility is included with Windows 7 to configure programs to believe that they are running with an older version of Windows: Choose Start ➤ Control Panel ➤ Programs, and then click Run Programs Made For Previous Versions of Windows.
XP Mode	The ability to run applications in Windows XP Mode (XPM) is included with Windows 7 Professional, Enterprise, and Ultimate. This is a virtual client (emulating Windows XP Professional with Service Pack 3), and you must download and install Windows Virtual PC to use it. This can be downloaded from the Windows Virtual PC site at: `http://windows.microsoft.com/en-US/windows7/install-and-use-windows-xp-mode-in-windows-7` You should have 2GB RAM and 15GB hard drive space for each virtual Windows instance.
Windows Defender	Windows 7 includes the Windows Defender antispyware program.
Windows Firewall	Windows 7 incorporates Windows Firewall, which can be used to stop incoming and outgoing traffic. There are only three basic settings: On, Off, and Block All Incoming Connections.

While most of the items in Table 16.2 are specifically listed in the objectives, you should also know these other key features of Windows 7:

Jump lists   This is a quick way to access files that you've been working on through their association with the application that has been using them. Right-click on the application and a list of current files appears.

Pinning to the Taskbar   The context menu for each application allows you to choose whether you want to pin (add) it to the Taskbar or remove it if it is already there.

Windows Taskbar   This has been redesigned to include thumbnail previews.

Snap   Also known as Aero Snap, this is a quick way to resize windows on the Desktop and work with side-by-side apps. Windows will remember sizes and locations of the apps and allow you to work with them much simpler than was possible in the past, allowing for true side-by-side multitasking.

HomeGroup   This is a simplified way to set up a home network. It allows you to share files and prevent changes from being made to those files by those sharing them (unless you give them permission to do so).

Windows Search   Instantly find anything on your PC as soon as you start typing into the search box.

Upgrades have been discussed in Chapter 13 and are covered in this, and the next two chapters as well. As you read, make sure you know the differences between three items for the exam:

In place upgrades: this is when the upgrade is done without removing the existing operating system (the opposite is a clean install)

Compatibility tools: These are used to keep legacy applications thinking they are running on a previous version of the operating system after you've upgraded

Windows upgrade OS advisor: These are Microsoft utilities, either called Upgrade Advisor (Windows 7) or Upgrade Assistant (Windows 8/8.1) that check your current configuration and report what you need to take into account (update, abandon, etc.) before upgrading to a newer OS.

Windows Touch   This feature adds touchscreen functionality to the operating system, allowing you to make selections without using a keyboard or mouse.

Libraries   You can logically (as opposed to physically) group files and folders that are not in the same location and make them appear as if they are. For example, suppose that you have to rewrite four chapters of a book. There can be one chapter stored in a folder beneath C:\BOOK, another beneath C:\REWRITES, and images beneath C:\USERS\PUBLIC\PICTURES, and all can be grouped into a library so that when you open C:\A_PLUS, all of the entities appear to be beneath it.

 Real World Scenario

ReadyBoost or ReadyDrive?

In addition to ReadyBoost, Windows offers a similar technology: ReadyDrive. You are not required to know about ReadyDrive for the exam, but it's a feature worth knowing about. Included with Windows Vista as well as Windows 7, ReadyDrive is the acceleration technology used with hybrid hard disk drives (H-HDD) that combines flash drives and mobile PC hard drives for better performance and battery life.

There have been problems with ReadyDrive. For example, when the first partition is small, the hybrid drive is not recognized.

When the technology works, the results are nothing short of impressive. When it does not work, however, its absence can be noticeable.

Installing Windows 7

Like every operating system, Windows 7 requires more (newer, better, and so forth) hardware than the previous version. If you are planning to install Windows 7 on an older machine, you will want to verify that you can do so before you start. Make sure that the hardware on which you plan to install Windows 7 can support the OS.

Checking Hardware Compatibility

The easiest way to see if your current hardware can run Windows 7 is to download and run the Windows 7 Upgrade Advisor, available at:

http://windows.microsoft.com/en-US/windows/downloads/upgrade-advisor

You can also always check hardware in the Windows 7 Compatibility Center at:

https://www.microsoft.com/en-us/windows/compatibility/compatcenter/home

---

If you are installing an operating system on more than one computer, it is always worth the effort to master an automated tool that can simplify this process. In the case of Windows 7, Microsoft has released the Microsoft Assessment and Planning (MAP) Toolkit, which can be downloaded from the Microsoft Download Center (www.microsoft.com/downloads). Using this tool, you can get an inventory of computers on your network and plan a rollout of this operating system. The current version of MAP (9.2) requires a dual core 1.5Hz or faster processor, 2GB of RAM, 1GB of free hard drive space, a network adapter card, and a graphics adapter that supports 1024×768 or higher resolution.

Windows 7 can be installed as an upgrade or a clean installation, which is accomplished with the Custom option (think custom = clean). When you choose Custom, you can choose whether or not to format the hard disk. If you choose not to format the hard disk, the old operating system is placed in a folder called WINDOWS.OLD; if you choose to format, the Custom option will erase your files, programs, and settings. On a standard, default installation, the \BOOT directory holds the boot file configuration for Windows.

The installation can be started from an installation disc or from a download (preferably to a USB drive). If the installation does not begin immediately on boot-up, look for the SETUP.EXE file and run it. When the Install Windows page appears, click Install Now.

You'll be asked if you want to get any updates (recommended) and to accept the license agreement. After you've done so, choose Custom (advanced) for the installation type and specify where you want to install Windows (C: is the most common). Follow the steps to walk through the remainder of the installation. It is highly recommended that after the installation is complete, you run Windows Update to get the latest system updates and drivers.

You will need to activate Windows 7. Activation is required, but registration is not. You have 30 days in which to do the activation or Windows 7 will stop working. All that you truly need to complete the process is the product key.

Upgrading to Windows 7

If you want to do an upgrade instead of a clean installation, then review the upgrade options in Table 16.3 (it is worth noting that a "No" does not mean that you can't buy the upgrade version of Windows 7 but rather that you can't keep your files, programs, and settings).

TABLE 16.3   Windows 7 upgrade options

Existing Operating System	Windows 7 Home Premium 32-bit	Windows 7 Home Premium 64-bit	Windows 7 Professional 32-bit	Windows 7 Professional 64-bit	Windows 7 Ultimate 32-bit	Windows 7 Ultimate 64-bit
Windows XP	No	No	No	No	No	No
Windows Vista Starter 32-bit	No	No	No	No	No	No
Windows Vista Starter 64-bit	No	No	No	No	No	No
Windows Vista Home Basic 32-bit	Yes	No	No	No	Yes	No
Windows Vista Home Basic 64-bit	No	Yes	No	No	No	Yes
Windows Vista Home Premium 32-bit	Yes	No	No	No	Yes	No
Windows Vista Home Premium 64-bit	No	Yes	No	No	No	Yes
Windows Vista Business 32-bit	No	No	Yes	No	Yes	No
Windows Vista Business 64-bit	No	No	No	Yes	No	Yes
Windows Vista Ultimate 32-bit	No	No	No	No	Yes	No
Windows Vista Ultimate 64-bit	No	No	No	No	No	Yes

There are additional versions of Windows Vista that are not shown in Table 16.3 because they do not offer an upgrade to Windows 7; that is, you must buy the full version of Windows 7. It should be noted that an easy way to remember the upgrade options for the exam is that you must have at least Windows Vista in order to be able to upgrade to Windows 7. In the real world, the Windows Vista machine should be running Service Pack 1 at a minimum, and you can always take an earlier OS and upgrade it to Vista SP1 and then upgrade to Windows 7.

Is the Operating System Current?

As of this writing, Service Pack 1 is the latest available service pack for Windows 7, Service Pack 2 is the latest available for Windows Vista, and Windows 8.1 is the latest update available for Windows 8. You can find the latest service packs at:

http://windows.microsoft.com/en-US/windows/downloads/service-packs

In the past, all service packs had been cumulative, meaning that you needed to load only the last one. Starting with XP SP3, however, all Windows service packs released have been incremental, meaning that you must install the previous one(s) before you can install the new one.

Microsoft created the Windows 7 Upgrade Advisor to help with the upgrade to this operating system. You can download the advisor from www.microsoft.com/downloads. It will scan your hardware, devices, and installed programs for any known compatibility issues. Once it is finished, it will give you advice on how to resolve the issues found and recommendations on what to do before you upgrade. The reports are divided into three categories: System Requirements, Devices, and Programs. Figure 16.4 shows the opening screen.

FIGURE 16.4   Run the Windows 7 Upgrade Advisor before beginning the upgrade of a machine.

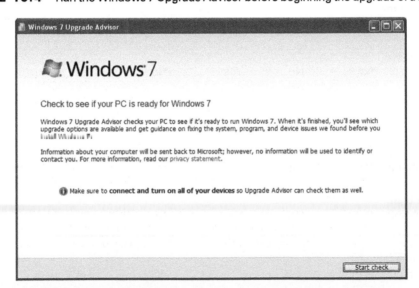

Figure 16.5 shows an example of a report generated by the Windows 7 Upgrade Advisor.

FIGURE 16.5   Incompatibilities are highlighted by the Windows 7 Upgrade Advisor.

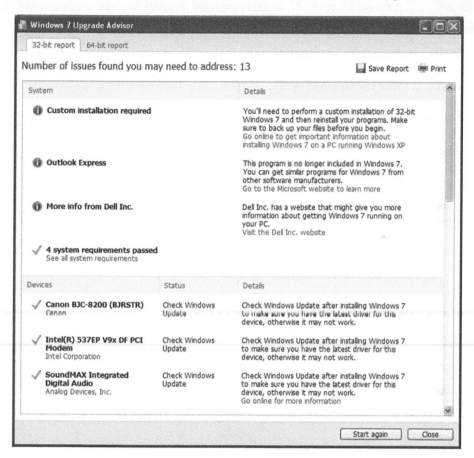

After all incompatibilities have been addressed, the upgrade can be started from an installation disc or from a download (preferably to a USB drive). If the setup routine does not begin immediately on boot, look for the SETUP.EXE file and run it. When the Install Windows page appears, click Install Now.

You'll be asked if you want to get any updates (recommended) and to accept the license agreement. After you've done so, choose Upgrade for the installation type and follow the steps to walk through the remainder of the installation. It is highly recommended that after the installation is complete, you run Windows Update to get the latest drivers.

Microsoft Windows User State Migration Tool (USMT) allows you to migrate user file settings related to the applications, Desktop configuration, and accounts. Version 4.0 works with Windows 7, but it is currently only available as part of the Windows Automated Installation Kit (WAIK). USMT 5.0 works with all of the migrations that CompTIA's exam covers, and more discussion of it can be found at the following location:

https://technet.microsoft.com/en-us/library/hh824913.aspx

Version 3.0 of USMT, which is not itself obsolete, worked with Windows Vista and XP, while previous versions, such as 2.6, also worked with Windows 2000.

If all you are doing is a simple migration from one OS to another, you do not need this tool, but it is invaluable during large deployments. Of course, you also don't need to use this tool if you chose the Upgrade option and are doing an in-place upgrade because user files and applications are preserved.

If you are migrating only a few accounts, Microsoft recommends Windows Easy Transfer (WET) instead of USMT. When you're transferring to Windows 7, a version of Windows Easy Transfer can be downloaded in either 32-bit or 64-bit versions for Windows Vista from www.microsoft.com/downloads.

Given a scenario, USMT would be used when you need to migrate a number of accounts and WET would be used if you're only transferring a few accounts. The Windows Upgrade Advisor, already mentioned in a few chapters by now, can check your current configuration and report what you need to take into account (update, abandon, etc.) before upgrading to a newer OS.

Upgrading Editions of Windows 7

Like Windows Vista, Windows 7 has the ability to upgrade at any time from one edition of the operating system to a higher one (for example, from Home Premium to Professional) using the Windows Anytime Upgrade utility in Control Panel (it can also be accessed by clicking the Start button and choosing All Programs. Scroll down the list and choose Windows Anytime Upgrade). Figure 16.6 shows the opening screen of this utility.

FIGURE 16.6   Change to a higher edition of Windows 7 using Windows Anytime Upgrade.

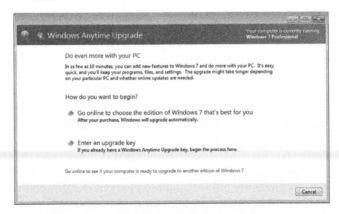

Installation/Upgrade Boot Options

You can begin the installation or upgrade process by booting from a number of sources. There are four in particular with which CompTIA wants you to be familiar: CD-ROM, DVD, USB, and PXE. The one most commonly used for an attended installation is the CD-ROM/DVD boot (they are identical). Because Windows 7 only comes on DVD, though, the CD-ROM option applies to older operating systems and not this one. You can boot a PC over the network (rather than from a DVD, USB, or hard disk) with Windows Preinstallation Environment (WinPE), which is a stub operating system that creates a *Pre-boot Execution Environment (PXE)*.

WinPE can be installed onto a bootable CD, USB, or network drive using the COPYPE .CMD command. This can be used in conjunction with a Windows deployment from a server for unattended installations and also to host the Windows Recovery Environment (WinRE).

As was discussed with other operating systems, you want to make certain that you use the latest driver software and Windows updates that are applicable for the operating system you are running. This can solve a great many problems with security holes as well as solve compatibility issues. Make certain, as well, that the boot drive is properly formatted and partitions are correct for your desired setup. Remember that a recovery partition, factory or otherwise, can be used to recover the operating system in the event of a failure.

The Windows 7 Boot Sequences

Both for the exam and for real life, you should know how to recognize common problems with the OS and make certain it is booting correctly. The sections that follow look at a number of topics related to keeping your OS booting and running properly.

Key Boot Files

Windows 7 requires only a few files, each of which performs specific tasks. These mirror the files required for Windows Vista and differ significantly from the files required for previous Windows operating systems. They are discussed next in the order in which they load:

BOOTMGR   The Windows Boot Manager (BOOTMGR) bootstraps the system. In other words, this file starts the loading of an OS on the computer.

BCD   The Boot Configuration Data (BCD) holds information about OSs installed on the computer, such as the location of the OS files.

WINLOAD.EXE   The program used to boot Windows 7. It loads the operating system kernel (NTOSKRNL.EXE).

WINRESUME.EXE   If the system is not starting fresh but resuming a previous session, then WINRESUME.EXE is called by the BOOTMGR.

NTOSKRNL.EXE   The Windows OS kernel.

System files   In addition to the previously listed files, Windows needs a number of files from its system directories (for example, SYSTEM and SYSTEM32), such as the hardware abstraction layer (HAL.DLL), session manager (SMSS.EXE), user session (WINLOGON.EXE), and security subsystem (LSASS.EXE).

Windows 7 Features

There are a number of features that make Windows 7 notable. In the following sections, we will look first at some of the tools and focus on the ones that you need to know for the A+ exam.

Tools in Windows 7

The tools that stand out in Windows 7, and that CompTIA expects you to know for the exam, include System Restore, Windows Defender, Windows Firewall, and Action Center. Each of these are discussed in the sections that follow.

System Restore

Chapter 13, "Operating System Basics," explored System Restore as it appears in all three versions of Windows. It allows you to restore the system to a previous point in time. This feature is accessed from Start ➢ All Programs ➢ Accessories ➢ System Tools ➢ System Restore, and it can be used to roll back as well as to create a restore point. Figure 16.7 shows the opening dialog box.

FIGURE 16.7   System Restore in Windows 7

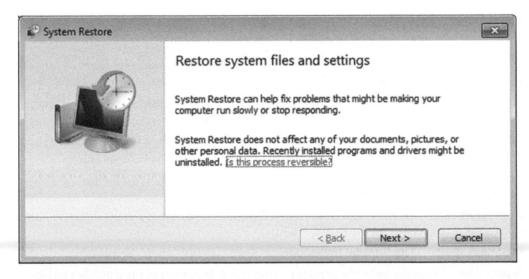

After clicking Next, pick a restore point to return to, as shown in Figure 16.8.

FIGURE 16.8   Choosing a restore point in Windows 7

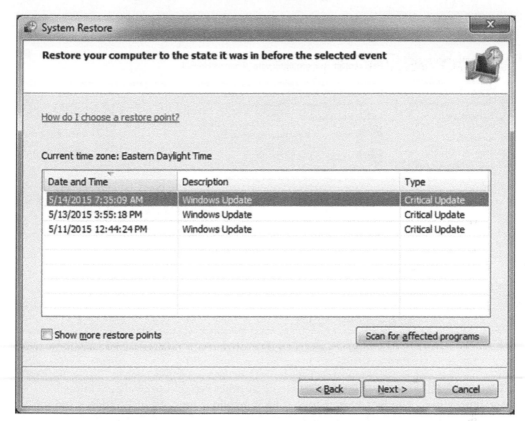

Windows Defender

Windows Defender can identify spyware, and it is included with all versions of Windows 7 (with small/large icons, choose Start ➤ Control Panel ➤ Windows Defender). As with similar programs, for Windows Defender to function properly, you need to keep the definitions current and scan on a regular basis.

Windows Firewall

Windows Firewall (with small/large icons, choose Start ➤ Control Panel ➤ Windows Firewall) is used to block access from the network, and in Windows 7, it is divided into separate settings for private networks and public networks as well as domain networks if you're connected to a domain (see Figure 16.9). If you are using Category view (instead of small/large icons), you have to click System and Security before getting to the Firewall.

FIGURE 16.9 Windows Firewall in Windows 7

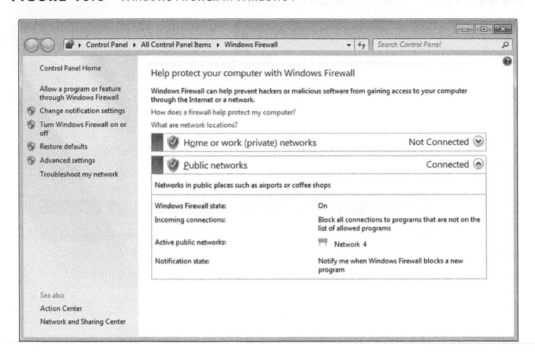

While host-based firewalls are not as secure as other types of firewalls, Windows Firewall provides much better protection than in previous versions of Windows and it is turned on by default. It is also included in the Security component of the Action Center (discussed in the next section) and can be tweaked significantly using the advanced settings. Once you click Advanced Settings, *Windows Firewall with Advanced Security* opens (see Figure 16.10).

Here you can configure inbound and outbound rules as well as import and export policies and monitor the security of your system. Monitoring is not confined to the firewall; you can also monitor security associations and connection security rules. In short, Windows Firewall with Advanced Security is an incredibly powerful tool that builds upon what Windows Vista started. Not only can this MMC snap-in do simple configuration, but it can also configure remote computers and work with Group Policy.

Firewall logging is not on by default in Windows 7. In Exercise 16.1, we will look at the firewall log settings in Windows 7 and turn them on.

FIGURE 16.10   Windows Firewall with Advanced Security in Windows 7

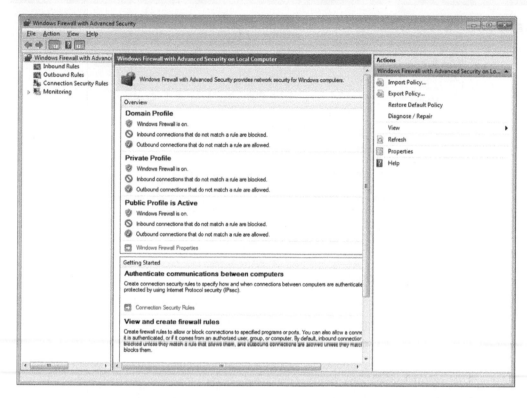

EXERCISE 16.1

Turning On Windows 7 Firewall Logs

1. From the Start menu, choose Control Panel ➢ System And Security ➢ Windows Firewall.

2. Click Advanced Settings.

3. Right-click Windows Firewall With Advanced Security On Local Computer and choose Properties under Actions on the right side.

4. Click Customize beneath Logging to open the Customize Logging Settings For The Domain Profile dialog box, as shown in Figure 16.11. Note that unless your computer is connected to a domain, the logging option will have no effect.

FIGURE 16.11 Windows Firewall custom logging options

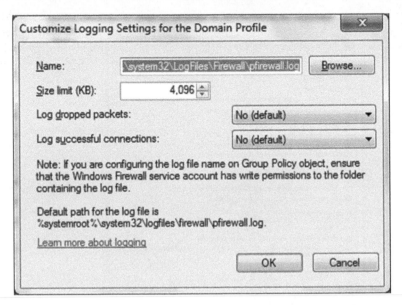

5. Change the setting for Log Dropped Packets to Yes; this will log information about why and when a packet was dropped. Note that you can also elect to change the setting on Log Successful Connections, but that can create quite a few more entries, and you'll need to check the log files more often; it logs why and when a connection was allowed.

6. Change Size Limit from the default of 4,096KB to 8,192KB. Note that this value is limited to sizes between 1KB and 32,767KB.

7. Click OK. As they occur, Events can now be found in Event Viewer beneath Applications And Services Logs (choose Microsoft, then Windows, and then choose Windows Firewall With Advanced Security).

Exceptions

Exceptions are configured as variations from the rules. Windows Firewall will block incoming network connections except for the programs and services that you choose to allow through. For example, you can make an exception for Remote Assistance to allow communication from other computers when you need help (the scope of the exception can be set to allow any computer, only those on the network, or computers from a custom list of allowed addresses that you create). Exceptions can include programs as well as individual ports.

Configuration

Most of the configuration is done as network connection settings. You can configure both ICMP and Services settings. Examples of ICMP settings include allowing incoming echo requests, allowing incoming router requests and redirects. Examples of services often configured include FTP Server, Post Office Protocol Version 3 (POP3), and Web Server (HTTP).

Enabling/Disabling Windows Firewall

In Windows 7, clicking Turn Windows Firewall on or off gives you control over the firewall for each location. While it is possible to choose to turn it off, it is not recommended: as the name implies, this turns Windows Firewall completely off. You can also toggle to block all incoming connections and to be notified when Windows Firewall blocks a new program.

Action Center

What was previously known as the Security Center has been modified in Windows 7 to become the Action Center (Start ➤ Control Panel ➤ Action Center). This interface (shown in Figure 16.12) still includes security, but it has been expanded to include such maintenance issues as problem reports and backup settings.

FIGURE 16.12   Action Center in Windows 7

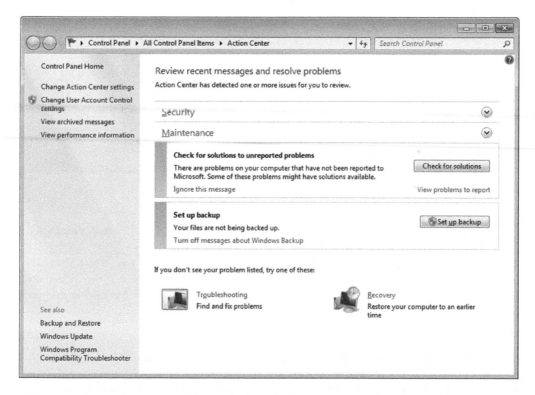

The Security settings show the status of, and allow you to configure, the firewall, Windows Update, virus protection, spyware and unwanted software protection, Internet security settings, UAC, and network access protection. The solutions portion of Maintenance rolls in the problem reporting features from earlier versions of Windows. In Windows 7, there are four options for error reporting settings that can be chosen:

- Automatically check for solutions (recommended)
- Automatically check for solutions and send additional data, if needed
- Each time a problem occurs, ask me before checking for solutions
- Never check for solutions (not recommended)

The setting that you want can be configured in Problem Report Settings (under Maintenance, click Settings). The administrator may choose to set one universal setting for the machine (not the default) or allow each user to make their own setting (the default), as shown in Figure 16.13.

FIGURE 16.13   Configuring Windows error reporting options in Windows 7

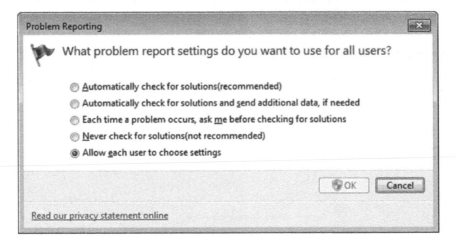

Windows 7 Administrative Tools

There are a number of system tools included with Windows 7 that you need to know for the exam. These administrative tools, discussed in the order they appear in the objectives, also include Windows Firewall and Advanced Security, previously covered in this chapter.

Local Users and Groups

You can use Computer Management to access Users and Groups. As an administrator, you can also configure the users and groups on a system in the Microsoft Management Console (MMC). Click Start, type **MMC** in the Search box, and press Enter. If Local Users And Groups is not visible in the left pane, choose File ➢ Add/Remove Snap-in, and then select Local Users And Groups from the list of possible snap-ins and click Add (or double-click on it). You can choose to manage the local computer or another computer (requiring you to provide its address). Figure 16.14 shows the default groups and explanations for each. The built-in groups for a domain are a superset of this set.

FIGURE 16.14   Default groups in Windows 7

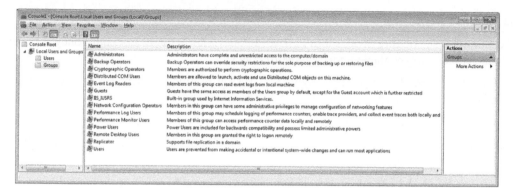

Local Users And Groups is not available for Windows 7 editions lower than Professional. In all other editions, you must manage user accounts using the User Accounts applet in Control Panel, and you cannot create or manage groups. The default users created are Administrator, Guest, and the administrative account created during the install.

Local Security Policy

Local Security Policy (choose Start ➤ Run and then enter **secpol.msc**) allows you to set the default security settings for the system. This feature is not available for Windows 7 in any editions other than Windows 7 Professional, Windows 7 Ultimate, and Windows 7 Enterprise. Figure 16.15 shows the utility. A scenario in which you would use this tool is when you want to change the default system settings for many security-related features hidden deep within the Registry.

FIGURE 16.15   Local Security Policy in Windows 7

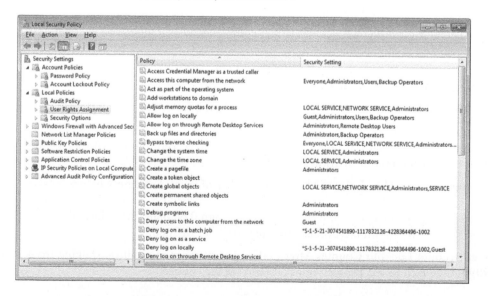

The following sections examine some of the Security Settings choices.

Account Policies

Account Policies further divides into Password Policy and Account Lockout Policy. The following choices are available under Password Policy:

Enforce Password History   This allows you to require unique passwords for a certain number of iterations. The default number is 0, but it can go as high as 24.

Maximum Password Age   The default is 42 days, but values range from 0 to 999.

Minimum Password Age   The default is 0 days (the password can be changed immediately), but values range from 0 to 998.

Minimum Password Length   The default is 0 characters (meaning no passwords are required), but you can specify a number up to 14.

Password Must Meet Complexity Requirements   The default is disabled. When this is turned on, the password must include at least three of the following elements: uppercase characters, lowercase characters, numerical characters, nonalphanumeric characters, and Unicode characters.

Store Password Using Reversible Encryption   The default is disabled. When enabled, it provides support for applications that require knowledge of the password.

Because the likelihood of laptops being stolen always exists, it's strongly encouraged that you use good password policies for this audience and security locks. Here's an example:

- Enforce Password History: 8 passwords remembered
- Maximum Password Age: 42 days
- Minimum Password Age: 3 days
- Minimum Password Length: 6 to 8 characters

The default for domain machines is that complexity requirements be enabled. It is a good idea, and accepted practice, to do so.

Account Lockout Policy

The Account Lockout Policy setting is divided into the following three values:

Account Lockout Duration   This is a number of minutes ranging from 1 to 99999. A value of 0 is also allowed here, and it signifies that the account never unlocks itself—administrator interaction is always required.

Account Lockout Threshold   This is the number of invalid attempts before lockout occurs. The default is 0 (meaning that the feature is turned off). The settings for invalid attempts range from 1 to 999. A number greater than 0 changes the values of the two associated options to 30 minutes; otherwise, they are "not defined."

Reset Account Lockout Counter After   This is a number of minutes, ranging from 1 to 99999, that each failed login attempt remains on the counter.

When you're working with a mobile workforce, you must weigh the choice of users calling you in the middle of the night when they've forgotten their password against keeping the system from being entered if the wrong user picks up the laptop. A good recommendation for a medium to low security environment may be to use a lockout after five attempts for a period of time between 30 and 60 minutes.

Local Policies Settings

The Local Policies section is divided into three subsections:

Audit Policy   The Audit Policy section contains nine settings; the default value for each is No Auditing. Valid options are Success and/or Failure. The Audit Account Logon Events entry is the one you should consider turning on for mobile users to see how often they log in and out of their machines. When auditing is turned on for an event, the entries are logged in the Security log file.

User Rights Assignment   The User Rights Assignment subsection of Local Policies is where the meat of the old System Policies comes into play. User Rights Assignment has many options, most of which are self-explanatory. Not Defined indicates that no one is specified for this operation. You can add groups and users. If you want to "remove" users or groups from the list, use the Remove button to do so. The Power User group has no more rights than a standard user in Windows 7; the group has only been left to provide backward compatibility.

Security Options   The Security Options section includes a great many options, which for the most part are Registry keys. The default for each is usually Not Defined.

System Configuration

The System Configuration tool (MSCONFIG.EXE) in Windows 7 is unchanged from Windows Vista. The five tabs it offers are General, Boot, Services, Startup, and Tools. The tools, and the executables associated with them, are as follows:

About Windows: WINVER.EXE

Change UAC Settings: USERACCOUNTCONTROLSETTINGS.EXE

Action Center: WSCUI.CPL

Windows Troubleshooting: CONTROL.EXE /NAME MICROSOFT.TROUBLESHOOTING

Computer Management: COMPMGMT.MSC

System Information: MSINFO32.EXE

Event Viewer: EVENTVWR.EXE

Programs: APPWIZ.CPL

System Properties: CONTROL.EXE SYSTEM

Internet Options: INETCPL.CPL

Internet Protocol Configuration: IPCONFIG.EXE

Performance Monitor: PERFMON.EXE

Resource Monitor: RESMON.EXE

Task Manager: TASKMGR.EXE

Command Prompt: CMD.EXE

Registry Editor: REGEDT32.EXE

Remote Assistance: MSRA.EXE

System Restore: RSTRUI.EXE

Each of these should be considered troubleshooting utilities that you can use to solve system problems. Know what they do and the executable associated with each to solve the majority of problems that you will encounter when working with Windows 7.

Component Services

Component Services is an MMC snap-in in Windows 7 that allows you to administer, as well as deploy, component services and configure behavior like security. Figure 16.16 shows an example of the interface (Start ➤ Control Panel ➤ Administrative Tools ➤ Component Services).

FIGURE 16.16   Component Services in Windows 7

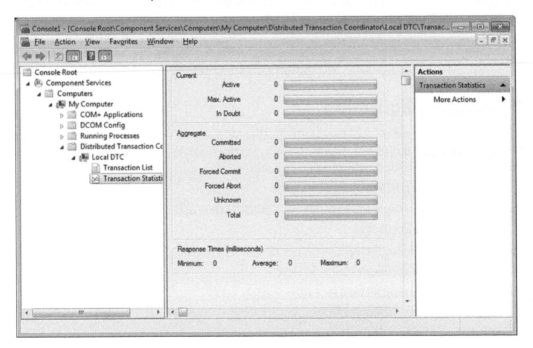

Data Sources

ODBC Data Source Administrator—Start ➤ Control Panel ➤ Administrative Tools ➤ Data Sources (ODBC)—allows you to interact with database management systems. Figure 16.17 shows an example of the screen.

FIGURE 16.17   Data Sources in Windows 7

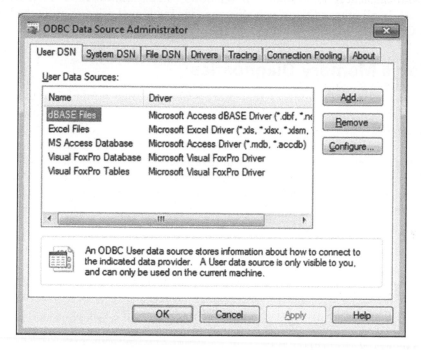

Database drivers that are added to the system will show up here and can be shared between applications.

Print Management

Carrying over from Windows Vista, Print Management (Start ➤ Control Panel ➤ Administrative Tools ➤ Print Management) allows you to manage multiple printers and print servers from a single interface (see Figure 16.18).

FIGURE 16.18   Print Management in Windows 7

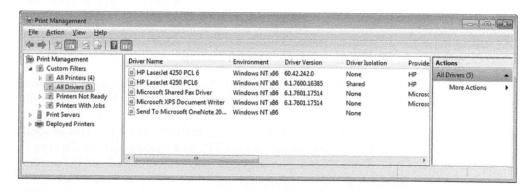

Print Management is not available for Windows 7 in any edition lower than Windows 7 Professional. In all other editions, you must manage individual printers using the Printers applet in Control Panel, and you are very limited in what you can manage.

Windows Memory Diagnostics

The Windows Memory Diagnostics Tool (Start ➤ Control Panel ➤ Administrative Tools ➤ Windows Memory Diagnostics) can be used to check a system for memory problems. For the tool to work, the system must be restarted. The two options that it offers are to restart the computer now and check for problems or to wait and check for problems on the next restart.

When the computer reboots, the test will take several minutes and the display screen will show which pass number is being run and the overall status of the test (percent complete). When the memory test concludes, the system will restart again and nothing related to it is apparent until you log in. If the test is without error, you'll see a message that no errors were found. If any issues have been detected, the results will be displayed.

Unique Control Panel Utilities

There are four Control Panel applets unique to Windows 7 of which you should be aware. One of these, Action Center, was addressed earlier in this chapter. The other three are discussed here and include HomeGroup, RemoteApp And Desktop Connections, and Troubleshooting.

HomeGroup

The purpose behind HomeGroup (Start ➤ Control Panel ➤ HomeGroup) is to simplify home networking and, more specifically, the sharing of files and printers. Windows 7 Starter can only join a HomeGroup, while all other editions of Windows 7 can both join and create a HomeGroup. The location from which you network must be set to Home.

Shared files can include libraries (a big feature of Windows 7). All computers participating in the HomeGroup must be running Windows 7 or Windows 8/8.1 (but not Vista), and the network cannot extend outside of the small group.

RemoteApp and Desktop Connections

This applet (Start ➤ Control Panel ➤ RemoteApp And Desktop Connections) in Windows 7 is used, as the name implies, to access remote computers and virtual machines made available over the network through port 3389 can run a remote application as if it were installed on the local machine. RemoteApp can be used directly to the host, and it can also be used through Remote Desktop Web Access, which uses HTTPS as a transport at the client end. The applications and virtual machines are hosted on Windows 2008 and 2008 R2 servers.

For the exam, remember that all versions of Windows 7 support outgoing connections but only Professional, Enterprise, and Ultimate can be used for hosting. To enable a remote connection, click Start, right-click Computer, click Properties, and then choose Remote Settings. You can now turn on Remote Assistance and/or Remote Desktop.

Remote Assistance is either on or off, while Remote Desktop offers three options:

- Don't allow connections to this computer
- Allow connections from computers running any version of Remote Desktop (less secure)
- Allow connections only from computers running Remote Desktop with Network Level Authentication (more secure)

Troubleshooting

This applet (Start ➢ Control Panel ➢ Troubleshooting) in Windows 7 is used, as the name implies, to provide a simple interface to use to attack many common problems. Figure 16.19 shows the opening screen.

FIGURE 16.19   The Troubleshooting applet in Windows 7

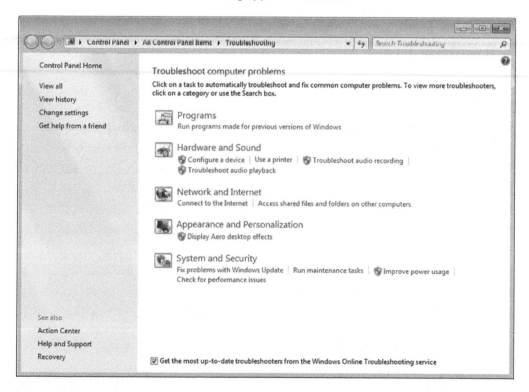

All links preceded by a shield require administrator permissions to run, and they are often tied to UAC prompts before they will continue. Most of the problems found will be "automatically fixed" without any prompts. For example, clicking the link Improve Power Usage on the machine shown in Figure 16.19 started the Power troubleshooter, which then fixed problems. Clicking to see the detailed report of what was done brings up the screen shown in Figure 16.20.

FIGURE 16.20   Report of the Power troubleshooter's changes

Note in Figure 16.17 the link Get Help From A Friend. Selecting this brings up Remote Assistance, allowing someone to connect to this computer. You can also offer to be the one helping another, as shown in Figure 16.21.

FIGURE 16.21   Windows Remote Assistance in Windows 7

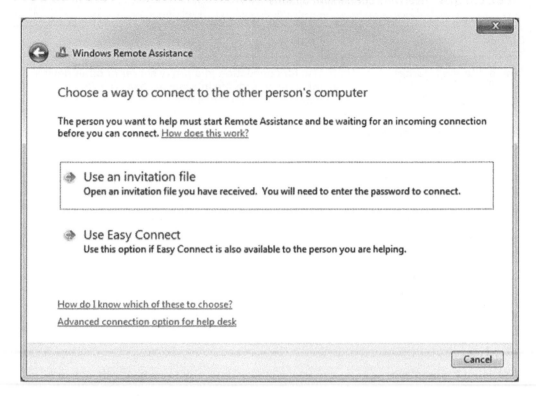

Networking and Windows 7

There are a number of things CompTIA expects you to know when it comes to the topic of networking and Windows 7. Most of the networking topics are covered in the chapters dedicated to that, and thus the discussion here is limited only to those topics specifically tied to Windows 7.

Connection option choices are shown in Table 16.4.

TABLE 16.4   Network connection options

Option	Purpose
Connect to the Internet	Use for connection to a proxy server or other device intended to provide Internet access. This includes wireless, broadband, and dial-up.
Set up a wireless router or access point	If the wireless device will be connected to this machine, this is the option to use.
Manually connect to a wireless network (this option is only visible if a wireless adapter is installed)	If you have a wireless network already in place and the device (router and so forth) is not directly connected to this machine, then use this option.
Set up a wireless ad hoc (computer-to-computer) network (this option is only visible if a wireless adapter is installed)	This is meant for peer-to-peer resource sharing, and it is typically a temporary connection.
Set up a dial-up connection	If you live in the middle of nowhere and the only way to access a network is by using a dial-up modem, then this is the option to select.
Connect to a workplace	If you need to connect to a virtual private network (VPN) from a remote location, this is the option to use.

A wireless wide area network (WWAN) connection is one that uses cellular to connect the host to the network. A wireless service provider (such as Verizon, AT&T, Sprint, or T-Mobile) will provide a card that is plugged into the host to make the cellular connection possible.

Regardless of which option you choose, you will need to fill out the appropriate fields for the device to be able to communicate on the network. With TCP/IP, required values are an IP address for the host, a subnet mask, an address for the gateway, and DNS information.

You also need to specify one of the types of locations for this network: Home, Work, or Public. If you choose one of the first two, *network discovery* is on by default, allowing you to see other computers and other computers to see you. If you choose Public, network discovery is turned off.

Configuring an Alternative IP Address in Windows

Windows 7, Windows Vista, and Windows 8/8.1 all allow the use of an alternate IP address. This is an address that is configured for the system to use in the event the first choice is not available. For an alternate configuration to be set, the first choice has to be dynamic—the tab becomes visible only when the General configuration is set to Obtain An IP Address Automatically, and the alternate is used only if the primary address cannot be found/used, such as when the DHCP server is down.

The Properties dialog box for each instance of IPv4, on any of the Windows operating systems on which this exam is focused, contains an Alternate Configuration tab. To make changes, you must click on it.

IP Addressing

Two radio buttons exist on the Alternate Configuration tab: Automatic Private IP Address and User Configured. The default is the first, meaning that the alternate address used is one in the APIPA range (169.254.*x.x*). Selecting User Configured requires you to enter a static IP address to be used in the IP Address field. The entry entered must be valid for your network in order for it to be usable.

Subnet Mask

When the User Configured radio button is chosen on the Alternate Configuration tab, you must enter a value in the Subnet mask field. This value must correspond with the subnet values in use on your network and work with the IP address you enter in the IP Address field.

DNS

When the User Configured radio button is chosen on the Alternate Configuration tab, you should enter values in the Preferred DNS Server and Alternate DNS Server fields. These entries are needed in order to translate domain names into IP addresses.

Gateway

When the User Configured radio button is chosen on the Alternate Configuration tab, you must enter a value in the Default Gateway field. This value must correspond with the subnet values and the IP address that you enter. This address identifies the router to be used to communicate outside the local network.

Network Card Properties

Like other devices, network cards can be configured to optimize performance. Configuration is done through the Properties dialog box for each card.

Half Duplex / Full Duplex / Auto

Duplexing is the means by which communication takes place:

- With full duplexing, everyone can send and receive at the same time. The main advantage of full-duplex over half-duplex communication is performance. NICs can operate twice as fast in full-duplex mode as they do normally in half-duplex mode.

- With half duplexing, communications travel in both directions but in only one direction at any given time. Think of a road where construction is being done on one lane—traffic can go in both directions but in only one direction at a time at that location.

- With auto duplexing, the mode is set to the lowest common denominator. If a card senses that another card is manually configured to half duplex, then it also sets itself to that.

Speed

You can configure whether the card should run at its highest possible setting or not. You often need to be compatible with the network on which the host resides. If, for example, you are connecting a workstation with a 10/100BaseT card to a legacy network, you will need to operate at 10MBps to match the rest of the network.

Wake-on-LAN

Wake on LAN (WoL) is an Ethernet standard implemented via a card that allows a "sleeping" machine to awaken when it receives a wakeup signal.

PoE

If the device that you are networking is in a remote location (such as a wireless access point in a ceiling or other place with no easy access to an electrical outlet), *Power over Ethernet (PoE)* is a handy technology to supply both power and an Ethernet connection. The purpose of Power over Ethernet (PoE) is pretty much described in its name: Electrical power is transmitted over twisted-pair Ethernet cable (along with data). A key advantage of PoE is that a UPS is required only in the main facility instead of at each device.

QoS

Quality of Service (QoS) implements packet scheduling to control the flow of traffic and help with network transmission speeds. No properties can be configured for the service itself.

Configuring Windows Networking

Given a scenario of configuring Windows networking on a client/desktop, many of the networking features and settings we've been discussing will apply. There are, however, a few more to be cognizant of:

HomeGroup vs. WorkGroup   As mentioned in Chapter 13, there are three types of networks to choose from: Workgroup, HomeGroup, and Domain. HomeGroups have been covered, but workgroups are those that utilize a peer-based model: there is no central controller and every computer has a set of user accounts. All computers are on the same subnet and there are typically very few computers (20 or less).

Domain Setup   As opposed to a HomeGroup or workgroup, with a domain one (or more) computer(s) act as a server and controls the security for the network. There can be many (think thousands) of computers on a domain and a user can access it from any machine as long as they have the credentials to do so whether or not they have an account on that individual workstation or not.

If you were to draw a line for network security, you would put a workgroup at one end and a domain at the other (with a HomeGroup as a hybrid between them). The type of security associated with a workgroup is share-level because it is based on the items on each computer that are shared. The type of security associated with a domain is user-level, requiring users to authenticate at the beginning of each session, and it is much more powerful than share-level.

Windows 7 System Performance and Optimization

Windows 7 went beyond Windows Vista in configurability, and it allows you to choose between four UAC settings:

- Always Notify

- Notify me only when programs try to make changes to my computer (the default)

- Notify me only when programs try to make changes to my computer (do not dim my desktop)

- Never Notify

To access the Change User Account Control settings, click Start ➤ Control Panel ➤ User Accounts ➤ Change User Account Control Settings. This opens the slider shown in Figure 16.22.

Encrypting File System (EFS) is available in the Professional, Enterprise, and Ultimate editions of Windows 7. It allows for the encryption/decryption of files stored in NTFS volumes. EFS can be used by all users (whereas BitLocker can be turned on only by administrators) and does not require any special hardware. While BitLocker benefits from the *Trusted Platform Module (TPM)*, it doesn't need it; it can also be operated using a USB key to store the encryption keys. Last, EFS can encrypt just one file, if so desired, while BitLocker encrypts the whole volume and whatever is stored on it. EFS can be used in conjunction with BitLocker to increase security further.

FIGURE 16.22   Changing UAC settings in Windows 7

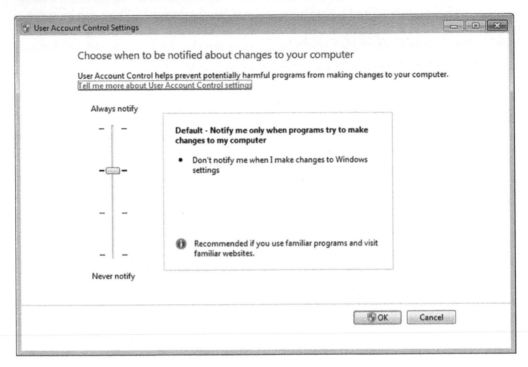

Given the appropriate scenario, there are many instances in which an administrator would want to access the User Accounts applet in the Control Panel (shown in Figure 16.23). Not to be confused with the similarly named User Account Control (UAC) settings that you can change from here, from this umbrella-like applet you can also change passwords, manage file encryption certificates and link online IDs.

FIGURE 16.23   The User Accounts applet in Windows 7

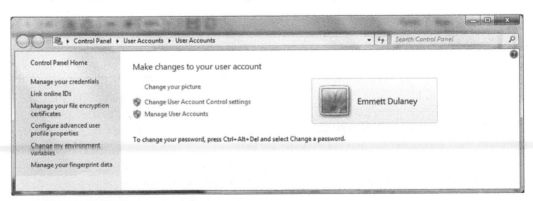

Given another scenario, it can be necessary to access the Programs and Features applet in the Control Panel (shown in Figure 16.24) to add or remove programs. From here, you can see update information, check out the version numbers of programs, the amount of space they are occupying, and run repairs.

FIGURE 16.24 The Programs and Features applet in Windows 7

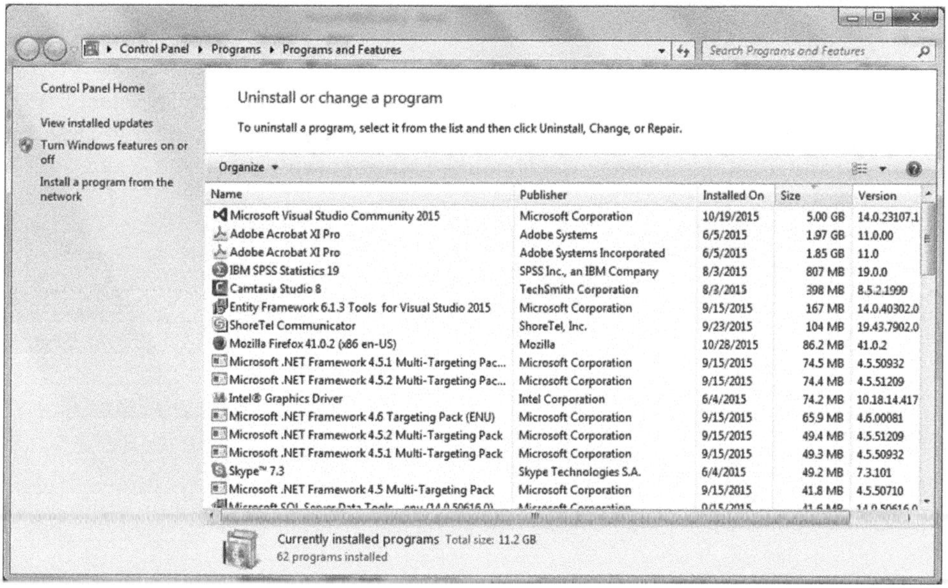

Summary

This chapter focused on Windows 7. This is one of the three Windows operating systems covered on the exam, and CompTIA expects you to be familiar with it and be able to answer questions on everything from installing it to managing it.

We looked at the various features of Windows 7, some that exist in other versions of Windows and some that are unique to this operating system. The latter category includes HomeGroup, Action Center, RemoteApp And Desktop Applications, and Troubleshooting.

Exam Essentials

Know what types of installations are possible with Windows 7.   You should know which operating systems can be upgraded to Windows 7 and which require a clean installation.

Understand upgrading.   You should know that a custom installation either wipes the old system or replaces the existing system, putting the old files into WINDOWS.OLD. Applications have to be reinstalled and user data has to be migrated from the old system using WET or USMT. An upgrade preserves the existing applications and the user data, moving them into the new system.

Know the editions of Windows 7.   Windows 7 Starter was created for netbooks. The retail channel options are Windows 7 Home Premium, Windows 7 Professional, and Windows 7 Ultimate. Windows 7 Enterprise is available only through volume licensing.

Know what Control Panel utilities are unique to Windows 7.   The Control Panel applets unique to Windows 7 are HomeGroup, Action Center, RemoteApp and Desktop Applications, and Troubleshooting. You should be familiar with the purpose and options of each.

Review Questions

The answers to the chapter review questions can be found in Appendix A.

1. Which editions of Windows 7 can create a HomeGroup? (Choose four.)
   A. Windows 7 Starter
   B. Windows 7 Home Premium
   C. Windows 7 Professional
   D. Windows 7 Enterprise
   E. Windows 7 Ultimate

2. What is the name of the file that runs if there are any gadgets placed on the Windows 7 Desktop?
   A. NTOS
   B. GADCONFIG
   C. GADGET
   D. SIDEBAR

3. Which of the following is used by BitLocker to be able to encrypt a drive?
   A. EFS
   B. TPM
   C. HPM
   D. Aero

4. Which feature of Windows 7 allows files and folders to be grouped logically and appear as if they are in the same location even when they are not?
   A. HomeGroup
   B. Touch
   C. Libraries
   D. Snap

5. As an administrator, you need to get an inventory of computers on your network and plan a rollout of Windows 7. Which tool can be used for this purpose?
   A. UDMT
   B. Microsoft Assessment and Planning (MAP) Toolkit
   C. USMT
   D. MigWiz

6. Which of the following editions of Windows Vista can be upgraded to Windows 7 Professional?
   A. Windows Vista Starter
   B. Windows Vista Home Basic

    C. Windows Vista Home Premium

    D. Windows Vista Business

    E. Windows Vista Ultimate

7. Which utility is shown in Figure 16.25?

FIGURE 16.25 One of the utilities available in Windows 7

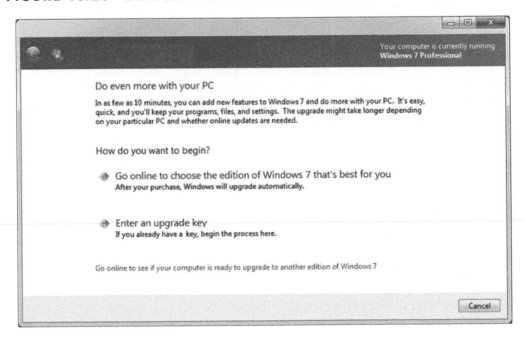

    A. Windows State Mover

    B. Windows Easy Transfer

    C. Windows Anytime Upgrade

    D. Windows Edition Roller

8. You need to do an installation of Windows 7 in a PXE environment. Which of the following can be used?

    A. WinLoad

    B. BOOTMGR

    C. WinPE

    D. WinResume

9. Which utility is shown in Figure 16.26?

FIGURE 16.26 One of the utilities available in Windows 7

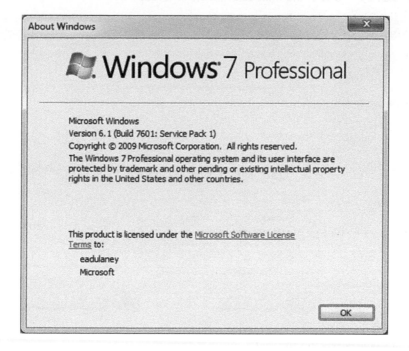

A. WINVER

B. MSINFO

C. MSCONFIG

D. SYSTEM32

10. Which editions of Windows 7 include BitLocker? (Choose two.)

    A. Windows 7 Starter

    B. Windows 7 Home Premium

    C. Windows 7 Professional

    D. Windows 7 Enterprise

    E. Windows 7 Ultimate

11. Where in Windows 7 can you manually create a restore point?

    A. System Restore option beneath System Tools

    B. System Protection tab of System Properties

    C. In Backup, beneath Administrative Tools

    D. Windows 7 does not allow for the manual creation of restore points

12. Which utility is shown in Figure 16.27?

FIGURE 16.27 One of the utilities available in Windows 7

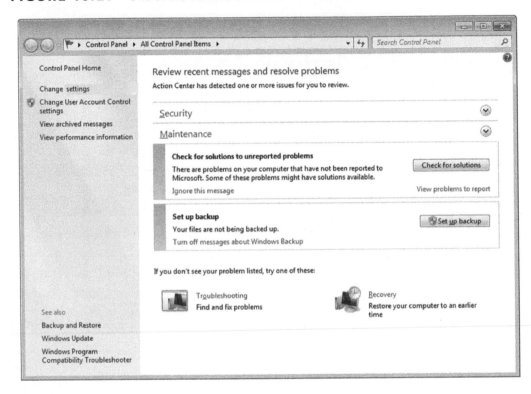

- **A.** Action Center
- **B.** Security Center
- **C.** HomeGroup
- **D.** Windows Vista Enterprise

13. After installing the operating system, what does Windows 7 require in order to curb software piracy?

- **A.** Certification
- **B.** Confirmation
- **C.** Activation
- **D.** Substantiation

14. What is the maximum number of physical CPUs supported by Windows 7 Enterprise edition?

- **A.** One
- **B.** Two
- **C.** Three
- **D.** Four

15. In Windows 7, what is the default setting for the UAC?

   A. Always notify

   B. Notify me only when programs try to make changes to my computer

   C. Notify me only when programs try to make changes to my computer (do not dim my desktop)

   D. Never notify

16. Which feature allows you to use free space on an SD card to speed up a system?

   A. ReadyDrive

   B. Shadow Copy

   C. ReadyBoost

   D. BitLocker to Go

17. Which utility is shown in Figure 16.28?

FIGURE 16.28   One of the utilities available in Windows 7

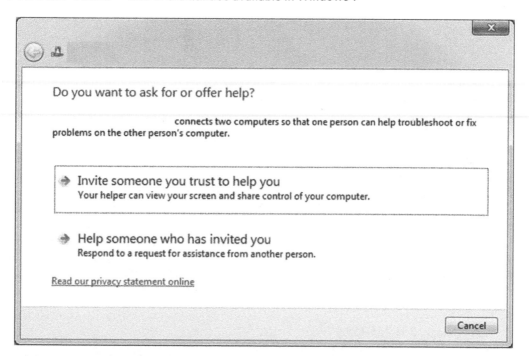

Do you want to ask for or offer help?

_____ connects two computers so that one person can help troubleshoot or fix problems on the other person's computer.

➡ Invite someone you trust to help you
Your helper can view your screen and share control of your computer.

➡ Help someone who has invited you
Respond to a request for assistance from another person.

Read our privacy statement online

Cancel

   A. Remote Control

   B. Remote Applications

   C. Remote Desktop

   D. Remote Assistance

18. Remote computers and virtual machines are made available with Windows 7 using which port?

A. 80

B. 139

C. 3389

D. 13742

19. Which directory on a standard Windows 7 installation holds the boot file configuration?

A. \BOOT

B. \START

C. \SYSTEM32

D. \WINDOWS

20. What is the maximum amount of RAM supported in the 64-bit Enterprise edition of Windows 7?

A. 8GB

B. 16GB

C. 128GB

D. 192GB

Performance-Based Question

You will encounter performance-based questions on the A+ exam. The questions on the exam require you to perform a specific task, and you will be graded on whether or not you were able to complete the task. The following requires you to think creatively in order to measure how well you understand this chapter's topics. You may or may not see similar questions on the actual A+ exam. To see how your answers compare to the authors', refer to Appendix B.

You have been sent to a client's Windows 7 workstation with specific directions to follow. They are using only IPv4, and they use DHCP for their normal configuration information. In the event that the DHCP server is not accessible, however, APIPA should not be used. An alternate configuration needs to be assigned with the following values:

IP address: 192.16.68.4

Subnet mask: 255.255.255.0

Default gateway: 192.16.68.1

How would you configure this?

Chapter

17

Working with Windows Vista

THE FOLLOWING COMPTIA A+ 220-902 EXAM OBJECTIVES ARE COVERED IN THIS CHAPTER:

✓ **1.1: Compare and contrast various features and requirements of Microsoft Operating Systems (Windows Vista).**

  ▪ Features: 32-bit vs. 64-bit

  ▪ Aero, gadgets, user account control, bit-locker, shadow copy, system restore, ready boost, sidebar, compatibility mode, administrative tools, defender, Windows firewall, security center

✓ **1.2: Given a scenario, install Windows PC operating systems using appropriate methods.**

  ▪ Types of installations: Upgrade, Clean install, Image deployment

✓ **1.4: Given a scenario, use appropriate Microsoft operating system features and tools.**

  ▪ Administrative: Local Users and groups, Local security policy, System configuration, Component services, Data sources, Print management, Windows memory diagnostics, Windows firewall, Advanced security

  ▪ Other: User State Migration Tool (USMT), Windows Easy Transfer

✓ **1.5: Given a scenario, use Windows Control Panel utilities.**

  ▪ Devices and Printers

✓ **1.6: Given a scenario, install and configure Windows networking on a client/desktop.**

  ▪ HomeGroup vs. Workgroup

  ▪ Home vs. Work vs. Public network settings

- Firewall settings: Exceptions, Configuration, Enabling/disabling Windows firewall

- Configuring an alternate IP address in Windows:

- IP addressing, Subnet mask, DNS, Gateway

- Network card properties:

- Half duplex/full duplex/auto, Speed, Wake-on-LAN, QoS, BIOS (on-board NIC)

Whereas previous chapters examined the unique Windows 8/8.1 and Windows 7 operating system features worth noting, this one does the same for Windows Vista. In many ways, Windows Vista was a vast departure from Windows XP, and it failed to live up to the expectations set for it. Although it was not widely adopted, you must be familiar with it for the CompTIA A+ 220-902 certification exam.

Some of the tools covered in this chapter have been addressed in the previous chapters for Windows 8/8.1, Windows 7, and operating systems in general (Chapter 13, "Operating System Basics," and Chapter 14, "Operating System Administration"), but you must know how they operate differently in Windows Vista.

Windows Vista Editions

Windows Vista was released in six different editions, four of which were made available in the retail channel: Windows Vista Home Basic, Windows Vista Home Premium, Windows Vista Business, and Windows Vista Ultimate. In addition to these, there is also Windows Vista Enterprise (offering more features than Business but fewer than Ultimate) and Windows Vista Starter (not marketed in countries such as the United States or the European Union, in which technology is more developed than in other places).

Table 17.1 offers a snapshot view of the five editions of Windows Vista made available domestically and some of the key features of each.

TABLE 17.1 Windows Vista editions and features

Edition	Maximum RAM Supported (in 64-bit Versions)	Maximum Physical CPUs Supported (Multiple Cores)	Notes
Home Basic	8GB	1	Lacks support for Aero, cannot join a Windows Server domain, does not support Shadow copies
Home Premium	16GB	1	Includes support for HDTV, cannot join a Windows Server domain, does not support Shadow copies

TABLE 17.1   Windows Vista editions and features *(continued)*

Edition	Maximum RAM Supported (in 64-bit Versions)	Maximum Physical CPUs Supported (Multiple Cores)	Notes
Business	128GB	2	Does not support parental controls, premium games disabled by default
Enterprise	128GB	2	Includes BitLocker, not available in retail or OEM channels (volume licensing only), premium games disabled by default
Ultimate	128GB	2	Includes BitLocker, available in retail and OEM channels

There are 32-bit and 64-bit versions available for each of the editions listed here. Table 17.2 lists a number of features associated with the Windows Vista operating system that you should know about for the exam, along with a brief description of each.

    If you don't know what edition of Windows Vista is running on a particular machine, you can click Start and type **winver** in the search box. The search results screen will identify the edition as well as the service pack installed.

TABLE 17.2   Windows Vista features

Feature	Description
Aero	The Aero interface was new with Windows Vista. The main difference between it and the previous Windows interface is the glass design that offers translucent windows.
Gadgets	These are mini-programs that can be placed on the Desktop, which allows them to run quickly and allows the user to personalize the PC. Commonly used gadgets are the Calendar, Clock, and news/weather feeds.
Sidebar	Gadgets can be placed on a bar known as the Sidebar that appears on the Desktop (Windows 7 kept the gadgets but did away with the Sidebar). The main selling point for using the Sidebar is that it can provide one location for common gadgets and be configured to be always visible.

Feature	Description
User Account Control (UAC)	New to Vista, UAC is intended to prevent unintentional/ unauthorized changes to the computer, either by prompting for permission or requiring the administrator password.
BitLocker	Referenced by CompTIA as "Bit-Locker," Microsoft calls it BitLocker, and it allows you to use drive encryption to protect files, including those needed for startup and logon.
Shadow Copy	The Volume Shadow Copy Service is used to create the copies that you can use should a file be accidentally deleted or overwritten.
ReadyBoost	This feature allows you to use free space on a removable drive (usually USB) as virtual memory and speed up a system. For the option even to be possible, at least 256MB of space must be available on the removable media. ReadyBoost is configured from the ReadyBoost tab of the Properties dialog box for the removable media device.
Compatibility Mode	The Program Compatibility Wizard was included with Vista to configure programs to believe that they are running with Windows XP or earlier versions of Windows: Choose Start ➤ Control Panel ➤ Programs, and then click Use An Older Program With This Version Of Windows.
Windows Defender	While available for other operating systems, Windows Vista was the first to ship with the Windows Defender antispyware program.
Windows Firewall	Windows Vista incorporates Windows Firewall, which can be used to stop incoming and outgoing traffic. There are three basic settings: On, Off, and Block All Incoming Connections.
Security Center	Windows Security Center provides a single interface for firewall settings, automatic updating, malware protection, and other security settings.

 Real World Scenario

Helpful or Just Plain Annoying?

One of the most derided features of Windows Vista is User Account Control (UAC). This feature was first introduced in Windows Vista, and it has carried on in Windows 7. While the purpose behind it is brilliant—to keep users from accidentally messing up their configuration settings—it turned out to be more of a source of frustration than ever anticipated.

continues

continued

Whenever a configuration change is possible—such as when you start a utility that has the ability to make a change to anything system related—the UAC either requires an administrator password or prompts the user to verify that they are sure they really want to go on. The problem lies not with the concept but with the annoyance of constantly having to respond to it. With Windows 7, there are four settings from which you can choose to tighten or loosen the hold UAC has on the system. In Windows Vista, it is either on or off.

While turning UAC off is not recommended, you can do so by choosing Start ➢ Control Panel ➢ User Accounts and clicking Turn User Account Control On Or Off. Naturally, UAC prompts you one last time to make sure that you really want to make the change. After confirming that you do, or entering the administrator password, clear the check box to turn UAC off.

Installing Windows Vista

As of this writing, it is pretty unlikely that you'll choose to install Windows Vista today since it is a fairly old operating system by technology standards. There are some situations in which you may have to do so: for example, if it needs to be reinstalled on a machine or used as an upgrade over an even older operating system. Regardless of any hypothetical situations, CompTIA wants you to know about it for the exam, starting with installing Windows Vista on a machine as a clean install or upgrading the existing operating system to Vista.

Clean Install

There are two methods of running a clean installation. Installing Vista over a previous operating system results in the user's data being moved to a folder called WINDOWS.OLD. The first option is to start the computer with the bootable Windows Vista DVD (CDs were available if you needed them) and begin the installation.

The second method—the one Microsoft recommends—is to run Setup from the DVD within your current Windows version. Once the DVD is inserted, the Setup program should automatically begin. If it does not, setup.exe can be manually run from the root folder and the menu will appear. On the menu, choose Install Now and then select Custom (Advanced) when the Which Type Of Installation Do You Want? screen appears. Answer the prompts to work through the steps and complete the installation.

If booting from the DVD, you will get the message *Press any key to boot from CD or DVD* upon startup, and at this point, you simply press a key and then begin the installation.

> **Windows Activation**
>
> To curb software piracy, Microsoft requires that each copy of Windows be *activated* (either by phone or via the Internet) after installation. Activation is the validation of the product key. Without activation, you can run the operating system, but only for a limited number of days. During that period of time, Windows will frequently remind you to activate the product.
>
> In addition, the activation records what kind(s) of hardware your system includes, and if three or more pieces change, it requires you to activate again. It's somewhat of a hassle on the part of a system owner if they are constantly upgrading systems. However, some types of Windows distributions don't require activation (such as those under volume license agreements with Microsoft).
>
> The activation process is simple. After installation is complete, a wizard pops up asking if you want to activate Windows. You can choose either the Internet or Phone option. If you have a connection to the Internet, the Activation Wizard only asks you which country you live in. No other personal information is required. You can then click Activate, and the Activation Wizard will send a unique identifier built from the different types of hardware in your system across the Internet to Microsoft's activation servers. These servers will send back a code to the Activation Wizard that activates your copy of Windows. The phone process is similar, but you must enter the code manually after calling Microsoft and receiving it.

Upgrading to Windows Vista

Whereas installation can typically be done over any existing OS, upgrading can only be done from an OS that is generally compatible with the one to which you're upgrading. In other words, the current operating system you are using determines the version of Windows Vista to which you can upgrade, if any. Table 17.3 lists the upgrade paths for each Windows Vista 32-bit version based on the existing operating system. Those listed as "No" must be clean installations.

 For the exam, recognize that no version of Windows older than Windows XP can be upgraded to Windows Vista.

TABLE 17.3   Windows Vista upgrade options

Existing Operating System	Vista Home Basic	Vista Home Premium	Vista Business	Vista Ultimate
Windows XP Home	Yes	Yes	Yes	Yes
Windows XP Professional	No	No	Yes	Yes

TABLE 17.3 Windows Vista upgrade options *(continued)*

Existing Operating System	Vista Home Basic	Vista Home Premium	Vista Business	Vista Ultimate
Windows XP Professional x64	No	No	No	No
Windows XP Media Center 2004/2005	No	Yes	No	Yes
Windows XP Tablet PC	No	No	Yes	Yes
Windows Vista Home Basic	N/A	Yes	No	Yes
Windows Vista Home Premium	No	N/A	No	Yes
Windows Vista Business	No	No	N/A	Yes
Windows Vista Ultimate	No	No	No	N/A

Note that Windows Vista Enterprise does not appear in the table because it is typically installed as a clean install. It can only be installed as an "upgrade" to Windows Vista Business. Also note that where N/A appears in the table, an upgrade is not possible, but a repair installation or clean installation can still be performed.

To begin the upgrade, insert the DVD. The Setup program should automatically begin (if it does not, run setup.exe from the root folder) and a menu will appear. On the menu, choose Install Now and then select Upgrade when the Which Type Of Installation Do You Want? screen appears. Answer the prompts to step through the upgrade. On a standard, default installation; the \boot directory holds the boot file configuration for Windows Vista.

You could once obtain CDs instead of the Windows Vista DVD from Microsoft, but they are no longer available.

Booting from the DVD is also possible, but it is recommended only if the method just described does not work. When you boot, you will get a *Press any key to boot from CD or DVD* message upon startup, and at this point, you simply press a key and begin the upgrade.

Transferring to Windows Vista

The *User State Migration Tool (USMT)* can be downloaded from Microsoft. It is intended to be used by administrators, and it requires a client computer connected to a Windows Server–based domain controller. It allows you to migrate user file settings related to applications, desktop configuration, and accounts for USMT 2.6. (USMT 3.0 does not require domain controller access except to transfer domain accounts.) More information on USMT can be found at the following location: http://technet.microsoft.com/en-us/library/cc722032(WS.10).aspx.

Windows Easy Transfer (WET) is also available for transferring items to Windows Vista (Start ➢ All Programs ➢ Accessories ➢ System Tools ➢ Windows Easy Transfer). This tool is intended for the one-time transfer of user settings, as well as applications and files, to Vista, whereas USMT is meant for wide-scale migrations. A key difference is that USMT allows transfers to be scripted whereas WET uses a GUI that requires user interaction.

As was discussed with other operating systems, you want to make certain that you use the latest driver software and Windows updates that are applicable for the operating system you are running. This can solve a great many problems with security holes as well as solve compatibility issues. Make certain, as well, that the boot drive is properly formatted and partitions are correct for your desired setup. Remember that a recovery partition, factory or otherwise, can be used to recover the operating system in the event of a failure.

The Windows Vista Boot Sequences

Both for the exam and for practical application, you should know how to recognize common problems with the OS and be able to make certain that it is booting correctly. The sections that follow look at a number of topics related to keeping your OS booting and running properly.

Key Boot Files

Windows Vista requires only a few files, each of which performs specific tasks. These files differ from the files for all previous Windows operating systems. These are discussed next in the order in which they load:

BOOTMGR   The Windows Boot Manager (BOOTMGR) bootstraps the system. In other words, this file starts the loading of an OS on the computer. It replaces NTLDR (used in previous operating systems) and is responsible for switching from real to protected mode during the boot process. The latter mode provides memory protection, multitasking, and other features that you expect from the operating system.

BCD   The Boot Configuration Data (BCD) file holds information about OSs installed on the computer, such as the location of the OS files.

WINLOAD.EXE   The program used to boot Windows Vista. It loads the operating system kernel (NTOSKRNL.EXE).

WINRESUME.EXE   If the system is not starting fresh but resuming a previous session, then WINRESUME.EXE is called by the BOOTMGR.

NTOSKRNL.EXE The Windows OS kernel. The solution to a corrupted NTOSKRNL.EXE file is to boot from a startup disk and replace the file from the setup disks or CD.

System files In addition to the previously listed files, Windows needs a number of files from its system directories (for example, SYSTEM and SYSTEM32), such as the hardware abstraction layer (HAL.DLL), session manager (SMSS.EXE), user session (WINLOGON.EXE), and security subsystem (LSASS.EXE).

We'll now look at the Windows Vista boot process from start to finish:

1. The system self-checks and enumerates hardware resources. The BIOS looks for the Master Boot Record.

2. The Master Boot Record (MBR) loads and finds the volume boot sector. The MBR finds the bootable partition and searches it for the NT boot sector of that partition.

3. The MBR determines the file system and loads BOOTMGR. Information in the boot sector allows the system to locate the system partition and to find and load the file located there into memory.

4. BOOTMGR checks to see if WINRESUME.EXE is needed.

5. BOOTMGR processes BCD.

6. BOOTMGR loads and runs WINLOAD.EXE.

7. WINLOAD.EXE loads NTOSKRNL.EXE and HAL.DLL. NTOSKRNL.EXE holds the OS kernel and also what's known as the executive subsystems. *Executive subsystems* are software components that parse the Registry for configuration information and start the needed services and drivers. HAL.DLL enables communication between the OS and the installed hardware.

8. The HKEY_LOCAL_MACHINE\SYSTEM Registry hive and device drivers are loaded, and control is transferred to NTOSKRNL.EXE to complete the boot process. It calls the WIN32K.SYS subsystem and the session manager SMSS.EXE.

9. WINLOGON.EXE loads. At this point, you are presented with the Logon screen. After you enter a username and password, you're taken to the Windows Desktop.

Windows Vista Features

There are a number of features that make Windows Vista an operating system worth noting. In the following sections, we will look first at some of the tools; we'll focus on the ones that you need to know for the A+ exam. By default, Vista displays a user-friendly screen for the Control Panel; clicking Classic View will show all of the available Control Panel items discussed in the following descriptions.

Tools in Windows Vista

The tools that stand out in Windows Vista include System Restore, Windows Defender, Windows Firewall, and Security Center. They are discussed in the sections that follow.

System Restore

System Restore, which was discussed in previous chapters, is arguably the most powerful tool in Windows Vista. It allows you to restore the system to a previous point in time. This feature is accessed from Start ➤ All Programs ➤ Accessories ➤ System Tools ➤ System Restore, and it can be used to roll back to as well as create a restore point. Figure 17.1 shows the opening screen of the System Restore dialog box.

FIGURE 17.1   System Restore in Windows Vista

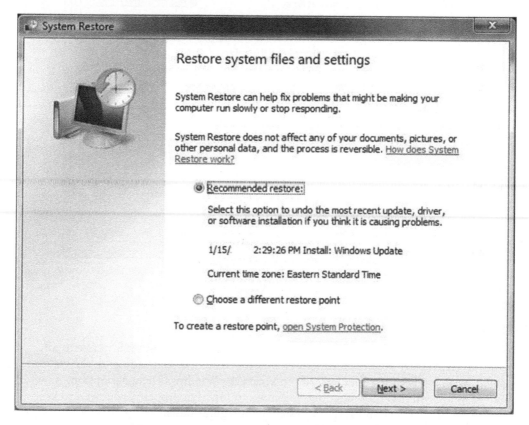

With Windows Vista, manually creating the restore point must be accomplished from the System Protection tab of System Properties (Start ➤ Control Panel ➤ System). Depending on the view that you are using, you may need to select System and Maintenance before you see the System option, as shown in Figure 17.2.

FIGURE 17.2   The option for creating a restore point in Windows Vista

Windows Defender

Windows Defender can identify spyware and unwanted software, and it is native to all versions of Vista (Start ➤ Control Panel ➤ Windows Defender). Depending on the view you are using, you may need to select Security to access the Windows Defender option. As with similar programs, in order for Windows Defender to function properly, you need to keep the definition files current and scan the system on a regular basis.

Windows Firewall

Windows Firewall (Start ➤ Control Panel ➤ Windows Firewall) is used to block access from the network (be it internal or the Internet). While host-based firewalls are not as secure as other types of firewalls, this was a great move in the right direction.

Figure 17.3 shows the opening screen of Windows Firewall in Windows Vista. Windows Firewall is turned on by default, and it is also included in the Security Center (discussed in the next section).

FIGURE 17.3   Windows Firewall can block unwanted traffic.

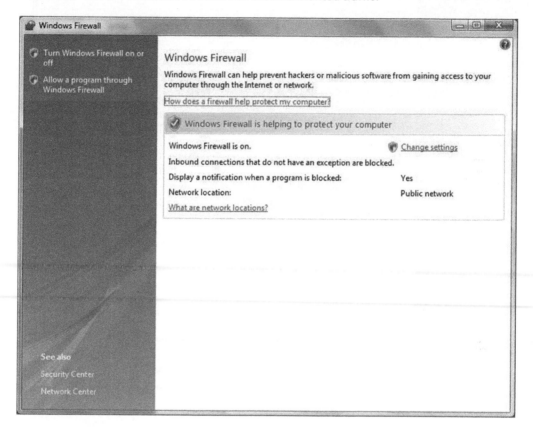

By default, Windows Firewall blocks incoming traffic. Clicking the Change Settings link opens the Windows Firewall Settings screen, which has three tabs: General, Exceptions, and Advanced. Using the Exceptions tab, you can configure what incoming traffic you want to allow through.

Security Center

Security Center (Start ➤ Control Panel ➤ Security Center) provides a single interface where you can administer Windows Firewall, Automatic Updates, Malware Protection, and other security settings. Figure 17.4 shows the opening screen.

FIGURE 17.4   Windows Security Center in Windows Vista

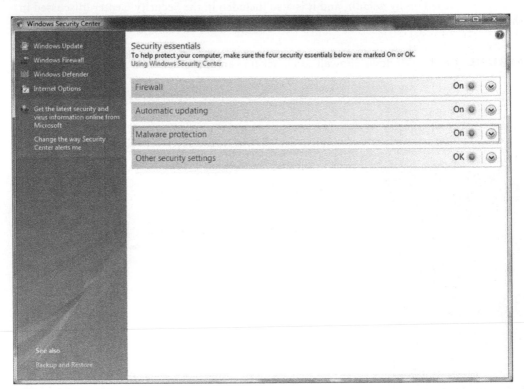

You can expand any of the four main categories to offer information on what is installed and make configuration changes. For example, as shown in Figure 17.5, if you expand Malware Protection and click Show Me The Antispyware Programs On This Computer, you can see that on this particular machine, there are three tools, and one of them—Windows Defender—is not turned on.

Windows Vista Administrative Tools

There are a number of system tools included with Windows Vista that you need to know about for the exam. These administrative tools, discussed in the order in which they appear in the objectives, also include Windows Firewall and Advanced Security, which was covered earlier in this chapter.

Users and Groups

As an administrator, you can configure the users and groups on a system in the Microsoft Management Console (MMC).

FIGURE 17.5 Antispyware programs on a sample machine

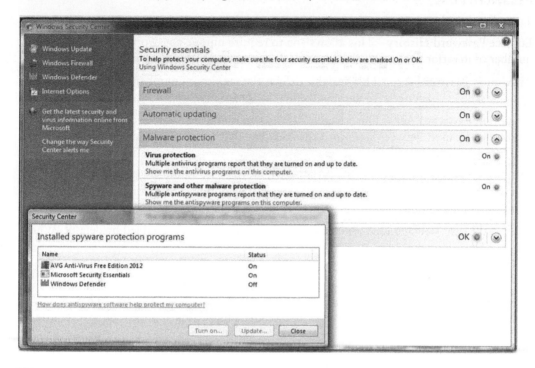

Start by clicking Start, typing **MMC** in the Search box, and pressing Enter. If Local Users And Groups is not visible in the left pane, choose File, then Add/Remove Snap-In, and then select Local Users And Groups from the list of possible snap-ins. You can choose to manage the local computer or another computer (which requires you to provide its address).

Local Users And Groups is not available for Windows Vista in any edition other than Windows Vista Business, Windows Vista Ultimate, and Windows Vista Enterprise. In all other editions, you must manage user accounts using the User Accounts applet in Control Panel, and you cannot create or manage groups.

Local Security Policy

To access the Local Security Policy tool, choose Start and then enter *secpol.msc* (or you can choose Control Panel ➢ Administrative Tools ➢ Local Security Policy). Local Security Policy allows you to set the default security settings for the system. This feature is not available for Windows Vista in any edition other than Windows Vista Business, Windows Vista Ultimate, and Windows Vista Enterprise.

The following sections examine some of the Security Settings options.

Account Policies

Account Policies further divides into Password Policy and Account Lockout Policy.

Password Policy

The following choices are available under Password Policy:

Enforce Password History   This allows you to require unique passwords for a certain number of iterations. The default number is 0, but it can go as high as 24.

Maximum Password Age   This variable defines the maximum number of days a password can be used. The default is 42 days, but values range from 0 to 999.

Minimum Password Age   This variable defines the minimum number of days that a password must be used between password changes. The default is 0 days, but values range from 0 to 999.

Minimum Password Length   This variable defines the least number of characters that must be used in a password. The default is 0 characters (meaning no passwords are required), but you can specify a number up to 14.

Password Must Meet Complexity Requirements   This setting is disabled by default. When it is turned on, the password must include at least three of the following criteria: uppercase characters, lowercase characters, numerical characters, nonalphanumeric characters, and/ or Unicode characters.

Store Password Using Reversible Encryption For All Users In The Domain   This setting is disabled by default. When it's enabled, it provides support for applications that require knowledge of the password.

Because the likelihood of laptops being stolen always exists, it's strongly encouraged that you implement strong password policies. Here's an example:

- Enforce Password History: 8 passwords remembered
- Maximum Password Age: 42 days
- Minimum Password Age: 3 days
- Minimum Password Length: 6 to 8 characters

Leave the other two settings disabled. Accepted practice is to insist that complexity requirements be enabled (and this is the default for domain machines).

Account Lockout Policy

The Account Lockout Policy setting is divided into the following three values:

Account Lockout Threshold   This is the number of invalid attempts before lockout occurs. The default is 0 (meaning that the feature is turned off). Invalid attempt settings range from 1 to 999. A number greater than 0 changes the values of the following two options to 30 minutes; otherwise, they are "not defined."

Account Lockout Duration   This is a number of minutes an account lockout lasts, ranging from 1 to 99999. A value of 0 is also allowed here and signifies that the account never unlocks itself; that is, administrator interaction is always required. When the number is greater than 0, the user must wait that many minutes before being allowed to try to log in again.

Reset Account Lockout Counter After   This is a number of minutes, ranging from 1 to 99999, that each failed login attempt remains on the counter. For example, if the value is set at 5, then after 5 minutes, one of the failed attempts is removed from the counter.

When you're working with a mobile workforce, you must weigh the choice of users calling you in the middle of the night when they've forgotten their password against keeping the system from being entered if the wrong user picks up the laptop. A good recommendation is to use a lockout after five attempts for a period of time between 30 and 60 minutes.

Local Policies

The Local Policies section is divided into three subsections: Audit Policy, User Rights Assignment, and Security Options. The Audit Policy section contains nine settings; the default value for each is No Auditing. When auditing is enabled, log entries are created for interactions with the item specified by the setting. Valid options are Success and Failure. The Audit Account Logon Events entry is the one that you should consider turning on for mobile users to see how often they log in and out of their machines.

When auditing is turned on for an event, the entries are logged in the Security log file.

The User Rights Assignment subsection of Local Policies is where the meat of what was once called System Policies comes into play. User Rights Assignment has many options, most of which are self-explanatory. Part of what is shown in the list of user rights are the defaults for who can perform each action; a value of Not Defined indicates that no one is specified for the corresponding operation.

The Security Options section includes a great many options which, for the most part, are representative of various Registry keys. The default for each is usually Not Defined.

System Configuration

The System Configuration tool (msconfig.exe) in Windows Vista is used to control the way the system behaves at startup, and it includes a number of tabs and options, as shown in Figure 17.6.

By clicking the Boot tab, you can see the configuration options for the BCD and make some minor changes, as shown in Figure 17.7. The Advanced Options button allows you to configure the number of processors, maximum memory, and global debug settings.

FIGURE 17.6 The System Configuration tool in Windows Vista

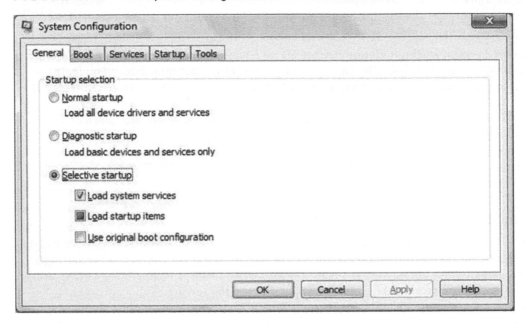

FIGURE 17.7 Options available on the Boot tab

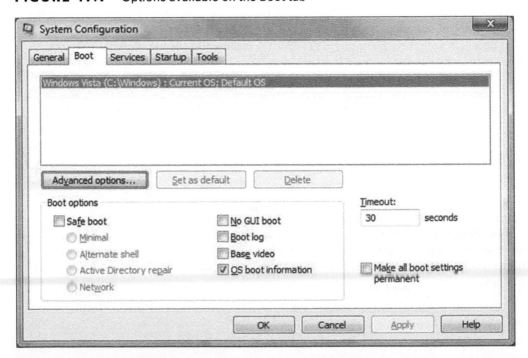

Component Services

Component Services is an MMC snap-in in Windows Vista that allows you to administer and deploy component services. It can be used to configure various settings, such as security settings. With this tool, it is possible for administrators to manage components while developers configure routine component and application behavior (object pooling, for example). Figure 17.8 shows an example of the interface.

FIGURE 17.8   Component Services

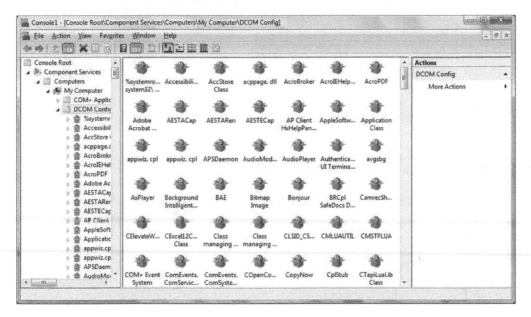

Data Sources

ODBC Data Source Administrator, accessed via Start ➤ Control Panel ➤ Administrative Tools ➤ Data Sources (ODBC), allows you to interact with database management systems. Figure 17.9 shows an example of the screen.

Database drivers that are added to the system will show up here and can be shared between applications.

Print Management

New to Windows Vista, Print Management (Start ➤ Control Panel ➤ Administrative Tools ➤ Print Management) allows you to manage multiple printers and print servers from a single interface. Print Management is not available for Windows Vista in any edition other than Windows Vista Business, Windows Vista Ultimate, and Windows Vista Enterprise. In all other editions, you must manage individual printers using the Printers applet in Control Panel, and you are very limited in what you can manage.

FIGURE 17.9 Data Sources in Vista

Windows Memory Diagnostics

The Windows Memory Diagnostics tool (Start ➤ Control Panel ➤ Administrative Tools ➤ Memory Diagnostics Tool) can be used to check a system for memory problems. For the tool to work, the system must be restarted. The two options that it offers are to restart the computer now and check for problems or to wait and check for problems on the next restart.

Upon reboot, the test will take several minutes and the display screen will show the number of the pass being run and the overall status of the test (percent complete). When the memory test concludes, the system will restart again and nothing related to it having run is apparent until you log in. If the test is without error, you'll see a message that no errors were found (see Figure 17.10). If any issues have been detected, the results will be displayed.

FIGURE 17.10 Memory test results

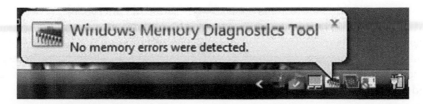

Distinctive Utilities

There are a number of Control Panel applets in Windows Vista of which you should be aware. These include Tablet PC Settings, Pen And Input Devices, Offline files, Problem Reports And Solutions, and Printers.

Tablet PC Settings

The Tablet PC Settings applet (Start ➢ Control Panel ➢ Tablet PC Settings) in Windows Vista can be used, as the name implies, to configure the device on which the operating system is installed to function as a true tablet. You can tweak handwriting recognition, handedness (left versus right), and other tablet-relevant settings.

Figure 17.11 shows the interface when Tablet PC Settings is first opened.

The Home Basic edition of Windows Vista does not support a tablet PC input panel, but all other editions of the operating system do.

FIGURE 17.11 Tablet PC Settings

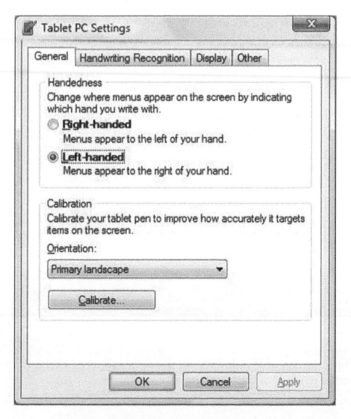

Pen and Input Devices

The Pen And Input Devices applet (Start ≻ Control Panel ≻ Pen And Input Devices) in Windows Vista is used in conjunction with the Tablet PC Settings applet. It is used to configure the pen and pointer options, as shown in Figure 17.12.

FIGURE 17.12 Pen And Input Devices settings

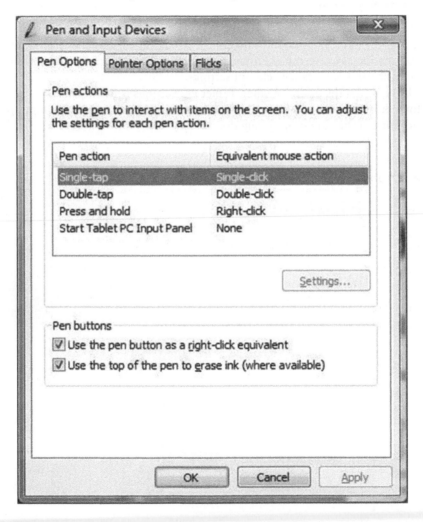

The Home Basic edition of Windows Vista does not support a tablet PC or have this applet, but all other editions of the operating system do.

Offline Files

Only some editions of Windows Vista (Business Ultimate and Enterprise) support offline files. Beginning with Windows 2000, Windows-based operating systems added the capability to work with resources that are "online" (accessed through the network or other connection) and "offline" (replicated copies of the resource stored locally). The key is to keep the files synchronized so that multiple copies of the same file stored in different locations match each other.

Windows Vista includes a Sync Center (Start ➤ Control Panel, then click Sync Center), as shown in Figure 17.13.

FIGURE 17.13 The Sync Center in Windows Vista is the primary interface for configuring synchronization.

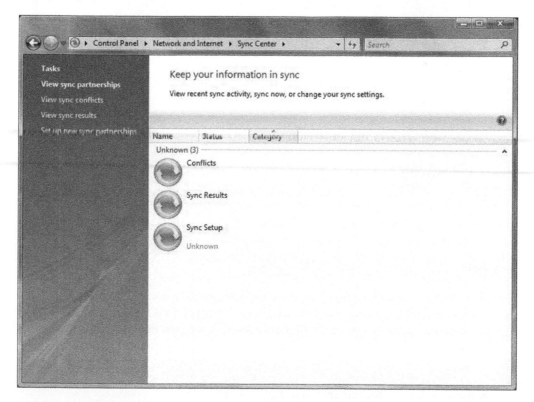

Sync partnerships can be set up with a large number of devices, ranging from a flash drive (as shown in Figure 17.14) to handheld devices. It is worth noting again that you cannot sync with network folders if you are using Windows Vista Starter, Home Basic, or Home Premium editions.

FIGURE 17.14   Establish a partnership with the device with which you want to sync in Sync Center.

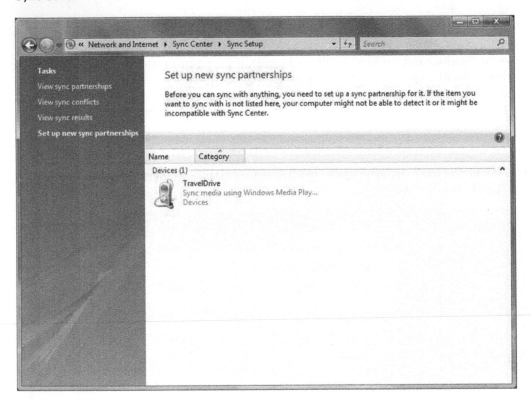

Problem Reports and Solutions

Building on the error reporting features offered in earlier versions of Windows, the Problem Reports And Solutions applet in Windows Vista (Start ➤ Control Panel ➤ Problem Reports And Solutions) can help solve problems on a particular machine (see Figure 17.15).

To configure (or disable) the feature, choose Change Settings and then Advanced Settings. On the Advanced Settings For Problem Reporting screen, click Change Setting to open a window similar to the one shown in Figure 17.16.

Your two major choices are to disable or enable error reporting. If you choose to disable it, you can still be notified when errors occur. Windows Vista offers the third choice of allowing each user to choose their settings. After choosing to enable error reporting, you can choose to report Windows operating system and/or program errors. By clicking a program's button, you can configure it to report errors. By default, all program errors from all programs are reported, but you can configure the reporting of errors on a program-by-program basis.

FIGURE 17.15   Problem Reports And Solutions in Windows Vista

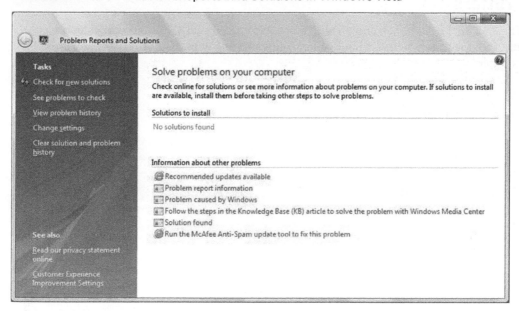

FIGURE 17.16   Windows error reporting options in Windows Vista

Printers

The Printers applet in Windows Vista (Start ➤ Control Panel ➤ Printers) provides a simple interface for adding a new printer or managing existing ones. Figure 17.17 shows an example.

FIGURE 17.17   The Printers applet in Windows Vista

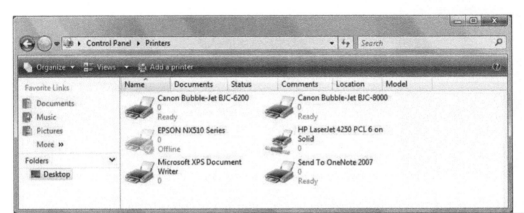

By right-clicking on any printer shown in the interface, you can choose to make it the default printer from the options menu that appears (in Figure 17.17, the check mark on the Epson NX510 indicates that it is the default printer). Clicking Add A Printer will start the Add Printer Wizard and allow you to add a network, wireless, or Bluetooth printer as well as one that is locally connected.

Networking and Windows Vista

There are a number of things CompTIA expects you to know when it comes to the topic of networking and Windows Vista. Most of the networking topics are covered in the chapters dedicated to that and thus the discussion here is limited to only those topics specifically tied to Windows Vista.

HomeGroups is a feature in Windows 7 and not Windows Vista, but you can easily configure almost any other type of network you want with Vista. By choosing the Network And Sharing Center (Start ➤ Control Panel ➤ Network And Sharing Center), you can choose to connect to an existing network, see (and manage) your current connections, and set up a new network. Choosing to set up a new network offers the choices shown in Figure 17.18.

The choices that are available are elaborated on in Table 17.4.

FIGURE 17.18 Creating a new network connection in Windows Vista

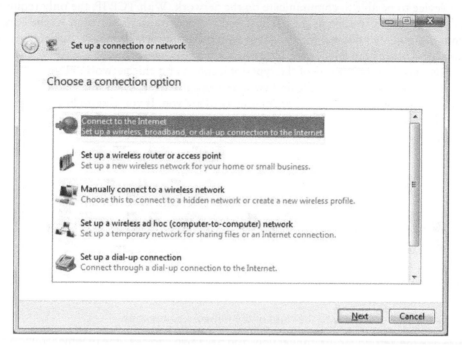

TABLE 17.4 Network connection options

Option	Purpose
Connect To The Internet	Use for connecting to a proxy server or other device intended to provide Internet access. This includes wireless, broadband, and dial-up.
Set Up A Wireless Router Or Access Point	If the wireless device will be connected to this machine, this is the option to use.
Manually Connect To A Wireless Network	If you have a wireless network already in place and the device (router, and so on) is not directly connected to this machine, then use this option.
Set Up A Wireless Ad Hoc (Computer-To-Computer) Network	This is meant for peer-to-peer resource sharing and is typically a temporary connection.
Set Up A Dial-Up Connection	If the way to access a network is by using a dial-up modem, then this is the option to select.
Connect To A Workplace	If you need to dial in to a virtual private network (VPN) from a remote location, this is the option to use.

Regardless of which option you choose, you will need to fill out the appropriate fields for the device to be able to communicate on the network. With TCP/IP, the only required values needed are an IP address for the host and a subnet mask to function. At the bare minimum, though, an address for the gateway and DNS information is recommended to be able to access other networks or the Internet.

You also need to specify one of the types of locations for this network: Home, Work, or Public. If you choose one of the first two, *network discovery* is on by default, allowing you to see other computers and other computers to see you. If you choose Public, network discovery is turned off. Exercise 17.1 walks you through the process of changing a network location type.

EXERCISE 17.1

Changing the Network Location Type in Windows Vista

1. Click the Start button, and choose Control Panel.

2. Choose Network And Sharing Center.

3. Click the Customize link to the right of the network connection.

4. Change the setting for the connection. You have two choices, one of which will already be selected:

   - Public

   - Private

5. Click Next.

6. Click Close and exit the Network And Sharing Center.

Network card properties that may be required include the speed at which the card will communicate and whether it is *half-duplex* (data going one direction at a time), *full-duplex* (data going both directions at the same time), or automatic. There may be extra features to configure, including *Wake on LAN (WoL)*, an Ethernet standard implemented via a card that allows a "sleeping" machine to awaken when it receives a wakeup signal. *Quality of Service (QoS)*, another extra feature, implements packet scheduling to control the flow of traffic and help with network transmission speeds. Figure 17.19 shows the QoS packet scheduler installed on a card. No properties can be configured for the service itself.

FIGURE 17.19   QoS scheduling on a network card in Windows Vista

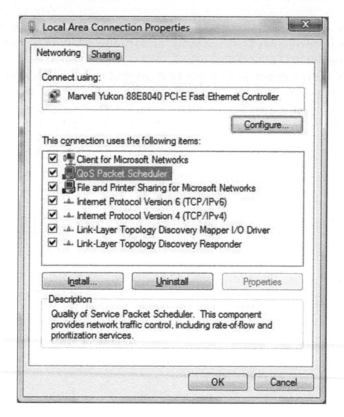

A network adapter built on the motherboard and integrated with it is known as an *on-board NIC* and is controlled by the BIOS. The BIOS is typically configured to look for and establish a connection automatically but that may not always be what you want. Given a scenario, you may want to disable the on-board NIC if it is experiencing problems or if it is slower than what can be obtained by adding another NIC to the machine. When this is the case, you can check manufacturer's documentation but typically it involves nothing more than disabling the NIC in the BIOS settings.

Vista System Performance and Optimization

Windows Vista introduced a number of features administrators should be aware of to understand how better to optimize a system. Some of these were mentioned at the beginning of the chapter, but only in passing. These include the *Aero* interface, the *User Account Control* feature, indexing, and *Sidebar*.

Aero

An acronym for *Authentic, Energetic, Reflective, and Open*, Aero differs from previous GUIs in that its windows are translucent and it provides the ability to create a 3D
stack of open windows and cycle through them (known as *Flip 3D*); while Flip 3D is
nice, it relies on a more important feature of Aero that provides live thumbnails of
each window, as demonstrated in Windows Flip (the standard task window) and on
the Taskbar. To configure Aero, right-click on the Desktop and choose Personalize
from the context menu, and then choose Window Color And Appearance, as shown in
Figure 17.20.

FIGURE 17.20   Configuring Aero

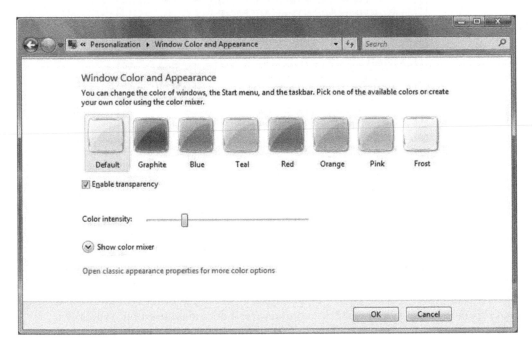

Here you can turn off the transparency as well as change the colors used for
windows. Aero can be turned off altogether by clicking Open Classic Appearance
Properties For More Color Options. This brings up the Appearance Settings dialog box
shown in Figure 17.21, from which you can choose to use Windows Standard, Windows
Classic, or another interface (choosing anything but the default of Windows Aero turns
Aero off).

FIGURE 17.21   Choosing an interface besides Aero

User Account Control

The User Account Control (UAC) feature was mentioned earlier in this chapter and has the sole purpose of keeping the user from running programs that could potentially pose a threat by requiring escalating privileges for many actions. While turning UAC off is an option, it is not a recommended option. If you have a program that you regularly run and do not want to be prompted about each time, you can right-click the icon for that program and then click Properties. Choose the Compatibility tab and then select the Run This Program As An Administrator check box. This will prevent the prompt from occurring each time you use the program.

> Operating system programs typically do not offer the choice to always run them as an administrator, and the privileges will stay grayed out on the Compatibility tab.

Indexing

Indexing services have existed since the early versions of Windows, and they allow the operating system to find files quickly by looking through a database of entries rather than having to start from scratch each time. The primary interface for configuring indexing is the Indexing Options applet in Control Panel. Figure 17.22 shows this interface for Windows Vista, and it differs from previous OS versions simply in the addition of the Pause button.

FIGURE 17.22 Configuring Indexing

The Advanced button takes you to the heart of the configuration. From here, you can choose whether to include encrypted files and what types of files to include in the index. Most meaningful is the ability to choose whether the index should include properties only (the default) or also include file contents. While choosing to include contents in the index greatly decreases search time, it can also slow the system down on a regular basis as it builds the index.

Sidebar

The Sidebar is a feature that allows easy access to gadgets. To configure the Sidebar, right-click on an area of it and choose Properties (if the Sidebar is not visible, click Start ➢ All Programs ➢ Accessories ➢ Windows Sidebar). This will bring up the dialog box shown in Figure 17.23.

FIGURE 17.23 Configuring the Sidebar

In addition to choosing Properties from the context menu, you can choose Close Sidebar, Bring Gadgets To Front, and Add Gadgets. To remove a gadget, right-click it and choose Close Gadget. You can also drag any gadget from the Sidebar directly onto the Desktop and drag them from the Desktop into the Sidebar as you wish.

Summary

This chapter focused on Windows Vista. Even though it is now an older Windows operating system, CompTIA expects you to be familiar with it and to be able to answer questions on everything from installing it to managing it.

We looked at the various features of Windows Vista, some that exist in other versions of Windows and some that are distinctive to this operating system. The latter category includes Tablet PC Settings, Pen And Input Devices, Offline Files, Problem Reports And Solutions, and Printers.

Exam Essentials

Know what types of installations are possible with Windows Vista.   You should know which operating systems can be upgraded to Windows Vista and which require a clean installation.

Understand upgrading.   You should know that a clean install does not preserve installed applications and will push old data files and settings into WINDOWS.OLD, while an in-place upgrade will preserve installed applications and settings.

Understand the Windows Vista boot process and order.   Know the purpose and role of BOOTMGR and BCD and how the boot process in Windows Vista differs from that of earlier versions of Windows.

Know what Control Panel utilities are notable in Windows Vista.   The Control Panel applets that stand out with Windows Vista are Tablet PC Settings, Pen And Input Devices, Offline Files, Problem Reports And Solutions, and Printers. You should be familiar with the purpose and options of each.

Understand what each of the following utilities are used for: System Restore, Windows Firewall, and Security Center.   System Restore is used to create, and revert back to, restore points. Windows Firewall limits traffic coming from the network to the host. Security Center provides a simple interface with which you may interact with virus scanners and other installed security software.

Review Questions

The answers to the chapter review questions can be found in Appendix A.

1. Which version of Windows Vista does *not* include offline folder capabilities?
   - **A.** Business
   - **B.** Enterprise
   - **C.** Home Premium
   - **D.** Ultimate

2. What is the first file used in the boot process of Windows Vista?
   - **A.** NTOSKRNL.EXE
   - **B.** CONFIG.SYS
   - **C.** AUTOEXEC.BAT
   - **D.** BOOTMGR

3. What is the maximum amount of RAM supported in the 64-bit Home Premium edition of Windows Vista?
   - **A.** 8GB
   - **B.** 16GB
   - **C.** 128GB
   - **D.** 256GB

4. Which of the following is an Ethernet standard implemented via a card that allows a "sleeping" machine to awaken when it receives a wakeup signal?
   - **A.** Sleep timer
   - **B.** WEP
   - **C.** Wake on LAN
   - **D.** WPA

5. Which editions of Windows Vista include BitLocker support? (Choose two.)
   - **A.** Business
   - **B.** Enterprise
   - **C.** Home Premium
   - **D.** Ultimate

6. Which Windows Vista feature allows you to recover from an accidental deletion or overwrite?
   - **A.** BitLocker
   - **B.** User Account Control

   C. Security Center

   D. Shadow Copy

7. You are migrating one stand-alone machine from Windows XP to Window Vista. Which of the following tools should you consider for transferring user state data and application files?

   A. Windows State Mover

   B. UDMT

   C. Windows Easy Transfer

   D. USMT

8. In Windows Vista, which of the following utilities can be used to see the edition and service pack installed on a system?

   A. `info`

   B. `spm`

   C. `winver`

   D. `msall`

9. Which utility is shown in Figure 17.24?

FIGURE 17.24　A Windows Vista utility

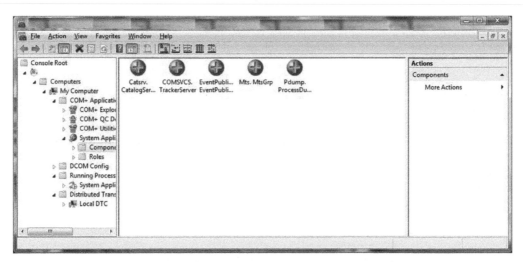

   A. Windows Memory Diagnostics

   B. Print Management

   C. Data Sources

   D. Component Services

10. Which of the following files is at the end of the boot process and presents the user with the Logon screen?

   A. SMSS

   B. WINLOGON

   C. HAL

   D. SIR

11. Where is the Windows Memory Diagnostics utility found in Windows Vista?

   A. In the Accessories folder

   B. In the System folder, beneath Accessories

   C. Beneath Administrative Tools

   D. Not available in Windows Vista

12. Which editions of Windows Vista support Local Security Policy (secpol.msc)? (Choose three.)

   A. Windows Vista Home Basic

   B. Windows Vista Home Premium

   C. Windows Vista Business

   D. Windows Vista Enterprise

   E. Windows Vista Ultimate

13. After installation of the Windows Vista operating system, what is required in order to curb software piracy?

   A. Certification

   B. Confirmation

   C. Activation

   D. Substantiation

14. What is the maximum number of physical CPUs supported by Windows Vista Business edition?

   A. One

   B. Two

   C. Three

   D. Four

15. Which utility is the System Configuration tool in Windows Vista?

   A. msinfo32.exe

   B. msconfig.exe

   C. sysconfig.cpl

   D. config.cpl

16. Which feature allows you to use free space on a removable drive (usually USB) to speed up a system?

    A. USB Speed

    B. Shadow Copy

    C. ReadyBoost

    D. Screamer

17. Spencer has dug out from the closet a legacy machine that is running Windows XP Professional. Since it is no longer supported, he wants to upgrade it to Windows Vista. Which of the following upgrades are possible? (Choose two.)

    A. Windows Vista Business

    B. Windows Vista Enterprise

    C. Windows Vista Home Premium

    D. Windows Vista Ultimate

18. Which of the following network locations disables network discovery in Windows Vista?

    A. Home

    B. Work

    C. Public

    D. Personal

19. Which directory on a standard Windows Vista installation holds the boot file configuration?

    A. \boot

    B. \start

    C. \system32

    D. \windows

20. What is the maximum amount of RAM supported in the 64-bit Ultimate edition of Windows Vista?

    A. 8GB

    B. 16GB

    C. 128GB

    D. 256GB

Performance-Based Question

You will encounter performance-based questions on the A+ exams. The questions on the exam require you to perform a specific task, and you will be graded on whether or not you were able to complete the task. The following requires you to think creatively in order to measure how well you understand this chapter's topics. You may or may not see similar questions on the actual A+ exams. To see how your answers compare to the authors', refer to Appendix B.

You are trying to troubleshoot a Windows Vista machine and think that memory may be an issue. How do you run the Windows Memory Diagnostics tool?

Chapter

18

Working with Mac OS and Linux

THE FOLLOWING COMPTIA A+ 220-902 EXAM OBJECTIVES ARE COVERED IN THIS CHAPTER:

✓ **2.1 Identify common features and functionality of the Mac OS and Linux operating systems.**

- Best practices: Scheduled backups, Scheduled disk maintenance, System updates/App store, Patch management, Driver/firmware updates, Antivirus/Antimalware updates

- Tools: Backup/Time Machine, Restore/snapshot, Image recovery, Disk maintenance utilities, Shell/Terminal, Screen sharing, Force Quit

- Features: Multiple desktops/Mission Controls, Key Chain, Spot Light, iCloud, Gestures, Finder, Remote Disk, Dock, Boot Camp

- Basic Linux commands: ls, grep, cd, shutdown, pwd vs. passwd, mv, cp, rm, chmod, mkdir, chown, iwconfig/ifconfig, ps, q, su/sudo, apt-get, vi, dd

The previous version of the CompTIA A+ certification exam (220-802) focused only on the Microsoft Windows operating system. Realizing that system administrators are dealing with a lot more than that in the workplace, the 220-902 exam expanded the coverage of operating systems to include the Mac OS and Linux.

This chapter looks at the non-Windows operating systems from the standpoint of what you need to know to pass the exam. All of the topics relevant to domain 2.1 of the 220-902 exam are covered, and a thorough overview of each topic is provided.

Best Practices

Regardless of the operating system in question, there are a number of best practices than an administrator should always follow. Depending on the operating system—and distribution, version, edition, and so on—it may be possible to perform operations with the utilities provided, or third-party utilities may be needed.

Scheduled Backups

Backups are duplicate copies of key information, ideally stored in a location other than the one where the information is currently stored. Backups include both paper and computer records. Computer records are usually backed up using a backup program, backup systems, and backup procedures.

The primary starting point for disaster recovery involves keeping current backup copies of key data files, databases, applications, and paper records available for use. Your organization must develop a solid set of procedures to manage this process and to ensure that all key information is protected.

Computer files and applications should be backed up on a regular basis. Here are some examples of critical files that should be backed up:

- Applications
- Appointment files
- Audit files
- Customer lists
- Database files
- Email correspondence

- Financial data
- Operating systems
- Prospect lists
- Transaction files
- User files
- User information
- Utilities

This list isn't all-inclusive, but it provides a place to start.

In most environments, the volume of information that needs to be stored is growing at a tremendous pace. Simply tracking this massive growth can create significant problems.

 An unscrupulous attacker can glean as much critical information from copies as they can from the original files. Make sure your storage facilities are secure, and it is a good idea to add physical security to the backup media as well.

You might need to restore information from backup copies for any number of reasons. Some of the more common reasons are listed here:

- Accidental deletion
- Application errors
- Natural disasters
- Physical attacks
- Server failure
- Virus infection
- Workstation failure

Types of Storage Mechanisms

The information you back up must be immediately available for use when needed. If a user loses a critical file, they won't want to wait several days while data files are sent from a remote storage facility. Several types of storage mechanisms are available for data storage:

Working copies *Working copy backups*, sometimes referred to as *shadow copies*, are partial or full backups that are kept at the computer center for immediate recovery purposes. Working copies are frequently the most recent backups that have been made.

Typically, working copies are intended for immediate use. They are usually updated on a frequent basis.

 Working copies aren't usually intended to serve as long-term copies. In a busy environment, they may be created every few hours.

Many filesystems used on servers include *journaling*. A *journaled file system (JFS)* includes a log file of all changes and transactions that have occurred within a set period of time (such as the last few hours). If a crash occurs, the operating system can check the log files to see which transactions have been committed and which ones have not.

This technology works well, allowing unsaved data to be written after the recovery, and the system is usually successfully restored to its pre-crash condition.

Onsite storage   *Onsite storage* usually refers to a location on the site of the computer center that is used to store information locally. Onsite storage containers are available that allow computer cartridges, tapes, and other backup media to be stored in a reasonably protected environment in the building.

> As time goes on, tape as a medium for backups is losing its popularity to other technologies.

Onsite storage containers are designed and rated for fire, moisture, and pressure resistance. These containers aren't *fireproof* in most situations, but they are *fire rated*: A *fireproof container* should be guaranteed to withstand damage regardless of the type of fire or temperature, whereas *fire ratings* specify that a container can protect the contents for a specific amount of time in a given situation.

If you choose to depend entirely on onsite storage, make sure that the containers you acquire can withstand the worst-case environmental catastrophes that could happen at your location. Make sure, as well, that they are in locations where you can easily find them after the disaster and access them (near exterior walls, on the ground floor, and so forth).

> General-purpose storage safes aren't usually suitable for storing electronic media. The fire ratings used for safes generally refer to paper contents. Because paper does not catch fire until 451° Fahrenheit, electronic media are typically ruined well before paper documents are destroyed in a fire.

Offsite storage   *Offsite storage* refers to a location away from the computer center where paper copies and backup media are kept. Offsite storage can involve something as simple as keeping a copy of backup media at a remote office, or it can be as complicated as a nuclear-hardened high-security storage facility. The storage facility should be bonded, insured, and inspected on a regular basis to ensure that all storage procedures are being followed.

Determining which storage mechanism to use should be based on the needs of the organization, the availability of storage facilities, and the budget available. Most offsite storage facilities charge based on the amount of space required and the frequency of access needed to the stored information.

While it is easy to see the need for security at any location where your files are stored, don't overlook the need for security during transportation as well.

Scheduled Disk Maintenance

When files are written to a hard drive, they're not always written contiguously, or with all of the data located in a single location. When discussing Windows, we talked about Disk Defragmenter, which has existed in almost all versions of Windows, and its ability to take file data that has become spread out over the disk and put it all in the same location, known as *defragmenting*. This decreases the time it takes to retrieve files and it should be done with every OS.

As opposed to FAT- and NTFS-based file systems, the file systems used on Mac OS and Linux rarely, if ever, need to be defragmented. Both ext3 and ext4 have on-the-fly defragmentation methods and implement file allocation strategies different than their traditional Windows counterparts.

System Updates/App Store

It is important to keep the operating system current and updated. Like Windows, many other operating systems include the ability to update automatically, and almost all can look for updates and tell you when they are available. In the Mac world, the App Store represents a location where you can also find updates.

For example, Figure 18.1 shows that a new version of iOS is available on an iPad. Figure 18.2 shows the reasons why the new version has been released, and it allows you to read about the changes and decide if you want to upgrade or not.

In most cases, unless a production machine would be negatively impacted, you should keep systems updated with the latest releases.

Patch Management

As a general rule, updates fix a lot of things and patches fix a few: multiple patches are rolled into updates. You can't always afford to wait for updates to be released and need to install patches—particularly security-related ones—when they are released. Bear in mind that if all of the security patches are not installed during installation, attackers can exploit the weaknesses and gain access to information.

A number of tools are available to help with patch management – the intentions behind some are better than others. For example, rather than probe a service remotely and attempt to find a vulnerability, the Nessus vulnerability scanner (www.tenable.com/products/nessus-vulnerability-scanner) will query the local host to see if a patch for a given vulnerability has been applied. This type of query is far more accurate (and safer) than running a remote check.

FIGURE 18.1 The Software Update feature informs you when a new version of iOS is available.

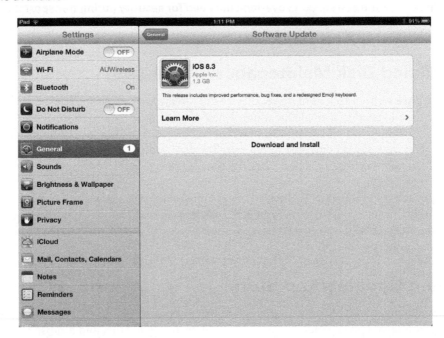

FIGURE 18.2 It is possible to learn more about the update before applying it.

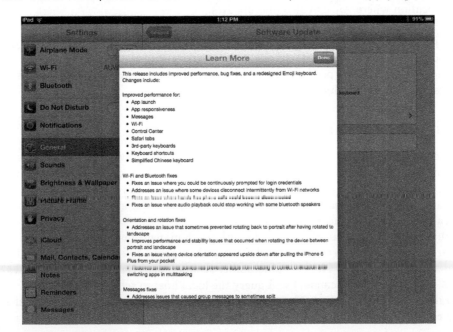

Depending on the variant of Linux you are running, apt (Advanced Package Tool) can be useful in getting the patches from a repository site and downloading them for installation. The most common command used with this tool is apt-get, which, as the name implies, gets the package for installation.

Driver/Firmware Updates

With any operating system, it is essential to keep the drivers and firmware updated. Always remember to back up your configurations (such as with routers) before making any significant changes—in particular, a firmware upgrade—in order to provide a fallback in case something goes awry.

Many network devices contain firmware with which you interact during configuration. For security purposes, you must authenticate in order to make configuration changes and do so initially by using the default account(s). Make sure that the default password is changed after the installation on any network device; otherwise, you are leaving that device open for anyone recognizing the hardware to access it using the known factory password.

Antivirus/Antimalware Updates

At one point in time, there were so few viruses outside the Windows world that users not running Windows felt safe without protection on their systems. A significant reason for the low amount of non-Windows malware was that the authors of such devious programs were focusing on Windows simply because it had the lion's share of the market: they wanted to inflict as much harm as possible with their code.

As other operating systems have increased in popularity, so too have the number of malware items written for them or that can affect them. Because of this, today it is imperative to have protection on every machine today. Additionally, this protection—in the form of definition files—must be kept current and up-to-date. Chapter 19 will discuss security and antivirus/anti-malware in more detail.

Tools

There are a number of tools to be aware of in Mac OS and Linux. Most of these have counterparts in the Windows world, and we'll make comparisons where they apply. More and more tools are released on a daily basis, but the ones CompTIA wants you to know are as follows:

Backup/Time Machine   As discussed in the previous section, backups are important. In the Mac OS X world, Time Machine is an application from Apple that can be used to make backups of various types (incremental, full, and so forth).

Restore/snapshot   Snapshots are archives of key files and settings as they exist at a moment in time—images. It is possible to take snapshots and restore them as needed.

Image recovery As a general rule only, images are typically larger than snapshots. You can take a snapshot of a project, and that will include all of the files associated with the project, while an image would include that and all files on the system at the time. Again, this is only a general rule as images can be granular as well, but typically snapshots are thought of as subsets of images.

Disk maintenance utilities There are a number of disk maintenance utilities available with, or for, Mac OS and Linux. The most important ones to know are du, which will show how much disk space is in use, df to see how much space is free, and fsck to check and repair disks.

Shell/Terminal The command-line interface in Linux is usually reached through a terminal session (though that need not always be the case). It is in this terminal session that you interact with the shell—the interpreter between the user and operating system. The most popular shell for Linux today is Bash (an acronym for Bourne Again Shell), but csh (C-shell), ksh (Korn shell), and a number of others are also in use. In the Mac OS X/iOS world, OpenSSH (open shell) is often downloaded and installed. The Mac OS X Terminal utility is also accessible by going to Applications ➤ Utilities ➤ Terminal.

Screen sharing This feature is built into Mac OS X, and it allows you to share your screen with others. While your screen is shared, the user of the other computer sees what you see and they can open, move, and close files as well as restart your system. It requires a Virtual Network Computing (VNC) connection.

Force Quit There are a few occasions where an application can become a runaway. When that happens with the Mac OS, you can use Force Quit to force it to close. Most devices, whether running Mac OS or iOS, offer similar options. With an iPad, for example, press the Home button twice quickly and a list of apps will appear at the bottom of the screen. Swipe to get to the one in question, then swipe up on its preview to close it.

Features

There are a number of Mac OS X features that CompTIA wants you to be aware of for the exam. You need not know the intricacies of each but rather of their existence and purpose. Be aware of the following features:

Multiple desktops/Mission Control It is possible to run a large number of things at one time, whether those things in question are apps or desktops. Apple's Mission Control is an easy way to see what is open and switch between applications. To access Mission Control, you can press the Mission Control key on an Apple keyboard, click the Mission Control icon in Dock (or Launchpad), or swipe up with three or four fingers on a trackpad. Once Mission Control is accessed, all open windows and spaces are shown—grouped by app— and you can choose between them.

Keychain   Keychain is a password management system from Apple. It allows you to store passwords for websites, mail servers, Wi-Fi, and so forth. There is an iCloud variant (iCloud Keychain) that keeps such information as Safari usernames/passwords and credit card information. Values stored in Keychain are kept current (changes are synced) to simplify resource access.

Spotlight   The search feature within Mac OS X is Spotlight, and a magnifying glass icon in the upper-right corner of the menu bar represents it (or you can press Command+space from any app). Spotlight can search for documents, images, apps, and so on. Recent versions include auto-complete features as well as suggestions for additional results (usually on Wikipedia, iTunes, and such).

iCloud   One of the best ways always to have the latest version of files, regardless of the device that you are using to access them, is to have them stored/accessed remotely. iCloud is Apple's answer to remote storage, and you can configure your Apple devices to place files there automatically, or use it for backup. Figure 18.3 shows iCloud configuration settings on an iPad.

FIGURE 18.3   Example of iCloud configuration settings on an iPad

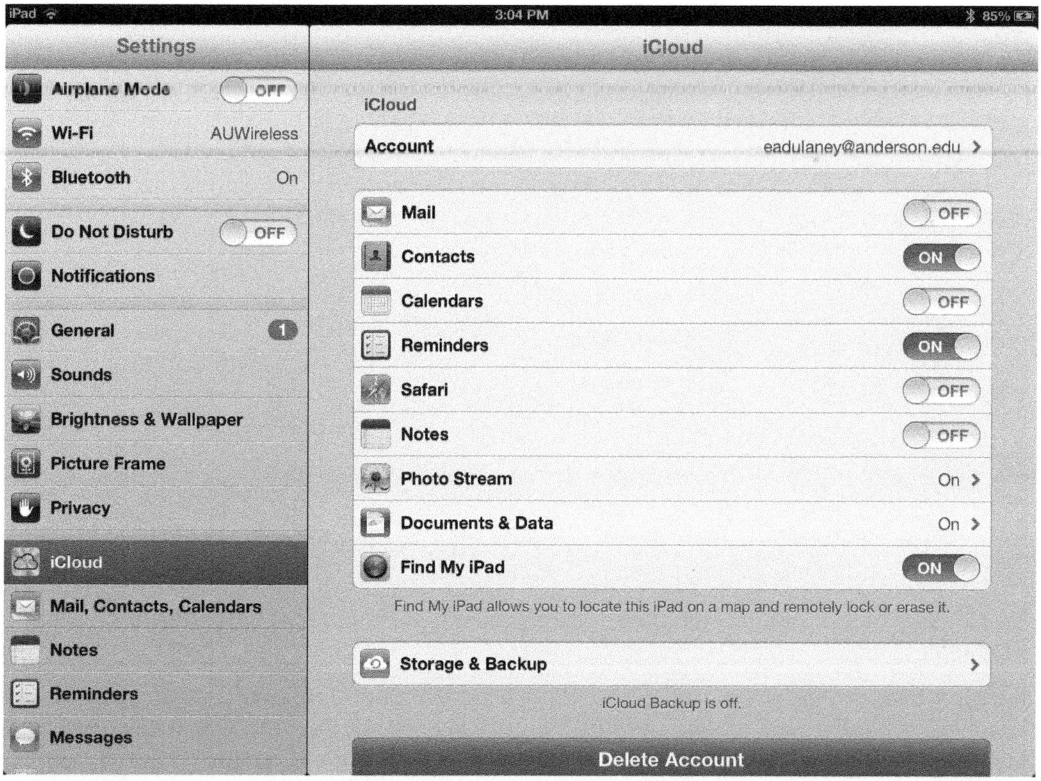

It should be noted that there can be cost associated with using iCloud. For example, the iPad shown in Figure 18.3 can access 5GB for free, but anything beyond that requires payment ($0.99/month for 20GB, $3.99/month for 200GB, $9.99/month for 500GB, or $19.99/month for 1TB at the time of this writing).

Gestures With Apple products, it is possible to scroll, tap, pinch, and swipe to interact with the Mac or other product in a way that is intended to be natural and intuitive. You can accept the default actions for these gestures, or you can configure them differently, as shown in Figure 18.4.

FIGURE 18.4 Example of the settings for default gestures on an iPad

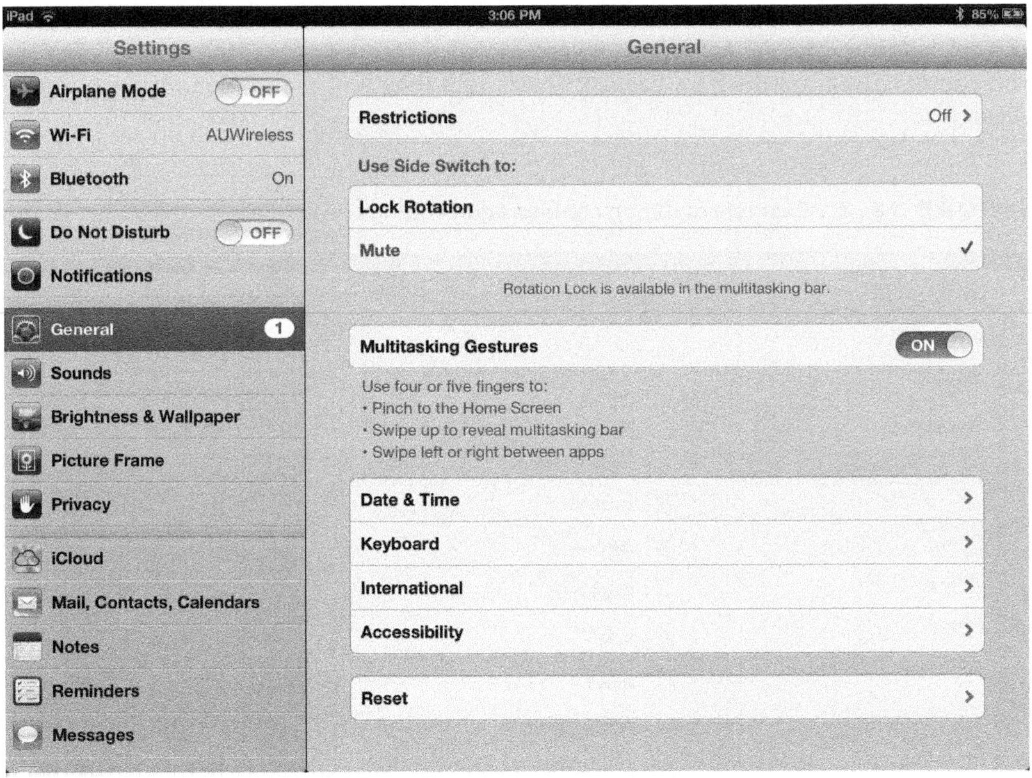

To see the basics of gestures on a Mac, visit: https://support.apple.com/en-us/HT204895.

Finder To use an analogy, Finder is to OS X what Windows Explorer is to Windows 7. It lets you browse through folders and find files, disks, apps and so on. You can change the view to see the entries with images, a list view, a column view, and so on.

Remote Disk   Officially called Remote Disc (disc with a *c*), this Mac OS X feature lets you access files on a CD or DVD installed in one machine on a remote machine. This is handy if you need to retrieve files from a disc and the workstation at which you are sitting does not have a built-in drive.

 The computer from which you are accessing a disc need not be running Mac OS X. It is also possible to access discs on a Windows computer if DVD or CD Sharing has been set up.

Dock   In Mac OS X, there is a bar of icons that runs along the bottom (or side, if so configured) of your screen. That set of icons is known as the dock, and it provides easy access to key apps that come with the Mac (such as Safari, Mail, Videos, and Music) or others that you choose to add there. To see the basics of the Dock on a Mac, visit `https://support.apple.com/en-us/HT201730`.

Boot Camp   As great as Mac OS X is, there are times when you need Windows—for compatibility purposes with apps, legacy data, and many others. Because of this, you can use Boot Camp to install Windows on a Mac computer and then choose between operating systems as you boot. The Mac computer must be Intel based, you have to have a 64-bit version of Windows, and you need a minimum of 30GB of free disk space to pull it off. For more details, visit `https://support.apple.com/en-us/HT201468`.

There are many other features of Mac OS X that make it a powerful operating system to use. The aforementioned features, however, are the ones that CompTIA wants you to be aware of for the exam. Make sure that you know the purpose of each as you prepare for the exam.

Basic Linux Commands

The best way to approach the following commands is to think about Microsoft Windows. That operating system offers a plethora of utilities for configuring the workstation and just in case they don't work, or you want to go about it the hard way, there are command-line utilities that can be used to accomplish similar tasks. The odds are good that you spend most of your time walking through graphical dialog boxes but you're familiar enough with the command-line utilities that you can use them when you need to.

Linux is the same way. There is an overabundance of graphical utilities that can be used to configure the system, and they differ based on the distribution and the graphical interface being used. In addition to these, there are command-line utilities that are available in every distribution that can be used to get the job done. Those command-line utilities are what we'll focus on here.

There is only one vendor for Windows (Microsoft), but there are many vendors for Linux (Red Hat, SuSE, Ubuntu—to name just three). Also, a new version of Windows is released only every few years (Windows Vista, Windows 7, Windows 8/8.1, Windows 10), but with Linux—especially because there are so many vendors—there are lots of versions. With Ubuntu, for example, the goal is to release a new version every six months. With all of the different distributions and versions, getting to the place where you can run command-line utilities can differ a bit. In almost every implementation of Linux, you can boot into a command-line mode, and the commands entered there can then be run. Better than that, though, the easiest way to get to the command line is to open a terminal (also called console) window. This allows you to interact with the shell where you can type commands to your heart's content. The default shell in many Linux distributions is Bash. When you open a terminal window or log in at a text console, the Bash shell is what prompts you for commands. When you type a command, the shell executes your command.

Understanding the Syntax of Shell Commands

Because a shell interprets what you type, knowing how the shell processes the text you enter is important. All shell commands have the following general format (some commands have no options):

```
command [option1] [option2] ... [optionN]
```

On a command line, you enter a command followed by zero or more options (or arguments). The shell uses a blank space or a tab to distinguish between the command and options. This means that you must use a space or a tab to separate the command from the options and the options from one another. If an option contains spaces, you put that option inside quotation marks. For example, to search for a name in the password file, enter the following grep command (grep is used for searching for text in files):

```
grep "Emmett Dulaney" /etc/passwd
```

When grep prints the line with the name, it looks like this:

```
edulaney:x:1000:100:Emmett Dulaney:/home/edulaney:/bin/bash
```

If you create a user account with your username, type the grep command with your username as an argument to look for that username in the /etc/passwd file. In the output from the grep command, you can see the name of the shell (/bin/bash) following the last colon (:). Because the Bash shell is an executable file, it resides in the /bin directory; you must provide the full path to it.

The number of command-line options and their formats depend on the actual command. Typically, these options look like X, where X is a single character. For example, you can use the -l option with the ls command. The command lists the contents of a directory, and the option provides additional details. Here is a result of typing **ls -l** in a user's home directory:

```
total 0
drwxr-xr-x 2 edulaney users 48 2015-09-08 21:11 bin
drwx-2 edulaney users 320 2015-09-08 21:16 Desktop
drwx-2 edulaney users 80 2015-09-08 21:11 Documents
drwxr-xr-x 2 edulaney users 80 2015-09-08 21:11 public_html
drwxr-xr-x 2 edulaney users 464 2015-09-17 18:21 sdump
```

If a command is too long to fit on a single line, you can press the backslash key (\) followed by Enter. Then continue typing the command on the next line. For example, type the following command (press Enter after each line):

**cat **
/etc/passwd

The cat command then displays the contents of the /etc/passwd file.

You can concatenate (that is, string together) several shorter commands on a single line by separating the commands with semicolons (;). For example, the following command changes the current directory to your home directory, lists the contents of that directory, and then shows the name of that directory.

```
 cd; ls -l; pwd
```

You can combine simple shell commands to create a more sophisticated command. For example, suppose you want to find out whether a device file named sbpcd resides in your system's /dev directory because some documentation says that you need that device file for your CD-ROM drive. You can use the ls /dev command to get a directory listing of the /dev directory and then browse through it to see whether that listing contains sbpcd.

Unfortunately, the /dev directory has a great many entries, so you may find it hard to find any item that has sbpcd in its name. You can, however, combine the ls command with grep and come up with a command line that does exactly what you want. Here's that command line:

```
ls /dev | grep sbpcd
```

The shell sends the output of the ls command (the directory listing) to the grep command, which searches for the string sbpcd. That vertical bar (|) is known as a pipe because it acts as a conduit (think of a water pipe) between the two programs—the output of the first command is fed into the input of the second one.

Discovering and Using Linux Commands

There are literally hundreds, if not thousands, of Linux commands that exist within the shell and the system directories. Fortunately, CompTIA asks that you know a much smaller number than that. Table 18.1 lists common Linux commands by category.

TABLE 18.1 Essential Linux commands

Command Name	Action
Managing Files and Directories	
cd	Change the current directory.
chmod	Change file permissions.
chown	Change the file owner and group
cp	Copy files.
ls	Display the contents of a directory.
mkdir	Create a directory.
mv	Rename a file and move the file from one directory to another.
rm	Delete files.
pwd	Display the current directory.
Processing Files	
dd	Copy blocks of data from one file to another (used to copy data from devices).
grep	Search for regular expressions in a text file.
Managing Files	
apt-get	Download files from a repository site.
ps	Display a list of currently running processes.
shutdown	Shut down Linux.
vi	Start the visual file editor.
Managing Users	
passwd	Change the password.

Command Name	Action
su	Start a new shell as another user (the other user is assumed to be root when the command is invoked without any argument).
sudo	Run a command as another user (usually the root user).
Networking	
ifconfig	View and change information related to networking configuration.
iwconfig	Similar to ifconfig, but used for wireless configuration.
Quitting	
q	While not a utility, the q command is often used to quit most interactive utilities. It is used, for example, to quit working in the **vi** editor.

Becoming root (Superuser)

When you want to do anything that requires a high privilege level (for example, administering your system), you have to become root. Normally, you log in as a regular user with your everyday username. When you need the privileges of the superuser, though, use the following command to become root:

su -

That's su followed by a space and the minus sign (or hyphen). The shell then prompts you for the root password. Type the password and press Enter.

After you've finished with whatever you want to do as root (and you have the privilege to do anything as root), type **exit** to return to your normal username.

Instead of becoming root by using the su - command, you can type **sudo** followed by the command that you want to run as root. In some distributions, such as Ubuntu, you must use the sudo command because you don't get to set up a root user when you install the operating system. If you're listed as an authorized user in the /etc/sudoers file, sudo executes the command as if you were logged in as root. Type **man sudoers** to read more about the /etc/sudoers file.

Managing Processes

Every time the shell executes a command that you type, it starts a process. The shell itself is a process, as are any scripts or programs that the shell runs. Use the ps ax command to see a list of processes. When you type **ps ax**, bash shows you the current set of processes. Here are a few lines of output from the command ps ax -cols 132 (the -cols 132 option is used to ensure that you see each command in its entirety):

```
PID TTY STAT TIME COMMAND
1 ? S 0:01 init [5]
2 ? SN 0:00 [ksoftirqd/0]
3 ? S< 0:00 [events/0]
4 ? S< 0:00 [khelper]
9 ? S< 0:00 [kthread]
19 ? S< 0:00 [kacpid]
75 ? S< 0:00 [kblockd/0]
115 ? S 0:00 [pdflush]
116 ? S 0:01 [pdflush]
118 ? S< 0:00 [aio/0]
117 ? S 0:00 [kswapd0]
711 ? S 0:00 [kseriod]
1075 ? S< 0:00 [reiserfs/0]
2086 ? S 0:00 [kjournald]
2239 ? S<s 0:00 /sbin/udevd -d
. . . lines deleted . . .
6374 ? S 1:51 /usr/X11R6/bin/X:0 -audit 0 -auth /var/lib/gdm/:0.Xauth -nolisten
tcp vt7
6460 ? Ss 0:02 /opt/gnome/bin/gdmgreeter
6671 ? Ss 0:00 sshd: edulaney [priv]
6675 ? S 0:00 sshd: edulaney@pts/0
6676 pts/0 Ss 0:00 -bash
6712 pts/0 S 0:00 vsftpd
14702 ? S 0:00 pickup -l -t fifo -u
14752 pts/0 R+ 0:00 ps ax—cols 132
```

In this listing, the first column has the heading PID, and it shows a number for each process. PID stands for *process ID* (identification), which is a sequential number assigned by the Linux kernel. If you look through the output of the ps ax command, you see that the init command is the first process and has a PID of 1. That's why init is referred to as the *mother of all processes.*

The COMMAND column shows the command that created each process, and the TIME column shows the cumulative CPU time used by the process. The STAT column shows the state of a process: S means that the process is sleeping, and R means that it's running. The symbols following the status letter have further meanings; for example < indicates a high-priority process, and + means that the process is running in the foreground. The TTY column shows the terminal, if any, associated with the process.

The process ID, or process number, is useful when you have to stop an errant process forcibly. Look at the output of the ps ax command, and note the PID of the offending process. Then use the kill command with that process number to stop the process. For example, to stop process number 8550, start by typing the following command:

```
kill 8550
```

Directory Navigation

In Linux, when you log in as root, your home directory is /root. For other users, the home directory is usually in the /home directory. For example, the home directory for a user logging in as edulaney is /home/edulaney. This information is stored in the /etc/passwd file. By default, only you have permission to save files in your home directory, and only you can create subdirectories in your home directory to organize your files further.

Linux supports the concept of a *current directory*, which is the directory on which all file and directory commands operate. After you log in, for example, your current directory is the home directory. To see the current directory, type the pwd command.

To change the current directory, use the cd command. To change the current directory to /usr/lib, type the following:

```
cd /usr/lib
```

Then to change the directory to the cups subdirectory in /usr/lib, type this command:

```
cd cups
```

Now if you use the pwd command, that command shows /usr/lib/cups as the current directory.

These two examples show that you can refer to a directory's name in two ways: with an absolute pathname or a relative pathname. An example of an absolute pathname is /usr/lib, which is an exact directory in the directory tree (think of the absolute pathname as the complete mailing address for a package that the postal service will deliver to your next-door neighbor). An example of a relative pathname is cups, which represents the cups subdirectory of the current directory, whatever that may be. (Think of the relative directory name as giving the postal carrier directions from your house to the one next door so that the carrier can deliver the package.)

If you type **cd cups** in /usr/lib, the current directory changes to /usr/lib/cups. However, if you type the same command in /home/edulaney, the shell tries to change the current directory to /home/edulaney/cups.

Use the cd command without any arguments to change the current directory back to your home directory. No matter where you are, typing **cd** at the shell prompt brings you back home. The tilde character (~) is an alias that refers to your home directory. Thus, you can also change the current directory to your home directory by using the command cd ~. You can refer to another user's home directory by appending that user's name to the tilde. Thus, cd ~superman changes the current directory to the home directory of superman.

A single dot (.) and two dots (..), often referred to as *dot-dot*, also have special meanings. A single dot (.) indicates the current directory, whereas two dots (..) indicate the parent directory. For example, if the current directory is /usr/share, you go one level up to /usr by typing the following:

```
cd ..
```

Directory Listings

You can get a directory listing by using the ls command. By default, the ls command, without any options, displays the contents of the current directory in a compact, multicolumn format. To tell the directories and files apart, use the -F option (ls -F). The output will show the directory names with a slash (/) appended to them. Plain filenames appear as is. The at sign (@) appended to a listing indicates that this file is a link to another file. (In other words, this filename simply refers to another file; it's a shortcut.) An asterisk (*) is appended to executable files. (The shell can run any executable file.)

You can see even more detailed information about the files and directories with the -l option. The rightmost column shows the name of the directory entry. The date and time before the name show when the last modifications to that file were made. To the left of the date and time is the size of the file in bytes. The file's group and owner appear to the left of the column that shows the file size. The next number to the left indicates the number of links to the file. (A *link* is like a shortcut in Windows.)

Finally, the leftmost column shows the file's permission settings, which determine who can read, write, or execute the file. This column shows a sequence of nine characters, which appear as rwxrwxrwx when each letter is present. Each letter indicates a specific permission. A hyphen (-) in place of a letter indicates no permission for a specific operation on the file. Think of these nine letters as three groups of three letters (rwx), interpreted as follows:

Leftmost group   Controls the read, write, and execute permission of the file's owner. In other words, if you see rwx in this position, the file's owner can read (r), write (w), and execute (x) the file. A hyphen in the place of a letter indicates no permission. Thus the string rw- means that the owner has read and write permission but not execute permission. Although executable programs (including shell programs) typically have execute permission, directories treat execute permission as equivalent to *use* permission: A user must have execute permission on a directory before they can open and read the contents of the directory.

Middle group   Controls the read, write, and execute permission of any user belonging to that file's group.

Rightmost group   Controls the read, write, and execute permission of all other users (collectively thought of as *the world*).

Thus a file with the permission setting rwx------ is accessible only to the file's owner, whereas the permission setting **rwxr--r--** makes the file readable by the world.

An interesting feature of the ls command is that it doesn't list any file whose name begins with a period. To see these files, you must use the ls command with the -a option, as follows:

```
ls -a
```

Most Linux commands take single-character options, each with a hyphen as a prefix. When you want to use several options, type a hyphen and concatenate (string together) the option letters, one after another. Thus ls -al is equivalent to ls -a -l as well as ls -l -a.

Changing Permissions and Ownership

You may need to change a file's permission settings to protect it from others. Use the chmod command to change the permission settings of a file or a directory. To use chmod effectively, you have to specify the permission settings. A good way is to concatenate letters from the columns of Table 18.2 in the order shown (who/action/permission). You use only the single character from each column—the text in parentheses is for explanation only.

TABLE 18.2   Letter codes for file permissions

Who	Action	Permission
u (user)	+ (add)	r (read)
g (group)	- (remove)	w (write)
o (others)	= (assign)	x (execute)
a (all)	s (set user ID)	

For example, to give everyone read access to all of the files in a directory, pick a (for *all*) from the first column, + (for *add*) from the second column, and r (for *read*) from the third column to come up with the permission setting a+r. Then use the set of options with chmod, like this:

chmod a+r *.

On the other hand, to permit everyone to execute one specific file, type this:

chmod a+x filename

Type **ls -l** to verify that the change took place.

Sometimes you have to change a file's user or group ownership for everything to work correctly. For example, suppose you're instructed to create a directory named cups and give it the ownership of user ID lp and group ID sys. You can log in as root and create the cups directory with the command mkdir:

mkdir cups

If you check the file's details with the ls -l command, you see that the user and group ownership is root root. To change the owner, use the chown command. For example, to change the ownership of the cups directory to user ID lp and group ID sys, type this:

```
chown lp.sys cups
```

Working with Files

To copy files from one directory to another, use the cp command. If you want to copy a file to the current directory but retain the original name, use a period (.) as the second argument of the cp command. Thus, the following command copies the Xresources file from the /etc/X11 directory to the current directory (denoted by a single period):

```
cp /etc/X11/Xresources .
```

The cp command makes a new copy of a file and leaves the original intact.

If you want to copy the entire contents of a directory—including all subdirectories and their contents—to another directory, use the command cp -ar sourcedir destdir. (This command copies everything in the sourcedir directory to destdir.) For example, to copy all of the files from the /etc/X11 directory to the current directory, type the following command:

```
cp -ar /etc/X11 .
```

To move a file to a new location, use the mv command. The original copy is gone, and a new copy appears at the destination. You can use mv to rename a file. If you want to change the name of today.list to old.list, use the mv command as follows:

```
mv today.list old.list
```

On the other hand, if you want to move the today.list file to a subdirectory named saved, use this command:

```
mv today.list saved
```

An interesting feature of mv is that you can use it to move entire directories (with all of their subdirectories and files) to a new location. If you have a directory named data that contains many files and subdirectories, you can move that entire directory structure to old_data by using the following command:

```
mv data old_data
```

To delete files, use the rm command. For example, to delete a file named old.list, type the following command:

```
rm old.list
```

Be careful with the rm command—especially when you log in as root. You can inadvertently delete important files with rm.

Working with Directories

To organize files in your home directory, you have to create new directories. Use the mkdir command to create a directory. For example, to create a directory named images in the current directory, type the following:

mkdir images

After you create the directory, you can use the cd images command to change to that directory.

You can create an entire directory tree by using the -p option with the mkdir command. For example, suppose your system has a /usr/src directory and you want to create the directory tree /usr/src/book/java/examples/applets. To create this directory hierarchy, type the following command:

mkdir -p /usr/src/book/java/examples/applets

When you no longer need a directory, use the rmdir command to delete it. You can delete a directory only when the directory is empty. To remove an empty directory tree, you can use the -p option, like this:

rmdir -p /usr/src/book/java/examples/applets

This command removes the empty parent directories of applets. The command stops when it encounters a directory that's not empty.

Networking Utilities

Just as you can use the ipconfig command to see the status of IP configuration with Windows, the ifconfig command can be used in Linux. You can get information about the usage of the ifconfig command by using ifconfig -help. The following output provides an example of the basic ifconfig command run on a Linux system:

```
eth0      Link encap:Ethernet   HWaddr 00:60:08:17:63:A0
          inet addr:192.168.1.101  Bcast:192.168.1.255  Mask:255.255.255.0
          UP BROADCAST RUNNING  MTU:1500  Metric:1
          RX packets:911 errors:0 dropped:0 overruns:0 frame:0
          TX packets:804 errors:0 dropped:0 overruns:0 carrier:0
          collisions:0 txqueuelen:100
          Interrupt:5 Base address:0xe400
```

```
lo          Link encap:Local Loopback
            inet addr:127.0.0.1  Mask:255.0.0.0
            UP LOOPBACK RUNNING  MTU:3924  Metric:1
            RX packets:18 errors:0 dropped:0 overruns:0 frame:0
            TX packets:18 errors:0 dropped:0 overruns:0 carrier:0
            collisions:0 txqueuelen:0
```

In addition to ifconfig, Linux users can use the iwconfig command to view the state of their wireless network. By using iwconfig, you can view such important information as the link quality, AP MAC address, data rate, and encryption keys, which can be helpful in ensuring that the parameters in the network are consistent.

Summary

This chapter provided an overview of operating systems other than Microsoft Windows. In particular, we looked at Mac OS X and Linux, and you learned about the features and various tools included with each that appear on the CompTIA A+ 220-902 exam.

There are best practices that administrators should follow regardless of which operating system(s) they are running, and we looked at those as well. The chapter concluded with an examination of some basic Linux commands and examples of most of them in use.

Exam Essentials

Be able to identify best practices.   Best practices help keep systems and data usable. Among the best practices to follow, it is important to schedule backups, schedule disk maintenance, keep systems up to date, and make sure antivirus/anti-malware definition files are current.

Know key Mac OS tools and features.   There are a number of tools and features included with Mac OS X that make it an attractive operating system to use. Among them are Mission Control, Keychain, Spotlight, Remote Disc, and Boot Camp.

Know the basic Linux commands.   Every version and distribution of Linux allows you to get to the command line in one way or another and interact with the shell. From there, you can give commands to navigate around (cd, pwd), to create and change file values (vi, chmod, chown), to run commands (su, sudo), and to do many other tasks.

Review Questions

The answers to the chapter review questions can be found in Appendix A.

1. Within a Linux terminal, you want to see all of the files on your system in long format (using the –l option), including any hidden files (which requires the –a option). Which command should you use?

    A. ls -a | ls -l

    B. ls -s; ls -l

    C. ls -la

    D. ls -a\ls -l

2. Which of the following allows you to install Windows on a Mac machine and choose between operating systems upon bootup?

    A. Keychain

    B. Mission Control

    C. Clicker

    D. Boot Camp

3. As part of your training program, you're trying to convince users to make backups on a regular basis. Which Apple app can be used to make backups of various types on a regular basis?

    A. Time Machine

    B. Trailer Horn

    C. Insurance Policy

    D. Father Time

4. Which of the following Linux commands/utilities can be used to edit a file?

    A. ps

    B. vi

    C. rm

    D. ls

5. Which of the following Linux commands/utilities can be used to edit a wireless connection's configuration settings?

    A. dd

    B. apt-get

    C. iwconfig

    D. pwd

6. Which of the following is a Mac OS X feature for password management?

   A. Spotlight

   B. Keychain

   C. Dock

   D. Gestures

7. The interpreter in Linux between the operating system and the user is known as the

   _____.

   A. Shell

   B. Translator

   C. Player

   D. Promoter

8. What type of backups are kept on site at the computer center for immediate recovery purposes?

   A. Man-in-the-middle

   B. Judicious copies

   C. Journal copies

   D. Working copies

9. Which of the following can be used in Linux to download patches for installation on a workstation?

   A. patchmaster

   B. shell/terminal

   C. apt-get

   D. hijack

10. Which of the following commands can be used to change the owner of a file to a new owner in Linux?

   A. chdir

   B. chmgr

   C. chown

   D. pwd

11. Which Linux utility can be used to check and repair disks?

   A. fsck

   B. chkdsk

   C. du

   D. dumgr

12. Your iPad has an application that will not stop running. What feature/tool can you use to stop it?

A. Kill

B. Force Quit

C. Task Manager

D. Treason

13. Which of the following is the most common shell used with Linux?

A. Dash

B. Cash

C. Bash

D. Sash

14. What is the name of the area at the bottom of a Mac OS X screen where, by default, a bar of crucial icons appears?

A. Foot

B. Shield

C. Taskbar

D. Dock

15. What key combination can you use to bring up Spotlight from within an app?

A. Control+Shift

B. Option+Tab

C. Command+space

D. Alt+Home

16. Which Linux command can be used to let you run a single command as another user?

A. sudo

B. su

C. passwd

D. ifconfig

17. Which of the following Linux commands will show you a list of running processes?

A. pr

B. pt

C. ps

D. pk

18. You are currently in a Linux terminal session and in directory /home/edulaney/documents/mail. Which command will take you to /home/edulaney/documents?

   A. cd .

   B. cd ..

   C. cd . . .

   D. cd ~

19. If the permissions for a file are rwxrw-r--, what permissions apply for a user who is a member of the group to which the owner belongs?

   A. Read, write, and execute

   B. Read and write

   C. Read only

   D. No access

20. What does the -p option with mkdir do?

   A. Prompts the user before creating files

   B. Prompts the user before creating subfolders

   C. Creates subfolders as well as folders

   D. None of the above

Performance-Based Question

You will encounter performance-based questions on the A+ exams. The questions on the exam require you to perform a specific task, and you will be graded on whether or not you were able to complete the task. The following requires you to think creatively in order to measure how well you understand this chapter's topics. You may or may not see similar questions on the actual A+ exams. To see how your answers compare to the authors', refer to Appendix B.

By default, not all files and folders in a Linux directory are shown when you do an ls listing. Entries that start with a period (.) are considered "hidden" and not shown. Try this command in your home directory, and then compare the result with what you see when you don't use the -a option:

1. Type **cd** to change to your home directory.

2. Type **ls -F** to see the files and directories in your home directory.

3. Type **ls -aF** to see everything, including hidden files.

Chapter

19

Security

THE FOLLOWING COMPTIA A+ 220–902 EXAM OBJECTIVES ARE COVERED IN THIS CHAPTER:

✓ **3.1   Identify common security threats and vulnerabilities.**

- Malware: spyware, viruses, worms, trojans, rootkits, ransomware
- Phishing
- Spear phishing
- Spoofing
- Social engineering
- Shoulder surfing
- Zero day attack
- Zombie/botnet
- Brute forcing
- Dictionary attacks
- Non-compliant systems
- Violations of security best practices
- Tailgating
- Man-in-the-middle

✓ **3.2   Compare and contrast common prevention methods.**

- Physical security: Lock doors, Mantrap, Cable locks, Securing physical documents/passwords/shredding, Biometrics, ID badges, Key fobs, RFID badge, Smart card, Tokens, Privacy filters, Entry control roster
- Digital security: antivirus/antimalware, firewalls, user authentication/strong passwords, multifactor authentication, directory permissions, VPN, DLP, disabling ports, access control lists, smart card, email filtering, trusted/untrusted software sources
- User education/AUP
- Principle of least privilege

✓ **3.3 Compare and contrast differences of basic Windows OS security settings.**

- User and groups: administrator, power user, guest, standard user

- NTFS vs. Share permissions: allow vs. deny, moving vs. copying folders and files, file attributes

- Shared files and folders: administrative shares vs. local shares, permission propagation, inheritance

- System files and folders

- User authentication: single sign-on

- Run as administrator vs. standard user

- Bit-locker

- Bit-locker-To-Go

- EFS

✓ **3.4 Given a scenario, deploy and enforce security best practices to secure a workstation.**

- Password best practices: setting strong passwords, password expiration, changing default user names/passwords, screensaver required password, BIOS/UEFI passwords, requiring passwords

- Account management: restricting user permissions, login time restrictions, disabling guest account, failed attempts lockout, timeout/screen lock

- Disable autorun

- Data encryption

- Patch/update management

✓ **3.5 Compare and contrast various methods for securing mobile devices.**

- Screen locks: fingerprint lock, face lock, swipe lock, passcode lock

- Remote wipes

- Locator applications

- Remote backup applications

- Failed login attempts restrictions

- Antivirus/antimalware

- Patching/OS updates

- Biometric authentication

- Full device encryption

- Multifactor authentication

- Authenticator applications

- Trusted sources vs. untrusted sources

- Firewalls

- Policies and procedures: BYOD vs. corporate owned, profile security requirements

✓ **3.6 Given a scenario, use appropriate data destruction and disposal methods.**

- Physical destruction: shredder, drill/hammer, electromagnetic (degaussing), incineration, certificate of destruction

- Recycling or repurposing best practices: low level format vs. standard format, overwrite, drive wipe

✓ **3.7 Given a scenario, secure SOHO wireless and wired networks.**

- Wireless specific: changing SSID, setting encryption, disabling SSID broadcast, antenna and access point placement, radio power levels, WPS

- Change default user names and passwords

- Enable MAC filtering

- Assign static IP addresses

- Firewall settings

- Port forwarding/mapping

- Disabling ports

- Content filtering/parental controls

- Update firmware

- Physical security

Think of how much simpler an administrator's life was in the days before every user had to be able to access the Internet. Think of how much simpler it must have been when you only had to maintain a number of dumb terminals connected to a minitower. Much of what has created headaches for an administrator since then is the inherent security risk that comes about as the network expands. As our world—and our networks—have become more connected, the need to secure data and keep it away from the eyes of those who can do harm has increased exponentially.

Realizing this, CompTIA added the security domain to the A+ exams a few years back. Security is now a topic that every administrator and technician must not only be aware of and concerned about, they must also be actively involved in implementing methods to enforce and monitor it. In the world of production, quality may be job one, but in the IT world, it is security.

This chapter looks at security primarily from the standpoint of what you need to know to pass the exam. All of the topics relevant to the security domain of the 220–902 exam are covered, and a thorough overview of each topic is provided.

A+ is not the only IT certification that CompTIA offers. Security+ is one of the more popular choices. The topics found in this chapter are a subset of what you need to know for that certification.

Common Prevention Methods

A great number of the security issues that plague networks today can be solved through the implementation of basic security elements. Some of those elements are physical (locked doors) and others are digital (antivirus software), but all share in common the goal of keeping problems out.

Six topic areas are key: physical security, digital security, user education, the principle of least privilege, email security, and VPNs. As you study for the exam, know the types of physical security elements that you can add to an environment to secure it. Know, as well, what types of digital security you should implement to keep malware at bay. Understand that the first line of defense is the user. You need to educate users to understand why security is important, and you need to impose the principle of least privilege to prevent them from inadvertently causing harm.

Physical Security

Physical security is a grab bag of elements that can be added to an environment to aid in securing it. It ranges from key fobs to retinal scanners. In the following sections, we will examine the list of components in the order in which CompTIA lists them.

Lock Doors

One of the easiest ways to prevent those intent on creating problems from physically entering your environment is to lock your doors and keep them out. A key aspect of access control involves *physical barriers*. The objective of a physical barrier is to prevent access to computers and network systems. The most effective physical barrier implementations require that more than one physical barrier be crossed to gain access. This type of approach is called a *multiple-barrier system*.

Ideally, your systems should have a minimum of three physical barriers. The first barrier is the external entrance to the building, referred to as a *perimeter*, which is protected by burglar alarms, external walls, *fencing*, surveillance, and so on. An *access list* or *entry control roster* should exist to identify specifically who can enter and can be verified by a guard or someone with authority. The second barrier is the entrance into the building, and it could rely upon such items as *ID badges* to gain access. The third barrier is the entrance to the computer room itself (and could require key fobs, or just keys to locks). Each of these entrances can be individually secured, monitored, and protected with alarm systems.

Think of the three barriers this way: (1) outer, such as a fence; (2) middle, such as guards, locks, and mantraps; and (3) inner, such as key fobs.

Although these three barriers won't always stop intruders, they will potentially slow them down enough so that law enforcement can respond before an intrusion is fully developed. Inside, a truly secure site should be dependent upon a *physical security token* for access to the actual network resources.

Tailgating

Tailgating refers to being so close to someone when they enter a building that you are able to come in right behind them without needing to use a key, a card, or any other security device. Many social engineering intruders needing physical access to a site will use this method of gaining entry. Educate users to beware of this and other social engineering ploys and prevent them from happening.

Using mantraps, which are devices such as small rooms that limit access to one or a few individuals, is a great way to stop tailgating.

Securing Physical Documents/Passwords/Shredding

The type and amount of information that can be gleaned from physical documents is amazing, even in the age when there is such a push to go paperless. *Dumpster diving* is a common problem that puts systems at risk. Companies normally generate a huge amount of paper, most of which eventually winds up in dumpsters or recycle bins. Dumpsters may contain information that is highly sensitive in nature (such as a password a user has written on a piece of paper because they haven't memorized it yet). In high-security and government environments, sensitive papers should either be shredded or burned. Most businesses don't do this. In addition, the advent of "green" companies has created an increase in the amount of recycled paper, which can often contain all kinds of juicy information about a company and its individual employees.

Biometrics

Biometric devices use physical characteristics to identify the user. Such devices are becoming more common in the business environment. Biometric systems include fingerprint/palm/hand scanners, retinal scanners, and soon, possibly, DNA scanners. To gain access to resources, you must pass a physical screening process. In the case of a hand scanner, this may include identifying fingerprints, scars, and markings on your hand. Retinal scanners compare your eye's retinal pattern to a stored retinal pattern to verify your identity. DNA scanners will examine a unique portion of your DNA structure to verify that you are who you say you are.

With the passing of time, the definition of *biometrics* is expanding from simply identifying physical attributes about a person to being able to describe patterns in their behavior. Recent advances have been made in the ability to authenticate someone based on the key pattern that they use when entering their password (how long they pause between each key, the amount of time each key is held down, and so forth). A company adopting biometric technologies needs to consider the controversy they may face (some authentication methods are considered more intrusive than others). The error rate also needs to be considered, along with an acceptance of the fact that errors can include both false positives and false negatives.

Badges

Badges can be any form of identification intended to differentiate the holder from everyone else. This can be as simple as a name badge or photo ID.

Smart cards are difficult to counterfeit, but they're easy to steal. Once a thief has a smart card, they have all the access the card allows. To prevent this, many organizations don't put any identifying marks on their smart cards, making it harder for someone to utilize them. A password or PIN is required to activate many modern smart cards, and encryption is employed to protect the card's contents.

Key Fobs

Key fobs are named after the chains that used to hold pocket watches to clothes. They are security devices that you carry with you; they display a randomly generated code that you can then use for authentication. This code usually changes very quickly (every 60 seconds is probably the average), and you combine this code with your PIN for authentication. RSA is one of the most well-known vendors of key fobs.

Multifactor Authentication

Anytime more than one item (factor) is needed to authenticate a user, this is known as multifactor authentication. It may take two, three, or four factors to authenticate, but as long as it is more than one, as the name implies, it is known as multifactor. One of the most common examples where this is used in everyday life is at the bank's ATM machine. In order to withdraw money, a user must provide a card (one card factor) and a PIN (a second factor). If you know the PIN number but do not have the card, you cannot get money from the machine. If you have the card but do not have the PIN number, you cannot get money from the machine.

RFID Badges and Smart Cards

A *smart card* is a type of badge or card that gives you access to resources, including buildings, parking lots, and computers. It contains information about your identity and access privileges. Each area or computer has a card scanner or a reader in which you insert your card. Radio frequency identification (RFID) is the wireless, no-contact technology used with these cards and their accompanying reader.

The reader is connected to the workstation and validates against the security system. This increases the security of the authentication process because you must be in physical possession of the smart card to use the resources. Of course, if the card is lost or stolen, the person who finds the card can access the resources it allows.

RSA Tokens

Physical tokens are anything that a user must have on them to access network resources, and they are often associated with devices that enable the user to generate a one-time password authenticating their identity. SecurID, from RSA, is one of the best-known examples of a physical token, and information on that series of products can be found at

www.emc.com/security/rsa-securid/rsa-securid-hardware-tokens.htm

Privacy Filters

Privacy filters are either film or glass add-ons that are placed over a monitor or laptop screen to prevent the data on the screen from being readable when viewed from the sides. Only the user sitting directly in front of the screen is able to read the data.

Digital Security

Whereas the topic of physical security, from CompTIA's standpoint, focuses on keeping individuals out, digital security focuses on keeping harmful data and malware out as well as on authorization and permissions. The areas of focus are antivirus software, firewalls, antispyware, user authentication/strong passwords, and directory permissions. Each of these is addressed in the sections that follow.

Antivirus and Anti-malware Software

The primary method of preventing the propagation of malicious code involves the use of *antivirus software*. Antivirus software is an application that is installed on a system to protect it and to scan for viruses as well as worms and Trojan horses. Most viruses have characteristics that are common to families of viruses. Antivirus software looks for these characteristics, or fingerprints, to identify and neutralize viruses before they impact you.

More than 200,000 known viruses, worms, bombs, and other malware have been defined. New ones are added all of the time. Your antivirus software manufacturer will work very hard to keep the definition database files current. The definition database file contains the currently known viruses and countermeasures for a particular antivirus software product. You probably won't receive a virus that hasn't been seen by one of these companies. If you keep the virus definition database files in your software up-to-date, you probably won't be overly vulnerable to attacks. Since viruses are a subset of malware, *anti-malware software* typically does everything that antivirus software does as well as identifying threats beyond just viruses. A lot of anti-malware software is marketed as antivirus software.

 The best method of protection is to use a layered approach. Antivirus software should be at the gateways, at the servers, and at the desktop. If you want to go one step further, you can use software from different vendors at each location to make sure that you're covered from all angles. You will need to avoid installing multiple antivirus scanners on any one machine, though, as they often don't play well together.

Firewalls

Firewalls are among the first lines of defense in a network. There are different types of firewalls, and they can be either stand-alone systems or included in devices such as routers or servers. You can find firewall solutions that are marketed as hardware only and others that are software only. Many firewalls, however, consist of add-in software that is available for servers or workstations.

 Although solutions are sold as "hardware only," the hardware still runs some sort of software. It may be hardened and in ROM to prevent tampering, and it may be customized, but software is present nonetheless.

The basic purpose of a firewall is to isolate one network from another. Firewalls are becoming available as appliances, meaning that they're installed as the primary device separating two networks. *Appliances* are freestanding devices that operate in a largely self-contained manner, requiring less maintenance and support than a server-based product.

Firewalls function as one or more of the following:

- Packet filter
- Proxy firewall
- Stateful inspection firewall

 To understand the concept of a firewall, it helps to know the origin of the term. In days of old, dwellings used to be built so close together that if a fire broke out in one, it could easily destroy a block or more before it could be contained. To decrease the risk of this happening, firewalls were built between buildings. The firewalls were huge brick walls that separated the buildings and kept a fire confined to one side. The same concept of restricting and confining is true in network firewalls. Traffic from the outside world hits the firewall and isn't allowed to enter the network unless it's invited.

The firewall shown in Figure 19.1 effectively limits access from outside networks while allowing inside network users to access outside resources. The firewall in this illustration is also performing proxy functions.

FIGURE 19.1   A proxy firewall blocking network access from external networks

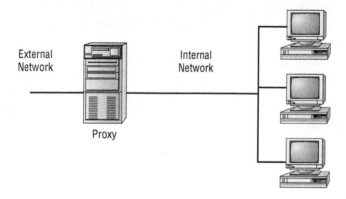

 Although firewalls are often associated with outside traffic, you can place a firewall anywhere. For example, if you want to isolate one portion of your internal network from others, you can place a firewall between them.

The following list includes discussions of three of the most common functions that firewalls perform:

Packet filter firewalls   A firewall operating as a *packet filter* passes or blocks traffic to specific addresses based on the type of application and the port used. The packet filter doesn't analyze the data of a packet; it decides whether to pass it based on the packet's addressing information. For instance, a packet filter may allow web traffic on port 80 and block Telnet traffic on port 23. This type of filtering is included in many routers. If a received packet request asks for a port that isn't authorized, the filter may reject the request or simply ignore it. Many packet filters can also specify which IP addresses can request which ports and allow or deny them based on the security settings of the firewall.

Packet filters are growing in sophistication and capability. A packet filter firewall can allow any traffic that you specify as acceptable. For example, if you want web users to access your site, then you configure the packet filter firewall to allow data on port 80 to enter. If every network were exactly the same, firewalls would come with default port settings hard-coded, but networks vary, so the firewalls don't include such settings (though Deny All is the most common default).

Proxy firewalls   A *proxy firewall* can be thought of as an intermediary between your network and any other network. Proxy firewalls are used to process requests from an outside network; the proxy firewall examines the data and makes rule-based decisions about whether the request should be forwarded or refused. The proxy intercepts all of the packages and reprocesses them for use internally. This process may include hiding IP addresses.

The proxy firewall provides better security than packet filtering because of the increased intelligence that a proxy firewall offers. Requests from internal network users are routed through the proxy. The proxy, in turn, repackages the request and sends it along, thereby isolating the user from the external network. The proxy can also offer caching, should the same request be made again, and it can increase the efficiency of data delivery.

A proxy firewall typically uses two network interface cards (NICs). This type of firewall is referred to as a *dual-homed* firewall. One of the cards is connected to the outside network, and the other is connected to the internal network. The proxy software manages the connection between the two NICs. This setup segregates the two networks from each other and offers increased security. Figure 19.2 illustrates a dual-homed firewall segregating two networks from each other.

FIGURE 19.2   A dual-homed firewall segregating two networks from each other

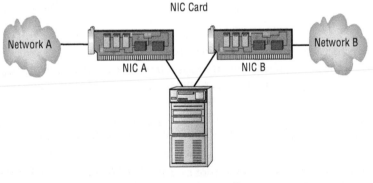

The proxy function can occur at either the application level or the circuit level. *Application-level proxy* functions read the individual commands of the protocols that are being served. This type of server is advanced and must know the rules and capabilities of the protocol used. An implementation of this type of proxy must know the difference between GET and PUT operations, for example, and have rules specifying how to execute them. A *circuit-level proxy* creates a circuit between the client and the server and doesn't deal with the contents of the packets that are being processed.

A unique application-level proxy server must exist for each protocol supported. Many proxy servers also provide full *auditing*, *accounting*, and other usage information that wouldn't normally be kept by a circuit-level proxy server.

Stateful inspection firewalls   *Stateful inspection* is also referred to as *stateful packet filtering*. Most of the devices used in networks don't keep track of how information is routed or used. After a packet is passed, the packet and path are forgotten. In stateful inspection (or stateful packet filtering), records are kept using a state table that tracks every communications channel and can deny packets that were not requested from the internal network. Stateful inspections occur at all levels of the network and provide additional security, especially in connectionless protocols such as *User Datagram Protocol (UDP)* and *Internet Control Message Protocol (ICMP)*. This adds complexity to the process. Denial of service (DoS) attacks present a challenge because flooding techniques are used to overload the state table and effectively cause the firewall to shut down or reboot. When multiple computers are aimed at the target, it is known as a distributed denial of service (DDoS) attack. A *smurf* attack attempts to use a broadcast ping (ICMP) on a network. The return address of the ping may be a valid system in your network. This system will be flooded with responses in a large network.

Antispyware

Just as antivirus software seeks out and stops viruses from entering and spreading, so too is the purpose of antispyware software. One thing separating spyware from most other malware is that it almost always exists to provide commercial gain. The operating systems from Microsoft are the ones most affected by spyware, and Microsoft has released Windows Defender and Security Essentials (as well as System Center Endpoint Protection for the enterprise) to combat the problem.

User Authentication/Strong Passwords

You can set up many different parameters and standards to force the people in your organization to conform. In establishing these parameters, it's important that you consider the capabilities of the people who will be working with them. If you're working in an environment where people aren't computer savvy, you may spend a lot of time helping them remember and recover passwords. Many organizations have had to reevaluate their security guidelines after they've invested great time and expense to implement high-security systems.

Enforcing authentication security, especially when supporting users, can become a high-maintenance activity for network administrators. On one hand, you want people to be able to authenticate easily; on the other hand, you want to establish security that protects your company's resources. In a Windows domain, password policies can be configured at the domain level using Group Policy objects. Variables that you can configure include password complexity and length and the time between allowed changes to passwords. A good password includes both upper- and lowercase letters as well as numbers and symbols. Educate users not to use personal information that one could easily guess about them, such as their pet names, anniversaries, or birthdays.

Directory Permissions

A bit later in this chapter, we will examine NTFS vs. Share permissions. Pay particular attention to Table 19.1 and Table 19.2. Most of the digital security at the directory permissions level is handled by NTFS, and there is not much that users can do to improve or change the security of the directory services deployed. However, you can ensure that they don't become a tool for an attacker bent on compromising your organization's security:

- Ensure that the most secure form of authentication encryption is used and supported by both the client and the authentication servers.

- Use encrypted software and protocols whenever possible, even for internal communications.

- Require users to change their password according to the company's password policy.

- Establish a minimum character limit for passwords. While many companies set the minimum at 8 characters, it is not uncommon to see this set at 16.

- Instruct users to never write their password down or, if they do, to divide it up into several pieces and store each in a different secure location (such as a home safe, a gun cabinet, a chemical supply locker, or a safe deposit box).

- Tell users to never share their password or logon session with another person; this includes friends, spouse, and children.

- Make sure users allow all approved *patch updates* to be installed onto their client. *Patch/update management* is an important part of basic security.

- Ensure that users copy all company data back to a central file server before disconnecting from a logon session.

- Users should back up personal data onto verified removable media.

- Users should never walk away from a logged-on workstation without first locking it (requiring a password to continue the session).

- Require users to employ a password-protected screensaver.

- Don't let users use auto-logon features.

- Encourage data encryption. This can be accomplished in any number of ways (including using BitLocker and EFS, which are discussed later in this chapter).

- Tell users to be aware of who is around them (and may be watching them) when they log on and when they work with valuable data.

- Users should never leave a company notebook computer, tablet computer, or smartphone in a position where it can be stolen or compromised while they are away from the office. *Cable locks* should be used to keep notebook computers securely in place whenever they are off site.

 Real World Scenario

Check the Movie Listings

Be wary of popular names or current trends that make certain passwords predictable. For example, during the first release of *Star Wars*, two of the most popular passwords used on college campuses were C3PO and R2D2. This created a security problem for campus computer centers.

A few years back, characters from the *Matrix* trilogy became popular passwords as those working in offices tried to live out their lives in fantasy. While you may truly like a movie or character that is popular at the moment, you need to understand that names associated with popular movies will be tried as password possibilities very quickly.

The protection of a directory service is based on the initial selection of a network operating system and its deployment infrastructure. After these foundational decisions are made, you need to understand fully the technologies employed by your selected directory services system and learn how to make the most functional, yet secure, environment possible. This will usually require the addition of third-party security devices, applications, services, and solutions.

User Education/AUP

The most effective method of preventing viruses, spyware, and harm to data is education. Teach your users not to open suspicious files and to open only those files that they're reasonably sure are virus free. They need to scan every disk, email, and document that they receive before they open it. You should also have all workstations scheduled to be scanned automatically on a regular basis.

Acceptable use policies (AUPs) describe how the employees in an organization can use company systems and resources, both software and hardware. This policy should also outline the consequences for misuse. In addition, the policy (also known as a *use policy*) should address the installation of personal software on company computers and the use of personal hardware such as USB devices.

Even secure workstations that do not contain traditional media devices (CD, DVD, and so forth) usually contain USB ports. Unless those ports are disabled, a user can easily connect a flash drive and copy files to and from it. Not only should you make every effort to limit USB ports, you should also have the use of such devices spelled out in the acceptable use policy to circumvent the "I didn't know" defense.

Every acceptable use policy today should include a section on smartphone usage (and even presence) within the workplace. Although a smartphone is a convenience for employees (they can now more easily receive and make personal calls at work), it can be a headache for the security administrator. Most smartphones can store files in the same way as any USB device, and they can be used to copy files to and from a workstation. Additionally, the camera feature on most phones makes it possible for a user to take pictures of things such as company documents, servers, and physical security implementation, among many other things that the company may not want to share. For this reason, most secure facilities have stringent restrictions on the presence of smartphones within the vicinity.

Make sure your acceptable use policies provide your company with adequate coverage regarding all acceptable uses of corporate resources.

Principle of Least Privilege

The concept of least privilege is a simple one: When assigning permissions, give users only the permissions they need to do their work and no more. This is especially true with administrators. Users who need administrative-level permissions should be assigned two accounts: one for performing nonadministrative, day-to-day tasks and the other to be used only when performing administrative tasks that specifically require an administrative-level user account. Those users should be educated on how each of the accounts should be used.

The biggest benefit to following this policy is the reduction of risk. The biggest headache with following this policy is trying to deal with users who may not understand it. Managers, for example, may assert that they should have a higher permission level than those who report to them, but giving those permissions to them also opens up all of the possibilities for inadvertently deleting files, misconfiguring resources, and so on.

A least privilege policy should exist, and be enforced, throughout the enterprise. Users should have only the permissions and privileges needed to do their jobs and no more. The ISO standard 27002 (which updates 17799) sums it up well: "Privileges should be allocated to individuals on a need-to-use basis and on an event-by-event basis, i.e., the minimum requirement for their functional role when needed." Adopting this as the policy for your organization is highly recommended.

Email Filtering

Email filtering, as the name implies, involves filtering email before passing it on. This can be done with messages intended both to enter and leave the network, and it can head off problems before they can propagate. One of the simplest filters is the spam filter included with most email programs. None of them are 100 percent efficient, and all suffer from false positives (identifying some email as spam that really isn't).

Virtual Private Networks

As networks grow beyond simple physical limitations (such as an office or a building) to include clients from all over the world, the need to secure data becomes paramount. One of the best methods of addressing this is to tunnel the data. Tunneling sends private data across a public network by placing (encapsulating) that data into other packets. Most tunnels are *virtual private networks (VPNs)*.

A VPN is a private network connection that occurs through a public network. A private network provides security over an otherwise unsecure environment. VPNs can be used to connect LANs together across the Internet or other public networks. With a VPN, the remote end appears to be connected to the network as if it were connected locally. A VPN requires either special hardware to be installed or a VPN software package running on servers and workstations.

Even though a VPN is created through the Internet or other public networks, the connection logically appears to be part of the local network. This is why a VPN connection that is used to establish a connection between two private networks across the Internet is considered a private connection or an extranet.

Though it is a few years old, the following blog provides a useful guide to different VPN tunnel types in Windows: http://blogs.technet.com/b/rrasblog/archive/2009/01/30/different-vpn-tunnel-types-in-windows-which-one-to-use.aspx

Common Security Threats

In the following sections, we discuss a number of very important topics that fall into the realm of the broad categories: social engineering and malware. We'll look at these topics as well as some of the reasons your network is vulnerable. The discussion is far from inclusive because troublemakers create new variants of malware and social engineering attacks on a regular basis. We will cover, however, everything CompTIA expects you to know for the exam.

Social Engineering

Social engineering is a process in which an attacker attempts to acquire information about your network and system by social means, such as talking to people in the organization. A social engineering attack may occur over the phone, by email, or in person. The intent is to acquire access information, such as user IDs and passwords. When the attempt is made through email or instant messaging, this is known as *phishing* (discussed later), and it's often made to look as if a message is coming from sites where users are likely to have accounts (eBay and PayPal are popular).

These are relatively low-tech attacks and are more akin to con jobs. Take the following example: Your help desk gets a call at 4:00 a.m. from someone purporting to be the vice president of your company. They tell the help desk personnel that they are out of town to attend a meeting, their computer just failed, and they are sitting in a FedEx office trying to get a file from their desktop computer back at the office. They can't seem to remember their password and user ID. They tell the help desk representative that they need access to the information right away or the company could lose millions of dollars. Your help desk rep knows how important this meeting is and gives the user ID and password over the phone. At this point, the attacker has just successfully socially engineered an ID and password that can be used for an attack.

Another common approach is initiated by a phone call or email from someone who pretends to be your software vendor, telling you that they have a critical fix that must be installed on your computer system. It may state that if this patch isn't installed right away, your system will crash and you'll lose all your data. For some reason, you've changed your maintenance account password and they can't log on. Your system operator gives the password to the person. You've been hit again.

In Exercise 19.1, you'll test your users to determine the likelihood of a social engineering attack. The steps are suggestions for tests; you may need to modify them slightly to be appropriate at your workplace. Before proceeding, make certain that your manager knows that you're conducting such a test and approves of it.

EXERCISE 19.1

Testing Social Engineering

1. Call the receptionist from an outside line when the sales manager is at lunch. Tell her that you're a new salesperson, that you didn't write down the username and password the sales manager gave you last week, and that you need to get a file from the email system for a presentation tomorrow. Does she direct you to the appropriate person or attempt to help you receive the file?

2. Call the human resources department from an outside line. Don't give your real name, but instead say that you're a vendor who has been working with this company for years. You'd like a copy of the employee phone list to be emailed to you, if possible. Do they agree to send you the list, which would contain information that could be used to try to guess usernames and passwords?

3. Pick a user at random. Call them and identify yourself as someone who works with the company. Tell them that you're supposed to have some new software ready for them by next week and that you need to know their password to finish configuring it. Do they do the right thing?

The best defense against any social engineering attack is education. Make certain that the employees of your company would know how to react to the requests presented here.

Password Attacks

Password attacks occur when an account is attacked repeatedly. This is accomplished by using applications known as *password crackers*, which send possible passwords to the account in a systematic manner. The attacks are initially carried out to gain passwords for an access or modification attack. There are several types of password attacks:

Brute-force attack   A *brute-force* attack is an attempt to guess passwords until a successful guess occurs. As an example of this type of attack, imagine starting to guess with *A* and then going through *z*; when no match is found, the next guess series goes from *AA* to *zz* and then adds a third value (*AAA* to *zzz*). Because of the nature of this routine, this type of attack usually occurs over a long period of time. To make passwords more difficult to guess, they should be much longer than two or three characters (Microsoft recommends eight as the minimum), be complex, and have password lockout policies.

Dictionary attack   A *dictionary attack* uses a dictionary of common words to attempt to find the user's password. Dictionary attacks can be automated, and several tools exist in the public domain to execute them. As an example of this type of attack, imagine guessing words and word combinations found in a standard English-language dictionary.

Hybrid   A *hybrid attack* typically uses a combination of dictionary entries and brute force. For example, if you know that there is a good likelihood that the employees of a particular company are using derivatives of the company name in their passwords, then you can seed those values into the values attempted.

Malware

We've all been battling malicious, invasive software since we bought our first computers. This software can go by any number of names—virus, malware, and so on—but if you aren't aware of its presence, these uninvited intruders may damage the data on your hard drive, destroy your operating system, and possibly spread to other systems.

Make certain your systems, and the data within them, are kept as secure as possible by using antivirus and antispyware programs. Doing so prevents others from changing the data, destroying it, or inadvertently harming it.

Man-in-the-Middle Attacks

Man-in-the-middle attacks clandestinely place something (such as a piece of software or a rogue router) between a server and the user, and neither the server's administrator nor the user is aware of it. The man-in-the-middle intercepts data and then sends the information to the server as if nothing is wrong. The server responds to the software, thinking it's communicating with a legitimate client. The attacking software continues sending information on to the server, and so forth.

If communication between the server and user continues, what's the harm of the software? The answer lies in whatever else the software is doing. The man-in-the-middle software may be recording information for someone to view later, altering it, or in some other way compromising the security of your system and session.

 A man-in-the-middle attack is an active attack. Something is actively intercepting the data and may or may not be altering it. If it's altering the data, the altered data masquerades as legitimate data traveling between the two hosts.

In recent years, the threat of man-in-the-middle attacks on wireless networks has increased. Because it's no longer necessary to connect to the wire, a malicious rogue can be outside of the building intercepting packets, altering them, and sending them on. A common solution to this problem is to enforce a secure wireless authentication protocol such as WPA2.

An older term that is now generically used for all man-in-the-middle attacks is *TCP/IP hijacking* even though they are not technically the same. TCP/IP hijacking involves the attacker gaining access to a host in the network and logically disconnecting it from the network. The attacker then inserts another machine with the same IP address. This happens quickly, and it gives the attacker access to the session and to all of the information on the original system. The server won't know this has occurred, and it will respond as if the client is trusted—the attacker forces the server to accept its IP address as valid. The hijacker will hope to acquire privileges and access to all of the information on the server. There is little you can do to counter this threat, but fortunately these attacks require fairly sophisticated software and are harder to engineer than a simple DoS attack.

Rootkits

Rootkits have become the software exploitation program du jour. Rootkits are software programs that have the ability to hide certain things from the operating system; they do so by obtaining (and retaining) administrative-level access. With a rootkit, there may be a number of processes running on a system that don't show up in Task Manager, or connections that don't appear in a Netstat display may be established or available—the rootkit masks the presence of these items. It does this by manipulating function calls to the operating system and filtering out information that would normally appear.

Unfortunately, many rootkits are written to get around antivirus and antispyware programs that aren't kept up-to-date. The best defense you have is to monitor what your system is doing and catch the rootkit in the process of installation.

Phishing

Phishing is a form of social engineering in which you simply ask someone for a piece of information that you are missing by making it look as if it is a legitimate request. An email might look as if it is from a bank and contain some basic information, such as the user's name. These types of messages often state that there is a problem with the person's account or access privileges. They will be told to click a link to correct the problem. After they click the link—which goes to a site other than the bank's—they are asked for their username, password, account information, and so on. The person instigating the phishing can then use this information to access the legitimate account.

One of the best countermeasures to phishing is simply to mouse over the Click Here link and read the URL. Almost every time, the URL is an adaptation of the legitimate URL as opposed to a link to the real thing.

The only preventive measure in dealing with social engineering attacks is to educate your users and staff never to give out passwords and user IDs over the phone or via email or to anyone who isn't positively verified as being who they say they are.

When you combine phishing with Voice over IP (VoIP), it becomes known as *vishing*, and it is just an elevated form of social engineering. While crank calls have been in existence since the invention of the telephone, the rise in VoIP now makes it possible for someone to call you from almost anywhere in the world, without the worry of tracing/caller ID/ and other features of land lines, and pretend to be someone they are not in order to get data from you.

Two other forms of phishing of which you should be aware are *spear phishing* and *whaling*, and they are very similar in nature. With spear phishing, the attacker uses information that the target would be less likely to question because it appears to be coming from a *trusted source*. Suppose, for example, you receive a message that appears to be from your spouse, and it says to click here to see that video of your children from last Christmas. Because it appears far more likely to be a legitimate message, it cuts through your standard defenses like a spear, and the likelihood that you would click this link is higher. Generating the attack requires much more work on the part of the attacker, and it often involves using information from contact lists, friend lists from social media sites, and so on.

 Trust is a key issue with security. There are *trusted software sources* that you know and work with all the time (such as Microsoft) and there are untrusted sources and you should differentiate between them. Likewise, there are trusted sites and untrusted sites, and you should similarly differentiate between them: Let common sense be your guide.

Whaling is nothing more than phishing, or spear phishing, for so-called "big" users, thus the reference to the ocean's largest creatures. Instead of sending out a To Whom It May Concern message to thousands of users, the whaler identifies one person from whom they can gain all of the data that they want—usually a manager or business owner—and targets the phishing campaign at them.

Shoulder Surfing

One form of social engineering is known as *shoulder surfing*, and it involves nothing more than watching someone when they enter their sensitive data. They can see you entering a password, typing in a credit card number, or entering any other pertinent information. The best defense against this type of attack is simply to survey your environment before entering personal data.

Spyware

Spyware differs from other malware in that it works—often actively—on behalf of a third party. Rather than self-replicating, like viruses and worms, spyware is spread to machines by users who inadvertently ask for it. The users often don't know they have asked for it but have done so by downloading other programs, visiting infected sites, and so on.

The spyware program monitors the user's activity and responds by offering unsolicited pop-up advertisements (sometimes known as *adware*), gathers information about the user to pass on to marketers, or intercepts personal data such as credit card numbers.

Viruses

Viruses can be classified as polymorphic, stealth, retrovirus, multipartite, armored, companion, phage, and macro viruses. Each type of virus has a different attack strategy and different consequences.

Estimates for losses due to viruses are in the billions of dollars. These losses include financial loss as well as lost productivity.

The following sections will introduce the symptoms of a virus infection, explain how a virus works, and describe the types of viruses you can expect to encounter and how they generally behave. We'll also discuss how a virus is transmitted through a network and look at a few hoaxes.

Symptoms of a Virus/Malware Infection

Many viruses will announce that you're infected as soon as they gain access to your system. They may take control of your system and flash annoying messages on your screen or destroy your hard disk. When this occurs, you'll know that you're a victim. Other viruses will cause your system to slow down, cause files to disappear from your computer, or take over your disk space.

Because viruses are the most common type of malware, the term *virus* is used in this section.

You should look for some of the following symptoms when determining if a virus infection has occurred:

-   The programs on your system start to load more slowly. This happens because the virus is spreading to other files in your system or is taking over system resources.

-   Unusual files appear on your hard drive, or files start to disappear from your system. Many viruses delete key files in your system to render it inoperable.

-   Program sizes change from the installed versions. This occurs because the virus is attaching itself to these programs on your disk.

-   Your browser, word-processing application, or other software begins to exhibit unusual operating characteristics. Screens or menus may change.

-   The system mysteriously shuts itself down or starts itself up and does a great deal of unanticipated disk activity.

- You mysteriously lose access to a disk drive or other system resources. The virus has changed the settings on a device to make it unusable.

- Your system suddenly doesn't reboot or gives unexpected error messages during startup.

This list is by no means comprehensive. What is an absolute, however, is the fact that you should immediately quarantine the infected system. It is imperative that you do all you can to contain the virus and keep it from spreading to other systems within your network, or beyond.

How Viruses Work

A virus, in most cases, tries to accomplish one of two things: render your system inoperable or spread to other systems. Many viruses will spread to other systems given the chance and then render your system unusable. This is common with many of the newer viruses.

If your system is infected, the virus may try to attach itself to every file in your system and spread each time you send a file or document to other users. Figure 19.3 shows a virus spreading from an infected system either through a network or by removable media. When you give removable media to another user or put it into another system, you then infect that system with the virus.

FIGURE 19.3   Virus spreading from an infected system using the network or removable media

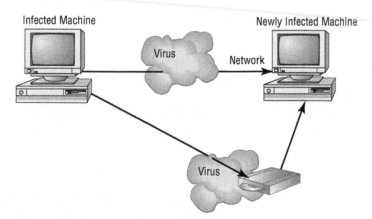

Many viruses today are spread using email. The infected system attaches a file to any email that you send to another user. The recipient opens this file, thinking it's something that you legitimately sent them. When they open the file, the virus infects the target system. The virus might then attach itself to all the emails that the newly infected system sends, which in turn infects the computers of the recipients of the emails. Figure 19.4 shows how a virus can spread from a single user to literally thousands of users in a very short period of time using email.

FIGURE 19.4 An email virus spreading geometrically to other users

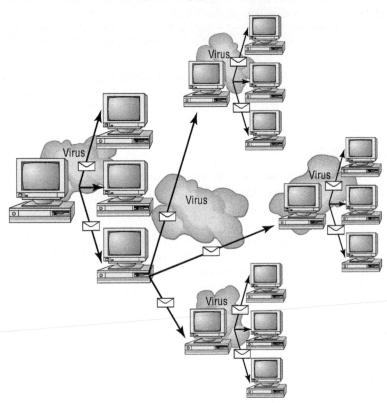

Types of Viruses

Viruses take many different forms. The following list briefly introduces these forms and explains how they work.

The best defense against a virus attack is up-to-date antivirus software installed and running. The software should be on all workstations as well as the server.

These are the most common types of viruses, but this isn't a comprehensive list:

Armored virus An *armored virus* is designed to make itself difficult to detect or analyze. Armored viruses cover themselves with protective code that stops debuggers or disassemblers from examining critical elements of the virus. The virus may be written in such a way that some aspects of the programming act as a decoy to distract analysis while the actual code hides in other areas in the program.

From the perspective of the creator, the more time that it takes to deconstruct the virus, the longer it can live. The longer it can live, the more time it has to replicate and spread to as many machines as possible. The key to stopping most viruses is to identify them quickly and educate administrators about them—the very things that the armor makes difficult to accomplish.

Companion virus   A *companion virus* attaches itself to legitimate programs and then creates a program with a different filename extension. This file may reside in your system's temporary directory. When a user types the name of the legitimate program, the companion virus executes instead of the real program. This effectively hides the virus from the user. Many of the viruses that are used to attack Windows systems make changes to program pointers in the Registry so that they point to the infected program. The infected program may perform its dirty deed and then start the real program.

Macro virus   A *macro virus* exploits the enhancements made to many application programs. Programmers can expand the capability of applications such as Microsoft Word and Excel. Word, for example, supports a mini-BASIC programming language that allows files to be manipulated automatically. These programs in the document are called *macros*. For example, a macro can tell your word processor to spell-check your document automatically when it opens. Macro viruses can infect all of the documents on your system and spread to other systems via email or other methods. Macro viruses are one of the fastest-growing forms of exploitation today.

Multipartite virus   A *multipartite virus* attacks your system in multiple ways. It may attempt to infect your boot sector, infect all of your executable files, and destroy your application files. The hope here is that you won't be able to correct all of the problems and will allow the infestation to continue. The multipartite virus depicted in Figure 19.5 attacks a system's boot sector, infects application files, and attacks Word documents.

FIGURE 19.5   A multipartite virus commencing an attack on a system

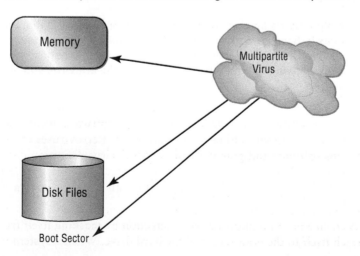

Phage virus   A *phage virus* alters programs and databases and the only way to remove this virus is to reinstall the programs that are infected. If you miss even a single instance of this virus on the victim system, the process will start again and infect the system once more.

Polymorphic virus   *Polymorphic viruses* change form to avoid detection. These types of viruses attack your system, display a message on your computer, and delete files on your system. The virus will attempt to hide from your antivirus software. Frequently, the virus will encrypt parts of itself to avoid detection. When the virus does this, it's referred to as *mutation*. The mutation process makes it hard for antivirus software to detect common characteristics of the virus. Figure 19.6 shows a polymorphic virus changing its characteristics to avoid detection. In this example, the virus changes a signature to fool antivirus software.

FIGURE 19.6   The polymorphic virus changing its characteristics

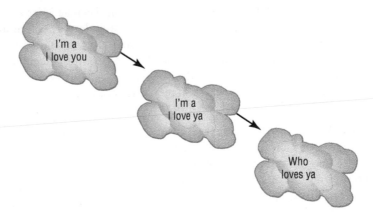

    A *signature* is an algorithm or other element of a virus that uniquely identifies it. Because some viruses have the ability to alter their signature, it is crucial that you keep signature files current, whether you choose to download them manually or configure the antivirus engine to do so automatically.

Retrovirus   A *retrovirus* attacks or bypasses the antivirus software installed on a computer. You can consider a retrovirus to be an anti-antivirus. Retroviruses can directly attack your antivirus software and potentially destroy the virus definition database file. When this information is destroyed without your knowledge, you would be left with a false sense of security. The virus may also directly attack an antivirus program to create bypasses for itself.

Stealth virus   A *stealth virus* attempts to avoid detection by masking itself from applications. It may attach itself to the boot sector of the hard drive. When a system utility or program runs, the stealth virus redirects commands around itself to avoid detection. An infected file may report a file size different from what is actually present. Figure 19.7 shows a stealth virus attaching itself to the boot sector to avoid detection. Stealth viruses may also move themselves from file A to file B during a virus scan for the same reason.

FIGURE 19.7   A stealth virus hiding in a disk boot sector

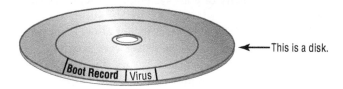

This is a disk.

Boot Record | Virus

Virus Transmission in a Network

Upon infection, some viruses destroy the target system immediately. The saving grace is that the infection can be detected and corrected. Some viruses won't destroy or otherwise tamper with a system; they use the victim system as a carrier. The victim system then infects servers, file shares, and other resources with the virus. The carrier then infects the target system again. Until the carrier is identified and cleaned, the virus continues to harass systems in this network and spread.

Present Virus Activity

New viruses and threats are released on a regular basis to join the cadre of those already in existence. From an exam perspective, you need only be familiar with the world as it existed at the time the questions were written. From an administrative standpoint, however, you need to know what is happening today.

To find this information, visit the CERT/CC Current Activity web page at www.us-cert.gov/current/current_activity.html. Here you'll find a detailed description of the most current viruses as well as links to pages on older threats.

Worms

A *worm* is different from a virus in that it can reproduce itself, it's self-contained, and it doesn't need a host application to be transported. Many of the so-called viruses that have made the news were actually worms. However, it's possible for a worm to contain or deliver a virus to a target system.

By their nature and origin, worms are supposed to propagate, and they use whatever services they're capable of using to do that. Early worms filled up memory and bred inside the RAM of the target computer. Worms can use TCP/IP, email, Internet services, or any number of possibilities to reach their target.

Trojans

Trojan horses are programs that enter a system or network under the guise of another program. A Trojan horse may be included as an attachment or as part of an installation program. The Trojan horse can create a back door or replace a valid program during installation. It then accomplishes its mission under the guise of another program. Trojan horses can be used to compromise the security of your system, and they can exist on a system for years before they're detected.

The best preventive measure for Trojan horses is to not allow them entry into your system. Immediately before and after you install a new software program or operating system, back it up! If you suspect a Trojan horse, you can reinstall the original program(s), which should delete the Trojan horse. A port scan may also reveal a Trojan horse on your system. If an application opens a TCP or UDP port that isn't supported in your network, you can track it down and determine which port is being used.

Ransomware

With *ransomware*, software—often delivered through a Trojan horse—takes control of a system and demands that a third party be paid. The "control" can be accomplished by encrypting the hard drive, by changing user password information, or via any of a number of other creative ways. Users are usually assured that by paying the extortion amount (the ransom), they will be given the code needed to revert their systems back to normal operations.

Spoofing

A *spoofing* attack is an attempt by someone or something to masquerade as someone else. This type of attack is usually considered an access attack. A common spoofing attack that was popular for many years on early UNIX and other timesharing systems involved a programmer writing a fake logon program. It would prompt the user for a user ID and password. No matter what the user typed, the program would indicate an invalid logon attempt and then transfer control to the real logon program. The spoofing program would write the logon and password into a disk file, which was retrieved later.

The most popular spoofing attacks today are IP spoofing, ARP spoofing, and DNS spoofing. With *IP spoofing*, the goal is to make the data look as if it came from a trusted host when it didn't (thus spoofing the IP address of the sending host).

With *ARP spoofing* (also known as *ARP poisoning*), the media access control (MAC) address of the data is faked. By faking this value, it is possible to make it look as if the data came from a networked device that it did not come from. This can be used to gain access to the network, to fool the router into sending to the device data that was intended for another host, or to launch a DoS attack. In all cases, the address being faked is an address of a legitimate user, and that makes it possible to get around such measures as allow/deny lists.

With *DNS spoofing*, the DNS server is given information about a name server that it thinks is legitimate when it isn't. This can send users to a website other than the one to which they wanted to go, reroute mail, or do any other type of redirection for which data from a DNS server is used to determine a destination. Another name for this is *DNS poisoning*.

Always think of spoofing as fooling. Attackers are trying to fool the user, system, and/or host into believing that they're something that they are not. Because the word spoof can describe any false information at any level, spoofing can occur at any level of network.

Another DNS weakness is *domain name kiting.* When a new domain name is issued, there is technically a five-day grace period before you must pay for it. Those engaged in kiting can delete the account within the five days and re-register it, allowing them to have accounts that they never have to pay for.

The important point to remember is that a spoofing attack tricks something or someone into thinking that something legitimate is occurring.

Zero-Day Attack

When a hole is found in a web browser or other software, and attackers begin exploiting it the very day it is discovered by the developer (bypassing the one-to-two-day response time that many software providers need to put out a patch once the hole has been found), it is known as a *zero-day attack* (or *exploit*). It is very difficult to respond to a zero-day exploit. If attackers learn of the weakness the same day as the developer, then they have the ability to exploit it until a patch is released. Often, the only thing that you as a security administrator can do, between the discovery of the exploit and the release of the patch, is to turn off the service. Although this can be a costly undertaking in terms of productivity, it is the only way to keep the network safe.

Several years ago, Stuxnet was found to be using a total of four zero-day vulnerabilities to spread from host to host:

www.symantec.com/connect/blogs/stuxnet-using-three-additional-zero-day-vulnerabilities

Zombie/Botnet

Software running on infected computers called zombies is often known as a *botnet*. Bots, by themselves, are but a form of software that runs automatically and autonomously. (For example, Google uses the Googlebot to find web pages and bring back values for the index.) *Botnet*, however, has come to be the word used to describe malicious software running on a zombie and under the control of a *bot-herder*.

Denial of service attacks—DoS and DDoS—can be launched by botnets, as can many forms of adware, spyware, and spam (via *spambots*). Most bots are written to run in the background with no visible evidence of their presence. Many malware kits can be used to create botnets and modify existing ones.

There is no universal approach to dealing with botnets, but knowing how to deal with various botnet types (all of which are described here) is important for exam preparation. Some can be easily detected by looking at a database of known threats, whereas others have to be identified through analysis of their behavior.

Non-Complaint Systems

One of the easiest ways to make your systems vulnerable and expose them to threats is to fail to keep them compliant. As an administrator, you should always follow security regulatory standards as well as compliance standards (such as ISO). One example of this approach is Cisco's SAFE:

www.cisco.com/en/us/td/docs/solutions/Enterprise/Security/SAFE_RG/SAFE_rg.html

The Security Control Framework is the backbone of SAFE, and unification is the underlying key (rather than a silo approach) to security. By being modular, it can incorporate all parts of the network, including the WAN, the extranet, the Internet, and the intranet.

Workstation Security Best Practices

The user represents the weakest link in the security chain, whether harm comes to them in the form of malware, social engineering, or simply avoidable mistakes. The workstation represents the digital arm of the user, and it must be properly and adequately secured to keep the user—and the network—protected.

The following sections will explore some of the more commonly implemented best practices in greater detail.

Setting Strong Passwords

One of the most effective ways to keep a system safe is to employ strong passwords and educate your users in the best practices associated with them. Many password-generation systems are based on a one-way hashing approach. You can't take the hash value and reverse it to guess the password. In theory, this makes it harder to guess or decrypt a password.

Passwords should be as long as possible. Most security experts believe a password of 10 characters is the minimum that should be used if security is a real concern. If you use only the lowercase letters of the alphabet, you have 26 characters with which to work. If you add the numeric values 0 through 9, you'll get another 10 characters. If you go one step further and add the uppercase letters, you'll then have an additional 26 characters, giving you a total of 62 characters with which to construct a password.

 Most vendors recommend that you use nonalphabetic characters such as #, $, and % in your password, and some go so far as to require it.

If you used a 4-character password, this would be $62 \times 62 \times 62 \times 62$, or approximately 14 million password possibilities. If you used 5 characters in your password, this would give you 62 to the 5th power, or approximately 920 million password possibilities. If you used a 10-character password, this would give you 62 to the 10th power, or 8.4×1017 (a very big number) possibilities. As you can see, these numbers increase exponentially with each position added to the password. The 4-digit password could probably be broken in a fraction of a day, while the 10-digit password would take considerably longer and much more processing power.

If your password consisted of only the 26 lowercase letters from the alphabet, the 4-digit password would have 26 to the 4th power, or 456,000, password combinations. A 5-character password would have 26 to the 5th power, or over 11 million, and a 10-character password would have 26 to the 10th power, or 1.4 × 1014. This is still a big number, but it would take considerably less time to break it.

Mathematical methods of encryption are primarily used in conjunction with other encryption methods as part of authenticity verification. The message and the hashed value of the message can be encrypted using other processes. In this way, you know that the message is secure and hasn't been altered.

Requiring Passwords and Expiration

Make absolutely certain that you require passwords (such a simple thing to overlook in a small network) for all accounts, and change the default passwords on system accounts (as well as the default user names where possible). Not only that, but configure password expiration on all accounts so that they have to be changed on a regular basis.

Add passwords on each system to basic input/output system (BIOS) and unified extensible firmware interface (UEFI) firmware.

Account Management

Given a security-related scenario, account management can take into account such settings as restricting user permissions, setting login time restrictions, disabling the guest account, locking an account after a certain number of failed attempts, and configuring a screen lock when the system times out after a certain length of inactivity. Each of these are discussed in the sections that follow.

Restricting User Permissions

When assigning user permissions, follow the principle of least privilege (discussed earlier): Give users only the bare minimum that they need to do their job. Assign permissions to groups rather than users, and make users member of groups (or remove them from groups) as they change roles or positions.

Add Login Time Restrictions

Configure user accounts so that logins can occur only during times that the user can be expected to be working. Preventing logins at 2:00 a.m. can be an effective method of keeping hackers from your systems.

Act on Failed Login Attempts

Configure user account settings so that there are a limited number of login attempts (three is a good number) before the account is locked for a period of time. Legitimate users who need to get in before the block expires can contact the administrator and explain why they weren't able to give the right password three times in a row, and nonlegitimate users will go away in search of another system to try to enter.

Changing Default Usernames

Default accounts represent a huge weakness because everyone knows they exist. When an operating system is installed—whether on a workstation or a server—certain default accounts are created. Knowing the names of those accounts simplifies the process of potential attackers accessing them because they only have to supply the password.

Disabling the Guest Account

When Windows is installed, one of the default accounts it creates is Guest, and this represents a weakness that can be exploited by an attacker. While the account cannot do much, it can provide initial access to a system and the attacker can use that to find another account or acquire sensitive information about the system.

To secure the system, disable all accounts that are not needed, especially the Guest account. Next, rename the accounts if you can (Microsoft won't allow you to rename some). Finally, change the passwords from the defaults and add them to the cycle of passwords that routinely get changed.

Screensaver Required Password

A screensaver should automatically start after a short period of idle time, and a password should be required before the user can begin the session again. This method of locking the workstation adds one more level of security.

There should be a screen lock/time-out setting configured on every workstation to prevent them from inadvertently becoming an open door to the network.

Disable Autorun

It is never a good idea to put any media in a workstation if you do not know where it came from or what it is. The simple reason is that said media (CD, DVD, USB) could contain malware. Compounding matters, that malware could be referenced in the AUTORUN.INF file, causing it to be summoned when the media is inserted in the machine and requiring no other action. AUTORUN.INF can be used to start an executable, access a website, or do any of a large number of different tasks. The best way to prevent a user from falling victim to such a ploy is to disable the autorun feature on the workstation.

Microsoft has changed (by default, disabled) the function on Windows so that it no longer acts as it previously did. The reason Microsoft changed the default action can be summed up in a single word: security. That text-based AUTORUN.INF file can not only take your browser to a web page, it can also call any executable file, pass along variable information about the user, or do just about anything else imaginable. Simply put, it is never a good idea to plug any media into your system if you have no idea where it came from or what it holds. Such an action opens up the user's system—and the network—to any number of possible risks. An entire business's data could be jeopardized by such a minuscule act if someone with elevated privileges placed a harmful CD into a computer at work.

Data Loss Prevention

Data loss prevention (DLP) systems monitor the contents of systems (workstations, servers, and networks) to make sure that key content is not deleted or removed. They also monitor who is using the data (looking for unauthorized access) and transmitting the data. DLP systems share commonalities with network intrusion prevention systems.

One of the best-known DLP systems is MyDLP, which started as an open-source solution to run on most Windows platforms. You can find MyDLP at www.mydlp.com. A large number of commercial programs are available for purchase, including Microsoft Forefront Identity Manager (www.microsoft.com/forefront/).

Tripwire is a great system for data protection. Tripwire monitors specific files to see if they have changed. If they have, the Tripwire system can either restore them or simply alert an administrator. There is both a commercial and an open-source version of Tripwire, and you can find more information at www.tripwire.org.

Working with Windows OS Security Settings

Every operating system offers security features and settings. While you need to know a little about Linux and Mac OS, the A+ exams focus primarily on Windows and the OS-specific security settings that you need to know to secure them.

The following sections will explore some of the more basic Windows OS security features and settings in more detail.

Users and Groups

There are a number of groups created on the operating system by default. The following sections look at the main ones.

Administrator

The *administrator* account is the most powerful of all: it has the power to do everything from the smallest task all the way up to removing the operating system. Because of the great power it holds, and the fact that it is always created, many who want to do harm will target this account as the one that they try to breach. To increase security, during the installation of the Windows operating systems in question, you are prompted for a name of a user who will be designated as the Administrator. The power then comes not from being called "Administrator" (the username might now be "edulaney," "eadulaney," or something similar) but from being a member of the Administrators group (notice the plural for the group and singular for the user).

Since members of the *Administrators* group have such power, they can inadvertently do harm (such as accidentally deleting a file that a regular user could not). To protect against this, the practice of logging in with an Administrators group account for daily interaction is strongly discouraged. Instead, we suggest that system administrators log in with a user account (lesser privileges) and change to the Administrators group account (elevated privileges) only when necessary.

Power User

Originally, Microsoft wanted to create a group in Windows that was not as powerful as the Administrators group, and that is how the *Power Users* group came into being. The idea was that membership in this group would be given read/write permission to the system, allowing members to install most software but keeping them from changing key operating system files. As such, it would be a good group for those who need to test software (such as programmers) and junior administrators.

The group did not work out as planned, and in Windows Vista, Windows 7, and Windows 8/8.1, the group has no more permissions than a standard user. The group is now only kept around for backward compatibility with Windows XP systems.

Guest

The *guest* account is created by default (and should be disabled) and is a member of the *Guests* group. For the most part, members of Guests have the same rights as Users except they can't get to log files. The best reason to make users members of the Guests group is to access the system only for a limited time.

 As part of operating system security, we usually recommend that you rename the default Administrator and Guest accounts that are created at installation.

Standard User

The User group is the default to which standard users belong. Members of this group have read/write permission to their own profile. They cannot modify system-wide Registry settings or do much harm outside of their own account. Under the principle of least privilege, users should be made a member of the Users group only unless qualifying circumstances force them to have higher privileges.

If you attempt to run some utilities (such as SFC) from a standard command prompt, you will be told that you must be an administrator running a console session in order to continue. Rather than opening a standard command prompt, choose Start ➤ All Programs ➤ Accessories, and then right-click Command Prompt and choose *Run As Administrator.* The UAC will prompt you to continue, and then you can run SFC without a problem.

NTFS vs. Share Permissions

The new technology file system (NTFS) was introduced with Windows NT to address security problems. Before Windows NT was released, it had become apparent to Microsoft that a new file system was needed to handle growing disk sizes, security concerns, and the need for more stability. NTFS was created to address those issues.

Although the file allocation table (FAT) file system was relatively stable if the systems that were controlling it kept running, it didn't do well when the power went out or the system crashed unexpectedly. One of the benefits of NTFS was a transaction tracking system, which made it possible for Windows NT to back out of any disk operations that were in progress when it crashed or lost power.

With NTFS, files, directories, and volumes can each have their own security. NTFS's security is flexible and built in. Not only does NTFS track security in ACLs, which can hold permissions for local users and groups, but each entry in the ACL can specify what type of access is given—such as Read & Execute, List Folder Contents, or Full Control. This allows a great deal of flexibility in setting up a network. In addition, special file-encryption programs were developed to encrypt data while it was stored on the hard disk.

Microsoft strongly recommends that all network shares be established using NTFS. Several current OSs from Microsoft support both FAT32 and NTFS. It's possible to convert from FAT32 to NTFS without losing data, but you can't do the operation in reverse (you would need to reformat the drive and install the data again from a backup tape).

If you're using FAT32 and want to change to NTFS, the convert utility will allow you to do so. For example, to change the E: drive to NTFS, the command is convert e: /FS:NTFS.

Share permissions apply only when a user is accessing a file or folder through the network. Local permissions and attributes are used to protect the file when the user is local. With FAT and FAT32, you do not have the ability to assign "extended" or "extensible" permissions, and the user sitting at the console effectively is the owner of all resources on the system. As such, they can add, change, and delete any data or file.

With NTFS as the file system, however, you are allowed to assign more comprehensive security to your computer system. NTFS permissions are able to protect you at the file level. Share permissions can be applied to the directory level only. NTFS permissions can affect users logged on locally or across the network to the system where the NTFS permissions are applied. Share permissions are in effect only when the user connects to the resource via the network.

Allow vs. Deny

Within NTFS, permissions for objects fall into one of three categories: allow, not allow, and deny. When viewing the permissions for a file or folder, you can check the box for Allow, which effectively allows the group selected to perform that action. You can also uncheck the box for Allow, which does not allow that group that action. Alternatively, you can check the Deny box, which prevents that group from using that action. There is a difference between not allowing (a cleared check box) and Deny (which specifically prohibits), and you tend not to see Deny used often. Deny, when used, trumps other permissions.

Permissions set on a folder are inherited down through subfolders, unless otherwise changed. Permissions are also cumulative: if a user is a member of a group that has Read permission and a member of a group that has Write permission, they effectively have both Read and Write permission.

Moving vs. Copying Folders and Files

When you copy a file, you create a new entity. When you move a file, you simply relocate it and still have but one entity. This distinction is important when it comes to understanding permissions. A copy of a file will generally have the permissions assigned to it that are placed on newly created files in the folder—regardless of what permissions were on the original file.

A moved file, on the other hand, will attempt to keep the same permissions as it had in the original location. Differences will occur if the same permissions cannot exist in the new location—for example, if you are moving a file from an NTFS volume to FAT32, the NTFS permissions will be lost. If, on the other hand, you are moving from a FAT32 volume to an NTFS volume, new permissions will be added that match those for newly created entities.

Folder copy and move operations follow guidelines that are similar to those with files.

File Attributes

Permissions can be allowed or denied individually on a per-folder basis. You can assign any combination of the values shown in Table 19.1.

TABLE 19.1 NTFS directory permissions

NTFS Permission	Meaning
Full Control	Gives the user all of the other choices and the ability to change permissions. The user can also take ownership of the directory or any of its contents.
Modify	Combines the Read & Execute permission with the Write permission and further allows the user to delete everything, including the folder.

TABLE 19.1   NTFS directory permissions *(continued)*

NTFS Permission	Meaning
Read & Execute	Combines the permissions of Read with those of List Folder Contents and adds the ability to run executables.
List Folder Contents	The List Folder Contents permission (known simply as List in previous versions) allows the user to view the contents of a directory and to navigate to its subdirectories. It does not grant the user access to the files in these directories unless that is specified in file permissions.
Read	Allows the user to navigate the entire directory structure, view the contents of the directory, view the contents of any files in the directory, and see ownership and attributes.
Write	Allows the user to create new entities within the folder.

Clicking the Advanced button allows you to configure auditing and ownership properties. You can also apply NTFS permissions to individual files. This is done from the Security tab for the file; Table 19.2 lists the NTFS file permissions.

TABLE 19.2   NTFS file permissions

NTFS Permission	Meaning
Full Control	Gives the user all of the other permissions as well as permission to take ownership and change permission
Modify	Combines the Read & Execute permission with the Write permission and further allows the user to delete the file
Read	Allows the user to view the contents of the file and to see ownership and attributes
Read & Execute	Combines the Read permission with the ability to execute
Write	Allows the user to overwrite the file as well as to change attributes and see ownership and permissions

By default, the determination of NTFS permissions is based on the *cumulative* NTFS permissions for a user. Rights can be assigned to users based on group membership and individually; the only time permissions do not accumulate is when the Deny permission is invoked.

Shared Files and Folders

You can share folders, and the files beneath them, by right-clicking on them and choosing Share With from the context menu. In Windows, the context menu asks you to choose with whom you want to share the folder or file. The options you see on the context menu will depend on the type of network to which you are connected—a domain, a workgroup, or a HomeGroup. If password-protected sharing is turned on (the default), the person accessing the share has to give a username and password to access the shared entity.

The Advanced Sharing settings will come up if you try to share something in one of the Public folders or make other changes. This interface can also be accessed through the Network and Sharing Center applet in the Control Panel, and it is used to change network settings relevant to sharing.

Administrative Shares vs. Local Shares

Administrative shares are created on servers running Windows on the network for administrative purposes. These shares can differ slightly based on which OS is running, but they always end with a dollar sign ($) to make them hidden. There is one for each volume on a hard drive (c$, d$, and so on) as well as admin$ (the root folder—usually c:\winnt), and print$ (where the print drivers are located). These are created for use by administrators and usually require administrator privileges to access.

Local shares, as the name implies, are those that are created locally. In Windows Vista, the icon for them shows two people to indicate the share.

Permission Propagation/Inheritance

Permissions are cumulative. A user who is a member of two groups will effectively have the permissions of both groups combined.

Inheritance is the default throughout the permission structure unless a specific setting is created to override it. A user who has Read and Write permissions in one folder will have that in all the subfolders unless a change has been made specifically to one of the subfolders.

System Files and Folders

System files are usually flagged with the Hidden attribute, meaning they don't appear when a user displays a directory listing. You should not change this attribute on a system file unless absolutely necessary. System files are required for the OS to function. If they are visible, users might delete them (perhaps thinking that they can clear some disk space by deleting files that they don't recognize). Needless to say, that would be a bad thing!

User Authentication

As mentioned in Chapter 14, one of the big problems larger systems must deal with is the need for users to access multiple systems or applications. This may require a user to remember multiple accounts and passwords. The purpose of a *single sign-on (SSO)* is to give users access to all of the applications and systems that they need when they log on. Single sign-on is both a blessing and a curse. It's a blessing in that once users are authenticated, they can access all of the resources on the network and browse multiple directories. It's a curse in that it removes the doors that otherwise exist between the user and various resources.

In the case of Kerberos, a single token allows any "Kerberized" applications to accept a user as valid. The important thing to remember in this process is that each application that wants to use SSO must be able to accept and process the token presented by Kerberos. Active Directory (AD) uses Kerberos v5 and a server that runs AD retains information about all access rights for all users and groups in the network. When a user logs on to the system, AD issues the user a globally unique identifier (GUID). Applications that support AD can use this GUID to provide access control.

Using AD simplifies the sign-on process for users and lowers the support requirements for administrators. Access can be established through groups, and it can be enforced through group memberships: all users log into the Windows domain using their centrally created AD account. On a decentralized network, SSO passwords are stored on each server and can represent a security risk. It's important to enforce password changes and make certain that passwords are updated throughout the organization on a frequent basis.

BitLocker and BitLocker To Go

You have to be careful, because CompTIA sometimes refers to the utility as "bit-locker" or "Bitlocker," while it is officially known as *BitLocker*. This tool allows you to use drive encryption to protect files—including those needed for startup and logon. This is available only with more complete editions of Windows 8 (Pro and Enterprise), Windows 7 (Enterprise and Ultimate), and Windows Vista (Enterprise and Ultimate).

For removable drives, *BitLocker To Go* provides the same encryption technology to help prevent unauthorized access to the files stored on them.

EFS

Encrypting File System (EFS) is available in most editions of Windows, and it allows for encryption/decryption of files stored in NTFS volumes. All users can use EFS, whereas only administrators can turn on BitLocker. It does not require any special hardware, while BitLocker benefits from having the Trusted Platform Module (TPM). As an additional distinction, EFS can encrypt just one file, if so desired, while BitLocker encrypts the whole volume and whatever is stored on it. Last, EFS can be used in conjunction with BitLocker to increase security further.

Mobile Device Security

Apple computers have a pretty decent reputation in the industry for being somewhat resistant to malware. Whether or not this is because of the relatively small installed base or the ease with which hackers penetrate "other" operating systems, this characteristic carries over to Apple's mobile devices. In fact, hackers don't seem to be as interested in attacking the legions of mobile devices as much as they have gone after the Windows operating system that drives the vast majority of laptops, desktops, and servers in the world. Nevertheless, attacks occur. Coupled with how easy mobile devices are to misplace or steal, it behooves users to have proactive monitoring and contingency plans in place.

The following sections detail the built-in security utilities that are common in today's mobile devices. Furthermore, for threats not covered by the software with which the devices ship, the protection available from third-party utilities is worth discussing.

Screen Locks

Apple and Android mobile devices include a requisite passcode locking mechanism that is off by default, but the user on the go is encouraged to enable a *passcode lock*. If your device acts more as a home computing device and rarely goes with you out the door, there is very little reason to set such a passcode, but knowing how to do so is important. Exercise 19.2 outlines the steps for creating a code for your iPhone. The same general concept for Android phones is presented in Exercise 19.3.

EXERCISE 19.2

Setting the Passcode Lock on an iPhone

1. Tap Settings.

2. Depending on iOS version, select either General or Touch ID & Passcode.

3. Select Passcode Lock.

4. Tap Turn Passcode On. If you'd like to use a passcode that requires use of the keyboard, you need to turn off the Simple Passcode switch. Otherwise, a simple four-digit PIN is required.

5. Enter the passcode of your choosing. The display will slide automatically, implying that you need to enter it a second time to confirm. Doing so sets the passcode.

6. Set the amount of time that must pass while the phone is asleep before the passcode will be required and whether the Erase Data feature should be enabled. Setting the Required Passcode field to Immediately requires entering the passcode each time the device wakes up.

Make note of the fact that there is a switch on the final screen mentioned in Exercise 19.2 that, when on, destroys all local data on the phone if incorrect passcodes are entered 10 times in a row. While this is recommended for users with phones that contain sensitive data and that are frequently taken into public venues or placed in compromising positions, the casual user should not turn this feature on unless they can be sure there will always be a recent backup available in iTunes.

Imagine a user's child or a mischievous, yet harmless, friend poking away at passcodes until the device informs them that it is being wiped clean. It's not for everyone. Restoring from a backup is easy enough, but will there be a recent backup available when disaster strikes? Apple performs a backup to the computer running iTunes that the iOS device syncs with. Conditions required for synchronization to occur are discussed later in this chapter.

Apple imposes cooling-off time-out periods of increasing duration, even if the Erase Data feature is disabled and you or someone else repeatedly enters the wrong code over multiple lockouts. The final penalty with the Erase Data feature disabled is that you cannot unlock the device until it is connected to the computer with which it was last synced.

EXERCISE 19.3

Setting the Passcode Lock on an Android Phone

1. Tap the Menu button.

2. Tap the Settings soft button.

3. Select Security from the Settings menu.

4. Tap Set Up Screen Lock from the Security menu.

5. Select Pattern from the Screen Unlock Security list.

6. Use your finger to draw a continuous pattern of four or more dots and then tap the Continue button.

7. Repeat the same pattern, and then tap the Confirm button.

8. Adjust the Lock Phone After field to set how long the device needs to be asleep before requiring the passcode.

When a passcode is set, Android devices take a less punitive approach to failed login attempts when compared to their Apple counterparts, where the static "destroy after 10 failed attempts" feature is your only option. Most Android systems have no adjustment for their default behavior, aside from turning off security.

The difference is that if waiting the time-out period won't help because you've forgotten the pattern or code, this device can tie your access back to the Google account you used when setting it up. This is also the account where you receive purchase notifications from the Market or Google Play, and it does not have to be a Gmail account (one of the benefits of the open-source nature of Android). If you remember how to log in to that account, you can still get into your phone. At least you can investigate the credentials to that account on a standard computer and return to the device to enter those credentials.

In addition to the commonly used passcode lock, other forms of screen locks include a *fingerprint lock*, *face lock*, or *swipe lock*. As the name implies, the first requires a fingerprint match to log in, the second a face match (both being *biometric authentication*), and the third a match to a prerecorded swipe.

Remote Wipes and Locator Applications

Should your work or personal mobile device disappear or fall into the wrong hands, it's always nice to have a backup plan for making sure that no company secrets or personal identifiers get misused by anyone who would use the information with ill will. Apple supplies a free app called Find My iPhone that, together with iCloud, allows multiple mobile devices and Macs to be located if powered on and connected to the Internet (via 4G, 3G, WiFi, Ethernet, and so on). The app allows the device to be controlled remotely to lock it, play a sound (even if audio is off), display a message, or wipe it clean.

Within a newer iPhone's Settings screen, you can find an iCloud settings page and select the Find My iPhone switch. With this switch off, the Find My iPhone app and iCloud web page will be unable to find your device.

On the login screen for the iPhone app, you must enter the iCloud account information that includes the device that you are attempting to control remotely.

Note that when you change the password for your Apple ID, it affects your iCloud account but does not transfer automatically within your device. Always remember to update your iCloud account information on each device when you update the associated Apple ID.

Although iCloud has its own settings page, you can also create an iCloud account—or change the settings—through the path Settings ➢ Mail, Contacts, Calendar.

The website's login page at www.icloud.com calls for the same credentials as the app requires. You are signing in with HTTPS, so your username and password are not traversing the Internet in the clear. With the switch in the iCloud settings screen set to off for all devices on your account, when you sign on to the app with your iCloud account credentials, you are met with a disabling switch message.

You do not need to go to the website if you have another device with the Find My iPhone app or borrow one from someone else. The device forgets your credentials when you log out, so the owner will not be able to control your device the next time they use the app.

After logging into the iCloud website, you can click the icon that matches the icon for the Find My iPhone app in iOS. Assuming that you've made it into the app on another device and your Find My iPhone feature is turned on in your missing device, the Info screen tells you that your device has been found and gives you options for the next step you take.

Tapping the Location button in the upper left shows you a map of where your device is currently located. You have three options for how to view the location: two-dimensional map, satellite, and a hybrid version where the two-dimensional street-name information is laid over the satellite view.

If you tap the Play Sound Or Send Message button on the Info screen instead of the Location button, the screen that pops up allows you to display a message remotely. You might consider first displaying a message without the sound, which is at maximum volume. Ask in the message to be called at another number. If you hear from someone in possession of your device, the hunt is over. Otherwise, send another message with the tone to get the attention of the nearest person. If you are at the reported location when you generate the sound, it can help you home in on the device.

If you do decide to use the remote-lock feature of the app, you'll have the opportunity to reconsider before locking it. You should have no issue with locking the device; doing so does not prevent you from using the app further. It simply makes sure that the device is harder to break into.

Should you decide to take the sobering step of destroying the contents of the device remotely, you get a solemn notice allowing you the opportunity to reassess the situation before proceeding. Sometimes there's just no other option.

For Android devices, the app called Lookout from Lookout Labs is a critically acclaimed application that performs some of the same functions as Apple's Find My iPhone, including the emission of an extremely loud scream. Google also provides the Android Device Manager app that has similar functionality.

 Real World Scenario

Uh-Oh. Where's My Phone?

During a recent visit to a car dealership, a prospective new car owner named Rotimi departed without his iPhone; at least, that's where Find My iPhone said it was. Luckily, he had the foresight to set up his free iCloud account and log that phone into it. Upon his return to the dealership, Rotimi was temporarily disheartened to find that no one had seen his phone.

It occurred to him that he had laid his phone down on the counter in the men's room as he was washing his hands. He didn't recall having it after that point. A cursory look around the facilities turned up nothing. The app was not accurate enough to tell him where exactly the phone was at the time it was located on the Find My iPhone website, which he checked from home. It did indicate that it was still somewhere at the dealership though.

Rotimi noticed that the salesperson assisting him had an iPhone. Upon recalling that fact, he asked her if she used the same app. She said she absolutely did. He asked if he could borrow her phone for a brief instant. She obliged, and Rotimi entered his iCloud credentials into the salesperson's app and proceeded to enter the message, "I'm in the showroom." He left the Play Sound switch on and tapped the Send button.

In less than 5 minutes, a manager that had been back at the loading dock came to the showroom with a story. He said he heard a disturbing noise coming from the dumpster, which was quite full and scheduled for pick-up the next morning. The trash bag containing Rotimi's phone was conveniently right at the top of the heap and easily retrieved by the manager.

Rotimi recalled being in a bit of a fluster as he left the men's room. He was about to finalize the terms of the deal he had been working on for more than an hour. In his haste to get back to the table, apparently his phone slipped from his hand as he was disposing of the wad of paper towels he used to dry his hands and the area around the sink that was quite wet and laced with liquid soap from a long day's use. Evidently, it's true that no good deed goes unpunished, but also the cliché "All's well that ends well" has a shred of truth. He owed this happy ending to the features of the Find My iPhone app and tells his story to anyone who will listen.

On an Android phone, the Lookout app automatically scans every app you install, performs a full scan of all of the apps on your device every week, and downloads the latest virus definitions regularly. Lookout Labs provides virus scanning of all apps on a regular basis in its Lookout product as well as in some of its more specialized offerings. Among these specialized apps, the company produces the Plan B app that boasts the ability to install itself after the device is lost, subsequently turning on location services remotely.

Remote Backup

Software companies like Lookout Labs also produce apps that are capable of backing up your device's contents over the Internet so that in case of a catastrophic failure, your information is easily restored to a new device. The app known as MyBackup Pro is designed exclusively for the purpose of backing up your data and storing the backup sets either locally on the device or remotely on the company's servers. You can choose the type of information to be backed up, and restoration is quite painless, resulting in your device returning to its predisaster state.

Apple iOS devices automatically back themselves up to the computer running iTunes that they sync with. In the sense that this backup exists on a system other than the iOS device, this can be considered a remote backup as well.

Operating System Updates

It's easy to forget that these tiny yet powerful mobile devices we've been talking about are running operating systems that play the same role as the operating systems of their larger brethren. As such, users must be careful not to let the operating systems go too long without updates. Occasionally, mobile devices will notify the user of an important update to the operating system. Too often, however, these notifications never come. Therefore, each user should develop the habit of checking for updates on a regular basis.

Not keeping up with software updates creates an environment of known weaknesses and unfixed bugs. Mobile devices operate on a very tight tolerance of hardware and software performance. Not maintaining the device for performance at the top of its game will tend to have more pronounced repercussions than those seen in larger systems.

For the iPhone, iPod Touch, and iPad, you can check for the most important level of updates by tapping Settings ➤ General ➤ Software Update. For the Android operating system, there are multiple updates that can be checked for manually. All of them are accessible by following Menu ➤ Settings ➤ System Updates. The resulting menu includes options for updating the firmware, the profile, the preferred roaming list (PRL), and the manufacturer's specific software.

Full Drive Encryption

BitLocker and BitLocker To Go were discussed a bit earlier in this chapter and they greatly enhance security by encrypting the data on drives (installed and removable, respectively) and helping to secure it from prying eyes. At a minimum, the same level of protection that you would apply to a desktop machine should be applied to a mobile device since it can contain confidential and personally identifiable information which could cause great harm in the wrong hands.

Android devices do not automatically encrypt data upon setting a passcode like iOS devices do.

Full drive encryption should be done on laptops and mobile devices and you should back up regularly to be able to access a version of it should something happen to the device itself.

Multifactor Authentication

Mutlifactor authentication was mentioned previously in this chapter and involves using more than one item (factor) to authenticate. An example of this would be configuring BitLocker encrypted flash drives so that when inserted into your laptop a passwords and smart card value must be given before the data is decrypted and available.

Authenticator Applications

The Authenicator app works with mobile devices to generate security codes that can keep accounts secure by requiring 2-step verification (a code from the app in addition to your account password). Available for use with Microsoft, Google, and other mobile devices, an account is usually added to it by entering a secret key or scanning a barcode.

Policies and Procedures

When it comes to mobile devices, there are two specific policies that should be created: one related to devices (and in particular, BYOD), and the other on profile security requirements. The BYOD policy needs to address differences in the support provided to the devices and those that are corporate owned. A common clause, for example, indicates that technical support is provided only to those devices used for legitimate corporate business but all devices are expected to be secured and the data on them protected.

As an administrator, you can choose settings for mobile devices under your purview and enforce profiles security requirements in various ways. In a given scenario, you may want to enforce settings for the entire organization and in others you may want to differ the settings based on organizational unit, role, or other group type. Among the settings you may want to enforce are those requiring encryption of drives and complex passwords.

Destruction and Disposal Methods

Think of all of the sensitive data written to a hard drive. Said drive can contain information about students, clients, users—about anyone and anything. That hard drive can be in a desktop PC, in a laptop, or even in a printer (many laser printers above consumer grade offer the ability to add a hard drive to store print jobs), and if it falls into the wrong hands, you can not only lose valuable data but also risk a lawsuit for not properly protecting privacy. An appropriate data destruction/disposal plan should be in place to avoid any potential problems.

Since data on media holds great value and liability, that media should never simply be tossed away for prying eyes to stumble upon. For the purpose of this objective, the media in question is hard drives, and there are three key concepts to understand in regard to them:

formatting, sanitation, and destruction. Formatting prepares the drive to hold new information (which can include copying over data already there). Sanitation involves wiping the data off the drive, while destruction renders the drive no longer usable.

While this objective is heavily focused on hard drives, it is also possible to have data stored on portable flash drives, backup tapes, CDs, or DVDs. In the interest of security, it is recommended that you destroy them before disposing of them.

Recycling or Repurposing Best Practices

For exam purposes, the best practices for recycling or repurposing fall beneath the categories of low-level formats (as opposed to standard formatting), overwrites, and drive wipes. Those are the very topics of the next few sections and we will explore each in detail.

Low-Level Format vs. Standard Format

There are multiple levels of formatting that can be done on a drive. A standard format, accomplished using the operating system's FORMAT utility (or similar), can mark space occupied by files as available for new files without truly deleting what was there. Such erasing—if you want to call it that—doesn't guarantee that the information isn't still on the disk and recoverable.

A low-level format (typically only accomplished in the factory) can be performed on the system, or a utility can be used to completely wipe the disk clean. This process helps ensure that information doesn't fall into the wrong hands.

The manufacturer performs a low-level format on integrated device electronics (IDE) hard drives. Low-level formatting must be performed even before a drive can be partitioned. In low-level formatting, the drive controller chip and the drive meet for the very first time and learn to work together. Because controllers are integrated into IDE drives, low-level formatting is a factory process. Low-level formatting is not operating system dependent.

Never perform a low-level format on IDE or SCSI drives! They're formatted at the factory, and you may cause problems by using low-level utilities on these types of drives.

The main thing to remember for the exams is that most forms of formatting included with the operating system do not actually erase the data completely. Formatting the drive and then disposing of it has caused many companies problems when individuals who never should have seen it retrieve the data using applications that are commercially available.

Hard Drive Sanitation and Sanitation Methods

A number of vendors offer hard drives with Advanced Encryption Standard (AES) cryptography built in, but it's still better to keep these secure hard drives completely out of the hands of others than to trust their internal security mechanisms once their usable life span has passed for the client. Some vendors include utilities to erase the hard drive, and if it is a Serial ATA (SATA) drive, you can always run HDDERASE, but you are still taking your chances.

In addition to HDDERASE, you can find a number of other software "shredders" by doing a quick Web search. It is important to recognize and acknowledge that many of these do not meet military or GSA specifications, and those specifications should be considered as guidelines to which you must also adhere when dealing with your own, or a client's, data. The only surefire method of rendering the hard drive contents completely eradicated is physical destruction.

Overwrite

Overwriting the drive entails copying over the data with new data. A common practice is to replace the data with 0s. A number of applications allow you to recover what was there prior to the last write operation, and for that reason, most overwrite software will write the same sequence and save it multiple times.

Drive Wipe

If it's possible to verify beyond a reasonable doubt that a piece of hardware that's no longer being used doesn't contain any data of a sensitive or proprietary nature, then that hardware can be recycled (sold to employees, sold to a third party, donated to a school, and so on). That level of assurance can come from wiping a hard drive or using specialized utilities.

Degaussing hard drives is difficult and may render the drive unusable.

If you can't be assured that the hardware in question doesn't contain important data, then the hardware should be destroyed. You cannot, and should not, take a risk that the data your company depends on could fall into the wrong hands.

Physical Destruction

Physically destroying the drive involves rendering the component no longer usable. While the focus is on hard drives, you can also physically destroy other forms of media, such as flash drives and CD/DVDs.

Shredder

Many commercial paper shredders include the ability to destroy DVDs and CDs. Paper shredders, however, are not able to handle hard drives, and you need a shredder created for just such a purpose: Jackhammer makes a low-volume unit that will destroy eight drives a minute and carries a suggested list price of just under $30,000.

Drill/Hammer

If you don't have the budget for a hard drive shredder, you can accomplish similar results in a much more time-consuming way with a power drill. The goal is to physically destroy the platters in the drive. Start the process by removing the cover from the drive—this is normally done with a Torx driver (while #8 does not work with all, it is a good one to try first). You can remove the arm with a slotted screwdriver and then the cover over the platters using a Torx driver. Don't worry about damaging or scratching anything—nothing is intended to be saved. Everything but the platters can be tossed away.

As an optional step, you can completely remove the tracks using a belt sander, grinder, or palm sander. The goal is to turn the shiny surface into fine powder. Again, this step is optional, but it adds one more layer of assurance that nothing usable remains. Always wear eye protection and be careful not to breathe in any fine particles that you generate during the grinding/destruction process.

Following this, use the power drill to create as small a set of particles as possible. A drill press works much better for this task than trying to hold the drive and drill it with a hand-held model.

Do You Really Want to Do it Yourself?

Even with practice, you will find that manually destroying a hard drive is time consuming. There are companies that specialize in this and can do it efficiently. One such company is Shred-it, which will pick it up and provide a chain-of-custody assurance and a certificate of destruction upon completion. You can find out more about what they offer at www.shredit.com.

Electromagnet (Degaussing)

A large electromagnet can be used to destroy any magnetic media, such as a hard drive or backup tape set. The most common of these is the degaussing tool. *Degaussing* involves applying a strong magnetic field to initialize the media (this is also referred to as *disk wiping*). This process helps ensure that information doesn't fall into the wrong hands.

Degaussing involves using a specifically designed electromagnet to eliminate all data on the drive, and that destruction also includes the factory prerecorded servo tracks. You can find wand model degaussers priced at just over $500 or desktop units that sell for up to $30,000.

Incineration

A form of destruction not to be overlooked is fire. It is possible to destroy most devices by burning them up and using an accelerant such as gasoline or lighter fluid to aid the process.

Be careful with any fire, and particularly those in which accelerants are used. Be sure that you are not burning anything capable of releasing toxic fumes and that you have the fire controlled and contained at all times.

Certificate of Destruction

A *certificate of destruction* (or certificate of recycling) may be required for audit purposes. Such a certificate, usually issued by the organization carrying out the destruction, is intended to verify that the asset was properly destroyed and usually includes serial numbers, type of destruction done, and so on.

Securing a SOHO Network (Wireless)

CompTIA wants administrators of small office, home office (SOHO) networks to be able to secure those networks in ways that protect the data stored on them. This objective looks at the security protection that can be added to a wireless SOHO network, while the one that follows examines similar procedures for a wired network.

A wireless network is not and never will be secure. Use wireless only when absolutely necessary. If you must deploy a wireless network, here are some tips to make some improvements to wireless security:

- Change the default SSID.
- Disable SSID broadcasts.
- Disable DHCP or use reservations.
- Use MAC filtering.
- Use IP filtering.
- Use the strongest security available on the wireless access point.
- Change the static security keys every two to four weeks.
- When new wireless protection schemes become available (and are reasonably priced), consider migrating to them.
- Limit the user accounts that can use wireless connectivity.
- Use a preauthentication system, such as RADIUS.
- Use remote access filters against client type, protocols used, time, date, user account, content, and so forth.
- Use IPSec tunnels over the wireless links.
- Turn down the signal strength to the minimum needed to support connectivity.
- Seriously consider removing wireless access from your LAN.

Change Default Usernames and Passwords

In addition to those created with the installation of the operating system(s), default accounts are also often associated with hardware. Wireless access points, routers, and similar devices often include accounts for interacting with, and administering, those devices. You should always change the passwords associated with those devices and, where possible, change the usernames.

If there are accounts that are not needed, disable or delete them. Make certain that you use strong password policies and protect the passwords with the same security that you use for users and administrators (in other words, don't write the router's password on an address label and stick it to the bottom of the router).

Changing the SSID

All radio frequency signals can be easily intercepted. To intercept 802.11a/b/g/n traffic, all you need is a PC with an appropriate 802.11a/b/g/n card installed. Many networks will regularly broadcast their name (known as an *SSID broadcast*) to announce their presence. Simple software on the PC can capture the link traffic in the wireless AP and then process this data to decrypt account and password information.

You should change the SSID—whether or not you choose to disable its broadcast or not— to keep it from being a value that many outsiders come to know. If you use the same SSID for years, then the number of individuals who have left the company or otherwise learned of its value will only increase. Changing the variable adds one more level of security.

Setting Encryption

The types of wireless encryption available (WEP, WPA, WPA2, and so forth) were discussed in Chapter 8, "Installing Wireless and SOHO Networks." It's important to remember that you should always enable encryption for any SOHO network that you may administer, and you should choose the strongest level of encryption you can work with.

Disabling SSID Broadcast

One method of "protecting" the network that is often recommended is to turn off the SSID broadcast. The access point is still there and can still be accessed by those who know of it, but it prevents those who are looking at a list of available networks from finding it. This should be considered a very weak form of security because there are still ways, albeit a bit more complicated, to discover the presence of the access point besides the SSID broadcast.

Enable MAC Filtering

Most APs offer the ability to turn on *MAC filtering*, but it is off by default. In the default state, any wireless client that knows of the existence of the AP can join the network. When MAC filtering is used, the administrator compiles a list of the MAC addresses associated with the users' computers and enters them. When a client attempts to connect, an additional check of the MAC address is performed. If the address appears in the list, the client is allowed to join, otherwise they are forbidden from so doing. On a number of wireless devices, the term *network lock* is used in place of *MAC filtering*, and the two are synonymous.

Adding port authentication to MAC filtering takes security for the network down to the switch port level and increases your security exponentially.

Antenna and Access Point Placement

Antenna placement can be crucial in allowing clients to reach the access point. For security reasons, you do not want to overextend the reach of the network so that people can get onto the network from other locations (the parking lot, the building next door, and so on). Balancing security and access is a tricky thing to do.

There isn't any one universal solution to this issue, and it depends on the environment in which the access point is placed. As a general rule, the greater the distance the signal must travel, the more it will attenuate, but you can lose a signal quickly in a short space as well if the building materials reflect or absorb it. You should try to avoid placing access points near metal (which includes appliances) or near the ground. They should be placed in the center of the area to be served and high enough to get around most obstacles.

Radio Power Levels

On the chance that the signal is actually traveling too far, some access points include *power level controls* that allow you to reduce the amount of output provided.

Power Value Information

A great source for information on RF power values and antennas can be found on the Cisco site at the following location:

www.cisco.com/c/en/us/support/docs/wireless-mobility/wireless-lan-wlan/23231-powervalues-23231.html

---

Assign Static IP Addresses

While DHCP can be a godsend, a SOHO network is small enough that you can get by without it issuing IP addresses to each host. The advantage to assigning the IP addresses statically is that you can make certain which host is associated with which IP address and then utilize filtering to limit network access to only those hosts.

WPS

WPS (Wi-Fi Protected Setup) can help secure the network by requiring new machines to do something before they can join the network. This often requires the user to perform an action in order to complete the enrollment process: press a button on the router within a short time period, enter a PIN number, or bring the new device close-by (so that near field communication can take place).

Securing a SOHO Network (Wired)

While a wired network can be more secure than a wireless one, there are still a number of procedures that you should follow to leave as little to chance as possible. Among them, change the default usernames and passwords to different values and secure the physical environment. You should also disable any ports that are not needed, assign static IP addresses, and use MAC filtering to limit access only to those hosts that you recognize.

Change Default Usernames and Passwords

Make sure the default password is changed after the installation of any network device. Failure to do so leaves that device open for anyone recognizing the hardware to access it using the known factory password.

In Windows, the Guest account is automatically created with the intent that it is to be used when someone must access a system but lacks a user account on that system. Because it is so widely known to exist, it is recommended that you not use this default account and create another one for the same purpose if you truly need one. The Guest account leaves a security risk at the workstation and should be disabled to deter those attempting to gain unauthorized access.

> Change every username and password that you can so they vary from their default settings.

Enable MAC Filtering

Limit access to the network to MAC addresses that are known and filter out those that are not. Even in a home network, you can implement MAC filtering with most routers and typically have an option of choosing to allow only computers with MAC addresses that you list or deny only computers with MAC addresses that you list.

> If you don't know a workstation's MAC address, use IPCONFIG /ALL to find it in the Windows-based world (it is listed as *physical address*) and ifconfig in UNIX/Linux.

Assign Static IP Addresses

Static IP addresses should be used (avoid having them dynamically issued by DHCP) on small office and home office networks to keep from issuing addresses to hosts other than those you recognize and want on the network.

Disabling Ports

Disable all unneeded protocols/ports. If you don't need them, remove the additional protocols, software, or services or prevent them (disable them) from loading. Ports not in use present an open door for an attacker to enter.

Many of the newer SOHO router solutions (and some of the personal firewall solutions on end-user workstations) close down the ICMP ports by default. Keep this in mind because it can drive you nuts when you are trying to see if a brand-new station/server/router is up and running.

Physical Security

Just as you would not park your car in a public garage and leave its doors wide open with the key in the ignition, you should educate users to not leave a workstation that they are logged in to when they attend meetings, go to lunch, and so forth. They should log out of the workstation or lock it: "Lock when you leave" should be a mantra they become familiar with. A password (usually the same as their user password) should be required to resume working at the workstation.

You can also lock a workstation by using an operating system that provides file system security. Microsoft's earliest file system was referred to as file allocation table (FAT). FAT was designed for relatively small disk drives. It was upgraded first to FAT-16 and finally to FAT-32. FAT-32 (also written as FAT32) allows large disk systems to be used on Windows systems.

FAT allows only two types of protection: share-level and user-level access privileges. If a user has write or change access to a drive or directory, they have access to any file in that directory. This is very unsecure in an Internet environment.

With NTFS, files, directories, and volumes can each have their own security. NTFS's security is flexible and built in. Not only does NTFS track security in *access control lists (ACLs)*, which can hold permissions for local users and groups, but each entry in the ACL can also specify what type of access is given. This allows a great deal of flexibility in setting up a network. In addition, special file-encryption programs can be used to encrypt data while it is stored on the hard disk.

Microsoft strongly recommends that all network shares be established using NTFS. While NTFS security is important, though, it doesn't matter at all what file system you are using if you log in to your workstation and leave, allowing anyone to sit down at your desk and use your account.

Because NTFS and share permissions are operating system specific, they were discussed in the chapters on operating systems.

Last, don't overlook the obvious need for physical security. Adding a cable to lock a laptop to a desk prevents someone from picking it up and walking away with a copy of your customer database. Every laptop case we are aware of includes a built-in security slot in which a cable lock can be added to prevent it from easily being carried off the premises.

When it comes to desktop models, adding a lock to the back cover can prevent an intruder with physical access from grabbing the hard drive or damaging the internal components. You should also physically secure network devices, such as routers, access points, and the like. Place them in locked cabinets, if possible, for if they are not physically secured, the opportunity exists for them to be stolen or manipulated in such a way as to allow someone unauthorized to connect to the network.

Wired and Wireless Security

Whether your SOHO network is wired or wireless, there are some basic security principles you want to keep in mind. The first is to configure firewall settings to block unwanted traffic. We've talked a lot about firewalls already and it is important to configure them to keep as many potential problems out as possible – turn off the ability to receive types of data that your users do not need and constantly monitor, tweak, and refine these settings.

Next, pay attention to port forwarding. On the router, the port configuration dictates what traffic is allowed to flow through. The router can be configured to enable individual port traffic in, out, or both and is referred to as port forwarding. If a port is blocked (such as 80 for HTTP or 21 for FTP), the data will not be allowed through, and users will be affected. Port forwarding is also known as port mapping and both are subsets of what a firewall does and the amount of tweaking they require to get right is about the same.

The basic premise behind content filtering is that some things are blocked – if a user attempts to go to a site that you do not want them to, for example, a message can appear telling them that access is denied. You can choose to block networks, types of sites, individual sites, or almost anything else on a granular level. While content filtering can be accomplished a number of ways, one of the most common is with parental controls (which are not available on a machine connected to the network through a domain). Within Windows 8.1, for example, choose User Accounts and Family Safety from the Control Panel then choose either to turn on Family Safety for a new child's account and then, after choosing or creating the account, you can configure options such as those shown in Figure 19.8.

FIGURE 19.8 Family Safety settings in Windows 8.1

Note that you can set time limits for computer usage, monitor sites they can access and control which apps can be run by this account.

Summary

In this chapter, you learned about the various issues related to security that appear on the A+ 220–902 exam. Security is a popular topic in computing, and the ways in which a troublemaker can cause harm increase regularly. Because of this, CompTIA expects everyone who is A+ certified to understand the basic principles of security and be familiar with solutions that exist.

In this chapter, you learned of security problem areas and issues that can be easily identified. Problem areas include viruses, Trojans, worms, and spyware. Security solutions include implementing encryption technology, using authentication, implementing firewalls, and incorporating security at many levels.

Security is a set of processes and products. For a security program to be effective, all of its parts must work and be coordinated by the organization.

Exam Essentials

Be able to describe why antivirus software is needed. Antivirus software looks at a virus and takes action to neutralize it based on a virus definition database. Virus definition database files are regularly made available on vendor sites.

Understand the need for user education. Users are the first line of defense against most threats, whether physical or digital. They should be trained on the importance of security and how to help enforce it.

Know the characteristics and types of viruses used to disrupt systems and networks. Several different types of viruses are floating around today. The most common ones are polymorphic viruses, stealth viruses, retroviruses, multipartite viruses, and macro viruses.

Know the various types of social engineering. Social engineering variants include shoulder surfing (watching someone work) and phishing (tricking someone into believing they are communicating with a party other than the one with whom they are communicating). Variations on phishing include vishing and whaling as well as spear phishing.

Understand the need for good passwords. Passwords are the first line of defense for protecting an account. A password should be required for every account and strong passwords should be enforced. Users need to understand the basics of password security and work to keep their accounts protected by following company policies regarding passwords.

Disable what you don't need. All accounts that are not in use—especially the guest account—should be disabled. You should also disable the Autorun feature to prevent it from running programs or commands that could inflict harm without your knowledge.

Understand the difference between standard and low-level formatting. Standard formatting uses operating system tools and marks the drive as available for holding data without truly removing what was on the drive (thus the data can be recovered). A low-level format is operating system independent and destroys any data that was on the drive.

Understand how to physically destroy a drive. A hard drive can be destroyed by tossing it into a shredder designed for such a purpose, or it can be destroyed with an electromagnet in a process known as degaussing. You can also disassemble the drive and destroy the platters with a drill or other tool that renders the data irretrievable.

Know the names, purpose, and characteristics of wireless security technologies. Wireless networks can be encrypted through WEP, WPA, and WPA2 technologies. Wireless controllers use service-set identifiers (SSIDs)—32-character case-sensitive strings—that must be configured in the network cards to allow communications. However, using ID string configurations doesn't necessarily prevent wireless networks from being monitored, and there are vulnerabilities specific to wireless devices.

Understand the basics of antenna placement and radio power levels. Antenna placement can be crucial in allowing clients to reach an access point. Place access points near the center of the area to be served and high enough to get around most obstacles. Know that power level controls allow you to reduce the amount of output provided.

Understand why ports should be disabled. Disable all unneeded protocols/ports. If you don't need them, remove them or prevent them from loading. Ports not in use present an open door for an attacker to enter.

Understand the purpose of MAC filtering. MAC filtering allows you to limit access to a network to MAC addresses that are known and filter out (deny access to) those that are not.

Review Questions

The answers to the chapter review questions can be found in Appendix A.

1. Which component of physical security addresses outer-level access control?
   - **A.** Perimeter security
   - **B.** Mantraps
   - **C.** Security zones
   - **D.** Strong passwords

2. You have a very small network in a home-based office, and you want to limit network access to only those hosts that you physically own. What should you utilize to make this possible?
   - **A.** Static IP addresses
   - **B.** Disabled DNS
   - **C.** Default subnet mask
   - **D.** Empty default gateway

3. As part of your training program, you're trying to educate users on the importance of security. You explain to them that not every attack depends on implementing advanced technological methods. Some attacks, you explain, take advantage of human shortcomings to gain access that should otherwise be denied. What term do you use to describe attacks of this type?
   - **A.** Social engineering
   - **B.** IDS system
   - **C.** Perimeter security
   - **D.** Biometrics

4. You're in the process of securing the IT infrastructure by adding fingerprint scanners to your existing authentication methods. This type of security is an example of which of the following?
   - **A.** Access control
   - **B.** Physical barriers
   - **C.** Biometrics
   - **D.** Softening

5. Which type of attack denies authorized users access to network resources?
   - **A.** DoS
   - **B.** Worm
   - **C.** Logic bomb
   - **D.** Social engineering

6. As the security administrator for your organization, you must be aware of all types of attacks that can occur and plan for them. Which type of attack uses more than one computer to attack the victim?

    A. DoS

    B. DDoS

    C. Worm

    D. UDP attack

7. A server in your network has a program running on it that bypasses authentication. Which type of attack has occurred?

    A. DoS

    B. DDoS

    C. Back door

    D. Social engineering

8. You've discovered that an expired certificate is being used repeatedly to gain logon privileges. Which type of attack is this most likely to be?

    A. Man-in-the-middle attack

    B. Back door attack

    C. Replay attack

    D. TCP/IP hijacking

9. A junior administrator comes to you in a panic. After looking at the log files, he has become convinced that an attacker is attempting to use a duplicate IP address to replace another system in the network to gain access. Which type of attack is this?

    A. Spoof

    B. Back door attack

    C. Worm

    D. TCP/IP hijacking

10. Which of the following is different from a virus in that it can reproduce itself, it's self-contained, and it doesn't need a host application to be transported?

    A. Worm

    B. Smurf

    C. Phish

    D. Trojan

11. A smurf attack attempts to use a broadcast ping on a network; the return address of the ping may be that of a valid system in your network. Which protocol does a smurf attack use to conduct the attack?

    A. TCP

    B. IP

    C. UDP

    D. ICMP

12. Your system log files report an ongoing attempt to gain access to a single account. This attempt has been unsuccessful to this point. What type of attack are you most likely experiencing?

    A. Password-guessing attack

    B. Back door attack

    C. Worm attack

    D. TCP/IP hijacking

13. One of the vice presidents of the company calls a meeting with the information technology department after a recent trip to competitors' sites. She reports that many of the companies she visited granted access to their buildings only after fingerprint scans, and she wants similar technology employed at this company. Of the following, which technology relies on a physical attribute of the user for authentication?

    A. Smart card

    B. Biometrics

    C. Mutual authentication

    D. Tokens

14. Your company provides medical data to doctors from a worldwide database. Because of the sensitive nature of the data you work with, it's imperative that authentication be established on each session and be valid only for that session. Which of the following authentication methods provides credentials that are valid only during a single session?

    A. Token

    B. Certificate

    C. Smart card

    D. License

15. Your help desk has informed you that they received an urgent call from the vice president last night requesting his logon ID and password. When talking with the VP today, he says he never made that call. What type of attack is this?

    A. Spoofing

    B. Replay attack

    C. Social engineering

    D. Trojan horse

16. Internal users suspect repeated attempts to infect their systems as reported to them by pop-up messages from their virus-scanning software. According to the pop-up messages, the virus seems to be the same in every case. What is the most likely culprit?

    A. A server is acting as a carrier for a virus.

    B. You have a caterpillar virus.

C. Your antivirus software has malfunctioned.

D. A DoS attack is under way.

17. You're working late one night, and you notice that the hard drive on your new computer is very active even though you aren't doing anything on the computer and it isn't connected to the Internet. What is the most likely suspect?

A. A disk failure is imminent.

B. A virus is spreading in your system.

C. Your system is under a DoS attack.

D. TCP/IP hijacking is being attempted.

18. You're the administrator for a large bottling company. At the end of each month, you routinely view all logs and look for discrepancies. This month, your email system error log reports a large number of unsuccessful attempts to log on. It's apparent that the email server is being targeted. Which type of attack is most likely occurring?

A. Software exploitation attack

B. Backdoor attack

C. Worm

D. TCP/IP hijacking

19. Upper management has decreed that a firewall must be put in place immediately, before your site suffers an attack similar to one that struck a sister company. Responding to this order, your boss instructs you to implement a packet filter by the end of the week. A packet filter performs which function?

A. Prevents unauthorized packets from entering the network

B. Allows all packets to leave the network

C. Allows all packets to enter the network

D. Eliminates collisions in the network

20. Which media is susceptible to viruses?

A. Tape

B. Memory stick

C. CD-R

D. All of the above

Performance-Based Question

You will encounter performance-based questions on the A+ exams. The questions on the exam require you to perform a specific task, and you will be graded on whether or not you were able to complete the task. The following requires you to think creatively in order to measure how well you understand this chapter's topics. You may or may not see similar questions on the actual A+ exams. To see how your answers compare to the authors', refer to Appendix B.

Pop-ups are proving to be a security concern—as well as an annoyance—throughout the office. Configure your Windows 7 machine to block pop-ups but to allow www.sybex.com through so you can access the material you are studying for the A+ exams.

Performance-Based Question

Chapter

20

Network Services, Cloud Computing, and Virtualization

THE FOLLOWING COMPTIA A+ EXAM 220-902 OBJECTIVES ARE COVERED IN THIS CHAPTER:

✓ **2.2 Given a scenario, set up and use client-side virtualization.**

- Purpose of virtual machines
- Resource requirements
- Emulator requirements
- Security requirements
- Network requirements
- Hypervisor

✓ **2.3 Identify basic cloud concepts.**

- SaaS
- IaaS
- Paas
- Public vs. Private vs. Hybrid vs. Community
- Rapid Elasticity
- On-demand
- Resource pooling
- Measured service

✓ **2.4 Summarize the properties and purpose of services provided by networked hosts.**

- Server roles
    - Web server
    - File server
    - Print server
    - DHCP server
    - DNS server
    - Proxy server
    - Mail server
    - Authentication server
- Internet appliance
    - UTM
    - IDS
    - IPS
- Legacy / embedded systems

Networks are oftentimes complicated structures. When users get on a network, they have expectations that certain services will be delivered, and most of the time they are unaware of the underlying infrastructure. As long as what they want gets delivered, they are content. In client-server networks, which you learned about in Chapter 6, "Networking Fundamentals," there are one or more servers that play unique roles in fulfilling client requests.

The traditional delivery method for services has been that the servers are on the same network as the clients. They might not be on the same LAN, but they are certainly administered by one company or one set of administrators. If clients on the network need a new feature, the network architects and administrators add the necessary server. This is still the most common setup today, but there's been a sharp growth in cloud computing and virtualization in the last several years. In essence, cloud computing lets networks break out of that model and have services provided by a server that the company doesn't own and so it's not under the company's direct control. Virtualization is an important technology in cloud computing because it removes the barrier of needing one-to-one relationships between the physical computer and the operating system.

In this chapter, we will talk about some key network services you will need to be familiar with as a technician. Servers will provide some services, and stand-alone security devices or Internet appliances will provide others. After that, we will dive into the world of cloud computing and virtualization, as it's a hot topic that will only become more important in the coming years.

Understanding Network Services

As you learned in Chapter 6, networks are made up of multiple types of devices operating together. There are different types of networks, such as peer-to-peer and client-server, and they are categorized based on the types of devices they support. Very simple, small networks can be peer-to-peer, where there are no dedicated servers. Most networks that you encounter in the business world will have at least one server though, and enterprise networks can easily have hundreds or even thousands of servers.

New network technicians won't be expected to manage large server farms by themselves, but they should be aware of the types of servers and other devices that will be on the network and their basic functions. Experienced technicians may be in charge of one or more servers, and they will need to be intimately familiar with their inner workings. As you gain more experience, you will find that there are advanced certifications in the market to prove your knowledge of servers and show off your skills to potential employers. For the A+ exam, you will need to know various server roles, the features of a few Internet security appliances, and the impact of legacy and embedded systems.

Server Roles

Servers come in many shapes and sizes, and they can perform many different roles on a network. Servers are generally named for the type of service they provide, such as a web server or a print server. They help improve network security and ease administration by centralizing control of resources and security; without servers, every user would need to manage their own security and resource sharing. Not everyone has the technical ability to do that, and even if they do, those types of responsibilities might not be part of what they are being asked to deliver at work. Servers can also provide features such as load balancing and increased reliability.

Some servers will be dedicated to a specific task, such as hosting websites, and they are called *dedicated servers*. *Nondedicated servers* may perform multiple tasks, such as hosting a website and serving as the administrator's daily workstation. Situations like this are often not ideal because the system needs more resources to support everything it needs to do. Imagine that you are the user of that computer and there is heavy website traffic. Your system could slow down to the point where it's difficult to get anything done! Servers can also perform multiple server-specific roles at the same time, such as hosting websites and providing file and print services. As you read through the descriptions of server roles, you will see that it makes more sense to combine some services than it does to combine others.

One important consideration network architects need to make when thinking about designing a network is where to place the server or servers. In Chapter 8, "Installing Wireless and SOHO Networks," we introduced the concept of a *demilitarized zone (DMZ)*, which is a network separated from the internal network by a firewall but also protected from the Internet by a firewall. Figure 20.1 shows an example.

FIGURE 20.1   A demilitarized zone (DMZ)

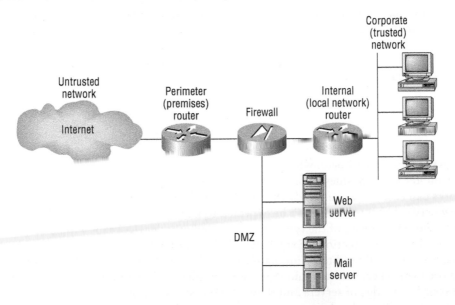

Figure 20.1 shows a DMZ managed by what is called a *three-pronged firewall*, which is called that because it has three network interfaces. You can see that the firewall has an Internet interface, an internal interface, and a DMZ interface. Another common configuration is a two-pronged firewall, with the DMZ in the middle of the two. In that setup, if an attacker wants to get to your internal network, they have to go through two separate fire-walls. Hopefully, you have your firewalls set up to make that task difficult on potential hackers!

In Figure 20.1, you see that the web and mail servers are in the DMZ and not on the internal network. This configuration can make it easier to manage the network but still provide great security. As a rule of thumb, any server that needs to be accessed by the outside world should be in the DMZ, and any server that does not need to be accessed from the Internet should be on the internal network, which is more secure. By the way, servers can play the role of firewalls too. It's not, however, on the list of objectives as a server role, and in practice it's best to separate other server roles from firewalls. In other words, if you intend to use a server as a firewall, then don't use it for any other types of services. Having services on the firewall itself just makes it easier for hackers to get to. There's no sense in making things easier for them. Now it's time to talk about specific server roles on a network.

Web Server

You've been on the Internet, right? That's probably a silly question to ask, because it seems like everyone is constantly connected to the Internet. Web-enabled smartphones and other mobile devices have made the connection seemingly persistent.

Whenever you visit a web page, you are making a connection from your device (the client) to a *web server.* To be more specific, a connection is requested by your Internet software (generally a web browser) using the *Hypertext Transfer Protocol (HTTP)* of the TCP/IP protocol suite. Your client needs to know the IP address of the web server, and it will make the request on port 80.

Secure connections are made using *Hypertext Transfer Protocol Secure (HTTPS)* and port 443.

The web server itself is configured with web hosting software, which listens for inbound requests on port 80 and/or port 443. Two of the most common web platforms are the open-source Apache and Microsoft's Internet Information Services (IIS), although there are a few dozen different packages available for use. Web servers provide content on request, which can include text, images, and videos, and they can also do things like run scripts to open additional functions, such as processing credit card transactions and querying databases.

Web servers often function as download servers too, meaning that they also use FTP. They listen for requests on TCP ports 20 and 21 as well.

Individuals or independent companies can manage web servers, but more often than not an Internet service provider or web hosting company that manages hundreds or thousands of websites manages them. In fact, one web server can be configured to manage dozens of smaller websites using the same IP address, provided it has sufficient resources to handle the traffic. On the flip side, huge sites such as Amazon.com and Google are actually made up of multiple web servers acting as one site. It's estimated that Google has over 900,000 servers, and Microsoft claims to have over one million servers!

If a company wants to host its own web server, the best place for it is in the DMZ. This configuration provides ease of access (after all, you *want* people to hit your web server) and the best security. The firewall can be configured to allow inbound port 80 and 443 requests to the DMZ but not to allow inbound requests on those ports to make it to the internal corporate network.

Contrast this to a situation where the web server is on the internal network. The firewall then has to let inbound port 80 connections through to the internal network so that Internet-based clients can get to the web server. However, that also means that inbound requests on port 80 can be sent to all internal computers, including non-web servers and even client computers. Hackers could then potentially take advantage of exploits using port 80 to attempt to gain illegitimate access to the network.

File Server

A *file server* provides a central repository for users to store, manage, and access files on the network. There are a few distinct advantages to using file servers:

- Ease of access to files for collaboration
- Centralized security management
- Centralized backups

File servers come in a variety of shapes and sizes. Some are as basic as Windows- or Linux-based servers with a large amount of internal hard disk storage space. Networks can also use *network attached storage (NAS)* devices, which are stand-alone units that contain hard drives, come with their own file management software, and connect directly to the network. If a company has extravagant data storage needs, it can implement a *storage area network (SAN)*. A SAN is basically a network segment, or collection of servers, that exists solely to store and manage data.

Since the point of a file server is to store data, it's pretty important to ensure that file servers have ample disk space. Some file servers also have banks of multiple optical drives for extra storage (letting users access files from optical media) or for performing backups. Processing power and network bandwidth can also be important to manage file requests and deliver them in a timely manner.

As far as location goes, file servers will almost always be on the internal network. You might have situations where a file server is also an FTP server, and in those cases the server should be on the DMZ. But in those cases, you will also want to ensure that the server does not contain highly sensitive information or other data that you don't want to lose.

Print Server

Print servers are much like file servers, except of course they make printers available to users. In fact, file servers and print servers are combined so often that you will see a lot of publications or tools refer to *file and print servers* as if they are their own category.

On its own, a *print server* makes printers available to clients over the network and accepts print requests from those clients. A print server can be a physical server like a Windows- or Linux-based server, a small stand-alone device attached to a printer (or several printers), or even a server built in to the printer itself. They handle the following important functions:

- Making printers available on the network
- Accepting print requests
- Managing print requests (in the print queue)
- In some cases, processing and storing print jobs

Figure 20.2 shows a simple stand-alone print server. It has an RJ-45 network connection and four USB ports to connect printers. Wireless print servers are easy to find as well.

FIGURE 20.2   A D-Link print server

Although the specific functionality will vary by print server, most of the time administrators will be able to manage security, time restrictions, and other options, including if the server processes the files and if the print jobs are saved after printing. An example is shown in Figure 20.3.

FIGURE 20.3   Printer management options

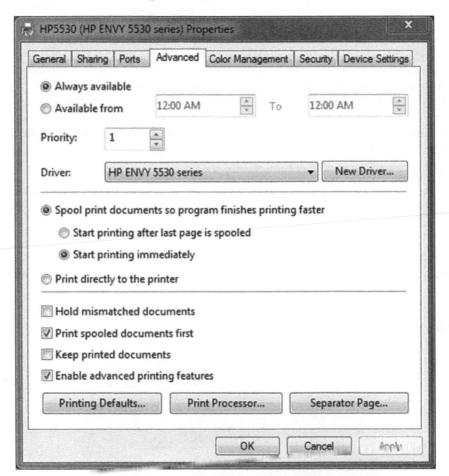

DHCP Server

Dynamic Host Configuration Protocol (DHCP) servers can make it easier to administer TCP/IP networks, which are pretty much every network out there today. DHCP servers are configured to provide IP configuration information automatically to clients, such as an IP address, subnet mask, default gateway, and the address of a DNS server.

DHCP Scopes

DHCP servers are configured with a *scope*, which contains the information that the server can provide to clients. DHCP servers need at least one scope, but they can also have more than one. The following items are typically included within the scope:

Address pool   This is the range of addresses that the server can give out to clients. For example, the pool may be configured to give out addresses in the range from 192.168.0.100 to 192.168.0.200. If all of the addresses are given out, then the server can't provide information to any new potential clients. The address pool configuration will also include the subnet mask if the network is using IPv4 addresses.

Lease durations   IP addresses given out by the DHCP server are leased to clients, and the lease has an expiration time. Before the lease expires, the client (if it's online) will typically renegotiate to receive a new lease. If the lease expires, then the address becomes available to assign to another client. If you have a situation where there are limited IP addresses but a lot of clients coming on and off the network frequently (say, a traveling sales force), you might want to shorten the lease times. The downside is that it will generate a bit more network broadcast traffic, as we will explain in just a bit.

Address reservations   Some IP addresses can be reserved for specific clients, based on the client's MAC address. This is particularly useful for devices that need to have a static IP address, such as printers, servers, and routers.

Scope options   These provide extra configuration items outside of the IP address and subnet mask. The most common items are the address of the default gateway (the router) and DNS servers. Other items might include the addresses of servers providing other functions, such as time synchronization, NetBIOS name resolution, telephony services, or the domain name (whatever.com) for the client to use.

 Real World Scenario

TCP/IP Configuration Choices

When configuring TCP/IP on a network, there are three choices for assigning IP addresses: manually, automatically using a DHCP server, and a hybrid approach.

The manual option takes the most work, and it really only works for smaller networks. The administrator needs to keep track of all of the addresses that have been assigned so that the same address doesn't end up being accidentally assigned to multiple computers. Duplicate addresses will cause communication problems. Most administrators have better things to do than to manage IP addresses manually.

continues

continued

DHCP is extremely convenient. The administrator sets up a scope and options and lets the server manage all of the IP addresses. For devices that need a static address, such as printers, servers, and routers, the administrator can configure address reservations based on their MAC addresses. That way, every time a specific printer comes online, it always receives the same address. This takes a bit of setup in the beginning, or when a new device is added, but is worth it in the long run. The DHCP server is then the single point of management for all IP addresses on the network. That makes administration and troubleshooting much easier.

The hybrid option is a combination of manual assignments and DHCP. For example, devices that need static IP addresses can be assigned manually, whereas clients get their information from a DHCP server. In a situation like this, the administrator might set a DHCP client pool address range for 192.168.0.100 to 192.168.0.200 and then use addresses 192.168.0.1 to 192.168.0.99 for static devices. The problem with this approach is that it requires extra administrative effort to manage the static addresses and ensure that the same address isn't assigned multiple times. In addition, say another administrator looks at the DHCP server and sees the scope. That administrator might or might not know that addresses lower than .100 are being used for static assignments and could increase the scope to include those addresses. Doing so will cause the DHCP server to hand out addresses that could conflict with devices that have been manually configured. So hybrid is an option, but it's not recommended.

The best option is to use the DHCP server to manage all IP addresses on the network.

How DHCP Works

DHCP clients need to be configured to obtain an IP address automatically. This is done by going into the network card's properties and then the TCP/IP properties, as is shown in Figure 20.4.

When the client boots up, it will not have an IP address. To ask for one, it will send a *DHCP DISCOVER* broadcast out on the network. If a DHCP server is available to hear the broadcast, it will respond directly to the requesting client using the client's MAC address as the destination address. The process is shown in Figure 20.5.

Notice that the DHCP DISCOVER and DHCP REQUEST messages are broadcasts, which means two important things. First, every computer on the network segment receives and needs to process the broadcast message. It's like snail mail that's addressed to "the current resident" at an address, and the computer is compelled to read it. Excessive broadcasts can dramatically slow network performance. Second, broadcasts do not go through routers. Thus, if the client and the DHCP server are on opposite sides of a router, there will be a problem. There are two resolutions. First, make the router the DHCP server. Second, install a *DHCP relay agent* on the subnet that doesn't have the DHCP server. It will be configured with the address of the DHCP server, and it will forward the request directly to the DHCP server on behalf of the client.

FIGURE 20.4   Configured as a DHCP client

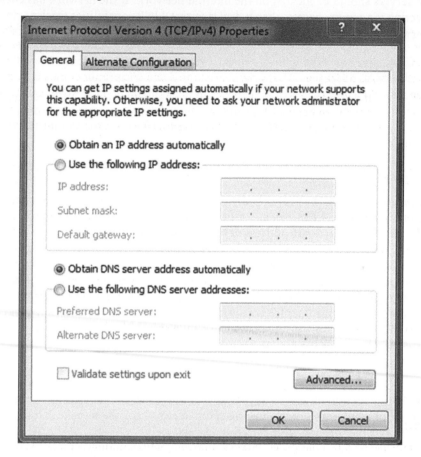

FIGURE 20.5   The DHCP request process

DHCP servers should be located on the internal network. If the network has clients that are connecting via remote access, then a device with DHCP capabilities (such as the Remote Access Service [RAS]) can be placed in the DMZ. DHCP uses UDP ports 67 and 68.

> **NOTE**
> If a Windows-based DHCP client is unable to reach a DHCP server, it will configure itself with an APIPA address (which we talked about in Chapter 7, "Introduction to TCP/IP"). Those addresses have the format 169.254.*x.x*.

DNS Server

DNS has one function on the network, and that is to resolve hostnames to IP addresses. As we discussed in Chapter 7, this has major implications. For a computer or phone to open a website, it needs to know the IP address of that website. The URL www.google.com means nothing to it. When a user enters the URL, the computer needs to figure out what the address is. The *DNS server* provides the answer, "That is 72.14.205.104." Now that the computer knows the address of the website that the user wants, it's able to go find it. DNS works the same way on an intranet (a local network not attached to the Internet) as it does on the Internet. The only difference is that instead of helping clients find www.google.com, it may help them find Jenny's print server or Joe's file server.

The DNS Server

If a company wants to host its own website, it also needs to maintain two public DNS servers with information on how to get to the website. (Two are required for redundancy.) An advantage of using ISPs or web hosting companies to host the website is that they are then also responsible for managing the DNS servers.

Each DNS server has a database, called a *zone file*, which maintains records of hostname to IP address mappings. Within a zone file, you will see information that looks something like this:

```
mydomain.com.    IN    SOA      ns.mydomain.com.      ;Start of Authority record
mydomain.com.    IN    NS       ns.mydomain.com.      ;name server for mydomain.com
mydomain.com.    IN    MX       mail.mydomain.com.    ;mail server for mydomain.com
mydomain.com.    IN    A        192.168.1.25          ;IPv4 address for mydomain.com
                 IN    AAAA     2001:db8:19::44       ;IPv6 address for mydomain.com
ns               IN    NS       192.168.1.2           ;IPv4 address for ns.mydomain.com
www              IN    CNAME    mydomain.com          ;www.mydomain.com is an alias
                                                       for mydomain.com
www2             IN    CNAME    www                   ;www2.mydomain.com is another
                                                       alias for mydomain.com
mail             IN    A        192.168.1.26          ;IPv4 address for mail.
                                                       mydomain.com
```

There are five columns of information presented. From left to right, they are as follows:

- The name of the server or computer, for example www.

- IN, which means Internet. (There are other options for this field, but for our purposes we will focus on Internet.)

- The record type. This example has SOA, NS, MX, A, AAAA, and CNAME. Table 20.1 explains some of the common record types.

- The address of the computer.

- Comments, preceded by a semicolon. In a file like this, the computer disregards everything after a semicolon. It's used to make notes for the administrator without affecting functionality.

TABLE 20.1   Common DNS record types

Type	Meaning
SOA	Start of Authority. It signifies the authoritative DNS server for that zone.
NS	Name Server. It's the name or address of the DNS server for that zone.
MX	Mail Exchanger. It's the name or address of the email server.
A	IPv4 host record.
AAAA	Called "quad A," it's the host record for IPv6 hosts.
CNAME	Canonical Name. It's an alias; it allows multiple names to be assigned to the same host or address.

The DNS server uses the zone file whenever a computer makes a query. For example, if you were to ask this DNS server, "Who is mydomain.com?" the response would be 192.168.1.25. If you ask it, "Who is www.mydomain.com?" it would look and see that www is an alias for mydomain.com and provide the same IP address.

If you are the DNS administrator for a network, you will be required to manage the zone file, including entering hostnames and IP addresses as appropriate.

DNS on the Internet

The Internet is really big. So big that there's no way one DNS server could possibly manage all of the computer name mappings out there. The creators of DNS anticipated this, and they designed it in a way that reduces potential issues. For example, let's say that you are looking for the website www.wiley.com. When the DNS server that your computer is configured to use is queried for a resolution, it will first check its zone file to see if it knows the IP address. If not, it then checks its cache to see if the record is in there. The cache is a temporary database of recently resolved names and IP addresses. If it still doesn't know the answer, it can query another DNS server asking for help. The first server it will ask is called a *root server*.

If you look back at the sample zone file shown earlier, you might notice that the first few rows contained mydomain.com. (the dot at the end, the *trailing dot*, is intentional). The Internet name space is designed as a hierarchical structure, and the dot at the end is the broadest categorization, known as "the root." The next level of the hierarchy are the top-level domains, such as .com, .net, .edu, .jp, and others. Below that are the second-level domains, like Google, Microsoft, and Yahoo. Below that there are subdomains (which are optional) and hostnames. Moving down, the levels in the hierarchy get more and more specific, until the name represents an exact host. Figure 20.6 shows an example.

FIGURE 20.6   Internet name hierarchy

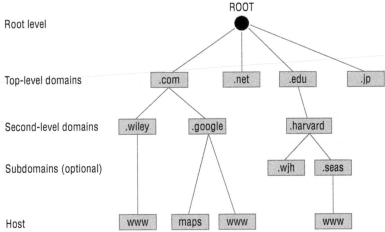

The Dot at the End of the Internet

You've probably used the Internet for quite some time, and you may be thinking, "Where did that trailing dot come from? I've never typed it into my browser." You're right.

As we said, the dot at the end represents the root. Without it, a domain name is not considered a *fully qualified domain name (FQDN)*, fit for Internet use. However, the dot is a convention that's implied when Internet browsers are used; users don't need to type it in. Even though it's omitted, the browser understands that it's technically looking for www.yahoo.com. and not www.yahoo.com with no terminal period. The Internet is an amazing place, isn't it?

There are 13 global root servers. All DNS servers should be configured to ask a root server for help. The root server will return the name of a top-level domain DNS server. The querying DNS server will then ask that server for help. The process continues, as shown in Figure 20.7, until the querying DNS server finds a server that is able to resolve the name www.wiley.com. Then the querying DNS server will cache the resolved name so that subsequent lookups are faster. The length of time that the name is held in cache is configurable by the DNS administrator.

> If you're curious, the list of root servers is maintained at www.iana.org/domains/root/servers, among other places.

FIGURE 20.7   The DNS name resolution process

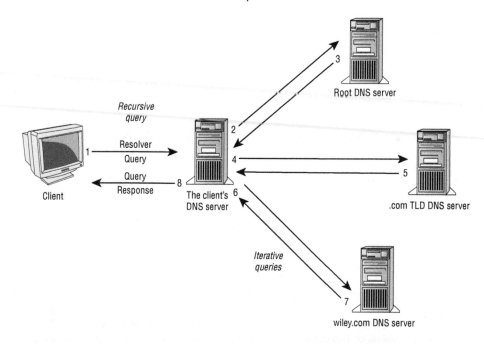

After looking at Figure 20.7, you might be amazed that the Internet works at all. If nothing else, it should explain why, if you visit a website you've never visited before, it can sometimes take longer than normal to load (provided no one else who uses your DNS server has visited the site recently either). The next time you visit that site, it will probably appear faster, if the name resolution is still held in cache.

   DNS servers for intranet use can be located inside all of the network firewalls. If it's being used for Internet name resolution, it's most effective to place it in the DMZ. DNS uses UDP or TCP port 53.

Proxy Server

A *proxy server* makes requests for resources on behalf of a client. The most common one that you will see is a web proxy, but you might run into a caching proxy as well. Exercise 20.1 shows you where to configure your computer to use a web proxy server in Windows 7.

EXERCISE 20.1

Configuring Windows 7 to Use a Proxy Server

1. If you are using Internet Explorer, click Tools ≻ Internet Options.

2. If you are using Google Chrome, open Internet Options by clicking the Menu icon (the box with the three horizontal bars to the right of the address bar) and choosing Settings ≻ Show Advanced Settings ≻ Change Proxy Settings.

3. Click the Connections tab and the LAN Settings button. You will open a screen similar to the one shown in Figure 20.8.

FIGURE 20.8   Enabling a proxy server

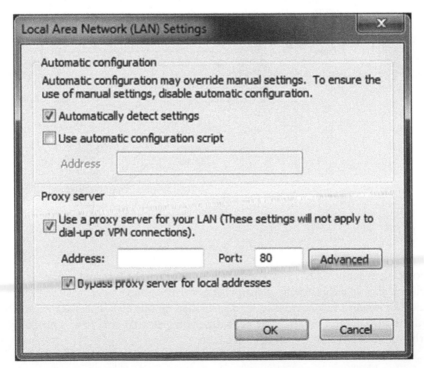

4. Check the top box under Proxy Server, and add the server's address and port number.

5. Click OK to save the settings, and close the window.

6. Click OK on the Internet Options dialog box to save the settings and close the window.

Let's use an example of a web proxy to illustrate how the proxy server process works. The user on the client computer opens a web browser and types in a URL. Instead of the request going directly to that website, it goes to the proxy server. The proxy then makes the request of the website, and it returns the requested information to the client computer. If it sounds to you like this slows down Internet browsing, you're right—it does. But there are three strong potential benefits to using a proxy.

First, the proxy server can cache the information requested, speeding up subsequent searches. (This is also the only function of a caching proxy, but caching-only proxies are most commonly configured to work on a local intranet.) Second, the proxy can act as a filter, blocking content from prohibited websites. Third, the proxy server can modify the requester's information when passing it to the destination, blocking the sender's identity and acting as a measure of security; the user can be made anonymous.

Keep in mind that if all of the traffic from a network must pass through a proxy server to get to the Internet, that can really slow down the response time. Make sure the proxy or proxies have ample resources to handle all of the requests. Figure 20.9 shows an example of a proxy server on a network.

FIGURE 20.9 A proxy server on a network

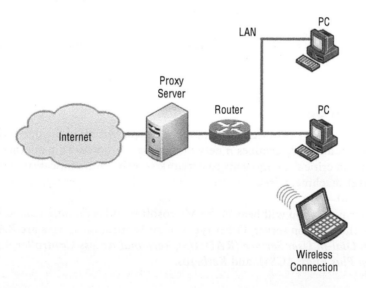

Mail Server

Email is critical for communication, and mail servers are responsible for sending, receiving, and managing email. To be a *mail server*, the computer must be running an email server package. The most popular ones are Microsoft Exchange, sendmail, Postfix, and Exim, although there are dozens of others on the market.

Clients access the mail server by using an email client installed on their systems. The most common corporate email client is Microsoft Outlook, but Apple Mail, IBM Notes (formerly Lotus Notes), and Thunderbird are also used. Mobile and Internet email clients (which are more popular than their corporate cousins) include the iPhone, iPad, and Android email clients, Gmail, Outlook.com, Apple Mail, and Yahoo! Mail.

In addition to sending and receiving email, mail servers often have anti-spam software built into them as well as the ability to encrypt and decrypt messages. Email servers are most often located in the DMZ. Table 20.2 lists the most important protocols to know for sending and receiving email.

TABLE 20.2 Important email protocols

Protocol	Port	Purpose
SMTP	25	Sending email and transferring email between mail servers.
POP3	110	Receiving email.
IMAP4	143	Receiving email. It's newer and has more features than POP3.

SMTP is a push protocol, whereas POP3 and IMAP4 are pull protocols.

Authentication Server

An *authentication server* is a device that examines the credentials of anyone trying to access the network, and it determines if network access is granted. Said another way, they are gatekeepers and critical components to network security. Authentication servers can be a dedicated server machine, wireless router or access point, Ethernet switch, or a remote access server (RAS).

A common term that you will hear in the Microsoft world is *domain controller*, which is a centralized authentication server. Other types of authentication servers are *RAS*, *Remote Authentication Dial-in User Service (RADIUS)*, *Terminal Access Controller Access-Control System Plus (TACACS+)*, and *Kerberos*.

The process will differ slightly between servers, but generally what happens is the user (or computer) trying to access the network presents credentials. If the credentials are deemed appropriate, the authentication server issues the user a security code or a ticket that grants them access to resources.

For most users, the required credentials are a username and password. To increase security, some systems require multiple items in addition to a username to authenticate users, such as a password and a security token. Such systems are said to support *multifactor authentication*. In multifactor authentication, the user is generally required to present two of these three items:

- Something they know, such as a password or a PIN.

- Something they have, such as a smart card or a PIN generated from an RSA security token (like the one shown in Figure 20.10).

- Something they are, which generally refers to biometrics. Examples include using fingerprints, facial recognition, and retinal scanners.

FIGURE 20.10   RSA SecureID token

Preserving the security of an authentication server is critical for network security. If an attacker breaches the authentication server, it can have catastrophic implications for the network. Therefore, most authentication servers should be securely tucked behind a firewall. To users who need remote access, RAS or RADIUS servers can be placed in a DMZ.

Internet Appliances

The definition of an *Internet appliance* is a device that makes it easy to access the Internet. The CompTIA A+ 220-902 exam objectives list three items under Internet appliances, and they are all related specifically to Internet security for networks as opposed to ease of Internet access. They are intrusion detection and prevention systems and unified threat management.

Intrusion Detection and Prevention Systems

Two Internet appliances that are closely related to each other are the *intrusion detection system (IDS)* and *intrusion prevention system (IPS)*. Both devices monitor network traffic and look for suspicious activity that might be the sign of a network-based attack. You can think of them as being somewhat analogous to antivirus (AV) programs. AV programs examine individual files looking for telltale signs of malicious content (called a *signature*). IDSs and IPSs look for signatures as well, but in network traffic patterns.

Both IDSs and IPSs are different from firewalls. Firewalls have specific sets of rules that allow or deny packets to enter a network, based on criteria such as the packet's origination or destination address, the protocol being used, or the source or destination ports. Their primary function is to block malicious traffic from entering the network in the first place. Firewalls may also have IDS or IPS software built in, or IDS and IPS devices can be stand-alone hardware devices.

An IDS is a passive device. It watches network traffic, and it can detect anomalies that might represent an attack. For example, if an attacker were to try to flood a network with traffic on a specific port, the IDS would sense that the additional traffic on that port was unusual. Then the IDS would log the anomaly and send an alert to an administrator. Note that it does nothing to prevent the attack; it simply logs relevant information pertaining to the attack and sends an alert.

By contrast, an IPS is an active device. It too monitors network traffic, but when it detects an anomaly, it can take actions to attempt to stop the attack. For example, if it senses suspicious inbound traffic on a specific IP port, it can shut the port down, block the sender, or reset the TCP connection. If the malicious stream of data is intended for one computer, it can prevent the attacking host from communicating with the intended victim computer or prevent the attacker from communicating with any computer. The specific actions it can take will depend on the device.

Both types of devices come in network-based varieties (NIDS and NIPS) and host-based varieties (HIDS and HIPS). As you might expect based on their names, the network-based versions are designed to protect multiple systems, whereas the host-based ones protect only one computer.

Unified Threat Management

The Internet is a wondrous place, but it's a scary one as well. It seems like for every video of puppies (or kittens) doing cute things, there are 10 hackers lurking in dark corners trying to steal identities or crash servers. It's an unfortunate reality of the Internet age. Software and hardware solutions have sprung up in response to various types of threats, and managing all of them can be a challenge. For example, a network needs a firewall, anti-malware and anti-spam software, and perhaps content filtering and IPS devices as well. It's a lot to deal with.

The goal of *unified threat management (UTM)* is to centralize security management, allowing administrators to manage all of their security-related hardware and software through a single device or interface. For administrators, having a single management point greatly reduces administration difficulties. The downside is that it introduces a single point of failure. If all network security is managed through one device, a device failure could be problematic.

UTM is generally implemented as a stand-alone device (or series of devices) on a network, and it will replace the traditional firewall. A UTM device can generally provide the following types of services:

- Packet filtering and inspection, like a firewall
- Intrusion protection service
- Gateway anti-malware
- Spam blocking
- Malicious website blocking (either prohibited or nefarious content)
- Application control

Many in the industry see UTM as the next generation of firewalls, and it's likely that its popularity will increase over the next several years.

Legacy and Embedded Systems

In regular human terms, legacies are considered a good thing. Most of us want to leave a legacy of some kind, whether it's within a community or organization or within our own families. A legacy is something that lives on far beyond a human life span.

If you mention the term *legacy system* in the computer world though, you are likely to be met with groans and eye rolls. It means that the system is old and hopelessly outdated by today's computing standards. Legacy systems are usually defined as those using old technology in one or more of the following areas:

- Hardware
- Software (applications or OS)
- Network protocols

Many legacy systems were state of the art when they were originally implemented in the 1970s or 1980s, but they haven't been upgraded or replaced. Today though, they are old and slow and specialized knowledge is required to maintain and operate them. For example, someone might need to know the Pick operating system (which came out in the 1970s), how to operate an IBM AS/400 or manage VAX, or how to configure the IPX/SPX network protocol. (Google these topics sometime!)

An *embedded system* is one that is critical in a process; other systems or processes depend upon it. For purposes of this section, we will treat legacy and embedded systems as one and the same because administrators face similar issues with both.

So why don't companies replace legacy systems? It's complicated. First, most companies don't have large IT budgets, and replacing legacy systems can be very expensive. This is especially true for many companies who see the systems providing reliable (if a bit slow) service. Why fix what's not broken? Second, the cost of failure of an upgrade could be catastrophic. The world's global financial systems are in many places supported by legacy systems. Messing up a migration in that context could be a career-limiting move. Third, the time it would take to test the new system, verify functionality, and roll out the implementation could be extensive. Time is money, and we already stated that IT budgets are generally tight.

Furthermore, it's challenging to find technicians and consultants who understand legacy systems. People move from company to company, or consultants retire and take their specialized knowledge with them. Someone who was a mid-20's computer whiz in 1975 is now in their mid-60's and probably looking forward to retirement. The cost to find someone knowledgeable on these systems can be high.

Speaking of high costs, finding replacement hardware can be difficult to impossible while being expensive at the same time. Eventually, the cost of maintenance might outweigh the cost of upgrading, but then again it might not.

 Real World Scenario

A Real Example of a Legacy System

Author's note: As fate would have it, one day after writing this section, one of my Facebook friends posted this link:

www.popularmechanics.com/technology/infrastructure/a16010/30-year-old-computer-runs-school-heat/

After reading the story, I had to edit this chapter to include it. The article does a great job of outlining the issues that network administrators face in the real world—namely, if it isn't broke, don't fix it!

So what's a network administrator to do? If possible, replacing or repurposing legacy systems can provide long-term benefits to a company. But also recognize the risk involved. If replacement isn't an option, then the best advice that we can give is to learn as much as you can about them. Hopefully, the system is based on established standards, so you can look them up on the Internet and learn as much as possible. If not, see what operating manuals you can track down, or pick the brain of those who understand how they operate. As challenging as legacy systems can be, you can make yourself quite valuable by being the expert on them.

A common administrative option is to try to isolate the legacy system as much as possible so that its lack of speed doesn't affect the rest of the network. This is usually much easier to do with hardware or protocols than with software. For example, the network might be set up with one segment that hosts the legacy systems or protocols.

One technology that is helping replace and update legacy systems is virtualization, which can obviate the need for one-to-one hardware-to-software relationships. We will cover virtualization in the next section.

Understanding Cloud Computing and Virtualization

The computer industry is one of big trends. A new technology comes along and becomes popular, until the next wave of newer, faster, and shinier objects come along to distract everyone from the previous wave. Thinking back over the past 20 years or so, there have been several big waves, including the rise of the Internet, wireless networking, and mobile computing.

Within each trend, there are often smaller ones. For example, the Internet was helped by modems and ISPs in the middle of the 1990s, and then broadband access took over. Wireless networking has seen several generations of faster technology, from the 11Mbps 802.11b, which at the time it came out was pretty cool, to 802.11ac, promising gigabit wireless. Mobile computing has been a long-lasting wave, first with laptop computers becoming more popular than desktops, and more recently with handheld devices (namely smartphones and tablets) essentially functioning like computers.

The biggest recent wave in the computing world is cloud computing. Its name comes from the fact that the technology is Internet based; in most computer literature, the Internet is represented by a graphic that looks like a cloud. It seems like everyone is jumping on the cloud (pun intended, but doesn't that sound like fun?), and technicians need to be aware of what it can provide and its limitations. The most important core technology supporting cloud computing is virtualization. We will cover both topics in the following sections.

Concepts of Cloud Computing

You hear the term a lot today—*the cloud*. What exactly is the cloud? The way it's named, and it's probably due to the word *the* at the beginning, it sounds like it's one giant, fluffy, magical entity that does everything you could ever want a computer to do. Only it's not quite that big, fluffy, or magical, and it's not even one thing.

Cloud computing is a method by which you access remote servers to store files or run applications for you. There isn't one cloud but hundreds of commercial clouds in existence today. Many of them are owned by big companies such as Microsoft, Google, HP, Apple, Netflix, and Amazon. Basically, they set up the hardware and/or software for you on their network, and then you use it.

Using the cloud sounds pretty simple, and in most cases it is. From the administrator's side, things can be a little trickier. Cloud computing involves a concept called virtualization, which means that there isn't necessarily a one-to-one relationship between a physical server and a logical (or virtual) server. In other words, there might be one physical server that virtually hosts cloud servers for a dozen companies, or there might be several physical servers working together as one logical server. From the end user's side, the idea of a physical machine versus a virtual machine doesn't even come into play, because it's all handled behind the scenes. We'll cover virtualization in more depth later in this chapter.

There are many advantages to cloud computing, and the most important ones revolve around money. Cloud providers can get economies of scale by having a big pool of resources available to share among many clients. It may be entirely possible for them to add more clients without needing to add new hardware, which results in greater profit. From a client company's standpoint, the company can pay for only the resources it needs without investing large amounts of capital into hardware that will be outdated in a few years. Using the cloud is often cheaper than the alternative. Plus, if there is a hardware failure within the cloud, the provider handles it. If the cloud is set up right, the client won't even know that a failure occurred. Other advantages of cloud computing include fast scalability for clients and ease of access to resources regardless of location.

The biggest downside of the cloud has been security. The company's data is stored on someone else's server and company employees are sending it back and forth via the Internet. Cloud providers have dramatically increased their security over the last few years, but this can still be an issue, especially if the data is highly sensitive material or personally identifiable information (PII). Also, some companies don't like the fact that they don't own the assets.

Now let's dive into the types of services clouds provide, the types of clouds, cloud-specific terms with which you should be familiar, and some examples of using a cloud from the client side.

Cloud Services

Cloud providers sell everything "as a service." The type of service is named for the highest level of technology provided. For example, if computing and storage is the highest level, the client will purchase infrastructure as a service. If applications are involved, it will be software as a service. Nearly everything that can be digitized can be provided as a service. Let's take a look at the three most common types of services offered by cloud providers, from the ground up:

Infrastructure as a Service   Let's say that a company needs extra network capacity, including processing power, storage, and networking services (such as firewalls) but doesn't have the money to buy more network hardware. Instead, it can purchase *infrastructure as a service (IaaS)*, which is a lot like paying for utilities—the client pays for what it uses. Of the three, IaaS requires the most network management expertise from the client. In an IaaS setup, the client provides and manages the software.

Platform as a Service   *Platform as a service (PaaS)* adds a layer to IaaS that includes software development tools such as runtime environments. Because of this, it can be very helpful to software developers; the vendor manages the various hardware platforms. This frees up the software developer to focus on building their application and scaling it. The best PaaS solutions allow for the client to export their developed programs and run them in an environment other than where it was developed. Examples of PaaS include Google App Engine, Microsoft Azure, Red Hat OpenShift, Amazon Web Services Elastic Beanstalk, Engine Yard, and Heroku.

Software as a Service (SaaS)   The highest of these three levels of service is *software as a service (SaaS)*, which handles the task of managing software and its deployment, and it includes the platform and infrastructure as well. This is the one with which you are probably most familiar, because it's the model used by Google Docs, Microsoft Office 365, and even storage solutions such as Dropbox. The advantage of this model is to cut costs for software ownership and management; clients typically sign up for subscriptions to use the software and can renew as needed.

Figure 20.11 shows examples of these three types of services. SaaS is the same as the Application layer shown in the figure.

```
https://commons.wikimedia.org/wiki/File:Cloud_computing.svg#/media/
File:Cloud_computing.svg
```

FIGURE 20.11   Common cloud service levels

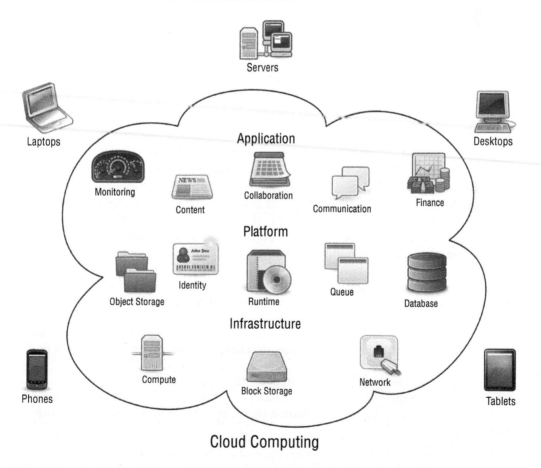

Although not included in the A+ objectives, other service levels also exist:

- Hardware as a service (HaaS), which is similar to IaaS but is more likely related specifically to data storage
- Communications as a service (CaaS), which provides things like voice over IP (VoIP), instant messaging, and video collaboration
- Network as a service (NaaS), which provides network infrastructure
- Desktop as a service (DaaS), which provides virtual desktops so that users with multiple devices or platforms can have a similar desktop experience across all systems
- Data as a service (also DaaS), which provides for multiple sources of data in a mash-up
- Business processes as a service (BPaaS), which is used to provide business processes such as payroll, IT help desk, or other services
- Anything/Everything as a service (XaaS), which is a combination of the services already discussed

The level of responsibility between the provider and the client is specified in the contract. It should be very clear which party has responsibility for specific elements should anything go awry.

Types of Clouds

Running a cloud is not restricted to big companies offering services over the Internet. Companies can purchase virtualization software to set up individual clouds within their own network. That type of setup is referred to as a *private cloud*. Running a private cloud pretty much eliminates many of the features that companies want from the cloud, such as rapid scalability and eliminating the need to purchase and manage computer assets. The big advantage, though, is that it allows the company to control its own security within the cloud.

The traditional type of cloud that usually comes to mind is a *public cloud*, like the ones operated by the third-party companies we mentioned earlier. These clouds offer the best in scalability, reliability, flexibility, geographical independence, and cost effectiveness. Whatever the client wants, the client gets. For example, if the client needs more resources, it simply scales up and uses more. Of course, the client will also pay more, but that's part of the deal.

Some clients have chosen to combine public and private clouds into a *hybrid cloud*. This gives the client the great features of a public cloud while simultaneously allowing for the storage of more sensitive information on the private cloud. It's the best of both worlds.

The last type of cloud to discuss is a *community cloud*. These are created when multiple organizations with common interests combine to create a cloud. In a sense, it's like a public cloud with better security. The clients know who the other clients are and, in theory, can trust them more than they could trust random people on the Internet. The economies of scale and flexibility won't be as great as with a public cloud, but that's the trade-off for better security.

Important Cloud Features

We've discussed several important cloud features to this point. The National Institute of Standards and Technology (NIST), a group within the United States Department of Commerce, has defined five essential characteristics of cloud computing. They are as follows:

On-demand self-service   This is one of the cloud's best features from an end user's standpoint. With *on-demand self-service*, users can access additional storage, processing, and capabilities automatically, without requiring intervention from the service provider.

Broad network access   This means that cloud capabilities are accessible over the network by different types of clients, such as workstations, laptops, and mobile phones, using common access software such as web browsers. The ability for users to get the data they want, when they want, how they want, is sometimes referred to as *ubiquitous access*.

Resource pooling   The idea of *resource pooling* is closely linked with virtualization, which we will cover shortly. The provider's resources are seen as one large pool, which can be divided up among clients as needed. Clients should be able to access additional resources as needed, even though the client may not be aware of where the resources are physically located. Typical pooled resources include network bandwidth, storage, processing power, and memory.

Rapid elasticity   We've talked about the ability to scale up resources as needed, and that is elasticity. In most cases, clients can get more resources instantly (or at least very quickly), and that is called *rapid elasticity*. For the client, this is a great feature because they can scale up without needing to purchase, install, and configure new hardware. Elasticity can also work backwards; if fewer resources are required, the client may be able to scale down and pay less without needing to sell hardware. You will hear some subscriptions with built-in elasticity referred to as *pay-as-you-grow* services.

Measured service   Most cloud providers meter clients' usage and then charge them for the services used. This type of setup is called *measured service*. Resource usage is monitored by the provider and reported to the client in a transparent fashion.

Using Cloud-Based Services

Up to this point, we have primarily focused on the characteristics that make up cloud computing. Now let's turn our attention to some practical examples with which users will probably be more familiar. The two types of cloud interaction we will cover are storage and applications. The next two sections will assume the use of public clouds and standard web browser access.

Cloud-Based Storage

Storage is the area in which cloud computing got its start. The idea is simple—users store files just as they would on a hard drive but with two major advantages. One, they don't need to buy the hardware. Two, different users can access the files regardless of where they are physically located. Users can be located in the United States, China, and Germany, and all of them have access via their web browser. This is particularly helpful for multinational organizations.

There is no shortage of cloud-based storage providers in the market today. Each one offers slightly different features. Most of them will offer limited storage for free and pre-mium services for more data-heavy users. Table 20.3 shows a comparison of some of the better-known providers. Please note that the data limits and cost can change; this table is provided for illustrative purposes only. Most of these providers offer business plans with unlimited storage as well for an additional cost.

TABLE 20.3   Cloud providers and features

Service	Free	Premium	Cost Per Year
Dropbox	2GB	1TB	$100
Apple iCloud	5GB	200GB	$48
Box	10GB	100GB	$60
Microsoft OneDrive	15GB	200GB	$48
Google Drive	15GB	1TB	$120

Which one should you choose? If you want extra features such as web-based applications, then Google or Microsoft is probably the best choice. If you just need data storage, then Box or Dropbox might be a better option.

NOTE   Nearly all client OSs will work with any of the providers, with the exception of Linux, which natively works only with Dropbox.

Most cloud storage providers offer synchronization to the desktop, which makes it so that you have a folder on your computer, just as if it were on your hard drive. And it's important to note that folder will always have the most current edition of the files stored in the cloud.

Accessing the sites is done through your web browser. Once you are in the site, managing your files is much like managing them on your local computer. In Figure 20.12, you can see the Google Drive interface, with three folders and two files in it.

FIGURE 20.12   Google Drive

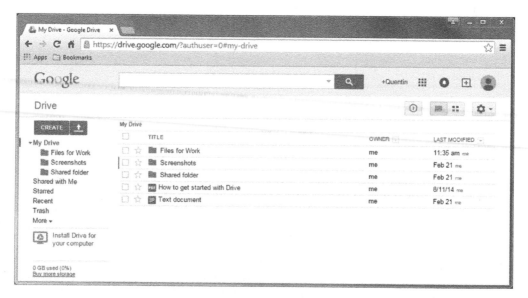

You have a few options for sharing a folder with another user. One way is to right-click the folder and choose Share ➤ Share (Figure 20.13). You'll be asked to enter their name or email address and to indicate whether they can view or edit the file. To share multiple items, you can check the boxes in front of folder names (as the box is checked in Figure 20.13) and then click the icon that shows a person and a plus sign right above the check box. That will take you to the same sharing menu, which asks for the name and email address.

FIGURE 20.13   Sharing a folder on Google Drive

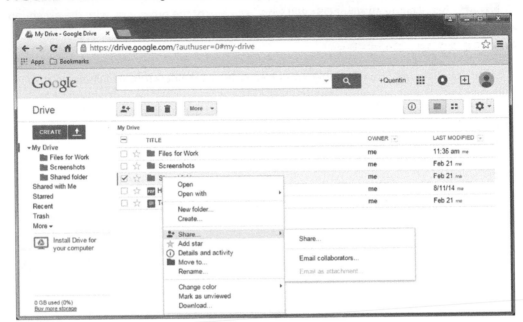

Cloud-Based Applications

Google really popularized the use of web-based applications. After all, the whole Chromebook platform, which has been very successful, is based on this premise! Other companies have gotten into the cloud-based application space as well, such as Microsoft with Office 365. The menus and layout are slightly different than PC-based versions of Office, but if you're familiar with Office, you can easily use Office 365, and all of the files are stored on the cloud.

Cloud-based apps run through your web browser. This is great for end users for a few reasons. One, your system does not have to use its own hardware to run the application. Two, different client OSs can run the application (usually) without worrying about compatibility issues.

To create a new document using Google Docs, you click the Create button shown on the left side of Figure 20.13 and then choose Document from the menu. It opens a new browser window with Google Docs, as shown in Figure 20.14.

When choosing a cloud provider, you may use any one you like. In fact, it's better if you experience the differences in how providers store files and let you manage and manipulate them before making your choice. Exercise 20.2 will give you experience with using cloud-based storage and applications, specifically Google Drive and its associated apps. This exercise will work best if you have someone with whom you can work. For example, in a classroom setting, you can partner with someone. If you are studying at home, you can create multiple accounts and get the same experience. You will just need to log off and on with your other account to see the shared files.

FIGURE 20.14 Google Docs

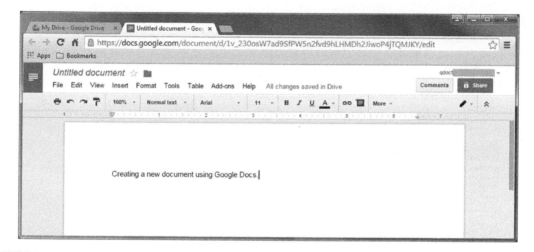

EXERCISE 20.2

Using Google's Cloud Services

1. Open Google at www.google.com.

2. If you do not already have a Google account, you will need to create one. With it, you use Google's online apps and storage as well as a Gmail account.

3. If you are doing this exercise on your own, create a second account to share files and folders with.

4. Once you're logged in, click the Apps icon in the upper-right corner. It's the one that has nine small squares (see Figure 20.15).

FIGURE 20.15 Google icons

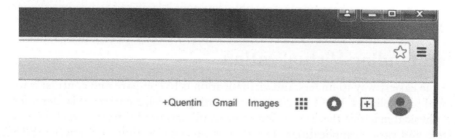

continues

EXERCISE 20.2 *(continued)*

5. In Apps, click Drive. This will open Google Drive, shown in Figure 20.16.

FIGURE 20.16 Google Drive

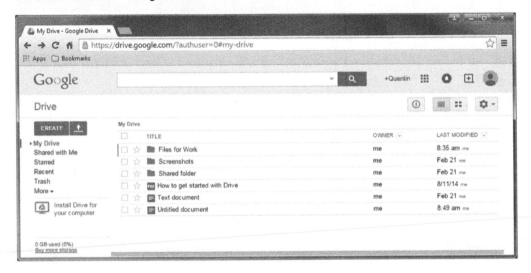

6. Create a folder and share it with another account. Also create a document or spreadsheet using Google's online software. How easy or difficult was it?

7. If necessary, log out and log in to the other account that you created to access the resources that were shared for you. How easy or difficult was it?

The newest trend in web applications and cloud storage is the streaming of media. Companies such as Netflix, Amazon, Pandora, Apple, and others store movies and music on their clouds. You download their client software, and for a monthly subscription fee, you can stream media to your device. It can be your phone, your tablet, your computer, or your home entertainment system. Before the advent of broadband network technologies, this type of setup would have been impossible, but now it is poised to become the mainstream way that people receive audio and video entertainment.

Understanding Virtualization

Perhaps the easiest way to understand virtualization is to compare and contrast it to more traditional technologies. In the traditional computing model, a computer is identified as being a physical machine that is running some combination of software, such as an operating system and various applications. There's a one-to-one relationship between the hardware and the operating system.

For the sake of illustration, imagine that a machine is a file server and now it needs to perform the functions of a web server as well. To make this happen, the administrator would need to ensure that the computer has enough resources to support the service (CPU, memory, network bandwidth), install web server software (Microsoft IIS or Apache, for example), configure the appropriate files and permissions, and then bring it back online as a file and web server. These would be relatively straightforward administrative tasks.

But now imagine that the machine in question is being asked to run Windows Server and Linux at the same time. Now there's a problem. In the traditional computing model, only one OS can run at one time, because each OS completely controls the hardware resources in the computer. Sure, an administrator can install a second OS and configure the server to dual-boot, meaning the OS to run is chosen during the boot process, but only one OS can run at a time. So if the requirement is to have a Windows-based file server and a Linux-based Apache web server, there's a problem. Two physical computers are needed.

Similarly, imagine that there is a Windows-based workstation being used by an applications programmer. The programmer has been asked to code an app that works in Linux, or Mac OS, or anything other than Windows. When the programmer needs to test the app to see how well it works, what does she do? Sure, she can configure her system to dual-boot, but once again, in the traditional computing model, she's limited to one OS at a time per physical computer. Her company could purchase a second system, but that quickly starts to get expensive when there are multiple users with similar needs.

This is where virtualization comes in. The term *virtualization* is defined as creating virtual (rather than actual) versions of something. In computer jargon, it means creating virtual environments where "computers" can operate. We use quotation marks around the word *computers* because they don't need to be physical computers in the traditional sense. Virtualization is often used to let multiple OSs (or multiple instances of the same OS) run on one physical machine at the same time. Yes, they are often still bound by the physical characteristics of the machine on which they reside, but virtualization breaks down the traditional one-to-one relationship between a physical set of hardware and an OS.

 Virtualization has been around in the computer industry since 1967, but it has only recently exploded in popularity thanks to the flexibility that the Internet offers.

The Purpose of Virtual Machines

We have already hit on the major feature of virtualization, which is breaking down that one-to-one hardware and software barrier. The virtualized version of a computer is appropriately called a *virtual machine (VM)*. Thanks to VMs, it is becoming far less common to need dual-boot machines today than in the past. In addition, VMs make technology like the cloud possible. A cloud provider can have one incredibly powerful server that is running five instances of an OS for client use, and each client is able to act as if it had its own individual server. On the flip side, cloud providers are able to pool resources from multiple physical servers into what appears to be one system to the client, effectively giving clients unlimited processing or storage capabilities (assuming, of course, that the provider doesn't physically run out of hardware!).

Virtual OSs can be powered on or off individually without affecting the host OS or hypervisor.

The underlying purpose of all of this is to save money. Cloud providers can achieve economies of scale, because adding additional clients doesn't necessarily require the purchase of additional hardware. Clients don't have to pay for hardware (or the electricity to keep the hardware cool) and can pay only for the services they use. End users, in the workstation example we provided earlier, can have multiple environments to use without needing to buy additional hardware as well.

The Hypervisor

The key enabler for virtualization is a piece of software called the *hypervisor*, also known as a *virtual machine manager (VMM)*. The hypervisor software allows multiple operating systems to share the same host, and it also manages the physical resource allocation to those virtual OSs. There are two types of hypervisors: Type 1 and Type 2, and they are illustrated in Figure 20.17.

FIGURE 20.17 Type 1 and Type 2 hypervisors

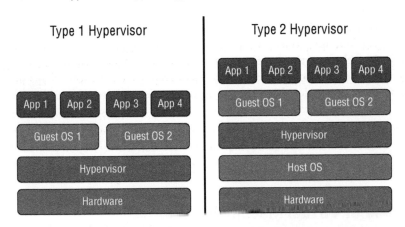

A *Type 1 hypervisor* sits directly on the hardware, and because of this, it's sometimes referred to as a *bare metal hypervisor*. In this instance, the hypervisor is basically the operating system for the physical machine. This setup is most commonly used for server-side virtualization, because the hypervisor itself typically has very low hardware requirements to support its own functions. Type 1 is generally considered to have better performance than Type 2, simply because there is no host OS involved and the system is dedicated to supporting virtualization. Virtual OSs are run within the hypervisor, and the virtual (guest) OSs are completely independent of each other. Examples of Type 1 hypervisors include Microsoft Hyper-V, VMware ESX, and Citrix XenServer.

A *Type 2 hypervisor* sits on top of an existing operating system, called the *host OS*. This is most commonly used in *client-side virtualization*, where multiple OSs are managed on the client machine as opposed to on a server. An example of this would be a Windows user who wants to run Linux at the same time as Windows. The user could install a hypervisor and then install Linux in the hypervisor and run both OSs concurrently and independently. The downsides of Type 2 are that the host OS consumes resources such as processor time and memory and a host OS failure means that the guest OSs fail as well. Examples of Type 2 hypervisors include Microsoft Virtual PC and Virtual Server, Oracle VirtualBox, VMware Workstation, and KVM.

Client-Side Virtualization Requirements

As you might expect, running multiple OSs on one physical workstation can require more resources than running a single OS. There's no rule that says a workstation being used for virtualization is required to have more robust hardware than another machine, but for performance reasons, the system should be fairly well equipped. This is especially true for systems running a Type 2 hypervisor, which sits on top of a host OS. The host OS will need resources too, and it will compete with the VMs for those resources. Let's talk about specific requirements now.

Resource Requirements

The primary resources here are the same as you would expect when discussing any other computer's performance: CPU, RAM, hard drive space, and network performance. From the CPU standpoint, know that the hypervisor can treat each core of a processor as separate virtual processors, and it can even create multiple virtual processors out of a single core. The general rule here is that the faster the processor the better, but really, the more cores a processor has, the more virtual OSs it can support in a speedy fashion. Within the hypervisor, there will most likely be an option to set the allocation of physical resources such as CPU priority and amount of RAM to each VM.

Some hypervisors require that the CPU be specifically designed to support virtualization. For Intel chips, this technology is called virtualization technology (VT), and AMD chips need to support AMD-V. In addition, many system BIOSs have an option to turn on or turn off virtualization support. If a processor supports virtualization but the hypervisor won't install, check the BIOS and enable virtualization. The specific steps to do this will vary based on the BIOS, so check the manufacturer's documentation. An example of what this might look like is shown in Figure 20.18.

Memory is always a big concern for computers, and virtual ones are no different. When you're installing the guest OS, the hypervisor will ask how much memory to allocate to the VM. This can be modified later if the guest OS in the VM requires more memory to run properly. Always remember, though, that the host OS requires RAM too. Thus, if the host

OS needs 4GB of RAM and the guest OS needs 4GB of RAM, the system needs to have at least 8GB of RAM to support both adequately.

FIGURE 20.18 Enabling virtualization in the BIOS

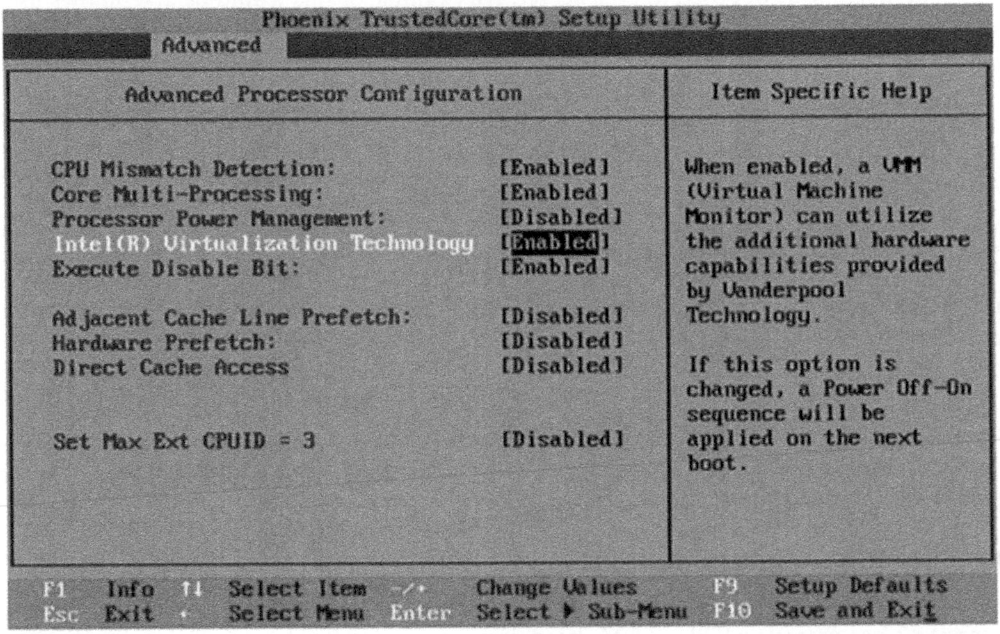

```
                    Phoenix TrustedCore(tm) Setup Utility
           Advanced

         Advanced Processor Configuration          │    Item Specific Help

                                                   │
    CPU Mismatch Detection:          [Enabled]     │  When enabled, a VMM
    Core Multi-Processing:           [Enabled]     │  (Virtual Machine
    Processor Power Management:       [Disabled]    │  Monitor) can utilize
    Intel(R) Virtualization Technology [Enabled]   │  the additional hardware
    Execute Disable Bit:             [Enabled]     │  capabilities provided
                                                   │  by Vanderpool
    Adjacent Cache Line Prefetch:    [Disabled]    │  Technology.
    Hardware Prefetch:               [Disabled]    │
    Direct Cache Access              [Disabled]    │  If this option is
                                                   │  changed, a Power Off-On
                                                   │  sequence will be
    Set Max Ext CPUID = 3            [Disabled]    │  applied on the next
                                                   │  boot.

    F1    Info   ↑↓   Select Item  -/+   Change Values    F9   Setup Defaults
    Esc   Exit   ←    Select Menu  Enter Select ▶ Sub-Menu F10  Save and Exit
```

Hard disk space works the same way as RAM. Each OS will need its own hard disk space, and the guest OS will be configured via the hypervisor. Make sure that the physical computer has enough free disk space to support the guest OSs.

Finally, from a networking standpoint, each of the virtual desktops will typically need full network access, and configuring the permissions for each can sometimes be tricky. The virtual desktop is often called a *virtual desktop interface (VDI)*, and that term encompasses the software and hardware needed to create the virtual environment. The VM will create a *virtual NIC* and manage the resources of that NIC appropriately. The virtual NIC doesn't have to be connected to the physical NIC; an administrator could create an entire virtual network within the virtual environment where the virtual machines just talk to each other.

That's not normally practical in the real world though, so the virtual NIC will be connected to the physical NIC. Configuring a virtual switch within the hypervisor normally does this. The virtual switch manages the traffic to and from the virtual NICs and logically attaches to the physical NIC. Figure 20.19 illustrates this. Network bandwidth is often the biggest bottleneck when running multiple virtual OSs.

FIGURE 20.19   Virtual NICs connecting to a physical NIC

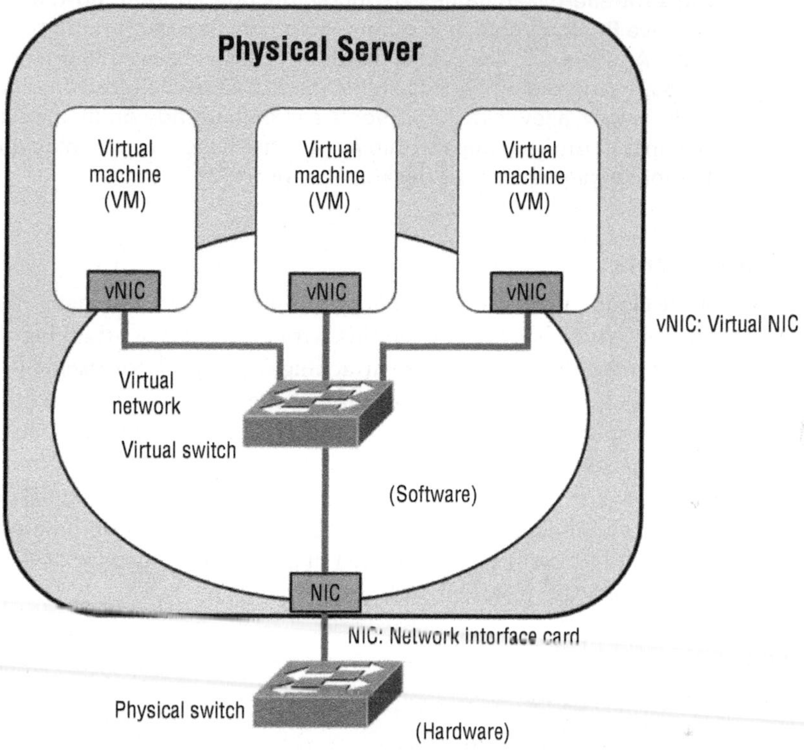

Physical Server

Virtual machine (VM)

Virtual machine (VM)

Virtual machine (VM)

vNIC

vNIC

vNIC

vNIC: Virtual NIC

Virtual network

Virtual switch

(Software)

NIC

NIC: Network interface card

Physical switch

(Hardware)

With Type 1 hypervisors, virtual desktops are often used with remote administration. This can allow a remote administrator to work on the workstation (to perform maintenance, for example) with or without the knowledge of the user sitting in front of the machine.

Emulator Requirements

Virtual machines are created to exist and function just like a physical machine. Because of that, all of the requirements that a physical machine would have need to be replicated by the hypervisor, and that process is called *emulation*. The terms *hypervisor* and *emulator* often get used interchangeably, although they don't mean the same thing. The hypervisor can support multiple OSs, whereas technically, an emulator appears to work the same as one specific OS. As for requirements, the emulator and the hypervisor need to be compatible with the host OS. That's about it.

Some mobile-based games are incredibly popular right now, and they do not have PC equivalents. In other words, you need to run them from iOS or the Android OS. Android is based on open-source code, meaning that there are Android emulators on the market. One such free emulator is Andy, at www.andyroid.net. People can install Andy on their desktops, and then install Android apps within Andy. That way, they can play their favorite mobile games on their desktop computer.

Security Requirements

In the early days of the cloud, a common misconception was that virtual machines couldn't be hacked. Unfortunately, some hackers proved this wrong. Instead of attacking the OS in the VM, hackers have turned their attention to attacking the hypervisor itself. Why just hit one OS when you can hit all of them on the computer at the same time? There have been a number of virtualization-specific threats that have cropped up focusing on the hypervisor, but updates have fixed the issues as they have become known. The solution to most virtual machine threats is to always apply the most recent updates to keep the system(s) current.

At the same time, all of the security concerns that affect individual computers also apply to VMs. For example, if Windows is being operated in a VM, that instance of Windows still needs anti-malware software installed on it.

 Real World Scenario

Setting Up and Using Client-Side Virtualization

If given a scenario on the A+ exam or faced with the situation in real life, you should be able to set up and show someone how to use client-side virtualization. Here are some sample steps to follow:

1. Determine the client needs for virtualization. For example, do they have a Windows or Mac client and need to run Linux? Or perhaps they have a Windows computer and want to run Mac OS X at the same time? Determine their needs, and then secure the additional OSs (including licenses, as appropriate) before beginning the installation.

2. Evaluate the computer to ensure that it can support the VM.

   a. Does the processor support virtualization?

   b. How much RAM does the computer have? Is it enough to meet the minimum requirements of all installed OSs?

   c. How much free hard drive space is there? It needs to be enough to install the hypervisor and the guest OS as well as to store any files that need to be stored from within the guest OS.

> **d.** Does the system have a fast enough network connection if the guest OS needs access to the network?
>
> **3.** Consider which hypervisor to use. Is there a version of the hypervisor that's compatible with the host OS?
>
> **4.** Consider security requirements. If the guest OS will be on the Internet, will it have proper security software installed?
>
> **5.** After all conditions are deemed sufficient, you can install the hypervisor and the guest OS. It will not affect the host OS, but it's always a good idea to back up the system first before installing any new major software packages!
>
> Exercise 20.3 will also give you hands-on experience installing a hypervisor and a guest OS.

Now that we have covered the key concepts behind client-side virtualization, it's time to practice. Exercise 20.3 will walk you through installing the Oracle VirtualBox hypervisor on a Windows 7 computer and then installing Lubuntu (a distribution of Linux). Normally, installing a second OS involves a relatively complicated process where you need to dual-boot your computer. You're not going to do that here. Instead, you will use the VirtualBox hypervisor that allows you to create a new virtual system on your hard drive and not affect your existing Windows installation. We promise you that this exercise will not mess up Windows on your computer! And when you're finished, you can just uninstall VirtualBox, if you want, and nothing will have changed on your system.

EXERCISE 20.3

Installing VirtualBox and Lubuntu on Windows 7

The first two steps are for preparation only. You need to download the Oracle VirtualBox and a version of Lubuntu. Really, any version of Linux is fine, but we'll point you to a 32-bit version of Lubuntu, which should minimize any compatibility issues. Depending on your network speed, the download could take an hour or more.

1. Download Oracle VirtualBox from www.virtualbox.org/wiki/Downloads. Select VirtualBox For Windows Hosts, unless, of course, you have a Mac, and then you need the one for OS X hosts. Save it to your desktop for ease of access.

2. Download Lubuntu from http://lubuntu.net/tags/download. There is a link on the left side for Lubuntu x86 CD. Choose that one. It will download a zipped file with an .iso extension. You will need that ISO file later; it will essentially act as a bootable CD for your OS installation.

Now you can begin the installation of VirtualBox.

3. Double-click the VirtualBox icon. If you get a security warning, click the Run button. Then click Next on the Setup Wizard screen.

continues

4. On the Custom Setup screen, click Next and then Next again. It will give you a warning about your network interfaces. Click Yes. (Your network connections will come back automatically.)

5. Click Install. This may take several minutes. (You might also need to clear another security warning box.)

6. Once the install is complete, click Finish. It's time to configure VirtualBox.

7. You might get a VirtualBox warning telling you that an image file is not currently accessible. That's fine. Click Ignore. You should see a screen similar to the one shown in Figure 20.20.

FIGURE 20.20   VirtualBox preconfiguration

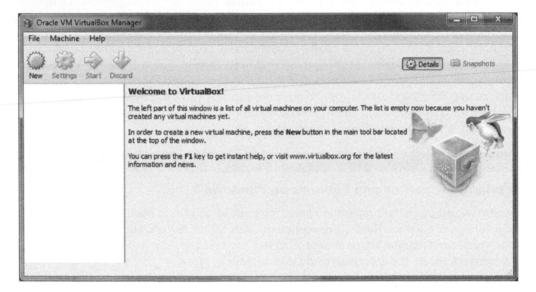

8. Click the blue New icon to create a new virtual machine. Give it a name. The Type and Version boxes aren't critical; they don't affect anything. If you type in Lubuntu for a name, it will automatically set Type to Linux and Version to Ubuntu (32 bit). Click Next.

9. In the Memory Size window, click Next.

10. In the Hard Drive window, the default option is Create A Virtual Hard Drive. Leave that option selected and click Create.

11. You will be prompted for what hard drive file type you want to create. Leave it on VDI and click Next.

12. On the next screen, either Dynamically Allocated or Fixed Size is fine. If you are low on disk space, go with Fixed Size. Click Next.

13. In the File Location And Size window, it's probably best to leave it at the default size of 8GB. Definitely don't make it any smaller. Click Create. Now you will see a screen like the one shown in Figure 20.21.

FIGURE 20.21   VirtualBox with a virtual drive

Great! You now have a virtual machine on your hard drive. Now you just need to put something on it, more specifically an OS.

14. Click the Settings button.

15. In the Lubuntu – Settings window, click the Storage icon on the left.

16. Under one of your controllers, you should see something that looks like a disc icon that says Empty. It should look like Figure 20.22.

continues

FIGURE 20.22 Lubuntu – Settings dialog

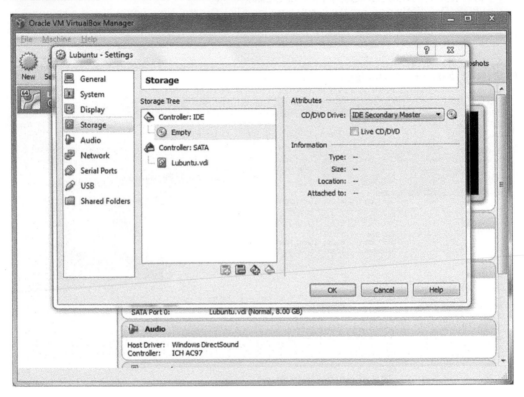

17. On the very right side of the window, you will have another disc icon with a little down arrow on it. Click that, and a menu will pop up. Select Choose A Virtual CD/DVD Disk File.

18. In the window that pops up, navigate to the directory where you stored the Lubuntu ISO file that you downloaded. Highlight the file, and then click Open.

19. Back on the Lubuntu – Settings dialog, your drive that was empty should now say Lubuntu. Click OK.

20. Now you are back to the Oracle VirtualBox Manager screen, With Lubuntu on the left highlighted, press the green Start arrow. This will begin installation of Lubuntu.

21. Choose a language and then, on the next screen, choose Install Lubuntu and press Enter.

22. Follow the Lubuntu installation process.

23. You will get to a screen similar to the one shown in Figure 20.23, which asks you for an installation type. It looks scary, but choose the Erase Disk And Install Lubuntu option. This will install it on the virtual disk that you created earlier with VirtualBox, and it will *not* wipe out your entire hard drive.

FIGURE 20.23   Installing Lubuntu

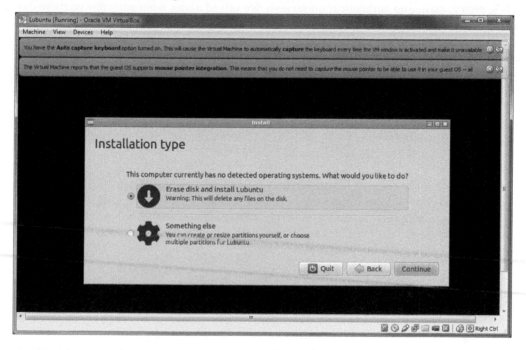

24. Continue with the installation process. When in doubt, choose the default and move to the next step.

25. When the installation is complete, click the Restart Now button.

Now that the installation is complete, play around in your new operating system! Some suggested additional exercises are included in the Chapter 20 performance-based question.

Summary

In this chapter, you learned about different server roles and technologies that work on local networks as well as ones that work on the Internet to make the cloud possible.

First, you learned about specific server roles. Options include web, file, print, DHCP, DNS, proxy, mail, and authentication servers. We talked about what each one of these does as well as where they should be located on the network, either inside the secure network or in the DMZ. In addition to servers, many networks will have Internet appliances dedicated to security, such as IDS, IPS, and UTM devices. Some networks also support legacy or embedded systems. While these systems are old and outdated, they often provide critical functionality on the network.

The next topic was cloud computing. Cloud computing has become one of the hottest topics in IT circles. There are several different types of services that cloud providers sell, such as IaaS, PaaS, and SaaS. There are also different types of clouds, such as public, private, community, and hybrid. Cloud computing is dependent upon virtualization.

Virtualization removes the barrier of there being a one-to-one relationship between computer hardware and an operating system. You learned about what virtualization does and the core piece of software, called the hypervisor. You also learned about requirements for client-side virtualization. The chapter finished with a long exercise on installing a hypervisor and Linux Ubuntu on a Windows computer.

Exam Essentials

Know the various roles that servers can play on a network.   Roles include web, file, print, DHCP, DNS, proxy, mail, and authentication server.

Understand where on the network various servers should be placed.   Every server should be secured behind a firewall, but some servers should be more secure and on an internal network, whereas others can be in the DMZ. The general rule of thumb is if users need to get on the server from the Internet, then it should be in the DMZ.

Understand how DHCP servers work.   DHCP servers assign IP addresses and configuration information to client computers. Clients request the information via broadcast. Each DHCP server has a scope with a configured range of available IP addresses. The server may also provide additional configuration information, such as the address of the default gateway (a router) and a DNS server.

Know what DNS servers do.   DNS servers resolve hostnames to IP addresses. Without them, finding your favorite websites on the Internet would be an incredibly challenging task!

Know the difference between an IDS and an IPS.   An intrusion detection system (IDS) is a passive device that monitors and logs network traffic for suspicious traffic that might indicate an attack is underway. An IPS monitors the network for the same activities, but it can take action to mitigate the attack.

Know the differences between SaaS, IaaS, and PaaS.   All of these are cloud terms. In infrastructure as a service (IaaS), the provider supplies the network infrastructure. In platform as a service (PaaS), software development tools and platforms are also provided. The highest level is software as a service (SaaS), where the provider supplies the infrastructure and applications.

Understand the purpose of virtual machines.   Virtual machines are designed to save providers and users money. They allow for multiple OSs to be installed on one computer.

Know what a hypervisor does.   The hypervisor is the most critical piece of software in virtualization because it allows for multiple guest OSs to be installed on one physical device.

Review Questions

The answers to the chapter review questions can be found in Appendix A.

1. Your company hosts its own web server, and it allows consumers to make purchases via the server. The help line has been getting complaints that users are unable to access the secure portion of the website. You open the site and it seems fine, although the secure portion where transactions are completed is inaccessible. What is the most likely cause?

   A. The firewall is blocking TCP port 80.

   B. The firewall is blocking TCP port 443.

   C. The security module of the web server is malfunctioning.

   D. The web server is down.

2. Your manager wants you to install a networked Internet appliance that that prevents network traffic–based attacks and includes anti-malware and anti-spam software. What should you install?

   A. NIPS

   B. NIDS

   C. UTM

   D. Proxy server

3. You are installing a file server for the accounting department. Where should this file server be located on the network?

   A. Outside of the firewall

   B. In the DMZ

   C. In the secure network

   D. On the router

4. You have been asked to identify the right type of cloud service to help the team of developers to provide programming elements such as runtime environments. Which service do you recommend?

   A. PaaS

   B. IaaS

   C. SaaS

   D. DaaS

5. Which of the following are services that a print server should provide? (Choose two.)

   A. Accepting print jobs from clients

   B. Turning off printers on demand

   C. Providing clients with the appropriate printer driver during installation

   D. Notifying users when the print job is complete

6. You are setting up a cloud contract with a provider. Your team needs the ability to increase capacity without intervention from the provider. What do you request?

    A. Rapid elasticity

    B. On-demand self-service

    C. Resource pooling

    D. Measured service

7. What type of server is responsible for preventing users from accessing websites with objectionable content?

    A. Proxy

    B. Web

    C. DHCP

    D. DNS

8. Your company wants to move to a cloud provider to be able to scale resources quickly, but it is concerned about the security of confidential information. Which of the following types of cloud models might be the most appropriate for your company?

    A. Public

    B. Private

    C. Community

    D. Hybrid

9. What does a DHCP server need to be configured with to operate properly?

    A. DNS server

    B. Scope

    C. Range

    D. DHCP relay agent

10. You have been asked to advise a group of several universities who want to combine research efforts and store data in the cloud. Which type of cloud solution might be best for them?

    A. Public

    B. Private

    C. Community

    D. Hybrid

11. When configuring a DNS server, which of the following must be created by the administrator?

    A. Zone file

    B. Hosts file

    C. Scope file

    D. DNS proxy

12. Your manager wants to use the cloud because everyone seems to be talking about it. What should you include when you are listing the benefits of using the cloud? (Choose all that apply.)

    A. Increased security

    B. Increased scalability

    C. Lower cost

    D. Improved reliability

13. You are configuring two email servers on your company's network. Which network protocol do the servers use to transfer mail to each other?

    A. POP3

    B. IMAP4

    C. SNMP

    D. SMTP

14. You have been asked to configure a client-side virtualization solution with three guest OSs. Each one needs Internet access. How should you configure the solution in the most cost-effective way?

    A. Three physical NICs

    B. One physical NIC, three virtual NICs, and one virtual switch

    C. One physical NIC, one virtual NIC, and three virtual switches

    D. One physical NIC, three virtual NIC, and three virtual switches

15. Which record type on a DNS server represents an IPv6 host?

    A. A

    B. MX

    C. CNAME

    D. AAAA

16. You have been asked to install Linux in a VM on a Windows 8 client. The Windows 8 client needs 4GB RAM and Linux needs 2GB RAM. How much RAM does the system need at a minimum?

    A. 4GB

    B. 6GB

    C. 8GB

    D. Unable to determine from the question

17. A computer using which of the following would be considered a legacy device? (Choose all that apply.)

    A. A 386 processor

    B. The IPX/SPX protocol

    C. An application developed in 1983

    D. Only 1GB RAM

18. You have been asked to set up client-side virtualization on an office computer. The host OS is Windows 7, and there will be three Windows 7 guest OSs. Which of the following is true about the need for antivirus security?

   A. The host OS needs an antivirus program, but virtual machines can't be affected by viruses.

   B. The host OS antivirus software will also protect the guest OSs on the VMs.

   C. Installing antivirus software on the virtual switch will protect all guest OSs.

   D. The host OS and each guest OS need their own antivirus software installed.

19. You have been asked by your manager to brief the group on security appliances. What is the difference between IDS and IPS?

   A. IDS is active, and IPS is passive.

   B. IDS is passive, and IPS is active.

   C. IDS monitors internal network traffic, and IPS monitors traffic coming in from the Internet.

   D. IDS monitors traffic coming in from the Internet, and IPS monitors internal network traffic.

20. You have been asked to set up client-side virtualization on a computer at work. The manager asks for a Type 2 hypervisor. What is the disadvantage of using that type of hypervisor?

   A. The guest OS will compete for resources with the host OS.

   B. The guest OS will be forced to a lower priortity with the CPU than the host OS.

   C. The guest OS will be forced to use less RAM than the host OS.

   D. The virtual guest OS will not be able to get on the physical network.

Performance-Based Question

You will encounter performance-based questions on the A+ exams. The questions on the exam require you to perform a specific task, and you will be graded on whether or not you were able to complete the task. The following requires you to think creatively in order to measure how well you understand this chapter's topics. You may or may not see similar questions on the actual A+ exams. To see how your answer compares to the authors', refer to Appendix B.

Using Lubuntu, perform the following administrative tasks:

1. Create a user account.

2. Manage the hard drives. See how much hard drive space is available. Determine what file system is used.

3. Create files and folders. Copy or move them from one location to another.

4. Create a desktop shortcut.

5. Configure accessibility options for users with special needs.

Chapter

21

Mobile Operating Systems and Connectivity

THE FOLLOWING COMPTIA A+ 220-902 OBJECTIVES ARE COVERED IN THIS CHAPTER:

✓ **2.5 Identify basic features of mobile operating systems.**

- Android vs. iOS vs. Windows
- Open source vs. closed source/vendor specific
- App source (play store, app store, and store)
- Screen orientation (accelerometer/gyroscope)
- Screen calibration
- GPS and geotracking
- WiFi calling
- Launcher/GUI
- Virtual assistant
- SDK/APK
- Emergency notification
- Mobile payment service

✓ **2.6 Install and configure basic mobile device network connectivity and email.**

- Wireless/cellular data network (enable/disable)
  - Hotspot
  - Tethering
  - Airplane mode

- Bluetooth
  - Enable Bluetooth
  - Enable pairing
  - Find device for pairing
  - Enter appropriate pin code
  - Test connectivity
- Corporate and ISP email configuration
  - POP3
  - IMAP
  - Port and SSL settings
  - Exchange, S/MIME
- Integrated commercial provider email configuration
  - Google/Inbox
  - Yahoo
  - Outlook.com
  - iCloud
- PRI updates/PRL updates/Baseband updates
- Radio firmware
- IMEI vs. IMSI
- VPN

✓ **2.7 Summarize methods and data related to mobile device synchronization.**

- Types of data to synchronize
  - Contacts
  - Programs
  - Email
  - Pictures
  - Music
  - Videos
  - Calendar
  - Bookmarks

- Documents
- Location data
- Social media data
- eBooks
- Synchronization methods
  - Synchronize to the Cloud
  - Synchronize to the Desktop
- Mutual authentication for multiple services
- Software requirements to install the application on the PC
- Connection types to enable synchronization

In Chapter 10, "Understanding Mobile Devices," we talked about the trend toward miniaturization in the computer industry. Devices that fit into the palm of your hand today are substantially more powerful than the bulky desktop systems of the 1990s, and those were exponentially more powerful than the room-sized supercomputers of the 1960s.

The movement toward smaller devices also creates new needs, specifically in the area of interaction with the devices—and that relates directly to the operating system. Remember that the OS is the interface between the hardware and the user, meaning that the OS needs to interpret user input and translate that into an action for the underlying hardware. Small mobile devices just don't have room for traditional input hardware, such as keyboards and mice, nor do small devices have the resources themselves to manage the overhead of full-blown workstation operating systems such as Windows 8. Touchscreen input is now standard fare; asking users to lug around a keyboard with their Android phone probably wouldn't go over too well.

Mobile operating systems have been created to match hardware requirements with the desired user experience. While some similar features exist, such as configuring network connectivity, they're handled in different places than on a workstation OS. And because of the size of the devices and different user needs, mobile operating systems have many different features that are not available on their workstation cousins.

This chapter focuses on mobile operating systems and connectivity. Specifically, we will cover mobile OS specifications and features, network connectivity and email, and device synchronization.

Understanding Mobile Operating Systems

We're not going to spend time in this chapter reviewing what an operating system does. Hopefully, that material was burned into your memory bank in the first six chapters of Part II of this book. What we will talk about are the major families of mobile OSs, unique facets of working with them, and specific mobile OS features about which you should be aware.

Comparing Mobile Operating Systems

The two most prolific mobile operating systems in the world by far are Google's Android and Apple's iOS. Both are produced by organizations that approach the market from the viewpoint of being a one-stop shop for almost everything their customers will need for their mobile computing and communications experience. Microsoft knows the size of the mobile market and wants its share too, so it produces Windows Phone. In terms of market share though, Android and iOS are completely dominant.

The two major mobile OS companies go about their quest for market domination in slightly different ways. Although they both provide a site for downloading applications compatible with their respective operating systems, Apple keeps its applications a little closer to the vest and manufactures its own handsets. Google prefers to let the developers dictate what applications are available to consumers and to let a wide variety of handset manufacturers produce the hardware on which its operating system runs. The following sections discuss these particulars as well as the proprietary nature of the operating systems.

Throughout this chapter, unless otherwise stated, it is assumed that no jailbreaking or rooting of your mobile device has been performed. Customizing devices in this way is outside the scope of the A+ exams.

Google Android

Google is the dominant global player in the mobile market with its *Android* OS. If you look at the smartphone market alone, Android has far more users thanks to a bigger presence in Asia than Apple has. Many sources claim that there are more Android installations than all other OSs in the world combined, and in 2014 Google itself claimed to have over one billion active monthly users.

Android started off as its own company and was purchased by Google in 2005. Like Google's Chrome OS, Android is Linux based. It's primarily installed on smartphones, but it is also found on specialized television, automobile, and wristwatch devices. It supports the use of touchscreen technology, much like other mobile devices. Figure 21.1 shows the Android 5.0 welcome screen.

Android was slightly later to the market than iOS, with Android 1.0 launching in 2008. Since its launch, though, it has quickly grown in popularity, and it is the top smartphone platform, thanks in large part to it being available on devices from several manufacturers, such as Samsung, LG, HTC, Sony, and Motorola, along with Google's own hardware. (Apple, much like it does with its OS X platform, restricts iOS to Apple hardware, which limits its potential installed base.) Highlights of Android versions and features are shown in Table 21.1.

FIGURE 21.1 Android 5.0 welcome screen

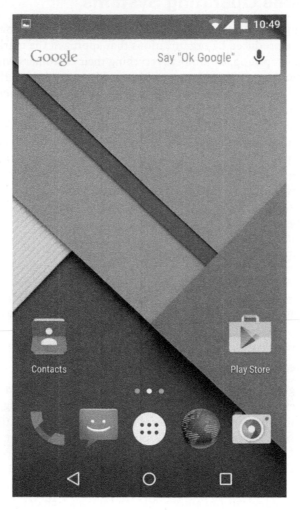

TABLE 21.1 Selected versions of Android OS

Version	Year	Name	Features
1.0	2008	(none)	Web browser, many Google apps, media player, Wi-Fi and Bluetooth support
1.5	2009	Cupcake	Widgets (mini apps that can be embedded in other apps and provide notifications), auto-rotation of screen
2.0	2009	Eclair	Microsoft Exchange email support, camera and keyboard improvements

Version	Year	Name	Features
2.2	2010	Froyo	Wi-Fi hotspot functionality, speed and memory optimizations
2.3	2010–11	Gingerbread	Support for multiple cameras, better power management, voice or video chat using Google Talk
3.0	2011	Honeycomb	First tablet-only version of Android
4.0	2011	Ice Cream Sandwich	Major improvements to "Holo" interface and system functionality
4.1	2012	Jelly Bean	Google Now personal assistant, swipe directly to camera, better clock, Bluetooth improvements
4.4	2013	KitKat	Wireless printing
5.0	2014	Lollipop	64-bit support, refreshed design

Moving forward, Android appears to be positioned to maintain its significant market presence due to the multi-vendor support it receives. The biggest question for Google relates to the future of Chrome OS and Android as separate operating systems. Many experts believe that they compete with each other, whereas Google says that's not the case. Over the next few years, it's possible that we could see a merging of the two into one platform.

Apple iOS

Apple is the second largest player in the mobile OS market with its iOS, running on the iPhone and iPad mobile platforms. Figure 21.2 shows the home screen of iOS 8.

The *iOS* system is built on the same foundation as Apple's desktop OS X, which was built on the Darwin distribution of UNIX. In fact, early marketing literature for the iPhone simply referred to the OS as a version of OS X. Later on it was renamed iPhone OS, but after the introduction of the iPad, it was shortened to iOS. Throughout their history, though, the workstation and mobile versions have been fairly different and not directly compatible with each other. Apps built for one would not work on the other, but Apple is working to change that.

The first generation of iOS was released in 2007, concurrently with the first iPhone. With this launch, Apple thrust itself into a very competitive mobile market, with a product that several pundits considered inferior to the established players. Apple got one thing very right, though, and that was the user experience. The iPhone was the first popular phone to have a touchscreen that you could use with your fingers and not a stylus, and it used pinch-to-zoom and intuitive finger swipes to navigate the screen. It had only a few built-in apps, such as Google Maps and the Safari web browser (and no way to develop new ones), but it played music, videos, and movies, which you could get from the already-established iTunes store.

FIGURE 21.2   iOS 8 home screen

Apple released newer versions with better features, often synchronized with the release of new hardware. One of the features it launched within a year of the first iOS release was the App Store, which featured thousands of useful third-party applications. While an app store seems like a given today, at the time it was revolutionary for the mobile market. Table 21.2 highlights some of the major enhancements.

TABLE 21.2   iOS versions and features

Version	Year	Features
1.0	2007	First finger-based touchscreen, iTunes connectivity, Safari web browser, onscreen virtual keyboard
2.0	2008	App Store for third-party apps, full email support for Microsoft Exchange
3.0	2009	Voice control; the ability to cut, copy, and paste; Spotlight search; landscape keyboard
3.2	2010	Support for iPad, including iPad resolutions and Bluetooth keyboards
4.0	2010	Multitasking, FaceTime video chat, ability to create folders on home screen for apps
5.0	2011	Siri, iCloud, iMessage
6.0	2012	Siri enhancements, Passbook, Facebook integration
7.0	2013	New visual interface, Control Center, iTunes Radio, biometric thumbprint scanner
8.0	2014	Widgets (so third-party apps can update you in the Notification Center); several app upgrades; family sharing of photos, calendars, and purchases

With the release of OS X Yosemite, Apple is trying to make the experience between workstation and mobile devices more seamless. Expect more of those types of efforts as Apple moves forward with new versions of iOS as well.

 Real World Scenario

Who's Really #1?

There's a lot of debate on the Internet and in the media about who is really the top player in the mobile space. Is it Android or iOS? Mark Twain is often quoted as saying, "There are three types of lies. Lies, damned lies, and statistics." In this case, the statistics can tell different stories, depending on how you slice them.

If you look at tablets, then iOS has the edge. If you limit the discussion to phones, then the market leader is clearly Android. In the United States, it's relatively close, but globally,

continues

continued

Android-based phones make up between 70 and 80 percent of shipments, depending on your data source.

Both platforms boast over one million apps in their respective application stores (App Store or Google Play). Internet usage (the number of searches, via NetMarketShare) favors iOS, as does business usage. Mobile usage alone (according to StatCounter) clearly favors Android. So it depends on whom you ask and how you ask the question. Regardless, both platforms are very successful, and they likely will be for the next several years.

Windows Phone

While Microsoft is the dominant player in the workstation PC market, it has a very small presence in the mobile world. The *Windows Phone* OS is manufactured by Microsoft, and it looks a lot like Windows 8 visually, using the same NT kernel and Metro start screen, as shown in Figure 21.3.

FIGURE 21.3 Windows Phone 8.1 start screen

Windows Phone start screen screenshot used with permission from Microsoft.

Microsoft started in the mobile space with Pocket PC back in 2000, mostly targeting corporate users and their mobile devices. In 2003, it changed the name to Windows Mobile, still targeting the same users. The software line was changed to Windows Phone in 2010, with a greater emphasis on phones and home users. Table 21.3 gives you a quick tour of Windows Phone versions.

TABLE 21.3 Windows Phone versions and features

Version	Year	Features
Windows Phone 7	2010	Based on Windows CE.
Windows Phone 8	2012	Uses Windows NT kernel; apps can theoretically work on both platforms seamlessly.
Windows Phone 8.1	2014	Interface upgrades, Cortana voice assistant, dropped requirements for physical Start and Search buttons on the device.

Windows 10 will provide additional support for mobile devices and further link Microsoft's workstation and mobile platforms together.

The biggest problem for Microsoft right now in the mobile space is its small market share. It maintains only about a 2 or 3 percent market share. Microsoft is aggressively pursuing licensing options to help drive its share upward, but it has a long way to go in a very entrenched market.

Source Code Classification

Source code is the programming code used in the creation of software. In the early days of personal computing, software was either free or for sale. Nothing has changed, except for the terms that we use to describe these two categories. Now software is either proprietary or *open source*. Proprietary software—also known as *closed-source* and *vendor-specific* software—is licensed to others for use but is kept within the control of the original publisher. Open-source software, on the other hand, is licensed to the developer community to be further developed, shared, and sometimes marketed, depending on the language of the licensing agreement. In any event, no money changes hands during the procurement of open-source software.

Google offers the Android operating system to the mobile community under an open-source license. Apple and Microsoft keep their mobile OSs closed source, and they manage all of the development and marketing of their operating systems.

Source of Applications

Apple, Google, and Microsoft maintain online sources for downloading applications written for their respective operating systems. Links can be supplied on the web pages of application publishers and marketers to forward customers to the locations where they can download their applications. More commonly, customers use an application on the mobile device—or on the computer used to synchronize software with the mobile device—to search for and download the application in which they are interested. Some apps are free, while others require payment to download, and still others are free to download and use or play but then charge you for additional in-app features.

Downloading Apps for iOS

Apple's *App Store* opened for business in 2008 just ahead of the introduction of the iPhone 3G, which was natively capable of accessing the App Store. The App Store was designed to market and serve applications created with the iOS and Mac software development kits (SDKs). The term *app* was coined long ago as shorthand for *application*, but in the period during the naming of Apple's store, the term saw a resurgence, and it is now mostly associated with mobile applications.

Apple requires annual fees from developers while Android requires only a one-time fee. Each app must be submitted to Apple for approval before being added by Apple to the App Store, which is the only way that they can be made available for installation. Note that any iPhone app can be run on Apple's line of iPads, but if an iPad-optimized app is available, iPad users should opt for these instead. If a user has an iPhone/iPod Touch and an iPad on the same Apple account, both classes of devices can install the same app after paying only once. The price, by the way, is the same for either platform.

A few months after the Apple App Store opened in 2008, Google's *Android Market* was launched and made available to users. In 2012, the Market and the Google Music service were combined to form *Google Play*, which took the place of both component services. Google does not guard apps for Android as closely as Apple guards its apps. In fact, you can use third-party utilities to find and download Android apps. You can also download them directly from the developer's website or use the Android SDK to create your own and install them yourself. Google does not approve apps before installation. Enterprises benefit from the resulting quick turnaround from in-house development to deployment for their proprietary apps. The downside is that without a central oversight team, not all apps are guaranteed to work properly. Google figures that the user community will weed out the bad apps through negative reviews.

NOTE   If you so desire, you can create iOS apps using the iOS SDK available at www.apple.com. Apps developed for iOS will have an .ipa (iOS App Store Package) filename extension. Apps developed with the Android SDK will have an .apk (application package file) extension.

Exercise 21.1 details the steps required to search for and download an app from the Apple App Store. This particular procedure downloads the Instagram app. If you already have this app, you can substitute any search criteria you like and adjust the remaining steps accordingly. The iPhone examples and exercises in this chapter reference procedures required for an iPhone 6 with iOS version 8.2.

EXERCISE 21.1

Downloading an App from the App Store

1. Find the App Store icon on the home screen, as shown in Figure 21.4.

FIGURE 21.4   App Store icon

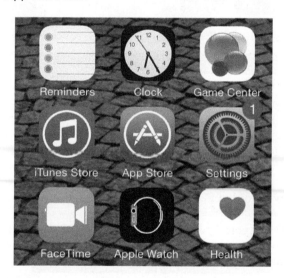

2. Tap the icon to open the app to the last page you visited.

3. Tap the magnifying glass search icon at the bottom, as shown in Figure 21.5.

FIGURE 21.5   Search icon

4. Type **instagram** in the search field, and tap the Search button on the keyboard.

5. Select the app from the list of search results. (In the case of Instagram, it will be the top one, as shown in Figure 21.6.

continues

FIGURE 21.6 Search results showing Instagram app

6. Tap the Get button to change it to an Install button.

7. Tap the Install App button in order to be asked for your Apple ID password.

8. Enter your password and tap OK. The app will install. After the installation, you can tap the Open button (where the Get and Install buttons were previously) or close the App Store and go back to the home screen.

9. Find the app's icon, and tap to open it.

10. To uninstall an app, tap and hold the icon until it starts shaking and has an *x* in the upper-left corner. Tap the icon again, and it will uninstall.

If your apps are ever updated in the App Store, the App Store icon will develop a little red badge (called a badge notification) in the upper-right corner with the number of apps that have updates ready for you to download, as shown in Figure 21.7.

FIGURE 21.7 Sixteen updates available

 You can turn badge notifications off by going into Settings ➢ Notifications ➢ App Store and turning off Allow Notifications or turning off Badge App Icon. Both options are shown (albeit enabled) in Figure 21.8.

FIGURE 21.8 App Store notifications

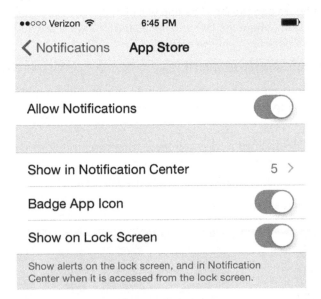

Downloading Apps for Android

Android apps are obtained from the Google Play Store. Exercise 21.2 walks you through the steps required to search for and download an Android app. The Android examples and exercises in this chapter mostly reference procedures used in Android 5.0.

EXERCISE 21.2

Downloading an App from the Google Play Store

1. Find the Play Store icon on the home screen or in Apps list. It will look like a shopping bag with a Play arrow on it, like the one shown in Figure 21.9.

FIGURE 21.9 Play Store icon

2. Tap the icon to open the Play Store. You may be asked to log in with your Gmail account. The Play Store is shown in Figure 21.10.

FIGURE 21.10   Google Play Store home page

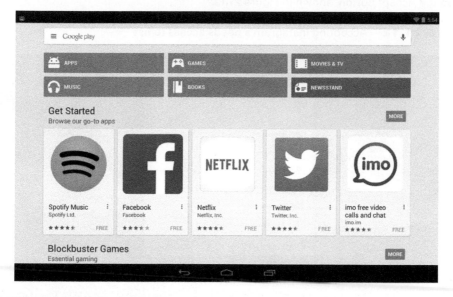

3. Tap the Apps button near the top.

4. Tap the magnifying glass in the upper-right corner to start a search.

5. Type in **instagram**, and a list with matching apps will auto-populate on the screen.

6. Tap the line with the Instagram icon on it, shown at the top of the list in Figure 21.11.

FIGURE 21.11   Searching for Instagram

continues

7. Tap the Install button.

8. Tap the Accept button, shown in Figure 21.12.

FIGURE 21.12 Accepting Instagram's needs access to list

9. Tap the Home button to leave Google Play. It's the center of the three buttons at the bottom. The other buttons are Back and Recents.

10. The app icon will appear on your home screen, as shown in Figure 21.13.

FIGURE 21.13 Instagram on the home screen

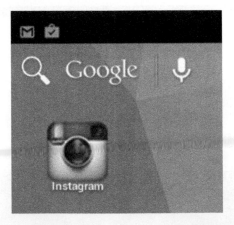

11. The app will also appear in the Uncategorized section of your apps (shown in Figure 21.14) when you tap the Apps button.

FIGURE 21.14 Uncategorized apps

Note that removing the icon from your home screen will not uninstall the app, but removing it from the Apps page will. To remove the app from either location, tap and hold the icon down. A menu option will appear above that says Remove or Uninstall.

Downloading Apps for Windows Phone

Windows Phone apps can be downloaded from the Windows Store. The icon for the store is shown in Figure 21.15.

FIGURE 21.15 Windows Store icon

Once in the store, you will see categories of apps as well as a search feature. An example is shown in Figure 21.16. You can also find the store at www.windowsphone.com/en-us/store.

FIGURE 21.16   Windows Store

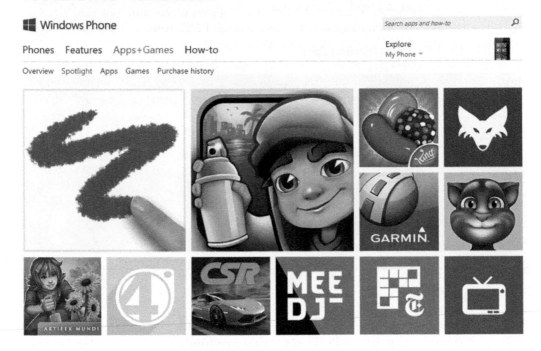

Understanding Sensors and Calibration

When most users first experience a mobile device, there is a lot of uncertainty on how to use them properly. There is no keyboard and no mouse. How can one possibly interact with this thing? If you have an iPhone, there's only one button on the front (called the Home button). Android devices have three or four buttons. New users have to get used to the functionality of a touchscreen in a hurry.

Mobile devices are built around a concept called *gesture-based interaction*, whereby users use their fingers and various movements to interact with their touchscreen. The good news is that the device doesn't require complicated interpretive dance patterns to work, although it has sensors built in that could detect your dance movements if you wanted it to. The device has several sensor components built in, and the operating system is built to take advantage of these sensors. We'll talk about the sensors more in a minute. The three gestures that most mobile OSs understand are tap, swipe, and pinch, and the sensors are part of a closely related concept called *kinetics*.

Tap   A tap of the finger is all that it takes to get a lot done on a mobile device. It's a bit like clicking on a Mac or double-clicking on a PC. Tapping an app's icon will open that app. In this manner, the user's finger acts a lot like the mouse pointer does on a PC.

Swipe   To swipe, the user presses their finger to the screen and then brushes it in a direction. It's almost like the gesture of turning a page in a book. Users will use this to move pages or scroll up or down. Swiping the finger up will scroll the page down, for example.

Pinch   By placing two fingers apart and then pinching them together (while touching the screen, of course), users can zoom out. Placing two fingers together and then slowly spreading them apart will zoom in. (It's kind of a reverse pinch.) This feature doesn't work in all apps, but it is particularly helpful when looking at maps.

Kinetics   Kinetics refers to the sense of motion. Mobile devices have an amazing array of kinetic sensors built in. For example, the iPhone 6 has a gyroscope, accelerometer, linear acceleration sensor, magnetometer, altitude sensor, and gravity sensor. These sensors let your device act like a GPS and compass, and they also detect movements such as tilting or shaking the device that many apps take advantage of. Most Android-based devices will have a similarly impressive list of sensors.

Now let's take a look at the specific features that the kinetic sensors enable. We will also discuss the concept of calibration, which is important for devices on which the screen is also the input device.

Screen Orientation

Most mobile devices can automatically detect their position and use the detected information to reorient the screen to match the orientation of the device. Most devices, especially handsets, are built to be used most often in an orientation that corresponds to the display of screen images in portrait mode (higher than wide). For screens of information that are displayed best in portrait mode, no change in orientation is required. Some devices, such as Apple's iPad, can even display images in portrait mode when the device is held upside down. This aids in collaboration with someone positioned across from you, which is more common with tablets than with handsets. For images that display best in landscape mode, merely turning most devices sideways reorients the screen image in landscape mode.

The method of detecting device orientation varies somewhat, but the following two popular methods exist and are presented here with their characteristic detection capabilities:

- Accelerometer: forward/backward, left/right, up/down
- Gyroscope: roll, pitch, yaw

Use of multiple or all methods by the same device increases the accuracy of orientation and positioning. The simple combination of an accelerometer and gyroscope, for example, makes for optimal orientation detection. The following sections detail the strengths previously listed beside the two methods.

Accelerometer

An *accelerometer* measures the acceleration—change in velocity, which is a function of speed and direction—of an object. This is one of the first kinetic sensors included in smartphones. For example, the original iPhone used only an accelerometer, and it was the only sensor used until the iPhone 4 added a gyroscope in 2011, which is discussed next.

Picture a smartphone lying flat on a desk. If you push the device in any of the four square directions—up, down, left, right—or diagonally without also rotating the phone on any of its various axes, the accelerometer will detect the precise movement. If you lift the phone up and then place it back down on the desk, the accelerometer can track this motion as well. These three axes (x, y, and z) of movement make up the totality of an accelerometer's capabilities.

Gyroscope

The accelerometer cannot detect if you lift any edge of the mobile device or give it a good spin as it lies flat on the desk. For these motions, a gyroscope is required. A *gyroscope* is a sensor that detects rotation around any of three axes, known as roll, pitch, and yaw.

For example, pick up the smartphone from the desk and hold it in your hand. Now, without changing the position of the absolute center of the phone, lift the left side upward, as if to flip the phone over toward the right, until the phone is face down and right side up in your hand. Then, flip it back in the reverse direction until it is face up again. A gyroscope would detect both of these motions as *roll*.

From the starting position, a gyroscope would sense a change in *pitch* if you lifted the top or bottom edge of the phone and flipped it toward the opposite end until the phone is once again face down, except that it is now also upside-down, in your hand.

If you place the phone back on the desk and give it a clockwise or counterclockwise spin, the gyroscope would detect such a rotation as *yaw*. These three new axes of movement complement those detected by the accelerometer, producing a high level of accuracy when detecting the device's orientation.

Positioning and Geolocation

Screen orientation is only part of the story. *Geolocation*, the relative and absolute positioning of your device from the viewpoint of the planet and space, is an important capability that allows effective navigation and access to personalized services and security features. Two technologies are used by most modern smartphones to accomplish positioning and geolocation:

- *Magnetometer:* compass heading
- *Global positioning system:* absolute position on the earth

Magnetometer

To detect the position of a device relative to a landmark on the planet, we use a compass. A *magnetometer* allows a device to sense magnetic fields, such as the one our planet exhibits at the magnetic north pole. Using a magnetometer, iPhones and Android devices allow for apps that act as compasses, giving you instantaneous access to the direction in which the top of your phone is pointing with respect to magnetic north. Orient the back (or the front, if you're lying down looking up) of your device as flat to the ground as possible to get the most accurate reading.

Global Positioning System

To detect the absolute position of a device with respect to the manmade latitude and longitude markings on the surface of the earth, triangulation is required. Using three satellites at a fixed distance above the earth's surface, devices with global positioning system (*GPS*) capability can determine their own absolute position. Add a magnetometer or use the change in GPS information over time and the compass heading of the device can also be determined. The magnetometer can detect the compass heading at all times when sources of magnetic interference are not present, and the GPS sensor can detect the heading in magnetic noise but only while in motion.

Many smartphones and other cellular-equipped devices use assisted GPS, which means they use information from the cellular network to help with geolocation. Assisted GPS is helpful when the satellite signals are being interfered with or partially blocked. When satellites are completely unavailable, cellular or Wi-Fi alone can be used to give slightly less accurate positioning. All Apple iOS products over all versions have supported geolocation over Wi-Fi. The Android operating system supports these forms of geolocation as well.

The Russian form of GPS, known as the Global Navigation Satellite System (GLONASS), was also first supported by the Apple iPhone 4S. Sony Ericsson was one of the first providers to bring GLONASS support to Android phones and tablets. Theoretically, GLONASS and GPS can be used in tandem to provide better positioning. In practice, however, access to three satellites in each system simultaneously is an issue. The upside is that satellite-based global positioning will be available in more parts of the world with newer devices.

Geotracking and Geotagging

Geolocation information collected by your mobile device can be used in various ways, some welcome and some less so. For example, you might perceive as a blessing being able to locate your child using real-time geolocation information from a phone that they are carrying. However, you might consider it a curse when someone else can locate your child in the same way.

In mid-2010, Apple added a controversial feature to iOS, starting with version 4, that collects your position and stores it locally on the phone in a file that is never harvested but reports it twice a day back to Apple. This *geotracking* feature has understandably come under scrutiny by privacy advocates.

You must jailbreak your iOS device—or in other words, gain full root access to its UNIX file system—to be able to find the file that holds the geolocation information, which can be used by forensic investigators and privacy invaders alike. Utilities exist, however, that can use the file to overlay the raw data on a world map, showing a visual record of the device's positioning over time, even months earlier.

Since the inception of its geotracking, Apple has progressively dialed down the amount of data that is collected by the iOS. Apple has also stopped allowing this information to be backed up and has begun encrypting the related file, as of iOS version 5, making casual access to the file and its contents impossible.

Geotagging uses similar information to add location information to various forms of media, such as photographs taken with the device and messages sent with the device. Many mobile devices also send geotagging information to social networking sites by default when updates are posted. Although often welcomed as a convenience by users with a pronounced Internet presence that would invariably identify their location anyway, geotagging is generally quite easy to disable on any given device for those who would rather not have their location automatically identified. Many parents, for example, would not want their children's current location advertised to the Internet.

Screen Calibration

Any device that, for input, relies on the user pressing against and flexing the outermost layer of material covering the screen occasionally requires the recalibration of the user's interface with the device's touch sensors. If the user places their finger squarely in the middle of an icon from the perspective of their visible interface but selects a different icon from the perspective of the sensors, the touch interface might require calibration. The need for recalibration varies between the two primary technologies used, resistive and capacitive. The following sections elaborate on this fact.

Resistive Touchscreens

The need for recalibration is expected in devices that use a resistive technology to detect touch. This is because they have an almost unperceivably flexible outer surface that eventually wears and changes over time due to repeated flexion. As a result, pressing the location where the image displays from the perspective of the user eventually generates an incorrect resistance based on the original calibration of the screen. Recalibration of resistive displays entails displaying an image with known touch points and asking the user to touch them all in succession. In this manner, the resistance across the entire screen is adjusted to compensate for the physical change in the outer surface.

Such devices are built using two layers of sturdy panels separated by an air pocket. One panel is flexible, usually made of plastic, and the other panel is often rigid, usually made of glass. Both panels are coated with indium tin oxide (ITO), which is conductive. When the user presses against the flexible outer surface, the two layers of ITO make contact and change the resistance detected by electrode strips along the edges of the panels. The computer is able to take the resistance reading from the electrodes and calculate two-dimensional coordinates.

Either a firm, often pointed, stylus or your fingernail is highly effective on resistive touchscreens. The optimal effect is achieved by applying pinpoint pressure to the outer surface without causing damage to the surface. Of course, damage is being caused, but on a minor level. Nevertheless, the cumulative damage caused by the required pressure is what leads to the need for calibration and eventual replacement of the screen or device.

Capacitive Touchscreens

With capacitive touchscreens, the same two layers of ITO as used with resistive screens are placed between two pieces of glass, resulting in a very smooth, silky surface to the touch. The same electrode placement is also used. The difference is in which electrical property the electrodes are monitoring. A uniform capacitive field can be projected through the top layer of glass. The faint electromagnetic charge of a human fingertip can change the capacitance to a measurable level at the point of contact. The device can calculate the two-dimensional coordinates of the point touched in the same manner that they are calculated from the changes in resistance for the resistive display.

The padded tip of the finger is the preferred method of touch for such displays. A stylus that emulates the fingertip and its electromagnetic charge can be used in place of the fingertip. Because of the physics involved, with capacitive interfaces, such as that used by all of Apple's mobile devices and many non-Apple devices, dry environments and other conditions favorable to the buildup of excess static electricity can lead to the touch sensors responding before the user's finger touches the surface. This phenomenon can be confused with poor calibration.

> Capacitive touchscreens need to detect an electromagnetic charge to function properly, and the human finger provides that. If you have ever tried to use a mobile phone with a capacitive touchscreen with a glove on (in winter, for instance), you will notice that it doesn't work.

However, because capacitive touchscreens do not wear as quickly as do resistive screens, due to the fact that the user does not apply pressure to complete a circuit, capacitive screens tend not to require recalibration. In fact, if you feel that you need to recalibrate an Apple display, there are more serious issues afoot. If neither restarting the device or performing a reset by holding the sleep and home buttons simultaneously solves the problem, it is likely that a certified Apple repair is in order because it is more probable that you have a hardware issue than a calibration issue.

Regardless of whether you have a resistive or capacitive display, or both, some devices give you the option to improve the ability of the computer to recognize how you personally actuate the sensors. Exercise 21.3 walks you through the procedure of recalibrating (actually retraining) the onscreen touch keyboard of the HTC EVO 4G running the Android operating system. Other Android devices may vary in their ability to be recalibrated or in the method of doing so.

EXERCISE 21.3

Recalibrating an Onscreen Android Keyboard

1. Tap the Menu button on the frame of the phone (not a soft button in this Android version).

2. Tap the Settings button in the menu, as shown in Figure 21.17.

FIGURE 21.17 Settings menu

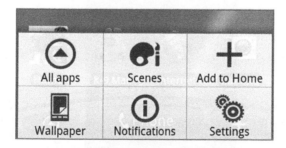

3. Scroll down to and tap the Language & Keyboard selection in the menu.

4. Tap the Touch Input selection in the menu.

5. Tap the Text Input selection in the menu.

continues

EXERCISE 21.3 *(continued)*

6.   Tap the Calibration Tool selection near the bottom of the menu, as shown in Figure 21.18.

FIGURE 21.18   Opening the Calibration tool

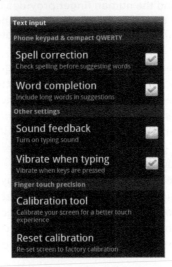

7.   Type the phrase shown as naturally as you can without thinking too much about the typing itself until you see the *Calibration is complete* message, as shown in Figure 21.19. Although typing with both thumbs is often the most effective method on such keyboards, just make sure that you are typing naturally.

FIGURE 21.19   Calibration complete

8.   Tap the Home button to leave the calibration tool.

Combination Touchscreens

Early resistive touchscreens were obvious to the touch. They had a matte finish that you could feel by running your fingertip across it. This finish made them more durable and allowed the use of a pointed stylus without the likelihood of the stylus sliding across the screen's surface, which would have resulted in less accuracy.

Many manufacturers migrated to a smoother surface and a stylus with a softer tip. With such a surface, some manufacturers created touchscreens that were both resistive *and* capacitive. If you used the stylus or your fingernail to press down on the screen, the resistive nature reacted. If you instead glided your fingertip or special capacitive stylus across the surface, the capacitive features of the display took over. Because the outer panel on the screen is flexible, frequent use of pressure to actuate the sensors would result in the need to recalibrate the screen.

Using Additional Mobile Operating System Features

The nature of mobile devices has clearly inspired the design of solutions for users on the move. As such, mobile operating systems have a number of features that are not standard on workstation OSs. The following sections cover some of the most important ones with which you should be familiar.

Launcher/GUI

Of course, mobile devices have a graphical user interface (GUI), as are common on PC OSs. The GUI on a mobile device is more limited in space though, so it contains a smaller number of items by default. On the home screen of the GUI, users will typically find a signal strength indicator for cellular and/or Wi-Fi signal strength, a battery level meter, a clock, and maybe a few more icons, such as the alarm clock or Bluetooth symbol. Otherwise, the home screen is devoted to icons, which the user can tap to open applications. The area of the screen with icons is known as the *launcher*. Its name makes sense because it's the area of the device from which applications are launched. Earlier in the chapter in Figure 21.1 and Figure 21.2, you could see the default launch screen for the Android and iPhone OSs.

The launcher sets the look and feel of the OS, because it's the screen that users are almost always looking at. As you might expect from the general approaches as to how Google and Apple run their businesses, they take very different stances on what users can or should do with their launchers.

Google wants users to be able to customize their experience, and because of this they allow users to change the look and feel of the launcher. Customized launchers are sometimes referred to as *home screen replacements*. To change your home screen, you simply download the launcher and install it just as you would any other Android app. There are over one hundred available; some of them are free and others are paid apps. Figure 21.20 shows four screen shots from Themer, which is a popular design launcher. A design launcher lets you pick from various themes that have been created by Android users. Other popular design launchers include Nova, Apex, Go Launcher EX, Dodol, and Buzz Launcher.

FIGURE 21.20   Four screen shots from Themer

A second classification of launchers is that of smart launchers, which will adapt and try to put the most relevant information in front of you. For example, it might give you the weather report or your daily schedule when you wake up in the morning. Popular smart launchers include Smart Launcher 3, EverythingMe, and Yahoo Aviate.

Apple, on the other hand, wants users to see the iOS look and feel, and it has historically made customizing the launcher incredibly difficult, other than letting the user choose backgrounds and wallpapers, create folders, and move some icons around. As of the middle of 2015 though, it looks like Apple has started softening its stance on launchers. An app called *Launcher*, which had initially been kicked out of the App Store, was allowed back in. Essentially, Launcher is just a widget that that lets you create shortcuts to apps that you commonly use (or contacts that you frequently call or text) and include them with the Notification Center. Since the approval of Launcher, other launchers have quickly sprung up in the App Store as well.

Virtual Assistant

Twenty years ago, the idea of asking your phone a question and having it answer you was the realm of science fiction. (Your friends might have asked, "Wait, do you mean asking a question of someone else on the other end of the phone?") Since the launch of Siri in 2011 and Google Now in 2012, that type of service is commonplace.

Siri and Google Now are examples of a *virtual assistant*, also called a *personal assistant*. You ask a question, and the phone uses its search feature to find an answer. It doesn't always give you the answer you want or even relevant information, but it will give you an answer. Microsoft introduced its own virtual assistant, Cortana, with Windows Phone 8.1. Windows 10 also has Cortana support.

Siri was first bundled with iOS 5 on the iPhone 4S in 2011. In iOS 8, Siri is enabled in Settings ➢ General ➢ Siri as shown in Figure 21.21. To start Siri, hold down the Home button for a few seconds until the phone beeps twice and Siri appears. To ask subsequent questions, just tap the microphone icon at the bottom of the screen, as shown in Figure 21.22. You can also configure Siri always to be in listening mode when plugged into a power source, so all you have to do is say, "Hey Siri," whenever you want to activate the service.

FIGURE 21.21 Siri settings

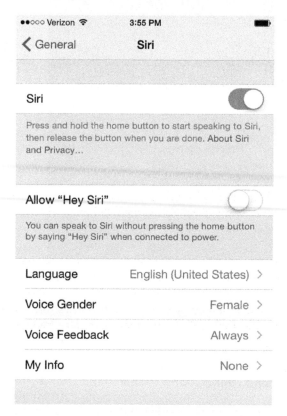

There are multiple virtual assistants available for Android; the default one is called Google Now, and you activate it by pressing the microphone button in the search bar and saying, "Ok Google," followed by your question. For Google Now to work, you must have Google app version 3.5 or newer with Android 4.4 or newer and Voice & Audio Activity turned on. Exercise 21.4 walks you through activating Google Now.

FIGURE 21.22 Use the microphone at the bottom to ask Siri a question.

Activating and Using Google Now

1. Make sure that you have the latest version of Google downloaded. If not, download and install it from the Play Store.

2. Enable Google Now by opening the Google app.

3. Enable voice detection by touching the menu icon in the upper-left corner and then choosing Settings ➢ Voice➢ "Ok Google" Detection.

4. Check the box next to From Google App.

5. To ask a voice question of Google Now, tap the microphone icon, shown in Figure 21.23. (If you tap the Google search, you have three options. One, type in a text question. Two, say "Ok Google." Three, tap the microphone icon.)

FIGURE 21.23   Google search and Google Now microphone

6.   Ask your question!

Much as with Siri, you can also enable Google Now to always listen (on most devices) by checking either the From Any Screen box or the Always On box within the Google Now settings. If Google Now isn't your favorite, you can choose other apps such as Dragon Mobile Assistant or Indigo Virtual Assistant.

Emergency Notification

Your mobile OS can provide alerts in the event of emergency situations. This is called *emergency notification*. By default, iOS has two types of notifications it can provide: AMBER alerts and Emergency alerts. An AMBER alert is issued when a child goes missing, and Emergency alerts warn of potential problems in a statement issued by a government agency. Alerts are regional, so, for example, if a child goes missing on the other side of the country, you should not receive an AMBER alert in that case. These alerts can be turned on or off in Settings ➤ Notifications under Government Alerts, as shown in Figure 21.24

FIGURE 21.24   Government alerts

Installed apps can provide emergency notifications as well. For example, you can download weather apps that provide a warning if there is a specific type of weather condition in your area, such as a severe storm or a flood. Those are also configured in Settings ➤ Notifications, but under the settings for that specific app.

In Android, notifications are managed in the Settings app under Wireless & Networks (tap More) ➤ Cell Broadcasts. Figure 21.25 shows an example of the configuration screen. Uncheck the boxes for the services that you no longer want.

FIGURE 21.25 Android emergency notification settings

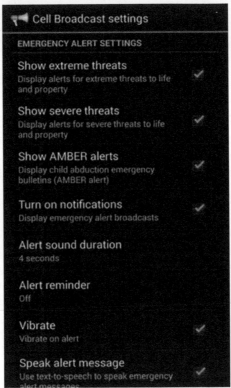

Wi-Fi Calling

Most mobile devices allow you to set up a calling plan with a wireless communications service provider to make voice calls. Sometimes, however, you will find yourself in a location with poor coverage and a weak signal, such as in rural areas or inside steel-and-concrete city buildings. The situation can be bad enough that calls are randomly dropped or you're unable to complete any calls at all.

This frustrating experience can be avoided if you're in an area where you have a Wi-Fi connection and your carrier supports *Wi-Fi calling*. The idea is similar to Voice over IP (VoIP) but it's wireless. When it's functioning properly, users won't even notice that the call has been switched from the cell network to the Wi-Fi network because such transitions should be seamless. Depending on your carrier and device, you may also be able to configure it to use Wi-Fi calling by default when you're connected to a Wi-Fi network.

As of the time of writing, only Sprint and T-Mobile support Wi-Fi calling in the United States, and neither company charges extra for it. Verizon and AT&T plan on adding Wi-Fi calling support in 2015. Not all devices are supported; check with your mobile provider to see which devices are able to use this service.

Apple iPhone 5c and newer support Wi-Fi calling, but it is turned off by default. To enable Wi-Fi calling, go to Settings ➢ Phone and turn it on. You will know that Wi-Fi calling is available if you see *Wi-Fi* after the carrier's name in the status bar.

Mobile Payment Service

As financial transactions are becoming more digitized, fewer people are carrying paper checks or even paper money. Debit and credit cards are accepted nearly everywhere, and merchants and card providers have made great efforts to make their use easier. For example, in some places you can just tap your card to a reader as opposed to having to swipe it (really, how lazy are we becoming?), and of course you can enter a PIN instead of needing to sign. If you can just tap a card and pay, why not allow people to pay with their mobile phones as well? Now you don't have to even carry a plastic card with you—just your phone.

The technology used to support financial transactions using a mobile device is called *mobile payment service*. Unlike many technologies that get a foothold in developed first-world countries, mobile payment services have gained the biggest traction in developing markets, where banks are scarce and their infrastructure is somewhat unreliable. Mobile phones are ubiquitous even in developing countries, so it's natural that they would be used to drive commerce there as well.

There are a few different ways that mobile payment services are implemented:

Text messages for services/products   With this method, the user sends an SMS or MMS text message to the merchant, often including a short code. The merchant receives the message, and a charge is applied to the user's phone bill or other online wallet.

You may have seen commercials asking to text a code to a certain number, such as "Text Yes or No to 12345 on your phone." Many times, those are free, other than possible text charges from the carrier, but those types of messages can be used for mobile transactions as well.

Direct mobile billing   When shopping online, the consumer may choose to have their mobile account charged directly. This must be enabled through the mobile provider before using it. In many cases, the user will also be required to supply a PIN and/or a password. The advantage of this method is that the user does not need to have or use a credit card, bank, or other online payment service (such as PayPal); the charge is directly applied to their phone bill.

Mobile web payments   As opposed to direct mobile billing, users of this method need to download an app that processes payments for them. In addition, it typically requires the user to process the payment through a bank, credit card, or online payment service. A PIN or a password is generally required.

Online wallets through companies such as PayPal, Amazon Payments, and Google Wallet are examples of apps that allow users to make mobile web payments.

Near field communication   Using near field communication (NFC), a user will simply move their device within range (about 4" or 10cm) of the merchant's receiver, and the payment will be processed. In most cases, a PIN is required. This method is of course used when the customer and merchant are in the same physical location. Charges are usually linked to a bank account, credit card, or online payment service.

Apple got into the NFC payment arena in 2014 with the launch of Apple Pay, which can be used from iPhones, iPads, and the Apple Watch. Users with iPhones with Touch ID simply need to get the phone within range of the receiving device and have their finger or thumb on the Touch ID button. The user will know that the payment has been processed when the phone vibrates and beeps once.

In 2015, Google introduced Android Pay, which is an update to the older Google Wallet app. The interesting history here is that Google Wallet pioneered the use of NFC for payments, but payment providers had not yet settled on standards. Google had the right idea but it was too early to market. Now it seems as though that Visa, MasterCard, and the big banks of the world are ready to embrace NFC, so now users have Apple Pay and Android Pay.

Mobile payments are popular today, and they will only increase in popularity in the coming years, much like e-commerce has exploded as an entity unto itself.

Network Connectivity and Email

Mobile devices like the iPhone and Android phones basically exist for their ability to connect to a network. No one is using their small mobile devices to crunch spreadsheets, write detailed presentations, or perform other tasks that are better suited for larger PCs and Macs. On the other hand, mobile devices are great for surfing the Internet, texting friends, taking pictures and sending them to friends, and listening to music. Each of these tasks requires a network connection, either wired or wireless, at some point.

Of course, mobile devices are well known for their cellular connectivity, including the ability to access data services over the cellular network. Many subscribers pay a premium for data access, and going over your limit on a data plan can be a very expensive mistake. To ease the expense involved in data-network access, nearly all manufacturers provide alternate access methods in their devices. For example, the service provider levies no additional expense for Wi-Fi or Bluetooth data access.

There are other cellular options on mobile devices with which you may be less familiar, though, such as hotspots and tethering and updating the firmware. In the following sections, we'll dive into those topics in some detail.

Connecting to a Wi-Fi network gives the mobile device access to resources on the network, such as printers, with the added bonuses of Internet access (assuming the wireless network has it), free texting, and perhaps Wi-Fi phone calls. Not only will this likely give the mobile user faster speeds than cellular, it also has the benefit of not counting against the data plan.

Bluetooth access to other devices is designed mainly for short-range communications, such as between the mobile device and a nearby computer with which it can exchange or synchronize data. Other applications of Bluetooth generally do not involve the exchange of data but rather the use of a nearby resource, such as a stereo system for the playback of the mobile device's audio media or a headset to make hands-free phone calls.

As you can see, there is a distinct advantage to being able to connect your mobile device to a noncellular network. Mobile devices will use Wi-Fi when connected instead of cellular for data operations. Android devices will ask you during an important update if you would like to use Wi-Fi only or if cellular is okay to use. Figure 21.26, for example, shows the Google Play Store Settings screen on an Android device that clearly offers the option to prohibit updates over anything other than Wi-Fi.

FIGURE 21.26   Google Play Store Settings screen

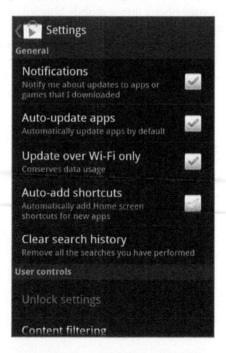

The following sections detail concepts relating to cellular networking and attaching to noncellular networks on iPhones and Android devices. Additionally, you will be introduced to the tasks required to establish email connectivity over these mobile units to corporate and ISP connections as well as integrated commercial providers.

Understanding Cellular Data Connections

Nearly every user of a mobile device knows how to get on the Internet. iOS users have the built-in Safari browser, and Android users have Google Chrome available. Getting online when you have a cellular connection is easy to do if the device has a data plan. Another great feature of mobile devices is that they can share their cellular data connections with other devices. It's basically the exact opposite of joining a mobile phone to a Wi-Fi network, which we will talk about later in this chapter. Next we will provide details on using hotspots and tethering, using airplane mode, and how data network updates are handled on mobile devices and cover a few key acronyms to know.

Using Mobile Hotspots and Tethering

If you have an iPhone with a data plan, you probably know how to get on the Internet. But imagine yourself in a situation where you're in an office building that doesn't have Wi-Fi and you need to send an important document from your laptop to a key client? What can you do?

One option may be to turn your phone into a mobile hotspot. A *mobile hotspot* lets you share your cellular Internet connection with Wi-Fi capable devices. The Wi-Fi enabled laptop in this example would look for the mobile phone's Wi-Fi network, join it, and then have Internet access. Enabling an iPhone to be a mobile hotspot is done via Settings ➢ Personal Hotspot. The personal hotspot screen is shown in Figure 21.27. A password to join the network is provided (and can be changed) as well as instructions on how to join.

FIGURE 21.27   Enabled personal hotspot

There are three downsides to using your mobile phone as a hotspot.

- *Speed*: Multiple devices are now using one cellular connection.

- *Cost*: You're using your cellular data plan, which could result in expensive charges if you go over your data limit. Unless you know that you have plenty of capacity in your plan, use a hotspot sparingly.

- *Security*: You may have noticed in Figure 21.27 that there was a password but no security options. iOS 7 and newer use WPA2 security, but of course any wireless network has the potential to be hacked. Older iOS versions were susceptible to brute force security attacks.

On Android, a mobile hotspot is enabled by checking the box next to Portable Wi-Fi Hotspot in Settings ➤ Wireless & Networks ➤ Tethering & Portable Hotspot. The option below that, Portable Wi-Fi Hotspot Settings, allows you to change the network SSID, security method (use WPA2!), and the password.

Some mobile providers limit the number of devices that can join the mobile hotspot. For example, Verizon limits it to five devices for a 3G phone and 10 devices for 4G LTE phones.

Finally, mobile providers sell small devices that are specifically used as mobile hotspots. Figure 21.28 shows a Verizon Wireless MiFi device. These types of devices will either use your existing mobile contract or will need to have an activation of their own.

FIGURE 21.28 Verizon Wireless MiFi

Tethering is when you have connected a device to a mobile hotspot. The term used to be reserved only for when you connected via USB cable, as opposed to connecting via wireless. Some devices will not function as a mobile hotspot but will allow you to tether a laptop (or other device) to it, so the mobile device can share the cellular Internet connection.

Using Airplane Mode

The *airplane mode* feature was named so because, for many years, no network signals were allowed on airplanes. Today, some airlines allow for in-flight Wi-Fi (for a nominal fee, of course), but the name of the feature still sticks. It's not restricted to airplane use though. If you're in a public area and suspect that someone is trying to hack your phone through the Wi-Fi or Bluetooth connection, airplane mode will quickly shut down all of your external connections.

The Android screen shots in this section are from Android (KitKat). Lollipop screens use the Material interface and offer airplane mode from the Quick Settings menu, which is two swipes down the screen.

To enable airplane mode in Android, open Settings and then tap More under Wireless & Networks (see Figure 21.29). Tap the check box next to Airplane Mode and you're all set.

FIGURE 21.29   Airplane mode in Android

You can get to airplane mode on an iPhone in a couple different ways. One is to open Settings, and it's the first option that you'll see (see Figure 21.30). When you slide it on, notice how all of the other connections are turned off.

The other way is to access it from the Control Center. You can do this from both the lock screen and the home screen. Simply swipe your finger up from the very bottom of the iPhone's touchscreen and you will get to the Control Center, similar to what's shown in Figure 21.31. Tap the airplane icon in the upper-left corner to enable airplane mode.

FIGURE 21.30   Airplane mode on iOS 8

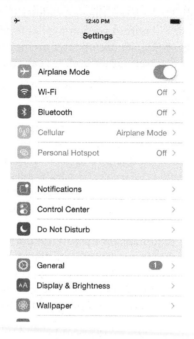

FIGURE 21.31   iPhone Control Center

Understanding Cellular Updates

When most people think of cellular updates, they probably think of an update to the operating system. Perhaps there's a new Android version available or iTunes is alerting them to download the latest incarnation of iOS. Those updates are normal, and completing them takes the active participation of the user. Other updates can occur too, and many of these are transparent to the user.

Before we talk about what those updates are, though, you must first understand that mobile phones don't just have one operating system. This might come as a surprise, but most mobile phones actually have three. Duties are split up between the operating systems, simply because there are so many specialized tasks for the phone to perform.

The first OS is pretty obvious. The other two are specialized OSs that handle specific functions for the device. These two OSs are very small, typically only a few hundred kilobytes in size, and they are referred to as *real-time operating systems (RTOSs)*. They are designed to be lightweight and fast, and *real-time* refers to their ability to minimize lag in data transfers.

First, there is a *baseband* OS that manages all wireless communication, which is actually handled by a separate processor. Some people will call the wireless communications chips in a mobile phone the radio or the modem. Consequently, you might hear about *radio firmware*, a radio firmware update, or a modem update. The last two terms are interchangeable with *baseband update*, which simply means an update of the baseband OS.

 Real World Scenario

Why Phones Need a Baseband OS

One question many students ask is, "Why does a mobile phone need three OSs?" It would seem that phones perform fewer functions than PCs do, and PCs run on one OS!

The answer is that it increases flexibility and reduces software development issues. Think about how many different types of mobile devices there are on the market, and then think about how many versions of each are available. We don't know the exact answer, but it's a large number. Without the baseband OS, the primary OS would need to know how to talk to every single type of radio hardware on the market. And when new hardware comes out, which happens frequently, the primary OS would need to know how to talk to it as well. This isn't feasible. Therefore, phones were designed with one additional layer, which is the baseband OS. The baseband OS knows how to talk to the radio hardware, but it also knows how to talk to the primary OS. When a new hardware chipset is deployed, the developers just need to make the new baseband OS talk to iOS or Android on one side and the new hardware on the other side.

Desktop OSs face similar issues, but Windows, Mac OS X, Linux, and others deal with this by using software drivers.

Second, a *subscriber identity module (SIM) OS* manages all data transfers between the phone and the SIM chip, which is a small memory chip that stores user account information, phone identification, and security data, and it is generally tied to a specific carrier.

These RTOSs are normally updated when a user updates an operating system, but occasionally the carrier will update them when the phone is not otherwise busy. Apple currently provides no way to update either RTOS manually on iOS devices. (Users can find information on how to jailbreak the phone online, but that voids all warranties and is not recommended.) There's more information available on how to update an RTOS on Android phones because Android is open source. Users or companies can provide newer versions of the baseband RTOS, and others can download and install them. Some will say that updating your baseband firmware can result in better reception, faster data throughput, and reduced battery usage. There is much Internet debate about the rewards versus the risks, though.

WARNING   A discussion of performing a manual update of an RTOS requires three warnings:

- Be sure that the upgrade comes from a reputable source. Look for reviews or comments to be sure that it delivers what you expect it to provide.

- Understand that performing this update will most likely void any warranty that you have.

- Always be sure to allow the updates to complete. Interrupting a firmware update in the middle is a nearly surefire way to *brick* your phone; that is, to make it inoperable.

Two other updates of which you should be aware are *PRI updates* and *PRL updates*. Product Release Instruction (PRI) contains settings for configuration items on the device that are specific to the network that it's on. The Preferred Roaming List (PRL) is the reference guide the phone uses to connect to the proper cell phone tower when roaming. Both PRI updates and PRL updates also normally happen when the primary OS on the phone is updated. Some carriers make these two easier to update manually than the RTOS on Android phones though. For example, on many Sprint devices, the user can dial ##873283# for a PRL update, and Verizon users can dial *228 for the same. As always, check with the carrier before attempting to perform these updates and to determine the exact procedure.

Key Acronyms to Know

The last section introduced a few new acronyms to know, such as PRI and PRL. There are a few others that you might see in relation to mobile phones that you should know too:

International Mobile Equipment Identity (IMEI)   This is a 15-digit serial number that is unique to each phone. If a phone is reported stolen, the IMEI will be declared invalid. The IMEI can be displayed on most phones by dialing *#06#. AT&T and T-Mobile were the first networks to use IMEI.

Mobile Equipment Identifier (MEID)   This is an alternate form of a serial number. It's identical to the first 14 numbers of the IMEI. Sprint and Verizon were the first to use MEIDs.

International Mobile Subscriber Identity (IMSI)   This is a unique 15-digit identifier that describes a specific mobile user and their network. It's composed of three elements:

  Mobile Country Code (MCC)   This is a three-digit code, such as 310 for the United States and 234 for the United Kingdom.

  Mobile Network Code (MNC)   This is a two- or three-digit code that identifies the carrier. Many carriers have multiple codes. For example, in the United States, 006 is a Verizon code, and 170 and 410 (among others) are AT&T.

  Mobile Station Identifier Number (MSIN   This is a sequential serial number.

Integrated Circuit Card Identifier (ICCID)   This is a 19- or 20-digit identifier for each SIM chip globally. It's like a serial number for the SIM card.

Secure Element Identifier (SEID)   This is a very long hexadecimal code that uniquely identifies the phone, and it is used in security applications, NFC, and features like Apple Pay.

Within iOS, you can find many of these numbers by choosing Settings ➢ General ➢ About and scrolling to the bottom, as shown in Figure 21.32. To find the same information in Android, go to Settings ➢ About Phone ➢ Status. Note that the About Phone page will often show the baseband version as well.

FIGURE 21.32   iOS phone information

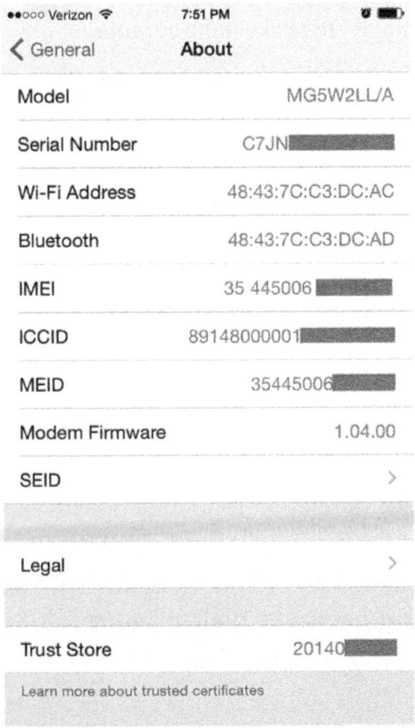

Establishing Wi-Fi Connectivity

Using a cellular network is great because you can connect from nearly anywhere. The downsides, though, are that the connection is slow compared to other connectivity methods, and you have to pay for the data you use. When within range of a secured Wi-Fi network, take advantage of the device's ability to use that network instead. Not only will it be faster, it will be free!

Before you can transfer data over a Wi-Fi network, you have to attach to the network in the same manner you would attach a laptop, for instance, to the same wireless network. You have to find the network by its service-set identifier (SSID) or you have to enter the SSID if it is not being broadcast. You must then satisfy any security requirements that might be in place, such as 802.1x authentication or security keys. Exercise 21.5 steps you through the procedure on an iPhone.

EXERCISE 21.5

Connecting an iPhone to a Wi-Fi Network

1. Tap the Settings app on the home screen.

2. Select Wi-Fi from the Settings menu, shown in Figure 21.33.

FIGURE 21.33 Settings menu

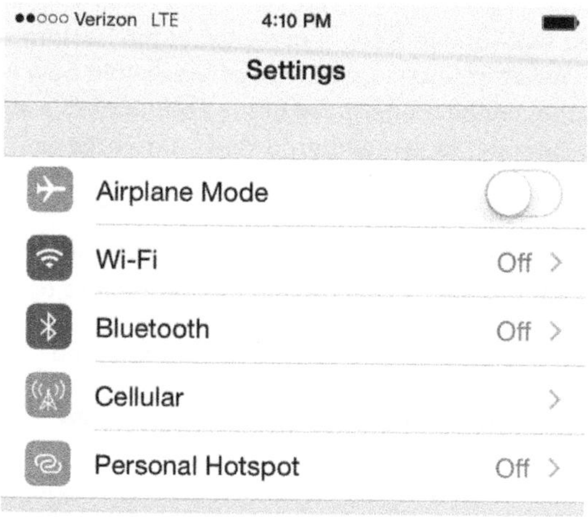

3. Swipe the Wi-Fi switch to the right to turn it on if it is off. Tapping switches also works to toggle them to the opposite state.

4. In the Choose A Network list, tap the name of the wireless network that you want to join.

5. Enter the password or key for the wireless network, if you are asked for one, and then tap the Join button. If it connects, it will move the network name to under the Wi-Fi switch and put a check next to it, as shown in Figure 21.34.

continues

EXERCISE 21.5 ***(continued)***

FIGURE 21.34 Wi-Fi settings with a network that's been joined

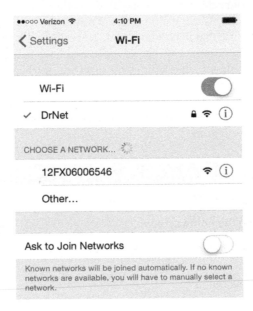

Also take note of the Ask To Join Networks switch at the bottom. Turning this off means that you will never be interrupted with offers to join new wireless networks that are in range of the device. Regardless of the setting of this switch, the device will still automatically reconnect to remembered Wi-Fi networks as they come into range.

6. Tap the Settings back button at the top left to return to the previous screen.

   Notice on this screen that the network you selected is now listed on the Settings page, as shown in Figure 21.35. If not, you are not connected to a Wi-Fi network.

FIGURE 21.35 Settings page with Wi-Fi network connected

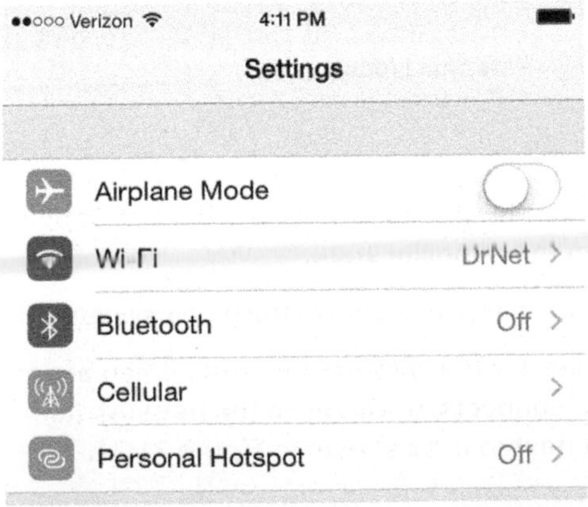

7. Click the hard Home button at the bottom in the frame of the phone to return to the home screen after noting that the network you joined is listed next to Wi-Fi on the menu.

You can use the Home button to return to the home screen at any time, but the app you leave will continue to remain open in the same screen as when you left it until you restart the iOS device or manually force the app to end.

Throughout this chapter, the practice of tapping successive back buttons in the upper-left corner of the screen, instead of clicking the Home button prematurely, will be referred to as *backing out of the app.*

A similar series of tasks is required when attaching an Android phone to the same type of network. Exercise 21.6 details that procedure.

EXERCISE 21.6

Connecting an Android Phone to a Wi-Fi Network

1. Tap the Menu button on the frame of the phone.

2. Tap the Settings button in the menu.

3. Select Wireless & Networks from the Settings menu.

4. Place a check in the box beside Wi-Fi in the Wireless & Networks menu (if it is unchecked), as shown in Figure 21.36.

FIGURE 21.36 Enabling Wi-Fi in Android

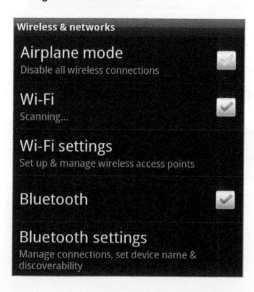

continues

5. Select Wi-Fi Settings from the Wireless & Networks menu to be taken to a screen with a list of wireless networks that are in range, like the ones shown in Figure 21.37.

FIGURE 21.37   Available Wi-Fi networks

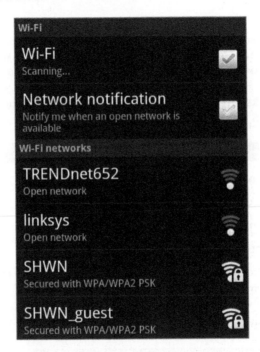

6. Tap the name of the wireless network that you want to join.

7. Enter the password or key for the wireless network, if you are asked for one, as shown in Figure 21.38, and then tap the Connect button.

8. Confirm that the network you selected connects successfully, as shown in Figure 21.39.

9. Tap the hard Home button to return to the home screen.

FIGURE 21.38   Enter a wireless password.

FIGURE 21.39   Connected to a Wi-Fi network

When your phone is connected to a Wi-Fi network, you don't need to use a cellular connection for data transfers. When connected to Wi-Fi, by default, apps will use the Wi-Fi connection for data. But if the connection gets dropped or you move out of Wi-Fi range, the device will use the cellular connection. This might be fine, but it also might not be what you want. If you want to ensure that the phone does not use cellular for data connections, you can disable that option. Exercise 21.7 walks you through the steps of how to do that on an iPhone. When the device is connected to a Wi-Fi network or when paired with a Bluetooth peer, data access will be possible. Otherwise, no data-network access will occur.

EXERCISE 21.7

Disabling Cellular Use for Data Networking on an iPhone

1. Tap the Settings app on the home screen.

2. Select Cellular from the Settings menu.

3. Turn off the switch labeled Cellular Data, which is shown in Figure 21.40.

FIGURE 21.40 Cellular Data setting

4. If you would like to keep cellular data usage enabled but not allow roaming into other providers' data networks, you can tap the Roaming button, shown in Figure 21.40 with a Voice Only tag. The Roaming screen, shown in Figure 21.41, allows you to turn off the Data Roaming switch.

FIGURE 21.41   Cellular roaming settings

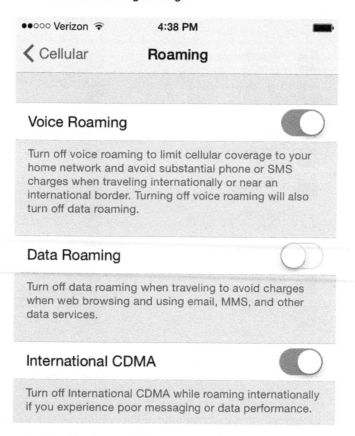

5. If you wish to disable cellular use just for a specific function or app, scroll down in the Cellular settings (or look for the app in the Settings page). You may be able to turn off the use of cellular data for that function or app alone. For example, Figure 21.42 shows the Use Cellular Data switch for several apps, all of which are currently enabled.

continues

FIGURE 21.42   Use Cellular Data settings for apps

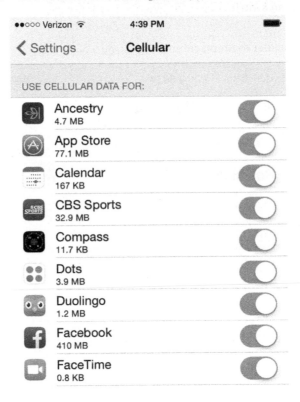

6. Back out of the Settings app, and then press the Home button.

     To disable cellular data in Android, go to Settings ➢ Data Usage (as shown in Figure 21.43) and turn the Mobile Data switch off. You will still be able to connect to the Internet using a Wi-Fi connection. Within Data Usage, you will also see options to view your mobile data usage and set a mobile data limit.

The final setting we will look at in relation to Wi-Fi networks is the *virtual private network (VPN)* configuration. A VPN is a secured network connection made over an unsecure network. For example, if you wanted to connect your phone to your corporate network over the Internet in order to read email, but you also wanted to secure the connection, you could use a VPN. To set up a VPN on an iPhone, go to Settings ➢ General ➢ VPN and tap Add VPN Configuration. You will see a screen similar to the one shown in Figure 21.44. Here you will need to choose the security protocol, provide a server name and user account name, and configure additional settings.

FIGURE 21.43   Data Usage in Android

FIGURE 21.44   Adding VPN configuration settings

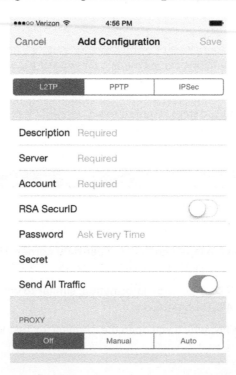

Once you have enabled the VPN, a new VPN option will appear on your Settings page, as shown in Figure 21.45. This will allow you to easily enable, disable, or configure the VPN.

FIGURE 21.45 VPN in Settings

 VPN connections can be made over cellular as well as over Wi-Fi.

Exercise 21.8 shows you the steps required to set up a PPTP or L2TP VPN connection in Android.

EXERCISE 21.8

Setting Up a VPN in Android

1. Open Settings ➢ Wireless & Networks, and tap More.

2. Tap VPN, and then tap the plus sign in the upper-right corner. This will open the Edit VPN Profile screen.

3. Enter the server's VPN configuration information, similar to what is shown in the example in Figure 21.46. Then tap Save.

4. Tap the name of the VPN, which will open the Connect To Test VPN screen, shown in Figure 21.47.

FIGURE 21.46   Edit VPN Profile screen

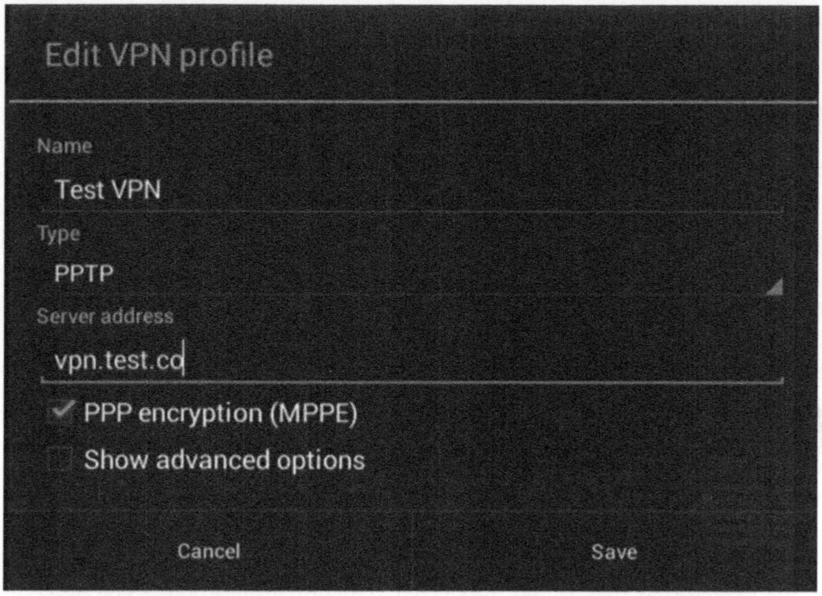

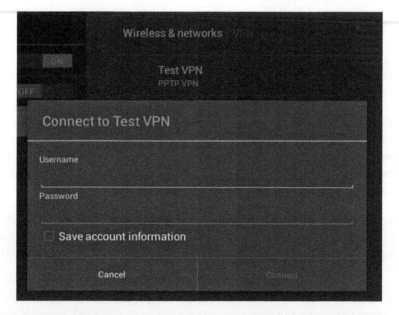

FIGURE 21.47   Connect To Test VPN screen

5.   Enter the username and password, and tap Connect.

Android also supports many apps that allow you to configure VPN connections, such as TunnelBear and Hola Free VPN. If your network uses an OpenVPN server, know that you have to install a third-party app (such as OpenVPN Connect) to create the VPN connection. Android does not natively support OpenVPN.

Establishing Bluetooth Connectivity

The IEEE 802.15 specifies wireless personal area networks (WPANs) that use Bluetooth for data-link transport. The concept is that certain paired devices will be capable of exchanging or synchronizing data over a Bluetooth connection, such as between a mobile device and a desktop or laptop computer.

In other cases, the Bluetooth pairing can be used simply to control one device with another, allowing information to flow bidirectionally, even if that transfer does not result in its permanent storage on the destination. Examples of this latter functionality include a Bluetooth headset for a cell phone, a Bluetooth-attached keyboard and mouse, and pairing a smartphone or MP3 player with a vehicle's sound system.

In general, connecting a mobile device to another device requires that both devices have Bluetooth enabled. Pairing subsequently requires that at least one of the devices be discoverable and the other perform a search for Bluetooth devices. Once the device performing the search finds the other device, a sometime-configurable pairing code must often be entered on the device that performed the search. The code must match the one configured on the device that was found in order for the pairing to occur. In some cases, this pairing will work in one direction only. Usually, it is the mobile device that should search for the other device. If both devices have the same basic capability and will be able to exchange data readily, then it's not as important which device performs the search. Regardless, the pairing code must be known for entry into the device that requests it.

The truth about pairing mobile devices with conventional computers is that the results are hit or miss. There's never any guarantee that a given pairing will be successful to the point of data transfer capability. Both devices must agree on the same Bluetooth specification. This turns out to be the easy part because devices negotiate during the connection. The part that is out of your control is what software services the manufacturer decided to include in their devices. If one device is not capable of file transfers over Bluetooth, then the pairing may go off without a hitch, but the communication process will stop there.

For example, in our Bluetooth pairing exercises, we use a MacBook Pro and an Android-based HTC EVO 4G. Given the MacBook, the Android, an iPhone, and an iPad from which we were able to choose, no other pairing among the four devices resulted in a file-transfer capability. Most users would assume that the Apple products would communicate with one another at a very high level, but alas, Bluetooth is not a technology that has received as much attention from Apple as, say, Wi-Fi. Third-party solutions that involve jailbreaking the iPhone do exist, however.

In Exercise 21.9, the steps are shown for how to connect an Android device to a MacBook Pro over Bluetooth and then to transfer a file back and forth between the two. This exercise is split into four sections so that you can concentrate on individual stages of the pairing and file sharing processes. Exercise 21.10 steps you through the process of pairing an iPhone with a vehicle in order to stream music to the vehicle's sound system. Note that the procedures shown here are based on the specific non-mobile devices used—a MacBook Pro and a 2013 Toyota. The procedure is roughly the same with other remote devices but will likely vary in the fine details.

EXERCISE 21.9

Pairing an Android Device with a MacBook Pro

Enabling Bluetooth and Pairing

1. On the Android, tap the Menu button.

2. Tap the Settings button.

3. Select Wireless & Networks from the Settings menu.

4. Select Bluetooth Settings in the Wireless & Networks menu.

5. Check the box next to Bluetooth in the Bluetooth Settings menu, as shown in Figure 21.48, if it is not already checked.

FIGURE 21.48   Bluetooth Settings menu

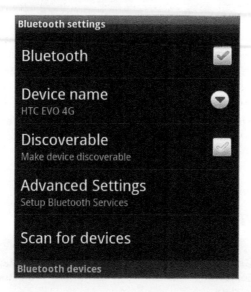

Note that you could have checked the Bluetooth box in the previous screen, but you would have needed to complete step 4 anyway to make the device discoverable or to scan for other devices. If this device does not scan for other devices or enable itself to be scanned by other devices, pairing cannot occur.

continues

6. Select Advanced Settings from the Bluetooth Settings menu.

7. Check the box labeled FTP Server, if it is not already checked. If the FTP server on the Android is not enabled, file transfers can still occur, such as pushing files back and forth between the devices, but you will not be able to browse the Android file system from the MacBook, which will also prevent your using the MacBook to pull files from the Android.

8. Tap the Back hard button to return to the Bluetooth Settings screen.

9. On the MacBook, click System Preferences in the Dock, shown in Figure 21.49.

FIGURE 21.49 Mac System Preferences

10. Click Bluetooth in the Internet & Wireless section of System Preferences, shown in Figure 21.50.

FIGURE 21.50 Internet & Wireless section

11. Check the box labeled On in the Bluetooth dialog (see Figure 21.51), if it is not already checked.

FIGURE 21.51 Bluetooth settings on a Mac

12. Click the Sharing Setup button at the bottom of the Bluetooth dialog.

13. Check the File Sharing and Bluetooth Sharing boxes in the Sharing dialog (see Figure 21.52), if not already checked, and click the onscreen back button (left arrow) to return to the Bluetooth dialog (or click the Bluetooth Preferences button at the bottom).

FIGURE 21.52 Enabling Bluetooth file sharing

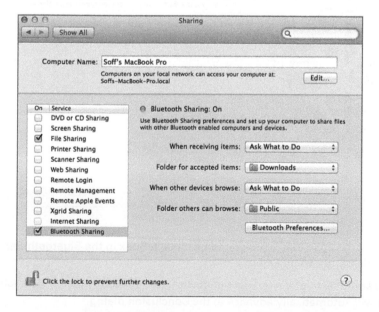

continues

Note the folders listed on the right side. The DOWNLOADS folder is set as the folder accessed by actions along the lines of "send via Bluetooth." The remote device cannot see the contents of this folder; it can only add to it. Any transfer to the folder set here must be approved on a file-by-file basis, or a box can be checked during the transfer to allow all. The PUBLIC folder is set as the one accessed by actions that mention "uploading" and "downloading." The remote device can actually see the contents of this folder.

14. On the Android device, check the box next to Discoverable. Note that scanning for devices to find the MacBook Pro is not helpful in this case. That would be useful for finding the car stereo system, for example.

15. On the MacBook, click the Set Up New Device button in the Bluetooth dialog.

16. Select the device that you want to pair from the list in the Bluetooth Setup Assistant, as shown in Figure 21.53, and click the Continue button.

FIGURE 21.53   Selecting a Bluetooth device to pair to

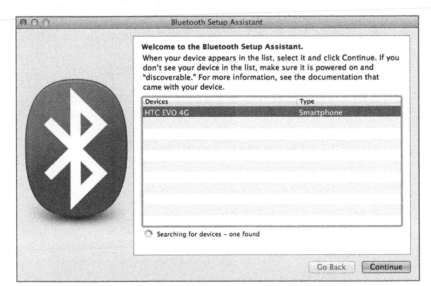

17. Make note of the code that is generated by the MacBook in the Bluetooth Setup Assistant dialog, shown in Figure 21.54.

When the approval to pair is granted on the Android device, the Bluetooth Setup Assistant will automatically advance to the Conclusion dialog.

FIGURE 21.54   Bluetooth pairing code

18. On the Android, compare the code in the pop-up generated (see Figure 21.55) when the MacBook Pro requests the pairing. If there is a match, tap the Pair button.

FIGURE 21.55   Confirm the passkey

continues

Notice that the MacBook's name has populated the Bluetooth Devices section behind the pop-up. This happens automatically when a remote device requests a pairing session.

19. On the MacBook, click the Quit button in the Bluetooth Setup Assistant to close that dialog and return your attention to the Bluetooth dialog.

20. Select the Android device—doing so is only necessary if multiple devices are found—and then click the gear icon (see Figure 21.56), revealing that there are options. We will refer to this menu as the Bluetooth task list.

FIGURE 21.56 Bluetooth task list

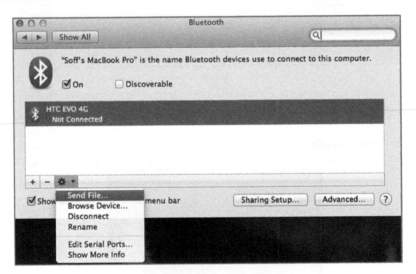

If you noticed that the Android device is not connected, this is the default behavior because FTP is used for the file transfers. FTP works in bursts over multiple successive connections. There is currently no need for a connection because data is not flowing.

MacBook: Transferring Files—Pulling from Android

1. Click Browse Device on the MacBook Bluetooth task list to produce a listing of the root file structure of the Android's SD card. This is the step that requires completion of step 7 of the section in this exercise, titled "Enabling Bluetooth and Pairing."

2. Navigate to a file to download to the MacBook.

3. Drag and drop the file to the location of your choice. Figure 21.57 shows a file dropped onto the Desktop.

FIGURE 21.57   Transferring a file

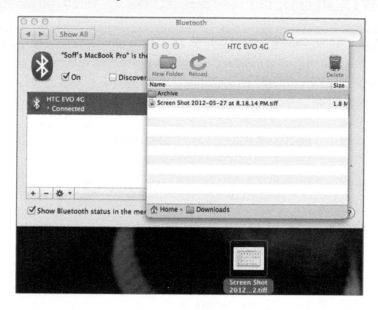

Notice that the Android is now shown as Connected. This will remain as long as you are browsing, and it will turn off in a matter of seconds after the browsing window is closed. The Connected state will also occur briefly when you push a file to the Android using Send File on the Bluetooth task list, which is discussed next.

Transferring Files—Pushing to Android

1. On the MacBook, click Send File on the Bluetooth task list to open the Finder, which is shown in Figure 21.58.

FIGURE 21.58   Selecting a file to send

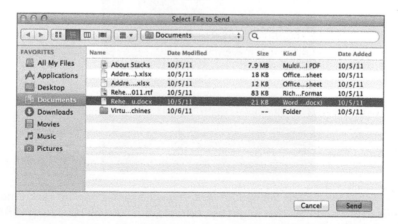

continues

EXERCISE 21.9 *(continued)*

2. Navigate to a file to upload to the Android.

3. Select the file, and then click the Send button. The result, as shown in Figure 21.59, indicates something that must be done on the Android.

FIGURE 21.59   Waiting for the Android

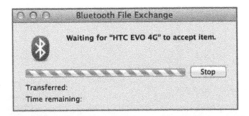

4. On the Android, check the box labeled Always in the pop-up, as shown in Figure 21.60, and tap Accept to start the transfer.

FIGURE 21.60   Authorizing the connection

If you do not check the box labeled Always, you will see this pop-up each time a file is pushed to the Android. That might be desirable, but you will have to confirm each transfer anyway, so checking the box makes each transfer a bit easier.

5. Use your finger to pull down—like a window shade—the status bar with the time on it, which is above the home screen on the Android. It will give you a notification screen like the one shown in Figure 21.61.

FIGURE 21.61   Notifications window

6. Tap the Bluetooth Share notification to begin the confirmation process.

7. Tap the Accept button in the resulting pop-up.

    The file pushed to the Android device is stored in a folder named BLUETOOTH that is created, if it doesn't already exist, under the top-level folder named DOWNLOADS. You might have to install an app to be able to view the local file structure of the Android. The image shown in Figure 21.62 is from an app called ES File Explorer, and it shows the transferred file on the SD memory card at /SDCARD/DOWNLOADS/BLUETOOTH.

FIGURE 21.62   Showing a transferred file

continues

Transferring Files—Pushing to and Pulling from MacBook

This procedure might require installing a third-party Android app, such as Bluetooth File Transfer. The Android operating system includes the functionality to put—or upload—files to the remote device, but not to get—or download—them. It also does not have a remote file browser built in.

Most apps have a remote or Bluetooth tab that acts as your browser tab to the remote device. With this tab, you can upload and download with MacBook approval required only during each new connection establishment phase, not for each file transferred. This is in contrast to transferring using the "send via Bluetooth" mechanism, in which case approval is required for each individual object transferred in addition to the initial approval. Figure 21.63 is an example of the approval that you have to give for "send via Bluetooth" transfers.

FIGURE 21.63 Approval needed for file transfer

Because "send via Bluetooth" transfers are placed in the "Accepted Items" folder from the Bluetooth Sharing dialog, you will find the transferred file in the DOWNLOADS folder, not the PUBLIC folder.

If you attempt to browse the MacBook's file system from the Android device, you will have to click the Allow button, shown in the pop-up in Figure 21.64, on the MacBook to allow browsing. Notice that the folder name is the name that was chosen earlier for the Browse field in the MacBook's Bluetooth Sharing dialog.

FIGURE 21.64 Allowing the Android to browse the Mac

In true FTP form, the Android device will display the MacBook's PUBLIC folder for the currently logged-in user as the root of a directory tree. If you upload from the Android device while browsing, it is this folder on the MacBook that will contain the transferred files.

The procedure in Exercise 21.10 is performed from the perspective of an iPhone pairing with a 2013 Toyota vehicle. The exact process for Bluetooth pairing will differ based on your mobile OS and the device to which you are connecting. In general, though, remember that these are the steps:

1. Turn on the Bluetooth hands-free device.
   a. Enable Bluetooth.
   b. Enable pairing.
2. Use your mobile device to locate and select the Bluetooth device.
3. Enter the Bluetooth device's passcode.
4. Confirm pairing on the Bluetooth device by pressing a button or a combination of buttons.
5. Test the connectivity.

EXERCISE 21.10

Pairing an iPhone with a Vehicle's Sound System

1. Enable Bluetooth pairing in the vehicle. It will often involve using menu or voice commands to begin the process.

2. Confirm that the vehicle's hands-free power is enabled. Hands-free power might be referred to in other ways, including simply as Bluetooth. Alternatively, the Bluetooth module in certain vehicles might be "always on" and not configurable. The key is to make sure that the vehicle is ready to accept incoming Bluetooth requests.

3. When the vehicle is ready, go into Settings ➤ Bluetooth on the iPhone, and slide the switch to enable Bluetooth, as shown in Figure 21.65. It found the car's multimedia system.

FIGURE 21.65 iPhone discovers the vehicle's multimedia system.

continues

EXERCISE 21.10 ***(continued)***

4. Tap the Car Multi-Media device. It will take you to the PIN screen.
5. Enter the four-digit PIN, as shown in Figure 21.66. (The car's setup program told me the PIN; your device documentation will tell you the default PIN, or you can try 0000.)

FIGURE 21.66 Entering the PIN

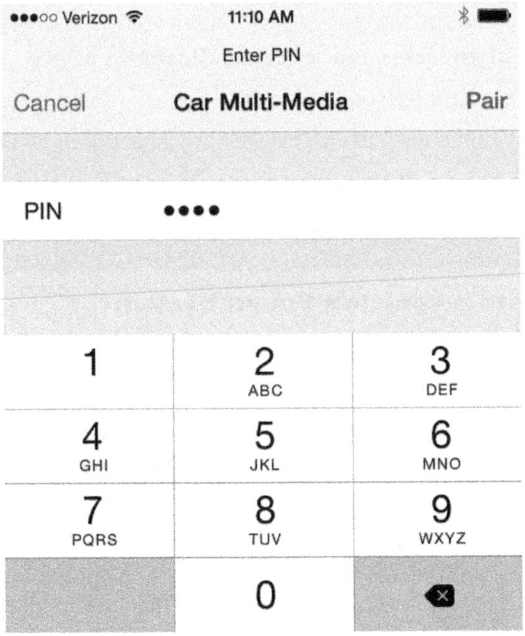

6. Tap Pair. The phone will show you that it's connected and ready for use, as shown in Figure 21.67.

   Bluetooth pairings in this list can be Connected, Not Connected (pairing was, however, successful), or Not Paired.
7. Confirm the iPhone's connection from the vehicle's perspective. If the vehicle has the ability to use the iPhone for voice calls, this feature might be presented to you automatically after pairing is complete. If so, this is a perfect way to confirm connectivity.

FIGURE 21.67   iPhone paired and ready for use

8. Switch to the vehicle's Bluetooth audio mode. The iPhone might still need to be "con-
    nected" for this use. The pairing allows you to select the connection feature in the
    vehicle and see the iPhone as a connection option. Depending on the vehicle, selecting
    the iPhone should cause music to begin playing either from its default playlist or the last
    position where playback was stopped over another output source, including the iPhone's
    internal speaker or headset jack. Future connection to the iPhone from this vehicle
    should be automatic when the vehicle's Bluetooth mode is selected, and the iPhone
    should begin playing from the point where it last stopped playing over any output
    source. The specific initial and subsequent interactions between the vehicle and iPhone
    may vary from this description.

Configuring Email Accounts

Because the vast majority of the world's email traffic flows over TCP/IP internetworks,
which includes the Internet, it is exceedingly simple to set up mobile devices to access email
accounts. Usually, the most difficult part is finding the server settings that are used only
during establishment of the connection, which tends to occur only once for each device.
The other big challenge is when users have the same devices and accounts for many years;

since they have not configured them in some time, it might be difficult for them to remember their usernames and passwords if needed.

When configuring mobile devices to access email, you will be attaching to one of two types of services. The first is an integrated commercial provider, which includes Google (Gmail), Yahoo!, Outlook.com, and iCloud email. The second is a corporate or ISP-based email service. Generally speaking, connecting to integrated commercial providers is quite easy and nearly automatic. Connecting to a corporate or ISP-based account usually involves a few more steps, but it shouldn't be too tricky if you know the proper server settings to input. In the following sections, we'll look at configuring email on a mobile device, settings to know for manual configuration, and special considerations for Exchange and S/MIME.

Mobile Internet Email Configuration

If your email is on a common web-based service, such as Gmail, Yahoo!, Outlook.com, or iCloud, configuring the email feature is pretty easy. Usually, your email address and password are all that are required. If, however, you have a corporate or ISP account or a custom domain, even if it's hosted and accessible through Gmail, Live, or the other popular services, you may need to take a few more steps to make a connection. For the purposes of trying out a commercial service, you can always make a dummy account on the service's website and play around with that if it helps you complete these exercises. Exercise 21.11 and Exercise 21.12 detail the basic steps required to configure a commercial email account on the iPhone and on an Android standard email client, respectively.

EXERCISE 21.11

Email Account Configuration on an iPhone

1. From the home screen, tap Settings and scroll down until you see Mail, Contacts, Calendars (see Figure 21.68).

FIGURE 21.68   Mail, Contacts, Calendars

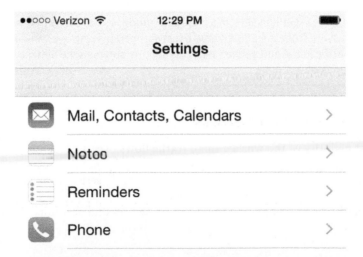

2. Tap Mail, Contacts, Calendars. It will show you accounts as well as the configuration settings for email, contacts, and calendars.

3. Tap Add Account (near the top), and it will show you a screen similar to the one shown in Figure 21.69.

FIGURE 21.69   Add Account

4. Note that if you have an email account with any of the listed services, you can tap it to configure your client. You will be asked for your username and password and, after entering this information, you should be done. It's as easy as that to add an account for a commercial provider. For this example, tap Other ➢ Add Mail Account. You will get a screen similar to the one shown in Figure 21.70. Here you can add your name, email address, password, and an optional description. Tap Next.

continues

FIGURE 21.70   Adding a new account

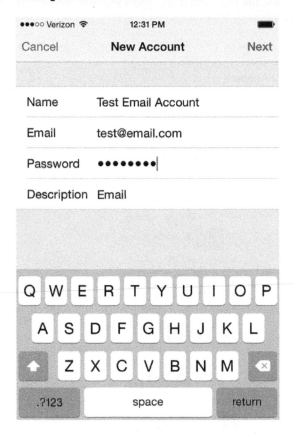

5. In the New Account screen (see Figure 21.71), choose IMAP or POP. We will get into the differences between the two in the next section, but if your server supports it, IMAP is preferable. Here you also configure the names of the incoming and outgoing mail servers. Many organizations will have one server handle both functions. Once you have entered the correct information, tap Next.

6. The iPhone will make connections to the server(s) to verify the username and password. If successful, you will get a screen asking which content you want to receive, similar to the one shown in Figure 21.72. Make your selections, and tap Save. It will add your account.

7. Now you can use the Mail icon on the home page to retrieve email. Note that you can have several email accounts configured to receive email in this app.

FIGURE 21.71 Configuring email servers

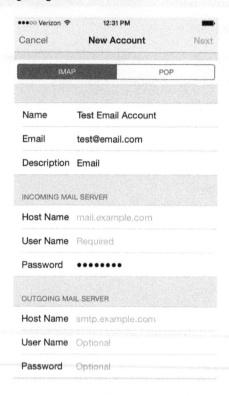

FIGURE 21.72 Email account content options

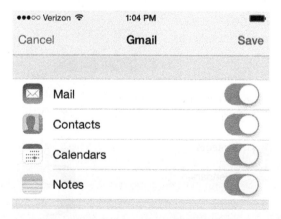

8. (Optional) To delete an account, repeat steps 1 and 2 in this exercise. On the Mail, Contacts, Calendars screen (see Figure 21.73), tap the account that you want to delete.

continues

FIGURE 21.73 Accounts list

9. (Optional) Tap Delete Account (see Figure 21.74) to remove it from this client. (The account name has been masked in this figure.)

FIGURE 21.74 Deleting an account

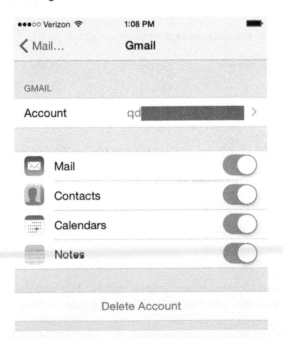

Exercise 21.12, as stated earlier, details the steps required for configuring an email account on an Android standard email client. If the Android device does not have the Mail app on the home screen, you can add it or run it directly from the All Apps list.

This exercise is written for the Gmail app that is not configured for any accounts. If accounts are already configured, from within the Mail app, tap the down arrow in the circle at the upper-left corner and then select New Account from the resulting pop-up, similar to the one shown in Figure 21.75.

FIGURE 21.75   Select New Account.

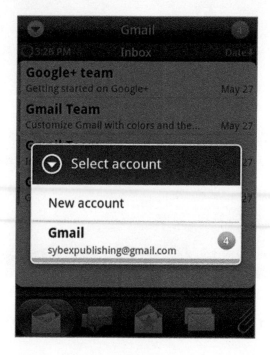

EXERCISE 21.12

Email Account Configuration in Android

Automatic Internet Email Configuration on an Android Phone

1. Tap Settings, and scroll down to the Accounts section on the left side. Tap Add Account (see Figure 21.76).

2. Tap the type of account that you want to add. For this example, choose Personal (IMAP).

3. Enter your email account name and tap Next.

continues

FIGURE 21.76   Add An Account screen

4. Enter your password and tap Next. You will get a screen similar to the one shown in Figure 21.77.

5. Note that the port is 143 because you chose IMAP. If you tap anywhere on the setting next to Security Type, you can change the security to SSL/TLS. That will automatically change the port number to 993. Tap Next. Android will contact the server and verify the server settings.

6. After verifying a connection to the server, you can choose account options like the ones shown in Figure 21.78. Choose the ones that you want and tap Next.

7. You will get an account confirmation page, where you can edit the account name that gets displayed as well as the name that gets displayed on outgoing messages (see Figure 21.79). Tap Next.

FIGURE 21.77   Incoming Server Settings screen

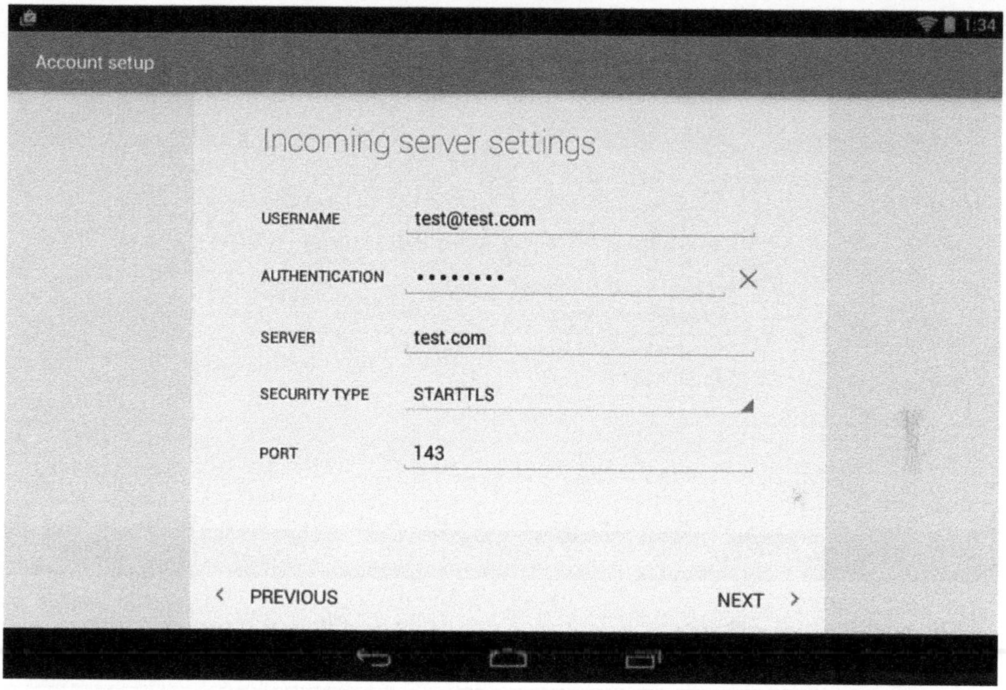

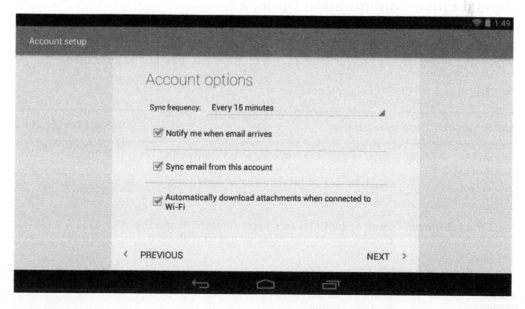

FIGURE 21.78   Email account options

continues

FIGURE 21.79 Account setup options

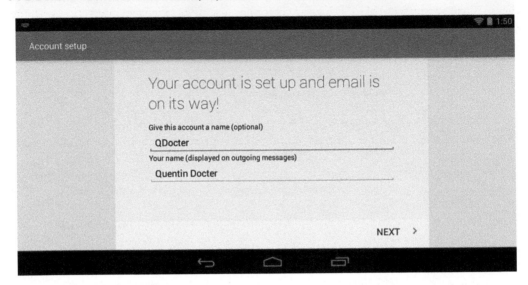

8. The new account will appear in your accounts list in Settings. You can access your email through the Gmail app on the home page.

Manual Email Configuration Options

In those situations when you find that your email client cannot automatically configure your email account for you, there are very often manual settings for the protocols required for sending and receiving emails. Table 21.4 details these protocols and their uses.

TABLE 21.4 TCP/IP mail protocols

Mail Protocol	Description	Default Port Number
Simple Mail Transfer Protocol (SMTP)	Used to communicate between client and server and between servers to send mail to a recipient's account. The key word is send, as this is a push protocol.	TCP 25
Post Office Protocol (POP)	Used to communicate between a client and the client's mail server to retrieve mail with little interaction.	TCP 110
Internet Message Access Protocol (IMAP)	Used to communicate between a client and the client's mail server to retrieve mail with extensive interaction.	TCP 143

In a TCP/IP network using only the protocols in Table 21.4 (there are other, less common options), you must always use SMTP for sending mail. You must decide between the use of POP and IMAP for interacting with the mail server to retrieve your mail with the client. When supported, IMAP is a clear choice because of its extensive interaction with the server, allowing the client to change the state or location of a mail item on the server without the need to download and delete it from the server. Many users who are familiar with Exchange might get the impression that Exchange is at work behind the scenes because of the ability to control items on the server from one client and then go to another local or web-based client and see the items in the exact same state as they left them in the previous client.

Conversely, POP limits client interaction with the server to downloading and deleting items from the server, not allowing their state to be changed by the client. In fact, the use of POP as your receive-mail protocol can lead to confusion because copies of the same items appear in multiple client locations, some marked as read and others unread. Additionally, where IMAP changes the state of a mail item on the server and leaves the item on the server for later access by the same or different client, POP settings must be configured *not* to delete the item from the server on download to each client. This, however, is what leads to the choice of multiple copies among the clients or only one client being able to download the item.

Most, if not all, Internet mail services require secure connections using Secure Sockets Layer (SSL) or Transport Layer Security (TLS). You might recognize these protocols from their use on TCP port 443 for the HTTPS protocol. The common port numbers listed in Table 21.4 are not secure and are not the best to use. Instead, the TCP port numbers in Table 21.5 are better to use for most webmail services for securing the protocols in Table 21.4. When you're establishing a manual email client connection, these are the ones that you are most likely to require.

TABLE 21.5 Secure mail ports

Mail Protocol	TCP Port Number
SMTP with SSL	465
SMTP with TLS	587
IMAP with SSL/TLS	993
POP with SSL/TLS	995

Additionally, you will need to know the server names for your service. Sometimes they are the same for inbound and outbound mail handling, but they may be different. Table 21.6 lists the servers in the United States for Gmail, Live (Hotmail), and Yahoo! Mail. Unless otherwise specified, the ports in Table 21.5 should be used for the protocols listed in Table 21.6.

TABLE 21.6   Secure mail servers for common webmail services

Service	Direction and Protocol	Server Name
Gmail	Outbound on SMTP with SSL or TLS	smtp.gmail.com
Inbound on IMAP with SSL	imap.gmail.com	
Inbound on POP with SSL	pop.gmail.com	
Outlook.com	Outbound on SMTP with SSL (port 25) or TLS (port 587)	smtp-mail.outlook.com
Inbound on IMAP with SSL	imap-mail.outlook.com (port 993)	
Inbound on POP with SSL	pop-mail.outlook.com	
Yahoo!	Outbound on SMTP with SSL	smtp.mail.yahoo.com
Inbound on IMAP with SSL	imap.mail.yahoo.com	
Inbound on POP with SSL	pop.mail.yahoo.com	

Exchange and S/MIME Considerations

Exchange is a proprietary client-server messaging platform from Microsoft. Many enterprises rely on Exchange for their entire suite of email services. Exchange connectivity to Internet mail services such as Outlook.com and Office 365 is steadily becoming more popular; it's a public form of the longstanding capability of enterprises to offer Exchange access to intranet users using Webmail over HTTP or through Outlook Web App (OWA).

The procedure for establishing connectivity to a Microsoft Exchange server is not much different from how you established connectivity to an Internet mail service. In fact, the same server can be configured to support Exchange. Microsoft Exchange servers support access by proprietary Exchange messaging as well as by the Internet mail protocols. When a mail client that does not support Exchange has to be used, or when an Exchange client account might cost the user money (as in the use of the newer public Exchange accounts), it is possible that the protocols and ports in Table 21.5 can be used to establish a connection.

When an Exchange or Exchange ActiveSync client is used in the enterprise, there is sometimes no need to supply information beyond the user's account name and password along with their email address. Sometimes, however, this is not enough to establish the connection. Unlike the need for picky details for an Internet mail connection, Exchange is likely to require only the server name to complete a manual configuration. When setting up the email clients (such as those you did in Exercise 21.11 and Exercise 21.12) to attach to Exchange, choose Exchange as the account type.

The last configuration option of which you should be aware is email encryption. Android and iOS both support the *Secure/Multipurpose Internet Mail Extensions (S/MIME)* standard for public key encryption.

If you can't decrypt email, it is most likely because S/MIME settings are not properly enabled on your email account, which means that you must install the certificate (and by extension, your private key) on your mobile device. Exercise 21.13 walks you through the general steps to enable S/MIME on iOS, using iOS 8 as an example. The exercise assumes that you already have obtained a security certificate through a certificate authority (CA).

EXERCISE 21.13

Enabling S/MIME on iOS 8

1. Transfer the security certificate to your iOS device. You need the `.p12` file; download it directly from your CA or email the `.p12` file to yourself.

2. Open the `.p12` file. iOS will automatically try to install it as a profile.

3. Click Install.

4. If you get a warning that the profile is unsigned, click OK.

5. Enter the passcode for the device, and then enter the passcode for the `.p12` file. Click Next.

6. Click Done to complete the certificate installation.

7. On your iOS device, open Settings ➢ Mail, Contacts, Calendars.

8. Tap Exchange, and then tap your email account.

9. At the bottom of your account settings, tap Advanced Settings.

10. Enable S/MIME, as shown in Figure 21.80.

FIGURE 21.80   Advanced Settings for email

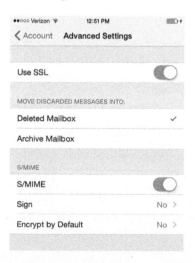

continues

11. Turn on Sign and Encrypt By Default, if you would like.

12. Back out of Advanced Settings.

Mobile Device Synchronization

Many users do not consider their mobile devices to be islands unto themselves. Instead, they treat their devices as an extension of their primary computing device that, even if it happens to be portable, stays at work or at home while the mobile computing device goes on the road with the user. However, because many of the same changes to a user's calendar, contacts, and personal files can be made from the mobile device as easily as from the primary computer, frequent synchronization of the two devices is in order. *Synchronization* is the act of mirroring all unique changes and additions from one device to the other.

In most cases, there are multiple options as to how the mobile device will connect to the computer system. Some connections allow synchronization; others do not. Common connections include over USB or FireWire, across Wi-Fi, and over a Bluetooth connection. While the wired serial connections tend to be the most reliable, the convenience of wireless connections and their automatic unattended synchronizations cannot be ignored.

Because each manufacturer of mobile devices must approach synchronization of data in the best manner for their devices, generalized discussions of data to be synchronized can *only* include the common types. The tabs in iTunes and their purpose are detailed in the next section, but the following list constitutes the most common types of data to be synchronized by all such utilities:

- Contacts
- Calendar
- Email
- Photos
- Music
- Videos
- Apps
- Bookmarks
- Documents
- Location data
- Social media data
- eBooks

Syncing Apple iOS Devices

Due to their size, Apple iOS devices have limited storage space, and they also have the potential to get lost (or stolen) somewhat easily. Because of this, it's smart to synchronize your device to a desktop or laptop computer (they will be collectively referred to as *desktop* in the rest of this section) and/or make backups of the device. The differences between the two concepts aren't that large. Synchronization means that the exact same copy of the data (music, pictures, contacts, or whatever) is on both the iOS device and the desktop. Backing up means taking whatever is on the phone at that time and ensuring that there's a duplicate stored elsewhere. Synchronization can often happen both ways, whereas backups are a one-way process. Apple provides two options for syncing and backing up: iTunes for desktops and iCloud for cloud-based backups.

Using iTunes

To sync a device with a desktop, iTunes must be installed on a compatible non-iOS computer. It's installed by default on Macs. The iOS devices will automatically sync each time they are connected by USB, and Wi-Fi in some cases, and they are recognized under the Devices section in the left frame of iTunes. The exception is when iTunes is set to prevent automatic synchronization. Figure 21.81 shows the dialog from iTunes attained by clicking Edit ➤ Preferences ➤ Devices. (You might need to press the Alt key to get the Edit menu to appear.) Notice that syncing is set to occur automatically because the Prevent iPods, iPhones, And iPads From Syncing Automatically check box is cleared.

FIGURE 21.81 Devices preferences in iTunes

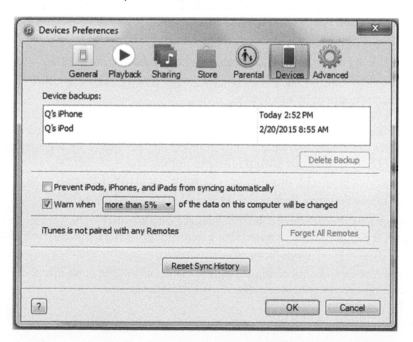

When synchronizing with a desktop, both the iOS and the desktop authenticate each other. This two-way authentication is called *mutual authentication*, and it lets multiple services on the iOS device communicate with the appropriate services on the desktop.

The iTunes options shown in this section are for version 12.0.1.26. Different versions may have slightly different configurations or menus.

The selection of what is to be synchronized is a task unto itself, but iTunes provides specific tabs on the left side of the interface for each class of data, as shown in Figure 21.82, under the Settings section. You can make very granular choices about what you want to sync. The following list gives the basic characteristics of each tab:

- *Summary*: This setting contains general information about the device, backup settings, and general sync options.

- *Apps*: This setting shows apps to be synced, their orientation on the different home screens, and documents, if any, available through apps that support file sharing.

- *Music*: This setting shows music to be synced and playlist, artist, album, and genre sections for making selections in partial syncing.

- *Movies*: This setting shows movies and video clips to be synced.

- *TV Shows*: This setting shows TV shows to be synced.

- *Podcasts*: This setting shows podcasts to be synced.

- *Books*: This setting shows books to be synced.

- *Photos*: This setting shows photos to be synced.

- *Info*: This setting shows contacts, calendars, mail, and bookmarks to be synced.

Below the Settings section, there is a section called On My Device that allows you to view what's currently stored on the device.

If the iOS device is running iOS version 5 or higher and the computer it syncs with is running iTunes version 10.5 or higher, you can sync your iOS device by using Wi-Fi. Besides these minimum version requirements, a few things have to come together before this will work. The following list outlines these requirements.

- You must enable Sync with this iPhone over Wi-Fi within iTunes. This is done from the Summary tab in Settings, as shown in Figure 21.83.

- Apple states that the iOS device must be plugged into a source of power before a sync will occur. It has been demonstrated that given enough battery power, the iOS device will sync without being plugged in.

- The iOS device should not be plugged into the USB port of the computer with which it syncs. USB synchronization overrides Wi-Fi synchronization.

FIGURE 21.82   iTunes synchronization categories

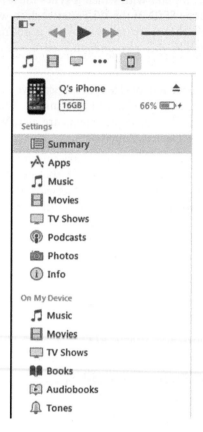

FIGURE 21.83   Enable sync over Wi-Fi

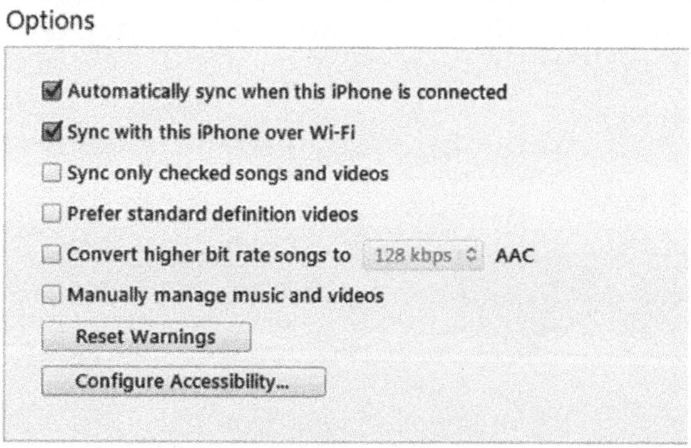

- The iOS device and the computer with which it syncs must be on the same Wi-Fi network, which means that the SSID of the Wi-Fi network to which they are attached is the same and you are sure that the wireless network is not misconfigured to produce a false positive result, such as with two unconnected WAPs configured with the same SSID.

- The computer with which the iOS device syncs must have iTunes running. Otherwise, the Sync Now button on the iOS device will be dimmed. When in this state, however, once iTunes is opened and all other requirements are met, Wi-Fi sync will begin automatically if not disabled in Devices Preferences.

For syncing over Wi-Fi to occur, it is not necessary to remove the wired connection of the computer running iTunes, if one exists. Although the computer will favor the use of the wired connection over the wireless link for regular network traffic, iTunes forces the communication to the iOS device to occur over the Wi-Fi link during establishment of the connection and synchronization.

If all of these conditions are met, you will be able to initiate synchronization from the iOS device. It's done through Settings ➤ General ➤ iTunes Wi-Fi Sync, as shown in Figure 21.84.

FIGURE 21.84 Sync Now option on an iPhone

••ooo Verizon 🛜   1:12 PM   🔋▸⚡

❮ General   iTunes Wi-Fi Sync

Automatically sync with iTunes on your computer when your iPhone is plugged in to power and connected to Wi-Fi.

Sync Now

Q-HP
Music

Last Sync: Today at 1:09 PM

You can tell when the device is syncing because the eject arrow to the right of the device name changes to the rotating sync icon, like the one in Figure 21.85. In Figure 21.85, you can also tell that this device is connected to the computer because the battery indicator is displayed. If it were syncing via Wi-Fi, the battery indicator would not be shown.

FIGURE 21.85   Device is syncing

If automatic synchronization is disabled in Devices Preferences, manual synchronization of an iOS device can be started by selecting the iOS device above the left frame in iTunes and then clicking the Sync button at the bottom-right corner of its Summary tab.

Using iCloud

So far, we've talked about syncing to the desktop, but we haven't mentioned an option that's becoming more popular, which is storing data on the cloud. Apple's version of the cloud is called iCloud, and it is available to all iOS users.

When a user creates an Apple ID, it's used to log into the iTunes store, but it can also be used for an iCloud account. Apple recommends that the same username be used for both, but it is not required. On the iOS device, it's easy to get to iCloud settings. Open the Settings app, and choose iCloud; the configuration page is shown in Figure 21.86.

At the top of the iCloud settings, it will show you what account you are using for iCloud (not pictured in Figure 21.86), the space available, and which types of data you are syncing or backing up. Simply slide the switch from off to on to turn on synchronization or backups. The default amount of storage space is 5GB; tapping Storage will give you an option to purchase more space if needed. Synchronization and backups will happen when the phone is plugged into a power source, locked, and connected to Wi-Fi.

FIGURE 21.86   iCloud configuration settings

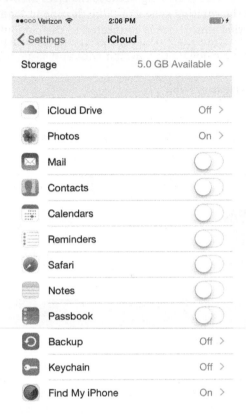

Syncing Android Devices

Just as with Apple's devices, mobile devices built for the Android operating system can be synced to a traditional computer. Apple's iTunes is proprietary and has been designated as the application that performs synchronization of iOS devices. In a similar way, manufacturers of Android devices have their own syncing utilities. Because this software and the connection methods allowed vary widely from one manufacturer to another, it is difficult to predict exactly what one manufacturer will offer in its utility and if each Android device it produces will interact the same way and over the same connections.

It should be assumed that, at a minimum, the same items that can be synced with iOS devices and iTunes can likely be synced for Android devices as well. What is also safe to assume is that no utility with the popularity and well-designed integration and features of iTunes exists for the Android market. Many manufacturers, however, create utilities that can tap into the playlists of iTunes and the data structures of Microsoft Outlook to obtain quite a bit of what they are looking for without the need to supply the same features in their own utilities. Don't be surprised when you see an Android device with an exact replica of a computer's iTunes playlist names as well as contents.

Many Android apps will use Google Drive as the preferred cloud storage location. Users can also elect to use Google Backup & Restore, but in general, the results are mixed and not quite as reliable as the iOS backup tools. Contacts are generally okay, but apps and settings may be hit or miss.

Software Installation Requirements

As with any software, minimum hardware and disk-space requirements exist for installing the software that allows synchronization of mobile devices. Any computer on which a user would install these software applications should have USB and Wi-Fi for connectivity. It never hurts to make sure, though. Here we'll outline the minimum requirements for installing iTunes and HTC Sync, a utility for the devices made by the popular manufacturer HTC.

Installation Requirements for iTunes

Apple's iTunes is available for Mac OS and Windows. The following sections list the hardware and software requirements for installing iTunes on each of these operating systems.

Windows Requirements

The following list details the minimum hardware requirements that a Windows machine must have in order to support the installation of iTunes version 12.2 (64-bit):

- 1GHz Intel or AMD processor
- 512MB of RAM
- To play standard definition video
    - Intel Pentium D processor
    - 512MB of RAM
    - DirectX 9.0–compatible video card
- To play 720p HD video, an iTunes LP, or iTunes Extras
    - 2.0GHz Intel Core 2 Duo processor
    - 1GB of RAM
    - Intel GMA X3000, ATI Radeon X1300, or NVIDIA GeForce 6150 video card
- To play 1080p HD video
    - 2.4GHz Intel Core 2 Duo processor
    - 2GB of RAM
    - Intel GMA X4500HD; ATI Radeon HD 2400; NVIDIA GeForce 8300 GS video card
- Screen resolution of 1024×768 or greater; 1280×800 or greater to play an iTunes LP or iTunes Extras
- 16-bit sound card and speakers
- Broadband Internet connection
- iTunes-compatible CD or DVD recorder (optional)

- Only certain versions of Windows support iTunes. The following list contains the software requirements for installing iTunes in Windows:
- Windows 7 or newer
- The iTunes 64-bit installer for 64-bit editions Windows 7 or Windows 8
- 400MB of available disk space

Mac Requirements

Apple includes iTunes in its operating system and on each of its new machines. Nevertheless, Apple publishes minimum hardware and software requirements for the installation of iTunes 12.2 on a Macintosh. The following list includes hardware requirements:

- Mac computer with an Intel processor
- 512MB of RAM
- To play 720p HD video, an iTunes LP, or iTunes Extras
  - 2.0GHz Intel Core 2 Duo processor
  - 1GB of RAM
- To play 1080p HD video
  - 2.4GHz Intel Core 2 Duo processor
  - 2GB of RAM
- Screen resolution of 1024×768 or greater; 1280×800 or greater to play an iTunes LP or iTunes Extras
- Broadband Internet connection
- Apple combo drive or SuperDrive (optional)

The Macintosh software requirements are shown in the following list:

- Mac OS X version 10.7.5; Apple Music requires OS X version 10.9.5.
- 400MB of available disk space.
- iTunes Extras requires OS X 10.10.3.

Installation Requirements for HTC Sync

A very popular manufacturer of mobile devices, HTC produces its own utilities for syncing its devices to your computer. Its popular HTC Sync Manager supports most HTC devices. Older devices with HTC Sense 3.6 or older need to use the HTC Sync app. Syncing with HTC Sync Manager requires a USB 2.0 connection.

The following list outlines the capabilities of HTC Sync Manager. Note the similarity to general syncing interests as well as to those specific to iTunes:

- Synchronize Outlook contacts and calendar or Outlook Express contacts
- Synchronize web browser bookmarks

- Install third-party Android applications
- Bring the following items to your phone:
    - Photos
    - Videos
    - Documents
    - Songs
    - Playlists

Because we are interested in establishing the basic functionality that allows synchronization to occur, let's take a look at the system requirements for installing HTC Sync Manager. You'll notice that they are in line with those for installing iTunes. HTC Sync Manager is supported for both PC and Mac.

This list specifies the minimum hardware requirements that a Windows machine must have to support the installation of HTC Sync Manager's current version:

- Intel or AMD dual-core processor, minimum 2GHz
- 2GB of RAM
- 1024×768 resolution video adapter and monitor
- 512MB of available free hard disk space
- USB 2.0

The software requirements in the following list are similar as well:

- Windows XP Home/Professional/Media Center Edition Service Pack 2 and 3 (32-bit)
- Windows Vista Ultimate/Enterprise/Business/Home Premium/Home Basic Edition (32-bit and 64-bit) Service Pack 1
- Windows 7 Ultimate/Professional/Home Premium/Home Basic Edition (32-bit and 64-bit)
- Microsoft Office Outlook 2003, 2007, 2010, or 2013 (32-bit and 64-bit)

For a Mac, here are the hardware requirements:

- Intel processor
- 512MB RAM
- 1024×768 resolution video adapter and monitor
- 100MB of available free hard disk space
- USB 2.0

The software requirements are in the following list:

- Mac OS X 10.6
- Microsoft Office for Mac 2011

NOTE If you use the older HTC Sync app, HTC reminds you to enable USB debugging to make sure that it works properly. This setting is for developers and for applications to gain a deeper access to the resources of the device. Most apps don't require it, but some, such as HTC Sync, cannot function properly or consistently without it. To make sure that USB debugging is enabled on your HTC Android device, select Settings ➢ Applications ➢ Development and check the box beside USB Debugging. You should disconnect and reconnect the device after making this change.

Summary

This chapter introduced you to mobile operating systems and specifically the two most popular mobile platforms: Apple's iOS and Google's Android. The primary concepts demonstrated in the course of this chapter included the basic features of the two operating systems, how to establish network connectivity and configure email clients, and how to synchronize mobile devices with conventional computer systems.

Exam Essentials

Be able to explain the differences and similarities between iOS and Android operating systems. Although all mobile devices inherently resemble one another, there are an ample number of distinct features that set each major platform apart from one another. It is important that you are able to discuss such differences as well as what is similar.

Know how to connect a mobile device to a wireless network. Wi-Fi networks have a strict set of guidelines for connectivity. This means that the procedure for connecting disparate devices is quite similar. However, each mobile operating system has its own sequence of screens and selections to make the connection to wireless networks. Familiarize yourself with the procedure in each platform.

Familiarize yourself with configuring email clients on mobile devices. Similar to the way that you can configure a laptop or desktop computer to access popular email services, you can configure mobile devices. Be able to interface automatically and manually with Internet mail services as well as with Exchange mail servers.

Know how to synchronize mobile devices with larger computer systems. Mobile devices are marvels of modern computing science, but their portability lends itself to loss and damage. Synchronization affords the user the ability to recover from even the most disastrous of circumstances. The key is to synchronize often, which should include the creation of full-system backups that are stored on a computer system separate from the mobile device and the ability to restore to the same or new mobile device if the need arises.

Review Questions

The answers to the chapter review questions can be found in Appendix A.

1. Which of the following is *not* a difference between iOS and Android?

   A. Android is not a proprietary operating system.

   B. You can download iOS apps from only one place.

   C. You can make a cellular phone call from all Android devices.

   D. It costs more to be a developer of iOS apps.

2. You want to create an Android application. Which of the following do you need to download and use?

   A. APK

   B. IPA

   C. SDK

   D. SPK

3. Bob's iPhone 4S cannot detect when he turns his device to the left and right like it's a steering wheel. Games and other apps that require this motion will not work correctly as a result. Which component has failed in Bob's phone?

   A. Gyroscope

   B. Accelerometer

   C. Magnetometer

   D. GPS

4. Which of the following is more likely to be associated with a resistive touchscreen versus a capacitive one?

   A. You won't have to apply as much pressure.

   B. You will need to recalibrate it.

   C. You will have to clean it more often for optimal functionality.

   D. You can use the pad of your finger instead of your fingernail.

5. Which of the following are text-messaging services used with mobile devices? (Choose two.)

   A. SMS

   B. SIP

   C. Androtext

   D. iOS Messaging

   E. MMS

6. Which of the following is *not* a valid reason to disable cellular data networking?

   A. You have a limited amount of data in your monthly plan.

   B. You have access to a reliable Wi-Fi signal.

    C. You are about to download an update to your phone.

    D. Your phone calls are going out over your carrier's cellular network.

7. Which of the following is a characteristic of Bluetooth?

    A. Bluetooth connections support wireless device control but not file transfers.

    B. Bluetooth is not yet a fully standardized protocol.

    C. Bluetooth connections do not reach as far as Wi-Fi connections.

    D. You must reboot paired devices to complete connection establishment.

8. What is the default TCP port number for SMTP?

    A. 25

    B. 110

    C. 143

    D. 995

9. Which mail protocol commonly uses TCP port 587?

    A. SMTP with SSL

    B. SMTP with TLS

    C. IMAP4 with SSL/TLS

    D. POP3 with SSL/TLS

10. You have enabled Wi-Fi calling on your new mobile device. You are on a cellular call within your Wi-Fi network's range and you lose the cellular signal. What happens to your call?

    A. It gets dropped.

    B. It will seamlessly switch over to Wi-Fi.

    C. The phone will beep at you and then switch to Wi-Fi.

    D. The phone will beep at you, and you need to tap Confirm to switch to Wi-Fi.

11. Which technology built into some mobile phones allows for the user to pass the phone close to a receiver to make an electronic payment, without the phone touching the receiver?

    A. Bluetooth

    B. APC

    C. RPS

    D. NFC

12. Which two communications technologies can you use to create a VPN connection?

    A. Bluetooth

    B. Wi-Fi

    C. Cellular

    D. NFC

13. Which software component of a mobile phone is responsible for managing all wireless communications?

    A. Either iOS or Android OS

    B. SIM OS

    C. Baseband OS

    D. Wireless OS

14. Which two of the following are examples of RTOSs?

    A. SIM OS

    B. Baseband OS

    C. iOS

    D. Android

15. Which standard is used to encrypt and decrypt email messages on mobile devices?

    A. SSL

    B. TLS

    C. MMS

    D. S/MIME

16. Which of the following are universally common items that are synced between a mobile device and a larger computer? (Choose three.)

    A. Office documents

    B. Contacts

    C. Operating system files

    D. Email

    E. Configuration settings

    F. Apps

17. Which of the following is *not* a requirement for installing iTunes on a Windows machine?

    A. A 1GHz processor or better

    B. 1GB of RAM or higher

    C. 400MB of available disk space

    D. Broadband Internet connection

18. Which of the following statements about configuring email access on a mobile device is true?

    A. Most Internet mail services offer an Exchange option.

    B. The TCP ports used for configuring access are usually standard port numbers.

    C. Most ports used for access are UDP ports.

    D. You must download third-party apps for connecting to email services.

19. Which of the following are disabled when airplane mode is switched on? (Choose all that apply.)

   A. Cellular

   B. Wi-Fi

   C. Bluetooth

   D. NFC

   E. Settings app

   F. Lock screen

20. You have a Verizon 4G mobile phone that you want to use as a mobile hotspot. How many connections are you allowed to support simultaneously on that device?

   A. 3

   B. 5

   C. 10

   D. 20

Performance-Based Question

You will encounter performance-based questions on the A+ exams. The questions on the exam require you to perform a specific task, and you will be graded on whether or not you were able to complete the task. The following requires you to think creatively in order to measure how well you understand this chapter's topics. You may or may not see similar questions on the actual A+ exams. To see how your answers compare to the authors', refer to Appendix B.

   Explain how to establish Wi-Fi connectivity on an Apple iPhone.

Chapter

22

Troubleshooting Theory, OSs, and Security

THE FOLLOWING COMPTIA A+ 220-902 EXAM OBJECTIVES ARE COVERED IN THIS CHAPTER:

✓ **4.1 Given a scenario, troubleshoot PC operating system problems with appropriate tools.**

- Common symptoms: Proprietary crash screens (BSOD/pin wheel), Failure to boot, Improper shutdown, Spontaneous shutdown/restart, Device fails to start/detected, Missing dll message, Services fail to start, Compatibility error, Slow system performance, Boots to safe mode, File fails to open, Missing NTLDR, Missing Boot Configuration Data, Missing operating system, Missing graphical interface, Missing GRUB/LILO, Kernel panic, Graphical interface fails to load, Multiple monitor misalignment/orientation

- Tools: BIOS/UEFI, SFC, Logs, System Recovery Options, Repair disks, Pre-installation environments, MSCONFIG, DEFRAG, REGSRV32, REGEDIT, Event viewer, Safe mode, Command prompt, Uninstall/reinstall/repair

✓ **4.2 Given a scenario, troubleshoot common PC security issues with appropriate tools and best practices.**

- Common symptoms: Pop-ups, Browser redirection, Security alerts, Slow performance, Internet connectivity issues, PC/OS lock up, Application crash, OS updates failures, Rogue antivirus, Spam, Renamed system files, Files disappearing, File permission changes, Hijacked email (Response from users regarding email, Automated replies from unknown sent email), Access denied, Invalid certificate (trusted root CA)

- Tools: Antivirus software, Antimalware software, Recovery console, Terminal, System restore/Snapshot, Pre-installation environments, Event viewer, Refresh/restore, MSCONFIG/ Safe boot

- Best practices for malware removal: 1. Identify malware symptoms, 2. Quarantine infected system, 3. Disable system restore (in Windows), 4. Remediate infected systems (a. Update antimalware software, b. Scan and removal techniques (safe mode, pre-installation environment)), 5. Schedule scans and run updates, 6. Enable system restore and create restore point (in Windows), 7. Educate end user

✓ **4.3 Given a scenario, troubleshoot common mobile OS and application issues with appropriate tools.**

- Common symptoms: Dim display, Intermittent wireless, No wireless connectivity, No Bluetooth connectivity, Cannot broadcast to external monitor, Touchscreen non-responsive, Apps not loading, Slow performance, Unable to decrypt email, Extremely short battery life, Overheating, Frozen system, No sound from speakers, Inaccurate touch screen response, System lockout

- Tools: Hard reset, Soft reset, Close running applications, Reset to factory default, Adjust configurations/settings, Uninstall/reinstall apps, Force stop

✓ **4.4 Given a scenario, troubleshoot common mobile OS and application security issues with appropriate tools.**

- Common symptoms: Signal drop/weak signal, Power drain, Slow data speeds, Unintended WiFi connection, Unintended Bluetooth pairing, Leaked personal files/data, Data transmission overlimit, Unauthorized account access, Unauthorized root access, Unauthorized location tracking, Unauthorized camera/microphone activation, High resource utilization

- Tools: Antimalware, App scanner, Factory reset/Clean Install, Uninstall/reinstall apps, WiFi analyzer, Force stop, Cell tower analyzer, Backup/restore (iTunes/iCloud/Apple Configurator, Google sync, One Drive)

✓ **5.5 Given a scenario, explain the troubleshooting theory.**

- Always consider corporate policies, procedures and impacts before implementing changes.

1. Identify the problem: Question the user and identify user changes to computer and perform backups before making changes.

2. Establish a theory of probable cause (question the obvious): If necessary, conduct external or internal research based on symptoms.

3. Test the theory to determine cause: Once theory is confirmed, determine next steps to resolve problem. If theory is not confirmed, re-establish new theory or escalate.

4. Establish a plan of action to resolve the problem and implement the solution.

5. Verify full system functionality and if applicable implement preventive measures.

6. Document findings, actions and outcomes.

Mentioning the words *troubleshooting theory* to many technicians can cause their eyes to roll back in their heads. It doesn't sound glamorous or sexy, and a lot of techs believe that the only way to solve a problem is just to dive right in and start working on it. Theories are for academics. In a way, they're right—you do need to dive in to solve problems because they don't just solve themselves. But to be successful at troubleshooting, you must take a systematic approach.

You may hear people say, "Troubleshooting is as much of an art as it is a science," and our personal favorite, "You just need to get more experience to be good at it." While there is an art to fixing problems, you can't ignore science. And if you need experience to be any good, why are some less experienced folks incredibly good at solving problems while their more seasoned counterparts seem to take forever to fix anything? More experience is good, but it's not a prerequisite to being a good troubleshooter. It's all about a systematic approach.

Applying a systematic approach to troubleshooting is key; systematic solutions also work well in preventing problems in the first place. Many of the computer problems that you stress over can be prevented.

Preventive maintenance tends to get neglected at many companies because technicians are too busy fixing problems. Spending some time on keeping those problems from occurring in the first place is a good investment of resources.

In this chapter, we'll look at the two systematic methods we just talked about. First we'll cover troubleshooting theory and the steps that you need to take to solve problems successfully. Then we'll look at some ways to help keep your systems running and in top shape.

Understanding Troubleshooting Theory

No matter how skilled you may be at troubleshooting, always consider corporate policies, procedures and impacts before implementing any changes.

When troubleshooting, you should assess every problem systematically and try to isolate the root cause. Yes, there is a lot of art to troubleshooting, and experience plays a part too. But regardless of how "artful" or experienced you are, haphazard troubleshooting is doomed to fail. Conversely, even technicians with limited experience can be effective troubleshooters if they stick to the principles. The major key is to start with the issue and whittle away at it until you can get down to the point where you can pinpoint the problem—this often means eliminating, or verifying, the obvious.

Although everyone approaches troubleshooting from a different perspective, a few things should remain constant. First, always back up your data before making any changes to a system. Hardware components can be replaced, but data often can't be. For that reason, always be vigilant about making data backups.

Second, establish priorities—one user being unable to print to the printer of their choice isn't as important as a floor full of accountants unable to run payroll. Prioritize every job and escalate it (or de-escalate it) as you need to.

Third, but perhaps most important, document everything—not just that there was a problem but also the solution that you found, the actions that you tried, and the outcome of each. In the next few sections, we'll take you through each step of the troubleshooting process.

Identifying the Problem

While this may seem obvious, it can't be overlooked: If you can't define the problem, you can't begin to solve it. Sometimes, problems are relatively straightforward, but other times they're just a symptom of a bigger issue. For example, if a user isn't able to connect to the Internet from their computer, it could indeed be an issue with their system. But if other users are having similar problems, then the first user's difficulties might just be one example of the real problem.

 Ask yourself, "Is there a problem?" Perhaps "the problem" is as simple as a customer expecting too much from the computer.

Problems in computer systems generally occur in one (or more) of four areas, each of which is in turn made up of many pieces:

- A *collection of hardware pieces* integrated into a working system. As you know, the hardware can be quite complex, what with motherboards, hard drives, video cards, and so on. Software can be equally perplexing.
- An *operating system*, which in turn is dependent on the hardware.
- An *application* or software program that is supposed to do something. Programs such as Microsoft Word and Microsoft Excel are bundled with a great many features.
- A *computer user*, ready to take the computer system to its limits (and beyond). A technician can often forget that the user is a very complex and important part of the puzzle.

Talking to the Customer

Many times, you can define the problem by asking questions of the user. One of the keys to working with your users or customers is to ensure, much like a medical professional, that you have good bedside manner. Most people are not as technically hip as you, and when something goes wrong, they become confused or even fearful that they'll take the blame. Assure them that you're just trying to fix the problem but that they can probably help because they know what went on before you got there. It's important to instill trust with your customer—believe what they are saying, but also believe that they might not tell you everything right away. It's not that they're necessarily holding back information; they just might not know what's important to tell.

Real World Scenario

Is the Power On?

It's a classic IT story that almost sounds like a joke, but it happened. A customer calls technical support because their computer won't turn on. After 20 minutes of trouble-shooting, the technician is becoming frustrated. . .maybe it's a bad power supply? The technician asks the user to read some numbers off of the back of their computer, and the user says, "Hold on, I need to get a flashlight. It's dark in here with the power out."

Help clarify things by having the customer show you what the problem is. The best method we've seen of doing this is to say, "Show me what 'not working' looks like." That way, you see the conditions and methods under which the problem occurs. The problem may be a simple matter of an improper method. The user may be performing an operation incorrectly or performing the operation in the wrong order. During this step, you have the opportunity to observe how the problem occurs, so pay attention.

Here are a few questions to ask the user to aid in determining the problem:

Can you show me the problem?   This question is one of the best. It allows the user to show you exactly where and when they experience the problem.

How often does this happen?   This question establishes whether this problem is a one-time occurrence that can be solved with a reboot or whether a specific sequence of events causes the problem to happen. The latter usually indicates a more serious problem that may require software installation or hardware replacement.

Has any new hardware or software been installed recently?   New hardware or software can mean compatibility problems with existing devices or applications. For example, a newly installed device may want to use the same resource settings as an existing device. This can cause both devices to become disabled. When you install a new application, that application is likely to install several support files. If those support files are also used by an existing application, then there could be a conflict.

Has the computer recently been moved?   Moving a computer can cause things to become loose and then fail to work. Perhaps all of the peripherals of the computer didn't complete—or weren't included in—the move, meaning that there's less functionality than the user expects.

Has someone who normally doesn't use the computer recently used it?   That person could have mistakenly (or intentionally) done something to make the computer begin exhibiting the irregular behavior.

Have any other changes been made to the computer recently?   If the answer is yes, ask if the user can remember approximately when the change was made. Then ask them to tell you approximately when the problem started. If the two dates seem related, there's a good chance that the problem is related to the change. If it's a new hardware component, check to see that it was installed correctly.

Be careful of how you ask questions so that you don't appear accusatory. You can't assume that the user did something to mess up the computer. Then again, you also can't assume that they don't know anything about why it's not working.

 Real World Scenario

The Social Side of Troubleshooting

When you're looking for clues as to the nature of a problem, no one can give you more information than the person who was there when it happened. They can tell you what led up to the problem, what software was running, and the exact nature of the problem ("It happened when I tried to print"), and they can help you re-create the problem, if possible.

Use questioning techniques that are neutral in nature. Instead of saying, "What were you doing when it broke?" be more compassionate and say, "What was going on when the computer decided not to work?" Frame the question in a way that makes it sound like the computer did something wrong, and not the person. It might sound silly, but these things can make your job a lot easier!

While it's sometimes frustrating dealing with end users and computer problems, such as the user who calls you up and gives you the "My computer's not working" line (okay, and what *exactly* is that supposed to mean?), even more frustrating is when no one was around to see what happened. In cases like this, do your best to find out where the problem is by establishing what works and what does not.

Gathering Information

Let's say that you get to a computer and the power light is on and you can hear the hard drive spinning but there is no video and the system seems to be unresponsive. At least you know that the system has power, and you can start investigating where things start to break down. (We sense a reboot in your future!)

The whole key to this step is to identify, as specifically as possible, what the problem is. The more specific you can be in identifying what's not working, the easier it will be for you to understand why it's not working and how to fix it. If you have users available who were there when the computer stopped working, you can try to gather information from them. If not, you're on your own to gather clues. It's like *CSI* but not as gory.

So now instead of having users to question, you need to use your own investigative services to determine what's wrong. The questions you would have otherwise asked the user are still a good starting point. Does anything appear amiss or seem to have been changed recently? What is working and what is not? Was there a storm recently? Can I reboot? If I reboot, does the problem seem to go away?

If a computer seems to have multiple problems that appear to be unrelated, identify what they are one at a time and fix them one at a time. For example, if the sound is not working and you can't get on the Internet, deal with those separately. If they seem related, such as not being able to get on the Internet or access a network file server, then one solution might solve both problems.

The key is to find out everything that you can that might be related to the problem. Document exactly what works and what doesn't and, if you can, why. If the power is out in the house, as in the story related earlier, then there's no sense in trying the power cord in another outlet.

Determining If the Problem Is Hardware or Software Related

This step is important because it determines the part of the computer on which you should focus your troubleshooting skills. Each part requires different skills and different tools.

To determine whether a problem is hardware or software related, you can do a few things to narrow down the issue. For instance, does the problem manifest itself when the user uses a particular piece of hardware (a DVD-ROM or a USB hard drive, for example)? If it does, the problem is more than likely hardware related.

This step relies on personal experience more than any of the other steps. Without a doubt, you'll run into strange software problems. Each one has a particular solution. Some may even require reinstallation of an application or the operating system. If that doesn't work, you may need to resort to restoring the entire system (operating system, applications, and data) from a data backup done when the computer was working properly.

Determining Which Component Is Failing (for Hardware Problems)

Hardware problems are usually pretty easy to figure out. Let's say that the sound card doesn't work. You've tried new speakers that you know do work, and you've reinstalled the driver. All of the settings look right, but it just won't respond. The sound card is probably the piece of hardware that needs to be replaced.

With many newer computers, several components such as sound, video, and networking cards are integrated into the motherboard. If you troubleshoot the computer and find a hardware component to be bad, there's a good chance that the bad component is integrated into the motherboard and the whole motherboard must be replaced—an expensive proposition, to be sure.

Laptops and a lot of desktops have components (network card, sound card, video adapter) integrated into the motherboard. If an integrated component fails, you may be able to use an expansion device (such as a USB or PC Card network adapter) to give the system full functionality without a costly repair.

Establishing a Theory

Way back when, probably in your middle school or junior high school years, you learned about the scientific method. In a nutshell, scientists develop a hypothesis, test it, and then figure out if their hypothesis is still valid. Troubleshooting involves much the same process.

Once you have determined what the problem is, you need to develop a theory as to why it is happening. No video? It could be something to do with the monitor or the video card. Can't get to your favorite website? Is it that site? Is it your network card, the cable, your IP address, DNS server settings, or something else? Once you have defined the problem, establishing a theory about the cause of the problem—what is wrong—helps you develop possible solutions to the problem.

Eliminating Possibilities

Theories can state either what can be true or what can't be true. However you choose to approach your theory generation, it's usually helpful to take a mental inventory to see what is possible and what is not. Start eliminating possibilities, and eventually the only thing that's left is what's wrong. This type of approach works well when it's an ambiguous problem; start broad and narrow your scope. For example, if the hard drive won't read, there is likely one of three culprits: the drive itself, the cable it's on, or the connector on the motherboard. Try plugging the drive into another connector or using a different cable. Narrow down the options.

A common troubleshooting technique is to strip the system down to the bare bones. In a hardware situation, this could mean removing all interface cards except those that are absolutely required for the system to operate. In a software situation, this usually means booting up in Windows Safe Mode so that most of the drivers do not load.

Once you have isolated the problem, slowly rebuild the system to see if the problem comes back (or goes away). This helps you identify what is really causing the problem and determine if there are other factors affecting the situation. For example, we have seen memory problems that are fixed by switching the slot containing the memory chips.

Using External Resources

Sometimes, you can figure out what's not working, but you have no idea why or what you can do to fix it. That's okay. In situations like these, it may be best to fall back on an old trick called reading the manual. As they say, "When all else fails, read the instructions." The service manuals are your instructions for troubleshooting and service information. Virtually every computer and peripheral made today has service documentation on the company's website, a DVD, or even in a paper manual. Don't be afraid to use them!

If you're lucky enough to have experienced, knowledgeable, and friendly co-workers, be open to asking for help if you get stuck on a problem.

Before starting to eliminate possibilities, check the vendor's website for any information that might help you. For example, typing in a specific error message on a vendor's website might take you directly to specific steps to fix the problem.

Testing Solutions

You've eliminated possibilities and developed a theory as to what the problem is. Your theory may be pretty specific, such as "the power cable is fried," or it may be a bit more general, like "the hard drive isn't working" or "there's a connectivity problem." No matter your theory, now is the time to start testing solutions. Again, if you're not sure where to begin to find a solution, the manufacturer's website is a good place to start!

Check the Simple Stuff First

This step is the one that even experienced technicians overlook. Often, computer problems are the result of something simple. Technicians overlook these problems because they're so simple that the technicians assume they *couldn't* be the problem. Here are some examples of simple problems:

Is it plugged in?   And plugged in at both ends? Cables must be plugged in at *both ends* to function correctly. Cables can easily be tripped over and inadvertently pulled from their sockets.

 Real World Scenario

"Is It Plugged In?" and Other Insulting Questions

Think about how you feel if someone asks you this question. Your likely response is, "Of course it is!" After all, you're not an idiot, right? You'll often get the same reaction to similar questions about the device being turned on. The problem is, making sure that it's plugged in and turned on are the first things that you should always do when investigating a problem.

When asking these types of questions, it's not what you say but how you say it. For example, instead of asking if it's plugged in, you could say something like, "Can you do me a favor and check to see what color the end of the keyboard plug is? Is that the same color of the port it's plugged into on the computer?" That generally gets the user at least to look at it without making them feel dumb. For power, something like, "What color are the lights on the front of the router? Are any of them blinking?" can work well.

Ask neutral and nonthreatening questions. Make it sound like the computer is at fault, not the user. These types of things will help you build rapport and you'll be able to get more information so that you can solve problems faster.

Is it turned on?   This one seems the most obvious, but we've all fallen victim to it at one point or another. Computers and their peripherals must be turned on to function. Most have power switches with LEDs that glow when the power is turned on.

Is the system ready?   Computers must be ready before they can be used. *Ready* means that the system is ready to accept commands from the user. An indication that a computer is ready is when the operating system screens come up and the computer presents you with a menu or a command prompt. If that computer uses a graphical interface, the computer is ready when the mouse pointer appears. Printers are ready when the Online or Ready light on the front panel is lit.

Do the chips and cables need to be reseated?   You can solve some of the strangest problems (random hang-ups or errors) by opening the case and pressing down on each socketed chip (known as *reseating*). This remedies the chip-creep problem, which happens when computers heat up and cool down repeatedly as a result of being turned on and off, causing some components to begin to move out of their sockets. In addition, you should reseat any cables to make sure that they're making good contact.

WARNING   Always be sure that you're grounded before operating inside the case! If you're not, you could create a static charge (ESD) that could damage components.

Check to See If It's User Error

User error is common but preventable. If a user can't perform some very common computer task, such as printing or saving a file, the problem is likely due to user error. As soon as you hear of a problem like this, you should begin asking questions to determine if the solution is as simple as teaching the user the correct procedure. A good question to ask is, "Were you *ever* able to perform that task?" If the answer is no, it means that they are probably doing the procedure wrong. If they answer yes, you must ask additional questions to get at the root of the problem.

If you suspect user error, tread carefully in regard to your line of questioning to avoid making the user feel defensive. User errors provide an opportunity to teach the users the right way to do things. Again, what you say matters. Offer a "different" or "another" way of doing things instead of the "right" way.

Restart the Computer

It's amazing how often a simple computer restart can solve a problem. Restarting the computer clears the memory and starts the computer with a clean slate. Whenever we perform phone support, we always ask the customer to restart the computer and try again. If restarting doesn't work, try powering down the system completely and then powering it up again (rebooting). More often than not, that will solve the problem.

Establishing a Plan of Action

If your fix worked, then you're brilliant! If not, you need to reevaluate and look for the next option. After testing solutions, your plan of action may take one of three paths:

- If the first fix didn't work, try something else.

- If needed, implement the fix on other computers.
- If everything is working, document the solution.

 Real World Scenario

Reboot First, Ask Questions Later

If you're running into a software problem on a computer, the first step (after understanding what the problem is and getting any relevant error messages written down or captured in a screen grab) should always be to reboot. Many times, the problem will go away and your work there is done. If it goes away, then it's no longer a problem!

Try, Try Again

So you tried the hard drive with a new (verified) cable and it still doesn't work. Now what? Your sound card won't play and you've just deleted and reinstalled the driver. Next steps? Move on and try the next logical thing in line.

> When trying solutions to fix a problem, make only one change to the computer at a time. If the change doesn't fix the problem, revert the system back to the way it was and then make your next change. Making more than one change at a time is not recommended for two reasons: One, you are never sure which change actually worked, and two, by making multiple changes at once, you might actually cause additional problems.

When evaluating your results and looking for that golden "next step," don't forget about other resources that you might have available. Use the Internet to look at the manufacturer's website. Read the manual. Talk to your friend who knows everything about obscure hardware (or arcane versions of Windows). When fixing problems, two heads can be better than one.

Spread the Solution

If the problem was isolated to one computer, this step doesn't apply. But some problems that you deal with may affect an entire group of computers. For example, perhaps some configuration information was entered incorrectly into the DHCP server, giving everyone the wrong DNS server address. The DHCP server is now fixed, but all of the clients need to renew their IP addresses.

Document the Solution

Once everything is working, you'll need to document what happened and how you fixed it. If the problem looks to be long and complex, we suggest taking notes as you're trying to fix it. It will help you remember what you've already tried and what didn't work. We'll discuss documenting in more depth in the section "Documenting the Work" later in this chapter.

Verifying Functionality

After fixing the system, or all of the systems affected by the problem, go back and verify full functionality. For example, if the users couldn't get to any network resources, check to make sure they can get to the Internet as well as to internal resources.

Some solutions may actually cause another problem on the system. For example, if you update software or drivers, you may inadvertently cause another application to have problems. There's obviously no way that you can or should test all applications on a computer after applying a fix, but know that these types of problems can occur. Just make sure that what you've fixed works and that there aren't any obvious signs of something else not working all of a sudden.

Another important thing to do at this time is to implement preventive measures, if possible. If it was a user error, ensure that the user understands ways to accomplish the task that doesn't cause the error to recur. If a cable melted because it was too close to someone's space heater under their desk, resolve the issue. If the computer overheated because there was an inch of dust clogging the fan…you get the idea.

Documenting the Work

Lots of people can fix problems. But can you remember what you did when you fixed a problem a month ago? Maybe. Can one of your co-workers remember something you did to fix the same problem on that machine a month ago? Unlikely. Always document your work so that you or someone else can learn from the experience. Good documentation of past troubleshooting can save hours of stress in the future.

Documentation can take a few different forms, but the two most common are personal and system based.

We always recommend that technicians carry a personal notebook and take notes. The type of notebook doesn't matter—use whatever works best for you. The notebook can be a lifesaver, especially when you're new to a job. Write down the problem, what you tried, and the solution. The next time you run across the same or a similar problem, you'll have a better idea of what to try. Eventually, you'll find yourself less and less reliant on it, but it's incredibly handy to have!

System-based documentation is useful to both you and your co-workers. Many facilities have server logs of one type or another, conveniently located close to the machine. If someone makes a fix or a change, it gets noted in the log. If there's a problem, it's noted in the log. It's critical to have a log for a few reasons. One, if you weren't there the first time it was fixed, you might not have an idea of what to try, and it could take you a long time using trial and error. Two, if you begin to see a repeated pattern of problems, you can make a permanent intervention before the system completely dies.

We've seen several different forms of system-based documentation. Again, the type of log doesn't matter as long as you use it! Often, it's a notebook or a binder next to the system or on a nearby shelf. If you have a rack, you can mount something on the side to hold a binder or notebook. For client computers, one way is to tape an index card to the top or side of the power supply (don't cover any vents!), so if a tech has to go inside the case, they can see if anyone else has been in there fixing something too. In larger environments, there is often an electronic knowledge base or incident repository available for use; it is just as important to contribute to these systems as it is to use them to help diagnose problems.

 Real World Scenario

If It Ain't Broke. . .

When doctors take the Hippocratic oath, they promise to not make their patients any sicker than they already are. Technicians should take a similar oath. It all boils down to "If it ain't broke, don't fix it." When you troubleshoot, make one change at a time. If the change doesn't solve the problem, revert the computer to its previous state before making a different change. Otherwise, you could cause more problems than you started with. There's no sense in making things more difficult than they need to be!

Troubleshooting Operating Systems

Windows is mind-bogglingly complex. Other operating systems are too, but the mere fact that Windows 7 has nearly 50 million lines of code (and over 2,000 developers worked on it!) makes you pause and shake your head.

Windows-based issues can be grouped into several categories based on their cause, such as boot problems, missing files (such as system files), configuration files, and virtual memory. If you're troubleshooting a boot problem, it's imperative that you understand the Windows boot process. Some common Windows problems don't fall into any category other than "common Windows problems." We cover those in the following sections, followed by a discussion of the tools that can be used to fix them.

Common Symptoms

There are numerous "common symptoms" that CompTIA asks you be familiar with for the exam. They range from the dreaded Blue Screen of Death (BSOD) to spontaneous restarts and everything in between. They are discussed here in the order in which they appear in the objective list.

Proprietary Crash Screens (BSOD/Pinwheel)/Kernel Panic

The *Blue Screen of Death (BSOD)*—not a technical term, by the way—is another way of describing the blue-screen error condition that occurs when Windows fails to boot properly or quits unexpectedly. Because it is at this stage that the device drivers for the various pieces of hardware are installed/loaded, if your Windows GUI fails to start properly, more likely than not the problem is related to a misconfigured driver or misconfigured hardware.

There are a few things that you can try if you believe that a driver is causing the problem. One is to try booting Windows in *Safe Mode*. In Safe Mode, Windows loads only basic drivers, such as a standard VGA video driver and the keyboard and mouse. Once in Safe Mode, you can uninstall the driver that you think is causing the problem. Another option is to boot into the last known good configuration. Doing this will revert the system drivers back to the state they were in during the last successful login. Bear in mind that the Last Known Good Configuration option is useful only if the user has not logged in again since the problem began occurring. If the problem is with a driver and the user has logged in since the driver went "bad," the last known good configuration will include the bad driver.

In the Apple world, the pinwheel is equivalent to BSOD, so named because the cursor turns into a pinwheel and does not let you do anything else. The only solution is to force a shutdown and reboot.

In the Unix/Linux world (which includes OS X), the equivalent crash is known as a kernel panic. This occurs when the operating system detects an error from which it cannot safely recover—rather than one app crashing, the whole system does. Solutions usually include updating hardware, firmware, software, and the OS itself. You can also check drives and RAM for errors that might be causing the crash and correct any problems that you uncover.

Failure to Boot

To troubleshoot boot problems, you must understand the Windows boot process. Windows requires only a few files to boot, each of which performs specific tasks. The main one, and the first one to load, is the one that bootstraps the system. In other words, this file starts the loading of an OS on the computer. While Windows 8/7/Vista uses BOOTMGR, CompTIA also wants you to know NTLDR, which is the equivalent file used by Windows XP and earlier Windows versions. Whichever of the two files the operating system uses, that file is responsible for switching from real to protected mode during the boot process.

Even though the only Windows operating systems mentioned in the objectives are Windows 8/8.1, Windows 7, and Windows Vista, CompTIA also lists files for earlier Windows versions in the objectives. Because of that, in addition to NTLDR, there are five other XP-era files with which you should be familiar:

BOOT.INI   Holds information about which OSs are installed on the computer. This file also contains the location of the OS files with Windows XP and earlier Windows operating systems. Windows 8/7/Vista use Boot

Configuration Data (BCD) in place of the BOOT.INI file, and it is configured with BCDEDIT.EXE.

NTDETECT.COM   In Windows XP, it parses the system for hardware information each time Windows is loaded. This information is then used to create dynamic hardware information in the Registry.

NTBOOTDD.SYS   On a Windows XP system with a SCSI boot device, this file is used to recognize and load the SCSI interface. On EIDE systems, this file is not needed and is not even installed.

NTOSKRNL.EXE   The Windows OS kernel. The solution to a corrupted NTOSKRNL .EXE file is to boot from a startup disk and replace the file from the setup media.

NTBTLOG.TXT   While not an executable file, this log file is very important; it holds the information collected if you choose to boot using the Boot Logging startup option.

System files come into the picture next. In addition to the previously listed files, all of which (except NTOSKRNL.EXE) are located in the root of the C: partition on the computer, Windows needs a number of files from its system directories (for example, system and system32), such as the hardware abstraction layer (HAL.DLL). In Windows 8/7/Vista, WINLOAD.EXE and WINRESUME.EXE replace NTLDR/NTDETECT.COM.

Numerous other dynamic link library (DLL) files are also required, but usually the lack or corruption of one of them produces a noncritical error, whereas the absence of HAL.DLL causes the system to be nonfunctional.

We'll now look at the Windows boot process. It's a pretty long and complicated process, but keep in mind that these are complex operating systems, providing you with a lot more functionality than older versions of Windows:

1. The system self-checks and enumerates hardware resources. Each machine has a different startup routine, called the POST (power-on self-test), which is executed by the commands written to the motherboard of the computer. Newer PnP boards not only check memory and processors, they also poll the systems for other devices and peripherals.

2. The Master Boot Record (MBR) loads and finds the boot sector. Once the system has finished with its housekeeping, the MBR is located on the first hard drive and loaded into memory. The MBR finds the bootable partition and searches it for the boot sector of that partition.

3. The MBR determines the file system and loads WINLOAD (or NTLDR). Information in the boot sector allows the system to locate the system partition and to find and load into memory the file located there.

4. WINLOAD/NTLDR switches the system from real mode (which lacks multitasking, memory protection, and those things that make Windows so great) to protected mode (which offers memory protection, multitasking, and so on) and enables paging. Protected mode enables the system to address all of the available physical memory. It's also referred to as *32-bit flat mode*. At this point, the file system is also started.

5. WINLOAD/NTLDR processes a file that resides in the root directory specifying what OSs are installed on the computer and where they reside on the disk. During this step of the boot process, you may be presented with a list of the installed OSs (depending on how your startup options are configured and whether you have multiple OSs installed). If you're presented with the list, you can choose an OS; if you don't take any action, the default selection is chosen automatically.

6. WINRESUME/NTDETECT.COM checks the system for installed devices and device configurations and initializes the devices it finds. It passes the information to WINLOAD/NTLDR, which collects this information and passes it to the kernel after this file is loaded.

7. The OS kernel loads the executive subsystems. *Executive subsystems* are software components that parse the Registry for configuration information and start needed services and drivers.

8. The HKEY_LOCAL_MACHINE\SYSTEM Registry hive and device drivers are loaded. The drivers that load at this time serve as boot drivers, using an initial value called a *start value*.

9. Control is passed to the kernel, and it initializes loaded drivers. It loads the Session Manager, which then loads the Windows subsystem and completes the boot process.

10. Winlogon loads. At this point, you are presented with the Logon screen. After you enter a username and password, you're taken to the Windows Desktop.

Improper Shutdown

Not shutting down properly can result in lost data from open applications or corrupted operating system files. Neither option is good.

You would think that people are pretty aware of how to shut down, but sadly that's not always true. When it comes to your own computers, always shut down properly. If you are a technician at a company, it's your responsibility to train all users on how to shut down properly as well.

Spontaneous Shutdown/Restart

Occasionally, a rogue system will begin automatically shutting down and/or restarting while in use. While it could be indicative of a hardware problem (malfunctioning motherboard, for example), it can also indicate a setting misconfiguration problem. Check the sleep settings for hibernation and disable those to see if it makes a difference. If the problem continues, start looking at drivers.

 On server systems, check to see if any of the services have a recovery setting configured to restart the computer if a service failure is encountered.

To begin ruling out possibilities, boot the system into Safe Mode and see if the problem continues. If the problem does not occur while in Safe Mode, then boot normally and begin testing what occurs as you eliminate drivers/devices one by one (sound, video, and so forth) until you find the culprit.

Device Fails to Start/Not Detected

When you are using Windows, you are constantly interacting with pieces of hardware. Each piece of hardware has a Windows driver that must be loaded in order for Windows to be able to use it. In addition, the hardware must be installed and functioning properly. If the device driver is not installed properly or the hardware is misconfigured, the device won't function properly.

If you have just updated a driver and the device isn't functioning, rolling back the driver installation can sometimes solve the problem. To roll back a driver, right-click on the device name in Device Manager and choose Properties. On the Drivers tab, click the Roll Back Driver button.

Missing DLL Message

The dynamic link library (DLL) files are required. (They were mentioned earlier in the section "Failure to Boot.") The problem of missing DLL files can also occur with applications when you attempt to start them, and the solution involves finding a copy of the DLL (online, on a backup, and so on) and replacing it. A great article on the topic can be found at the following location:

www.makeuseof.com/tag/how-to-fix-missing-dll-file-errors/

Within the Windows toolkit, the best utility to use to tackle this problem is the System File Checker (SFC).

Service Fails to Start

Once you have an application successfully installed, you may run into a problem of getting it to start properly. This problem can come from any number of sources, including an improper installation, a software conflict, or system instability. If your application was installed incorrectly, the files required to run the program properly may not be present, and the program can't function without them. If a shared file that's used by other programs is installed, installation of the wrong (usually older) version can cause conflicts with other programs already installed. Finally, if one program causes a general protection fault (GPF), it can result in memory problems that can destabilize the system and cause other programs to crash. The solution to these problems is to uninstall and reinstall the offending application, first making sure that all programs are closed.

Real World Scenario

Did You Reboot Your Computer?

Quick quiz: You just got an error in Windows, and it appears that you are on the verge of a crash (of your application or the whole system). What do you do?

The first thing is to write down any error messages that appear. Then save your work (if possible) and reboot your computer.

Anyone who has called tech support, or who has been a tech support person, knows how demeaning the question, "Did you restart your computer?" can seem. Most people respond with an indignant, "Of course!" when the reality is they might or might not have actually done it.

Whenever there's a software problem, always, always reboot the computer before trying to troubleshoot. Often, the problem will disappear, and you'll have just saved yourself half an hour of frustration. If the same problem reappears, then you know that you have work to do.

Why does rebooting help? When an application is running, it creates one or more temporary files that it uses to store information, and it also stores information in memory (RAM). If a temporary file or information in RAM becomes corrupted (such as by application A writing its information into application B's memory space), the original application can have problems. Rebooting will clear the memory registers and most often remove problematic temporary files, thus eliminating the issue.

It might sound trite, but the first axiom in troubleshooting software really is to reboot. Even if the user says they did, ask them to reboot again. (Tell them you want to see the opening screen for any possible error messages, or make up another good excuse.) If the problem doesn't come back, it's not a problem. If it does, then you can use your software skills to fix it.

Compatibility Error

Device drivers are software programs that tell the operating system how to work with the hardware. When you purchase a hardware device, odds are that it's been in that box for a while. By the time it gets made, packaged, stored, delivered to the store, stored again at the retailer, and then purchased by you, it's entirely likely that the company that made the device has updated the driver—even possibly a few times if there have been a lot of reported problems.

If Microsoft does not digitally sign your device driver—that is, it hasn't been tested for *compatibility* with your version of Windows—then you will get a warning message when you attempt to install it. You can tell Windows to continue the installation, and most of the time this doesn't cause any problems. Be aware, though, that if the driver isn't signed or isn't compatible, this means that there could be problems with it after you complete the installation. We've installed dozens of unsigned drivers without problems, but we've also run across a few that didn't work as advertised.

In Windows, the User Account Control (UAC) feature has the sole purpose of keeping the user from running programs that could pose a potential threat if the user's privileges were equal to that of Administrator. While turning UAC off is an option, it is not a recommended one. If you have a program that you regularly run and do not want to be prompted each time, you can right-click the icon for that program and then click Properties. Choose the Compatibility tab and then select the Run This Program As An Administrator check box. This will prevent the prompt from occurring each time you use the program.

You are typically not able to set the UAC feature for operating system programs, and the privileges will stay grayed out on the Compatibility tab.

Slow System Performance

Over time, systems seem to run slower than they once did. This can be due to a plethora of drivers, lots of background processes, memory hogs, or many other possibilities. The first place to turn for help to troubleshoot this problem is the Performance Troubleshooter.

In Windows, choose Start ➢ Control Panel ➢ Troubleshooting ➢ Check For Performance Issues (under System And Security). The Performance Troubleshooter will look for common problems, such as more than one virus detection program running, multiple users logged into the same machine, visual settings affecting performance, and so on.

If no problems are found, then take the usual steps: deleting programs that are never run, removing items from startup, defragmenting the hard drive, and so on. Disk Cleanup can help you free up space by deleting unneeded files.

Boots to Safe Mode

At times, a system will become corrupted to the point where it will only boot into Safe Mode and not allow a normal boot. While a hardware issue can cause this, it can often be associated with a damaged/missing driver. To address the problem, boot into the Recovery Console and scan for problems. You can choose to boot to the last known good configuration or resort to the recovery DVD.

File Fails to Open

When a file fails to open, it is often due to corruption. The corruption can be caused from improperly shutting down the application or system. The best solution to this problem is to recover the file from a backup.

Missing *NTLDR*

The NTLDR loader file is a key component of the Windows XP boot process and the system will not boot without it. Occasionally, a message that the file is missing will occur if you change your active partition (which may be done if you are dual-booting with another operating system, such as Windows 7, for example). A BOOT.INI file that points to the wrong location can also trigger this message. In this case, the problem is not with the NTLDR file at all but rather with the misconfigured BOOT.INI.

The file can be retrieved from the Recovery Console or from bootable media (recovery DVD, repair disk, and so on).

> Windows 8, Windows 7, and Windows Vista use the BOOTMGR instead, and a similar message that this file is missing will appear. To resolve this problem, you can boot into System Recovery Options and choose Startup Repair (or type **BOOTREC /FIXBOOT** at the command prompt).

Missing Boot Configuration Data

Different versions of Windows use different files to identify what operating systems are installed and where their boot files can be found. With Windows XP and earlier versions (something you need to know only because NTLDR is an objective), the text file BOOT.INI is used to identify the operating systems installed, their locations, and the boot options to use. This text-based file can be (re)created using any text editor. When it is missing or damaged, you can recover it by booting into the Recovery Console.

Windows 8, Windows 7, and Windows Vista use the Windows Boot Configuration Data (BCD) file instead, and a similar message that this file is missing will appear. To resolve this problem, you can boot into System Recovery Options and choose Startup Repair (or type **BOOTREC /REBUILDBCD** at the command prompt).

Missing Operating System

The first thing to check when it's reported that an operating system is missing is that there is no media in the machine (DVD, CD, and so on), which the system is reading during boot prior to accessing the hard drive. If that is the case, remove the media and reboot (down the road, change the BIOS settings to boot from the hard drive before any other media).

If there is no removable media attempting to boot, then turn to the installation DVD (you may have to set the BIOS to use the DVD drive as your primary boot device) or to the Windows Repair CD. In Windows 8/8.1, Windows 7, and Windows Vista, go to System Recovery Options and choose Startup Repair.

Missing Graphical Interface/GUI Fails to Load

Occasionally, the Windows graphical user interface (GUI) won't appear. The system will hang just before the GUI appears. Missing or corrupt files cause this, and the best tool to turn to here is the Windows Repair CD or the installation DVD. In Windows, go to System Recovery Options and choose Startup Repair.

Missing GRUB/LILO

If you are using GRUB (GRand Unified Bootloader) or LILO (LInux LOader) as a multiboot loader, you can encounter problems if they become corrupted or deleted. To solve these problems, you need to re-create the loader (and reconfigure it for your system) to be able to use it.

If the problem is just an invalid boot disk message, try removing any media in the machine (DVD, CD, and so on) that the system is reading during boot prior to accessing the hard drive and reboot. If that solves the problem, change the BIOS settings to make the hard drive the primary boot device. Two great references on solving GRUB/LILO errors can be found at the following locations:

https://kb.acronis.com/content/1686 or http://sourceforge.net/p/boot-repair/home/Home/

www.aboutlinux.info/2005/11/how-to-repair-corrupt-mbr-and-boot.html

Multiple Monitor Misalignment/Orientation

The ability to stretch the desktop across multiple monitors is a great feature, but it is one that can also be difficult to fix if the display settings are not working properly. In Windows, go to Display Settings and choose the appearance you want for your system. From this configuration interface, you can choose the orientation and whether you want to extend or mirror the displays. Fine-tuning is particularly critical when all of the monitors are not the same size.

Operating System Tools

Many of the tools needed for troubleshooting appear in the objectives pertaining to the operating systems as well. Chapter 13, "Operating System Basics," and Chapter 14, "Operating System Administration," introduced and discussed many of the operating system tools. To avoid needless repetition, only new information or topics not fully covered previously are addressed here.

BIOS/UEFI

First-line tools include the system basic input/output system (BIOS) and Unified Extensible Firmware Interface (UEFI) firmware. Keeping the most current versions of firmware on these devices can sideline a plethora of problems.

SFC

The purpose of this utility is to keep the operating system alive and well. SFC.EXE automatically verifies system files after a reboot to see if they were changed to unprotected copies. If an unprotected file is found, a stored copy of the system file overwrites it.

Storing system files (some of which can be quite large) in two locations consumes a large amount of disk space. When you install an operating system, make sure that you leave ample hard drive space for growth on the drive where %systemroot% resides.

Only users with administrative permissions can run SFC. It also requires the use of a parameter. The valid parameters are as follows:

Parameter	Function
/OFFBOOTDIR	Allows you to set the location of an offline boot directory that can then be used for offline repair
/OFFWINDIR	Allows you to set the location of an offline Windows directory that can then be used for offline repair
/SCANFILE	Specifies a file to be scanned and repaired if needed
/SCANNOW	Checks system files now and repairs any problems found
/VERIFYFILE	Specifies a file to be scanned but not repaired if errors are found
/VERIFYONLY	Specifies that files are scanned but not repaired if errors are found

Logs

Log files are created to record significant events. Those events can range from system problems to just normal user activity. It is the former on which you should focus when troubleshooting PC operating system problems. Windows includes Event Viewer (discussed in a later section) for the purpose of looking at log files and identifying problems.

System Recovery Options

System Recovery Options allows for troubleshooting system problems (the Recovery Console served a similar purpose with Windows XP and earlier versions of Windows). Once you've booted into the Recovery Options, you can use a number of command-line commands to fix issues. Two of the most important commands are BOOTREC /FIXBOOT and BOOTREC /FIXMBR to work with the Master Boot Record. The utility BOOTCFG does a job similar to BOOTREC /REBUILDBCD, and it is a bit easier to work with.

Repair Disks

If you want to recover your computer and bring it back to the point where it was when it was new (minus any files that you added since purchasing the machine), you can use the recovery CD set or DVD. With Dell computers, for example, this is known as the Reinstallation DVD, and it accompanies each machine shipped. It can only be used to reinstall the operating system on the machine. After the Reinstallation DVD finishes, you must then use a similar DVD to reinstall the applications that were on the machine when it shipped.

WARNING   Use the recovery sets only when nothing else seems to work and you are ready to start from scratch.

In Windows, you can create a system repair disc from the Backup And Restore interface (beneath the Control Panel options for System And Security). The system repair disc can be used to boot the computer, and it will contain the system recovery tools. Windows 8/8.1 added Refresh and Restore options as well.

Pre-installation Environments

The Windows Pre-installation Environment (Windows PE) is a minimal Win32 OS that is running the Windows kernel and is intended as a stub that can be run on a machine to allow it to begin an installation. As such, you can think of it as a bootable OS for the Windows Recovery Environment or for installation deployment through System Center Configuration Manager (SCCM), Systems Management Server (SMS), or Windows Deployment Services (WDS). This is the operating system booted into when recovery or installation is necessary.

The technical reference for Windows PE can be found at the following location: http://technet.microsoft.com/en-us/library/dd744322(WS.10).aspx

MSCONFIG

This utility helps troubleshoot startup problems by allowing you to selectively disable individual items that are normally executed at startup. There is no menu command for this utility; you must run it with the Run command (on the Start menu). Choose Start ➢ Run, and type **MSCONFIG**. It works in most versions of Windows, although the interface window is slightly different among versions.

On the boot tab of the tool, you can choose Safe Boot and then opt for a minimal configuration, and alternate shell, Active Directory repair, or to have networking enabled.

DEFRAG

When you save files to a hard drive, Windows will generally write the file into the first available space on the disk. So let's say that you create an Excel spreadsheet and save it. It will be written to the disk. Next, you create a dozen new Word documents and save them as well. Then you go back and add a ton of data to your spreadsheet. Now the Excel file is much bigger. Instead of moving it all to a space on the hard drive big enough to handle the file, Windows will keep part of the file in its original location and write the rest of the data to another available space on the hard drive. When a file is in several places on a disk, it's called a *fragmented file*. Excessive fragmentation of your files can slow down your computer's performance.

Defragmenting a disk involves analyzing the disk and then consolidating fragmented files and folders so that they occupy a contiguous space, thus increasing performance during file retrieval. In Windows, there are a few different ways that you can get to the Disk Defragmenter:

- In Windows 8/7/Vista, click Start and type **defrag** into the Start Search box. Choose Disk Defragmenter from the Programs list.

- In Windows, open Computer or My Computer, right-click on a hard drive, choose Properties, select the Tools tab, and click Defragment Now.

- Start typing defrag in Windows 8 at the Start Screen, choose Defragment, and optimize your hard drives (see Figure 22.1).

FIGURE 22.1   Disk Defragmenter

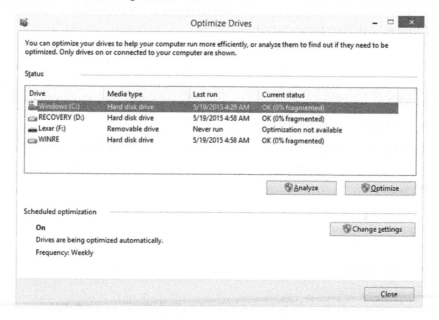

Clicking Change Settings gives you options for scheduling defragmentation, as shown in Figure 22.2.

FIGURE 22.2   Schedule optimization

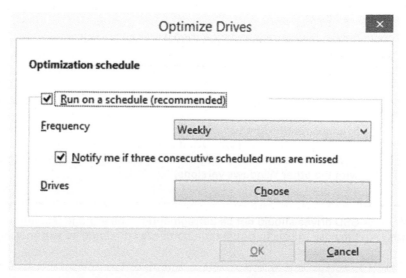

Microsoft recommends that you enable scheduled defragmentation. If you want to defragment immediately, click the Defragment Now button.

There are two versions of Disk Defragmenter: a command-line version and a Windows version that runs from within Windows. The Windows version is located on the System Tools submenu on the Start menu (Start ➤ All Programs ➤ Accessories ➤ System Tools ➤ Disk Defragmenter). In Exercise 22.1, you will run the Disk Defragmenter in Windows 7.

EXERCISE 22.1

Running Disk Defragmenter in Windows 7

1. Choose Start ➤ All Programs ➤ Accessories ➤ System Tools ➤ Disk Defragmenter.

2. If you are prompted by UAC to continue, choose to do so. The Disk Defragmenter utility will appear.

3. Click the Defragment Now button. This will work only if this is the first time the tool has been used. If you have already used it, you have the Analyze option available and can pick a drive and then click Defragment Disk.

4. Choose the disks to defragment and click OK.

5. Exit Disk Defragmenter.

These are some of the available switches for the command-line version (DEFRAG.EXE):

/A	Analyze only
/C	Defrags all disks
-F	(Vista only) Force defragmentation even if disk space is low
/V	Verbose output

In an interesting anomaly, with Windows Vista, you precede the switches with a hyphen (-), and with Windows 7/0/0.1, it needs to be a slash (/). Thus -a and /a are the same, but the former works in Vista and the latter works with the other Windows versions.

SSD drives should not be defragmented. The storage management system they use makes this operation pointless and doing so will shorten the life of the device.

REGSVR32

REGSVR32.EXE, known as the REGSVR32 tool, allows you to register and unregister modules and controls for troubleshooting purposes. It is often associated with Internet Explorer, but it can be used with any control or module. The command-line syntax is REGSVR32 DLLNAME, and Figure 22.3 shows the options that are available with it.

FIGURE 22.3   REGSVR32 options

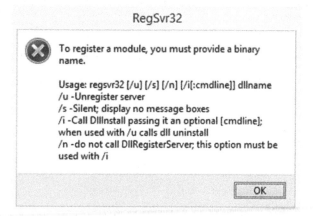

REGEDIT

The Registry Editor is used to change values and variables stored in a configuration database known as the Registry. This centralized database contains environmental settings for various Windows programs along with registration information, which details the types of filename extensions associated with applications so that when you double-click a file in Windows File Explorer, the associated application runs and opens the file.

The Registry Editor, shown in Figure 22.4, enables you to make changes to the large hierarchical database that contains all of Windows's settings. These changes can potentially disable the entire system, so they should not be made lightly.

There is no menu command for the Registry Editor. You must run it with the Run command. REGEDIT is the name of the program. Windows also includes a second Registry Editor program called REGEDT32. But in recent versions of the OS, this has been nothing more than a link to REGEDIT.

WARNING   The Registry holds great power, but it can also cause great harm. Never edit the Registry without being completely sure about what you're doing.

FIGURE 22.4   The Registry Editor

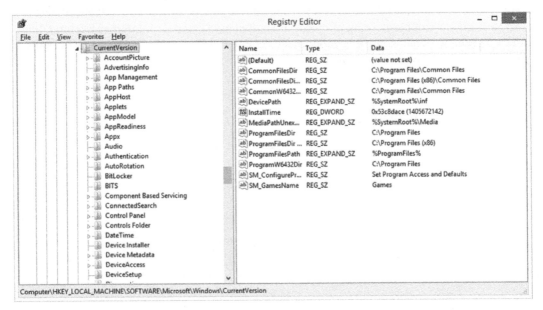

Event Viewer

This utility provides information about what's been going on with the whole system to help you troubleshoot problems. Event Viewer shows warnings, error messages, and records of things that have happened successfully. It's found in all current versions of Windows (which include Windows 8/8.1, Windows 7, and Windows Vista). You can access it through Computer Management, or you can access it directly from the Administrative Tools in Control Panel.

Safe Mode

If when you boot Windows won't load completely (it hangs or is otherwise corrupted), you can often solve the problem by booting into Safe Mode. *Safe Mode* is a concept borrowed from Windows 95 wherein you can bring up part of the operating system by bypassing the settings, drivers, or parameters that may be causing it trouble during a normal boot. The goal of Safe Mode is to provide an interface with which you're able to fix the problems that occur during a normal boot and then reboot in normal mode.

To access Safe Mode, you must press F8 when the operating system menu is displayed during the boot process. You'll then see a menu of Safe Mode choices, as listed in Table 22.1. Select the mode into which you want to boot.

With Windows 8/8.1, booting into Safe Mode is just plain hard. One method of so doing is described at

`https://support.microsoft.com/en-us/kb/2809468`

You can also employ the Advanced Startup Options as described at

`http://pcsupport.about.com/od/windows-8/a/open-advanced-startup-options-windows-8.htm`.

TABLE 22.1   Windows Advanced Boot Options

Choice	Loaded
Safe Mode	Provides the VGA monitor, Microsoft mouse drivers, and basic drivers for the keyboard (storage system services, no networking).
Safe Mode With Networking	Same as Safe Mode, but with networking.
Safe Mode With Command Prompt	Same as Safe Mode, but without the interface and drivers/services associated with it.
Enable Boot Logging	Creates NTBTLOG.TXT in the root directory during any boot.
Enable VGA Mode	Normal boot with only basic video drivers. In Windows, this option is called Enable Low-Resolution Video.
Last Known Good Configuration	Uses the last backup of the Registry to bypass corruption caused during the previous session.
Disable Automatic Restart On System Failure	Disables automatic restarting and is helpful when troubleshooting.
Debugging Mode	Sends information through the serial port for interpretation/troubleshooting at another computer.
Start Windows Normally	Bypasses any of the options here.
Return To OS Choices Menu	Gives you an out in case you pressed F8 by accident.

You need to keep a few rules in mind when booting in different modes:

- If problems don't exist when you boot to Safe Mode but do exist when you boot to normal mode, the problem isn't with basic services/drivers.
- If the system hangs when you load drivers, the log file can show you the last driver it attempted to load, which is usually the cause of the problem.
- If you can't solve the problem with Safe Mode, try the Last Known Good boot, System Restore, or System Image Recovery (if it is Windows 8/8.1, you can also try Refresh/Restore).

Command Prompt

The command prompt has been mentioned numerous times in this chapter, and it is the environment in which you can run many troubleshooting utilities. Typing **CMD** at the Run prompt on the Start menu can start this. Figure 22.5 shows an example of the command prompt interface.

FIGURE 22.5   The command prompt interface

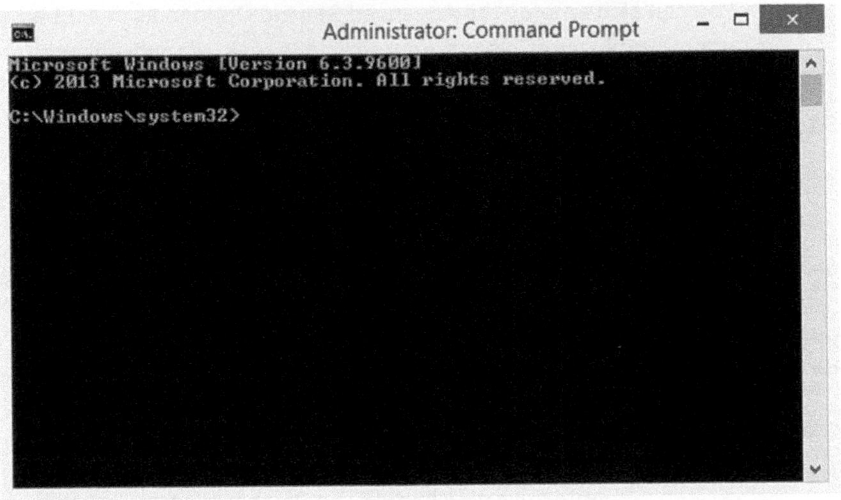

If you will be regularly running commands as Administrator, you can create an icon on the desktop for the executable (CMD.EXE) and configure on the Advanced section of the Shortcut tab to run the program as Administrator in Windows 7 and Windows Vista. Windows 8 already gives you the option of Command Prompt (Admin).

Uninstall/Reinstall/Repair

When a problem pops up with the Windows 8 operating system, you can boot into the Windows Recovery Environment (Windows RE) and repair it by choosing to refresh, reset, or restore it. Refreshing it keeps personal files and settings along with the default apps and those that you installed from the Windows Store.

Resetting reinstalls Windows and deletes all your personal files and settings. Restoring allows you to just undo recent system changes.

Depending on the type of repair operation you perform, you may or may not need the Windows 8 product key to continue.

Troubleshooting Security Issues

Many viruses will announce that your system is infected as soon as they gain access to it. They may take control of your system, flash annoying messages on your screen, or destroy your hard disk. When this occurs, you'll know that you're a victim. Other viruses will cause your system to slow down, cause files to disappear from your computer, or take over your disk space. The Windows Action Center, shown in Figure 22.6, can show you what security measures are set on your system.

FIGURE 22.6 The Windows Action Center offers a quick glimpse of current protection settings.

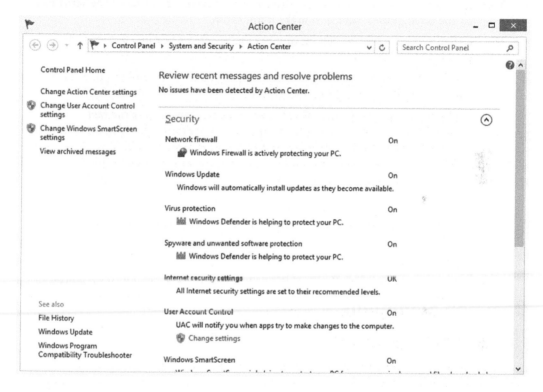

 Viruses are the most common type of malware. In this section, we use the term virus to refer to many types of malware.

You should look for some of the following symptoms when determining if a virus infection has occurred:

- The programs on your system start to load more slowly. This happens because the virus is spreading to other files in your system or is taking over system resources.

- Unusual files appear on your hard drive, or files start to disappear from your system. Many viruses delete key files in your system to render it inoperable.

- Program sizes change from the installed versions. This occurs because the virus is attaching itself to these programs on your disk.

- Your browser, word processing application, or other software begins to exhibit unusual operating characteristics. Screens or menus may change.
- The system mysteriously shuts itself down or starts itself up, and a great deal of unanticipated disk activity occurs.
- You mysteriously lose access to a disk drive or other system resources. The virus has changed the settings on a device to make it unusable.
- Your system suddenly doesn't reboot or gives unexpected error messages during startup.
- You notice an *X* in the system tray over the icon for your virus scanner, or the icon for the scanner disappears from the system tray altogether.

This list is by no means exhaustive. What is an absolute, however, is the fact that you should immediately quarantine the infected system. It is imperative that you do all that you can to contain the virus and keep it from spreading to other systems within your network and beyond. Many enterprises have a no-tolerance (zero tolerance) policy for infected systems, and they are always physically destroyed.

It cannot be overstated that establishing security policies and procedures, updating your operating systems, updating your applications, and updating your network devices are all good measures to take to help eliminate potential security problems.

Common Symptoms

There are a number of common symptoms CompTIA expects you to know for the 220–902 exam when it comes to security issues. Many of these issues also appear in other CompTIA certification exams, namely Security+. Rest assured that for the 220–902 exam, you do not need to know the content as well as you would if you were preparing for the Security+ exam.

Pop-Ups

Pop-ups (also commonly known as popups) are both frustrating and chancy. When a user visits a website and another instance (either another tab or another browser window) opens in the foreground, it is called a pop-up; if it opens in the background, it is called a pop-under. Both pop-ups and pop-unders are pages or sites that you did not specifically request and may only display ads or bring up applets that should be avoided.

Pop-up blockers are used to prevent both pop-ups and pop-unders from appearing. While older browsers did not incorporate an option to block pop-ups, most newer browsers, including the latest versions of Internet Explorer, now have that capability built in.

Browser Redirection

Pharming is a form of redirection in which traffic intended for one host is sent to another. This can be accomplished on a small scale by changing entries in the hosts file and on a large scale by changing entries in a DNS server (poisoning). In either case, when a user attempts to go to a site, they are redirected to another. For example, suppose Illegitimate Company ABC creates a site to look exactly like the one for Giant Bank XYZ. The pharming is done (using either redirect method) and users trying to reach Giant Bank XYZ are tricked into going to Illegitimate Company ABC's site, which looks enough like what they are used to seeing that they give their username and password data.

As soon as Giant Bank XYZ realizes that the traffic is being redirected, it will immediately move to stop it. But while Illegitimate Company ABC will be shut down, it was able to collect data for the length of time that the redirection occurred, which could vary from minutes to days.

Security Alerts

Users have plenty of real viruses and other issues to worry about. Yet some people find it entertaining to issue phony threats disguised as *security alerts* to keep people on their toes. Some of the more popular hoaxes that have been passed around are the Good Time and the Irina viruses. Millions of users received emails about these two viruses, and the symptoms sounded awful.

Both of these warnings claimed that the viruses would do things that are impossible to accomplish with a virus. When you receive a virus warning, you can verify its authenticity by looking on the website of the antivirus software you use, or you can go to several public systems. One of the more helpful sites to visit to get the status of the latest viruses is the CERT organization (`www.cert.org`). CERT monitors and tracks viruses and provides regular reports on this site.

Though the names are similar, there is a difference between cert.org and us-cert.gov. While the latter is a government site for the United States Computer Emergency Readiness Team, the former is a federally funded research and development center at Carnegie Mellon University.

When you receive an email that you suspect is a hoax, check the CERT site before forwarding the message to anyone else. The creator of the hoax wants to create widespread panic, and if you blindly forward the message to co-workers and acquaintances, you're helping the creator accomplish this task. For example, any email that includes "forward to all your friends" is a candidate for hoax research. Disregarding the hoax allows it to die a quick death and keeps users focused on productive tasks. Any concept that spreads quickly through the Internet is referred to as a *meme*.

Identifying a Hoax

Symantec and other vendors maintain pages devoted to bogus hoaxes. Symantec's site is located at

www.symantec.com/business/security_response/threatexplorer/risks/hoaxes.jsp

You can always check there to verify whether an email you've received is indeed a hoax.

Slow Performance

Slow performance was addressed previously in this chapter in relation to operating system issues. Viruses, worms, and other malware can slow performance because they rob resources from the other applications and services forced to share them.

Internet Connectivity Issues

If your computer is hooked up to a network, you need to know when your computer is not functioning properly on the network and what to do about it. In most cases, the problem can be attributed either to a malfunctioning network interface card (NIC) or improperly installed network software. The biggest indicator in Windows that some component of the network software is nonfunctional is that you can't log on to the network or access any network service. To fix this problem, you must first fix the underlying hardware problem (if one exists) and then properly install or configure the network software.

PC/OS Lock Up

It is obvious when a system lockup occurs. The system simply stops responding to commands and stops processing completely. System lockups can occur when a computer is asked to process too many instructions at once with too little memory. Usually, the cure for a system lock-up is to reboot. If the lockups are persistent, it may be a hardware-related problem instead of a software problem.

Remember that there are two universal solutions to Windows problems: rebooting and obtaining an update from the software manufacturer. If neither of these solutions work, it could be hardware causing the problem.

 Real World Scenario

Dr. Watson?

Earlier versions of Windows included a special utility known as Dr. Watson that intercepted all error conditions and, instead of presenting the user with a cryptic Windows error, displayed a slew of information that could be used to troubleshoot the problem. Windows 8/7/Vista do not include Dr. Watson for debugging but instead have rolled that functionality into the program called Problem Reports And Solutions.

Application Crash

When an application crashes, you want to isolate the cause of the crash—it could be a compatibility issue, hardware, or a host of other problems—and solve it. One step to take early on is to look for updates/patches/fixes to the application released by the vendor. Be sure to try these updates on a test machine first before rolling them out to all, and verify that they do address the problem and not introduce new ones.

OS Update Failures

Failed updates for Windows—assuming that connectivity issues do not cause them—can often be traced to setting misconfigurations. These settings can also cause the operating system to report that an update needs to be installed when it has already been installed. The best solution is to find the error code being reported in Windows Update Troubleshooter, solve the problem, and download the update.

For information on addressing this problem with both Windows Update and Microsoft Office, see the knowledge base article at http://support.microsoft.com/kb/906602.

Rogue Antivirus

One of the more clever ways of spreading a virus is to disguise it so that it looks like an antivirus program. When it alerts the user to a fictitious problem, the user then begins interacting with the program and allowing the rogue program to do all sorts of damage. One of the more tricky things for troublemakers to do is to make the program look as if it came from a trusted source—such as Microsoft—and mimic the Windows Action Center interface enough to fool an unsuspecting user.

Microsoft offers a page on fake virus alerts that can be shared with employees to help educate them about rogue security software at the following location:

www.microsoft.com/security/pc-security/antivirus-rogue.aspx

Spam

While *spam* is not truly a virus or a hoax, it is one of the most annoying things with which an administrator must contend. Spam is defined as any unwanted, unsolicited email, and not only can the sheer volume of it be irritating, it can often open the door to larger problems. For instance, some of the sites advertised in spam may be infected with viruses, worms, and other unwanted programs. If users begin to respond to spam by visiting those sites, then viruses and other problems will multiply in your system.

There are numerous antispam programs available, and users as well as administrators can run them. One of the biggest problems with many of these applications is false positives: they will occasionally flag legitimate email as spam and stop it from being delivered. You should routinely check your spam folders and make sure that legitimate email is not being flagged and held there.

Just as you can, and must, install good antivirus software programs, you should also consider similar measures for spam. Filtering the messages out and preventing them from ever entering the network is the most effective method of dealing with the problem. Recently, the word *spam* has found its way into other forms of unwanted messaging beyond email, giving birth to the acronyms SPIM (spam over Instant Messaging) and SPIT (spam over Internet Telephony).

Renamed System Files/Disappearing Files/Permission Changes/ Access Denied

Creators of malware have a number of methods by which they can wreak havoc on a system. One of the simplest ways is to delete key system files. When this occurs, the user can no longer perform the operation associated with the file, such as print, save, and so on. Just as harmful as deleting a file is to rename it or change the permissions associated with it so that the user can no longer access it or perform those operations.

Hijacked Email

One of the easiest ways to spread malware is to capture the email contacts of a user and send the malware as an attachment to all of those in their circle. The recipient is more likely to open the attachment because it seemingly comes from a trusted source. It is important that you scan all email, both internal and external, and identify problems before they spread. Be wary of responses from users regarding email that they haven't sent and watch for automated replies from unknown sent email. As good as your malware detection may be, one of the best things to do to prevent these types of attacks from being successful is to educate users of what to watch out for, how to respond, and how to get a hold of you as quickly as possible.

Invalid Certificate

PKI, or public key infrastructure, was discussed in Chapter 21, and it relies upon digital certificates for security. An invalid certificate usually means that the certificate that you have has expired. If this is the case, renew the certificate—or get one that is valid—and the problem will correct itself.

Security Tools

A number of the security tools that fall beneath this objective have already been discussed. These include Recovery Console, pre-installation environments, Event Viewer, and MSCONFIG/Safe boot. Refresh/Restore was also discussed earlier in the chapter, and the sections that follow focus on topics not yet addressed.

Antivirus Software

This type of preventive maintenance is absolutely critical these days if you have a connection to the Internet. A *computer virus* is a small, deviously ingenious program that replicates itself to other computers, generally causing those computers to behave abnormally. Generally speaking, a virus's main function is to reproduce. A virus attaches itself to files on a hard disk and modifies those files. When a program accesses the files, the virus can infect the program with its own code. The program may then in turn replicate the virus code to other files and other programs. In this manner, a virus may infect an entire computer.

When an infected file is transferred to another computer (via disk or download), the process begins on the other computer. Because of the frequency of downloads from the Internet, viruses can run rampant if left unchecked. For this reason, antivirus programs were developed. They check files and programs for any program code that shouldn't be there and either eradicate it or prevent the virus from replicating. An antivirus program is generally run in the background on a computer, and it examines all of the file activity on that computer. When it detects a suspicious activity, it notifies the user of a potential problem and asks the user what to do about it. Some antivirus programs can also make intelligent decisions about what to do. The process of running an antivirus program on a computer is known as *inoculating* the computer against a virus.

> For a listing of most of the viruses that are currently out there, refer to Symantec's AntiVirus Research Center (SARC) at www.symantec.com/security_response/.

> You may notice that a lot of the language surrounding computer viruses sounds like the language that we use to discuss human illnesses. The moniker virus was given to these programs because a computer virus functions much like a human virus, and the term helped to anthropomorphize the computer a bit. Somehow, if people can think of a computer as getting sick, it breaks down the computer phobia that many people have.

There are two categories of viruses: benign and malicious. Benign viruses don't do much besides replicate themselves and exist. They may cause the occasional problem, but it is usually an unintentional side effect. Malicious viruses, on the other hand, are designed to destroy things. Once a malicious virus (for example, the Michelangelo virus) infects your machine, you can usually kiss the contents of your hard drive goodbye.

To prevent virus-related problems, you can install one of any number of antivirus programs (Norton AntiVirus or McAfee VirusScan, for example). These programs will periodically scan your computer for viruses, monitor regular use of the computer, and note any suspicious activity that might indicate a virus. In addition, these programs have a database of known viruses and the symptoms each one causes.

> Antivirus databases should be updated frequently (about once a week, although more often is better) to keep your antivirus program up-to-date with all the possible virus definitions. Most antivirus programs will automatically update themselves (if configured properly) just as Windows Update will update Windows, provided the computer has a live Internet connection. It's a good idea to let them automatically update, just in case you forget to do it yourself.

Anti-malware Software

There are many other forms of malware in addition to viruses. While a true antivirus program will scan for viruses, anti-malware programs are a superset of virus scanners and will look for more than just traditional viruses. One program included with Windows that falls into this category is Windows Defender, which is mainly a spyware detector (and incorporates Microsoft Security Essentials, or MSE, with it as of Windows 8 and later).

As with similar programs, for Windows Defender to function properly, you need to keep the definitions current and scan on a regular basis. In Exercise 22.2, you'll run Windows Defender (shown in Figure 22.7).

FIGURE 22.7   Windows Defender can identify security threats.

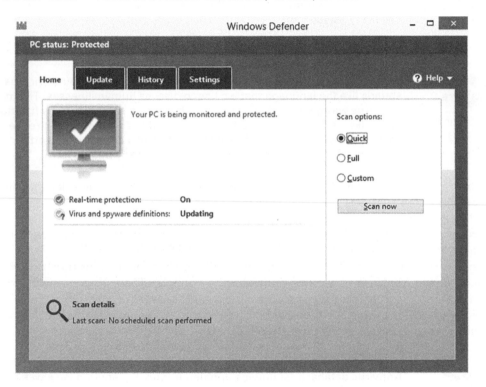

EXERCISE 22.2

Run Windows Defender in Windows 7

1. Choose Start ➤ Control Panel, then type **Security** and choose Windows Defender.

2. If you are prompted that Defender is not configured, choose to turn it on (this will bring up a UAC prompt to continue if UAC is toggled on).

3. From the drop-down list next to Help (a question mark in a blue circle), choose Check For Updates (again, if UAC is toggled on, you will be prompted to continue).

4. Click Scan.

5. Upon completion, the message "Your computer is running normally" should appear within the frame labeled No Unwanted Or Harmful Software Detected. If anything else appears, resolve those issues.

6. Exit Windows Defender.

Terminal

The terminal, or command prompt, allows you to interact with the system at the command line. In UNIX/Linux environments, this is where you interact with the shell and run many of the commands discussed in Chapter 18, "Working with Mac OS and Linux."

System Restore/Snapshot

There are times when bad things happen to good computers. No matter how hard you've tried to keep a system running flawlessly, your computer crashes. There are several ways to get your computer back up and running, but many of them (such as reinstalling the operating system) take a lot of time. System Restore was added to Windows, and it allows you to create restore points to make recovery of the operating system easier.

A *restore point* is a copy, or *snapshot*, of your system configuration at a given point in time. It's like a backup of your configuration but not necessarily your data. Restore points are created in one of three ways. One, Windows creates them automatically by default. Two, you can manually create them yourself. Three, during the installation of some programs, a restore point is created before the installation (that way, if the install fails, you can "roll back" the system to a preinstallation configuration). Restore points are useful for when Windows fails to boot but the computer appears to be fine otherwise or if Windows doesn't seem to be acting right and you think it was because of a recent configuration change.

To open System Restore, click Start ➢ All Programs ➢ Accessories ➢ System Tools ➢ System Restore. By clicking Next, you can choose a restore point.

You'll notice that checkpoints are included in the list of restore points along with backups that you have performed.

> If you need to use a restore point and Windows won't boot, you can reboot into Safe Mode. After Safe Mode loads, you will have the option to work in Safe Mode or to use System Restore. Choose System Restore, and you'll be presented with restore points (if any) that you can use.

Creating a restore point manually is easy to do using the System Restore utility. In Exercise 22.3, we'll walk you through the process of creating a restore point in Windows Vista.

Creating a Restore Point in Windows Vista

1. Open System Restore by clicking Start ➤ All Programs ➤ Accessories ➤ System Tools ➤ System Restore.

2. Click the Open System Protection link. (You can also get to System Protection by right-clicking My Computer, choosing Properties, and then selecting the System Protection tab. This is the method to use with Windows 7.)

3. Choose the disk or disks for which you want to create restore points, and then click Create.

4. Type a description to help you identify the restore point, and then click Create.

5. Within a minute, you will be presented with a confirmation screen with the time, date, and name of your restore point.

Best Practices for Malware Removal

Rounding out this chapter is a discussion of the best practices for malware removal. The best way to think of this is as a seven-item list of what CompTIA wants you to consider when approaching a possible malware infestation. The following discussion presents the information that you need to know in just that fashion.

1. **Identify malware symptoms.** Before doing anything major, it is imperative first to be sure that you are dealing with the right issue. If you suspect malware, then try to identify the type (spyware, virus, and so on) and look for the proof needed to substantiate that it is indeed the culprit.

2. **Quarantine infected system.** Once you have confirmed that malware is at hand, then quarantine the infected system to prevent it from spreading the malware to other systems. Bear in mind that malware can spread in any number of ways, including through a network connection, email, and so on. The quarantine needs to be complete enough to prevent any spread.

3. **Disable System Restore (in Windows).** This is a necessary step because you do not want to have the infected system create a restore point—or return to one—where the infection exists.

4. **Remediate infected systems.** The steps taken here need to be dependent upon the type of malware with which you're dealing, but they should include updating anti-malware software with the latest definitions and using the appropriate scan and removal techniques. The latter can include booting into Safe Mode, booting to a pre-installation environment, and so on.

5. **Schedule scans and run updates.** The odds of the system never being confronted by malware again are slim. To reduce the chances of it being infected again, though,

schedule scans and updates to run regularly. Most anti-malware programs can be configured to run automatically at specific intervals, but should you encounter one that does not have such a feature, you can run it through Task Scheduler.

6. **Enable System Restore and create a restore point (in Windows).** Once everything is working properly, it is important once again to create restore points should a future problem occur and you need to revert back.

7. **Educate the end user.** Education should always be viewed as the final step. The end user needs to understand what led to the malware infestation and what to avoid, or look for, in the future to keep it from happening again.

Together, these seven steps offer a best practices approach to confronting malware removal.

Troubleshooting Mobile Issues

As mobile devices have been rapidly replacing the desktop and laptop machines that used to rule the workplace, the equipment an administrator must maintain has now evolved to cover a plethora of options. This section focuses on common mobile OS and application issues and some of the tools that can be used to work with them. A subsequent section will look at the same topics with more of a focus on security.

The following symptoms of problems are common with mobile OSs and applications:

- **Dim display.** Light can quickly drain a battery on a mobile device, and thus most of them include the ability to dim the display both manually and automatically after a period of inactivity. While you normally want these actions, if the settings are incorrect, the screen can be too dim to work with. Check the settings on the device to see if it possible to brighten the screen and/or keep it from automatically dimming within a short period of time.

- **Intermittent wireless.** There are a number of causes why intermittent wireless connections can occur, but the two most common are lack of a good signal, and interference. Increasing the number of repeaters, or being closer to them, can address the lack of a good signal. Interference can be addressed by reducing the number of devices competing for the same channel.

- **No wireless connectivity.** A common cause for lack of wireless connectivity is for a device to be in airplane mode. Make sure your device is not in that mode, and do a hard reboot if necessary.

- **No Bluetooth connectivity.** Lack of Bluetooth connectivity is often caused when a device is not turned on and/or has an improper setting for discoverabilty. Make sure the device is turned on and discoverable (checking manufacturer's documentation if necessary).

- **Cannot broadcast to an external monitor.** Connecting a mobile device, such as a phone, to a television or monitor should not be problematic as long as auto-detection is working. If auto-detection is disabled, or just not working, then you may need to configure the output device manually.

- **Nonresponsive touchscreen.** If your touchscreen becomes nonresponsive with a mobile device, try some basic steps: first, remove any added case or screen protector that may have been put on your device and then clean the screen (use a lint-free cloth). Next, unplug your device and restart it (forcing it to restart, if necessary).

- **Apps not loading.** If an app does not load, try rebooting (forcing the device to restart, if necessary). If that does not work, attempt to reload the app and be sure to check the vendor's site for any similar problems (and solutions) encountered by others.

- **Slow performance.** Slow performance is often related to RAM. Look for any apps that are running and can be closed, and add more RAM if possible.

- **Unable to decrypt email.** Mail decryption depends upon certificates, and problems can occur when those certificates expire or you have a configuration problem (which can accompany upgrades). To address the problem, try reimporting S/MIME certificates and deleting/importing them from the source.

- **Extremely short battery life.** Batteries never last as long as you would like. Apple defines *battery life* as the amount of time a device runs before it needs to be recharged (as opposed to *battery life span*, which is the amount of time a battery lasts before it needs to be replaced). Tips for increasing battery life include keeping OS updates applied (they may include energy saving patches), avoiding ambient temperatures that are too high or too low, letting the screen automatically dim, and turning off location-based services. You should also disconnect peripherals and quit applications not in use (Wi-Fi, for example, uses power when enabled, even if you are not using it to connect to the network).

- **Overheating.** When most mobile devices get too warm, they will tell you that they need to cool down before they can continue to be used and they will automatically take measures to protect themselves (turning off features, closing apps, and so on). One of the best ways to avoid overheating is to avoid ambient temperatures that are too hot or too cold: avoid having the device in direct sunlight for extended time periods, in a hot car on a summer day, or on top of a heat source. When the device does overheat, you can often help it cool down quicker by removing any protective case that may be there—and putting it back on later.

- **Frozen system.** If the system is frozen—not responding to a single thing—try to force a restart. For example, press and hold the Sleep/Wake and Home buttons an iPhone for at least 10 seconds until you see the Apple logo. If the restart does not work, try plugging the device in and letting it charge (an hour or more is recommended) and try restarting again.

- **No sound from speakers.** Occasionally, a device can be unknowingly put into silent mode, and this will keep sound from coming to the speakers, headphones, or other connected devices. When troubleshooting, always check to see that silent mode is not enabled and restart the device if necessary.

- **Inaccurate touchscreen response.** To solve problems with inaccurate touchscreen responses, start by cleaning the screen, as discussed earlier, and rebooting the device.

- **System lockout.** Being locked out of a system can be a frustrating experience. The lockout can be the result of the device being disabled, forgetting the passcode, or any of a number of other possibilities. Apple outlines how to approach this for the iPhone, iPad, or iPod Touch at `https://support.apple.com/en-us/HT204306`.

There are a number of tools—really just techniques—that can be used to approach these common problems:

- **Hard reset**. A hard reset should always be done as a last resort. With Apple's iPhone, iPad, and iPod Touch, forcing a restart on the device is done by pressing and holding the Sleep/Wake and Home buttons for at least 10 seconds until you see the Apple logo.

- **Soft reset**. Not as forceful as a hard reset, a soft reset keeps the data of running applications. With Apple's iPhone, iPad, or iPod Touch, press and hold the Sleep/Wake button until the red slider appears, and then drag the slider to turn the device off. Next, press and hold the Sleep/Wake button again until you see the Apple logo.

- **Close running applications**. With most smartphones, iPads, and so on, you do not need to close running applications unless there is a problem. When there is, press the Home button two times and then find the desired application (sliding between choices, if necessary). Hold your finger on the application for 2 seconds, and the icon for it will start to shake with a minus symbol on the top left of it. Press the icon again, and it will close the app.

- **Reset to factory default**. When you need to get to a safe state—such as when you are disposing of a device or assigning it to a new user—you can reset it to factory default settings. To do this, tap Settings and then General. Scroll down until you see the Reset option and choose it. Tap Erase All Content And Settings. At this point, the iPhone or iPad will ask you to confirm the reset, and when you tap OK, it will start the process.

- **Adjust configurations/settings**. Configurations and settings need to be personalized to the user using the device. Except for apps, choosing Settings on the device usually does this, followed by finding the areas that you want to modify and then making the desired changes and saving them.

- **Uninstall/reinstall apps**. Apps that are not used should be removed from a device to free up resources: the last thing you need is apps to continually update when they are ones you never use. Occasionally, an app may need to be reinstalled to correct problems with its configuration.

- **Force stop**. When an app is unresponsive, you can do a force stop to close it. With iOS, press the Home button twice quickly and small previews of your recently used apps will appear. Swipe left to find the app that you want to close, and then swipe up on the app's preview to close it using a force stop.

This list constitutes the "tools" CompTIA wants you to be familiar with for the common mobile OS and application issues section of the exam.

Troubleshooting Mobile Security Issues

While the preceding section—and its corresponding objectives—looked at mobile devices and focused on common OS and application issues, this one builds on that and focuses on security-related issues. Once again, it looks at common symptoms and tools, differing only in that there is more of a focus on security. It needs to be pointed out, though, that CompTIA is stretching the definition of the word *security* to include more than many would: a fair number of the issues that appear in this section would easily have fit in the last section.

> In addition to the A+ certification, there is also CompTIA Mobility+, and the topics here are a subset of what you will find there. The exam for it covers mobile device management, troubleshooting, security, and network infrastructure.

The following list includes common symptoms of problems with mobile OS and applications security issues:

- **Signal drop/weak signal.** Weak signals are a common culprit behind dropped signals. Before engaging in communication, signal strength on the device should be evaluated. If the signal is low (for example, no bars), then change location (step outside, drive out of the tunnel, exit the elevator, and so forth) and try for a better signal. A low battery can affect signal strength, so keep the battery charged as much as possible.

- **Power drain.** While apps, usage, and so on can contribute to power drain, one of the biggest offenders is the search for a signal. If the antenna is not able to perform at its peak, it can reduce its efficiency, which causes it to search more for a signal. Make sure that nothing is impeding the performance of the antenna.

- **Slow data speeds.** Slow data speeds can be caused by too much interference, as pointed out earlier in this chapter. Try changing the channel on Wi-Fi routers to less-used channels and performance should increase.

- **Unintended Wi-Fi connection.** When autoconnect is enabled on devices, it is possible for them to seek out open Wi-Fi networks and try to connect to them automatically. This setting should be disabled for all devices because an untrusted connection is a possible place for a DNS or man-in-the-middle attack to occur.

- **Unintended Bluetooth pairing.** When anonymous devices are allowed to connect to Bluetooth-enabled devices, this is known as *unintended Bluetooth pairing* and it represents a security threat. Mobile security policies should be created and enforced to prevent this from occurring.

- **Leaked personal files/data.** When authorized users access devices through unintended connections or unauthorized users access absconded devices, they can access the data on the device. Every firm should have a policy for protecting data (encryption) and dealing with leaks when they occur.

- **Data transmission overlimit.** Going over the limits on data plans can be symptomatic of a hacked account. Closely monitor account usage.

- **Unauthorized account access.** Unauthorized account access can give users access to personal files and data to which they should not have access. Closely monitor account usage.

- **Unauthorized root access.** Security holes in mobile device operating systems can leave back doors into which users can get unauthorized root access. The majority of these holes are closed by patches and upgrades as soon as they are discovered, so be sure to keep operating systems current.

- **Unauthorized location tracking.** While location-based data can be very valuable when you are using maps and trying to find sites, it can also give away sensitive information if accessed by someone who should not have it. You can optimize your battery life and protect yourself by turning off Location Services. On an iPhone, turn it off in Settings ➤ Privacy ➤ Location Services. There you will see each app listed along with its permission setting. Apps that recently used Location Services have an indicator next to the on/off switch, and you can configure them accordingly.

- **Unauthorized camera/microphone activation.** The camera and microphone can be activated remotely and allow a troublemaker to spy on you. It is suggested that, when not in authorized use, you cover the camera and microphone to keep them from providing any data if they are remotely accessed.

- **High resource utilization.** High resource utilization can be a telltale sign that a device is running more than you think it should be—perhaps the drives are being searched or the camera is recording your every move. Monitor for high resource usage, and if it's discovered, find out what is causing it and respond appropriately.

There are a number of tools—or techniques—that can be used to approach these common problems. Some of them have been discussed before in this chapter and are not in the following list (factory reset/clean install, uninstall/reinstall apps, and force stop). Those that remain are as follows:

- **Anti-malware.** As has been pointed out several times in this chapter, keep malware definitions current and run scanning programs on every device.

- **App scanner.** Similar to anti-malware, an app scanner looks for problems with apps. On an Android phone, for example, the Lookout app automatically scans every app that you install, performs a full scan of all of the apps on your device every week, and downloads the latest definitions regularly.

- **Wi-Fi analyzer.** This is a tool that can show you the Wi-Fi channels, and it can be useful in problem detection.

- **Cell tower analyzer.** What the Wi-Fi analyzer can do for Wi-Fi, the cell tower analyzer can do for cell towers—showing a graphical representation of traffic and signals.

- **Backup/restore.** Because problems tend to happen no matter how careful you may be, it is important to back up devices and be able to restore from those backups after an incident. Some services exist beyond just giving you a place to store backups. In the Apple world, there is iTunes/iCloud/Apple Configurator. The latter simplifies mass configuration and deployment on iPhone, iPad, and iPod Touch, and it is intended for use by schools, businesses, and institutions. In the Google world, there is Google Sync, which allows you to sync your phone, desktop, and tablet devices. Last, in the Microsoft world, there is OneDrive, which has been discussed previously.

As with so many issues involving troubleshooting, common sense is most important. Using logic and a systematic approach, you can often identify and correct small problems before they become large ones.

Summary

This chapter addressed systematic approaches to working with computer problems as well as troubleshooting operating systems and resolving security-related issues. In our discussion of troubleshooting theory, you learned that you need to take a systematic approach to problem solving. Both art and science are involved, and experience in troubleshooting is helpful but not a prerequisite to being a good troubleshooter. You learned that in troubleshooting, the first objective is to identify the problem. Many times, this can be the most time-consuming task!

Once you've identified the problem, you need to establish a theory of why the problem is happening, test your theory, establish a plan of action, verify full functionality, and then document your work. Documentation is frequently the most overlooked aspect of working with computers, but it's an absolutely critical step!

Next we discussed operating system troubleshooting issues. First, we looked at common trouble symptoms and followed that by discussing tools that can be helpful in solving problems.

Finally, we looked at security troubleshooting issues. Again, we started by looking at common issues and then turned to tools. The discussion concluded by looking at the best practices for malware removal.

Exam Essentials

Know the steps to take in troubleshooting computers.   First identify the problem. Then establish a theory of probable cause, test your theory, establish a plan of action to resolve the problem, verify full system functionality, and finally, document your findings.

Understand how to talk to the customer.   Questions should be nonaccusatory and neutral in tone. Seek to understand what happened, but be careful not to blame the users because they may become defensive and not give you the information that you need to solve the problem.

Know how to create restore points.   Restore points in Windows can be created through the System Restore utility and the System Protection tab.

Review Questions

The answers to the chapter review questions can be found in Appendix A.

1. In Windows, which utility is responsible for finding, downloading, and installing Windows service packs?

    A.   Update Manager

    B.   Service Pack Manager

    C.   Download Manager

    D.   Windows Update

2. Which boot mode loads only basic drivers?

    A.   Limited Mode

    B.   Safe Mode

    C.   Feature Mode

    D.   Windows Mode

3. Which BOOTREC option can be used in Windows to rebuild the boot configuration file?

    A.   /FIXBOOT

    B.   /REBUILDBCD

    C.   /FIXBCD

    D.   /FIXMBR

4. What is the first step in the troubleshooting process?

    A.   Document findings

    B.   Identify the problem

    C.   Establish a theory

    D.   Verify functionality

5. Which tool do you use to create a restore point in Windows?

    A.   Backup

    B.   System Restore

    C.   Restore Point

    D.   Emergency Repair

6. Which of the following operating systems use the BOOT.INI file during boot?

    A.   Windows XP

    B.   Windows Vista

    C.   Windows 7

    D.   Windows 8/8.1

7. One of the users you support has a Windows 7 laptop that continues to shut down and restart spontaneously. What should you try first?

   A. Swap the motherboard.

   B. Begin disabling drivers one by one until you find the culprit.

   C. Disable the sleep settings for hibernation.

   D. Reinstall Windows 7.

8. Windows 7 includes a feature called a _____, which is a copy of your system configuration that can be used to roll back the system to a previous state if a configuration error occurs.

   A. Restore point

   B. Repair point

   C. Rollback point

   D. Registry point

9. Which of the following are used to prevent pop-unders from appearing?

   A. Anti-malware utilities

   B. Pop-up blockers

   C. Phishing sites

   D. Antivirus software

10. In general, how often should you update your antivirus definitions?

    A. Once a week.

    B. Once a month.

    C. Once a year.

    D. Antivirus definitions do not need to be updated.

11. One of your users claims that their hard drive seems to be running slowly. What tool can you use to check to see how fragmented the hard drive is?

    A. Disk Analyzer

    B. Disk Cleanup

    C. Disk Defragmenter

    D. CHKDSK

12. You want to ensure that your computer receives automatic updates to Windows and other Microsoft products. Which tool will take care of this for you?

    A. Windows Update

    B. Microsoft Update

    C. System Update

    D. None of the above

13. Which of the following programs could be considered anti-malware?

  A. Windows Defender

  B. Microsoft Monitor

  C. System Watchdog

  D. None of the above

14. Which of the following allows you to register and unregister modules and controls for troubleshooting purposes?

  A. REGSVR32

  B. SFC

  C. FIXBOOT

  D. FIXMBR

15. Which of the following can you do to help eliminate security problems? (Select all that apply.)

  A. Establish security policies and procedures.

  B. Update your operating systems.

  C. Update your applications.

  D. Update your network devices.

16. Internal users are seeing repeated attempts to infect their systems as reported to them by pop-up messages from their virus scanning software. According to the pop-up messages, the virus seems to be the same in every case. What is the most likely culprit?

  A. A server is acting as a carrier for a virus.

  B. You have a worm virus.

  C. Your antivirus software has malfunctioned.

  D. A DoS attack is under way.

17. Which of the following tools can you use to delete temporary Internet files and other unneeded files to free up disk space?

  A. Disk Analyzer

  B. Disk Cleanup

  C. Disk Defragmenter

  D. CHKDSK

18. Which of the following tools automatically verifies system files after a reboot to see if they were changed to unprotected copies?

  A. DAZR

  B. NTLDR

  C. REGEDIT

  D. SFC

19. To open System Restore, click Start ➤ All Programs ➤ Accessories, and then what?

    A. Advanced

    B. System Tools

    C. Backup

    D. TCP/IP

20. Which utility is shown in Figure 22.8?

FIGURE 22.8 A Windows-based utility

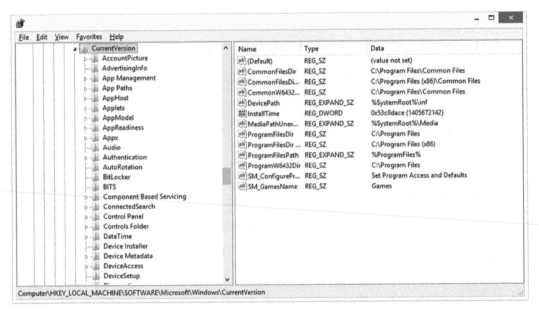

    A. REGEDIT

    B. REGSRV32

    C. MSCONFIG

    D. Event Viewer

Performance-Based Question

You will encounter performance-based questions on the A+ exams. The questions on the exam require you to perform a specific task, and you will be graded on whether or not you were able to complete the task. The following requires you to think creatively in order to measure how well you understand this chapter's topics. You may or may not see similar questions on the actual A+ exams. To see how your answers compare to the authors', refer to Appendix B.

List, in order, the seven best practice steps associated with malware removal.

Chapter

23

Understanding Operational Procedures

THE FOLLOWING COMPTIA A+ 220-902 EXAM OBJECTIVES ARE COVERED IN THIS CHAPTER:

✓ **5.1 Given a scenario, use appropriate safety procedures.**

- Equipment grounding
- Proper component handling and storage
    - Antistatic bags
    - ESD straps
    - ESD mats
    - Self-grounding
- Toxic waste handling
    - Batteries
    - Toner
    - CRT
- Personal safety
    - Disconnect power before repairing PC
    - Remove jewelry
    - Lifting techniques
    - Weight limitations
    - Electrical fire safety
    - Cable management
    - Safety goggles
    - Air filter mask
- Compliance with local government regulations

✓ **5.2 Given a scenario with potential environmental impacts, apply the appropriate controls.**

- MSDS documentation for handling and disposal
- Temperature, humidity level awareness, and proper ventilation
- Power surges, brownouts, blackouts
  - Battery backup
  - Surge suppressor
- Protection from airborne particles
  - Enclosures
  - Air filters/Mask
- Dust and debris
  - Compressed air
  - Vacuums
- Compliance to local government regulations

✓ **5.3 Summarize the process of addressing prohibited content/activity, and explain privacy, licensing, and policy concepts.**

- Incident response
  - First response
    - Identify
    - Report through proper channels
    - Data/device preservation
  - Use of documentation/documentation changes
  - Chain of custody
    - Tracking of evidence/documenting process
- Licensing / DRM / EULA
  - Open source vs. commercial license
  - Personal license vs. enterprise licenses
- Personally Identifiable Information
- Follow corporate end-use policies and security best practices

✓ **5.4 Demonstrate proper communication techniques and professionalism.**

- Use proper language—avoid jargon, acronyms, slang when applicable
- Maintain a positive attitude / Project confidence
- Actively listen (taking notes) and avoid interrupting a customer
- Be culturally sensitive
    - Use appropriate professional titles, when applicable
- Be on time (if late contact the customer)
- Avoid distractions
    - Personal calls
    - Texting / Social media sites
    - Talking to co-workers while interacting with customers
    - Personal interruptions
- Dealing with a difficult customer or situation
    - Do not argue with customers and/or be defensive
    - Avoid dismissing customer's problems
    - Avoid being judgmental
    - Clarify customer statements (ask open-ended questions to narrow the scope of the problem, restate the issue or question to verify understanding)
    - Do not disclose experiences via social media outlets
- Set and meet expectations/timeline and communicate status with the customer
    - Offer different repair/replacement options if applicable
    - Provide proper documentation on the services provided
    - Follow up with customer/user at a later date to verify satisfaction
- Deal appropriately with customers' confidential and private materials
    - Located on a computer, desktop, printer, etc.

Every day at work, we do what it takes to get the job done. As IT professionals, we have millions of facts crammed into our heads about how various hardware components work and what software configuration settings work best for our systems. We know which servers or workstations give us constant trouble and which end users need more help than others. We are counted on to be experts in knowing *what* to do to keep computers and networks running smoothly. And even though we don't tend to think about it overtly, we need to be experts in *how* we get things done as well. Even though the *how* might not be top of mind for you every day (hopefully you don't go to work every day thinking "Okay, don't get killed by a monitor" or "Let's see if I can be nice to someone today"), but it should be integrated into your work processes. Operational procedures define the *how*, and they provide guidance on the proper ways to get various tasks accomplished.

In this chapter, we will start off by talking about safety, which includes your safety and the safety of your co-workers, as well as environmental concerns. Observing proper safety procedures can help prevent injury to yourself or to others.

Our discussion about the environment is two sided. The environment affects computers (via things like dust, sunlight, and water), but computers can also potentially harm the environment. We'll consider both sides as we move through this chapter.

Next, we will cover some legal aspects of operational procedures. These include licensing of software, protection of personally identifiable information, and incident response.

In the final part of this chapter, we'll switch to discussing professionalism and communication and focus on topics that you need to know for your exam study. Applying the skills learned here will help you pass the exam, but on a more practical level, it will help you become a better technician and possibly further advance your career.

Understanding Safety Procedures

The proliferation of computers in today's society has created numerous jobs for technicians. Presumably that's why you're reading this book: You want to get your CompTIA A+ certification. Many others who don't fix computers professionally do like tinkering with them as a hobby. Years ago, only the most expert users dared to crack the case on a computer. Oftentimes, repairing the system meant using a soldering iron. Today, thanks to the cheap parts, computer repair is not quite as involved. Regardless of your skill or intent, if you're going to be inside a computer, you always need to be aware of safety issues. There's no sense in getting yourself hurt or killed—literally.

As a provider of a hands-on service (repairing, maintaining, or upgrading someone's computer), you need to be aware of some general safety tips, because if you are not careful, you could harm yourself or the equipment. Clients expect you to solve their problems, not make them worse by injuring yourself or those around you. In the following sections, we'll talk about identifying safety hazards and creating a safe working environment.

Identifying Potential Safety Hazards

Anything can be a potential safety hazard, right? Okay, maybe that statement is a bit too paranoid, but there *are* many things, both man-made and environmental, that can cause safety problems when you're working with and around computers.

Perhaps the most important aspect of computers you should be aware of is that not only do they *use* electricity, they also *store* electrical charge after they're turned off. This makes the power supply and the monitor pretty much off-limits to anyone but a repairperson trained specifically for those devices. In addition, the computer's processor and various parts of the printer run at extremely high temperatures, and you can get burned if you try to handle them immediately after they've been in operation.

Those are just two general safety measures that should concern you. There are plenty more. When discussing safety issues with regard to PCs, let's break them down into four general areas:

- Computer components
- Electrostatic discharge
- Electromagnetic interference
- Natural elements

Computer Components

As mentioned earlier, computers use electricity. And as you're probably aware, electricity can hurt or kill you. The first rule when working inside a computer is always to make sure that it's powered off. So if you have to open the computer to inspect or replace parts (as you will with most repairs), be sure to turn off the machine before you begin. Leaving it plugged in is usually fine, and many times it is actually preferred because it grounds the equipment and can help prevent electrostatic discharge.

There's one exception to the power-off rule: you don't have to power off the computer when working with hot-swappable parts, which are designed to be unplugged and plugged back in when the computer is on. Most of these components have an externally accessible interface (such as USB devices or hot-swappable hard drives), so you don't need to crack the computer case.

The Power Supply

Do not take the issue of safety and electricity lightly. Removing the power supply from its external casing can be dangerous. The current flowing through the power supply normally follows a complete circuit; when your body breaks the circuit, your body becomes part of that circuit. Getting inside the power supply is the most dangerous thing you can do as an untrained technician.

The two biggest dangers with power supplies are burning or electrocuting yourself. These risks usually go hand in hand. If you touch a bare wire that is carrying current, you could get electrocuted. A large-enough current passing through you can cause severe burns. It can also cause your heart to stop, your muscles to seize, and your brain to stop functioning. In short, it can kill you. Electricity always finds the best path to ground. And because the human body is basically a bag of saltwater (an excellent conductor of electricity), electricity will use us as a conductor if we are grounded.

Although it is possible to open a power supply to work on it, doing so is *not* recommended. Power supplies contain several capacitors that can hold *lethal* charges *long after they have been unplugged!* It is extremely dangerous to open the case of a power supply. Besides, power supplies are pretty cheap. It would probably cost less to replace one than to try to fix it, and this approach would be much safer.

In the late 1990s, a few mass computer manufacturers experimented with using open power supplies in their computers to save money. We don't know if any deaths occurred because of such incompetence, but it was definitely a very bad idea.

Current vs. Voltage: Which Is More Dangerous?

When talking about power and safety, you will almost always hear the saying, "It's not the volts that kill you, it's the amps." That's mostly true. However, an explanation is in order.

The number of volts in a power source represents its potential to do work. But volts don't do anything by themselves. Current (amperage, or amps) is the force behind the work done by electricity. Here's an analogy to help explain this concept: Say you have two boulders. One weighs 10 pounds and another weighs 100 pounds, and each is 100 feet off the ground. If you drop them, which one will do more work? The obvious answer is the 100-pound boulder. They both have the same potential to do work (100 feet of travel), but the 100-pound boulder has more mass and thus more force. Voltage is analogous to the distance the boulder is from the ground, and amperage is analogous to the mass of the boulder.

This is why you can produce static electricity on the order of 50,000 volts and not electrocute yourself. Even though this electricity has a great potential for work, it does very little work because the amperage is so low. This also explains why you can weld metal with 110 volts. Welders use only 110 (sometimes 220) volts, but they also use anywhere from 50 to 200 amps!

If you ever have to work on a power supply, for safety's sake you should discharge all capacitors within it. To do this, connect a resistor across the leads of the capacitor with a rating of 3 watts or more and a resistance of 100 ohms (Ω) per volt. For example, to discharge a 225-volt capacitor, you would use a 22.5kΩ resistor (225 volts times 100Ω = 22,500Ω, or 22.5kΩ).

The Monitor

Other than the power supply, the most dangerous component to try to repair is a computer monitor, specifically older-style cathode-ray tube (CRT) monitors. In fact, we recommend that you *do not* try to repair monitors of any kind.

To avoid the extremely hazardous environment contained inside the monitor—it can retain a high-voltage charge for hours after it's been turned off—take it to a certified monitor technician or television repair shop. The repair shop or certified technician will know the proper procedures for discharging the monitor, which involve attaching a resistor to the flyback transformer's charging capacitor to release the high-voltage electrical charge that builds up during use. They will also be able to determine whether the monitor can be repaired or whether it needs to be replaced. Remember, the monitor works in its own extremely protected environment (the monitor case) and may not respond well to your desire to try to open it.

 WARNING A CRT is vacuum sealed. Be extremely careful when handling a CRT. If you break the glass, it will implode, which can send glass in any direction.

Even though we recommend not repairing monitors, the A+ exam may test your knowledge of the safety practices to use if you ever you need to do so. If you have to open a monitor, you must first discharge the high-voltage charge on it by using a *high-voltage probe*. This probe has a very large needle, a gauge that indicates volts, and a wire with an alligator clip. Attach the alligator clip to a ground (usually the round pin on the power cord). Slip the probe needle underneath the high-voltage cup on the monitor. You will see the gauge spike to around 15,000 volts and slowly reduce to 0 (zero). When it reaches zero, you may remove the high-voltage probe and service the high-voltage components of the monitor.

 WARNING Do *not* use an ESD strap when discharging the monitor; doing so can lead to a fatal electric shock.

Working with LCD monitors or any device with a fluorescent or LCD backlight presents a unique safety challenge. These types of devices require an *inverter*, which provides the high-voltage, high-frequency energy needed to power the backlight.

The inverter is a small circuit board installed behind the LCD panel that takes DC power and converts (inverts) it for the backlight. If you've ever seen a laptop or handheld device with a flickering screen or perpetual dimness, it was likely an inverter problem. Inverters store energy even when their power source is cut off, so they have the potential to discharge that energy if you mess with them. Be careful!

The Case

One component that people frequently overlook is the case. Cases are generally made of metal, and some computer cases have very sharp edges inside, so be careful when handling them. You can, for example, cut yourself by jamming your fingers between the case and the frame when you try to force the case back on. Also of particular interest are drive bays. Countless technicians have scraped or cut their hands on drive bays when trying in vain to plug a drive cable into the motherboard. Particularly sharp edges can be covered with duct tape—just make sure that you're covering only metal and nothing with electrical components on it.

The Printer

If you've ever attempted to repair a printer, you might have thought that there was a little monster in there hiding all of the screws from you. Besides missing screws, here are some things to watch out for when repairing printers:

- When handling a toner cartridge from a laser printer or page printer, do not turn it upside down. You will find yourself spending more time cleaning the printer and the surrounding area than fixing the printer.
- Do not put any objects into the feeding system (in an attempt to clear the path) when the printer is running.
- Laser printers generate a laser that is hazardous to your eyes. Do not look directly into the source of the laser.
- If it's an inkjet printer, do not try to blow in the ink cartridge to clear a clogged opening—that is, unless you like the taste of ink.
- Some parts of a laser printer (such as the EP cartridge) will be damaged if you touch them. Your skin produces oils and has a small surface layer of dead skin cells. These substances can collect on the delicate surface of the EP cartridge and cause malfunctions. Bottom line: Keep your fingers out of places where they don't belong!
- Laser printers use very high voltage power sources to charge internal components, which can cause severe injuries.
- Laser printers can get extremely hot. Don't burn yourself on internal components.

 Using an egg carton (or other container with small compartments) is a great way to store and keep track of screws that you take out of a device when you're working on it.

When working with printers, we follow some pretty simple guidelines. If there's a messed-up setting, paper jam, or ink or toner problem, we will fix it. If it's something other than that, we call a certified printer repairperson. The inner workings of printers can get pretty complex, and it's best to call someone trained to make those types of repairs.

The Keyboard and Mouse

Okay, we know that you're thinking, "What danger could a keyboard or mouse pose?" We admit that not much danger is associated with these components, but there are a couple of safety concerns that you should always keep in mind.

First, if your mouse has a cord, it can catch on something, causing items to fall off of a desk, or it might even be long enough that someone can trip over it, so make sure that it's safely out of the way. Second, you could short-circuit your keyboard if you accidentally spill liquid into it. Keyboards generally don't function well with half a can of cola in their innards!

Electrostatic Discharge

So far, we've talked about how electricity can hurt people, but it can also pose safety issues for computer components. One of the biggest concerns for components is *electrostatic discharge (ESD)*. For the most part, ESD won't do serious damage to a person other than provide a little shock. But little amounts of ESD can cause serious damage to computer components, and that damage can manifest itself by causing computers to hang or reboot or fail to boot at all. ESD happens when two objects of dissimilar charge come into contact with one another. The two objects exchange electrons in order to standardize the electrostatic charge between them. This charge can, and often does, damage electronic components.

 CPU chips and memory chips are particularly sensitive to ESD. Be extremely cautious when handling them.

When you shuffle your feet across the floor and shock your best friend on the ear, you are discharging static electricity into their ear. The lowest static voltage transfer that you can feel is around 3,000 volts; it doesn't electrocute you because there is extremely little current. A static transfer that you can *see* is at least 10,000 volts! Just by sitting in a chair, you can generate around 100 volts of static electricity. Walking around wearing synthetic materials can generate around 1,000 volts. You can easily generate around 20,000 volts simply by dragging your smooth-soled shoes across a carpeted floor in the winter. (Actually, it doesn't have to be winter. This voltage can occur in any room with very low humidity—like a heated room in wintertime.)

 Relative humidity has a significant impact on the electricity you generate. Walking around can generate 1,500 volts at 65 to 90 percent relative humidity, but it can produce 35,000 volts if the relative humidity is in the 10 to 25 percent range.

It makes sense that these thousands of volts can damage computer components. However, a component can be damaged with less than 300 volts! This means that if a small charge is built up in your body, you could damage a component without realizing it.

Do you have long hair or (gasp!) have to wear a tie when fixing computers? Tie it back. Letting long hair or dangling cloth get inside an open computer case is asking for trouble because both are notorious for carrying and conducting static electricity.

The good news is that there are measures that you can implement to help contain the effects of ESD. The first and easiest item to implement is the antistatic wrist strap, also referred to as an ESD strap. We will look at the antistatic wrist strap, as well as other ESD prevention tools, in the following sections.

Antistatic Wrist Straps

To use the ESD strap, you attach one end to an earth ground (typically, the ground pin on an extension cord) or the computer case and wrap the other end around your wrist. This strap grounds your body and keeps it at a zero charge. Figure 23.1 shows the proper way to attach an antistatic strap. There are several varieties of wrist straps available. The one in Figure 23.1 uses a banana clip, while others use alligator clips and are attached to the computer case itself.

FIGURE 23.1   One possible way to use an ESD strap

Pin connects to ground pin
(small round hole) or
earth ground

ESD strap

Outlet

  Real World Scenario

ESD Symptoms

Symptoms of ESD damage may be subtle, but they can be detected. One of the authors relates this experience:

"When I think of ESD, I always think of the same instance. Several years ago, I was working on an Apple Macintosh. This computer seemed to have a mind of its own. I would troubleshoot it, find the defective component, and replace it. The problem was that as soon as I replaced the component, it failed. I thought maybe the power supply was frying the boards, so I replaced both at the same time, but to no avail.

"I was about to send the computer off to Apple when I realized that it was winter. Normally this would not be a factor, but winters where I live are extremely dry. Dry air promotes static electricity. At first I thought my problem couldn't be that simple, but I was at the end of my rope. So, when I received my next set of new parts, I grounded myself with an antistatic strap for the time it took to install the components, and prayed while I turned on the power. Success! The components worked as they should, and a new advocate of ESD prevention was born."

For an antistatic wrist strap to work properly, the computer must be plugged in but turned off. When the computer is plugged in, it is grounded through the power cord. When you attach yourself to it with the wrist strap, you are grounded through the power cord as well. If the computer is not plugged in, there is no ground and any excess electricity on you will just discharge into the case, which is not good.

An ESD strap is a device that is specially designed to bleed electrical charges away *safely*. It uses a 1 megohm resistor to bleed the charge away slowly. A simple wire wrapped around your wrist will not work correctly, and you could be electrocuted!

Never wear an ESD strap if you're working inside a monitor or inside a power supply. If you wear one while working on the inside of these components, you increase the chance of getting a lethal shock.

ESD Antistatic Mats

It is possible to damage a device by simply laying it on a bench top. For this reason, you should have an ESD mat in addition to an ESD strap. This mat drains excess charge away from any item coming in contact with it (see Figure 23.2). ESD mats are also sold as mouse/keyboard pads to prevent ESD charges from interfering with the operation of the computer. Many wrist straps can be connected to the mat, thus causing the technician and any equipment in contact with the mat to be at the same electrical potential and eliminating ESD. There are even ESD bootstraps and ESD floor mats, which are used to keep the technician's entire body at the same potential.

FIGURE 23.2   Proper use of an ESD antistatic mat

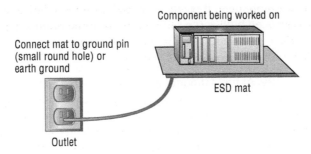

Component being worked on

Connect mat to ground pin
(small round hole) or
earth ground

ESD mat

Outlet

Antistatic Bags for Parts

Antistatic bags are important tools to have at your disposal when servicing electronic components because they protect the sensitive electronic devices from stray static charges. By design, the static charges collect on the outside of these silver or pink bags rather than on the electronic components.

WARNING   Unlike antistatic mats, antistatic bags do not "drain" the charges away, and they should never be used in place of an antistatic mat.

You can obtain the bags from several sources. The most direct way to acquire antistatic bags is to go to an electronics supply store and purchase them in bulk. Most supply stores have several sizes available. Perhaps the easiest way to obtain them, however, is simply to hold on to the ones that come your way. That is, when you purchase any new component, it usually comes in an antistatic bag. After you have installed the component, keep the bag. It may take you a while to gather a collection of bags if you take this approach, but eventually you will have a fairly large assortment.

Self-Grounding

First of all, we recommend that you include a grounding strap in your technician toolkit so you're never without it. But we also realize that things happen and you might find yourself in a situation where you don't have your strap or an ESD mat. In cases like that, you should self-ground.

Self-grounding is not as effective as using proper anti-ESD gear, but it makes up for that with its simplicity. To self-ground, make sure the computer is turned off but plugged in. Then touch an exposed (but not hot or sharp!) metal part of the case. That will drain electrical charge from you. Better yet is if you can maintain constant contact with that metal part. That should keep you at the same bias as the case. Yes, it can be rather challenging to work inside a computer one-handed, but it can be done.

Additional Methods

Another preventive measure that you can take is to maintain the relative humidity at around 50 percent. Don't increase the humidity too far—to the point where moisture begins to condense on the equipment. Also, use antistatic spray, which is available commercially, to reduce static buildup on clothing and carpets.

 If you don't have any antistatic spray, you can always use the "Downy solution." In a spray bottle, combine one part water with one part liquid fabric softener. Mist areas such as carpet and clothing that cause problems. If used regularly, it will keep static away and keep your office smelling nice too!

Vendors have methods of protecting components in transit from manufacture to installation. They press the pins of integrated circuits (ICs) into antistatic foam to keep all of the pins at the same potential. In addition, most circuit boards are shipped in antistatic bags, as discussed earlier.

 Antistatic foam looks a lot like Styrofoam. However, there are huge differences between the two. While antistatic foam helps reduce the transfer of electricity, Styrofoam does not. Styrofoam holds a charge on its surface quite easily. Have you ever tried to get some of those small packing "peanuts" off your hands? Be careful to not mix the two up, lest you fry your components.

At the very least, you can be mindful of the dangers of ESD and take steps to reduce its effects. Beyond that, you should educate yourself about those effects so that you know when ESD is becoming a major problem.

Electromagnetic Interference

When compared to the other dangers that we've discussed in this chapter, *electromagnetic interference (EMI)*, also known as *radio frequency interference (RFI)* when it's in the same frequency range as radio waves, is by far the least dangerous. EMI really poses no threats to you in terms of bodily harm. What it can do is to make your equipment or network malfunction.

EMI is an unwanted disturbance caused by electromagnetic radiation generated by another source. In other words, some of your electrical equipment may interfere with other equipment. Here are some common sources of interference:

Network devices   The popularity of wireless networking devices has introduced the possibility of interference. Some of the most popular wireless networking standards, 802.11b/g/n, use the 2.4GHz range for transmissions. Bluetooth devices happen to use the same frequency. In theory, they won't interfere with each other because they use different modulation techniques. In practice, interference between the two types of devices can happen.

Magnets   Magnets work by generating an electromagnetic field. It might make sense, then, that this field could cause electromagnetic interference. For the most part, you don't need to worry about this unless you have huge magnets at work. Do note, however, that many motors use magnets, which can cause interference. For example, one of our friends used to have his computer on the opposite side of a wall from his refrigerator. Whenever the compressor kicked in, his monitor display would become wavy and unreadable. It was time to move his home office. Another common culprit is a desk fan. Put a desk fan next to a monitor and turn the fan on. What happens to the display? It will become wavy. This is another example of EMI.

Cordless phones   Cordless phones can operate at a variety of frequencies. Some of the more common ones are 900MHz, 1.9GHz, 2.4GHz, and 5.8GHz. Many of these are common ranges for computer equipment to operate in as well.

Microwave ovens   Microwave ovens are convenient devices for heating food and beverages. The radiation they generate is typically in the 2.45GHz range, although it can vary slightly. If a microwave is being used near your computer, you'll often see a distorted display just as if a fan or motor were being run next to your computer. You may also experience interference with wireless network communications.

 Copper wires are susceptible to EMI. Fiber-optic cables, which use light to transmit data, are not susceptible to EMI.

Natural Elements

Computers should always be operated in cool environments away from direct sunlight and water sources. This is also true when you're working on computers. We know that heat is an enemy of electrical components. Dirt and dust act as great insulators, trapping heat inside components. When components run hotter than they should, they have a greater chance of breaking down faster.

It pretty much should go without saying, but we'll say it anyway: Water and electricity don't mix. Keep liquids away from computers. If you need your morning coffee while fixing a PC, make sure that the coffee cup has a tight and secure lid.

Water and Servers Don't Mix

This situation happened at a company where one of the authors used to work. The building needed some roof repairs. Repairs went on for several days, and then the weekend came. It just so happened that the area on which they were working was over the server room. That weekend was a particularly rainy one, and of course no one was in the office over the weekend.

Monday morning came, and the IT staff arrived to find that the server room was partially flooded. Rain had come in through weaknesses in the roof caused by the maintenance and had flooded through the drop ceiling and into the server room. Nearly half a million dollars of equipment was ruined.

Although this is an extreme example, it illustrates an important point: Always be aware of the environment in which you're working, and be alert to potential sources of problems for your computer equipment.

Creating a Safe Workplace

Benjamin Franklin was quoted as saying, "An ounce of prevention is worth a pound of cure." That sage advice applies to a lot in life and certainly to computer safety. Knowing how to work with and handle computer equipment properly is a good first start. It's also important to institutionalize and spread the knowledge, though, and to make sure that your company has the proper policies and procedures in place to ensure everyone's safety.

Moving Computer Equipment

We've already talked about some of the hazards posed by computer parts. Many times it's the more mundane tasks that get us though, such as moving stuff around. One of the most common ways that IT employees get hurt is by moving equipment in an improper way. Changing the location of computers is a task often completed by IT personnel, and you can avoid injury by moving things the right way.

To ensure your personal safety, here are some important techniques to consider before moving equipment:

- The first thing to check for always is that it's unplugged. There's nothing worse (and potentially more dangerous) than getting yanked because you're still tethered.
- Securely tie the power cord to the device, or remove it altogether if possible.
- Remove any loose jewelry and secure long hair or neckties.
- Lift with your legs, not your back (bend at the knees when picking something up, not at the waist).
- Do not twist when lifting.
- Maintain the natural curves of the back and spine when lifting.
- Keep objects close to your body and at waist level.
- Push rather than pull if possible.

The muscles in the lower back aren't nearly as strong as those in the legs or other parts of the body. Whenever lifting, you want to reduce the strain on those lower-back muscles as much as possible. If you want, use a back belt or brace to help you maintain the proper position while lifting.

CRT monitors can be heavy. (Thank goodness for flat screens!) When lifting and carrying any type of monitor, always keep the glass face toward your body. The front of the monitor is the heaviest part, and you want the heavy part closest to your body to reduce strain on your muscles.

If you believe that the load is too much for you to carry, don't try to pick it up! Get assistance from a coworker. Another great idea is to use a cart. It will save you trips if you have multiple items to move, and it saves you the stress of carrying components.

When moving loads, always be aware of your surrounding environment. Before you move, scout out the path to see whether there are any trip hazards or other safety concerns such as spills, stairs, uneven floors (or ripped carpet), tight turns, or narrow doorways.

Using Appropriate Repair Tools

A big part of creating a safe working environment is having the right tools available for the job. There's no sense implementing a sledgehammer solution to a ball-peen hammer problem. Using the wrong tool might not help fix the problem, and it could very possibly hurt you or the computer in the process.

Most of the time, computers can be opened and devices removed with nothing more than a simple screwdriver. But if you do a lot of work on PCs, you'll definitely want to have additional tools on hand.

Computer toolkits are readily available on the Internet or at any electronics store. They come in versions from inexpensive (under $10) kits that have around 10 pieces to kits that cost several hundred dollars and have more tools than you will probably ever need. Figure 23.3 shows an example of a basic 11-piece PC toolkit. All of these tools come in a handy zippered case, so it's hard to lose them.

FIGURE 23.3 PC toolkit

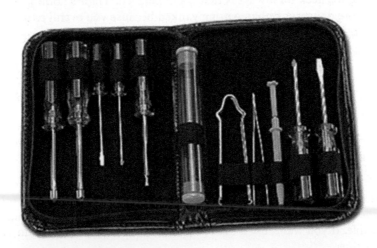

Looking at Figure 23.3, from left to right you have two nut drivers (¼″ and ³⁄₁₆″), a ⅛″ flat screwdriver, a #0 Phillips screwdriver, a T-15 Torx driver, a screw tube, an integrated circuit (IC) extractor, tweezers, a three-claw retriever, a #1 Phillips screwdriver, and a ³⁄₁₆″; flat screwdriver. A favorite of ours is the three-claw retriever because screws like to fall and hide in tiny places. While most of these tools are incredibly useful, an IC extractor probably won't be. In today's environment, it's rare to find an IC that you can extract, much less find a reason to extract one.

The following sections look at some of the tools of the PC troubleshooting trade.

Screwdrivers

Every PC technician worth their weight in pocket protectors needs to have a screwdriver. At least one. There are three major categories of screwdrivers: flat-blade, Phillips, and Torx. In addition, there are devices that look like screwdrivers, except that they have a hex-shaped indented head on them. They're called hex drivers, and they belong to the screwdriver family.

Whenever picking a screwdriver, always keep in mind that you want to match the size of the screwdriver head to the size of the screw. Using a screwdriver that's too small will cause it to spin inside the head of the screw, stripping the head of the screw and making it useless. If the screwdriver is too large, on the other hand, you won't be able to get the head in far enough to generate any torque to loosen the screw. Of course, if the screwdriver is way too big, it won't even fit inside the screw head at all. Common sizes for Phillips-head screws are 000, 00, 0, 1, 2, and 3. When dealing with Torx screws, the two most common sizes are T-10 and T-15.

When tightening screws, you don't need to make them so tight that they could survive the vibrations of an atmospheric reentry. Snug is fine. Making them too tight can cause problems when loosening them, which could cause you (or someone else not so strong) to strip the head. Using an electric screwdriver is fine if you have one. The only problem with them is that they tend to be larger than manual screwdrivers and can be difficult to get inside a case.

Using magnetic-tipped screwdrivers is not recommended. Many computer disks contain magnetically coded information, and the magnetic tip of a screwdriver could cause a problem. Keep a retrieving tool handy instead, just in case you drop a screw.

Antistatic Wrist Straps

We've already talked about these, but they are important, so we'll mention them again. An antistatic wrist strap is essential to any PC technician's arsenal. They don't typically come with smaller PC toolkits, but you should always have one or two handy.

Other Useful Tools

PC techs also commonly carry the following tools:

Pliers   Pliers are useful for a variety of tasks, especially gripping something. Long-nose or needle-nose pliers extend your reach.

Wire cutters   Wire cutters come in a variety of forms but are primarily used for cutting cables. It's not likely that you'll need any sort of heavy-duty metal cutters.

Strippers   If you are making your own network cables or fixing them, having a cable stripper (and crimper) is essential.

Mirrors   Mirrors are handy inside tight spaces. Many techs like to use a dentist-style mirror because of its compact size and good reach.

Flashlight   Never underestimate the utility of a good flashlight. You never know what your lighting situation will be like when you're at a repair site. Smaller flashlights with good output are great to have because they can fit into tight spaces.

Compressed air   For as much as computers and dust don't get along, it sure seems like they are attracted to each other. In all seriousness, computer components are powered by electricity, which causes the components to have a slight electrical charge. Dust is also electrically charged, so it's attracted to computer components. Compressed air can help you clean off components, especially in hard-to-reach places.

 Be judicious about your use of compressed air. Often, you will find yourself just blowing the dust from one part of a computer to another.

Multimeter   If you're having power issues, a multimeter is an invaluable tool that measures electrical current, voltage, and resistance. You'll also hear of voltmeters, and while the two have somewhat different functions, both of them can be used to troubleshoot power problems. Using a voltmeter, you can see if a computer power supply is producing the right amount of current for the devices that depend on it.

Safety goggles and air filter masks   We've mentioned dust before, and you will occasionally encounter large amounts of it when working inside computers. If you're using compressed air to blow dust out, it could easily get into your eyes or lungs. You don't want to breathe the stuff, and in some environments (like machine shops), you don't know what types of hazardous materials are mixed in with that dust. You don't need a big army-grade gas mask, but a small respirator will help considerably.

Creating a Safe Work Environment

We've already talked about some work environment issues. For example, don't put a computer next to the break room sink, and keep computers out of direct sunlight (even if the desk location is great). A few other things to watch out for are trip hazards, atmospheric conditions, and high-voltage areas.

Cables are a common cause of tripping. If at all possible, run cables through drop ceilings or through conduits to keep them out of the way. If you need to lay a cable through a trafficked area, use a cable floor guard to keep the cables in place and safe from crushing. Floor guards come in a variety of lengths and sizes (for just a few cables or for a lot of cables). Figure 23.4 shows a cable guard.

FIGURE 23.4   Floor cable guard

Another useful tool to keep cables under control is a cable tie, like the ones shown in Figure 23.5. It's simply a plastic tie that holds two or more cables together. They come in different sizes and colors, so you're bound to find one that suits your needs.

FIGURE 23.5   Cable ties

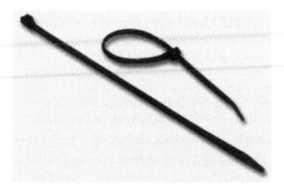

 In a pinch, and without a floor cable guard, you can use tape, such as duct tape, to secure your cables to the floor. This is recommended only as a temporary fix for two reasons. First, it's not much less of a trip hazard than just having the cables run across the floor. Second, duct tape doesn't protect the cables from being crushed if people step on them or heavy objects are moved over them.

Exercise 23.1 is a simple exercise that you can modify and use as needed. Its purpose is to illustrate common office hazards that you may not have realized were there.

EXERCISE 23.1

Finding Trip Hazards

1. Walk around the server room and count how many cables are lying on the floor.

2. Walk around the client areas and see how many cables are lying on the floor or are exposed underneath cubicles.

Maybe you're fortunate and don't find any, but odds are that you found at least one area with exposed cables that should not be exposed. You can reapply this exercise for other dangerous items, such as exposed wires and exposed sharp edges.

Atmospheric conditions you need to be aware of include areas with high static electricity or excessive humidity. This is especially important for preventing electrostatic discharge, as we've already discussed.

Finally, be aware of high-voltage areas. Computers do need electricity to run, but only in measured amounts. Running or fixing computers in high-voltage areas can cause problems for the electrical components and can cause problems for you if something should go wrong.

Implementing Safety Policies and Procedures

The Occupational Safety and Health Act states that every working American has the right to a safe and healthy work environment. To enforce the act, the Occupational Safety and Health Administration (OSHA) was formed. OSHA covers all private-sector employees and post office workers. Public-sector employees are covered by state programs, and federal employees are covered under a presidential executive order. In a nutshell, OSHA requires employers to "provide a workplace that is free of recognized dangers and hazards."

There are three overarching criteria to a safe work environment:

▪ The company and its employees have identified all significant hazards in the work setting.

▪ Preventive measures have been taken to address each significant hazard.

▪ The company and its employees understand how to respond to accidents or near-miss accidents if or when they occur.

The following sections explore specific responsibilities and how to create a safe work environment plan.

Always ensure that your company's safety policies and procedures comply with all government regulations.

Employer and Employee Responsibilities

Maintaining workplace safety is the responsibility of employers as well as employees. Here are some of the important responsibilities of employers:

- Provide properly maintained tools and equipment.
- Provide a warning system, such as codes or labels, to warn employees of potential hazards or dangerous chemicals.
- Post the OSHA poster in a prominent location.
- Keep records of workplace injuries or illnesses.
- Continuously examine workplace conditions to ensure OSHA compliance.

It's also the responsibility of the employee to help maintain a safe work environment. Specifically, employees are charged with the following tasks:

- Read and understand OSHA posters.
- Follow all employer-implemented health and safety rules and safe work practices.
- Use all required protective gear and equipment.
- Report hazardous conditions to the employer.
- Report hazardous conditions that the employer does not correct to OSHA.

As you can see, employers and employees need to work together to keep the workplace safe. It is illegal for an employee to be punished in any way for exercising their rights under the Occupational Safety and Health Act.

 Real World Scenario

Play It Safe with Common Sense

When you're repairing a PC, do not leave it unattended. Someone could walk into the room and inadvertently bump the machine, causing a failure. Worse, they could step on pieces that may be lying around and get hurt. It is also not a good idea to work on the PC alone. If you're injured, someone should be around to help if you need it. Finally, if you're fatigued, you may find it difficult to concentrate and focus on what you are doing. The most important safety measure to remember when you are repairing PCs is to pay close attention to what you are doing.

Safety Plans

We recommend that your company create and follow a workplace safety plan. Having a safety plan can help avoid accidents that result in lost productivity, equipment damage, and employee injury or death.

A good safety plan should include the following elements:

- A written document that states, among other things, who is responsible for implementing and managing the plan
- Systematic periodic inspections to identify workplace hazards

- Procedures for eliminating hazards once identified
- Processes for investigating the cause of accidents, injuries, or illnesses
- A safety and health training program specific to the job duties performed
- A system for employees to communicate safety or health concerns without fear of reprisal
- A system to ensure that employees comply with safety and health rules
- A system to maintain safety and health records, including steps taken to implement accident prevention initiatives

It might seem like a laundry list of items to consider, but a good safety program needs to be holistic in nature for it to be effective.

Many companies also incorporate rules against drug or alcohol use in their safety and health plans. Specifically, employees are not allowed to come to work if under the influence of alcohol or illegal drugs. Employees who do come to work under the influence may be subject to disciplinary action up to and including termination of employment.

After your safety plan has been created, you need to ensure that all employees receive necessary training. Have each employee sign a form at the end of the training to signify that they attended, and keep the forms in a central location (such as with or near the official safety policy). In addition to the training record, you should make available and keep records of the following:

- Safety improvement suggestion form
- Accident and near-accident reporting form
- Injury and illness log
- Safety inspection checklist
- Hazard removal form
- Material safety data sheets

Safety rules and regulations will work only if they have the broad support of management from the top down. Everyone in the organization needs to buy into the plan or it won't be a success. Make sure that everyone understands the importance of a safe work environment, and make sure that the culture of the company supports safety in the workplace.

Incident Management

Accidents happen. Hopefully, they don't happen too often, but we know that they do. Details on how to handle accidents are a key part of any safety plan so that when an accident does happen, you and your co-workers know what to do. Good plans should include steps for handling a situation as well as reporting an incident. We will cover incident response in more detail later in this chapter. Two major classifications of accidents are environmental and human.

ENVIRONMENTAL ACCIDENTS

When related to computers, environmental accidents typically come in one of two forms: electricity or water. Too much electricity is bad for computer components. If lightning is striking in your area, you run a major risk of frying computer parts. Even if you have a surge protector, you could still be at risk.

The best bet in a lightning storm is to power off your equipment and unplug it from outlets. Make the lightning have to come inside a window and hit your computer directly in order to fry it.

WARNING   Those cheap $10 surge suppressors will fry right along with your computer. And don't be fooled—most power strips do *not* protect against power surges.

Water is obviously also bad for computer components. If there is water in the area and you believe that it will come in contact with your computers, it's best to get the machines powered off as quickly as possible. If components are not powered on but get wet, they may still work after thoroughly drying out. But if they're on when they get wet, they're likely cooked. Water + electronic components = bad. Water + electronic components + electricity = *really* bad.

Many server rooms have raised floors. Although this serves several purposes, one is that equipment stored on the raised floor is less susceptible to water damage if flooding occurs.

HUMAN ACCIDENTS

Human nature dictates that we are not infallible, so of course we're going to make mistakes and have accidents. The key is to minimize the damage caused when an accident happens.

If a chemical spill occurs, make sure the area gets cordoned off as soon as possible. Then clean up the spill. The specific procedure on how to do that depends on the chemical, and that information can be found on material safety data sheets (MSDSs). Depending on the severity of the spill or the chemical released, you may also need to contact the local authorities. Again, the MSDS should have related information.

Physical accidents are more worrisome. People can trip on wires and fall, cut or burn themselves repairing computers, and incur a variety of other injuries. Computer components can be replaced, but that's not always true of human parts (and it's certainly not true of lives). The first thing to keep in mind is always to be careful and use common sense. If you're trying to work inside a computer case and you see sharp metal edges inside the case, see whether the metal (or component on which you are working) can be moved to another location until you finish. Before you stick your hand into an area, make sure that nothing is hot or could cut you.

When an accident does happen (or almost happens), be sure to report it. Many companies pay for workers' compensation insurance. If you're injured on the job, you're required to report the incident, and you might also get temporary payments if you are unable to work because of the accident. Also, if the accident was anything but minor, seek medical attention. Just as victims in auto accidents might not feel pain for a day or two, victims in other physical accidents might be in the same position. If you never report the accident, insurance companies may find it less plausible that your suffering was work related.

Real World Scenario

Fire Safety

Repairing a computer isn't often the cause of an electrical fire. However, you should know how to extinguish such a fire properly. Four major classes of fire extinguishers are available, one for each type of flammable substance: A for wood and paper fires, B for flammable liquids, C for electrical fires, and D (metal powder or NaCl [salt]) for flammable metals such as phosphorus and sodium.

The most popular type of fire extinguisher today is the multipurpose, or ABC-rated, extinguisher. It contains a dry chemical powder (for example, sodium bicarbonate, monoammonium phosphate) that smothers the fire and cools it at the same time. For electrical fires (which may be related to a shorted-out wire in a power supply), make sure the fire extinguisher will work for class C fires. If you don't have an extinguisher that is specifically rated for electrical fires (class C), you can use an ABC-rated extinguisher.

Understanding Environmental Controls

It is estimated that more than 25 percent of all of the lead (a poisonous substance) in landfills today comes from consumer electronics components. Because consumer electronics (televisions, DVRs, Blu-ray players, stereos) contain hazardous substances, many states require that they be disposed of as hazardous waste. Computers are no exception. Monitors contain several carcinogens and phosphors as well as mercury and lead. The computer itself may contain several lubricants and chemicals as well as lead. Printers contain plastics and chemicals such as toners and inks that are also hazardous. All of these items should be disposed of properly.

Remember all those 386 and 486 computers that came out in the late 1980s and are now considered antiques? Maybe you don't, but there were millions of them. Where did they all go? Is there an Old Computers Home somewhere that is using these computer systems for good purposes, or are they lying in a junkyard somewhere? Or could it be that some folks just cannot let go and have a stash of old computer systems and computer parts in the dark depths of their basements? Regardless of where they are today, all of those old components have one thing in common: they are hazardous to the environment.

On the flip side, the environment is also hazardous to our computers. We've already talked about how water and computers don't mix well, and that's just the beginning. Temperature, humidity, and air quality can have dramatic effects on a computer's performance. And we know that computers require electricity; too much or too little can be a problem.

With all of these potential issues, you might find yourself wondering, "Can't we all just get along?" In the following sections, we will talk about how to make our computers and the environment coexist as peacefully as possible.

Managing the Physical Environment

Some of our computers sit in the same dark, dusty corner for their entire lives. Other computers are carried around, thrown into bags, and occasionally dropped. Either way, the physical environment in which our computers exist can have a major effect on how long they last. It's smart to inspect the physical environment periodically in order to ensure that there are no working hazards. Routinely cleaning components will also extend their useful life, and so will ensuring that the power supplying them is maintained as well.

Maintaining Power

As electronics, computers need a power source. Laptops can free you from your power cord leash for a while, but only temporarily. Power is something that we often take for granted until we lose it, and then we twiddle our thumbs and wonder what people did before the Internet. Most people realize that having too much power (a power surge) is a bad thing because it can fry electronic components. Having too little power, such as when a *blackout* occurs, can also wreak havoc on electrical circuits.

> Power blackouts are generally easy to detect. Power sags without a complete loss, called a *brownout*, are also very damaging to electrical components but oftentimes go unnoticed.

Power strips come in all shapes and sizes and are convenient for plugging multiple devices into one wall outlet. Most of them even have an on/off switch so that you can turn all of the devices on or off at the same time. A simple one is shown in Figure 23.6.

FIGURE 23.6   A power strip

Don't make the mistake of thinking that power strips will protect you from electrical surges, though. If you get a strong power surge through one of these $10 devices, the strip and everything plugged into it can be fried. Some people like to call power strips "surge protectors" or "surge suppressors," but power strips do nothing to protect against or suppress surges.

Devices that actually attempt to keep power surges at bay are called *surge protectors*. They often look similar to a power strip so it's easy to mistake them for each other, but protectors are more expensive, usually starting in the $25 range. They have a fuse inside them that is designed to blow if it receives too much current and not to transfer the current to the devices plugged into it. Surge protectors may also have plug-ins for RJ-11 (phone), RJ-45 (Ethernet), and BNC (coaxial cable) connectors as well. Figure 23.7 shows a surge protector.

FIGURE 23.7 Surge protector

The best device for power protection is called an *uninterruptible power supply (UPS)*. These devices can be as small as a brick, like the one shown in Figure 23.8, or as large as an entire server rack. Some just have a few indicator lights, while others have LCD displays that show status and menus and come with their own management software.

FIGURE 23.8 An uninterruptible power supply

Inside the UPS is one or more batteries and fuses. Much like a surge suppressor, a UPS is designed to protect everything that's plugged into it from power surges. UPSs are also designed to protect against power sags and even power outages. Energy is stored in the batteries, and if the power fails, the batteries can power the computer for a period of time so that the administrator can then safely power it down. Many UPSs and operating systems will also work together to power down a system automatically (and safely) or switch it to UPS power. These types of devices may be overkill for Uncle Bob's machine at home, but they're critically important fixtures in server rooms. UPSs can accommodate several different devices; the number depends on the size and power rating. The model shown in Figure 23.9 has three plugs for battery backup and surge protection, and another three outlets for surge protection only.

FIGURE 23.9   The back of a UPS

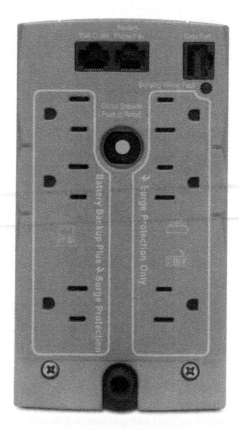

The UPS should be checked periodically as part of the preventative maintenance routine to make sure its battery is operational. Most UPSs have a test button you can press to simulate a power outage. You will find that batteries wear out over time, and you should replace the battery in the UPS every couple of years to keep the UPS dependable.

Managing the Environment

Sometimes we can't help how clean—or unclean—our environments are. A computer in an auto body shop is going to face dangers that one in a receptionist's office won't. Still, there are things that you can do to help keep your systems clean and working well. We're going to break these concepts down into two parts. In the first, we'll look at common issues you should be aware of, and in the second, we'll discuss proper cleaning methods.

Avoiding Common Problems

In a nutshell, water and other liquids, dirt, dust, unreliable power sources, and heat and humidity aren't good for electronic components. Inspect your environment to eliminate as many of these risks as possible. Leaving your laptop running outside in a rainstorm? Not such a good idea. (Been there, done that.)

Computers in manufacturing plants are particularly susceptible to environmental hazards. One technician reported a situation with a computer that had been used on the manufacturing floor of a large equipment manufacturer. The computer and keyboard were covered with a black substance that would not come off. (It was later revealed to be a combination of paint mist and molybdenum grease.) There was so much diesel fume residue in the power supply fan that it would barely turn. The insides and components were covered with a thin, greasy layer of muck. To top it all off, the computer *smelled terrible*!

Despite all this, the computer still functioned. However, it was prone to reboot itself every now and again. The solution was (as you may have guessed) to clean every component thoroughly and replace the power supply. The muck on the components was able to conduct a small current. Sometimes, that current would go where it wasn't wanted and zap!—a reboot. In addition, the power supply fan is supposed to partially cool the inside of the computer. In this computer, the fan was detrimental to the computer because it got its cooling air from the shop floor, which contained diesel fumes, paint fumes, and other chemical fumes. Needless to say, those fumes aren't good for computer components.

Computers and humans have similar tolerances to heat and cold, although computers like the cold better than we do. In general, anything comfortable to us is comfortable to a computer. They don't, however, require food or drink (except maybe a few RAM chips now and again)—keep those away from the computer.

 It's bad practice to eat, drink, or smoke around your computer. Smoke particles contain tar that can get inside the computer and cause problems similar to those just described.

Computers need lots of clean, moving air to keep them functioning. One way to ensure that the environment has the least possible effect on your computer is always to leave the blanks in the empty slots on the back of your box. These pieces of metal are designed to keep dirt, dust, and other foreign matter out of the inside of the computer. They also maintain proper airflow within the case to ensure that the computer does not overheat.

You can also purchase computer enclosures to keep the dust out—just make sure that they allow for proper air ventilation. Many times these devices use air filters in much the same way a furnace or a car engine does.

Cleaning Systems

The cleanliness of a computer is extremely important. Buildup of dust, dirt, and oils can prevent the various mechanical parts of a computer from operating. Cleaning them with the right cleaning compounds is equally important. Using the wrong compounds can leave residue behind that is more harmful than the dirt that you are trying to remove.

Most computer cases and monitor cases can be cleaned by using mild soapy water on a clean, lint-free cloth. Do *not* use any kind of solvent-based cleaner on monitor screens because doing so can cause discoloration and damage to the screen surface. Most often, a simple dusting with a damp cloth (moistened with water) will suffice. Make sure that the power is off before you put anything wet near a computer. Dampen (don't soak) a cloth in mild soap solution and wipe the dirt and dust from the case. Then wipe the moisture from the case with a dry, lint-free cloth. Anything with a plastic or metal case can be cleaned in this manner.

WARNING   Don't drip liquid into any vent holes on equipment. Monitors in particular often have vent holes in the top.

Additionally, if you spill anything on a keyboard, you can clean it by soaking it in distilled, *demineralized water* and drying it off. The extra minerals and impurities have been removed from this type of water, so it will not leave any traces of residue that might interfere with the proper operation of the keyboard after cleaning. The same holds true for the keyboard's cable and its connector.

The electronic connectors of computer equipment, on the other hand, should never touch water. Instead, use a swab moistened in distilled, *denatured isopropyl alcohol* (also known as electronics or contact cleaner and found in electronics stores) to clean contacts. Doing so will take oxidation off the copper contacts.

Finally, the best way to remove dust and debris from the inside of the computer is to use compressed air instead of vacuuming. Compressed air can be more easily directed and doesn't easily produce ESD damage as a vacuum could. Simply blow the dust from inside the computer by using a stream of compressed air. However, make sure to do this outside so that you don't blow dust all over your work area or yourself. Also be sure to wear safety goggles and use an air mask. If you need to use a vacuum, a nonstatic *computer vacuum* that is specially made for cleaning computer components is recommended. Their nozzles are grounded to prevent ESD from damaging the components of the computer. A computer vacuum is pictured in Figure 23.10.

FIGURE 23.10   A computer vacuum

One unique challenge when cleaning printers is spilled toner. It sticks to everything and should not be inhaled—it's a carcinogen. Use an electronics vacuum that is designed specifically to pick up toner. A normal vacuum's filter isn't fine enough to catch all of the particles, so the toner may be circulated into the air. Normal electronics vacuums may melt the toner instead of picking it up.

 If you get toner on your clothes, use a magnet to get it out (toner is half iron).

Table 23.1 summarizes the most common cleaning tools and their uses.

TABLE 23.1   Computer cleaning tools

Tool	Purpose
Computer vacuum	Sucking up dust and small particles.
Mild soap and water	Cleaning external computer and monitor cases.
Demineralized water	Cleaning keyboards or other devices that have contact points that are not metal.
Denatured isopropyl alcohol	Cleaning metal contacts, such as those on expansion cards.

Tool	Purpose
Monitor wipes	Cleaning monitor screens. Do not use window cleaner!
Lint-free cloth	Wiping down anything. Don't use a cloth that will leave lint or other residue behind.
Compressed air	Blowing dust or other particles out of hard-to-reach areas.

Periodically cleaning equipment is one of the easiest ways to prevent costly repairs, but it's also one of the most overlooked tasks. We're often too busy solving urgent crises to deal with these types of tasks. If possible, block out some time every week for the sole purpose of cleaning your equipment.

Handling and Disposing of Computer Equipment

Each piece of computer equipment that you purchase offers a manual, usually found online. Detailed instructions on the proper handling and use of that component can be found in the manual. In addition, many manuals give information on how to open the device for maintenance or on whether you should even open the device at all.

If you have the luxury of having paper manuals, don't throw them away. Keep a drawer of a file cabinet specifically for hardware manuals (and keep it organized!). You can always look up information on the Internet as well, but having paper manuals on hand is useful for two reasons:

- You may need to fix something when Internet access isn't readily available (router problems, anyone?).
- Some companies are required to keep hardware documentation in case of an audit (such as for ISO 9000–compliant organizations).

In the following sections, we'll cover two topics: using safety documentation and following safety and disposal procedures.

Using Safety Documentation

Besides your product manuals, another place to find safety information is in *material safety data sheets (MSDSs)*. MSDSs include information such as physical product data (boiling point, melting point, flash point, and so forth), potential health risks, storage and disposal recommendations, and spill/leak procedures. With this information, technicians and emergency personnel know how to handle the product as well as respond in the event of an emergency.

MSDSs are typically associated with hazardous chemicals. Indeed, chemicals do not ship without them. MSDSs are not intended for consumer use; rather, they're made for employees or emergency workers who are consistently exposed to the risks of the particular product.

The United States *Occupational Safety and Health Administration (OSHA)* mandates MSDSs only for the following products:

- Products that meet OSHA's definition of *hazardous* (it poses a physical or health hazard)
- Products that are "known to be present in the workplace in such a manner that employees may be exposed under normal conditions of use or in a foreseeable emergency"

One of the interesting things about MSDSs is that OSHA does not require companies to distribute them to consumers. Most companies will be happy to distribute one for their products, but again, they are under no obligation to do so.

If employees are working with materials that have MSDSs, those employees are required by OSHA to have "ready access" to MSDS sheets. This means that employees need to be able to get to the sheets without having to fetch a key, contact a supervisor, or submit a procedure request. Remember the file cabinet drawer that you have for the hardware manuals? MSDSs should also be kept readily accessible. Exercise 23.2 helps you find your MSDS sheets and get familiar enough with them to find critical information.

EXERCISE 23.2

Finding MSDS Sheets

1. Locate the MSDS sheets in your workplace. You might have to ask a manager. (Do you even have them?)

2. Find one for a product in which you're interested.

3. Are there any potential health effects listed for this item? What are they?

4. What is the proper disposal procedure for this item?

It's not likely that you're going to memorize or need to memorize everything on an MSDS sheet. The key is knowing where to find them and knowing how to find information in them quickly. If you have a spill of a potentially dangerous chemical, the last thing you need to do is spend your time is figuring out how to handle the spill without causing injury to yourself or others.

At this point, you might stop to think for a second, "Do computers really come with hazardous chemicals? Do I really need an MSDS?" Consider this as an example: oxygen. Hardly a dangerous chemical, considering we need to breathe it to live, right? In the atmosphere, oxygen is at 21 percent concentration. At 100 percent concentration, oxygen is highly flammable and can even spontaneously ignite some organic materials. In that sense, and in the eyes of OSHA, nearly everything can be a dangerous chemical.

If you are interested in searching for free MSDSs, several websites are available, such as www.msds.com. Many manufacturers of components will also provide MSDSs on their websites.

The sections within an MSDS sheet will be the same regardless of the product, but the information inside each section changes. Here is a truncated sample MSDS for ammonium hydrogen sulfate.

```
**** MATERIAL SAFETY DATA SHEET ****

Ammonium Hydrogen Sulfate
90009

        **** SECTION 1—CHEMICAL PRODUCT AND COMPANY IDENTIFICATION ****

MSDS Name: Ammonium Hydrogen Sulfate
Catalog Numbers:
     A/5400
Synonyms:
     Sulfuric acid, monoammonium salt; Acid ammonium sulfate; Ammonium
     acid sulfate.

        **** SECTION 2—COMPOSITION, INFORMATION ON INGREDIENTS ****

CAS#      Chemical Name               %     EINECS#
7803-63-6 Ammonium hydrogen sulfate   100 % 232-265-5
          Hazard Symbols: C
          Risk Phrases: 34

        **** SECTION 3—HAZARDS IDENTIFICATION ****

                    EMERGENCY OVERVIEW
Causes burns. Corrosive. Hygroscopic (absorbs moisture from the air).

Potential Health Effects
     Skin:
               Causes skin burns.
     Ingestion:
 May cause severe gastrointestinal tract irritation with nausea, vomiting,
and possible burns.
     Inhalation:
 Causes severe irritation of upper respiratory tract with coughing, burns,
breathing difficulty, and possible coma.

        **** SECTION 4—FIRST-AID MEASURES ****

     Skin:
 Get medical aid immediately. Immediately flush skin with plenty of water for at
least 15 minutes while removing contaminated clothing and shoes.
     Ingestion:
```

Do not induce vomiting. If victim is conscious and alert, give 2-4 cupfuls of milk or water. Never give anything by mouth to an unconscious person. Get medical aid immediately.

Inhalation:

Get medical aid immediately. Remove from exposure and move to fresh air immediately.

If not breathing, give artificial respiration. If breathing is difficult, give oxygen.

**** SECTION 5—FIREFIGHTING MEASURES ****

**** SECTION 6—ACCIDENTAL RELEASE MEASURES ****

General Information: Use proper personal protective equipment as indicated in Section 8.

**** SECTION 7—HANDLING and STORAGE ****

Handling:

Wash thoroughly after handling. Wash hands before eating. Use only in a well-ventilated area. Do not get in eyes, on skin, or on clothing. Do not ingest or inhale.

Storage:

Store in a cool, dry place. Keep container closed when not in use.

**** SECTION 8—EXPOSURE CONTROLS, PERSONAL PROTECTION ****

Engineering Controls:

Use adequate general or local exhaust ventilation to keep airborne concentrations below the permissible exposure limits.

Respirators:

Follow the OSHA respirator regulations found in 29 CFR 1910.134 or European Standard EN 149. Always use a NIOSH or European Standard EN 149 approved respirator when necessary.

**** SECTION 9—PHYSICAL AND CHEMICAL PROPERTIES ****

Physical State: Solid
Color: White
Odor: Not available

**** SECTION 10—STABILITY AND REACTIVITY ****

Chemical Stability:

Stable under normal temperatures and pressures.

```
Conditions to Avoid:
Incompatible materials, dust generation, exposure to moist air or water.

           **** SECTION 11—TOXICOLOGICAL INFORMATION ****

RTECS#:
     CAS# 7803-63-6: BS4400500

           **** SECTION 12—ECOLOGICAL INFORMATION ****

           **** SECTION 13—DISPOSAL CONSIDERATIONS ****
```

Products which are considered hazardous for supply are classified as Special Waste, and the disposal of such chemicals is covered by regulations which may vary according to location. Contact a specialist disposal company or the local waste regulator for advice. Empty containers must be decontaminated before returning for recycling.

```
           **** SECTION 14—TRANSPORT INFORMATION ****

           **** SECTION 15—REGULATORY INFORMATION ****

European/International Regulations
     European Labeling in Accordance with EC Directives
          Hazard Symbols: C
          Risk Phrases:
                    R 34  Causes burns.
          Safety Phrases:
  S 26  In case of contact with eyes, rinse immediately with plenty of water and
seek medical advice. S 28  After contact with skin, wash immediately with…

           **** SECTION 16—ADDITIONAL INFORMATION ****

MSDS Creation Date:  6/23/2004  Revision #0 Date: Original.
```

Following Proper Disposal Procedures

It is relatively easy to put old components away, thinking that you might be able to put them to good use again someday, but doing so is not realistic. Most computers are obsolete as soon as you buy them. And if you have not used them recently, your old computer components will more than likely never be used again.

We recycle cans, plastic, and newspaper, so why not recycle computer equipment? The problem is that most computers contain small amounts of hazardous substances. Some countries are exploring the option of recycling electrical machines, but not all have enacted appropriate measures to enforce their proper disposal.

Some countries are ahead of others on the recycling issue. For example, the United Kingdom introduced the Waste Electrical and Electronic Equipment (WEEE) Regulations in 2013, which puts an obligation on manufactures to provide disposal methods for items they manufacture. Consumers can insist that manufactures take back dangerous waste and electrical and electronic equipment. Many local governments also provide e-waste programs and disposal centers.

Regardless of manufacturer or community programs, we can take proactive steps as consumers and caretakers of our environment to promote the proper disposal of computer equipment:

- Check with the manufacturer. Some manufacturers will take back outdated equipment for parts (and may even pay you for them).

- Properly dispose of solvents or cleaners (as well as their containers) used with computers at a local hazardous waste disposal facility.

- Disassemble the machine and reuse the parts that are good.

- Check out businesses that can melt down the components for the lead or gold plating.

- Contact the Environmental Protection Agency (EPA) for a list of local or regional waste disposal sites that accept used computer equipment. The EPA's web address is www.epa.gov.

- Check with the EPA or at www.msds.com to see if what you are disposing has a Material Safety Data Sheet (MSDS). These sheets contain information about the toxicity of a product and whether it can simply be disposed of as trash. They also contain lethal-dose information.

- Check with local nonprofit or education organizations that may be interested in using the equipment.

- Check out the Internet for possible waste disposal sites. Table 23.2 lists a few websites that we came across that deal with disposal of used computer equipment. A quick web search will likely locate some in your area.

TABLE 23.2   Computer recycling websites

Site Name	Web Address
Computer Recycle Center	www.recycles.com
Computer Recycling Center	www.crc.org
RE-PC	www.repc.com
Tech Dump	www.techdump.org

Following the general rule of thumb of recycling your computer components and consumables is a good way to go. In the following sections, we'll look at four classifications of computer-related components and proper disposal procedures for each.

Batteries

The EPA estimates that there are over 350 million batteries purchased annually in the United States. One can only imagine what the worldwide figure is. Batteries contain several heavy metals and other toxic ingredients, including alkaline, mercury, lead acid, nickel cadmium, and nickel metal hydride.

Never burn a battery to destroy it. That will cause the battery to explode, which could result in serious injury.

When batteries are thrown away and deposited into landfills, the heavy metals inside them will find their way into the ground. From there, they can pollute water sources and eventually find their way into the supply of drinking water. In 1996, the United States passed the Battery Act to address two issues: to phase out the use of mercury in disposable batteries and to provide collection methods and recycling procedures for batteries.

There are several countries around the world with battery recycling programs. Information on battery recycling in the United States can be found at www.ibm.com/ibm/environment/products/battery_us.shtml. You can also find information on the Mercury-Containing and Rechargeable Battery Management Act at www.epa.gov/osw/hazard/recycling/battery.pdf.

There are five types of batteries most commonly associated with computers and handheld electronic devices: alkaline, nickel cadmium (NiCd), nickel metal hydride (NiMH), lithium ion (Li-ion), and button cell.

Alkaline batteries　Alkaline batteries have been incredibly popular portable batteries for several decades now. Before 1984, one of the major ingredients in this type of battery was mercury, which is highly toxic to the environment. In 1984, battery companies began reducing the mercury levels in batteries, and in 1996, mercury was outlawed in alkaline batteries in the United States. Still, it's strongly recommended that you recycle these batteries at a recycling center. Although newer alkaline batteries contain less mercury than their predecessors, they are still made of metals and other toxins that contaminate the air and soil.

Nickel cadmium (NiCd)　Nickel cadmium is a popular format for rechargeable batteries. As their name indicates, they contain high levels of nickel and cadmium. Although nickel is only semitoxic, cadmium is highly toxic. These types of batteries are categorized by the EPA as hazardous waste and should be recycled.

Nickel metal hydride (NiMH) and lithium ion (Li-ion)　Laptop batteries are commonly made with NiMH and lithium ion. Unlike the previous types of batteries that we have discussed, these are not considered hazardous waste, and there are no regulations on recycling them. However, these batteries do contain elements that can be recycled, so it's still a good idea to go that route.

Button cell These batteries are named so because they look like a button. They're commonly used in calculators and watches as well as portable computers. They often contain mercury and silver (and are environmental hazards due to the mercury) and need to be recycled.

You may have noticed a theme regarding disposal of batteries: recycling. Many people just throw batteries in the trash and don't think twice about it. However, there are several laws in the United States that require the recycling of many types of batteries, and recycling does indeed help keep the environment clean. For a list of recycling centers in your area, use your local yellow pages (under Recycling Centers) or do an Internet search.

If you're ever exposed to the electrolyte (the inside "juice") of the battery, immediately flush the exposed area with water. If it gets on your eye, immediately contact a physician and wash the eye for 15 minutes.

Display Devices

Computer monitors (CRT monitors, not LCDs) are big and bulky, so what do you do when it's time to get rid of them? As we mentioned earlier in this chapter, monitors have capacitors in them that are capable of retaining a lethal electric charge after they've been unplugged. You wouldn't want anyone to set off the charge accidentally and die. But the thing that we didn't mention earlier, which is important now, is that most CRT monitors contain high amounts of lead. Most monitors contain several pounds of lead, in fact. Lead is very dangerous to humans and the environment and must be dealt with carefully. Other harmful elements found in CRTs are arsenic, beryllium, cadmium, chromium, mercury, nickel, and zinc.

If you have to dispose of a monitor, contact a computer recycling firm. It's best to let professional recyclers handle the monitor for you.

 Real World Scenario

How *Not* to Dispose of Your Monitors

This story comes from the technical support division of a now-defunct major computer manufacturer, which used a lot of computers at its own facility. At one time, the company had as many as 500 technicians working the phones. So you can imagine that they burned out a lot of equipment.

Here's how they disposed of dead monitors. An IT staff member would take the monitor out to the dumpster and bring along a sledgehammer. Setting the monitor on its back, he would take one good swing at the glass panel with the hammer to shatter the screen. (This was done, by policy, to ensure that no one would want to go out to the dumpster and try to salvage the dead monitor.) After spraying glass everywhere, he picked up the monitor and threw it in the dumpster.

One employee made an observation that it probably wasn't good to be spreading glass all over the parking lot by shattering monitors. That advice was taken, and the sledgehammer was retired. Instead, an IT staff member would use a permanent black marker and draw all over the screen (again, so no one would want to try to salvage it), and again, it was thrown in the dumpster.

In our enlightened state today (as opposed to the mid-1990s), we can see how this was not a good plan for disposing of broken monitors. In fact, many states today have laws prohibiting the disposal of computer monitors in trash bins. This is a good law because, with the amount of harmful elements in monitors, they're every bit the environmental hazard as are batteries.

Laser Printer Toner

Toner cartridges should be recycled as well. PC recycling centers will take old toner cartridges and properly dispose of them. The toner itself is a carcinogen, and the cartridges can contain heavy metals that are bad for the environment.

Chemical Solvents and Cans

Nearly every chemical solvent that you encounter will have a corresponding MSDS. On the MSDS for a chemical, you will find a section detailing the proper methods for disposing of it. Chemical solvents were not designed to be released into the environment because they could cause significant harm to living organisms if they're ingested. If in doubt, contact a local hazardous materials handler to find out the best way to dispose of a particular chemical solvent.

Cans are generally made from aluminum or other metals, which are not biodegradable. It's best always to recycle these materials. If the cans were used to hold a chemical solvent or otherwise hazardous material, contact a hazardous materials disposal center instead of a recycling center.

Always be sure that you are following all applicable laws and regulations when disposing of computer equipment!

Understanding Policies, Licensing, and Privacy

Many of the operational procedures that we've discussed up to this point have been about safety—yours, computer equipment, and the environment. You've also heard us touch on regulations a bit, as in always be sure to comply with local government regulations. In the following sections, we focus more on the legal side of things. Not understanding legal requirements is not a justifiable defense in a court of law. Considering that IT professionals often deal with software licensing and personally identifiable information, or sometimes encounter prohibited activity or have to deal with a security incident, it's best that you understand the general principles related to these concepts.

Managing Software Licenses

When you buy an application, you aren't actually buying the application. Instead, you're buying the right to use the application in a limited way as prescribed by the licensing agreement that comes with it. Most people don't read these licensing agreements closely, but suffice it to say, they're pretty slanted in favor of the software manufacturer.

Don't like the terms? Too bad. No negotiation is allowed. If you don't accept the *end-user license agreement (EULA)*, your only recourse is to return the software for a refund. (Most vendors will refuse to take back an opened box. Still, the software manufacturer is required to take it back and refund your money if you reject the licensing. This is true of programs purchased online as well.)

NOTE   Many companies rely upon *digital rights management (DRM)* to protect digital assets such as online photos or videos. DRM is not as established as licensing agreements are, but you should still respect the property of the owners of digital content.

Although the majority of the applications that you acquire will probably be commercial products, there are a number of alternatives to commercial software sales. Here are some of the license types that you may encounter:

Freeware   *Freeware* is software that is completely free. On a small scale, you can get such software from download sites such as www.download.com or from the creator's personal website. Large companies like Google and Microsoft also sometimes offer products for free, because it serves the company's interests to have lots of people using their software. Examples include Google Chrome and Microsoft Internet Explorer. Freeware doesn't include source code, and users aren't allowed to modify the application.

Open Source   *Open-source software* is freer than free: not only is the application free, but the source code (code used by programmers) is also shared to encourage others to contribute to the future development and improvement of the application. OSs such as Linux and applications like OpenOffice fit this category. Open-source software can't be sold, although it can be bundled with commercial products that are sold.

Shareware   *Shareware* is software that provides a free trial, with the expectation that you'll pay for it if you like it and decide to keep it. In some cases, a shareware version isn't the full product; in other cases, it expires after a certain amount of time. Some shareware provides a full and unlimited version, with payment requested on the honor system.

Multiuser   This is commercial software that you're allowed to install on more than one computer. For example, some versions of Microsoft Office allow you to install the same copy on two or three PCs.

Single User   This is commercial software for which the license restricts installation to a single PC. A common misconception is that a single-user license allows you to install the software on more than one computer as long as you use only one instance at a time, but that's not accurate. Commercial products sometimes have activation systems that lock the software to a specific PC once it's installed, so you can't install it elsewhere. Microsoft Office is a good example of commercial software.

Concurrent   This license allows the software to be installed on many PCs but used concurrently by a smaller number. For example, you may have 1,000 computers with the application installed, but only 100 users can use it simultaneously. This is useful in situations in which everyone needs to have an application available but the application gets very little actual use.

Corporate, Campus, or Site   These are enterprise licenses, which permit an organization to install the application on an agreed-upon number of PCs. For example, a school may buy a site license of an antivirus program and allow all students to download and install it freely to ensure that the school's network remains virus free. Microsoft calls this a volume license key.

If you buy any sort of commercial software, you will receive a *product key*, which you will need to enter during installation or the first time the application is opened. The product key might be emailed to you, or it could be located on the physical media if you got an installation CD-ROM or DVD. Figure 23.11 shows an example of a product key.

FIGURE 23.11   Microsoft product key

In a corporate environment, license management is a critical responsibility. The company may spend thousands or even millions of dollars on software licenses; money could be wasted on unused licenses, or if the company's computers have unlicensed software, it could result in huge fines. Ignorance is not a legal excuse in this area.

To avoid these problems, it may be best for your company to purchase a software asset management tool, such as Microsoft's Software Asset Management (www.Microsoft.com sam), License Manager by License Dashboard (www.licensedashboard.com), or FlexNet Manager by Flexera Software (www.flexerasoftware.com). In general, here are the steps to take for proper license management:

1. Build a database of all licenses owned by your company. This includes what type of license it is, license numbers, and expiration date, if any.

2. Perform an inventory of all licensed software installed on your computers. This can be quite an effort.

3. Compare the license list to the install base.

4. For any gaps where you have unlicensed software, either remove the software or procure licenses.

Because of the potential for heavy fines, many companies prohibit the installation of software on client computers unless specifically authorized by a manager or the IT department.

 Real World Scenario

How Do I Buy the Right Licenses?

Consider this situation: After talking to your boss about software licenses, you decide to investigate the office productivity software on your department's computers. You are unable to find proper documentation that the correct software licenses were purchased, leading you to wonder whether the company has the right licenses. Your boss wants to avoid any potential legal issues and asks you to go buy enough copies of the latest version of Microsoft Office for the 20 users in your department. What do you do?

The first question to ask yourself is do all 20 people use their computers at the same time? If not, then you might be able to purchase a concurrent license for fewer than 20 users. If there's the possibility of all 20 users needing Office at once, then you'll definitely need licenses for everyone. You might purchase a corporate license as well. Now that you have figured out what to buy, how do you do it?

One option is to go to the local computer store, load up 20 boxes of Office (if they have that many in stock), and trudge up to the cashier. A second option is to go to Microsoft's volume licensing site at www.microsoft.com/licensing/about-licensing/office.aspx

to learn about purchasing multiple licenses. Microsoft will direct you to an authorized reseller so that you can purchase them; the authorized reseller will email you the list of license numbers to use when installing the software. Now you need just one physical (or downloaded) copy to perform the installation.

Managing Sensitive Information

As an IT manager, you will very likely have access to information that you will need to keep closely guarded. For example, you might have access to username and/or password lists, medical or educational records, addresses and phone numbers, or employee records. It's your responsibility to ensure that sensitive information does not get released into the wrong hands. On the flip side, you may encounter information that's sensitive because it's prohibited or illegal. You need to know how to react in those situations as well.

Working with Personally Identifiable Information

Personally identifiable information (PII) is anything that can be used to identify an individual person on its own or in context with other information. This includes someone's name, address, other contact information, the names of family members, and other details that people would consider private.

PII should always be kept confidential and secure. It seems like every few months or so, we see news stories of data breaches at big companies resulting in stolen credit card data or username and contact lists. This information finds its way into hacker's hands and causes millions of people grief and monetary damages. Be sure that this information is properly secured and can be accessed only by authorized personnel.

Dealing with Prohibited Content/Activity

This is a situation that no one really wants to deal with, but it happens more often than we would care to admit. A computer you are fixing has content on it that is inappropriate or illegal, or you see someone on your network performing an action that is against policy or laws. How you respond in such a situation can have a significant bearing on your career, the other people involved, and, depending on the situation, the well-being of your company. The lynchpin to dealing with *prohibited content* or activity is to have a comprehensive policy in place that covers appropriate behavior. After that, it's a matter of executing the proper steps per the plan when something happens.

Creating a Prohibited Content Policy

As mentioned previously, creating a policy is the most important part of dealing with prohibited content or actions. Without a policy in place that specifically defines what is and what isn't allowed, and what actions will be taken when a violation of the policy occurs, you don't really have a leg to stand on when a situation happens.

What is on the policy depends on the company for which you work. Generally speaking, if something violates an existing federal or local law, it probably isn't appropriate for your network either. Many companies also have strict policies against the possession of pornographic or hate-related materials on company property. Some go further than that, banning personal files such as downloaded music or movies on work computers. Regardless of what is on your policy, always ensure that you have buy-in from very senior management so that the policy will be considered valid. Here are some specific examples of content that might be prohibited:

- Adult content
- Content that advocates violence against an individual, group, or organization
- Unlicensed copyrighted material
- Content related to drugs, alcohol, tobacco, or gambling
- Content about hacking, cracking, or other illegal computer activity
- Violent or weapons-related content

A good policy will also contain the action steps to be taken if prohibited content or activity is spotted. For example, what should you do if you find porn on someone's work laptop?

The policy should explicitly outline the punishment for performing specific actions or possessing specific content. The appropriate penalty may very well be based upon the type of content found. Something that is deemed mildly offensive might result in a verbal or written warning for the first offense and a more severe sentence for the second offense. If your company has a zero-tolerance policy, then employees may be terminated and possibly subject to legal action.

Finally, after the policy has been established, it's critical to ensure that all employees are aware of it and have proper training. In fact, it's highly recommended that you have all employees sign a disclosure saying they have read and understand the policy and that the signed document be kept in their human resources file. Many companies also require that employees review the policy yearly and re-sign the affidavit as well.

Handling Specific Situations

If you have your policy in place, then your *incident response* plan should be relatively scripted. It might not be easy to deal with, but the steps you should take should be outlined for you. Because we talk about professionalism in this chapter, this is a good time to remind you that people will be looking at your reaction as well as your actions. If you see prohibited content and start giggling and walk away, that probably doesn't reflect well on you. Always remember that others are watching you.

The specific steps that you take will depend on your policy, but here are some general guidelines:

Follow your policies exactly as they are written. Yes, we've already said this several times. It's crucial that you do this. Not following the policies and procedures can derail your case against the offender and possibly set you up for problems as well.

If you are the first responder, get a verifier.   Your first priority as the first responder is to identify the improper activity or content. Then you should always get someone else to verify the material or action so that it doesn't turn into a situation of your word against someone else's. Immediately report the situation through proper channels.

Preserve the data or device.   The data or device should immediately be removed from the possession of the offending party and preserved. This will ensure that the data doesn't mysteriously disappear before the proper parties are notified.

Use documentation.   Document everything that could be relevant to the situation. Many companies have standard documentation that is used in incident response in order to be sure that the responder captures important information and does not forget to ask critical questions or look for vital clues.

Follow the right chain of custody.   The removed materials should be secured and turned over to the proper authorities. Depending on the situation, materials may be held in a safe, locked location at the office, or they may need to be turned over to local authorities. Have a documented procedure in place to follow, given a situation. Always document the findings and who has custody of the offensive materials.

Once this first part is complete, then it's a matter of levying the right punishment for the infraction.

Situations involving prohibited content or activities are not easy to address. The accused person might get angry or confrontational, so it's important always to have the right people there to help manage and defuse the situation. If you feel that the situation is severe enough and are worried about your own personal safety, don't be afraid to involve the police if needed. While the situation needs to be handled, there's no sense in putting yourself in direct danger to do so.

Always be sure to follow government regulations as well as corporate end-user policies and security best practices when dealing with sensitive information.

Demonstrating Professionalism

As a professional technician, you need to possess a certain level of technical competence or you'll quickly find yourself looking for work. Technical ability alone isn't enough though; there are many people out there with skills similar to yours. One thing that can set you apart is acting like a true professional and building a solid reputation. As the noted investor Warren Buffet said, "It takes 20 years to build a reputation and 5 minutes to ruin it. If you think about that, you'll do things differently."

You could probably break down professionalism a hundred different ways. For the A+ 220-902 exam, and for the purposes of this chapter, we're going to break it down into two critical parts: communication and behavior.

Good communication includes listening to what the user or manager or developer is telling you and making certain that you understand completely: approximately half of all communication should be listening. Even though a user or customer may not fully understand the terminology or concepts, that doesn't mean they don't have a real problem that needs to be addressed. You must, therefore, be skilled at not only listening but also at translating.

Professional behavior encompasses politeness, guidance, punctuality, and accountability. Always treat the customer with the same respect and empathy that you would expect if the situation were reversed. Likewise, guide the customer through the problem and the explanation. Tell them what has caused the problem that they are currently experiencing and the best solution for preventing it from reoccurring in the future.

Communicating with Customers

The act of diagnosis starts with the art of customer relations. Go to the customer with an attitude of trust: Believe what the customer is saying. At the same time, retain an attitude of hidden skepticism; *don't* believe that the customer has told you everything. This attitude of hidden skepticism is not the same as distrust, but just remember that what you hear isn't always the whole story, and customers may inadvertently forget to provide some crucial detail.

One of the best ways to become proficient in communicating with customers is to put yourself in the shoes of the novice user. None of us are experts in every field, so think of an area where you are weak—auto repair or home repair, for example—and imagine how you would want a professional in that area to communicate with you.

For example, a customer may complain that their CD-ROM drive doesn't work. What they fail to mention is that it has never worked and that they installed it. On examining the machine, you realize that they mounted it with screws that are too long and that these prevent the tray from ejecting properly.

Here are a few suggestions for making your communication with the customer easier:

Use proper language.   End users are very likely to be less computer literate than you—that's why you are there to fix the problem! Therefore, they might not know computer acronyms, slang, or jargon. In fact, the excessive use of computer terms might make them feel stupid (and make the situation uncomfortable) or make you seem aloof. It's always best to start off with basic terms, such as "Where does it plug into?" If the user answers, "Oh, it's an eSATA SSD," then you know you have the freedom to use more technical terms. Users with computer knowledge will often let you know. Users with little knowledge may be afraid to tell you that they don't understand something because they don't want to look dumb.

Have the customer reproduce the error.   The most important part of this step is to have the customer show you what the problem is. The best method we've seen of doing this is to ask, "Show me what 'not working' looks like." That way, you see the conditions and methods under which the problem occurs. The problem may be a simple matter of doing an operation incorrectly or performing the operation in the wrong order. During this step, you have the opportunity to observe how the problem occurs, so pay attention.

Identify recent changes. The user can give you vital information. The most important question is, "What changed?" Problems don't usually come out of nowhere. Was a new piece of hardware or software added? Did the user drop some equipment? Was there a power outage or a storm? These are the types of questions that you can ask a user in trying to find out what is different.

If nothing changed, at least outwardly, then what was going on at the time of the failure? Can the problem be reproduced? Is there a workaround? The point here is to raise as many questions as you need to ask in order to pinpoint the source of the trouble.

Use the collected information. Once the problem or problems have been clearly identified, your next step is to isolate possible causes. If the problem cannot be clearly identified, then further tests will be necessary. A common technique for hardware and software problems alike is to strip the system down to bare-bones basics. In a hardware situation, this could mean removing all interface cards except those absolutely required for the system to operate. In a software situation, this may mean disabling elements within Device Manager.

Generally then, you can gradually rebuild the system toward the point where the trouble started. When you reintroduce a component and the problem reappears, you know that component is the one causing the problem.

Customer satisfaction goes a long way toward generating repeat business. If you can *meet* the customer's expectations, you will most likely hear from them again when another problem arises. However, if you can *exceed* the customer's expectations, you can almost guarantee that they will call you the next time a problem arises.

 Real World Scenario

Communication Is Key

Marriages disintegrate when couples do not communicate effectively, or so many experts proclaim. Communication is ranked as one of the most important skills needed to make a marriage work. The same can be said for business partnerships—it is important to make certain that you are listening to your customers, whether they are truly customers in the traditional sense of the word or internal users that you support. You also need to listen carefully to managers and vendors and make sure that you understand them before beginning a project.

Similarly, you need to make certain that the parties in question understand what you are saying to them. It isn't acceptable to resort to the "But I told you . . ." excuse when customers or partners aren't pleased with the results. Making certain that they understand what you are telling them is as equally important as making certain that you understand what they are telling you.

Customer satisfaction is important in all communications media—whether you are on site, providing phone support, or communicating through email or other correspondence. If you are on site, follow these rules:

- When you arrive, immediately look for the person (user, manager, administrator, and so on) who is affected by the problem. Make sure the user knows you are there, and assure that person that you will do all you can. Project a positive attitude and confidence that you can resolve their problem.

- Listen intently to what your customer is saying, and avoid interrupting them. Make it obvious that you are listening and respecting what they are telling you. If there is a problem with understanding the client, go to whatever lengths you need to in order to remedy the situation. Look for verbal and nonverbal cues that can help you isolate the problem. Taking notes is also helpful. Make sure to say something to the user like, "I'm listening, and I am going to write down a few notes just too to make sure I remember everything."

- Share the customer's sense of urgency. What may seem like a small problem to you can appear to your customer as if the whole world were collapsing around them.

- Be honest and fair with the customer and try to establish a personal rapport. Explain what the problem is, what you believe is the cause, and what can be done in the future to prevent it from recurring.

- Handle complaints as professionally as possible. Accept responsibility for errors that may have occurred on your part, and never try to pass the blame elsewhere. Avoid arguing with a customer; it serves no purpose. Resolve the customer's anger with as little conflict as possible. Remember, the goal is to keep the customer and not to win an argument.

- When you finish a job, notify the user that you have finished. Make every attempt to find the user and inform them of the resolution. If it is impossible to find them, leave a note explaining the resolution. You should also leave a means by which the customer can contact you should they have a question about the resolution or a related problem. In most cases, you should leave your business number and, if applicable, your cellphone number in case the customer needs to contact you after hours. Notification should also be given to both managers—yours and the user's—that the job has been completed.

If you are providing phone support, keep these guidelines in mind:

- Always answer the telephone in a professional manner, announcing the name of the company and yourself.

- Using the customer's name can help build rapport. Using it in every sentence can sound condescending, but using it once in a while can make you seem more personable.

- Make a concentrated effort to ascertain the customer's technical level and communicate at that level, not above or below it.

- The most important skill that you can have is the ability to listen. You have to rely on the customer to describe the problem accurately. They cannot do that if you are second-guessing or jumping to conclusions before the whole story is told. Ask broad questions to begin, and then narrow them down to help isolate the problem. It is your job to help extract the description of the problem from the user. For example, you might ask the following questions:

- Is the printer plugged in?

- Is it online?

- Are there any lights flashing on it?

- Complaints should be handled in the same manner that they would be handled if you were on site. Make your best effort to resolve the problem and not argue. Again, your primary goal is to keep the customer.

- Close the incident only when the customer is satisfied that the solution is the correct one and the problem has gone away.

- End the telephone call in a courteous manner—thanking the customer for the opportunity to serve them is often the best way.

Talking to the user is an important first step in the troubleshooting process. Your first contact with a computer that has a problem is usually through the customer, either directly or by way of a work order that contains the user's complaint. Often, the complaint is something straightforward, such as "There's smoke coming from the back of my monitor." At other times, the problem is complex, and the customer does not mention everything that has been going wrong. Regardless of the situation, always approach it calmly and professionally, and remember that you only get one chance to make a good first impression.

 Real World Scenario

Communication Is Everywhere

Almost every profession stresses the importance of good communication, and IT industry positions are no different. Jamie Walters, founder and chief vision and strategy officer for Ivy Sea, Inc., and Sarah Fenson, Ivy Sea's guide to client services, wrote an article for Inc.com on steps to smooth conversations (www.inc.com/articles/2000/08/20000.html) that included this advice:

- Don't take things personally. If someone acts inappropriately toward you, just react in a calm manner. They are likely responding that way because of outside factors.

- Admit when you don't know the answer to something. It's okay to defer to somebody else or tell the user or customer that you'll have to look into their complaint and will get back with them as soon as possible.

continues

continued

- It is better to validate someone's feeling or respond to the information that they have given to you than to react to them. For instance, if somebody complains that a help ticket has not been handled in a timely manner, tell them that you understand how they feel and will look into it instead reacting in a defensive manner.

- Don't let your personal opinions or feelings get in the way of the real complaint. Try to put yourself in the user's or customer's shoes.

- Be sympathetic. If you need a user to leave their laptop with you overnight, tell them that you realize it's frustrating and apologize.

- Try to provide a solution from which you both can benefit. Look for commonalities between you and the client, and work to find a solution that is agreeable to both of you.

- Try to be as informative as possible when discussing a solution to their problem. Most people are uncomfortable with change, so explaining the benefits of a particular solution might help ease this discomfort.

- Try to keep a positive attitude and be optimistic.

- Always work on your listening skills!

Using Appropriate Behavior

Critical to appropriate behavior is to treat the customer, or user, the way you would want to be treated. Much has been made of the Golden Rule—treating others the way you would have them treat you. Six key elements to this, from a business perspective, are punctuality, accountability, flexibility, confidentiality, respect, and privacy. The following sections discuss these elements in detail.

Punctuality

Punctuality is important and should be a part of your planning process: If you tell the customer that you will be there at 10:30 a.m., you need to make every attempt to be there at that time. If you arrive late, you have given them false hope that the problem will be solved by a set time. That can lead to anger because it can appear that you are not taking the problem seriously. Punctuality continues to be important throughout the service call and does not end with your arrival. If you need to leave to get parts and return, tell the customer when you will be back, and be there at that time. If for some reason you cannot return at the expected time, alert the customer and tell them when you can return.

Along those same lines, if a user asks how much longer the server will be down and you respond that it will up in five minutes only to have it down for five more hours, the result can be resentment and possibly anger. When estimating downtime, always allow for more time than you think you will need just in case other problems occur. If you greatly underestimate the time, always inform the affected parties and give them a new time estimate. To use an analogy that will put it in perspective, if you take your car to get an oil change and the counter clerk tells you it will be "about 15 minutes," the last thing you want is to be still sitting there four hours later. If you ever feel that you won't be able to meet the timeline you proposed, communicate that as quickly as possible. It's better to over-communicate than it is to have them wondering where you are.

Exercise 23.3 is a simple drill that you can modify as needed. Its purpose is to illustrate the importance of punctuality.

EXERCISE 23.3

Understanding Punctuality

1. Consider this scenario: You call someone important in your life—your spouse, a parent, an in-law, or a close friend—and tell them that you have something very important that you need to discuss. You give that person no other details, but ask them to meet you in exactly one hour at a location familiar to both of you.

2. Now imagine that you waited two hours before showing up.

3. What would be that person's reaction? How would that person feel about having to wait for you? What kind of an impact would it have on the person's mood and behavior?

This is an interaction with someone who matters in your life. Imagine how it would affect a customer who does not know you. Punctuality can go a long way toward keeping dialogue pleasant between two parties.

Accountability

Accountability is a trait that every technician should possess. When problems occur, you need to be accountable for them and not attempt to pass the buck to someone else. For example, suppose you are called to a site to put a larger hard drive into a server. While performing this operation, you inadvertently scrape your feet across the carpeted floor, build up energy, and zap the memory in the server. Some technicians would pretend the electrostatic discharge (ESD) never happened, put the new hard drive in, and then act completely baffled by the fact that problems unrelated to the hard drive are occurring. An accountable technician would explain to the customer exactly what happened and suggest ways of proceeding from that point—addressing and solving the problem as quickly and efficiently as possible.

Accountability also means that you do what you say you're going to do, ensure that expectations are set and met, and communicate the status with the customer. Here are some examples of ways to be accountable:

- Offer different repair or replacement options if they're available.
- Provide proper documentation on the services that you provided.
- Follow up with the customer at a later date to ensure satisfaction.

The last one is the most overlooked, yet it can be the most important. Some technicians fix a problem and then develop an "I hope that worked and I never hear from them again" attitude. Calling your customer back (or dropping by their desk) to ensure that everything is still working right is an amazing way to build credibility and rapport quickly.

Flexibility

Flexibility is another trait that's as important as the others for a service technician. You should respond to service calls promptly and close them (solve them) as quickly as you can, but you must also be flexible. If a customer cannot have you on site until the afternoon, you must make your best effort to work them into your schedule around the time most convenient for them. Likewise, if you are called to a site to solve a problem and the customer brings another problem to your attention while you are there, you should make every attempt to address that problem as well. Under no circumstances should you give a customer the cold shoulder or not respond to additional problems because they were not on an initial incident report.

You should always follow the express guidelines of the company for which you work as they relate to flexibility, empowerment, and other issues.

It's also important that you are flexible in dealing with challenging or difficult situations. When someone's computer has failed, they likely aren't going to be in a good mood and that can make them a "difficult customer" to deal with. In situations like these, keep in mind the following principles:

Avoid arguing or being defensive.   Arguing with the customer—about anything—is only going to make the situation worse. The customer may be mad and may be yelling at you, but don't argue back, act defensive, or take their comments personally. Try to defuse the situation by calmly reminding them that you're here to help and you want to understand what's going on so you can do that. They may need to vent for a bit, so let them to do that. Just focus on doing what you need to do to resolve the problem.

Don't minimize their problems.   While the customer's problem might seem trivial to you, it isn't to them. Treat the problem as seriously as they're treating it. Keep in mind that facial expressions and body language are also important. If someone tells you their problem and you look at them like they're delusional, they're probably going to pick up on that, which can make the situation worse.

Avoid being judgmental.   Don't blame or criticize. As stated earlier, just focus on what needs to happen to fix the problem. Accusing the user of causing the problem does not build rapport. Even seemingly innocent statements such as "What did you do to the computer?" can be considered judgmental and put the customer on the offensive. Stick with more neutral language, such as "Can you help me understand what happened?"

Focus on your communication skills.   If you have a difficult customer, treat it as an opportunity to see how good a communicator you really are. (Maybe your next job will be a foreign ambassador!) Ask nonconfrontational, open-ended questions. "When was the last time it worked?" is more helpful than "Did it work yesterday?" or "Did you break it this morning?" These can help you narrow down the scope of the problem.

Another good tactic here is to restate the issue or question to verify that you understand. Starting with "I understand that the problem is. . ." and then repeating what the customer said can show empathy and proves that you were listening. If you have it wrong, it's also a good opportunity to let your customer correct you so that you're on track to solve the right problem.

Confidentiality

The goal of *confidentiality* is to prevent or minimize unauthorized access to files and folders and disclosure of data and information. In many instances, laws and regulations require confidentiality for specific information. For example, Social Security records, payroll and employee records, medical records, and corporate information are high-value assets. This information could create liability issues or embarrassment if it fell into the wrong hands. Over the last few years, there have been a number of cases in which bank account and credit card numbers were published on the Internet. The loss of confidence by consumers due to these types of breaches of confidentiality can far exceed the actual monetary losses from the misuse of this information.

Confidentiality entails ensuring that data expected to remain private is seen only by those who should see it. Confidentiality may be implemented through authentication and access controls.

As a computer professional, you are expected to uphold a high level of confidentiality. Should a user approach you with a sensitive issue—telling you their password, asking for assistance obtaining access to medical forms, and so on—it is your obligation as a part of your job to make certain that information goes no further.

Confidential materials on workspaces and printers should always be protected.

As part of confidentiality, don't ever disclose work-related experiences via social media. You might have had a terrible day and really want to say something like, "Wow, the people at XYZ company sure are insufferable morons!" but just don't do it. It's not professional, and it could expose you to legal action.

Respect

Much of the discussion in this chapter is focused on respecting the customer as an individual. However, you must also respect the tangibles that are important to the customer. While you may look at a monitor that they are using as an outdated piece of equipment that should be scrapped, the business owners may see it as a gift from their children when they first started their business.

Treat the customers' property as if it had value and you will win their respect. Their property includes the system on which you are working (laptop/desktop computer, monitor, peripherals, and the like) as well as other items associated with their business. Avoid using the customer's equipment, such as telephones or printers, unless it is associated with the problem you've been summoned to fix.

Another way to show respect is to focus on the task at hand and avoid distractions. For example, you should avoid the following:

- Personal calls
- Texting or social media sites
- Talking to co-workers while interacting with customers
- Personal interruptions

As for texting or talking to co-workers, there may be times that it's appropriate for you to do based on the situation. The key is to find the right time to do it and, if appropriate, tell the customer what you are doing. For example, after gathering information, you might say something like, "Do you mind if I give my co-worker Jen a quick call? The other day she told me about a situation she had that sounded exactly like this and I want to see if her fix worked well." But then make the call quick and business-focused.

 The Customer Respect Group, www.customerrespect.com, measures the behavior of corporations and the respect they give to customers through their websites. Such items as privacy, responsiveness, attitude, simplicity, transparency, and business principles are combined to create a Customer Respect Index (CRI) ranking. The items they rank in the online world are just as important in the offline world and mirror those presented here.

Respecting the customer is not rocket science. All you need to do—for this exam and in the real world—is think of how you would want someone to treat you. Exercise 23.4 explores this topic further. This exercise, like Exercise 23.3, can be modified to fit your purpose or constraints. Its goal is to illustrate the positive power of the unexpected.

EXERCISE 23.4

Surprise Someone

1. Pick a random, toll-free number used for business solicitation and call it.

2. Chat with the operator for a few moments about the company's product or service, and then ask to speak to the supervisor.

3. When the supervisor comes on, commend the operator with whom you have been speaking for the job that he or she has done.

It is likely the operator became confused when you asked to speak to the supervisor; this almost always occurs only in a negative situation. How did the operator handle the request? Did it change the tone of the communication that was taking place? Did they fulfill your request even though they feared they could lose from it? Did the supervisor respond by expecting negative comments? How was the positive information you offered accepted?

Ideally, this illustrated the importance of staying professional and keeping the channel of communication open even in a tough situation. You should be able to adapt this to the workplace when a customer asks to speak to your superior or has another request that is difficult for you to fulfill.

One last area to consider that directly relates to this topic is that of ethics. *Ethics* is the application of morality to situations. While there are different schools of thought, one of the most popular areas of study is known as normative ethics, focusing on what is normal or practical (right versus wrong and so on). Regardless of religion, culture, and other influences, there are generally accepted beliefs that some things are wrong (stealing, murder, and the like) and some things are right (for example, the Golden Rule). You should always attempt to be ethical in everything you do because it reflects not only on your character but also on the company for which you work.

Privacy

While there is some overlap between confidentiality and privacy, privacy is an area of computing that is becoming considerably more regulated. As a computing professional, you must stay current with applicable laws because you're often one of the primary agents expected to ensure compliance.

Although the laws provide a minimal level of privacy, you should go out of your way to respect the privacy of your users beyond what the law establishes. If you discover information about a user that you should not be privy to, you should not share it with anyone, and you should alert the customers that their data is accessible and encourage them—if applicable—to remedy the situation. This includes information that you see on their computer, on their desk, on printers, or anywhere else in their facility.

 **Real World Scenario**

A Little Goes a Long Way

The following examples of respecting and disrespecting the customer come from one of the authors' own experiences:

"My wife and I were in an unfamiliar part of Chicago without ready access to a vehicle when we started to get hungry. I am a meat-and-potatoes man, and I rarely take a chance on anything else. There were no restaurants of that type around, however, and we wound up at an Asian grill. Expecting not to like the buffet, we ordered a side of lettuce wraps

continues

continued

and then two buffets and drinks. As it turned out, I liked the buffet a great deal, and I went back through the line many times. We also liked the drinks and got several of those. Everything was great, except the waiter forgot to bring the lettuce wraps. I dismissed it and made a mental note to inform the waiter when he brought the bill and have him deduct them from our tab. Instead, the manager brought the bill over when we were finished eating, and he had scribbled on it 'no charge.' When I asked him why, he apologized that no one brought the wraps and said he hoped we would come back another time. I was beside myself with disbelief and thanked him profusely, and since then I have told many people about that restaurant, describing it as the best place in Chicago I know of to eat.

"In a very different situation, while driving home one night, the 'low tire pressure' dashboard light came on. Upon inspection, I could hear the right-rear tire hissing. I drove to a tire store and explained the situation. I had used this same tire store over the past 14 years for tires, oil changes, exhaust, maintenance, and a number of other things on the vehicles I've owned. The manager came out and said that they found a nail in the tire. They removed the nail, patched the tire, and charged me $13. I was delighted, expecting it to cost much more, and so I paid the bill and went on my way. The next morning, I woke up to find the right-rear tire completely flat. I canceled the morning's appointment, filled the tire with an air compressor, and drove back to the tire store. Shortly, the manager came out and told me that they found another nail in that tire; they were going to eat the $13 on this one, but it had better not happen again. I could not believe the insinuation—that I was driving about looking for nails to hit with that one tire just so I could spend my morning taking them for $13! Instead of offering the possibility that they had overlooked a nail the previous night, apologizing for the inconvenience, or anything of that sort, he shifted the responsibility to me. Needless to say, I have not been back since, and all of my repair business is now done elsewhere."

These two examples illustrate two different approaches to treating the customer. In the first example, the customer is well respected and treated better than expected. In the second example, the customer is disrespected and is treated as an inconvenience. Given the lifetime value of customers, it is always better to respect them—and retain them—than to dismiss them offhandedly.

Putting It All in Perspective

Whether you are dealing with customers in person or on the phone, there are rules to which you should adhere. These were implied and discussed in the previous sections, but you must understand them and remember them for the exam:

▪ Use proper language and avoid using jargon, abbreviations, and acronyms. Every field has its own language, and outsiders feel lost when they start hearing it. Put yourself in the position of someone not in the field and explain what is going on by using words they understand.

- Maintain a positive attitude and tone of voice, and project confidence. The customer is counting on you to fix their problem. The last thing they want is for you to sound defeated when you hear about the problem.

- Listen to your customers and take notes. Allow them to complete their statements and avoid interrupting them. People like to know that they are being heard, and as simple an act as it is, this can make all of the difference in making them feel at ease with your work. Everyone has been in a situation where they have not been able to explain their problem fully without being interrupted or ignored. It is not enjoyable in a social setting, and it is intolerable in a business setting.

- Be culturally sensitive. Some people may have a language barrier that makes it difficult to explain their problem. (Think about how much computer language you learned in your high school language courses!) Others may have different habits or practices in their workplace. Be respectful of their world. In some cases, using the appropriate professional titles is a sign of respect, and not using them is an insult.

- Be on time. If you're going to be late, be sure to contact your customer. Not doing so indicates that you think their problem isn't important.

- Avoid distraction and/or interruptions when talking with customers. You need to make them feel that their problem is important and that it has your full attention. Distractions can include personal calls, texting or social media, talking to coworkers, and other personal interruptions.

- Exercise patience with difficult customers and situations:
  - Avoid arguing with customers and/or becoming defensive.
  - Do not minimize customers' problems. While it may be a situation you see every day, it is a crisis to them.
  - Avoid being judgmental and/or insulting or calling the customer names.
  - Clarify the customer's statements and ask pertinent questions. The questions you ask should help guide you toward isolating the problem and identifying possible solutions. Don't be afraid to nod, ask questions, and repeat to the customer what you think they are saying to make sure that you understand it correctly.
  - Don't vent about customers on social media.

- Set and meet—or exceed—expectations and communicate timelines and status. Customers want to know what is going on. They want to know that you understand the problem and can deal with it. Being honest and direct is almost always appreciated.

- Deal appropriately with confidential materials. Don't look at files or printouts that you have no business looking at. Make sure the customer's confidential materials stay that way.

Summary

This chapter covered four areas of operational procedures that you should integrate into your work:

- Safety procedures
- Environmental controls
- Licensing, policies, and sensitive materials
- Professionalism and communication

First we looked at the importance of safety procedures. Safety is about protecting you from harm as well as protecting your computer components from getting damaged. We outlined some methods to apply safe working environment policies and procedures and identified potential safety hazards. Included were preventing electrostatic discharge (ESD) and electromagnetic interference (EMI), creating a safe work environment, and handling computer equipment properly.

Safety involves you and your coworkers, but it also includes environmental issues. The environment can have a harmful effect on our computers, but computers can also greatly harm the environment. You also need to be familiar with material safety data sheets (MSDSs) and their importance as well as proper disposal procedures for batteries, display devices, and chemical solvents and cans. These items need to be kept out of the environment because of the damage that they can cause.

Understanding potential legal issues is important too, because failure to follow certain procedures can expose you or your company to legal proceedings. Make sure that all of the software on your computers is legal and licensed and that the computers contain no illegal or prohibited materials. You may also need to protect personally identifiable information, depending on the type of data you have. When incidents happen, you need to know how to respond properly to mitigate the issue.

Finally, we moved on to professionalism and communication. You should treat your customers as you would want to be treated and let them know that you respect them and their business through your actions and behavior.

Exam Essentials

Know which computer components are particularly dangerous to technicians. The most dangerous are the power supply and the monitor. Both are capable of storing lethal charges of electricity, even when unplugged. You also need to be aware of parts that get incredibly hot, such as the processor, which can cause severe burns if touched.

Understand where to find safety information regarding chemicals. You can find this information on a material safety data sheet (MSDS). An MSDS might not have come with your purchase, but most suppliers will gladly supply one if requested.

Know which tool to use for which job.   The majority of computer repair jobs can be handled with nothing more than a Phillips-head screwdriver. However, you might need cutters, extra light, or a mirror for some jobs. Avoid using magnetically tipped tools.

Understand methods to help prevent ESD.   One of the biggest and most common dangers of electronic components is electrostatic discharge (ESD). There are several methods that you can employ to help avoid ESD problems, such as grounding yourself; using an antistatic wrist strap, bag, or mat; and controlling the humidity levels.

Know proper disposal procedures for used computer parts, batteries, and chemical solvents.   The specific disposal procedure depends on the item. However, the safe answer is always to recycle the component and not throw it in the trash bin.

Know the differences between license types.   Open-source applications don't require a purchased license, whereas commercial applications do require a purchased license. Some licenses are personal licenses, meaning they are for use by one person on one computer, while others are enterprise licenses, meaning they can be used on multiple computers at the same time.

Use good communication skills.   Listen to your customers. Let them tell you what they understand the problem to be, and then interpret the problem and see if you can get them to agree to what you are hearing them say. Treat your customers with respect, whether they be end users or colleagues, and take their issues and problems seriously.

Use job-related professional behavior.   The Golden Rule should govern your professional behavior. Six key elements to this, from a business perspective, are punctuality, accountability, flexibility, confidentiality, respect, and privacy.

Understand how to handle prohibited content or activity.   First, always have policies and procedures in place to deal with prohibited content or activity. When an incident happens, follow the procedures, report through proper channels, preserve the data or device, and follow the chain of custody.

Review Questions

The answers to the chapter review questions can be found in Appendix A.

1. You are troubleshooting a computer that is experiencing random reboots and phantom problems. You reboot the system, and the problems seem to disappear. What should you do?

    A. Replace the motherboard.

    B. Boot clean.

    C. Replace the power supply.

    D. Open the cover, clean the inside of the computer, and reseat all cards and chips.

2. You have a failed CRT monitor that you must dispose of safely. Which of the following is used to discharge voltage properly from the unplugged computer monitor?

    A. Antistatic wrist strap

    B. Screwdriver

    C. High-voltage probe

    D. Power cord

3. One of your coworkers just spilled a chemical solvent in a warehouse, and you have been asked to help clean it up. Which of the following must contain information about a chemical solvent's emergency cleanup procedures?

    A. OSHA

    B. MSDS

    C. Product label

    D. CRT

4. You are purchasing an inkjet printer cartridge for home use, which you know has an MSDS. How do you obtain the MSDS for this product?

    A. The store is required to give you one at the time of purchase.

    B. It's contained in the packaging of the printer cartridge.

    C. You are not legally allowed to have an MSDS for this product.

    D. Visit the website of the printer cartridge manufacturer.

5. In the interest of a safe work environment, which of the following should you report? (Choose two.)

    A. An accident

    B. A near-accident

    C. Dirt on the floor inside a building

    D. Rain forecasted for a workday

6. What is the approximate minimum level of static charge for humans to feel a shock?

    A. 300 volts

    B. 3,000 volts

    C. 30,000 volts

    D. 300,000 volts

7. Your work environment has been unusually dry lately, and several components have been damaged by ESD. Your team has been asked to be extra careful about ESD damage. Which of the following measures can be implemented to reduce the risk of ESD? (Choose two.)

    A. Using an antistatic wrist strap

    B. Using an antistatic bag

    C. Wearing an antistatic hair net

    D. Shuffling your feet

8. Which of the following are OSHA requirements for a safe work environment that must be followed by employers? (Choose two.)

    A. Attend yearly OSHA safe work environment seminars.

    B. Provide properly maintained tools and equipment.

    C. Have an OSHA employee stationed within 5 miles of the facility.

    D. Display an OSHA poster in a prominent location.

9. Your office just added 20 new workstations, and your manager has put you in charge of configuring them. The users need to have Microsoft Office installed. What should you do to install Microsoft Office properly on these computers?

    A. Ensure that the company has the proper licenses to install 20 additional copies.

    B. Agree with the open-source license agreement during installation.

    C. Use the personal license key from an existing system to install Office on the new computers.

    D. Follow normal installation procedures; nothing else needs to be done.

10. Your office is moving from one floor of a building to another, and you are part of the moving crew. When moving computer equipment, which of the following are good procedures to follow? (Choose two.)

    A. Lift by bending over at the waist.

    B. Carry monitors with the glass face away from your body.

    C. Use a cart for heavy objects.

    D. Ensure that there are no safety hazards in your path.

11. You have four AA alkaline batteries that you just removed from a remote-control device. What is the recommended way to dispose of these batteries?

    A. Throw them in the trash.

    B. Incinerate them.

    C. Take them to a recycling center.

    D. Flush them down the toilet.

12. During a routine hard drive replacement, you have discovered prohibited material on a user's laptop computer. What two things should you do first? (Choose two.)

    A. Destroy the prohibited material.

    B. Confiscate and preserve the prohibited material.

    C. Confront the user about the material.

    D. Report the prohibited material through the proper channels.

13. While working on a user's system, you discover a sticky note attached to the bottom of the keyboard that has their username and password written on it. The user is not around, and you need to verify that the network connection is working. What should you do?

    A. Log in, verify access, and log out.

    B. Log in and stay logged in when you are finished.

    C. Text the user.

    D. Log in and change the user's password.

14. You promised a customer that you would be out to service their problem before the end of the day but have been tied up at another site. As it now becomes apparent that you will not be able to make it, what should you do?

    A. Arrive first thing in the morning.

    B. Wait until after hours and then leave a message that you were there.

    C. Call the customer and inform them of the situation.

    D. Send an email letting them know that you will be late.

15. A customer is trying to explain a problem with their system. Unfortunately, the customer has such a thick accent that you are unable to understand their problem. What should you do?

    A. Just start working on the system and looking for obvious errors.

    B. Call your supervisor.

    C. Ask that another technician be sent in your place.

    D. Apologize and find another user or manager who can help you translate.

16. You have been trying to troubleshoot a user's system all day long when it suddenly becomes clear that the data is irretrievably lost. Upon informing the customer of this, he becomes so angry that he shoves you against a wall. What should you do?

    A. Shove the user back, only a little harder than he shoved you.

    B. Shove the user back, only a little easier than he shoved you.

    C. Try to calm the user down, and leave the site if you cannot.

    D. Yell for everyone in the area to come quickly.

17. A customer tells you that a technician from your company who was there on a service call spent three hours on the phone making personal calls. What should you do with this information?

    A. Nothing.

    B. Inform your manager.

    C. Talk to the technician personally.

    D. Ask the customer to prove it.

18. You arrive at the site of a failed server to find the vice president nervously pacing and worrying about lost data. What should you do?

    A. Offer a joke to lighten things up.

    B. Downplay the situation and tell him that customers lose data every day.

    C. Keep your head down and keep looking at manuals to let him know that you are serious.

    D. Inform him that you've dealt with similar situations and will let him know what needs to be done as soon as possible.

19. You're temporarily filling in on phone support when a caller tells you that he is sick and tired of being bounced from one hold queue to another. He wants his problem fixed, and he wants it fixed now. What should you do?

    A. Inform him up front that you are only filling in temporarily and won't be of much help.

    B. Transfer him to another technician who handles phone calls more often.

    C. Try to solve his problem without putting him on hold or transferring him elsewhere.

    D. Suggest that he call back at another time when you are not there.

20. At the end of the day, you finish a job only to find that the user you were doing it for had to leave. What should you do? (Choose two.)

    A. Clean up and leave no evidence that you were there.

    B. Leave a note for the user detailing what was done and how to contact you.

    C. Notify the user's manager and your own manager that you have finished.

    D. Put the system back to its original state.

Performance-Based Question

You will encounter performance-based questions on the A+ exams. The questions on the exam require you to perform a specific task, and you will be graded on whether or not you were able to complete the task. The following requires you to think creatively in order to measure how well you understand this chapter's topics. You may or may not see similar questions on the actual A+ exams. To see how your answers compare to the authors', refer to Appendix B.

    Recently, one of your office co-workers tripped on a power cord and injured himself. What should you do to find potential trip hazards in your office? Once the hazards are identified, what actions should you take?

Appendix A

Answers to Review Questions

Chapter 1: Motherboards, Processors, and Memory

1. A. The spine of the computer is the system board, otherwise known as the motherboard. On the motherboard, you will find the CPU, underlying circuitry, expansion slots, video components, RAM slots, and various other chips.

2. C. DDR SDRAM is manufactured on a 184-pin DIMM. DIMMs with 168 pins were used for SDR SDRAM. The SIMM is the predecessor to the DIMM, on which SDRAM was never deployed. DIMMs with 240 pins are used for DDR2 and DDR3 SDRAM.

3. B. Remember the 8:1 rule. Modules greater than but not including SDR SDRAM are named with a number eight times larger than the number used to name the chips on the module. The initials *PC* are used to describe the module, the initials *DDR* are used for the chips, and a single-digit number after PC and DDR is used to represent the level of DDR. The lack of a single-digit number represents DDR as long as the number that is present is greater than 133 (such as PC1600). Otherwise, you're dealing with SDR (such as PC133). This means that PC3-16000 modules are DDR3 modules and are populated with chips named DDR3 and a number that is one-eighth of the module's numeric code: 2000.

4. D. The ITX motherboard family consists of smaller boards that fit in standard or miniature cases and use less power than their larger counterparts.

5. A. The lower-end Core i7 desktop (nonmobile) processors call for the LGA 1156 socket, but the 9xx series requires the LGA 1366 socket.

6. B. ZIF sockets are designed with a locking mechanism that, when released, alleviates the resistance of the socket to receiving the pins of the chip being inserted. Make sure that you know your socket types so that the appearance of a specific model, such as Socket 1366, in a question like this does not distract you from the correct answer. Only LGA would be another acceptable answer to this question because with a lack of pin receptacles, there is no insertion resistance. However, no other pin-layout format, such as SPGA, addresses issues with inserting chips. LPGA might have evoked an image of LGA, leading you to that answer, but that term means nothing outside of the golfing community.

7. B. The Northbridge is in control of the local-bus components that share the clock of the frontside bus. SATA and all other drive interfaces do not share this clock and are controlled by the Southbridge.

8. A. A hard drive stores data on a magnetic medium, which does not lose its information after the power is removed and can be repeatedly written to and erased.

9. C. This processor requires an AM3 socket. The only other version of Phenom II was for the AM2+, and it is not compatible with DDR3 RAM.

10. B. Soft power is the feature whereby the front power button acts as a relay to initiate various system power changes, depending on the duration that the button is held.

11. B, F. DIMMs used in desktop motherboard applications have one of three possible pin counts. SDR SDRAM is implemented on 168-pin modules. DDR SDRAM and 16-bit RIMMs are implemented on 184-pin modules. DDR2 and DDR3 are implemented on 240-pin modules with different keying. Dual-channel RIMM modules have 232 pins. Modules with 200 and 204 pins are used in the SODIMM line, and there are no modules with 180 pins.

12. C, D. Both the CPU and BIOS have to be designed to support virtualization in hardware.

13. D. Most motherboards have a jumper or similar momentary closure mechanism that will allow you to clear the CMOS memory of any user settings and cause the BIOS to use factory defaults, including no user or supervisor passwords.

14. A. The easiest solution that works to cool your CPU is to connect the four-pin connector into the three-pin header. The missing pin allows you to control the speed of the fan. Without it, the fan will run at top speed, which is fine, albeit a little noisier. The heat sink alone should not be relied upon for proper cooling of modern CPUs.

15. D. The PCIe 1.1 specification provided 250MBps of throughput per lane per direction. With the 2.x versions of PCIe, this rate was doubled to 500MBps. As a result, each v2.0 lane is capable of a combined 1GBps. A x16 slot consists of 16 lanes, for a total bidirectional throughput of 16GBps.

16. C. The reset button causes the computer to return to nearly the same point it is in when you power it on, but without the need for power cycling. Using Restart in the Start menu does not reboot as deeply as the reset button. Hibernation is a power state that completely removes power after saving the contents of RAM to the hard drive; pressing the power button is required to resume the session in the same manner as starting the computer after a complete shutdown. The power button cannot be used as a method of restarting the system.

17. B. None of the options are required, but a UPS is by far the most helpful among the answers in that loss of power during this procedure can range from annoying to devastating.

18. A. These CPUs integrate the graphics-processing unit. The Core i7 before them integrated the memory controller, eliminating the FSB. Math coprocessors have been integrated since the 80486DX.

19. D. Pentium 4 processors are always mated with memory mounted on DIMMs.

20. B. Although technically all of the slots listed could be used for video adapters, PCIe excels when compared to the other options and offers technologies such as SLI, which only make PCIe's advantage more noticeable.

Chapter 2: Storage Devices and Power Supplies

1. B. A conventional HDD contains discs called platters, on which data is stored magnetically through read/write heads by way of a magnetic coating.

2. A. A conventional hard disk drive system consists of the hard disk and its often-integrated controller as well as a host adapter to gain access to the rest of the computer system. The drive interface is a common component of the controller and host adapter.

3. D. A fixed number of clusters is supported by each operating system, leading to a corresponding maximum volume size. If the maximum NTFS cluster size of 64KB is used, NTFS can support a single-volume size of 64KB less than 256TB. When a cluster size of one sector, or 512 bytes (1/2KB), is used, the maximum volume size reduces to 2TB.

4. C. Solid-state disks (SSDs) are capable of replacing conventional HDDs, contingent upon cheaper components and higher capacities.

5. B. A solid-state hybrid drive incorporates the features of both conventional magnetic-only hard drives and solid-state drives. As a result, the performance of an SSHD exceeds that of a hard drive but costs less than the equivalent-sized SSD. A dual-drive option still requires the purchase of a full-sized SSD. Adding the cost of the SSD and the HDD, the dual-drive solution does not satisfy the requirement of an affordable technology.

6. B. Blu-ray discs have a single-sided, single-layer capacity of 25GB. The best the other options achieve is no more than roughly 17GB.

7. A. Hot-swappable devices can be removed while the power to the system is still on. Warm-swappable devices need to be stopped in the operating system before being removed. The term has nothing to do with the heat level of the device.

8. C. Power supplies and AC adapters use standard wall outlets for an input of AC voltage, which they convert to the DC voltages required by the components to which they supply power.

9. A, C, D, E, F. A PC's power supply produces +3.3VDC, +5VDC, −5VDC, +12VDC, and −12VDC from a 110VAC input.

10. D. PC power supplies accept alternating current as input and produce direct current for the internal components. Europe requires the voltage selector switch be set at the higher setting. SATA drives most often use a specific power connector that is not compatible with the Molex connector used by PATA drives. Legacy AT-based motherboards called for P8 and P9 connectors; ATX motherboards have a newer 20- or 24-pin single power connector.

11. C. Today's hard drives, regardless of their rpm, have standard internal power connections. Each of the other options are valid concerns when installing an internal drive.

12. A. Although inefficient as an interactive medium, sequential tape-based storage continues to be developed in increasing capacities. Tape remains the best choice for frequently backing up large amounts of data for redundancy and archival purposes.

13. A. The *e* in eMMC stands for *embedded*. MultiMediaCard memory cards were modified to be able to be embedded on circuit boards in small or inexpensive devices. The eMMC module acts as solid-state form of secondary storage, performing similar functions to the HDDs and SSDs of larger or more expensive systems.

14. D. 12,000 rpm HDDs were once produced in low quantities but were never common.

15. B. Personal computers do not have permanently installed power supplies. Like other electrical and electronic components, power supplies can and do fail on a regular basis. Permanently mounting a power supply to a chassis would be a disservice to the consumer. You should consider the cumulative power needs of your installed components, and you might have to obtain adapters and splitters if you do not have enough or you have the wrong types of connectors coming from the power supply.

16. B. The red stripe on the cable indicates pin 1.

17. C. One drawback to dual-rail power supplies is that despite the fact that they supply more cumulative power, they offer less power on each individual rail than the single rail of other power supplies. As a result, it is easier to overdraw one of the two rails than it is to overdraw a single-rail power supply's rail because the two rails do not combine their power but instead offer it separately, thus reducing the relative output of each individual rail.

18. B. Hybrid drives are named for their inclusion of traditional hard drive technology as well as newer solid-state technology. Hybrid systems can be all in one or comprise one drive of each technology. Special software is needed to optimize the hybrid drive's usage and performance.

19. D. Each concept applies to both HDDs and SSDs except for platter spin rates. Revolutions per minute (rpm) measurements refer to drives with moving parts. SSDs have none.

20. A. Power supplies are rated in watts. When you purchase a power supply, you should make sure the devices inside the computer do not require more wattage than the chosen power supply can offer. The voltage is fairly standard among power supplies, and it has nothing to do with the devices connected to the power supply. Amperage and resistance are not selling points for power supplies.

Chapter 3: Peripherals and Expansion

1. D. A PS/2 port is also known as a mini-DIN 6 connector.

2. D. The USB 2.0 spec provides for a maximum speed of 480 megabits per second (Mbps—not megabytes per second, or MBps).

3. C. Touchscreens are used as standard displays, making them output devices, but they are also used as input devices because they translate the user's touch to a point on a two-dimensional plane, which is then transferred to the software interface to replace such stimuli as the combination of a mouse movement and click. Webcams, motion sensors, and touchpads are used only for input.

4. C. The IEEE 1394 standard provides for greater data transfer speeds, increased power, and the ability to send memory addresses as well as data through a serial port. USB 3.0 proves to threaten more competition in these areas, but USB 2.0 could not compare to the overall performance of IEEE 1394.

5. B. USB hubs are used to connect multiple peripherals to one computer through a single port. They support data transfer rates as high as 12Mbps, or 1.5MBps (for USB 1.1, which is the option listed here).

6. D. The IEEE 1284 standard specifies that the ECP parallel port use a DMA channel and that the buffer be able to transfer data at higher speeds to printers.

7. C. The description 5.1 refers to six channels of audio. The 5 in the name refers collectively to the single center channel, the right and left front channels, and the right and left rear channels. The 1 in the name refers to the single LFE channel connected to the subwoofer.

8. A. Intel and Apple collaborated on Thunderbolt to add PCIe to VESA's DisplayPort and to make the resulting interface smaller and less expensive to connect.

9. C. HDMI is a digital interface and cabling specification that allows digital audio to be carried over the same cable as video.

10. C. Such a connection should not be made. DVI-I cables act like universal cables; they can connect two DVI-A interfaces or two DVI-D interfaces with adapters. Natively, they are used to connect two DVI-I interfaces, both of which are configured as either analog or digital. They are unable to convert the analog signal to a digital one, however. Analog and digital DVI interfaces are too disparate to interconnect.

11. B. Biometric input devices scan a physical trait of the user, such as voice, fingerprint, and retina, for authentication purposes when the user attempts to access computer systems and other property.

12. D. KVM switches are ideal when you have multiple computers situated near one another and do not want to commit the extra desk space to each computer having its own keyboard, mouse, and monitor.

13. C. MIDI devices use a 5-pin DIN connector similar to the one used with the original AT keyboard.

14. B. A video capture card is used to convert raw video input to a format that can be shared electronically. Although many TV tuner cards provide this functionality, it is their video-capture component that gives them this capability. Any adapter that is strictly a TV tuner cannot capture video.

15. A. Multimedia input devices, not standard input devices, use 1/8″ jacks. Standard input devices include human interface devices, such as keyboards and mice. The other three options can be used for such devices.

16. C. Network interface cards are considered to be a form of communications adapter.

17. B. Interfaces such as USB ports are considered input/output ports. If you have to add USB capability to a computer, an I/O adapter with USB ports on it would meet the need.

18. A. Modems have RJ-11 jacks to provide an interface to the Public Switched Telephone Network (PSTN). The modular jacks that Ethernet NICs have are known as RJ-45 jacks.

19. C. A trackball is a sort of stationary upside-down mouse that has the ball for movement detection on the top of the device along with the keys. The ball is actuated by the thumb or fingers, not by moving the device along a flat surface or mouse pad. Trackballs are ideal where desk space is limited. Touchpads feature a touch-sensing surface with no ball for movement, while *trackpad* is a rarer term meaning the same.

20. B. VGA signals are analog, uncompressed, component signals that carry all of the video information for all three components of the original RGB signal.

Chapter 4: Display Devices

1. C. LCDs do not have electron guns that are aimed by magnets as CRTs do. This difference makes LCDs more compatible with nearby speaker magnets. Additionally, the cathode ray tube for which CRT monitors are named is a rather bulky component, requiring more desk space to accommodate the CRT's cabinet. Projectors are not common personal display devices; they are used more in group environments. HDMI is a standard for connecting display devices, not a type of display device.

2. B, E. Early LCD monitors featured one or more fluorescent bulbs that were used to produce light that shone through the LCD panel. Modern LCD monitors have LED panels to generate the light, the advantage being that there is now a separate LED for each picture element instead of a common light source for the entire monitor.

3. D. The maximum allowable refresh rate does tend to be affected by the resolution you choose in the operating system. The refresh rate is most often expressed in cycles per second (Hz), not millions of cycles per second (MHz). You must usually select the refresh rate that you want from the display settings dialogs, not through the monitor's built-in menu system, although the monitor can often tell you the refresh rate that you're using. Finally, both the monitor and adapter must agree on the refresh rate you select. If either device does not support a particular refresh rate, such a rate cannot be used.

4. C. TN-based LCDs are less expensive and offer better response times for the money. TN, not IPS, technology suffers from color shifts when viewed at wide angles.

5. A. The amount of memory installed on a graphics adapter is directly related to how many pixels can be displayed at one time and how many colors the pixels can be set to. Monitors don't have memory installed in them. LCDs, not CRTs, have a single, fixed resolution called the native resolution. You might be limited to a particular refresh rate because the resolution is too high, but the refresh rate is automatically adjusted down, if necessary, when you select a resolution.

6. B. SXGA has a resolution of 1280 × 1024. Consult Table 4.2 for the resolutions that characterize other technologies.

7. **D.** Although the *Q* stands for *quad,* the pixel count for each axis is only doubled, resulting in four times as many total pixels.

8. **A.** Contrast ratio is a selling point for LCDs. Higher contrast ratios mean darker blacks and brighter whites. The measure of luminance between adjacent pixels is known as contrast, not contrast ratio.

9. **D.** Both OLED and plasma displays use electrodes to excite the material in a sealed chamber to produce light. Each in its own way uses that light to create red, green, or blue light within individual subpixels. All LCD panels form images that require an external light source to view.

10. **C, E.** Older LCD panels might have employed passive-matrix addressing for their pixels, resulting in a poorer viewing angle than that created by active-matrix LCD panels. Additionally, privacy filters intentionally limit the angle of screen visibility by changing the light's polarization when viewed from the side. Antiglare filters might unintentionally do the same thing.

11. **B.** Although it's true that you must start with the Display Settings dialog box, which ironically shows a single tab labeled Monitor, and that you subsequently click the Advanced Settings button, the Monitor properties tab is where you select the refresh rate. The Adapter tab in those same properties pages has no selection for refresh rate.

12. **A.** Unplugging the power to the projector before the projector's fan has had the opportunity to cool the unit and stop running on its own can lead to expensive repairs on the projector or to the cost of replacing the projector outright.

13. **D.** Safe Mode disables as many nonessential drivers and services as possible. One of the nonessential drivers it disables is the driver for the graphics adapter. Windows uses its standard VGA driver to control the graphics adapter while you are in Safe Mode. Another reason for defaulting back to standard VGA is that you might have a corrupt or incorrect driver for your adapter.

14. **C.** If your monitor allows you to change the resolution, it might not actually allow you to change the resolution. As confusing as that sounds, your monitor might maintain its optimal hardware resolution, such as an LCD's native resolution, and force you to scroll to see any pixels created by the chosen software resolution that it cannot fit on the hardware screen at that particular moment.

15. **A.** An LCD's native resolution is the single, fixed resolution that provides optimal clarity.

16. **D.** The multimonitor feature allows two monitors to display exactly the same thing (clone) or to extend your Desktop onto the second monitor. There is no need to use one adapter to achieve this result. In fact, the two adapters don't even have to use the same expansion-bus architecture. The two cards must, however, use the same graphics-adapter driver.

17. **A.** Active matrix is a superior technology to passive matrix. Dual scan is merely an enhanced form of passive matrix, but it is not on par with active matrix. Dual matrix isn't an LCD type.

18. B. Dividing 16 by 10 produces a value of 1.6. Dividing the first number of a 16:10 resolution by the second number always results in 1.6. Resolutions with a 4:3 aspect ratio produce the value 1.333, while 5:4 resolutions such as 1280 × 1024 produce the value 1.25.

19. C. Regardless of how high the refresh rate, which measures the total number of all screens of information that is displayed per second, is on a monitor, only the number of unique frames in the content being played back during each second is considered when computing frame rate. Each frame represents a complete screen of information.

20. B. A lumen is a unit of measure for the total amount of visible light that the projector gives off, based solely on what the human eye can perceive.

Chapter 5: Custom Configurations

1. A. Graphics design and CAD/CAM design workstations do not require a fast hard drive because the artist works with static images that do not stream from the drive. However, RAM is needed to hold the highly detailed, sometimes 3D, artwork before saving, and a powerful processor is required for implementing complex algorithms on a small amount of information during rendering. High-end video is necessary for assisting in the rendering and display of the images.

2. D. A/V editing workstations require specialized audio and video cards and large and fast hard drives, and they also benefit from dual monitors. A fast NIC, extra RAM, and a faster than normal processor do not support the requirements of A/V editors.

3. B. Virtual machines do not imply virtual processing. The data storage, processing cycles, and RAM usage are all real. The separate hard drive and chassis for each operating system are virtual. The other answers all have at least one fundamental problem with their logic. CPU cores are not installed in virtual machines but in CPU packages within physical machines. CPU cores do not take over for each other. There is no fault tolerance among them. Storing data is the job of RAM, which should also be maximized for virtualization workstations.

4. A. The processors found in a gaming PC are many, and the CPU is often overclocked. Such a configuration generates too much heat for conventional cooling to dissipate before the system is damaged. These machines don't have unusual hard-drive requirements. The cooling has no effect on external controllers, and sound cards don't generate much heat, but analog would certainly generate more than digital.

5. C. Home theater PCs are based on the mini-ITX motherboard and have their own form factor, HTPC, a more compact form factor than chassis made for micro-ATX boards.

6. B. Thick clients are standard desktop PCs. They stand in contrast to systems with specialized requirements, such as the remaining options.

7. D. Although not all thin clients are devoid of local processing capability, some are. High-resolution graphics are not a requirement, but thin clients do require a system unit with a NIC.

8. C. Optimally, the server should communicate across a link that is the aggregate of all client links, but at the very least, the server's link should be a faster one to alleviate the potential bottleneck when all clients try to access the server simultaneously.

9. D. Quite simply, the rendering of 2D and 3D graphics makes use of complex algorithms that need all of the processing power they can get to remain usable. CAD workstations deal with static images, not streaming video. Manufacturing equipment is generally slower than computers used for the design phase. CAD workstations call for high-end video, which includes graphics adapters with GPUs often more powerful than the system's CPU.

10. A. Editors of this type of media have numerous controls and timelines to track. These constructs often lie along the bottom of the application and run horizontally. Subsequent monitors allow the editor to spread out without shrinking the view excessively.

11. B. Maximum RAM and CPU cores are the primary requirements for such systems. Although there are multiple guest operating systems, generally there is but one host to those guests. File sharing may be a service the administrator decides to offer, and multiple NICs might prove advantageous with virtual machines that are popular among the clients, but these workstations do not require either.

12. B. Gaming PCs are not known for requiring fault tolerance or data persistence. RAID arrays, therefore, are generally not included. The other components are a benefit for gaming PCs, however.

13. A. A/V editing workstations require video enhancements and a hard drive capable of storing a large quantity of data and accessing it quickly. The other system types require faster or more plentiful processors.

14. C. Because of its exceptional capabilities of digital video and audio output as well as its potential for support of future standards, HDMI is the home-theater video output technology of choice. Neither DVI nor component video (YCbCr and YPbPr) can make the same claims. WUXGA is a resolution of 1920 × 1200 and not a video output technology.

15. D. These standard systems do not have any special requirements, only that they can run Windows and desktop applications.

16. C. Clients request services of servers. Thin clients can request software services from their servers, whether in the form of running the software and passing the results to the client or passing the code of the software to the client to be executed by its processor and kept only in RAM.

17. B. Additional RAM in the home server PC offers no advantage for the performance of the server past a certain point. The tasks the server is asked to perform do not require high performance.

18. A, D. Virtualization and graphic design workstations benefit from as much RAM as can be installed. Home theater PCs and gaming PCs do not require a large amount of temporary storage of instructions and data. They are more about the rapid movement of graphical data toward an output device.

19. A. The Windows 7 computer can be built as a normal system with a 2TB or 3TB drive. WHS 2011 needs a home server PC. A type of CAD/CAM workstation capable of CNC crafts the rims. A home theater PC is an ideal choice to take the place of both the BD player and DVR.

20. B. The clients of the home server PC that use the server for streaming video content might benefit from enhanced video, but the server will not.

Chapter 6: Network Fundamentals

1. D. Companies that want to ensure the safety and integrity of their data should use fiber-optic cable because it is not affected by electromagnetic or radio-frequency interference. Even though some copper cables have shielding, they are not immune to EMI or RFI. This eliminates twisted-pair and coaxial. CSMA/CD is an access method, not a cable type.

2. C. The IEEE 802.3 standard originally specified a bus topology that uses coaxial baseband cable, and it can transmit data up to 10Mbps.

3. C. It is the responsibility of the Transport layer to signal an "all clear" by making sure that the data segments are error free. It also controls the data flow and troubleshoots any problems with transmitting or receiving data frames.

4. B. Carrier Sense Multiple Access with Collision Detection (CSMA/CD) specifies that the NIC pause before transmitting a packet to ensure that the line is not being used. If no activity is detected, then it transmits the packet. If activity is detected, it waits until it is clear. In the case of two NICs transmitting at the same time (a collision), both NICs pause to detect and then retransmit the data.

5. A. The Open Systems Interconnection (OSI) model is used to describe how network protocols should function. The International Organization for Standardization (ISO) designed the OSI model.

6. D. A hub or a switch is at the center of a star topology. A NIC is a network card, which each computer must have to be on the network. Bridges and routers are higher-level connectivity devices that connect network segments or networks together.

7. C. Fiber-optic cable can span distances of several kilometers because it has much lower attenuation, crosstalk, and interference as compared to copper cables.

8. A. Routers are designed to route (transfer) packets across networks. They are able to do this routing, determining the best path to take, based on the internal routing tables that they maintain.

9. D. A peer-to-peer network has no servers, so all of the resources are shared from the various workstations on which they reside. This is the opposite of a client-server network, in which the majority of resources are located on servers that are dedicated to responding to client requests.

10. A. Bluetooth networks are often called wireless personal area networks (WPANs).

1222 Appendix A • Answers to Review Questions

11. **A, C, D.** In a star network, all systems are connected using a central device such as a hub or a switch. The network is not disrupted for other users when more systems are added or removed. The star network design is used with today's UTP-based networks.

12. **A.** For areas where a cable must be fire retardant, such as in a drop ceiling, you must run plenum-grade cable. Plenum refers to the coating on the sleeve of the cable, not the copper or fiber within the cable itself. PVC is the other type of coating typically found on network cables, but it produces poisonous gas when burned.

13. **D.** The local connector (LC) is a mini form factor (MFF) fiber-optic connector developed by Lucent Technologies. If it helps, think of LC as "Little Connector."

14. **A.** If you need to make a connection that is 5 kilometers long, then you are limited to fiber-optic cable, specifically SMF. The two common SMF standards are 10GBaseER and 10GBaseEW. (Think of the *E* as *extended*.) A *T* designation in an Ethernet standard refers to twisted pair. SR and LR are fiber standards that do not stretch for 5 kilometers.

15. **C.** In a mesh network, the number of connections is determined by the formula $(x \times (x - 1)) \div 2$. With seven computers, that amounts to 21 connections.

16. **B.** A crimper can attach connectors to the end of a network cable. A punch-down tool will attach a cable to a wiring frame such as a 110 block. Cable testers will see if the cable works properly after you've created it. A loopback plug is for testing network cards.

17. **B.** The job of a firewall is to block unwanted network traffic. Firewalls do this by using a list of rules called an access control list (ACL). Routers connect networks to each other. Internet appliances give the user Internet access. A network attached storage (NAS) device is like a dedicated file server.

18. **A.** The two RG standards used for cable television are RG-6 and RG-59. Of the two, RG-6 is better and can handle digital signals. RG-59 is for analog signals only. RG-8 is thicknet coax, and RG-58 is thinnet coax.

19. **C, D.** Bridges and switches are Layer 2 devices. Hubs work at Layer 1, and routers work at Layer 3. Note that some switches are called multilayer switches, and they will work at Layer 3 as well.

20. **B.** Multimode fiber (MMF) can transmit up to 550 meters, depending on the Ethernet specification. Other standards using MMF can transmit only up to 300 meters. If you need to transmit up to 40 kilometers, you will need to use single-mode fiber (SMF).

Chapter 7: Introduction to TCP/IP

1. **B.** A Dynamic Host Configuration Protocol (DHCP) server provides IP configuration information to hosts when they join the network. A Domain Name System (DNS) server resolves hostnames to IP addresses. A domain controller may provide login authentication, but it does not provide IP configuration information. There is no IP configuration server.

2. B. Class A addresses have a first octet between 1 and 126, Class B between 128 and 191, and Class C between 192 and 223. With a first octet of 171, this is a Class B address.

3. A. HTTP uses port 80. HTTPS uses 443, Telnet 23, and POP3 110.

4. D. An IPv6 interface is not limited in the number of addresses that it can be assigned, although there could be limitations based upon practicality.

5. A, B, C. An IPv6 address contains 128 bits, written in eight 16-bit fields represented by four hexadecimal digits. Option A contains all eight fields expressed in full. Option B is an IPv4 address expressed in IPv6 form. Option C is the same address as option A, but written in accepted shorthand. Option D is not valid because the double colons (::) can be used only once within an address.

6. A. DNS servers resolve hostnames to IP addresses. On the Internet, a DNS server needs to have a public IP address. The address 10.25.11.33 is in a private address space, so that address would not be valid for a DNS server on the Internet.

7. D. The address assigned to the computer is an APIPA address. Microsoft client computers (and others) will configure themselves with an address in this range if they are unable to reach a DHCP server.

8. C. Simple Mail Transfer Protocol (SMTP) is responsible for sending email. IMAP4 and POP3 both receive email. SNMP is a network management protocol.

9. D. Remote Desktop Protocol (RDP) works on port 3389. DNS works on port 53, IMAP4 works on 143, and LDAP works on 389.

10. C, D. The two protocols that work at the Host-to-Host layer are TCP and UDP. IP and ARP both work at the Internet layer.

11. A, D. TCP is a connection-oriented protocol that establishes virtual circuits and acknowledges delivery of packets. Because of these features, it has higher overhead than UDP and is a little slower.

12. B. The HTTP protocol is inherently unsecure, but the HTTPS protocol is secure. (SSH and SFTP are secure as well, but they are not protocols used to connect to websites.)

13. A. The router is your doorway out into other networks, and it is known in TCP/IP terms as the default gateway. Without this configuration option, you will not be able to get to external networks.

14. A, B. The only mandatory IPv4 configuration items are an IP address and a subnet mask. If you are not connecting to another network, you do not need a default gateway. DNS servers resolve hostnames to IP addresses, but they are not mandatory.

15. D. IMAP4 and POP3 are the two protocols that are used for email delivery. Of the two, only IMAP4 provides security features. SMTP sends email. SNMP is a network management protocol.

16. B. The Secure Shell (SSH) was developed as a secure alternative to Telnet. SMB is Server Message Block, which is a network file system. SNMP is for network management. SFTP is designed for secure file downloads. It's a secure alternative to FTP, not a replacement for Telnet.

17. A. Telnet uses port 23. SSH uses port 22. FTP uses ports 21 and 20. DNS uses port 53.

18. E. IPv6 does not have broadcasts. IPv6 does have multicasts, which are a bit like targeted broadcasts. FF00:: is the first part of a multicast address.

19. A. DNS is typically known as a name resolver on the Internet, but it will work on private networks as well. DNS resolves hostnames to IP addresses. DHCP automatically configures clients with IP address information. FTP is for file downloads. APIPA is a process used to assign clients a private IP address automatically when they can't reach the DHCP server.

20. C. The Address Resolution Protocol (ARP) resolves IP addresses to hardware (MAC) addresses. RARP does the reverse—it resolves MAC addresses to IP addresses. DNS resolves hostnames to IP addresses. DHCP automatically configures TCP/IP clients.

Chapter 8: Installing Wireless and SOHO Networks

1. B, D. Both 802.11b and 802.11g operate in the 2.4GHz range and use similar transmission standards. Many devices on the market are listed as 802.11b/g, meaning they will work with either system. Alternatively, 802.11a and 802.11ac operate in the 5GHz range.

2. C. A service-set identifier (SSID) is the unique name given to the wireless network. All hardware that is to participate on the network must be configured to use the same SSID. Essentially, it is the network name. When you are using Windows to connect to a wireless network, all available wireless networks will be listed by their SSID.

3. A, C. The two technologies that 802.11ac employs to achieve high throughput are channel bonding and MIMO. Channel bonding is the combination of multiple smaller channels into one large channel for greater bandwidth. MIMO is enhanced over 802.11n to allow for more multiple inputs and outputs. 802.11ac also uses beamforming, but that helps the range, not the throughput.

4. C. WEP was the original encryption standard developed for Wi-Fi networks, but it is easily hacked. WPA is an upgrade, but WPA2 is more secure and incorporates the entire 802.11i standard. SAFER+ is used to encrypt Bluetooth communications.

5. C. QoS level 5 is designated for interactive voice and video, with less than 100ms delay. Level 1 is for background applications and is low priority. Level 4 is known as controlled load, which is lower priority than interactive voice and video. Level 6 only has 10ms latency but is reserved for control traffic.

6. A, B. You should always change the default administrator name and password as well as the default SSID when installing a new wireless router. Enabling encryption is also a good idea, but WPA and WPA2 are better options than WEP. The channel has nothing to do with security.

7. A. Of the options listed, DSL provides the fastest speed. DSL can easily provide 12Mbps downloads. Dial-up is limited to 56Kbps, and BRI ISDN (128Kbps) and PRI (about 1.5Mbps) don't even come close. Satellite is also much slower than DSL.

8. D. Network Address Translation (NAT) allows users to have a private IP address and still access the Internet with a public IP address. NAT is installed on a router and translates the private IP address into a public one for the user to access the Internet. DHCP assigns IP configuration information to clients. DNS resolves hostnames to IP addresses. A DMZ is an area on a network between an external router and an internal router.

9. C. There are 14 communication channels in the 2.4GHz range, but only the first 11 are configurable. The three non-overlapping channels are 1, 6, and 11.

10. A, C, D. Three standards listed—802.11ac (1300Mbps), 802.11g (54Mbps), and 802.11n (600Mbps)—give users the required throughput.

11. B. To join the network, client computers need to find the SSID, ensure that the security settings are correct (to match the router), and enter the security passphrase. As an administrator, you should have configured this passphrase to be different than the router's administrator password.

12. B. Infrared is limited to about 1 meter, with a viewing angle of about 30 degrees. Most Bluetooth devices can transmit up to 10 meters. WiMAX has a maximum range of about 5 miles. Satellite signals can travel from the surface of the Earth to a small metal can orbiting the planet.

13. B, C. Dial-up Internet is archaic by today's standards, but it is widely available (anywhere there is phone service) and it's generally lower in cost than other Internet access methods. It's definitely not high speed, and its security is really no different than that of broadband Internet access methods.

14. B. WEP could use a 64-bit or 128-bit security key, but it was a static key. TKIP introduced a dynamic per-packet key. AES and CCMP came after TKIP.

15. D. The good news is that 802.11g is backward compatible with 802.11b. The bad news is if you run in a mixed environment, all devices that communicate with the WAP (or router) will be forced to slow down to accommodate the older technology.

16. D. MAC filtering is a security option that can specify that only computers with specific MAC (hardware) addresses can access the network. Port forwarding is a feature of firewalls. WPS is an easy setup mechanism for wireless networks. SSID is the wireless network name.

17. B. The set of rules for access on a firewall is called an access control list (ACL). An SLA is an agreement on service level for QoS. Default deny is a good policy for firewalls because it doesn't let any traffic through. A DMZ is a subnet located between an external network router and an internal router.

18. C. If your router is using AES, the clients will need to use WPA2. TKIP is a protocol utilized by WPA. WEP is the weakest of the encryption options.

19. A. Bluetooth also operates in the 2.4GHz range.

20. D. Basic rate interface ISDN (BRI ISDN) provides two separate 64Kbps B channels for data transmissions. These channels can be combined to increase throughput. A PRI ISDN uses 23 B channels. DSL, cable, and satellite do not offer multiple dedicated digital channels.

Chapter 9: Understanding Laptops

1. D. Laptop service manuals can be obtained from the manufacturer's website. It's very rare that paper service manuals are shipped with the laptop. Pressing F1 while in Windows will open Windows Help, and pressing F2 on many laptops during the system boot will take you into the BIOS.

2. B. By and large, compromises always must be made when comparing laptops to desktops. Although laptops can be used as desktop replacements, their performance is almost always lower than comparably priced desktops.

3. A, B. The components of an LCD screen are the inverter, screen, and backlight. The video card is also a key component of the LCD system. A CRT is a different technology than LCD.

4. C. The Touchpoint point stick was released with the IBM ThinkPad series of laptops.

5. B. A DC adapter converts the DC output from a car or airplane accessory power plug into the DC voltages required by your laptop.

6. C. DDR2 MicroDIMMs can have 172 or 214 pins.

7. C. USB is used most often in laptops as an expansion bus for external peripherals. Although parallel and PS/2 ports allow for connection of external peripherals, they are not as flexible or widely used for expansion as USB.

8. A. Your best bet is to turn off your wireless connection immediately in order to sever the tie between your laptop and the public network. This is done using the Wi-Fi toggle.

9. C. Sometimes the only way to ensure that equipment doesn't walk away is to lock it down physically. Laptops come equipped with holes for cable locks that can be used to secure them to a desk or other workstation.

10. C. The backlight won't really affect the viewing angle of the laptop. What you should look for is a laptop that uses LCD IPS technology, which offers a wider viewing angle than does TN.

11. A. The ExpressCard bus brings USB 2.0, USB 3.0, and PCIe to the small-form-factor computing industry. CardBus is an older technology that supports USB 1.1 and PCI only. Mini PCI *is* PCI, not PCIe.

12. C. The user needs a digitizer, which takes input from the device, such as drawn images, and converts them into electronic images on the computer.

13. D. Thunderbolt 2 provides for speeds up to 20Gbps. USB 3.1 only supports speeds up to 10Gbps.

14. A. A docking station made specifically for its associated brand and model of laptop can host desktop components permanently, regardless of whether the laptop is attached to the docking station. When the laptop's portability is not required, but instead use of the desktop components is the priority, attaching the laptop to the docking station makes such components available to the laptop without separately attaching each component.

15. D. The processor can reduce how fast it's working, which is called throttling, to help conserve battery life.

16. B. Think of wattage as a "bucket" of power that the attached device can draw on. A bigger bucket simply holds more power but does not force the power on the device. Less wattage is not advised, however. Voltage can be thought of as the pressure behind the power to the device. Anything but the proper voltage is dangerous for the device. When you replace a laptop's AC adapter, you should match the voltage ratings of the original adapter. This also means that you should use an adapter with a fixed voltage if that matches the characteristics of the original; otherwise, obtain one that automatically switches voltages at the levels needed.

17. C. Battery calibration for Li-ion batteries allows the powered device to drain the battery's power before recharging. Battery exercising is the initial charging and discharging of nickel-based batteries so that they will function as expected. You should never short a battery's terminals, and replacement is a last resort, used when any battery has reached the end of its life.

18. D. Laptop hard drives commonly have a 2½″ form factor. The most common form factor for desktop hard drives is 3½″. Laptop hard drives use the same drive technologies as their desktop counterparts, such as serial and parallel ATA. As with desktop hard drives, laptop hard drives are available in both solid-state and conventional varieties. Unlike desktop hard drives, laptop hard drives do not have separate power connectors.

19. B. A USB Bluetooth adapter should do the trick. Replacing the laptop is a much more expensive proposition.

20. C. SODIMM and MicroDIMM are the common laptop small-form-factor memory standards. Of the two, MicroDIMM is smaller.

Chapter 10: Understanding Mobile Devices

1. C. Most mobile devices today use capacitive touch screens, which allow the user to use their finger as an input device.

2. A. Apple created a new OS for its watch called WatchOS. It's very similar to iOS 8.

3. A. *Multi-touch* simply means that the touch screen can accept multiple inputs from different parts of the screen at the same time. This allows for functionality such as

pinch to zoom. It could mean that multiple people are using the touch screen at once, but it does not have to mean that.

4. C. Google Glass uses augmented reality (AR) technology, which is common on heads-up types of displays.

5. D. GRiDPad was the first commercial tablet released, in 1989. None of the others were released until at least the year 2000.

6. B. The iPhone 5 was the first iPhone to use the Lightning connector. iPhone 6 uses it as well.

7. A. Tablets generally have a screen size between 7″ and 12″. Phablets are between 5″ and 7″, and smartphones are smaller than phablets. GPS touch screens are usually around the same size as the screens on smartphones.

8. B. Most mobile Bluetooth accessories are Class 2 devices, which have a maximum functional range of 10 meters.

9. B. The app store for Android-based devices is Google Play. iOS devices download apps from the App Store.

10. C. Near field communication (NFC) has a maximum range of about 10 centimeters. Wi-Fi depends on the standard, but it usually has a range of 30 meters or more. Bluetooth Class 2 devices can operate at about 10 meters, and infrared (IR) has a maximum range of about 1 meter.

11. B. Phablets are larger than smartphones but smaller than tablets. Typically, a phablet will have a screen size of from 5″ to 7″.

12. D. Infrared has an operational range of about 1 meter. Near field communication (NFC) has a maximum range of about 10 centimeters. Wi-Fi depends on the standard, but it usually has a range of 30 meters or more. Bluetooth Class 2 devices can operate at about 10 meters.

13. B, C. e-Readers that use electrophoretic ink (E Ink) have a longer battery life than tablets and are easier to read in bright light conditions.

14. D. Tethering is when a Wi-Fi enabled device attaches to a cellular device to get on the Internet. The cellular device is usually called a mobile hotspot.

15. B. GPS uses 24 satellites. There are 32 GPS satellites in space, but the extra 8 are backups.

16. C. The three speeds supported by NFC are 106Kbps, 212Kbps, and 424Kbps.

17. A. GLONASS is the Russian version of GPS. Galileo is European, BDS is Chinese, and IRNSS is Indian.

18. D. NFC uses Simple NDEF Exchange Protocol (SNEP) in peer-to-peer mode. It's based on LLCP.

19. C. It's the receiver's job to perform triangulation to determine its position based on data received from the satellites.

20. D. Micro SDXC cards can hold up to 2TB. SDHC cards can hold up to 32GB, and standard SD cards can hold up to 4GB.

Chapter 11: Installing and Configuring Printers

1. **A.** Because the toner on the drum has a slight negative charge (–100VDC), it requires a positive charge to transfer it to the paper; +600VDC is the voltage used in an EP process laser printer.

2. **C, D.** A page printer is a type of computer printer that prints a page at a time. Common types of page printers are the laser printer and the inkjet printer.

3. **D.** The rate of transfer and the ability to recognize new devices automatically are two of the major advantages that currently make USB the most popular type of printer interface. However, it is the network printer interface that allows the printer to communicate with networks, servers, and workstations.

4. **D.** Dot-matrix printers are impact printers and therefore can be used with multipart forms. Daisy-wheel printers can be used with multipart forms as well.

5. **A.** The writing step uses a laser to discharge selected areas of the photosensitive drum, thus forming an image on the drum.

6. **B, D.** Of those listed, only PostScript and PCL are page-description languages. There is no PDL or PageScript.

7. **A.** For the toner (which has a charge of –600VDC) to be transferred from the print drum (which has a charge of –600VDC) to the paper, there must be a positive, or opposite, charge of greater difference to break the –600VDC charge from the drum.

8. **B.** In an inkjet printer, the ink cartridge is the actual print head. This is where the ink is expelled to form letters or graphics. Toner cartridges are used by laser printers to store toner. A daisy wheel is the device that impacts the letters on the paper in a daisy-wheel printer. Paper trays are the storage bins in laser printers and inkjet printers that allow the pickup rollers to feed the paper into the printer.

9. **D.** The correct sequence in the EP print process is processing, charging, exposing, developing, transferring, fusing, and cleaning.

10. **D.** There are nine standard assemblies in an electrophotographic process printer. Early laser printers using the electrographic process contained the nine standard assemblies. Newer laser printers do not require an ozone filter and contain only eight standard assemblies.

11. **A, B, D.** An electrophotographic (EP) laser printer toner cartridge includes the toner, print drum, and cleaning blade. The laser is usually contained within the printer, not within the toner cartridge.

12. **A.** After a laser has created an image of the page, the developing roller uses a magnet and electrostatic charges to attract toner to itself and then transfers the toner to the areas on the drum that have been exposed to the laser. The toner is melted during the fusing stage. The laser creates an image of the page on the drum in the writing stage.

An electrostatic charge is applied to the paper to attract toner in the transferring stage, which happens immediately after the developing stage.

13. A, C, D. Printers can communicate via parallel, serial, USB, infrared, wireless, and network connections.

14. C. If a printer is using out-of-date or incorrect printer drivers, the printer may produce pages of garbled text. The solution is to ensure that the most recent printer drivers are downloaded from the manufacturer's website.

15. B. The daisy-wheel printer gets its name because it contains a wheel with raised letters and symbols on each "petal."

16. A. The high-voltage power supply is the part of the laser printer that supplies the voltages for charging and transferring corona assemblies.

17. C. The transfer corona assembly gets the toner from the photosensitive drum onto the paper. For some printers, this is a transfer corona wire, and for others, it is a transfer corona roller.

18. D. Developing happens after exposing. The correct order is processing, charging, exposing, developing, transferring, fusing, and cleaning.

19. B. The fuser assembly presses and melts the toner into the paper. The transfer corona transfers the toner from the drum to the paper. The printer controller circuitry converts signals from the PC into signals for the various printer assemblies. The paper transport assembly controls the movement of the paper through the printer.

20. A. Firmware upgrades for laser printers are downloaded for free from the manufacturer's website. A technician does not need to install a new chip because firmware is upgraded via software. It's unlikely that the manufacturer will send you the upgrade on a CD; it will refer you to its website to download it.

Chapter 12: Hardware and Network Troubleshooting

1. A, B. Two helpful things to try are toggling the video output function key (usually Fn+F8) and plugging an external monitor into the laptop. Removing the display is possible but not recommended. Powering the system off and back on isn't likely to correct the problem.

2. C. Discolored areas on the board are often caused by overheating. This can be the result of power surges.

3. A. The NET USE command allows you to connect to shared resources such as shared drives and printers on the network.

4. C. Every computer has a diagnostic program built into its BIOS called the power-on self-test (POST). The BIOS is the software stored on the CMOS chip. DNS is Domain Name Service, which in networking resolves hostnames to IP addresses.

5. B. The IPCONFIG command is perhaps the most used utility in troubleshooting and network configuration. The IPCONFIG /RENEW command will send a query to the DHCP server asking it to resend and renew all DHCP information. For a more detailed look at the IPCONFIG command, type **IPCONFIG /?** at the command prompt.

6. B. If print jobs are seemingly getting "stuck" in the printer queue, you should stop and restart the print spooler service. There is no Printer Troubleshooting utility that will diagnose printer problems. Deleting and reinstalling is not necessary.

7. A, D. Heat sinks and fans are commonly used to cool components within a PC. Compressed air can be used to blow out small particles or dust. Freon is a coolant used in some air conditioners, but it is not typically used for personal computers.

8. B. The manufacturer's website is the first place you should go for information on your products, including troubleshooting information. Many years ago, manufacturers would provide paper manuals with their products, but that's almost unheard of today unless you download a PDF version from the website. Server logs can show error codes, but they won't tell you how to fix anything.

9. A. The most likely cause is a groove or a scratch in the EP drum. Toner is collecting in that groove or scratch, and then it is being deposited onto the page.

10. B. It has to be a problem with the LCD display. If it were the video card, the display would appear warped and fuzzy on the external monitor as well. While many motherboards contain video circuitry, this answer is not specific enough. If the video driver were corrupted, you would have the same problem on all displays.

11. A. If an ink cartridge is faulty or develops a hole, it can release excessive amounts of ink, which will lead to smearing. A corrupt print driver would result in printing garbage. Inkjet printers do not have a fuser. Excessive humidity may cause smearing, but it wouldn't cause the disbursement of too much ink.

12. B. The ipconfig utility can be used with Windows to see the networking configuration values at the command line. It is one of the most commonly used command-line utilities that can be used in troubleshooting and network configurations. To view IP configuration information, use the IPCONFIG /All command.

13. C, D. Seeing images from previous print jobs is a phenomenon called ghosting. It's most likely due to a bad erasure lamp or a broken cleaning blade.

14. D. It may well be that the video card is dead. Different BIOS manufacturers use different beep codes, though, so you'll want to look it up to be sure. If the motherboard was dead or the BIOS weren't functioning, you wouldn't get to the POST routine, so you wouldn't get a beep code.

15. B. Tracert is a Windows command-line utility that enables you to verify the route to a remote host. It is often used in the troubleshooting process to verify the path a data packet takes toward its final destination.

16. C. The only components that typically make noise are the ones that have moving parts, such as fans and hard drives. In most cases, a rhythmic ticking sound will be something that's generated by the hard drive.

17. C. If there is a consistent blank space, it likely means that a pin is not firing properly and the print head needs to be replaced. If the print ribbon were old, you would have consistently faded printing. If the ribbon were not advancing properly, you would get light and dark printing. If the wrong driver is installed, you will get garbage.

18. A. If a laptop won't power up on battery, always try to use AC power. You never know when a battery could have failed. If the user had a spare and didn't have an AC power cord, trying a spare might work, but trying AC power is the best bet. There is no battery power switch on laptops.

19. D. Loopback plugs are used to test the sending and receiving ability of network cards. Wireless locators find wireless network signals. Cable testers validate cables, and toner probes are used to trace a cable from one end to the other.

20. C. A RAID 0 array is also known as disk striping. RAID 0 actually decreases your fault tolerance versus one hard drive because there are more points of failure. You need to replace the drive, and hopefully you had it backed up so that you can restore the data.

Chapter 13: Operating System Basics

1. B, C. To open a command prompt, you can use CMD or COMMAND.

2. D. A driver is extremely specific software written for the purpose of instructing a particular OS on how to access a piece of hardware.

3. C. You can increase the Taskbar's size by moving the mouse pointer to the top of it, pausing until the pointer turns into a double-headed arrow, and then clicking and dragging. Keep in mind that in Windows XP, you have to unlock the Taskbar first by right-clicking on it and deselecting Lock The Taskbar.

4. A. FAT32 does not have as many options as NTFS, such as Encryption and Compression, which are attributes available only on NTFS partitions.

5. B, C. The Windows File Explorer program can be used to copy and move files and to change file attributes.

6. D. Standard permissions, unlike special permissions, have been grouped together to make it easier for administrators to assign permissions.

7. B. The shell is a program that runs on top of the OS and allows the user to issue commands through a set of menus or some other graphical interface.

8. C. To run any program, select Start ➤ Run and type the name of the program in the Open field. If you don't know the exact name of the program, you can find the file by clicking the Browse button. Once you have typed in the executable name, click OK to run the program.

9. D. Multithreading offers the ability for a single application to have multiple requests in to the processor at one time.

10. B. All deleted files are placed in the Recycle Bin. Deleted files are held there until the Recycle Bin is emptied. Users can easily recover accidentally deleted files from the Recycle Bin.

11. D. To turn off a Windows 7 machine, select Start ➤ Shut Down, and choose Shut Down. This will turn off the computer.

12. D. The minimum amount of memory recommended for Windows 8.1 is 1GB for 32-bit installations and 2GB for 64-bit installations.

13. B. The minimum amount of free hard drive space recommended for the installation of Windows Vista Home Basic is 15GB.

14. B. The minimum recommended memory for a 32-bit installation of Windows 7 is 1GB.

15. C. In Windows, a quick way to access Help is to press the F1 key.

16. B. The Sidebar existed only in Windows Vista and provided a quick interface that allowed you to access common utilities such as the headlines.

17. C. The system tray is located on the right side of the Taskbar.

18. A. In addition to right-clicking on the Desktop, you can access the Display Properties settings by using the Display icon under Control Panel (as long as you are not using Category view in some versions).

19. B. The interface included with Windows Vista is called Aero.

20. C. The minimum recommended memory for a 64-bit installation of Windows 7 is 2GB.

Chapter 14: Operating System Administration

1. B. The GPUPDATE utility is used to update Group Policy settings and replaces some of the functionality that previously existed with SECEDIT.

2. D. In Windows, CDFS is the file system of choice for CD media.

3. C. The SHUTDOWN.EXE utility can be used to schedule a shutdown (complete or a restart) locally or remotely.

4. A. The BOOTREC /FIXBOOT command can be used to write a new boot sector.

5. D. ExFAT is a proprietary file system created by Microsoft for use with large flash drives.

6. D. The TASKLIST utility will list all running processes at the command line.

7. B. Virtual memory settings are accessed through the Performance tab or area of the System applet in the Control Panel.

8. D. Services can be started automatically or manually or be disabled.

9. D. You can use Task Manager to deal with applications that have stopped responding.

10. B. MSTSC can be used to configure a remote connection.

11. A. The screen shot shows DxDiag with the name of the utility purposely obscured.

12. A. Device Manager is used in Windows to configure all hardware resources about which Windows is aware.

13. B. The Backup utility provided with Windows 7 and Windows Vista versions of Windows has different levels of functionality. In Windows 8, this could be done with File History.

14. D. The SFC command will run System File Checker. The /SCANNOW option will scan files, and SFC automatically repairs files that it detects as corrupted.

15. C. The operating system boots from the active partition. Active partitions must be primary partitions, but a primary partition does not have to be active. (There can be up to four primary partitions per hard drive.)

16. B. There are five basic hives in the Windows Registry: HKEY_CLASSES_ROOT, HKEY_CURRENT_USER, HKEY_LOCAL_MACHINE, HKEY_USERS, and HKEY_CURRENT_CONFIG. HKEY_LOCAL_MACHINE stores information about the computer's hardware. HKEY_CURRENT_MACHINE, HKEY_MACHINE, and HKEY_RESOURCES do not exist.

17. C. GPT is replacing the MBR in 64-bit versions of the Windows operating system.

18. A. Windows Disk Defragmenter rearranges files on your hard disk so that they occupy contiguous spaces (as much as possible).

19. B. The /MIR switch can be used with ROBOCOPY to mirror a complete directory tree.

20. D. The DxDiag utility (DirectX Diagnostics) is used to test DirectX functionality. Telnet is used to establish a remote connection, Msinfo32 shows configuration settings and Ping can let you know if a remote host can be reached.

Chapter 15: Working with Windows 8/8.1

1. D. The Windows 8 interface was originally called Metro. It is now more commonly referred to as the Windows 8 UI.

2. A, B. Only the Pro and Enterprise versions support BitLocker and EFS.

3. A. The minimum hardware requirements for a 32-bit installation are 1GHz (or faster) processor, 1GB RAM, 16GB hard drive space, and a DirectX 9 graphics device with WDDM driver.

4. B. For 64-bit installations, 2GB RAM and 20GB hard drive space represent the minimum requirements.

5. C. OneDrive is the online/cloud storage account that comes with your Microsoft account.

6. D. File Explorer is the new name for Windows Explorer.

7. A. The Windows Store is an online site where you can download apps, games, software, and so on. Windows 8 or higher is required to use the Windows Store.

8. D. Charms are controls that are available on the side of the screen. They consist of Search, Share, Start, Devices, and Settings.

9. C. Within PowerShell, you can write script files based on the .NET programming framework.

10. B. Windows 7 Ultimate can be upgraded to Windows 8 Pro.

11. D. Windows Upgrade Assistant can evaluate your current system and determine if it can be upgraded to Windows 8.

12. A. The Microsoft Deployment Toolkit (commonly called MDT) simplifies the process and reduces the time each install takes.

13. C. If you install Windows on a system with multiple hard drives, you can use disk-part to make sure images are pointing to their intended drives.

14. B. Windows To Go can be used to boot Windows 8 from flash drives.

15. C. Microsoft recommends that WinSAT.exe be used with the formal option to optimize Windows for the SSD. (This reduces the number of write operations Windows makes.)

16. D. By definition, a system partition is one that contains the hardware-specific files needed to load Windows.

17. A. Only Windows 8 Enterprise includes the Windows To Go feature.

18. C. The refresh repair option keeps personal files and settings along with the default apps and those that you installed from the Windows Store.

19. A. The Windows 8 product key is a 25-character code used for Windows activation.

20. D. The system partition usually appears as 0, but the system can assign different numbers and different computers with identical hardware configurations that can have different disk numbers assigned to them.

Chapter 16: Working with Windows 7

1. B, C, D, E. While all editions of Windows 7 can join a HomeGroup, only Home Premium, Professional, Enterprise, and Ultimate can create one.

2. D. Even though Windows 7 does not have Sidebar (a feature that lived and died with Windows Vista), the file that runs for gadgets is SIDEBAR.EXE.

3. B. BitLocker uses (if it is present) the Trusted Platform Module (TPM).

4. C. Libraries allow files and folders to be grouped logically and appear as if they are in the same location even when they are not.

5. B. The Microsoft Assessment and Planning (MAP) Toolkit can be used to get an inventory of computers on your network and plan a rollout of the new operating system.

6. D. Only Windows Vista Business can be upgraded to Windows 7 Professional.

7. C. The utility shown is Windows Anytime Upgrade, which can be accessed from Control Panel. Portions of the screen that would reveal the name of the utility have been hidden in the screen shot.

8. C. Windows Preinstallation Environment (WinPE), is a stub operating system that creates a Pre-boot Execution Environment (PXE).

9. A. The utility shown is WINVER. This utility will show the operating system, the edition, and the service pack installed on any Windows operating system.

10. D, E. Only Windows 7 Enterprise and Windows 7 Ultimate support BitLocker drive encryption.

11. B. In Windows 7 (and Windows Vista), the ability to do this has been moved to the System Protection tab of System Properties.

12. A. The Action Center replaces the Security Center (which existed in Vista) and adds the Maintenance portion.

13. C. Windows 7 requires the installation to be followed by a process known as product activation to curb software piracy.

14. B. The maximum number of physical CPUs supported by Windows 7 Enterprise edition is two.

15. B. The UAC default in Windows 7 is "Notify me only when programs try to make changes to my computer."

16. C. The ReadyBoost feature allows you to use free space on a removable drive (such as an SD card) to speed up a system.

17. D. The utility shown is Windows Remote Assistance. Portions of the utility that show its name have been obscured in the screen shot.

18. C. When remote computers and virtual machine utilities are used in Windows 7 networking, port 3389 is the default port used.

19. A. On a standard, default installation, the \BOOT directory holds the boot file configuration for Windows 7.

20. D. The Professional, Enterprise, and Ultimate editions support 192GB. The maximum amount of RAM supported by Home Premium is 16GB. The Starter edition supports only 2GB.

Chapter 17: Working with Windows Vista

1. C. The two biggest modifications to offline folders in Windows Vista are the inclusion of the Sync Center and the restriction of offline file support to the Business, Enterprise, and Ultimate versions.

2. D. The first file used in the Windows Vista boot process is BOOTMGR.

3. B. The maximum amount of RAM supported by 64-bit Home Premium is 16GB. The Business, Enterprise, and Ultimate editions support 128GB. The Home Basic edition supports only 8GB.

4. C. Wake on LAN is an Ethernet standard implemented via a card that allows a "sleeping" machine to awaken when it receives a wakeup signal.

5. B, D. Only the Enterprise and Ultimate editions of Windows Vista include support for BitLocker.

6. D. Shadow Copy is a Windows Vista feature that allows you to recover from an accidental deletion or overwrite.

7. C. For just one machine, Windows Easy Transfer should be used for transferring user state data and application files. For a mass rollout across a network, USMT can be used.

8. C. In Windows Vista, and all Windows versions with which you need to be familiar for the A+ exam, the winver utility can be used to see the edition and service pack installed on a system.

9. D. The utility shown is Component Services (with the name of the utility obscured). This MMC snap-in allows you to deploy and administer component services.

10. B. WINLOGON presents the Logon screen and wraps up the boot process.

11. C. The Windows Memory Diagnostics utility (Start ➤ Control Panel ➤ Administrative Tools ➤ Memory Diagnostics Tool) can be used to check a system for memory problems.

12. C, D, E. Only the Business, Enterprise, and Ultimate editions of Windows Vista support Local Security Policy (secpol.msc).

13. C. Windows Vista requires the installation to be followed by a process known as product activation to curb software piracy.

14. B. The maximum number of physical CPUs supported by Windows Vista Business edition is two. Both Home Basic and Home Premium editions support only one, while Business, Enterprise, and Ultimate support two.

15. B. The System Configuration tool is msconfig.exe in Windows Vista.

16. C. The ReadyBoost feature allows you to use free space on a removable drive (usually USB) to speed up a system.

17. A, D. Windows XP Professional can only be upgraded to Windows Vista Business and Windows Vista Ultimate.

18. C. When the network location is set to Public, network discovery is disabled. Network discovery is enabled for both Home and Work. There is no such location as Personal in Windows Vista.

19. A. On a standard, default installation, the \boot directory holds the boot file configuration for Windows Vista.

20. C. The 64-bit Enterprise, and Ultimate editions support 128GB. The maximum amount of RAM supported by Home Premium is 16GB. The Home Basic edition supports only 8GB.

Chapter 18: Working with Mac OS and Linux

1. C. The command ls -la will show all files (including hidden ones) in long-listing format.

2. D. Boot Camp can be used to install a 64-bit version of Windows on a Intel-based Mac and then let you choose which operating system to use upon bootup.

3. A. Time Machine is an application from Apple that can be used to make backups.

4. B. The vi utility is a visual editor that can be used to edit files.

5. C. There is a utility called ifconfig that is used to see and edit network configuration files. It has a counterpart, iwconfig, that works with wireless connection configuration files.

6. B. The Keychain app is used for password management.

7. A. The shell serves as the interpreter between the OS and the user. A number of different shells are available.

8. D. Working copies are backups kept on site at the computer center for immediate recovery purposes.

9. C. The apt-get utility command can be used in Linux to download files, including patches.

10. C. The chown utility is used to change the owner from one person to another.

11. A. The fsck utility can be used to check and repair disks in Linux.

12. B. Force Quit exists for the purpose of stopping those runaway applications when they pop up.

13. C. The Bash shell (borne again shell) is the most popular one included with Linux distributions.

14. D. The area at the bottom of the screen is known as the Dock.

15. C. The Command+space sequence is used to access Spotlight from within an app.

16. A. The sudo command is used to run a command as another user, and the default user is root.

17. C. The ps command will show running processes on your system.

18. B. To change to the parent directory of the one you are in, use two periods (..) with the cd command.

19. B. The middle set of three permissions applies to the group. In this case, the value is rw-, which means read and write permission only (not execute).

20. C. This option is used to create the folders as well as subfolders, making the parent so to speak.

Chapter 19: Security

1. A. The first layer of access control is perimeter security. Perimeter security is intended to delay or deter entrance into a facility.

2. A. The advantage to assigning the IP addresses statically is that you can make certain which host is associated with which IP address and then utilize filtering to limit network access to only those hosts.

3. A. Social engineering uses the inherent trust in the human species, as opposed to technology, to gain access to your environment.

4. C. A fingerprint scanner, or any device that identifies a person by a physical trait, is considered a biometric security control.

5. A. Although the end result of any of these attacks may be denying authorized users access to network resources, a DoS attack is specifically intended to prevent access to network resources by overwhelming or flooding a service or network.

6. B. A distributed denial of service (DDoS) attack uses multiple computer systems to attack a server or host in the network.

7. C. In a back door attack, a program or service is placed on a server to bypass normal security procedures.

8. C. A replay attack attempts to replay the results of a previously successful session to gain access.

9. D. TCP/IP hijacking is an attempt to steal a valid IP address and use it to gain authorization or information from a network.

10. A. A worm is different from a virus in that it can reproduce itself, it's self-contained, and it doesn't need a host application to be transported.

11. D. A smurf attack attempts to use a broadcast ping (ICMP) on a network. The return address of the ping may be that of a valid system in your network. This system will be flooded with responses in a large network.

12. A. A password-guessing attack occurs when a user account is repeatedly attacked using a variety of passwords.

13. B. Biometrics relies on a physical characteristic of the user to verify identity. Biometric devices typically use either a hand pattern or a retinal scan to accomplish this.

14. A. Tokens are created when a user or system successfully authenticates. The token is destroyed when the session is over.

15. C. Someone trying to con your organization into revealing account and password information is launching a social engineering attack.

16. A. Some viruses won't damage a system in an attempt to spread into all of the other systems in a network. These viruses use that system as the carrier of the virus.

17. B. A symptom of many viruses is unusual activity on the system disk. The virus spreading to other files on your system causes this.

18. A. A software exploitation attack attempts to exploit weaknesses in software. A common attack attempts to communicate with an established port to gain unauthorized access.

19. A. Packet filters prevent unauthorized packets from entering or leaving a network. Packet filters are a type of firewall that block specified traffic based on IP address, protocol, and many other attributes.

20. D. All of these devices can store and pass viruses to uninfected systems. Make sure that all files are scanned for viruses before they're copied to these media.

Chapter 20: Network Services, Cloud Computing, and Virtualization

1. B. For secure transactions, the web server should be using HTTPS, which uses port 443. If non-secure portions of the website work, then the server is fine. It's most likely that the firewall is blocking inbound traffic on port 443.

2. C. It sounds like the manager wants a unified threat management (UTM) device. They are designed to be one-stop network protection devices.

3. C. If the data on the server does not need to be accessed via the Internet, then the server should be in the most secure place possible, which is inside the firewall(s) in the secure network.

4. A. Platform as a Service (PaaS) is probably the right level of service for the developer team. It provides infrastructure like IaaS, and it also supplies needed programming elements.

5. A, C. Print servers should make printers available to clients and accept print jobs. They also process print jobs and manage print priorities. Finally, they provide client computers with the right print drivers when the clients attempt to install the printer.

6. B. The ability to expand services without provider intervention is called on-demand self-service.

7. A. A proxy server can be configured to block access to websites that contain potentially dangerous or inflammatory material.

8. D. A hybrid cloud provides the best of public and private clouds. You get the scalability and cost effectiveness of a public cloud but the security that you need for important files on the private portion of the cloud.

9. B. Every DHCP server needs to have a scope, which is the range of addresses available to clients, as well as other options that it can give to client computers.

10. C. When multiple organizations with similar objectives want to combine efforts in a cloud, the best choice is generally a community cloud. This allows for the flexibility and scalability normally found in a public cloud, but it also limits the number of users to a smaller, trusted group.

11. A. DNS server records are contained in the zone file, which must be configured by administrators. A hosts file is an alternative to using DNS (but that does not work well when scaling to the Internet). A scope is created on DHCP servers.

12. B, C, D. Cloud solutions are great for enhancing scalability and reliability while generally lowering costs. The biggest issue with cloud computing is security.

13. D. The Simple Mail Transfer Protocol (SMTP) is used to transfer email between servers.

14. B. Each virtual machine will use its own virtual NIC. The virtual NICs will communicate with a virtual switch managed by the hypervisor. The virtual switch will communicate with the physical NIC.

15. D. The quad A record is used to represent IPv6 hosts. IPv4 hosts need an A record. The CNAME record is used if one host has alias (multiple) names. MX is for a mail server.

16. B. There needs to be enough RAM to support both OSs, so the answer is 6GB. More is better though!

17. A, B, C. Legacy systems are ones that use older hardware, software, or network protocols that are not commonly used today. A system with only 1GB RAM might be underpowered, but that in and of itself does not make it a legacy system.

18. D. Each instance of the OS you are running requires its own security software.

19. B. IDS devices are passive. They will detect, log, and perhaps send an alert, but that's it. An IPS can take active steps to shut down an attack if it detects one. Both devices will monitor internal network traffic as well as incoming traffic.

20. A. A Type 2 hypervisor sits on top of an existing OS, meaning that OSs installed in VMs will compete for resources with the host OS. The amount of resources available to a guest OS can be configured. Virtual OSs can get on the physical network if configured properly.

Chapter 21: Mobile Operating Systems and Connectivity

1. C. The operating system installed is independent of the mobile device's ability to make cellular calls. Both Android and iOS devices are potentially capable of making them.

2. C. To develop an app, you need a software development kit (SDK). The app package will have an .apk filename extension when it's developed.

3. A. Three gyroscopes are used to detect roll, pitch, and yaw. The problem is with the gyroscope that detects yaw. The accelerometer would be suspect if the iPhone were not detecting flat movement to the side or forward and backward. The magnetometer can only help with compass headings, and the GPS helps with geographical positioning.

4. B. Resistive touchscreens require pressure to actuate them, while capacitive ones do not and instead can be actuated by the fleshy part of the human finger. Body oils, moisture,

and dirt are not as detrimental to the effectiveness of resistive screens as they are to capacitive screens.

5. A, E. SMS is the most widely supported text-messaging service across all platforms and service providers. MMS is another text messaging technology.

6. D. Phone calls will always be sent out over the cellular network by default. In situations like that, data transfers may still be using a Wi-Fi connection. Whenever you have a reliable Wi-Fi signal available, which you do not pay for "as you go," you should feel free to disable your cellular access to data networking. The wireless network is often faster and does not cost you anything to use. If data networking works better when you leave the cellular network available as a fallback, you can choose to disable it only for certain large downloads or disable it completely until the download is complete. Unless you are particularly sensitive to the situation or know that data is going out over your cell access, you might not need to disable the cellular data-networking feature.

7. C. The range of Bluetooth connections is considered short compared to Wi-Fi connections. Bluetooth is a fully standardized protocol that supports file transfers using FTP. Rebooting, or even restarting, paired devices is not a requirement for Bluetooth connection.

8. A. SMTP sends mail to the server at TCP port 25. POP3 uses port 110. IMAP4 uses 143, and POP3 uses port 995 securely over SSL or TLS.

9. B. SMTP with TLS uses port 587 by default. With SSL, SMTP uses port 465. IMAP4 with SSL/TLS uses port 993, while POP3 with SSL/TLS uses port 995.

10. B. When Wi-Fi calling is enabled, calls will seamlessly switch from cellular to Wi-Fi if you are within range of a Wi-Fi network of which you are a member.

11. D. The technology that allows a phone to pass near a receiver to make an electronic payment is near field communication (NFC).

12. B,C. You can create virtual private network (VPN) connections on a mobile device using Wi-Fi or cellular network connections.

13. C. Each mobile phone has a separate processor that manages wireless communications, also known as radio communications or baseband communications. There is a baseband OS that manages this, and it works with the primary OS on the phone.

14. A, B. The two real-time OSs (RTOSs) that mobile phones have are the baseband OS and the SIM OS.

15. D. S/MIME is the public key encryption standard used for encrypting and decrypting email.

16. B, D, F. The items most often able to be synchronized are contacts, apps, email, photos, music, and videos.

17. B. iTunes will run on a computer with 512MB of RAM. 1GB is not required unless you want to play 720p high-definition videos.

18. B. Mail access uses standard secure or insecure TCP ports, not UDP ports. Exchange access to such mail services is not unheard of, but it is exceedingly rare. Mobile devices tend to have email clients built in.

19. A, B, C, D. Airplane mode disables all radio communications, including cellular, Wi-Fi, Bluetooth, and NFC. It does not affect the opening of any other apps or the lock screen.

20. C. 4G Verizon devices functioning as mobile hotspots can support up to 10 concurrent connections. 3G devices can support only five.

Chapter 22: Troubleshooting Theory, OSs, and Security

1. D. Windows Update automatically (by default) finds, downloads, and installs service packs and other Windows updates. None of the other options are real utilities.

2. B. Safe Mode loads only basic drivers, such as a standard VGA video driver and the keyboard and mouse.

3. B. Windows uses the Windows Boot Configuration Data (BCD) file instead of the BOOT.INI file. This can be rebuilt with the /REBUILDBCD option.

4. B. The first step is to identify the problem. Once you have done that, you should (in order) establish a theory of probable cause, test the theory, establish a plan of action to resolve the problem, verify full system functionality, and document your findings.

5. B. The System Restore tool is used to create restore points. Backup creates backups of your hard drive. You can use Backup to create copies of your configuration (like a restore point) along with other data, but to create a restore point specifically, use System Restore. There are no Restore Point or Emergency Repair tools.

6. A. Only Windows XP uses the BOOT.INI file. Newer versions of Windows use the Boot Configuration Data (BCD) file.

7. C. Check the sleep settings for hibernation, and disable those first to see if that makes a difference. If it does not, then you can begin disabling drivers and making other changes.

8. A. Windows can use restore points to roll back the system configuration to a previous state. None of the other options exist.

9. B. Pop-up blockers are used to prevent both pop-ups and pop-unders from appearing. While older browsers did not incorporate an option to block pop-ups, most new browsers, including the latest versions of Internet Explorer, now have that capability built in.

10. A. It's critical to keep your antivirus software up-to-date, so you should update your definitions at least once per week.

11. C. Disk Defragmenter will analyze the hard drive to determine how fragmented it is, and it will allow you to defragment it. There is no Disk Analyzer tool. Disk Cleanup can help you free up space by deleting unneeded files. Check Disk (CHKDSK) can help you find problems on the hard drive, but it does not look for fragmentation.

12. A. Windows Update downloads patches for the Windows operating system and other Microsoft products.

13. A. Windows Defender is an anti-malware program. It checks for harmful, or unwanted, software installed on the machine.

14. A. The REGSVR32 tool (REGSVR32.EXE) allows you to register and unregister modules and controls for troubleshooting purposes.

15. A, B, C, D. Establishing security policies and procedures, updating your operating systems, updating your applications, and updating your network devices are all good measures to take to help eliminate potential security problems.

16. A. Some viruses won't damage a system in an attempt to spread into all of the other systems in a network. These viruses use that system as the carrier of the virus.

17. B. Disk Cleanup can help you free up space by deleting unneeded files. Disk Defragmenter will analyze the hard drive to determine how fragmented it is, and it will allow you to defragment it. There is no Disk Analyzer tool. Check Disk (CHKDSK) can help you find problems on the hard drive, but it does not delete files.

18. D. SFC automatically verifies system files after a reboot to see if they were changed to unprotected copies.

19. B. To open System Restore, click Start ➤ All Programs ➤ Accessories ➤ System Tools ➤ System Restore.

20. A. The figure shows REGEDIT, but the name of the utility has been purposely obscured.

Chapter 23: Understanding Operational Procedures

1. D. When a computer is experiencing random reboots and phantom problems that disappear after reboot, you should open the cover, clean everything (if it's dirty), and reseat all of the cards and chips. Some components could have gunk on them that carries an electrical charge or could have experienced "chip creep," where they slowly work themselves out of their sockets.

2. C. A high-voltage probe is designed to release the electricity from high-voltage components, which are found in the back of CRT computer monitors. Wearing an antistatic wrist strap when working on a computer monitor can cause the stored-up electric current to be released through your body, which could result in serious injury or death!

3. B. The Material Safety Data Sheet (MSDS) contains information about chemical properties, including what to do if an accident occurs.

4. D. Companies are not legally required to provide MSDSs to consumers. However, most will do so if you ask for them. The best place to look is the manufacturer's website.

5. A, B. Accidents and near-accidents should always be reported. Dirt isn't usually a safety issue. Rain could be, but hopefully it wouldn't affect the inside of your building.

6. B. Most people can feel an electric shock at about 3,000 volts. However, computer equipment can be damaged with as little as 300 volts.

7. A, B. Antistatic wrist straps, bags (for parts), and floor mats can all help reduce the risk of ESD. There are no antistatic hair nets (but if you have long hair, it's best to tie it back so that it doesn't come in contact with computer parts). Shuffling your feet on the floor will actually increase the risk of ESD.

8. B, D. Private-sector employers are required by OSHA to maintain a safe work environment. This includes maintaining tools and equipment, keeping records of accidents, and displaying a safety information poster.

9. A. Before installing new commercial software, ensure that the proper licenses are in place. An enterprise license is most likely appropriate in a situation like this, but you need to make sure that the parameters of your enterprise license agreement allow for the installation of this many new computers.

10. C, D. You should always lift with your legs, not your back. This means bending at the knees and not the waist. Monitors should be carried with the glass face toward your body. Using carts for heavy objects is a good idea, as is ensuring that your path is free of safety hazards, such as trip hazards.

11. C. Alkaline batteries should always be recycled. Throwing them in the trash means that they'll end up in a landfill, where they can contaminate the environment. Burning batteries is always a bad idea because they will explode.

12. B, D. If you encounter prohibited material, you should confiscate and preserve the material and report it through the correct channels. Confronting the issue directly with the user before you have established a proper case could cause problems.

13. C. You should page the user and let them know that they need to verify access. You also should tell them that you saw the sticky note and highly recommend that they change their password and not write it down. Logging in to the system using the information you found would be violating the privacy of that user and should not be done. Further, logging in with someone else's information makes you a potential scapegoat for any data that is corrupted or missing until the user changes the password.

14. C. While calling and sending email are both solutions to this situation, calling the customer provides an immediate means of communication. Inform the customer of the situation, and offer to be out there at your first opportunity, which will hopefully be first thing in the morning.

15. D. While there is no perfect solution to problems of this type, the best solution is to find someone else who can mediate and help you understand the problem.

16. C. Physical abuse violates respect and should be avoided at all costs. You should try to calm the user down. If you cannot do this, you should leave the site immediately and not return until it is safe to do so. You may also want to report the incident to your management so that they're aware of the situation.

17. B. The customer is expressing a concern that she was not shown respect by a technician from your company. You should apologize and make your manager aware of the situation. Unless you are a supervisor, which is not implied in the question, you should not personally talk to the technician about the issue.

18. D. You should always act with confidence and in a manner similar to how you would want to be treated if you were in the customer's situation—ignoring, downplaying, and joking about the vice president's obvious concerns are very poor choices.

19. C. The best solution is to meet the customer's needs and solve his problem. If that means that you have to summon additional help or resources, you should do so.

20. B, C. You should leave a note for the user explaining what you did and include your contact information. You should also notify your manager and the user's manager that you have completed your task.

Appendix B

Answers to Performance-Based Questions

Chapter 1: Motherboards, Processors, and Memory

Answer to Performance-Based Question 1

Here is how to remove a DIMM and replace it with another one:

1. Pull the tabs on either end of the DIMM away from the DIMM.

2. Pull the loose DIMM straight out of the slot and away from the motherboard.

3. Ensure that the locking tabs are completely opened and out of the way of the slot.

4. Align the module's notch with the tab or tabs in the slot.

5. Insert the new DIMM straight down into the slot.

6. Apply firm and even pressure downward until the locking tabs automatically snap into place.

7. Nudge the tabs inward toward the module to make sure that they are tight.

Answer to Performance-Based Question 2

The components are labeled in the following illustration.

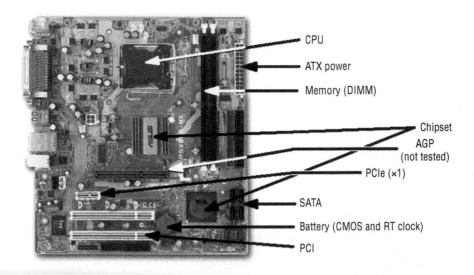

Chapter 2: Storage Devices and Power Supplies

Here are the steps to remove a power supply from a computer chassis:

1. Remove the power source from the system.
2. Ground yourself and the computer to the same source of ground.
3. Remove the cover from the system.
4. Locate the power supply.
5. Follow all wiring harnesses from the power supply to their termini, disconnecting each one.
6. Remove any obstructions that appear as if they might hinder removal of the power supply.
7. Locate and remove the machine screws on the outside of the case that are used to secure the power supply.
8. Pull the power supply out of the case.

Chapter 3: Peripherals and Expansion

Based on the connectors, here are the connections to make:

1. Plug the VGA cable into the blue, DE15 interface.
2. Plug the USB cable into the gray, flat 4-pin interface.
3. Plug the mouse into the green, mini-DIN-6 interface.
4. Plug the keyboard into the purple, mini-DIN -6 interface.
5. Plug the speaker into the green, 3.5mm TRS interface.

Chapter 4: Display Devices

Here is how to extend a display onto a second monitor and adjust their orientation with respect to each other:

1. Right-click a blank portion of the Desktop.
2. Click Screen Resolution.

3. Click on the picture of the monitor with the number 2 on it.

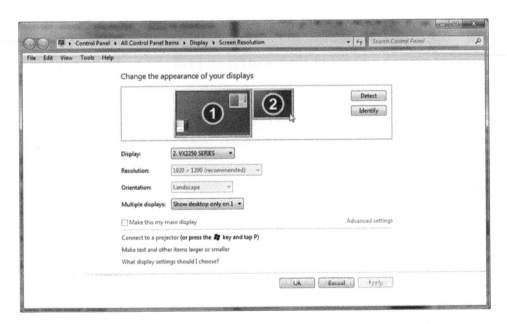

4. Pull down the menu labeled Multiple Displays; select Extend These Displays.

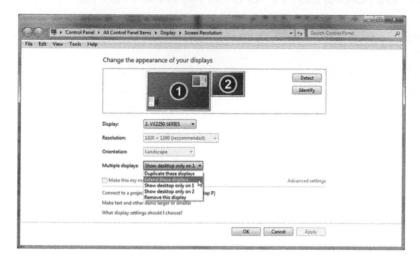

5. Click Keep Changes in the pop-up dialog that results.

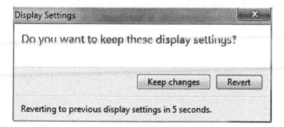

6. Click and drag the second monitor to the desired virtual position around the primary monitor.

7. Click OK to save the changes and exit, or click Cancel to exit without saving the changes.

Chapter 5: Custom Configurations

These are the steps to set up video streaming from one Windows 7 computer to another in the same house:

1. Run Network And Sharing Center.
2. Click the Change Advanced Sharing Settings link in the left frame.
3. Expand the Home Or Work configuration section.
4. Click the Choose Media Streaming Options link.
5. Change desired Blocked buttons to Allow.
6. Open Windows Media Player and switch to Library mode, if necessary.
7. Ensure that streaming is enabled.
8. On the remote system, start Windows Media Player.
9. Expand the remote library that you just shared under Other Libraries to play music, watch videos or recorded TV, and view pictures.

Chapter 6: Network Fundamentals

Possible answers for examples of physical network topologies could include bus, ring, star, mesh, and hybrid. The simplest topology, and the one that uses the least amount of cable, is a bus. It consists of a single cable that runs to every workstation, as shown in the following illustration.

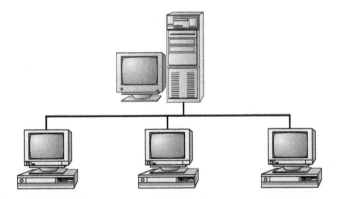

In a star topology, shown in the next illustration, each network device branches off a central device called a hub or a switch, making it easy to add a new workstation. If the hub or switch fails, the entire network fails.

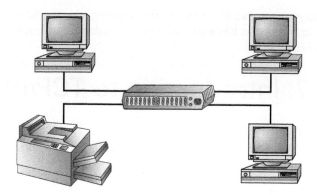

In a physical ring, each computer connects to two other computers, joining them in a circle and creating a unidirectional path where messages move from workstation to workstation. These are very rarely implemented.

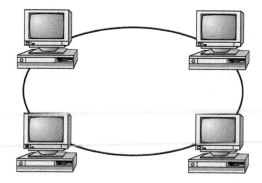

The mesh topology is the most complex in terms of physical design. In a mesh, each device is connected to every other device as shown in the following illustration. This provides redundancy but costs more to implement.

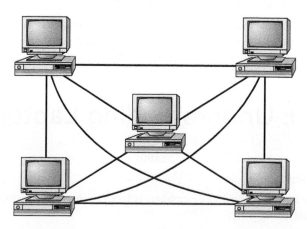

A hybrid topology combines two or more other topologies into one network. An example might be a server room that has a partial mesh for redundancy but the clients are all connected to switches in a star.

Chapter 7: Introduction to TCP/IP

Here's how to use Internet Explorer to connect using FTP:

First open Internet Explorer. Then, in the address window, type the following:

`ftp://jsmith:getfiles@ftp.domain.com`

Chapter 8: Installing Wireless and SOHO Networks

Here are the steps to install a PCI network card for a Windows 7 desktop:

1. Power off the PC.
2. Remove the case and the metal or plastic blank covering the expansion slot opening.
3. Insert the new expansion card into the open slot.
4. Secure the expansion card with the screw provided.
5. Put the case back on the computer and power it up.
6. Windows Plug and Play (PnP) should recognize the NIC and install the driver automatically. It may also ask you to provide a copy of the necessary driver if it does not recognize the type of NIC that you have installed.
7. If Windows does not start the installation routine immediately, open Control Panel in Small Icon or Large Icon view, and choose Devices And Printers and then Add A Device. Choose the NIC and continue the installation.
8. After installing a NIC, you must hook the card to the network using the appropriate cable (if you're using wired connections). Attach a patch cable to the connector on the NIC and to a port in the wall (or connectivity device), thus connecting your PC to the rest of the network.

Chapter 9: Understanding Laptops

Here is how to replace a hard drive on the example laptop computer:

1. Turn off the computer.
2. Disconnect the computer and any peripherals from their power sources, and remove any installed batteries.

3. Locate the hard drive door and remove the screw holding it in place.

4. Lift the hard drive door until it clicks.

5. Slide the hard drive out to remove it.

6. Remove the two screws holding the hard drive to the hard drive door.

7. Attach a new hard drive to the hard drive door.

8. Slide the new hard drive back into the hard drive bay.

9. Snap the hard drive door back into place, and insert and tighten the screw to hold the door in place.

Chapter 10: Understanding Mobile Devices

The five steps to pair a Bluetooth device are:

1. Turn on the Bluetooth device.
    a. Enable Bluetooth.
    b. Enable pairing.
2. Use your mobile device to locate and select the Bluetooth device.
3. Enter the Bluetooth device's passcode.
4. Confirm pairing on the Bluetooth device by pressing a button or a combination of buttons.
5. Test connectivity.

Chapter 11: Installing and Configuring Printers

Here are some example steps to take to clean an inkjet printer. The process for starting the cleaning cycle on inkjet printers can vary, and some printers have both quick and deep-clean cycles. Always check your documentation for steps specific to your printer.

1. Power on the printer, and open the top cover to expose the area containing the print cartridges.
2. Initiate a self-cleaning cycle.
3. When the print head moves from its resting place, pull the AC power plug.
4. Locate the sponge pads on which to apply the cleaning solution.
5. Using the supplied syringe, apply the cleaning solution to the sponge pads until they are saturated.
6. Plug the printer back into the wall outlet and turn it on. The print heads will park themselves.
7. Turn the printer off. Let the solution sit for at least three hours.
8. Power the printer back on, and run three printer cleaning cycles. Print a nozzle check pattern (or a test page) after each cleaning cycle to monitor the cleaning progress.

Chapter 12: Hardware and Network Troubleshooting

Here is how to stop and restart the print spooler in Windows 7:

1. Open Computer Management, and navigate to Services by right-clicking the Computer icon and choosing Manage. If necessary, click the arrow next to Services And Applications to expand the list.

2. Find the Print Spooler service.

3. Stop the spooler service. There are several ways that you can do this:

   - Right-clicking on the service and choosing Stop
   - Clicking the Stop square above the list of services
   - Using the More Actions menu on the right

4. Restart the spooler by right-clicking on the service and choosing Start or by clicking the Start arrow above the list of services.

5. Close Computer Management.

Chapter 13: Operating System Basics

Given the information that you need to collect, the easiest method is to use the System applet in Control Panel

1. Click Start.

2. Select Control Panel.

3. Choose System.

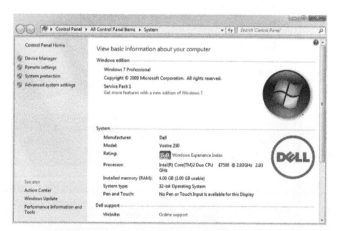

4. Write down the information for every item except the information related to the paging file.

5. Click Advanced System Settings. The System Properties dialog box appears.

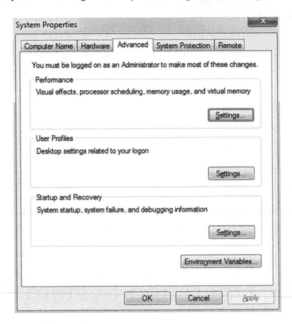

6. Click the Settings button beneath Performance, and choose the Advanced tab.

7. Write down the paging file information.
8. Click OK to exit the Performance Options dialog box.
9. Click OK to exit System Properties.
10. Close the System applet.

 The `msinfo32.exe` (System Information) tool presents all of this informa-tion in one screen.

Chapter 14: Operating System Administration

To check to see what background processes are running, and the resources they are using, open Task Manager. Do this by pressing Ctrl+Alt+Del and selecting Start Task Manager. You can also press Ctrl+Shift+Esc.

Once in Task Manager, click the Processes tab. It will also be helpful to check the Show Processes From All Users box if it is not already checked. Click the CPU column header to sort by CPU usage. If a process is taking up a considerable amount of CPU time, you can highlight it and click End Process to shut it down. You can also sort by memory used and shut down processes that look to be using excessive amounts of memory. Note that shutting down critical processes may cause Windows to lock up or otherwise not work properly, so be careful what you choose to terminate. Note as well that right-clicking on one of the pro-cesses offers the End Process Tree option—a useful option when the process being killed is associated with others.

Chapter 15: Working with Windows 8/8.1

To write a PowerShell script to find other scripts in a user profile directory and all of its subdirectories, you need the environment variable $home. While there are a number of ways of writing this script, one possibility from Technet is as follows:

```
Get-ChildItem -Path $home\* -Include *.ps1 -Recurse
```

Chapter 16: Working with Windows 7

To configure the TCP/IP values given in Windows 7:

1. Choose Start ➢ Control Panel ➢ Network And Sharing Center.

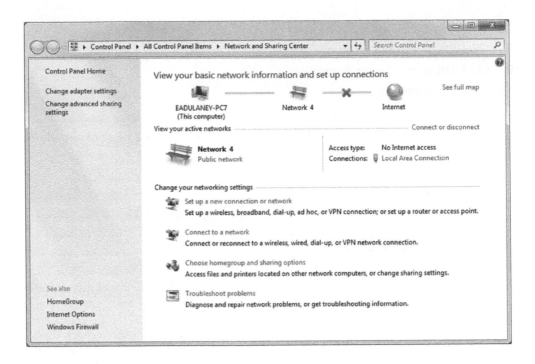

2. Click Change Adapter Settings. A screen similar to the one in the next screen shot will appear.

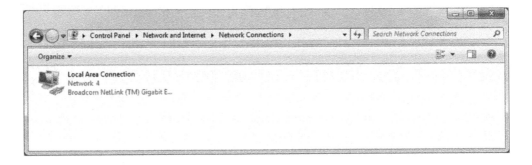

3. Right-click the connection icon and choose Properties.

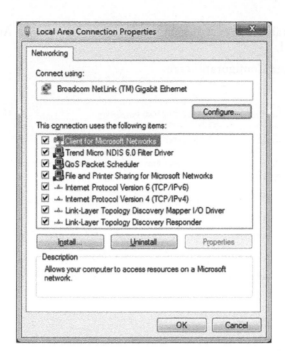

4. Click Internet Protocol Version 4 (TCP/IPv4), and then click the Properties button.

5. On the General tab, make certain that the Obtain An IP Address Automatically radio button is selected.

6. Click the Alternate Configuration tab.

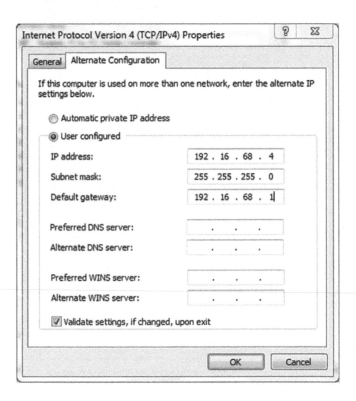

7. Click the User Configured radio button.

8. Enter the three values given for the IP address, the subnet mask, and the default gateway.

9. Click OK to close the dialog box. Click Close to exit the Local Area Connection Properties dialog box. Click the close icon in the upper-right corner of the Network Connections window.

Chapter 17: Working with Windows Vista

Here are the steps needed to run the Windows Memory Diagnostics tool:

1. Choose Start ➢ Control Panel ➢ Administrative Tools.

2. Choose Memory Diagnostics Tool.

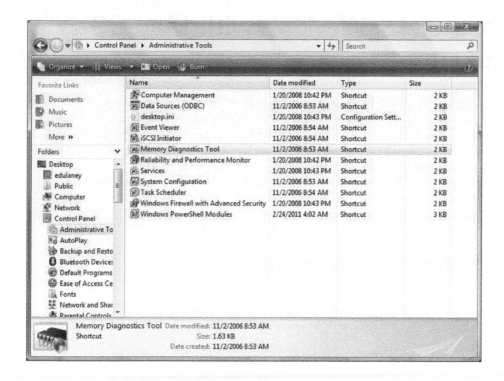

3. Click Restart Now And Check For Problems.

4. Upon reboot, the test will take several minutes and the display screen will show which pass number is being run and the overall status of the test (percent complete).

Chapter 18: Working with Mac OS and Linux

The listing you see when typing these commands will differ based on such factors as the system, the directory, your permissions, and the files/subdirectories present, but in all cases, there will be entries present with the –a option that do not appear in the display without it. Among those listings that now appear are a single period (representing the present directory) and a double period (representing the parent directory).

If there are any files or directories starting with a period, they will now appear where they did not before. The easiest way to "hide" a file or directory in Linux is to start the name of it with a period, and thus it will not show up in a listing unless the –a option is used.

Chapter 19: Security

Here is how to block pop-ups but allow them from one specific website:

1. Click Start ➤ Control Panel ➤ Internet Options.

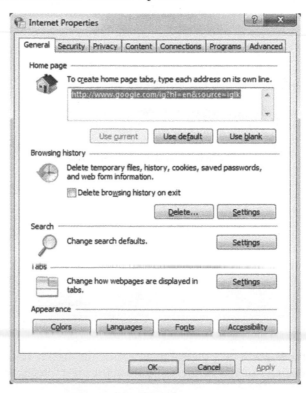

2. Click the Privacy tab.

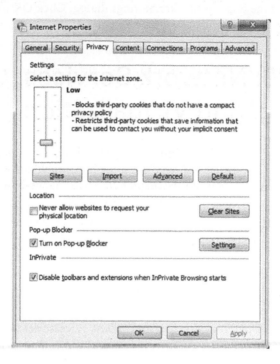

3. Click the Turn On Pop-Up Blocker check box, and then click the Settings button.

4. Type in the address **www.sybex.com** and click Add.

5. Click Close to exit the Pop-Up Blocker Settings dialog. Click OK to exit Internet Properties.

Chapter 20: Network Services, Cloud Computing, and Virtualization

Using Lubuntu will probably feel very similar using Windows. The interfaces have quite a few similarities in terms of navigation. Here are some hints on where you can find the utilities you need to complete the steps in the Chapter 20 performance-based question:

1. **Creating a user account.** You can do this by clicking the launcher (it looks like a button with a bird on it), about where you would expect the Start button to be in Windows, and then choosing System Tools ➤ Users And Groups. Click the Add button to create a new user.

2. **Managing storage space.** Open the launcher, and choose Preferences ➤ Disk Utility. This one won't work exactly like the one in Windows because it's on a virtual hard drive.

3. **Manipulating files.** Open the launcher, and choose Accessories ➤ File Manager, or you can choose File Manager using the icon to the right of the launcher. Once File Manager opens, you can right-click files to perform your tasks,

4. **Creating a shortcut.** Right-click the desktop, and choose Create New ➤ Shortcut.

5. **Configuring accessibility options.** As of now, Lubuntu does not offer the types of accessibility options Windows offers. The developer is committed to accessibility, but it has not yet developed these capabilities. For more information, see

https://wiki.ubuntu.com/Lubuntu/Developers/Accessibility

Maybe you can help!

Chapter 21: Mobile Operating Systems and Connectivity

Here are the steps to connect an iPhone to a Wi-Fi network:

1. Tap the Settings app on the Home screen.

2. Select Wi-Fi from the Settings menu.

3. Swipe the Wi-Fi switch to the right to turn it on if it is off. You can also tap switches to toggle them to the opposite state.

4. In the Choose A Network list, tap the name of the wireless network that you want to join.

5. Enter the password or key for the wireless network, if you are asked for one, and then tap the Join button. If it connects, the network name will appear under the Wi-Fi switch with a check mark next to it.

Chapter 22: Troubleshooting Theory, OSs, and Security

There are seven best practice steps associated with malware removal. Some of these steps, such as educating the end user, apply with almost every troubleshooting venture. In order, the seven steps are as follows:

1. Identify malware symptoms.

2. Quarantine infected system.

3. Disable system restore (in Windows).

4. Remediate infected systems:

    a. Update antimalware software.

    b. Scan and removal techniques (safe mode, pre-installation environment).

5. Schedule scans and run updates.

6. Enable system restore and create restore point (in Windows).

7. Educate end user.

Chapter 23: Understanding Operational Procedures

Here are some steps to take to look for trip hazards and eliminate them:

1. Walk around the server room, and count how many cables are lying on the floor.

2. Walk around the client areas, and see how many cables are lying on the floor or are exposed underneath cubicles.

3. Devise a plan to secure the cables and prevent them from being hazards. For example, purchase and install floor guards, use cable ties, or install conduit as necessary to secure all loose cables.

Index

Numbers

568A wiring standard, 279–280
568B wiring standard, 279–280

A

A+ certification. *See also test topic by name*
    Cisco series, 317
    CompTIA Network+ Study Guide
        (Lammle), 318
    Mobility+ test, 1140
    Network+ test, 249, 317
    Security+ test, 896, 1128
Absolute Software, 29
AC adapters
    for laptops, 426
    as power supplies, 107–108
accelerometers, 1023
acceptable use policies (AUPs), 905
access control list (ACL)
    for firewall config., 288, 383, 1222
    for LDAP changes, 304
    NTFS tracking in, 917, 943
access points, network
    antenna placement, 941
    defined, 285
    installing wireless, 371–373
access rosters, 897
accidents, 1168–1170
Account Lockout Policy, 806–807, 842
account management, 921
Account Policies, 806, 841–842
accountability, 1197
Action Center applet
    security settings in, 1127
    Windows, 720, 767
    Windows 7, 803–804
active cooling, 58

Active Directory (AD), 755, 921
active hubs, 286
active matrix LCD screens, 187
active matrix OLED (AMOLED) screens,
    191
active partition, 751
ad hoc networks, 529
adapter cards. *See* expansion cards
adapters
    cell phone, 123, 253
    in cooling air paths, 232
    display, 205
    DVI-to-HDMI, 150
    DVI-to-VGA, 148
    Ethernet over power, 288–289
    HDMI-to-VGA, 151
    laptop USB, 420
    PCI, 13
    PS/2-to-USB, 147
    USB-to-Ethernet, 121, 122
address autoconfiguration, 318–319
administration, network
    in client-server model, 260
    name and password, 376
    in peer-to-peer systems, 259
    Quality of Service (QoS) strategy,
        384–385
    Registry edit restriction by, 732
    rootkit attacks as, 910
    security compliance by, 920
    shares by, 754, 920
    static IP addressing by, 315
administration, Windows
    A+ exam topics, 707–708
    best practices, 868–873
    command prompt diagnostics, 721–730
    Control Panel interface, 709–721
    disk management, 749–752
    MMC tools, 739–746
    overview of, 707–709

practice test on, 757–760, 1233, 1259
Task Manager tool, 734–739
Windows 7, 804–810
Windows Vista, 840–846
Administrator account, 916
Adobe, 526
Adobe Acrobat, 530
Advanced Attributes options, 695–697
Advanced Configuration Power Interface
(ACPI), 748
Advanced Encryption Standard (AES), 340
Advanced Power Management (APM), 748
Advanced Sharing, 920
Advanced tab (Control Panel), 718–720
Advanced Technology Extended (ATX)
motherboards, 6, 7, 69
advanced video resolutions, 207–211
adware, 912
Aero interface
Windows 7, 787
Windows Vista, 830, 856–857
AFP (Apple Filing Protocol), 302
air filters, 1164
air flow, 57, 1174
airborne particles, 576
airplane mode, 409, 602, 1039
AirPrint, 545
alcohol, denatured isopropyl, 1175
alerts
government-issued, 1033–1034
from hardware devices, 579
operating system, 579
security, 1129
system failure, 719
alkaline batteries, 1183
All Programs submenu, 678–680
allocation units, 76–77
Allow vs. Deny, 918
alpha connectors, 142–143
alternating current (AC), 99
Amazon Kindle, 472
Amazon.com, 958
AMBER alerts, 1033
ammonia, 556
ammonium hydrogen sulfate, 1179–1181
amperage, 1152
analog interface, 185

analog sound jacks, 136–137
Android devices
airplane mode, 1040
app development, 1007
Bluetooth pairing, 1057–1067
connectivity troubleshoots, 602
disabling cellular data, 1052
email configuration, 1075–1078
Google Now, 1031–1033
keyboards onscreen, 1027–1028
market share, 1007, 1011–1012
mobile hotspots, 1039
mobile payment via, 488, 1036
passcode locks, 930, 931
phone locator app, 933, 934
service and repair to, 458
smart watches, 477
smartphones, 466–467
syncing, 1088–1089
touchscreen calibration, 1027
VPN configuration, 1054–1056
Wi-Fi connection, 1047–1050
Android operating system
app downloads, 1018–1021
Google Cloud Print support, 549
for Kindle Fire, 472
OS emulators, 990
overview of, 1007–1009
on phablets, 470
practice test on, 1092–1096
on tablets, 463
Android Pay, 1036
Andy, 990
antenna placement, 941
antiglare filters, 189
anti-malware software
layered applications, 900
for mobile devices, 1141
and NAT use, 318
overview of, 899–900, 1133
updates, 873
Windows Vista, 839
antispam programs, 1131
anti-spyware, 903
anti-static devices, 1156–1158, 1163
antivirus software
layered applications, 900

need for, 914
overview of, 899–900, 1132–1133
rogue, 1131
updates, 873
anycast IPv6 addresses, 320
app scanners, 1141
App Store, 871, 1014, 1015
Apple
  app development, 1007
  Apple Watch, 477–479, 1036
  Bonjour, 544
  iOS. *See* iOS operating system
  iPad, 463, 1009
  iPhone. *See* iPhone
  launcher options, 1029
  mobile payment options, 1036
  mouse, 158
  multi-touch technology, 459
  phablets, 470
  remote backups, 934
  security, 921
  service and repair to, 458
  Siri, 1030–1032
  syncing devices, 1083–1087
  Thunderbolt and, 155, 421–422
  troubleshooting, 1111
Apple MacBook Pro, 155
Apple Pay, 488, 1036
AppleTalk, 302
appliances, firewall, 900
Application Layer
  defined, 267
  in OSI diagram, 268
  protocols, 301–306
  proxy firewalls, 902
applications
  Android vs. iOS, 1012
  backing up, 868–869
  cloud-based, 982–983
  crashing, 1130–1131
  defined, 663
  device compatibility, 464
  downloading, 1014–1022
  Google, 1007
  Google Glass, 484
  hard/software requirements, 222
  icons for, 680–685

Launcher, 1030
load fails, 604
mobile device locator, 931–934
mobile payment, 1035
network sharing of, 258
password crackers, 908
pinned to Start menu, 765
printer compatibility with, 539–540
troubleshooting
  A+ exam topics, 1098
  failures to start, 1114
  symptoms, 1137–1139
  tools, 1139–1142
  typical issues, 1101
virtual printing, 526
Windows 8 access, 768–769
windows for, 685
apt (Advanced Package Tool), 873
archiving files, 695
ARM (Advanced RISC Machine), 765
armored virus, 914–915
ARP (Address Resolution Protocol), 301,
  308
ARP spoofing, 918
artwork, digitizing, 166
aspect ratio, 209
asymmetric DSL (ADSL), 344, 345–346
Asynchronous DRAM (ADRAM), 45
AT connector, 100–101, 145
AT&T, 283
ATI Crossfire, 231
ATSC (Advanced Television Systems
  Committee), 209
ATSC 480i/480p, 210
ATSC 720p, 210
attributes, file, 695
ATX power connectors
  12V 2.1 PCIe connector, 105
  12V 2.x connector, 104
  12V connector, 102, 103
  12V P4 connector, 104
  defined, 23
audio jacks, 31
audio setup
  for audio/video editing, 226
  for gaming, 231–232
  for home theater PCs, 234

laptop adjustment keys, 408
  speakers, 174
  surround sound channels, 136–137
audio/video editing workstations, 225–227
audio/video jacks, 132–133
Audit Policy, 807
auditing, 902
augmented reality (AR), 482
authentication of users, 754–755, 833, 920
authentication server, 970–971
Authenticator app, 935
auto duplexing, 815–816
Automatic Private IP Addressing (APIPA)
  defined, 318–319
  for NIC setup, 365
  troubleshooting issues with, 633
autorun, disabling, 914–915

B

back end computer, 251
Backblaze, 591
Background tab, 673
backlight displays
  faulty, 599
  LCD, 429
  LED, 212
back-off times, 332
backside bus (BSB), 10
Backup utility, 753, 873
backups
  defined, 1083
  drive, 753
  home data, 236
  laptop devices for, 406
  Linux and Mac OS, 868–869
  mobile security, 1141
  for Registry restores, 732
  remote, 934
  and screen lock wipes, 930
  tape, 89
badges, ID, 897, 898
barcode readers, 165–166
bare metal hypervisor, 986
baseband frequency, 157
baseband OS, 1042
baseband update, 1042
Bash shell, 878

basic rate interface (BRI), 348
basic storage, 751
batteries
  calibrating, 425
  chargers/packs, 491
  laptop
    Li-ion and NiMH, 1183
    swollen battery, 597–598
    troubleshooting, 596
    types of, 424–425
  mobile device, 1138
  recycling, 1183
BCD, 776, 797, 835
BD-R discs, 85
BD-RE discs, 85
BD-ROMs, 79, 80–81, 85
bearer (B) channel, 348
beep code, 580
behavior, professional,
  1196–1202
BellSouth, 464
benign viruses, 1133
beta connectors, 143
bias voltage, 521
binary system, 309–310
biometric devices, 167, 898
BIOS (basic input/output system)
  ACPI support, 748
  boot sequence, 581
  chip overview, 24–26
  controlling onboard NIC, 865
  as firmware routine, 23
  flashing the BIOS
    how to, 27–28
    for laptops, 446
    upgrades via, 581
  POST diagnostics, 579–580
  POST process, 26–28
  troubleshooting, 1118
  video memory sharing, 428
BIOS boot screens, 27
BitLocker
  encryption by, 26, 921
  full drive encryption, 934–935
  To Go, 921, 934–935
  Windows 7, 789
  Windows Vista, 831
BlackBerry
  decline of, 468–469

as early smartphone, 465–466
10 OS, 469
blackouts, 1171
Blåtand, King Harald, 253
Blue Screen of Death (BSOD), 584, 1110,
    1111
Bluetooth
    connectivity
        mobile setups, 486–487, 1056–1069
        troubleshooting, 602, 1137
    defined, 253
    devices, 253, 361
    pairing
        Android/MacBook, 1057–1067
        defined, 486
        requirements, 1056
        unintended, 1140
    printer interface, 529
    USB adapter, 420
    versions and data rates, 360–361
Bluetooth Special Interest Group
    (SIG), 253
Blu-ray
    Disc Association, 85
    HDMI cables for, 149
    issue identification, 593
BNC connector, 274
bonding, 348
Bonjour, 544–545
Boot Camp, 877
boot partition, 776
boot sequence
    BIOS settings, 581
    dual-booting, 719
    for multiple OS access, 774
    OS upgrades via, 773
    restore point access in, 691
    Safe Mode, 1111, 1116, 1124
    secondary drive boot, 581–582
    by system ROM, 50
    troubleshooting
        failure to boot, 589, 1111–1113
        loaders, 1117
        missing config. data, 1117
    Windows 7, 798–799
    Windows 8, 776–777
    Windows Memory Diagnostics, 810
    Windows Vista, 835–836, 860

BOOT.INI, 1111
BOOTMGR
    troubleshooting via, 1111
    Windows 7, 797
    Windows 8/8.1, 776
    Windows Vista, 835
BOOTREC command, 721–722
bot-herders, 919
botnet, 919
Box, 980
BRI ISDN lines, 348–349
bridges, 286
brightness
    and contrast ratios, 211–212
    in projection systems, 193–194
broadband, 157, 341
brownouts, 1171
browser redirection, 1128
brute-force password attacks, 908
buffered (registered) memory modules
    (RDIMMs), 42–43
burners, storage disc, 82–85
bursting, 141
bus architecture, 9–10, 14
bus topology, 262, 265
button cell batteries, 1184
buttons, mouse, 159
BYOD, mobile device policies, 935

C

cable locks, 431, 904, 944
cable modems, 346–348
cable testers, 636–637
cables
    common peripheral, 134–146, 178
    comparison chart, 282
    EMI-sensitive, 1160
    floor guard for, 1165
    network
        installing, 370–371
        topology setup, 261, 264
        troubleshooting, 631
        types of, 272–284
    pricing, 284
    printer interface, 528–529
    reseating, 1107

troubleshooting
    CPU/motherboard, 582–583
    tools, 635–639
    unplugged, 1106
  video display, 146–157
cache
  DNS server checks to, 965
  as key PC component, 16–19
  for multicore processors, 223
CAD/CAM design workstations, 223–224
calibration, inkjet, 511, 532–534
caliper, paper, 551
Call of Duty series, 230
camcorders, 172–173
cameras
  digital, 172–173
  smart, 476–477, 1141
campus software licenses, 1187
Canon, 513
capacitative touchscreens, 1026–1027
capacitators
  distended, 583
  safety around, 586, 1152
capacitive interfaces, 175
CardBus PC card, 416
carriage belt, 508
carriage motor, 507
cartridges, printer
  refilling, 610
  replacing, 552, 553
  troubleshooting
    inkjet, 610–612
    laser, 618, 619–621
cases, 398, 1154
cat command, 879
cathode ray tubes (CRTs), 189, 1153, 1164
CATV F connector, 157
CD burners, 82
cd command (Linux), 883
CD command (Windows), 722–723
cd cups command, 883
cd images command, 887
CD-R drives, 82
CD ROM File System (CDFS), 750
CD-ROMs
  data storage in, 79
  troubleshooting, 577, 593
CD-RW drives, 82, 593

cells, memory, 40
cellular adapters, 123
cellular data connections
  disabling, 1050–1052
  mobile options, 1037–1044
cellular hotspots, 123, 354
Cellular WAN, 352
central processing unit. *See* CPU (central
  processing unit)
centralized processing, 251
CERT website, 1129
certificate of destruction, 939
channels
  bonding, 335
  configuring wireless router, 378–379
  wireless communication, 333–335
characters per second (cps), 504
charge coupled devices (CCDs), 163
charging, EP print, 518–519, 614
charging corona, 518
Charms, 766
chemicals
  ammonium hydrogen sulfate, 1179–1181
  MSDS sheets, 1177–1178
  safe disposal of, 1185
  spilled, 1169
chipsets
  chip creep, 577
  cooling, 55, 58
  ESD dangers, 1155
  generational, 44
  interface diagram, 12
  memory, 40
  overheated, 586
  reseating, 1107
  structure of, 32
  types of, 10–12
CHKDSK command, 727–728
chmod command, 885
Chrome OS, 1008
Chromebooks, 395, 396
CIDR (classless inter-domain routing),
  312–314, 317
CIFS (Common Internet File System), 302
circuit-level proxy, 902
Class A, B, and C networks, 311, 317
clean installs
  vs. upgrading, 769

Windows 7, 792
Windows 8/8.1, 778
Windows Vista, 832, 833
cleaning
computers, 1174–1177
in EP printing, 522–523, 614
inkjet cycle, 512
laptop keyboards, 600
solutions for printers, 554–555
client computers
in network installations, 363
virtualization requirements, 987–991
virtualization setups, 990–991
workstations as, 256
client software, 256
client-server resource model, 260–261
clock frequency, 36, 45–48
closed source code, 664, 1013
cloud computing
A+ exam topics, 953
administration of, 975–976
applications, 982–984
cloud features, 979
cloud types, 978–979
data storage
Android options, 1088
iCloud, 1087
OneDrive, 765
providers of, 980
VPNs, 906–907
practice test on, 996–1001, 1240, 1266
printing from the cloud, 546–550
services, 976–978
virtualization-enabled, 227
clusters (allocation units), 74, 76–77
CMOS battery
CR2032, 25
function of, 29
replacing, 444–446
Coax RG types, 273
coaxial cables
networking via, 272–274
overview of, 156–157
RCA, 144
coaxial jacks, 133
code division multiple access (CDMA), 352
cold cathode fluorescent lamp (CCFL), 429
cold-swappable devices, 59

collision, data, 269
Color Graphics Adapter (CGA), 206, 209
color palette
post-VGA, 208, 211
pre-VGA standards, 205, 206
troubleshooting video, 594
VGA, 206, 207
combination touchscreens, 1029
COMMAND column, 882
command-line interface
directory management, 723
IP address renewal, 644–645
Linux shell commands, 878–879
MS-DOS as a, 721
OS diagnostics via, 707–708, 721–730
troubleshooting prompt, 1125–1126
commands. *See also commands by name*
for network troubleshoots, 639–652
OS diagnostic, 721–730
standard vs. administrator privilege,
730
commercial software, 1187
common access cards (CACs), 169
communications
professionalism in, 1192–1196
protocols, 299
rules of network, 265–269
wireless channels of, 333–335
communications adapter, 120
communications ports, 422
community clouds, 979
companion virus, 915
compasses, 1024
compatibility, 1115
Compatibility Mode
Windows, 681
Windows 7, 790
Windows Vista, 831
compatibility tools, 791
Component Services, 808, 845
component video, 151–153
composite video, 153
compressed air, 1164
compression, file, 696, 750
CompTIA Network+ Study Guide
(Lammle), 318
Computer icon, 683
Computer Management Console, 739–740

computer name, 716–717
computerized numerical control (CNC)
    systems, 224
concentrators, 143
concurrent software installs, 1187
confidentiality, 1199
connectivity devices, 285–288
connectivity issues, 630–635
connectors
    characteristics of, 126–134
    coaxial, 274–276
    common ports and, 135–136
    F-connector, 276
    fiber-optic, 283
    keyboard and mouse, 146
    network, 272–284
    power. *See* power connectors
    RCA cable, 144
    for syncing mobile devices, 484–486
    twisted-pair, 278–279
    types of, 113–115
    USB 2.0 and 3.0, 140
    video display cables and, 146–157
contention-based access, 269
contrast ratio, 189, 211, 213
Control Panel
    access via filenames, 711
    configuring microphones, 173
    Windows, 708, 709–721
    Windows 7, 810–813, 817
    Windows Vista, 847–852, 860
controllers, hard drive, 72
conversation, professional, 1192, 1195
converters, 156
cooling systems
    for gaming, 232
    laptop, 400–401, 443
    in projectors, 194
    troubleshooting
        fixes by fail type, 586–587
        mobile devices, 597, 1138
        symptoms, 575–576
    types of, 54–63
cooperative multitasking, 664
COPY command, 724–725
copying files/folders, 918
cordless phones, 1160
Core 2 processors, 35

Core Solo processors, 35
corona roller, 517
corona wire, 517
corporate policies, 1100
Cortana, 1030
cp command, 886
CPU (central processing unit)
    component matching, 36
    cooling
        common methods, 59–63
        fan, 55
        in gaming setups, 232
    enhancements
        gaming, 230–231
        graphic and CAD/CAM, 223
        virtualization, 228
    identifying, 34
    memory choices, 48–49
    memory communication with, 11
    overview of, 31–33, 63
    practice test on, 65–68
    processor sockets and, 19–22
    troubleshooting
        fixes by fail type, 582–583
        symptoms, 567–568, 575–582
    virtualization requirements, 987
credit card readers, 491
crimpers, 635
crossover cable, 280
CSMA/CA access methods, 332
CSMA/CD standard, 269
CUDA (Compute Unified Device
    Architecture), 225
custom PC configurations
    A+ exam topics, 219–220, 221
    audio/video editing workstations,
        225–227
    for gaming, 230–232
    graphic and CAD/CAM workstations,
        223–224
    home server PCs, 236–241
    home theater PCs, 232–235
    list of common, 219–221
    practice test on, 241–246, 1219–1221,
        1252
customer relations, 1191–1203
CutePDF, 526
cylinders, hard drive, 74, 75–76

D

daisy chain networks, 144, 155
daisy-wheel printers, 503–504
data
    backups. *See* backups
    cloud-sent, 976
    data loss prevention (DLP), 915
    destruction
        mobile wipes, 930–934
        physical methods, 935–939
    drives, 226
    intercept attacks, 909
    non-cellular vs. cellular use, 1037
    privacy, 1199
    sensitive, 1189–1191
    synchronization, 1082
    third-party recovery, 593
    VPN tunneling of, 906
data link layer
    bridge work at, 286, 287
    defined, 267
    in OSI diagram, 268
data rates
    Bluetooth, 360–361
    cable modem, 346–347
    dial-up, 342
    DSL, 344
    Ethernet standards, 357
    for expansion slots, 13
    FireWire cable, 143
    4G vs. 3G, 353
    HDD speeds, 77
    module throughput and, 45–48
    near field communication, 487–488
    NIC, 271
    optical drive, 82
    PCIe, 15, 16
    QoS strategy to aid, 385
    satellite, 350–351
    Thunderbolt interface, 155
    troubleshooting slow, 634
Data Source Administrator
    Windows 7, 808–809
    Windows Vista, 845, 846
databases, antivirus, 1133
Date And Time applet, 712
daughterboards, 400

DC adapters, 426
DC Power Supply (DCPS), 516
DDR memory slots, 18
DDR SDRAM, 46
DDR2/DDR3 SDRAM, 47–48
decryption, 604
dedicated servers, 255, 956
defaults
    accounts, 914
    changing, 914, 940, 942
    default allow, 383
    default deny, 288, 383
    masks, 317
Defender, Windows
    Windows 7, 790, 799
    Windows Vista, 831, 838
defragmenting disks
    function of, 753–754
    how to, 1120–1122
    importance of, 871
    Windows 7, 1122
degaussing, 938
DEL command, 723
Dell Latitude C640, 435
Dell Streak 5, 470
demilitarized zone (DMZ)
    authentication servers in, 971
    defined, 288, 382
    and server placement, 956
    three-pronged firewalls, 957
denial of service (DoS) attacks, 920
Deny vs. Allow, 918
Department of Defense (DOD) model, 300–301
Department of Defense (DOD), U.S., 473, 474
Deployment Toolkit, 773
desktop computers. *See also* personal computers (PCs)
    Bluetooth pairing with, 1056
    LCD screens, 185
    restart to troubleshoot, 1107
    software development, 1042
    vs. laptops
        expansion slots, 12
        hard drives, 404
        portability issue, 368
        power supplies, 107

pros and cons, 396–398
   SODIMM chips, 402–403
wireless card installation, 368
workstations as, 256, 257
desktops
  cloud sync to, 981
  multiple computer, 874
  virtual, 988
  Windows
    icon, 684
    overview of, 671–674
    remote connection to, 720
destruction, data, 935–939
developing, EP print, 520–521, 614
developing roller, 521
device connector types, 127
Device Manager tool, 228, 739
DHCP (Dynamic Host Configuration
  Protocol)
  defined, 302
  enabling, 615
  function of, 314–316
  scopes, 961
DHCP DISCOVER broadcast, 962
DHCP REQUEST broadcast, 962, 963
DHCP servers
  configurations without, 365
  enabling, 377
  function of, 960–964
  TCP/IP config. via, 962
  wireless routers as, 367
dial-up connections, 341, 342
dictionary attacks, 909
die (silicon wafer), 19
digital cameras, 172–173
digital interface, 185
digital rights management (DRM), 157, 1186
digital security, 899–905
digital/analog sound in/out, 135
digitizers, 166–167, 430
digitizing tablets, 166
DIMM (dual inline memory module)
  buffered and unbuffered, 42–43
  overview of, 50–53
  types of, 16–17
DIR command, 728–729
direct current (DC), 99

directories
  for file organization, 692
  Linux, 883–884
  NTFS permissions, 918–919
  security of, 903–905
direct-sequence spread spectrum
  (DSSS), 338
disable execute bit, 38
discs
  burning storage, 82–85
  Linux/Mac OS access to, 877
  repairing, 1119–1120
Disk Defragmenter, 753–754
disk management
  Disk Management utility, 751–752
  filesystems and, 749–751
  overview of, 749
Disk Management utility
  managing drives, 94, 751
  mapping drives, 754
disk mirroring (RAID 1), 88, 592
disk striping (RAID 0), 87, 227
DISKPART command, 726, 774
disks
  defragmenting, 753–754, 871
  Linux/Mac OS tools, 874
  management of, 94, 749–752
  prepping for storage, 749–752
display adapters, 205
display devices
  A+ exam topics, 183
  connectors for, 178
  environmental effects on, 212
  e-reader, 471–472
  for gaming, 231
  as input/output devices, 174
  laptop, 426–431, 440
  practice test on, 213–217, 1217, 1249
  safe disposal of, 1184–1185
  safety around, 1153, 1157
  settings adjustment, 195–204
  troubleshooting
    failed printer, 624
    multiple monitors, 1118
    symptoms, 569
    for video issues, 598–599
  types of, 184–194, 212

using multiple
  for audio/video editing, 225
  Dual View, 202
  settings for, 202–204, 217
video issues, 594
DisplayPort, 153–154, 421
disposal of equipment, 1177–1186
distended capacitors, 583
distributed processing, 251
DIX connector, 274
DLL (dynamic library link), 1114
DNS (Domain Name System) servers
  domain name kiting, 919
  function of, 302, 314–316
  manual configuration of, 367
  overview of, 964–968
  security attacks, 918–919
  Windows 7 IP config., 815
dock, icons, 877
docking stations, 422–424, 491
Docter, Quentin, 257
domain controller, 261, 970
Domain Setup, 817
domains, 261, 816
dongles, 420
dot-matrix printers
  overview of, 504–505
  troubleshooting, 608–609
double-sided memory, 41
draft quality prints, 505
DRAM (dynamic random access memory),
  43, 44–49
DRAM-based SSDs, 78
drive activity light, 31
drive gears, dot-matrix printers, 609
drivers
  configuring printer, 532–534
  defined, 663
  detecting new hardware, 447
  Linux/Mac OS updates, 873
  NIC, 272
  print server, 542
  signing, 717, 718, 746
  software, 1042
  troubleshooting
    compatibility errors, 1115
    mis-installed, 1114
    printer, 607, 622

drives
  backing up, 753
  BitLocker encryption, 789
  disposal methods, 935–939
  drive interfaces, 134–135
  hard drives. *See* hard drives
  and RAID, 85–86
Dropbox, 980
DSL connections, 343–346
D-subminiature connectors,
  127–128
dual in-line package (DIP), 32
Dual View, 202
dual voltage options, 100
dual-booting, 719, 985
dual-channel memory, 41
dual-drive storage, 79
dual-homed firewall, 902
dual-rail architecture, 99
dual-scan displays, 187, 188
dumb terminals, 235
Duo processors, 35
duplexing
  printer assembly, 513, 518
  RAID 1, 88
  USB 2.0 and 3.0 capacities, 141
  Windows 7 NIC, 815–816
durability of components, 397
dust, 576
DVD burners, 83–85
DVD Forum, 84
DVD+RW Alliance, 84
DVD-ROMs
  burning, 83
  characteristics of, 85
  defined, 80
  issue identification, 593
  unusual noise from, 577
DVI (Digital Visual/Video Interface)
  cables, 147–149
  characteristics of, 147–149
  consumer call for, 147
DVI-A connector, 148
DVI-A interface, 185
DVI-D connector, 148
DVI-I connector, 148
DVI-to-HDMI adapter, 150
DVI-to-VGA adapter, 148

Dvorak Simplified Keyboard, 162–163
DVR machines, 177
DxDiag (DirectX Diagnostic) tool, 745–746
dynamic disk, 752
dynamic frequency selection (DFS), 335–336
Dynamic Network Address Translation
        (DNAT), 380
dynamic ratio, 212
dynamic storage, 751

E

E Ink, 471
E Ink Holdings, Inc., 472
editing the Registry, 731, 732
effective clock rate, 36
802.11 networks
    as built into laptops, 422
    devices for, 338–339
    modulation techniques, 337–338
    standards, 331–337, 387
    upgrading laptop cards, 439
802.11a standards, 332–333
802.11ac standards, 335–337
802.11b standards, 333
802.11g standards, 333–334
802.11n standards, 334
802.3 CSMA/CD (Carrier Sense Multiple
        Access with Collision Detection), 269
electrocution
    anti-static strap hazards, 1157
    from capacitors, 583, 586, 1152
    from components, 1151–1155
    from desktop PCs, 577
    from inverters, 429, 440
    from power supplies, 99, 516
    via stored electricity, 1151
electromagnet drive destruction, 938
email
    encryption, 1081–1082
    filtering, 906
    hijacked, 1132
    mobile configurations, 1069–1082
    phishing, 907–908, 910
    protocols, 970
    S/MIME setup, 604–606
    viruses, 914

embedded MultiMediaCard (eMMC),
        92–93
embedded systems, 973–974
emergency notifications, 1033
EMI (electromagnetic interference), 371,
        1159–1160
employees
    responsibility of, 1166–1167
    safety plan for, 1168
employer responsibilities, 1166–1167
emulation, 989–990
encryption
    access point, 372
    BitLocker, 921
    in digital rights management, 157
    drive, 26
    email, 1081–1082
    enabling wireless router, 377
    Encrypting File System (EFS), 817, 921
    full drive encryption, 934–935
    of geotracking, 1025
    of GPS signals, 474–475
    NFC as lacking, 488
    via HTTPS, 303
    Windows 7 network, 817
    Windows Advanced Attributes options,
        696–697
    of wireless networks, 339–340, 940
endpoints, 143
endspan PoE devices, 289
enduser license agreement (EULA), 1186
energy density, 424
engine self-test, 623
Enhanced Graphics Adapter (EGA),
        206, 210
enterprise licenses, 1187
enterprise networks
    Quality of Service (QoS) strategy, 384–
        385
    tape backups, 89
    WPA choices, 340, 378
enterprise servers
    file sharing, 240
    multiple, 955
    vs. home servers, 236
entry control rosters, 897
envelope feeders, 559
Environment Variables button, 718

environmental issues
    accidents, 1168–1169
    display degradation, 212
    hazardous waste, 1170, 1177–1186
    managing physical, 1171–1177
    water, 1160, 1169
    workplace safety, 1164–1170
EP (electrophotographic) printing
    overview of, 518–524, 613–614
    printers using, 513
EPS12V power connectors, 102, 104
erasable PROM (EPROM), 50
Erase Data feature, 931
erasing discs, 82
e-readers, 471–473
ergonomic keyboard, 162
Ericsson headset, 253
error-correcting code (ECC), 41
errors. *See also* alerts
    laser printer codes, 624
    memory, 40–41
    OS reinstallation following, 709, 732
    recreating, 1192–1193
    user, 1107, 1108
    Windows 7, 804
    Windows Vista reports, 850
eSATA cards, 120, 135, 226
ESD (electrostatic discharge)
    component damage from, 1155–1159
    static eliminator strip, 517, 617
Ethernet
    cables, 277
    common standards, 357
    interfaces
        adapters for, 121
        commonality of, 135
        for home servers, 240–241
        for printers, 528–529
    naming standards, 273
    splitters, 279
    USB capacity extension, 122
    Wake on LAN (WoL), 816
Ethernet over power, 288–289
ethics, 1201
even parity, 40
Event Viewer tool, 739, 1124
Exchange, 1080
executive subsystems, 1113

EXIT command, 729
EXPAND command, 729
expansion cards
    A+ exam topics, 113–116
    blank slots, 576
    installing/configuring, 113, 117–126
    for laptops, 414–422
    practice test on, 178–182, 1215, 1249
    replacing laptop, 438–439
expansion slots, 12–16
expiration, password, 921
Explorer, 693–694
exposing (writing), EP print, 520, 614
ExpressBus, 415
ExpressCard, 414–415
ExpressCard/34, 415, 416
ExpressCard/54, 415, 416
Extended File Allocation Table (ExFAT), 750
Extended File System (ext), 750–751
Extended Graphics Array (XGA), 208, 210
extenders, 285
extranet connections, 907

F

failure, system, 719
fanless cooling, 61–63
fans
    common symptoms, 575–576
    CPU, 59
    projector, 194
    types of, 54–58
FAT32, 750, 917
fault tolerance, 236, 264
F-connector, 276
feeder, printer, 558–559
fencing, 897
fiber-optic cables, 280–284
fiber-optic Internet, 349–350
Fiber-to-the-Home (FTTH) service, 349
Fiber-to-the-Node (FTTN) service, 350
fieldreplaceable units (FRUs), 439
file allocation table (FAT), 749–750, 917
File Explorer. *See* Explorer
file servers, 255, 958–959
files
    backing up, 868–869

corrupt, 1116
disk storage for, 749
formats, 749–750
Linux navigation, 884
locking, 252
management of, 691–698
moving vs. copying, 918
permissions
   Linux, 884, 885
   NTFS, 697–698, 917–919
   propagation, 920
print sharing, 240
printing to, 525–527
sharing, 919–920
signs of infected, 1132
syncing offline, 849–850
system, 920
virus signature, 916
filtering, MAC, 940–941, 942
Find My Phone app, 932, 933
Finder, 876
Fingerworks, 459
finishers, printer, 559
FiOS, 349
fire, electrical, 1170
fire ratings, 870
fireproof data storage, 870
firewalls
   configuring wireless, 384
   DMZ management, 957
   Firewall applet, 720
   function of, 381, 383
   network-based, 383
   overview of, 900–903
   as security device, 288
   types of, 383
   UTM, 973
   Windows 7, 790, 798–803
   Windows Vista, 838–839, 860
FireWire (IEEE 1394) cables, 142–144
FireWire (IEEE 1394) ports, 130, 135
FireWire 400 interface, 142, 143–144
FireWire 800 interface, 142
FireWire cards, 120
firmware
   defined, 23
   Linux/Mac OS updates, 873

printer upgrades, 558
   SOHO install updates, 376
Fitbit, 480–482
Fitbit Flex, 480
Fitbit Surge, 481–482
fitness monitors, 479–482
flash drives, 777
flash memory, 89, 90–95
flash-based SSDs, 78
flashing the BIOS
   how to, 27–28
   for laptops, 446
   upgrades via, 581
flatbed scanners, 163–164
flexibility, 1197–1198
FlexNet Manager, 1188
fluorescent lights, 371
Folder Options applet, 714–716
folders
   in the cloud, 981, 982
   managing, 692
   moving vs. copying, 918
   NTFS permissions, 917–919
   sharing, 919–920
   system, 920
Force Quit tool, 874
force stop, 1139
form factors
   CPU, 32
   flash memory, 90, 92, 94
   home theater PC, 233, 234
   laptop, 399, 402, 403, 417
   memory, 17, 50, 53
   motherboard, 6–8, 124
   power supply, 106
   storage devices, 81, 97
FORMAT command, 724, 751
formatter boards, 622
formatting
   files, 749–750
   low-level vs. standard, 936
   storage discs, 82
   in Windows 8 upgrades, 772
/? command, 729
4G technology, 353
4G LTE (Long-Term Evolution), 353
fragmented files, 1120

frame rate, 199, 213
frames, laptop, 398
freeware, 1186
frequencies
    clock frequency, 36
    DSL vs. phone, 345
    EMI interference, 1159–1160
    for expansion slots, 13
    GPS transmission, 474
    wireless channel, 333–335, 378–379
frequency-hopping spread spectrum (FHSS),
    337
front end computer, 251
front intake fan, 54
front panel connectors, 29–30
front stereo channel, 137
frontside bus (FSB), 9–10
frozen system, 604, 1138
FSB speed, 36, 46–47
FTP (File Transfer Protocol), 301, 303
full drive encryption, 934–935
full duplexing, 815–816, 854
full format, 751
Full Speed USB, 138
full-duplex communication, 271
Function (Fn) key, 407, 599
function keys, 161–162
fusing, EP print, 522, 614
fusing assembly, 517–518, 621

G

gadgets
    Windows, 675
    Windows 7, 788
    Windows Vista, 830
Galaxy Note, 470
game pads, 168, 491
games, mobile, 990
gaming graphics, 16
gaming PCs
    fiber-optic connections for, 350
    overview of, 230–232
    propagation delay to, 351
Garmin Nuvi GPS, 475
Gateway field, 815

geolocation, 1024, 1025
gesture-based interaction, 1022
Gestures, 876
ghost cursors, 600
ghosting, 621
Gigabit Ethernet, 335, 357, 414
gigabit NIC, 240–241
glasses-mounted computer, 482
Global Navigation Satellite System
    (GLONASS), 1025
Global Navigation Satellite Systems (GNSSs),
    473–474
Global System for Mobile Communications
    (GSM), 352
globally unique identifier (GUID), 755, 921
Gmail, 1070, 1075
goggles, safety, 1164
Google
    Android OS. See Android operating
        system
    cloud services, 546–549, 982–984
    Docs, 982, 983
    Drive, 980, 981, 1088
    email services, 1070
    Glass, 482–484
    launcher options, 1029
    Now, 1030
    Play Store, 1018
    Wallet, 1036
    web servers, 958
government alerts, 1033
GPRESULT command, 728
GPS (global positioning system)
    on mobile devices, 1024–1025
    overview of, 473–475
    troubleshooting, 606–607
GPT disk, 752
GPUPDATE command, 728
graphic design workstations, 223–224
graphical user interface (GUI)
    defined, 664
    failures to load, 1117
    mobile, 1029
graphics adapter
    for audio/video editing, 225
    defined, 118
    for home theater PCs, 234

Graphics Device Interface (GDI), 530
graphics mode, 206
graphics processing units (GPUs)
    enhancements to, 224
    for gaming, 231
    integrated, 38
grep command, 878
GRiD Systems GRiDPad, 461
grounding, 1156–1159
groups, managing, 804–805, 921
GRUB (Grand Unified Bootloader),
    1117–1118
GSmartControl, 590
Guest account, 914, 916
gyroscopes, 1024

H

hacking, 318, 957
half duplexing
    configuring, 815–816, 854
    vs. full, 271
half self-test, 623
hard drives
    anatomy of, 72–77, 108
    connectors, 134–135
    destruction methods, 935–939
    Disk Management of, 751
    installing printer, 558
    laptop, 403–404
    optimizing, 753–754
    replacing laptop, 435–437
    specialized, 226–227
    speeds, 77
    troubleshooting
        failure metrics, 591
        fixes by fail type, 588–593
        symptoms, 568
    uncoupling, 226
    virtual memory on, 18
    virtualization requirements, 987, 988
hardware. *See also components by name*
    acceptable use policies (AUPs), 905
    compatibility, 665–669, 792
    Control Panel Hardware tab, 717–718
    custom configurations, 221–222
    destruction/disposal of, 937–939, 1177–1186

firewalls, 288, 382, 900–903
laptop
    basic components, 398–431
    replacing external, 446–447
    replacing internal, 434–446
MAC addresses, 271
network, 270–284
print servers, 542
safety moving, 1161–1162
troubleshooting
    A+ exam topics, 567–572
    common symptoms, 575–582, 1104
    methods for, 1101, 1105
    misconfigured, 1114
    practice test on, 1230–1232, 1257
    symptom list, 567–572
upgrades, 27–28, 446
for virtualization work, 698
Hardware Compatibility List (HCL), 666
hardware-assisted virtualization, 699
hazardous waste, 1170, 1177–1186
HD DVD, 149
HDDERASE, 937
HDMI (High-Definition Multimedia
    Interface)
    1.3, 1.4, and 2.0, 149–150
    cables, 149, 150
    characteristics of, 149–151
    consumer call for, 147
    for gaming, 232
    for home theater PCs, 234
HDMI-to-VGA adapter, 151
head carriage, 506–507
headers, 135, 266
headsets, 482–484, 490
heat pipes, 62
heat sinks
    function of, 54
    increasing efficiency of, 59–60
    laptop, 400–401
    motherboard chipset, 11
    processor socket, 19–20
    removal of, 60
    troubleshooting
        fixes by fail type, 586
        symptoms, 575–576
helium cooling systems, 63
Help and Support command, 679

HELP command, 729
Hercules Graphics Card (HGC),
   206, 209
Hewlett-Packard
   HP ePrint, 549–550
   HP LaserJet, 622–626
   laser printers, 513
   Photosmart Plus, 545
   Photosmart printer, 90, 91
   Tablet PC, 462
hibernation state, 748
hierarchical addressing, 308, 309
high bit-rate DSL (HDSL), 344
High Speed HDMI cables, 149, 150
High Speed USB 2.0, 130, 138
high-voltage power supply (HVPS), 515–516,
   619
high-voltage probes, 1153
hijacked email, 1132
hives, Registry, 731
HKEY_CLASSES_ROOT, 731
HKEY_CURRENT_CONFIG, 731
HKEY_CURRENT_USER, 731
HKEY_LOCAL_MACHINE, 731, 1113
HKEY_USERS, 731
hoaxes, security, 1129
home office networks. *See* SOHO wireless
   networks
home screen replacements, 1029
home server PCs, 236–241
home theater PCs, 232–235
HomeGroups
   configuring Windows networking,
      816–817
   Windows 7, 237, 790, 810
   Windows Vista, 852
hops, 144
host bus adapter (HBA), 72
host ID, 310
host OS, 987
host-based firewalls, 383
hostname-to-IP-address pairs, 315
hosts
   address assignation, 941
   emulator compatibility, 989
   hypervisor shares of, 986, 987
   IP address, 308–309
Host-to-Host layer, 301, 306–308

hotspots, mobile
   defined, 354
   how to enable, 1038–1039
   overview of, 488–490
hot-swappable devices
   booting Windows from, 776
   defined, 95
   for laptops, 446
HTC
   Dream, 466
   EVO 4G, 1056
   HTC Sync, 1090–1092
   TouchFLO, 460
HTTP (Hypertext Transfer Protocol), 301,
   303, 957
HTTPS (Hypertext Transfer Protocol
   Secure), 303–304, 957
hubs
   broadcast function, 285–286
   central, 263
   vs. switches, 287
   WAP, 338
human-caused accidents, 1169
humidity and ESD, 1155, 1159
hybrid attacks, 909
hybrid clouds, 978
hybrid drives, 78–79
hybrid hard drives, 405
hybrid TCP/IP configuration, 962
hybrid topology, 265
Hyper-Threading Technology (HTT), 33
hypervisor
   defined, 698, 986–987
   hacks, 990

I

IBM
   advanced video resolutions, 207–208
   Simon Personal Communicator, 464, 465
iCloud
   configuration settings, 1088
   data storage, 1087
   email configuration, 1070
   Find My Phone app, 932
   iPad configuration, 875–876
ICMP (Internet Control Message Protocol),
   301, 308, 903

Icy Sea Inc., 1195
ID badges, 897, 898
IDE (integrated drive electronics) drives, 86, 936
identity theft, 372
IEEE 1394 (FireWire) cables, 142–144
IEEE 1394 (FireWire) ports, 130
IEEE 802.11 standards. *See* 802.11 networks
ifconfig command, 632, 887–888
image deployment, 773
image recovery tool, 874
IMAP (Internet Message Access Protocol), 304, 1078
IMAP4, 304
impact paper, 504
impact printers, 503–513
Improve Power Usage, 812
incident response, 1168–1169, 1190
incineration, drive, 938–939
Indexing Service, 695, 858–859
Infrared Data Association (IrDA), 131–132, 362
infrared networks, 361–363, 487
infrared ports, 131–132
infrastructure, 253
Infrastructure as a Service (IaaS), 976
infrastructure mode, 529
init process, 882
injury, repetitive strain, 169
ink cartridges, 506, 552
inkjet printers, 505–513
inoculation, virus, 1133
in-place upgrades, 770, 791
in-plane switching (IPS), 185, 186, 429
input devices
    applet, 848
    common, 158–170
    mobile methods, 459–460
    multimedia, 170–173
    and output devices, 173–177
    overview of, 157–173
    practice test on, 178–182
    troubleshooting mobile, 599–600
Institute of Electrical and Electronics Engineers (IEEE)
    creation of 802 standards, 268
    creation of WLAN standards, 332
insurance, compensation, 1169

Integrated Circuit Card Identifier (ICCID), 1044
integrated drive electronics (IDE) drives, 86
integrated GPU, 38
integrated print servers, 542
Intel
    motherboard chipsets, 10
    Pentium M chip, 401
    Processor Identification utility, 37
    Thunderbolt collaboration, 155
Intel Core 2 Quad Q9650 processor, 48
Intel Core i7-990X Extreme Edition processor, 49
Intel i7 Extreme Edition processor, 229
interlaced technology, 208
internal network connections, 356–363
International Mobile Equipment Identity (IMEI), 1043
International Mobile Subscriber Identity (IMSI), 1044
International Mobile Telecommunications Advanced (IMT-Advanced) standards, 353
Internet
    appliances, 971–973
    DNS interactions with, 966–967
    dot at the end, 966
    as network public side, 288
    and network security, 971–973
    pharming, 1128
    virtualization via, 985
Internet access
    choosing internal, 356–363
    connection types, 329–330, 341–356
    firewalls as filtering, 900–901
    prevalence of, 331
    provider availability, 355–356
    security risks in, 896
    shared connections, 380–381
    troubleshooting
        no connectivity, 319
        printer connectivity, 615
        and security, 1130
    via cellular hotspots, 123
    via web servers, 957
Internet Control Message Protocol (ICMP), 301, 308, 903
Internet layer, 308
Internet Options applet, 714

Internet Protocol (IP), 308
intrusion detection, 25, 972
intrusion prevention system (IPS), 972
inverse multiplexing, 348
inverters, 429, 440, 1153
I/O (input/output) ports, 582–583
I/O cards, 120
IOS (Internetwork Operating System), 90
iOS operating system
    airplane mode, 1041
    app downloads, 1014–1017
    App Store, 871
    Cloud Print support, 549
    connectivity troubleshoots, 602–603
    emulators, 990
    geotracking by, 1025
    on iPads, 463
    on iPhones, 466
    market share, 1007, 1011–1012
    overview of, 1009–1011
    practice test on, 1092–1096
    S/MIME enables, 1081–1082
    S/MIME setup, 604–606
    syncing devices, 1083–1087
    versions of, 1011
    VPN configuration, 1054–1056
IP addresses
    assigning static, 941, 943
    binary system, 309–310
    CIDR, 312–314
    configuring alternative, 814–815
    as hierarchical, 308–309
    IPCONFIG command, 641–643
    IPv4 address classes, 310–312
    Network Address Translation, 379–380
    network and host IDs, 310
    public vs. private, 316–318
    renewal in Windows 7, 643–644
    resolving hostnames to, 315
    troubleshooting, 633
IP spoofing, 918
iPad, 463, 1009
IPCONFIG /ALL
    defined, 641
    output, 642–643
    to renew IP addresses, 644–645
    troubleshooting via, 634
    for workstation address, 942

IPCONFIG command
    in IPv4-IPv6 networks, 321, 322
    as a mobile hotspot, 488–489
    switches, 641–642
    troubleshooting via, 319, 631, 633
iPhone. *See also* iOS operating system
    Apple Watch pairings, 479
    disabling cellular data, 1050–1052
    email configuration, 1070–1074
    Find My Phone app, 932
    5c, 1035
    operating system, 1009
    overview of, 466
    pairing with vehicles, 1067–1069
    passcode locks, 930
    size history, 468
    Wi-Fi connection, 1045–1047
    wired connectors, 486
IPv4 addressing
    communication via, 310–312
    patterns, 309
    vs. IPv6, 319, 320
IPv4-IPv6 networks, 321
IPv6 addressing, 319–322
ISDN (Integrated Services Digital Network), 348–349
ISP (Internet service provider), 341, 1070
iTunes syncing, 1083–1087, 1089
ITX motherboards, 8

J

jailbreaking
    for Bluetooth connectivity, 1056
    and geolocation, 1025
    mobile OSs, 1007
jams, printer, 608–609
Jawbone, 480
journaled file system (JFS), 870
joysticks, 168
jump lists, 790

K

Kensington lock, 431
Kerberos, 754–755, 920, 970

kernel panic, 1111
key fobs, 898
keyboards
    backlights for, 410
    BlackBerry, 468–469
    cables, 145–146
    installation, 163
    interface, 133–134
    laptop
        overview of, 407–410
        ports, 422
        replacing, 441–442
    layouts, 161–162
    PC, 161–163
    safety around, 1155
    troubleshooting
        laptop, 599–600
        power issues via, 578
    wireless, 146, 158
Keychain, 875
Kindles, 472
kinetic sensors, 1023
KitKat, 1040
Kobo, 472
KVM (keyboard/video/mouse) switch, 175

L

labels, printing, 609
Lammle, Todd, 318
land grid array (LGA), 20–21, 33
lands, 33
lanes, 14
language, professional, 1192, 1195
laptops
    A+ exam topics, 393–394
    Bluetooth pairing with, 1056
    building your own, 397
    cable locks, 431–432
    components, 398–431
        cases, 398
        display, 185, 394, 426–431
        hardware, 393
        input devices, 406–414
        keyboards, 407–410
        memory, 17, 402–403
        motherboards/processors, 399–401

    pointing devices, 159–161, 410–414
    replacing external, 446–447
    replacing internal, 434–446
    storage devices, 403–405
    expansion ports, 414–422
    external monitors for, 202
    portability of, 457
    power systems, 424–427
    practice test on, 448–453, 1226, 1254
    troubleshooting
        dis-/reassembly, 432, 434–447
        fixes by fail type, 595–607
        and warranty voids, 433
    vs. desktops, 396–398
laser printers
    overview of, 513–524
    PS vs. PDL driver software, 531
    routine maintenance, 614
    toner disposal, 1185
    troubleshooting, 613–626
laser scanning assembly, 515
Last Known Good Configuration option,
    732, 1111
latency, 350, 351
launcher, 1029
Launcher app, 1030
Layer 2 Logical Link Control Protocol
    (LLCP), 488
layers, OSI model, 266–267
LCD (liquid crystal display) screens
    contrast ratios, 211–212
    cutoff switch, 598
    failed printer, 624
    laptop, 426, 440
    native resolution, 211
    overview of, 185–189
    practice test on, 213
    refresh rate adjustment, 195
    vs. OLED displays, 191
LDAP (Lightweight Directory Access
    Protocol), 304
League of Legends, 230
Leap Motion Controller, 169
least privilege principle, 906
LED (light emitting diode) displays
    backlighting from, 189
    for laptop displays, 429
    vs. OLED displays, 191

leftmost directory group, 884
legacy systems, 973–974
legal issues, 1186–1191
letter quality (LQ), 504
Level 1, 2, and 3 caches, 19
libraries, 791
License Manager, 1188
licenses, software, 1186–1189
lightning, 1169
Lightning connector, 486
Li-ion battery, 425
LILO (LInux LOader), 1117–1118
link local addresses, 321
links, 14
Linksys EA3500 wireless router, 373–379
Linux
    A+ exam topics, 664, 867
    as Android OS base, 1007
    basic commands, 877–888
    best admin. practices, 868–873
    cloud options, 981
    on early mobile devices, 477
    Extended File System (ext), 750–751
    features, 874–877
    on-the-fly defrags, 871
    Network File System, 750
    network operating system, 258
    practice test on, 888–892, 1238, 1264
    print server drivers, 542, 544
    terminal prompt, 1135
    tools, 873–874
    troubleshooting, 1111
    updating, 871–873
liquid cooling systems, 60–61, 586
lithium ion (Li-ion), 1183
Live sign in, 767
load-reduced DIMMs (LRDIMMs), 43
local area networks (LANs)
    defined, 250
    history of, 251–252
    speed of, 254–255
local connector (LC), 284
local network printing, 542–545
Local Policies, 807, 843
Local Security Policy
    Windows 7, 805–807
    Windows Vista, 841–843
local shares, 754, 920

Local Users And Groups tool
    overview of, 739
    Windows 7, 804–805
    Windows Vista, 840–841
location, network, 854
Location Services, 1141
locking doors, 897
locks, cable, 431, 904, 944
log files, 1119
Logical Link Control (LLC), 269
logical partition, 751
logins, user
    Find My Phone app, 932
    security for failed attempts, 921–922
LoJack, 29
Lollipop, 1040
Lookout Labs, 933, 934
loopback addresses, 312
loopback plugs, 638
low-level format, 936
LowSpeed USB, 138
LPR protocol, 544
ls command
    for directory listing access, 884
    overview of, 878, 879
ls /dev command, 879
Lubuntu, 991–995
Lucent Technologies, 284
luggable computers, 185, 395
luma (Y), 152
lumens, 193
lux, the, 193

M

M.2 expansion cards, 417–419
MAC addresses
    barcode readers of, 165
    cloning, 381
    defined, 269, 271
    filtering, 940–941, 942
    resolving conflicts, 633
    security issues, 378
    spoofing attack, 918
MAC Filtering tab, 378
Mac OS
    A+ exam topics, 664, 867

best admin. practices, 868–873
features, 874–877
on-the-fly defrags, 871
network operating system, 258
practice test on, 888–892, 1236, 1264
print server drivers, 542, 544
sync requirements, 1090
tools, 873–874
updates, 871–873
Mac OS X, 549, 876
MacBook Pro, 410, 1057–1067
macro virus, 915
Magellan, 475
magnetometer, 1024
magnets, 1160
mail servers, 970–971
mainframe computers, 251
maintenance station, 506
malicious viruses, 1133
malware
anti-. *See* anti-malware software
defined, 909
infection symptoms, 912–913, 1127–1128
known, 899
removal of, 1136–1137
man-in-the-middle attacks, 909
mantraps, 897
manual email setup, 1078–1080
manual TCP/IP configuration, 961
mark parity, 40
master boot record (MBR), 27, 1112
Master File Table (MFT), 749–750
mats, antistatic, 1157–1158
maximize/minimize buttons, 685, 688
MD command, 722–723
measured service, 979
media access, 141, 157
Media Access Control (MAC) sublayer, 269
media streaming, 237
memes, 1129
memory. *See also* RAM (random access
memory)
A+ exam topics, 3–4
app fails to load, 604
banks, 39–40
characteristics of, 38–43
cooling, 55, 58
CPU choices, 48–49

flash memory, 90–95
inserting/removing, 53, 68
laptop modules, 402–403
mobile cards, 492
packaging, 50–54
practice test on, 65–68, 1212, 1248
printer upgrades, 556–557, 616
replacing laptop, 435–438
resolution requirements, 202
slots, 16–19
troubleshooting
symptoms, 583
Windows diagnostics tool, 810, 846
types of, 43–54
upgrading, 428
video memory sharing, 428
worms, 917
mesh topology, 264–265
Metro UI, 765
metropolitan area network (MAN), 251,
254
Micro ATX motherboards, 7
MicroDIMM, 403
microHDMI connector, 151
microphones
defined, 173
laptop, 430
unauthorized access of, 1141
microSD cards, 90
Microsoft
BitLocker. *See* BitLocker
CIFS protocol, 302
cloud services, 982
Exchange, 1080
OS tools, 708
PixelSense technology, 460
printing to PDF, 527
RRAS (Routing and Remote Access
Service), 342
smart watches, 477
Tablet PC, 462
virtual memory, 18
web servers, 958
Microsoft Assessment and Planning (MAP)
Toolkit, 792
Microsoft Deployment Toolkit (MDT), 773
Microsoft Disk Operating System
(MS-DOS)., 721

Microsoft Surface Pro 3, 463
Microsoft Windows User State Migration
    Tool (USMT), 796
microwaves, 1160
middle directory group, 884
MIDI (Musical Instrument Digital Interface)
    devices, 171–172, 226
midspan PoE devices, 289
MiFi, 1039
MIMO, 335
mini DisplayPort (MDP), 154, 421
Mini PCIe technology, 415–417, 438
minicomputers, 251
mini-DIN 6 connector, 133–134
miniHDMI connector, 151
miniSD cards, 90
Mission Control, 874
mkdir command, 885, 887
MMC (Microsoft Management Console)
    Windows, 739
    Windows 7, 804
    Windows Vista, 840
mobile devices
    A+ exam topics, 455–456
    accessories, 456, 490–492
    characteristics of, 455, 458–460
    connectivity
        Bluetooth, 1056–1069
        cellular data, 1037–1044
        email, 1069–1082
        Wi-Fi, 1045–1056
    email configuration, 1069–1082
    emergency alerts, 1033–1034
    hand-held, 461–477
    operating systems. See mobile operating
        systems
    OS updates, 934
    OS-based games, 990
    passcode locks, 930–931
    payments via, 1035–1036
    policies and procedures, 935
    ports, 455
    practice test on, 492–497, 1227, 1256
    printing from, 545
    remote wipes, 931–934
    security of, 929–934
    service and repair to, 458
    Tablet PC Settings applet, 847

    as technological edge, 457
    touchscreens, 1022–1029
    troubleshooting
        common issues, 1137–1139
        fixes by fail type, 595–607
        security, 1139–1142
        symptoms, 570–571
    virtual assistants, 1030–1033
    wearable, 477–484
    Wi-Fi calling via, 1034–1035
    wired connections, 484–486
    wireless connections, 486–490
Mobile Equipment Identifier (MEID), 1044
mobile hotspots. See hotspots, mobile
mobile operating systems. See also Android
    operating system; iOS operating system
    A+ exam topics, 1003–1005
    Android. See Android operating system
    app downloads, 1014–1022
    iOS. See iOS operating system
    jailbreaking, 1007, 1025
    launchers, 1029–1030
    practice test on, 1092–1096, 1241, 1266
    smart watches, 477, 478
    troubleshooting
        A+ exam topics, 1098
        practice test on, 1142–1146
        symptoms, 1137–1139
        tools, 1139–1142
    updates to, 934, 1042–1043
    Windows Phone, 1012–1013
mobile payment service, 1035–1036
Mobility+ test, 1140
modems
    adapters for, 120
    defined, 123–124, 285
    DSL, 343
    Internet shares, 381
Molex connectors, 101–102
monitors. See display devices
Monochrome Display Adapter (MDA),
    206, 209
motherboards
    A+ exam topics, 3–4
    audio setup, 226
    components of
        BIOS and POST, 24–28
        bus architecture, 9–10

chipsets, 10–12
CMOS/CMOS battery, 29
CPU/processor sockets, 19–22, 32–38
expansion slots, 12–16
firmware, 23
front-/top panel connectors, 29–31
identifying, 5–6
list of common, 8–9
memory slots/cache, 16–19
safety issues, 1151–1155
connectors
fan, 55–57
on- and off-board, 134–135
power, 23, 101
error messages, 580
expansion cards matching, 117
form factors, 6–8
with integrated NIC, 121
laptop, 399–400
practice test on, 63, 65–68, 1212, 1248
riser technology for, 124
supported modules, 44
troubleshooting
fixes by fail type, 582–583
symptom list, 567–568
symptoms, 575–582
motion sensors, 168–169
motion smoothing, 190
mouse, computer
cables, 145–146
click options in Windows, 672
installation, 163
interface, 133–134
laptop
fails and fixes, 600
options, 410–414
ports, 422
overview of, 158–159
safety around, 1155
wireless, 146, 158
Mouse applet, 160
mouse pad, 158
moving files/folders, 918
MSCONFIG
Boot tab in Windows 7, 743
General tab in Windows 7, 742
Services tab in Windows 7, 743
Startup tab in Windows 7, 744
Tools tab in Windows 7, 744
MSCONFIG.EXE, 807, 843, 1120
MSDS (Material Safety Data Sheets), 1177, 1178
Msinfo32 tool, 745
MSTSC (Remote Desktop Connection), 745–748
multiboot installation, 773, 774
multicast IPv6 addresses, 320
multi-channel memory systems, 41–42
multicore architecture, 35
multicore processor, 223
multifactor authentication, 899, 935, 971
multimedia adapters, 119
multimedia input devices, 169–173
multimeters, 635–636, 1164
multimode fiber cable, 281
Multimonitor Taskbars, 766
multipartite virus, 915
multiple-barrier security systems, 897
multithreading, 665
multi-touch technology, 459
multiuser software, 1187
mutation, virus, 916
mutual authentication, 1084
mv command, 886
My Computer icon, 678
MyBackup Pro, 934
MyDLP, 915

N

naked DSL, 346
name, network, 376
NAT (Network Address Translation), 316, 318
National Television System Committee (NTSC) signal, 153
native resolution, 211, 213
navigation, GPS, 473
NBTSTAT command, 647
near field communication (NFC), 487–488, 1036
near letter quality (NLQ), 505
Nessus vulnerability scanner, 871

NET command, 648–651
NET SHARE command, 649–651
NET USE command, 754
netbooks, 396
netboots, 777
NETDOM command, 651
NETSTAT command, 646–647
network, defined, 250
Network Access layer, 301
network adapters, 120, 865
Network Address Translation (NAT),
    379–380
network attached storage (NAS), 958
network discovery, 814, 854
Network File System (NFS), 750
Network icon, 683
network ID, 310
network interface card (NIC)
    characteristics of, 270–272
    configuring, 365–367, 368
    gigabit, 240
    integrated, 121
    printer upgrades to, 557–558
    for proxy firewalls, 902
    troubleshooting, 631–632
    Windows 7 install, 364–365
    Windows 7 properties, 815–816
    wireless, 122
    workstation install, 256
network layer, 267, 268
network locks, 941
network operating system (NOS)
    in client-server model, 260
    as necessary component, 254
    popular systems, 258
network terminator, 348
Network+ test, 249, 317
networks. *See also* wired networks; wireless
    networks
    A+ exam topics, 247–248, 630
    administration of. *See* administration,
        network
    architecture devices, 248
    attacks on unsecured, 369
    auxiliary devices, 288–289
    booting Windows from, 777
    cables and connectors, 247

communication rules, 265–269
components of, 254–261
configuring Windows networking,
    816–817
connectivity devices, 285–288
defined, 250, 664
firewalls. *See* firewalls
hardware, 270–289
installations
    cost of, 360
    how to do, 364–373
    practice test on, 387–391
    pre-planning, 341, 363–364
internal connections, 356–363
laptop connectivity, 409
mobile device
    A+ exam topics, 1003–1005
    Bluetooth, 1056–1069
    cellular data, 1037–1044
    email, 1069–1082
    smart cameras, 477
    test on, 1092–1096, 1240
    troubleshooting, 600–607
    Wi-Fi, 1045–1056
names and passwords, 376
NTFS shares, 917
practice test on, 290–295, 1221, 1252
for printers
    configuring pools, 537
    educating users, 541
    installing/sharing, 542–550
remote OS upgrades from, 773
resource access
    efficient forms of, 258–261
    install plans for, 363
    server-managed, 255
    shared, 257–258
responsibilities, 258
security, 971–973
servers. *See* servers
speed capacities, 254
TCP/IP. *See* TCP/IP (Transmission
    Control Protocol/Internet Protocol)
with thin clients, 235–236
topologies, 143, 261–265
troubleshooting
    A+ exam topics, 567–572

EMI, 1159
fixes by fail type, 630–635
practice test on, 1257
sharing solutions, 1108
software for, 639–652
symptom list, 567
test on, 1230–1232
tools for, 635–639
types of, 248, 250–254
virtualization needs, 987, 988
virus spread via, 913–914
Windows 7 options, 812
Windows Vista options, 852–855
New Low-Profile Extended (NLX)
motherboard, 124
New Technology File System (NTFS)
Advanced Attributes options, 695
directory security by, 903
file permissions, 697
Master File Table (MFT), 749–750
vs. share permissions, 917–919
for wired networks, 943
New York Times, 471
Next Generation Form Factor (NGFF), 417
NFC Data Exchange Format (NDEF), 488
nickel cadmium (NiCd) batteries, 1183
nickel metal hydride (NiMH) batteries, 1183
NICs (network interface cards), 865
Nintendo Wii, 168
Nitro PDF, 526
nitrogen cooling systems, 63
NLE software, 226
no-execute (NX) bit, 38
noise, unusual, 577, 588
nondedicated servers, 255, 956
non-parity memory, 39
Northbridge chipsets, 10
notebook computers, 395
Novell, 251
NSLOOKUP command, 651–652
NTBOOTDD.SYS, 1112
NTBTLOG.TXT, 1112
NTDETECT.COM, 1112, 1113
NTLDR, 1111, 1117
NTOSKRNL.EXE
in troubleshooting boot, 1112
Windows 7, 797
Windows 8, 776

Windows Vista, 836
NTT DoCoMo, 465
NVIDIA
Control Panel, 200, 201
CUDA, 225, 226
liquid cooling system, 232, 233
SLI, 16, 231
video card, 1089

O

Occupational Safety and Health
Administration (OSHA), 1166, 1178
odd parity, 40
odors and smoke, 578
off-board hard disk connectors, 134–135
Office 365, 982
offline file syncing, 849–850
offsite storage, 870
OLED (organic light emitting diode)
displays, 190–192
onboard hard disk connectors, 134–135
onboard NIC, 865
on-demand self-service, 979
OneDrive, 765
onsite storage, 870
open access point, 372
Open Computing Language (OpenCL), 225
open source code, 664
open-source software, 1186
OpenXPS (OXPS), 527
operating systems. *See also systems by name*
A+ exam topics, 660–661, 664
administration of Windows. *See*
administration, Windows
alerts, 579
booting, 776
compatibility
hardware, 222, 665–669
printers, 539–540
defined, 662–663
emulators, 989–990
file storage, 1118
guest/host virtualization use, 227–228
identifying, 678
installing multiple, 774
locked up, 1130

mobile. *See* mobile operating systems
network client software, 256
for networks. *See* network operating
    system (NOS)
practice test on, 1232, 1257
security settings, 915–921
server vs. workstation, 257
supporting Cloud Print, 549
system requirements, 665–669
terms and concepts, 664–665
for thin clients, 236
troubleshooting
    symptoms, 1101, 1110–1118
    test on, 1143, 1243, 1267
    tools for, 1118–1126
update failures, 1131
variables, 718–719
virtual, 698, 985–986
operational procedures
A+ exam topics, 1147–1149
environmental control, 1170–1186
legal issues, 1186–1191
practice test on, 1204–1209, 1244, 1267
professionalism, 1191–1203
for safety, 1150–1170
optical storage drives
forms of, 79–85
for laptops, 406
practice test on, 108
troubleshooting, 593
USB optical drives, 420
option ROMs, 26
orientation rotation, 427
orthogonal frequency division multiplexing
    (OFDM), 338
OS X operating system, 1009
OS X Yosemite, 1011
OSI (Open Systems Interconnection) model
overview of, 266–268
vs. DOD model, 300
Outlook, 1070
output devices
input/output devices, 175–177
list of, 173–175
practice test on, 178–182
overclocking, 575
overwriting drives, 937
ozone, 518, 555

P

packet filter firewalls, 901
page printers, 513–518
page-description language (PDL), 529–531
PAGEFILE.SYS, 18
paging files, 18
Palm, Inc., 477
paper
    feed sensors, 510
    feeder, 508, 509
    jams
        dot-matrix, 609
        inkjet, 612
        laser printer, 616–617
    quality of, 551
    shredding, 898
    transport assembly, 516
    tray
        inkjet, 509, 510
        upgrades, 558–559
Parallel ATA (PATA), 86, 593
parallel communications, 9
parallel computer systems, 9
parallel print interface, 528
parity checking, 39–40
partitions, 751, 776
parts bag, antistatic, 1158
passcode locks, 930–931
passive cooling, 58, 61–63
passive hubs, 286
passive matrix OLED (PMOLED) displays,
    191
passive-matrix LCD screens, 187–188
Password Policy, 806, 842
passwords
    attacks on, 908–909
    changing default, 940, 942
    Keychain, 875
    mobile screen lock, 930
    network, 376
    requiring, 921
    screensaver, 914
    securing, 898
    setting system defaults, 806
    strong, 903, 904, 920–921
    for user authentication, 755
patch cable, 279, 631

patch management
  Linux and Mac OS, 871
  and social engineering attacks, 907–908
  user education on, 904
patch panels, 286
pathnames, absolute and relative, 883
paths, file, 692
pay-as-you-go-services, 979
payments
  credit card readers, 491
  mobile options, 1035
  on NFC, 488
Pb signal, 152–153
PCI Express (PCIe) expansion slots, 14–15,
  118
PCI-Extended (PCI-X) expansion slots, 14
PCMCIA (Personal Computer Memory Card
  International Association), 414
PDF files, 526
PDPs (plasma display panels), 189–190
peer-to-peer network, 259–260, 261
Peltier cooling elements, 62
Pen And Input Devices applet, 848
Pentium processors
  heat sinks for, 19
  in laptops, 401
  Pentium M chip, 401
performance
  cache as improving, 19
  Computer Management tool, 740
  faulty. *See* troubleshooting
  laptop vs. desktop, 397
  network interface card, 270
  optimizing hard disk, 753–754
  Performance Monitor tool, 740–741
  Performance tab, 718
  slow mobile device, 604, 1138
  slow PC, 1116, 1130
  uncoupling drives for, 226
  virus symptoms and, 1127
Peripheral Component Interconnect (PCI)
  expansion slots, 13
peripheral devices. *See also device by name*
  A+ exam topics, 113–116
  booting Windows from, 776
  data destruction methods, 936
  interfaces for, 134
  port authentication, 941

practice test on, 178–182, 1215, 1249
  types of, 115–116
permissions, user, 921
persistence technology, 29
personal area network (PAN), 251, 253–254
personal assistant, 1030–1033
personal computers (PCs). *See also* desktop
    computers
  components of, 5
  custom configurations. *See* custom PC
    configurations
  home theater PCs, 232–235
  laptop vs. desktop, 396–398
  locked up, 1130
  networking history, 251
  peripheral interfaces, 134
  portability of, 395
  restart to troubleshoot, 1107
  syncing Apple devices to, 1083
  toolkit, 1162
  un-networked, 249–250
personalization, Desktop, 673
phablets, 469–471
phage virus, 916
pharming, 1128
phase-change cooling, 62
Philips, 363
phishing, 907, 910–911
phone communications, 345
photography, digital, 172
photosensitive laser printer drum, 514
Photosmart Plus, 545
physical layer, 268
physical layer (OSI model), 267
physical security, 896–889
pickup rollers, 508, 509
pickup stepper motor, 508
piconet, 253, 361
piezoelectric effect, 36
PII (personally identifiable information),
    1189
pin grid array (PGA) for CPUs, 20, 33
PING command, 632, 640–641
ping of death, 641
ping time, 351
pinwheel, 1111
piracy, media, 157, 833
pixel addressing, 187

pixels
   aspect ratio of, 209
   "dead," 594
   resolution and video memory, 202
plasma displays, 189–190
plastics, laptop, 398
Platform as a Service (PaaS), 976
platters, hard drive, 74, 77
plenum cable, 370
Plug and Play system
   expansion card recognition, 119, 126
   safe device removal, 717
   storage device recognition, 95, 96
   Universal Plug and Play, 380
   USB technology as, 138
point sticks, 413–414
pointer drift, 600
pointing devices, 410–414
point-to-multipoint connections, 351
point-to-point infrared use, 362
Point-to-Point Protocol (PPP), 342
policies
   mobile devices, 935
   troubleshooting and, 1100
polymorphic viruses, 916
polyvinyl chloride (PVC), 272
POP (Post Office Protocol)
   function of, 1078, 1079
   POP3, 304, 305
   at Process Layer, 301
pop-ups, 1128
Port Address Translation (PAT), 318, 379
port forwarding, 380, 383
port numbers, 306, 307
port replicators, 422, 424
portable computers, 395, 396
portable document scanner, 165
ports
   assignment of, 383
   authentication of, 941
   common, 135–136
   defined, 126
   disabling, 943
   secure mail, 1079
   triggering, 383
POST (power-on self-test) routine
   boot process, 1112
   overview of, 26–28

   troubleshooting via, 579–580
POST cards, 580
PostScript, 530
POTS (plain old telephone service), 342
power
   to CMOS memory chip, 28
   density, 424
   electrical fire, 1170
   ensuring it is on, 1102, 1106
   hazards. *See* electrocution
   level controls, 941
   lights, 29–30
   maintaining, 1171–1173
   -saving states, 748–749
power adapters, 426
power buttons, 29–30
power circuits, 511
power connectors
   defined, 23
   for fans, 55–57
   types of, 100–106
Power Options applet, 720
Power over Ethernet (PoE) technology
   for ceiling installations, 372
   PoE injectors, 289
   for Windows 7 networks, 816
power strips, 1171
power supplies
   A+ exam topics, 71
   AC adapters as, 107–108
   anti-static strap hazards, 1157
   exhaust fans, 54
   laptop, 424–427
   PoE technology, 289
   power connectors, 100–106, 108
   practice test on, 109–112, 1214, 1249
   printer, 532, 613
   replacing, 106–107, 108
   safety around, 99, 1151–1153
   troubleshooting
      fixes by fail type, 584–587
      laptop/mobile device, 596–598
      laser printer, 614–615
      odors and smoke, 578
      symptoms, 567–568, 575–582
      visible damage, 579
   USB 2.0 and 3.0, 141–142
   voltage ratings, 99–100

Power User account, 916
PowerShell, 766
Pr signal, 152–153
Precise Positioning Service (PPS), 474
preemptive multitasking, 665
presentation layer, 267, 268
pre-VGA standards, 205
PRI (Product Release Instruction) updates, 1043
prices
    DSL discounts, 345–346
    Internet comparisons, 355
    laptop vs. desktop, 396
    legacy system replacement, 974
    mobile hotspot, 1039
    networking cable, 284, 349
    virtualization to reduce, 985, 986
primary (extended) partition, 751
primary rate interface (PRI), 348
print buffer, 512
print head
    alignment, 611
    defined, 503
    in dot-matrix printers, 505
    in inkjet printers, 506
Print Management, 809–810, 845
print queue, 626–628
print servers
    AirPrint, 542
    defined, 255
    functions of, 959–960
    security issues, 550
print sharing, 240
print spooler, 629–630
printed circuit boards (PCB), 5–6
printer banks, 363
Printer Command Language (PCL), 530
printer drivers, troubleshooting, 607
Printer Properties dialog, 534–538
printers
    A+ exam topics, 500–501
    cloud printing, 546–550
    control circuits, 511
    controller assembly, 518
    daisy-wheel, 503–504
    defined, 502
    dot-matrix, 504–505
    environmental issues, 555–556
    inkjet, 505–513

    installing local, 532–541
    installing networked, 542–550
    interfaces
        components, 527–529
        overview of, 527–5332
        software, 529–532
    laser, 513–518
    maintenance how-to, 550–556
    memory card slots, 91–92
    practice test on, 560–565, 1229, 1256
    safety around, 1154
    technology options, 500
    thermal, 524
    troubleshooting
        dot-matrix, 608–609
        garbage prints, 531, 532, 622
        inkjet, 610–613
        install issues, 607
        job managment, 626–630
        laser, 613–626
        symptoms, 571–572
    upgrading, 550, 556–559
    virtual, 525–527
Printers applet, 852–853
privacy
    filters, 188
    laws, 1201–1202
    public printer issues, 550
    smart headset invasions, 484
    upholding, 1199
private clouds, 978
private IP addresses, 316–318, 379–380
private side, firewall, 288, 382
PRL (Preferred Roaming List) updates, 1043
problem identification, 1101–1104
Problem Report Settings, 804
Problem Reports And Solutions applet, 850–851
procedures
    mobile devices, 935
    troubleshooting and, 1100
process identification (PID), 882
Process/Application layer, 301–306
processing, EP print, 518, 614
processor sockets
    chip creep, 577
    for CPUs, 19–22
    matching components, 36

processors
 A+ exam topics, 3–4
 laptop, 400–401
 multicore processors
  for graphic and CAD/CAM
    design, 223
  for virtualization work, 228
 practice test on, 1212–1213, 1248
 in-printer, 530
 removing/replacing laptop, 443–444
 throttling, 401
product keys, 1187
professionalism, 1191–1203
Program and Features applet,
  Windows 7, 819
program windows, 685
programmable ROM (PROM), 50
programs. *See* applications
prohibited content, 1189
projection systems, 192–194, 569
propagation delay, 350, 351
proprietary docking ports, 424
proprietary power connectors, 105
protective covers, 491
proxy firewalls, 901–902
proxy servers, 968–969
ps ax command, 881, 882
PS/2 cables, 145–146
PS/2 ports
 for laptops, 422
 overview of, 133–134
 photo of, 135–136
PS/2-to-USB adapter, 147
public clouds, 978
public IP addresses, 316–318, 379–380
public key encryption, 604–606
public key infrastructure (PKI), 1132
public side, firewall, 288, 382
Public Switched Telephone Network
  (PSTN), 120
punch-down tools, 638
punctuality, 1196–1197
PXE-initiated boot, 773, 797

Q

q command, 881
Quad processors, 35

Quad XGA (QXGA), 209, 210
Qualcomm, 352
Quality of Service (QoS) strategy
 function of, 384–385
 Windows 7, 816
 Windows Vista, 854, 855
quarantines, 1128, 1136
quick format, 751
Quick Launch, 675
Quick Response (QR) codes, 166
QWERTY layout, 161

R

radar interference, 335
radio firmware, 1042
RADIUS servers, 378, 970
RAID (Redundant Array of Independent
  Disks)
 creating RAID volumes, 752
 hardware types, 87–88
 for home servers, 241
 to increase drive capacity, 227
 troubleshooting, 568, 591–593
RAID 0 (disk striping)
 creating RAID volumes, 752
 defined, 87–88
 to increase drive capacity, 227
 points of failure, 592
RAID 1 (disk mirroring), 88, 592, 752
RAID 10 (RAID 1+0), 88, 593
RAID 5, 88, 593, 752
RAID 6, 88
RAM (random access memory). *See also*
  memory
 characteristics of, 38–43
 component matching, 36
 CPU choices, 48–49
 for gaming, 231
 maximizing, 224, 228–229
 MicroDIMM, 403
 practice test on, 65–68
 resolution requirements, 202
 slots, 16–19
 for thick clients, 222
 troubleshooting, 567, 575–582
 virtualization needs, 987–988

ransomware, 918
rapid elasticity, 979
RAS (Remote Access Service), 342
Raster Image Processor (RIP), 518
raster line, 518
rasterizing, 518
RAW (Standard TCP/IP Port Monitor)
 protocol, 544
RC-5 protocol, 363
RCA cables, 144
RCA jacks, 132
RCA plugs, 132
RCO jacks, 119
RD command, 722–723
RDP (Remote Desktop Protocol), 305
read/write heads, 74
ReadyBoost
 Windows 7, 789, 791
 Windows Vista, 831
ReadyDrive, 791
real-time operating systems (RTOSs), 1042,
 1043
rear exhaust fan, 54
rear projection systems, 192
rear stereo channel, 137
rebooting
 for software issues, 1108, 1115
 as universal solution, 1104, 1107, 1130
receivers, GPS, 475
Recent Items submenu, 679
recordable storage discs, 82–85
recovery partition, 774, 776
Recycle Bin, 684–685
recycling
 best practices, 936
 computer equipment, 1181–1185
 ink and toner, 553, 1185
Red Hat, 877
redirection of browsers, 1128
redundancy, 236
refresh rate
 adjusting, 195–199
 for plasma displays, 190
 and soap-opera effect, 190
refreshing OS installations, 774
Region And Language Options, 713–714
registered ports, 307
Registry, Windows, 731–732

Registry Edit, 1123–1124
REGSVR32 tool, 1123
reinstalling Windows, 1126
remote controls, 363
remote data wipes, 931–934
Remote Desktop Connection (MSTSC),
 745–748
Remote Desktop Protocol (RDP), 302
Remote Desktop Web Access, 810–811
Remote Disk, 877
Remote tab, 720
RemoteApp, 810–811
removable storage devices, 89
repairs
 discs for, 1119–1120
 of OS installs, 774
 tools for, 432, 433, 1162
 Windows, 1126
repeaters, 285
repetitive strain injuries (RSIs), 169
repurposing, best practices, 936
Research In Motion (RIM), 465, 468–469
reset button, 30
Reset CMOS jumper, 24
resistive interfaces, 175
resistive touchscreens, 1026
resolutions
 adjusting display, 199–202
 advanced video, 207–211
 graphic adapter for special, 226
 and memory size, 205
 native resolution, 211
 practice test on, 213
resource access
 acceptable use policies, 905
 and antenna placement, 941
 cloud pooling for, 979
 QoS strategy to aid, 385
 via Bluetooth, 1037
 via operating systems, 662–663
resource pooling, 979
respect, 1199–1200
responsiveness issues, 603–607
restarting computers, 1107
restores. *See also* System Restore
 from backups, 869
 Linux/Mac OS tools, 873
 mobile security, 1141

of OS installs, 774
restore points, 690–691, 732
of windows, 688
retrovirus, 916
RF Explorer, 639
RF power values, 941
RFI (radio frequency interference), 1159
RFID (Radio Frequency Identification)
    badges, 899
RGB separation, 151–152
ribbon, inked, 503, 505, 552
right-clicking, 159
rightmost directory group, 884
ring topology, 262–263
riser cards, 124–125
RJ (registered jack) connector, 128, 278
RJ-11 connectors, 128, 278
RJ-45 connectors, 128, 278
rm command, 886–887
rmdir command, 887
roaming, data, 1051
ROBOCOPY command, 726
ROM (read-only memory), 43, 50
ROM BIOS chip, 24
root, becoming, 881, 883
root directory, 692, 749
root file access, 1025
root servers, 966–967
rootkits, 910
routers
    on the DSL line, 344
    function of, 287–288
    ping blocks on, 641
    shared Internet connections, 381
    wireless
        configuring, 373–380, 385–386
        installs, 371–373, 385–386
routing tables, 287
RSA tokens, 899, 971
Run command, 679–680

S

Safe Mode boot, 1111, 1116, 1124–1125
Safely Remove Hardware, 95, 447
safety. *See also* electrocution
    accidents, 1168–1170
    burns from fried parts, 585
    hardware disposal, 1170, 1177–1186
    hazards, 1151–1161
    with power supplies, 99
    practice test on, 1204–1209
    procedures, 1150–1170
    via attentiveness, 1167
    workplace, 1161–1170
Samsung
    Galaxy Note, 470
    Gear watch, 477
    micro USB chargers, 485
    NX500 camera, 476
sanitation, hard drive, 936–937
SATA (serial ATA) drives
    for graphic design, 226
    headers, 73, 135
    overview of, 85, 86–87
    power connectors, 105–106
    sanitation of, 937
SATA 1.5Gbps, 86
SATA 3Gbps, 86
SATA 6Gbps, 86
satellite Internet, 350–352
satellites, GPS, 473
satisfaction, customer, 1194–1195
scalability, 976
Scalable Link Interface (SLI), 16, 231
scan line, 518
scanners, 163–165
scatternets, 254
scheduled backups, 868–869
scientific method, 1105
screen calibration, 1026–1029
screen locks, 930–931
screen orientation, 1023
Screen Saver tab, 673, 674
Screen Sharing utility, 874
screens, laptop, 429
screensaver passwords, 914
screwdrivers, 433, 1163
screws, stripping, 433, 1163
Scythe Ninja, 61
SDR SDRAM, 45
sealing, 26
Search menu, 679, 790
secondary storage, 460
secret self-test, 623

sectors, hard drive, 74, 75
Secure Boot, 26
Secure Digital (SD) cards, 90
Secure Sockets Layer (SSL), 1079
security
   A+ exam topics, 893–895
   Apple Pay, 488
   attacks
      common threats, 907–920
      on iOS, 489
      NAT hacks, 318
      on NFC networks, 488
      on unsecured networks, 369
      via public Wi-Fi, 409
   authentication server, 971
   of backups, 869
   BIOS system role in, 26
   cable locks, 431–432
   on the cloud, 976
   data disposal methods, 935–939
   in data transport, 871
   digital preventions, 899–905
   document, 898
   email filtering, 906
   false alerts, 1129
   file permissions, 697
   firewalls. *See* firewalls
   home network, 372
   hotspot, 1039
   infrared network, 362
   Internet appliances for, 971–973
   least privilege principle, 906
   Linux/Mac OS updates, 873
   management of, 255
   mobile device, 929–934
   patch management, 871
   persistence technology, 29
   physical preventions, 896–889
   practice test, 945–950, 1239, 1264
   public printers, 550
   quarantines, 1128
   risks
      Google Glass, 484
      outdated firmware, 376
      reducing user, 905, 906
      SSID broadcasts, 634, 940
      SSO passwords, 755
      unsecured networks, 369

      UPnP, 380
   setting system defaults, 805–807
   troubleshooting
      A+ exam topics, 1097
      fix tools, 1132–1136
      malware removal, 1136–1137
      practice test on, 1142–1146, 1243–1244, 1267
      symptoms, 1127–1132
   trust issues in, 911
   user education on, 905
   via HTTPS, 303–304
   via webcam use, 170
   virtualization needs, 990
   Windows settings, 915–921
   in wired networks, 358
   wireless network
      protocols, 339–340, 387
      risks, 359, 939
   for workstations, 920–923
Security Center
   as Action Center, 720, 803
   Windows Vista, 831, 840, 860
Security Options, 807, 843
Security+ test, 896
Selective Availability (SA), 474
self-grounding, 1158–1159
self-tests, 622–623
sensitive data, 1189–1191
separator pads, 508, 509, 612
serial print interface, 528
Server Message Block (SMB), 302
server-based networks, 261
servers
   A+ exam topics, 954
   antivirus software for, 914
   data intercept attacks, 909
   in email configuration, 1079–1080
   home server PCs, 236–241
   management tips, 955
   network, 255–256, 363
   practice test on, 995–1001
   print servers, 542
   roles/types of, 956–971
   for thin clients, 235–236
   user authentication, 755
   vs. workstations, 257
   water safety for, 1160

service call tips, 1191–1202
service packs, 794
Services tool, 740
service-set identifier (SSID), 332
SERVICES.MSC, 740
session layer (OSI model), 267
set-top box (STB), 177
SFC command, 726–727, 1118–1119
SFTP (Secure File Transfer Protocol), 305
shadow copies, 869
Shadow Copy Service, 789, 831
Shared Folders tool, 739
ShareNet, 251
shares
    administrative vs. local, 754
    NTFS, 917–919
    printer, 537–539
    for wired networks, 943
shareware, 1187
shell commands (Linux), 874, 878
shell program, 664
shielded twisted-pair (STP), 277
shielding, 140
shortcuts, Windows, 680
shoulder surfing, 911
Show Hidden Files/Folders, 715–716
shredders, drive, 937
Shred-it, 938
Shut Down command, 680
SHUTDOWN command, 722
shutdown state, 749, 1113–1114
side stereo channel, 137
Sidebar
    Windows 7, 788
    Windows Vista, 830, 859–860
signal (D) channel, 348
signal modulation techniques, 337–338
signature files, 916
signatures, malicious, 972
Simple NDEF Exchange Protocol (SNEP),
    488
Simple Service Discovery Protocol, 380
simultaneous multithreading (SMT), 33
Single Connector Attachment (SCA), 95
single point of failure, 262–263
single sign-on (SSO), 754–755, 920
single user software, 1187
single-channel memory, 41, 42

single-mode fiber (SMF) cable, 281
single-sided memory, 41
Siri, 1030–1031
site license, 258
64-bit operating system, 665
64-bit processors, 37, 786, 830
Skandier, Toby, 194
slate mode, 462
sleep modes, 401
sleep state, 748
SLI, 16, 231
slowdown modes, 401
S.M.A.R.T (Self-Monitoring, Analysis, and
    Reporting Technology), 589–591
smart cameras, 476–477
smart cards
    overview of, 899
    readers, 169–170, 420
smart TV, 176–177
smart watches, 477–479
smartphones
    barcode scanning, 165–166
    characteristics of, 463–469
    leading OS platform, 1011–1012
    multiple OSs for, 1042
    as portable computers, 395
    as security risk, 905
    Wi-Fi calling, 1034
SMB (Server Message Block), 305
S/MIME settings, 604–606, 1081–1082
smoke, 578
smoking, 1174
SMTP (Simple Mail Transfer Protocol), 301,
    305, 1078
smurf attacks, 903
snap tool, 790
snapshot, system, 1135
sneakernet, 250
SNMP (Simple Network Management
    Protocol), 305–306
soap-opera effect (SOE), 190
social engineering
    defined, 907–908
    phishing as, 910–911
    physical barriers to, 897
sockets. *See* processor sockets
SODIMM (small outline DIMM)
    defined, 17

for laptops, 402–403, 438
overview of, 53–54
software. *See also* operating systems
acceptable use policies, 905
custom configurations, 221
development, 227, 1042
for digital security, 899–905
firewalls, 288, 382, 900–903
hypervisor, 986–987
licenses, 1186–1189
malware, 909
for network clients, 256
NLE, 226
OS compatibility with, 222
Print function, 512–513
printer interface, 529–532
rootkits, 910
sound, 137
source code, 1013
sync requirements, 1089–1092
as tech issue source, 1104
troubleshooting
for hard drives, 588
for printers, 607
rebooting for, 1115
S.M.A.R.T, 589–591
trusted sources, 911
Software Asset Management, 1188
SOHO wired networks, 942–945
SOHO wireless networks
A+ exam topics, 329–330
configuring, 373–381
firewalls, 382–384
installing, 363–373
internal connections, 356–363
Internet connections, 341–356
practice test on, 387–391, 1224, 1254
routers, 385–386
security for, 939–942
solenoid, 503
solid-state drives (SSDs)
booting Windows from, 777
laptop, 404–405
for mobile devices, 460
overview of, 77–79
solid-state hybrid drives (SSHD), 78–79
Solo processors, 35
solution tests, 1105–1107

sound card jacks, 136–137
sound cards, 119
source code, 664, 1013
Southbridge chipsets, 11–12
space parity, 40
spam, 1131
spambots, 920
S/PDIF (Sony/Philips Digital Interface)
for gaming, 232
for home theater PCs, 234
implementing, 133
transmission quality, 119
speakers
for mobile devices, 490
troubleshooting, 606, 1138
spear phishing, 911
speed, processor, 36
splitter, coax, 275
spoofing attack, 918–919
spooler, print, 629–630
sports, watching, 190
Spotlight, 875
Sprint, 1034
spyware, 903, 911–912
square connector, 283
SRAM (static random access memory), 43, 49
SSH (Secure Shell), 306
SSID (service-set identifier)
configuring, 373, 374, 376
disabling broadcast, 940
not found, 634
security issues, 339, 940
SST certification, 304
stabilizer bar, 508
standard formatting, 936
Standard HDMI cables, 149
standard peripheral power (Molex)
connectors, 101–102
standard permissions, 697
Standard Positioning Service (SPS), 474
standard SSDs (solid state drives), 77–78
standard thick client, 222
star topology
to network peripherals, 143
overview of, 262–263
pros and cons, 265
Start menu
overview of, 676–678

as Taskbar item, 674
   Windows 8/8.1, 766, 768
Startup And Recovery options, 719
STAT column, 882
stateful inspection firewalls, 902
static charge, 1107
static IP addressing, 315
static shock, 1155–1159
static-charge eliminator strip, 517, 617
status light indicators, 578, 596
stealth virus, 916–917
stepper motor
   defined, 507
   problems, 609, 612
stereo minijacks, 137
storage area network (SAN), 958
storage devices
   A+ exam topics, 71
   for backups, 869–870
   basic and dynamic drives, 751
   the cloud, 765, 980–982, 1087
   configuring/installing/removing, 95–98,
      108
   drive interfaces and RAID, 85, 87–88
   file servers as, 958–959
   flash memory, 90–95
   laptop, 403–405
   mobile SSDs, 460
   optical, 79–85
   preparing disks for storage, 749–752
   recognition of, 95
   removable, 89
   SATA drives, 86–87
   solid-state drives, 77–79
   test on, 109–112, 1214, 1249
   troubleshooting, 588–593
straight-tip fiber-optic connectors, 283
streaming
   home server, 237–240
   USB supports, 141
Stuxnet, 919
su - command, 881
submarining, 188
subnet masks, 310, 316, 815
subscriber connector (SC), 283
subscriber identity module (SIM), 1043
subwoofer channel, 137
Super AMOLED displays, 192

Super AMOLED Plus displays, 192
Super VGA (SVGA), 207–208, 210
Super XGA (SXGA), 210
SuperSpeed USB 3.0, 130, 138, 139
supervisor password, 26
surge protectors, 1171
surround sound setup, 136–137
SuSE, 877
swap files, 18
switches, 263, 287
swollen battery, 597–598
SXGA+, 210
Symantec's AntiVirus Research Center
      (SARC), 1133
symmetric DSL (SDSL), 344
symmetric multiprocessing (SMP), 33
synchronization
   Android device, 1088–1089
   Apple device, 1083–1087
   defined, 1082
   software requirements, 1089–1092
Synchronous DRAM (SDRAM), 45
syncing devices, 484, 1004–1005
System applet, 716–720
system boards. *See* motherboards
System Configuration tool
   Windows 7, 807–808
   Windows Vista, 843–844
system files, 920
system partition, 776
System Protection tab, 720
System Recovery Options, 722, 1119
System Restore
   creating restore points, 690–691
   post-infection, 1135
   Windows 7, 798–799
   Windows Vista, 837–838, 860
System Startup, 719
system tray, 674

T

T1 connections, 254
Tablet PC Settings applet, 847
tablets
   characteristics of, 461–463
   leading OS platform, 1011–1012

as portable computers, 395
vs. e-readers, 472–473
TACACS+, 970
tailgating, 897
tape backup devices, 89
Task Manager, 734–739
Task Scheduler tool, 741–742
Taskbar
overview of, 674–676
Windows 7, 790
TASKKILL command, 721
TASKLIST command, 722
TCP printing, 543–544
TCP/IP (Transmission Control Protocol/
Internet Protocol)
A+ exam topics, 297–298
APIPA, 318–319
configuration options, 961
email protocols, 1078–1080
hijacking, 910
HTTP of, 957
IP addressing, 308–322
properties and protocols, 298
structure of, 300–308
test on, 323–328, 1224, 1254
troubleshooting, 319
TCP/IPv4, 366, 367
technology, progress of, 456, 975
Telnet, 306
TEMP variables, 719
temperatures, and BIOS shutdown, 25
Temporal Key Integrity Protocol (TKIP), 340
10Base2, 273
10Base5, 273
terminal adapters, 348
terminal prompt, 1135
Terminal utility, 874
test page printing, 539, 626, 630
tethering, 354, 490, 1038–1039
text mode, 206
thermal paste, 59–60
thermal printers, 524
thermoelectric coolers (TECs), 62
thick clients, 222
thicknet coax, 274
thin clients, 235–236
ThinkPads, 413
thinnet coax, 274

32-bit flat mode, 1112
32-bit operating system, 665
32-bit processors
defined, 37
Windows 7 for, 786
Windows Vista for, 830
threats, security, 907–920
3D model production, 224
3G mobile technology, 352
throttling
in desktops, 35
in laptops, 401
Thunderbolt cards
eSATA similarity, 227
for input/output, 120
interface for, 154, 155–156
for laptops, 421
Thunderbolt-to-DVI converter, 156
TIME column, 882
Time Machine, 873
time zone changes, 712
T-Mobile, 1034
token, network, 269
Token Ring, 263
tokens, security, 899
TomTom, 475
toner. *See also* cartridges, printer
cartridge, 514, 618
cleaning up, 1176
for laser printers, 513
probes, 636
recycling laser, 523, 1185
replacing, 552, 553
shipping printers without, 515
tools
laptop disassembly, 432, 433
safety via proper, 1162–1164
top panel, 29–30
topology, networking
forms of, 143, 261–265
practice test on, 295
Torx drivers, 433, 938
Toshiba, 133
TOSLINK interface, 133
TouchFLO, 460
touchpads, 159–161, 411–413
touchscreens
iPhone, 1009

nonresponsive, 604
overview of, 175, 414
resistive and capacitive, 462
sensor calibration, 1022–1029
software interfaces, 459–460
troubleshooting, 1138
Windows 7, 791
TRACERT (trace route) command, 645
trackballs, 410
tracks, hard drive, 74, 75
tractor feed, 503
Tracy, Dick, 477
trailing dot, 966
transfer corona assembly, 516–517, 619
transferring, EP print, 521–522, 614
transformers, 511
transport layer (OSI model), 267, 268
Transport Security Layer (TSL), 1079
tray, printer, 558–559
tree topology, 143–144
triangulation, 474
trip prevention, 1165, 1166
triple-channel memory, 41
Trojan horses, 304, 918
troubleshooting. *See also specific component by name*
    A+ exam topics, 1097
    documenting fixes, 1109–1110
    establishing theory, 1105–1107
    grounding during, 1107
    identifying problems, 1101–1104
    mobile devices, 1137–1139
    plan of action, 1107–1109
    practice test on, 652–658, 1142–1146
    road maps for, 434
    security
        mobile device, 1139–1142
        symptoms, 1126–1137
        test on, 1243–1244, 1267
    testing function, 1109
    tips for effective, 573–574
    tools, 1162–1164
    via sequential changes, 1110
Troubleshooting applet, 810–811
Trusted Platform Module (TPM), 26, 817
tunneling, VPN, 907
TV, 349, 363
TV tuner cards, 120, 235

TWAIN drives, 163
twisted nematic (TN) screens, 185–186, 429
twisted-pair cables, 276–280
Type 1 hypervisor, 986, 988
Type 2 hypervisor, 986, 987
Type A USB connector, 138
Type A USB converter, 142
Type B HDMI interface, 151
Type B USB connector, 138
Type B USB converter, 142
Type C HDMI interface, 151
Type D HDMI interface, 151

U

ubiquitous access, 979
Ubuntu, 877, 878
UDP (User Datagram Protocol), 301, 903
UEFI (Unified Extensible Firmware
    Interface), 24, 1118
UHD 4K, 210
Ultra XGA (UXGA), 209
unattended installation, 773
unbuffered (unregistered) memory modules
    (UDIMMs), 42–43
unicast IPv6 addresses, 320
Unicode, 713
unified threat management (UTM), 972–973
UNII (Unlicensed National Information
    Infrastructure), 336
uninstalling Windows, 1126
United States Department of Defense (DOD),
    473, 474
Universal Plug and Play (UPnP), 380
Universal Product Code (UPC) barcodes, 166
UNIX, 1009, 1025, 1135
unshielded twisted-pair (UTP), 277
Upgrade Assistant (Upgrade Advisor), 791–
    792, 796
upgrading
    options for, 791
    vs. clean installs, 769–770, 778
    to Windows 7, 792–796
    Windows 7, 796–797
up-plugging, 16
UPS (uninterruptible power supply),
    1172–1173

USB (Universal Serial Bus) cables, 137–142
USB (Universal Serial Bus) ports
   characteristics of, 129
   commonality of, 135
   defined, 32–33
   for laptops, 419–420
   for printer interface, 528
   as security risk, 905
USB 2.0
   cable lengths, 140
   chart of USB speeds, 138
   differences from 3.0, 140–142
   ports, 130
USB 3.0
   cable lengths, 140
   chart of USB speeds, 138
   differences from 2.0, 140–142
   interface color coding, 139
   ports, 130
USB 3.1, 227
USB A to B converters, 142
USB card readers, 93, 420
USB cards, 120
USB devices
   debugging, 1092
   flash drives, 90, 94
   recovery drives, 775
   safe removal of, 446, 447
   to sync mobile devices, 485
   USB printer installation, 540–541
USB hubs, 139–140
USB Micro-B connector, 139
USB NIC, 270
USB optical drives, 420
USB-to-Ethernet adapters, 121, 122
use policies, 905
User Account Control
   settings, 1116
   Windows 7, 788, 817–818
   Windows Vista, 831–832, 857–858
User Accounts applet, Windows 7, 818
User Datagram Protocol (UDP), 903
user password, 26
User Rights Agreement, 807
User Rights Assignment, 843
User State Migration Tool (USMT), 796, 835
usernames, 940, 942

users
   as aid in problem ID, 1101–1103
   authenticating
     for security, 903
     server for, 970–971
     single sign-ons, 754–755, 920
   Control Panel variables, 718–719
   data intercept attacks, 909
   default accounts for, 916–917
   errors by, 1107, 1108
   failed login attempts, 914
   groups and, 804–805, 840–841
   least privilege principle, 906, 921
   migrating settings, 796, 835
   multiple networked, 252
   profiles, 719
   as security risks, 920
   as tech issue source, 1101
   training
     on printers, 540, 541
     in security, 905, 908, 910, 943
     in shutdowns, 1113
USMT (User State Migration Tool), 796, 835
utilities
   Control Panel, 709–721
   icons for, 680–685
   minimizing, 688
UTP cables, 277

V

vacuum, computer, 1175
vampire taps, 274
variable length subnet masking (VLSM), 317
vehicle/iPhone Bluetooth setups, 1067–1069
vender-specific software, 1013
Verizon, 349, 1039
Verizon Wireless MiFi device, 1039
very high bit-rate DSL (VDSL), 344, 345
VGA interface, 185
VGA mode, 594
VGA standards
   characteristics of, 206–207
   DVI as superior to, 148
   pre- and post-, 205
   replacing, 146
   technology comparison chart, 210

VGA/USB switch, 176
video adjustments, 408
video capture devices, 172
video cards
    chipset fan, 55
    defined, 118
    laptop, 427–428
    troubleshooting
        identifying issues, 593–595
        laptop/mobile device, 598–599
        symptoms, 569
    upgrading laptop, 439–440
    video capture cards, 120
video display cables, 146–157
video display unit (VDU), 184
Video Electronics Standards Association
    (VESA), 154, 421
video enhancements
    for audio/video editing, 225
    for gaming, 231
    for graphic and CAD/CAM design, 224
    for home theater PCs, 234
video gaming console, 491
video jacks, 132–133
video memory, 202, 428
video standards
    non-adjustable characteristics, 211–212
    post-VGA and advanced, 207–211
    pre-VGA and VGA, 205–207
virtual assistant, 1030–1033
virtual desktop interface (VDI), 698, 988
virtual FAT (VFAT), 750
virtual machine manager (VMM),
    986–987
virtual machines (VM)
    purpose of, 985–986
    RAM required for, 229
    resources for, 227–228
    updates to, 698
virtual memory, 18, 584
virtual NIC, 988–989
virtual printers, 525–527
virtual private networks (VPNs)
    configuring Android, 1054–1056
    configuring iOS, 1052–1054
    as security measure, 906–907
VirtualBox, 991–995

virtualization
    A+ exam topics, 953
    client requirements, 987–991
    in cloud computing, 975
    function of, 984–986
    hypervisor, 986–987
    practice test on, 996–1001, 1240, 1266
    setting up, 990–991
    support, 37
    Windows options, 698–699
    workstations for, 227–229
viruses
    CERT website, 1129
    defined, 1132
    infection symptoms, 1127–1128
    rogue antivirus as, 1131
    types of, 912–917
vishing, 911
Vizplex, 472
VMware Player, 698
voice communications, 345
VoIP industry, 165, 911
voltage
    lethal, 1152
    matching laptop to regional, 425–426
    of PC power supplies, 100, 107
volts direct current (VDC), 99

W

Wake on LAN (WoL), 816, 854
walk-up infrared use, 362
Walters, Jamie, 1195
warm-swappable devices, 95
warranties, 433
waste, hazardous, 1170, 1177–1186
watches, smart, 477–479
WatchOS, 478
water safety, 1160, 1169
wattage of power supplies, 99
wearable technology, 477–484
weather
    satellite signal interference, 350
    -station radar, 335
web servers, 957–958
webcams, 170, 430

weight, paper, 551
well-known ports, 307
WEP.*x*, 339
WET (Windows Easy Transfer), 796, 835
whaling, 911
wide area networks (WANs)
   defined, 250, 252–253
   speed of, 254–255
Wide Ultra XGA (WUXGA), 209
widescreen displays, 209
Widescreen XGA (WXGA), 210
Wi-Fi
   Alliance, 373
   devices, 253
   802.11 standards, 331–339
   laptop antenna, 431
   mobile configuration, 1045–1056
   mobile security, 1140, 1141
   phone calls via, 1034
   printer interface, 529
   syncing over, 1086
Wi-Fi Protected Access (WPA), 340
Wi-Fi Protected Access 2 (WPA2), 340
Wi-Fi Protected Setup (WPS), 942
wildcards, 694
Windows
   Action Center, 1127
   activating, 833
   administration. *See* administration,
      Windows
   All Programs submenu, 678–680
   Anytime Upgrade utility, 796
   battery life support, 597
   command-line diagnostics, 721–730
   configuration Registry, 731–732
   Control Panel, 709–721
   Defender
      overview of, 1134
      Windows 7, 790, 799, 1134
      Windows Vista, 838
   Desktop, 671–674
   features of, 699–701
   file management, 691–698
   Firewall applet, 720, 790, 799
   Firewall with Advanced Security, 800,
      801
   Google Cloud Print support, 549
   hardware requirements, 665–669

icons, 680–685
Media Player, 237
Memory Diagnostics, 810, 846
mobile operating system, 463
mouse click options, 672
network operating systems, 259
practice test on, 702–706
Print To XPS option, 527
program windows, 685–688
restore points, 690–691
security settings, 915–921
service packs offered, 794
smartphones, 467
Start menu, 674, 676–678
sync requirements, 1089–1090
Taskbar, 674–676
troubleshooting
   security, 1127
   symptoms, 1110–1118
   tools for, 1118–1126
   universal solutions, 1130
updates, 689–690
upgrade utility, 669
user interface (UI), 669–685
Windows 7
   A+ exam topics, 783–784
   administrative tools, 804–810
   All Programs submenu, 678–680
   boot sequences, 797–798
   Control Panel utilities, 810–813
   Desktop, 671–674
   disabling touchpads, 411–413
   Disk Management utility, 752
   editions of, 785–787
   features of, 699–701, 787–791, 798–804
   installing, 791–796
   interface, 669–670
   IP address renewal, 643–644
   Lubuntu/VirtualBox installs, 991–995
   media streaming setup, 237–240
   MSCONFIG tabs, 742–744
   multiple monitor settings, 202–204, 213
   networking options, 813–816
   performance optimization, 817–819
   practice test on, 819–825, 1235, 1259
   print spooler management, 629–630
   printer additions, 532–534
   printer configuration, 534–539

proxy server config., 968
refresh rate adjustment, 195–198
resolution adjustment, 200–202
Start menu, 676–677
system requirements, 667, 669
Taskbar, 674
TCP printing installation, 543–544
Upgrade Assistant, 794–795
upgrading, 796–797
USB printer installation, 540–541
Windows 7 Enterprise, 785, 786
Windows 7 Home Basic, 785
Windows 7 Home Premium, 785, 792
Windows 7 Professional, 785, 786, 792
Windows 7 Starter, 785
Windows 7 Ultimate, 785, 786, 792
Windows 8 Enterprise, 764, 770
Windows 8 Pro, 764, 770
Windows 8 RT
    ARM processor, 765
    defined, 764
    no upgrade options to, 770
Windows 8/8.1. *See also* Windows
    A+ exam topics, 763
    All Programs submenu, 678–680
    boot methods, 776–777
    Desktop, 671–674
    editions of, 764–769, 778
    features of, 699–701
    installing, 769–775, 778
    interface, 670–671
    practice test on, 778–782, 1234–1235,
        1259
    Start menu, 676, 678
    system requirements, 667, 669, 764
    Taskbar, 674
    Upgrade Assistant, 770–772
    upgrade options, 770
Windows Display Driver Model (WDDM),
    202
Windows Easy Transfer (WET),
    796, 835
Windows File Explorer. *See* Explorer
Windows Phone, 1012–1013, 1021–1022
Windows Preinstallation Environment
    (WinPE), 797, 1120
Windows Store, 766, 1021–1022
Windows To Go (WTG), 777

Windows Vista. *See also* Windows
    A+ exam topics, 827–828
    administrative tools, 840–846
    All Programs submenu, 678–680
    boot sequences, 835–836
    editions and features, 836–840
    features of, 699–701, 829–832
    installing, 832–835
    restore point creation, 1136
    Sidebar, 676
    system requirements, 668
    Taskbar, 674
    test on, 860–865, 1236, 1262
    upgrade options, 792–793
Windows Vista Business, 793, 829, 834
Windows Vista Enterprise, 829, 834
Windows Vista Home Basic, 793, 829, 834
Windows Vista Home Premium, 793, 829, 834
Windows Vista Ultimate, 793, 829, 834
Windows XP
    Home, 833
    Media Center, 834
    Run box, 303
    upgrade options, 792–793
    wireless connectivity, 368
Windows XP Professional, 833, 834
Windows XP Tablet PC, 834
WINDOWS.OLD, 832
WINDOWS.OLDIPCONFIG, 832
WINLOAD.EXE
    troubleshooting via, 1112
    Windows 7, 797
    Windows 8/8.1, 776
    Windows Vista, 835
winlogon, 1113
WINRESUME.EXE
    troubleshooting via, 1112, 1113
    Windows 7, 797
    Windows 8/8.1, 776
    Windows Vista, 835
winver command, 787
wipes, data, 931–934, 938
Wired Equivalent Privacy (WEP), 339–340
wired networks. *See also* networks
    conflicts with wireless, 601–602
    installing, 356–359
    for mobile devices, 484–486
    SOHO security, 942–945

for SOHO use, 356–359
troubleshooting
    A+ exam topics, 569–570
    common symptoms, 630–634
    tools for, 635–652
wired printer interfaces, 528–529
wireless access point (WAP), 338, 371
wireless LAN (WLAN), 332, 359
wireless networks. *See also* networks
    A+ exam topics, 329
    as built into laptops, 401
    configuring connection, 368–370
    conflicts with wired, 601–602
    802.11 standards, 331–339
    internal connections, 359–363
    laptop settings, 409
    locator tool, 639
    for mobile devices, 486–490
    for printer interface, 529
    router configuration, 373–380
    security
        data intercepts, 909–910
        encryption, 339–340
        SOHO networks, 939–942
    smartphone capacities, 464
    test on, 1224–1226, 1254
    troubleshooting
        A+ exam topics, 569–570
        common symptoms, 630–635
        laptop/mobile, 600–603, 1137
        software, 639–652
    upgrading laptop cards, 439
    vs. wired, 331, 356
wireless personal area network (WPAN),
    253
wireless print interface, 529
wireless printers, connection issues, 607
wireless routers
    installs, 371–373, 385–386
    shared Internet connections, 381
wireless wide area network (WWAN), 814
wiring standards, 568A and 568B, 279–280
work groups, 816–817
workgroups, 259, 260
working copy backups, 869
workplace safety, 1162–1170
workstations
    acceptable use policies, 905

antivirus software on, 914
custom. *See* custom PC configurations
MAC address ID, 942
network, 256–257
OS upgrades via, 773
security practices, 920–923, 943
vs. servers, 257
World of Warcraft, 230
worms, 917
WPA2, 910
WPA2 Enterprise, 378
WPS (Wi-Fi Protected Setup), 942
WQUXGA, 210
WQXGA, 210
wrist straps, anti-static, 1156, 1163
writing
    to disk process, 753
    in EP printing, 520, 614
    hard drive failure in, 588
    overwriting drives, 937

X

x64 operating systems, 665
x64 processors, 765
x86 operating systems, 665
x86 processors, 765
XCOPY command, 725–726
Xerox, 513
XP Mode, 790
XPS (Open XML Paper Specification) files,
    527

Y

Yahoo! 1070

Z

zero configuration networking, 318–319
zero insertion force (ZIF) sockets, 20
zero-day attack, 919
ZIF sockets, 443, 444
zombies, 919
zone files, 964

Comprehensive Online Learning Environment

Register on Sybex.com to gain access to the comprehensive online interactive learning environment and test bank to help you study for your CompTIA A+ certification.

The online test bank includes:

- **Assessment Test** to help you focus your study to specific objectives
- **Chapter Tests** to reinforce what you learned
- **Practice Exams** to test your knowledge of the material
- **Digital Flashcards** to reinforce your learning and provide last-minute test prep before the exam
- **Searchable Glossary** gives you instant access to the key terms you'll need to know for the exam

Go to `http://sybextestbanks.wiley.com` **to register and gain access to this comprehensive study tool package.**